New England Colleges 2006

Concept Development
Jim Balzer, Adam Burns, and Chris Mason

Cover Design
McGinty

Development
Kristen Burns, Christina Koshzow, Chris Mason, and Kimberly Moore

Editing
Adam Burns, Kristen Burns, Omid Gohari, Christina Koshzow, Kevin Nash, Joey Rahimi, and Luke Skurman

ISBN # 1-59658-504-8
© Copyright 2005 College Prowler
All Rights Reserved
Printed in the U.S.A.
www.collegeprowler.com

Special thanks to: Roland Allen, Chris Babyak, Babs Carryer, Jared Cohon, The Donald H. Jones Center for Entrepreneurship, Bill Ecenberger, Thomas Emerson, Mark Exler, Daniel Fayock, Julie Fenstermaker, Andy Hannah, Paul Kelly, David Koegler, LaunchCyte, Dave Lehman, Bert Mann, Jerry McGinnis, McGinty, Glen Meakem, Abu Noaman, Gabriela Oates, Tim O'Brien, Jon Reider, Kyle Russell, Bob Sehlinger, Andrew Skurman, Barbara Skurman, Terry Slease, Daniel Steinmeyer, Team Evankovich, Tri Ad Litho, Lauren Varacalli, Larry Winderbaum, Jacque Zaremba, and the College Prowler student authors.

College Prowler™
5001 Baum Blvd.
Suite 750
Pittsburgh, PA 15213

Phone: 1(800) 290-2682
Fax: 1(800) 772-4972
E-mail: info@collegeprowler.com
Website: www.collegeprowler.com

College Prowler™ is not sponsored by, affiliated with, or approved by the colleges covered herein.

College Prowler™ strives faithfully to record its sources. As the reader understands, opinions, impressions, and experiences are necessarily personal and unique. Accordingly, there are, and can be, no guarantees of future satisfaction extended to the reader.

© Copyright 2005 College Prowler. All rights reserved. No part of this work may be reproduced or transmitted in any form or by any means, including but not limited to, photocopy, recording, or any information storage and retrieval systems, without the express written permission of College Prowler™.

Welcome to College Prowler

During the writing of College Prowler's guidebooks, we felt it was critical that our content was unbiased and unaffiliated with any college or university. We think it's important that our readers get honest information and a realistic impression of the student opinions on any campus—that's why if any aspect of a particular school is terrible, we (unlike a campus brochure) intend to publish it. While we do keep an eye out for the occasional extremist—the cheerleader or the cynic—we take pride in letting the students tell it like it is. We strive to create a book that's as representative as possible of each particular campus. Our books cover both the good and the bad, and whether the survey responses point to recurring trends or a variation in opinion, these sentiments are directly and proportionally expressed through our guides.

College Prowler guidebooks are in the hands of students throughout the entire process of their creation. Because you can't make student-written guides without the students, we have students at each campus who help write, randomly survey their peers, edit, layout, and perform accuracy checks on every book that we publish. From the very beginning, student writers gather the most up-to-date stats, facts, and inside information on their colleges. They fill each section with student quotes and summarize the findings in editorial reviews. In addition, each school receives a collection of letter grades (A through F) that reflect student opinion and help to represent contentment, prominence, or satisfaction for each of our specific categories. Just as in grade school, the higher the mark, the more content, more prominent, or more satisfied the students are with the particular category.

Once a book is written, additional students serve as editors and check for accuracy even more extensively. Our bounce-back team—a group of randomly selected students who have no involvement with the project—are asked to read over the material in order to help ensure that the book accurately expresses every aspect of the university and its students.

This same process is applied to the 200-plus schools College Prowler currently covers. Each book is the result of endless student contributions, hundreds of pages of research and writing, and countless hours of hard work. All of this has led to the creation of a student information network that stretches across the nation to every school that we cover. It's no easy accomplishment, but it's the reason that our guides are such a great resource.

When reading our books and looking at our grades, keep in mind that every college is different and that the students who make up each school are not uniform—as a result, it is important to assess schools on a case-by-case basis. Because it's impossible to summarize an entire school with a single number or description, each book provides a dialogue, not a decision, that's made up of different topics and hundreds of student quotes. In the end, we hope that this guide will serve as a valuable tool in your college selection process. Enjoy!

OMID GOHARI ○ CHRISTINA KOSHZOW ○ CHRIS MASON ○ JOEY RAHIMI ○ LUKE SKURMAN ○
Founders of College Prowler™

What is a College Prowler *Off the Record* Guidebook?

Explore the School of your Dreams—Without Setting Foot on Campus!
Over 100,000 books are in circulation (and counting, fast!), with each guidebook providing a comprehensive, honest, in-depth portrayal that is dedicated to one school. Every college is a unique experience, therefore, each college has an entire book dedicated to it.

55,000 Students Share Their Opinions
To maintain objectivity, we have refused investment from colleges. Instead, we let the students tell it like it is and fill each guide with over 300 student responses, both positive and negative.

Students Rank 200 Colleges in 200 Guides
Our rankings represent student happiness, prominence, and satisfaction for each respective category. The higher the grade, the happier, the more prominent, or the more satisfied students are with the particular category. The ranking process is in the hands of current students and recent graduates the entire time.

Students Speak Out About:
- Academics
- Athletics
- Campus Dining
- Campus Housing
- Campus Strictness
- Computers
- Diversity
- Drug Scene
- Facilities
- Girls
- Greek Life
- Guys
- Local Atmosphere
- Nightlife
- Off-Campus Dining
- Off-Campus Housing
- Parking
- Safety & Security
- Transportation
- Weather

200 Writers Dig for the Details You Care About
College Prowler has quotes from students about drugs on campus, Greek life, diversity, campus strictness and many other categories that don't usually pop up in traditional college guides. These quotes and categories are here to provide a helpful assessment of what's really happening on each campus. By including important, relevant facts and stats, like the average SAT score or the cost of a parking permit, you get a detailed look at the unique culture of each college.

It's like having an older friend show you around campus.

OMID GOHARI ○ CHRISTINA KOSHZOW ○ CHRIS MASON ○ JOEY RAHIMI ○ LUKE SKURMAN ○
Founders of College Prowler™

New England Colleges 2006

About This Book
College Prowler's line of over 200 guidebooks, each focusing on an individual school, have already become student favorites by providing unbiased, insider information on colleges and universities across the nation. You now hold in your hands the updated *New England Colleges* 2006 compendium—all 34 of our New England guidebooks collected in a single, easy-to-use reference, with plenty of advice on attending college in the northeastern states. Whether as a starting point in the college search, or as a side-by-side comparison of a few favorite schools, this book is designed especially for the prospective student searching for that perfect school.

Going to School in New England
Nearly half of New England's 860,000-plus college students attend private institutions, as opposed to about one-quarter of students nationally. This statistic is just one of many not-so-subtle indicators that the educational experience in all six New England states is more private and exclusive than other regions of the United States. Whether attending a small liberal arts school in Maine, one of the region's historic Ivy League institutions, or one of many affordable, quality public or state schools, a coveted New England education will open many doors after all is said and done. Watch out for similar compendiums from College Prowler on California, the Ivy League, and the Southern States.

OMID GOHARI ◯ CHRISTINA KOSHZOW ◯ CHRIS MASON ◯ JOEY RAHIMI ◯ LUKE SKURMAN ◯
Founders of College Prowler™

www.collegeprowler.com

Did You Know?

Visit our Website at: *www.collegeprowler.com* and find out how you can enter our annual essay contest to win a $500 college scholarship. While you're at it, check out rankings on top colleges across the nations, or order one of our in-depth, school-specific, student-written guides. Go ahead, get your prowl on!

Save 10% Now!

Order Online
Save 10% on your entire order!
www.collegeprowler.com

→ Enter coupon code **NEW ENGLAND**

→ The Truth About America's Top Colleges

OMID GOHARI ○ CHRISTINA KOSHZOW ○ CHRIS MASON ○ JOEY RAHIMI ○ LUKE SKURMAN ○
Founders of College Prowler™

NEW ENGLAND SCHOOLS
Table of Contents

How to Use This Book 1

What's In This Book 2

New England Educational System 4

At a Glance 11

Colleges In Depth

New England Public Schools

University of Connecticut 24

University of Massachusetts 50

University of New Hampshire 80

University of Rhode Island 110

University of Vermont 137

NESCAC

Bates College 160

Bowdoin College 187

Colby College 213

Connecticut College 243

Middlebury College 269

Trinity College 300

Tufts University 326

Wesleyan University 357

Williams College 387

The Five College Consortium

Amherst College 412

Mount Holyoke College 439

Smith College.. 472

> You'll find the University of Massachusetts in the New England Public Schools section. Look for an upcoming College Prowler title on the other consortium school, Hampshire College, at *www.collegeprowler.com*.

The Ivy League

Brown University.. 498

Dartmouth College 525

Harvard University 556

Yale University 586

> There are eight Ivy League schools in total, but only four are located in New England. Find out more about the other four universities—Cornell, Columbia, Princeton, and the University of Pennsylvania—at *www.collegeprowler.com*.

New England Private Schools

Babson College 616

Bentley College 642

Boston College 668

Boston University 694

Brandeis University 726

College of the Holy Cross 753

Emerson College 777

MIT 803

Northeastern University 830

Providence College 856

Rhode Island School of Design 884

Wellesley College 909

Wheaton College 940

New England Weather Map 970

Report Card Summary

Academics 971

Local Atmosphere 972

Safety & Security 973

Computers	974
Facilities	975
Campus Dining	976
Off-Campus Dining	977
Campus Housing	978
Off-Campus Housing	979
Diversity	980
Guys	981
Girls	982
Athletics	983
Greek Life	984
Drug Scene	985
Campus Strictness	986

Financial Aid 987

Students with Special Needs 989

New England Admissions Counseling 998

Words to Know 999

About the Authors 1002

How to Use This Book

Self-Assess
First, decide what's important to you. Are you a party animal or straight-laced? Club kid? Homebody? Do you want to go Greek? Numbers and rankings can never provide the final answer, which is why College Prowler guidebooks are divided into sections covering everything from academics to dining. It might be helpful to make some notes detailing what each category means to you. It's your four years—make the most of it!

Find the Schools
Dive into our in-depth sections, pages 24-969, where detailed, school-by-school information is provided in over 20 distinct sections. Browse student quotes, statistics, and the authors' editorials. Find out why those schools you've got your eye on scored well in one category and poor in another. Just like the original College Prowler guidebooks, each school's section provides its own unique dialogue to help you discover if the college is right for you.

Check the Grades
Check out our report card summaries, pages 971-986, for those aspects of college life that matter most. These summaries provide a side-by-side review of the schools, organized by section, with all 34 colleges right at your fingertips. Get a sense for which colleges suit you best—it couldn't be easier to find a school. We're confident we've provided an accurate comparison and a great starting point for your college search.

Get the Guide
Now that you've narrowed your choices, check out the expanded College Prowler guidebooks—180 pages of inside information on each school with even more student quotes, key admissions statistics, and advice on everything from dorm life to the local club scene. A great companion for those campus visits, College Prowler guidebooks are your last stop in the college search process. For more info check out *www.collegeprowler.com*.

What's In This Book?

> The following paragraphs explain what's included in each section of this book.

School Systems
New England offers strong and often oppositional academic opportunites in both the public and private systems. The "New England Education System" section explains the different options available—public vs. private, the Ivy League, Boston area colleges, and so on. It's a great introduction to the academic scene of the Northeast.

Admissions Contacts
Not only does New England offer a rich and varied collection of universities to choose from, it also offers an astounding number of schools. The "At a Glance" section offers a few key pieces of information—not only on those colleges covered in-depth by College Prowler's individual guidebooks, but also several others we thought were worth a mention. It's information that can get you started on discovering those hidden gems.

Student Perspectives
"Colleges In Depth" is the most important section of this book, a highlight of our *Off the Record* guidebooks with honest, inside information, straight from the students' mouths. The last four sections, "Overall Experience," "The Inside Scoop," "Finding a Job or Internship," and the school's "Best & Worst" don't have grades. They're your chance to look at the school as a whole again. Even if the school is missing something you consider a must-have, it might compensate or really shine in another area. Get a sense of what your fellow students would be like, find out about a school's unique traditions or hidden drawbacks, and discover the opportunities available after graduation. You probably won't have the opportunity to visit every college that grabs your attention. Consider this a preview without ever having to leave your seat.

The Weather Forecast
The "New England Weather Map," located towards the back of the book, will tell you all you need to know when packing that suitcase.

Rankings
The report card summaries offer a side-by-side category comparison of the 34 schools. Flip to the summaries and check out two schools side by side, or compare the grades in one section to another. This section will help remind you where a school stands in the grand scheme. It's easy to move back and forth with each new question, so use this section as a worksheet and a quick index.

Financial Advice
The "Financial Aid" section of this book offers advice and resources to get you started on finding the funds to pay for your education. The good news is that nearly 70 percent of students receive financial aid in some form. Not only is federal aid (FAFSA) available to those who qualify, there are also New England-specific awards available to state residents. While the process of applying for aid can be confusing and sometimes discouraging, many students who believe they don't qualify in fact do.

Students with Special Needs
Those with special needs should check out the "Students With Special Needs" section, which lists contact info and services available for individual schools.

Admissions Counselors
If you're still having problems deciding, it might be a good idea to look into admissions counseling. The counseling section of this book can get you connected to New England counselors as well as College Prowler Counseling.

Glossary
Learn a few new words to stay in the know.

Author Bios
Each college's section was written by its own student author. Good luck with your college search—maybe you'll be the next student to write a College Prowler guidebook!

New England Educational System

The following paragraphs explain the different sorts of schools available in New England.

New England Public Schools

Unless one considers community colleges, there are significantly fewer public colleges and universities than private schools in the New England region. According to the New England Board of Higher Education, New Englanders invest $159 per-capita in state support of public higher education, compared with $217 nationally. This is often attributed to the region's wealth of private institutions.

- **Versatile**
  Don't let the statistics mislead you; New England's all-inclusive public college system is committed to providing affordable, life-long learning and also emphasizes the importance of leadership, service, civic responsibilities, ethical development, and international education.

- **Dynamic**
  Nearly 75 percent of New England public school students participate in some sort of campus club or organization, and more than a third are involved in organized sports. Public service and social activism are also proud traditions at many New England area public schools.

- **Competitive**
  Both the men's and women's basketball teams at The University of Connecticut won national titles for basketball in 2003-2004, the University of Rhode Island recently opened a 7,700 seat sports arena (The Thomas M. Ryan Center), and the University of Massachusetts has a variety of nationally-competitive athletic teams. New England public schools excel at athletics, and student athletes who attend New England public schools are often champions both in the classroom and on the playing field.

Check out www.collegeprowler.com for complete College Prowler guidebooks on:

- University of Connecticut
- University of Massachusetts
- University of New Hampshire
- University of Rhode Island
- University of Vermont

NESCAC

The New England Small College Athletic Conference (NESCAC) is made up of a group of 11 highly-selective liberal arts colleges and universities: Amherst College, Bates College, Bowdoin College, Colby College, Connecticut College, Hamilton College, Middlebury College, Trinity College, Tufts University, Wesleyan University, and Williams College.

- **Organized**
  NESCAC members are usually more restrictive than other NCAA Division III schools with regard to length of season, number of games, and post-season competition. With member institutions sponsoring an average of nearly 30 varsity programs, NESCAC provides more than 7,500 opportunities for participation in intercollegiate competition at the Division III level.

- **Diligent**
  NESCAC believes that student athletes are students first. Unlike more competitive Division I state schools, there's no academic escape hatch for athletes—no "Basket Weaving" or "Swimming Pool Management." No slipping through the cracks, if NESCAC has a say in it.

- **Respectable**
  Attendance policies for classes are the same as for other students and alternative arrangements must be made to avoid conflicts with games. Professors are expected to end classes by a certain time so that there is no conflict with practices. Execution comes down to the coaches, athletes, and professors working together to ensure that education and athletics have a healthy balance.

Check out *www.collegeprowler.com* for complete College Prowler guidebooks on:

- Amherst College
- Bates College
- Bowdoin College
- Connecticut College
- Colby College
- Hamilton College
- Middlebury College
- Trinity College
- Tufts University
- Wesleyan University
- Williams College

The Five College Consortium

If the big city buzz of Boston doesn't seem like your cup of tea, the bordering towns of Amherst, South Hadley, and Northampton provide more than 30,000 undergraduate students with a laid-back learning environment in a small-town setting. The Five College Consortium provides an extraordinarily rich set of academic and cultural resources to its students. The consortium is intended to draw upon the resources of five area colleges: Amherst, Hampshire College, Mount Holyoke, Smith, and The University of Massachusetts (at Amherst).

- **Collective**
  Students enrolled at one of the consortium schools may choose from more than 6,000 courses at any of the five colleges with essentially no bureaucratic difficulties, and at no extra charge. Consortium students have access to more than eight million library volumes and the academic facilities of all five campuses.

- **Accessible**
  Faculty and staff enjoy being part of a college community with five times the number of colleagues and events. Each of the five colleges is within 12 miles of one another and it is not uncommon for students to have groups of friends on each of the five campuses.

- **Diverse**
  The colleges enroll students from nearly every state and from more than 50 countries. Students are admitted without regard to financial aid, and each admitted student is guaranteed financial aid equal to financial need. The schools' generous endowments, meanwhile, allow them to provide students with some of the most state-of-the-art facilities in the nation.

Check out www.collegeprowler.com for complete College Prowler guidebooks on:

- Amherst College
- Mount Holyoke College
- Smith College
- University of Massachusetts

The Ivy League

The origin of the name "Ivy League" is somewhat obscure, but it is said to have arose from a now-defunct football league formed by the eight Ivy League universities. Year after year New England's Ivy League institutions (Brown, Dartmouth, Harvard, and Yale) rank amongst the best schools in America. Rankings aside, these schools have long carried a certain aura of elitism and prestige. There are four other Ivy League schools located outside New England.

- **Selective**
  New England's four Ivy League schools each have between 4,000-6,000 undergrads. Compared to other private institutions in the region, these are very small numbers. Students admitted are usually very bright, very wealthy, or both.

- **Demanding**
  Some of the most notable political figures and brightest minds of our day have failed to do well while enrolled in Ivy League institutions. Senator Ted Kennedy was expelled from Harvard for cheating on a Spanish examination. Ever hear of Harvard dropout Bill Gates? Of course, some Ivy League notables actually do graduate and go on to have prominent, successful careers: for instance President George W. Bush (Yale '68), John F. Kennedy Jr. (Brown '83), and Edward Norton (Yale '91).

- **Prestigious**
  Being that the majority of Ivy League students come from upper-class backgrounds, many Ivy League students are less worried about their own job prospects, and can take a more relaxed attitude towards their education. Students coming from less fortunate backgrounds may have a tougher time adjusting. In the words of one of College Prowler's Ivy League authors, "The toughest thing about the Ivy Leagues is not getting in. It is getting over them."

Check out *www.collegeprowler.com* for complete College Prowler guidebooks on:

- Brown University
- Cornell University
- Columbia University
- Dartmouth College
- Harvard University
- Princeton University
- Yale University

New England Private Schools

New England's private colleges and universities are older than the United States itself. For more than three centuries, New England's private institutions have prepared students for full lives, productive careers, and active citizenship.

- **Prominent**
  A Bachelor's degree from just about any private New England school will undoubtedly turn the heads of a great number of employers in the professional work force.

- **Accommodating**
  There are no "typical" private school students in New England, just as there is no "typical" private school experience. There are numerous liberal arts schools in the region as well as schools of business, arts and design, technical, and all-girls schools.

- **Expensive**
  Private schools do not receive tax revenues, but instead are funded through tuition, fundraising, donations, and private grants. Total yearly tuition fees, including room and board, now average more than $35,000 at New England's private four-year colleges compared to just over $14,000 for state residents attending public four-year campuses. The comparable national figures are $27,516 for students at four-year private campuses and $11,354 for state residents at public four-year campuses.

Check out *www.collegeprowler.com* for complete College Prowler guidebooks on:

- Babson College
- Bentley College
- Boston College
- Boston University
- Brandeis University
- College of the Holy Cross
- Emerson College
- MIT
- Northeastern University
- Providence College
- The Rhode Island School of Design
- Wellesley College
- Wheaton College

Boston Area Colleges

The town of Boston has been described as a "College Mecca," and with over 50 colleges and universities in the surrounding area educating over a quarter of a million students, it could very well be the most well-rounded, student-oriented learning environment in the country (if not the world). In the words of one student, "Boston has so many people, you meet a new friend, see a new teacher, a new student, a new RA, and a new enemy day in and day out." Boston College, Boston University, Emerson, Harvard, MIT, and Tufts are just a few of the top-tier private institutions that you'll find in the Boston area.

- **Historic**

  No city in the United States is more deeply entwined in its historical roots than Boston, and no city has preserved more of its original buildings as memorials to America's past. Yet, Boston maintains a youthful, contemporary atmosphere that small, isolated college towns simply cannot provide.

- **Hip**

  During the school months, a third of the people in Boston are under the age of 25. Boston is fairly clean and efficient, described by many teachers and students as a "walking town," and absolutely bursting with character.

- **Happening**

  Some Boston colleges are self-contained islands within a city, such as Boston College whose 120-acre Gothic-style campus is bounded by hedges and a double row of oak trees. Others spread over city blocks, such as Boston University and Northeastern University. Downtown theaters, shopping, the financial district, and Fenway Park are all a walk or a subway ride away from many surrounding universities. On a spring day, you will find many students boating, jogging, sunning along the Charles River, or shopping and sightseeing in the city's cultural district.

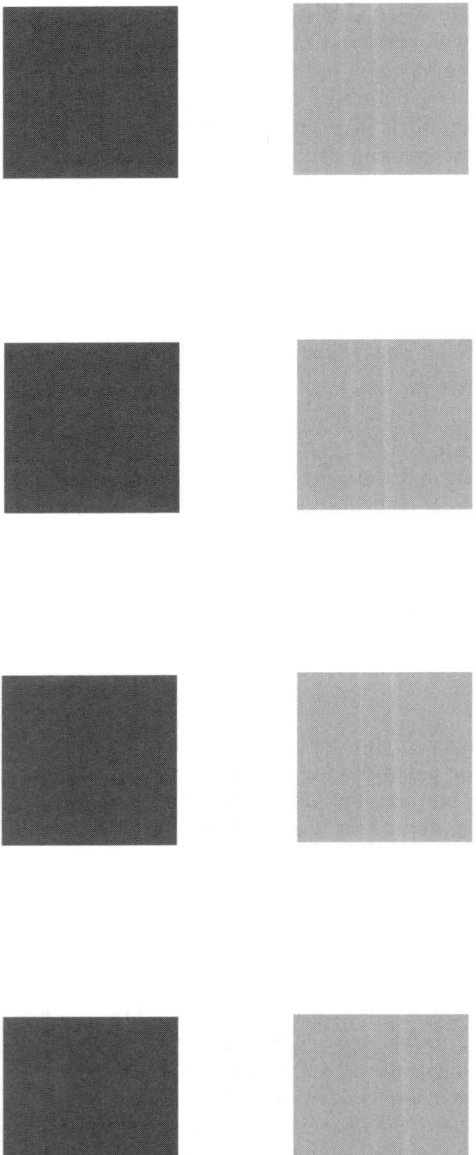

New England Community Colleges

A community college can be an ideal choice for a student who might not be financially, academically, or personally ready to attend a four year university. New England's community colleges are somewhat numerous in certain areas (Massachusetts has 23) and in short supply in others (Rhode Island only has one—the Community College of Rhode Island).

- **Accomodating**

  Many students in the New England area attend community colleges to prepare for a career or to start on a four-year degree.

- **Inexpensive**

  Community colleges are publicly supported two-year colleges that offer an affordable variety of programs for students. Many students choose to earn their first two years of schooling at a New England area community college for a fraction of what they would pay at other colleges. Then, as juniors, they move to finish their bachelor's degree at another public or private institution.

- **Transferable**

  Students can work towards an associate degree in hundreds of academic and technical fields. After completion, students can transfer to a college or university to complete a baccalaureate degree or look for a job in their area of training. Many of the most popular certificate programs revolve around the health professions and high-technology fields.

NEW ENGLAND COLLEGES
At a Glance

Over a hundred schools are listed below, with important information for the prospective student. Check out the in-depth sections to find out even more.

Schools in Connecticut

College	Website	Phone	Tuition	Acceptance Rate	Application Deadline	Setting	GPA	SAT
Albertus Magnus College	www.albertus.edu	(800) 578-9160	$16,858	96%	Rolling	Suburban	2.7	800 – 1040
Central Connecticut State University	www.ccsu.edu	(860) 832-2278	$7,672 in-state, $14,406 out-of-state	55%	May 1	Suburban	N/A	940 – 1120
Charter Oak State College (CT)	www.cosc.edu	(860) 832-3800	$960 in-state, $1,225 out-of-state	N/A	N/A	N/A	N/A	N/A
Connecticut College	www.conncoll.edu	(860) 439-2200	$39,975	35%	January 1	Suburban	N/A	1205 – 1390
Eastern Connecticut State University	www.easternct.edu	(860) 465-5286	$5,704 in-state, $12,438 out-of-state	59%	Rolling	Suburban	N/A	940 – 1120
Fairfield University	www.fairfield.edu	(203) 254-4100	$27,935	49%	January 15	Suburban	3.4	1110 – 1280
Holy Apostles College and Seminary	www.holyapostles.edu	(860) 632-3033	$3,600	N/A	N/A	Urban	N/A	N/A
Paier College of Art	www.paierart.com	(203) 287-3031	$11,200	N/A	N/A	Urban	N/A	N/A
Quinnipiac University	www.quinnipiac.edu	(800) 462-1944	$22,500	52%	Rolling	Suburban	3.4	1050 – 1220

Get the guide at *collegeprowler.com*

Schools in Connecticut

College	Website	Phone	Tuition	Acceptance Rate	Application Deadline	Setting	GPA	SAT
Sacred Heart University	www.sacred-heart.edu	(203) 371-7999	$21,990	68%	Rolling	Suburban	3.3	990 – 1150
Southern Connecticut State University	www.southernct.edu	(203) 392-5656	$5,492 in-state, $12,226 out-of-state	61%	June 1	Urban	N/A	870 – 1058
St. Joseph College	www.sjc.edu	(860) 232-4571	$21,970	68%	Rolling	Suburban	N/A	870 – 1000
Teikyo Post University	www.teikyo-post.edu	(203) 596-4500	$18,800	66%	Rolling	Suburban	2.3	N/A
Test School								
✓ Trinity College	www.trincoll.edu	(860) 297-2180	$31,940	36%	January 15	Urban	N/A	1210 – 1410
United States Coast Guard Academy	www.cga.edu	(800) 883-USCG	$3,000	7%	March 1	Suburban	3.8	1170 – 1330
University of Bridgeport	www.bridgeport.edu	(203) 576-4552	$19,450	84%	Rolling	Urban	2.7	750 – 980
✓ University of Connecticut	www.uconn.edu	(860) 486-2000	$7,308 in-state, $19,036 out-of-state	53%	February 1	Rural	N/A	1080 – 1260
University of Hartford	www.hartford.edu	(860) 768-4296	$23,480	64%	Rolling	Suburban	N/A	970 – 1160
University of New Haven	www.newhaven.edu	(800) DIAL-UNH	$21,696	67%	Rolling	Suburban	3.0	910 – 1130
✓ Wesleyan University	www.wesleyan.edu	(860) 685-3000	$31,650	27%	January 1	Urban	N/A	1290 – 1460

Get the guide at collegeprowler.com

Schools in Connecticut

College	Website	Phone	Tuition	Acceptance Rate	Application Deadline	Setting	GPA	SAT
Western Connecticut State University	www.wcsu.edu	(203) 837-9000	$5,661 in-state, $12,395 out-of-state	55%	Rolling	Urban	N/A	870 – 1070
Yale University	www.yale.edu	(203) 432-9316	$29,820	11%	December 31	Urban	N/A	1380 – 1580

Schools in Massachusetts

College	Website	Phone	Tuition	Acceptance Rate	Application Deadline	Setting	GPA	SAT
American International College	www.aic.edu	(413) 205-3201	$18,000	77%	Rolling	Urban	2.9	830 – 1010
Amherst College	www.amherst.edu	(413) 542-2328	$31,360	18%	December 31	Rural	N/A	1320 – 1540
Anna Maria College	www.annamaria.edu	(508) 849-3360	$20,335	88%	Rolling	Rural	2.6	830 – 1040
Art Institute of Boston	www.aiboston.edu	(617) 585-6700	$18,710	77%	Rolling	Urban	3.0	940 – 1150
Assumption College	www.assumption.edu	(888) 882-7786	$22,425	79%	March 1	Urban	3.2	980 – 1170
Atlantic Union College	www.atlanticuc.edu	(978) 368-2235	$12,780	36%	August 1	Rural	N/A	N/A
Babson College	www.babson.edu	(781) 239-5522	$28,832	37%	January 15	Suburban	N/A	1170 – 1320
Bay Path College	www.baypath.edu	(413) 565-1331	$18,440	82%	Rolling	Suburban	3.0	910 – 1100
Becker College	www.beckercollege.edu	(877) 523-2537	$17,200	83%	Rolling	Urban	N/A	N/A
Benjamin Franklin Institute of Tech	www.bfit.edu	(617) 423-4630	$12,500	91%	September 1	Urban	N/A	N/A

Get the guide at collegeprowler.com

Schools in Massachusetts

College	Website	Phone	Tuition	Acceptance Rate	Application Deadline	Setting	GPA	SAT
Bentley College	www.bentley.edu	(781) 891-2244	$25,544	46%	February 1	Suburban	N/A	1100 – 1270
Berklee College of Music	www.berklee.edu	(800) 237-5533	$23,480	78%	Rolling	Urban	N/A	N/A
Boston Architectural Center	www.the-bac.edu	(617) 585-0123	$8,220	89%	Rolling	Urban	2.9	N/A
Boston College	www.bc.edu	(617) 552-3100	$29,396	31%	January 3	Suburban	N/A	1230 – 1400
Boston Conservatory	www.bostonconservatory.edu	(617) 912-9153	$22,740	43%	N/A	Urban	N/A	N/A
Boston University	www.bu.edu	(617) 353-2300	$30,402	52%	January 1	Urban	3.5	1220 – 1380
Brandeis University	www.brandeis.edu	(781) 736-3500	$31,072	44%	January 15	Suburban	N/A	1250 – 1440
Bridgewater State College	www.bridgew.edu	(508) 531-1237	$5,248 in-state, $11,388 out-of-state	72%	February 15	Suburban	2.9	920 – 1110
Cambridge College	www.cambridgecollege.edu	(800) 877-4723	N/A	N/A	N/A	Urban	N/A	N/A
Clark University	www.clarku.edu	(508) 793-7431	$28,265	63%	February 1	Urban	3.4	1090 – 1300
College of the Holy Cross	www.holycross.edu	(508) 793-2443	$29,686	42%	January 15	Suburban	N/A	1210 – 1350
Curry College	www.curry.edu	(800) 669-0686	$21,530	68%	Rolling	Suburban	N/A	893 – 1067
Dean College	www.dean.edu	(508) 541-1508	$21,380	74%	Rolling	Suburban	2.4	780 – 960

Get the guide at collegeprowler.com

Schools in Massachusetts

College	Website	Phone	Tuition	Acceptance Rate	Application Deadline	Setting	GPA	SAT
Eastern Nazarene College	www.enc.edu	(617) 745-3732	$17,439	40%	Rolling	Suburban	N/A	920 – 1180
Elms College (College of Our Lady of the Elms)	www.elms.edu	(800) 255-3567	$19,970	90%	Rolling	Suburban	2.7	860 – 1140
✓ Emerson College	www.emerson.edu	(617) 824-8600	$23,380	48%	January 15	Urban	3.5	1110 – 1300
Emmanuel College	www.emmanuelcollege.edu	(800) 860-8800	$9,600	49%	August 1	Rural	N/A	N/A
Endicott College	www.endicott.edu	(978) 921-1000	$18,428	48%	Rolling	Suburban	N/A	970 – 1110
Fitchburg State College	www.fsc.edu	(978) 665-3144	$4,588 in-state, $10,668 out-of-state	60%	April 1	Urban	2.9	920 – 1110
Framingham State College	www.framingham.edu	(508) 626-4500	$4,740 in-state, $10,820 out-of-state	55%	February 15	Suburban	3.1	950 – 1140
Gordon College	www.gordon.edu	(800) 343-1379	$21,448	78%	Rolling	Suburban	3.6	1110 – 1310
Hampshire College	www.hampshire.edu	(413) 559-5471	$30,978	55%	February 1	Rural	3.5	1160 – 1360
✓ Harvard University	www.college.harvard.edu	(617) 495-1551	$30,620	10%	January 1	Urban	N/A	1400 – 1590
Hebrew College	http://hebrew-college.edu	(800) 866-4814	N/A	N/A	N/A	Suburban	N/A	N/A
Hellenic College	www.hchc.edu	(617) 731-3500	$14,700	N/A	Rolling	Urban	N/A	N/A

Get the guide at *collegeprowler.com*

Schools in Massachusetts

College	Website	Phone	Tuition	Acceptance Rate	Application Deadline	Setting	GPA	SAT
Lasell College	www.lasell.edu	(617) 243-2225	$18,500	75%	Rolling	Suburban	2.5	850 – 1030
Lesley University	www.lesley.edu	(617) 349-8800	$21,275	77%	Rolling	Urban	3.0	960 – 1130
Longy School of Music	www.longy.edu	(617) 876-0956	$20,115	100%	Rolling	Urban	N/A	N/A
Massachusetts College of Art	www.massart.edu	(617) 879-7222	$6,400 in-state, $17,700 out-of-state	53%	February 15	Urban	3.2	980 – 1180
Massachusetts College of Liberal Arts	www.mcla.edu	(413) 662-5410	$5,397 in-state, $14,342 out-of-state	67%	Rolling	Rural	2.9	930 – 1160
Massachusetts College of Pharmacy and Health Sciences	www.mcp.edu	(800) 225-5506	N/A	76%	March 1	Urban	3.3	950 – 1140
MIT	web.mit.edu	(617) 253-4791	$30,800	16%	January 1	Urban	3.9	1410 – 1560
Massachusetts Maritime Academy	www.maritime.edu	(800) 544-3411	$4,463 in-state, $14,943 out-of-state	74%	Rolling	Suburban	2.8	950 – 1140
Merrimack College	www.merrimack.edu	(978) 837-5100	$22,100	60%	February 1	Suburban	3.3	1020 – 1160
Montserrat College of Art	www.montserrat.edu	(978) 921-4242	$19,650	83%	Rolling	Suburban	2.7	880 – 1150
Mount Holyoke College	www.mtholyoke.edu	(413) 538-2023	$30,938	52%	January 15	Suburban	3.7	1210 – 1370

Get the guide at collegeprowler.com

Schools in Massachusetts

College	Website	Phone	Tuition	Acceptance Rate	Application Deadline	Setting	GPA	SAT
Mount Ida College	www.mountida.edu	(617) 928-4535	$17,671	80%	Rolling	Suburban	2.6	730 – 940
New England Conservatory of Music	www.newengland-conservatory.edu	(617) 585-1101	$26,300	38%	Rolling	Urban	N/A	N/A
Newberry College	www.newberry.edu	(800) 845-4955	$17,470	58%	Rolling	Urban	N/A	820 – 1090
Nichols College	www.nichols.edu	(800) 470-3379	$20,810	82%	Rolling	Rural	2.3	810 – 1000
✓ Northeastern University	www.northeastern.edu	(617) 373-2200	$26,990	47%	February 15	Urban	N/A	1120 – 1300
Pine Manor College	www.pmc.edu	(617) 731-7104	$14,544	71%	Rolling	Urban	2.4	690 – 890
Regis College	www.regiscollege.edu	(866) 438-7344	$20,500	87%	Rolling	Suburban	3.0	800 – 1060
Salem State College	www.salemstate.edu	(978) 542-6200	$5,283 in-state, $11,423 out-of-state	82%	Rolling	Suburban	2.8	840 – 1050
School of the Museum of Fine Arts	www.smfa.edu	(617) 369-3626	$23,290	76%	Rolling	Urban	N/A	993 – 1185
Simmons College	www.simmons.edu	(800) 345-8468	$24,490	68%	March 1	Urban	3.1	1000 – 1190
Simon's Rock College of Bard	www.simons-rock.edu	(413) 528-7312	$30,687	46%	July 1	Rural	N/A	N/A
✓ Smith College	www.smith.edu	(413) 585-2500	$29,156	52%	January 15	Urban	3.8	1150 – 1370
Springfield College	www.springfieldcollege.edu	(413) 748-3136	$20,360	74%	April 1	Urban	N/A	930 – 1120

Get the guide at collegeprowler.com

Schools in Massachusetts

College	Website	Phone	Tuition	Acceptance Rate	Application Deadline	Setting	GPA	SAT
St. John's Seminary	www.sjs.edu	(617) 254-2610	N/A	N/A	N/A	Urban	N/A	N/A
Stonehill College	www.stonehill.edu	(508) 565-1373	$23,008	49%	January 15	Suburban	3.5	1110 – 1270
Suffolk University	www.suffolk.edu	(617) 573-8460	$19,870	82%	March 1	Urban	2.9	940 – 1090
✓ Tufts University	www.tufts.edu	(617) 627-3170	$30,969	26%	January 1	Suburban	N/A	1250 – 1420
✓ University of Massachusetts–Amherst	www.umass.edu	(413) 545-0222	$9,008 in-state, $17,861 out-of-state	82%	January 15	Suburban	3.3	1030 – 1240
University of Massachusetts–Boston	www.umb.edu	(617) 287-6100	$4,012 in-state, $9,378 out-of-state	55%	August 11	Urban	3.0	940 – 1140
University of Massachusetts–Dartmouth	www.umassd.edu	(508) 999-8605	$7,802 in-state, $14,484 out-of-state	71%	Rolling	Suburban	3.1	970 – 1150
University of Massachusetts–Lowell	www.uml.edu	(978) 934-3931	$7,891 in-state, $15,004 out-of-state	62%	Rolling	Urban	3.1	1000 – 1180
✓ Wellesley College	www.wellesley.edu	(781) 283-2270	$29,796	41%	January 15	Suburban	N/A	1260 – 1450
Wentworth Institute of Technology	www.wit.edu	(617) 989-4000	$15,700	70%	Rolling	Urban	N/A	N/A
Western New England College	www.wnec.edu	(413) 782-1321	$19,950	76%	Rolling	Suburban	3.1	960 – 1160

Get the guide at
collegeprowler.com

Schools in Massachusetts/Maine

College	Website	Phone	Tuition	Acceptance Rate	Application Deadline	Setting	GPA	SAT
Westfield State College	www.wsc.mass.edu	(413) 572-5218	$4,857 in-state, $10,937 out-of-state	66%	March 1	Suburban	2.9	940 – 1100
Wheaton College	www.wheaton-college.edu	(508) 286-8251	$30,580	43%	January 15	Suburban	3.5	1130 – 1290
Wheelock College	www.wheelock.edu	(617) 879-2206	$22,500	67%	Rolling	Urban	2.9	940 – 1160
Williams College	www.williams.edu	(413) 597-2211	$29,990	21%	January 1	Rural	N/A	1310 – 1510
Worcester Polytechnic Institute	www.wpi.edu	(508) 831-5286	$29,730	71%	February 1	Urban	3.6	1180 – 1370
Worcester State College	www.worcester.edu	(508) 929-8040	$4,574 in-state, $10,654 out-of-state	56%	June 1	Urban	2.9	900 – 1080
Bates College	www.bates.edu	(207) 786-6000	$39,900	31%	January 15	Urban	N/A	1270 – 1410
Bowdoin College	www.bowdoin.edu	(207) 725-3100	$31,626	24%	January 1	Suburban	3.9	1290 – 1440
Colby College	www.colby.edu	(207) 872-3168	$39,800	34%	January 1	Urban	N/A	1270 – 1420
College of the Atlantic	www.coa.edu	(800) 528-0025	$23,961	69%	February 15	Rural	N/A	1090 – 1320
Husson College	www.husson.edu	(207) 941-7100	$11,050	97%	Rolling	Urban	3.1	790 – 1000
Maine College of Art	www.meca.edu	(800) 639-4808	$22,343	87%	Rolling	Urban	3.2	960 – 1170
Maine Maritime Academy	www.maine-maritime.edu	(207) 326-2206	N/A	68%	July 1	Suburban	N/A	920 – 1130
St. Joseph's College	www.sjcme.edu	(207) 893-7746	$19,615	79%	Rolling	Suburban	3.1	880 – 1110

Get the guide at collegeprowler.com

www.collegeprowler.com

Schools in Maine/New Hampshire

College	Website	Phone	Tuition	Acceptance Rate	Application Deadline	Setting	GPA	SAT
Thomas College	www.thomas.edu	(800) 339-7001	$15,520	73%	Rolling	Rural	2.7	830 – 1030
Unity College	www.unity.edu	(207) 948-3131	$16,190	89%	Rolling	Rural	3.0	870 – 1110
University of Maine - Augusta	www.uma.edu	(207) 621-3185	$4,665 in-state, $10,305 out-of-state	92%	August 30	Urban	N/A	N/A
University of Maine - Farmington	www.umf.maine.edu	(207) 778-7050	$5,150 in-state, $11,840 out-of-state	72%	Rolling	Rural	N/A	950 – 1160
University of Maine - Fort Kent ME	www.umfk.maine.edu	(207) 834-7600	$4,514 in-state, $10,154 out-of-state	86%	Rolling	Rural	N/A	N/A
University of Maine - Machias ME	www.umm.maine.edu	(888) 468-6866	$4,115 in-state, $10,115 out-of-state	82%	August 15	Rural	N/A	840 – 1040
University of Maine - Orono ME	www.umm.maine.edu	Phone: (207) 581-4090	$6,394 in-state, $15,784 out-of-state	76%	Rolling	Rural	3.2	970 – 1190
University of Maine - Presque Isle ME	www.umpi.maine.edu/cms/index.php	(207) 768-9532	$4,460 in-state, $10,400 out-of-state	87%	Rolling	Rural	2.9	N/A
University of New England ME	www.une.edu	(207) 283-0171	$20,875	97%	Rolling	Rural	3.1	920 – 1140
University of Southern Maine ME	www.usm.maine.edu	(207) 780-5670	$5,468 in-state, $13,598 out-of-state	72%	Rolling	Urban	3.0	940 – 1130
Colby-Sawyer College NH	www.colby-sawyer.edu	(800) 272-1015	$23,310	82%	Rolling	Rural	2.9	920 – 1110
College for Lifelong Learning NH	www.cll.edu	(603) 228-3000	$4,563 in-state, $5,043 out-of-state	N/A	N/A	Urban	N/A	N/A

Schools in New Hampshire

College	Website	Phone	Tuition	Acceptance Rate	Application Deadline	Setting	GPA	SAT
Daniel Webster College	www.dwc.edu	(800) 325-6876	$21,630	77%	Rolling	Suburban	N/A	970 – 1190
Dartmouth College	www.dartmouth.edu	(603) 646-2875	$30,465	18%	January 1	Rural	3.7	1330 – 1530
Franklin Pierce College	www.fpc.edu	(800) 437-0048	$22,510	87%	Rolling	Rural	N/A	905 – 1110
Keene State College	www.keene.edu	(603) 358-2276	$6,920 in-state, $13,360 out-of-state	71%	April 1	Urban	2.9	910 – 1100
New England College - NH	www.nec.edu	(800) 521-7642	$21,944	97%	Rolling	Rural	N/A	810 – 1020
Plymouth State University	www.plymouth.edu	(603) 535-2237	$6,240 in-state, $12,290 out-of-state	71%	April 1	Rural	2.8	860 – 1060
Rivier College	www.rivier.edu	(603) 888-1311	$19,825	77%	August 30	Suburban	N/A	790 – 1050
Southern New Hampshire University	www.snhu.edu	(603) 645-9611	$19,314	71%	Rolling	Suburban	2.9	867 – 1079
St. Anselm College	www.anselm.edu	(603) 641-7500	$23,350	71%	Rolling	Suburban	3.1	1020 – 1200
Thomas More College of Liberal Arts	www.thomasmorecollege.edu	(603) 880-8308	N/A	N/A	Rolling	Suburban	N/A	N/A
University of New Hampshire	www.unh.edu	(603) 862-1360	$9,226 in-state, $20,256 out-of-state	69%	February 1	Rural	N/A	1010 – 1230
University of New Hampshire at Manchester	N/A	N/A	N/A	N/A	N/A	Urban	N/A	N/A

Get the guide at collegeprowler.com

Schools in Rhode Island

College	Website	Phone	Tuition	Acceptance Rate	Application Deadline	Setting	GPA	SAT
Brown University	www.brown.edu	(401) 863-2378	$31,334	16%	January 1	Urban	N/A	1290 – 1500
Bryant College	www.bryant.edu	(800) 622-7001	$23,580	59%	February 15	Suburban	3.2	1010 – 1170
Johnson and Wales University	www.jwu.edu	(401) 598-2310	$17,460	85%	Rolling	Urban	3.0	810 – 1040
Providence College	www.providence.edu	(401) 865-2535	$23,639	53%	January 15	Urban	3.4	1110 – 1300
Rhode Island College	www.ric.edu	(800) 669-5760	$4,270 in-state, $10,910 out-of-state	73%	May 1	Suburban	N/A	890 – 1090
Rhode Island School of Design	www.risd.edu	(401) 454-6300	$27,975	35%	February 15	Urban	3.3	1090 – 1310
Roger Williams University	www.rwu.edu	(401) 254-3500	$21,778	80%	Rolling	Suburban	3.0	980 – 1160
Salva Regina University	www.salve.edu	(888) 467-2583	$22,200	55%	Rolling	Urban	3.2	990 – 1140
University of Rhode Island	www.uri.edu	(401) 874-7100	$6,752 in-state, $18,338 out-of-state	70%	February 1	Rural	N/A	1010 – 1200

Schools in Vermont

College	Website	Phone	Tuition	Acceptance Rate	Application Deadline	Setting	GPA	SAT
Bennington College	www.bennington.edu	(800) 833-6845	$31,070	68%	January 1	Rural	3.5	1140 – 1350
Burlington College	www.burlingtoncollege.edu	(800) 862-9616	$14,170	72%	August 9	Urban	N/A	N/A
Castleton State College	www.castleton.edu	(800) 639-8521	$6,146 in-state, $13,086 out-of-state	70%	Rolling	Rural	N/A	860 – 1070
Champlain College	www.champlain.edu	(800) 570-5858	$13,850	63%	Rolling	Urban	2.9	1000 – 1130
College of St. Joseph	www.csj.edu	(802) 773-5900	$13,200	94%	Rolling	Rural	N/A	750 – 1010

Get the guide at collegeprowler.com

Schools in Vermont

College	Website	Phone	Tuition	Acceptance Rate	Application Deadline	Setting	GPA	SAT
Goddard College	www.goddard.edu	(800) 468-4888	$9,080	N/A	Rolling	Rural	N/A	N/A
Green Mountain College	www.green-mtn.edu	(802) 287-8208	$21,134	60%	Rolling	Rural	2.8	890 – 1140
Johnson State College	www.johnson-statecollege.com	(800) 635-2356	$5,980 in-state, $12,920 out-of-state	38%	Rolling	Rural	N/A	N/A
Lyndon State College	www.lsc.vsc.edu	(802) 626-6413	$7,056 in-state, $13,996 out-of-state	94%	Rolling	Rural	2.5	800 – 950
Marlboro College	www.marlboro.edu	(800) 343-0049	$25,740	82%	February 15	Rural	3.3	1100 – 1340
Middlebury College	www.middlebury.edu	(802) 443-3000	$40,400	23%	January 1	Rural	N/A	1370 – 1490
Norwich University	www.norwich.com	(800) 468-6679	$19,650	71%	Rolling	Rural	2.9	930 – 1170
Southern Vermont College	www.svc.edu	(802) 447-6304	$12,498	71%	Rolling	Rural	N/A	810 – 1000
St. Michael's College	www.smcvt.edu	(800) 762-8000	$25,535	67%	February 1	Suburban	N/A	1020 – 1210
Sterling College	www.sterlingcollege.edu	(802) 586-7711	N/A	95%	Rolling	Rural	2.9	940 – 1265
University of Vermont	www.uvm.edu	(802) 656-3370	$10,226 in-state, $23,866 out-of-state	75%	January 15	Urban	N/A	1060 – 1250
Vermont Technical College	www.vtc.edu	(802) 728-1445	$11,096 in-state, $13,986 out-of-state	61%	Rolling	Rural	3.0	890 – 1130

Get the guide at collegeprowler.com

University of Connecticut

1232 Storrs Rd., Storrs, CT 06268
www.uconn.edu   (860) 486-3137

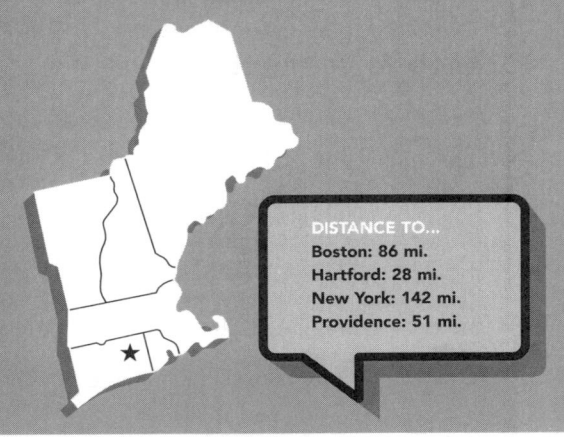

DISTANCE TO...
Boston: 86 mi.
Hartford: 28 mi.
New York: 142 mi.
Providence: 51 mi.

"When you come to the University of Connecticut, you're part of a community."

Total Enrollment:
14,332

Acceptance Rate:
53%

Tuition:
$7,308 in-state, $19,038 out-of-state

Top 10% of High School Class:
30%

SAT Range
Verbal	Math	Total
530 – 620	550 – 640	1080 – 1260

SAT II
Not required

Most Popular Majors:
16% Business
16% Social Sciences
7% Psychology
6% Health Professions
5% Engineering

Students Also Applied To:*
Boston College
Boston University
Northeastern University
University of Massachusetts–Amherst
University of Rhode Island

*For more school info check out www.collegeprowler.com

Table of Contents

Academics	25
Local Atmosphere	27
Safety & Security	28
Computers	29
Facilities	31
Campus Dining	32
Off-Campus Dining	34
Campus Housing	35
Off-Campus Housing	37
Diversity	38
Guys & Girls	39
Athletics	41
Greek Life	42
Drug Scene	43
Campus Strictness	44
Overall Experience	46
The Inside Scoop	47
Finding a Job or Internship	48
The Best & Worst	49

College Prowler Report Card

Academics	B
Local Atmosphere	D+
Safety & Security	A-
Computers	B
Facilities	A-
Campus Dining	B-
Off-Campus Dining	C
Campus Housing	B+
Off-Campus Housing	B
Diversity	D
Guys	B+
Girls	B
Athletics	A
Greek Life	B-
Drug Scene	A-
Campus Strictness	B-

Academics

There are many schools within the University itself, and some schools are better than others. Expect to be taking general education classes during your freshman year and part of the first semester of your sophomore year. There are a lot of requirements, but the gen-ed classes are set categorically so that within each category (i.e., Western culture, literature) there is a plethora of classes to choose from. Get an early freshman orientation date in order to secure more options. If you're coming in with a major, most of your classes will be pre-decided for you, but don't miss the opportunity to take a class that sounds interesting within the categories that are still open.

Undecided freshman come in under the exploratory major (ACES). Entering under the ACES program is good, as the advisors are friendly, always available, and always know of the latest developments regarding requirements (which general education classes can't be used for which majors, etc.). Since you'll be taking a slew of required classes anyway, ACES is a good way to figure out what you might be interested in majoring in; it allows you to take whatever sounds cool and still fulfills requirements. The only downside is that with some programs, you may have to stay an extra year. Look into this ahead of time, but it's no different than getting into your junior year of school having taken only biology classes, and then deciding you want to switch to English—you'll be here awhile.

The Lowdown
ON ACADEMICS

Degrees Awarded:
Associate, Bachelor, Master, Doctorate

Undergraduate Schools:
College of Agriculture and Natural Resources, School of Allied Health, School of Business, School of Engineering, College of Continuing Studies, School of Family Studies, School of Fine Arts, College of Liberal Arts and Sciences (CLAS), Neag School of Education, School of Nursing, School of Pharmacy, Ratcliffe Hicks School of Agriculture

Full-time Faculty:
865

Faculty with Terminal Degree:
95%

Student-to-Faculty Ratio:
17:1

Average Course Load:
5 courses

AP Test Score Requirements:
Possible credit for scores of 4 or 5

IB Test Score Requirements:
Possible credit for scores of 3 or higher

Best Places to Study:
Library and dorm study lounges

Did You Know?

The school is growing and improving by leaps and bounds in every way, thanks to state grants through the UConn 2000 and 21st Century UConn programs. UConn has received over 2.3 billion dollars to date to improve everything from facilities to infrastructure, and the improvements it has made are highly visible. Actually, most students would argue that, during this transitional period, improvements have been too visible, as there are construction sites everywhere.

Students Speak Out
ON ACADEMICS

The College Prowler Take
ON ACADEMICS

"I get the feeling that professors don't care that much about their students, but more about their research or experiments. For the most part, my classes are interesting, except Psychology 132—that was painful."

Q "Most teachers and TAs are enthusiastic individuals that do their best to **make learning enjoyable**. However, every once in a while you'll get one that is clearly just running through the syllabus in an attempt to get back to whatever research they are doing."

Q "Teachers are very helpful if you seek them out. **Most classes are big**—between 40 to 150 people."

Q "Personally, I find the professors to be elusive. **Most just have TAs teach** for them."

Q "I have had a few excellent teachers, and also a few that were not so great, but there are **more good than bad**. Most are fair and knowledgeable, but it changes depending on the types of classes, though. The main problem is not understanding a teacher or teaching assistant. This happens sometimes, but not always, with math or science classes."

Q "Most of my professors aren't bad. **The TAs can be difficult**. I have nothing against them personally, but it's just hard to understand some of them."

Some professors are wonderful, energetic, and excited to teach material they love. Some professors don't even speak English. College means diversity, right? There are simply too many students at UConn for a student to expect routine one-on-one attention as an underclassman. The professors have office hours, and most are very accommodating but will never approach you. When you delve further into your major, classes will become progressively smaller. Use www.myprofessorsucks.com every time you open up the registration guide. It's an invaluable resource for choosing classes.

The College Prowler™ Grade on
Academics: B

A high Academics grade generally indicates that professors are knowledgeable, accessible, and genuinely interested in their students' welfare. Other determining factors include class size, how well professors communicate, and whether or not classes are engaging.

Want the 411 on academics at UConn? For a detailed listing of all academic clubs on campus, check out the College Prowler book on UConn available at *collegeprowler.com*.

Local Atmosphere

The Lowdown
ON LOCAL ATMOSPHERE

Region:
Northeast

City, State:
Storrs, Connecticut

Setting:
Rural

Distance from Boston, MA:
1 hour, 30 minutes

Distance from New York, NY:
2 hours, 51 minutes

Major Sports Teams:
Wolfpack (hockey), Suns (WNBA)

Students Speak Out
ON LOCAL ATMOSPHERE

"[Around] UConn, Storrs is the town. It has a bad reputation for being a drinking school, but, at least for me, there is much more to do."

"We're in **the middle of nowhere**. No other universities are present in Storrs, to my knowledge. Stay away from the smelly cows. Visit Jorgensen, Gampel for a game, or even the new IMAX when it opens."

"The atmosphere is very quaint. ECSU is nearby in Willimantic. I'd stay away from certain parts of Willimantic, but **it's really pretty out here** and a nice place to be outdoors."

"The town is pretty small. Manchester is 25 minutes away, and it has a mall, restaurants, movie theater, shopping, and stuff like that. You can buy a bus ticket on campus for five dollars, round trip. I can't really think of anything to stay away from, except maybe Willimantic, which is the nearest big city. It's really **rundown, poor, and not a fun place** to go."

"Well, **Storrs is a cow town**; it's a 15- to 20-minute drive from the highway to the campus that seems to last forever. There's nothing in the town, except some stores and restaurants. The closest university is Eastern Connecticut State, which is about 20 minutes away, but it's a small school of 8,000 students."

The College Prowler Take
ON LOCAL ATMOSPHERE

The local atmosphere is rural and quaint—words that should be setting off alarms. There's a reason that every time someone mentions local atmosphere to a campus tour-guide, the words "New York and Boston are pretty close," are somewhere in their carefully-worded response. UConn is Storrs, and the surrounding area is very beautiful but empty. Mansfield and the sketchy Willimantic offer more options, but only students with cars or friends that have them will be able to go whenever they like. Hartford is less than a half hour away and opens up a slew of options for the weekend, but the driving situation is the same. The local atmosphere is redeemed by all there is to do on campus. UConn is isolated, and most of the nights you go out, you'll probably end up somewhere on campus.

The College Prowler™ Grade on

Local Atmosphere: D+

A high Local Atmosphere grade indicates that the area surrounding campus is safe and scenic. Other factors include nearby attractions, proximity to other schools, and the town's attitude toward students.

Safety & Security

The Lowdown
ON SAFETY & SECURITY

Number of UConn Police:
21

Phone:
(860) 486-4800

Safety Services:
Escort Service and Shuttle Service

Health Center Office Hours:
8:30 a.m. – 5:00 p.m., Monday through Friday; 24/7 care for acute illnesses and injuries, except weekend evenings and nights

Students Speak Out
ON SAFETY & SECURITY

Q "UConn has its own squad of state troopers, and its own fire and EMT station. There are always tons of police around, and there's an emergency call system all over campus. You can see the call-boxes anywhere on campus, and just push a button for help. The campus is **very well-lit in most places**. Buses run almost all the time to get you to where you need to go, and you can call Safe Rides if they aren't running. They'll pick you up and take you anywhere on campus, 24/7."

Q "There are a few incidents every year, without a doubt. But, there are buses that run until midnight on weekdays, and **there is an escort service that is pretty much always available**. Most dorms are locked at night, and many are locked all day. So, while there are a few unfortunate incidents, it's generally safe, and there are plenty of resources in terms of protecting yourself on campus."

Q "There's a police station on campus. They are all jerks. They wrongly arrest people all the time and have the highest arrest rate in the state of Connecticut for DUIs [Driving Under the Influence] and marijuana charges. I know for a fact that **they have arrested people for DUIs when they weren't even driving the car**. As for marijuana charges, they would charge a whole crowd with possession when only one person would have a dime bag on them. Plus, last year, there were about three people who got robbed at gunpoint on campus, and the cops never caught them."

Q "Security on campus is wonderful. There are **hundreds of alert poles across campus**. There is an escort service provided by the University and campus police. The buildings are always locked after 7 p.m., and almost all of the buildings require a swipe of the student's ID to enter the building. Only students who live in those specific buildings can enter."

{ "Overall it's pretty lax. We have campus police, but you have to be in range to call them."

Q "Security has been kind of an issue lately, although **I don't feel unsafe at all**. I mean, being a female, there's always a few more worries, but if you don't put yourself in bad situations, you won't have problems."

Did You Know?

The police department is required to publish reports on incidents and crime statistics, which can be found online at www.police.uconn.edu/ucr.html.

The College Prowler Take
ON SAFETY & SECURITY

For all that's been done to ensure safety on campus, security should have a better rep. It's hard to go anywhere without seeing a blue-light station, like those incorporated on many other college campuses. As is demonstrated by the UConn police Website, there are sizable amounts of verified larceny and burglary reports, but there aren't many other crimes, besides alcohol-related ones. The campus is in a small town, and the majority of students report feeling safe. Escort services are available to shuttle students across campus at night, and the whole the campus is well-lit, including paths.

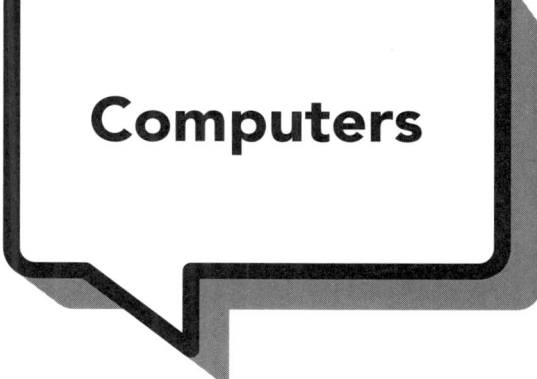

Computers

The Lowdown
ON COMPUTERS

High-Speed Network?
Yes

Number of Labs:
26

Numbers of Computers:
1,318

Operating Systems:
PC/Mac

Wireless Network?
Only in business and engineering buildings

Charge to Print?
Only in the library—15 cents a page

Free Software:
Symantec AntiVirus Corporate Edition

24-Hour Labs:
Ecology and Evolutionary Biology Building, ITS Building, Library Pathobiology & Vet Science Building, School of Pharmacy, the Psychology Building

The College Prowler™ Grade on
Safety & Security: A-

A high grade in Safety & Security means that students generally feel safe, campus police are visible, blue-light phones and escort services are readily available, and safety precautions are not overly necessary.

Students Speak Out
ON COMPUTERS

{ "Having your own computer is best because the labs aren't open when you really need them. They always close so early."

Q "The network is fast, but the five gigabyte quota for external traffic really is a pain for people like me. **Computer labs aren't always crowded** because of how they started charging for printing this semester. It's ten cents a page, I think, so bringing your own computer and printer is a good idea."

Q "The network has to be the best thing ever. You are constantly online and can download songs in, like, three seconds. It's really handy. The computer labs usually aren't that crowded, but **I definitely found it helpful to have a computer**. It's all a matter of preference, though. Once you go to school, you realize that Instant Messenger is your savior and allows you to keep in touch with everyone, minus the phone bills."

Q "Pretty much everyone has their own computer. **Each room has a phone line and two Internet connections**, which are really fast, so it usually makes sense to have your own. Some computer labs are crowded, while others are almost always empty. You just have to know which ones to go to and when."

Q "Bringing your own computer is not a must, but it is a key means of communication. Instant Messenger is one way that almost everyone keeps in contact. Computer labs are often open, but they are run by student workers who can be less than reliable. I like to write at 3 a.m., and **the labs aren't open that late**, so it was a necessity for me to have my computer up here. I did have it go down for a few months, though, and I never had a problem finding a computer to use in the labs. Printing is free in the labs, so that's nice."

Did You Know?

To ensure network integrity, ResNet scans for computers that are vulnerable to exploitation (or that have already been exploited), and then blocks them from accessing the network. ResNet also has a workshop in the New Haven building, where people can bring their computers to be fixed to work on our network, free of charge.

The College Prowler Take
ON COMPUTERS

You can survive at UConn without a computer the same way you could survive if you were stranded on a deserted island without one. It's possible, but it's probably not going to be a whole lot of fun. While there are accessible labs scattered around campus that have free printing, you'll probably feel very isolated not having one in your dorm. The University's housing and class registration have gone digital, so having a computer for those things is a plus. Also, most of the teachers require papers to be typed. Doing a paper at a lab can be more efficient because you won't have any distractions, but it won't be as comfortable as rolling out of bed on a Saturday morning and into your computer chair. If you work at night, a computer is an absolute requirement.

The College Prowler™ Grade on
Computers: B

A high grade in Computers designates that computer labs are available, the computer network is easily accessible, and the campus' computing technology is up-to-date.

Facilities

Favorite Things to Do
SUBOG-sponsored events are usually a good time, and feature prizes as incentive for hibernating students to come out of their dorms. An e-mail sent to every student's Husky Mail account called "The Focus" informs students about weekly events.

Students Speak Out
ON FACILITIES

The Lowdown
ON FACILITIES

Libraries:
1

Bowling on Campus?
No

Bars on Campus:
Huskies, Teds

Student Center:
The Student Union (the SU)

Athletic Center:
Guyer Gym, Greer Field House

Movie Theatre on Campus?
Yes.

Coffeehouse on Campus?
Not in the traditional sense, but all of the cafés listed in the dining section are set up like coffeehouses.

Popular Places to Chill
When it's cold, the dorms and study lounges are the places to be, but when it gets warmer, the lawns are dotted with students on blankets. Once the SU is finished, it should fill a gap in the campus community.

{ **"The athletic facilities are amazing, it's very nice. The Student Union is a great place to sit and talk with friends and the academic facilities are very good as well."**

Q "They are getting better, and there have been lots of renovations. There's **a new student union**; it has fast food places, a movie theatre, and shops. The gym is really nice, although it's usually crowded around spring break or summer (bathing suit weather). The library has also been redone. There are definitely some nice things here."

Q "The athletic facilities are excellent. The field house has free-weight rooms, plenty of exercise machines, a pool, basketball and volleyball courts, and an indoor track. There are also outdoor fields for the teams and IM [intramural] sports. There are **some good computer rooms**. The Student Union is all right, but it's being completely redone, along with plenty of other buildings, with a movie theater and all kinds of cool new stuff. It's being done in phases. There's always construction, but the campus is looking really nice."

Q "There's a field house where you can go to swim, work out, play sports, or do whatever. They have a track field, hockey rink, football field, rugby field, polo field, and a few practice fields. Most of the computers are up-to-date and pretty nice. The newer classrooms are nice, with all sorts of computers, technology, and the like. The older ones are being renovated. The **Student Union was recently rebuilt**. The same goes for the bookstore. They have a good library here. It's a nice place to study or hang out."

Q "The facilities are very good. **The library is open until midnight**, but there is a place called Bookworms in the library, which is open 24 hours. The field house and gym are open from 6 a.m. until midnight and are often full. The student center is fine. I don't use it too much, but there are some cool things."

Q "Everything is beautiful on campus. They already renovated a lot of the buildings and just got tons of money to redo more of them. They have a bunch of plans. **The campus is big and beautiful**."

Campus Dining

The College Prowler Take
ON FACILITIES

The Lowdown
ON CAMPUS DINING

Since UConn is a public university, it receives funding from the state. The programs UConn 2000 and 21st Century UConn have poured over two-billion dollars into the school to improve the campus and infrastructure. The changes have launched UConn ahead of a lot of other higher education institutions and are very visible. There is a running joke on campus that UConn stands for "University of Construction," because of all the new buildings constantly going up. Even with all the positive alterations that have been completed on campus within the past few years, it cannot be ignored that there is still work to be done. Once the Student Union gets past its numerous delays, it should be spectacular and will improve the overall perspective of UConn's facilities in a positive way.

Freshman Meal Plan Requirement?
Yes

Meal Plan Average Cost:
$1,500

Student Favorites:
W.E.B.B. Site, Jonathan's, Papa Gino's, Bookworms Café

Regarding your meal plan, there's a difference between meals and points. For meals, you'll typically go through an average of 175 per semester, depending on how much you eat. Points are prepaid cash and are worth more than paper money at the University-run cafés. The best meal plan for first semester students is 250 meals plus 80 points. See what you use, then adjust if needed for the second semester.

24-Hour On-Campus Eating?
No, but there are two 24-hour convenience stores a block away from campus, near the Shippee and Buckley dorms and the Northwest dorms.

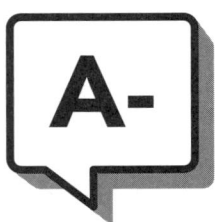

The College Prowler™ Grade on
Facilities: A-

A high Facilities grade indicates that the campus is aesthetically pleasing and well-maintained; facilities are state-of-the-art, and libraries are exceptional. Other determining factors include the quality of both athletic and student centers and an abundance of things to do on campus.

Students Speak Out
ON CAMPUS DINING

"The food on campus is pretty good. There are a bunch of places you can order out from late at night that will get you things like pizza, Chinese, calzones, Friendly's, Subway, Blimpie's, and buffalo wings."

Q "I personally like some of the food a lot, although, like everyone, I get tired of it. **South Campus and Northwest have the best dining halls**. They're both equal in quality, and the dining halls are new. South is more crowded, but it has a better variety. There's also a deli, a Papa Gino's, and Jonathan's, which is a fast food place. You can use your meal plan, and they're great for stocking up on drinks and snacks for your room."

Q "Some people complain about the food here, but I really like it. The best cafe to eat in is South, as they have a grill chef, pizza, Chinese, pasta, and lots of other stuff everyday. North has a good café, too. All the cafés are **buffet-style eating**, so there are always plenty of choices. The school has its own bakery, where you can order cakes and cookies whenever you want. They also make their own ice cream, which is absolutely amazing, and you can have all you want at every meal."

Q "The café is **kind of nasty**, but you'll find that on many campuses. They do offer other places on campus where you can use your meal plan."

Q "Dining hall food does not compare to home-cooked meals. The only good thing about them is that it's 'buffet' every single day—which can be dangerous. South is the best place to eat, but **be prepared to wait 15 minutes for mashed potatoes and chicken**."

Q "The food is good! I mean, **it's not what you get at home**, but it's good for campus food. I've been to two other schools, and the food hasn't been nearly as good, nor had such a large selection."

Did You Know?
In Towers Dining Hall, the conveyer that you place your tray on after you're done eating is past the staff member, beyond his view. It's the easiest place to steal a tray from, if you want to snag one to go sledding. Just make sure you return it afterwards!

The College Prowler Take
ON CAMPUS DINING

Food on campus is really good, with the exception of a few of the dining halls. South and Towers are usually rated the best, with Northwest close behind. North and Buckley are usually held as the worst. Though you can eat at any dining hall with your card, the majority of students will find themselves using all their meals at one dining hall. Why? Because the one next to your dorm is closer than the good ones, and, for the average college student, apathy outweighs decadence by a ratio of exactly 38,000 to 1. Besides, while there are quite a few dining halls, most of them serve similar things.

The College Prowler™ Grade on
Campus Dining: B-

Our grade on Campus Dining addresses the quality of both school-owned dining halls and independent on-campus restaurants as well as the price, availability, and variety of food.

Off-Campus Dining

The Lowdown
ON OFF-CAMPUS DINING

Best Pizza:
Sgt. Pepperoni's

Best Chinese:
Chang's Garden

Best Breakfast:
Husky Bean

Best Wings:
Wings Express

Best Healthy:
The Co-op Deli

Late-Night Food Specials:
Wing's Express

Best Place to Take Your Parents:
C.O. Jones, Margarita's, Macaroni Grill

Student Favorites:
Wings Express, DP Dough, C.O. Jones, Angelinos, Kathy John's, Chang's Garden, Wings Over Storrs, Sgt. Pepperoni's, Domino's

Students Speak Out
ON OFF-CAMPUS DINING

"There are a lot of takeout places for pizza, wings, calzones, grinders, or Chinese. You would need to have a car to get to any real restaurants."

"There are lots of decent places around campus, granted you have a car. Manchester, has a mall and **a bunch of chain restaurants** around, such as the Olive Garden, Chili's, and Macaroni Grill. There are also some good non-chains that are nearby."

"The best place to eat off campus is Wings Over Storrs. If you ever need a late-night meal, hit that spot up. There are two pizza places a little bit down the road, depending where you live. Also, there is **a place that sells calzones** called DP Dough that's pretty good."

"There are a couple of restaurants around campus that are yummy. **It's not food like you could get in a big city**, but it's good. Sgt. Pepperoni's has good pizza, and Wings Over Storrs is great for wings and sandwiches."

"It takes a little while to get really good stuff off campus, but there are closer things off campus, like Margarita's and Applebee's. There are also **places that deliver right to the dorm until two or three in the morning**."

"There are **not too many restaurants on campus**. There's a Friendly's that's just off, otherwise you can drive 10 minutes to Angelino's for great Italian and Ruby Tuesday's, or go five minutes to Margarita's—a college hangout place—or Willington Pizza."

Fun Fact
During the warmer months, some of the dining halls will close for lunch or dinner and, instead, cater outdoor events that usually include some sort of cultural theme, with music and international dishes.

The College Prowler Take
ON OFF-CAMPUS DINING

Despite being out in the middle of nowhere, there are several restaurants in relatively close proximity to campus. C.O. Jones is a great spot to grab Mexican, and Starbucks is right off campus in the same area near the music building and the Buckley and Shippee dorms. Of the restaurants that deliver to your dorm, Sgt. Pepperoni's, DP Dough, Wings Express and Domino's are the favorites. The website *www.campusfood.com* is a vital part of dorm existence, if you set up an account, and *www.needfoodnow.com* is pretty helpful, too. Although there is diversity in off-campus eating, there are only a few restaurants just off campus. The rest you'll need a car to get to.

The College Prowler™ Grade on
Off-Campus Dining: C

A high Off-Campus Dining grade implies that off-campus restaurants are affordable, accessible, and worth visiting. Other factors include the variety of cuisine and the availability of alternative options (vegetarian, vegan, Kosher, etc.).

Campus Housing

The Lowdown
ON CAMPUS HOUSING

Undergrads on Campus:
75%

Number of Dormitories:
60

Dormitories
Most dorms do not stand alone, but are set up in what is referred to as a "quad." A quad is a group of buildings arranged around a central lawn, and sometimes a dining hall. There is a map of the locations of the residence halls on the ResLife Website: *www.reslife.uconn.edu*.

Cleaning Service?
Yes. Housekeeping services keep the dorms consistently clean; janitors and grounds crews keep the rest clean.

Students Speak Out
ON CAMPUS HOUSING

"North has a good location, but the dorm rooms are pretty rundown. If you're a freshman, I'd definitely try getting into Northwest; or South, if you're an upperclassman."

The College Prowler Take
ON CAMPUS HOUSING

Q "The new freshmen dorms are pretty nice, although they're substance-free. They just redid them, and I got to live in them the first year they were open. As far as niceness and cleanliness, they are the best. **I would stay away from Towers, East, and Buckley**; they are basically the most inconvenient dorms."

Q "North Campus, or 'the Jungle,' has had a reputation of a party area, but I lived there this year, and I'm glad I did. They aren't the nicest dorms, but the atmosphere was great. The dorms all together are pretty much the same for underclassmen in levels of niceness. I mean, **they aren't anything spectacular**; it's just, pretty much, what you'd expect dorms to be."

Q "You definitely don't want Towers. They slapped a pretty new face on the buildings a few years ago, but the inside is still nasty. **It's dark and small, and it smells**. I swear every floor has this weird smell. Hilltop, McMahon, and South are really nice, but as a freshman, you can pretty much count on having no chance of getting into any of those. I didn't even have a chance this year."

Q "Avoid dorms where **the smell radiates out the door**. Most in Towers are okay."

Northwest or Towers are the best communities for freshmen on campus. Some students complain that Northwest is like another year of high school, but you can't beat it for making friends. The Towers dorms are a bit far, but they have a beautiful new dining hall and buses that run frequently to most parts of campus. The dorms are another facet of campus that has benefited from the massive amounts of state funding, so most of them are pristine. The furniture ranges from dorm to dorm. In some dorms, such as Northwest, it's nice and can be arranged in many different ways.

Did You Know?

Due to an extreme shortage in housing, which sparked a massive amount of controversy in the spring of 2004, upperclassmen are subjected to a lottery. The school has offered $500 each to any students willing to triple up.

If you live in Northwest, you have a four-hour community service requirement you have to complete before November. Since you have to do something, do "Northwest Fall Fest." It's a festival held for students, but only students volunteering to run it show up. This results in hours of pool and Ping-Pong tournaments populated by volunteers. Executing the largest sacrilege in community service history, I won $10 in a best-of-three pool match while I was knocking off my four hours.

The College Prowler™ Grade on
Campus Housing: B+

A high Campus Housing grade indicates that dorms are clean, well-maintained, and spacious. Other determining factors include variety of dorms, proximity to classes, and social atmosphere.

Off-Campus Housing

The Lowdown
ON OFF-CAMPUS HOUSING

Undergrads in Off-Campus Housing:
35%

Average Rent for a 2BR Apartment:
$500/month

Popular Areas:
Hilltop Apartments, Charter Oak Apartments

Best Time to Look for a Place
During the housing selection, as the best ones are found through ResLife

For Assistance Contact
Department of Residential Life
(860) 486-2926
www.uconn.edu/housing.html

Students Speak Out
ON OFF-CAMPUS HOUSING

Q "I'd say it's worth it by junior year. For the first couple of years, **it's nice to live in a dorm community** and meet people."

Q "There are some apartments off campus, but they aren't very nice and are **significantly more expensive than the dorms**. They do have free bus service to and from campus during the day, though."

Q "It depends. I lived in **the brand new Hilltop Apartments** off campus, and they were right there and very nice. Most of the other apartments have a bus that goes to them, but they aren't as well-kept."

Q "Off-campus housing can easily be found, but **I would highly recommend living on campus**, at least for your freshman year. The people you meet in the halls that first year are integral in establishing friendships and strong habits for survival."

The College Prowler Take
ON OFF-CAMPUS HOUSING

Since UConn is out in the middle of nowhere, most of the off-campus apartments are out in the woods. The off-campus apartments vary from horrible, to mediocre, to truly awe-inspiring. Everyone agrees that the Hilltop Apartments are where it's at. Do your research if you think that off-campus living is for you, and make sure that both the lifestyle and place of residence match your needs.

"Some awesome apartments have recently gone up. There are other apartments that are decent, but I don't know too much about them. Hilltop Apartments are definitely the best."

The College Prowler™ Grade on
Off-Campus Housing: B

A high grade in Off-Campus Housing indicates that apartments are of high quality, close to campus, affordable, and easy to secure.

Diversity

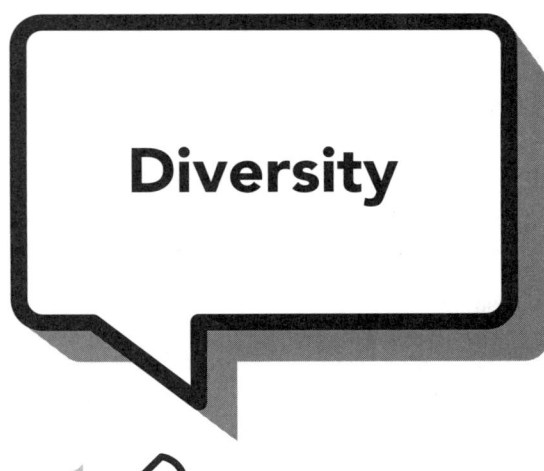

Political Activity

Students at UConn are generally apathetic about political issues, although the liberal school newspaper, *The Daily Campus*, has a commentary section that is always a fun read over breakfast. Unless the government reinstates prohibition, it's doubtful there will be any political-based, on-campus riots. There are clubs for both Democrats and Republicans on campus, and the women's rights groups are also pretty active. UConn PIRG is the environmental group on campus, funded by a small optional fee added to every student's tuition bill. They work diligently to challenge the state's legislation on issues regarding Connecticut's environment, and volunteer to keep it clean.

The Lowdown
ON DIVERSITY

African American: 5%

Asian American: 6%

Hispanic: 5%

Native American: 0%

White: 83%

International: 1%

Out-of-State: 23%

Gay Tolerance

The Rainbow Center (*www.rainbowcenter.uconn.edu/index.html*) is the organization on campus dedicated to creating a positive environment for the lesbian, gay, bisexual, transgender, queer, and questioning people at the University of Connecticut. To quote their Website: "Surveys conducted at the University of Connecticut have found that gay, lesbian, bisexual, transgender, queer, and questioning students, faculty, and staff often feel isolated and unsupported. Some have experienced harassment; many fear negative consequences if others were to learn of their sexual orientation. Many feel that they have few safe places in which to acknowledge who they are and share their experiences, both positive and negative." The Rainbow Center is working to promote gay tolerance, but the campus is definitely not as open-minded about gay rights as they would like it to be.

Minority Clubs

There are over 30 ethnic-based clubs on campus, but some minority clubs are larger than others. The African American and Asian clubs are probably the most visible on campus, and usually participate in events such as those sponsored by SUBOG. Though there are many minority organizations, they are not a large part of the social scene on campus.

Most Popular Religions

Almost every religious club dedicated to a particular religion listed on the school's Website is Christian, and that says it all. There are several churches right on campus, along North Eagleville Road. Campus Crusade for Christ (CCC) is an active Christian organization and the most visible on campus. There is also a Jewish, Muslim, and Buddhist presence on campus.

Students Speak Out
ON DIVERSITY

"UConn isn't very diverse. Everyone kind of melts together and becomes part of the UConn community, but the amount of cultural diversity is not very visable."

"It seems pretty diverse. I've met **many different types of people**. The University is trying to make the campus more tolerant."

- "The campus is **sort of diverse**, but it is mainly Caucasian."
- "There are lots of different people, and there are also the normal types of discrimination. **People here are very homophobic**—it's kind of ridiculous."
- "It is fairly diverse. However, **certain majors are, or seem to be, segregated**—not by University design, just by interest."

The College Prowler Take
ON DIVERSITY

Though UConn's efforts to enhance cultural and geographic diversity resulted in a 27 percent increase in the number of minority freshmen in recent years, the campus is predominately, if not overwhelmingly, white. Also, it must be taken into consideration that all numbers regarding percentages of minorities include the satellite campuses in areas that have more minorities. Though there are students from everywhere in the world, and those students comprise a significant percentage of the student body, their cultural influence is lacking. This is certainly not to say that students from all races and walks of life are not friends with each other, or that the general population is racist, but diversity will never jump out at you when you walk out of your dorm. This is evident by the way most students answer the question: most believe that diversity simply means seeing people from other races on campus.

The College Prowler™ Grade on
Diversity: D

A high grade in Diversity indicates that ethnic minorities and international students have a notable presence on campus and that students of different economic backgrounds, religious beliefs, and sexual preferences are well-represented.

Guys & Girls

The Lowdown
ON GUYS & GIRLS

Women Undergrads: 52%

Men Undergrads: 48%

Birth Control Available?
Yes, check with the Department of Health Services.

Social Scene
UConn is a social explosion. Everyone has their own group, more or less, and, with such a diverse array of personalities, compatibility is almost guaranteed.

Hookups or Relationships?
Because the underclassman social scene on campus mainly consists of dancing and drinking at off-campus parties, it would seem that hooking up is the thing to do. That wouldn't be far from the truth, as there are many single people, but there is also a good percentage of relationships. It seems that at UConn, most people are dating seriously or looking to by their junior year.

Dress Code
The dress for the most part is preppy: A&F is huge. Jeans and a tight T-shirt are pretty standard for girls, while the guys tend to go with jeans, or cargo pants, and a sweatshirt.

Students Speak Out
ON GUYS & GIRLS

The College Prowler Take
ON GUYS & GIRLS

{ "It is a big school, so there's a bit of everything. There are a lot of 'fake' people, but some are nice."

Q "The frat boys can be jerks, but most I've met are cool and attractive. **Sorority girls are mostly rude**, but I've met a lot of nice and pretty girls."

Q "There's **a lot of really annoying people**, but I had no trouble meeting people I liked. It's such a big school that there are all sorts of people hanging around."

Q "The people at UConn are definitely great. **There's a great mix**. I haven't really met anyone who wasn't friendly. Generally, people are open and very friendly, and if they aren't, either they don't go to UConn, or they just plain suck. Either way, these types of people are few and far between."

Q "**I met a wonderful guy the day classes began** in August. He became a great friend, whom I fell in love with. He's gorgeous, perfect, and truly the person of my dreams. Now we're engaged. Enough said."

Q "The people here are conceited. Everybody thinks they are better than everybody else. There are decent amounts of hot girls, but most have bad personalities or play games. Personally, I think **all the guys here are nerds**; they both look and act that way. The guys seem ugly, but then again, I really can't judge them."

UConn is a very attractive campus. The biggest problem on campus is meeting people you're potentially compatible with, and the best way to do it is to get involved in activities that interest you. It's not a real good idea to date people on your floor, and you're probably not going to find dates in class, so activities are your best option. With 250 clubs, find something you enjoy, and try to make a few friends doing it. Who knows, maybe you'll get a relationship out of it.

The College Prowler™ Grade on
Guys: B+

A high grade for Guys indicates that the male population on campus is attractive, smart, friendly, and engaging, and that the school has a decent ratio of guys to girls.

The College Prowler™ Grade on
Girls: B

A high grade for Girls not only implies that the women on campus are attractive, smart, friendly, and engaging, but also that there is a fair ratio of girls to guys.

Did You Know?

The most prevalent STD on the University of Connecticut campus is HPV (genital warts).

Athletics

The Lowdown
ON ATHLETICS

Men's Varsity Teams:
Basketball
Baseball
Cross Country
Football
Golf
Ice Hockey
Soccer
Swimming and Diving
Tennis
Track and Field

Women's Varsity Teams:
Basketball
Cross Country
Field Hockey
Ice Hockey
Lacrosse
Rowing
Soccer
Softball
Swimming and Diving

Men's Club Sports:
Baseball
Crew
Cycling
Ultimate Frisbee
Wrestling
Kayaking
Lacrosse
Pistol and Rifle
Polo
Roller Hockey
Rugby
Sailing
Ski
Soccer
Volleyball

Women's Club Sports:
Cycling
Equestrian
Field Hockey
Ultimate Frisbee
Ice Hockey
Lacrosse
Morgan Drill Team
Pistol and Rifle
Polo
Rugby
Sailing
Figure Skating
Ski
Tennis
Volleyball

Intramurals (IMs):
Basketball
Spring Ice Hockey
Inner Tube Water Polo
Spring Bowling League
Wallyball
Swimming
Flag football
Soccer
Volleyball
Tennis Doubles
Tennis Singles
Softball
Running
Track and Field
Fall Bowling
Fall Sand Volleyball
Fall Ice Hockey
Great Pie Race
Badminton Singles
Badminton Doubles
Racquetball Singles

Athletic Division
NCAA Division I

School Mascot
Jonathan the Husky Dog

Overlooked Teams
The varsity track team is highly overlooked, along with field hockey and soccer. These sports tend to take the backseat to the high-profile sports, such as football and basketball, even though they're incredibly competitive.

Students Speak Out
ON ATHLETICS

"Sports are big. The intramurals are competitive, and UConn basketball is really big. They also recently opened up a football stadium."

"Basketball pretty much runs the school—the games are really fun to go to. The other sports such as soccer, football, [and] baseball have a following, but they're definitely not as popular as basketball. Intramurals are definitely fun, and there are a bunch of different leagues. So, depending on how competitive you want it to be, there's pretty much a league that caters to everyone, which is cool. If you're just going to have fun, you don't have to play against people whose lives revolve around that sport."

Q "I know that you know about the men and women's basketball teams. The girls are always ranked number one, and the men are normally ranked in the twenties and won the championship in 1999 [and 2004]. I guess **our soccer teams are ranked high also**. The IM sports are pretty big."

Q "Sports are a big part of UConn. I've gone to all the men's basketball games, and some women's games, and it's a blast. There are **a lot of really good teams** here, and they're fun to watch. For all of us who can't quite play at a Division I level, intramurals [IMs] are also big. They have a lot of IM sports, and a bunch of people I know participate."

The College Prowler Take
ON ATHLETICS

Athletics at UConn are huge. One of the most prominent, and intimidating, places on campus is Gampel Pavilion: the dome that hosts men's and women's basketball. The newly built Rentschler Field is the new football stadium that seats over 40,000 people, which was built for the football team. Most of the traditions on campus are embedded in the athletic program. Intramural sports are all encompassing and offer something for everyone of any skill level that wishes to get involved. If you want to get involved with an intramural sport, head over to the field house and check the message board early in the semester. They fill up quickly, so if it's something you want to do, make it a priority the first week you're on campus to look into it.

The College Prowler™ Grade on
Athletics: A

A high grade in Athletics indicates that students have school spirit, that sports programs are respected, that games are well-attended, and that intramurals are a prominent part of student life.

Greek Life

The Lowdown
ON GREEK LIFE

Number of Fraternities:
24

Number of Sororities:
7

Students Speak Out
ON GREEK LIFE

"**I'm not in a frat, but a few of my roommates have been in one, and they seemed to enjoy it. I've been to a couple of decent frat parties, but it's not like you need to be a part of Greek life to fit in or have fun.**"

Q "The Greek life at UConn is there, but I don't think it really dominates. I mean, I've been to some frat parties, but **there really isn't a 'frat row'** like some other big campuses. I mean, they're present, but not really that big."

Q "**Frat life doesn't dominate.** I know a couple people in frats, and they're just involved with it, it's not their life at all. I don't know many people in search of a fraternity or sorority."

Q "Greek life isn't too dominating. They have parties, but **they are not big shots**. Some people might think they are better than everyone else because they are in a frat or sorority. I knew some people like that."

Q "The fraternities are really poor, in terms of quality of character. **The sororities are cool**, though. I know a few of the ladies in the sororities, and they are really nice."

Q "Greek life is good here. I have been in a fraternity since my freshman year, and I have to say I have enjoyed it. **The Greeks throw the best parties**. Greek life isn't as big here as other schools, but it is getting bigger."

The College Prowler Take
ON GREEK LIFE

Most of the fraternities on campus are service- or academic-based, and don't throw parties. Also, a large majority also focus on volunteering, which makes them a good way to get involved in the community, while enjoying the benefits of Greek life. However, the frats that are socially-based are known to throw the biggest parties. Some of the houses are fraternities and some are not, but the house parties are well-attended by freshman and sophomores. At UConn, Greek life is something students go out and find if they want to. It's not an overwhelming facet of the school's social structure.

The College Prowler™ Grade on
Greek Life: B-

A high grade in Greek Life indicates that sororities and fraternities are not only present, but also active on campus. Other determining factors include the variety of houses available and the respect the Greek community receives from the rest of the campus.

Drug Scene

The Lowdown
ON DRUG SCENE

Most Prevalent Drugs on Campus:
Alcohol and marijuana

Drug Counseling Program:
The HEART program

Students Speak Out
ON DRUG SCENE

{ "The drug scene exists. Alcohol and pot are prevalent, but more stuff is around, underground."

Q "The drug scene isn't that prevalent. There have been **some pretty decent busts**, but you definitely won't walk down the hall and be swamped with drugs. Pot is definitely common among UConn students."

Q "I don't really use drugs. Plenty of people smoke pot, but not so many that it's bothered me. Unfortunately, **we had a student who overdosed on heroin this year**, but that's more the exception than the rule. I've never been around any serious drug use."

Q "Ecstasy and pot are both present, depending on where you live. **Dealers come and go all the time,** because of the cops. Watch out for narcs. I wouldn't say there is too much drug use on campus, though."

Q "Drugs are not that big on campus, at least from my perspective. Marijuana is probably the most prominent narcotic. **There have been incidents with cocaine and heroin,** but those were one-time incidents."

Q "Although there are **strict rules** against it, many kids still do what they want."

The College Prowler Take
ON DRUG SCENE

Though it may be naïve to believe that drugs aren't present on campus, you can certainly gain that impression from living in the dry dorms. The rules are stringent against drug use, and students caught engaging in illegal activity are placed on a wait-list for housing. Although alcohol is present in all of the dorms, and marijuana can be found with connections, the drug scene is not prominent. Marijuana is the most prevalent drug used on campus by far, and relatively easy to acquire, but you won't see it if you don't want to. Willimantic is home to some off-campus students and is known for drug problems. The drug scene can best be described as "private."

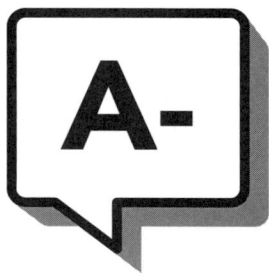

The College Prowler™ Grade on
Drug Scene: A-

A high grade on Drug Scene indicates that drugs are not a noticeable part of campus life; drug use is not visible, and no pressure to use them seems to exist.

Campus Strictness

The Lowdown
ON CAMPUS STRICTNESS

What Are You Most Likely to Get Caught Doing on Campus?

DWI/DUI, parking illegally, plagiarism, noise violations, smoking pot in the dorms, drinking in the substance-free dorms

Students Speak Out
ON CAMPUS STRICTNESS

"The police are pretty cool if you've been drinking but aren't visibly drunk. If you're causing a disruption, though, they'll nail you."

Q "Around here, UConn has a bit of a reputation as a party school. **The school is trying to crack down on the drinking,** but we're not sure if we should take it seriously or as a joke. Northwest dorms are substance-free since it's freshmen housing. They're trying to make Towers and North Campus substance-free next year as well, but no one really believes they can enforce it. There's a smoke-free dorm in every complex."

Q "The campus is not too strict. A lot of the time, they can't control us, because there are so many people doing things. **You have to be careful about drugs**, though. Some resident assistants [RAs] are cool, but others will get you in trouble if you do anything wrong."

Q "Well, there has been quite the crackdown this year with drugs, but it really depends on the situation. I know someone who got arrested for marijuana, but they ended up getting community service and having to take a drug awareness class. Then again, other people have been all-out arrested and tossed in jail for the same thing. My word of advice is to **be very careful around campus police**—they change their views, constantly."

Q "There were several drug busts two weeks before classes ended, and as an RA, I documented over 100 people for underage drinking. It was much higher than the average, but the point is, **some RAs are less likely to ignore drinking**, while others are more likely; it's all luck."

Q "Campus police are strict on drinking by minors and drugs, but **it's easy not to get caught**. Don't drink outside or on the street. If you're drinking or doing drugs in the dorms, just make sure the door is shut, or there are no RAs around. In the dorms, it always helps if you're less noisy, too, since it attracts more attention if you are noisy."

The College Prowler Take
ON CAMPUS STRICTNESS

Overall, what you'll be able to get away with will be determined by those responsible for your punishments. If your RA is really strict, you'll be written up for noise violations, having alcohol, and, especially, any drug use. Test the waters with your RA before doing things you could get in trouble for. If you don't respect that your RA has a job to do, they'll be stricter with you; getting to know them is a good idea. The campus police will tell you that they won't arrest you for being drunk, only for causing a disturbance or underage possession. Don't be afraid to walk home directly from an off-campus party and go past the police, as long as you don't still have alcohol on you. The campus is strict enough to keep people happy and safe, but things are loose enough to leave you in control of your own partying destiny.

Want to know how far you can go with partying on campus? Find out what you can and can't get away with in the College Prowler book on UConn available at *www.collegeprowler.com*.

The College Prowler™ Grade on
Campus Strictness: B-

A high Campus Strictness grade implies an overall lenient atmosphere; police and RAs are fairly tolerant, and the administration's rules are flexible.

Overall Experience

Q "I loved UConn. When I graduated last week, I cried for hours because I know I will never be as happy as I was these last four years. The people I have met, and the memories I have made, will be with me always; **I don't regret anything, for a second.**"

Q "I like it a lot, but it gets a little dull, with **barely any cultural outlets nearby**. If you can deal with not much in the winter, besides indoor sports, drinking in the dorms, and snowball fights, you'll be fine."

Students Speak Out
ON OVERALL EXPERIENCE

The College Prowler Take
ON OVERALL EXPERIENCE

"UConn wasn't my first choice last year, but I am glad I went here. I wouldn't go anywhere else. It's kind of in the middle of nowhere, but at the same time, it's between any city you'd ever want to go to."

Q "It just felt right for me to go to UConn, and I can say right now that I couldn't be happier with my decision. The school is great academically, and it's getting better. **The state just gave us like $1.6 billion to do construction** and improve the school, overall. I know it's the plan of the state to make UConn a top-10 public school in the country. Plus, we have a good sports program, and the parties on and off campus are ridiculous. There are always parties going on every weekend, and the parties off campus aren't far at all. Everything is located within a mile of campus, so it's pretty easy to get around."

Q "I'm very happy here. I've never regretted coming to UConn. It is a nice mix of academics, athletics, and social aspects. **I feel like I'm getting a good education**. I am pretty involved around campus and enjoying myself."

Q "I love my school. Yeah, it has its problems, but the people you end up hanging with are great. There is **something here for everyone**."

For many students, UConn wasn't a first choice, but after discovering all it had to offer, few students can imagine themselves having ended up anywhere else. There is, literally, something for everyone. The University of Connecticut is a very large school. With over 10,000 undergraduates, you will not have your opportunities handed to you. For example, in high school and at smaller colleges, it's common for a music teacher to do some recruiting. At the University of Connecticut, you could be Charlie Parker and stay hidden. This applies to every aspect of campus life. If you don't go out and get what you want, you'll sit idly in your dorm room doing little more than class work, and you'll meet few people other than those on your floor. Motivation is, at UConn, either a most fervent asset or your most cankerous liability. No one will make your college experience for you, and you are guaranteed to get out only as much as you put in. Joining one of the 250-plus clubs on campus is the best way to get involved, and there is something for everyone. From ballroom dancing to fencing, and a wide array of activities, from martial arts to the marching band, there is no excuse to ever be bored. Most have been very happy with their college experience, but some have been overwhelmed at the 200-plus students in their freshmen seminars. Make sure you fit, before plunging headlong into the deep blue sea that is a large research university like UConn.

The Inside Scoop

The Lowdown
ON THE INSIDE SCOOP

School Spirit
At every college, the student running naked and/or drunk across the quad garners more attention than the student in the library. School spirit is very prominent on campus, and sports are one of the largest attractions, but that scene isn't for everyone. There are students who live and breathe Husky sports, those who couldn't care less, and everything in between. Love it or ignore it, you can't avoid seeing the Husky-mania.

Traditions
Spring Weekend
Thousands of students from UConn and the surrounding schools come out to party each night of Spring Weekend for concerts and widespread inebriation. Each night of the weekend holds an official, or unofficial, campus event in either one of the giant parking lots, on campus or at the off-campus apartments.

Midnight Madness
Midget Madness is a pep rally held in Gampel Pavilion to kick off the first official practice of the men's basketball season.

Rubbing Jonathan's Nose
Rubbing the nose of the Husky mascot, Jonathan, whose statue resides in front of Gampel Pavillion, is considered good luck for exams.

Ooze-ball
Ooze-ball is volleyball played in mud during the senior week festivities.

Football
Due to the recent completion of the new field in Hartford, the old traditions were left behind, but UConn is in the process of forming new ones.

Winter Weekend
SUBOG sponsors a full weekend of entertaining events which usually include a dance, a big name concert, and other, smaller events. Last year, Dashboard Confessional played an acoustic show, which was attended by the guys' families.

Things I Wish I Knew Before Coming to UConn:
- It is widely rumored that an approximate 60 percent of the campus has HPV (genital warts).
- Communicate with your roommate about what you're each bringing; you don't need two microwaves.
- Orientation is actually horrible for everyone.
- Don't buy 300 meals.

Tips to Succeed at UConn:
- Research your professors at either http://myprofessorsucks.com or www.ratemyprofessors.com/index.jsp.
- Utilize the library.
- Utilize WebCT, which is the online resource for all of your classes. Its usefulness varies from class to class; it can be accessed from the *students.uconn.edu* Web page.
- Go to your professors' office hours and participate in class. If they can pick your face out of a crowd, it will help you later on.
- In the bigger classes, grading will be formulaic. Figure out what they want, and give it to them to the best of your ability.
- Go. To. Class. It doesn't matter if you don't know what's going on. In giant lectures, it's very easy to get lost, and the professors aren't motivated to help you if you haven't attended. Don't count on getting other people's notes too often or as a rule—only in emergencies. The things you absorb in class, and would write down, are individual.
- Use your Husky Mail account.

Finding a Job or Internship

The Lowdown
ON FINDING A JOB OR INTERNSHIP

Career Center Resources & Services:
ExpLORE program, career counseling, Career Cafés and career cairs (Schedules are online at www.career.uconn.edu), internships, cooperative education, job shadowing community service, summer/part-time jobs, on-campus recruiting program

Alumni Services
Continuing Education; Interfolio, which is an online credential and reference service; Drake Beam Morin, which offers extensive, career development opportunities, such as networking and career consultation; Discover Me, a personality-based recruiting service on the Internet; Resume Referral, which maintains a referral database that employers may access.

The Alumni Center
The Alumni Center is the headquarters for any of the 162,000 alumni returning to Storrs, and the hub for the many services the alumni association offers. The building also houses the Husky Heritage Sports Museum and a library, which features books by UConn alumni.

Major Alumni Events
The Alumni Center sponsors over 300 events, the largest of which are Senior Week, the Reunion Weekend, Homecoming, and numerous awards ceremonies such as the Awards Gala.

Alumni Publications
MemberExtra! and *The MemberExtra! Magazine*

UConn has a top-notch Career Services department, whose mission is to help students network with the plethora of businesses that are constantly in touch with the school. Though they see mostly students in their junior year who've finally gotten around to going, they target first- and second-year students in an attempt to start the process early.

Advice
Though by now it borders on redundancy, you have to take the initiative. The earlier you go to the office, the earlier they can begin to make you marketable. They offer the ExpLORE program, which can help undergraduates of any semester or state of confusion about their major, to begin to explore career options. The program gets you early access to career fairs, contact information for job leads, helps you write resumes, and promotes networking. Enrollment meetings are in February and March.

Did You Know?
Famous UConn Alumni:
Fred Contrata (Class of '90), CFO of Zurich Global Energy, Bermuda

Kirstie Alley and Meg Ryan, famous actresses (both did not graduate from UConn)

The Best & Worst

The Ten BEST Things About UConn:

1. Basketball!
2. Spring Weekend
3. Football at the new stadium
4. 6,000 members of the opposite sex
5. Academic and technological support
6. It feels like both a rural community and a developed city
7. Intramural sports
8. State tuition
9. Location (in between New York and Boston)
10. Snow (when it starts)

The Ten WORST Things About UConn:

1. Parking
2. Math teachers
3. Construction
4. The "Wind Tunnel Effect"
5. New England weather in general
6. Lots of competition
7. Foreign TAs
8. STDs—eek!
9. Location (middle of nowhere)
10. Snow (when it won't end)

University of Massachusetts

181 President's Drive, Amherst, MA 01003-9291
www.umass.edu   (413) 545-0222

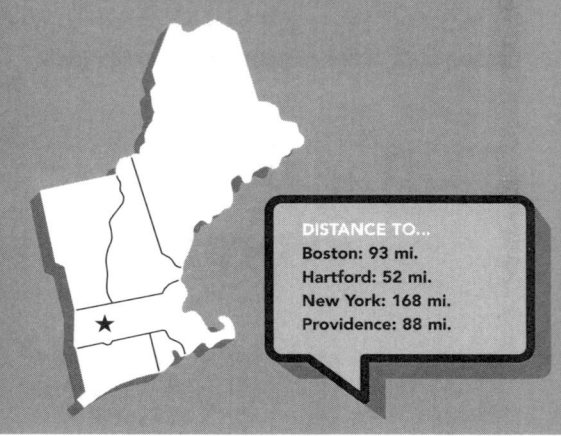

DISTANCE TO...
Boston: 93 mi.
Hartford: 52 mi.
New York: 168 mi.
Providence: 88 mi.

"Just because everyone in the world appears to go to UMass, it doesn't mean UMass is for everyone in the world."

Table of Contents

Academics	51
Local Atmosphere	53
Safety & Security	54
Computers	56
Facilities	57
Campus Dining	59
Off-Campus Dining	60
Campus Housing	62
Off-Campus Housing	64
Diversity	65
Guys & Girls	67
Athletics	69
Greek Life	71
Drug Scene	72
Campus Strictness	74
Overall Experience	75
The Inside Scoop	77
Finding a Job or Internship	78
The Best & Worst	79

Total Enrollment:
17,379

Acceptance Rate:
82%

Tuition:
$9,008 in-state, $17,861 out-of-state

Top 10% of High School Class:
16%

Average GPA:
3.3

SAT Range

Verbal	Math	Total
520 – 630	510 – 610	1030 – 1240

SAT II
Not Required

Most Popular Majors:
19% Social Sciences
14% Business
9% Communications
7% Psychology
5% Engineering

Students Also Applied To:*
Boston University, Northeastern University, Boston College, University of New Hampshire

* For more school info check out www.college.prowler.com

College Prowler Report Card

Academics	B
Local Atmosphere	C
Safety & Security	B
Computers	C+
Facilities	B-
Campus Dining	C+
Off-Campus Dining	B+
Campus Housing	B-
Off-Campus Housing	C
Diversity	C-
Guys	A-
Girls	A-
Athletics	B
Greek Life	B+
Drug Scene	B-
Campus Strictness	A-

Academics

The Lowdown
ON ACADEMICS

Degrees Awarded:
Associate, Bachelor, Master, Doctorate

Undergraduate Schools:
Commonwealth College Honors Program, School of Education, College of Engineering, Graduate School, College of Humanities and Fine Arts, College of Natural Resources and the Environment, College of Natural Sciences and Mathematics, School of Nursing, Isenberg School of Management, School of Public Health and Health Sciences, College of Social and Behavioral Sciences

Full-time Faculty:
1,218

Faculty with Terminal Degree:
94%

Student-to-Faculty Ratio:
18:1

Average Course Load:
5 courses

AP Test Score Requirements:
Possible credit for scores of 3 or higher

IB Test Score Requirements:
Not looked at for admissions purposes, only placement

Best Places to Study
Library, Campus Center, and empty classrooms

Sample Academic Clubs
Alchemists Anonymous, ALANA Nursing Association, Alpha Lambda Delta, Art History Club, Boltwood Project, Chamber Choir, Debate Team, Environmental Horticultural Club, Hotel Managers, Institute of Industrial Engineers, International Relations Club, Investment Club, Macintosh Users Group, National Society of Black Engineers, National Society of Collegiate Scholars, NSSLHA, Philosophical Society, Pre-Vet and Animal Science Club, Society of Hispanic Professional Engineers, Society of Physics Students, Society of Women Engineers, Sport Managers of Color, Student Film Society, Student Nurses Association, Student Society of Arboriculture, Student Sports Managers, Wildlife Society, Women in Sports Management

Did You Know?

UMass alumni are high achievers. They count among their ranks an astronaut, a Nobel Prize winner, Pulitzer Prize winners, four MacArthur "Genius" award recipients, state and federal lawmakers, Olympic athletes, several Fortune 500 CEOs, and scores of influential scholars, scientists, and engineers.

The University of Massachusetts Medical School's primary care education is listed among the top 10 percent of the nation's 125 medical schools, according to several national scholarly reviews.

Students Speak Out
ON ACADEMICS

The College Prowler Take
ON ACADEMICS

"The teachers at my school are unbelievable! The general education professors I've had have been decent, for the most part, and many of the University's faculty have won awards for their teaching and research."

Q "**Professors at UMass are a mixed bag.** You could get a total idiot, or a complete genius. I have lucked out with teachers, but others haven't been so lucky. The teachers within your major are bound to be good, but don't expect too much out of general education courses."

Q "One important thing to consider, before you go to UMass, is the registration process. Before this year, getting into the classes you wanted was not a problem. However, this year, and probably for a couple of years to come, **registering will be very difficult** for people because some teachers were cut, and the classes seem to be filling up very quickly."

Q "It's hard to generalize about the faculty at UMass. **Some of them are amazing** and really care about the students. On the other hand, I've had some really terrible professors who are obviously only here for research. A lot of introductory classes have more than 400 students, but there are usually small discussion sections with a graduate TA. I've never had a TA who wasn't really helpful."

Q "My experience has been that **professors tend to be condescending**. I don't know if that is especially the case at UMass, but I have had a lot of teachers whose egos get in the way of their teaching."

Q "**People always talk about how important it is to have a diverse student body**, which is true, but I also think it is important to have a diverse faculty, and UMass does. The point is to get as many points of view as possible."

Many of the students polled feel as though the faculty at UMass are more than capable of doing their jobs. Unfortunately, the combination of budget cuts and enrollment procedures have left many students unable to register for the classes they need. Despite the overwhelmingly large, general education courses that each student must satisfy, the breadth and scope of these courses are such that students who have not yet picked a major get exposed to fields that they might not have considered. Conversely, due to UMass's size, students are sure to experience varying degrees of quality among the faculty.

UMass teachers are very good at making themselves available and ensuring that students are able to get help frequently and on an individual basis. Whether through e-mail, office hours, or weekly tutoring sessions, students can readily access teachers at any point in the semester if they are falling behind. Teacher evaluations, conducted at the end of each semester by the students, are taken quite seriously by the faculty, which helps keep the class formats up-to-date and of a high quality. One strength that UMass possesses over most other schools is the Five College Interchange. This program allows students to take courses at any one of the four colleges in the immediate area, for no additional charge. These colleges include; Hampshire, Holyoke, Smith, and Amherst.

The College Prowler™ Grade on
Academics: B

A high Academics grade generally indicates that professors are knowledgeable, accessible, and genuinely interested in their students' welfare. Other determining factors include class size, how well professors communicate, and whether or not classes are engaging.

Local Atmosphere

Students Speak Out
ON LOCAL ATMOSPHERE

"You can definitely tell the locals from the outsiders, but there is a mutual respect because both groups have to be here. Amherst is lovely."

Q "**We are in the 'Five College' circuit**, with Amherst College, Mount Holyoke, Smith, and Hampshire, all less than 20 minutes away. UMass offers the Five College Interchange option of taking classes at any of the surrounding schools, for no additional charge."

Q "**The center of Amherst is right outside of UMass's campus**, in reasonable walking distance. It's always hopping. There are shops, a mall, and a movie theater a quick bus ride away. I personally enjoy quaint little Amherst. It feels old-fashioned."

Q "In every way, **Amherst is a college town**. All the businesses are dependent on the colleges around them, but it's a very nice atmosphere. Down near Smith College is Northampton, and the bus goes right there. It's a great town with a lot of history, culture, and some very nice restaurants. Everyone loves the movie theater, where the shows are only five dollars."

Q "It's like any place really, it's all what you make of it. I didn't want to come here right after high school, but I didn't get into any of the Boston schools, not like I could afford them. Amherst grew on me, and now **I'm glad that I'm not in a big city**."

Q "Amherst is a small town with two colleges—UMass and Amherst College. Northampton is about five, or six, miles down the road. It's a trendy town with lots of shops, restaurants, and music halls. The Northhampton district is lively, while **Amherst is more laid-back**."

The Lowdown
ON LOCAL ATMOSPHERE

Region:
Northeast

City, State:
Amherst, Massachusetts

Setting:
Suburban

Distance from Boston:
2 hours

Distance from New York:
3 hours

Points of Interest:
Downtown Amherst and Northampton

City Websites:
www.amherstcommon.com
www.amherstarea.com

Did You Know?

One way to tell a local from an outsider in Amherst is the way they pronounce Amherst. Outsiders say "Am-herst," while locals say "Am-erst."

The College Prowler Take
ON LOCAL ATMOSPHERE

Amherst is a lively college town that clearly demonstrates New England's characteristic atmosphere. The richness and volume of culture in Amherst, and nearby Northampton, exemplify exactly what people usually associate with the word "college." During semesters, Amherst gets crowded and takes on the likeness of a metropolis; however, during summer and winter breaks, Amherst could pass for any other rural farming community. The visible relationship between native Amherst residents, businesses, and the surrounding schools is one of the synergistic benefits of going to UMass. As previously mentioned, five major colleges are in the immediate area: Mount Holyoke College, Amherst College, Hampshire College, Smith College, and of course, the University of Massachusetts. Therefore, during the school year, Amherst is an exciting town.

The College Prowler™ Grade on
Local Atmosphere: C

A high Local Atmosphere grade indicates that the area surrounding campus is safe and scenic. Other factors include nearby attractions, proximity to other schools, and the town's attitude toward students.

Safety & Security

The Lowdown
ON SAFETY & SECURITY

Number of UMass Police:
350

Phone:
(413) 545-2121

Health Center Office Hours:
Open 24 hours a day during the semester, and from 8 a.m. to midnight during summer and winter breaks

Safety Services:
Emergency phones located all across campus (a.k.a. "blue-phones," or "call-boxes"), Rape Defense classes (RAD), walking escorts, campus shuttle

Did You Know?

The most read section of the *UMass Daily Collegian* is the police log section, which records any arrests that took place on campus.

The UMass police department commonly patrols campus by horseback.

Students Speak Out
ON SAFETY & SECURITY

"Every dorm building has security 'check-ins' on the weekends—you have to have a dorm sticker on your student card, or be signed in by someone who lives in the building, to get in."

Q "Be aware of your surroundings, and **always walk with someone else at night**. The campus is pretty well-lit, and there are 'call boxes' along the paths. As a nursing major, I spent many long nights at the library but made sure that I always walked home with friends."

Q "Security has been really good the last couple of years, but with the recent budget cuts, **the escort service was eliminated**. The escort service was a van driven by a campus police officer that made stops around campus from 5 p.m. to 3 a.m. It was incredibly reliable, but it's gone, replaced with buses that run later, into the wee hours of the morning."

Q "Occasionally, non-students come onto campus and cause problems, but there isn't any way to prevent that. The only time I have ever felt nervous was walking around at night, both during the week and on the weekends. Just be aware of your surroundings, and **lock your dorm room**."

Q "Honestly, **security and safety need improvement**. There have been attacks and rapes on campus just this spring, but they're improving security. There are a lot of resources to use, if you're willing to help yourself."

Q "My freshmen year, I heard about these people who were all dressed up, and came to a Northeast building telling people to leave for an hour so they could fumigate. Then, when the students got back, all of their valuable stuff was gone. **What a great idea for a robbery**!"

The College Prowler Take
ON SAFETY & SECURITY

A strong focus is placed on safety and security, both on and off campus at UMass. Colleges, in general, tend to have very high crime rates, and when theft occurs at UMass, it is usually nonviolent and involves microscopes, car stereos, and books. Certain areas of UMass experience more crime than others, a statistic that inevitably coincides with population size. These areas include Southwest, parking lots, and the many off-campus apartment complexes. Students can take many steps to protect themselves from crime, such as walking with friends, walking in well-lit areas, being vocal, locking doors, never leaving a personal item unattended, carrying a cell phone, and remaining alert at all times. Between the Amherst Police Department and the UMass Police Department, most students seem to feel safe on campus.

The College Prowler™ Grade on
Safety & Security: B

A high grade in Safety & Security means that students generally feel safe, campus police are visible, blue-light phones and escort services are readily available, and safety precautions are not overly necessary.

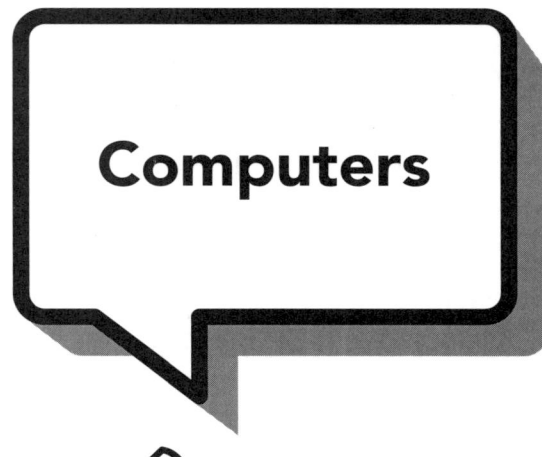

Computers

Students Speak Out
ON COMPUTERS

The Lowdown
ON COMPUTERS

High-Speed Network?
Yes

Wireless Network?
Yes

Number of Labs:
11

Average Number of Computers:
25

24-Hour Labs:
Yes, residential labs

Charge to Print?
Depends on the lab. Library labs have free printing.

Operating Systems:
2 Mac labs, 9 PC labs

{ "**Definitely bring your own computer to campus. It is much easier, and some classes send you e-mail or require you to do some homework on the Web.**"

Q "**The computer network is generally awesome**. Each room has two Ethernet ports, so you and your roommate can each have your own account. Some computer labs are busy, while others aren't at all. If you can bring at least a laptop with an Ethernet card, you'll be golden, because you can do nearly anything from your room."

Q "**Computer labs are rarely crowded**, unless there is a class using the computers. There are always computers available in the library."

Q "The dorm Internet connections are great—**two LAN connections in each room**! Two dorms on campus have computer labs, as well as the Research Center and the library. They're usually pretty empty."

Q "Setting up my computer account for the computer in my room was the biggest headache, except that I didn't even have a choice, because most of my classes required us to do homework on the Internet. The computer labs in the library **offer free printing**, but sometimes they are so busy, not to mention the hike it takes to get from my room to the library. The Internet is fast around here; on the other hand, the computers in the dormitory labs are extremely old and outdated. One good thing about living in the dorms, though, is that you always know someone with a computer, and usually a printer. Even with all this said, I recommend any new students bring their own."

Q "Considering how old some of the buildings are at UMass, the Internet hookups are pretty decent. The library computers are useful, but you have to figure out when there will be classes held at them so you can avoid that. I **never really had any major problems** concerning the computers here."

Facilities

The College Prowler Take
ON COMPUTERS

Ironically, UMass has a very reputable computer science program, yet disappointing computer resources for everyone else. Relying on campus computer labs is risky, because they have bizarre hours and get extremely packed. On the bright side, UMass does have excellent Internet access through Ethernet connections. Getting a mandatory OIT account is relatively easy and cheap, but if anything goes wrong, it can take days before you actually get to speak with a live customer service representative. The Office of Information Technologies is wretchedly understaffed, a problem that is only compounded at the beginning of each semester, when all the students are trying to get squared away at the same time. The library labs probably have the nicest computers, and free printing, which is huge. Regardless of whether you are going to live on or off campus, bring your own computer. If you don't have one, and can't afford to purchase a new one, just sell your car—because you won't need that.

The Lowdown
ON FACILITIES

Student Center:
Lincoln Campus Center

Athletic Centers:
William D. Mullins Center, Boyden Gymnasium, Totman Gymnasium

Libraries:
W.E.B. Dubois Library, Biological Sciences Library, Physical Sciences and Engineering Library, AIMS Film/Video Library

Movie Theatre on Campus?
No

Bowling on Campus?
No

Bar on Campus?
Yes. Blue Wall Pub, the University Center

Coffeehouse on Campus?
Yes. Bluewall Coffeehouse, at the University Center

Favorite Things to Do:
Intramural sports, party, join one of over 200 registered student organizations, go on a hike, go to the Holyoke mall

Popular Places to Chill:
Campus Pond, dorms, student union

The College Prowler™ Grade on
Computers: C+

A high grade in Computers designates that computer labs are available, the computer network is easily accessible, and the campus' computing technology is up-to-date.

# Students Speak Out
ON FACILITIES

# The College Prowler Take
ON FACILITIES

"There are lots of computer labs around campus, in places like the English building and the library. The student union and the campus center usually offer a lot."

"**The athletic facilities could be better**, but the student center has a lot of stuff in it, and people always hang out there."

"I really like the campus center, where there is a big store, **a bunch of places to eat**, lots of different clubs to join, and places to study. The library is huge—it's over 20 stories high."

"The campus center and student union are right in the middle of campus and offer many different things, like dining areas, crafts centers, a campus store, and campus tables to advertise the different **student organizations**."

"**The facilities on campus are kind of a mixed bag**: there are some old-fashioned, typical New England-style buildings, and there are some hideous, modern, concrete buildings."

"For a while, the campus was really ugly because of **all the construction going on in front of the Fine Arts Center**. It really depends. UMass has a lot of facilities. The Mullins Center is great, and there is always something happening there. But the gyms for the students are awful, and you'll be lucky if you don't have to stand in line for a treadmill. If you want to see what the nicer UMass facilities are, just take a look at the brochure!"

To a new student, the sheer number and range of facilities at UMass is impressive, and a little intimidating. Overall, the general feeling is that UMass facilities are well-maintained, and offer us students everything we need, and most of what we want. Many of the buildings could use a face-lift, as they appear to have been designed by an architect who lived in communist Russia. The pulse of UMass is located in the campus center, where vendors and student organizations compete against each other for your fickle attention. This complex, which includes the student union, accommodates everything from cafeterias to a mini Wal-Mart known as the University Store. The best advice for anyone contemplating enrollment at UMass, whose decision rests solely on the condition of its facilities, is to deliberate as to whether or not the building housing their major is one they can tolerate spending a lot of time in.

The College Prowler™ Grade on
Facilities: B-

A high Facilities grade indicates that the campus is aesthetically pleasing and well-maintained; facilities are state-of-the-art, and libraries are exceptional. Other determining factors include the quality of both athletic and student centers and an abundance of things to do on campus.

Campus Dining

The Lowdown
ON CAMPUS DINING

Freshman Meal Plan Requirement?
Yes

24-Hour On-Campus Eating?
No

Student Favorites:
People's Market, Blue Wall

Meal Plan Average Cost:
Three options: Basic ($1,206.50 per semester), Value ($1,256.50 per semester), Deluxe ($1,288 per semester)

Did You Know?
It is cheaper to get an off-campus apartment and buy groceries than it is to pay for room and board. As a freshmen and sophomore, you must live in the dorms and get a meal plan unless you live within a 40-mile radius of UMass and commute … hint hint.

Students Speak Out
ON CAMPUS DINING

"There are several good places to eat on campus. The most popular places are The Blue Wall and Coffee Shop. The student union has the People's Market—a great place to grab coffee, juice, and bagels."

Q "I found the dining commons to be fine my first two years at UMass. I ate at the Franklin dining hall, but **by junior year, I was sick of it** and just bought food for my room."

Q "Personally, I think the DCs [dining commons] are pretty good—**I've had worse**. When I eat on campus, I go for Hampshire or Berkshire. Berkshire has the greatest stir-fry. You can get something to eat at the Blue Wall or at People's Market, too—both are great places."

Q "I'll be honest—**the dining commons food sucks**. It's mandatory to eat there for your first two years, which is a huge pain in the butt. We have a few good places on campus, though. The Hatch, Blue Wall, and Greenough Sub Shop are the most common favorites. They serve things ranging from soups and salads, to pizza and subs. Your campus meal plan swipes you into these places. The Hatch is the best place to eat on campus, though few freshmen know this valuable fact."

Q "**The dining halls on campus offer standard campus food**. They're buffet-style, with full salad bars, pasta, and deli areas. There are also some other places on campus to eat. The Blue Wall in the campus center is good."

Q "Basically, the dining hall food on campus sucks. Fortunately, for us, there's a program called 'Off-Campus Meal Plan' [OCMP]. **You can pay extra money to put food from off-campus restaurants on a special card they issue**. It's kind of expensive, but definitely worth it. A couple of good places to eat on campus are not included in the basic meal plan—the Hatch in the basement of the student union is a good one."

The College Prowler Take
ON CAMPUS DINING

UMass dining commons are nothing special. Although, considering the number of people they feed everyday, Food Services keeps the shelves stocked and the cafeterias relatively clean. They have foods for breakfast, lunch, and dinner that are cooked everyday, like pizza, pasta, and salad, and entrees that change every day. If you want a little variety, your best bet is to eat at one of the many cafeterias located all across campus. The best spots are the Newman Center and the Hatch, where you can find anything from Mexican to Asian at reasonable prices. Students have the option of purchasing off-campus meal plans, which allow them to dine at many of the restaurants located near campus. Regardless of what you like, and no matter how picky an eater you are, somewhere on campus you will find something you like.

Off-Campus Dining

The Lowdown
ON OFF-CAMPUS DINING

The College Prowler™ Grade on
Campus Dining: C+

Our grade on Campus Dining addresses the quality of both school-owned dining halls and independent on-campus restaurants as well as the price, availability, and variety of food.

Best Pizza: Antonio's

Best Chinese: China Inn

Best Breakfast: Black Sheep Deli

Best Wings: Wings

Best Healthy: Bueno Y Sano, Banana Rama

Late-Night, Half-Price Food Specials:
None

Best Place to Take Your Parents: The Pub

24-Hour Eating:
None

Closest Grocery Stores:
Stop and Shop
456 Russell St (RTE 9)
Hadley, MA
(413) 253-3227

Did You Know?

As a meal plan option, you can purchase OCMP (Off-Campus Meal Plan), which most off-campus restaurants will accept. However, it really only makes sense to get OCMP if you own a vehicle, or if you don't mind taking the bus.

A company known as Delivery Express (413-549-0077) will deliver food from any of Amherst's restaurants to you.

Students Speak Out
ON OFF-CAMPUS DINING

"Amherst and Northampton are great for dining out. There are several restaurants in the area that range in price as well as the types of food they offer."

"**Restaurants off campus are all very good**. There is Judie's, in the center of Amherst—very good food, but very expensive. The center of town is also home to Antonio's, a popular pizza joint, and Amherst Brewing Company, a very good restaurant which I have been to multiple times. It's your typical, grill-type restaurant with nightly specials."

"Restaurants off campus are usually really good and fairly cheap. Since Amherst attracts a lot of people from all over, there is a wide variety of places to eat, from pizza places to Thai and Indian. **Most of them accept OCMP**. There are also a ton of late-night delivery places, delivering everything you could ever want. If the place you want doesn't deliver, you can call Delivery Express. They will go to any restaurant in the Amherst area and pick it up for you."

"**Ninety percent of the businesses in Amherst are restaurants**, and ninety percent of those have great food—in fact, that is why I came to UMass."

"**Antonio's is, hands down, the best pizza** place ever. They come up with slices you could never imagine on your own. Wings has awesome chicken, and the Sub is the best sub place I've ever eaten at. Amherst Brewing Company is slightly expensive, but it's really good and has live music all the time. Fifteen minutes outside campus is Northampton, a small city with some of the best restaurants in the state, not to mention the four-plus music venues and a great music scene."

The College Prowler Take
ON OFF-CAMPUS DINING

The restaurants off campus are amazing, and most of them deliver. Another great part about Amherst restaurants is that they are fun places to hang out. They are always playing good music, and most have beautiful murals on the walls. On the weekends, they stay open very late to cater to the many people walking around town. As a freshman at UMass, you may learn which restaurants to eat at in town before you even know where the dining commons are.

The College Prowler™ Grade on
Off-Campus Dining: B+

A high Off-Campus Dining grade implies that off-campus restaurants are affordable, accessible, and worth visiting. Other factors include the variety of cuisine and the availability of alternative options (vegetarian, vegan, Kosher, etc.).

Campus Housing

Room Types
Coed dorms (89%), women's dorms (6%), men's dorms (1%), sorority housing (2%), fraternity housing (2%), single-student apartments, married-student apartments, special housing for disabled students, special housing for international students, other housing

Students Speak Out
ON CAMPUS HOUSING

The Lowdown
ON CAMPUS HOUSING

"The dorms aren't as bad as people make them out to be. They are a little small, but living there is a great way to meet people."

Undergrads on Campus:
59%

Number of Dormitories:
41

Number of University-Owned Apartments:
345

Available for Rent:
Mini-fridge with microwave

Cleaning Service?
Bathrooms and hallways, almost every day

You Get:
Closet/wardrobe, bookcases, desk, chair, cable TV, Ethernet, local phone, dresser, window shade

Bed Type:
Twin extra-long (39"x80"); some lofts, some bunk-beds

Also Available: Single sex, special interest options

Q "The dorms are decent, but **stay away from Sylvan**. Southwest is my personal favorite, but only to visit. Sylvan is suite-style, so you're living with five or six other people. Southwest is a huge, concrete mess—the general rule of thumb is that you go there to party, but not to live. I've lived in Central all three years, and I loved it. It's located near just about everything, and the dorms are nice and made of brick."

Q "Sylvan sucks, Northeast is quiet, and **Orchard Hill is nice and quiet**. Central has a bit of a drug culture, but they're very open-minded and laid-back. Southwest is a big party area with tall towers, and the people there are pretty shallow. I lived in a low-rise in Southwest for two years, and I thought it was pretty fun. I will probably be an RA in Central in a year or so, because Central is pretty cool."

Q "There are five areas on campus: Central, Southwest, Sylvan, Northeast, and Orchard Hill. I have lived in Central for three years, and think that it is the nicest area on campus. Northeast and Orchard Hill are also pretty nice. I'd avoid Sylvan because the rooms can get a little small, and Southwest because it's just a lot of concrete stairwells and such, which kind of creeps me out."

Q "Some dorms are nice and some are not. **There are five areas, each with a distinct feel to them**. Southwest is the urban center of campus. There are five high-rises going up 22 floors, and 11 low-rises with four floors each. About a quarter of the students at UMass live there. I think it's supposed to be the most densely populated city block in the world, but it doesn't seem crowded. I live there, and it's a lot of fun. At least once during the year, there is a riot in Southwest—not people breaking everything, but celebrations when the Patriots or Red Sox win, or when the Yankees lose. Everyone here hates the Yankees."

Q "**Northeast has the biggest and cleanest dorms**, but the social life is really bad. It's far away from everything, so if you like a fun, social life and a clean dorm, or you want to be close to everything, live in Southwest in a low-rise. Be sure you don't live in a tower; they suck."

Did You Know?

According to a survey taken in 2003 on *Lazystudents.com*; 75 percent of the 840 college students polled answered "yes" to an online question asking, "Do you pee in the shower?" In other words, bring flip-flops!

The College Prowler Take
ON CAMPUS HOUSING

UMass has five major clusters of dormitories. Each cluster has buildings that are worth avoiding, either because the rooms are too small, or because you won't be able to get work done in your room. Overall, many think Central and Orchard Hill have the best dorms, although Southwest has "Z rooms" that are worth checking out. Living in one of the Southwest towers can be a grueling experience, depending on what floor you are banished to.

UMass is good about placing students in the buildings that they have requested. Unfortunately, because UMass enrolls more students than there is room for, freshmen will rarely, and only under special circumstances, get a single. Not to mention that when the dorm rooms run out, a handful of students have to stay in the Campus Center Hotel until a spot opens up. Much of how you perceive living on campus has to do with your roommate, so if you get stuck with someone whose behavior isn't compatible with your own, change rooms immediately, and keep your fingers crossed.

The College Prowler™ Grade on
Campus Housing: B-

A high Campus Housing grade indicates that dorms are clean, well-maintained, and spacious. Other determining factors include variety of dorms, proximity to classes, and social atmosphere.

Off-Campus Housing

Students Speak Out
ON OFF-CAMPUS HOUSING

"There are lots of off-campus options, and some are even cheaper than living on campus. Most are right on the bus routes, making it easy to get around."

Q "Off-campus housing is pretty good. There are a lot of places to choose from, but you have to really try hard to get a place. **They are affordable for the most part**—if you are in a four-bedroom place with four people, it will run you about $350 to $400 a month [each]."

Q "**Housing off campus is somewhat hard to find**, but all of it is very close to campus. If you don't have a car, there are buses that will take you right to your living area, whether you live in North Amherst, South Amherst, Northampton, or Sunderland."

Q "There are many options for off-campus housing, but you can't move off campus until junior year. **There are plenty of nice places to live at very affordable prices**. There are plenty of parties out there, too."

Q "**You're required to live on campus your first two years at UMass**. After that, most people choose to move off campus. There are tons of affordable apartments, houses, and condos, either within walking distance of campus, or on the bus route."

Q "If you are smart, **off-campus housing can be much cheaper** than living in the dorms."

The Lowdown
ON OFF-CAMPUS HOUSING

Undergrads in Off-Campus Housing:
41%

Best Time to Look for a Place:
Early summer

For Assistance Contact:
Commuter Services and Housing Resource Center
Web: www-ims.oit.umass.edu/~cshrc
Phone: (413) 545-0865
Fax: (413) 545-3633
E-mail: cshrc@stuaf.umass.edu

COLLEGE PROWLER™

Need help finding the right spot for your new, dorm-free abode? For a detailed listing of local rent and utility prices, check out the College Prowler book on UMass available at *www.collegeprowler.com*.

The College Prowler Take
ON DIVERSITY

Off-campus housing is very similar to living in the dorms, except that you get a bathroom and kitchen that you share with three people as opposed to 30. Actually, if you get off the meal plan and move off campus after your freshman and sophomore year, it can be much cheaper. On the down side, you have to worry about the hassle of getting to class, which basically leaves you with two options: you can either take the bus, which is relatively convenient, or drive your own car, which is relatively inconvenient. The parking lots are far from the classrooms, and you have to purchase a parking permit.

Brandywine is a nice, off-campus place to live, but you can also find apartments that are near UMass and on the bus route, a very convenient situation. Another option that won't leave much in your bank account is to get a house, an alternative that sometimes requires more than four roommates. Excluding the parking issue, the off-campus option is recommended in order to save money and have a quieter place to study than the dorm rooms.

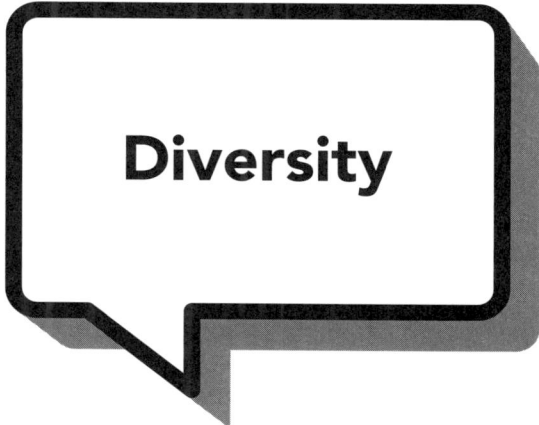

Diversity

The Lowdown
ON DIVERSITY

African American: 4%

Asian American: 7%

Hispanic: 3%

Native American: 1%

White: 84%

International: 1%

Out-of-State: 17%

Minority Clubs
The office of ALANA Affairs (African, Latino/a, Asian/Pacific Islander, and Native American) is a multicultural and educational support agency that exists to serve the needs of UMass's minority population. Universal access to education is a strong theme at UMass, and groups such as ALANA work towards reaching that goal. ALANA is a conglomeration of over 20 minority clubs that remain very active on campus by holding rallies, speeches, and other events to address and solve any problems facing students of an ethnic minority. ALANA can be reached online at *www.umass.edu/alana*.

The College Prowler™ Grade on
Off-Campus Housing: C

A high grade in Off-Campus Housing indicates that apartments are of high quality, close to campus, affordable, and easy to secure.

Most Popular Religions

If there is a "popular" religion on campus, it is probably Christianity. However, there are also registered student organizations on campus that reflect a few other religions. These groups can be found on the UMass website at www.umass.edu/religious_affairs, and include, Alliance Christian Fellowship, Athletes in Action, Campus Crusade for Christ, Chabad House, Christian Faculty Ministry, Episcopal Chaplaincy, First Baptist Church, Hillel House, Intervarsity Christian fellowship, Jewish Affairs, Mercy House, Muslim Students Association, Navigators Christian Ministry, United Christian foundation, Upside down/ International Church of Christ. Despite the number of religious groups, religion plays a minor role at UMass, and is not exceptionally visible on campus.

Political Activity

The town of Amherst, including the students from the University of Massachusetts, is a very politically active place. Most people here are of the liberal persuasion, and will not hesitate to discuss, or argue, any important issue. Many political candidates campaign throughout the year at the various UMass auditoriums. The Student Government Association (SGA) has a very strong presence on campus, and is known for effectively involving students.

Gay Tolerance

The homosexual community at UMass is quite prevalent. Once a year, a rally is held at the student union to discuss issues pertaining to their lifestyle. In fact, Mary Lyon Hall in the Northeast residential area, has a floor where gay, lesbian, bisexual, and transgender students can choose to live together. Also, the Stonewall Center (413-545-4824), a gay, lesbian, bisexual, and transgender educational resource center, offers various information that caters to the homosexual community.

Economic Status

Just about every economic class is represented at UMass. At any given moment, you could see an El Camino and a Lincoln Navigator stopped at the same red light. The students at nearby Amherst College are very affluent, while UMass students, on average, illustrate a more accurate depiction of middle-class America.

Students Speak Out
ON DIVERSITY

"The campus is really diverse. You can learn a lot from other people, racially and culturally, if you make an effort to do so."

"**Groups tend to form around people from the same ethnic groups**. It's understandable, but with more diversity, there'd be more unity."

"**You are almost guaranteed to meet someone from every race at UMass**. You'll meet many people from different cultures—it's great. There are several groups for different cultural backgrounds and sexual orientations, and any type of discrimination is totally unacceptable. Be prepared to come to UMass with an open mind."

"**Diversity was somewhat of an issue before the budget cuts came along**. The minorities on campus had rallies last year, saying not enough minorities were accepted into UMass. It seems to me like there is plenty of diversity."

"**The diversity on this campus is a point of pride**. There are all kinds of people and very little blatant racism. People are cool with most crowds out here."

"At a big school like this, you are bound to have classmates and teachers that are from another country. **Most people here are very accepting of foreigners**, but some have a very narrow view of the world. I'm sure that those people can be found in any country, though."

The College Prowler Take
ON DIVERSITY

UMass is fairly diverse, and there are many cultural groups to get involved with on campus. You certainly have the opportunity to meet and become friends with many people from different countries at UMass, and you are unlikely to observe, or experience, any type of racism. The quality of education at any school increases with the level of diversity, and UMass definitely benefits from this reality. Professors here frequently take advantage of this situation to explore the relevancy of others cultures to our own lives—September 11th likely served as a catalyst, in this respect. Although predominantly a white population, 28 different countries are currently represented by the students here. The diversity this campus offers, despite being in the middle of such a non-diverse region, is an important theme at UMass.

The College Prowler™ Grade on
Diversity: C-

A high grade in Diversity indicates that ethnic minorities and international students have a notable presence on campus and that students of different economic backgrounds, religious beliefs, and sexual preferences are well-represented.

Guys & Girls

The Lowdown
ON GUYS & GIRLS

Women Undergrads: 51%

Men Undergrads: 49%

Birth Control Available?
Yes, at University Health Services, or from the resident assistants

Social Scene
Contrary to what you might expect from a big school, students at UMass can easily form groups of close friends, and network on all areas of campus. Because of a common living situation or class schedule, students often find themselves interacting with the same people on a daily basis. In general, the people enrolled at UMass are very friendly, and, as freshmen, they are probably just as eager to make new friends as you are.

Hookups or Relationships?
The wide array of personalities here make this question pretty subjective. If you are looking for your future husband, or wife, at a frat party, you will need all the luck in the world. Then again, if you are looking for just one night of company, you probably won't find your lusty companion in the library. Roughly 75 percent of the relationships that begin at UMass are not altogether serious, and, therefore, end at UMass.

Dress Code
All shapes and sizes. Although, I think the frat guys have a mandatory Abercrombie & Fitch dress code.

The College Prowler Take
ON GUYS & GIRLS

Students Speak Out
ON GUYS & GIRLS

{ "People at UMass range from hippies and frat guys, to jocks and nerds. There are a lot of attractive people here, and I'm sure you could find someone that suits your taste."

Q "**We're a pretty good-looking campus**, but beauty is only skin deep. There are lots of ditsy girls and jock boys who completely fill the stereotypes, but there are also plenty of good-looking, nice people."

Q "There are so many guys that **it's always easy to find one you like**. In my case, I see a new hot guy every day! It's always nice to look. I have mixed feelings about the girls here—some are cool, but some are snotty."

Q "**There are people from all walks of life** and with many different personalities on campus. I'm sure you won't have any trouble making friends. There are a lot of good-looking people here, but of course there are some ugly ones, too. Everyone is very accepting, though."

Q "Personally, **I never had any trouble finding attractive guys on campus**. There are jocks, hippies, and gangster types. Depending on what area of campus you live in, you'll probably be exposed to different types of people. In general, UMass has a pretty attractive student population."

Q "**UMass women are very easy on the eyes**, and they are a dime a dozen. Most of them have their heads on straight, but some you'd swear do not belong in college."

Without a doubt, at UMass there are some remarkable student bodies and more than enough attractive people to go around. More women than men enroll at UMass every year, so for guys, the odds are looking pretty good. But, girls don't make out too poorly here, either. If, however, you want to see a lot of people who all dress, talk, and behave the same way, look no further than any frat or sorority. By simply walking around campus, one can observe some truly beautiful young men and women. Dozens of possibilities exist for meeting people to become romantically involved with, but it always seem to happen when you least expect it, right?

The College Prowler™ Grade on
Guys: A-

A high grade for Guys indicates that the male population on campus is attractive, smart, friendly, and engaging, and that the school has a decent ratio of guys to girls.

The College Prowler™ Grade on
Girls: A-

A high grade for Girls not only implies that the women on campus are attractive, smart, friendly, and engaging, but also that there is a fair ratio of girls to guys.

Athletics

Most Popular Sports
Basketball, football

Overlooked Teams
Men and Women's Swimming, Alpine Skiing

Fields
Intramural soccer/softball/football/field hockey fields, Baseball field, Tennis courts, Football practice field, Curry Hicks Field, Warren P. McGuirk Alumni Stadium, Soccer field

School Mascot:
Minuteman

Athletic Division:
NCAA Division I

Conference:
Atlantic 10, Hockey East

Getting Tickets:
Free for students, as long as you show up with your student ID

The Lowdown
ON ATHLETICS

Men's Varsity Teams:
Alpine Skiing
Baseball
Basketball
Cross Country
Diving
Football
Ice Hockey
Lacrosse
Soccer
Swimming
Tennis
Track and Field (outdoor)

Women's Varsity Teams:
Alpine Skiing
Basketball
Crew
Cross Country
Diving
Field hockey
Lacrosse
Soccer
Softball
Swimming
Tennis
Track and Field (indoor)
Track and Field (outdoor)

Club Sports For Men
Bicycle Racing, Fencing, Lacrosse, Rowing, Rugby, Volleyball

Club Sports For Women
Bicycle Racing, Fencing, Ice Hockey, Rugby

Intramurals
Basketball, Field Hockey, Flag Football, Ice Hockey, Soccer, Softball, Swimming, Tennis, Track and Field, Ultimate Frisbee, Volleyball, Walleyball, Wrestling

Students Speak Out
ON ATHLETICS

"**Football and basketball are the biggest varsity sports on campus.** Intramural (IM) sports are very popular, too. They are a great way to make friends and have some fun."

"**Sports are very big on campus**, but they have come under the knife with the budget cuts. Everyone loves football and Midnight Madness—the first night the basketball team starts practice for the season—is a big deal. Our teams really aren't that good, even with our enthusiasm."

"Varsity sports are fairly big on campus, but **not as big as they used to be**. UMass basketball was once quite the event, but they have definitely tailed off in recent years."

Q "**The football team sucks**, and not many people go to see the games. If they do, it's to see the marching band—no joke. The marching band is incredible! I'm not too sure about intramural sports, because a lot of them were eliminated because of the budget cuts."

Q "**I play two intramural sports every semester and love them**. This year we won the softball tournament, which had, like, 64 teams! Varsity sports aren't as big as they were, which means that you can get awesome seats to just about any game. I think Dr. J went to school here."

Q "**UMass has a lot of nationally-competitive varsity teams,** that practically no one knows about. People only care about the men's basketball and football teams. The Red Sox are more popular here than the Minutemen."

The College Prowler Take
ON ATHLETICS

Surprisingly, varsity sports on campus are not very big, especially when compared to universities of a similar size, like UConn or some Boston schools. A lot of the less popular sports are now done away with. You'll never have a problem finding a seat at a football or basketball game, and all tickets for sporting events are free for students. The Dr. J glory days—or, for that matter, the Marcus Camby glory days—have long since passed. But, intramural sports here are big. They're also a great distraction from your homework.

Need help choosing a club sport that fits your personality? For a detailed listing of all club sports on campus, check out the College Prowler book on UMass available at *collegeprowler.com*.

The College Prowler™ Grade on
Athletics: B

A high grade in Athletics indicates that students have school spirit, that sports programs are respected, that games are well-attended, and that intramurals are a prominent part of student life.

Greek Life

Students Speak Out
ON GREEK LIFE

"**The social scene at UMass is dominated primarily by off-campus parties. They aren't far—when they say 'off campus,' it usually means about two miles.**"

💬 "**Greek life is all right**, but it's mostly washed-up jocks and losers. Freshmen love it, but after your first year, you kind of get sick of it. There are tons of parties at off-campus apartments, so once the fraternities lose their value, there are still parties to go to."

💬 "Compared to a lot of schools, **Greek life is very unpopular**. It's terrible to say, but it's the 'freshman thing' to do. The frat houses are a place for underage people to party and drink. Sororities are viewed as snobby, but I know plenty of girls in them who are sweethearts. Fraternities and sororities at UMass are definitely looked down upon, but the people who are in them love being Greek."

💬 "Even though I am not in a fraternity, I'd say **Greek life plays a big role in the campus community**. Some of the brothers are always doing community service and are active in student government, but others are just there to drink their college lives away. If you intend to join a fraternity or sorority, you could probably find one that fits your lifestyle."

💬 "**There are rumors about the Greek system being eliminated** within the next couple of years, so if you're really interested in joining a frat, you may want to research that before you decide to come to UMass. If you're not interested in going Greek, there's definitely not any pressure to do so."

💬 "Fraternities and sororities are pretty good at making their presence known on campus, because of all the community work they do. I almost joined a frat, but then I saw the frat houses. **They're complete dumps.**"

The Lowdown
ON GREEK LIFE

Number of Fraternities:
21 (11 houses)

Number of Sororities:
12 (7 houses)

Percent of Undergrad Men in Fraternities: 6%

Percent of Undergrad Women in Sororities: 5%

Multicultural Colonies
Multicultural Greek Council (comprised of: Gamma Phi Sigma, Pi Delta Psi, Lambda Pi Chi, Sigma Lambda Upsilon, Lambda Upsilon Lambda, Sigma Psi Zeta), African Student Association, Afrik-Am, Ahora, Arab Students Association, Asian American Student Association, Black Student Union, Boricuas Unidos, Cambodian Student Association, Cape Verdean Student Alliance, Casa Dominicana, English Speaking Caribbean Association, Haitian American Students Association, Japan America Club, Jewish Student Union, Korean Student Association, Native American Students Association, Persian Student Organization, Pride Alliance, Russian Student Organization, Student Association for the Multicultural Brazilian Alliance, South Asian Students Association, Taiwanese Student Association, Vietnamese Student Association, Wazobia Group

The College Prowler Take
ON DRUG SCENE

Greek life does not dominate the social scene, but it is a large part of it. Some of the frats and sororities are very involved with the local community and school projects, and some are not. Every freshman will experience their share of frat parties, and some will tire of it much quicker than others—perhaps even after the first weekend! For the amount of Greek organizations on campus, you'd think they would be more visible, although, from time to time, they will host events and make their presence known. Because there are so many, it is likely that the frats at UMass play a larger role in campus life than at most other universities, but you certainly won't be overwhelmed if you don't want to be.

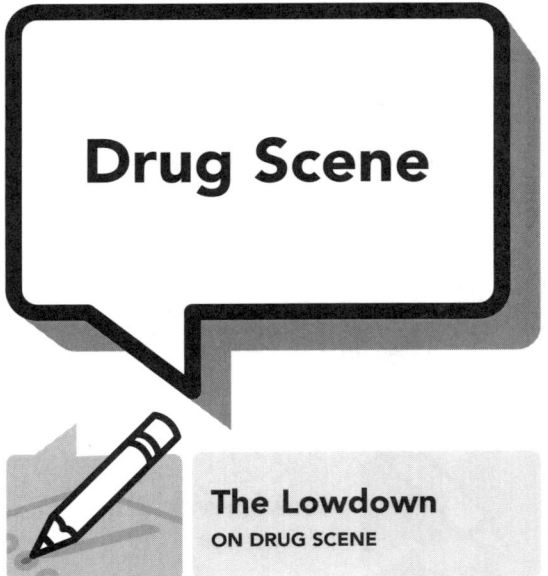

Drug Scene

The Lowdown
ON DRUG SCENE

Most Prevalent Drugs on Campus:
Alcohol and marijuana

Drug Counseling Programs
The Drug and Alcohol Education program offers general information, referrals, training and peer workshops, and can be found on campus through University Health Services. They can be reached at (413) 577-5181.

The Residential Education Alcohol program provides general information, referral, and multi-session alcohol education programs for UMass students. This program is located in the Moore lobby. For more information, call (413) 545-0137.

Other drug and alcohol programs that occur on campus include, Alcoholics Anonymous (413-532-2111), Alanon (413-253-5261), Adult Children of Alcoholics/Dysfunctional Families (413-545-2337), and Narcotics Anonymous (413-538-7479).

The College Prowler™ Grade on
Greek Life: B+

A high grade in Greek Life indicates that sororities and fraternities are not only present, but also active on campus.
Other determining factors include the variety of houses available and the respect the Greek community receives from the rest of the campus.

Students Speak Out
ON DRUG SCENE

The College Prowler Take
ON DRUG SCENE

"**Drugs are decreasing in popularity on campus, but they'll probably always be present. The drug of choice is marijuana, but you will sometimes find acid, ecstasy, and amphetamines being used.**"

Q "**There are not too many drugs around**. The dorm area, Central, is the biggest area for the drug crowd, though it's also one of the nicest dorms. There's weed, shrooms, and acid—stuff like that—but it's mostly drinking."

Q "**There's no peer pressure, and drugs are pretty private**. If you do it, everyone's fine with it, but if you don't, you're fine, too. It's no big deal—there's no epidemic and there definitely isn't a drug problem."

Q "There's lots of pot, but that's about it. **You'll run into Ecstasy here and there**, but it's not like we have coke heads or heroin addicts running around."

Q "You can always find people who do what you're into. Just stay away from the people you need to. It's a huge place, so **it won't be hard to avoid things you don't like**. I haven't met too many people who have real problems."

Q "**The drug scene here is very noticeable, especially the use of weed**. A lot of people here smoke weed, and it isn't hard to get. Once in a while you will see people doing coke, or pills like OxyContin and Vicadin, at a party, but it is all very avoidable. Although, if you don't want to be around drugs, I suggest not living in Southwest or Central."

Excessive drug use on campus has not recently been a concern. The UMass newspaper (*The Daily Collegian*) prints arrests that were made the day before, and the number-one cause of arrests on campus is drugs (specifically, weed), whether involving students, non-students, or both. Even so, the number of drug-related arrests on campus, given the number of students, is unexpectedly low. Drugs can be found at UMass, but in no way are they unavoidable. Once in a great while you may smell the odor of marijuana in a dormitory hallway, but almost never will you come across someone doing a harder drug. Either this is because drug users at UMass are few in number, or because they are very clandestine about their behavior—but which is it?

The College Prowler™ Grade on
Drug Scene: B-

A high grade on Drug Scene indicates that drugs are not a noticeable part of campus life; drug use is not visible, and no pressure to use them seems to exist.

Campus Strictness

Students Speak Out
ON CAMPUS STRICTNESS

"You can get away with a lot. I've had several incidents on campus where I've been drinking and never got caught. If you do get caught, though, the penalties are pretty severe."

Q "**Police aren't too tolerant about drugs**, but they know we're all college students, and they're pretty laid-back about drinking. The dorms have policies prohibiting underage drinking in residential areas, but the policies are seldom enforced."

Q "You can drink and smoke all you like in your dorm, as long as you're not an idiot about it. **Just towel your door, keep alcohol covered, and don't flaunt anything**. The resident assistants know that most kids do illegal things, but as long as you don't make it obvious to them and keep relatively quiet, you can do whatever you want."

Q "The police say they're strict, but **a lot of stuff goes on that they don't know about**. We're not a dry campus, so if you're 21, you can bring a certain amount of alcohol into the dorms."

Q "Underage drinking on campus is kind of like drinking at your parents' house while they are away. **If they find out**, **you're screwed**, but if not, it will be an awesome time."

Q "**You really have to try to get in trouble**. If you are doing something illegal, there are many ways to avoid detection. The RAs are relatively understanding; they are students, too, and don't want to be held responsible for someone hurting themselves or others on their floor. If you are lucky, your room won't be right next to one."

The Lowdown
ON CAMPUS STRICTNESS

What Are You Most Likely to Get Caught Doing on Campus?

Using a fake ID, possession of an open container of alcohol, driving with alcohol in your car when under 21, driving under the influence of drugs and/or alcohol, making a lot of noise in your apartment or dorm room, parking illegally

For even more student opinions on the demeanor of campus security and police, check out the College Prowler book on UMass available at www.collegeprowler.com.

The College Prowler Take
ON CAMPUS STRICTNESS

UMass is not strict by any means. Certain behavior may or may not get you in trouble if you get caught. The penalties for doing something serious, like selling drugs, are severe, but if you get caught with a beer in your room, you might only have to go to an alcohol education class. If you get caught again, the punishment stiffens, and so on. But, really, UMass authorities, including the RAs, are good about focusing on what's important—safety. One thing RAs crack the whip about is playing with the fire extinguishers that are located on each floor, so don't do that—even though it's really fun.

However, do not assume that behavior you can get away with on campus is behavior you can get away with at the frats, apartments, or anywhere else off campus. Amherst police don't tolerate student hijinks as much as UMass police do. Campus strictness is not overwhelming at UMass by any means; the main concern is that students remain safe.

The College Prowler™ Grade on
Campus Strictness: A-
A high Campus Strictness grade implies an overall lenient atmosphere; police and RAs are fairly tolerant, and the administration's rules are flexible.

Overall Experience

Students Speak Out
ON OVERALL EXPERIENCE

"**I am absolutely happy with this school.** I think it's a great place with lots of opportunities, if you decide to make the most of things. Despite some of the recent budget cuts, I am really happy here."

Q "**UMass really feels like home** to me. It's like living in a city, with so many people here, and I think it's more like real life. I still have a group of friends, and I don't feel lost in the crowd at all. There are always events happening on campus, so you'll never get bored. The academics are also pretty good. Overall, it's a nice place to go to school."

Q "**It's hard for me to say what my overall experience was at UMass.** I absolutely loved it as a freshman, but I was really sick the first semester of last year, so I associated some bad things with being there. Just the same, I had a ton of fun, and met a lot of amazing people. I am genuinely sad to leave. Right now things at UMass are a little uncertain because of budget cuts, but they're expected to smooth out the problems within the next couple of years. In the meantime, getting into classes will probably be a huge pain. You should make sure the major you are interested in is not slated to be cut if the budget decreases continue."

💬 "In the beginning, **I didn't like it because I wasn't very outgoing**, and you have to be at any big school. It's easy to slip through the cracks if you're not. My advice is to join clubs and other activities right away. I am on the ski team, and I'm having the time of my life. I love UMass now, and I definitely can't wait for next semester. There are so many good things that go on. My only concern is the budget cuts. You should definitely investigate, so you know if the major you want will still be here."

💬 "UMass is a great school. **I definitely feel as though I got my money's worth**. Like anything, you get out of it what you put into it. The people here are all right, and the teachers are really good. I went on exchange my junior year and had such a great time, and all for the same price you pay at UMass. I highly recommend that everyone exercise their option of going on exchange at some point. And if you do, look for a school that provides things that UMass doesn't, or can't. Overall, I'm glad I went to school here, even if my parents couldn't find me at my graduation because there were so many people."

💬 "I learned a lot here, about a lot of things. What you learn at college doesn't all come from a textbook. It's funny, because your senior year you think 'I can't wait to get out of here,' but once you finally graduate you think, 'What now? **I wish I was still in school!**' It's a mixed bag really, but overall, I am glad that I went to UMass. I will leave with many good memories."

The College Prowler Take
ON OVERALL EXPERIENCE

The overall experience at UMass tends to be a very positive one. But many students wish that certain things were handled differently, particularly the recent budget cuts. However, UMass's financial situation will surely improve over time, and may never even affect current prospective students. An education at UMass will enrich your life: You will learn things you never even dreamed of and meet unique and diverse people that will become friends for life.

Despite the bad parking, unpredictable weather, and crummy campus dining, no one ever says that they hate UMass. If you work hard, and don't let yourself get too distracted by all the parties, you will avoid the main pitfall that plagues students fresh out of high school. Many aren't used to such responsibility—or such a large school—and get a bit carried away. Try to keep a level head. Going to UMass and experiencing such a multifaceted institution will open doors for you. If anything, the size of UMass provides students with more resources and options than they would have elsewhere. If you come here, take advantage of them—and have fun!

The Inside Scoop

The Lowdown
ON THE INSIDE SCOOP

UMass Slang:
Know the slang, know the school. The following is a list of things you really need to know before coming to UMass. The more of these words you know, the better off you'll be.

The Bowl: Orchard Hill area where people congregate

The Cage: Curry Hicks Athletic Field

Cluster F@#ked: A student who has to report to the cluster office because they got caught doing something

The Cluster Office: Every three dorms or so have a "headquarters" where students can obtain different objects or services. This is also where students have to report when they get in trouble.

The DC: Dining Commons (cafeteria)

The Fart Center: Fine Arts Center

Frat Row: The street between campus and Amherst Center where most of the frats are located

Grinder: A submarine sandwich/hoagie

Haigis Mall: Area in front of the Fine Arts Center, not really a mall

The Horseshoe: A wrap-around road in Southwest near the basketball courts

Puffer's: Puffer's Pond, a popular swimming hole near campus

The Quad: Campus Pond or the Northeast Quad

Rape Trails: Various trails around campus, through secluded spots, that students sometimes take as short cuts, at their own risk

Round Robin: A drinking event that occurs in the dorms

Shotgun: A method of chugging a beer straight from the can. The tab gets cracked slightly and a large hole to guzzle from is cut in the side of the can.

Whitless/Sh*tmore: The Whitmore Administration building

Wicked: Very

The Zoo: UMass!

UMass Urban Legends
Every year, the rumor that Bill Cosby is going to speak at graduation gets circulated around the entire campus.

If your roommate commits suicide, you will be granted straight As for that semester.

School Spirit
The school spirit at UMass is not what it used to be, partially because the athletic department has been downsized over the last couple years. However, certain sporting events are still a big draw at UMass, like Midnight Madness and the homecoming football game.

Traditions
Streaking
Fall and spring streaking happens each semester before finals. As a way to blow off steam, and get a break from studying, hundreds of UMass students run butt-naked through the Northeast Quad at night.

Finding a Job or Internship

Things I Wish I Knew Before Coming to UMass:

- Lost or stolen dorm room keys cost $160 dollars to replace. Ouch.
- If you are unable to register for a course online, or via telephone, you can still approach the professor and ask him or her to be admitted.
- Fake IDs do not work well here.
- Buying anything but the most basic and inexpensive meal plan is a complete waste of money.
- How to manage my time better.
- Instead of buying your textbooks at the Textbook Annex, it makes more sense to either split the cost with someone else in the class, buy the books online (www.amazon.com), or see if the library has what you need.
- Just because you need a course doesn't mean you will get it.
- Going on exchange for a semester or two is comparable in cost to attending UMass for that same amount of time.
- Don't skip orientation!
- One bad grade can really bring down your cumulative GPA. And averages are hard to recover.

Tips to Succeed at UMass:

- Go to class—sounds like common sense but still very important, and not as common as you'd think.
- Work hard and play hard, but balance these things in your life.
- Take every extra credit opportunity you can. Don't be lazy!
- Keep an assignment book, write down and mark off all of your assignments.
- Do an internship.
- Try to develop a schedule for studying.

The Lowdown
ON FINDING A JOB OR INTERNSHIP

Many students who graduated in the spring of 2003 had trouble finding jobs. When the economy is bad, not only are companies not hiring, but they don't offer very exciting positions. Students can search for jobs and post their resumes with the Campus Career Network, although, limiting yourself to only one job source is not advisable during tough times.

Advice

It is my Belief that your ability to get a job after graduation relies heavily on how much experience you have. For this reason, I suggest that at some point during your four years at UMass, or however long it takes you to graduate, find and complete an internship that has some correlation with what you plan on doing after school. Also, make connections and do some serious networking, it's all about who you know and what you know.

The Best & Worst

The Ten BEST Things About UMass:

1. Wild parties
2. Compassionate, knowledgeable teachers
3. Low tuition cost
4. Variety of majors to choose from
5. Great library
6. Career Services
7. Sweet location
8. Student resources
9. Quality of education
10. The campus pond

The Ten WORST Things About UMass:

1. Budget cuts
2. No parking
3. Office of Information Technology
4. Expensive textbooks
5. Poor campus food
6. Far walks to get to class
7. Ugly buildings
8. Registering for classes
9. Somewhat bad reputation
10. Shanty dormitories

University of New Hampshire

Thompson Hall, Durham, NH 03824
www.unh.edu   (802) 656-3370

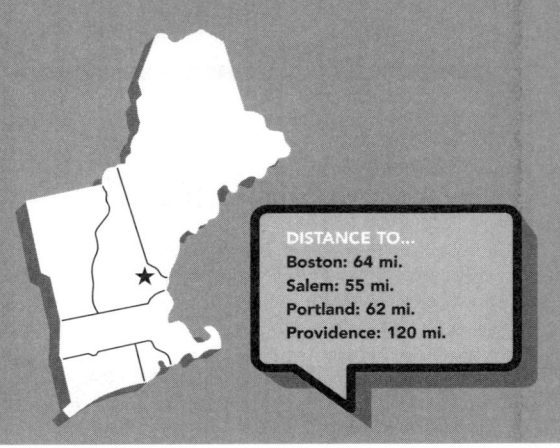

DISTANCE TO...
Boston: 64 mi.
Salem: 55 mi.
Portland: 62 mi.
Providence: 120 mi.

"This vintage campus is quite a sight among the farms and hayfields that surround it."

Total Enrollment:
10,700
Acceptance Rate:
69%
Tuition:
$9,226 in-state, $20,256 out-of-state
Top 10% of High School Class:
20%
SAT Range
Verbal	Math	Total
500 – 610	510 – 620	1010 – 1230

Most Popular Majors:
15% Business
15% Social Sciences
10% Health Professions
7%   English Language and Literature/letters
7%   Communications

Students also applied to:*
Northeastern University
Syracuse University
University of Connecticut
University of Massachusetts–Amherst
University of Vermont

*For more school info check out www.collegeprowler.com

Table of Contents

Academics	81
Local Atmosphere	83
Safety & Security	84
Computers	86
Facilities	87
Campus Dining	89
Off-Campus Dining	91
Campus Housing	92
Off-Campus Housing	94
Diversity	96
Guys & Girls	97
Athletics	99
Greek Life	101
Drug Scene	102
Campus Strictness	104
Overall Experience	105
The Inside Scoop	106
Finding a Job or Internship	108
The Best & Worst	109

College Prowler Report Card

Academics	B-
Local Atmosphere	B
Safety & Security	A
Computers	B-
Facilities	B+
Campus Dining	B
Off-Campus Dining	B-
Campus Housing	B+
Off-Campus Housing	B-
Diversity	D-
Guys	B-
Girls	B
Athletics	B+
Greek Life	C+
Drug Scene	C-
Campus Strictness	C-

Academics

The Lowdown
ON ACADEMICS

Degrees Awarded:
Associate, Bachelor, Master, Post-Master's Certificate, Doctorate

Undergraduate Schools:
College of Engineering and Physical Sciences, College of Liberal Arts, College of Life Sciences and Agriculture, School of Health and Human Services, Thompson School of Applied Sciences, Whittemore School of Business and Economics

Full-time Faculty:
588

Faculty with Terminal Degree:
92%

Student-to-Faculty Ratio:
14:1

Average Course Load:
4 courses

AP Test Score Requirements:
Possible credit for scores of 3, 4, or 5

IB Test Score Requirements:
Possible credit for scores of 5, 6, or 7 (on a higher level)

Special Degree Options
Cross-registration, double major, English as a Second Language (ESL), exchange student program (domestic), honors program, independent study, internships, student-designed major, study abroad, teacher certificate program

Sample Academic Clubs
American Sign Language Club, Earth Science Club, Mock Trial Club, National Society of Minorities in Hospitality, Pre-Vet Club, Society of Woman Engineers

Best Places to Study
Dimond Library, Memorial Union Building

Did You Know?

The University's international research opportunities program (IROP) was the first of its kind. Now, it serves as a model for others nationwide.

UNH ranks in the top 30 educational institutions nationwide, and in the top two in New England, in funding from the National Aeronautics and Space Administration (NASA).

Students Speak Out
ON ACADEMICS

"**Some teachers can be very good, and some tend to be rather boring and unprofessional. The same thing goes for classes.**"

"**Most of the teachers try and make themselves available to students** by making office hours. If you can't make it to their office hours, they're usually good about making an appointment to see you. All of the classes I have taken, with the exception of Economics and Propaganda, have been interesting."

Q "From what I've heard, it varies from department to department, but all of the teachers that I have had have been wonderful. Obviously, **teaching methods vary**, and some are more effective to me than others, but teachers are always available during office hours to help you. Also, in a lot of cases, there are teaching assistants [TAs] around. Contrary to popular belief, the professors and TAs really do want to see you succeed."

Q "**Some are the best I've ever had; some are the worst**. There are always study groups and lots of support from the Center for Academic Research [CFAR], if you're having trouble. CFAR is great, and you can read comments from students about teachers, if you want to know who to look out for."

Q "Get to know your teachers, and **they'll definitely help you out** in the future. Even though it's a big school, the large classes can feel small when you get to know the professor and some of the other students."

Q "Teachers are usually pretty friendly, [but] some seem more involved with their research at UNH than their classes. **Most of my classes are interesting, but some aren't**."

The College Prowler Take
ON ACADEMICS

Every student has their favorite teacher and their most despised teacher. Most students at UNH agree that the teachers that are good at their jobs make up for the others. Although a large percentage of teachers at UNH are also doing research, and therefore may not have as much time for students as they would like, they still seem to have a lot of compassion for the students and are always willing to help those who really want it and need it. All UNH teachers post office hours and devoutly stick to them. Take advantage of this. If a teacher's office hours don't coincide with your daily schedule, other appointments are also available.

At every college, there are classes that you may not like very much. With all the course requirements given out today (at almost all national universities), it is a given that you'll probably have to take some classes that you have little or no interest in. UNH is no different. The lecture classes tend to be in the hundreds, and every student has a set of general education requirements to reach before graduation. Within the requirements, though, there is a lot of variation in what classes you can choose, and most are fairly small in class size. If you need help, the Center for Academic Research (CFAR) is more than willing to give advice on what courses and professors to take, and can even show you student quotes and opinions (much like the quotes in this guidebook) that will give you a better idea of what direction you should take.

The College Prowler™ Grade on
Academics: B-

A high Academics grade generally indicates that professors are knowledgeable, accessible, and genuinely interested in their students' welfare. Other determining factors include class size, how well professors communicate, and whether or not classes are engaging.

Local Atmosphere

Students Speak Out
ON LOCAL ATMOSPHERE

"**The town is almost exclusively centered around the college. There are no other universities in town. It's a very small town with not much to do in Durham.**"

Q "**There are no other universities here**. Durham is a one street town."

Q "The town we are in is **very quaint and quiet**. It's a great town if you're an earthy type of person. There are many outdoor activities available. There really isn't anything in the area to stay away from, although there are many pretty things, like the waterfall on the path in the college woods."

Q "**Newington and Portsmouth are 10 minutes away**, with nice restaurants and theaters. If you're in the mood for some sun, the ocean is only 20 minutes from campus."

Q "I love Durham! **UNH is a big school in a quaint town**. Downtown Durham runs right through the campus, so you see students sitting outside coffee shops or just hanging out at the restaurants all the time. New Hampshire is really beautiful, and there are a lot of things to do in the area."

Q "The town is pretty accepting of the college because **we give the shops and restaurants most of their business**. There are no nearby colleges, and there's nothing too exciting going on in town."

The Lowdown
ON LOCAL ATMOSPHERE

Region:
Northeast

City, State:
Durham, New Hampshire

Setting:
Rural/Small Town

Distance from Portsmouth:
10 minutes

Distance from Boston:
45 minutes

Points of Interest:
NH seacoast

Major Sports Teams:
You'll be rooting for the Boston teams: Boston Bruins (NHL), Boston Celtics (NBA), New England Patriots (NFL), New England Revolution (MLS), Boston Red Sox (MLB)

City Websites:
www.ci.durham.nh.us

The College Prowler Take
ON LOCAL ATMOSPHERE

Durham, New Hampshire is the ideal hometown for the University of New Hampshire. It is probably safe to say that the two are dependent on one another. The students love everything about the town, while many Durham shops stay in business because of UNH students. The rural atmosphere also makes for a comfortable and serene learning environment. Durham itself consists of a collection of small suburbs close to the campus, and the vast farming fields that surround it. There is a definite distinction between the college students and the so-called locals. The night life belongs solely to the students. If it weren't for the campus, Durham would probably be boring, to say the least.

Safety & Security

The Lowdown
ON SAFETY & SECURITY

The College Prowler™ Grade on

Local Atmosphere: B

A high Local Atmosphere grade indicates that the area surrounding campus is safe and scenic. Other factors include nearby attractions, proximity to other schools, and the town's attitude toward students.

Number of UNH Police:
15

Phone:
(603) 862-1427

Health Center Office Hours:
Monday, Tuesday, Thursday, Friday: 7:30 a.m. - 4:30 p.m.
Wednesday: 7:30 a.m. - 7:30 p.m.
Saturday and Sunday: 12 noon - 4 p.m.
Labor Day, Veteran's Day, & Martin Luther King Day: 12 noon - 4 p.m.
Summer and Semester Breaks,
M - F: 8 a.m. - 4:30 p.m.

Safety Services:
Security escort service, SAFE rides, fire safety, Sexual Harassment and Rape Prevention Program (S.H.A.R.P.P.)

Students Speak Out
ON SAFETY & SECURITY

"The security system is pretty good. There are safety lights and emergency call-boxes at regular intervals, and campus security patrols the campus."

Q "I don't know a lot about campus security, because it has never really been an issue, which I guess is a good thing. UNH is a place where walking around at night could be potentially scary, because there are not a lot of people out, and there are a lot of wooded paths. But, **there are lights with emergency call-boxes and panic buttons** that can be seen from all over, and you really just get a sense of security on campus."

Q "Security is good. There are **24-hour lock downs** in residence halls, two full-size police forces at all times, two-minute response time at emergency call-boxes, student security officers, bike cops, and more."

Q "There have been **incidents of Peeping Toms** before on campus, but most problems have been resolved. We have security call-boxes around campus, which makes me feel safe."

Q "**Security at UNH is extreme**. It's a safe environment, and I feel fine walking across campus at night, or in the afternoon. You can always call for a free escort if you feel unsafe."

Q "**UNH takes safety and security very seriously**. Each student must use an ID to get into his or her dorm at night-time. It's very reassuring. There are many student activist groups that make safety a priority, like S.H.A.R.P.P., which is our rape prevention center."

The College Prowler Take
ON SAFETY & SECURITY

Since UNH is a small campus in a small town, it is much safer here than it would be on a large campus in a large city. However, no place—not even Durham—is completely and entirely safe. Most recently, the campus has dealt with a couple of stalking cases. But, overall, there haven't been any serious problems. It would be illogical to let a few isolated cases deter you from realizing how safe Durham really is. The campus police have a great relationship with the students and care about their safety a whole lot. And, when the safety of the students is compromised, the students are never left in the dark. The campus has an emergency light system in place to help security personnel with keeping students safe. With the recent problems with terrorism, all dormitories have been locked 24 hours a day, seven days a week. The campus is fairly safe, and most students probably don't think twice about a walk alone to their car at night.

The College Prowler™ Grade on
Safety & Security: A

A high grade in Safety & Security means that students generally feel safe, campus police are visible, blue-light phones and escort services are readily available, and safety precautions are not overly necessary.

Computers

The Lowdown
ON COMPUTERS

High-Speed Network?
Yes

Wireless Network?
Yes

Number of Labs:
7

Numbers of Computers:
208

Free Software:
Adobe Acrobat 5.0, Adobe Acrobat Reader 5.1, Adobe Photoshop 7.0, McAfee VirusScan 4.5, Microsoft Access 2000, Microsoft PowerPoint 2000, Microsoft Word X, Matlab 6.5 R13, WS-FTP95 LE, Mozilla 1.2, AppleWorks 6.2.4.

24-Hour Labs:
McConnell 104, Kingsbury 128, Kingsbury 317 (Unix)

Charge to Print?
Yes

Operating Systems:
Windows (157 computers), Macintosh (51 computers), Linux (16 computers)

Students Speak Out
ON COMPUTERS

"All labs are usually crowded, and it helps to have your own computer."

Q "I don't know anybody who doesn't have their own computer, so I would definitely recommend it. The network is great, and **every student has their own high-speed Internet connection**, and there are multiple clusters across campus where students can use facilities if it is more convenient for them."

Q "**Computers that allow printing are always crowded**. We get fast Internet connection, though, and you can check out laptops in the library to use."

Q "I would definitely suggest bringing your own computer. **It's a hassle to haul all your schoolwork to the clusters**. The clusters are never full, and there is always a free computer on campus. There is one computer cluster that is open 24 hours a day, which is helpful. The clusters have both Macs and PCs, which is a plus. The computer network in the dorms is very fast. I am very satisfied with our network on campus."

Q "I would recommend bringing your own computer, as **there are only two labs open 24 hours**. They get very crowded around midterms and finals, and it is nearly impossible to get in."

Q "If you want to bring a computer and your only choice is an old one with old programs, don't bother. **UNH uses all the newest programs**, and all the professors will ask you to use them, as well."

The College Prowler Take
ON COMPUTERS

Although the number of labs might be a bit small for the amount of people at UNH, there is always at least one open. Most of the students bring their own computer just because it makes their life easier in the end. College is not completely impossible without a computer, though. UNH tries very hard to keep the computer programs updated. Also, the student network is fast and efficient, and very rarely malfunctions or shuts down completely. So, even if you don't have the convenience of your own personal computer, the ones provided for you are more than adequate. Overall, the computers available on campus are top of the line and the services the campus offers are very helpful.

Facilities

The Lowdown
ON FACILITIES

The College Prowler™ Grade on
Computers: B-

A high grade in Computers designates that computer labs are available, the computer network is easily accessible, and the campus' computing technology is up-to-date.

Student Center:
The Memorial Union Building (MUB)

Athletic Center:
The Whittemore Center/Hamel Recreation Center, and the field house

Libraries:
2

Movie Theatre on Campus?
There are two movie theater auditoriums in the Memorial Union Building.

Bowling on Campus?
No

Bar on Campus?
On Main Street there is Murphy's Tin Palace, Scorpions, and Libby's Bar & Restaurant.

Coffeehouse on Campus?
In the Memorial Union Building, there is the Panache Café. On Main Street, the local favorite is Breaking New Grounds (BNG).

Popular Places to Chill:
Main Street, Murphy's Tin Palace, Breaking New Grounds

Favorite Things to Do:
If you're looking to kill a few minutes between classes you can find plenty do in the Memorial Union Building, such as studying with a fresh coffee or milkshake. There is a large billiards room on the ground floor where you can always find a table. If you have more time on your hands, the MUB has events scheduled every day, including a lecture series, musical performances, comedians, and club meetings.

Students Speak Out
ON FACILITIES

"UNH has a wonderful gym that offers aerobics, workout facilities, an indoor tack, racquet ball, saunas, and basketball. The student center is pretty big; it is a nice place to go for dinner, too."

"The facilities are all pretty nice. UNH is in the process of building a new dorm and dining hall, which will be awesome! **The gym on campus is really amazing**—it's packed at times, but we have a lot of kids here. We have an indoor track, and the gym equipment is pretty much all new. The computer centers are located all over campus and are really nice. If there is anything you need, there are different places to help you in the student center. The people are really nice and offer to help with everything."

"All of our facilities are very nice. **The student center doesn't have a ton in it**, but it's got the typical pool tables and living rooms that students need. Our athletic facilities are beautiful. So beautiful, in fact, that the gym is always crowded."

"UNH just built an awesome new workout facility. It's **free to all students**—a lot of schools don't have that perk. Most of the buildings are pretty new and very clean, with new equipment. Some lecture halls are old, but still nice."

"The student athletic center is very nice and popular, [with] good equipment and facilities. The computers are also pretty new. The student center [MUB] is a great building with a ton of different things to do. There are **movie theatres, retail food operations, the mail room, meeting rooms [and] lounges**, student activity offices. The list goes on and on. It is also a beautiful building."

"**The facilities on campus are top-of-the-line**. The new dining hall has really good food and a nice atmosphere. There is the MUB, which is basically the student union, which is nice and has many things to do in it. The on-campus gym is really nice. They're always adding new equipment to it. The gym is air-conditioned, too, which is a plus. We also have an indoor ice rink for ice skating and activities during the winter. We have a year-round indoor pool. We also have basketball and tennis courts to use."

The College Prowler Take
ON FACILITIES

The UNH campus offers a lot to its students. They have recently renovated the athletic centers, library, and numerous dorms. In 2003, the campus opened the new $26 million dollar dining hall, Holloway Commons, and the new dorm, Mills Hall. Mills Hall is a suite-style dorm with five- to eight-person suites with deluxe bathrooms and a living room in each. UNH has plans for more renovations to all its dorms. A multi-story parking garage may also be on the administration's agenda for the near future. Until more space is available, most students work around the crowded times at the gym or the pool. Overall, the students at UNH seem generally happy with the facilities provided for them.

Campus Dining

The Lowdown
ON CAMPUS DINING

Freshman Meal Plan Requirement?
No

24-Hour On-Campus Eating?
Campus Convenience and Store 24

Student Favorites:
Holloway Commons and Campus Convenience

Meal Plan Average Cost:
$1,123 – $1,165

The College Prowler™ Grade on
Facilities: B+

A high Facilities grade indicates that the campus is aesthetically pleasing and well-maintained; facilities are state-of-the-art, and libraries are exceptional. Other determining factors include the quality of both athletic and student centers and an abundance of things to do on campus.

Students Speak Out
ON CAMPUS DINING

"The food isn't that great, but there are a lot of places around campus that are good to eat. There's a commons building in the center of campus known as the MUB, and there are all kinds of places to eat there."

Q "Compared to most schools, **our dining halls are pretty good**. We have unlimited meal plans and a wide variety of foods at the dining hall. In addition to whatever the main course is for the night, we always have pizza, stir-fry, salad bars, sandwich bars, soups, grilled food, and many other things to choose from. I eat a lot better at school than at home. Besides the three dining halls, we have a couple of cafe-like places where you can buy food to take out with you. It's convenient for people who are always going to and from classes."

Q "Any dining hall pretty much stinks. **They have their good days**, but they're not too great overall. On campus, Joe's Pizza is always popular for party nights. Domino's, JP's Subs, and Durham House of Pizza are all pretty good, and Stat's has awesome ice cream."

Q "The dining halls suck, but I'm sure that is the same everywhere. On campus, there isn't really too much besides some pizza places and a restaurant called **Benjamin's, where they have good food**. My favorite place to eat is the MUB [Memorial Union Building], where they have a food court with Chinese food, pizza, sandwiches, Taco Bell, and other fast food."

Q "**The dining halls are surprisingly not bad**. We just got a new dining hall, which I enjoy a lot. The MUB has a food court in it that has many places to go. There is a sub shop, a burger place, a Taco Bell, a Chinese food stop, and a counter for vegetarian fare."

Q "**We all complain about the food** at UNH, but the school has won many awards for their cuisine. It's actually very good. People complain because, like any other school, it can get old. The good thing is, that if you don't always want to go to the dining hall, the MUB has good food and you can use your meal plan there. You can also use Cats Cache at most downtown restaurants."

The College Prowler Take
ON CAMPUS DINING

UNH Dining Services tries very hard to please as many students as it can and has won numerous awards for its efforts. The students who complain about the UNH campus food selection ought to realize that dining hall food is produced in mass quantity. In the process of making large amounts of food, it may lose some of its flavor, hence the awful reputation that dining hall food has universally received—not just here, but everywhere. Students should, however, try to keep things in perspective in this department. Overall, UNH Dining Services genuinely goes out of its way to please the students in any way that they can. Things could be a lot worse!

The College Prowler™ Grade on
Campus Dining: B

Our grade on Campus Dining addresses the quality of both school-owned dining halls and independent on-campus restaurants as well as the price, availability, and variety of food.

Off-Campus Dining

Students Speak Out
ON OFF-CAMPUS DINING

"There aren't too many restaurants off campus, but two that come to mind are the Portsmouth Brewery and the Muddy River Smoke House."

Q "Durham is very small. There are a couple of places to eat downtown, such as Durham House of Pizza, Wildcat Pizza, and JP's Eatery. There are a couple bars downtown, including Libby's, the Tap Room, and some others. **Newingtown, about a 15-minute car ride away, has more places to eat and a mall**."

Q "Just off campus, **there are many coffee shops** and pizza places worthy of going to. I recommend Joe's New York Style Pizza."

Q "If you take a 10-minute drive, there are the typical, casual restaurants like **Applebee's, TGI Friday's, and the Olive Garden**. Benjamin's is right in town, walking distance from campus, serves everything, and is really good."

Q "Durham is pretty small, so **there aren't many places to eat** there, but the take-out food is great up here. Durham doesn't have many great restaurants—mostly little places for pizza or subs. There are some actual restaurants, but the towns nearby are better."

Q "As far as off-campus restaurants, there is a variety of food in Durham, including **the best pizza in the world**, grinders or subs, cheap Italian, fine Italian, bagels, coffee, and ice cream. For more variety, Portsmouth is a short car or bus ride away and has some of the best food in New England, located right on Portsmouth's coastal harbor!"

The Lowdown
ON OFF-CAMPUS DINING

Best Pizza:
Joe's New York Style Pizza

Best Chinese:
China Buffet

Best Breakfast:
The Bagelry

Best Wings:
Murphy's Tin Palace

Best Healthy:
Pauly's Pockets

Late-Night, Half-Price Food Specials:
$1 pizza at Durham House of Pizza after 11 p.m.

Best Place to Take Your Parents:
Libby's Bar and Grill

Student Favorites:
Durham House of Pizza, Libby's Bar and Grill, Murphy's Tin Palace

The College Prowler Take
ON OFF-CAMPUS DINING

The town of Durham is small, and unfortunately, so is the selection of restaurants. Most students don't have the time or money to go to the better places further off campus. So, most of the time, you will see students hanging out at the local bars and sub shops during the day. There are plenty of fancy restaurants in Portsmouth that are worth visiting as well—it's just a matter of getting a bunch of friends together and spending a night on the town.

The College Prowler™ Grade on
Off-Campus Dining: B-

A high Off-Campus Dining grade implies that off-campus restaurants are affordable, accessible, and worth visiting. Other factors include the variety of cuisine and the availability of alternative options (vegetarian, vegan, Kosher, etc.).

Campus Housing

The Lowdown
ON CAMPUS HOUSING

Undergrads on Campus: 50%

Number of Dormitories: 20

Number of University-Owned Apartments: 3

You Get:
Bed, desk and chair, bookshelf, dresser, closet or wardrobe, window coverings, cable TV jack, Ethernet or broadband Internet connections, free campus and local phone calls.

Bed Type:
Single in all University-owned rooms.

Also Available:
Themed Housing: Chem-Free, The Clubhouse, Multicultural Living, Community Service, Whittemore School of Business, First Year Student Experience, Honors Program, International Living, Living in Harmony, Academic, Outdoor Experiential Education, Performing Arts, Science and Engineering, Tomorrows Educators, Visual Arts, Wired, and All-Female.

Cleaning Service?
In all dorms and campus apartments only, usually a couple of times a week.

Room Types

Singles: These are rather small depending on which dorm. They come with bed, desk, chair, and closet.

Doubles: These are the most common rooms in the dorms and have everything for two people.

Triples: There are also a common room in freshman dorms.

Forced Triple: Double rooms fit for three people. This is due to a shortage of space in the dorms, but they are broken up within the first few months of school as new spots open up.

Quads: Four person rooms, which are usually study lounges turned into dorm rooms.

Suites: Mills Hall is the only suite dorm. Suites hold five to eight students. They have common living areas with furniture and a private bathroom with showers.

Apartments: There are two on-campus apartment complexes (Woodsides and Gables). They range from four- to six-person apartments and include a full-size living room, dining table, and kitchen area.

Students Speak Out
ON CAMPUS HOUSING

"Some of the dorms are better than others. I would avoid Stoke Hall. Hubbard Hall is very nice (the rooms are bigger than most), and Congreve Hall has a very good location."

Q "**Some dorms are nice, and some dorms are not so nice**. As freshmen, you may choose to live in an all-freshman dorm or somewhere else. Your typical room has two people, two beds, desks, etc. It's hard getting used to living in such a small space with another person, but dorm life is really great—you get to know so many new people. As upperclassmen, it becomes easier to get into nicer dorms, such as the suite-style dorms or the on-campus apartments."

Q "**If you can get into Congreve or Mills, go for it**. They're brand new. I would stay away from the freshmen dorms like Christiansen, Williamson, and Stoke. They are huge, crowded, and usually dirty. The dorms in the upper quad are nice, and the rooms are a good size. Englehart is the chem-free dorm, and there are many other themed dorms."

Q "The dorm you choose depends on what you want out of school. If you want to be able to walk out your door and onto frat row, you should stay in the biggest dorm, Stoke. Williamson and Christiansen are far away from the parties but close to the school. **The Gables is in the middle of nowhere** but there are no RAs, so you can have parties and stuff without anyone watching you."

Q "Overall, **the dorms are a good size**, and there aren't many problems. Freshmen dorms are kind of far from classes, but they are nice because all the residents are freshmen. You'll have some of the best times of your life here!"

Q "Most of the dorms are pretty nice. **I've seen better at other schools**, but they're not bad at UNH. Definitely live in freshmen dorms for freshman year. They're not as nice as some of the others, but you'll want the experience to be with other people who are going through the same things you are."

The College Prowler Take
ON CAMPUS HOUSING

UNH has dorms to suit everyone's style. Whether you're a double major in biology and mathematics who wants nothing more then a quiet living space to study that's in close proximity to the science and math buildings, or a party-animal jock whose sole purpose in life is to be drunk and at the center of attention, there is probably a dorm for you. There are large freshmen dorms that aren't as pretty as the other dorms (Christiansen, Williamson, Stoke), but the people you meet and the relationships you form are hard to come by anywhere else. Once again, whatever your style, you can find a place to fit in at UNH.

Off-Campus Housing

The Lowdown
ON OFF-CAMPUS HOUSING

The College Prowler™ Grade on
Campus Housing: B+

A high Campus Housing grade indicates that dorms are clean, well-maintained, and spacious. Other determining factors include variety of dorms, proximity to classes, and social atmosphere.

Undergrads in Off-Campus Housing:
60%

Average Rent for a Studio Apartment:
$150 - $200/month

Average Rent for a One-Bedroom Apartment:
$300 - $350/month

Average Rent for a Two-Bedroom Apartment:
$400 - $500/month

Popular Areas:
Main Street in Durham, Dover, Newmarket

Best Time to Look for a Place:
At the start of the second semester, for the next year.

 ## Students Speak Out
ON OFF-CAMPUS HOUSING

 ## The College Prowler Take
ON OFF-CAMPUS HOUSING

{ "Living off campus is definitely worth it. Newmarket and Dover are great places, and the bus system makes it all that much easier."

Q "There is a lot of off-campus housing, but **it goes quickly and is very expensive** in Durham. Many students live in the dorms until junior year, and if they do not move into the on-campus apartments, Gables or Woodsides, they try to live outside of Durham in Dover, Lee, or Newmarket because it is cheaper."

Q "A lot of people like off-campus housing because **you don't have to deal with as much authority**, and there are a lot of really nice apartments out there. There is housing available in surrounding communities, such as Dover and Newmarket, as well as in Durham. However, living off campus makes everything a lot less convenient. When you are living on campus, everything is right here at your fingertips."

Q "If you can get an apartment right in downtown, it's nice but very expensive. **I would stay on campus through my sophomore year**, though. They offer on-campus apartments for students, too. If you have a car and don't mind a drive, getting an apartment in Dover might not be a bad idea, although it is more detached from the whole 'college' feeling."

Q "**Off-campus housing is difficult to get** and costs as much as it does to live on campus, but it is close to campus and offers more freedom."

Q "It seems **people are always looking for roommates off campus**. I think it's kind of hard to get an apartment in Durham, but many students get apartments in Dover and Newmarket, the two surrounding towns. There are plenty of options for an apartment."

UNH is surrounded by small rural towns, with the exception of Portsmouth. Most students who choose to live off campus move to the neighboring towns of Dover and Newmarket. Rent prices in those towns are very reasonable. A house for five people could range anywhere from $1,000 to $2,000 depending on certain amenities. Through the UNH website, students can search for off-campus housing relatively easy. Most renters in these towns welcome students. Shuttles frequently run out to these two towns and make for an easy 10- or 20-minute commute to campus. Living in Durham itself is a much sought after treasure, as you are able to still walk to school and be close to the atmosphere of UNH. Finding a place to live in Durham is not easy, but it's not impossible.

The College Prowler™ Grade on
Off-Campus Housing: B-

A high grade in Off-Campus Housing indicates that apartments are of high quality, close to campus, affordable, and easy to secure.

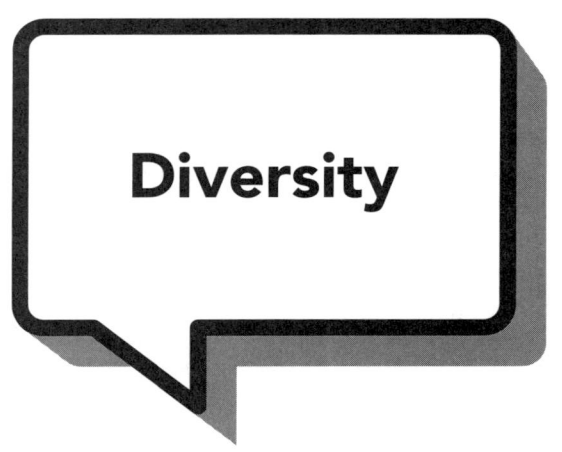

Diversity

Gay Tolerance
UNH is very accepting of gay culture. Gay organizations are very prominent on campus, and they hold many events tailored specifically toward gay awareness and the gay community.

Economic Status
The economic status tends to lean more toward the upper-class, with many students from rich, prominent towns in southern New Hampshire and Massachusetts. However, UNH is a state school, and there are many "blue collar" students as well.

The Lowdown
ON DIVERSITY

Students Speak Out
ON DIVERSITY

African American: 1%

Asian American: 2%

Hispanic: 1%

Native American: 0%

White: 95%

International: 1%

Out-of-State: 42%

Minority Clubs
The Office of Multicultural Students Association (OMSA) holds numerous events to help raise awareness of student minorities and to give minorities a great way to meet people.

Most Popular Religions
UNH has a very active Christian Fellowship and Jewish organization, and new groups are popping up every year.

Political Activity
UNH tends to be very politically active, especially around the Presidential primaries.

"UNH is about 99.999 percent white."

"**Different races are present**. There's an international dorm and a Spanish-speaking one. The people you meet are so different from high school people. There are no cliques—everyone is family, and no one is judged. There are gays, different religions, different majors, and so on. You'll meet so many totally different, really cool people."

"**UNH is fairly diverse**, but it generally reflects the state of New Hampshire itself."

"The campus isn't that diverse by the statistics they give students, but then again, **I've met a diverse group of people**. I had one girl on my floor from Japan, and I also have many African American friends from the football team."

"Not too diverse, and it seems more like **they segregate the diversity through theme floors**, rather than integrating them with the general student population."

"**Diversity is a work in progress for UNH**. They are trying to implement new programs to increase diversity on campus. There are plenty of clubs that encourage diversity, so it's there if you want it."

The College Prowler Take
ON DIVERSITY

UNH administration has long been assigned the difficult task of trying to bring diversity to a small campus in the middle of New England. Generally, New Hampshire is not a state that appeals to minority students. This may never change. Many would have to travel great distances to come here and, consequently, would be far from their own cultures. On the other hand, most of the multicultural students here are actually longtime New Hampshire residents. While it's true that UNH may never become a poster school for diversity, students and administration alike continue the attempt to diversify the campus. There is a long way to go.

The College Prowler™ Grade on
Diversity: D-

A high grade in Diversity indicates that ethnic minorities and international students have a notable presence on campus and that students of different economic backgrounds, religious beliefs, and sexual preferences are well-represented.

Guys & Girls

The Lowdown
ON GUYS & GIRLS

Women Undergrads: 57%

Men Undergrads: 43%

Birth Control Available?
Yes, in the Health Services Department.

Social Scene
Every student at UNH desires to make the most out of their college experience. Almost everyone is friendly to some extent. Every weekend, there is a party to be found or an event where people can meet others, but mostly, people meet at the fraternity parties. Outside of parties, classes and the library are the next best thing. Study partners are a great way to meet prospective lovers or just good friends.

Hookups or Relationships?
With the large Greek party presence on the weekends, the bulk of student relationships begin as random hookups, but relationships seem to be found where students meet and interact. Most random hookups from frat parties tend to evolve into relationships as well (some more serious than others).

Dress Code
The Greek look can range from hipster casual with the fake authentic trucker hat, to a Polo shirt with stone washed jeans. Pink seems to be coming back as a guy color. The next biggest fashion trend is complete abandonment of trends. In other words, the less you seem to care about appearance (to a certain extent of course) the more desired you'll be by the opposite sex. The dirtier your hair is, the more "original" you'll seem. It's beginning to be all about originality at UNH. Birkenstocks, in some cases, are a must. Due to the colder climates the closed-toed Birks are the best. Another popular trend is the classical grunge skater garb. When it comes to fashion, basically anything goes at UNH.

Students Speak Out
ON GUYS & GIRLS

"**The guys can be rather, well, thick-headed, and some of the girls are ditsy. But, I've found lots of very intelligent, cool people. And yes, there are lots of hot women.**"

"**The guys and girls are both really nice**. If you need help with something, I wouldn't feel bad walking up to a stranger to ask a question. I think that most of the guys on campus are okay looking, some are better than others. We have a fair share of hippies, too, and to me, they seem dirtier than the rest of the population."

"There are large variations in the people at UNH. **We have a lot of hippies**, but also a lot of the preppy, Abercrombie type, and the 'pretty-boy' type. For the most part, the campus is very much 'all-American.' I think there are lots of hot guys here, as long as you like all-American boys."

"In general, **UNH is a very nice-looking campus**. The guys are hot, but there are a lot of jerks. There are also a lot of awesome guys, too, so it all depends on who you involve yourself with. I think that most girls at UNH are very friendly and chill. I have met some of my best friends here, and I think that it's a very friendly and accepting campus."

"There are cute guys and girls, but, unfortunately, **girls outnumber guys three-to-one**, or something like that."

"Whatever your type, you'll find them at UNH. Both the guys and the girls are attractive. **There are 18- to 23-year-olds everywhere**, so of course you'll be drooling—I know I was!"

The College Prowler Take
ON GUYS & GIRLS

Ah yes, the ultimate question on any prospective student's mind. Are the girls and guys hot? The answer at UNH is "yes" and "no." This is the answer anyone will give because of the wide variety of students attending UNH. Since the school is fairly large, there is every type of beauty imaginable. There are the traditional pretty-boys and sorority girls, as well as the sporty types, the smart types, the girls- and guys-next-door, the dirty hippies, rugged mountain men, and those who certainly won't be gracing the cover of the next *YM* magazine. Anyway that you look at it, there is someone for everyone. It's safe to say that, in the looks department, the guys and girls at UNH won't disappoint.

The College Prowler™ Grade on
Guys: B-

A high grade for Guys indicates that the male population on campus is attractive, smart, friendly, and engaging, and that the school has a decent ratio of guys to girls.

The College Prowler™ Grade on
Girls: B

A high grade for Girls not only implies that the women on campus are attractive, smart, friendly, and engaging, but also that there is a fair ratio of girls to guys.

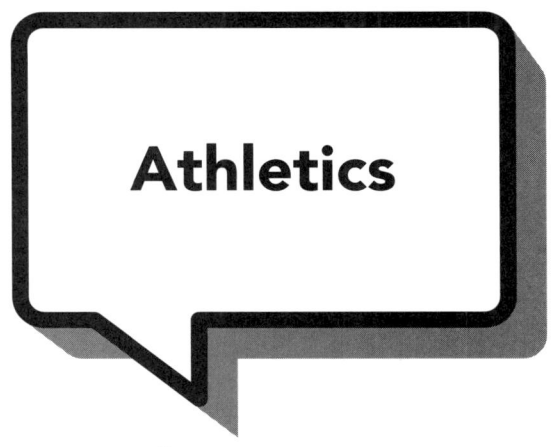

Athletics

The Lowdown
ON ATHLETICS

Men's Varsity Teams:
Hockey
Basketball
Soccer
Football
Indoor/Outdoor Track
Skiing
Tennis
Cross Country
Swimming/Diving
Lacrosse

Women's Varsity Teams:
Basketball
Crew
Field Hockey
Volleyball
Gymnastics
Ice Hockey
Indoor Track
Lacrosse
Outdoor Track
Skiing
Soccer
Swimming/Diving
Tennis

Club Sports:
Aikido
Archery
Baseball
Crew (men's)
Cycling
Dance
Fencing
Golf (men's)
Golf (women's)
Judo
Lacrosse
Rifle
Rugby
Sailing
Shotokan Karate
Softball
Tae Kwon Do
Volleyball
Wrestling

Intramurals:
Indoor/Outdoor Soccer
Kickball
Softball
Flag Football
Broomball
Volleyball
Off-season 5-on-5 basketball
Women's Field Hockey
Ultimate Frisbee
Golf
Billiards
Basketball
Hockey
Floor Hockey
Dodgeball
Table Tennis
Tennis
Racquetteball
4-on-4 Flag Football
Track and Field

Most Popular Sports
Hockey, soccer, football, women's lacrosse, field hockey, ultimate Frisbee

Overlooked Teams
Tennis, skiing, volleyball, swimming

Fields
Memorial Field (short turf), Upper Field (long turf), Boulder Field, track and field, football, soccer, rugby, baseball

School Mascot
Wild E. Cat

Athletic Division
Division I in the majority of sports

Getting Tickets
Tickets to almost all sports are free to students and very easy to get, even for the men's hockey games.

Students Speak Out
ON ATHLETICS

The College Prowler Take
ON ATHLETICS

"**Intramural sports are big on campus. A lot of times, people play on an intramural team with their floor or residence hall. As far as varsity sports, UNH students take a lot of pride in the hockey team. Games usually always sell out.**"

Q "**Varsity sports are pretty big**. Ice hockey is huge for girls and guys. Football is doing well, and so are men's and women's basketball. I play basketball, and we had huge crowds this year. The sports community is awesome. We all support each other—it's great."

Q "Intramural sports are very popular at UNH. **Many dorms start their own leagues for a variety of sports**. One of the most popular intramural sports is 'broomball,' which is played on the ice hockey rink. Varsity sports are big when the team is good. Our hockey team has been really good and has gone far in the past. Hockey games are always fun to go to. Football is pretty popular, as well as rugby and soccer."

Q "UNH is huge in sports. **They are so much fun to root for**, especially our nationally-ranked hockey team. Even if you're not into sports, you'll enjoy all the good-looking athletes."

Q "Both varsity and intramurals are huge! **Our hockey team is incredible**, so basically the whole school goes to watch them play. Intramurals are always going on, from volleyball, to floor hockey, to soccer. There is always an intramural team to play on."

Q "I would say, besides men's hockey, **the second-most popular sport is ultimate Frisbee**. There are always people playing it somewhere on campus."

If you like hockey, UNH is most definitely your place. UNH is home to the Wildcats, who have been a perennial powerhouse in Division I hockey for a long time. Unfortunately, hockey tends to overshadow many other varsity sports that the University has to offer. UNH is competitive in football, soccer, track and field, volleyball, basketball, alpine skiing, and also boasts one of the best intramural programs in New England. Intramural sports are a big deal to the students of UNH. While those who win don't get any endorsements or signing bonuses, they do get a T-shirt and just about all the respect you could ever need. Overall, the students at UNH aren't about big national titles, but more about the students getting their chance to show off some skills. Although, the students still save time to cheer the Wildcats hockey team to the national championship each year.

The College Prowler™ Grade on
Athletics: B+

A high grade in Athletics indicates that students have school spirit, that sports programs are respected, that games are well-attended, and that intramurals are a prominent part of student life.

Greek Life

Students Speak Out
ON GREEK LIFE

"**I'm a sorority sister here, and the Greek system is the largest student organization. But, it doesn't dominate the school by any means. The Greek system works very closely with the school and I love it! Go Greek!**"

Q "**The fraternities get a lot of hassle** from the school administration, but they aren't that out of control here."

Q "**The fraternities get a lot of hassle** from the school administration, but they aren't that out of control here."

Q "**The Greek life doesn't dominate the social scene**, but it's a huge part of UNH because it's where a lot of kids party. The frat parties are always filled with kids who aren't Greek, and there are millions of on-campus and off-campus apartments where people party."

Q "I think UNH is the number 11 party school in the nation, number two for binge drinking, and number two for petty drug usage. **Partying is huge here**, but there are also awesome academic programs. People work hard and party hard. The frats have a lot to do with that."

Q "Some of the frats are **definitely like "Animal House**," but they are all different."

Q "**Greek life is big on campus**, a lot of people pledge sororities or fraternities. They do have parties and such, but it doesn't dominate the social scene by any means."

Q "**The Greek houses are all in one general area of the campus**, on what we call 'frat row,' and yeah, it does dominate the social scene. There are parties down there almost every night of the weekend. Greek life is very popular on campus, and the Greeks get involved a lot to help out."

The Lowdown
ON GREEK LIFE

Number of Fraternities:
12

Number of Sororities:
5

Percent of Undergrad Men in Fraternities:
5%

Percent of Undergrad Women in Sororities:
5%

Fraternities on Campus:
12

Sororities on Campus:
5

The College Prowler Take
ON GREEK LIFE

With all the Greek houses being very close to campus and all in the same general area, it is hard for most students to ignore Greek life on the weekends. Overall, the amount of students in the Greek system is small. However, there are always parties on the weekends and "frat row" is where most students enjoy going. The Greek system at UNH is large enough to satisfy those who really want to become involved without shutting out those who choose not to. Not being Greek won't kill your social life, but pledging can make it a lot easier to meet people and keep up with the party scene. Many students who join fraternities and sororities say that the Greek system at UNH made their experience twice as good, and the people they met are friends for life.

The College Prowler™ Grade on
Greek Life: C+

A high grade in Greek Life indicates that sororities and fraternities are not only present, but also active on campus. Other determining factors include the variety of houses available and the respect the Greek community receives from the rest of the campus.

Drug Scene

The Lowdown
ON DRUG SCENE

Most Prevalent Drugs on Campus:
Marijuana

Liquor-Related Arrests:
102

Drug-Related Arrests:
38

Drug Counseling Programs:
Alcohol and other drug (AOD) services are offered by the Office of Health Education and Promotion (OHEP), including AOD education, assessment, intervention, counseling, and referral for UNH students on a voluntary or mandatory basis, as well as training and consultation for UNH staff and faculty.

Students Speak Out
ON DRUG SCENE

"There's a heck of a lot of weed. There are other drugs, but unless you do them, you rarely see them. Everything is behind closed doors. There a lot of kids that use Ritalin and Adderall to stay awake."

Q "**UNH is a big pot school**. I'm not into that, but if you are this is the school for you. It's very easy to get almost anything you want."

Q "I don't ever see people doing drugs besides weed. **I've heard of people doing Ecstasy and cocaine**, but it was no one I knew or saw. I am not really sure about this because I try to stay away from it."

Q "There are drugs present at UNH, just as if you went to any other campus. Pot is always big, no matter where you go, but on the other hand, I don't want you to think that we are a bunch of hippies who just smoke up all day long. There are probably some that actually will do that, but academically they don't last long. For the most part, **it's pretty much under control**."

Q "I'm not aware of any over-usage of any drug on campus, other than marijuana. **I know of a lot of people that smoke**. Alcohol is definitely the number-one substance used on campus."

Q "Drugs are a big issue with the police, as is underage drinking and transportation of alcohol. **If you drink somewhere private, you'll probably be fine**. Just carry alcohol in a backpack."

The College Prowler Take
ON DRUG SCENE

Although drug use is basically out in the open, it's rarely a hassle to the students. Some students aren't exposed to any drug use at all. The general consensus is that drugs are basically there if you want them to be. At UNH, the harder drugs are much less prevalent, and very few cases have been cited. Recently though, a campus convenience store was busted for selling weed and some harder drugs over the counter. The store has since been closed by local authorities. Overall, UNH is a fairly harmless school when it comes to drugs, but ultimately, the choice is up to the students.

The College Prowler™ Grade on
Drug Scene: C-

A high grade on Drug Scene indicates that drugs are not a noticeable part of campus life; drug use is not visible, and no pressure to use them seems to exist.

Campus Strictness

The Lowdown
ON CAMPUS STRICTNESS

What Are You Most Likely to Get Caught Doing on Campus?

Trying to sneak into bars while underage, inciting or participating in a riot, getting in a fight at the local bar, drinking in public, parking in a no-parking spot, mouthing off to a police officer, smoking weed in college woods or your dorm room

Students Speak Out
ON CAMPUS STRICTNESS

"Campus police suck, but only if you're stupid. If you stumble around outside drunk, they'll arrest you if you're underage. They do have a tendency to break up parties if they get too big and out of control."

Q "**There are always campus police driving around at night**. They don't usually bother you, though. If you're stumbling and being stupid, they might pull you aside and ask you what's going on, but they're usually harmless."

Q "**UNH is very strict about drinking since it's a dry campus**. This doesn't mean that UNH students listen to the rules, but you can easily lose housing for getting caught with alcohol or drugs in the dorms. If you have an open beer can outside, you will be arrested on the spot. It's pretty strict, but people still seem to get away with it, anyway."

Q "**Supposedly, this is a dry campus**. Police are out every night patrolling the streets for drunken teenagers. However, I have yet to hear of anybody being arrested. UNH housing is another story. Drinking in your room is grounds for eviction. They're not kidding around."

Q "They are very strict about underage drinking on campus. At the beginning of the year, **they will make an example of you** and evict you from the dorm system on your first offense."

Q "**Campus police can be a pain in the butt**, but just don't do anything stupid, and you'll be fine. There are plenty of arrests that happen every weekend from drug- or alcohol-related problems, but only the silly people get caught. Just be responsible, and you won't have to worry. Don't have open containers in the dorms or walk down the street after drinking, and you'll be fine. If you're being obvious and obnoxious, you'll get in trouble. There are cops around frat row Thursday through Saturday nights, but there are fewer at the apartments."

COLLEGE PROWLER™

Want to know how to avoid the authorities on campus? Check out the College Prowler book on UNH for more student responses on how to have a good time without getting busted, available at www.collegeprowler.com.

The College Prowler Take
ON CAMPUS STRICTNESS

The campus police don't seem to bother the students at UNH very much. As long as you are not acting like a fool, or putting yourself and others in danger, you'll be given free reign over your activities on and around campus. Campus police seem to realize that it is a college campus and they have to pick and choose their battles. Two things that campus police don't tolerate are drug offenses and underage drinking, especially in the dorms. Some local officers are even infamous for evicting students from the dorms on the first offense: all the more reason to drink intelligently and responsibly. Overall, students at UNH can enjoy their college experiences if they are smart about their actions.

The College Prowler™ Grade on
Campus Strictness: C-

A high Campus Strictness grade implies an overall lenient atmosphere; police and RAs are fairly tolerant, and the administration's rules are flexible.

Overall Experience

Students Speak Out
ON OVERALL EXPERIENCE

"At first, I was unsure of coming to UNH because I live so close. Once I got the chance to meet people and get to know the campus, I was hooked. **The people make it great.**"

Q "I am very pleased with my decision to attend UNH. **The campus is just so pretty, calm, and laid-back**, and everything is at your disposal. UNH really gives students a chance to shape their own experiences. Classes, parties, friends, drugs, sororities—they are all there for you to mold into whatever you want. Nothing is forced; it all just floats around your head like puzzle pieces, and it is your job to put that puzzle together."

Q "I was accepted to all the schools I applied to, but I chose UNH because **it was the one I could afford**. To be honest, it wasn't my first choice. Let me tell you, though, that I had a great time while I was there. The school is wonderful, and I had a good time."

Q "There are times that **the University makes you feel more like a number than a person**, and the business aspect of the school can be overpowering. You definitely know the administration is out to make as much money as possible, but the school is wonderful."

The Inside Scoop

The Lowdown
ON THE INSIDE SCOOP

Q "**I had a lot of trouble adjusting to college life my freshman year**, as a lot of students do. But after being here for two years, I have come to love UNH as my home. All of the experiences that I've had here have helped me to grow as a person, and I'm sure that UNH will provide me with many more. The people here are great; the students are so down-to-earth. When it comes down to it, I can't imagine myself anywhere other than here."

Q "I hear a lot of people complaining that **UNH is kind of a boring school**, but I don't ever really have a problem finding plenty of things to do. Plus, the people are all awesome here."

The College Prowler Take
ON OVERALL EXPERIENCE

Most students did not pick UNH as their first choice. Some felt wary because they felt that UNH was too close to home, others because the school was too far away. However, many of these same students will tell you that they learned to appreciate UNH and its well-rounded course curriculum, spectacular seasons, local "college town" atmosphere, and myriad activities for students of all ages. The campus also encourages students to explore all that they have to offer through many different organizations, including the American Students Association, several fraternities and sororities, and the National Society of Minorities in Hospitality. Although the campus has its short-comings in some areas, the effort of the administration is greatly evident through recent renovations of several dormitories (Mills, Congreve) and on-campus facilities (Holloway Commons, Whittemore Center). A very open and accepting environment seems to carry over to the non-student residents of Durham as well. This is obvious from the amount of specials by local businesses geared toward UNH students. The Durham House of Pizza would certainly not sell many one-dollar slices of pizza after midnight if it weren't for the students!

The town of Durham revolves around the students and vice-versa. Most students will agree that just about everyone they meet on campus has a great personality—not to mention being very good-looking as well! This atmosphere provides a very pleasant and encouraging campus that genuinely leaves the college experience at UNH up to the students to mold for the best.

UNH Slang:
Know the slang, know the school. The following is a list of things you really need to know before coming to UNH. The more of these words you know, the better off you'll be.

The MUB: The Memorial Union Building; the main student center on campus

The Whitt: The Whittemore Center, which houses the hockey rink and the student athletic center

PCAC: Paul Creative Arts Center. This is home to the Art Majors

Webcat: The schools online network for registering for classes, checking grades, and other personal information

CampCo: The Campus Convenience store

24: The convenience store 24

Fireplace room: A room in the MUB where students mainly sleep on couches

T-Hall Lawn: The lawn in front of Thompson Hall that is home to numerous lounging students in the spring

Boulder Field: A field on campus property that has a giant boulder in the middle of it; This is also the unofficial Frisbee field

The DUMP: The local grocery store also known as the Durham Market Place

Zylas: The P.K. Zylas store where you can find just about anything you will ever need for college life

The Greens: A group of apartments on Madbury Street, where weekend parties are very frequent

The Ghetto: A group of apartment notorious for being very cheap and very dirty, to say the least

Frat Row: Also known as Madbury Road, and is where all the fraternity and sorority houses are found

Kurt's Lunch Box: The guy who sells late-night snacks and sandwiches out of a trailer which can be found behind Mills Hall

College Woods: The area of woods behind the athletic fields and Boulder Field

Things I Wish I Knew Before Coming to UNH:

- Walking 10 miles a day is something you better get used to.
- Ultimate Frisbee means more to some people than life itself.
- The fourth floor of the library has the most comfortable chairs to read in.
- Find anyway possible to bring your car to school.
- Laundry baskets make great sleds.
- Sprint is the only cell phone service that works in this area. Period.

Tips to Succeed at UNH:

- Work really hard your first year to get your GPA up high, because it's incredibly hard to raise it once it goes down.
- Meet with your professors and get to know them well. You will always do better than if you didn't.
- It's a good idea to know what you want to study by the end of sophomore year.
- Join all the student groups you can in your freshman year and find people that you really have a connection with.
- Don't take 8 a.m. classes—you will never go to them.
- Buy your books a week early.

UNH Urban Legends

Congreve Hall is supposedly haunted by the ghost of a student from the early 1900s.

Stoke Hall, a dorm, was supposedly constructed to be easily demolished with dynamite.

It is said that if you do the deed with a special someone in the old wagon on top of Wagon Hill before you graduate, you will have good luck for the rest of your life. You also have to stay there overnight.

School Spirit

UNH school spirit is strong in areas such as sports. UNH's biggest team is the men's hockey team. They have made it to numerous Division I Final Fours and a few championship games. This high-caliber team brings out the heckler in everyone. The UNH fans are regarded as some the harshest fans in college hockey. Original cheers include much profanity, sexuality, and personal attacks on opposing teams and their fans. However, the fans do it all for their team and hold much pride in them, win or lose. Outside of sports, UNH pride is fairly strong. Students here generally seem proud to be a Wildcat. Everyone owns at least one UNH sweatshirt and lives in it through the winter months.

Traditions

At the men's hockey games, there are many traditions. The most popular one is throwing a dead fish onto the ice after the first goal of every home game.

"White-out the Whitt" is a hockey tradition where fans wear white to one of the men's home hockey games.

Boulderfest is the UNH version of Woodstock. Activities include all-day Frisbee, music, food, and a huge bonfire. This event happens every year as an end-of-the-year celebration.

"Stoke Wreath Lighting" is a tradition where the Stoke Hall staff constructs a giant wreath out of pine bows and Christmas lights and hangs it from the building with a crane. There is a ceremony to officially light up the wreath, where warm food and music kick off the holiday spirit.

Finding a Job or Internship

Advice
Have a good idea of what you want to study before you get to UNH. The sooner you know, the sooner you can start planning and talking with your advisor. This also gives you plenty of time to explore options. Most importantly, don't worry: it's not the end of the world if you don't know how to plan your life right off the bat. It is better to take the time to find out what you really want in life.

Career Center Resources & Services
Jobline, W.O.R.K. (Wildcat Online Recruiting Kit), job fairs, internships, on-campus recruiting, career mentor network

The Lowdown
ON FINDING A JOB OR INTERNSHIP

The best way to find an internship at UNH is through your major. Many of the majors offer senior internships for credit. Some internships are paid, and most are required. The UNH Career Center takes great pride in setting students up with numerous job opportunities. Students also are assigned an advisor in their specific major who can provide the best help with internships in that particular major. The campus also holds numerous job fairs for specific majors as well, which are open to anyone in those majors and provide direct contact with employers. The Career Center is located in Hood House next to the MUB.

COLLEGE PROWLER™

Need to know the ins and outs concerning life after UNH? Find out about all job and internship resources on campus at *www.collegeprowler.com*.

The Best & Worst

The Ten BEST Things About UNH:

1. The men's hockey team!
2. Outdoor barbecues
3. The country scenery
4. The ocean beaches
5. $1 pizza
6. Thompson Hall lawn on a warm spring day
7. Broomball competitions
8. Kurt's Lunch Box
9. Smoothies from the coffee shop
10. The "On The Spot" column in the student newspaper

The Ten WORST Things About UNH:

1. The bell tower (rings every 30 minutes)
2. No parking!
3. The lack of holidays
4. Mud season
5. The wind
6. Traffic on Main Street
7. The confusing layout of Holloway Commons
8. Winter parking ban
9. Price of books at the UNH Bookstore
10. New meal plans

University of Rhode Island

Kingston, RI 02881
www.uri.edu (401) 874-7000

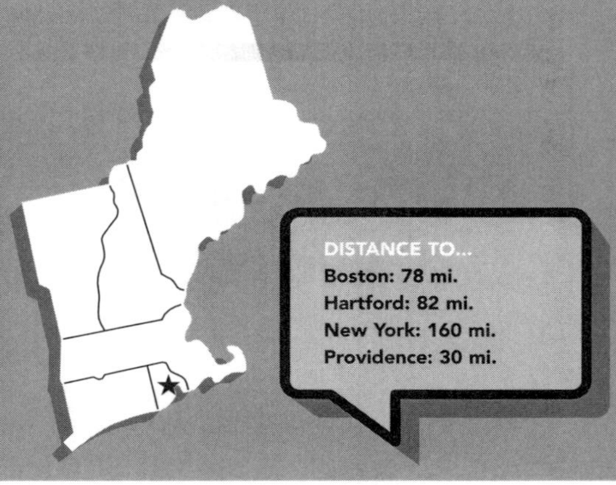

DISTANCE TO...
Boston: 78 mi.
Hartford: 82 mi.
New York: 160 mi.
Providence: 30 mi.

"It is not particularly hard to get into, so a lot of people have low expectations towards the academic credibility of the school."

Total Enrollment:
9,429

Acceptance Rate:
70%

Tuition:
$6,752 in-state, $18,338 out-of-state

Top 10% of High School Class:
19%

Acceptance Rate:
70%

Tuition:
70%

SAT Range
Verbal	Math	Total
500 – 590	510 – 610	1010 – 1200

SAT II
Not required

Most Popular Majors:
9% Communications
9% Psychology
6% Human Development and Family Studies

Students Also Applied To:*
University of Massachusetts, Boston University, University of Connecticut, University of Delaware
*For more school info check out www.collegeprowler.com

Table of Contents

Academics	111
Local Atmosphere	112
Safety & Security	114
Computers	115
Facilities	117
Campus Dining	118
Off-Campus Dining	120
Campus Housing	121
Off-Campus Housing	123
Diversity	124
Guys & Girls	125
Athletics	127
Greek Life	129
Drug Scene	130
Campus Strictness	131
Overall Experience	132
The Inside Scoop	133
Finding a Job or Internship	135
The Best & Worst	136

College Prowler Report Card

Academics	B
Local Atmosphere	B
Safety & Security	A-
Computers	B-
Facilities	A-
Campus Dining	C+
Off-Campus Dining	B+
Campus Housing	B-
Off-Campus Housing	A-
Diversity	D
Guys	A-
Girls	A
Athletics	A-
Greek Life	C+
Drug Scene	C+
Campus Strictness	B-

Academics

Special Degree Options
Dual-Degree Program: Master of Community Planning and Jurist Doctrine, Engineering Master of Science and Diploma, Master in Science in Labor Relations, and Human Resources and Juris Doctrine

Sample Academic Programs
Honors Program, Study Abroad, Office of Internship and Experimental Education, National Student Exchange, ROTC, Community Service Opportunities

The Lowdown
ON ACADEMICS

Did You Know?
Are you undecided? URI offers around 200 undergraduate, graduate, and degree programs so students are not limited in their studies.

Degrees Awarded:
Bachelor, Post-Bachelor Certificate, Master, First Professional, and Doctorate

Undergraduate Schools:
College of Arts and Sciences, College of Continuing Education, College of Business Administration, College of Engineering, College of Environment and Life Sciences, College of Human Science and Services, College of Nursing, College of Pharmacy, College of Graduate School of Oceanography, University College, University Library

Full-time Faculty:
93.3%

Faculty with Terminal Degree:
90%

Student-to-Faculty Ratio:
18:1

Average Course Load:
12-19 credits

AP Test Score Requirements:
Possible credit for scores of 3, 4, 5

Best Place to Study
Library

Students Speak Out
ON ACADEMICS

"All my classes are hands-on. If I miss one, I usually need someone to explain what we did. I really do benefit a lot from going to class, so I try not to ever miss it."

"I'm an engineering student, and every lecture that I have has over 200 people in it. Most people don't need to go to these lectures. **You have to go about 50 percent of the time**, and you'll be able to do fine in the class. Teachers can't take attendance with that many people, so participation won't affect your grade that much."

"I'm a business major, and **I have group projects in pretty much all my classes**. I'm in small classes, and I've never had a TA (teacher's assistant). Classes usually have the same kids in them because it's all the same major."

Q "I was undecided at first. I started taking all my general education requirements until I finally decided to be an English major. I was behind in the program because just about **every major has their own curriculum**. The best way to keep on schedule is to know your major going into college."

Q "The easiest A you'll get, and **the most pointless class, is URI 101**. All freshmen are required to take it, and it's just a course about URI. It's a waste of time, but I guess it's supposed to get you involved with the school."

Local Atmosphere

The College Prowler Take
ON ACADEMICS

The Lowdown
ON LOCAL ATMOSPHERE

Teachers are an important aspect in everyone's academic career. If you have good teachers, you'll be pushed to do well. Since URI is a pretty big school with around 10,000 undergraduate students, classrooms range in size. Students will find themselves in lectures with over 500 students, classrooms with less then 20 students, and everywhere in between. There's less of a chance to connect with professors in large classes. Within a smaller classroom setting, there's more of an opportunity to build a personal relationship. However, no matter how big your class is, every teacher makes themselves available to all students. Teachers encourage students to contact them by having office hours, writing them e-mails, and some even give out their home phone numbers. It's up to the students to contact the teachers.

One of the most frustrating things that students deal with is not being able to get into classes that they need. There was only a 34 percent graduation rate for the entering class in 1997. Taking four to six years to graduate is not uncommon for most URI students.

Region:
South County

City, State:
Kingston, Rhode Island

Setting:
Rural

Distance from Providence:
40 minutes

Distance from Boston:
1.5 hours

Points of Interest:
Beaches: Narragansett State Beach, Scarborough State Beach, Block Island

Closest Shopping Malls or Plazas:
Belmont Market, Kingston Emporium, Mariner Square

Closest Movie Theatre:
Entertainment Cinemas
30 Village Square Drive
South Kingston, RI 02881
(401) 793-8008

Major Sports Teams:
Boston Bruins, Boston Red Sox, New England Patriots

The College Prowler™ Grade on
Academics: B

A high Academics grade generally indicates that Professors are knowledgeable, accessible, and genuinely interested in their students' welfare. Other determining factors include class size, how well professors communicate, and whether or not classes are engaging.

City Websites:
www.visitrhodeisland.com; www.rhody.com

Fun Facts about Rhode Island:

1. "Dumb and Dumber," shot in Providence, helped introduce the big blue bug to the rest of the world. The 58-foot-long bug is the world's largest bug, which sits on the roof of New England Pest Control.

2. "Outside Providence," starring Shawn Hatosy, Alec Baldwin, and Amy Smart was filmed on the URI campus in 1999.

3. Rhode Island is the birthplace of Newport Storm beer, a brewery started by four friends and their common love of beer.

Students Speak Out

"Narragansett is a college town. My whole neighborhood is practically URI kids. It's fun because there's always something to do. I'm always running into kids at Stop & Shop or Cumby's."

Q "I live off campus in Narragansett. Half of the people that I run into who live there year-round are pretty friendly, but the other half hate college kids because of all the parties. **They like to call the cops on you**, even if you only have a couple people over because they think it will turn into a party."

Q "The local shopping is basically shopping plazas. The closet mall is in Warwick, about 20 minutes away. **There are plenty of restaurants and bars around**. As for shopping, it is mainly independently-owned stores or local shops."

Q "**I wish that Wal-Mart was closer.** It took me a while to get used to having to get on the highway just to run some errands. I guess I just need to explore Narragansett better to find the hidden treasures. I do find the 24-hour CVS helpful, though."

Q "Rhode Island is small. It makes it easier because **there are, like, two main roads that lead to everything**. All the local shopping is pretty much together in the same area. If you just keep driving down the same street, you'll run into something that you're looking for."

The College Prowler Take
ON LOCAL ATMOSPHERE

The local atmosphere is a huge part of the overall URI atmosphere. College students have taken over the local community and have made it their own. With most students living off campus and in local towns, the atmosphere of Narragansett is similar to what you would find on campus. Narragansett is your average town, but URI students make it stand out. Over the years, they've single-handedly turned this summer town into a year-round paradise.

There are a lot of restaurants and bars throughout town, along with shopping and entertainment. There are shopping plazas and independently-owned stores all around. There's a movie theatre close by as well as a bowling alley. Even the grocery stores are taken over by URI students in Narragansett. The local atmosphere lacks a mall and major commercial companies.

Since Narragansett is a beach town, there are a lot of fishing, boating, and camping sites around town. This offers students something a little different than what you'd find in a city atmosphere.

The College Prowler™ Grade on
Local Atmosphere: B

A high Local Atmosphere grade indicates that the area surrounding campus is safe and scenic. Other factors include nearby attractions, proximity to other schools, and the town's attitude toward students

Safety & Security

Students Speak Out
ON SAFETY & SECURITY

"I see cop cars parked outside of buildings and dorms. I think police are mostly worried about illegal parking, especially during the day."

Q "I have to walk back to my car alone after a late class, but I've never felt scared. **The campus is well-lit**, and I just take major pathways as opposed to shortcuts."

Q "**I hate walking around at night**. I live on campus, and when I walk to my car at night or to other dorms, I usually go with someone. I don't think that it's particularly unsafe, I just don't want to put myself in an uncomfortable situation."

Q "The major thing that I worry about on campus is my car. The parking lot is pretty far away from my dorm, so I can't keep an eye on it. It does make me feel better that **there are security cameras in the parking lots**, but they only do so much. I don't know if police patrol the lots at night or what."

Q "I think the dorms are pretty safe. There are security cameras in the new dorm and where I live in Barlow. I heard that someone once got in trouble by the RAs for running around the halls and knocking on doors and just being stupid. So, I think **the dorms are pretty safe**."

The Lowdown
ON SAFETY & SECURITY

Number of URI Police:
19

Phone:
(401) 874-2121

Safety Services:
Campus Escort, SafeRide/SafeWalk, Rape Crisis Center, Campus Emergency Phones,

Health Services:
Orthopedics, Dermatology, Internal Medicine, Gynecology, Psychiatry, Pharmacy, Nutritionist, Complete physicals and Basic medical services, Immunizations, X-ray lab, Birth control

Health Center Office Hours:
The Potter Building, home to Health Services is open Monday thru Friday, 8 a.m. to 8 p.m. and Saturdays and Sundays from 10 a.m. to 6 p.m.

Did You Know?

Rhode Island was ranked the 19th safest state in 2001 by the *Morgan Quitno Press*.

The College Prowler Take
ON SAFETY & SECURITY

Most students can agree that they feel safe on campus. All people on campus have a reason for being there. There are predominately students, faculty, staff, or visitors found treading through campus. URI is not in the middle of a city or surrounded by other main attractions; it's just a college campus. This limits the amount of outsiders from coming on campus. This setting allows students to feel safe and free to walk around campus without having to worry about any outside elements getting in.

Students feel that all the safety precautions, like emergency phones and escorts, make them feel more comfortable on campus, especially at night. Since the campus is large, well-lit areas are essential for providing safety once the sun goes down. There are some safety measures that students can do on their own to help ensure their safety. Students are encouraged to walk in groups at night, and they should not let anyone into the resident halls. All residents need an ID in order to enter the dorms. However, people do get in without them by the help of fellow students. Security cameras have been installed in new dorms throughout campus and in parking lots. Police patrol the campus, and are there 24 hours, seven days a week. A close eye is kept on students, and the University is doing all it can to provide safety for students.

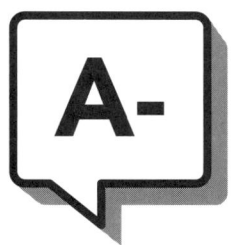

The College Prowler™ Grade on
Safety & Security: A-

A high grade in Safety & Security means that students generally feel safe, campus police are visible, blue-light phones and escort services are readily available, and safety precautions are not overly necessary.

Computers

The Lowdown
ON COMPUTERS

High-Speed Network?
Yes

Wireless Network?
Yes

Number of Labs:
2 student labs, 3 instructional labs, 2 multimedia labs

Numbers of Computers:
1,716

24-Hour Labs:
None

Charge to Print?
Yes, students need to purchase a Copico Card, which works like debit card. Black and white printing costs nine cents and color printing costs 75 cents per copy.

Did You Know?

The HELIN catalog, an online library for URI that allows students to search the Kingston Library and all other university libraries in Rhode Island, has been updated and more information has been added to help students in their research.

Students Speak Out
ON COMPUTERS

{ "I've never had a problem with the Internet access on campus. I'm always able to get on, and stay on, for as long as I want. I never get kicked off, and it runs pretty fast."

Q "I don't know what I would do without a computer. **I live on the Internet and AIM.** If I didn't have a computer, it would be annoying to have to walk up to the library to go to the lab. It's just more convenient to have your own."

Q "**I bought my computer through the URI computer store** when I was freshman. They had it all set up for me when I moved in. I didn't have to do anything. Wherever I had a problem with it, they were there to fix it."

Q "Even though I don't get as much work done in my room, **I can go at my own pace** and not have to worry about trying to print and paying for paper and ink every time I need to hand something in."

Q "If you go to any other computer that isn't in a lab at school, **it's so slow**. The computer lab in the library was full one time, so I went upstairs to one of the random computers. It was so slow and made all kinds of noises, like it was really struggling. I don't even know why they're there. I guess if you're desperate, use them, but they're really bad."

The College Prowler Take
ON COMPUTERS

Computers are an important part of college life. Students use computers to surf the web and talk to friends through instant messaging. Not much school work gets done in the labs. Although the computer labs are there for students to get work and research done, or for those who don't own their own computer, they are more likely to be used for amusement. Most students have their own computers and printers, so most of their work is being done in their rooms or at home. Students also rarely take their laptops around campus. There is a wireless network, but it's limited to particular areas on campus like the library and certain classrooms. All dorms have Internet access, and most students love it and never have problems getting online.

URI is not the most technically-advanced school, but it does offer all the necessary equipment.

The College Prowler™ Grade on
Computers: B-

A high grade in Computers designates that computer labs are available, the computer network is easily accessible, and the campus' computing technology is up-to-date.

Facilities

The Lowdown
ON FACILITIES

What Is There to Do?
Students study at the library, meet with friends at the Union, workout at the gym, go shopping, or grab something to eat at the Emporium. There are workshops on diversity, art exhibits, and concerts. Venders are also known to come to URI and set up "mini malls," selling various items such as posters, jewelry, and clothes.

Movie Theatre on Campus?
There is no movie theatre directly on campus; however, different organizations will sometimes hold movie nights where students are able to view movies for a discounted price.

Libraries:
University Library, Kingston

Student Center:
The Memorial Union

Athletic Center:
Boss Ice Arena, Keaney Gym, Ryan Center

Bar on Campus?
URI is a dry campus and there is no bar.

Bowling on Campus?
No

Favorite Things to Do:
Most students like to hang out at Union during the week. There are pool tables and an arcade for students to enjoy. Kids also hang out on the quad, which is a grassy area in the middle of campus. On nice days people play Frisbee, sunbathe, or just relax. Plays are performed at the URI Theatre, guest speakers come, comedians perform, and concerts are held.

Popular Places to Chill:
The Student Union, The "Reserves" at the library (the only place they allow students to talk and eat), the quad on nice days, dorm rooms and lounges, The Emporium

Coffeehouse on Campus?
Yes. 1930 Coffee House, The Memorial Union Daily Grind Coffee Cart, Reserves in the library

Students Speak Out
ON FACILITIES

"**I like when The Ryan Center has concerts. It's a great, new building. It's much better than Keaney, where all the events used to be.**"

Q "There are plenty of food places up at the emporium that deliver down to the dorms. **The Union has a lot of stuff**. The bookstore is there, and so are some food places and a convenience store. I also go to the information center a lot to buy a newspaper or stamps, stuff like that. Everything you need could be found on campus, except beer."

Q "The campus is pretty big, so **people tend to stick to one part**."

Q "I'm glad we have the Emporium. There are a bunch of fast restaurants up there, and **most of them deliver to the dorms**. There's a CVS, bookstore, coffee shops, tanning place, and a salon; it's really convenient."

> "**I have everything I need on campus.** Food, books, supplies; whenever I need something I just go to the Union or the Emporium. I feel like Wal-Mart and those places are far away. I can usually get what I need right here on campus."

The College Prowler Take
ON FACILITIES

URI has a lot to offer their students. Since there is a high volume of commuters, it's good to have a place to go to during down time and in between classes. The Union is one of the most popular places for students on campus. Both residents and commuters enjoy and benefit from all that the Union has to offer. Students can get food, play games, get their hair done, join or learn about student organizations, or just hang out, all in one building. It is a great resource to have for all students and even faculty. Most students who live on campus feel that they do not need to go off campus to find what they are looking for. Just about everything is accessible through campus facilities. The Emporium is another place that has a lot of stores and eateries for students to enjoy. Since the URI campus is in a somewhat remote area, they need to have a variety of things available.

There are little complaints about the lack of activities or things to do while on campus. The campus has a lot of new attractions, like the Ryan Center, which holds a lot of sporting events and concerts. Also, the gym is a great retreat for students who have some extra time and want to workout. With all the facilities on campus, students have just about everything they need all within walking distance.

The College Prowler™ Grade on
Facilities: A-

A high Facilities grade indicates that the campus is aesthetically pleasing and well-maintained; facilities are state-of-the-art, and libraries are exceptional. Other determining factors include the quality of both athletic and student centers and an abundance of things to do on campus.

Campus Dining

The Lowdown
ON CAMPUS DINING

Freshman Meal Plan Requirement?
All students who live on campus are required to have a meal plan.

Meal Plan Average Cost:
There are two different meal plans offered at URI. The Points Plan is more equivalent to money; each point is worth one cent in the dining halls. The average cost of a Points Plan is $1,646 per semester, earning students 50,350 points. The Board Plan is based on meals per week. The average cost of a Board Plan is $1,560 per semester, allowing 15 meals a week.

Other Options:
Students can set up a Ram Account, which is accepted at many places on campus. The Ram Account is a savings account that students can deposit money into. Students are able to use their URI ID as a credit card at participating restaurants, the bookstore, vending machines, and laundry rooms in resident halls.

Student Favorites:
Ronzio's, Kingston Pizza, Bagelz, International Steakhouse, Spikes

Students Speak Out
ON CAMPUS DINING

The College Prowler Take
ON CAMPUS DINING

"I get grossed out by some of the food. The cooks look unhappy to be there, and I don't know what they're putting into the food. They just glob in onto trays."

Q "There's a lot of variety. They offer a little bit of everything, so you can usually find something that you like. Also, **most of the food is pretty traditional**. You can't really make a bad turkey sandwich or ruin a bowl of salad."

Q "I wish some of the meals were healthier, specifically the hot meals. They usually serve chicken nuggets or something fried for lunch and dinner. And it seems like **all the hot vegetables are soaked in butter** or oil."

Q "**I can totally see how people get the 'Freshman 15**.' They have a lot of desserts and fatty or fried foods. Who's going to have a salad when there's pizza and burgers and fries? Even their cereal choices are all sugar, like Lucky Charms and Frosted Flakes. There's no Total or anything healthy."

Q "During the holidays, they have special dinners. They decorate and have special meals, like steak and gourmet side dishes. **They make it all fancy**. It's fun, and good."

Q "**I wish there was more of a fruit variety**. There are always apples, bananas, and sometimes pears. But where's the oranges or pineapples, peaches and plums?"

Dining halls are not places that produce gourmet meals. They are there to provide a minimal amount of nourishment for students. Roger Williams and Butterfield dining halls are both buffets, and students have to have their IDs swiped before entering, deducting one meal or a designated number of points. Students are then free to get whatever they want and as much of it as they want. The all-you-can-eat factor is a definite plus when it comes to dining. If you try something and don't like it, students can go up and try something else. The quality is not the greatest, but there are a lot of options that can't really be messed up. Sandwiches are one meal that is pretty much a guaranteed fulfillment, so they are a popular meal of choice. Having multiple dining halls allows students to find their favorites and not be stuck with one option. Although most students complain about the food, they learn to live with it. Most agree that it could be a lot worse; you learn to adjust to the food preparation and taste.

The College Prowler™ Grade on
Campus Dining: C+

Our grade on Campus Dining addresses the quality of both school-owned dining halls and independent on-campus restaurants as well as the price, availability, and variety of food.

Off-Campus Dining

Students Speak Out
ON OFF-CAMPUS DINING

"You can take your parents to any of the restaurants around town. They're all pretty nice and different from the average Chili's or Friday's."

The Lowdown
ON OFF-CAMPUS DINING

Best Pizza:
Kingston Pizza

Best Chinese:
New Dragon

Best Breakfast:
Bluebird Cafe

Best Wings:
Casey's Grill and Bar

Best Healthy:
Pick Pocket, Subway

Late-Night Food Specials:
Fat Jacks, Kingston Pizza

Best Place to Take Your Parents:
Charlie O's, Coast Guard House, and Cucina and Twist

24-Hour Eating:
None

Student Favorites:
The Mews, Casey's, Charlie O's, Kingston Pizza

Closest Grocery Store:
Cumberland Farms
90 Fortin Road

"There are a lot of places to eat around town. I hardly go out to dinner because I can't afford it. **A lot of the restaurants are also popular bars**. Either there is a separate bar or dining room, or after a certain time the restaurant turns into more of a bar scene."

"My friends and I have our spot—The Mews. There are a lot of choices, anything from salads to sandwiches, to pizza and pasta. Plus they have a huge beer and drink menu. **The price isn't bad** either, and the atmosphere is chill."

"**I wish there was a 24-hour diner** or something around. I think the latest places stay open is 1 or 2 a.m. Cheap and 24-hours, you can't really beat that for a poor college kid."

"Being on the beach, there's a lot of good seafood restaurants. And you have the hidden gems like Aunt Carrie's. **You can always get a great bowl of clam chowder** wherever you go out to dinner in Rhode Island. It's fantastic!"

Fun Fact:
Ever substitute vinegar for ketchup? Rhode Islanders like to dip their french fries in vinegar for a taste of something different.

The College Prowler Take
ON OFF-CAMPUS DINING

Food is important to all college kids. Most students don't get cooked meals like at home, so going out to eat makes food taste that much better. The good thing about off-campus dining is the selection. There is a variety of restaurants all within the same area. There are hardly any chain restaurants nearby except for fast food places like McDonalds, Burger King, Taco Bell, and KFC, but you can hardly call that dining. Most of the restaurants have a laid-back atmosphere, and people rarely complain about service and quality. College students can go out for a nice meal for a decent price and come home satisfied. Some restaurants have bars that are also popular with students. If you like your meal that much, you could just head over to the bar and get a good seat before the rest of URI shows up for their night out. Places like this include The Mews, Casey's and Charlie O's.

Overall, students enjoy the off-campus dining options. Although there are a lot of places to choose from, they all offer similar menus. There are American, Italian, Chinese, and seafood places, but that's about it. Some students complain about the lack of a healthy restaurant, Subway is probably the healthiest, and that's just a shame. Students do like how there are a lot of places that deliver and are open late, but they are still waiting for a 24-hour hot spot.

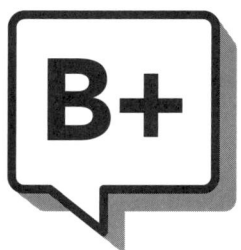

The College Prowler™ Grade on
Off-Campus Dining: B+

A high off-campus dining grade implies that off-campus restaurants are affordable, accessible, and worth visiting. Other factors include the variety of cuisine and the availability of alternative options (vegetarian, vegan, Kosher, etc.).

Campus Housing

The Lowdown
ON CAMPUS HOUSING

Room Types:
Standard resident halls are constructed by having either small or large corridors of rooms with a common bathroom. Two room, suite-style resident halls have two rooms connected by a private bathroom. Four room suite-style resident halls group four individual rooms with two private bathrooms per floor.

Best Dorms:
Barlow, Butterfield, Bresseler, Browning, Weldin

Worst Dorms:
Merrow, Tucker

Undergrads on Campus:
41%

Number of Dormitories:
19

Number of University-Owned Apartments:
2, University Terrace and North Village Apartments

Bed Type:
Twin beds; there's an option of bunking beds and ordering loft beds.

Cleaning Service?
Cleaning services are only offered in public areas and common bathrooms in resident halls.

You Get
Twin bed, desk and chair, closet or wardrobe some with a dresser, cable TV, internet access, free local and on-campus phone line

Also Available
Tucker is the wellness dorm. There are sorority and fraternity houses on campus along with the Rainbow Diversity house.

Students Speak Out
ON CAMPUS HOUSING

"I live in Weldin, and I meet new people all the time. The corridor-style hallways are nice, and the community bathrooms are good meeting places. I also like that it's all freshmen."

"Even though the older dorms aren't that nice; **the rooms are more private**, and you basically have your own bathroom. Kids don't get in much trouble because they aren't as strict. Plus, the balcony rooms are pretty cool."

"I lived in Coddington my sophomore year. The first day I moved in, **we had a bee infestation**. I woke up to buzzing the whole first week and we probably had to kill around 50 bees. Apparently, they were getting in through one of the vents. I was not happy, and after that I hated the old dorms. They're just gross."

"Our toilet got clogged once because my roommate decided to flush a bunch of paper towels. To make a long story short, it leaked down to the two floors below us. The girls were pissed. **It's always exciting living in the dorms**!"

"Sophomore year, I was in a triple with two other friends. It got a little tight at times, but we managed. Plus, **we got a good discount on housing for tripling up**. It was worth it. The three of us spend most of our time together anyways, so why not benefit from it?"

The College Prowler Take
ON CAMPUS HOUSING

There's a wide range of dorms that students can live in, and there are pros and cons to each one. A couple of dorms were recently developed, and the older ones are slowly being renovated. Although the new dorms, like Barlow, Weldin, Bresseler, and Butterfield, are nicer, cleaner, and in the center of campus, they are more strict. It is harder for students to drink and be loud in the newer dorms. The older dorms like Coddington, Dorr, and Burnside allow students to get away with a lot more, but they also have to put up with poor living conditions.

All the resident halls differ from each other. Some buildings have balcony rooms and private bathrooms, while others have air conditioning and community bathrooms. There are two students per room, and when there's a housing shortage, they'll squeeze three in a room. However, those students sharing a room with three other people do get compensation. Housing and Residential Life does make it easy for students to switch rooms if they are not satisfied with the living conditions or roommate situation. No matter which dorm you live in, you will have a good time.

The College Prowler™ Grade on
Campus Housing: B-

A high Campus Housing grade indicates that dorms are clean, well-maintained, and spacious. Other determining factors include variety of dorms, proximity to classes, and social atmosphere.

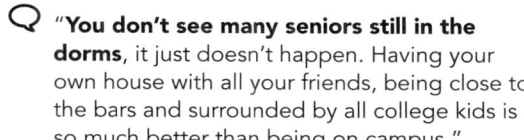

Off-Campus Housing

Q "**You don't see many seniors still in the dorms**, it just doesn't happen. Having your own house with all your friends, being close to the bars and surrounded by all college kids is so much better than being on campus."

Q "**I hate my neighbors**. We live next to this old couple who complain about every little thing we do. The first weekend we moved in, the cops came to our house at 9 p.m. because there were five cars in the driveway, three of which were ours. I guess the neighbors thought we were having a party. The cop was really nice, though. He apologized and knew it was all a misunderstanding."

The Lowdown
ON OFF-CAMPUS HOUSING

Undergrads in Off-Campus Housing:
59%

Best Time to Look for a Place:
Students start looking for off-campus housing as early as October and as late as the summer months. The earlier you start, the more options you'll have.

Average Rent for a Two-Five Person House:
$500/month for each person, not including utilities.

Popular Areas:
Bonnet Shores, Narragansett Pier, Scarborough Beach, Eastward Look

The College Prowler Take
ON OFF-CAMPUS HOUSING

Living off campus is definitely worth it. After sophomore year, most students get tired of living in a one-room dorm and head off campus. The cost of living off campus is about the same as living on campus, but every house is different. The average rent per resident is anywhere between $450 - $500 a month. The part that gets expensive is buying food, gas, and utilities. Even though there are more bills to be paid, there is more independence. Campus is about 10 miles away and takes about 20 minutes to get there. However, people who live "Down the Line," as it is referred to by students, are closer to the beach, bars, and restaurants. Since Narragansett is a beach town, families who have their summer houses here rent them out from September to May to URI students. Anywhere from two to 10 people can live in a house together.

Living off campus definitely has its perks. You have more freedom to do the things you like and not get into trouble. Finding a house is convenient and well worth it.

Students Speak Out
ON OFF-CAMPUS HOUSING

"Just about everyone moves off campus after their sophomore year. I like the freedom and independence. Plus, you aren't restricted to one tiny room for two people."

A-

The College Prowler™ Grade on
Off-Campus Housing: A-

A high grade in Off-Campus Housing indicates that apartments are of high quality, close to campus, affordable, and easy to secure.

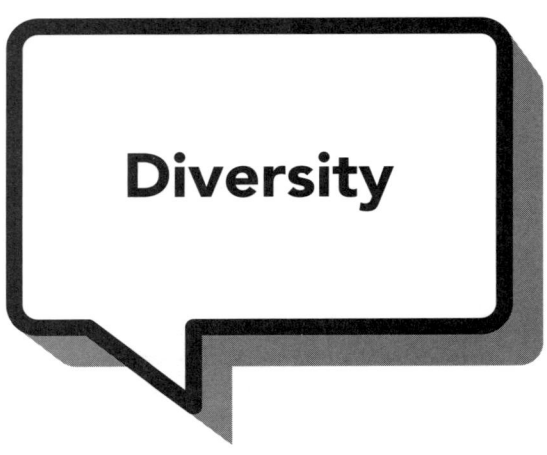

Diversity

Economic Status

URI is mostly middle-class students. There is little poverty in the surrounding communities, and most out-of-state and in-state students are able to afford the tuition.

Minority Clubs

There are a number of minority student organizations at URI. The Asian Student Association conducts community services and other social events. Hillel is a center for Jewish life that explores and develops Jewish identity. Cape Verdean Student Association (CVSA), Latin American Students Association (LASA), Native American Students Association (NASA), Cultural Italian American Organization, Students Organized Against Racism (SOAR), and NAACP URI chapter all deal with race and ethnicity.

The Lowdown
ON DIVERSITY

African American: 4%
Asian American: 3%
Hispanic: 4%
Native American: 0%
White: 89%
International: 0%
Out-of-State: 39%

Students Speak Out
ON DIVERSITY

Political Activity

Rhode Island is, for the most part, a democratic state. Most students and staff members are pretty liberal in their political views. Protests are rarely held, and most students are usually apathetic towards politics. Students are concerned, but they keep their opinions to themselves.

Gay Tolerance

The acceptance of gays is growing at URI due to certain organizations' awareness and education. Diversity Week is held each year, which is a workshop of different events that promote diversity, including homosexuality. There are also student organizations, such as Students for Social Change and Gay, Lesbian, Bisexual, Transgender Association (GLBTA), for all students to join. The Rainbow Diversity house is a living community that gives students the opportunity for social change by taking classes in a diverse environment.

"The school is predominantly white. I don't think it's that diverse, but there are other races here."

"There are a lot of minority groups on campus. **The Multicultural Center is always putting on events** to support and educate minorities. They have a Diversity Week and a lot of teachers encourage students to go to the events. Some give extra credit for it, and I think all freshmen are required to go to an event for URI 101. It's a good learning experience, and they make it really fun. There are poetry readings, concerts, and lectures."

"A lot of Rhode Island is Indian land, just listen to the names of the town—Narragansett. I think **there's a big Indian population in Charleston**, so it's pretty diverse."

"No one comes from the same background, and everyone has a different life history. Diversity could be something as simple as different gender and different personalities, to different races and classes. **I think there's a mix on campus**, just like there is a mix in the United States."

💬 "**People judge you more on where you're from**, your hometown and state, rather than your race. People have more to say about where you're from than about your ethnic background."

The College Prowler Take
ON DIVERSITY

Diversity is not a major part of the student body. There are, however, a variety of races, ethnicities, religions, and classes that attend URI. Students are not afraid to promote and show their pride for all their differences. Although the campus might not be that diverse, there are a lot of organizations that promote awareness and educate people about cultural differences. Diversity Week is a great example of this. Students get the chance to experience events outside of their normal, everyday lives. This is important in the understanding of social, moral, and physical differences.

Even though URI is not an overwhelmingly diverse university, it is very accepting of diversity. Minorities should not feel threatened or intimidated by the dominant white race on campus. Students are open-minded and fair in their attitudes towards diversity, and URI and the surrounding community are unprejudiced.

The College Prowler™ Grade on
Diversity: D

A high grade in Diversity indicates that ethnic minorities and international students have a notable presence on campus and that students of different economic backgrounds, religious beliefs, and sexual preferences are well-represented.

Guys & Girls

The Lowdown
ON GUYS & GIRLS

Women Undergrads: 56.5%

Men Undergrads: 43.5%

Birth Control Available?
Yes, it is available by appointment at the Women's Clinic. A full exam is required before prescribing birth control, and women have a choice as to what form they would like, either pills, patch or shots. Birth control prescriptions can be picked up directly at the Health Services Pharmacy, or at local pharmacies. The price ranges for birth control start at $10 to $30 a pack.

Social Scene
Students are naturally outgoing and charismatic. Everyone is looking forward to having a good time, and people are always willing to show you one. Students embrace the social scene with open arms. Like all schools, URI has its share of cliques, but no one is completely shut out. Sports teams interact with one another as well as fraternities, sororities, and other student organizations and clubs. Even if you don't belong to a particular group, it isn't hard to make some friends. Whether you meet people in your classes, within your major, or just from the living situation, URI is a social school filled with outgoing students who like a good balance between work and play.

Hookups or Relationships?

Most college students are usually too immature, too horny, or too promiscuous to have a steady relationship in college. College is supposed to be the best time of a person's life. With that said, most students don't want to be tied down in relationships.

Best Place to Meet Guys/Girls

Students have a lot of luck finding hotties on and off campus. On campus, students can find love at first sight anywhere from the gym, to the library. The more social places on campus, like the Union, dining halls and resident halls, are also places that you can run into your next crush. As for off campus, the bars, parties, and restaurants can definitely help you meet the guy or girl of your dreams. Since URI students have taken over the local towns, the chance that you would meet a fellow URI student is pretty much a guarantee. URI is a very social college, and meeting new people is not hard. The real challenge is trying to find that special someone and keep them all to you.

Top Three Places to Find Hotties

1. The Gym
2. The Union
3. Bars/Parties

Top Places to Hook up

1. Off-Campus Parties
2. Frats
3. Dorm Room Parties
4. Parking Lots
5. Bathroom/Shower

Dress Code

There is no particular dress code at URI. During the day, for the most part, students dress causal—jeans and a t-shirt, or sweats. The fashion basically depends on the mood a person is in or by the comfort that they desire. The same person may wear sweats one day and a skirt and heels the next. Labels are more important for girls. A lot of girls want nice clothes and show off their sense of style. No matter what mood you're in, students try to stay in style, and there will always be people flaunting the newest fashion trends. Guys are generally not impressed as much by fashion, just as long as you look presentable.

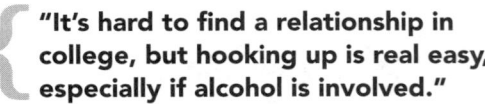

Students Speak Out
ON GUYS & GIRLS

"It's hard to find a relationship in college, but hooking up is real easy, especially if alcohol is involved."

"I had a boyfriend going into college, and I broke up with him within the first week I got here. There are so many hot guys, **I wanted to be single**!"

"There are a lot of hotties at URI. **There's a girl for every guy, and every type of girl is here**. You have your brains, your athletes, your party girls, shy girls, small girls, fat girls, tall girls, short girls, all girls. You are bound to find one you like."

"Frat guys are really cocky. **They think they're so cool** and have the most amazing parties. I try to stay away from the whole frat scene."

"It's hard to have a relationship here because **there is so much temptation**. Part of me wishes that I was in a relationship because it would be more satisfying and fulfilling. But then again, it would be hard to trust someone because there is such a temptation to cheat."

"I always see couples on campus, holding hands and walking to class together. **I thought nobody dated in college**. Is it just me?"

The College Prowler Take
ON GUYS & GIRLS

URI is a hot school. Students can potentially meet the guy or girl of their dreams just about anywhere on campus, as well as off campus. There are no limits to where you can meet attractive people of the opposite sex. The student body at URI is also pretty vain, and girls and guys both aim to impress the opposite sex. Most students develop a crush without even looking for one. A lot of students take pride in their looks and want to show off their best assets. There is no stereotypical guy or girl on campus; just a wide variety of looks and personality. There's a lot of competition, though. Guys are aggressive and will go after what they want, while girls just want to be impressed and swept off their feet.

Love on campus can be a little tricky. Even if you aren't interested in a relationship, chances are you want some love and affection. Relationships may not be at the top of students' lists of things they want, but hookups are. Casual sex is not an uncommon thing at URI. Alcohol might play a small part in this by lowering the tension and liberating one's true self. If you're looking for love, you might not be successful at URI. If you are looking for a casual open relationship, congratulations. You've hit the jackpot.

The College Prowler™ Grade on
Guys: A-

A high grade for Guys indicates that the male population on campus is attractive, smart, friendly, and engaging, and that the school has a decent ratio of guys to girls.

The College Prowler™ Grade on
Girls: A

A high grade for Girls not only implies that the women on campus are attractive, smart, friendly, and engaging, but also that there is a fair ratio of girls to guys.

Athletics

The Lowdown
ON ATHLETICS

Athletic Division:
NCAA Division I, Division I-AA for football

Conference:
Atlantic 10 Conference

Men's Teams
Baseball
Basketball
Cross Country
Football
Golf
Soccer
Swimming
Tennis
Track and Field

Women's Teams
Basketball
Cross Country
Field Hockey
Gymnastics
Rowing
Soccer
Softball
Swimming
Tennis
Track and Field
Volleyball

Club Sports	**Intramurals**
Crew	Badminton
Equestrian	Basketball
Hockey	Billiards
Lacrosse	Bowling
Roller Hockey	Flag Football
Rugby	Floor Hockey
Sailing	Golf
Skiing	Ice Hockey
Synchronized Swimming	Soccer
	Softball
Ultimate	Tennis
Volleyball	Volleyball

Fields
Bill Beck Field, Meade Stadium, URI Soccer Complex, URI Softball Complex

School Mascot
Ram

Getting Tickets
All URI students get free admission to all home games with a valid student ID. Students can easily get tickets right before a game. Sold-out sporting events only happen during playoffs.

Most Popular Sports
Men's Basketball

Overlooked Teams
Women's Basketball, Volleyball

Best Place to Take a Walk
South County Bike Path

Gyms/Facilities
Boss Ice Arena

The Boss Ice Arena, home of Rhode Island's Men's and Women's club ice hockey teams, opened in September 2002. It holds 2,500 people and is open to the public all year round.

Keaney Gymnasium

Keaney Gymnasium is the primary home to the URI Volleyball team. The complex holds 3,385 spectators and was renovated in 1990. There is a workout room that students are allowed to use as long as they have their ID.

Gyms/Facilities (Continued...)
Mackel Field House

Mackel Field House opened in 1991 and is an important athletic facility. Mackel has a new indoor track, gymnastics trainings and competition area, a weight room and fitness center and four newly-restored basketball courts. Men's and Women's Indoor Track & Field Championships are held in Mackel each year.

Students Speak Out
ON ATHLETICS

{ "Games are never sold out, and you don't have to pay for tickets. Basketball is big."

Q "I did flag football my freshman year, and it was great. I met a lot of cool people, and **it gave me a chance to be competitive**. Now I live off campus and don't have the time for it."

Q "I like going to the football games. **Homecoming is the best**. A lot of people show up, and it's always a good time."

Q "I love being an athlete. **All my friends are on my team**, and we spend all of our time together. College just wouldn't be the same if I didn't do a sport. Even if we don't win, I still love going out there and playing."

Q "Fans go nuts at the basketball games. The whole cheering section down in front **paints their bodies** and goes crazy during the games. It's good to see that sort of school spirit."

Q "Being an athlete definitely has its advantages. Teachers know if you're on a team and miss class for traveling. **They let you make things up**. Also, you're known on campus. It's cool."

Q "I have never gone to any games at URI. **I'm not a sports fan**, and I don't need to waste my time. I don't even know what teams are good."

The College Prowler Take
ON ATHLETICS

Athletics is an important part of campus life to a lot of students. Whether they are players or spectators, sports are popular at URI. Even though games may not be selling out in the box office, students do show their support. Rhode Island has a lot of pride and this little state has a lot of big dreams. Many of the sports facilities are new, like the Ryan Center and the Boss Ice Arena. This will hopefully attract more people to the games and get people more excited about URI sports.

Basketball is probably the most popular sport at URI. They now play in the Ryan Center and students can get tickets at any time. Midnight Madness is an event that starts the season off. It is the official first day of practice, and the students go out to support their team. Dance routines are performed by dance teams and other special guests and entertainers come out to hype up the crowd.

The College Prowler™ Grade on
Athletics: A-

A high grade in Athletics indicates that students have school spirit, that sports programs are respected, that games are well-attended, and that intramurals are a prominent part of student life.

Greek Life

The Lowdown
ON GREEK LIFE

Number of Fraternities: 7

Number of Sororities: 7

Percent of Undergrad Men in Fraternities: 10%

Percent of Undergrad Women in Sororities: 10%

Students Speak Out
ON GREEK LIFE

"The Greek system at URI isn't that big. Joining a sorority or fraternity doesn't really matter much. You could still have a good college experience without going Greek."

Q "**I hate rush**. All the sororities try to go out and recruit girls. Just leave me alone."

Q "I don't really understand the whole Greek life. **What exactly do they do**? Whenever I drive by a frat house, they're outside playing sports, or they're in the middle of the road with a bucket asking for donations for something. They don't seem very productive."

Q "I've gone to a couple of frat parties and **they were fun**. If you're a girl, they'll let you in without a problem. I think they make some guys pay. Its typical, but I can't complain."

Q "I was all about being in a sorority when I first got to URI. I'm glad I'm in a sorority, and **I've made some great friends**. I live in a sorority house with 40 other girls. We always have a good time."

The College Prowler Take
ON GREEK LIFE

Greek life makes up a small percentage of URI. Most students involved in a fraternity or sorority are glad that they joined and have a positive message to say about their experiences. Students not involved in Greek life are not complaining. Greeks certainly do not rule the school or the social scene. It is a good way to make friends and keep active on campus. It is, however, not the only way to survive life on campus. They are not a dominant group, but if you're looking to join an organization, check them out.

URI has a large population and Greeks only make up 10 percent of it. To outsiders, Greek life seems like a lame excuse to make some friends who are exactly the same as you. To members, it is a support team and family. Individuals need to decide on their own if Greek life is right for them.

The College Prowler™ Grade on
Greek Life: C+

A high grade in Greek Life indicates that sororities and fraternities are not only present, but also active on campus. Other determining factors include the variety of houses available and the respect the Greek community receives from the rest of the campus.

Drug Scene

The Lowdown
ON DRUG SCENE

Most Prevalent Drugs on Campus:
Alcohol, marijuana, caffeine, and cocaine

Liquor-Related Referrals: 104

Liquor-Related Arrests: 0

Drug-Related Referrals: 0

Drug-Related Arrests: 36

Drug Counseling Programs:
Substance Abuse Services, Memorial Union
(401) 874-5413

Students Speak Out
ON DRUG SCENE

"I think there's a good amount of drugs on campus, especially pot. I know some kids who do coke as well. I don't think there's any pressure, though. They aren't that important."

Q "I wouldn't know where to go if I wanted to get drugs. **I don't know who is selling or whom to trust**, so I don't deal with them. If someone offers me a hit, I'll take it, but I wouldn't buy it."

Q "**URI had a rep of being a party school**. When I decided to come here, everyone was like, you're going to URHigh. Then, when I got here, I didn't really run into that many drugs. People drink, and I come across an occasional pot smoker, but other than that, nothing."

Q "The kids across the hall from me would smoke pot everyday. They would do it in there rooms, on the balcony, or take a ride in their car. **They never got caught**."

Q "**No one cares** if you smoke or not. It's not going to get you more friends."

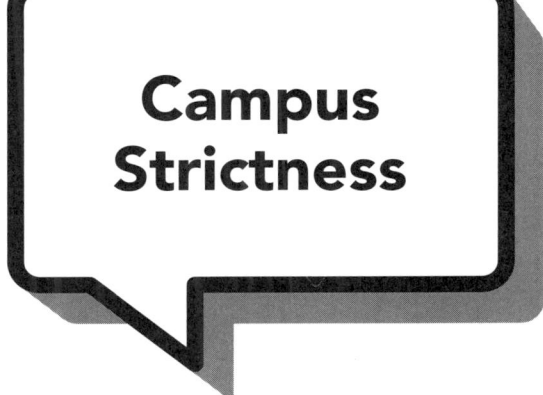

Campus Strictness

The College Prowler Take
ON DRUG SCENE

You may be oblivious to the drug scene at URI, but it is there. Most students don't promote the fact that they do drugs or know people who do. It is not something that they brag about, but it is something that is being done. It is, however, very easy to ignore and dismiss. If you don't want to get involved with the drug scene, you won't have to. Many people don't come in contact with drugs because they are simply not looking for them. The most popular drug for students would have to be alcohol, and it is legal for most students. URI is a party school and underage drinking and drinking on a dry campus is bound to happen. Students like to party and drink, especially on the weekends. Although, you can always find someone ready to rage any night of the week.

Marijuana and cocaine are the only drugs that students are willing to admit they use, or know people who use them. Although drugs are used at URI, they aren't in popular demand, and there's no pressure to do them.

The Lowdown
ON CAMPUS STRICTNESS

What Are You Most Likely to Get Caught Doing on Campus?
Underage drinking, speeding, parking illegally, making too much noise in dorm rooms, not cleaning dorm room bathrooms, smoking, public rowdiness, fighting

Students Speak Out
ON CAMPUS STRICTNESS

"Sophomore year I got parking tickets 'like whoa.' I probably got about six tickets that year, and I couldn't protest any of them."

Q "**We always got in trouble for the noise**. Our room was right above the dorm room director's, and she would come up all the time to ask us to lower our music and keep it down. We never got written up, just verbal warnings. I'm sure if we were drinking or something, then we'd have gotten written up."

The College Prowler™ Grade on
Drug Scene: C+

A high grade in the Drug Scene indicates that drugs are not a noticeable part of campus life; drug use is not visible, and no pressure to use them seems to exist.

Q "**I got written up by my RA** one time because I didn't clean the bathroom by a certain day. I thought that was pretty crazy."

Q "If you get caught smoking pot on campus, you get arrested. It happened to one of my friends. **He got arrested and charged with possession** and had to go to court. I think he had to pay a fine or do community service."

Q "Definitely don't walk around campus or your dorm with beer in your hand. You'll get in trouble. It's happened to me. **They don't care if you're drunk**, you just can't be drinking."

The College Prowler Take
ON CAMPUS STRICTNESS

URI students agree that no one is off the hook when it comes to campus strictness. If you get caught doing something you aren't supposed to be doing, you will get in trouble for it. Although students complain about getting in trouble, that only means that the police are doing their job. Students realize that there are consequences for their actions and some students really have to watch out. Not only do the campus police watch after URI students, the local police do as well. It is clear to students that the police are on the lookout for any wrongful behavior.

Having a school with a large party scene, officials need to keep students safe. It is their job, and students seem to be understanding of that. Cooperation is key when it comes to a run-in with the law. But, no matter how hard you beg and plead, you will get in trouble.

The College Prowler™ Grade on
Campus Strictness: B-

A high Campus Strictness grade implies an overall lenient atmosphere; police and RAs are fairly tolerant, and the administration's rules are flexible.

Overall Experience

Students Speak Out
ON OVERALL EXPERIENCE

"I love URI. I wouldn't want to go anywhere else. I like the size, the people, and the variety of classes. There is something for everyone."

Q "I'm from Rhode Island, and half my high school goes here. I've stayed friends with a lot of them, so **I feel like I never really went off on my own**. I still hang out with a lot of my high school friends because they either go here or somewhere close by. I kind of regret not going somewhere else and getting the chance to meet all new people."

Q "There are some things that I don't like about URI. I can't graduate in four years because I can never get into the classes that I need to take. **It's frustrating being behind** and knowing that there is nothing you can do about it."

Q "URI is kind of in the middle of nowhere. When I came to visit my senior year (in high school) I didn't like where the campus was. We were driving forever on this long, empty road and then, all of a sudden, there's URI. I didn't know what I was going to do if I left campus. Now I realize that **there is a lot of stuff to do off campus**, it just takes a little while to get there."

Q "Academics are an important part of URI, and so is the social life. I like to think that there is an equal amount of both. **I'm happy here**."

The College Prowler Take
ON OVERALL EXPERIENCE

When most people think about URI, they think party school. The stigma of being one of the nation's biggest party schools has become infamous with URI. What most people don't know is that this notorious reputation has slowly died down. There is a lot less partying and drinking on campus after it went dry. Students come here expecting an endless line of parties, but they are sadly mistaken. Security has cracked down. This doesn't mean that there is no partying here. Students just have to venture off campus to find it.

Many students are happy with their choice of making URI their home for higher education. Students agree that there is an equal balance of academics and social life. Students are expected to do well and have many opportunities to succeed. The biggest part of college is learning to adjust and knowing what is out there. URI is a friendly environment and most students feel happy to be here. Academics are the biggest challenge, and getting into the right classes is often an obstacle. There are a lot of organizations and events that engage students throughout the year. Overall, students have a positive experience at URI. There is something for everyone.

The Inside Scoop

The Lowdown
ON THE INSIDE SCOOP

URI Slang: Know the slang, know the school. The following is a list of things you really need to know before coming to URI The more of these words you know, the better off you'll be.

Ro-Jo's: Roger Williams Dining Hall
The Butt: Butterfield Dining Hall
Down the line: Referred to as off-campus living
The Quad: A grassy area in the middle of campus
The Cigar: The school newspaper
BISC: Biological and Science Center
Bonnet: Area for off campus housing
SK: South Kingston
Old Eastward Look: Popular neighborhood for college kids
New Eastward Look: Popular neighborhood for college kids
Ragin': Slang for partying/drinking
Rippin': Slang for partying/drinking
'Gansett: Short for Narragansett
The Ghetto: The older dorms down by the gym; Coddington, Burnside, Dorr and Ellery
The Union: The Student Memorial Union
Projo: *The Providence Journal*
E-Campus: Online class registration

Things I Wish I Knew Before Coming to URI:

- It takes a while to walk to class, so make sure you leave early.
- Most students graduate in five years.
- Here, knowing your major is better than being undecided.
- You have to take at least 15 credits a semester to graduate on time.
- Frats are only fun the first week of school.
- You will need a car.
- You may never learn your teachers name or get to know some of your professors.
- You will need to go to class.
- You will get parking tickets.

Tips to Succeed at URI:

- Go to your advisor.
- Know all the classes that you need to take for your major.
- Join a club, organization, or sport.
- Get to know your teachers.
- Keep up with the work.
- Learn to manage your time.
- Go to class.
- Don't get in the habit of taking naps.

School Spirit

Rhode Island has a lot of pride, and that is something that encourages students. One of the first things that new students learn when they come to URI is the fight song. "We're Rhode Island born and we're Rhode Island breed and when we die we'll be Rhode Island dead so go go Rhode Island, Island U-R-I!" Students are forced to sing it with enthusiasm, and it really gets everyone going. Most students are proud to be at URI, and you can always find someone wearing school sweat shirts, pants and T-shirts.

Traditions

12th Night

The newest tradition for URI is called 12th Night. It was held on the twelfth day of classes to welcome all students back to school by adding some fun into their busy schedules. The event was held in the center of campus, on the quad. Games like bungee jumps and an air-walk obstacle course were set up. Students enjoyed other activities like rock wall climbing, jousting, a mechanical bull, and boxing, along with student organizations and venders selling jewelry and other goods. There was also a band that entertained students on their way to and from classes.

Midnight Madness

Midnight Madness is a great sports tradition at URI. Every October, students flock to the Ryan to celebrate the beginning of the basketball season. It is a huge event that attracts more than just sports fans at URI. The celebration includes dance performances by the Flava Unit and the Ramettes. Comedians and hypnotists are also known to show up and entertain the crowd before the practice begins. The crowd really goes wild when the players are introduced by the coaches. This tradition is a great part of URI and the athletic department.

Freek Week

Freek Week was started by the Greek system. It is an annual event that invites new and interested students to join a fraternity or sorority. The whole Greek system goes out and tries to recruit new members by inviting them to different social events and meetings.

Finding a Job or Internship

The Lowdown
ON FINDING A JOB OR INTERNSHIP

Career Center Resources & Services

BEACON is an online service that provides full-time, on campus, and work study job and internship listings for students. BEACON allows students to view company job listings, post their resumes online, and sign up for on-campus interviews. Student use BEACON to find on-campus jobs as well as off-campus jobs.

URI Career Services
228 Roosevelt Hall
90 Lower College Road
Kingston, RI 02881
(401) 874-2311

The Office of Internships and Experiential Education
90 Lower College Road, Suite 12
University of Rhode Island
139 Roosevelt Hall
Kingston, RI 02881
(401) 874-2160

The Office of Internships and Experimental Education is a great resource. The URI internship program allows students to get credit for their job experience in their field of study. There are over 400 placement sites throughout Rhode Island and students have a great opportunity for gaining job experience and earning credits at the same time.

Advice

Look into all your resources. The teachers themselves will be able to give you great advice and help when looking for an internship. Many advisors are able to help as well. Job fairs are important to go to as well and they are held throughout the year, each with a focus on a different major. Workshops are held to help develop skills needed in order to get a job, such as how to take an interview and how to write a fantastic resume.

Famous URI Alumni:
- Christine Amanpour, Class of '83, CNN chief international correspondent
- Robert D. Ballard, Class of '75, Oceanographer, discoverer of the Titanic (1985)
- Tom Ryan, Class of '75, CEO/President of CVS

The Best & Worst

The Ten BEST Things About URI:

1. Being by the beach
2. Parties
3. All the people you meet
4. Off-campus housing
5. Lots to do, even in the middle of nowhere
6. Taking over local communities
7. Seeing cows on the way to school
8. Proximity to everywhere in Rhode Island
9. Concerts at the Ryan Center
10. Free admission to all sporting events

The Ten WORST Things About URI:

1. Parking
2. Registering for classes
3. Not getting into classes that you need
4. Walking up one big hill everyday
5. Overcrowded shuttles
6. Rainy days
7. Taking five years to graduate
8. Cops
9. Traffic
10. Squirrels all over campus

University of Vermont

South Prospect Street, Burlington, VT 05405-0160
www.uvm.edu   (802) 656-3370

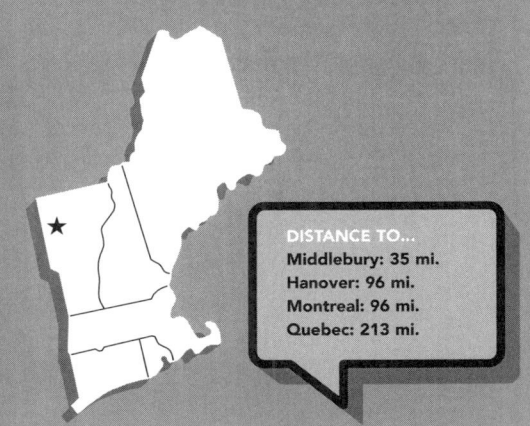

DISTANCE TO...
Middlebury: 35 mi.
Hanover: 96 mi.
Montreal: 96 mi.
Quebec: 213 mi.

"It is like an epicenter. UVM is within a day's drive of New York, Boston, the Atlantic Ocean, and Canada."

Total Enrollment:
7,768
Acceptance Rate:
75%
Tuition:
$10,226 in-state, $23,866 out-of-state
Top 10% of High School Class:
21%

SAT Range
Verbal	Math	Total
530 – 620	530 – 630	1060 – 1250

ACT Range
Verbal	Math	Total
N/A	N/A	22-27

Most Popular Majors:
10% Business Administration and Management
9%   Psychology
8%   English Language and Literature
7%   Political Science and Government

Students Also Applied To:*
Boston College
Boston University
University of Connecticut
University of Massachusetts–Amherst
University of New Hampshire

*For more school info check out www.collegeprowler.com

Table of Contents

Academics	138
Local Atmosphere	139
Safety & Security	141
Computers	142
Facilities	144
Campus Dining	145
Off-Campus Dining	146
Campus Housing	148
Off-Campus Housing	149
Diversity	150
Guys & Girls	151
Athletics	153
Greek Life	154
Drug Scene	155
Campus Strictness	156
Overall Experience	157
The Inside Scoop	158
Finding a Job or Internship	159
The Best & Worst	159

College Prowler Report Card

Academics	B-
Local Atmosphere	A-
Safety & Security	A-
Computers	B+
Facilities	B+
Campus Dining	B+
Off-Campus Dining	A-
Campus Housing	B
Off-Campus Housing	B
Diversity	D
Guys	B
Girls	B+
Athletics	B-
Greek Life	B-
Drug Scene	C+
Campus Strictness	D+

Academics

Did You Know?
UVM stands for Universitas Viridis Montis, or "University of the Green Mountain"—the name in which it was originally chartered.

Students Speak Out
ON ACADEMICS

The Lowdown
ON ACADEMICS

Degrees Awarded:
Associate, Bachelor, Master, Doctorate

Undergraduate Schools:
Agriculture & Life Science, Arts & Science, Education-Social Service, Engineering-Mathematics, Nursing-Health Sciences, Business Administration, Natural Resources

Full-time Faculty:
974

Faculty with Terminal Degree:
88%

Student-to-Faculty Ratio:
14:1

Average Course Load:
15 credits

AP Test Score Requirements:
Possible credit for scores of 4 or higher.

Best Places to Study:
Billing's Student Center, University Green (weather permitting)

Sample Academic Clubs:
Cycling Club, Outing Club, Student Government, Literary Magazine, Music Ensembles

"Like any school, you will have both bad teachers and good ones. Most professors were easy to get in to see and to get extra help from."

Q "Professors at UVM are interesting people, and, in many cases, approachable and receptive. My own experience has been limited to teachers within the school of Arts and Sciences, primarily humanities, but **I've encountered a lot of professors with a great commitment to teaching**. Few have expressed their own work and research as more important and urgent than our education, at least in the classroom."

Q "The **quality of the teaching totally depends on your major**. I'm a chemistry major—I know it doesn't sound like much fun, but my teachers were awesome. I took Spanish, too, but I really didn't care for my professor."

Q "Let's just say that some are really, really good and **some are just plain bad**! If you find out that you have a bad teacher, you can often switch to another section within the first two weeks of the semester."

Q "I think that at UVM, the quality of your teachers **depends on the effort that you make to get to know them**. If you want to get to know them, they are there to help, but they won't put that much effort into getting to know you unless you make the first move."

Q "The professors at UVM are excellent. Not only do they provide you with a quality education, they also serve as mentors and friends for the students. **I've only had good experiences with my educators**; they've been one-in-a-million."

The College Prowler Take
ON ACADEMICS

When a professor really enjoys an area of study, he or she will almost undoubtedly be an emphatic and effective teacher. Similarly, those eager to learn will be more successful when the material, and/or the teacher, excites and engages them. And indeed, this appears to be the case at UVM, where both professors and students approach their jobs with enthusiasm and dedication.

The professors at the University of Vermont are primarily good-natured and sincere in their quest to share knowledge. Given that UVM is one of the lowest paying universities in the country, most students feel these professors are not in it for the money. Like Vermont itself, especially Burlington, UVM teachers are often in a class of their own. A laid-back attitude takes precedence over high-strung, fast-paced living. Professors here definitely possess personality, and reflect a variety of backgrounds, which results in many refreshing and original approaches to teaching. Some bring with them stories and life experiences from as far away as South Africa, China, Russia, or India, while others were reared right here in New England. Even though nearly all UVM professors are exceptionally qualified in their respective fields and hold degrees from prestigious universities, most still take the time to learn your name, and on occasion, become your friend.

The College Prowler™ Grade on
Academics: B-

A high Academics grade generally indicates that professors are knowledgeable, accessible, and genuinely interested in their students' welfare. Other determining factors include class size, how well professors communicate, and whether or not classes are engaging.

Local Atmosphere

The Lowdown
ON LOCAL ATMOSPHERE

Region:
Northeast

City, State:
Burlington, Vermont

Setting:
City

Distance from Boston:
3 hours

Distance from NYC:
4.5 hours

Distance from Montreal:
2 hours

Points of Interest:
Lake Champlain, Church, Robert Hull Fleming Museum, Ben & Jerry's Factory, Shelburne Museum, ECHO at the Leahy Center for Lake Champlain, Flynn Theatre, Restaurants Galore, Burlington Bike Path, Long Trail

Major Sports Teams:
Burlington does not have any major sports teams.

Students Speak Out
ON LOCAL ATMOSPHERE

{ "Vermont and UVM are really laid-back; people are super chill. I absolutely love it here, and I don't want to be anywhere else."

Q "The atmosphere is great. It's Vermont! Burlington has a few other universities in the area; their presence is mostly a positive thing. The **commercial downtown area is beautiful**, but the surrounding area—Vermont's natural setting—can be a nice place to visit, too. Check out Centennial Woods."

Q "The atmosphere is excellent. It is **definitely populated mostly by college students** during the academic year. Stuff to stay away from—nothing, really. Some of the stuff to visit includes Shelburne, Church Street, Lake Champlain, Smuggs, Stowe, Mount Mansfield, Camel's Hump, Magic Hat Brewery, the Intervale, New Alpha Baptist Church, Flynn Theater, Higher Ground, and the New England Culinary Institute."

Q "I would have to say that **Burlington definitely has a cool environment**, but I wish there were more 'real' people that I could relate to here. Granted, I'm a music major—there honestly aren't that many people who are as dedicated to music as I am, but I still feel a slight bit of alienation from this crowd."

Q "All I can say is: Burlington, city of the future! I am not a Vermonter, New Englander, or from the East Coast, and the atmosphere here in Burlington, and Vermont, is the reason I came to UVM. The tolerance, the crunchiness, the happiness, and the unabashed liberal and free spirit provide the necessary background for a college student: an **atmosphere in which everything and anything is accepted**."

Q "Burlington is a fantastic place to go to college. The community's relationship with UVM is pretty good; distinguishing locals from those associated with the University is almost arbitrary. The **downtown area is always bustling with students**, street performers, and regular people, too."

Q "There are a couple of other colleges in the area, St. Michaels College and Champlain College. **Meeting students from these schools around town is less common** than meeting UVM students, given the comparatively dominant size of UVM's population. Burlington and the surrounding area have a lot to offer. Of course, the easy access to the ski mountains, as well as the Long Trail and other parts of the Green Mountain National Parks is a huge bonus."

The College Prowler Take
ON LOCAL ATMOSPHERE

With majestic, rolling fields, golden stalks sweeping in the wind, and the Green Mountains hailing brilliantly in the background, Vermont is a sublime vision for those who love rural landscape and the cycle of the seasons. Those who come to Burlington, though, will find a small, but lively, city in the midst of the natural beauty. This is an obvious advantage for those who enjoy outdoor activities, such as skiing, hiking, or biking. Vermont boasts arguably the best region on the East Coast for outdoor activities. At UVM, you can engage in numerous outdoors activities and revel in the majesty of the Green Mountains. Nearby, the winter months give rise to the East Coast's best skiing at Killington and Stowe—the only Eastern rivals to Rocky Mountain skiing. The progressive community of both UVM and Burlington gives a revived, or rekindled, sense of place and proves that big things come in little states.

The College Prowler™ Grade on

Local Atmosphere: A-

A high Local Atmosphere grade indicates that the area surrounding campus is safe and scenic. Other factors include nearby attractions, proximity to other schools, and the town's attitude toward students.

Safety & Security

The Lowdown
ON SAFETY & SECURITY

Number of UVM Police:
33

Phone:
(802) 656-3470

Safety Services:
Blue Light Phones, Safe Ride, RAD, Property Registration

Students Speak Out
ON SAFETY & SECURITY

"We did have two girls that were assaulted once, but it was late, and they were walking alone, which was a really stupid thing for them to do. Overall, I'd say it's pretty safe here."

Q "UVM maintains a very safe campus. However, should a problem arise, **we have 'blue-lights' stationed all over campus**. At the push of a button, a UVM officer will be at your service. UVM also has a fully-trained police squad that is on duty 24/7. Our campus is very safe and secure. You'll always feel comfortable here."

Q "I've **never felt unsafe on campus**; there are security personnel and emergency phone boxes around campus. It is not easy to get into most of the dorms if you don't live in them. Not all of the dorms are like that, though. Mine wasn't, but I still felt safe."

Q "I personally feel **profoundly secure and safe on campus**, enough so to walk around alone anytime from midnight 'till 5 a.m. and not be worried. In case there ever is a problem though, there are security call-boxes all over the place, so maybe there are some people that feel unsafe."

Q "You don't hear much about bad things happening on campus. Safe Ride is a mode of transportation for people who need rides home late at night. **UVM also has its own police force** which regularly patrols campus. If you're a good kid, they'll leave you alone."

Q "For the most part, UVM's campus, as well as Burlington itself, feels **safe and manageable**. Incidents are generally well-publicized and security is dependable, although perhaps campus police should be less discipline-oriented and more approachable with safety concerns."

The College Prowler Take
ON SAFETY & SECURITY

Many students love the secure feeling they get from having award-winning police services on campus. Many others, however, feel that the University police are an overbearing burden on their consciences. More often than not, the students' perception of police really just comes down to their fear of getting caught. Those with nothing to hide are apt to have nothing to fear, while those sidestepping the law behind closed doors usually feel a bit more wary. Regardless of direct campus involvement, UVM naturally avoids many of the problems that exist at other colleges and universities that are set in cities. With little crime in the Burlington vicinity, there is little to fear from the outside community. So, as far as safety is concerned, it is a safe and comfortable place.

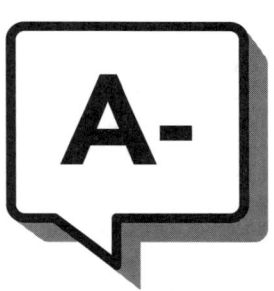

The College Prowler™ Grade on
Safety & Security: A-

A high grade in Safety & Security means that students generally feel safe, campus police are visible, blue-light phones and escort services are readily available, and safety precautions are not overly necessary.

Computers

The Lowdown
ON COMPUTERS

High-Speed Network?
Yes

Wireless Network?
Yes

Number of Labs:
7

Numbers of Computers:
685

24-Hour Labs:
Yes

Charge to Print?
Usually 10 cents per page

Operating Systems:
Windows XP, Mac OSX, UNIX, Windows 2000

Free Software:
Norton Anti Virus, Adobe Acrobat Reader, Eudora, etc.

Did You Know?

Ben Affleck attended his first semester of school at the University of Vermont back in 1990.

Students Speak Out
ON COMPUTERS

"Computer availability gets a little tight during finals. I would bring your own computer. They have many great labs, but nothing compares to doing your homework in your own space."

Q "I definitely recommend having a computer and a printer because it is just a pain in the butt not to have them. I also **definitely recommend using Ethernet** because the school Ethernet connection offers quick Internet access and keeps your phone lines free, which your roommate will appreciate."

Q "Most **students do bring their own computers**. Every dorm room is equipped with high speed Internet. The network itself is generally pretty reliable. Since there are few labs located on the residential campuses, having a computer is convenient and common. Though labs do become crowded around finals, as a rule, if you have to wait at all, it won't be for too long."

Q "The computer network is usually very fast and very good. **There are a lot of computers on campus**, but I think that you'll find that you want your own computer in your room. When we aren't doing work and stuff, we play games on our computers, or talk to people online. It's also very helpful to have your own computer for late-night papers and research."

Q "The school's pretty well-equipped where computers are concerned, but it helps to have your own if you can get one. The **computer labs get pretty crazy at the end of the semester**, so it's nice to have your own computer and not have to deal with that. It also depends on your major and how much you'll actually need to use one."

Q "If you can, you should definitely bring your own computer. It's just a whole lot more convenient, especially on cold, snowy days when you don't want to hike over to the computer labs. It's **usually pretty easy to find a computer somewhere** on campus unless it's finals week."

The College Prowler Take
ON COMPUTERS

In this world of rapidly increasing, technological advancements, computers are becoming more essential. From daily business affairs to cash registrars, computers are everywhere and UVM is no exception. It is not surprising then that nearly all students, as well as the University, recommend bringing your own computer. The University has an Ethernet connection which provides students with almost instantaneous results. They also provide at least one port per student living on campus—meaning everyone gets more than his or her fair share of Internet usage. Moreover, the Internet is "free," for the low, low cost of your college tuition! But, at any rate, Internet use is unlimited and widely available around campus. If you have your own computer, it is best to bring it. Without a doubt, you will be thankful in the long run.

The College Prowler™ Grade on
Computers: B+

A high grade in Computers designates that computer labs are available, the computer network is easily accessible, and the campus' computing technology is up-to-date.

Facilities

The Lowdown
ON FACILITIES

Athletic Center:
Patrick Gymnasium

Libraries:
Bailey-Howe Library

Coffeehouse on Campus?
Cyber Café and Waterman Café

Student Center:
Billings Student Center,
ALANA Student Center

Popular Places to Chill:
Main Green, Redstone Field,
Cook Commons

Bar on Campus?
No

Bowling on Campus?
No

Theatre on Campus?
Royal Tyler Theatre

Q "Most classrooms are nice, and the dining areas are clean. People hang out all over the place. The lobby of your complex will have Ping-Pong tables and stuff, but **most people hang out in their rooms** or halls."

Q "The athletic center is really nice and has pretty much anything you could want from a climbing wall to a swimming pool. I don't know much about the computers, but **the buildings are all really nice**, and there is an ample amount of places for students to gather and do whatever they want to do."

Q "The facilities are nice, especially the gym and weight room. The **student center is rather impersonal and complex-like**. It feels more like a maze than a place to go hang out."

The College Prowler Take
ON FACILITIES

The University of Vermont is a fairly large school and there are a number of facilities available to all students, faculty, and staff. While some enjoy a morning run around the track, others may prefer to work out in the fitness center and enjoy the panoramic view of the sun burning away at the frost. Likewise, students may prefer to study among their peers in the library, or immerse themselves in a book near the fireplace in Billings. UVM is also building a new student center to compliment the already-existing Billings Student Center—home to numerous places to study, the University radio station, and club spaces, as well as the *Vermont Cynic,* the school's newspaper.

Students Speak Out
ON FACILITIES

{ "The student center is a great place to study; it has big, comfy couches. The athletic facilities are also great; they are accessible."

B+

The College Prowler™ Grade on
Facilities: B+

A high Facilities grade indicates that the campus is aesthetically pleasing and well-maintained; facilities are state-of-the-art, and libraries are exceptional. Other determining factors include the quality of both athletic and student centers and an abundance of things to do on campus.

Campus Dining

The Lowdown
ON CAMPUS DINING

Freshman Meal Plan Requirement?
Yes

Meal Plan Average Cost:
$2,216

Places to Grab a Bite with Your Meal Plan:
Harris-Millis, Simpsons, Simpson Store, Cook Commons, Alice's, The University Marché

24-Hour On-Campus Eating?
Not yet (but there are possible plans to build one within the next year)

Student Favorites:
Marché, Cook Commons

Did You Know?

The quality of life in Burlington was recently ranked among the top 10 cities in the country.

Students Speak Out
ON CAMPUS DINING

{ **"If you're vegetarian, like me, you'll find that UVM is probably more accommodating than most schools."**

Q "The food on campus is great. The system that UVM employs allows for a wide variety of choices for any kind of eater. **We have two major dining halls** in which you can use your dining points at the door and then eat all you want from the typical offerings of pizza, French fries, hamburgers, garden burgers, a salad bar, bagels, breads and lunch meats, soup, pasta, grilled cheese, cereal, and a meal that changes for most of the day. In the morning, they offer waffles, bacon, sausage, potato tots or hash browns, omelets, and other breakfast foods."

Q "Besides the dining halls, **UVM also has food-court-type places** where your food is made to order. These places include the Round Room, which offers a wide variety of sandwiches made on your choice of bread; The Underground, which is similar to Subway; and Cook Commons—located on the main campus—which offers a rotating selection of Chinese food, fast food, a 'homemade' food place, and wraps, which are really good."

Q "The food is atrocious in the dining halls, except for the occasional, clean salad bar. I ate in the Harris-Millis dining hall maybe 25 times all year, and I lived in that very complex! That's how bad it is. Instead, I would amble on over to the Marché at the Living/Learning Center where the selection is a bit fresher and wider, but constant and never-ever!-changing. **Thank God for downtown Burlington**. I will give credit, however, to UVM Dining Services for catering very well to the vegans and vegetarians all across campus."

Q "**Most of the food is fattening**, but you will find lots of vegetarians here, so there's also lots of organic, healthy food. They have made improvements to the on-campus dining and there are some new places opening up."

Q "The food is decent, but **not great**. This year I used the carte blanche meal program, which I honestly wouldn't recommend. This gives you unlimited blocks which allows you to eat at any cafeteria meal as many times as you desire. I found that an all-points plan is more efficient. It allows you to eat anywhere on campus and even allows you to order pizza."

The College Prowler Take
ON CAMPUS DINING

The University of Vermont receives high marks from a lot of students as far as the quality and taste of food. Where it loses points, however, is in the generally overpriced nature of the food, the often unchanging menu at several of the dining facilities, and the noticeable lack of Kosher options (except during Passover). The food is not meant to be the best food you've ever had—it is there so you won't starve to death. Though it probably does not beat your mom's home cooking, UVM does have a better than average food program.

B+

The College Prowler™ Grade on
Campus Dining: B+

Our grade on Campus Dining addresses the quality of both school-owned dining halls and independent on-campus restaurants as well as the price, availability, and variety of food.

Off-Campus Dining

The Lowdown
ON OFF-CAMPUS DINING

Late-Night Food:
Kountry Kart Deli

Best Pizza:
Leonardo's

Best Chinese:
Kwan's Chinese Food

Best Breakfast:
Penny Cluse Café

Best Wings:
Big Daddy's

Best Healthy:
Stone Soup

Best Sushi:
Sakura

Best Place to Take Your Parents:
'O' on the waterfront

Students Speak Out
ON OFF-CAMPUS DINING

"My friends and I usually hit the cheaper places like Halverson's— a cute and good bar-and-grill-type place, where your average meal is about seven dollars."

Q "Burlington is a great little city. No matter where you go on Church Street, you will be able to find a delicious meal within your desired price range. **We are also home to Ben & Jerry's**, the world's best ice cream!"

Q "If you or your parents put money on your Catscratch account with your ID card, you can order from so many places! **You can even order from Dunkin' Donuts** if you want. It's a really great thing."

Q "I could write a novel on eating out in Burlington. Burlington, and the surrounding area, hosts a plethora of excellent restaurants. **Anything on or around Church Street is a sure bet**. NECI, the restaurant affiliated with the New England Culinary Institute, is the perfect place to take the parents—or to be taken to by the parents, as the case may be. Halverson's is a personal favorite—cozy with a pretty basic menu."

Q "I recommend the California Burger. For the adventurous eaters who like a little ethnic variety, check out the Pacific Rim for very unique dishes at good prices, the Sunday brunch at the Indian restaurant, and Parima's interior design is as amazing as the Thai cuisine. Oh, and **all-you-can-eat pizza and wings at Manhattan Pizza** is possibly the coolest thing in the world."

Q "There are great restaurants in Burlington. I like the **Five Spice Cafe**, the Vermont Pub and Brewery, the India House, and Wind Jammer. Big Daddy's is good for late-night munchies. It's open for delivery until 2 a.m."

Q "City Market is the place to go for salad and everything else, I guess. **City Market is Burlington culture at its finest**, and you'll love every second of it. The food is incredibly delicious and fresh, and it's a prime place for people-watching, too. I have never had a bad meal downtown, and, while it can be pricey, it is worth it. If you are with guests and want to impress them with elegance, go to "O," the new restaurant on the waterfront for great ambience. One cannot go wrong with sushi, Thai, or, of course, Ben and Jerry's!"

The College Prowler Take
ON OFF-CAMPUS DINING

More than anything else, students at UVM cannot get over Burlington's plethora of restaurants and eateries. Nearly every type of cuisine, from almost every part of the world, is represented here, and it's one of the things that drives the college community into Burlington and keeps them coming back for more. In a town with so many places to eat, it is hard for most students to pick an absolute favorite. As far as choosing a place, one student put it perhaps most appropriately: "The best way is to experience them all." Even though Burlington is a small town, there is a big-city feel when it comes to the numerous food establishments.

The College Prowler™ Grade on
Off-Campus Dining: A-

A high Off-Campus Dining grade implies that off-campus restaurants are affordable, accessible, and worth visiting. Other factors include the variety of cuisine and the availability of alternative options (vegetarian, vegan, Kosher, etc.).

Campus Housing

> "**Living/Learning Center is a dorm designed with suites** that have their own balconies and two bathrooms for five or six people. The other dorms don't offer much variety in setup."

> "UVM offers **less dorm options than a lot of colleges**. Freshman and sophomore year, everyone is required to live on campus in dorm rooms, with extremely limited access to suites and virtually no campus apartments exist."

> "If you want a single, go to Converse. **If you are more academic, try for Wright Hall**. If you tend to be on the more hippie/crunchy side, go to Living/Learning where you will be part of a community 24/7, all year long. If you want to party constantly, try everything else."

The Lowdown
ON CAMPUS HOUSING

Undergrads on Campus:
51%
Room Types:
Single, Double, Triple

The College Prowler Take
ON CAMPUS HOUSING

UVM housing options span a few different campuses—Main Campus, the Athletic Campus (also called East Campus), and Redstone Campus are the most popular. UVM's recent investment in the campus that used to be Trinity College, located just across the road from UVM's Main Campus, has increased the availability of on-campus housing, especially for transfer students. Most people try to avoid Main Campus more than anywhere else because the rooms are small and cramped; although, the students who get "stuck" on Main Campus are not always disappointed. While UVM does not offer many alternatives to the basic dorm room, with the notable exception of Living/Learning, the required two years of on-campus housing allows students to develop important ties to UVM, both socially and individually.

Students Speak Out
ON CAMPUS HOUSING

> "Dorms are dorms. I got stuck in a triple first semester on Redstone Campus, which is primarily the campus where the upperclassmen live. I wasn't particularly happy over there."

> "The **dorms with the smallest rooms are Chittenden, Buckham, and Wills**; most people dread living there. You never can tell, though. I lived in Wills for what turned out to be my greatest year of college. I loved every minute of being in Wills. The 'nice' dorms are Christie, Wright, and Patterson."

> "Live in Harris [or] Millis your first year. I lived there my first year, and I thought it was great. **Athletic Campus is the place to be during your freshman year**, and Redstone Campus is the place to be for your sophomore year."

The College Prowler™ Grade on
Campus Housing: B

A high Campus Housing grade indicates that dorms are clean, well-maintained, and spacious. Other determining factors include variety of dorms, proximity to classes, and social atmosphere.

Off-Campus Housing

The Lowdown
ON OFF-CAMPUS HOUSING

Undergrads in Off-Campus Housing:
48%

Average Rent for a Studio Apartment:
$500

Average Rent for a One-Bedroom Apartment:
$700

Average Rent for a Two-Bedroom Apartment:
$1,200

Popular Areas:
Anywhere in the proximity of campus

Best Time to Look for a Place:
Six months prior to desired move-in date or earlier

Students Speak Out
ON OFF-CAMPUS HOUSING

{ "I'm in the midst of trying to acquire off-campus housing. There's quite a bit of it available, but you should start looking for it early—unlike me."

Q "Moving off campus is definitely worth it. Between Main Campus and downtown, the hill is densely-populated with **big, old houses transformed into apartments**."

Q "After sophomore year, almost everyone moves off campus. You can walk to anything in Burlington. **Houses are everywhere**."

Q "The group of housing located near campus in Burlington is both expensive and of poor quality. **Housing is in demand here**, even without college students, so it's tough."

Q "**You can't live off campus until you are a junior**. But if you plan on living off campus, you need to start looking for friends to live with and a place to stay no later than February of your sophomore year."

Q "Housing in Burlington is **fairly expensive**, and sometimes it's hard to get a good location because all of the students want to live between UVM and downtown, Burlington."

The College Prowler Take
ON OFF-CAMPUS HOUSING

With few exceptions, UVM makes you wait until you are a junior to live off campus, but when the time comes to move into an apartment, students often find it to be a pleasant change of pace from dormitory life. If you begin looking early enough, off-campus housing is convenient, fun, and certainly well worth it. While most students jump at the opportunity to live in an apartment with their friends somewhere off campus, not all elect to do so. Some stay because they enjoy the proximity of living on campus, while others are wary of the stress it may take to move away—bills, groceries, landlords, etc. Burlington is pressed for housing, so look early and make arrangements with friends for living together.

The College Prowler™ Grade on
Off-Campus Housing: B

A high grade in Off-Campus Housing indicates that apartments are of high quality, close to campus, affordable, and easy to secure.

Diversity

Students Speak Out
ON DIVERSITY

The Lowdown
ON DIVERSITY

African American: 1%

Asian American: 2%

Hispanic: 2%

Native American: 0%

White: 94%

International: 1%

Out-of-State: 62%

Minority Clubs
ALANA (African, Latino/a, Asian, and Native American)

Political Activity
Political activity on campus has a noticeable presence. There is a Socialist Club, a College Democrats Club, and a College Republicans Club. These organizations bring speakers to campus, promote related causes to the UVM community, and provide a link to local and national political organizations.

Gay Tolerance
UVM is a tolerant place where people of all sexual orientations are accepted. Not surprising, since Vermont was the first state to have implemented gay civil unions and is reputed for being a progressive, liberal place.

"There is definitely a lack of diversity on campus and in Vermont in general. Maybe that's part of the reason everyone is required to take a Race and Ethnicity class and a Non-European Cultures class."

Q "The campus **isn't racially diverse at all**. There are very few minorities present, and white is definitely the dominant population, which kind of sucks. While there is a lack of racial diversity, there is diversity in other areas. People are very liberal, and there is a large, visible gay and lesbian community."

Q "UVM is not very diverse. There are only **four percent of us non-white students** in the entire school, which is like 400, but that includes faculty and international students. Those four percent of us are pretty tight, though."

Q "UVM, like Vermont, has a fairly homogenous population. Ethnically, **a lot of white faces are in every classroom**, and foreign students are a novelty. Diversity of sexual orientation is perhaps more prominent, not surprising given the liberal nature of the state. There are some active organizations supporting diversity though—ALANA as well as LGBTA."

Q "It's extremely **diverse in thought, tolerance, ideas, intellectually, etc.**, but not at all diverse in race and ethnicity, but we are trying—[for example] UVM's relationship with Christopher Columbus High School."

Q "It's not as culturally diverse as it could be, but there are students representing many ethnic backgrounds and about 50 different countries. The diversity here **stems from peoples' different upbringings and thoughts**. You'll get into some great conversations at UVM. It's a very liberal place."

The College Prowler Take
ON DIVERSITY

Racial diversity is an area that most UVM students agree needs for improvement. Those surveyed commented that the lack of diversity is something many students dislike about UVM. In spite of this, many of these same students also commented on their awareness of the University's diversity with respect to progressiveness and individual thought, as well as the strong presence of the gay community. It is important to remember that diversity is not limited to skin color. Religious, sexual, political, and racial diversity are important to a diverse community. Unfortunately, at UVM, we may have three out of four, but that is not good enough. The school is actively pursuing the expansion of ethnic and racial diversity here on campus.

The College Prowler™ Grade on
Diversity: D

A high grade in Diversity indicates that ethnic minorities and international students have a notable presence on campus and that students of different economic backgrounds, religious beliefs, and sexual preferences are well-represented.

Guys & Girls

The Lowdown
ON GUYS & GIRLS

Women Undergrads:
57%

Men Undergrads:
43%

Hookups or Relationships?
Both

Dress Code:
Nearly anything and everything

Students Speak Out
ON GUYS & GIRLS

{ "Everyone is nice and generally laid-back. The guys are cute and the girls are sweet. You'll find your group."

"The guys would seem to be **either potheads or preppies**, if you were to generalize. There are lots of skateboarding, skiing, and snowboarding bums, but they're a pretty accepting lot most of the time. They're also good looking most of the time, although some can be kind of grungy, with dreadlocks all over the place. The girls are pretty nice and accepting as well."

Q "Well, let's just say that you can find **quite a variety of guys, from dreads, to preps, to jocks**. So, it depends on your type of guy. Personally, I'm into the preps and jocks, and I find them quite hot! Dating isn't popular on campus at all. It's mostly just random hookups at parties or something."

Q "Perhaps the biggest misconception about UVM's student population is the omnipresence of hippies hugging every tree. They're definitely here, but so are the rest of us. Neither guys nor girls can really be pigeonholed at UVM. **Dreadlocks and crew cuts are equally as likely to be pot-heads**, active members of clubs and organizations, and friends with one another. We do have a physically active student population, providing for a fairly fit and attractive crowd."

Q "My boyfriend says the girls are decent, and I met him here, so I guess the men are good. I know that, on my floor alone, I made some of my best friendships. **No one is snotty, rude, or judgmental**, and I think that that's the best thing about UVM people. On my recruiting visit for soccer, everyone was so friendly. I didn't hear one bad thing about UVM from the students the entire time that I was here. When I signed to play here I told everyone that, 'the people sold the place to me.'"

Q "You will find that, in general, everyone on campus is pretty laid-back and down-to-earth. We all take pride in our school and everyone seems to get along, no matter what. **We all have common interests and connections**, whether it happens to be our common interest in music, snowboarding, or whatever. You will make friends and acquaintances in no time at all. There are many hot guys at UVM. Were you interested in girls, too? I mean, there are many attractive people, in general."

The College Prowler Take
ON GUYS & GIRLS

It is unanimous that both the guys and the girls at UVM are attractive. If anything is missing, it is the mental and emotional connections between people in relationships. Once you go to college, the freedom allocated to students often results in lots of sexual expression. Hooking up and having fun seem to be the trends at UVM and the rest of the country. There are certainly people in serious relationships, but many people at UVM want nothing more than a casual, physical relationship.

The College Prowler™ Grade on
Guys: B

A high grade for Guys indicates that the male population on campus is attractive, smart, friendly, and engaging, and that the school has a decent ratio of guys to girls.

The College Prowler™ Grade on
Girls: B+

A high grade for Girls not only implies that the women on campus are attractive, smart, friendly, and engaging, but also that there is a fair ratio of girls to guys.

Who's hot and who's not on campus? Check out the College Prowler book on UVM to find out, available at *www.collegeprowler.com*.

Athletics

Students Speak Out
ON ATHLETICS

> "Certain sports are bigger than others. Hockey and basketball are pretty big. IM sports seem fun."

The Lowdown
ON ATHLETICS

Women's Teams:
Basketball
Cross Country
Field Hockey
Ice Hockey
Indoor Track
Outdoor Track
Lacrosse
Swimming
Skiing
Soccer
Softball
Tennis

Men's Teams:
Basketball
Baseball
Cross Country
Golf
Ice Hockey
Lacrosse
Swimming
Skiing
Soccer
Tennis

Club Sports
13 (e.g., Cycling, Swimming)

Intramurals (IMs)
14 (e.g., Frisbee, Lacrosse)

Fields
Soccer field, Rugby field, Redstone Field, Football field (although there is no team)

School Mascot
Catamount

Athletic Division
Division I

Conference
America East Conference

Getting Tickets
(802) 656-4410

> "**Sports are very big at UVM**, especially basketball and hockey. There are many different sports to choose from to play and to watch. The gym has a large pool, as well as tennis courts, racquetball courts, a hockey rink, a weight room, and a dance room."

> "UVM tends to attract students of the independent spirit rather than those into school spirit. However, there are plenty of jocks at UVM. Hockey is huge on campus and is widely supported. UVM skiing is Division I, second in the entire nation, and the number-one team in the East—the ski team finished second only to the University of Utah at nationals. Most students don't even know this. That in itself suggests how big sports are at UVM."

> "UVM has no football team, but **our hockey team is a big deal**, and so is our basketball team, and I think the soccer team has done well. One of the things that kind of sucks about UVM is school spirit. We do lack a bit in that department, but it's hard when the school doesn't promote varsity sports that much."

> "Varsity sports are big, with hockey, basketball, and skiing being the dominant sports. The **IM sports are pretty big**, too, with a whole host of teams to play with and sports to play. It's also pretty low-key, so it's lots of fun."

> "Sports **aren't that big**. I referee some IM sports and play in some other ones. However, they are fun, and it's definitely worthwhile to participate in them. I was a member of varsity swimming for two months but found it too difficult to manage my time with all of my classes and stuff."

The College Prowler Take
ON ATHLETICS

Some varsity sports are much bigger than others. As far as intramurals go, there are a great number of possibilities. There probably exists an IM sport for every varsity sport—sometimes more. So, if you don't make the cut for varsity, you always have the opportunity to play the club sport. While UVM has not typically drawn the best athletes from across the country, its reputation as a competitive Division I school is increasing and starting to bring in more athletes at the top of their game.

The College Prowler™ Grade on
Athletics: B-

A high grade in Athletics indicates that students have school spirit, that sports programs are respected, that games are well-attended, and that intramurals are a prominent part of student life.

Greek Life

The Lowdown
ON GREEK LIFE

Number of Fraternities:
10

Number of Sororities:
5

Percent of Undergrad Men in Fraternities:
3%

Percent of Undergrad Women in Sororities:
2%

Students Speak Out
ON GREEK LIFE

"If you make friends with people who aren't in fraternities or sororities and live off campus, you'll still have plenty of great opportunities to party. Also, if you play a sport, you can count on knowing about plenty of parties."

Q "I'm a sister in Alpha Delta Pi, a small and selective sorority that exists all over the nation. **Greek life is only five percent of the campus**, that's about 500 kids, but the party scene is dominated by Greeks, at least for me. Were you to join, it'd make the campus much smaller—the Greek community rocks!"

Q "Thank God it does not dominate social life. Greek life offers **a great sense of community and partying**, but only for the five percent of the students of the University of Vermont who actually take part in it."

Q "**Greek life is a big thing at UVM**, but if you don't choose to be a part of it, there are plenty of other ways to have a good time. I find that Greek life at UVM doesn't dominate the social scene, but it gives UVM a good party atmosphere."

Q "Greek life does exist on this campus, but it is not the only form of social activity. If you want to go to a frat party on the weekends, you'll always be able to find one. However, **there's always something else to do**."

The College Prowler Take
ON GREEK LIFE

The people who join Greek life usually want to join, and so they are likely to enjoy it. The 95 percent who do not belong to Greek organizations, though, do not miss a beat on anything happening. It is one of those things that most students agree is only there if you want it to be. There is not huge pressure to join a fraternity or sorority, and there is not a high demand for recruits, simply because the presence is not that large. If you want to be a frat boy or a sorority girl, you can, but there will not be as much focus or support as there may be at other universities. Regardless of this, however, by pledging you will still become a member of the house and, hopefully, make lifelong friends.

The College Prowler™ Grade on
Greek Life: B-

A high grade in Greek Life indicates that sororities and fraternities are not only present, but also active on campus. Other determining factors include the variety of houses available and the respect the Greek community receives from the rest of the campus.

Drug Scene

The Lowdown
ON DRUG SCENE

Most Prevalent Drugs on Campus:
Alcohol and marijuana

Liquor-Related Violations:
369

Drug-Related Violations:
194

Drug Counseling Programs:
Alcohol & Drug Services

Students Speak Out
ON DRUG SCENE

"**If you want to avoid drugs and drinking and can't stand people who choose to use them, you should live in a substance-free dorm or on a substance-free floor.**"

Q "UVM definitely has **a reputation for being strict**. It is really easy to get away with smoking and drinking in the dorms, especially if you're quiet. A cop isn't allowed to enter your room without your consent, unless he or she has a reason for doing, so that saves a lot of people!"

Campus Strictness

Students Speak Out
ON CAMPUS STRICTNESS

Q "The kids here are chill. **Hardcore drugs really don't have a popular status** at UVM. I came from a school where frat parties consisted of kids shooting up and sniffing crack for fun. I had to get away from that kind of atmosphere."

Q "I heard that the administration is trying to crack down on the pot smoking, but I would say that **it's easier to get drugs than to get alcohol** if you're under 21. Frat parties have alcohol, though."

Q "**Marijuana is used rabidly and marginalizes** many of the individuals who are at UVM for the actual education, not the marijuana. President Fogel is in the midst of changing UVM back to being a public flagship university."

Q "**Pot is smoked by a lot of students**. Other drugs are around; mushrooms and LSD come in waves."

"A lot of people smoke in their rooms. If that's not for you, request a roommate who does not smoke. It'll make your life easier!"

Q "UVM often has security guards roaming the halls of campus facilities during the night on all days of the week, but even more so on the weekends. There are also **many police cars that drive around campus** on the weekends, when students are likely to be out."

Q "Most of the officers I've encountered have been very nice, though **I do know students who've had problems with them**."

Q "**Campus police are Vermont state police**, so you need to be careful about what you do."

Q "Campus police suck. **They have no regard for students' rights** and really come down hard on the students. The detoxification program is even worse. The best thing to do is to not be stupid. Don't ever walk home alone, and don't party in the dorms, ever. It's stupid, and you will get caught."

Q "The **UVM police are very strict about drinking in the dorms** if you're underage. If you're over 21, you can drink in the dorms. There is basically no tolerance for drugs, and it seems to be a constant topic of debate."

The College Prowler Take
ON DRUG SCENE

As with any college campus, there will be drugs and alcohol, and there will be students who use either, both, or none. And that pretty much sums up UVM as well. Marijuana is the most prevalent illegal substance, along with alcohol. Like many students say, though, how much you choose to partake is up to you. There are risks involved with drugs and alcohol, and you should be conscious of them before you make a decision. But keep in mind, this is Vermont, and it is a very liberal state. Pot is very common not only here, but in the surrounding Burlington community. It is just important to remember that regardless of whether you engage in drugs and alcohol or not, you must learn to balance your work with your play.

The College Prowler™ Grade on
Drug Scene: C+

A high grade on Drug Scene indicates that drugs are not a noticeable part of campus life; drug use is not visible, and no pressure to use them seems to exist.

The College Prowler Take
ON CAMPUS STRICTNESS

The level of strictness on campus leaves some students aggravated and feeling as though their rights are being violated. Other students, meanwhile, like the added feeling of security provided by increased police presence and firmness. Whatever the belief, common sense will keep you out of trouble and prevent you from having to answer to the law. As already mentioned, campus police are stricter than they used to be. They are more lenient about alcohol offenses than they are marijuana charges, but if you're irresponsible, you are asking for trouble.

The College Prowler™ Grade on
Campus Strictness: D+

A high Campus Strictness grade implies an overall lenient atmosphere; police and RAs are fairly tolerant, and the administration's rules are flexible.

Overall Experience

Students Speak Out
ON OVERALL EXPERIENCE

"**I would recommend getting involved in the school community. It makes such a difference in your overall experience. I'm a member of ADPI and the Greek community.**"

Q "UVM is a lot of fun and has great academics. There is always something to do and somewhere to go to just get away. Being from the area myself, **I sometimes get bored with the town**, but with Montreal being only an hour away, there is always a whole new place to explore. I highly recommend it, and perhaps I'll see you on campus."

Q "There's plenty of really fun stuff to do around Burlington—**cool bars, restaurants, Church Street, and outdoors stuff like hiking and camping**. Burlington's right on beautiful Lake Champlain. The Adirondacks and the Green Mountains are really close to Burlington. Montreal is only about an hour-and-a-half away; the drinking age in Montreal is 18—very crazy and very fun."

Q "**I do wish that I was not at UVM**. Like I said before, I'm from New York, a little outside the city, and I miss the city life."

> "Ambivalence. I love New England and Vermont, especially Burlington, and **I love to ski, which is why I came to UVM.** I have had an extremely positive experience academically and socially—although, I'm looking forward to meeting people more on my wavelength as I progress each semester."

> "**I might be happier at a bigger school**, where there are probably more down-to-earth people, as opposed to all of the stereotypical, superficial, hippie UVM people you find here. I might be a tad bit unhappy about where I am."

The Inside Scoop

The College Prowler Take
ON OVERALL EXPERIENCE

The Lowdown
ON THE INSIDE SCOOP

Students are in agreement that the University of Vermont is a remarkable place to go to school. The refreshing environment and lovely surroundings mesh well with the progressive, laid-back city of Burlington. One particular area students wished to see improvement in is an increase in the amount of racial diversity at UVM. Perhaps the coming years will bring a more diverse application pool snf allow students to learn in a more varied and culturally-aware environment. And, while less consequential factors such as parking or Greek life were neither praised nor abhorred, the most important aspects of college, such as academics, atmosphere, and housing, consistently achieved superior rankings from the students.

Compared with most other state universities, the University of Vermont offers a very competitive educational experience in an unbeatable setting. The University of Vermont houses provocative and diverse thoughts, mixed with a dedicated student body and the additional flair of Burlington. The verdict is in: UVM is a beautiful school with a rigorous academic curriculum in a place that many people come to enjoy and continue to love.

Tips to Succeed at UVM:
- Major in something you will enjoy.
- Set aside time for friends.
- Have fun learning.
- Make an effort to get involved.
- Introduce yourself to professors, and put a face with the name.

Finding a Job or Internship

The Lowdown
ON FINDING A JOB OR INTERNSHIP

It is best to check in with the Career Center. They can help you write a resume and network with a variety of people in various fields.

Career Center Resources & Services
www.uvm.edu/~career/
(802) 656-3450

The Best & Worst

The Ten BEST Things About UVM:

1. The weather (if you are a skier)
2. Spectacular scenery
3. Laid-back people
4. Outstanding professors
5. Progressive student body
6. Safe and thriving city locale
7. Accessibility to Montreal, Canada
8. The assortment of local music, art, and food
9. Easy access to the great outdoors
10. Great skiing nearby

The Ten WORST Things About UVM:

1. The weather (cold, unpredictable winters)
2. Parking (or lack thereof)
3. Strict policies
4. 6 a.m. registration
5. Few on-campus housing alternatives
6. Lack of school spirit
7. Students can be cliquey
8. Lacking diversity
9. Fun things might distract from schoolwork
10. School work might distract from fun things

Bates College

23 Campus Avenue, Lewiston, ME 04240
www.bates.edu   (207) 786-6000

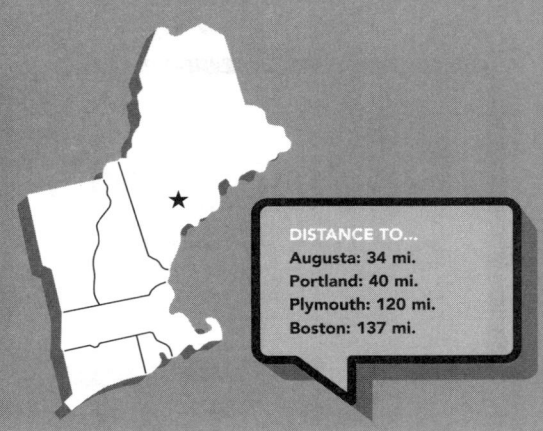

DISTANCE TO...
Augusta: 34 mi.
Portland: 40 mi.
Plymouth: 120 mi.
Boston: 137 mi.

"The first coeducational college in New England, Bates College was founded in 1855 by Maine abolitionists."

Total Enrollment:
1,746
Acceptance Rate:
37%
Tuition:
$28,832
Top 10% of High School Class:
65%
Top 25% of High School Class:
92%
SAT Range
Verbal	Math	Total
630 – 700	640 – 710	1270 – 1410

Most Popular Majors:
31% Social Sciences
13% Biological and Biomedical Sciences
8% Psychology
6% English Language and Literature/Letters
6% Foreign Languages and Linguistics

Students Also Applied To:*
Colby College, Middlebury College, Darmouth College, Williams College

*For more school info check out www.collegeprowler.com

Table of Contents

Academics	161
Local Atmosphere	163
Safety & Security	164
Computers	166
Facilities	167
Campus Dining	169
Off-Campus Dining	170
Campus Housing	172
Off-Campus Housing	173
Diversity	175
Guys & Girls	176
Athletics	178
Greek Life	179
Drug Scene	180
Campus Strictness	182
Overall Experience	183
The Inside Scoop	184
Finding a Job or Internship	185
The Best & Worst	186

College Prowler Report Card

Academics	A-
Local Atmosphere	C-
Safety & Security	A
Computers	B+
Facilities	B-
Campus Dining	B
Off-Campus Dining	C+
Campus Housing	B
Off-Campus Housing	C
Diversity	D-
Guys	B-
Girls	B
Athletics	C+
Greek Life	N/A
Drug Scene	C
Campus Strictness	B+

Academics

The Lowdown
ON ACADEMICS

Degrees Awarded:
B.A. and B.S.

Full-time Faculty:
163

Faculty with Terminal Degree:
91%

Student-to-Faculty Ratio:
10:1

Average Course Load:
4 courses

Best Places to Study:
Pettengill Hall (study areas and department lounges), Ladd Library, and The Ronj

Sample Academic Clubs:
The Garnet literary magazine. Student-run newspapers (*The Student* and *The John Galt Press*), Geology Club, Brooks Quimby Debate Council, Bates Information Technology Club. Bates Investors Club, Chess Club. Economics Society

AP Test Score Requirements:
Possible credit for scores of 4 or 5

IB Test Score Requirements:
Possible credit for scores of 6 or 7

Combined degree programs
3-2 liberal arts/engineering programs with Case Western Reserve University, Columbia University, Dartmouth College, Rensselaer Polytech Institute, and Washington University-St. Louis. Individual interdisciplinary majors, double majors, and Honors Program are also available.

Study Abroad
More than 200 juniors study off campus each year, and since 1990, Bates students have studied in over 70 countries. Students need to have at least two semesters of a language to study in a country where that language is spoken. If the language isn't offered at Bates, there is no language requirement. The Colby-Bates-Bowdoin programs are taught by faculty from each of the three schools and take place in London, England, Quito, Ecuador, and Capetown, South Africa each year. There are also several opportunities for travel during Short Term. Past programs include a theater program in Hungary, a Shakespeare program in London, and art programs in Europe.

Did You Know?
One of the most unique aspects of Bates is its calendar. The five week, Short Term in spring enables students to focus on a single course, often one that they would not be able to take otherwise. Sample Short Term courses include: Planetarium Production (students conceive, write, and produce planetarium shows for public presentation) and Bates Theater Abroad (students produce a play in a theater outside the United States).

During Short Term, the Student Activities Office runs an Experimental College, which consists of a variety of non-credit extra-curricular courses, such as bartending, yoga, ballroom dancing, knitting, and basic car mechanics.

Students Speak Out
ON ACADEMICS

"Professors, for the most part, are serious about their fields. They have studied their subjects in depth and continue to do so. Some of my classes are interesting and some aren't."

Q "Short of living on campus, the professors are as involved with students and their lives as can be. It isn't unusual to find pairs of students and professors sharing a Chai at the student center cafeteria, affectionately called 'The Den.' As I found my way through the academic world at Bates, **I've forged extremely close ties with two professors**, one in my own department, and another in a department in which I'm not minoring. This is typical as the years go by, and comes in handy once thesis time rolls by."

Q "Classes are as interesting as you make them, because **you'll rarely find a professor who isn't up to par**. In my three years thus far, I've yet to find a class where I was thoroughly displeased at the professor's performance—my interest in the subject, or lack thereof, has mostly been a deterrent for me continuing in the same class!"

Q "Overall, **the teachers have been pretty solid**. But honestly, some profs could not be any worse at their jobs. Classes are interesting, but I would have liked to see more diversity and not just standard courses one could find at any college."

Q "As a whole, the classes that I've taken that weren't to fulfill my general education were more interesting than my classes that I had to take to satisfy requirements. One of the things about the professors that bothers me is that **they all seem to have very similar political and social views**. Sometimes I feel like I'm only getting one politically correct perspective when I should be getting many, even if they aren't necessarily views that everyone agrees with."

Q "I think the teachers here are pretty good. They usually know what they're talking about, and when there's something they don't know, they are willing to admit it. Most importantly, I have almost always felt like they care about the students. For the most part, they have led interesting classes, although sometimes I feel like **they rely too much on old teaching methods** that aren't very engaging."

The College Prowler Take
ON ACADEMICS

Most Bates professors are experts in their fields, and they generally bring a high degree of enthusiasm to the classes they teach. The school's small class sizes and high teacher-to-student ratio ensure that students are able to develop close relationships with their professors. This encourages an atmosphere of mutual respect; many professors will ask their students to call them by their first name, and often professors request that students aid them in research projects. Students are usually deeply involved in their courses. Participation is not only encouraged, but often required. Probably the biggest issue surrounding Bates academics at the moment is that of general education (GE) requirements. In order to graduate, students must fulfill these requirements. Students who are taking courses simply to fulfill GE requirements compete for places with students who are taking the courses for their majors or because they're genuinely interested in the subjects. Aside from the GE requirements, students have few complaints.

The College Prowler™ Grade on
Academics: A-

A high Academics grade generally indicates that professors are knowledgeable, accessible, and genuinely interested in their students' welfare. Other determining factors include class size, how well professors communicate, and whether or not classes are engaging.

Local Atmosphere

Students Speak Out
ON LOCAL ATMOSPHERE

"**The atmosphere in Lewiston is stuffy. It's obvious to me that most people who live in Lewiston don't like upper-middle class students, so I try to be as friendly and polite as possible.**"

Q "Having a liberal arts school where many of the students are upper-middle class to upper-class creates an interesting dynamic in a town like Lewiston. **In recent years, Lewiston has experienced the loss of its major industries** and businesses, which has created economic problems and much visible poverty. This causes rifts between the two groups. Bates actively tries to reach out to the community through service-learning and other initiatives, which will hopefully improve our community relations."

Q "I like Lewiston and Auburn, but most students don't. I took a Short Term on writing the history of Lewiston and found the local history to be really interesting. It's basically a defunct mill town that thrived and attracted a variety of immigrant groups to the area. Now that the mills are barely functional, the economy has collapsed, and the local scenery proves it. There isn't a lot to do apart from going to the movie theater, going out for a crappy meal, or going to one of three bars. However, **many interesting communities, including Portland, are nearby** for evening or day trips."

Q "This town is a black hole! **An ex-student was stabbed to death a block away** from where I live, so not only is it boring as all hell, but it's unsafe. The major attraction in Lewiston is the Super Wal-Mart, which is, apparently, the second largest, single retail store in America. There is nothing for college-age kids, and the nearest city with bars and clubs is an hour away. Also, you must have a car to get around. It might be a good place if you're interested in hiking, but even the good hiking trails are about a half an hour away."

The Lowdown
ON LOCAL ATMOSPHERE

Region:
Northeast

City, State:
Lewiston, Maine

Setting:
Small City

Distance from Portland:
45 minutes

Distance from Boston:
3 hours

Points of Interest:
Thorncraig Bird Sanctuary, Bates Mill (including Creative Photographic Arts Center of Maine), Androscoggin River Walk Railroad Park, Lost Valley Recreational Area, Lewiston-Auburn Public Theater, The Franco-American Heritage Collection, Acadia National Park, The Atrium Gallery, The Androscoggin Historical Society Museum, and The Shaker Museum

Major Sports Teams
Lewiston MAINEiacs (hockey) and Portland SeaDogs (baseball)

City Websites
http://ci.lewiston.me.us/
www.auburnmaine.org/
www.androscoggincounty.com
www.mainetoday.com/

The College Prowler Take
ON LOCAL ATMOSPHERE

Though the city of Lewiston is probably the biggest drawback about going to Bates, Lewiston probably isn't quite as bad as most students make it out to be. While there honestly isn't that much to do in Lewiston, Portland is less than an hour's drive from campus. For students who don't have cars, the school runs a bus that goes to the Old Port about once a month. The area surrounding Lewiston is nice as well, with ski areas and good spots for hiking. The Outing Club organizes numerous trips to local hiking spots, and there are deals on seasonal passes for Batesies at local ski areas. If you're interested in outdoor winter sports, including snowball fights, Bates is a great school. If you're interested in spending a lot of time hanging out in a booming urban metropolis, you might be happier somewhere else. The relationship between students and "townies" is generally very poor, since most people from Lewiston resent the spoiled rich kids going to Bates. It isn't safe for students to walk around the city alone at night, and the rape and stabbing that took place a few years ago didn't help matters. For those who are interested in Franco-American or mill town history, Lewiston-Auburn is a treasure trove of information, but, mainly, Bates students try to avoid the town as much as possible.

Safety & Security

The Lowdown
ON SAFETY & SECURITY

Number of Security Personnel:
15

Phone:
Security: (207) 786-6254

Emergency:
(207) 786-6111

Phone:
(207) 786-6199

Health Center Office Hours:
24 hours a day (during school sessions)

Safety Services:
Whistle Alert program, security phones, (RAD) Rape Defense classes, Self Defense classes, Safe Walk, SafeRide shuttle, Security alerts

The College Prowler™ Grade on

Local Atmosphere: C-

A high Local Atmosphere grade indicates that the area surrounding campus is safe and scenic. Other factors include nearby attractions, proximity to other schools, and the town's attitude toward students.

Students Speak Out
ON SAFETY & SECURITY

"While security is not as strict about alcohol as other schools, they do their job, and I think students feel safe. In spite of the few recent events at Bates, I think most students feel ok on campus."

Q "The first thing that comes to mind when thinking of Bates security [officers] is how incredibly friendly they are. Unlike other schools, **students are happy to welcome security into their rooms and parties**, knowing almost all the officers by name. You get the 'we're in this together' feeling from security personnel, and it builds a sense of community and responsibility when it comes to each other's safety."

Q "It seems odd to say that I feel safe on a campus that experienced a murder and a rape within two months of one another. But **I have always felt reasonably safe here**. I also think most colleges are inherently at-risk environments. I've locked my doors and not traveled downtown at night and have been lucky, so I feel fairly safe."

Q "Bates has its own campus security that both patrols and responds to emergency situations. It has Safe Walk and SafeRide programs so students do not have to walk alone from buildings on campus at night. **All dorms have call-boxes**, so people can call up to a friend's room in a different dorm. Electronic access devices have also been installed."

Q "**The past few years have been pretty shocking**, as one student was violently raped in an academic building and another murdered by a local. Despite these frightening events, I find that Bates students are a lot more threatening than townies. I think the school has a problem with mutual respect right now, and there is an alarmingly high incidence of date rape on campus."

Did You Know?

Bates students are issued whistles as first-years. When a whistle is blown, those nearby are supposed to blow their own whistles and run towards the original whistle, as well as to notify security. There is a $75 fine for blowing a whistle without cause.

The College Prowler Take
ON SAFETY & SECURITY

Bates is a small campus and most students describe it as "self-contained." Some of the college-owned houses spread into the city, but generally Batesies opt to reside right on their well-lit, well-patrolled campus. Security officers definitely make their presence felt, although not in an imposing way. Most security personnel are friendly and more than willing to chat, or even hang out, with students. Since the rape and murder which occurred several years ago, security at Bates has become much more stringent. The school is installing Proximity Cards, which will only allow students to enter residential buildings. Also, it is now necessary for students to show their ID cards in order to enter certain buildings after 7 p.m. While security may be stricter in light of recent events, security members are still very friendly and approachable.

The College Prowler™ Grade on
Safety & Security: A

A high grade in Safety & Security means that students generally feel safe, campus police are visible, blue-light phones and escort services are readily available, and safety precautions are not overly necessary.

Computers

Did You Know?
Study areas and the library have Ethernet ports so students with laptops can access the Internet from all over campus.

Bates uses Web-based registration and grading.

The Lowdown
ON COMPUTERS

High-Speed Network?
Yes

Wireless Network?
No

Charge to Print?
No

Number of Labs:
7

Numbers of Computers:
1,150

Operating Systems:
PC and Mac

24-Hour Labs:
Coram Library

Free Software:
Illustrator, PageMaker, Photoshop, Type Manager Lite, Telnet, Canvas, ChemOffice Ultra, Choices CT, Word perfect, Datasim, Dreamweaver, EndNote, Ethnograph, Fetch, Filemaker Pro, EVIEWS, FrontPage, HyperCard, Maple V, Mathematica, MatLAB, Meeting Maker, Minitab, Prism ProCite, SAS, SigmaPlot, SPSS, StorySpace, and Virex

Students Speak Out
ON COMPUTERS

"A computer of your own isn't necessary to have, although it's a great convenience. During finals and midterms, the computer labs can get very crowded, but other than that, they seem to be fairly empty."

Q "I'd say bring your own computer. There are a few computer labs, but they can be busy, particularly around exam time. Sometimes, **the people in the labs are pretty loud**, which makes concentrating on writing a paper somewhat difficult."

Q "The network at Bates sucks. **It used to be fast but is now overloaded**. The labs have new computers but get extremely crowded during finals."

Q "I find the computer network at Bates very reliable compared to other schools, and there are quite a few computer labs on campus, as well as Internet hookups in the library for people with laptops. Around midterm and final times, the computer labs are fairly crowded, so **you have to plan ahead if you need to use a computer**. Most students bring their own computers and rely on them for e-mail and also to do work. I would recommend it."

Q "The computer network is so incredibly extensive and accessible that students often say that they'll be crippled when they go out into the real world because they'll lack an advanced system such as Bates'! **The network administrators are always available and helpful**, and the storage space is abundant."

Q "Access speed and intra-network facilities are impeccable. **There are plenty of computer labs**, with a roughly even distribution between Macs and PCs. Though computers are readily available throughout most of the year, during exam weeks they can be hard to find, even at two in the morning. I recommend bringing your own computer. You can make use of the many Internet ports throughout campus and find your own little corner in the library."

The College Prowler Take
ON COMPUTERS

With the exception of exam times, it's usually easy to find a computer in one of Bates' labs. During exams, every building on campus is packed, and study space is as coveted as billboard space in Times Square. Despite the availability of computers, most students opt to bring their own because it is much more convenient to have a computer, especially late at night when most labs are closed.

It helps to have your own computer, but it is not necessary to buy one from the school. Computer labs are often filled with students who actually own computers and are simply seeking an environment with fewer distractions. When students absolutely have to get a paper done, sometimes it helps to work anywhere but in their own room. In these cases, the computer labs are really handy. However, there is nothing like typing a paper in the comfort of your own room while wearing your favorite Garfield pajamas and eating Doritos.

The College Prowler™ Grade on
Computers: B+

A high grade in Computers designates that computer labs are available, the computer network is easily accessible, and the campus' computing technology is up-to-date.

Facilities

The Lowdown
ON FACILITIES

Movie Theatre on Campus?
There's no large theater, but films are shown in the Olin Arts Center.

Bowling on Campus?
No

Bar on Campus?
The Den (that's the campus restaurant) operates as a pub on weekend evenings.

Coffeehouse on Campus?
Yes, the Ronj, a student-run coffeehouse on Frye Street.

Student Center?
Not really, but plans for a student center are underway.

Athletic Centers
Alumni Gymnasium, Davis Fitness Center, Clifton Daggett Gray Athletic Building, Merrill Gymnasium, Tarbell Pool, Underhill Arena, Wallach Tennis Center

Library
George and Helen Ladd Library

What Is There to Do?
Check out the Andrew Wyeth exhibit. The Wyeth exhibit was organized by his granddaughter, a Bates student, at College Museum of Art—a member of Maine Art Museum Trail—and hosts more than 22,000 visitors a year.

Students Speak Out
ON FACILITIES

{ "The facilities at Bates are very nice. The athletic center, including the pool, a new track, the ice rink, and new tennis courts, is great. I think the gym and cardio room could use improvement, though."

Q "While the student center is still on the drawing board, all other facilities on campus are ample and in excellent condition. **Our maintenance department does an excellent job** of keeping everything clean and new. Facilities for athletics, computers, and dorms all have separate maintenance branches that are responsible for keeping things working, and as a result, we rarely suffer from a lack of upkeep."

Q "**The gym is lacking in equipment**. I think there's one treadmill and two bikes for a student body of 1,700. The student commons has very little in the way of extra facilities, besides the dining hall and bookstore. The dining hall is excellent. It is open almost all day and provides a variety of food options."

Q "The facilities here are pretty good. The classrooms are great, there are nice desks and the latest computer technology so teachers can give Power Point presentations, show videos, or even connect to the Internet on a big screen. **The computer labs are very nice**, too, with new flat screen monitors, but they are often crowded and noisy."

Q "We have **no student center**, though we have a student activities office that plans many events on campus, and students hang out at the on-campus restaurant, 'The Den.'"

Q "Most facilities here are nice on the outside. But, with the notable exceptions of the buildings less than 10 years old, **most buildings are slightly dilapidated inside**. We have no student center and probably won't for a while."

Students Speak Out
ON FACILITIES

Bates doesn't have a student center, which is a heated issue for many students. Currently, there are plans to build one, but nothing is set in stone, and it could be some time before construction even begins. In the meantime, Chase Hall serves as a sort of student center. It houses the dining hall, post office, bookstore, and game room. There are several new gym facilities, but most of the personal training equipment is somewhat outdated, and there are nowhere near enough machines for everyone who wants to work out. People often go to the gym at odd hours to make sure they'll actually manage to get on one of the school's archaic machines.

The quality of facilities at Bates depends largely on the age of the building. Some of the classrooms have almost space-age technology, with remote controls for lights, projection screens, and even window shades. Other classrooms are not so fortunate, and look like they haven't been renovated since they were built, decades ago. Some rooms are not big enough for the classes that meet in them; it's not unheard of for students to have to sit on the floor if they arrive after all the seats have been taken. To be fair, the school is making efforts to improve matters.

The College Prowler™ Grade on
Facilities: B-

A high Facilities grade indicates that the campus is aesthetically pleasing and well-maintained; facilities are state-of-the-art, and libraries are exceptional. Other determining factors include the quality of both athletic and student centers and an abundance of things to do on campus.

Campus Dining

The Lowdown
ON CAMPUS DINING

Freshman Meal Plan Requirement?
Yes

24-Hour On-Campus Eating?
No

Student Favorites:
The Den

Meal Plan Average Cost:
The meal plan is part of the Bates comprehensive fee.

Students Speak Out
ON CAMPUS DINING

{ "The food is excellent here. However, it can be very hard to find a table in the one-and-only dining hall on campus. They could definitely use a second dining hall, but the food in the one they have is pretty good."

Q "Commons, the one dining hall at Bates, has its share of good and bad days. It has a wide variety of food, but rarely do I find more than two or three things that are 'good.' **Campus dining has gotten tiresome** now that I am a senior, but I was blown away by the quality and variety of foods to eat as a freshman. The servers are very friendly, and I've never had to go hungry."

Q "We have one dining hall, Commons, which serves possibly some of the best food that colleges have to offer. I have visited many colleges and other large universities, and it is always a pleasure to come back to food at Bates. Apart from the food being absolutely amazing, the one thing that sets Bates dining aside is the enthusiasm and kindness of the dining staff. They are **motivated, eager to keep us happy, and proud to serve the food** that they make everyday. Everything is fresh and labeled appropriately for every kind of preference that diners may have."

Q "I like Commons food. I think that it is **pretty good in terms of college meals** and you can always find something to fill up on. How can you beat an all-you-can-eat buffet every day?"

Q "I think the Bates dining service is great! The staff is incredibly friendly, and they are very sensitive to the needs of the students. **There is even a vegan bar** and a special fridge that includes soy milk and veggie burgers. I'm grateful that my college provides healthy food options (along with the pizza and ice cream), unlike other universities, which only offer fast food garbage. Now that's how you gain the 'Freshman 15'!"

Q "There are upsides and downsides to eating at Bates. **The food is good, but there is only one dining hall**, so it can feel very repetitive after a while. As far as the meal plan goes, it's nice to be able to eat as often as you want, but it can be frustrating, since you can't choose a smaller meal plan if you're only eating two meals a day."

The College Prowler Take
ON CAMPUS DINING

Considering there is just the one dining hall, Commons, Bates Dining Services brings a lot of variety to each meal. There is a pasta bar, a vegan bar, a sandwich bar, a salad bar, a cereal bar, a pizza bar, the main dining line, and the Marche station, which provides alternative hot food or dessert options. Additionally, the Silo serves soup and sandwich lunches on weekdays. The food that Bates Dining Services provides is generally very well-prepared, and there are a number of healthy options as well. The advantage of having a single dining hall is that you always see someone you know. The disadvantage is seating. Commons can get very crowded between 5:30 and 6:30 p.m., which makes it almost impossible to find a table. Lunches can get pretty crowded as well, especially between noon and 12:30 p.m. The Napkin Board ensures that students actually have a lot of say in what Commons serves, and it isn't unusual to see an item appear in the dining hall only a short time after students jot it down. Students have unlimited meals, which can be a big advantage if you stop by Commons six times a day for coffee, but is also frustrating for students who only eat one or two meals in the dining hall a day. On the whole, Bates Dining Services is outstanding, especially considering how small the school is.

Off-Campus Dining

The Lowdown
ON OFF-CAMPUS DINING

Discount Food Specials:
Domino's Bates Special

Best Pizza:
Pat's Pizza

Best Chinese:
Chopsticks

Best Breakfast:
The Slamma

Best Wings:
Gipper's Sports Grill

Best Healthy:
Nezinscot Farm

Best Place to Take Your Parents:
DaVinci's

24-Hour Eating:
Denny's, Dunkin Donuts

Student Favorites:
DaVinci's, Chopsticks, Domino's, Margaritas, and Pat's Pizza

The College Prowler™ Grade on
Campus Dining: B

Our grade on Campus Dining addresses the quality of both school-owned dining halls and independent on-campus restaurants as well as the price, availability, and variety of food.

Students Speak Out
ON OFF-CAMPUS DINING

The College Prowler Take
ON OFF-CAMPUS DINING

{ "Surprisingly, there is a good amount of places to go eat off-campus. You just have to know how to find them. DaVinci's and Thai Dish are good, and Portland is only 50 minutes away."

Q "The Lewiston restaurant scene has improved since I was a freshman. Nothing But The Blues Café is a short walk away and is very good. DaVinci's is the classic Parents' Weekend, family Italian restaurant. Thai Dish is **remarkably good for a Thai restaurant in central Maine**, but stay away from the Chinese restaurants around Lewiston."

Q "There are some restaurants that are frequented by Bates students—DaVinci's, Thai Dish, and Margaritas, to name a few. All of them have **specials for Bates students**. There are some favorite brunch places, too—the Slamma and Wen & Shirls, which are especially popular on Sunday mornings."

Q "**There aren't too many restaurants off campus**. My favorite is DaVinci's. I think students tend to frequent Margaritas, Pat's Pizza, Chopsticks, and Applebee's."

Q "For crappy Tex-Mex, try Margaritas. For a juicy steak you can't afford, go to the Black Watch. Decent Asian restaurants in the area include Thai Dish, Thai Elephant, and Chopsticks. If you're looking for the coffee shop feel, and an expensive, but good, sandwich, head to Austin's. **Pat's Pizza is cheap**, has a vegetarian menu, and offers a variety of different appetizers. If you want an organic, farm-fresh breakfast, go to Nezinscot Farm in Turner."

Q "The off-campus restaurants range from great to less-than-impressive. DaVinci's is a popular Italian sit-down place, Margaritas for Mexican food, Chopsticks for Chinese, Thai Dish for, well, Thai food. **I personally like the fast food more in Lewiston**. Amato's is a great Italian take-out place, and Russell Street Variety makes a lot of great American food. Both are really cheap, really fast, and really good."

Restaurants in the Lewiston-Auburn area run the gamut from awful to really good. The favorite is definitely DaVinci's, which has a great atmosphere, delicious food, and more than reasonable prices. During Parents' Weekend, the waiting list at DaVinci's can get up to two hours long. Chopsticks Chinese restaurant has a very classy dining room and decent food, and Margaritas is often frequented by Bates students. Students who are under 21 go for the food, and students who are of age go for the food and the moderately-priced mixed drinks. Another very popular restaurant among Batesies is Russell Street Variety, which is about a two-minute walk from Adams Hall. Students can phone in orders and walk over 15 minutes later to get cheap and delicious pizzas, calzones, or subs. Domino's and Papa John's, the two pizza delivery places in the area, are also popular, especially late at night. Also, Portland boasts a number of ethnic restaurants that Lewiston lacks.

The College Prowler™ Grade on
Off-Campus Dining: C+

A high Off-Campus Dining grade implies that off-campus restaurants are affordable, accessible, and worth visiting. Other factors include the variety of cuisine and the availability of alternative options (vegetarian, vegan, Kosher, etc.).

Campus Housing

Did You Know?
The great majority of Bates students live on campus. On-campus housing is guaranteed to students all four years. Only a limited number of seniors rent apartments off-campus. This is intended to foster a sense of community.

The Lowdown
ON CAMPUS HOUSING

Students Speak Out
ON CAMPUS HOUSING

Undergrads on Campus: 90%

Residence Halls: 11

Houses: 25

Apartments: 0

"When it comes to quality of living, Page is bad—really, really bad. The Village, however, is good. Parker is okay. Some of the houses are really nice, as well."

"The dorms are **overcrowded and generally get trashed a lot**. John Bertram and the Village are dorms with suites, and Rand is a nice dorm if you don't want to live in a suite. They all get loud except for the Bill, which is chem-free."

Cleaning Service?
Bathrooms are usually cleaned once a day during the week, but not on Saturdays or Sundays. Common areas (kitchens and lounges) are cleaned periodically, but it is the responsibility of the students to keep them respectfully neat.

"Dorms at Bates are great as long as you aren't expecting to live in a palace. They all have wonderful, sweet custodians who empty trash and clean the hallways and bathrooms. **The dorms get really dirty on the weekends**, especially in the first-year dorms, with lots of spilled beer and vomit in the hallways."

You Get
Bed, desk and chair, bookshelf (usually supplied, and if not, shelves are available upon request), waste basket, dresser, closet, window coverings, Ethernet connection, free campus and local phone calls.

"All dorms are very well-kept and most are very nice to live in. The majority of housing at Bates, though, is in **Victorian houses**, which are very popular. It may be a smart move to choose 'chem-free' dorms or houses to live in if you want your living space to be free of alcohol consumption, or to chose a 'quiet' dorm if you'd like a peaceful setting at all times."

Also Available
Bates has female-only and male-only houses available. There are several chemical-free buildings on campus and a number of quiet houses and dorms. There is also themed housing available. Some examples of themed houses include the Russian House, the Fine Arts House, the Performance House, the Human Rights House, and the Mentoring/Leadership House.

> "Some of the dorms are nice, but avoid Page. Parker can be a fun place for freshman. **The Village seems to be pretty nice**, but, in my experience, the houses are the best bet. You can get to know your house-mates and the rooms in the houses are quite nice, usually. Nash is a great house, as is FSU. Off-campus housing is nice for those more independent types, but it can get kind of remote."

Off-Campus Housing

The College Prowler Take
ON CAMPUS HOUSING

Dorms range from the spectacular to the squalid, and, obviously, the higher your class rank, the better your dorm will be. The Village is new and has excellent suites for juniors and seniors. John Bertram (JB) and Rand are nice, although they are party dorms and are noisier and dirtier than the designated quiet dorms such as Adams and Williams Hall (The Bill). First-year students should avoid Page and aim for Parker, or, if they're looking for chem-free housing, The Bill. Other students choose to live in one of the houses or Hedge Hall, which create very tightly-knit groups of friends but make it harder for students to meet a lot of people.

The Lowdown
ON OFF-CAMPUS HOUSING

Undergrads in Off-Campus Housing:
10%

Popular Areas:
Wood Street, Vale Street

Best Time to Look for a Place:
Winter semester of junior year

Average Rent for a Studio Apartment:
$400/month

Average Rent for a 1BR Apartment:
$470/month

Average Rent for a 2BR Apartment:
$525/month

For Assistance Contact
Erin Foster, Director of Housing
Phone: 786-6215
E-mail: efoster@bates.edu
There is a message board about off-campus housing in Chase Hall.

The College Prowler™ Grade on
Campus Housing: B

A high Campus Housing grade indicates that dorms are clean, well-maintained, and spacious. Other determining factors include variety of dorms, proximity to classes, and social atmosphere.

Students Speak Out
ON OFF-CAMPUS HOUSING

"I'm living off-campus next year. Because I'm not on financial aid, it costs a little less, if not about the same. People who live off-campus can elect to continue their meal plan, if they choose."

Q "Students are required to live on campus until their senior year, and then a select number are allowed off campus. I think it is fairly easy to find off-campus housing, though **it is more expensive**, and people end up living on one of the side streets bordering the campus anyway."

Q "You can only live off campus your senior year. **Some find the independence comforting**, while many choose to stay on campus. In my opinion, staying on campus is far more convenient since you are closer to all the campus resources and in the cold winter days, you won't have to walk as far to get to class!"

Q "Only a fraction of seniors are allowed to live off campus. **There is very cheap housing available in Lewiston**, and it's usually close by. Living off campus is nice because you are allowed more independence. You can cook your own meals, have more space, and receive special cable and phone services. The downsides to living off-campus are slow Internet access, living further from campus, and, potentially, not living with all your friends."

Q "I think one unusual asset at Bates is the fact that it is difficult to get off-campus housing. Having almost all Bates students on campus really promotes a sense of community and continuity. As a senior, I couldn't be more excited to be living right in the middle of campus. **There's enough time after college to live in an apartment**. Dorm life only happens for four years."

Q "Bates students aren't allowed to live off campus until their senior year, and even then, they must apply to live in their own apartments. This is stupid because campus housing is overcrowded as it is. Off-campus housing is available, but **students need to be organized about applying for it**."

The College Prowler Take
ON OFF-CAMPUS HOUSING

The fact is, the majority of Bates students live on campus. A percentage of seniors may apply to live off campus, but they must live within a mile of the school. Considering the amount of snow Maine gets every winter, living more than a mile away would be an inconvenience. It's not too difficult to get housing off campus, and it ends up costing about the same as living in the dorms. Students who elect to live off campus can continue with the meal plan, and many do. There are advantages and disadvantages to off-campus living. It is a lot more work to organize renting an apartment, you have to go further to get to classes, and you're not connected to the Bates computer network. On the other hand, off-campus students are more independent, and are able to better prepare themselves for life after Bates. After three years of living in dorms, many students are ready to live in an apartment of their own.

The College Prowler™ Grade on
Off-Campus Housing: C

A high grade in Off-Campus Housing indicates that apartments are of high quality, close to campus, affordable, and easy to secure.

Diversity

The Lowdown
ON DIVERSITY

African American: 2%

Asian American: 3%

Hispanic: 2%

Native American: 0%

White: 87%

International: 6%

Out-of-State: 88%

Political Activity
The campus is overwhelmingly liberal, and many students are politically active. Several times a year, buses take students to protests in larger cities, and Bates students can often be seen distributing leaflets outside chain stores such as the Gap. The school also has a small Republican element, which organizes lectures and manages Bates' conservative newspaper, *The John Galt Press*.

Gay Tolerance
The community is very accepting of gay students, and OUTfront, the on-campus student group, is very popular. Each year, members of OUTfront and other students gather to fill the footpaths on the quad with colorful drawings and statements done in sidewalk chalk, expressing support for Bates' gay, lesbian, bisexual, and transgender community.

Economic Status
The student body contains representatives from many different economic groups. However, a majority of students are from wealthy families. This has led to some tension between Bates students and Lewiston "townies." On campus, differences between students' economic backgrounds are hardly noticed, especially since many wealthy students choose to hold jobs on campus.

Minority Clubs
Bates has a multi-cultural center which is affiliated with the school's 11 cultural and ethnic groups. These include Amandla!, which aims to promote understanding of African culture; the American Indian Awareness Organization; the Francophone Club; Solidariad Latina; and the Women of Color Group. The Bates International Club is very popular and active, as is the Jewish Cultural Community.

Students Speak Out
ON DIVERSITY

{ **"'Diversity' is a word that Bates students will never understand, unless they are from Boston or New York."**

Q "There are students from all over the world who attend Bates, but it is a school in Maine, and **the minority population is not large**. Bates recruits for diversity, but for the most part, students are white, upper-middle class, and live 20 minutes outside of Boston."

Q "There are many different types of people with different interests. However, this campus is about **as white as Wonderbread**."

Q "Bates is not very diverse, but if you look, you can find some diversity. There's a whole lot of diverse students on campus, but you have to make some effort to find them. Some clubs and organizations help, but **it's very easy to look at this school and see only white kids**."

> "Bates is not diverse at all. There is **a unified community of international students**, but there is not a lot of racial or ethnic diversity. The increasing cost of a private education discourages the American middle and upper-middle class from attending a school like Bates, over their state universities. Most of my friends are either really rich, (i.e., live next door to Angelina Jolie), or are on a lot of financial aid and from more rural areas."

The College Prowler Take
ON DIVERSITY

A number of students at Bates weren't able to visit the school before they came here and were surprised by the uniformity of the student body. Even students who aren't minorities, but who are used to living in a more diverse environment, sometimes feel uncomfortable in such a homogenous student body. A few have expressed regrets at coming to Bates because they feel so out of place. Bates is a small, private, liberal arts college in northern New England, and the unfortunate result is a lack of diversity. However, despite the small numbers of minorities on campus, the International Club and other minority clubs are a definite presence. Many students, not just internationals or minorities, attend events organized by these clubs, such as the International Fashion Show and the Asian Dinner. Considering its location and its size, Bates is about as diverse as you'd expect it to be—that is to say, not very diverse at all.

The College Prowler™ Grade on
Diversity: D-

A high grade in Diversity indicates that ethnic minorities and international students have a notable presence on campus and that students of different economic backgrounds, religious beliefs, and sexual preferences are well-represented.

Guys & Girls

The Lowdown
ON GUYS & GIRLS

Women Undergrads: 51%

Men Undergrads: 49%

Birth Control Available?
Yes, women may go to the Health Center and meet with a nurse practitioner, who gives them a prescription for birth control that can be filled at a number of locations in the area.

Social Scene
Students most often meet people while participating in clubs or sports. In their first year, students will make many of their new friends in their own dorms, but older students tend to stay with their established groups and interact with their dorm-mates mostly on a smile-and-say-hi level. This also goes for classes; students will sit with the friends they already have, rather than making friends with others in the class. Parties are obviously another way students interact socially, but, most often, people at parties are too drunk to remember their "new best friends" the morning after. Many Bates students are very passionate about their interests, so they tend to hang out with people who have similar likes and concerns. This has led to a Breakfast Club-style social situation on campus, with hippies, preppies, and jocks mainly socializing only with others in their groups.

Hookups or Relationships?

There is no middle ground in the Bates dating scene. Couples are either "just hooking up" or involved in serious relationships with wedding bells chiming faintly in the distance. Casual dating is almost unheard of, perhaps because of the difficulty of going on actual dates (many students don't have cars, and taking the school shuttle to see a movie with your date is hardly romantic, and meeting in the dining hall is even less so). But, with so many students partying on the weekends, hookups are common. Considering the intense friendships so many students develop at Bates, it is no surprise that serious relationships are just as prevalent.

Students Speak Out
ON GUYS & GIRLS

"Anyone who is choosing colleges based on how attractive the people are would probably not choose Bates. Students here do have fun with each other, though."

Q "Batesies are a friendly bunch; supportive, too. They are **ambitious, intelligent, and involved**. Batesies care. They care about their classes, their work, their activities, the environment, the community, and their friends."

Q "There are some hot guys on campus, but when you get to know their personalities, **you're left feeling disappointed**. But I think that is the same everywhere. There are many different types of guys. You've got your meathead, beer-chugging jock, you've got your greasy, smelly hippy, and you've got your nerdy smart guys. And there's probably a few other types thrown in there, too."

Q "**The guys and girls here are all drunks**! I found a great group of guys, and the girls, well, they're all right. But, I heard a rumor that 60 percent of Batesies marry Batesies."

Q "The guys and girls are often **hippies who don't shower**, so I'd have to say they're not that hot."

Q "I don't understand it, but every year it seems as though the crops of **first-years are getting better and better looking**. On the flip side, they also seem to be getting snobbier and more shallow, so that kind of sucks."

The College Prowler Take
ON GUYS & GIRLS

Bates is a small campus, and before too long, students will be able to recognize just about everyone they pass. And, because the school is so small, pretty much everybody knows everybody else's business. Drunken hookups are common, and some people don't even bother to get out of the hallway before they start messing around. Oftentimes, hall-mates know everyone else's "secret code" that students write on the whiteboard to alert their roommate they have a guest in the room, so even those who fool around in their own rooms don't have all that much privacy. Nearly everyone on campus is familiar with the "walk of shame" back to their rooms the morning after. Some people choose to run, hoping no one will see them. Batesies do tend to be attractive physically, but some people have complained about the general shallowness of the students on campus.

The College Prowler™ Grade on
Guys: B-
A high grade for Guys indicates that the male population on campus is attractive, smart, friendly, and engaging, and that the school has a decent ratio of guys to girls.

The College Prowler™ Grade on
Girls: B
A high grade for Girls not only implies that the women on campus are attractive, smart, friendly, and engaging, but also that there is a fair ratio of girls to guys.

Athletics

Most Popular Sports

The Bates football team is something of a joke, but the school's basketball team is very popular, often playing for a full house. Lacrosse games are also very well-attended. Intramural (IM) teams, particularly basketball and hockey, are popular, with many students participating in them and going to matches. The Outing Club has a large membership; many students take advantage of the hiking opportunities available in Maine.

The Lowdown
ON ATHLETICS

Athletic Division:
Division III

Conference:
New England Small College Athletic Conference (NESCAC)

School Mascot:
Bobcat

Men's Varsity Teams:
Cross Country
Football
Golf
Rowing
Soccer
Basketball
Alpine Skiing
Nordic Skiing
Squash
Swimming
Diving
Track and Field
Baseball
Lacrosse
Tennis

Women's Varsity Teams:
Cross Country
Field Hockey
Golf
Rowing
Soccer
Tennis
Volleyball
Basketball
Alpine Skiing
Nordic Skiing
Squash
Swimming
Diving
Track and Field
Lacrosse
Softball

Getting Tickets

All Bates sporting events are free, and there is seldom any difficulty finding seats, even at major games.

Students Speak Out
ON ATHLETICS

"A lot of students are involved in sports, and a lot aren't. There's an Outing Club, which organizes hikes, rock climbing, skiing, and more."

Q "Sports are not huge on campus, although if you want to participate, there is certainly an opportunity. I guess there is **a whole scene for which sports is a big deal**, but it is by no means pervasive. It's not like you are an outsider if you don't go to football games."

Q "Varsity sports are **a big part of Bates**, as are IM sports. I think the majority of students here have participated in either a varsity or IM sport. And if they haven't, they've probably been to a sporting event to cheer on their friends."

Q "Varsity sports aren't really very big, because **we're not that good**. IM sports are popular, especially in May when it is nice out."

Q "**Bates isn't at the top of the pancake stack** when it comes to sports. We are more like the soggy one on the bottom. Although, I hear that our lacrosse team is good."

Q "Varsity sports are not that big. If we had some better-than-decent teams maybe they would be. IM sports are **big for those who participate in them**, but I didn't notice them too much when I wasn't playing."

The College Prowler Take
ON ATHLETICS

Not to say that athletics aren't important at Bates, but academics always take top priority. Thus, varsity sports at Bates are Division III and probably always will be. While this has led to a low profile concerning athletics at Bates, there is certainly no lack of opportunities for students to play. Between varsity, IM, and club sports, students with almost any level of interest can find something that suits them. Bates also offers a number of PE courses, such as yoga, ballroom dancing, indoor climbing, and RAD self-defense for women. Four PE credits are required to graduate, and these can be satisfied by taking PE courses or by participating in other sporting options. Sorry guys, beer-pong is not included!

The College Prowler™ Grade on
Athletics: C+

A high grade in Athletics indicates that students have school spirit, that sports programs are respected, that games are well-attended, and that intramurals are a prominent part of student life.

Greek Life

The Lowdown
ON GREEK LIFE

Number of Fraternities: 0

Number of Sororities: 0

Students Speak Out
ON GREEK LIFE

"We don't have any frats. Actually, I wish we did. Then all the 'frat boy types' would be removed from the general population."

Q "There is no Greek life, but **house parties often imitate it**."

Q "There are no frats or sororities at Bates, although **Moulton House sometimes seems like a sorority**."

Q "There is **no Greek life at Bates**, and I love that. People are much more social."

Q "Bates is a small college and doesn't allow exclusive organizations, so there are no fraternities or sororities. **Students are all the more social for it**."

Q "Thank holy God there is no Greek life at Bates, and there never has been. **It was one of the major factors in my application process**, and I am still overjoyed that Bates has a proud tradition of barring fraternities. The dorm parties at Bates are just as good as frat parties at other schools that my friends attend."

Did You Know?

Bates was founded on principles of egalitarianism; it was the first coed college in New England and has never discriminated based on race, religion, national origin, or sex. Bates has never had fraternities or sororities either, because these institutions are contradictory to the school's ideals.

Drug Scene

The Lowdown
ON DRUG SCENE

The College Prowler Take
ON GREEK LIFE

Most Batesies are fairly indifferent to the idea of having Greek organizations. The school is full of very opinionated individuals, and yet the issue of having fraternities and sororities has yet to rear its head. Some Bates students graduate without ever having gone to a frat party, and most don't seem to regret that in any way. Greek life is a non-issue at Bates. It seems unlikely that the college will ever have fraternities or sororities, which is something Batesies aren't going to lose any sleep over. As for excessive partying and binge drinking, they lose plenty of sleep over that!

Liquor-Related Referrals: 111

Liquor-Related Arrests: 18

Drug-Related Referrals: 22

Drug-Related Arrests: 16

Most Prevalent Drugs on Campus:
Alcohol and marijuana

Drug Counseling Programs

The Health Center can arrange a free two hour session at St. Mary's Chemical Dependency Program, which involves testing, evaluation, a counseling session, and recommendation for further action, if needed.

There are two licensed, registered substance abuse counselors on the Health Center staff, and each student is entitled to four free counseling sessions each year.

Student resident coordinators and junior advisors receive training dealing with problems arising from substance abuse.

The College Prowler™ Grade on
Greek Life: N/A

A high grade in Greek Life indicates that sororities and fraternities are not only present, but also active on campus. Other determining factors include the variety of houses available and the respect the Greek community receives from the rest of the campus.

 ## Students Speak Out
ON DRUG SCENE

 ## The College Prowler Take
ON DRUG SCENE

"There is a huge abuse of Adderall here, and most people who party also smoke pot regularly. I know a handful of people who also do harder drugs, like coke."

Q "There is quite a bit of pot on campus, and I am sure every other drug imaginable, but **the harder drugs are not visible**. Most people party with alcohol or marijuana."

Q "It is there if you look for it. **Pot and alcohol are pretty ubiquitous**. You don't have to look all that hard for those. Harder stuff can be found if you're looking for it. It will not be shoved in your face, though. It's not like they're selling heroin in the library!"

Q "I've never done drugs, and neither have any of my friends. Most Batesies have a heavy workload and, therefore, **don't have time for that**."

Q "My freshman year, I lived in Page, and when you walked down the hall, all you could smell was pot and the incense that students used to cover it up. It was **totally disgusting**. Sometimes it seems like half the kids at this school smoke weed every day."

Q "Actually, it's the same on every U.S. campus. You can always find someone selling drugs. Anyway, it's not my lifestyle, so I don't know a whole lot about it."

Bates is like most other colleges as far as drugs go. A majority of the campus drinks, a significant number of the students have at least tried marijuana, and more than a few are regular smokers and are less inclined to be secretive about doing so. Marijuana is definitely present, and you'd be hard-pressed to walk through the dorms without smelling pot. For students who don't want to get involved in the drug scene, there are a variety of chem-free housing options—smoking and drinking are even prohibited within 20 feet of these buildings! There's no social stigma attached to people who smoke marijuana, probably because so many people do smoke. Another reason for this, is that the students who choose to smoke pot still have to keep up with Bates' challenging curriculum, so few people really abuse the drug.

The College Prowler™ Grade on
Drug Scene: C

A high grade on Drug Scene indicates that drugs are not a noticeable part of campus life; drug use is not visible, and no pressure to use them seems to exist.

Want to know more about drugs on campus? For more student opinions, check out the College Prowler book on Bates at *www.collegeprowler.com*.

Campus Strictness

The Lowdown
ON CAMPUS STRICTNESS

What Are You Most Likely to Get Caught Doing on Campus?
Parking illegally, making too much noise in your dorm during quiet hours, bringing food or drink in the library, playing drinking games—especially beer pong—in the hallways, drinking hard alcohol, walking around campus with an open container, having illegal appliances in your dorm room

Students Speak Out
ON CAMPUS STRICTNESS

"Security isn't overly concerned with recreational drug use and doesn't care about beer drinking. Hard liquor isn't allowed, but most people still drink it in their own rooms."

Q "Campus drinking policies are ridiculous. They encourage clandestine drinking by **not allowing us to have unregistered, un-checked kegs**. Instead, people seem to double up on drugs and hard liquor. They don't check our rooms or anything, but they'll take hard alcohol away and give you a strike."

Q "Very few people receive strikes for substance use, and mainly what happens behind closed doors is unnoticed. The campus has a **no-tolerance policy for drugs and hard alcohol**, and drinking games are technically not allowed either."

Q "Campus security is **not very strict**. However, the Lewiston police have recently become more active on campus regarding drinking and other foul play."

Q "Security on campus is getting **stricter and stricter as the years go on**. One day we'll all be chained to our desks—well, probably not."

The College Prowler Take
ON CAMPUS STRICTNESS

Drinking is permitted in dorms, provided they aren't chem-free. If security catches someone drinking outside, they'll ask the student to pour his or her drink out and then let the student go. In other ways, Bates can be fairly strict. Rooms are checked over breaks, and students who forget to hide their illegal appliances or cable-stealing wires and boxes can get in trouble. Bates is very strict about parking; illegally parked cars are nearly always ticketed and even towed.

The College Prowler™ Grade on
Campus Strictness: B+

A high Campus Strictness grade implies an overall lenient atmosphere; police and RAs are fairly tolerant, and the administration's rules are flexible.

Overall Experience

Students Speak Out
ON OVERALL EXPERIENCE

Q "Going here has been pretty good. I've had problems, but I think I would have found things wrong with any school I'd gone to. I'm a skeptic, I guess."

Q "Bates has a great many problems to address. We have a small endowment, a terrible social atmosphere—the largest problem—and very little diversity of race, class, and geographic location. **Everything here can seem overwhelmingly homogenous**. At times, I have wished that I were somewhere else, but I also believe that many problems facing Bates are faced by other colleges. The most important things about Bates—the classes, the professors, the academic environment, and the relationships that I've forged—I couldn't imagine being any better."

Q "In high school, my big complaint in life was that I learned nothing from school and more from my peers. Now, I feel the reverse. Academically, I feel challenged by my classes and professors, especially now that I know how to pick good classes. However, **I don't feel challenged by my peers**. I would've done better in a more intellectually-driven school."

Q "I liked it here the first two years, although sometimes I wish I would've gone to a bigger school. Now that I'm back for my senior year, I know I would have chosen a different place. Not that it's a bad school. I know I'm getting a good education; it's just that **it's not exactly right for me**. There are just too many negatives in the surrounding environment."

The College Prowler Take
ON OVERALL EXPERIENCE

Bates students vary greatly in their opinions of their school. Some feel that Bates is a great school and wouldn't dream of having gone to another school. Others spend their four years at Bates wishing they were someplace else. Bates is a very unique school, and for the people it suits, it's amazing. Other people, who were looking for a different college experience, are less happy with the school. Bates does provide its students with a number of opportunities and, considering its size, resources, and class options, tries hard to accommodate every student. However, it is a small school in a small city and doesn't have all the same resources that are available at larger universities. The student body isn't characterized by diversity, so if the people who go to Bates aren't your type, it's easy to feel frustrated and out of place.

Whether you love Bates or hate it, when you graduate, you'll have a degree from one of the most selective liberal arts schools in the country. That definitely counts for something. Before you decide which school you want to go to, you need to be very sure what you want from a college. If you're looking for an intimate atmosphere, a close-knit campus, and an academically-challenging school, you'll probably enjoy Bates. If you want a big university with a diverse student body and an exciting city nearby, you might be better off somewhere else. Overall, Bates is a good school, with an amazing faculty and a very strong academic program, and even students who might wish they were somewhere else will leave the school with a valuable degree and a unique learning experience.

The Inside Scoop

The Lowdown
ON THE INSIDE SCOOP

School Spirit
Many students at Bates are passionate, but few of them are passionate about Bates. People who play sports have lots of school spirit, but others remain fairly apathetic. Most students busy themselves by rallying for causes such as saving the rainforests or stopping third-world sweatshops, rather than devoting their energies to school spirit. There are a number of students who are proud to be Batesies, but many students look at the school as simply a means of getting a degree from a small, private liberal arts college. Certainly, Bates is a selective school, and students are proud to have gotten in, but this has more to do with "personal pride" in their own accomplishments than pride in the school itself. Still, the school store does a brisk trade in clothing and supplies with the Bates logo; students are certainly not ashamed to be Batesies.

Traditions
The Puddle Jump

One of Bates' more interesting traditions is the St. Patrick's Day Puddle Jump. Every year, dozens of zany students take a dip in the water through a hole that is cut in the ice. Some bold souls even do this in their birthday suits. Polar Bear Club eat your heart out!

Senior Pub Crawl

In the spring, seniors form teams, choose silly costumes for their teams (Vikings, Smurfs, etc.) and go on a pub crawl through Lewiston. At the end, everyone comes to Bates and jumps in The Puddle.

The Daily Jolt
The Daily Jolt is a student-run website that provides information and amusement to Batesies. It has links to the official Website, as well as events listings, a cross-campus forum, humorous quotes from professors, and horoscopes.

Winter Carnival
Bates Winter Carnival brings a bit of cheer to the fierce Maine winters. There is a snow sculpture contest and a number of other competitions.

Things I Wish I Knew Before Coming to Bates:
- Sign up for a science class (or two) your freshman year.
- Get your PE credits out of the way as soon as possible.
- There is nothing to do in Lewiston.
- Don't buy your computer or bed linen from the school.
- Bring a PC if you can (if anything goes wrong with an iMac no one will know how to help you).
- Call your roommate before you get to campus (you both might show up with refrigerators).
- Bring a Hot Pot (they're indispensable).

Tips to Succeed at Bates:
- The main doors in Pettengill are push, not pull, when you're going out.
- Don't jump in The Puddle (no matter how drunk you are).
- Take at least one late-night trip up Mount Andrews (from that distance, even Lewiston looks pretty).
- Pettigrew and Pettengill are two very different buildings.
- Don't take any 8 a.m. classes, unless you really have to.
- Don't travel in massive groups on Friday nights.
- Remember that your computer is for doing work, not just chatting on AIM, checking your e-mail, and playing Snood.
- Take classes that actually interest you.
- Be prepared to work harder than you've ever had to before.
- Don't ever hesitate to ask questions if you don't understand what's going on.
- Take advantage of the small class sizes and establish a personal relationship with some of your professors.

Finding a Job or Internship

The Lowdown
ON FINDING A JOB OR INTERNSHIP

Advice

Bates has an excellent career services department, but it's up to you to use it. Every year, the Office of Career Services sends students a newsletter detailing all the steps they should take that year in order to prepare for life after Bates. The information is also posted on the OCS website. It's important to follow those steps and to attend the relevant lectures and fairs. If you have any questions at all, it's very easy to call or e-mail OCS and set up an appointment to meet with a counselor.

Career Center Resources & Services:
eRecruiting, campus employment, career counseling, career workshops, graduate school advising, e-mailed alerts to job/internship opportunities, career testing, alumni career advice, network, career library, employer resources, help guides, internship programs, Year-By-Year at Bates, graduate school fair, online job searching resources, and recruiting

Average Salary Information

The following information represents the salaries or yearly incomes of Bates alumni from one, 10, and 25 years after graduation. These are divided by percentages of alumni in each income bracket.

Starting Salaries

Salary	Percentage of the alumni surveyed
Over $50,000	5%
$50,000-$40,000	2%
$35,000-$40,000	11%
$30,000-$35,000	24%
$25,000-$30,000	28%
$20,000-$25,000	7%
Under $25,000	23%

10 Years Later

Salary	Percentage of the alumni surveyed
Over $500,000	1.5%
$250,000-$500,000	1.5%
$100,000-$240,000	22%
$50,000-$100,000	42%
$25,000-$50,000	25%
Under $25,000	8%

25 Years Later

Salary	Percentage of the alumni surveyed
Over $500,000	3%
$250,000-$500,000	9%
$100,000-$250,000	38%
$50,000-$100,000	36%
$25,000-$50,000	12%
Under $25,000	2%

The Best & Worst

The Ten BEST Things About Bates:

1. Strong academic programs
2. Lick-It and Gala
3. The Strange Bedfellows improv comedy group
4. Dollar Chai Nights at the Ronj
5. The Bates computer network
6. Hanging out on the quad in nice weather
7. Snowball fights and sledding
8. The intimate professors
9. The Blue Goose
10. Late night breakfasts

The Ten WORST Things About Bates:

1. Finding a parking spot
2. Six months of winter
3. Lewiston
4. People playing beer-pong outside your room at 4 a.m.
5. No cable in dorm rooms
6. Ultra-strict GE requirements
7. The persistent smell of pot
8. Overly-politically correct staff and students
9. Only one dining hall
10. The Bates Bubble

Bowdoin College

5000 College Station, Brunswick, Maine 04011
www.bowdoin.edu   (207) 725-3100

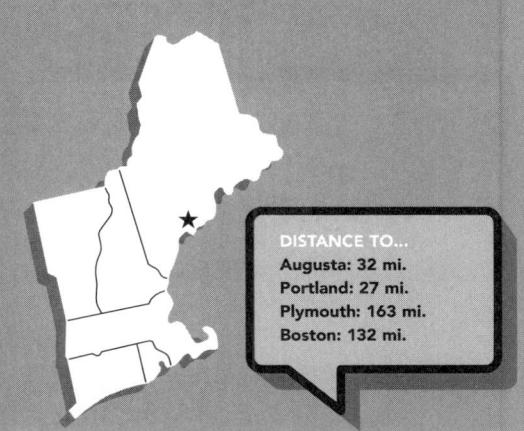

DISTANCE TO…
Augusta: 32 mi.
Portland: 27 mi.
Plymouth: 163 mi.
Boston: 132 mi.

"The retention rate and school reviews show the students' approval."

Table of Contents

Academics	188
Local Atmosphere	190
Safety & Security	191
Computers	193
Facilities	194
Campus Dining	196
Off-Campus Dining	197
Campus Housing	199
Off-Campus Housing	200
Diversity	201
Guys & Girls	203
Athletics	204
Greek Life	206
Drug Scene	207
Campus Strictness	208
Overall Experience	209
The Inside Scoop	210
Finding a Job or Internship	211
The Best & Worst	212

Total Enrollment:
1,640

Acceptance Rate:
24%

Tuition:
$31,626

Top 10% of High School Class:
72%

Average GPA:
3.9

SAT Range
Verbal	Math	Total
640 – 730	650 – 710	1290 – 1440

Most Popular Majors:
17% Political Science and Government
10% English Language and Literature
10% Biology
10% Economics
9%   Sociology

Students Also Applied To:*
Amherst College, Colby College
Dartmouth College, Middlebury College
Williams College

*For more school info check out www.collegeprowler.com

College Prowler Report Card

Academics	A
Local Atmosphere	C+
Safety & Security	A+
Computers	B+
Facilities	B
Campus Dining	A
Off-Campus Dining	B
Campus Housing	A
Off-Campus Housing	C
Diversity	C
Guys	A-
Girls	C+
Athletics	B+
Greek Life	N/A
Drug Scene	B
Campus Strictness	B+

Academics

The Lowdown
ON ACADEMICS

Degrees Awarded:
Bachelor

Undergraduate Schools:
Bowdoin College is an undergraduate school only.

Full-time Faculty:
154

Faculty with Terminal Degree:
152 (99%)

Student-to-Faculty Ratio:
9.9 to 1

Average Course Load:
4 courses

AP Test Score Requirements:
Varies by department, but usually a score of 4 or 5

IB Test Score Requirements:
Varies by department, but usually a score of 5 or higher

Best Places to Study:
Hatch, HL, and Smith Union

Special Degree Options

Accelerated program, double major, domestic exchange student program (12 College Exchange is Amherst, Connecticut, Dartmouth, Mount Holyoke, Smith, Trinity, Vassar, Wellesley, Wheaton, or Williams Colleges, or Wesleyan University), independent study, liberal arts/career combination, student-designed major, study abroad, teacher certification program, first-year experiences, service learning, senior capstone, writing in the disciplines, undergraduate research, internships, 3-2 engineering degree programs with California Institute of Technology and Columbia University, and 3-3 law degree program with Columbia University Law School

Sample Academic Clubs

African American Society, Architects & Designers, BALA (aquatic), Bowdoin Business Club, Brunswick Power and Light Art Club, Chemistry Demonstration Team, Computer Science Club, Crafts Center, Debate Team, Digital Underground, Fashion Design Club, Film/Video Society, Huntington Club (ornithology), Kamerling Society (American Chemical Society), Literary Society, Math Club, Meditation and Buddhist Studies, Neuroscience Journal Club, Peucinian Society, Poeting, Polar Consulting Group, Student Government

Did You Know?

14,000: Number of objects in the Bowdoin Museum of Art's collection, ranging from the art of the ancient world to the art of today.

7,405: Number of bottles of chemicals in Druckenmiller Hall.

917: Number of different titled text books that the Textbook Annex ordered last spring semester.

273: Number of different courses offered last spring semester.

209: Number of years men have studied at Bowdoin.

Over 100: Number of approved study-abroad programs. The options are endless for Bowdoin students.

Students Speak Out
ON ACADEMICS

The College Prowler Take
ON ACADEMICS

"Some professors are too concerned with themselves. They can come across as arrogant, rather than confident. Other than that, the overall faculty is awesome!"

Q "The professors I've had have been excellent. I've also had some great classes. **It's really nice to be given the chance to get to know my professors intimately** as an undergraduate. I've found it easy to meet with my professors, and most have set aside time to meet with students each week, outside of class."

Q "The professors spend ample time with students in order to answer any questions they might have. **Classes are stimulating and provoke a great deal of thought**. To help students do well, professors conduct nightly study sessions."

Q "The faculty is as diverse, if not more so, than the student body. **Professors come from all across the world** to teach at Bowdoin. The humanities and sciences are rich at Bowdoin, and so are the sciences."

Q "I found the teachers here at Bowdoin available, but **not approachable**. It was almost as if they acknowledged that they should form some type of relationship with their students, to the satisfaction of what the syllabus claims, at least, but made little efforts to make themselves approachable. I assume that if you really wanted to speak to them about matters beyond the classroom you could, but the students are expected to take the initiative."

Q "There are many good professors, but you need to be smart and find out who they are. If you just pick any professor without researching first, you may well end up with some who are boring or disorganized. Also, some of the departments have many great professors while other departments aren't as good. On the whole, though, I'd say **the teachers are good**. I find that my classes are as interesting as the professor makes them, but I also have to be prepared to be engaged and interested."

Receiving help and support from your professors 24/7 at Bowdoin is the norm. They want to see you succeed and will do their best to offer what constructive criticism they can. Professors grace the student union (Smith Union), the dining halls, the gyms, the guest lectures, and so on, to gain better access to their students. The faculty invites their students to dinner or ice cream at their homes. They hire their students to baby-sit their kids. Not only that, they also share their glory; some professors have been known to sign their students on as co-authors in their professional journal writings.

Bowdoin professors are invited to speak at many bigger universities about their research. The small student-to-faculty ratio of 10 to one allows them to cap enrollment at 50 students per class (less than five percent of classes enroll more than 40 students). Although they are leaders in their fields, the professors in the math and science departments can be a bit antisocial and difficult to work with. On occasion, you might find a language barrier with a professor. Expect a heavy workload. Many say you will receive a graduate level education as an undergraduate. Despite the hard work, recent grads that go on to graduate school say that, except for medical school, their studies seem easier than what they experienced at Bowdoin. Many alumni feel that the Bowdoin faculty inspired them to feel empowered to do anything they put their minds to.

The College Prowler™ Grade on
Academics: A

A high Academics grade generally indicates that professors are knowledgeable, accessible, and genuinely interested in their students' welfare. Other determining factors include class size, how well professors communicate, and whether or not classes are engaging.

Local Atmosphere

Students Speak Out
ON LOCAL ATMOSPHERE

"Brunswick is a very small town, which seems separate from the college. I've found that one can live on campus and still not have contact with Maine culture, if that is what you want from your time at Bowdoin."

The Lowdown
ON LOCAL ATMOSPHERE

Region:
Cumberland County, Maine

City, State:
Brunswick, Maine

Setting:
Suburban

Distance from Portland:
35 minutes

Distance from Boston:
2 hours

Distance from New York City:
6 hours

Distance from Montreal:
6 hours

Points of Interest:
State and national parks (Popham's Beach, Bailey Island Bridge, Eagle Island), museums (art, maritime history, arctic exploration, and civil war hero Joshua Chamberlain), coastline, mountains, restaurants, ski areas, outdoor activities, cultural festivals, and arts community

Major Sports Teams:
Pirates (hockey) and Sea Dogs (baseball)

City Websites:
www.maineguide.com/brunswick, www.brunswickme.org, www.cityofbath.com, www.freeportmaine.com, and www.ci.portland.me.us

Q "Brunswick is a very college-friendly town. It's easy to walk to the center of town. There are a lot of great restaurants and cafés, an independent movie theater, a grocery store, a drug store, and CD/DVD stores. It's a very convenient location. Also, Cook's Corner is a five-minute drive and has **all the conveniences**, like Walmart, Staples, Starbucks, chain restaurants, and a movie theatre. Freeport is just 10 minutes away and is home to the LL Bean headquarters. Freeport is also home to around 100 different outlets. Portland, Maine's major city, is just 30 minutes away."

Q "Brunswick is a small town. **There are many small shops and restaurants**, a nearby ocean, and a couple of other small colleges within an hour away. The University of Maine at Orono is two hours away, and Cook's Corner has everything a student might need in regards to shopping, restaurants, and a movie theater."

Q "I find the atmosphere in Brunswick, at least in the central part of town, friendly. I come from a very big and crowded city, so I feel a little strange when there is almost no one except me on the streets in the middle of the day, but I guess this is more of a cultural difference between Europe and the U.S. I still have not gotten around enough to know something specific in Maine to visit or stay away from. However, I definitely recommend **taking trips to the woods, beaches, and lakes**."

Q "Maybe it's because I'm a minority student, or that I adorn the usual Bowdoin apparel on a daily basis, but it is obvious that I am not a local. Anyhow, **people in town are friendly** and generally interested in the fact that you're from the college. Other universities are not present. I personally think the giant staircase out by Bailey Island is a must go for the students. It's a date spot, and it's awesome."

Q "The town is **quiet, peaceful, and safe**. Because other schools are too far away and Bowdoin is a bubble in itself, the presence of universities around the area is almost unknown. Be sure to visit the beaches and hike in the mountains. If you are not an outdoorsy person in some way, don't go to Maine, period."

The College Prowler Take
ON LOCAL ATMOSPHERE

The quaint little town of Brunswick offers a New England feel, with antique stores, boutiques, and restaurants dotting Maine Street. Brunswick's tranquil location creates a warm setting with tree-lined streets, open parks, bed and breakfasts, nice shopping stores, eateries, and much more. Like much of New England, Brunswick boasts an amazing fall season, that features breathtaking changes of colors, cool temperatures, beautiful sunsets and sunrises, and an amazing sense of serenity. Bowdoin's campus is nestled into the town of Brunswick, close to the middle school, high school, hospitals, downtown areas, shopping, and the ocean. Students at Bowdoin find comfort in their tranquil surroundings. They enjoy the calm ocean air that breezes over campus, the chirps of the local fauna, and the aroma of the indigenous flora. Students comment that the town, at times, doesn't offer enough variety for their busy lifestyles, but Brunswick's close proximity to Freeport, Augusta, Lewiston, Bath, and Portland makes Bowdoin a choice school for any prospective or current student.

The College Prowler™ Grade on

Local Atmosphere: C+

A high Local Atmosphere grade indicates that the area surrounding campus is safe and scenic. Other factors include nearby attractions, proximity to other schools, and the town's attitude toward students.

Safety & Security

The Lowdown
ON SAFETY & SECURITY

Number of Bowdoin Police:
15

Phone:
(207) 725-3314 (non-emergency)
(207) 725-3500 (emergency)

Health Center Office Hours:
Monday through Friday, 8:30 a.m. to 5:00 p.m., except for Wednesday when the Health Center is open from 9:30 a.m. to 5:00 p.m.

Safety Services:
Brunswick Taxi Service (on weekends); escort service; shuttle buses; whistle program; self-defense classes; 24-hour foot, vehicle and bicycle campus patrol; emergency call-boxes; lighted pathways/walks; emergency alert program; informal discussions; pamphlets, posters, films; residences are locked 24 hours a day; and a staffed communications center is available around the clock.

Did You Know?

The Bowdoin campus remains the only school in the area without any major crimes (Bates had a stabbing a few years ago and Colby had a murder).

The crime index (the lower the index, the safer the town/city) according to www.city-data.com for Brunswick is 125.3. The national average is 330.6. Lewiston's crime index is 295.5, Waterville's crime index is 220.0, Middlebury's crime index is 297.2, and Boston has a crime index of 562.7. (The cities/towns mentioned are home to schools that many prospective students tend to consider.)

Students Speak Out
ON SAFETY & SECURITY

"Personally, I feel very safe on and around, campus. Campus security can often be seen making their rounds."

"Campus security is always out and about; they're **very responsive**. I feel very safe. However, the main campus is poorly-lit at night."

"Fortunately, I haven't had any run-ins with security, but, from what I've heard, they could do a **much better job of arriving on time** and giving people rides."

"It seems fairly safe in Brunswick. **There are emergency phones all over the place**, and the grounds are well-lit. Any person who bothers students, or seems out of place is immediately reported via e-mail to all members of the campus community."

"Although Brunswick is not a very threatening place, I feel like when an incident occurs, **security keeps the campus informed** and takes the appropriate action to follow up and investigate the situation."

"Security is wonderful—**they really care about the safety of the students**. They manage to be extremely vigilant without being omnipresent and are generally very friendly and polite. There are many blue-light emergency phones across the campus. The Safe Ride service is another great program."

The College Prowler Take
ON SAFETY & SECURITY

Because both the Bowdoin campus and the student body are relatively small, everybody knows everybody else. When anyone who shouldn't be on campus is there, it becomes obvious to students and security alike. It is a bit sad, but townies are easily identifiable because they do not blend in with our private college. Campus security can seem a bit obsessive with parking, but they definitely keep the Bowdoin campus safe. They keep faculty, students, and administration alert to any suspicious behavior. The blue-light stations and yellow call-boxes all over campus offer a sense of security and assurance that nothing bad will happen to the students here. If students voice concern, the directors of security are more than willing to listen and do what they can to make appropriate changes.

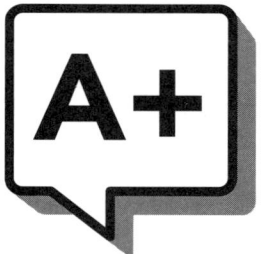

The College Prowler™ Grade on
Safety & Security: A+

A high grade in Safety & Security means that students generally feel safe, campus police are visible, blue-light phones and escort services are readily available, and safety precautions are not overly necessary.

Computers

Students Speak Out
ON COMPUTERS

"It's helpful to bring your own computer to campus. The labs tend to fill up around finals time. On a normal day, it is pretty easy to get a computer to use in the lab."

The Lowdown
ON COMPUTERS

High-Speed Network?
Yes

Wireless Network?
Yes

Number of Labs:
25 computer centers/labs

Numbers of Computers:
302

24-Hour Labs:
Hatch Science Library Lab, Kanbar Hall, and Coles Tower

Charge to Print?
None

Operating Systems:
PC, Mac, and Unix

Free Software:
Adobe Reader, Aladdin Stuffit Expander, Better Telnet, Cisco Telnet, Fetch, Internet Explorer, Meeting Maker, Microsoft Access, Microsoft Excel, Microsoft Powerpoint, Microsoft Publisher, Microsoft Visio, Microsoft Windows, Microsoft Word, Netscape Messenger, Sophos, WinZip, and WS_FTP LE

Q "You **definitely need your own computer**. During the day and early night, most computers in the labs and libraries are taken. However, late at night, the labs are a good place to crank out a paper, they are less noisy than dorms at that hour."

Q "Computer labs are only overly crowded during exam periods. Having one's own computer is always more convenient, even though computer labs may be open 24/7. I had a semester without the Internet last year, and it was very inconvenient when it came to receiving assignments in the middle of the night via e-mails, or having to go to the lab to research something on the Internet while it's snowing outside. On the other hand, **many students who have computers still go to labs** to write papers and avoid distractions."

Q "Coming from suburban America, I'm familiar with what most colleges are like. Bowdoin is not completely wireless, like some Ivies or engineering schools, but for a school with Bowdoin's focus, it does pretty well by **offering wireless in the [Smith] Union, libraries, and on the lawns**. A lot of schools of Bowdoin's size don't offer anything high-tech at all, and the computer labs look old and outdated. Bowdoin's labs are state-of-the-art, with Apple and PC monitors to suit all tastes."

Q "Everyone owns their own computer, and you should, too! Once November rolls around, there is no way you will want to walk to the library to use a public computer. **Computer labs get crowded around crunch times**, like midterms, reading period, and finals, but can often be totally deserted on nights and weekends. The network generally performs great, although the firewall can present problems depending on your software, and the network often has inexplicable down time."

Q "Our wireless network could be better. **Computer labs are adequate**. But keep in mind that winters are brutally cold, and if you want to save yourself from the frigid walk, a computer in the comfort of your dorm would be preferable."

The College Prowler Take
ON COMPUTERS

Bowdoin does its best to provide the latest technology to the student body. With high-speed Internet connection in dorm rooms, library study spaces, classrooms, the student union, and just about everywhere else on campus, there will never be a place you can't check your e-mail. There is a rumor that students at Bowdoin check their e-mail every six minutes; this would make sense with the busy lifestyle of the average Polar Bear. Although IT and CIS collectively manage several big computer labs, most students recommend bringing either a laptop or desktop computer to campus to offer convenience and avoid trekking through campus in two feet of snow. However, most students agree that having a computer at Bowdoin isn't a necessity. Many students get along fine without one, though.

The College Prowler™ Grade on
Computers: B+

A high grade in Computers designates that computer labs are available, the computer network is easily accessible, and the campus' computing technology is up-to-date.

Facilities

The Lowdown
ON FACILITIES

Movie Theatre on Campus?
Yes

Bowling on Campus?
No

Bar on Campus?
Yes, Jack Magee's Pub

Coffeehouse on Campus?
Yes, the Café

Student Center:
Smith Union (the Union, SU)

Athletic Center:
Sargent and Morrell Gymnasiums, Watson Fitness Center, Farley Field House, Lubin Family Squash Center, Greason Swimming Pool, and Dayton Ice Arena

Libraries:
11 (Hawthorne-Longfellow Library, Beckwith Music Library, Hatch Science Library, Pierce Art Library, Special Collections & Archives, Government Documents, Language Media Center, African American Center Library, Women's Resource Center Library, Career Planning Center Library, Susan Dwight Bliss Room)

Popular Places to Chill:
Smith Union, The Pub, Hatch, and The Tower

Students Speak Out
ON FACILITIES

"I think Bowdoin's facilities are well-equipped for a college of its size."

Q "The **facilities could be better**, but they could also be worse. Enough said."

Q "The architecture here is beautiful. From Hubbard Hall and the Art Museum to the newly constructed [Farley] Field House—**each building carries a distinct ambience**. They are welcoming, soothing, and pleasant inside and out. There are many updated computer labs and a number of places for students to mingle or study quietly."

Q "Computer centers, library, and student centers are all state-of-the-art, well-kept, and clean. Most athletic facilities can't rival other league schools in terms of size and beauty. **Bowdoin has many overcrowded locker rooms**. This is because there's only one indoor facility for spring teams to train in the pre-season, while the winter teams are going through their regular seasons."

Q "I love our facilities! The athletic facilities are great. **The dining halls are clean and pretty**. The big dining hall is beautiful and spacious, and the small dining hall is a cozy place that begins to feel like your very own dining room after awhile. The student center is very cool with multiple levels, a café, a pub, space for dancing or concerts and, on the balcony, there are little tables for studying."

Q "We have the **prettiest student union in the country**, as far as I'm concerned. The libraries have great resources, and most of them have wireless access. The athletic facilities do not always schedule hours well for non-athletes, but are, overall, pretty good. The workout rooms in the Union are really good to have when it's cold out and you don't want to travel to the field house."

The College Prowler Take
ON FACILITIES

On its 200-acre campus, Bowdoin pampers its student body with six athletic centers, two dining halls, a convenience store, a pub and grill, computer labs, music library, science library, general purpose library, special collections department, government document collection, and much more. Students agree that the facilities available to them are more than adequate for a school of Bowdoin's size. The Olympic-sized pool, hockey rink, squash courts, two basketball courts, climbing wall, indoor track, indoor and outdoor tennis courts, a separate Outing Club building, a dance studio, and an aerobics room are all available for use by the Bowdoin community year round. With more than 116 buildings on campus offering over 1.8 million square feet of floor space, Bowdoin students won't grow claustrophobic by any means. You'll see a little of everything at Bowdoin.

The College Prowler™ Grade on
Facilities: B

A high Facilities grade indicates that the campus is aesthetically pleasing and well-maintained; facilities are state-of-the-art, and libraries are exceptional. Other determining factors include the quality of both athletic and student centers and an abundance of things to do on campus.

Campus Dining

Students Speak Out
ON CAMPUS DINING

"After 20 weeks, the food becomes 'eh,' but compared to what my friends at bigger universities are served, it's still top-notch!"

*"The food at Bowdoin is excellent. **There are two dining halls with different menus for each meal**. There are lots of great vegetarian and vegan options. They also serve great theme and holiday dinners—it's very good!"*

*"**Our food is number one in the nation**: what more can I say? The variety at Moulton Union and Thorne Hall is incredible. They meet the needs of a variety of eaters, from vegetarian to vegan to carnivores. The dining halls are spacious and comforting. They offer a good break from the continuous stress of the day."*

*"During winter recess, I went home and my mom made me a great dinner. I told her that it was **almost as good as the food I ate at Bowdoin**. The food they serve is just that good—my mom is a great cook."*

*"Parents count the days until **Parents' Weekend because they cannot wait to enjoy the Bowdoin cuisine**—it's that good. They feel like they are entering a four-star restaurant. Parents have been known to say, 'Where was that kind of food when we were in college?'"*

*"Most of the time, the food here is great. They have the greatest salad dressing options I know. They are so tasty; sometimes dining services can make bad choices, but they deserved to be number one for best college food. **The selection is huge**."*

The Lowdown
ON CAMPUS DINING

Freshman Meal Plan Requirement?
Yes

24-Hour On-Campus Eating?
No

Meal Plan Average Cost:
$4,431

Student Favorites:
Thorne and Jack Magee's Pub

Did You Know?

Bowdoin was ranked number two in the nation for best dining hall food. Among Ivy League or NESCAC schools, Bowdoin offers one of the best meal plan options for the money.

The lighting in Thorne dining hall was the gift of a successful alumni who requested his donation be used for the "artistic betterment" of the campus. The lights flash rhythmically, and with varied colors.

The College Prowler Take
ON CAMPUS DINING

Feel free to dig in! Yes, believe the hype. Bowdoin dining is quite spectacular. All first-years purchase the 19-meal plan, which basically translates into a lot of good food, a lot of the time. This makes students' transitions easier, and gaining the "Freshman 15" much, much easier. Many students across campus joke that they spend more time in the dining halls then they do in classes. Meal time at Bowdoin also provides a great time for students to socialize and relax after a hectic day of classes. Dining services are aware that students use this time to cool down, and they do their best to offer a variety of options to suit every student's desires.

Off-Campus Dining

The Lowdown
ON OFF-CAMPUS DINING

The College Prowler™ Grade on
Campus Dining: A

Our grade on Campus Dining addresses the quality of both school-owned dining halls and independent on-campus restaurants as well as the price, availability, and variety of food.

Best Pizza:
Benzoni's and Griff's Pizza

Best Chinese:
Bangkok Garden

Best Breakfast:
Wild Oats Bakery

Best Wings:
Domino's

Best Healthy:
Little Lads (vegan)

Best Place to Take Your Parents:
Cook's Lobster House

Late-Night Eating:
Most of the places around Bowdoin will close around 9 p.m., but the pizza stores will usually be open to deliver until 1 a.m. on weekdays and 2 a.m. on weekends. At Cook's Corner, there is a McDonald's, Wendy's, and a Burger King that is usually open late. Hannaford's, less than a mile from campus, is open until 3 a.m. Other than that, there aren't many options if you have the late-night munchies.

24-Hour Eating:
No

Student Favorites:
Scarlet Begonias, Benzoni's, Fat Boy's (seasonal), Shere Punjab, and Thai Dish

Did You Know?

During the spring and summer, a lot of vendors set up on Maine Street with a variety of tasty food to try.

The edible inhabitants of the ocean are only four miles from campus and often make it to your plate in the dining hall.

Cody's is a popular ice cream shop that hoards of Bowdoin students visit in May, when it opens up for the summer season. Students wait all year to get such flavors like Java Bean, Crunch, or The Mainer.

Students Speak Out
ON OFF-CAMPUS DINING

"Every type of fast food chain is within a mile, as well as Applebee's, Friendly's, a couple sports bars, and numerous other fancy eateries."

"There are some fine restaurants off-campus. **My favorites are Bombay Mahal** for Indian, Wild Oats Bakery & Café, Big Top Deli, Bohemian Coffee House, and Scarlet Begonia's for Italian."

"Surprisingly, the **Thai restaurants here are good**. It's worth a try and, who knows, maybe you'll be taking your date there every time you get the chance to eat off campus."

"I am amazed by the number of restaurants in downtown Brunswick. For such a small town, there is **a very good selection**."

"For being a small and overwhelmingly white town, Brunswick has a good array of choices when it comes to restaurants. We've got at least two Indian and three Thai places, along with **a few Chinese restaurants**, several American-style places, a sub-par Mexican place, and surely one of the only Irish-Mexican restaurants in the world. Good spots are Scarlet Begonias—tiny, but famous for its pizza and pasta—Shere Punjab, and Bangkok Garden."

"Off-campus **restaurants are good to excellent**. However, with the great on-campus food, I don't venture out that often."

The College Prowler Take
ON OFF-CAMPUS DINING

The overall consensus of the student body is that off-campus dining is good, but could be better. Most of the really good establishments around do not stay open late, so night owls who eat after 9 p.m. are often left hungry. With such amazing on-campus dining options, many students only wander off campus once in a while when they need a change in their daily routine. On the whole, you won't be seeing the majority of the student body eating off campus in an attempt to avoid bad food—that just isn't the case at Bowdoin. Overall, though, the wide selection of eateries in Brunswick, not to mention Bowdoin's close proximity to restaurants in neighboring towns and cities, offer more than enough variety for a number of tastes.

The College Prowler™ Grade on
Off-Campus Dining: B

A high Off-Campus Dining grade implies that off-campus restaurants are affordable, accessible, and worth visiting. Other factors include the variety of cuisine and the availability of alternative options (vegetarian, vegan, Kosher, etc.).

Campus Housing

Students Speak Out
ON CAMPUS HOUSING

"Hyde has a bad reputation, but it's undeserved. Just because someone is chemical-free—alcohol-free, mostly—doesn't mean that they can't have a social life."

Q "Housing at Bowdoin is great. Pretty much everything but Chamberlain doubles are sought after. On the plus side; the **Chamberlain doubles are brand new**, so they are nice, even if they are insanely small."

Q "The new dorms are technologically advanced, awesome, and clean. The renovated dorms are nice and spacious. The old dorms that are left un-renovated for decades may seem unlivable, but man, **there's just class and history all around you**—it's amazing."

Q "I liked Hyde. Even though it's wooden and very old, it has its own charm. I also like Howell, but that is because most of my friends and boyfriend live there. That's one perk of living in a social house [old frat]; **a huge group of friends can try to live together**."

Q "**Dorms vary in quality from mediocre to excellent**. I'm not a fan of Brunswick because of the noise. Howell is a very pretty house—it is chemical and substance-free—and Stowe Inn is also nice."

Q "Most dorms aren't exactly grand, but they do have their own flair. **Many upperclassmen dorms almost guarantee a single or double-room arrangement**, like Howard, Chamberlain, and The Tower. It's fair to warn you that The Tower vaguely resembles a parking garage made for people."

The Lowdown
ON CAMPUS HOUSING

Undergrads on Campus:
91.6%

Number of Dormitories:
28

Number of University-Owned Apartments:
5

Available for Rent:
No

Cleaning Service?
Yes, in public areas only

Bed Type:
Twin extra-long (all beds)

Room Types:
Singles, doubles, triples, quads

You Get:
Bed, desk, chair, dresser, high-speed Internet, cable television, telephone, couches (in suites), mirror, etc.

Also Available:
Chemical/Substance-Free Housing (Hyde, Howell, Howard, Burnett, and Boody)

Did You Know?

Coles Tower, when first built, stood as the tallest building in Maine. Now it's ranked third.

The College Prowler Take
ON CAMPUS HOUSING

Bowdoin is one of the few schools in the country that guarantees spacious housing to all of its students for all four years. First-years at Bowdoin get to live in rooms better than many upperclassmen get at competing schools. There are six dorms, more commonly referred to as "The Bricks." Residential Life is always doing its best to look out for new property to buy and renovate into housing; they kind of have to in order to keep up with the aforementioned, four-year-housing guarantee. In the event that nothing satisfies your needs, you can always petition the Residential Life office to let you live off campus. But, usually the only people to venture off campus will be seniors looking for a break from campus life and a little independence. Students at Bowdoin love the options, and, with the lottery system, Residence Life keeps things as fair as they can by giving seniors first priority.

Off-Campus Housing

The Lowdown
ON OFF-CAMPUS HOUSING

Undergrads in Off-Campus Housing: 8.4%

Best Time to Look for a Place: Winter or spring for the following fall

Average Rent for a Studio Apartment: $750 per semester

Average Rent for a One-Bedroom Apartment: $1,000-$1,300 per semester

Average Rent for a Two-Bedroom Apartment: $1,600-$2,300 per semester

Popular Areas: Harpswell (ocean-front houses for rent)

For Assistance Contact:
The Residential Life Office
www.bowdoin.edu/reslife/
Phone: (207) 725-3255
E-mail: kpacelli@bowdoin.edu

The College Prowler™ Grade on
Campus Housing: A

A high Campus Housing grade indicates that dorms are clean, well-maintained, and spacious. Other determining factors include variety of dorms, proximity to classes, and social atmosphere.

Students Speak Out
ON OFF-CAMPUS HOUSING

{ "A respectable amount of students live off campus. I'm not sure how it works with financial aid, though." }

- Q "**Ninety percent of us stay on campus** for all four years, but if someone wants to move off campus, there are great coastal homes."

- Q "Housing **off campus is only a dream for most sophomores**. Sophomores at Bowdoin get screwed worse than any other students in terms of housing."

- Q "Senior year, **I lived, like, one minute off campus**. We rented some space in the house of an older woman. It was nice and comfortable. If you want to live off campus, then possibilities are there."

The College Prowler Take
ON OFF-CAMPUS HOUSING

Diversity

The Lowdown
ON DIVERSITY

Although most students decide to stay on campus their senior year (the housing lottery favors them and the possibilities are amazing), the students that decide to live off campus can find excellent oceanfront homes to rent for close to what they would pay to live on campus. The only downside to this is that you have to travel from your off-campus housing to campus, and take care of your own meals. Unlike many schools, at Bowdoin you need to live on campus for three years, unless you travel abroad for part of your junior year. You can petition to live off campus with a group of your friends before your senior year, but, to be honest, permission from Residence Life is rarely granted. Students who decide to live off campus tend to enjoy themselves, mostly due to an increased sense of independence and an escape from everyday Bowdoin life.

African American: 5%

Asian American: 10%

Hispanic: 5%

Native American: 1%

White: 76%

International: 3%

Out-of-State: 87%

Minority Clubs
African American Society, Anokha, Asian Student Association, Caribbean Student Alliance, Circolo Italiano, Hawaii Ohana, International Club, Korean-American Students Association, Latin American Student Association, Russian Club

Most Popular Religions
Protestant/Christian, Roman Catholic, Episcopal, Jewish, Buddhist, Islamic, Hindu

The College Prowler™ Grade on
Off-Campus Housing: C

A high grade in Off-Campus Housing indicates that apartments are of high quality, close to campus, affordable, and easy to secure.

Political Activity

About five to 10 percent of the student body participates directly in student government each year (Student Executive Board and Student Congress). Student political groups include Amnesty International, Bowdoin College Democrats, Evergreens, The Bowdoin Forum, Global Help, the Bowdoin Patriot, Bowdoin College Republicans, Bowdoin Students for Democratic Socialism. Nearly half of the student body considers themselves to be "liberal."

Gay Tolerance

Gay & Lesbian Studies Program, Bowdoin Gay/Straight Alliance, a Queer Resource Center.

Economic Status

No clubs exist on campus that favor the affluent or the subsistent. However, the social houses tend to get a reputation for attracting a similar crowd that would be interested in fraternity life and tend to have a higher socioeconomic population.

Students Speak Out
ON DIVERSITY

Q "The students on the cover of our brochures look pretty similar to our actual students, but admissions actually attracts a pretty diverse student body."

Q "I've learned that **the campus is more diverse now than it has ever been**."

Q "Bowdoin is much more diverse than it was in 1794, but it's still **just a bunch of middle-class, white kids**."

Q "It seems like many of the **minorities stick together** so you notice them, but considering their visibility, the campus doesn't seem like it is only 70 percent white."

Q "Well, it is **not very diverse** here. People who identify themselves as some sort of minority frequently hold endless, and completely futile, diversity meetings."

Q "I have found it to be fairly diverse and have enjoyed getting to know people of many different backgrounds. Some are international students; many are Americans whose heritage is that of another culture, as well as that of the U.S.. There are city kids, kids from public schools and private schools, and students with different religious and social views. I've **enjoyed learning from friends with backgrounds different from mine**."

The College Prowler Take
ON DIVERSITY

Diversity at Bowdoin is often misconstrued simply as the need to be racially varied. It seems, at times, that admissions works too hard to shift away from a predominately white school. Bowdoin is a private school in New England, comprised of a student body of over 1,600 students. Fifty percent of these students are not geographically located in the Northeast. Fifty percent of Bowdoin students are from public schools, and 30 percent of Bowdoin students are minorities. Thirty percent says a lot about the trend that Bowdoin is following. The idea that a school that once fed off private prep schools has such a high percentage of minority students is startling to some. But how does one actually define diversity? Beyond the preppy façade, the students at this school all offer something special. They each have their own story of how they became who they are and what aspirations they have for the future.

The College Prowler™ Grade on
Diversity: C

A high grade in Diversity indicates that ethnic minorities and international students have a notable presence on campus and that students of different economic backgrounds, religious beliefs, and sexual preferences are well-represented.

Guys & Girls

The Lowdown
ON GUYS & GIRLS

Women Undergrads:
49.5%

Men Undergrads:
50.5%

Birth Control Available?
Yes. You can get most anything at the Dudley Coe Health Center, and condoms are available in on-campus housing.

Social Scene
The social scene at Bowdoin is dictated by the athletes and a select few other organizations. The rest of campus tends to attend parties that these organizations throw. With 60 percent of the student body being involved in sports on campus and 75 percent once being involved in a varsity sport in high school, the parties on campus resemble frat parties even though the Greek system no longer exists at Bowdoin. The pressure and mischievous behavior that once may have existed during the golden age of fraternities no longer exists now. Students are very accepting of each other's decision as to whether to participate or abstain from drinking.

Hookups or Relationships?
In past years, the scene on campus seemed to be one of random hookups after parties, but in the last year, there seems to be a developing trend of relationships forming all around campus. The statistic that 60 percent of the student body will marry another Bowdoin student penetrates into people's conversations, but no one knows if this statistic is accurate or not.

Dress Code
Students at Bowdoin stick to a variety of preppy looks (yes, there are such things). Some examples are hardcore preppy, prep jock, prep earthy, prep public school, prep-without-a-clue, and prep wannabe. Flipped up collars, pink polos, yellow and pink pants, plaid shorts, and penny loafers can commonly be seen by those pulling off the hardcore Republican preppy look. The older you become at Bowdoin, the preppier your class will seem. Distinct forms of dress that existed your first-year will start to blend together as people become more "prepped out." When you step onto campus you will think you stepped into an American Eagle and Abercrombie catalog, minus the naked people running around (except during initiation). A lot of the student body will wear Adidas, Nike, Bauer, Easton, Puma, Helly Hanson, and other athletic labels.

Students Speak Out
ON GUYS & GIRLS

> "Girls are pretty much generic here. Guys offer very little variety. However, on the upside, overall, they are of an above-average, quality breed for guys."

Q "Being a guy, I'll speak about the girls. I feel we are **not known for having hot girls**. However, many girls that come here in their freshmen year are girls who were not used to much attention at their high schools, but now find themselves among the 'relatively' good-looking people on campus. They all get carried away with this new attention."

Athletics

The Lowdown
ON ATHLETICS

Q "If girls draped in Abercrombie, Gap, American Eagle, Ralph Lauren, and other name brands are your type, then this is your school. With close to **50 percent of the student body coming from private schools**, the campus is definitely not eclectic."

Q "With so many athletes, the guys work out to stay competitive, and with such activity, good bodies come along with it. **Guys here, on the whole, are better looking than the girls**."

Q "I don't like how some **guys dress so uber-preppy with pink pants and popped up collars**. I'm from California, and I guess I don't understand the preppy phenomenon. Overall, though, the guys are excellent to look at. What I don't like is how everyone is so body conscious. It seems like everybody works out."

Q "It's **a very 'jocky' school**. Once spring comes and people start to shed the heavy clothing, there are a good number of hot people, but it's no Southern state school."

Men's Teams:	Women's Teams:
Baseball	Basketball
Basketball	Cross Country
Cross Country	Field Hockey
Football	Golf
Golf	Ice Hockey
Ice Hockey	Lacrosse
Lacrosse	Rugby
Sailing	Skiing
Skiing	Soccer
Soccer	Softball
Squash	Squash
Swimming	Swimming
Tennis	Tennis
Indoor Track	Indoor Track
Outdoor Track	Outdoor Track
	Volleyball

The College Prowler Take
ON GUYS & GIRLS

Finding a blonde-haired, blue-eyed, hockey player with good grades, or a brunette with green eyes, who is a soccer team captain and a neuroscience major, will not be difficult at Bowdoin. Does this sound like the school you want to attend? The Bowdoin men might be some of the hottest any college in New England offers. If you think the South harbors the best looking students, take a moment and look at the Bowdoin students, before you rule the North out. You need to remember that Bowdoin is a very athletic school.

The College Prowler™ Grade on
Guys: A-

A high grade for Guys indicates that the male population on campus is attractive, smart, friendly, and engaging, and that the school has a decent ratio of guys to girls.

The College Prowler™ Grade on
Girls: C+

A high grade for Girls not only implies that the women on campus are attractive, smart, friendly, and engaging, but also that there is a fair ratio of girls to guys.

Most Popular Sports

The athletic program at Bowdoin can be considered quite popular. With 60 percent of the student body participating in either a varsity sport, club sport, or intramural sport, staying active remains a priority. Soccer, field hockey, lacrosse, basketball, and ice hockey draw big crowds.

Fields
Pickard Fields, Whittier Field, and Farley Fields

Getting Tickets
If you attend Bowdoin, you will not need to purchase tickets. By showing your student ID, you can get into any game that requires an entrance fee. The fee to the public is pretty reasonable. Except for games against major rivals like Middlebury and Colby, it should not be too hard to get tickets.

Athletic Division:
NCAA Division III

Conference:
New England Small College Athletic Conference (NESCAC)

School Mascot:
Polar Bear

Students Speak Out
ON ATHLETICS

"You can tell by how the student body carries themselves, what they wear, and how they talk, that sports are big on campus."

Q "Varsity sports are big here. For those not playing varsity, they can play either club or intramural sports. **IMs are popular because there are three different levels**: A, B, and C, ranging from beginner to expert."

Q "It is said that about **65 percent of the student body plays at least one varsity sport**. Many athletes exist on campus. Some sports receive much more attention than others. IM sports are very popular, with all sorts of kids engaging in all sorts of sports, from a bowling league to water polo."

Q "Varsity sports are not a huge deal like at some Division I schools, but at the peak of their seasons there is **considerable enthusiasm and attendance at hockey and basketball games**. IM sports seem to be popular."

Q "Varsity sports are big at Bowdoin. The illustrious **Varsity Row is kept behind closed doors most of the time**. That says a lot about how students view the head coaches here."

The College Prowler Take
ON ATHLETICS

Varsity sports play an integral part in students' lives at Bowdoin. More than 35 percent of the student body plays an intercollegiate sport. The school spirit for each team is amazing. Even the less-than-stellar football squad has their enthusiastic fans each game. Men's ice hockey and lacrosse bring in big crowds. What the Harvard-Yale game is to the Ivy League, the Middlebury-Bowdoin and Colby-Bowdoin games are to the NESCAC. Playing a varsity sport at Bowdoin is serious. The NESCAC is considered one of the premier collegiate Division III leagues in the country, with a coaching staff that makes the all-time best rankings with Division I coaches. Many athletes that come to Bowdoin probably could play at a Division I school if it were not for their size, or their desire for a balanced lifestyle.

The College Prowler™ Grade on
Athletics: B+

A high grade in Athletics indicates that students have school spirit, that sports programs are respected, that games are well-attended, and that intramurals are a prominent part of student life

Greek Life

The Lowdown
ON GREEK LIFE

Number of Social Houses:
6

Percent of Men in Social Houses:
12.2%

Percent of Women in Social Houses:
6.4%

Social Houses on Campus:
Baxter House, Helmreich House, Howell House, Ladd House, Macmillan House, and Quinby House

Did You Know?

Every fall, Ladd House hosts a campus-wide party called "The Luau." Bowdoin abolished on-campus Greek systems in 1997 and established a new college house system.

Bowdoin College just finished acquiring the last of the nine fraternity houses that existed in 2000 when the transition was complete.

It looks like a fund will be created to increase the house budgets by double. The fund will be around $2 million.

Students Speak Out
ON GREEK LIFE

"No Greek life exists anymore; there's the college house system, instead. They have a presence, but it's not at all unreasonable."

Q "Social house life is an **acquired taste**, and certainly not for me."

Q "There are **no fraternities or sororities** at Bowdoin, and I think the school is all the better for it."

Q "Instead of Greek Life, we've got the **house system**. It's kind of like having only six frats on campus, except there is no rush and everyone belongs to at least one of them"

The College Prowler Take
ON GREEK LIFE

The Greek system has not existed at Bowdoin in any form since 2000. The college house system replaced Greek row. It's a six-house system that is matched with first-year housing to assist the proctors in transitioning first-years to the social life on campus. The houses existed as fraternities before Bowdoin decided that the fraternity system hindered admissions from attracting the best student body possible. Less than 20 percent of the student body participates in this housing option. Unlike the Greek system, the Residential Life office controls the houses by playing a role in who lives in the house. However, they give each house a budget to plan its own programming for itself, its affiliated first-years, and the community.

The College Prowler™ Grade on
Greek Life: N/A

A high grade in Greek Life indicates that sororities and fraternities are not only present, but also active on campus. Other determining factors include the variety of houses available and the respect the Greek community receives from the rest of the campus.

Drug Scene

Q "I **don't know much about drugs here** except that it exists. Marijuana is somewhat common; as far as other drugs, I don't know."

Q "I've **never heard of any hard drugs** here. I've certainly never seen any."

The College Prowler Take
ON DRUG SCENE

The Lowdown
ON DRUG SCENE

Once upon a time, Bowdoin had a slight reputation for chemical research in drugs, but today our campus is more known for having its fair share of alcoholic beverages and marijuana. Although some hardcore drugs may be used on campus, it is definitely kept private and hidden from the main stream of campus life. The pressure to participate is relatively tame. Students at Bowdoin respect the wishes of other students, and will not put them in situations they are not comfortable with.

Most Prevalent Drugs on Campus:
Alcohol, marijuana

Drug Counseling Programs:
If such counseling is needed, the Health Center will refer you to the Counseling Services office, and they make the appropriate recommendations to rehabilitation centers.

Students Speak Out
ON DRUG SCENE

"**It's mostly weed at Bowdoin, but there is definitely some harder stuff going around underground.**"

Q "There's **a lot of pot**—I'm not aware of other heavy drug use."

Q "It's **healthy from what I can tell**. I haven't come across heroin, like at my high school, so that's pretty nice."

Q "It exists, but you can do what you want with it. The drug scene here is **not as big as it is at other schools**. It's not like they're selling crack in the library!"

The College Prowler™ Grade on
Drug Scene: B

A high grade on Drug Scene indicates that drugs are not a noticeable part of campus life; drug use is not visible, and no pressure to use them seems to exist.

Campus Strictness

💬 "They are all **about our safety**! They aren't ridiculous about making sure no one drinks. Security checks parties to make sure people are safe and being responsible, but not to make sure that only 21-year-olds drink. It's nice because we don't go overboard."

💬 "They are **lenient and understanding** in terms of drinking, at least. Drugs are a different story."

💬 "They aren't very strict at all. **They seem to look the other way as much as they can**, but if it's blatant that you are breaking the rules, they'll send you to one of the deans. They don't tolerate breaking the Honor Code."

The Lowdown
ON CAMPUS STRICTNESS

The College Prowler Take
ON CAMPUS STRICTNESS

What Are You Most Likely to Get Caught Doing on Campus?

Carrying an uncovered countainer filled with alcohol; parking your car in a lot other than where your decal designates it to be; violating the Honor Code; stealing the dorm name signs on the building; stealing food from the dining halls; if you're under 21, holding an alcoholic bevarage while on campus in a residential building; consuming hard alcohol (it is banned on campus)

The deans, campus security, and residential life officers give students a lot of room to be individuals. The school usually will not come down on you unless your drinking or drug use causes you to become violent or disturb those around you. The proctors and resident advisors make it clear, in most cases, that if they can't see blatant disregard of policy, they will not get you in trouble. People with open containers will be written up by campus police, but they are just trying to keep you out of trouble with the Brunswick Police Department. The administration and faculty want students to believe that they enforce the Honor Code, and they remind students of its importance in all things, whether it is doing homework, preparing for labs, taking exams, running for student government, etc.. The threat that the deans and faculty use to keep students honest is that if they violate any policy, they will go up in front of the Judicial Board.

Students Speak Out
ON CAMPUS STRICTNESS

"They aren't too strict, as far as I know. If you are in your room and not too loud, they won't bother you, but they might break up a noisy party."

💬 "If you don't give them rise for concern, you're fine. But if you do, watch out! **They'll raid with a vengeance**."

The College Prowler™ Grade on
Campus Strictness: B+

A high Campus Strictness grade implies an overall lenient atmosphere; police and RAs are fairly tolerant, and the administration's rules are flexible.

Overall Experience

Students Speak Out
ON OVERALL EXPERIENCE

"At Bowdoin, you'll find great academics, great friends, great food, and great accommodations. I have complaints, but overall, it has been a good experience."

Q "Going to school here is a mixed bag. I've met very nice kids, but the **typical day and lifestyle is so repetitive**. I have my days when I question my stay at Bowdoin, but then others, I couldn't be more psyched."

Q "I wouldn't go anywhere else. I love Bowdoin, and in some ways—totally unconnected with homework and examinations—**I look forward to going back after every vacation** and starting every new year."

Q "With so much opportunity and so many great people, I always feel like I could have done more, but, considering my maturity, I feel **I gained a lot from my education** at Bowdoin. Even though I may not have loved the school while experiencing it, I love it now and would recommend it to anyone. You become more of a unique person by attending this small institution."

Q "Overall, I have had a wonderful experience. I've met lots of interesting and awesome people here. Advising from the faculty could be better, but then again, I should be more willing to take the initiative, too. **I don't want to be anywhere else besides inside this Bowdoin bubble**—where the food is always good, Colby is forever despised, and everything is generally in good condition."

Q "It's been a good ride. Because of the field I want to go into, **I'm very glad that the professors are willing to help me** with independent studies since there aren't many classes that target my chosen career path."

The College Prowler Take
ON OVERALL EXPERIENCE

Like any teenager or early 20-something, it's easy for Bowdoin students to spout out complaints, but, when it comes down to it, most students here are glad that they made the decision to attend college in Brunswick, Maine. Students realize that attending college is not just about attending classes, participating in sports, and partying on weekends; it is about doing everything with passion and determination and the ability to give back. A startling number of students spend some time teaching before going on to graduate school or accepting employment at a company, because they want to share the type of education they received.

Bowdoin is the first choice for many students; they are drawn to the school's small size and the intimacy that exists between the administrators, faculty, coaches, alumni, and students. They also love the available resources, the convenient suburban location, and accessibility to bigger metropolitan areas, and the school's overall reputation. Like at any college, students go through hardships here, and some might question whether they made the right choice, but, in the end, they usually decide that they did. The high retention rate and positive reviews of the school are a testament to that. School pride among students and alumni is intense. Being a Polar Bear is about more than hating the Panther or the Mule, it is about honoring one's faculty, one's coaches, one's past, one's future, and the experience one shared with one's peers. Alumni defend their school's history and reputation because they believe their overall experience was unlike any other. The rigorous demands, the Maine weather, the busy schedules, and the challenge to do well all become part of an education at Bowdoin that you will never forget.

The Inside Scoop

The Lowdown
ON THE INSIDE SCOOP

School Spirit

Students who attend Bowdoin believe in their school, its mission, the faculty, their president, their architecture, their town, their mascot, and their reputation. Most of the students who attend this college wanted to be here and did not come because it was their safety school. Students are proud of the work they do, the majors they choose, the sports they play, the social houses they live in, the involvement they put on their resumes, and the stories they share with interviewers at graduate schools and companies. Whether you are a biology, chemistry, psychology, neuroscience, visual arts, history, sociology, or government major, you are proud of the work and time you spent on all your classes, and proud to say you earned your degree at Bowdoin College. It's not uncommon to see students wearing Bowdoin hats, T-shirts, sweatshirts, sandals, gym pants, rings, etc. The students want people to know they attend this fine school in Brunswick.

Spirit at Bowdoin for athletic teams is strong when it comes to games against rivals. Students turn out for games against Middlebury, Colby, Bates, and other league rivals. When sports teams are just playing regulation games against non-league teams, students appear apathetic and disinterested. Students are very proud of how the varsity teams perform and rank in national polls, but teams like tennis attract a very small fan base. Bowdoin Student Government plans barbecues at games and bus service to away games against rivals.

Traditions

Chapel Bells
After two years of renovation, Bowdoin started the chimes again on September 20, 2004 at 8 a.m.—it chimes every 15 minutes.

Polar Bear
Bowdoin's pride and joy is the mascot, the Polar Bear. The Polar Bear makes its appearance at athletic events to rally school support.

Ivies
During the last week of April, the tradition is to start drinking on Wednesday in classes, and keep going through the weekend, to celebrate the school's decision to reject an invitation from the Ivies to join them.

Lobster Run
Every fall before classes, the students meet at the Farley Fields to enjoy a lobster feast, with all the trimmings. To end the festivities, students participate in a 5K run around the athletic fields to celebrate the start of classes; at the finish line are several students dressed as lobsters to congratulate you on your participation.

Want to know more about crazy traditions and urban legends on campus? Check out the College Prowler book on Bowdoin available at *www.collegeprowler.com*.

Things I Wish I Knew Before Coming to Bowdoin:

- How to decorate a dorm room
- How to live with other people
- How to dress for the different temperatures
- How to manage time wisely
- How to choose classes and professors wisely
- How to not overextend myself
- How to stay healthy without mom and dad watching over
- How to do laundry
- How to live without a car
- How to ask for help when in trouble
- That everyone here is a fan of the Boston Red Sox and New England Patriots
- How smart and capable everyone else is
- How to work out regularly
- A Pre-Orientation trip is a MUST!
- Campus is not as dry as the administration would like

Finding a Job or Internship

The Lowdown
ON FINDING A JOB OR INTERNSHIP

Life after college can be a scary concept to ponder, but the Career Planning Center at Bowdoin College does its best to make the transition easier for graduating seniors. With consortiums set up with numerous other respectable schools, and an online database better than many big universities, Bowdoin makes hundreds, if not thousands, of different job listings accessible to students. The staff at the Career Planning Center on campus cares about your worries, needs, and future, and will spend as much time as needed to set up a desirable plan for your future.

For those not graduating, Bowdoin CPC organizes and lists thousands of internships and jobs that both Bowdoin and other schools have found. With a solid reputation with other schools, top law firms, and prestigious companies, if you want a job, internship, or research opportunity, it's there for you to take. The staff offers a wide range of workshops and clinics to help students get off on the right foot so that no opportunity will be squandered.

Student experiences with finding a job or internship while in college vary, but what remains the same are the resources available to them anytime throughout their four years at Bowdoin.

Advice

Just like everything in life, start early, plan your time and prospects well, and continue working hard, without procrastination. If you do this, the opportunities will come your way. Utilize the staff's help, the workshops, the campus visits, the recruitment days, and all that the Career Planning Center makes readily available to you. It might be hard to realize there is life after Bowdoin, but it is important to remember that you need to set things up for yourself; you can't stay in college forever, and if you can, you probably don't need the Career Planning Center to help you find a job!

Career Center Resources & Services

Campus employment, career counseling, career workshops, resource center, graduate school advising, career center announcement board: www.bowdoin.edu/cpc/ (upcoming events, campus interview postings, job fair announcements, etc.), eBear, Liberal Arts Career Network, Spotlight on Careers, Vault, career search, off-campus interviewing fairs, graduate school fair

The Best & Worst

The Ten BEST Things About Bowdoin:

1. Supportive faculty and administration
2. Dining hall food and service people
3. Cook's Corner, Freeport, Portland, and Boston
4. Huge Outing Club program
5. Housing available for all four years
6. Ivies Weekend!
7. Taking classes on Coles Tower's 16th floor
8. Amazing athletic team
9. Good-looking male student body
10. Greatest mascot in our league: the Polar Bear!

The Ten WORST Things About Bowdoin:

1. Long winter
2. Extremely preppy campus
3. Towed without warning
4. Brunswick goes to bed at 8 p.m.
5. No public transportation
6. 25 percent of the campus comes from Mass.
7. Hooking-up too much leads to awkwardness
8. Football team ranked worst by *SI*
9. Existence of the J-Board
10. Cliquey student body

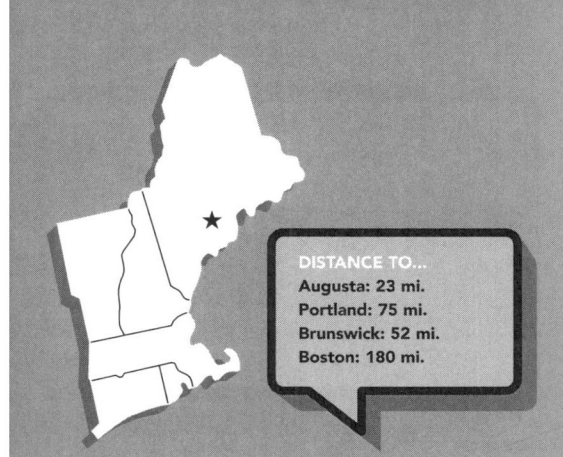

DISTANCE TO...
Augusta: 23 mi.
Portland: 75 mi.
Brunswick: 52 mi.
Boston: 180 mi.

> "At Colby, it's perfectly okay to be undecided on your major, your career goal, and even your classes for next semester."

Total Enrollment:
1,768

Acceptance Rate:
34%

Tuition:
$39,800

Top 10% of High School Class:
62%

SAT Range
Verbal	Math	Total
630 – 710	640 – 710	1270 – 1420

ACT Range
Verbal	Math	Total
26-30	26-30	27-30

Most Popular Majors:
13% English Literature
13% Biology/Biological Sciences
13% Economics
10% Political Science and Government
8% History

Students Also Applied To:*
Bates College, Bowdoin College, Dartmouth College, Middlebury College, Williams College

*For more school info check out www.collegeprowler.com

Table of Contents

Academics	214
Local Atmosphere	215
Safety & Security	217
Computers	218
Facilities	220
Campus Dining	221
Off-Campus Dining	223
Campus Housing	224
Off-Campus Housing	226
Diversity	228
Guys & Girls	230
Athletics	231
Greek Life	233
Drug Scene	234
Campus Strictness	236
Overall Experience	237
The Inside Scoop	239
Finding a Job or Internship	241
The Best & Worst	242

College Prowler Report Card

Academics	B+
Local Atmosphere	C-
Safety & Security	B+
Computers	B-
Facilities	B
Campus Dining	A-
Off-Campus Dining	B+
Campus Housing	C-
Off-Campus Housing	D
Diversity	D+
Guys	C+
Girls	B+
Athletics	C+
Greek Life	N/A
Drug Scene	B+
Campus Strictness	C-

Academics

Students Speak Out
ON ACADEMICS

> "Generally, courses are as interesting as you make them. Students have so much liberty to choose their own classes. It would be ridiculous to take a class you didn't find interesting."

Q "In four years, I don't think I've had one professor who didn't really care, not only about the class and the material they were teaching, but about me as a student and as a person. Professors are generally wonderful with office hours, and it is not uncommon to be given their house and cell phone numbers. **Many host class dinners at their houses**."

Q "The professors at Colby, in general, are extremely **knowledgeable, approachable, reputable, and honest**. Many of them are involved in other aspects of student life, and classes, for the most part, are interesting. Of course, you always have a class or two that you don't like, but no school is perfect. On the whole, Colby has excellent professors."

Q "Teachers are all different, of course, but **all of them are highly-qualified**. Some teachers are super-organized, and others are scattered. I've never had one that I hated too much. Classes are interesting, depending on how much you like the subject. I hate math, but when I took Math as a Liberal Art, I still found myself interested in much of the subject matter. There are plenty of options for requirements, so it shouldn't be hard to find something to fit your likes and dislikes."

Q "**The professors are always willing to help out students**. Yes, some of them might be a little boring or a little weird, but they are nice people once you make the effort to get to know them. Small classes are generally more interesting than the big lectures since more discussion takes place between the students and the professor."

The Lowdown
ON ACADEMICS

Degrees Awarded:
Bachelor

Full-time Faculty:
158

Faculty with Terminal Degree:
95%

Student-to-Faculty Ratio:
11:1

Average Course Load:
4 courses

Special Degree Options:
None

AP Test Score Requirements:
Possible credit for scores of 4 or 5

IB Test Score Requirements:
Possible credit for scores of 5, 6, or 7

Best Places to Study:
Library, Pugh Center, Mary Low Coffeehouse, Spa

Sample Academic Clubs:
Computer Club, Debate Team, Student Women in Science, Psychology, Biology (Raging Species), Chemistry, Economics, Geology, Philosophy

The College Prowler Take
ON ACADEMICS

Colby is a liberal arts school through and through. While we haven't eliminated core requirements entirely, like some of the more progressive schools, we have whittled them down to a handful of "distribution requirements." All Colby students take an introductory English course as freshmen and then have the rest of their time at school to take one class each in arts, historical studies, literature, quantitative reasoning, and social sciences. These are completely easy to fulfill, though. You can test out with AP scores, and if you still need to fulfill requirements, you can take courses like Math as a Liberal Art. Colby also features a unique 4-1-4 semester schedule. Students take four classes in the fall and the spring, and one class during January, called Jan-Plan. This is another chance to fulfill credits, or take interesting and unique courses, like The Psychology of Nazi Germany, Sanskrit, or German Fairy Tales in Popular Culture, for example.

The students are pretty much in agreement here: Colby's faculty is a pivotal part of academic life, and they make the time here worthwhile. Caring and accessible, not to mention really, really smart, the professors are definitely one of Colby's biggest draws. Upperclassmen are always willing to rave about their favorite teachers, so talking to them is a great way to get a handle on which teachers are Colby legend and which can be skipped, making it even easier to ensure a good academic experience. Academics, in general, are strong here. The English, government, and biology departments are especially lauded.

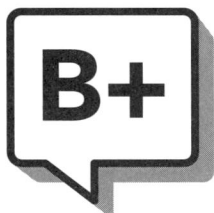

The College Prowler™ Grade on
Academics: B+

A high Academics grade generally indicates that professors are knowledgeable, accessible, and genuinely interested in their students' welfare. Other determining factors include class size, how well professors communicate, and whether or not classes are engaging.

Local Atmosphere

The Lowdown
ON LOCAL ATMOSPHERE

Region:
Northeast

City, State:
Waterville, Maine

Setting:
Small town

Distance from Portland:
1.5 hours

Distance from Boston:
3.5 hours

Points of Interest:
Waterville Opera House, Railroad Square Cinema (Waterville); Maine State Museum, Old Fort Western (Augusta); Belgrade Lakes, L.L. Bean and the 50+ outlet stores (Freeport); Reid State Park (Georgetown); Owls Head Transportation Museum (Owls Head)

City Websites:
www.watervillemainstreet.org
www.ci.waterville.me.us

Major Sports Teams:
Portland Pirates (Hockey), Portland Sea Dogs (Minor League baseball)

Students Speak Out
ON LOCAL ATMOSPHERE

The College Prowler Take
ON LOCAL ATMOSPHERE

"Waterville is a large town, but some may call it a small city. It has a wide variety of fast food restaurants, and, of course, Wal-Mart, K-Mart, Shaw's, and Hannaford."

Q "**It seems a little bleak at first**, but you get used to it. It contains everything you need in a college town. Too much time can be spent meandering the aisles of Wal-Mart, for lack of other recreational outlets. If you become tired of flipping through the multiple Olsen-twins calendars, people-watching can provide hours of solid entertainment. If nothing else, you may be able to spot the next suitable contestants for 'The Swan.'"

Q "The town we technically live in, and I say technically because campus is separated from the town, is a depressed Maine town, and **our relationship with the people of Waterville is not at its best**. There is another college in town, but I don't know of any socializing that occurs between the two schools."

Q "Not too many people spend that much time in Waterville. If you go off campus, it's usually to Portland, Freeport, Sugarloaf [the ski mountain], or to other mountains to hike or climb. But **Waterville provides everything we need**: great pizza, pharmacies, hospitals, and a few awesome places to take the parents."

Q "The campus is rather isolated in our own '**Colby Bubble**.' It's nice to go downtown to get off campus for a while and get coffee at Jorgenson's. If you want to do any serious clothing shopping, though, you need to go to Augusta or Freeport."

Q "Colby is a small school, and the atmosphere is what you would expect. **It feels like a small community**. People know people and care about what happens on campus. There are plenty of places to visit in the community if you like to volunteer, like the soup kitchen, animal shelter, and school. There are other schools nearby—Bowdoin and Bates, along with Thomas College."

Waterville is typically viewed as a tiny, quaint, and somewhat impoverished, town. It is definitely a far cry from the Main Street college towns of many universities. While it provides Colby students with what they need, it is definitely not an attraction. Most students see a divide between the school and the town, although the Colby Volunteer Center and groups like the South End Coalition are working hard to improve relations. Most students, though, accept its flaws and find ways to enjoy getting off the hill every now and then.

The College Prowler™ Grade on

Local Atmosphere: C-

A high Local Atmosphere grade indicates that the area surrounding campus is safe and scenic. Other factors include nearby attractions, proximity to other schools, and the town's attitude toward students.

Safety & Security

Students Speak Out
ON SAFETY & SECURITY

"Security is completely adequate and a bit bothersome on the weekends, but there hasn't been a time when I've felt unsafe while on campus."

The Lowdown
ON SAFETY & SECURITY

Number of security officers:
13

Phone:
(207) 872-3345

Health Center Office Hours:
Nurse coverage: 24 hours
Clinic hours: Monday-Friday 8 a.m.-4 p.m.

Safety Services
Jitney Service (transportation within Waterville), courtesy rides by security officers, Colby Check (property identification and marking), lost and found, safety whistles, party checks, emergency safety advisories

Q "In my three years at Colby, **I have never felt unsafe or threatened** by anything. Colby does an excellent job of making students feel secure. My only complaint about security is that they are often too interested in breaking up parties and fining students."

Q "**I've never felt in danger at Colby**. Security works incredibly hard to keep us safe and is always in the process of improving their equipment and methods. There's a student escort system, so no one has to walk anywhere by themselves. All you have to do is call the security office and ask for the escort to walk you wherever you're going."

Q "Security is pretty willing to help when you need it. **You can call for an escort at any time**, and while they may not always be incredibly prompt, they'll always come and drive you where you need to go. Also, everyone is given whistles that they may use."

Q "**There is good security on campus**. I have always felt safe. The 2003 homicide was a very random, tragic occurrence."

Q "**The security is always present**. Security officers are constantly patrolling in their cars; I see someone from the staff several times a day. I can honestly say there were only one, or two, times throughout the school year that I didn't feel safe."

The College Prowler Take
ON SAFETY & SECURITY

It's a testament to how much Colby students trust security that everyone seems to feel completely safe on campus, even after the tragic (and well-remembered) death of a student a few years ago. Colby's isolated location is certainly a reason for this sense of safety. Also, Colby security is very visible and well-known. Most students can tell you the name, and nickname, of at least one security officer, and it's not uncommon for students to stop and chat with whichever officer is prowling around outside dances. Also, students trust each other. Most feel comfortable leaving their books and bags in the library while they meet friends at a dining hall for dinner, and there are very few reports of stolen items. If you lose something, chances are you'll either find it right where you left it or get a phone call from the person who found it.

Computers

The Lowdown
ON COMPUTERS

High-Speed Network?
Yes

Wireless Network?
In the library only

Number of Labs:
5

Numbers of Computers:
77

24-Hour Labs:
Miller Street

Charge to Print:
No

Operating Systems:
PC, Mac

The College Prowler™ Grade on
Safety & Security: B+

A high grade in Safety & Security means that students generally feel safe, campus police are visible, blue-light phones and escort services are readily available, and safety precautions are not overly necessary.

Free Software
Nothing's free, but Microsoft Word is covered by tuition. Also, Colby has purchased several software packages for download, including Oracle Calendar, EndNote 7, SOPHOS, Fetch 4.03 (for Mac OS X only), Better Telnet (for Mac only) and TeraTerm (for Windows only).

Students Speak Out
ON COMPUTERS

"Although I have always had a laptop in my room, I have found that I do most of my work in Colby's computer labs. They are rarely crowded, and it is often easier to concentrate there than in a noisy dorm."

Q "**Yours will die as soon as you plug it in**. Don't download anything, and get good antivirus protection. ITS really doesn't help at all, sadly."

Q "I would definitely bring my own computer. There are great labs, but **they are not open 24-hours**, and they're often crowded."

Q "**The computer labs are usually crowded** at crunch times, like midterms and finals, but besides that, you can always find a spot. Most people do have their own computers, and since everyone is given Ethernet in their room, it is definitely nice. If you don't own one, I don't think it would be a huge problem."

Q "I'd recommend having your own computer. The library labs are usually only full around finals, but **the student network does allow for easy transfer of viruses**. Our student computer services, though, are incredibly helpful about ridding your computer of viruses when need be."

Q "**The network is abysmal**. Any virus you see making waves on the news, Colby has. And they will all kill your network connection intermittently until ITS finally gets around to fixing the computers of those that are too stupid to fix them themselves."

The College Prowler Take
ON COMPUTERS

There are plenty of computers sprinkled throughout campus for general use, although the labs can get quite crowded around finals. Many students bring computers, but it's up to you to decide if you want a laptop or a desktop, a PC or a Mac. Colby only has wireless Internet in Miller Library, so you do have to plug in when you're in your dorm. Usually this works pretty well, and it's great to be able to send files quickly over the network. It's not foolproof, though, and the network has an ugly tendency to fail during the most critical times (like finals). Having your own computer is definitely a nice convenience, especially because nobody wants to be walking from their room to a computer lab at 2 a.m. in a blinding snowstorm. It is also more convenient for those who are just plain lazy and don't feel like going to the lab.

The College Prowler™ Grade on
Computers: B-

A high grade in Computers designates that computer labs are available, the computer network is easily accessible, and the campus' computing technology is up-to-date.

Facilities

Students Speak Out
ON FACILITIES

"Colby is uber-pristine—they take great care of all the facilities and buildings and are always trying to offer the best to students. If anything falls below par, they re-do it."

"**The student center looks plastic and fake**. The math and physics building looks like a prison, but the rest of the campus is beautiful."

"**The library has too many steps**. It's like a Himalayan trek getting to the third floor of Miller, and by then, one is too tired to study and instead slumps into those comfy chairs and has a three hour nap—or so I've heard."

"The facilities are awesome, and the athletic center is great. I use the gym all the time, and honestly, it is the nicest one I've been to. **The pool is wonderful, as are the basketball court, hockey rink, track, and aerobics room**. There's a writers' center for people who want help with term papers or anything written. I've used it, and it's great. The health center is wonderful, too. The nurses there can help you with anything."

"The student center is not a popular place to hang out. It's a nice building, but for some reason, **people don't really seem to use it**, besides getting their mail. The academic buildings, libraries, laboratories, and gym are all very nice."

"**The athletic center is amazing and huge**. There is a pool, ice hockey rink, a basketball court, a weight room with awesome equipment, an indoor track, and an exercise [and] yoga room. As for the student center—I love it. I hang out there a lot whenever I don't want to be confined to my room or someone else's."

The Lowdown
ON FACILITIES

Movie Theatre on Campus?
No, but some lecture rooms are used to show films on a pretty regular basis.

Bowling on Campus?
No

Bar on Campus?
The Blue Light Pub in Cotter Union

Coffeehouse on Campus?
Mary Low Coffeehouse on the first floor of the Mary Low dorm

Favorite Things to Do
While Colby students are usually content to talk to each other wherever they happen to meet in between classes, Colby's facilities are put to good use as well. The gym is popular, especially in the late afternoon and early evening. When the weather is nice, students flock outdoors to Johnson Pond or one of the many grassy, sunny spots. In the evenings, the on-campus pub is typically packed, even during the week.

The College Prowler Take
ON FACILITIES

Some students claim to have chosen to come to Colby because all the buildings match. The buildings and landscaping are definitely top quality, and the view from the Miller Library steps is nothing short of breathtaking. The athletic center is well-liked and well-used—sometimes a little too well-used. It's quite a challenge to find an exercise machine after classes get out in the late afternoon. And, although Miller Library is very picturesque and well-lit, most students choose not to study there, instead favoring the brighter, more welcoming Olin Science Library. Cotter Union is a huge building and includes Page Commons (for dances, lectures, and other big events), the Pugh Center, the Spa, the Pub, the on-campus post office, mailboxes, and an ATM. You'll need to use it, eventually.

Campus Dining

The Lowdown
ON CAMPUS DINING

Freshman Meal Plan Requirement?
Yes

24-Hour On-Campus Eating?
No

Student Favorites:
The Spa, the Pub

Meal Plan Average Cost:
Included in tuition

The College Prowler™ Grade on
Facilities: B

A high Facilities grade indicates that the campus is aesthetically pleasing and well-maintained; facilities are state-of-the-art, and libraries are exceptional. Other determining factors include the quality of both athletic and student centers and an abundance of things to do on campus.

Students Speak Out
ON CAMPUS DINING

"The food on campus is great; there are no complaints here. Of the three dining halls on campus, I only eat at Foss. There is great food—it's fresh and always has vegetarian options."

Q "**All of the dining halls are good**. Where you eat says a lot about you. I like that they all have good salad bars, and there is always fresh fruit. The desserts are dangerous, though. Beware: there are so many, and they all taste so good!"

Q "The food on campus is extraordinarily good. **All three dining halls serve different, high-quality, food**. Just be careful to know exactly what you're eating at Foss, or you might get a nasty surprise. After a year or so the food can get a little monotonous, but there's huge potential for mixing the foods to keep things interesting. My favorite is cutting up the Sunday night chicken fingers into a salad, and pairing it with a mug full of root beer and a scoop of ice cream. Creativity is the difference between dorm food and cuisine."

Q "The food honestly is really good. And yes, I am talking about the dining halls. It's all-you-can-eat, three meals a day, seven days a week. I think it makes a huge difference that we have such good food—**life is more enjoyable**."

Q "The food is amazing—**I never get sick of it**. Foss has, hands down, the best atmosphere and really the most quality food, including the best salad bar. Dana and Bob's are fairly tasty, too, but not quite as exciting. The omelet and grilled cheese bars are amazingly one-of-a-kind."

Q "Eventually I grew tired of the food, but I can't complain. I am grateful for the variety. Also, **the dining halls are spacious, but can get crowded sometimes**. The dining halls are very well-kept by an amazing team of dedicated and diligent dining hall staff members."

The College Prowler Take
ON CAMPUS DINING

Dining is integral to Colby social life, and the individual characteristics of the three dining halls are part of what defines campus politics. Tables in the dining halls are big, as they are meant for large groups of friends, and they usually end up overcrowded anyway. Lots of social interaction happens over dining-hall food, and it's not too much of a stretch to say that friendships have formed and ended due to dining-hall preference.

The College Prowler™ Grade on
Campus Dining: A-

Our grade on Campus Dining addresses the quality of both school-owned dining halls and independent on-campus restaurants as well as the price, availability, and variety of food.

Off-Campus Dining

Students Speak Out
ON OFF-CAMPUS DINING

"**Pad Thai is absolutely delicious, and they love Colby kids. The Last Unicorn is a great place for parents. Silver Street has the best meat, and Bread Box is very tasty.**"

Q "**There are a couple great Thai places**, a few seafood places, a good soul-food place, and a couple nice, traditional American restaurants. Colby students have a peculiar, and rather unanimous, affection for Pad Thai."

Q "There are a few really good restaurants in town: Pad Thai, which is the most popular place for Thai food; Freedom Café, which has excellent food that tends to be Southern and homemade; the Breadbox Café, a really nice little place with a great atmosphere and amazing food; Jorgenson's, an adorable little café with sandwiches and a huge variety of coffees; and **Big G's, which has excellent and enormous sandwiches and breakfasts**."

Q "For a small town, **Waterville has this covered**! We've got Big G's for huge and creative sandwiches—try the Zonker Harriss—Asian Café and Pad Thai for all things Asian, and Freedom Café for huge portions of truly excellent Southern cooking."

Q "Pad Thai is good, **Waterville House of Pizza is a good place to order from at 1 a.m.**, and The Last Unicorn and Freedom Café are good places to go with the 'rents."

Q "**There is a ton of great restaurants**. You just have to know how to get to them since they're not right next to the highway."

The Lowdown
ON OFF-CAMPUS DINING

Best Pizza:
Waterville House of Pizza, Spanky's Pizza

Best Asian:
Pad Thai, Asian Café

Best Breakfast:
Big G's

Late-Night, Student Specials:
Waterville House of Pizza, Spanky's Pizza

Best Place to Take Your Parents:
Bread Box Café, the Last Unicorn, the Freedom Café

Student Favorites:
Big G's, Bread Box Café, Freedom Café, Gifford's Ice Cream, Grand Central Café, Pad Thai, Spanky's Pizza, Waterville House of Pizza

The College Prowler Take
ON OFF-CAMPUS DINING

You'll be hard-pressed to find a Colby student who doesn't have an inexplicable, and undying, love for Pad Thai. The small, often crowded, hole-in-the-wall Thai restaurant is easily the most popular in Waterville, which is quite the accomplishment in a city full of great restaurants. The food is definitely Waterville's biggest attraction (we sure don't have shopping). Although restaurants are often far from campus, or difficult to find (Big G's is particularly elusive), students are always willing to venture into the Waterville wilds to find great food. On-campus dining halls are great, but they get old, and Waterville rises to meet the needs of bored and hungry Colby students. The popular spots get crowded, and continual eating out will burn holes in your wallet, but in a city that often has little to offer Colby students, the off-campus dining scene is pretty phenomenal.

Campus Housing

The Lowdown
ON CAMPUS HOUSING

Undergrads on Campus:
94%

Number of Dormitories:
25

Number of University-Owned Apartments:
One building

Bed Type:
Twin extra-longs, which can be lofted if you ask nicely.

Available for Rent
Mini-fridge

Cleaning Service?
In the public bathrooms

You Get:
Bed, dresser, closet, desk, chair, as many Ethernet connections as there are people in the room, telephone jack, cable TV jack

Also Available:
Chem-free living, quiet living

The College Prowler™ Grade on
Off-Campus Dining: B+

A high Off-Campus Dining grade implies that off-campus restaurants are affordable, accessible, and worth visiting. Other factors include the variety of cuisine and the availability of alternative options (vegetarian, vegan, Kosher, etc.).

Room Types

Residence Halls have a variety of rooms. Singles, doubles, two-room doubles, one- or two-room triples, quads, five-person suites, and six-person suites are all available. Quads, five-person, and six-person suites have their own bathrooms, as do a few doubles and triples. For the most part, though, students living in singles, doubles, and triples share a central bathroom located near their rooms. Seniors may elect to live in on-campus apartments, which include a variety of really luxurious suites (including a two-story six-person suite).

Did You Know?

AMS is brand-new building, and Averill and Johnson were recently renovated.

Students Speak Out
ON CAMPUS HOUSING

"Chem-free dorms are nice because you don't have to deal with people puking in the bathrooms. Avoid Williams. It has a nice sense of community, but is not too exciting."

Q "**The dorms totally vary**. There are old frat houses and new buildings that feel like hotels—each has its ups and downs. The frat row dorms are kind of on the shabby side, but are more social. The new dorms have nice bathrooms, but can be less social."

Q "**The dorms are comfortable, but there are some that are tiny**. Dorms on frat row don't have the best bathrooms. All are equipped with one or more common rooms, kitchens, televisions, and vending machines. The laundry rooms are not bad, but can be a hassle if there is only one for the 28 people in a dorm."

Q "The dorms are really great. **Almost no one lives off campus**. Foss, Mary Low, Coburn, AMS, Averill, and Johnson are the nicest buildings. West Quad, East Quad and Johnson have the best location. The frat row dorms are indisputably the worst buildings; Heights isn't far behind. Frat row, Hillside, and Foss all have bad locations. The senior apartments are the best, but they're only open to seniors."

Q "Since the remodeling and revamping of the dorms on campus, there really aren't any dorms that are truly awful. **Heights is ugly, but it has two-room doubles** and is close to a dining hall. The Hillside dorms, or 'ugly white buildings,' aren't so hot, but the rooms are big. Frat row has smaller rooms, but isn't bad for location."

Q "The dorms do vary, but overall, they tend to be very nice. Of course, the newest, or newly renovated, dorms, like AMS, Foss, Woodman, Averill, and Johnson, are all beautiful inside. The college has recently renovated the small dorms on frat row, which tend to have smaller rooms and older facilities. **The Hillside dorms are not quite as nice**, but they are very social and a lot of fun to live in."

COLLEGE PROWLER™

Want to find a dorm that best fits your personality? For a detailed listing of all dorms on campus, check out the College Prowler book on Colby available at www.collegeprowler.com.

The College Prowler Take
ON CAMPUS HOUSING

Dorms are pretty hit-or-miss. There aren't really any phenomenal rooms, but nothing's too abysmal, either. Dorms are renovated on a 20-year rotating schedule, so no building is more than 20-years old, and something is always being updated. Every building has its ups and downs, and people tend to become very devoted to the building they live in. Chem-free is a surprisingly popular living option and carries no stigma whatsoever. Many claim that one of the best things about Colby's housing system is that everyone lives together. All buildings are coed by room, rather than by floor, and there is no themed housing or freshman housing. Freshmen live with seniors, live with guys, live with girls, live with international students, and live with Mainers. The people living in the dorms are often what make them special and unique.

The College Prowler™ Grade on
Campus Housing: C-

A high Campus Housing grade indicates that dorms are clean, well-maintained, and spacious. Other determining factors include variety of dorms, proximity to classes, and social atmosphere.

Off-Campus Housing

The Lowdown
ON OFF-CAMPUS HOUSING

Undergrads in Off-Campus Housing:
6%

Average Rent for a House:
$250-$350/month (10- and 12-month leases)

Popular Areas:
On the lakes

Best Time to Look for a Place:
Fall of junior year (if you want to live off campus as a senior)

Students Speak Out
ON OFF-CAMPUS HOUSING

"Get heat and all utilities included, if possible. My roomies and I ended up paying $300 or more a month for heating oil—ouch."

Q "Most students live on campus. **The people I know who live off campus either really love it, or really hate it**. They all appreciate the freedom from college rules, but at the same time rant about the rent."

Q "**Some of the off-campus housing is convenient**, but a lot of the houses are more than a 10-minute drive from campus. I would rather live on campus."

Q "I understand it to be very difficult, mostly because you have to have a car and find roommates who want to live off campus. **Roommates are hard to find** because it's a lot more fun to live on campus. For one thing, you can always go back to your room between classes. The best part about living on campus is being immersed in everything. Your best friends are just down the hall, and you can find something to do at the drop of a hat."

Q "**Students usually stick to on-campus housing until senior year**. This is one of my favorite aspects of Colby—everyone is always on campus. By senior year, you can choose to live off campus and experience something new."

Q "Most people live on campus, and if you want to live off campus, **you have to apply to do so**. It's really crucial that you have a car because there are not too many houses immediately surrounding the college. I prefer living at school—you can always go to the parties off-campus, and it seems more practical to live a five-minute walk away from classes."

The College Prowler Take
ON OFF-CAMPUS HOUSING

Most people (especially underclassmen) see off-campus living as a party scene, and that's about it. Colby students tend to live on campus. Off-campus housing is unique. There aren't apartments; instead, houses are rented year after year by Colby students. Off-campus housing is included in the housing lottery at the end of the year, and it's rare that sophomores qualify to live off campus. Typically, only a few seniors actually rent houses (although there's been an increasing number in past years). Students who feel trapped on campus, or who want a break from the rules and security, will move into houses their senior year. The school does not really publicize this alternate living option, and those who want to escape campus life typically prefer on-campus alternatives, like the senior apartments or the co-op.

The College Prowler™ Grade on
Off-Campus Housing: D

A high grade in Off-Campus Housing indicates that apartments are of high quality, close to campus, affordable, and easy to secure.

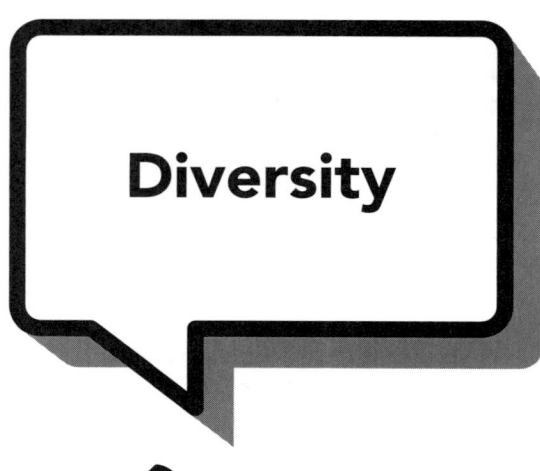

Diversity

The Lowdown
ON DIVERSITY

African American: 2%

Asian American: 5%

Hispanic: 3%

Native American: 0%

White: 83%

International: 7%

Out-of-State: 87%

Most Popular Religions
There are some prevalent Christian organizations on campus. The Colby Christian Fellowship (CCF) and the Newman Council (a Catholic organization) are well-attended clubs that host a few very prominent campus events. The Jewish population is quite large as well.

Political Activity
Although many students would identify themselves as left-leaning, the conservatives on campus are very vocal and well-organized. There is a handful of very vocal, very liberal activist-types who go to protests and organize campus events. Racial awareness week and social class awareness week are particularly notable, as well as the extremely well-organized diversity conference. Many students, though, are politically inactive.

Gay Tolerance
In general, the campus is very supportive of gay rights but tends to get uncomfortable if things get too loud.

Economic Status
Most Colby students seem to come from very well-off backgrounds. Although the school is economically diverse, these differences aren't easy to see. This contributes to the (perhaps erroneous) perception of the school as entirely populated by rich, white New Englanders.

Students Speak Out
ON DIVERSITY

"Anyone who speaks out is ostracized, blamed for increasing student tensions, and usually has their name splattered all over the *Digest of Civil Discourse* and the joke *Echo*."

Minority Clubs
The Pugh Center, located within the student center building, houses many diversity-oriented clubs. Students Organized Against Racism (SOAR), Students Organized for Black and Hispanic Unity (SOBHU), The Bridge (gay-straight alliance), and all the religious groups are a few of the 20 or so clubs that have offices and safe spaces in the Pugh Center. The Pugh Community Board works to facilitate dialogue between these groups, and bring speakers and events to campus.

Q "Trying to find a person of color at Colby is **like the search for rainbow marshmallows in a bowl of Lucky Charms**. You spot a few falling into the bowl as you're pouring, but when you set your mind to finding as many as you can, none turn up."

Q "**A lot of students are upper-class**, New England, white kids, but Colby tries very hard to make a diverse campus. The Pugh Center hosts many clubs dedicated to diversity."

Q "**Diversity is a ridiculous issue**. Colby claims to be 'diverse,' and in some ways it is. For example, there are a lot of people from other countries, and there are domestic students from across the nation. But if you are thinking of diversity as only skin color, you are not going to find a very broad range at Colby."

Q "Diversity's a funny thing—I never think of it unless someone brings it up, which is strange since I applied here as a minority. **Colby has a reasonable amount of diversity**, but more wouldn't hurt. Colby is making a strong effort to diversify, though."

Q "**Colby is diverse by Maine standards**, but there is a definite rift between minority groups and the privileged white kids on campus."

The College Prowler Take
ON DIVERSITY

The question of diversity is complex at Colby. We have a large population of international students, and minorities are very vocal. The campus is pretty polarized between the activist types and the non-political kids. The Foss/Mary Low side of campus tends to be more politically aware and diverse, or at least more aware of diversity. Social class has been a particular topic of concern lately—many people see Colby as very elitist. All these diversity-related issues, though, are pretty actively brought to light. Although the campus is working very hard to create a more diverse atmosphere, minorities continue to feel marginalized, and the people who speak out on their behalf often end up feeling ostracized. This creates an intense atmosphere sometimes—discussions and demonstrations on campus can feel pretty heated. But continual efforts to introduce more diversity and alleviate tensions are definitely to be applauded.

The College Prowler™ Grade on
Diversity: D+

A high grade in Diversity indicates that ethnic minorities and international students have a notable presence on campus and that students of different economic backgrounds, religious beliefs, and sexual preferences are well-represented.

Guys & Girls

Students Speak Out
ON GUYS & GIRLS

"I feel that the Colby students are generally attractive. The dating scene is interesting. You are either dating, which means you are practically married, or you're just hooking up. It is very hard to find an in between."

The Lowdown
ON GUYS & GIRLS

Women Undergrads: 53%

Men Undergrads: 47%

Birth Control Available?
Yes, $10 per pack at the Garrison-Foster Health Center.

Hookups or Relationships?
Either/or, but casual dating is almost unheard of. Colby students tend to either hook-up very randomly and very frequently, or get involved in intense and long-term relationships.

Dress Code
"Collars up" is practically a mantra at Colby. The typical Colby student wears khakis or Nantucket reds, a polo shirt with an upturned collar (two, in complimentary pastels, to be really trendy), and flip-flops. Girls accessorize with pearls and hair-ribbons, guys might pull out a hemp or shell necklace. Nalgene bottles are key, decorated with stickers proclaiming a love of Guster and skiing.

Q "One can find pretty attractive women and pretty loud and annoying girls. **Colby has an online dating service called 'Mulematch'**—use it at your own discretion."

Q "**We have a very attractive campus**. Everyone is so friendly. When I first came here I was struck that everyone smiled at you, even if you didn't know who they were. Although, all the Ralph Lauren, Tiffany's heart bracelets, and pastel matching seemed a little over-the-top."

Q "Walking around Colby is a little like walking into a J. Crew catalog. Upturned collars, Northface and Patagonia fleece, and **a good, healthy dose of preppiness** are the general atmosphere. We've also got a handful of hippies, but punks are rarely seen on Mayflower Hill."

Q "**Guys tend to be sophomoric and socially moronic**—despite how intelligent they are. Their potential starts to show senior year, but until then, they act like idiots. Most Colby girls, despite how shallow or ignorant they can seem, are, overall, smart and sweet. All you have to do is spend five minutes talking with them, and you'll see that there's gold in them all. And the girls are hot, plain and simple."

Q "**I think the girls are much more attractive than the boys**. Many of the girls are 'naturally pretty,' and do not try to emulate Britney Spears. For the most part, they dress on the more conservative side and in a respectable manner. I think that it is difficult to meet guys on this campus. You can meet people at parties, but I wish there was some other type of social interaction during the week where people could meet on sober terms."

The College Prowler Take
ON GUYS & GIRLS

Most people choose to come to Colby because of the friendliness of Colby students. Colby folks smile at each other, make conversation easily, and are overwhelmingly optimistic. Alcohol is definitely a huge part of the social scene, though, and can get to be a bit much at times. Great chem-free living is very important for people who aren't into the drinking scene. "Work hard, play hard," is the phrase that embodies social life at Colby. Classes are rigorous and homework does pile up, but for most students, weekends are sacrosanct. Many take partying almost as seriously as they take their studies, discussing pre-game techniques avidly before class. The small campus means you get to know people very quickly. This is good and bad—if you develop a negative reputation, you can easily be ostracized, and there are definitely cliques. They might smile at each other and talk during class, but you'll rarely see the activist kids at the same parties as the jocks on weekends (or during the week!).

The College Prowler™ Grade on
Guys: C+

A high grade for Guys indicates that the male population on campus is attractive, smart, friendly, and engaging, and that the school has a decent ratio of guys to girls.

The College Prowler™ Grade on
Girls: B+

A high grade for Girls not only implies that the women on campus are attractive, smart, friendly, and engaging, but also that there is a fair ratio of girls to guys.

Athletics

The Lowdown
ON ATHLETICS

Men's Varsity Teams:
Cross Country Track
Football
Golf
Soccer
Alpine Skiing
Basketball
Hockey
Indoor Track
Nordic Skiing
Squash
Skiing
Baseball
Crew
Lacrosse
Outdoor Track
Tennis

Women's Varsity Teams:
Cross Country
Field Hockey
Golf
Soccer
Volleyball
Alpine Skiing
Basketball
Ice Hockey
Indoor Track
Nordic Skiing
Squash
Swimming
Crew
Lacrosse
Outdoor Track
Softball
Tennis

Club Sports

Ballroom Dance, badminton, Cheer Club, cycling, equestrian, fencing, rugby (men's and women's), Tai Chi Julebu, men's volleyball, sailing ultimate Frisbee, Woodsmen's Team (coed; this involves axes and chain saws)

Intramurals

Field hockey, soccer (competitive and recreational), flag football (competitive and recreational), Broomball, basketball (five-on-five and three-on-three), triathlon, Home Run Derby, softball (competitive and recreational)

Most Popular Sports
Hockey, lacrosse, broomball, ultimate Frisbee, campus golf (not a real sport, but very popular regardless)

Fields
Synthetic track, 50 acres of fields (includes football, soccer, and lacrosse), 10 tennis courts, cross-country running and ski trails, and a lumberjack area.

Getting Tickets
Is not a problem. The football game against Bates, and the hockey game against Bowdoin are well-attended, but crowds don't tend to grace Colby's athletic fields.

Athletic Division:
NCAA Division III

Conference:
NESCAC

Overlooked Teams:
Football, badminton, squash, rugby

School Mascot:
A white mule. This mascot originated in 1923, when Colby students decided they were tired of being referred to as the dark horse competitors in athletics.

Students Speak Out
ON ATHLETICS

"The campus is very active—that means everything from gym, to varsity sports, to skiing, to hiking. The skiing and crew teams are good, but the other teams don't really match up to the schools we compete against."

Q "Because Colby is so small, it sometimes feels as though **almost everyone plays a sport**. Colby is a very athletic and outdoorsy school. Most students are active in some way."

Q "**Varsity sports are very popular**, but not enough people watch the games. Intramural sports are very popular and are so much fun. Everybody plays broomball—it's the most fun you'll ever have while getting the crap kicked out of you."

Q "There's a significant group that plays varsity sports, but an equally significant one that doesn't. The interaction between these groups is fairly good. If you play a varsity sport, there's a strong tendency to get sucked in and have few friends outside the team. **Intramural sports are popular**. Not everyone wants to play sports, but for those who do, there's a sport and a level for anyone."

Q "**Varsity sports are pretty big**, but if you are used to a big crowd at football games, you are not going to find it at Colby. You will get to know a lot of the players, so it's fun to watch your friends. Intramurals are really big. I have played soccer and softball recreationally, but you can also play competitively."

Q "**The student body can be easily excited by school rivalries**. The Colby-Bates football game and the Colby-Bowdoin hockey game are famous. Around the time of the Colby-Bates football game, you see many students wearing 'Buck Fates' T-shirts."

The College Prowler Take
ON ATHLETICS

Colby isn't well-known for its mighty, athletic prowess. "Real" sports don't get too much attention here, certainly not as much as they do at major universities with big football teams. Lacrosse and soccer can be pretty popular, and hockey games are comparatively well-attended. The Bates football rivalry and the Bowdoin hockey rivalry boost the attendance at those games as well. But, despite the lack of emphasis on varsity sports, Colby students are outdoorsy and athletic. The intramural teams, known as "I-play sports," are more popular than the varsity sports and are a great way to get to know people outside of your dorm and your classes. Although varsity sports do not define life at Colby, students are far from lazy armchair-dwellers.

The College Prowler™ Grade on
Athletics: C+

A high grade in Athletics indicates that students have school spirit, that sports programs are respected, that games are well-attended, and that intramurals are a prominent part of student life.

Greek Life

The Lowdown
ON GREEK LIFE

Number of Fraternities:
0

Number of Sororities:
0

Percent of Undergrad Men in Fraternities:
0

Percent of Undergrad Women in Sororities:
0

Multicultural Colonies:
None

Did You Know?

In case you didn't recognize from the abundance of zeros above, Colby has no Greek life.

There are rumors of secret frats at Colby, but if the rumors are true, no one is speaking up about them. Some swear the secret frats exist; others claim they're nothing but Colby legend.

Students Speak Out
ON GREEK LIFE

{ "We don't have any Greek life—oh, except for those secret frats, but they're secret, so I can't tell you."

Q "We have **no Greek Life here**, and I think we're all the better for it."

Q "If you're college life is based on how many beers you can bong and how many friends you can buy, then **Colby probably isn't the place for you**."

Q "There is no Greek life here—unless you count **philosophy class**."

The College Prowler Take
ON GREEK LIFE

Fraternities and sororities were abolished in 1984 because they were associated with excessive drinking, segregation, hazing, and sexual assault. Currently, there has been heated debate about establishing multicultural housing. Many people think that establishing multicultural housing will take Colby back to the days of exclusion and separatism. Others say that problems of discrimination were not felled by the banning of Greek life, and multicultural housing is intended to remedy problems of discrimination.

The College Prowler™ Grade on
Greek Life: N/A

A high grade in Greek Life indicates that sororities and fraternities are not only present, but also active on campus. Other determining factors include the variety of houses available and the respect the Greek community receives from the rest of the campus.

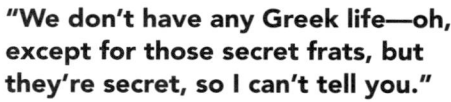

Drug Scene

The Lowdown
ON DRUG SCENE

Most Prevalent Drugs on Campus:
Marijuana, "study drugs" (Ritalin and Adderall, for example)

Liquor-Related Referrals: 0

Liquor-Related Arrests: 15

Drug-Related Referrals: 0

Drug-Related Arrests: 0

Drug Counseling Programs:
Substance Counselor

Phone:
(207) 872-3394

Services:
Confidential counseling and evaluations.

Maine General Hospital Substance Abuse Services:

Phone:
(207) 872-4140

Services:
Emergency services, inpatient treatment, partial hospitalization, outpatient services, intensive outpatient day and evening services, adolescent services

Students Speak Out
ON DRUG SCENE

The College Prowler Take
ON DRUG SCENE

"When it comes time to turn papers in, kids stick a bunch of Ritalin up their noses and turn things in late."

"**The illegal drug scene is, overall, weak and deeply underground**. Everyone knows someone who smokes pot, and someone else who smokes up all the time, but no one will try to pressure you to. Alcohol is everywhere. It's rare for there to be pressure to drink, but it does happen. Binge drinking is really common."

"**There is a lot of pot**, but if you are not into it, no one cares one way or the other. You can easily have fun without it. There are more hardcore drugs scattered around, but I have never come in contact with them."

"There are a good number of pot smokers and not much else. **Most people just drink**."

"The only fun drugs you can easily obtain are marijuana and ADD medication. **Sadly, prescription meds are difficult to come by**, and I have not yet seen cocaine. If this is what you are looking for, try a city university."

"**Colby kids do love their weed**, but besides that, drugs are not a huge presence."

There is no cocaine in the bathrooms for Colby students. We may be reliant on alcohol for fun, but drug use is rare and kept quiet. Marijuana is the biggest illicit vice; certain dorms never really lose that stoner smell. Hard drug use does exist, and those who are looking for drugs know where to find them. Almost everyone has heard tales of the local tattoo and piercing parlor, where the piercing artists deal coke and heroin on their days off, but you would have to be actively looking for drugs to come in contact with them. Study drugs can be a problem, though. People who are on prescription drugs have had problems with friends or acquaintances looking to buy their medicine for an extra paper-writing boost. Oh, and don't forget about alcohol—yes, it is a drug, and it seems to be the drug of choice, so the drug scene is probably no different than any other school.

The College Prowler™ Grade on
Drug Scene: B+

A high grade on Drug Scene indicates that drugs are not a noticeable part of campus life; drug use is not visible, and no pressure to use them seems to exist.

Campus Strictness

The Lowdown
ON CAMPUS STRICTNESS

What Are You Most Likely to Get Caught Doing on Campus?

Drinking alcohol from an open container in the hallways, underage drinking, having too many people in a dorm room, illegally possessing a Colby table (frequently stolen as Beer Die or Beirut tables), making too much noise during quiet hours, propping doors open

Students Speak Out
ON CAMPUS STRICTNESS

"A lot of people say security is too strict; I say they aren't strict enough. One time I was working in Miller Library, and I had to clean up beer bottles left by drunken students."

Q "They try to make it a priority to keep the use of drugs and alcohol **regulated to a healthy standard**."

Q "**If security decides to bust you, you're not going to get out if it**. They usually give pretty fair warning for drinking, though. I've seen them standing in the hallway outside a party, not doing anything, just reminding students of their job. As long as the party you're at isn't busted, they won't do anything about you if you're underage and drunk."

Q "Security is **really strict about the open container policy**. No one, regardless of age, can have open alcohol outside of the place where they got it. Basically, security gives a pretty wide berth, but there is a definite line, and you don't want to even try to walk it."

Q "Security is not very strict at all. **Underclassmen can even get alcohol without much of a problem**. The only violation you'll get is having an open container in a non-approved area."

Q "**They are becoming much more strict about the drinking**, and this is pissing off the student body. People still manage to party, but the number of complaints are growing."

Q "**Campus security has been tightening up recently**, and coming up with more consequences for getting caught. There is a very strict open-container policy with a hefty fine, and there is also a strict underage drinking fine. As long as you stay in your room, keep the door closed, and turn the music down, you'll be fine."

Want to know the 411 on campus strictness? For more student responses, check out the College Prowler book on Colby at *collegeprowler.com*.

The College Prowler Take
ON CAMPUS STRICTNESS

Colby does seem to be getting stricter about drinking and partying. The administrative take on partying is still pretty much, "Students are going to drink and party, so we should make sure they don't end up in the hospital or in jail." However, to avoid getting in trouble with the police, hefty open-container fines have added to the strictness of security. Don't walk around the halls with an open can of beer. If you do, you're pretty much asking for trouble. Strictness can vary from dorm to dorm, and from night to night, as well. Most people know at least one security guard fairly well, which is a good way to avoid getting a citation. Most students think that security has gotten tighter on campus, especially with regards to partying and drinking. It has become more difficult to have huge parties on campus, and increased harshness has led to a bigger, off-campus party scene. But most agree that, especially in comparison to friend's schools, Colby students are pretty lucky.

The College Prowler™ Grade on
Campus Strictness: C-

A high Campus Strictness grade implies an overall lenient atmosphere; police and RAs are fairly tolerant, and the administration's rules are flexible.

Overall Experience

Students Speak Out
ON OVERALL EXPERIENCE

"**Academically, Colby surpasses all expectations. Classes are great, teachers are amazing, and the workload is manageable if you forgo sleep; but socially, Colby seems to be drastically stunted.**"

Q "Life at Colby tends to revolve, like many other colleges, around alcohol. School events without alcohol are generally poorly attended, **alcohol-free parties are generally abandoned early in the night in favor of alcoholic ones**, and the only mass movement that the entire campus seemed to participate in was the 'Take Back Doghead' riot that incurred thousands of dollars worth of property damage. This is especially unfortunate, considering the administration crackdown on alcohol that is leaving the campus full of angry, white kids from outside of Boston who want their booze and are willing to do anything for it."

Q "Overall, my experience has been pretty good. It's different from where I came from, which I guess is what I was looking for. **I wish I was somewhere else**—don't we all?—but I don't know where yet, so I'll just stay here for now."

Q "**I came to Colby because the people here are second-to-none**. When I came to visit during the spring of my high school senior year, I was overwhelmed by how incredibly welcoming and kind everyone was. Thanks to my overnight host, I met so many different kinds of people, and they were all awesome."

Q "This year, I reconnected with a few of the people I spent a lot of time with on my first visit to campus, and we became friends. When I was here, my host had someone taking me around every minute, and they were all eager to help, funny, nice, easygoing, and wonderful. **I fell in love with the school before I left the next day**, and I still am in love."

Q "I love it at Colby. It seems like everyone is just so happy to be there and loves this school as much as I do. **Everyone is always looking for fun things to do, and more cool people to meet**. The people at this school are what make it so amazing. They are down-to-earth and love what they're doing."

Q "My overall experience has been great. **I'm glad I traveled this far to attend college**. I do not wish I were anywhere else—the environment is a great place to study and be. The people are wonderful and helpful."

The College Prowler Take
ON OVERALL EXPERIENCE

Colby students love Colby. While they can always find something to complain about—the weather, the town, the lack of diversity, and the homework—they tend to be happy that they chose Colby. Most cite the academics and the friendly atmosphere. Classes and professors are undeniably wonderful, and the student body tends to be happy, friendly, and optimistic.

There are definitely things about Colby that should change. The school is not for everyone. The diversity issue is pretty serious, and causes the most friction on campus. Being up on Mayflower Hill all the time can drive you crazy if you can't find a way to get into town every now and then. And even when you can get into town, unless you're eating or seeing movies, there's not much to do. The near-constant drinking can overwhelm some people. And the school really needs to work on a system of underground tunnels, so we don't have to walk around outside in the winter. The campus, though, is bolstered by the student body's seemingly endless stores of energy and optimism, and most people have a positive Colby experience.

The Inside Scoop

The Lowdown
ON THE INSIDE SCOOP

Colby Slang:
Know the slang, know the school. The following is a list of things you really need to know before coming to Colby. The more of these words you know, the better off you'll be.

Beer Die: Colby's own drinking game. It involves stolen tables, dice, and a bunch of plastic cups.
Beirut: The second most popular drinking game. It's a lot like beer die, except with ping-pong balls instead of dice.
Bob's: Short for Robert's Union; this building houses Bob's dining hall, the campus bookstore, the student newspaper offices, and the campus radio station.
Bro: Colby's president William "Bro" Adams. Even he calls himself Bro.
Buck Fates: A clever play on words. Colby's biggest rivalry is with Bates College in (sort of) nearby Lewiston.
The Co-op: The first-floor rooms of Mary Low. They have a kitchen and a 100-meal-per-semester meal plan.
The Digest: This refers both to the *Digest of General Announcements*, and the *Digest of Civil Discourse*. These are e-mails Colby students get every day. On the *Digest of General Announcements* students can post information about upcoming events, lost and found items, rides needed, etc.. The *Digest of Civil Discourse* is a place where people can bring up things that bother them.
The Echo: The student newspaper
The Fishbowl: A study area in Cotter Union

Frat Row: The row of small dorms lining the walkway between the library and Bob's. They used to be fraternities.
HRs: Head Residents. They keep the dorms running smoothly.
Jan-plan: January. This is the time of year when you have class for eight hours a week and drink or ski the rest of the time.
The Pub: Technically called the Blue Light Pub. It's what it sounds like, an on-campus pub open only to students over 21.
SGA: Student Government Association
The Spa: You can't get your nails done at the Spa. It's the only non-dining-hall food on campus. It's open when the dining halls aren't and has good food that you actually have to pay for.
The Street: A big hallway underneath Miller Library. It's full of couches to study (or nap) on, is open 24-hours, and is always heated, making it a nice way to avoid the cold in the winter.

Colby Urban Legends
There is a blue light on top of Miller Library. According to Colby myth, the light will only go out when a virgin graduates.

Secret fraternities—maybe they exist, and maybe they don't.

School Spirit
While varsity sports might not be huge, Colby spirit is alive and well. Some people are apathetic, but rivalries with Bates and Bowdoin, as well as common feelings about Brown, can incite even the least spirited students to bouts of chanting. Many students feel that Colby's traditions, especially the Doghead St. Patrick's Day party, and the last day of class events, are being eliminated. These perceived injustices have led to some of the biggest displays of school spirit all year. Pretty much every car has a Colby sticker on it, and athletes love to wear their Colby gear. Students are proud of "Beer Die," and take offense when insults are leveled at the school. An article in Yale's newspaper describing Colby students as immature lushes prompted immediate outcry. The school spirit at Colby is not overwhelming or football-driven, but it is definitely present and palpable.

Traditions

The Miller Steps
The steps leading to Miller Library are a symbolic beginning and end to life at Colby. One of the first things new students do, after dumping all their stuff into their dorm rooms and meeting their roommate, is go to the steps with their parents to listen to a welcome to Colby speech. Commencement ceremonies also take place on the steps.

Champaign Toast
On the last day of classes, seniors gather on the Miller Steps (surprise, surprise) to toast the school. This sounds like a perfectly respectable and mature thing to do, until you realize that the seniors aren't toasting with glasses, they're toasting with multiple bottles. Waterville's liquor stores actually sell out of champagne in the days before the toast—many students end up going to Augusta. In the past, this toast has been followed by a swim in Johnson Pond, but this was forbidden two years ago.

Doghead
Doghead is a huge party that takes place the weekend closest to St. Patrick's Day. It's usually held at an off-campus house, and people wake up as early as 4 a.m. to start drinking. Recently, the police heard in advance about the party, and it ended up being cancelled, but the party moved on campus. Everyone started drinking before breakfast and partied all weekend.

Mr. Colby
This is an amazingly well-attended, beauty pageant featuring men rather than women. Mr. Colby is a great opportunity for the men of Colby to show off their assets (and sense of humor). Runners-up are crowned Mr. Bates and Mr. Bowdoin.

A cappella
As at many New England liberal arts schools, a cappella groups are well loved at Colby. We have six a cappella groups and they are all amazing. Shows and invites draw huge crowds.

Cafeteria Tray Sledding
Colby is situated on a big hill in the middle of Maine; so obviously, sledding is popular here. While people can get pretty creative about coming up with things to sled on, your college experience isn't complete until you've stolen a cafeteria tray and slid down Chapel Hill. Be careful—trays go really, really fast.

Loudness
The first and last weekend of each semester are called Loudness weekends. Bands perform and activities are planned. The first Loudness is especially great, because classes are just starting, and no one is too bogged down with homework yet. The end-of-semester Loudnesses typically feature stress-busting activities to help people get through finals.

Things I Wish I Knew Before Coming to Colby:
- Waterville is not a typical college town, and it's not too close to campus.
- Speaking of not too close to campus, the airport's an hour and a half away.
- It's totally not weird to talk to random people in the first week of classes—in fact, that's how you'll make the most new, and lasting, friendships.
- Freshmen get to have cars on campus.
- Two things that could be potentially nerdy but aren't are pearls and chem-free living.
- The work will be hard, but the parties will be hard, too.

Tips to Succeed at Colby:
- Don't be afraid of the upperclassmen—they're your most valuable resource.
- Don't be afraid of the professors—they're good resources, too.
- Go to office hours or after class study sessions.
- Read the *Digest*. Or, at least skim it.
- Wear your collar up.
- Don't puke in your first month.
- Work hard, play hard!

Finding a Job or Internship

Career Center Resources & Services
eRecruiting with Experience eRecuiting Network, Vault, eChoices, fellowship directory, Alumni director, career counseling

Workshops
Resume writing, cover letter writing, interviewing, summer jobs and career planning

Alumni Publications

Colby Magazine
The Colby Magazine is free to current students and alumi. It is published four times a year and is available online at *www.colby.edu/colby.mag*.

The Lowdown
ON FINDING A JOB OR INTERNSHIP

Career Services can help you with everything, from finding a summer job, to finding a career after college. We have no pre-med, pre-law, or business majors, but if you're looking into a future in those fields, Career Services tends to be very helpful. There's an extensive Career Services library with lots of books about lots of subjects, and the counselors and faculty tend to be more than willing to talk to the students. While they have services for freshmen and sophomores, they do tend to cater to the upperclassmen a bit more.

Famous Colby Alumni:
Doris Kearns Goodwin (Class of '64), Pulitzer Prize-winning author/historian.

Annie Proulx (Class of '57), Winner of the National Book Award and the Pulitzer Prize; author of *The Shipping News*.

Advice
eRecruiting is a great tool for finding a job or internship, especially for summer jobs. Even if it can't help you find the perfect employment, it can at least give you some fresh, new ideas. Start getting into the Career Services offices as a freshman. They'll send a few e-mails and things, but as a youngster, they won't pursue you too actively. Go to resume writing and interviewing workshops because they are ridiculously helpful.

The Best & Worst

The Ten BEST Things About Colby:

1. The professors are great
2. Everyone's friendly
3. There's something to do every weekend
4. It's really easy to get involved
5. Nine out of 10 people are hot!
6. Security is easygoing
7. Hefty Endowment
8. The campus is gorgeous
9. Differing opinions are respected
10. Liquor flows like water on the weekends

The Ten WORST Things About Colby:

1. Weather, weather, weather!
2. It's sometimes completely dead on campus
3. Cheap beer
4. The Jitney
5. Music at dances and concerts
6. No cities to be found
7. Small size leads to a vast rumor mill
8. Student apathy
9. Cliques and status symbols
10. Liquor flows like water on the weekends

Connecticut College

270 Mohegan Ave., New London, CT 06320-4196
www.concoll.edu   (860) 439-2000

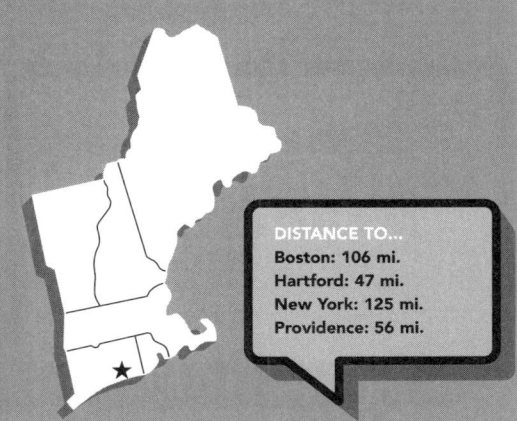

DISTANCE TO...
Boston: 106 mi.
Hartford: 47 mi.
New York: 125 mi.
Providence: 56 mi.

> "This is a great school for students who don't know what they want to major in."

Table of Contents

Academics	244
Local Atmosphere	246
Safety & Security	247
Computers	249
Facilities	250
Campus Dining	252
Off-Campus Dining	253
Campus Housing	255
Off-Campus Housing	256
Diversity	257
Guys & Girls	259
Athletics	260
Greek Life	262
Drug Scene	263
Campus Strictness	264
Overall Experience	265
The Inside Scoop	266
Finding a Job or Internship	267
The Best & Worst	268

Total Enrollment:
1,750

Acceptance Rate:
35%

Tuition:
$39,975

Top 10% of High School Class:
46%

SAT Range
Verbal	Math	Total
603 – 695	602 – 695	1205 – 1390

SAT Requirements
The SAT-I is optional. Students are required to either submit the results of any three SAT-II subject tests or the ACT.

Most Popular Majors:
11% Economics
10% English Language and Literature
10% Political Science and Government
10% Psychology
8% History

Students Also Applied To:*
Middlebury College, Skidmore College, Trinity College, Tufts University, Vassar College

*For more school info check out www.collegeprowler.com

College Prowler Report Card

Academics	B+
Local Atmosphere	C-
Safety & Security	A-
Computers	C
Facilities	B
Campus Dining	B+
Off-Campus Dining	B
Campus Housing	B+
Off-Campus Housing	D
Diversity	D
Guys	C+
Girls	A-
Athletics	B
Greek Life	N/A
Drug Scene	B-
Campus Strictness	B+

Academics

The Lowdown
ON ACADEMICS

Degrees Awarded:
Bachelor, Master

Full-time Faculty:
149

Faculty with Terminal Degree:
89%

Student-to-Faculty Ratio:
11:1

Average Course Load:
4 courses

Best Places to Study:
Library, arboretum,
your dorm's common room

Sample Academic Clubs:
Astronomy Club, Film Society, French Club

Undergraduate Schools:
There is only one school at Connecticut College—the college of liberal arts and sciences.

AP Test Score Requirements
Possible credit for scores of 4 or 5

IB Test Score Requirements
Possible credit for scores 5 or greater

Special Degree Options

As a liberal arts school, Conn wholeheartedly supports interdisciplinary studies and has several interdisciplinary majors, including medieval studies and neuroscience. In addition, it is fairly easy for students to design their own major or minor, as long as it meets with the faculty's approval. Examples of recent self-designed majors are meteorology and comparative European cultures.

One major that Conn lacks is engineering, but it makes up for it by offering a 3/2 engineering program with Boston University and Washington University in St. Louis. Students in this program spend three years at Connecticut College and two years at the other institution. After five years, the student is awarded a B.A. in physics from Conn, and a B.S. in engineering from the other institution.

Conn has four prestigious and exclusive Interdisciplinary Centers that award its members a certificate at graduation. Graduating from one involves taking courses based around a theme, performing a summer internship, and completing a final integrative project. The four centers are the Ammerman Center for Arts & Technology, the Goodwin-Niering Center for Conservation Biology and Environmental Studies, the Holleran Center for Community Action and Public Policy, and the Toor Cummings Center for International Studies and the Liberal Arts. Also, a certificate program in museum studies is offered through the art history department.

General Education Requirements

Students are required to take seven core general education (GE) classes in different areas. Unless you've tested out of an area through an AP test, there's no way out of taking a class in subjects you might absolutely despise. You can, however, cheat the system a little. Look for the classes that students half-derogatorily, half-lovingly call Math for Jocks or Chemistry for Poets—these classes are your easy way out of a requirement.

Did You Know?

Years ago, exam-bound students used to rub an oversized bust of Dante Aligheiri for good luck. Apparently, this was a fate worse than the Inferno for Dante, who mysteriously disappeared, only to turn up roughly 10 years later across campus. It soon vanished again, and was later found hiding in Cro's basement. Today, it resides in the CISLA office in Fanning hall, away from students' sticky fingers.

Conn has self-scheduled finals. This means that students choose from a list of available times and then take their final exams, unproctored. This helps relieve some (although certainly not all) of the stress toward the end of the semester.

Students Speak Out
ON ACADEMICS

"The professors at Conn each has his or her individual story. You'll take a class for a month and find out that your professor lived in New Sudan for six months and wrote about the behavioral patterns of native tribes."

Q "One English teacher likes to have free time, so we can share with him our take on current events and the craziness from the weekend before. Another teacher says the most profound things about simple literature. Another teacher started and ended class exactly on the times designated, and covered the exact materials that she set out to cover in the syllabus. **I'd say classes are interesting**."

Q "The majority of teachers are engaging and top-notch, but I have had some professors who seemed to care more about their own academic pursuits than teaching. The classes are interesting, but for a school that has **one of the highest tuition levels in the country**, I expect the best teachers."

Q "The professors at Conn are very knowledgeable, and they take a personal interest in their students from day one. **Some classes can be pretty boring**, especially intro levels and GEs, but overall, the classes are very interesting. It's all a matter of picking classes in areas that interest you."

The College Prowler Take
ON ACADEMICS

Often referred to as a "Little Ivy," Connecticut College has strong and innovative academic programs. Rather than follow a predetermined list of classes, students are encouraged to actively plan out their education at Conn. Some of the special options include designing a major, developing a concentration, participating in a certificate program, or writing an honors thesis. Every freshman is assigned a faculty advisor and a student advisor to assist with these decisions. Because of Conn's small size, there aren't many huge lecture hall-style classes. Students usually get to know the professors in their major(s) very well, which makes it easy to seek out help after class or fall into research and intern positions. Professors are clearly exuberant about the subjects they teach, and shy away from monotonous lectures in order to get students to participate in class. The assignments are challenging and usually involve a lot of writing.

The College Prowler™ Grade on
Academics: B+

A high Academics grade generally indicates that professors are knowledgeable, accessible, and genuinely interested in their students' welfare. Other determining factors include class size, how well professors communicate, and whether or not classes are engaging.

Local Atmosphere

Students Speak Out
ON LOCAL ATMOSPHERE

"New London is a great place for volunteer work, but students don't leave campus for anything else. There are a few really fun shops and cafés; they just aren't very accessible."

Q "New London is not a nice college town. There isn't much to do, and it's **not the safest place to be at night**. The Coast Guard Academy and Mitchell College are both in New London. The CGA is across the street and has a good relationship with Conn. There are some nice parks and beaches to visit in the area, and both Foxwoods and Mohegan Sun are within 20 minutes. There are also a fair amount of stores and restaurants, including a mall five minutes away. You need to look hard to find good places to go, though."

Q "Conn itself is very isolated. **It's pretty easy to get bored** if you can't get off campus at least once a week. Having a car, or knowing friends with cars, is a necessity to being content. I enjoyed the surrounding area. Downtown New London has some nice restaurants, and there are beaches in the area and lots of restaurants, bowling, ice-skating, roller-skating, the mall, other shopping, and Mystic."

Q "The city of New London is growing and prospering, but there is little interaction between the college and the city. The Coast Guard Academy is across the street, and cadets are on the college campus every weekend looking for drinks and girls to entertain them for the evening. There is no known interaction between Connecticut College and Mitchell College, a community college in New London. **There are a number of little restaurants, bars and clubs in New London**, some of which should be visited regularly while others you learn to stay away from, based on your own personal preference. The Roadhouse, a small bar downtown, has karaoke and is a popular spot for the students over 21. Downtown New London alone at night is not the place to be."

The Lowdown
ON LOCAL ATMOSPHERE

Region:
Northeast

City, State:
New London, Connecticut

Setting:
Small city, suburban

Distance from Hartford:
45 minutes

Distance from Providence:
1 hour

Distance from Boston:
2 hours

Points of Interest:
Lyman Allen Museum, United States Coast Guard Academy, New London Ledge Lighthouse, Ocean Beach, Harkness Memorial State Park, Mystic Pizza, Mystic Aquarium, Mystic Seaport, Tao House Museum, Foxwoods Casino, Mohega Sun Casino

City Websites:
http://ci.new-london.ct.us
www.newlondongazette.com
www.theday.com

Q "The town of New London is pretty dead at first glance. There are a few spots, but most of the entertainment is found on campus. There are a number of good restaurants in the surrounding areas. **Mystic is a great, quaint location**—as well as Ocean Beach—both 10 to 15 minutes away."

Q "New London is a great town; a lot more **culture and interesting things go on in the city** than students know about. I wish people would take more advantage of them. Waterford, Mystic, and other surrounding towns provide nice restaurants."

Safety & Security

The College Prowler Take
ON LOCAL ATMOSPHERE

The Lowdown
ON SAFETY & SECURITY

New London's claim to fame—its once booming whaling industry—won't make any students (aside from a few scrimshaw fans) rush to Conn. Nevertheless, New London does have a few draws. First, history buffs will appreciate the many historical homes, monuments, and museums nearby. Second, the city has all the goods that college students need, including a grocery store, a mall, bars, restaurants, movie theaters, and a Staples. After the errands are done, however, New London doesn't offer that much in the way of an exciting scene. The drawbacks to New London include safety issues at night and its isolation from campus. Other than students who venture into the city several times a week to do community service, there aren't that many students who consider investing much of their time in New London.

Number of Conn Police:
Full-time officers and dispatchers: 16
On-call officers: 6

Phone:
Emergencies: x1111
Non Emergencies: x2222

Campus Safety Hotline:
(860) 439-5200 (used to anonymously report criminal activities)

Health Center Office Hours:
Monday-Thursday, 8:30 a.m.-7 p.m.
Friday, 8:30 a.m.-5 p.m.
Appointments start at 9 a.m.

Safety Services:
Safewalk and night escorts on request, emergency phones, blue-lights

The College Prowler™ Grade on
Local Atmosphere: C-

A high Local Atmosphere grade indicates that the area surrounding campus is safe and scenic. Other factors include nearby attractions, proximity to other schools, and the town's attitude toward students.

Did You Know?

As part of a campus-wide effort to renounce a series of anonymously committed, racist acts on campus over the past few years, campus safety keeps a log of any bias incidents on Conn's intranet and immediately reports the situation and all actions taken to the campus community.

While on their rounds, campus safety officers find a ton of lost items. Everything from earrings to disks carrying that all-important term paper can be exhumed at the lost and found in campus safety's headquarters, Nicols House.

Students Speak Out
ON SAFETY & SECURITY

"Security is okay, but I wouldn't trust campus safety with my life. I feel safe and don't mind walking by myself to and from places at night."

Q "I think most students are more scared about campus safety breaking up parties than they are of intruders. As a woman, I really don't feel threatened walking around campus late at night. **Never once was I scared** that I would be in danger, and plus, because we're far away from downtown New London, the campus is isolated. No one ever comes up here."

Q "Often, students get to know and become friendly with individual campus safety officers. **There are very few emergency lights and phones** on campus, but there is no real need for them. Campus safety patrols at night and offers a ride service for students who do not feel comfortable walking across campus alone at night. I never felt uncomfortable walking across campus alone, at 3 a.m.."

Q "My experience with campus safety was really **the only bad experience I had at Conn**. They all seem to resent the students, and their obvious disdain for me made me feel more unsafe than the possibility of New Londoners coming on campus. They are never helpful and act put out whenever you need anything."

Q "Not much security is needed at Conn. People are free to enter the campus during the day, but only students, faculty, and staff can at night. The campus safety officers are **friendly and willing to help**."

Q "Generally, since Conn's campus is secluded from the rest of New London, it is **a safe place to be**. However, there are not enough campus safety officers patrolling at night, or enough emergency call-boxes. The lighting on campus is also very poor in some areas."

The College Prowler Take
ON SAFETY & SECURITY

Aside from a few isolated incidents of crime (usually perpetrated by New Londoners) and numerous student liquor referrals, Conn is a pretty safe and quiet school. Campus safety officers patrol around the clock and maintain a high profile on campus. The single biggest threat to safety on campus is that students always leave the entrances to their dorms propped open. Every so often, this leads to a completely unnecessary, and avoidable, breach in security. Fortunately, campus safety is vigilant and just a phone call away. The main paths and parking lots are sufficiently lit at night, but it never hurts to exercise caution when walking around campus in the wee hours of the morning.

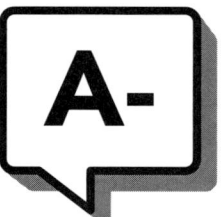

The College Prowler™ Grade on
Safety & Security: A-

A high grade in Safety & Security means that students generally feel safe, campus police are visible, blue-light phones and escort services are readily available, and safety precautions are not overly necessary.

Computers

Charge to Print?
Yes. Conn recently instituted this rule in order to save paper. Fortunately, the first 200 pages each semester are free.

Did You Know?
Camelweb, Conn's intranet, is the one-stop place to find up-to-date information on everything from the menus in the dining halls, to upcoming campus events.

The Lowdown
ON COMPUTERS

High-Speed Network?
Yes

Wireless Network?
Yes

Number of Labs:
5

Numbers of Computers:
355

24-Hour Labs:
None

Operating Systems:
PC, Mac, UNIX

Free Software:
Access, Adobe CS, Appleworks, Atajo, AudoCad LT, ChemDraw Pro, CodeWarrior IDE, CommonSpace, CricketGraph, DeltaGraph, Dreamweaver, EndNote, FileMaker Pro, Finale, Fireworks, Flash, Freelance Graphics, GoLive, HiLighter, HyperResearch, HyperStudio, Illustrator, Lotus Freelance Graphics, Macromedia suite, Mathematica, Metapop, Microsoft Access, NJ Star Chinese, NJWin CJK Multilingual Viewer, Pagemill, Photoshop, Psychism, Quark Xpress, RAMAS Metapop, SAS, S-Plus, SPSS

Students Speak Out
ON COMPUTERS

"The network is awful—half the time it doesn't work. The computer labs are always packed, not just during finals, and if you don't bring a computer, you won't be able to do work."

Q "The computer network isn't great. **Viruses take down the network wicked easily**. Computer labs aren't overcrowded every day, but it can often be difficult to find an available computer; especially around exam time. You should definitely bring your own computer."

Q "Although it's not necessary, **most people bring their own computers**. The labs are good for when you need to go to the library and buckle down and actually work! However, they sometimes can be crowded, especially on the dreaded Sunday nights."

Q "The network is good and works most of the time. During peak times, **labs are crowded**, but you can always find a computer to use; a personal computer is easiest, though."

Q "Definitely have your own computer in your room. During finals, the library gets crazy, so **it's nice to have a backup work place**. The computer network is the moodiest, most fickle part of campus, but I feel like we aren't any different from other colleges."

Facilities

Q "There are only a few computer labs [and] stations, all in the library, which are crowded during the evenings, midterms, and finals. At those times, it is sometimes impossible to find a free computer to work on. Definitely bring your own computer—a laptop, if possible—to work in your room, or any of the other places on campus. **The network gets better every year**, but there are still problems with it, especially the small e-mail server, which crashes with each instance of a new computer virus. For the most part, problems are fixed very quickly, but they are still a nuisance."

The College Prowler Take
ON COMPUTERS

The Lowdown
ON FACILITIES

Despite its best efforts, Conn is lacking in computer infrastructure. Internet brownouts are fairly common and can be devastating when you're in the middle of a research paper due the next day. When this happens, you can always head over to the library workstations, or one of five computer labs, but you'll find that many of your fellow students are doing the same. During high use times—usually 15 minutes before classes and several hours after dinner—the computer labs are packed. Although grumbles about the network frequently make their way into student conversations, the network runs smoothly most of the time.

Bowling on Campus?
No

Bar on Campus?
Cro-bar, Crosier Williams Student Center

Coffeehouse on Campus?
Coffee Grounds, first floor, Katharine Blunt House

Libraries:
Three

Student Center:
Crosier Williams Student Center

Athletic Center:
Christoffers Rowing/Training Complex, Dayton Arena, Dawley Field, Luce Field House, Lott Natatorium Silfen Track & Field Complex

Popular Places to Chill:
Oasis snack shop, Shain library first floor, Coffee Grounds, College Green, Harris

The College Prowler™ Grade on
Computers: C

A high grade in Computers designates that computer labs are available, the computer network is easily accessible, and the campus' computing technology is up-to-date.

Movie Theatre on Campus?

No. While there is no devoted space solely for showing films, there is a student-run film society, which uses a large projection screen in a lecture hall. Its members show second-run movies, as well as classics, on a projection screen in a lecture hall.

Favorite Things to Do

Conn students de-stress between classes by hanging out in Harris or heading down to the fitness center. In the afternoon, varsity, club, and intramural sports take the stage, and most students' attention, away from other activities. At night, there is usually a plethora of meetings and the ubiquitous "Dessert and Dialogue," an invitation for students to get together in a dorm's common room for a dialogue with a special guest moderator. Past subjects of these talks have ranged from ruminations on body image to dissections of Super Bowl commercials.

Students Speak Out
ON FACILITIES

"The library is nice, and the inter-college exchange system gives students access to even more resources. The athletic complex is too far away, and there isn't a good place for non-athletes to work out."

Q "The athletic complex is very large with a swimming pool, gym—this is too small and often overcrowded, however—track, hockey rink, and huge arena with over four basketball courts. There are also racquetball courts, and the Thames River is used for rowing and sailing. **The student center is a good size and the hub of the social scene.** People flock to it on Saturday nights for food, dancing, and Cro-Bar. Although the library is ugly on the outside and doesn't fit into the rest of the campus, it is sufficient and has four floors. Some of the classrooms are nicer than others, which also goes for the buildings."

Q "The athletic center is **small, overcrowded, and run-down**. It's also too hot; they need to put on the air conditioning more. The classrooms are kind of run-down, too. Most of them have really old, uncomfortable desks."

Q "Conn sometimes is **a little bit behind, technologically**. Its Internet connection has many problems, and people want to be able to use their ID cards in more places than just the snack shop and dining hall. The older dorms, while beautiful from the outside, are often troublesome on the inside."

Q "The athletic facilities are a little below par, but they are redoing the entire complex. The student center is great. You never feel crowded, there are always tons of events, and there is a snack shop and a bar. The library is fine; it's where you do your work. **The classrooms are always nice.** I'm an English major, so classrooms don't really matter to me. I'm sure classroom space is much more important if you're a bio major, or something."

The College Prowler Take
ON FACILITIES

The student center at Conn, known as Cro, is the heart of campus activity and the best place to look for students or professors between classes. Cro is versatile, and includes a bar, snack shop, mailroom, convenience store, dance studios, and meeting space among its facilities. Fortunately, the building is fairly new, and everything is well-kept. To see Connecticut College at its finest, one only needs to head towards South Campus. Sandwiched in between the South Campus dorms and several academic buildings is the College Green. From soccer matches and Harvestfest booths in the fall, to heated pickup games of ultimate Frisbee in the spring, College Green always hums with activity.

The College Prowler™ Grade on
Facilities: B

A high Facilities grade indicates that the campus is aesthetically pleasing and well-maintained; facilities are state-of-the-art, and libraries are exceptional. Other determining factors include the quality of both athletic and student centers and an abundance of things to do on campus.

Campus Dining

The Lowdown
ON CAMPUS DINING

24-Hour On-Campus Eating?
No

Student Favorites:
Harris Dining Hall

Meal Plan Average Cost:
Included in the comprehensive fee

Freshman Meal Plan Requirement?
Yes. All students are required to have the full meal plan (20 all-you-can-eat meals a week), unless they live off campus or in specialty housing. Even specialty housing residents must have reduced meal plans.

Students Speak Out
ON CAMPUS DINING

"We have innumerable options in the main dining hall, but the smaller ones are the best for the atmosphere. We also have an all-vegetarian dining hall—Freeman—that does make-your-own stir-fry twice a week."

Q "The dining halls are **the greatest things ever**! Every time my family comes up to visit, all they want to do is eat in Harris. I seriously believe CC has the best food of all my friends' colleges and all the colleges I visited senior year."

Q "The food in the dining halls is pretty good, especially compared with other schools. People complain about the food, but really, it is probably in the upper tier of dining halls for a college its size. The main dining hall, Harris, gives you the most options—it is what you make of it. Other dining halls have **vegetarian or alternative options**."

Q "The food is what you make of it. There are a lot of options, but even with the variety, **dining hall food gets boring and unappetizing after a time**. It's important to be creative. There are smaller dining halls to satisfy everyone's needs: there's a vegan [and] vegetarian hall that has a great make-your-own stir-fry night; a sandwich and salad hall open for lunch; an international hall where multi-language conversations are encouraged; and smaller dining halls serving the same food as the main dining hall in a smaller, more intimate environment."

Q "The food on campus is fair. There is usually something you can eat at each meal. Some meals are definitely better than others, however. The amount of choice is adequate, but more food options should be made available since eating at Conn becomes monotonous. The dinning halls are nice, and the staff is courteous. There are a few different dining halls that cater to people's tastes. There is **a vegetarian dining hall, a foreign language dining hall, and a deli**. Most people dine in Harris, the main dining hall on campus. Harris can get very crowded, so go to dinner early if you are going with a big group."

Q "Food from the dining halls is definitely not the reason students attend Conn. However, there is a plenitude of food from which to select and create your own meals, which is **the best bet for tastiness and healthiness**. Harris is the main dining hall and the place to find anyone and everyone on campus."

Did You Know?

Food scraps and unusable leftovers are collected and given to Secchiaroli & Sons, a local piggery, to be utilized as pig food.

Off-Campus Dining

The College Prowler Take
ON CAMPUS DINING

Connecticut College features centralized dining, which means that one dining hall, Harris Refectory, serves all-you-can-eat, buffet-style breakfast, lunch, and dinner to most of the campus. This near-monopoly allows Harris to stay open from 7:30 a.m. to 7:30 p.m., with only a 90-minute break in the afternoon to prepare for dinner. By and large, the food is much better than average college fare, although it probably will still make you miss Mom's cooking. Students are locked into a meal plan at Conn, so there's no reason not to take advantage of it. At least you'll have variety. If you have any special requests—even if it's just to request your favorite cereal—you can drop them a "Napkin Note," and you'll have a response in about two weeks. Of course, you can't always get what you want, but it's nice to know that your input is taken into consideration.

The Lowdown
ON OFF-CAMPUS DINING

24-Hour Eating: Rosie's Diner

Best Breakfast: Kitchen Little

Best Chinese: Golden Wok

Best Japanese: Little Tokyo, Zhang's

Best Healthy: Pat's Kountry Kitchen

Best Indian: A Taste of India

Best Italian: Paul's Pasta, Bravo Bravo, Olio Italian Restaurant

Best Mexican: Margaritas

Best Pizza: The Plum Tomato, Pizza Cucina, Alforno Brick Oven Ristorante

Best Thai: Bangkok City Thai Restaurant

Best Wings: Bank Street Roadhouse

Best Place to Take Your Parents: Bravo Bravo, Go Fish, Bee and Thistle Inn, Timothy's Restaurant

Late-Night, Half-Price Food Specials: Margaritas

The College Prowler™ Grade on
Campus Dining: B+

Our grade on Campus Dining addresses the quality of both school-owned dining halls and independent on-campus restaurants as well as the price, availability, and variety of food.

Students Speak Out
ON OFF-CAMPUS DINING

The College Prowler Take
ON OFF-CAMPUS DINING

{ "The restaurants are great, but they're hard to get to. I don't have a car, so I stay on campus."

Q "There are lots of great restaurants in the area. Bangkok City, Little Tokyo, and Northwest Indian restaurant are great ones in downtown New London. **Mystic has some cute places**, like the famous Mystic Pizza. Gridlock Grille on Colman Street has a good selection of lots of American things."

Q "Overall, the restaurants off campus are pretty good. Plum Tomato is **a very popular place for college students** to get great pizza and socialize with friends."

Q "**There are great restaurants in New London** and the surrounding areas. In Mystic, Zhang's and Margaritas are great. In New London, there's Bangkok City and Captain's Pizza."

Q "There are tons of good restaurants off campus: Zhang's if you like sushi and Japanese food, Margaritas if you're into Mexican, and **Go Fish for awesome seafood**. If your wallet is a little fuller, and you want something fancy, go for Buckley House, Bravo Bravo, and the Daniel Packer Inne."

Q "There are a good number of great restaurants. These include Margaritas, Paul's Pasta, Indian places, the Plum Tomato, Angelica's—a really cute café—**along with the usual** Chili's, Outback Steakhouse, and Applebee's."

From casual eateries to romantic tables for two, New London and the surrounding towns have some excellent restaurants. When students get tired of cafeteria food, they flock to local favorites like the Plum Tomato and Margaritas, or order MSG-laden noodles from Golden Wok. There are cuisines for every palette and budget in New London County, and no one escapes Conn without finding a new favorite restaurant. When parents show up to visit, there are plenty of good places to splurge (their treat, of course). If you're more into chains than the local restaurants, New London also offers a nice variety. Applebee's, Chili's, and Outback Steakhouse are popular student-favorites that give students a menu that they might be more familiar with. Still, though, you should try new things and at least give local places a chance.

The College Prowler™ Grade on
Off-Campus Dining: B

A high Off-Campus Dining grade implies that off-campus restaurants are affordable, accessible, and worth visiting. Other factors include the variety of cuisine and the availability of alternative options (vegetarian, vegan, Kosher, etc.).

Hungry? For a listing of all the best spots for local grub check out *Connecticut College—Off the Record*, available at *www.collegeprowler.com*.

Campus Housing

Did You Know?
Due to a recent change in Connecticut legislation, all of Conn's dorms are smoke-free.

Knowlton House served as an apartment for male visitors back when Connecticut College was an all-female school.

The Lowdown
ON CAMPUS HOUSING

Students Speak Out
ON CAMPUS HOUSING

Undergrads on Campus:
1,852

Number of Dormitories:
23

You Get:
Bed, desk and chair, dresser, mirror, closet or wardrobe, shade, cable, TV jack, Ethernet connection, phone, free campus and local phone calls

"All the dorms are pretty much the same. You will have the time of your life in any dorm, so long as you are with your friends. The people make the dorms great."

Number of University-Owned Apartments
Zero—although some dorms have the word "apartment" in their names, they are really just glorified dorms.

Available for Rent
Nothing. Connecticut College used to partner with a micro-fridge rental company before it went under.

Cleaning Service?
Public areas and bathrooms are cleaned once a day. Bathrooms are typically not cleaned on weekends, meaning that if you live in a party dorm, you could end up sidestepping vomit and beer cans on your way to brush your teeth. Students in co-ops and apartment-style living arrangements do not have access to the cleaning services.

"The dorms are really nice for the most part. I tend to like the older, homier ones, like Katharine, Blunt, Harkness, and Windham. The Plex dorms, like Morrisson and Park, are really clean and also come with air conditioning, but they can feel like a hospital. **Dorms to avoid include Lazrus**, which doesn't fit in with the other dorms at all—I can't see my parents paying forty grand a year for me to live there. Others include Marshall and Hamilton, which are in need of a renovation."

"The most popular dorms are either the newer dorms in the Plex, because they have air conditioning, better Internet access, and are generally nicer, or the Central Campus dorms, like Plant and Branford, because of their great location. Lazrus has the honor of the most-feared dorm. It has a kitchen and **a generally good community atmosphere**, but the rooms are boxes, and it is not very aesthetically pleasing. South Campus is also popular because of the social scene, although the location is furthest from the main dining hall."

Q "The dorms are great. Some of the bathrooms aren't that great. Really, there are no bad rooms, although **most people say to stay away from the old Plex dorms**. Even if you get one of those, you'll see that they have their charm, and a lot of people really like them."

Q "The majority of the dorms are really nice. New Plex is new, but somewhat hospital-like. **Old Plex is old, but tons of fun** and a great place to party. Besides that, all the dorms are really nice and very community-oriented, especially with people from all four grades living together in one place."

Off-Campus Housing

The College Prowler Take
ON CAMPUS HOUSING

The Lowdown
ON OFF-CAMPUS HOUSING

Connecticut College is a residential campus, with approximately 96 percent of its students living on campus. As such, there is a wide variety of living options. Dorms are located all over campus, and where you'll live depends a great deal on what area suits you best. North Campus features a community of six dorms; Central is at the heart of the campus, next to the library and student center; and South is right by College Green, Conn's most heavily-trafficked, and widely-used, open space. In addition, there is a lot of specialty housing at Conn. From substance-free housing in Blackstone, to the apartment-style setup of Abbey, you're sure to find an arrangement that feels like home.

Undergrads in Off-Campus Housing:
4%

Popular Areas:
Stonington, Norwich

Average Rent for a Studio Apartment:
$650/month

Average Rent for a 1BR Apartment:
$775/month

Average Rent for a 2BR Apartment:
$1,000/month

Best Time to Look for a Place:
Summer before first semester

The College Prowler™ Grade on
Campus Housing: B+

A high Campus Housing grade indicates that dorms are clean, well-maintained, and spacious. Other determining factors include variety of dorms, proximity to classes, and social atmosphere.

Students Speak Out
ON OFF-CAMPUS HOUSING

"Live on campus. That is the best way to meet people and not have to worry about transportation. Most everyone is on campus, so why would you want to be somewhere else?"

Q "Unfortunately, there really isn't any off-campus housing. That's one of the few problems with housing at Conn—**there aren't very many options for upperclassmen** who'd like to live in something other than a dorm room."

Q "There is **hardly any off-campus housing**. There's only River Ridge, and that's only offered to a few people. It's cut off from everyone."

Q "Because it's a summer vacation hot spot, I know a bunch of kids who **rented summer vacation homes for nothing during the school year**. In fact, many homeowners actually like having Conn students take care of their houses during the winter months. But you really don't have to live off campus."

The College Prowler Take
ON OFF-CAMPUS HOUSING

Connecticut College is definitely not a commuter school. With guaranteed housing for four years, and good odds of getting a single after freshman year, very few students even consider hunting through the local classifieds. Social life really revolves around on-campus events, and there are meetings, sporting events, and lectures at all different times of the day. It would be difficult for a student to be very involved in campus life while living off campus. The urge to stay on campus is reinforced by the fact that the immediate area offers no great housing options and can be a dangerous area in which to live.

The College Prowler™ Grade on
Off-Campus Housing: D

A high grade in Off-Campus Housing indicates that apartments are of high quality, close to campus, affordable, and easy to secure.

Diversity

The Lowdown
ON DIVERSITY

African American: 4%

Asian American: 3%

Hispanic: 4%

Native American: 0%

White: 80%

International: 9%

Out-of-State: 84%

Minority Clubs
It's impossible to miss Conn's minority groups; they constantly sponsor lectures, dialogues, dances, parties, and vigils. The current minority groups are ATLAS, CCASA, I-Pride, La Unidad, Umoja, and the USSC.

Most Popular Religions
Most students are not outwardly religious, but there is a sizable population of Christians. Catholic masses, Protestant worship services, and Baptist Bible study are held every week, as well as a Shabbat dinner for the Jewish community. Other religions include Hinduism, Islam, and Paganism.

Political Activity

The political temperature of Connecticut College is decidedly liberal, but many students are apathetic and apolitical. The most active political groups are the College Democrats, the College Republicans, and the outspoken CC LEFT.

Gay Tolerance

The campus is very accepting of all sexual orientations and transgender and questioning students. A student group called Sexual Orientations United for Liberation (SOUL) acts as a supporting group for its members.

Economic Status

Conn is a very expensive school, so most students come from well-to-do backgrounds. Some of the students drive nicer cars than the faculty.

Students Speak Out
ON DIVERSITY

{ "We need to keep working on being a better place for students of color, not just working at getting more of them on campus."

"Diversity is **a big issue on our campus**. I suppose there could be more diversity, but this could happen best if students integrated more, instead of choosing to separate themselves and exclude white students."

"Ninety percent of the students are **white, upper-middle-class, and rich**. Ten percent fit in other categories, although there has been a recent push for a more diverse campus."

"It's diverse but not overly diverse. There's a huge population of one very specific type of person: **preppy, wealthy, snobby, white people**. But, if you look deeper, there's a fairly large, international student population. They are very interesting and intelligent people. I had a great time meeting international students at Conn."

"The campus could be more diverse. The typical student is **WASPy but friendly**. Look out for preppy, rich, white kids in nice cars. Still, the campus is diversifying, and students do intermingle with those different than them. It is not a divided school in terms of friend groups."

The College Prowler Take
ON DIVERSITY

Diversity is difficult to measure at Connecticut College. While the school can't boast a high percentage of non-white students like some of its peer institutions, the spirit of diversity is at the heart of the Conn experience. There are dialogues, lectures, and presentations on topics ranging from affirmative action, to white privilege, to the experience of interracial dating on campus. The cultural groups are completely inclusive in their memberships and are strong forces on campus. There is even talk of including a diversity class in the general education requirements, which would require students to take a class about another culture before they graduate. Simply put, Conn values diversity and is aware of the importance of race and culture in students' education.

The College Prowler™ Grade on
Diversity: D

A high grade in Diversity indicates that ethnic minorities and international students have a notable presence on campus and that students of different economic backgrounds, religious beliefs, and sexual preferences are well-represented.

Guys & Girls

Hookups or Relationships?
Hookups abound at Conn. If you're looking for them, all you need to do is to stumble to a Cro dance after the liquor starts flowing. An influx of Coast Guard Cadets looking for some action increases your chances. Of course, it is possible to start lasting relationships at Conn. Almost every month *CC: Magazine* brings news of two Conn graduates who have decided to tie the knot. It would seem that in the wild, Camels mate for life.

Students Speak Out
ON GUYS & GIRLS

The Lowdown
ON GUYS & GIRLS

Women Undergrads: 60%

Men Undergrads: 40%

Birth Control Available?
Yes. A wide range of contraceptives, including the morning-after pill and contraceptive counseling are available in the Health Services building. Free condoms are available in the lobby, or by request through the mail.

Social Scene
Most students are outgoing and like to spend a good deal of time away from their dorm. The real problem with Conn's smallish social scene is that it can get cliquey, real fast. When students get bored of the repetitive dances at Cro, they tend to go out less and meet fewer people, until most weekends are spent with the same friends at the same parties. This is compounded by the student body's general reluctance to try new things or fully engage themselves in the wide spectrum of social events offered by the SAC.

Dress Code
There is no escaping the fact that Conn is a preppy school. At times, it feels like J.Crew and Abercrombie & Fitch are the school's uniform.

"The guys are a bit small and skinny, overall, but there are more nice guys than hot guys. The girls are hot, and they work at it."

"There are definitely more girls than guys on campus—it's about a 60 to 40 ratio. The guys are **either rich jerks or nice dorks**, but sometimes you can find good ones. The girls are good-looking, and a good amount dress from a Gap or J.Crew catalog."

"The guys are not so hot and not so tall. The girls are skinny and attractive. Just **your average New England NESCAC crowd**. We have a good mix, so you can find 'your crowd' at CC without looking too hard. It feels just like high school, but on a college campus."

"**The girls are either very hot or very not.** There are plenty of cool guys around; it's all about finding your little group of friends that you fit in with."

"Everyone is gorgeous. Oh, I'm sorry, I mean the girls are. The unfortunate cycle that happens is that the ratio of every hot guy to every hot girl is about one to six. This means the hot guys become egomaniacs. **Conn girls are some of the hottest around**. Unfortunately, with beauty sometimes comes shallowness, cockiness, and snobbery."

"I think that there are **more good-looking girls than guys**. This may be because I have a boyfriend already, so I'm not looking at any boys in particular."

The College Prowler Take
ON GUYS & GIRLS

Maybe it's Connecticut College's history as a former all-girl's school, or maybe just pure chance, but the ratio of guys to girls is about 40 to 60. Translation: guys have good odds here for a love connection, or at least a hookup. More often than not, Conn students aren't looking for long-term relationships, but serious relationships can develop from random hookups. Dances at Cro provide more than ample opportunity for both sexes to find a one-night fling or potential hookup buddy. If you like to take it slow in relationships, however, Conn may not be the place for you. Its small size and plentiful, single rooms could effectively make you roommates with your new boyfriend/girlfriend before you know it.

The College Prowler™ Grade on
Guys: C+

A high grade for Guys indicates that the male population on campus is attractive, smart, friendly, and engaging, and that the school has a decent ratio of guys to girls.

The College Prowler™ Grade on
Girls: A-

A high grade for Girls not only implies that the women on campus are attractive, smart, friendly, and engaging, but also that there is a fair ratio of girls to guys.

Athletics

The Lowdown
ON ATHLETICS

Varsity Teams:
Basketball
Crew
Cross Country
Field Hockey
Ice Hockey
Indoor Track & Field
Lacrosse
Outdoor Track & Field
Sailing
Soccer
Squash
Swimming & Diving
Tennis
Volleyball
Water Polo
Sailing

Club Sports:
Badminton
Baseball
Cricket
Equestrian
Golf
Hockey (Men's and Women's)
Lacrosse (Men's and Women's)
Martial Arts
Mountain Biking
Rugby (Women's)
Ski Team
Snowboard and Ski Club
Soccer (Men's and Women's)
Softball
Synchronized Ice Skating
Ultimate Frisbee Team
Water Polo

Intramurals:
Basketball (Three-on-Three)
Coed Beach Volleyball (Two-on-Two and Six-on-Six)
Flag Football
Floor Hockey
Racquetball
Six-a-side Soccer
Softball
Squash
Team Tennis
Coed Volleyball

Athletic Division:
Sailing and Water Polo: Division I, all other sports: Division III

Conference:
NESCAC (New England Small College Athletic Conference), Collegiate Water Polo Association

School Mascot:
Camel

Getting Tickets
If you want to root on the Camels at home, just show up at a game. Sporting events at Conn are typically under-attended, so tickets aren't necessary.

Most Popular Sports
The soccer teams use College Green as their homefield, which is great real estate for drawing spectators from the nearby South Campus dorms. Even on a rainy day, students can catch the game from their windows. Crew is a popular sport in the fall, but many rowers drop out in the spring due to the time and dedication the sport demands.

Students Speak Out
ON ATHLETICS

"Because the student body isn't very big, a lot of students participate in varsity and/or intramural sports. Our varsity teams are all right, and the intramural sports are pretty fun and change every few weeks."

Q "Intramural sports are bigger than varsity. **Lots of people play intramurals**. Since it's Division III, athletic events aren't that well-attended. The most successful sports are water sports."

Q "Most students play a varsity or intramural sport. However, spectator attendance at games is, generally, fairly low. **We have no football team**. However, sports are an important component of Conn's culture."

Q "Varsity sports are big, but they're not overwhelming. People go to the games but aren't obsessive. **Intramurals and club sports are huge**, especially ultimate Frisbee and women's rugby."

Q "Varsity hockey, lacrosse, and soccer are sports that students watch. **A lot participate** in intramurals, most specifically soccer, floor hockey, ice hockey, and broom ball."

The College Prowler Take
ON ATHLETICS

Even though Conn is a Division III school, athletics are vital to campus life. Once afternoon classes finish up, it seems like the whole school suits up for practice, or gets ready for a workout. Conn competes in the NESCAC (New England Small College Athletic Conference) against a difficult roster of opponents, featuring the likes of Colby and Trinity. The Camels typically don't get a lot of fan support at home, which is a shame, because all sporting events are free and easily accessible. Varsity sports steal the headlines in the *College Voice*, but one could argue that intramural and club sports are the real backbone of athletics at Conn.

The College Prowler™ Grade on
Athletics: B

A high grade in Athletics indicates that students have school spirit, that sports programs are respected, that games are well-attended, and that intramurals are a prominent part of student life.

Greek Life

"It would be nice to have a more actively-planned social scene, but the lack of Greeks allows students to intermingle much more on the same playing field, with no presumptions. The school is so small that **Greek life would be silly**. It works well the way it is."

Did You Know?

Connecticut College has a study abroad program called SATA Greece, which sends a group of students and a professor to study in Athens for a semester. That's about as Greek as the school gets.

The Lowdown
ON GREEK LIFE

Number of Fraternities: 0

Number of Sororities: 0

Students Speak Out
ON GREEK LIFE

"I love that we don't have Greek life. It makes socializing so much easier, and it also eliminates the stereotypical frat boy or sorority sister."

"**Who needs frats** when you have sports teams? A lot of our kegs and activities relate to clubs and sports on campus. That makes our party life so much more inclusive and fun."

"One of the reasons I came to Conn was because it doesn't have Greek life. You could argue that it helps people make friends, but I think **Greek life increases irresponsible drinking** and intolerance of others."

"I chose this place because it didn't have frats. **Hockey and lacrosse teams try to act like frats**, but, thankfully, they're not given housing for it. Some girls act like sorority girls."

The College Prowler Take
ON GREEK LIFE

Don't come to Connecticut College looking for "Animal House." Conn is simply too small to support a Greek system. In addition, Conn students typically don't fit the frat brother/sorority sister mold. Of course, there are trade-offs to a ban on Greek life. On the positive side, students feel that the social scene is more inclusive without it. The school puts on concerts and dances every week, which usually draw a sizable crowd of drunken students looking for a good time. As students get older, they adopt a "been there, done that," attitude toward the school-sponsored, costume parties and luaus. A Greek system on campus would give students another alternative on weekend nights. Keg parties hosted by sports teams and a cappella groups attempt to fill this void with varying levels of success.

The College Prowler™ Grade on
Greek Life: N/A

A high grade in Greek Life indicates that sororities and fraternities are not only present, but also active on campus. Other determining factors include the variety of houses available and the respect the Greek community receives from the rest of the campus.

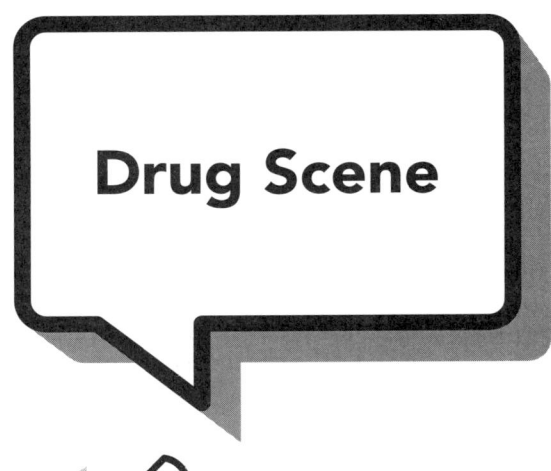

Drug Scene

Q "Drinking is a significant part of our social life. There are not a ton of drugs coming into Conn, but it's **not hard to find marijuana, coke, and maybe 'shrooms**."

Q "**Pot is widely used**, but that's about it for the vast majority of students."

Q "Eh, a lot of pot—like every other campus. Booze, of course. **Students hit up pills to keep themselves awake** during crunch time, but nothing more serious than that."

Q "Drugs of all sorts are popular. Smoking is the most popular pastime. There is no pressure; **people are chill**, and drugs are not an issue."

The Lowdown
ON DRUG SCENE

Liquor-Related Referrals: 316

Liquor-Related Arrests: 0

Drug-Related Referrals: 32

Drug-Related Arrests: 0

Most Prevalent Drugs on Campus:
Caffeine, alcohol, marijuana, Ritalin

Student Counseling Services
Phone: (860) 439-4587
Services: Free and confidential evaluation, individual and group counseling, crisis intervention services, outreach and consultation to the college community, referral to off-campus clinicians for specialized and/or intensive treatment

The College Prowler Take
ON DRUG SCENE

Without a doubt, Conn's poison of choice is alcohol. Students hit the bottle pretty hard on Thursdays and Saturdays, and the bottle hits back, necessitating a full day to nurse hangovers from each bacchanalian night. Pot is also available on campus and widely-used, but students who get high are far more discrete. In fact, if you're not seeking out people to smoke up with, the only encounter with pot you're likely to have is the occasional telltale scent emanating from some stoner's room. Harder drugs are far less visible and less popular, but they can be acquired. All-in-all, if alcohol is discounted, Conn has a minor drug scene, but it's really not that visible in the day-to-day goings on of the campus.

Students Speaks Out
ON DRUG SCENE

"Drugs never seemed to be an enormous problem or anything. I, personally, hardly ever see people doing drugs."

The College Prowler™ Grade on
Drug Scene: B-

A high grade on Drug Scene indicates that drugs are not a noticeable part of campus life; drug use is not visible, and no pressure to use them seems to exist.

Campus Strictness

The Lowdown
ON CAMPUS STRICTNESS

What Are You Most Likely to Get Caught Doing on Campus?
Parking illegally; underage drinking; stealing from the library; breaking quiet hours in the dorms; having candles and incense sticks in your dorm; smoking pot; running around on rooftops of buildings; sneaking into a dining hall without an ID; running stop signs; cheating on an exam or plaigerizing

Students Speak Out
ON CAMPUS STRICTNESS

"**If you are somewhat quiet and discreet about your activities at night, then you are fine. It's only when you go out of control, or annoy other people, that you really get in trouble.**"

Q "The campus police are not particularly strict about drugs and drinking. **They give you many warnings** before you get in trouble. This is because they are too lazy to properly do their jobs. Conn has strict rules about drugs and alcohol, but they aren't properly enforced."

Q "The main thing the campus police are worried about is safety, so they pretty much leave you alone. But, **they also will randomly enforce the rules**, which is kind of annoying."

Q "I've never heard any complaints about campus safety confiscating drugs, other than one or two stories about marijuana and smoking paraphernalia. **Underage students will usually have their drinks confiscated** and will be written up to be brought to 'trial' in front of the student-run Judiciary Board [or J-Board], where punishments are doled out based on the severity of the actions."

Q "There is a bar on campus for of-age students to safely drink without the risk of having to drive back to campus. **Kegs and other alcohol parties are hosted every weekend**, but there are strict guidelines surrounding those—who can throw a party, how much alcohol can be purchased, how many non-alcoholic drinks must be purchased, etc.—and there is a course (KEG 101) that of-age students must take before they can throw a party in a public area and serve alcohol."

Q "Recently, **campus safety has been very strict with drinking**, but that has more or less stopped. They found if they allow kegs, and stay a little laid-back, that students are less likely to do other recreational drugs, binge drink with hard alcohol in their rooms before going out, or leave campus and find themselves in even more dangerous situations, like drinking and driving. In order to help this issue last year they made an 'alcohol task force,' made up of both students and faculty to make drinking safer on campus."

Q "The level of strictness depends on which campus security officer catches you. **They just want you to be safe**. Some of them are complete jerks and treat us like babies that cannot be responsible, and others are really cool about drinking and partying. It really depends, but they are usually fair."

The College Prowler Take
ON CAMPUS STRICTNESS

Conn students love a good party, and it's no secret to campus safety (or anyone else) that underage drinking is par for the course on a typical Thursday, Friday, or Saturday night. Fortunately, campus safety generally will not hassle students who are drinking responsibly. They will, however, put the kibosh on excessively raucous parties and parties that spill out into the halls of dorms. If you are cooperative with them, the campus safety officers will let you get away with a warning nine times out of 10 (although they might make you pour out your screwdriver).

The College Prowler™ Grade on
Campus Strictness: B+

A high Campus Strictness grade implies an overall lenient atmosphere; police and RAs are fairly tolerant, and the administration's rules are flexible.

Overall Experience

Students Speak Out
ON OVERALL EXPERIENCE

"**I don't really fit in at Conn, but I know so many kids that love it more than anything. I think I would have been happier at a bigger school.**"

Q "I loved my time at Conn and had a great time while I was there. Throughout my four years, I made many friends with whom I am still in touch, and professors whom I will always talk to and update on my post-Conn life. I never wished I had gone anywhere else, but I did take advantage of studying abroad for a semester and would recommend doing so to everyone. Conn is a bubble on a hill, and it is very important for one to experience the outside world. Your time at Conn is what you make it out to be—if you don't do anything, you will be miserable. But if you find people, clubs, and organizations that you enjoy, **you will have an unbelievable experience**."

Q "I have to say that I was lucky enough to find my core group of friends during freshman year. **It was a fun four years that I'll never forget**. If I could have gone to Yale or Harvard, speaking from a career standpoint, I wouldn't have come here. However, CC was good to me, and I wish I could do it all over again."

Q "Sometimes **I wish I had gone to a bigger school** in a bigger city, but, on the whole, there's no place I'd rather be than Conn College."

Q "I love it. I would never want to be anywhere else. Once you find your group of friends, you are set. **It really is a great place to learn**. The weather keeps you on your toes. The teachers either make you laugh or push you really hard. The sports are fun and up-and-coming. The kegs keep you happy, the food keeps you full. Who wouldn't want all that?"

The College Prowler Take
ON OVERALL EXPERIENCE

Overall, students enjoy their experience at Conn. Some of the reasons cited include the amazing professors, strong academic programs, small size of the school, and the beautiful campus. This is a great school for students who don't know what they want to major in. Conn's general education requirements make it mandatory to take a variety of courses, and faculty are always available to advise students. Because of this, many come to Conn a *tabula rasa*, unsure of what to study, and leave as knowledgeable practitioners in a field that they genuinely enjoy. The most common complaint among students who don't like Conn is its small size. Because of this, it's important to visit overnight, or at least take a tour of campus.

Despite the restricted social scene, most students find a core group of friends and have an unforgettable four years. Besides, with a willingness to try new things, students should never be bored on campus. There are so many opportunities to get involved in athletics, music, academics, and student organizations that everyone should be able to find something that he or she enjoys. The Conn experience can be as much, or as little, as you make of it. It's all up to you.

The Inside Scoop

The Lowdown
ON THE INSIDE SCOOP

School Spirit
School spirit certainly isn't always rampant at Conn, but it does occasionally bubble to the surface. For example, students can be spotted wearing shirts supporting Conn's football team and it's almost 100-year undefeated streak. The mere fact that Conn has never had a football team does nothing to damper the students' zeal. Another great place to observe school spirit is in the opening ritual of Camelympics, an annual competition between dorms. Conn students go to dinner wearing team uniforms and sit with their dorms. Each team then tries to psyche the others out by hurling taunts, and the occasional food item, across the cafeteria.

Traditions
Alternative Highs Month

In an effort to curb drug use and underage drinking, the Student Activities Committee created Alternative Highs Month, a series of daily events in April. At each substance-free event, students collect raffle tickets for a drawing at the end of the month. Past prizes have included a skydiving lesson and a white water rafting trip.

Camel Cabaret

Camel Cabaret is Conn's spring talent show. Each dorm sends one act and is allowed to include their adopted faculty and staff. A panel of faculty, student, and staff judges award cash prizes and bragging rights to the top competitors.

Festivus

Like its assumed *Seinfeld* namesake, Festivus is a nondenominational holiday in December for "the rest of us" (although sadly there is no Festivus Pole). Students start the night by exchanging gifts with their "Secret Snowflakes" at a dorm party, then dress up and head over to Cro, which is, quite possibly, the largest venue ever to celebrate Festivus. Typical events include a dance and live music. Each year, students get to take home personalized souvenirs, like snow globes or ornaments with their pictures in them.

Senior Week

Senior Week marks the culmination of four challenging and (hopefully) successful years at Connecticut College. Themed parties, some on campus and some off, are thrown every night, and there are various trips and functions during the day. A one-time payment ($100 for past Senior Weeks) is necessary to take part in the festivities, but the memories are well worth it.

Things I Wish I Knew Before Coming to Connecticut College:

- COOP (Conn's Outdoor Orientation Program) is worth considering if you're into outdoorsy activities. You'll make some friends before school even starts.
- Orientation might seem silly and pointless, but it's a great way to meet people and make first impressions.
- The official Connecticut College mascot has one hump—don't buy camel dolls/decorations with two!
- Taking time to seriously plan out the layout of your room with your roommate(s) is not just a girl thing. Do it.
- Unless you know exactly what you want to major in, take four classes your first semester that have nothing to do with one another. You might find something you love.
- Connecticut College is a really preppy school.
- Many students would rather complain about the social life than try doing something different.
- Depending on how involved you are, the school can either seem like the hub of the universe or a desert island.

Finding a Job or Internship

The Lowdown
ON FINDING A JOB OR INTERNSHIP

Making the transition from the familiar surroundings of Connecticut College to the alien "real world" can be daunting. Luckily, the CELS (Career Enhancing Life Skills) office is available to help from the moment you first arrive on campus.

The CELS office offers a four-year program that takes students from the first tentative steps of planning a career, to senior year job-search assistance. Each semester, students are required to attend professional development seminars that teach job search techniques, networking skills, and resume formatting. The highlight of the program is a stipend of $3,000 to fund any internship of each student's choice between the summer of his junior and senior year. During senior year, students must complete a short, integrative paper summarizing what they have learned throughout the program.

Sign up for the program, even if you know exactly what you want to do with your life. It's the easiest way on campus to get a funded internship. Then, make sure you attend all the seminars. Sure, they're a pain, but if you don't go, the school will take away your funding. It's best not to burn bridges. You can always drop out of the program, but if you miss a seminar or other requirement, you probably won't be allowed back in. Plus, the ePortfolio is something you'll have, even after you graduate, and is a handy tool for writing resumes.

The Best & Worst

The Ten BEST Things About CC:

1. Outstanding professors
2. Student-faculty research opportunities
3. Honor Code/self-scheduled final exams
4. Single rooms (usually) after freshman year
5. Floralia
6. Funded summer internship available through various programs
7. The arboretum
8. Simple meal plan with good food
9. Campus-wide emphasis on conservation and ecology
10. Shared governance

The Ten WORST Things About CC:

1. Insularity
2. Restricted and predictable social scene
3. Internet brownouts
4. Not very diverse
5. Lack of public transportation
6. Poor off-campus housing options
7. Apolitical students
8. The overactive student rumor mill
9. Arctic-like winds from Long Island Sound
10. Freshman registration

Middlebury College

Middlebury, VT 05753
www.middlebury.edu   (802) 443-3000

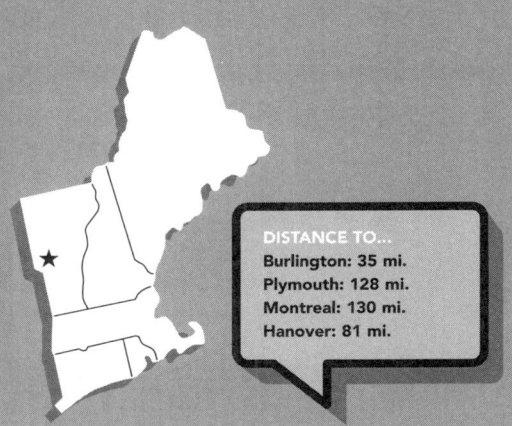

DISTANCE TO...
Burlington: 35 mi.
Plymouth: 128 mi.
Montreal: 130 mi.
Hanover: 81 mi.

"Coming to Middlebury is a throwback to the antiquated, yet charming, days of 1920s brick storefronts."

Total Enrollment:
2,399
Acceptance:
23%
Tuition:
$40,400
Top 10% of High School Class:
77%
SAT Range
Verbal	Math	Total
690 – 750	680 – 740	1370 – 1490

ACT Range
Verbal	Math	Total
N/A	N/A	28-32

SAT II Requirements
Writing, one quantitative science (Math, Chemistry, or Physics), and one additional test selected by the applicant.

Most Popular Majors:
13% Economics
7% English Language and Literature/Letters
6% International Relations and Affairs; Psychology; Political Science and Government

Students Also Applied To:*
Darmouth College, Williams College, Amherst College, Brown University, Bowdoin College
*For more school info check out www.collegeprowler.com

Table of Contents

Academics	270
Local Atmosphere	272
Safety & Security	274
Computers	275
Facilities	277
Campus Dining	279
Off-Campus Dining	280
Campus Housing	282
Off-Campus Housing	284
Diversity	286
Guys & Girls	287
Athletics	289
Greek Life	291
Drug Scene	293
Campus Strictness	294
Overall Experience	296
The Inside Scoop	297
Finding a Job or Internship	299
The Best & Worst	299

College Prowler Report Card

Academics	A
Local Atmosphere	C+
Safety & Security	A-
Computers	B+
Facilities	A
Campus Dining	A-
Off-Campus Dining	B-
Campus Housing	B+
Off-Campus Housing	D+
Diversity	D
Guys	B+
Girls	A-
Athletics	B+
Greek Life	N/A
Drug Scene	B
Campus Strictness	B+

Academics

The Lowdown
ON ACADEMICS

IB Test Score Requirements
Students who have completed the full IB Diploma with a total of 36 or more points, including at least three higher-level grades of six or seven, are eligible for sophomore standing. Students having fewer than 36 points, or fewer than three scores of six or higher, may receive two course credits for each higher-level examination passed with a score of six or seven. No credit is awarded for standard level exams.

Best Places to Study
Great Hall in Bicentennial Hall, lounges at ends of Bicentennial Hall corridors, Grill, Juice Bar, Battell Beach, deck outside Rehearsals Café, Ross Commons Lounge

Sample Academic Clubs
French Club, Geology Club, Middlebury College Speech and Debate Union, Pre-Med Society, Philomathesian Club, Psychology Club

Degrees Awarded:
Bachelor, Master, Doctorate

Undergraduate Schools:
Liberal Arts

Full-time Faculty:
98%

Faculty with Terminal Degree:
97%

Student-to-Faculty Ratio:
11:1

Average Course Load:
4 courses/term

Special Degree Options:
Joint-Major, Design-Your-Own Major, Special Focus-Related Subject, Pre-Medical Program

AP Test Score Requirements:
Possible credit for scores of 4 or 5 (3 for AB or BC Calculus)

Did You Know?
MiddKid.com, a local student site, offers online course evaluations. You can use this site to reference classes you're thinking of taking, so you can see how other students have rated the teacher and material. Check out *www.middkid.com/eval* for more information.

The first black graduate of any United States college was Alexander Twilight, who received his diploma from Middlebury in 1823. Twilight Hall was renovated and named after him in 1986.

Students Speak Out
ON ACADEMICS

"The teachers are laid-back, and all have projects and research of their own. They make class fun by talking about their research, using real-life examples, and bringing in interesting, and often famous, speakers."

Q "There are good and bad teachers at every school, but I've found that the overwhelming majority of my professors have been fantastic and are ones that I want to work with over and over again. **The classes are a mixed bunch like the teachers**, but in most cases, if you are choosing a class that sounds really interesting to you, it will live up to your expectations."

Q "Middlebury is widely recognized for having some of the most engaging professors and class discussions. Most Middlebury professors present even the most mundane class material in a way that promotes **active, involved, and thought-provoking discussions**."

Q "The teachers are generally **well-regarded in their fields**, and class sizes are small. Not all courses are equally engaging, however. I tend to avoid the introductory courses and go straight to intermediate or upper-level classes."

Q "I find the professors and the teaching to be excellent. **Classes are small**, and the professors are just that—professors, not teaching assistants. For the most part, the faculty is very responsive, though some of the older professors still do not use e-mail. Almost all are very interested in getting to know and work with me. I have been satisfied with all but one of my classes, as they are all very interesting and engaging. I noticed this when comparing Middlebury's classes to those of the school abroad I studied at."

Q "The professors are very **accomplished, but also very approachable**. They really take an interest in their students. I've had several professors invite the class over to his or her house for a meal and an informal discussion. I also find my classes interesting."

The College Prowler Take
ON ACADEMICS

The professors at Middlebury College are incredibly intelligent people—sometimes too intelligent for their own flowering egos. Some are quirky, most have led extremely interesting lives, all are published, and a few cloud their accomplishments with preening tales of Harvard Law School and the RAND Think Tank. Due to the fact that they have led such lofty academic lives, however, they know all the right people. As a result, students often times have the occasion to listen to renowned scholars, poets, politicians, and scientists from home and abroad. Don't get the wrong idea, though—most professors don't spend the entire time preaching from the soapbox in medium- to small-sized classes, so be prepared to participate in discussion. The sooner you embrace the scholarly hubris, the better.

The primary reason that most students come to Middlebury is for the academics. Although introductory classes tend to be a bit overcrowded, this is cured quickly into your college career. Even in the biggest classes, your professors are approachable. At Middlebury, you'll find economics professors who have led intriguing lives. Discovering that your math professor used to be a Latin American pop star is not an uncommon event—some dive into extraordinary pursuits simply to add flavor to their credentials. You will be disappointed, however, if you think you'll have a rich social life, especially on the weekdays. All that will be blossoming on your calendar from Monday to Friday will be work, work, and harder work.

The College Prowler™ Grade on
Academics: A

A high Academics grade generally indicates that professors are knowledgeable, accessible, and genuinely interested in their students' welfare. Other determining factors include class size, how well professors communicate, and whether or not classes are engaging.

Local Atmosphere

Did You Know?

Want to find out what's going on around Middlebury? Check out www.middlebury.edu/calendars/ for events and calendars aimed at everything from this week to the whole year.

The Lowdown
ON LOCAL ATMOSPHERE

Region:
Northeast

City, State:
Middlebury, Vermont

Setting:
Small town

Distance from Burlington:
40 minutes

Distance from Boston:
3.5 hours

Distance from New York:
5 hours

Points of Interest:
Ben and Jerry's Factory (Burlington), Shelburne Museum (Shelburne), Snow Bowl (Middlebury College Ski Mountain), Breadloaf (College Cross-Country Ski Area and Mountain Campus, Home of the Breadloaf School of English and the Breadloaf Writers Conference)

City Websites:
www.vtliving.com/towns/middlebury, www.city-data.com/city/Middlebury-Vermont.html, www.middlebury.govoffice.com/

Major Sports Teams:
None

Students Speak Out
ON LOCAL ATMOSPHERE

{ **"What Middlebury lacks in entertainment and culture, it makes up for in coziness and charm."**

Q "This is very much a 'college town,' in every sense of the word—**there is very little here other than the college**, a movie theater, some small restaurants, and stores, that mostly catering to the college community. UVM [University of Vermont] is in Burlington, but I've found that the social scenes rarely overlap. Try to stay away from the freezing cold weather. In terms of stuff to visit, the Ben and Jerry's factory is always a lot of fun because you get free samples, and the Vermont Teddy Bear Company can be entertaining."

Q "Middlebury is a quaint, little, New England town. I'm from a big city, and I think it's just adorable. There are no other colleges in town. **The main street is lined with little gift shops**. I always enjoy an occasional walk into town."

Q "**The town of Middlebury is adorable, but it's pretty dead**. The closest university is 45 minutes away, as is the closest city. Definitely stay away from Angela's Pub on weeknights, unless you're looking for a fight, but check out the bar at Two Brothers Tavern for awesome, reasonably-priced food, and a fun atmosphere often dressed up with live music."

Q "Middlebury [College] maintains positive relations with the town, and the two exist symbiotically, as the college employs a very large percentage of the town's population. **A large proportion of hockey game spectators are residents of the town**, and between plays at a recent NESCAC men's championship game, the commentators even congratulated the high school girls' hockey team for their record. Being Vermont, the Ben and Jerry's beside Otter Creek is a popular destination for visitors, so don't forget that either."

Q "**There is not a whole lot in town**. It seems as though it was built up around the school since almost everyone in the town has some connection or other to the college, itself. The closest universities are up in Burlington, about a half an hour away, so we don't have much contact with them. There isn't really anything to stay away from here, and there isn't really much aside from shops and restaurants, either. However, there are quite a few museums in the area, and if you have a car, there are lots of places to visit between a half an hour and an hour's drive away."

The College Prowler Take
ON LOCAL ATMOSPHERE

No matter what exotic tidbits or intriguing locales we attempt to haggle out of this town, in the end, we still wind up with good ol' Middlebury—a small, antique doll house of a village, dotted with restaurants and shops that all close between 5 p.m. and midnight, and a smattering of snow-covered, cobblestone streets. It's quiet, it's quaint, and it can feel suffocating at times. On the other hand, the atmosphere caters well to those more inclined toward outdoor activities—particularly winter sports, hiking, and swimming. The Middlebury experience feels similar to being inside a cozy penny-candy store, or an old-fashioned piggy bank. It's a trinket of a town, really. If you're a country bumpkin, a lover of the magnificent outdoors, or are simply anxious to be liberated from the noise and pollution of the city, Middlebury is definitely the place for you.

The College Prowler™ Grade on

Local Atmosphere: C+

A high Local Atmosphere grade indicates that the area surrounding campus is safe and scenic. Other factors include nearby attractions, proximity to other schools, and the town's attitude toward students.

Safety & Security

The Lowdown
ON SAFETY & SECURITY

Number of Middlebury College Police:
26, including 11 full-time officers

Phone:
(802) 443-5911 or (802) 443-5133

Health Center Office Hours
24 hours a day during academic year; during the summer, hours are 8:30 a.m. – 4:30 p.m. on weekdays and 12 p.m. – 4 p.m. on weekends.

Safety Services
Rape Aggression and Defense Program (RAD), MiddRides, Midd Watch Program, Bicycle Registration, Safety Escorts, Safety Alerts, Emergency Call Boxes, Access Card System (to enter campus buildings, in effect after 11 p.m.), Lighting Tours, Commons Residential Associates (CRAs), Residential Assistants (RAs), and Junior Counselors (JCs).

Did You Know?
MiddRides, a bus designed to save students from their own aimless, drunken debauchery, now offers cookies to its passengers (as long as they aren't tossing some of their own).

Students Speak Out
ON SAFETY & SECURITY

"Middlebury is a safe place. Campus security is generally lenient, and there isn't much of a crime problem. They only started locking the dorms a few years ago."

Q "**The Public Safety department has a healthy relationship with the students**, providing assistance and support, as well as enforcing appropriate behavior. The rural setting of Middlebury provides a very safe, undisturbed environment to the extent that 'blue-lights' have never been necessary."

Q "**We feel kind of bad for security officers on campus**. They have nothing better to do than ride around in minivans and break up relatively docile parties at two in the morning—a pretty cushy job, if you ask me."

Q "Security has beefed itself up this year, especially with underage drinking. They are also a pain when it comes to parking tickets, and **it's easy for them to ticket** since the junior and senior parking lots are usually filled, leaving upperclassmen no place to park. Other than that, they're fairly reasonable."

Q "The campus is really safe, and **most students don't even lock their doors**. Occasionally, rooms are broken into, but that is a rarity and usually occurs during a drunken weekend night, anyway. I have always felt safe on campus."

Q "**The campus needs to improve its outdoor safety**. All dorms are now locked at night, where, before, you could get in anywhere, at any time. Now, all students have access cards to get into all dorms. There are not enough lights on campus and there is no blue-light system. Security was always good about giving rides if asked, and there is a late-night shuttle system around campus."

The College Prowler Take
ON SAFETY & SECURITY

Don't be fooled—although the campus seems to be crawling with cops from dusk 'til dawn, most people don't see a bit of crime at Middlebury in their entire four-year stay. What security is really scouring the campus for are illegally parked cars, underage drinking, unregistered parties, and drugs. In short, it's not you that's in danger—it's your Honda, your Heineken, and your herb that you need to keep a close eye on. The college does, however, lock its dormitories and all other buildings after 11 p.m., as there have been a few cases of theft in the past couple of years. Drunken vandalism of facilities and dorms also occurs on occasion.

Computers

The Lowdown
ON COMPUTERS

High-Speed Network?
Yes

Wireless Network?
Yes (in specific locations)

Number of Labs:
12

Numbers of Computers:
195

24-Hour Labs:
Bicentennial Hall 116/117 (must be inside before doors lock at 1 a.m.), Voter 104/105, Voter West

Charge to Print:
No

Operating Systems:
Mac OS, Windows

The College Prowler™ Grade on
Safety & Security: A-

A high grade in Safety & Security means that students generally feel safe, campus police are visible, blue-light phones and escort services are readily available, and safety precautions are not overly necessary.

Students Speak Out
ON COMPUTERS

The College Prowler Take
ON COMPUTERS

{ "The computer labs aren't often crowded. There's no need to bring your own computer; there is enough to go around on campus."

Q "**Definitely bring your own computer**, if only for the convenience of dorm room Internet access. The college has a deal with Dell where you can buy computers through the school, and financial aid students even get a discount that is proportional to their aid package. Labs get really crowded around exam time, but, otherwise, there are more than enough to go around. The network is pretty good; it occasionally acts up, but no more than anywhere else."

Q "I have always liked having my own computer just because it makes it possible to check e-mail and write papers in my dorm. However, **I've never had any problems with computer labs being overcrowded** when I've had to print things out. I definitively recommend bringing your own computer for convenience, but if that's not an option, there are so many available computers open in 24-hour computer labs that it's not a problem if you don't."

Q "Bringing your own computer is certainly the norm, but **I have gone without a computer for almost a year**, and I've never had problems gaining access to a computer."

Q "Computer labs are pretty accessible on campus, **except during exam periods**. I've really enjoyed having my own computer, which has allowed me to work in my room."

Q "**The computer network is fast**, and the school is gradually moving toward a wireless connection. I would recommend bringing your own computer to campus, though you can always find an open computer in one of the labs. But, the labs can get noisy. I would recommend a laptop, since there are some great wired places around campus where you can work and have a change of scenery."

Middlebury sports a fully-functional, wired network in all of the residence halls and academic buildings, as well as in computer labs dotted throughout campus; a wireless network is being expanded. Considering the size of the school, Middlebury has more than enough computers to go around—both Macs and PCs. All of the lab computers are in good condition and connected to the network. Even with the availability of computers and 24-hour labs, however, you should still consider bringing your own. Internet access in your dorm, which is included in your comprehensive tuition fee, is the key to indulging in your obsessive e-mail, IM habits, and endless games of Snood (which hones one's vital procrastination skills). Middlebury has so many computers, relative to the number of students, that you will almost never have to worry about getting access. The exception would be finals week, when you may have to try a few computer labs before you track down a vacant cubby.

The College Prowler™ Grade on
Computers: B+

A high grade in Computers designates that computer labs are available, the computer network is easily accessible, and the campus' computing technology is up-to-date.

Facilities

The Lowdown
ON FACILITIES

Movie Theatre on Campus?
No

Bowling on Campus?
No

Bar on Campus?
No, but Middlebury is working on selling beer at The Juice Bar.

Coffeehouse on Campus?
Yes, The Juice Bar, McCullough Social Space

Student Center:
McCullough Social Space

Athletic Center
Chip Kenyon '85 Arena, Memorial Field House (includes Pepin Gymnasium and Nelson Recreation Center), fitness center, natatorium, the Field House bubble (indoor track, squash, and tennis courts)

Libraries
Three on Main Campus (one more in the works, which is slated to be completed in the fall of 2005), one on Breadloaf Campus

Favorite Things to Do
Before you judge Middlebury students, you should know that getting hammered at social houses and dancing half-naked at McCullough parties isn't all we enjoy doing. During one of our favorite nights of the year, we boast much more class than that—when we get drunk in our best duds. Nothing goes better with shots of Jim Beam than a sharp tie, a velvet dress, and a slew of silver streamers. Midd kids also tend to gravitate towards student plays, which normally go up in the Hepburn Zoo, and Free Movie Fridays held in Sunderland International Language Center's main auditorium. Student talent shows are also a must; yet, to the dismay of some, they often don't present any opportunity for heckling. Mainly, Middlebury is the ideal locale for enjoying outdoor activities, from swimming in Lake Dunmore, to skiing at Breadloaf.

Popular Places to Chill
The Grille, The Juice Bar, Battell Beach (on a warm, dry day), the Great Hall in Bicentennial Hall

Students Speak Out
ON FACILITIES

"**Everything is new and has probably been built within the last five or 10 years. Needless to say, the facilities are gorgeous.**"

Q "**The sports facilities could be the envy of Division I schools**. There's been a real building binge in recent years, which has produced top-rate facilities from a new hockey arena, to a fresh student center."

Q "I think that Middlebury's facilities are unparalleled by any comparable liberal arts school. Recent additions include **an ice hockey arena, workout facilities, a dining hall, and new senior housing**. The college is still working on other additional housing, and a new library. Construction is always active on campus, providing students and alums with a visible indication of how their tuition dollars are being spent."

Q "**I don't think many colleges could rival the facilities Middlebury provides its students**. The athletic facilities are amazing, both for sports teams and for working out on your own. The student center is a convenient meeting place, with great food available at The Grille as an alternative to the dining halls. Unfortunately, I don't think the McCullough Social Space is as much of a gathering point for the students as the college intends it to be. Functions there, such as late-night dances, are poorly attended, as students often prefer to stay in their dorms to party."

Q "The facilities are all really nice and new. I don't often go to the athletic complex, but when I do, it is always clean and has everything you could ever want. **The computers are all fairly new and work well**. They are scattered around campus, so you can usually find one. The student center is nice and has everything that you might really need as well—a store, restaurant, study room, social hall, mailroom, and other stuff. The buildings are really confusing until you get familiar with them, but you will adapt quickly."

Q "Middlebury's facilities are unbelievably beautiful. **I especially appreciate The Grille**, which is a nice, alternative place for studying and meeting friends."

The College Prowler Take
ON FACILITIES

At first glance, Middlebury College is overwhelming—not in size, but in the fact that it has so much to do that it seems like you'll never get the time to take full advantage of it. While you've got the opportunity to spend your days at MIddlebury swimming in the pool, running on the pristine rubber track, checking out concerts at The Juice Bar, and spending a lot of time in BiHall's observatory, you'll never have the time to do everything you want. However, if only in response to being surrounded by 2,500 other busybodies, you'll fill your days with as many worthwhile activities as possible. There are plenty of options.

The College Prowler™ Grade on
Facilities: A

A high Facilities grade indicates that the campus is aesthetically pleasing and well-maintained; facilities are state-of-the-art, and libraries are exceptional. Other determining factors include the quality of both athletic and student centers and an abundance of things to do on campus.

Campus Dining

Students Speak Out
ON CAMPUS DINING

"The food on campus is really outstanding, especially at The Grille. However, if you want to eat in the dining halls, there is always a variety of choices—particularly at Ross."

The Lowdown
ON CAMPUS DINING

Freshman Meal Plan Requirement?
Yes

Meal Plan Average Cost:
$2,440/year

24-Hour On-Campus Eating?
No, but The Grille and the Juice Bar are both normally open until 2 a.m..

Student Favorites:
Ross Dining Hall, The Grille, Hamlin on Sunday nights

Did You Know?
Middlebury won the Ivy Award a couple years ago for serving up some of the best college food in the country.

A few times per semester, Proctor and Ross Dining Halls sponsor special events which offer outdoor and indoor cuisine matching the theme of the night. Rodeo Night is a student favorite, featuring barbecue beef, ribs, root beer, cotton candy, and a staff dressed in chaps and spurs.

Q "Middlebury has **won various awards for the quality of its food**, and three dining halls provide uniquely enjoyable dining experiences. The highlight of food at Midd is The Grille and the Juice Bar—a popular stop for food, coffee, and smoothies."

Q "I am quite content with the food on campus. **Middlebury supports local farmers** and offers organic vegetables in its salad bars. Its dining staff isn't afraid to try creative dishes, and usually that's not a problem."

Q "**Ross dining rules**! The food is above average in all Middlebury dining halls, but Ross always has great selections. Visitors are consistently in awe of the quality of food that we get there."

Q "Outstanding food—in fact, Middlebury won the prestigious Ivy Award for food. **Sorry if I sound like a public relations agent, but the food is incredible**. One will not go hungry. Ross has great pizza; Proctor has the best salad bar; and one can enjoy pizza and burgers at Freeman and Hamlin, which is a longer walk, but will help you burn some calories. Be sure to go either before 6 p.m. or after 6:30 p.m. for supper to avoid the crowds. The special events are fun, too. My advice to future students: leave the cups in the dining halls!"

Q "Right now, there are four dining halls on campus, and in the coming years, more will be built, and the older ones will be closed. Ross has the best food by far. It's worth the crowds to eat there. **I want Middlebury Dining Services to make their carrot cake for my wedding**—it's the best I've ever had!"

The College Prowler Take
ON CAMPUS DINING

The students have spoken, and the verdict is that the food here undoubtedly surpasses the standard. How many other college students can choose between fried calamari, fresh stir-fry, grilled chicken, and three varieties of pizza for lunch? Or between flank steak, pork tenderloin and mashed potatoes, and a decent vegetarian lasagna and spinach strudel for dinner? Students have the opportunity to fill out comment cards, suggesting how the dining hall services and food might be improved—and most times, they get their way. One cook even claimed he would look into getting lobster bisque for breakfast.

Off-Campus Dining

The Lowdown
ON OFF-CAMPUS DINING

Best Pizza:
Green Peppers, Neil and Otto's Best

Best Chinese:
Panda House

Best Breakfast:
Steve's Park Diner, Tully and Marie's, Middlebury Inn, Otter Creek Bakery

Best Wings:
Mister Up's

Best Healthy:
Starry Night Café, Natural Food Co-op, American Flatbreads

Best Place to Take Your Parents:
Dog Team Tavern, Fire and Ice, Storm Café

Late-Night, Half-Price Food Specials:
Mister Up's: 35-cent wings after 9 p.m., Two Brothers' Tavern: $1 off everything on Sundays

24-Hour Eating:
None

Student Favorites:
Starry Night Café, Dog Team Tavern, Mary's (in Bristol), Mister Up's, Storm Café, Taste of India, American Flatbreads, Noonie's

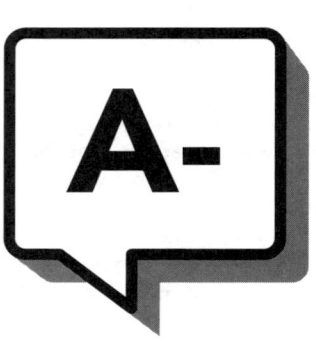

The College Prowler™ Grade on
Campus Dining: A-

Our grade on Campus Dining addresses the quality of both school-owned dining halls and independent on-campus restaurants as well as the price, availability, and variety of food.

Fun Facts

Vermont takes pride in its locally grown and raised products, and therefore serves them up as frequently as possible. Take advantage of fresh Vermont foods—mix and match the organic with the typically fatty college food.

Middlebury has three chain "restaurants"—Subway, McDonald's, and Dunkin' Donuts. Should Middlebury's incorrigible cuteness become irritating, these are your venues for suburban escape.

Want to know where Middlebury student go to get the best grub off campus? Check out the complete College Prowler book on Middlebury available at www.collegeprowler.com.

Students Speak Out
ON OFF-CAMPUS DINING

"**The restaurants off-campus are average. My favorites are Taste of India, Steve's Park Diner for breakfast, and Storm Café.**"

Q "There are tons of little restaurants around the Middlebury area. Some good ones are the Dog Team Tavern, Tully and Marie's, the Bobcat Café, and **Mary's in Bristol, which is just outside of Middlebury**."

Q "The restaurants in town are useful for an infrequent night out, although **they're much better for when your parents are in town**. Fire and Ice and the Dog Team Tavern are my favorite places."

Q "**There is a surprising number of restaurants off campus**, ranging from casual Mister Up's, to the more upscale Fire and Ice. But, you may only want to go to the latter if your parents are paying."

Q "Off-campus restaurants are very good, but some are pricey. **Mister Up's is relaxed and has a nice atmosphere**; American Flatbread is the hottest thing in town, and the wait is long. Amigo's is good. I think that Tully and Marie's is overrated. If you want to mingle with the real locals, go to Rosie's or Steve's Park Diner for breakfast, or Green Peppers Pizza for dinner. And who can forget Ben and Jerry's?"

Q "**High-quality food at reasonable prices is somewhat limited off campus**, especially for dinner. Given the small size of the town, however, there is a good variety of restaurants, including those with good Indian and Mexican food. Go to Otter Creek Bakery for a yummy breakfast or lunch. Angela's, Two Brothers, and Mister Up's are good restaurants/bars in town. If you have a car, go to the Dog Team Tavern for the sticky buns."

The College Prowler Take
ON OFF-CAMPUS DINING

What Middlebury lacks in nightlife and "hustle and bustle factor" it makes up for in off-campus dining. The town of Middlebury boasts nearly every type of cuisine you might crave—except sushi, which you'll have to make the trip to Burlington for. If you're really looking for some low-class fun, there's always McDonald's on Route 7. Middlebury is no fast food hub, though; it purposefully shies away from the commercialized, fast food establishments to preserve its "antique New England charm."

Most of Middlebury's greatest restaurants are pricey. For such a small town, it boasts some skilled chefs and savory dishes—and they come at a price. For those living on a small stipend, you may find Middlebury lacking in variety. It's best to eat on campus most of the time and save up for a couple marvelous meals a month at one of Middlebury's upscale establishments, where you can enjoy local recipes, wine, and tasty steak or seafood.

Campus Housing

The Lowdown
ON CAMPUS HOUSING

Undergrads on Campus: 97%

Number of Dormitories: 17

Number of University-Owned Apartments:
9 (5 of which are townhouses)

Room Types
Student choices include singles, doubles, two-room doubles, and suites.

Singles
Most students live in singles, which will likely be a shoebox-sized room all to yourself. Some singles, however, are quite large. Bathrooms are shared by the entire hall, typically 15 other students.

Doubles
Mostly freshmen are assigned to doubles (a room shared with one other person). Once again, students in this living situation use the hall bathrooms, and there are normally two or three of them, sometimes coed.

Triples
A room shared with two other people. Triples are rare and normally inhabited by freshmen. Students who live in triples will use hall bathrooms.

The College Prowler™ Grade on
Off-Campus Dining: B-

A high Off-Campus Dining grade implies that off-campus restaurants are affordable, accessible, and worth visiting. Other factors include the variety of cuisine and the availability of alternative options (vegetarian, vegan, Kosher, etc.).

Two-Room Doubles
Student will share a sink, or half-bathroom, with one other person, but is allotted a single room separated by a thin wall from his or her "sink mate's" room.

Suites
Typically three to five students, usually each with his or her own room, will share a bathroom, common living space, and a kitchen.

Apartments/Townhouses
Located both on and off-campus, they include mostly single bedrooms, which afford lots of privacy, a kitchen, a living room, and one or two bathrooms. Apartments and townhouses normally accommodate three to five people.

Student Houses
Located on and off campus, though off-campus options are limited. Students living in houses typically reside with three to four others and share a couple of bathrooms, a large living room, a kitchen, and sometimes even a dining room. Most students will claim a room to themselves, and some rooms are big enough to convert into doubles.

Available for Rent
Micro-fridge (mini fridge and microwave), small refrigerator, small microwave

Cleaning Service?
The cleaning service covers public spaces in all Middlebury housing, including on-campus housing, apartments, and suites. The service does not take care of individual rooms. Bathrooms, halls, and other public spaces are cleaned five days a week.

You Get
Bed, desk, and chair, bookshelf (attached to the desk), dresser, closet or wardrobe, Internet connections, free campus and local phone calls, window shades

Bed Type
Twin extra-long beds (39" x 80") are most common. Some houses have lofts, and some rooms (particularly those designed for freshmen) have bunk-able beds.

Also Available
Substance-free housing, special-interest housing, language houses

Did You Know?
Middlebury also provides a laundry service for those of you too preoccupied or unmotivated to walk down to the laundry facilities. The price can be steep, however, depending on how often you have your laundry picked up. The average cost is around $300, where students will typically have their dirty duds fetched every Thursday.

Students Speak Out
ON CAMPUS HOUSING

"The freshman dorms aren't great, but the options are good for upperclassmen. I like to avoid the new dorms and stick with the older ones that are right in the heart of campus."

"**All our housing is pretty good**. There's not much difference between the dorms in terms of physical quality, but there are huge social differences. You'll pick up on these differences by word of mouth right away."

"The dorms vary. Most upperclassmen live in spacious singles. **Many people prefer the 'new dorms'**—Milliken, Hadley, Kelly, and Lang—for their modern amenities, but I'm a fan of the older buildings because they've got charm. Either way, you can't go wrong."

"The dorms are outstanding. Middlebury is currently working on **the 'Commons' system, which is controversial**. All rooms are nice; both singles and suites are plentiful. Ross Commons has the best variety of housing, while Brainerd is seriously lacking. The new Atwater Complex will be outstanding. Freshmen are placed in Allen, Battell, Stewart, Milliken, and some in Hepburn, which is generally an upperclassmen hall. Of these, Allen or Milliken are probably the best. Stewart has same-sex halls."

Q "Most of the dorms are nice and spacious, and **the new La Force suites look really comfortable**. The older dorms, like Pearsons and Forest, have lots of charm, but not a lot of privacy."

Q "The dorms are a really mixed bunch. Some of the newer ones, like Ross, are absolutely lovely, while others, like Coffrin, are less pleasant. Overall, **the rooms are comfortable**."

The College Prowler Take
ON CAMPUS HOUSING

If you can shack most kids up in on-campus housing and keep them relatively satisfied for four years, you must be doing something right. From the outside, all the dorms are almost uniformly impressive, granite castles. On the inside, they're pretty plush, too, with cozy amenities to boot. Freshmen rooms, and some sophomore rooms, are just big enough for you and your stuff. Junior and senior rooms, however, will not only fit you and your stuff, but allow your guests a bit of room to breathe at an impromptu party as well. If you're lucky, you may even get to live in a house or a suite your senior year. Every dorm has a kitchen, at least one TV or study lounge, a bike room, and someone to clean up after your unfortunate Friday night boozing accidents in the bathroom. Regardless of your rooming situation, Middlebury is leaps and bounds ahead of other colleges when it comes to "luxurious" student living.

The College Prowler™ Grade on
Campus Housing: B+

A high Campus Housing grade indicates that dorms are clean, well-maintained, and spacious. Other determining factors include variety of dorms, proximity to classes, and social atmosphere.

Off-Campus Housing

The Lowdown
ON OFF-CAMPUS HOUSING

Undergrads in Off-Campus Housing:
Number limited to approximately 60 students (not including students taking only two classes during their last semester of college).

Average Rent for a Studio Apartment:
$300-$400/month

Average Rent for a One-Bedroom Apartment:
$500-$650/month

Average Rent for a Two-Bedroom Apartment:
$700-$850/month

Popular Areas
Court Street, Battell Block, Cornwall, Weybridge, Ripton, in-town Middlebury

Best Time to Look for a Place
January, right before February class graduates; and mid-May, right before regular class graduates

For Assistance Contact
The College, itself, can answer questions about participating in the off-campus draw to obtain off-campus housing. Students must find housing on their own if they are drawn.

Students Speak Out
ON OFF-CAMPUS HOUSING

"As for off-campus housing, there isn't much of a choice since there isn't much available. I think it's better to live on campus, anyway."

Q "**Only a limited number of seniors can apply to live off campus**. Middlebury is a residential college, and I fully support the off-campus housing limits. Life revolves around the college campus anyway."

Q "**The vast majority of students live on campus for all four years**, and getting approved for off-campus housing is a hassle. Generally, the farthest people move off campus is to a social house or other interest-based house, all being college-owned."

Q "Housing off campus is practically nonexistent. They don't really allow very many people to live off campus, and even then it's only seniors. The College tries to encourage everyone to stay on campus, which is actually quite convenient since **it gets cold during the winters in Vermont**, and a long hike from your apartment to campus is not always an appealing option."

Q "There really isn't much housing off campus until senior year, and **it's difficult to find anything like a student apartment** in Middlebury. This really isn't a problem though, since there are very few people who do, or who want to, live off campus."

Q "**You are not allowed to live off campus until senior year**, and even then, you have to go through a lottery to be able to live off campus. It is probably not worth doing this, as most of the dorms are quite nice, and the college is opening more senior housing on campus, which means suites, houses, etc.."

The College Prowler Take
ON OFF-CAMPUS HOUSING

Most students are so locked into the Middlebury College bubble that they hardly notice that housing, let alone an entire community, exists off campus. Even those who are aware of life beyond campus limits have to enter a draw to score off-campus housing, and the quota is limited to approximately 60 students per year. Given this, and the fact that on-campus housing options are typically so appealing, students rarely have the desire to leave their dorms. But, the town of Middlebury and the surrounding areas are certainly host to some rather cozy housing options.

Furthermore, most are not outrageously overpriced and admittedly do afford students the chance to escape the frenetic academic lifestyle once classes have let out for the day. The fact remains, however, that it is difficult to obtain off-campus housing, and often not worth the sweat and tears, as you will have to spend precious study and play time driving to class, lectures, organization meetings, and on-campus performances.

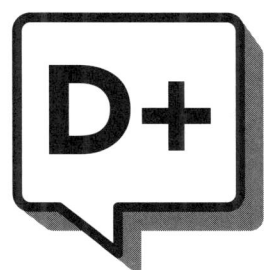

The College Prowler™ Grade on
Off-Campus Housing: D+

A high grade in Off-Campus Housing indicates that apartments are of high quality, close to campus, affordable, and easy to secure.

Diversity

The Lowdown
ON DIVERSITY

African American: 3%

Asian American: 7%

Hispanic: 5%

Native American: 1%

White: 76%

International: 8%

Out-of-State: 94%

Political Activity
Middlebury boasts a score of diverse political groups. Yet, surprisingly, it manages to avoid major confrontations between Democrats and Republicans—groups tend to fight their battles in a civilized forum. Although the majority of students are generally thought of as politically and socially liberal, throngs of conservatives make their presence known. In fact, many tag Middlebury as a "conservatively liberal" school.

Gay Tolerance
The rumor has it that Middlebury becomes more tolerant of homosexuality each year. The Middlebury Open Queer Alliance (MOQA), which hosts campus events annually, is establishing a more prominent presence on campus. More students than ever are "coming out." This past fall, MOQA received a surprisingly low amount of intolerant slander.

Economic Status
Between all of the stingy students, the granola-crunching longhairs who can only afford half a flannel, and the pretentious brownnosers who join theater only to learn how modesty is feigned, you wouldn't guess that 65 percent of Middlebury students do not receive grant aid. That said, there are still a great number of kids who need aid, a great number who need aid and do not receive it, and a handful sailing on a full ride. Although many affluent students play the part of the rich kid, you would never know others had a dime by the down-to-earth way they carry themselves.

Minority Clubs
Middlebury is host to an overwhelming number of minority organizations. Examples include the International Student Organization (ISO) Cultural Show, the RIDDIM World Dance performance in the spring, and the African American Alliance (AAA) Fashion Show. Students who attend these showcases are eclectic and encouraging groups. Acceptance of people from all backgrounds is often celebrated in the most unsuspecting places—even in a small, rural, New England town.

Most Popular Religions
The most visible religious groups on campus seem to be Protestant praise and Bible study groups. However, Catholic groups are also quite prominent, as well as the Jewish organization, Hillel.

Students Speak Out
ON DIVERSITY

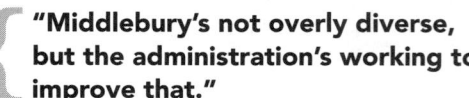

"Middlebury's not overly diverse, but the administration's working to improve that."

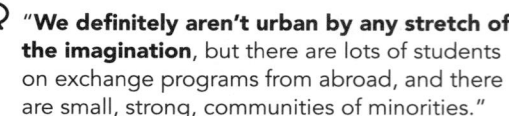

"**We definitely aren't urban by any stretch of the imagination**, but there are lots of students on exchange programs from abroad, and there are small, strong, communities of minorities."

Q "Middlebury is pretty diverse; **it just depends on who you hang out with**. There are plenty of opportunities to meet more than your typical, American college student. Actually, the percentage of international students here is relatively high, compared to other colleges."

Q "Like most New England liberal arts colleges, **Middlebury is predominantly white**, but there are also substantial numbers of African Americans and Asians. International students also constitute a large portion of the student body, and they are often the most interesting and fun groups to hang out with. Unfortunately, minorities often tend to stick together, so it requires some effort to be part of a diverse group of friends."

Q "**Middlebury's campus isn't very diverse**. However, the number of nationalities represented at Middlebury is impressive."

The College Prowler Take
ON DIVERSITY

It's evident that admissions is attempting to make Middlebury a more diverse campus, ethnically. However, this trend is diminished by the fact that many minority students tend to stick together for support. The key is to try to meet many different people as soon as you arrive, before everyone becomes obstinately separated into close-knit groups of "diverse" and "non-diverse" students. In addition to an impressive number of international students, Middlebury also boasts students from many states; however, most of these are from the New England area or the West Coast.

The College Prowler™ Grade on
Diversity: D

A high grade in Diversity indicates that ethnic minorities and international students have a notable presence on campus and that students of different economic backgrounds, religious beliefs, and sexual preferences are well-represented.

Guys & Girls

The Lowdown
ON GUYS & GIRLS

Women Undergrads: 51%

Men Undergrads: 49%

Birth Control Available?
Yes. Condoms and dental dams are free, readily available, and come in all flavors, colors, and sizes, at Parton Health Center and in some bathroom dormitories. Female students who have had a women's health exam may also obtain a prescription for birth control pills that can be filled at the nearby pharmacy. The birth control shot and patch are also available options, as well as emergency contraception upon an examination and a pregnancy test.

Social Scene
The most common "type" at Middlebury is the "da Vinci," who's competitive at everything. The one thing larger than the amount of alcohol we consume, however, is our academic conscience. It's not that it's hard to find someone who's interested in you at Middlebury; it's just difficult to convince him or her that you're worth one hour per night over his or her chemistry book. You think you're special because you took a family vacation to Europe with your parents in the sixth grade and toughed out NOLS in Alaska last summer. But, the guy next to you will be a double-major in ancient Buddhist scriptures and biology with a focus in complex cell structures, and a minor in astrophysics.

Hookups or Relationships?

If you consider a serious relationship as one grind session to "Bootylicious" at a McCullough dance party, passing out in a sweat-drenched heap back in some stranger's dorm room, and a "please don't call me tomorrow," then Middlebury's your place to find true love. There's a lot of hooking up—therefore, by default, there are a lot of singles. Many of the girls are involved in long-distance relationships, yet students who date among the Middlebury crowd are rare.

Dress Code

Most people will tell you that it's hard to distinguish Middlebury students from a J. Crew ad, and while that might be true, we've still got our share of crunchy kids and casual dressers. Some dress this way for the sake of originality alone, while others simply like the feel of sweatpants and hairy legs beneath hand-woven, hemp-skirts.

As for the outdoorsy dressing crowd, you have to ask yourself if it's better to be the guy who wears chamois shirts, smells like fish, and was raised on the Appalachian Trail, or the guy who wears North Face and grew up in Manhattan. The latter type is way more common.

Students Speak Out
ON GUYS & GIRLS

{ "Midd kids are infamous, not only for wearing J. Crew, but also for looking like J. Crew models. At Middlebury, it certainly doesn't seem like blond hair or blue eyes is a recessive trait."

Q "As for the guys and the girls, this is a decent-sized school, so you can probably find pretty much any type of person that you're looking for to hang out with. Sadly, however, **there's not much of a dating scene**. You're either single, doing random hookups, or in the 'Middlebury marriage.' If one of these categories suits you, you'll definitely be able to find people of a similar persuasion around Middlebury."

Q "People always say that Middlebury is a college for 'beautiful people,' and compared to the average American population, Middlebury students are, in general, very attractive. There are plenty who break the mold, but **most students are quite cookie-cutter looking**. I'd describe people as mostly preppy and sporty looking. Dating at Middlebury is a lot different from the way relationships work in the real world, and you don't find many couples that began their relationship in a traditional way. I'd say that most guys are on the immature side and are generally out to have a good time."

Q "Time for a confession: **I came to Middlebury partially because there are so many hot girls here**. Yes, there is a stereotypical Middlebury student—beautiful, intelligent, usually wealthy, a good dresser, and athletic to some extent. There are a lot of students who came from prep, boarding, or magnet schools. With that said, a lot of people can be pretentious, so look for the genuine and interesting people. If this says anything, I met my girlfriend at Middlebury and am living the 'Middlebury married couple' legend to this day."

Q "**People at Middlebury are uniformly beautiful**. This is both wonderful and discouraging, and I would say you have to be pretty comfortable with yourself to fit in here. You could lose yourself in comparisons to those jogging girls, or those fit, Nordic skiers. Dating is hard to come by at Middlebury. Most kids are too busy studying to form relationships, and one-night stands are not infrequent."

Q "Midd is full of beautiful people, but I found it's just like anywhere else. **There are groups of friends based on activities**. The football team and the social houses tend to stick together for example, and there are boundaries between different groups. However, the boundaries can get blurry since everyone has friends from their dorm, from their major, from other classes, and from activities. Then, there is the stereotype that Midd grads marry other Midd grads!"

Athletics

The College Prowler Take
ON GUYS & GIRLS

If one opinion sounds off more loudly than any other, it's that we think we're pretty hot. This could mean that we're arrogant, but we like to call it honesty. True, people here often seem as if they were cut and pasted off of the pages of Abercrombie and Patagonia catalogs, but at least those catalogs are full of models—right? As for personality, students tend to have lots of it, or at least make it seem like they do.

The Lowdown
ON ATHLETICS

The College Prowler™ Grade on
Guys: B+

A high grade for Guys indicates that the male population on campus is attractive, smart, friendly, and engaging, and that the school has a decent ratio of guys to girls.

The College Prowler™ Grade on
Girls: A-

A high grade for Girls not only implies that the women on campus are attractive, smart, friendly, and engaging, but also that there is a fair ratio of girls to guys.

Men's Varsity Teams:
Alpine Skiing
Baseball
Basketball
Cross Country
Football
Golf
Hockey
Indoor Track
Lacrosse
Nordic Skiing
Soccer
Swimming & Diving
Tennis
Track & Field

Women's Varsity Teams:
Alpine Skiing
Basketball
Cross Country
Field Hockey
Golf
Hockey
Indoor Track
Lacrosse
Nordic Skiing
Soccer
Softball
Squash
Swimming & Diving
Tennis
Track & Field
Volleyball

Getting Tickets

The only tickets that seem to be in relatively high demand are tickets to men's ice hockey games. You may need to purchase tickets ahead of time if you're looking to attend the NESCAC championships. Normally, students never have a problem getting into regular season games, even at the last minute. Tickets are free for students and cost $2 during the NESCAC finals.

Club Sports:
Coed Competitive Cheerleading
Crew
Cricket
Cycling
Equestrians
Figure Skating
Fly Fishing
Free Heelers (Telemark Skiing)
Middlebury Mountain Club (MMC)
Rugby
Sailing (MCSC)
Ski Patrol
Snowboarding
Squash
Triathlon Club
Ultimate Frisbee
Water Polo
Wrestling

Intramurals (IMs):
Touch Football
Soccer
Volleyball
Golf
Home Run Derby
Three-on-Three Basketball
Basketball
Broomball
Ice Hockey
Snow Football
Indoor Soccer
Skiing
Squash
Tennis
Softball
Lacrosse
Indoor Wiffle Ball
Disc Golf

Most Popular Sports

It only makes sense that Vermont's top teams would be involved in the cold sports like Nordic and Alpine skiing and ice hockey.

Fields

Ralph Myhre golf course, softball field, Peter Kohn Field, Forbes baseball field

Athletic Division:
NCAA Division III

Conference:
NESCAC

Overlooked Teams:
The women's ice hockey team is continually under-praised for all of the national championships it has won.

School Mascot:
The Panther

Students Speak Out
ON ATHLETICS

"Sports are important at Middlebury, but students who don't play sports aren't shunned or beaten. I think there's a pretty healthy balance among the student body."

Q "**Varsity sports are huge**, bigger than IMs. Probably half the campus plays a varsity sport."

Q "People pay the most attention to the men's varsity hockey team. **Middlebury has Division I skiing**. Field hockey, soccer, and lacrosse are great programs. These varsity sports are very demanding. Many partake in intramural sports like broomball and rugby to avoid the time crunch. Ultimate Frisbee is also popular. The Mountain Club is also popular."

Q "Sports, whether varsity, club, or IM, are big here; **it's an active, athletic campus**. Not as many people play sports, however, as Middlebury's reputation might suggest."

Q "I didn't realize it when I applied, but Middlebury really is a jock school! Athletics are quite popular, and many students play a sport. Even if they aren't involved officially, Midd kids are known for **taking advantage of the surrounding mountains** to ski and hike."

Q "All sports are pretty big, and **there isn't much distinction between varsity and IM sports**. There are also lots of clubs and student organizations to join as well."

The College Prowler Take
ON ATHLETICS

Not to toot our own horn, but beep, beep—Middlebury is home to some of the best sports teams in Division III. Men's ice hockey reigns supreme as far as student popularity. Football is surprisingly not as popular as many other sports, but our team can still play with the best of them. If you want to train in some of the most state-of-the-art athletic facilities in the country, Middlebury's your school. If you want to play with some of the most driven, hard-working, and talented athletes in the country, Middlebury's your school. And if you simply want to take part in an IM here or there, Middlebury has plenty of those, too. When it comes to athletics, it would suffice to say we've got it all—except for a Division I standing in most sports.

Greek Life

The Lowdown
ON GREEK LIFE

The College Prowler™ Grade on
Athletics: B+

A high grade in Athletics indicates that students have school spirit, that sports programs are respected, that games are well-attended, and that intramurals are a prominent part of student life.

Number of Social Houses:
6

Percent of Undergrad Men in Social Houses:
Less than 6%

Percent of Undergrad Women in Social Houses:
Less than 5%

Social Houses on Campus:
5

Multicultural Colonies:
Language houses often hold dinners with the appropriate dishes and other such events to commemorate the countries in which their "language of choice" is spoken. Thus far, there are French, Italian, German, Russian, Chinese, Portuguese, Spanish, and Japanese houses.

Students Speak Out
ON GREEK LIFE

The College Prowler Take
ON GREEK LIFE

{ **"There is no Greek life on campus per se, but there are several social houses that throw big parties and host rush for students."**

"**There is absolutely no Greek life here.** Instead, we have social houses, which are the equivalent of coed fraternities and sororities, but very few people are in them."

"Social houses play a pretty big role in campus life, but **if you're not a member, you won't be shunned**. Most of the houses are pretty welcoming, and if you're 'anti-social houses,' there's a lot of non-social house stuff to do on the weekends."

"**If you are interested in the Greek system, go elsewhere**. The school has pretty much suffocated the system due to all of the problems. The houses are now coed and tightly regulated. Don't get me wrong, I still think the houses are an important part of the community, but they are not as vital as they are at other schools, and they are losing popularity."

"**Middlebury has social houses**. However, one can have a very active social life without ever attending a social house party."

"The social houses do not dominate social life on campus. They can **provide a good opportunity to meet people** and have a tight social circle, but life can be equally satisfying as a non-member. Parties are usually not limited to members, so it's not necessary to rush to take part."

Fraternities and sororities were "outlawed" over ten years ago at Middlebury—that is, until they were reborn under the name "social houses," a much more innocuous-sounding title. Rushing is not nearly as life threatening as it used to be, and any daunting initiation stunts are overshadowed by sugarcoated photos in the student newspaper of rushers sharing spaghetti dinners with older members. The large majority of students do not join social houses, and it is not necessary to join to attend the parties. Even better, no student is ever turned away from a party due to their age. You will be stamped with a smiley face at the door if you're over 21, and with an "X" if you're underage. However, the "X" stamp does not necessarily mean that you will be denied the privileges that come with a smiley stamp. But, if your first criterion in searching for a college is a rampant, old-fashioned Greek scene, Middlebury would not be the school for you.

The College Prowler™ Grade on
Greek Life: N/A

A high grade in Greek Life indicates that sororities and fraternities are not only present, but also active on campus. Other determining factors include the variety of houses available and the respect the Greek community receives from the rest of the campus.

Drug Scene

Students Speak Out
ON DRUG SCENE

{ "I haven't seen any drug use on campus. It's not my scene, and it's also not in my face."

Q "Like on any college campus, **people do a lot of pot**. Other than that, I haven't really encountered much of a drug scene, and it has certainly never been a problem."

Q "**A lot of drinking and smoking goes on here due to the stress**. People smoke marijuana, and there are some other hard drugs that appear once in a while. No-Doz and caffeine are popular, but there are plenty of people who do not use drugs."

Q "Alcohol is the drug of choice at Middlebury. As at any college, **binge drinking happens**. Although other drugs are present, they are not nearly as prevalent as alcohol."

Q "Pot is everywhere. Coke is in a lot of places. If you know where to go, **you can find just about any drug you want**, but if you don't know it's there, you won't notice it. It's there if you want it to be, but it's not in your face."

Q "Like anywhere, the drugs are here if you're looking for them, but not in your face if you're not. Pot smoking is fairly common, and **a few kids use other drugs**, but for almost everyone, alcohol is the drug of choice."

The Lowdown
ON DRUG SCENE

Most Prevalent Drugs on Campus:
Alcohol, marijuana, caffeine, No-Doz, Ritalin, speed, cocaine

Liquor-Related Referrals: 854

Liquor-Related Arrests: 1

Drug-Related Referrals: 128

Drug-Related Arrests: 6

Drug Counseling Programs

Substance Use and Abuse Assessment

Phone: (802) 443-5141

Services: Confidential consultation and assessment of student's addiction to alcohol. Provides referrals to area hospitals and counseling centers, if necessary.

Groups

Phone: (802) 443-5141

Services: Discussion groups facilitated through the Counseling Staff Center include "Alcohol and Other Drugs," "Feeling Good/Doing Well," "Children of Alcoholics Group," "Substance Use Group," and more.

The College Prowler Take
ON DRUG SCENE

In brief, the word on the drug scene at Middlebury is "covert." You can be here for four years without witnessing one drug deal, or one person doing hard drugs at a party, though you may smell things here and there. The essence of the social house experience is cheap beer. Hard drugs can be found, but they are not prevalent by any stretch of the imagination. Basically, if you want marijuana, it's easily obtainable, and if you want hard drugs, those can be found as well, though they are not nearly as prominent. Even if you have fallen in with the drug crowd, inadvertently or not, most Middlebury students strive to be individualists. Therefore, students here will respect your desire to abstain if you're not into experimenting. At a school so focused on academics and achievement, rest assured there are many Middlebury students who don't spend their time or money on drugs.

The College Prowler™ Grade on
Drug Scene: B

A high grade on Drug Scene indicates that drugs are not a noticeable part of campus life; drug use is not visible, and no pressure to use them seems to exist.

Campus Strictness

The Lowdown
ON CAMPUS STRICTNESS

What Are You Most Likely to Get Caught Doing on Campus?

Underage drinking, illegal drug use, possession of a narcotic, parking illegally, streaking, bike theft, hanging Christmas lights in dorm rooms, hanging tapestries on ceiling or decorations on sprinklers (fire hazards), burning candles or incense, carrying around open containers of alcohol on campus, making too much noise in a dorm

Students Speak Out
ON CAMPUS STRICTNESS

{ "Campus police aren't that strict about drugs, drinking, and stuff like that, unless you blatantly shoot up in front of them or something."

Q "The campus police are pretty **strict about enforcing the drug and alcohol policies**, but they aren't out to get you. They are really just there to take care of potential problems when they arise."

Q "**We've just revised our underage-drinking policies**, and they're laxer than ever. There aren't great consequences for drinking on campus. Vermont liquor laws are strict, so off-campus drinking for those under 21 is not common. Campus security officers are usually willing to look the other way when kids are just having a good time on campus, as long as you're not being too rowdy."

Q "The security guards tend to be pretty nice if you're not doing anything horribly wrong. They will issue citations for drinking without blinking an eye, but **most people take pride in their citations**. They have to knock before entering your room if you're having a party, so you learn when to drop your drink. And when you're of age, they'll never bother you."

Q "**The campus security is seen as more of a nuisance than anything else**. Repeat offenders will get into trouble, but mostly, there are a lot of 'slaps on the wrist.' A lot of partying is now fleeing campus to avoid security."

Q "The policy around drugs and drinking seems **pretty relaxed**. I think people can get away with a lot when it comes to substances."

The College Prowler Take
ON CAMPUS STRICTNESS

Middlebury's campus is not host to screaming hoards of whistleblowing security officers and/or Robocops by any means. Quite frankly, you'll get away with drinking, and perhaps even more, if you are halfway discreet about it. Oftentimes, security officers are too busy busting parking offenders and criminal Christmas-light-stringers, to be bothered with all the underage debauchery that goes on around here. Everyone knows that parties run rampant, particularly on weekends, and security hardly has the numbers to make a dent in all the chicanery. If you are stupid about breaking policy, however, you will—and deserve to be—caught.

Acts of vandalism and bike theft (or "borrowing," as we like to call it) are considered more serious offenses and are punished accordingly. If you're one of those people incorrigibly in love with illegal substances, at least make an attempt to keep the use of them in your room by closing the door. Security knows what pot smells like, too, and will not buy the "medicinal purposes" argument. That's already been tested.

Want to know how not to get caught on campus? For more student opinons on how to avoid a run-in with the campus po', check out the College Prowler book on Middlebury available at *www.collegeprowler.com*.

The College Prowler™ Grade on
Campus Strictness: B+

A high Campus Strictness grade implies an overall lenient atmosphere; police and RAs are fairly tolerant, and the administration's rules are flexible.

Overall Experience

Q "I wonder what it would have been like to go to college in a city, but **I don't regret coming to Middlebury College** in the least. Middlebury is a beautiful, intensive place to spend four years, and I've met a lot of interesting people here."

Q "Honestly, **I can't see myself being happy anywhere else**. It took some time to adjust to the intensity of Middlebury—the academics are certainly nothing to sneeze at. But looking at my experience from the tail end, I see how well everything has worked out. I think finding that balance is the key to enjoying life at Middlebury."

Students Speak Out
ON OVERALL EXPERIENCE

The College Prowler Take
ON OVERALL EXPERIENCE

"My experience has been very good, overall. The campus is very sheltered, which feels limiting sometimes, but I believe it's actually very good in the end for learning and academics."

Q "Sometimes I wish I'd gone somewhere where I would have had more free time, but when I think about the opportunities that are open to me because I went to Middlebury and excelled in such a rigorous academic environment, I'm happy that I stuck it out! **Middlebury is a great place brimming with talented and fun people** and a generally friendly and helpful staff. I would come here again, if I had to choose."

Q "I've had an unbelievable time at Middlebury. **I'm glad I choose a small, liberal arts college over a university**. I've really benefited from the tight community and academic rigor. Looking back, I made the right choice."

Q "I definitely feel like I made the right decision by coming to Middlebury because I love the atmosphere of the small school where **you know all of your professors**, are comfortable approaching them, and talking with them about any problems you're having."

Most people you talk to who are still in school at Middlebury are more than satisfied with their "college experience," or else they wouldn't be doling out $40K a year to come here. The academics are outstanding, though you may wonder where they'll take you later. Students often wish they toiled less at the books and more at the booze, but the pristine facilities tend to distract us from indulging in too much scholastic misery. Professors are brilliant, witty, and sympathetic, although there are some haughty bumps in the road. The on-campus social scene is lively and shot through with school spirit.

Middlebury provides an incredibly varied experience—an opportunity to stick your paintbrush in all shades of colors, so to speak. Students who spent 18 years in Nowheresville, Iowa watching PBS will leave Middlebury with seven different areas of study, exposure to at least 10 different foreign countries, and stories of rock climbing in New Zealand under their belts. Sure, you'll inevitably take a class or two that feels like the bane of your existence for a semester, and you will cringe at the titanic tuition bill every month, but the people you'll meet and the places you'll go will set your experience apart from those of other students in your high school's graduating class. The daunting ambitions of others around you will provide a constant challenge to your own motivations, actions, and thoughts.

The Inside Scoop

The Lowdown
ON THE INSIDE SCOOP

Middlebury College Slang:
Know the slang, know the school. The following is a list of things you really need to know before coming to Middlebury College. The more of these words you know, the better off you'll be.

CFA: Center for the Arts

Comps: Comprehensive exams in various subjects taken exclusively by seniors.

The Dungeon: The basement of Allen Hall, brimming with rowdy hoards of freshmen boys.

Febism: Jealousy or hatred of Febs—students who matriculate in February.

IM Sports: Intramural sports, which are much more low-key and less time consuming than varsity sports.

ITS: Information Technology Services, located in Voter Hall.

The Loft: The comfy space up one flight of stairs in the library; conducive to sleep and hooking-up.

The Monastery: The all-girls top floor of Stuart Hall. They are all pretty snobbish.

The Nunnery: The fourth floor of Allen Hall; once again, all girls known to be prudes.

Open Container: An open alcoholic beverage on public property, subject to a citation.

The Pit: The basement of Stewart Hall, also teeming with stereotypical freshmen boys.

RUDI: Random Unidentified Drunk Injury

Adirondack Circle: Parking circle at the top of College Street and in front of the Adirondack House.

The Zoo: The small theater space couched in the third floor of Hepburn Hall.

Traditions

Like a Prayer

One of the spiciest, most scandalous traditions that Middlebury students adhere to is taking one's shirt off during "Like a Prayer" by Madonna. Considering the fact that the song is played as the grand finale of nearly every college dance bash, there will be plenty of room for half-nudity.

Winter Procession

For all of you avid ski bums, what could be more exciting than combining your favorite hobby with finishing that grueling college career? How about receiving your diploma at the bottom of a ski mountain? At the end of January, every February student will ski down the college's Snow Bowl during procession. The college chooses a bunny slope for this event, so have no fear if you're a Santa Barbara novice.

Waking the President

Revenging their financial woes after four years at a pricey private school, students march down to the president's door at 5 a.m. on graduation day to ask him whether or not the procession will take place outside that year. They also entreat him to join the graduating seniors for breakfast at Steve's Park Diner.

Swim Team Streakers

Every spring, the new freshmen swimmers are forced to endure an initiation process, which often entails eating a live fish, and, most times, streaking across campus and through McCullough Social Space.

Polar Bearing

As soon as Lake Dunmore thaws, all the intrepid (and possibly half-witted) students take to the icy waters at midnight every Thursday for a dip—naked. Remember where you place your clothes and towel before you jump in, or you'll be sorry when you come out.

Middlebury College "Rural" Legends

- Middlebury was ranked *Playboy*'s hottest campus in 1998.
- Middlebury was ranked one of *Playboy*'s top 10 biggest party schools.
- Steven Spielberg toured the campus when he was checking out colleges for his son.
- One time, someone put Ecstasy in the punch at a party in the Chateau.

School Spirit

Middlebury College is just small enough to foster a substantial amount of school spirit. It is particularly prominent during ice hockey games and around Winter Carnival time; yet it's sustained the whole year through, with kids donning Middlebury logos, Middlebury apparel, and sweatshirts that represent their commons. Sometimes Middlebury kids can come off as a bit too pretentious about their school.

Tips to Succeed at Middlebury College:

- Check your voice mailbox and e-mail at least five times per day.
- Don't panic if you don't get all of your reading done—you never will.
- Never cheat—you risk being expelled.
- Take a variety of classes to probe your potential interests.
- Do your homework yourself to learn the material—this isn't high school anymore.
- Maintain contact with at least one or two professors for reference purposes.
- Keep on track with your major by staying in touch with your advisor.
- Seek off-campus and on-campus employment as soon as you arrive!

Things I Wish I Knew Before Coming to Middlebury College:

- Tuition has been climbing at a rate of approximately $2,000 dollars per year.
- It is essential to bring long underwear and any other winter clothing you can scrounge up to Middlebury. You can never have enough.
- It would behoove you to bring flannel sheets, unless you plan on sharing your bed with your roommate to stay warm.
- Do not be wooed by honey-tongued book salesmen. Go to all of your classes first before buying the books from them, and find out which ones the professor actually plans on using. Next, look for used editions first, ask friends if you can borrow a copy of their book if he or she took the same course last term, and check Amazon for better deals than the college book store offers.
- Structure your time so that you can be involved in as many activities as possible outside of academics, making sure to incorporate sleep somewhere into the equation. Try something you never had the opportunity to be a part of during high school, but again, don't max out, fail out, or drop out because you've gotten yourself in over your own ambitious head.
- Before enrolling in a class, ask around about the professor's reputation. Visit *www.middkid.com* to hear what the students have to say about certain professors.
- There are many discounted trips, lectures, and artistic performances sponsored by the college. Take advantage of these as much as you can.
- Hepburn Hall has that deceptively classic charm and is centrally located to boot. Do not be misled. Unless you get a room on the fifth floor, you'll be stuck with crumbling furniture and a room the size of a shoebox.
- If you're interested in engineering, meteorology, or some other specific scientific field, do not come to Middlebury unless you plan to go to graduate school later on to narrow your academic focus.

Finding a Job or Internship

The Lowdown
ON FINDING A JOB OR INTERNSHIP

The college's Career Service Office provides a few helpful services to get you started: MiddNet provides a list of Middlebury alumni volunteers working in a variety of different fields, with their contact information. MoJo, a list of job opportunities and employer information, is also a useful tool, which the Office trumpets from your first day to your last day on campus.

Advice:
Although the Career Services Office can seem obnoxiously helpful and intimidating, it is a valuable tool if you know how to use it. Attend its classes on how to write a resume and cover letter if you're unsure (or simply look at a sample online); go to its seminar on how to succeed at an interview; post your resume and academic and contact information on MoJo to increase your visibility to employers; and, most importantly, search MoJo for current internship and job postings—many are great opportunities. The Career Service Office also provides information on scholarship and grant opportunities, and has set up MiddNet—an incredibly useful inroad to your prospective career path. Alumni are generally eager to assist current Middlebury students.

The Best & Worst

The Ten BEST Things About Middlebury:

1. Athletic facilities
2. McCullough dance parties
3. Winter Carnival
4. Bicentennial Hall observatory and lab facilities
5. Ross food
6. Chicken Parmesan night
7. Ben and Jerry's ice cream
8. Small class sizes
9. Helpful and compassionate professors
10. The Snow Bowl

The Ten WORST Things About Middlebury:

1. Pretentiousness
2. Overly-competitive students
3. Overachievers
4. Security and parking
5. The transcript office
6. The study abroad office
7. Frigid winter temperatures
8. Chickpeas in every dish at Proctor
9. The overwhelming workload
10. The nearest nightlife is 45 minutes away

Trinity College

300 Summit Street, Hartford, CT 06106
www.trincoll.edu   (860) 297-2180

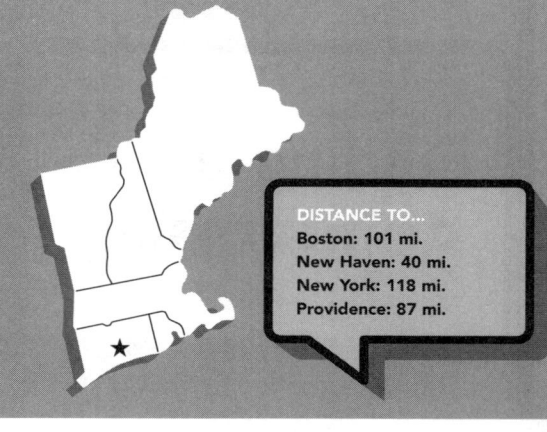

DISTANCE TO...
Boston: 101 mi.
New Haven: 40 mi.
New York: 118 mi.
Providence: 87 mi.

"The one thing everyone seems to have in common at Trinity is a fierce loyalty to this imperfect place."

Total Enrollment:
2,001

Acceptance Rate:
36%

Tuition:
$31,940

Top 10% of High School Class:
51%

SAT Range
Verbal	Math	Total
590 – 700	620 – 710	1210 – 1410

ACT Range
Verbal	Math	Total
24-29	24-29	25-29

Most Popular Majors:
16% Political Science and Government
12% Economics
10% History
9% English Language and Literature
7% Psychology

Students Also Applied To:*
Boston College, Brown University, Georgetown University, Tufts University, Wesleyan University

*For more school info check out www.collegeprowler.com

Table of Contents

Academics	301
Local Atmosphere	303
Safety & Security	304
Computers	306
Facilities	307
Campus Dining	309
Off-Campus Dining	310
Campus Housing	312
Off-Campus Housing	313
Diversity	315
Guys & Girls	316
Athletics	318
Greek Life	319
Drug Scene	321
Campus Strictness	322
Overall Experience	323
The Inside Scoop	324
Finding a Job or Internship	325
The Best & Worst	325

College Prowler Report Card

Academics	B+
Local Atmosphere	C-
Safety & Security	C
Computers	B-
Facilities	B
Campus Dining	B-
Off-Campus Dining	B+
Campus Housing	B+
Off-Campus Housing	D
Diversity	D
Guys	B+
Girls	B+
Athletics	B-
Greek Life	B-
Drug Scene	B-
Campus Strictness	A-

Academics

Best Places to Study

The library has been recently remodeled and now has enough Internet connections for every student in the school and a café in the center. The Cave, one of the school-run eating venues, is furnished with a coffee bar and couches. In warmer weather, nothing beats studying out on the quad, although Frisbees may fly in your direction.

Did You Know?

Trinity College offers 37 different majors and over 970 different courses on its 100-acre campus.

The Lowdown
ON ACADEMICS

Degrees Awarded:
Bachelor, Master

Undergraduate Schools:
College of Arts & Sciences, School of Education, School of Professional Studies

Full-time Faculty: 196

Faculty with Terminal Degree: 91%

Student-to-Faculty Ratio: 9:1

Sample Academic Clubs:
Tutorial College, Guided Studies, The Cities Program

Special Degree Options:
Five-year B.S./M.S. electrical/mechanical engineering program with Rensselaer-Hartford

AP Test Score Requirements:
Possible credit for scores of 4 or higher

IB Test Scores:
May be used for credit and/or placement

Students Speak Out
ON ACADEMICS

"The teachers can be a bit egotistical, but, they are always there for you and listen to what you have to say. The interesting classes are the challenging ones headed by teachers who are really into what they teach."

"By and large, Trinity's professors exude enthusiasm and considerable expertise in their respective subjects. In every department, there are professors whose classes fill up rapidly, and who have the ability to make any subject fascinating, whether it is Shakespeare or business and finance. However, the quality of teaching is variable, and there are a limited number of professors that students may want to avoid. **The Trinity student body is quite candid with their opinions**, and incoming students will find it helpful to discuss professor options with older students."

"For the most part, **the teachers at Trinity are very helpful and enthusiastic** about their work. I have yet to come across a professor that is not enthralled in the subject matter they teach or does not go beyond the call of duty to help his or her students."

The College Prowler Take
ON ACADEMICS

Q "I think that **Trinity's professors are one of its most valuable assets.** The professors work hard to challenge their students, but they are always willing to help. My one complaint would be that Trinity is beginning to focus more on the price tag associated with good teaching rather than the value it brings to the college as a whole. Several of the teachers I had last year will no longer be working at Trinity due to budget cuts."

Q "The Tutorial College program was created by members of Trinity's faculty who wanted to inspire dedicated sophomores to develop lasting relationships with their professors, taking the opportunity to not only learn, but, perhaps, teach. The program requires professors to **read and explore areas beyond their expertise**, which they do, happily, in order to further the experience of their students. These few faculty members are a microcosm of the dedicated professors that Trinity employs."

Q "Due to the size of the student population, professors are able to take a more personal interest in students that a larger student body wouldn't permit. **The ability to form personal relationships with your teachers** allows you to become a stronger student, confident in the knowledge that your teachers are always available. The strength of the faculty and its commitment to the development of the students as people, not merely chair holders, is evident by the freshman seminar program and the faculty-inspired, Tutorial College."

Q "I know a professor who really wanted to stay at Trinity last year but couldn't because of **unreasonable administration policies**—she was offered, and accepted, the position of chair of her department at an Ivy League school. Luckily, our administration is now changing."

The majority of professors at Trinity are great, however, like at any school, there are a few not-so-great ones mixed in, as well. At Trinity, because the school and class sizes are so small, students receive a lot of individual attention. Students definitely sign up for classes, not necessarily because of any specific interest in the subject, but because of the professor teaching it. In several classes, professors have been known to bring in cake or beer, or to invite students to a get-together at their house—one professor even cooked his students a three-course meal to enjoy during class time! Not only are many of the professors at Trinity personable and social with the students, but a number of them have received grant awards from organizations such as the National Endowment of the Arts and NASA. When passing each other on the main path across campus, you can always see students greeting professors as they would their friends.

As for finding classes interesting, Trinity students almost always do. In addition, because all faculty members teach both introductory and advanced courses in their discipline, there is a unique opportunity for students to take a favorite professor repeatedly, which helps to foster great relationships between the students and faculty. Unfortunately, during the 2002-2003 school year, we lost several great professors due to unreasonable budget cuts.

The College Prowler™ Grade on
Academics: B+

A high Academics grade generally indicates that professors are knowledgeable, accessible, and genuinely interested in their students' welfare. Other determining factors include class size, how well professors communicate, and whether or not classes are engaging.

Local Atmosphere

Students Speak Out
ON LOCAL ATMOSPHERE

"Trinity is located in Hartford, which is a small city. There are other colleges around, but Trinity students tend to stay on campus or explore the downtown area."

Q "A lot of students get intimidated by the Hartford ghetto, which is right by Trinity, but there are **a lot of opportunities to make a difference** in Hartford, and there are a lot of fun things in town if you look for them. Too many people stay stuck on campus. Maybe the campus is its own little world and it can be a prison, but don't let it be."

Q "**Hartford is often seen as the 'downside' of going to Trinity**. However, by the time a student has reached his or her junior year, it becomes obvious that the city adds much to the experience of college. Students are able to secure internships at the capitol or perform in local bars and clubs. The problems facing Hartford have created an opening for Trinity and its students to become a part in the reinvention of the city."

Q "Trinity is located in the heart of Hartford, Connecticut. The evidence of a once illustrious and successful community is found in the large Victorian houses on the streets surrounding Trinity, but the neighborhood is now poor and can be off-putting if prospective students and their parents are not warned. However, Hartford does offer cultural spots, such as the Wadsworth Atheneum and the Mark Twain House. Furthermore, only 15 minutes away, West Hartford has students forgetting the grittiness of the Trinity area with its excellent restaurants and small specialty stores. Students do not feel isolated because **there are several excellent schools close by**."

The Lowdown
ON LOCAL ATMOSPHERE

Region:
New England

City, State:
Hartford, Connecticut

Setting:
Downtown

Distance from Boston:
1 hour 45 minutes

Distance from New York City:
2 hours

Major Sports Teams:
The Hartford Wolf Pack, a professional hockey organization

City Websites:
www.enjoyhartford.com
hartford.about.com
www.thecityofhartford.com
www.clubct.com/hartford.htm

> "The capital city we're set in isn't the friendliest of towns, and although there are several other universities nearby, Trinity tends to keep itself isolated. Visit Hartford's beautiful old buildings, museums, and theatres when the weather isn't so great, and its parks when it's nice out. **Visit NYC and Boston every chance you get**."

The College Prowler Take
ON LOCAL ATMOSPHERE

The local atmosphere is not the best. While Hartford is a surprisingly cultural town (check out the Mark Twain House, the plays at the Hartford Stage Company, or the Atheneum—the oldest public museum in the country), it is not very student friendly. However, it is possible to take a tour of the country's oldest State House or visit the ancient burial grounds before taking in a Broadway show at one of the local theaters.

There is not much to see in downtown Hartford, which always surprises people, seeing how it is the capital of Connecticut. The downtown area does consist of several pretty buildings, though many are now boarded up. Students will sometimes joke that their favorite thing about downtown Hartford is the train station, with two-hour trains to New York and Boston. There are things to do and places to go if you search hard enough; but, while gaining an appreciation of Hartford is possible, it does take a genuine effort on the part of the student.

The College Prowler™ Grade on
Local Atmosphere: C-

A high Local Atmosphere grade indicates that the area surrounding campus is safe and scenic. Other factors include nearby attractions, proximity to other schools, and the town's attitude toward students.

Safety & Security

The Lowdown
ON SAFETY & SECURITY

Number of Safety Officers
21 campus safety officers; three dispatchers and three administrative personnel work in the Safety Department, alongside security guards at Ferriss Athletic center. Campus safety officers are not police, although they have received formal police or security training. The nearest police station is two blocks from campus.

Phone:
(860) 297-2222

Health Center Office Hours:
Monday – Friday, 8:30 a.m. – 5:30 p.m.; Saturday, noon – 4 p.m.

Health Center Website:
www.trincoll.edu/StudentLife/HealthSafety/HealthCenter

Safety Services:
More than 50 emergency call-boxes across campus

Did You Know?
In addition to health services provided at Trinity, students also have access to the Trinity Counseling Center, where they can seek out assistance and treatment for a number of mental health issues.

Students Speak Out
ON SAFETY & SECURITY

"Trinity is not in a very good neighborhood, so there are a number of crimes caused by local residents. On campus, crime occurrences are far less than at other schools."

Q "Muggings occur on campus every year, sometimes at gunpoint. Unfortunately, in the fall semester of the 2002-2003 school year, a student was **stabbed outside his dormitory building in the early morning** by an assailant from the neighborhood. Due to incidents like this, campus safety added more officers to their staff, and the school requested that Hartford police department squad cars be stationed around the perimeter. Trinity has taken steps, which it hopes will improve campus safety, beyond adding to the manpower."

Q "Trinity is a generally safe school. It is an open campus, meaning that **people from the surrounding neighborhood may enter at any time**. Instead of decreasing safety, this policy actually helps the relationship between the school and the outside community. Campus safety officers are available 24 hours a day, and there are many emergency call boxes located around the campus. However, students need to exercise common sense, and most students choose not to walk alone at night."

Q "Trinity students access their dorm rooms via codes, which in the past were also their means of access to their dorm building. Trinity feared that students were giving out their codes, and that people seeking access to the buildings were guessing at codes, so the code system was removed from the outer doors of the dorms. Instead, students use their **ID cards to open the doors** to their dorms."

Q "I usually feel safe on campus. I have never had any problems, although each year **several muggings occur on campus**. For those who don't feel comfortable walking, Trinity runs several shuttles around campus and the Hartford area."

The College Prowler Take
ON SAFETY & SECURITY

Reading the quotes above may give you the idea that there are very different opinions about the safety of Trinity campus. In general, however, students agree on the basic facts. We are in the center of a large urban area. There is crime. The muggings that occur each year usually happen to freshman walking alone at night. Don't walk alone at night. This is typical of most college campuses located in urban areas. If you use common sense and use the shuttle instead of walking alone at night, chances are you will usually feel safe, despite the crime that occurs on campus.

The College Prowler™ Grade on
Safety & Security: C

A high grade in Safety & Security means that students generally feel safe, campus police are visible, blue-light phones and escort services are readily available, and safety precautions are not overly necessary.

Computers

Students Speak Out
ON COMPUTERS

"Trinity has recently updated its computer labs, which are very efficient and up-to-date. The computer labs can be crowded during certain periods of time, such as during finals."

Q "**Computer labs are never overcrowded**, but that's because just about everyone brings their own computer. The network has its problems once in a while—they all do—but the problems are not serious, and they never last long."

Q "It is recommended that students bring their own computers, though it is far from necessary. The computer center in the library is **open 24 hours a day** and has multiple labs for student use. There are both PC and Mac computers."

Q "The computing help desk is located within the library and can help you set up your computer, get online, or fix any problems that come up during the semester. There are also computers available in the library, and printing facilities are located there as well. If you bring a laptop, there are **desks with Internet access and outlets available in the library** so that you can continue working there."

Q "In the main computing center, there are two large computer labs that service both IBM compatibles and Macintosh computers. There are **two main printers that students have access to**, both from the computer labs and from their own dorm rooms."

Q "For those students who are able to bring their own computer, the Trinity network serves as a great resource that is **fast, fairly reliable, and easy to use**. Many professors are now using the Trinity network to post assignments and to receive papers. In addition, with the installation of a new wireless network, students are able to take laptop computers anywhere on campus without having to worry about connection cords or plugs."

The Lowdown
ON COMPUTERS

High-Speed Network?
Yes

Number of Labs:
One

Numbers of Computers:
Around 325 available to students

24-Hour Labs:
The computer center is open 24 hours a day

Operating Systems:
Apple LS 10.2, Windows XP Professional

Free Software:
Many Microsoft programs, including Office, Windows, Front Page, Outlook, etc.

Wireless Network?
It's available on about half the campus so far, including the library and the quad.

Charge to Print?
Each student is given an account with 25 dollars on it already; after that, it is 14 cents per one-sided page and seven cents per side on a double-sided page (14 cents per piece of paper, regardless of the amount of print on it).

The College Prowler Take
ON COMPUTERS

Trinity's network access is fast and up-to-date. There are several wireless Internet locations, with more being set up, but, for the most part, we use DSL cords to connect. The connection is fast—songs download from KaZaA in a split-second. Students here strongly recommend that new students bring their own computer, although it is not a crisis if you have to use the computers in the lab. The labs are open 24 hours a day, and there are almost always enough computers for everyone to use.

The College Prowler™ Grade on
Computers: B-

A high grade in Computers designates that computer labs are available, the computer network is easily accessible, and the campus' computing technology is up-to-date.

Facilities

The Lowdown
ON FACILITIES

Athletic Centers:
Ferris Athletic Center, Jessee/Miller Field and George A. Kellner Squash Center

Libraries:
Trinity College Library and Watkinson Library

Student Center:
Not really. Mather Hall pretends to be one, but it is filled with administrative offices and students don't really meet there.

Popular Places to Chill:
The Bistro, The Cave, and the quad

Movie Theatre on Campus?
Yes, Cinestudio. (860) 297-2463

Bowling on Campus?
No

Bar on Campus?
No, although The Tap is directly across the street from the south side of campus.

Coffeehouse on Campus?
Yes, there is a coffee shop in the Gallows Hill bookstore with delicious coffee.

Arts Center
The Austin Arts center has one main auditorium, two performance centers, and an art gallery, as well as many studio classrooms. It houses various art events. (860) 297-2330.

Favorite Things to Do
Sunbathe on the quad in the spring, meet friends for dinner at The Bistro, or grab a smoothie between classes at The Bistro.

Students Speak Out
ON FACILITIES

{ "The only thing that wasn't nice was the library, but it's been totally renovated, and it's awesome. There's no good student center, and it would be nice if the dorms had kitchens."

Q "There is no student union, though Mather Hall attempts to be one. **Mather contains a game room**, not often populated with students, two of the dining facilities, an excellent coffee shop known as The Underground, and offices for community service and student activities. Unfortunately, the office aspect of Mather tends to deter students from hanging out there as they would a more conventional student union, but the administration has made an effort to figure out what the students want, in terms of a real student center."

Q "Many facilities have been recently renovated and are really nice. The new library is gorgeous. The study area is actually conducive to studying, which can be a good or bad thing. There are **comfortable leather chairs and great lighting**. There is also a 24-hour coffee shop. The athletic facilities are comprehensive, and the squash courts are the best in the country. If you don't know what squash is when you come to Trinity, you will very soon after."

Q "The athletic center in **very nice,** although expect to wait a while for a free treadmill."

Q "Overall, the facilities on campus are clean, well-maintained, and up-to-date. The center houses the school bookstore, the mailroom, two different dining options and several auditoriums/conference rooms for guest speakers and performances. The Ferris Athletic Center houses the main gyms, the swimming pool, the tank rooms, squash courts, and the fitness room. With **a state-of-the-art fitness room**, both athletes and non-athletes are able to take advantage of the new equipment and spacious areas to exercise."

The College Prowler Take
ON FACILITIES

The new library is fantastic. It boasts plenty of new places to study, many with sweeping views of campus, and a study lounge around a large fireplace for those chilly winter days and nights! In the basement, there is a newly-renovated computer lounge, and the librarians are all eager to help you however they can. But, the new library aside, overall, when one thinks about the facilities, it becomes clear just how small a school Trinity really is. Don't expect any big, university-type size or efficiency here. Also, the lack of an "official" student center at Trinity is a problem for many, but, in a sense, students agree that the whole campus is our student center.

The College Prowler™ Grade on
Facilities: B

A high Facilities grade indicates that the campus is aesthetically pleasing and well-maintained; facilities are state-of-the-art, and libraries are exceptional. Other determining factors include the quality of both athletic and student centers and an abundance of things to do on campus.

Campus Dining

The Lowdown
ON CAMPUS DINING

Freshman Meal Plan Requirement?
Yes

Meal Plan Average Cost:
$2,510 per semester

24-Hour On-Campus Eating?
Call for pizza.

Student Favorites
Some people like The Bistro for its small-restaurant atmosphere, and some like The Cave for its location. No one really likes Mather, but they eat there because of the meal plans. Mather also has the best variety of all three places, and you can always get staples there: a bagel and cream cheese, cereal, or a PB&J.

Did You Know?

For Halloween, the cafeteria is decorated, and we get free candy. Last year, there was also a table set up to make your own caramel-covered apples (they were delicious).

Students Speak Out
ON CAMPUS DINING

"The food on campus is barely digestible, and The Cave serves all fried food, but people think that The Bistro is nice."

Q "There are three dining halls on campus. The main eating area is Mather, which offers a wide variety of foods. It is either a hit or miss at Mather, as some nights are satisfying, and others leave one wondering what the meal planners could possibly have been thinking. The Cave is located in the basement of Mather and has a grill, a sandwich bar, and a salad bar. It is best used as a lunch area, or as a place to grab a quick meal. **The Bistro feels cleaner than Mather or The Cave,** and it offers excellent sandwich and smoothie options, as well as a grill and a salad bar."

Q "Mather, the main dining hall, tends toward the heavier and, unfortunately, fried variety. However, it does have **a fabulous pasta bar** where you can get vegetables sautéed and then add pasta, pick your sauce, and end up with a fairly healthy, tasty meal. Mather also has a vegetarian section."

Q "The Bistro is Trinity's 'restaurant-like' dining facility. Although there is no table service, and students mostly eat off plastic plates, The Bistro offers **the best food on campus by far**. With specialty sandwiches, Au Bon Pain soups, smoothie drinks, and a full salad bar, The Bistro stands as a student's most tasty option."

Q "Food is usually **somewhere between awful and decent**. It varies. The main dining hall isn't good, but I love The Bistro, and the meal plans are really pretty flexible."

> "Food on campus is decent. The main place to eat, Mather, is all-you-can-eat. It's got everything from a salad and pasta bar, to featured items like meat and fish. The menu gets boring after a while, and the food can often be overcooked. The two other options, The Cave and The Bistro, are good for a change. **The Bistro is by far the best place to eat** with a gourmet-like menu."

The College Prowler Take
ON CAMPUS DINING

Don't expect gourmet food at Trinity, but expect enough quality to get by. The three dining centers, Mather, The Cave, and The Bistro, are all operated by Chartwell's, which means that they aren't in competition with one another, resulting in often-mediocre food. Mather, the main cafeteria, has a wide variety, with vegetarian selections, a grill, and specials each night. The food is cooked for the masses, though, and can be rather bland; however, you can always find cereal or a homemade bagel with good cream cheese. Students should consider campus dining the same way they should consider the local atmosphere. If you come to Hartford expecting NYC, you will be disappointed—and so, too, if you come to Trinity expecting gourmet grub, you will be disappointed and will miss out on all that the school has to offer.

The College Prowler™ Grade on
Campus Dining: B-

Our grade on Campus Dining addresses the quality of both school-owned dining halls and independent on-campus restaurants as well as the price, availability, and variety of food.

Off-Campus Dining

The Lowdown
ON OFF-CAMPUS DINING

Student Favorites
Goldroc Diner, open late, is great for late-night/early-morning meals. It's great to go to after a party or in the middle of an all-nighter, or whenever you get a craving for really unhealthy, really delicious food and a fun diner atmosphere.

Best Pizza
Programmed into the speed dial of my cell phone is Breto's Pizza, (860) 278-4334. They make delicious pizza and are open to special orders, if you can understand their accents. They are open late (many students order as late as 3 a.m.). Some people prefer Campus Pizza, however; it is just across the street from campus.

Students Speak Out
ON OFF-CAMPUS DINING

> "There are many good restaurants off campus. A few of my favorites are City Steam, Black Eyed Sally's, Pastis, and TGI Friday's."

> "I like going into downtown Hartford with my parents because **it can be expensive**, but there are some really nice restaurants on Park Street, which is the Spanish-speaking community. Most people just order pizza or Chinese food, though."

Q "One of the main advantages of going to school in a city is the restaurants. Besides all the chain restaurants you can imagine, some of the best restaurants are Trout Brook, for hamburgers and a beer; Spice, for Indian; Lemongrass, for Thai; and Restaurante Bricco, for a nice, romantic meal. **I could go on for hours** about all the local restaurants."

Q "Timothy's is just across Zion Street, to the west of Trinity. The fare is **pretty exotic**, with a spinach and feta quesadilla and great burgers, making it equally friendly to carnivores as well as the vegetarians. However, the real draw of Timothy's is the Black Magic Cake. The luscious chocolate cake with chocolate frosting and a scoop of vanilla ice cream is, well, magical."

Q "One of Hartford's most valuable assets is the good food that you can find around every corner. Within the city, **you can find almost any type of cuisine**, ranging from Greek to Italian, to Mexican, to Japanese, to anything your taste buds desire. Some of the most notable restaurants that Trinity students like to frequent include Timothy's, a small family-owned restaurant across that street from campus that offers unique, home-made dishes, and Tapas, a great Greek restaurant. Also, there is Puerto Vallarta, a Spanish restaurant in the heart of West Hartford, and Max's Downtown, a more pricey option that offers excellent dining for special occasions."

Did You Know?

If you take in nothing else from this book, please remember this when finals roll around: The Krispy Kreme donut store is open until 1 a.m. A perfect plan for a night of cramming is to stop by the donut store around midnight, pick up a dozen donuts (or several dozen if you plan to share with friends), and plenty of coffee.

In addition, a favorite place to eat or just to get a snack and coffee, is Cosi—along with great coffee and home made Italian sandwich bread, they also have a "make-your-own-s'mores" desert option. Delicious!

The College Prowler Take
ON OFF-CAMPUS DINING

Trinity students tend to stick pretty close to campus for most aspects of daily life, with one large exception—we eat out. Hartford has great dining. The city itself is populated with people from all different cultural backgrounds, and that fact is shown off superbly by the off-campus restaurant choices. There is everything from expensive restaurants for special treats (Max's Downtown), to everyday restaurants with great food (Timothy's—don't forget to try the chocolate cake). The great restaurants are not easy to get to without a car, and the neighborhoods they are in are not always the most charming.

The College Prowler™ Grade on
Off-Campus Dining: B+

A high Off-Campus Dining grade implies that off-campus restaurants are affordable, accessible, and worth visiting. Other factors include the variety of cuisine and the availability of alternative options (vegetarian, vegan, Kosher, etc.).

Campus Housing

Students Speak Out
ON CAMPUS HOUSING

"One of the advantages of Trinity is that you are guaranteed housing all four years, so you never have to worry, no matter how bad your housing lottery number is."

Q "Most dorms are very comfortable. All rooms are equipped with an Internet connection, cable, and phone lines. Freshmen dorms tend to be the ones to avoid, such as Little and North. All upperclassman dorms are **good places to live**."

Q "If you are considering requesting a dorm freshman year, request Jones. It's close to everything, is the cleanest, and has the best lounge compared to other frosh dorms. It also has a big screen TV and vending machines. It is **comparatively further away from the frat party scene**, but you will be thanking your lucky stars that everyone's on the other side of campus when you have to stay in on a Saturday night to finish up a term paper."

Q "The most sought-after dorms are really those on North Campus, mainly for the placement. Because of this, these dorms tend to be senior dorms. Vernon, which is connected to the Barn [Vernon Social Center], is **a 21-and up-dorm**, which means that the issue of alcohol in the dorm is completely eradicated."

Q For the most part, the dorms are clean, well-functioning, and in good condition. However, the dorms at Trinity are nothing to brag about. The rooms for freshmen and sophomores are small and cramped, with linoleum floors and fluorescent lights. **The juniors and seniors have better housing options with large, carpeted rooms** and furnished common areas. The newest dorms on campus, the Summit Suites, are the housing option most prized by students. The rooms are brand new, with carpet, lighting fixtures, individual bathrooms, common areas, kitchens, and discussion rooms. Although these rooms are most often enjoyed by juniors and seniors, sophomores in Tutorial College are housed in the Summit East suites."

The Lowdown
ON CAMPUS HOUSING

Undergrads on Campus:
94%

Number of Residence Halls:
27

Students who live off campus:
6%

Available for Rent:
Mini-refrigerators

Cleaning Service?
In public areas only

You Get
Every dorm room comes equipped with a telephone jack, a cable television connection (we get about 50 channels), and an Ethernet outlet. Per student, each room has a bed, mattress, desk, chair, and a wardrobe or a chest of drawers. Triples and quads with common rooms include stuffed furniture and coffee tables. Rooms with kitchens include a fridge, a stove, a breakfast table, and chairs. There are washers and dryers usually within each dorm building (it is $2 to wash and dry one load). Most dorms also have study lounges.

Also Available
Health dorm (smoke- and substance-free), community service dorm, quiet dorm

> "Sophomores generally congregate in an area known as **the 'sophomore slums,'** because of its close vicinity to the surrounding neighborhood. These dorms are like little apartments, with either one or two bedrooms, a common room, a kitchen, and private bathroom. Juniors and some sophomores live in the center of campus in the 'concrete jungle' that contains Jackson, Wheaton, Smith, and Funston dormitories. These dorms house quads consisting of four single bedrooms, a common room, and single bathroom."

Off-Campus Housing

The College Prowler Take
ON CAMPUS HOUSING

No matter where you live, you do okay with housing at Trinity. Every dorm room comes pretty well-equipped, with furniture, a telephone jack, and Internet and cable TV connections. While two of the freshman dorms, Little and Frobb, come across as rather small and unkempt, most other dorms are considered "good" or "bad," based primarily on location. The center of campus, circling the quad, is a prime location, although these are the oldest buildings on campus. The newest dorms on campus are the Summit dorms, close to the computing center but not much else. Most students spend all four years living on campus. Because there is plenty of housing, you will almost always be able to find a nice place to live.

The Lowdown
ON OFF-CAMPUS HOUSING

Undergrads in Off-Campus Housing:
6%

Popular Areas:
Right off Trinity's campus

Average Rent for a Studio Apartment:
$700/month

Average Rent for a 1BR Apartment:
$800/month

Average Rent for a 2BR Apartment:
$1,000/month

Best Time to Look for a Place:
Places can be found on pretty short notice.

For Assistance Contact:
hartford.forrent.com/search/
www.hartford.americasapartments.com/
www.apartment.com

The College Prowler™ Grade on
Campus Housing: B+

A high Campus Housing grade indicates that dorms are clean, well-maintained, and spacious. Other determining factors include variety of dorms, proximity to classes, and social atmosphere.

 ## Students Speak Out
ON OFF-CAMPUS HOUSING

 ## The College Prowler Take
ON OFF-CAMPUS HOUSING

> "In no way is housing off campus worth it. That'd be my advice."

Q "There are off-campus housing options, but not many students choose to explore them, mostly due to security reasons and convenience. Primarily, residential students attending Trinity live on campus in one of the dormitories, or in a themed house—i.e., a fraternity, sorority, society, multicultural house, or the community service house. Being situated in a city, crime and vandalism are a major problem that the school and its students have to deal with. With these concerns in mind, **most students feel the safest living on campus** and having the resources of the college always at hand."

Q "If dorms do not appeal to a student, there are houses for rent along Allen Place, which is technically off campus, but really considered part of it, just as Crescent Street is. Since **there really are no bad dorms and there is usually enough room**, students have no need to go beyond these options for off-campus housing. However, if a student did want a place farther away from campus, there really is not a lot of opportunity. The neighborhood in which Trinity is situated is not the safest, and parking on campus is limited."

Q "Next door to the 'sophomore slums' are apartment buildings that tend to be occupied by Trinity students. Usually, students do not move off campus until their junior or senior year, and **they often move into these apartments on Crescent Street**."

Q "The only off-campus housing that students elect is on Allen Place, which may as well be on campus because of how close it is. The two sorority houses are located on Allen Place as well as the 'hippie house.' In general, off-campus housing is **not an option that many students explore**."

Q "Off-campus housing is rare. **I wouldn't think it's very safe**. Entering my senior year, I don't know anyone who is living off campus."

Those who live off campus, for the most part, live directly off campus—no more than a block away from the dorms. You don't save much money by renting an off-campus apartment, and you miss out on important things like an Ethernet connection, cable TV, and convenience and safety benefits. Because they live so close to campus, most students who live off campus don't lose out on much of the community feel of Trinity, nor do they receive a greater feeling of independence or individuality. The only real reason to live off campus is if you live in a sorority or fraternity house. Each year, several people will also rent houses or apartments on Crescent Street, which is the same street that houses the "sophomore slums."

The College Prowler™ Grade on
Off-Campus Housing: D

A high grade in Off-Campus Housing indicates that apartments are of high quality, close to campus, affordable, and easy to secure.

Diversity

Economic Status
Most students at Trinity seem to be from upper- or upper-middle-class families. Some students complain about all the "rich kids."

Students Speak Out
ON DIVERSITY

The Lowdown
ON DIVERSITY

White: 83%

African-American: 5%

Asian-American: 6%

Hispanic: 5%

International: 1%

Native American: 0%

Out-of-state students: 79%

Political Activity
Democrats and liberal Republicans seem to be about evenly matched on Trinity's campus. Most students vote in the elections, and a good amount attend debates beforehand to learn about the different candidates for Student Government positions and their ideas for the school.

Gay Tolerance
Trinity is, for the most part, a tolerant community. EROS is a Trinity club open to any student interested in GLTB rights issues.
www.trincoll.edu/orgs/eros

"The parties at the cultural houses are not as well-attended [as other parties] by Trinity students, since many of the white students do not appear comfortable going to these houses."

Q "Trinity has said that diversity is one of its focal points, but **many minority students find themselves dissatisfied** with Trinity's efforts. The Multicultural Affairs Committee [MAC] has batted around this issue for years and often feels that nothing is really happening. Minority students tend to sit together in the dining hall and voice concerns that they are not welcome at other tables."

Q "It's **not a diverse campus**, but my group of friends is really diverse, and yours will be, too, if you're open."

Q "Trinity is often criticized for the uniformity of its students and the small number of minority students who feel welcome at its doors. One of the least appealing aspects of Trinity is the homogeny of its population. Most Trinity students are white, middle- to upper-class Americans who are intelligent and looking for a school where they will be challenged, but will also have a chance to party and let loose on the weekends. **Many administrators have tried to tackle the diversity issue** by enticing more minority students to look at Trinity as a viable option, but their efforts have yet to be seen around campus."

Q "Recently, Trinity has dealt with **issues of racial profiling** by campus safety officers toward students on campus."

> "Trinity is not well known for its diversity. At a quick glance, it seems that **everyone looks the same**. However, with a closer look, it is clear that diversity does exist at Trinity. Communities such as the Men of Color Alliance, Hillel, La Voz Latina, and Encouraging Respect of Sexualities [EROS] all support non-uniformity as well as help students feel comfortable in a relatively homogenous environment."

The College Prowler Take
ON DIVERSITY

The general consensus among Trinity students is that there is diversity on campus, but that there is not much interaction between ethnic and cultural groups. The majority of Trinity students seem to be upper-middle-class, white, and American. However, the cultural clubs are relatively active around campus. Problems like racial profiling by campus safety officers, and a lack of interaction between students of different backgrounds, have been talked about a lot recently. While these are unfortunate situations that should not exist in the first place, the fact that they are being aired so much in the open does prove that the real majority of Trinity students are concerned about these trends and are eager to see them end.

The College Prowler™ Grade on
Diversity: D

A high grade in Diversity indicates that ethnic minorities and international students have a notable presence on campus and that students of different economic backgrounds, religious beliefs, and sexual preferences are well-represented.

Guys & Girls

The Lowdown
ON GUYS & GIRLS

Women Undergrads: 51%

Men Undergrads: 49%

Birth Control Available?
Yes, different types are available from the Health Center.

Social Scene
On the weekends, we rarely leave campus. There are always loads of parties on campus, whether school-sponsored, or sponsored by a social or cultural club. There are also many dorm room and frat parties (22 percent of girls and 27 percent of men join a Greek organization while at Trinity). There are several bars in Hartford, such as The Brickyard, Bourbon Street, The Pig's Eye and The Tap, but usually the campus parties are more fun. There is heavy drinking at many of the parties, but it isn't necessary to drink a lot to have fun. The Underground coffeehouse has live music and open mic nights, and The Bistro also has live music and comedy shows.

Hookups or Relationships?
There are more random hookups than serious relationships, although it really depends on what an individual student is looking for.

Students Speak Out
ON GUYS & GIRLS

"The guys are jerks and the girls are hot. Every stuck-up, tanned, skinny inch of them tells you that they know it, too."

Q "The girls are hot, really hot. When spring rolls around, I **just look around and thank God**."

Q "These people are gorgeous. Just about everyone is in spectacular shape and works to stay that way, and **people really care about how they dress**. This can distract you from your studies, but it means that you are forced to show your professors respect by not showing up in pajama pants."

Q "Trinity students are best characterized as preppy. Walking around campus, you will definitely see **upturned collars, Nantucket Reds, and flip-flops**, but with each new class that passes through, the style changes. For a long time, Trinity was known for attracting good-looking males and females of the middle- and upper-class. However, as more students who are interested in the school for its educational opportunities (rather than the crowd it is known to attract), filter in, the school is beginning to form a new face. It is pretty hard to go to a Friday night party or to take a walk down the Long Walk without bumping into someone whom you find attractive."

Q "Trinity is known as a 'beautiful people campus.' The typical Trinity look for girls is **bright, flowered Lily Pulitzer dresses**, pearl earrings, designer jeans, Polo shirts with the collar flipped up, and CK Bradley accessories. The typical Trinity male wears jeans or khakis and purple or pink polo shirts with the collar also flipped up. Both sexes wear flip-flops through November and start up again in early March. Although it seems that Trinity is overrun with white Anglo-Saxon Protestants, there is diversity on campus and not everyone hails from Greenwich, Connecticut. Different groups of people abound at Trinity, and it is simply up to the individual to find his or her niche."

Q "The guys and the girls can be pretty preppy, with flipped up collars on their Polo shirts to prove it. This can be funny to those who aren't used to it, but does nothing to detract from how **genuinely nice** people at Trin can be."

The College Prowler Take
ON GUYS & GIRLS

Trin students care about their looks. Bright colors are everywhere, and most every guy and girl on campus owns a pink polo shirt. The "dress code" is very New England and preppy. That said, if you don't enjoy wearing ribbons in your hair, or pearl earrings to the gym, nobody will really care all that much. The guys and girls are, to use an overused but appropriate word, pretty nice. You will be able to find a social group where you feel that you belong. Hookups are, in general, more common than relationships. Trinity has a reputation as a party school, and it is not undeserved. Guys and girls lose some points for their lack of diversity and a tendency towards cliquishness.

The College Prowler™ Grade on
Guys: B+

A high grade for Guys indicates that the male population on campus is attractive, smart, friendly, and engaging, and that the school has a decent ratio of guys to girls.

The College Prowler™ Grade on
Girls: B+

A high grade for Girls not only implies that the women on campus are attractive, smart, friendly, and engaging, but also that there is a fair ratio of girls to guys.

Athletics

Intramurals (IMs):
Flag Football
Soccer
Physical Fitness
Squash
Tennis
Aerobics
Rugby
Volleyball
Basketball
Softball
Indoor Soccer

Athletic Division
Division III

School Mascot
Bantam (looks like a chicken, sometimes called a cock, those who don't attend the school may think that the Bantam is an unfortunate choice—but we Trinity students like our mascot).

Getting Tickets
You don't really "get" tickets at Trinity. In the fall and spring, you sit on a sloping hill overlooking the fields and cheer on the various teams. You wander into the Jessee/Miller Field to watch football, or you grab a seat on the bleachers to watch softball.

The Lowdown
ON ATHLETICS

Men's Varsity Teams:
Basketball
Rowing
Ice Hockey
Lacrosse
Soccer
Squash
Tennis
Baseball
Football
Cross Country
Track and Field
Swimming and Diving
Wrestling
Golf

Women's Varsity Teams:
Basketball
Rowing
Ice Hockey
Lacrosse
Soccer
Squash
Tennis
Softball
Field Hockey
Cross Country
Track and Field
Swimming and Diving
Volleyball

Students Speak Out
ON ATHLETICS

{ **"Varsity sports at Trinity are pretty much ignored by those not actually playing them."**

Q "Sports come in and out of fashion at Trinity. When our athletic teams are doing well, the stands are packed, but when the scores are not as high, **most students find something else to occupy their free time**. However, to the students who are involved with the athletic programs, sports are a big part of their everyday lives."

Q "Tons of people play varsity sports. Squash, football, and basketball get spectators. Nothing else really does. **We are five-time national champions in squash** and undefeated for the past five years. Intramural sports have a small, but very loyal, membership of enthusiastic people."

Club Sports
Alpine skiing, cheerleading, equestrian sports fencing, riflery, rugby, sailing, ultimate Frisbee, volleyball, water polo

Q "Homecoming at Trinity **tends to revolve around the tailgating,** rather than the 'big game.'"

Q "Just about everyone is on a team or knows someone who is. Teams get T-shirts made with their team name, and nicknames, for the players on the backs. A few years ago, **a team was even sponsored—given T-shirts to wear—by a strip club in Providence**. This team ended up winning their league and sending the club a Trinity Intramural Champs T-shirt, which everyone on a winning team receives and wears with pride for the rest of their time at Trinity."

The College Prowler Take
ON ATHLETICS

Greek Life

The Lowdown
ON GREEK LIFE

Stuck in Division III, we aren't the biggest sports school—although Trinity does recruit squash players from all over the world. Our football team doesn't get much notice. However, that doesn't mean that our homecoming celebration isn't one of the biggest of the year. Our gym is more than adequate, and nearly everyone on campus works out in the weight room. Intramural sports are great. Although our sports teams, with the major exception of squash, may not get much recognition, they are still a big part of the school. There is a lot of heart in the Trinity sports teams—illustrated by the pride students show in their mascot, the Bantam. Bantam may be just another word for chicken or cock, but we love him anyway.

Undergrad Men in Fraternities: 27%

Undergrad Women in Sororities: 22%

Recognized Greek Letter Organizations: About four to seven, at any given time

Students Speak Out
ON GREEK LIFE

"I would not say that the frat parties dominate the social scene, but they make up a big part of it. There are at least five main frats, and they are all pretty different from each other, which is nice."

The College Prowler™ Grade on
Athletics: B-

A high grade in Athletics indicates that students have school spirit, that sports programs are respected, that games are well-attended, and that intramurals are a prominent part of student life.

Q "Trinity does not have a large Greek population and prevents rushing and pledging during a student's freshman year. However, **everyone knows someone who is in a fraternity or sorority**, because the campus is related more closely than by six degrees."

Q "Although not many Trinity students actually belong to fraternities or sororities, **Greek life definitely plays a large role in the social scene** on campus. On Friday and Saturday nights, most students flee to the fraternity houses, either for themed parties such as 'Toga Night' or just some late-night drinking. In addition to throwing parties, members of the Trinity Greek Council facilitate community service projects and educational opportunities for students."

Q "Greek life is present at Trinity, but it definitely does not dominate the social scene. **Kappa Kappa Gamma is the only sorority that is nationally-recognized**. Ivy, the other sorority, was previously Tri Delta. Psi Upsilon and Alpha Delta are the two nationally-recognized fraternities, and Saint Anthony's Hall, better known as "The Hall," is a fraternity with both men and women members. Cleo is an all-inclusive literary society that provides an alternative social scene from the mainstream. In general, the sorority parties are held off campus and are closed to the public, while the fraternities are better known for the publicly open 'Late Night.'"

Q "Most fraternities throw a party each semester, which is authorized. They also throw parties that are completely unauthorized. Among the authorized parties is Psi Upsilon's 'Tropical,' which takes place at the beginning of the school year. Grass skirts and Hawaiian shirts seem to appear out of nowhere on Trinity's campus the night of Tropical. On the Saturday of Spring Weekend, St. Anthony's Hall sponsors 'Hallapalooza,' **a day-long series of concerts on The Hall's property**. It's a little pricey, but loads of fun."

The College Prowler Take
ON GREEK LIFE

Greek life is there. Take advantage of it if you want—you will find yourself with some great friends and fun parties. Ignore it if you want—you will still have plenty to do on the party nights. Greek life is pretty visible, but not in a bad way. If you chose to partake in it, that is fine, and if you chose not to, well, that is fine, too. Most sororities do not throw parties that are open to the public, but the fraternities all do, and for every different personality type, there is a fraternity party.

The College Prowler™ Grade on
Greek Life: B-

A high grade in Greek Life indicates that sororities and fraternities are not only present, but also active on campus. Other determining factors include the variety of houses available and the respect the Greek community receives from the rest of the campus.

Drug Scene

Q "Although most students find their partying limit with alcohol, there are pockets of students who rely heavily on drugs for their weekend festivities. Although the most abused drug appears to be marijuana, Trinity **students have been found in possession of cocaine, heroin, and Special K**. Several years ago, Trinity lost two students to a drug overdose, and since then, students have begun to wise up and party with a little more caution."

Q "Although the former president, Dick Hersh, tried to institute several new college policies to crack down on the consumption of alcohol on campus, the party scene still seems to be thriving on **kegs, hard alcohol, and common college drugs** [i.e. marijuana, Adderall, etc.]."

The Lowdown
ON DRUG SCENE

Liquor-Related Campus Citations:
143

Liquor-Related Arrests by Hartford Police:
6

Drug-Related Campus Citations:
44

Drug-Related Arrests by Hartford Police:
12

Most Prevalent Drugs on Campus:
Alcohol, marijuana, caffeine, cocaine

The College Prowler Take
ON DRUG SCENE

You won't find prevalent hardcore drug use. Marijuana is around, but there's not too much of the harder stuff. However, the alcohol abuse can get pretty outrageous. Some students will blow off steam on the weekends by getting very, very drunk. There is a student organization called T-Cert, made up of EMT-certified volunteer students, and their weekends tend to be pretty busy for reasons other than their social schedules: they are frequently called when a student overdoes with alcohol and they arrive quickly to take care of the student.

Students Speak Out
ON DRUG SCENE

"Drugs are readily available, especially pot. But, not too many people do drugs. There is a small 'drug crowd,' but there's no pressure to do any."

Q "Rumors and stories indicate that marijuana is easily available to any student with the money to purchase it and that **cocaine is always able to be found** on campus."

Q "There's nothing about Trinity that makes it **any worse than any other college**."

The College Prowler™ Grade on
Drug Scene: B-

A high grade on Drug Scene indicates that drugs are not a noticeable part of campus life; drug use is not visible, and no pressure to use them seems to exist.

Campus Strictness

The Lowdown
ON CAMPUS STRICTNESS

What Are You Most Likely to Get Caught Doing on Campus?
Drinking in a "freshman" dorm, parking illegally, having candles in your room, throwing snowballs off the roof of your dorm

Students Speak Out
ON CAMPUS STRICTNESS

"Campus policy on drinking has been more strictly enforced recently, since Trinity has been gaining a reputation as a party school. Alcohol is taboo in freshmen dorms, no matter what the age of the occupant is."

Q "Underage students cannot walk around campus with alcohol, or they run the risk of getting written up. After a certain number of these write-ups, **a student can lose the right to housing**, or be punished more severely by the Dean of Students."

Q "Most campus safety officers will, at most, tell a student to dump out their beer or to throw away their cup rather than write them up and pass their name along to the dean. As long as students are partying in a fairly reasonable manner, **the campus safety officers will leave them be**. It seems as though their objective is more to protect students from intruders and bad situations than to be the drinking police."

Q "We are going through presidents pretty quickly at the moment, unfortunately. As I began my senior year, Trinity welcomed its fourth president in four years. They all seem to have different attitudes towards drinking on campus. For the most part, the drinking is **tolerated in moderation**, which is as it should be; people at college will drink, and it is better that they stay on campus than drive into unsafe areas of Hartford and then drive home."

The College Prowler Take
ON CAMPUS STRICTNESS

Students who are resident assistants (RAs) are allowed to write people up for drinking and will sometimes have little power trips, but the campus safety officers are, for the most part, pretty reasonable. For the most part, the Trinity administration is good about understanding that it is better that students drink in the sheltered atmosphere of Trinity, with friends, a bed, and even EMT-trained students close by, than for them to drive to an unsafe bar in the middle of the city, drink too much (as, face it, most freshmen do at least once), and then, to cap off the night, drive (swerve) home. There are even times when campus safety officers really should be a little tougher.

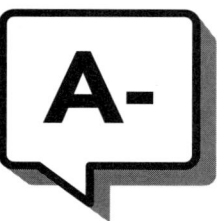

The College Prowler™ Grade on
Campus Strictness: A-

A high Campus Strictness grade implies an overall lenient atmosphere; police and RAs are fairly tolerant, and the administration's rules are flexible.

Overall Experience

Students Speak Out
ON OVERALL EXPERIENCE

"My parents wish I was closer to home, but I'll fight to stay at Trinity because it's the right place for me and I've found a way to make it my home."

Q "Trinity is **a good place to hide from reality** for four years, but I wouldn't mind being abroad or in California."

Q "My first year at Trinity was a big adjustment. Coming from a public high school and being submerged in a crowd of boarding school graduates, I was overwhelmed with the preppy clothes, the boarding school drugs, and the elitist attitude. I definitely had thoughts of transferring. But, during my second year, I found a group of students that I automatically clicked with. Being such a small school, Trinity is **all about groups, cliques, and finding your own niche**. Once that happens, the rest just falls into place. My academic experience so far has been intense and challenging, while my social life blurs into one big party scene. Although it's nice to take a break from campus every so often, either for Thanksgiving, spring break, or the end of the semester, I always look forward to returning to Camp TrinTrin."

Q "Trinity is a small school, and as such **it can get on one's nerves**. However, Trinity became my home within the first semester I was there."

Q "In a quiz that was created by a Trinity student and distributed through our AIM profiles, this student tested how 'Trin' we were. One of the questions that you had to answer as true to get a point toward being 'Trin' was that you had **talked about transferring every day of your freshman year**. I answered true to that question. Since then, however, I have viewed a trying freshman year as the key to a wonderful experience. The reasons I went to Trinity are not the reasons I stayed. The people, the professors, and the opportunities are all aspects of the school that can only be explained in a brochure, never experienced in all their glory."

Q "My overall experience at Trinity has been wonderful. I had a rocky start freshman year and seriously considered transferring, but I gave it one more chance, and it worked out for me. I found a group of friends with whom I was very compatible, and we have all developed close ties with each other. I have experimented with several majors and **have found the faculty supportive and helpful** as I explored my intellectual interests. Although Trinity is not a utopia by any means, I am thankful that I did not go anywhere else."

The College Prowler Take
ON OVERALL EXPERIENCE

Everyone seems to experience a similarly difficult freshman year, but that can be expected wherever one goes. News flash for any incoming freshman: Trinity is not perfect, but no place really is. Once you accept that, you can begin settling down, growing comfortable, and viewing this imperfect little oasis in the middle of Hartford as home for the next four years. As a kid, you can't wait for summer vacation, but in college, you can't wait for the beginning of September and the chance to go back to school.

The Inside Scoop

The Lowdown
ON THE INSIDE SCOOP

Trinity Slang
Know the slang, know the school. The following is a list of things you really need to know before coming to Trinity. The more of these words you know, the better off you'll be.

The Barn – Vernon Social Center
Club "V" – Vernon Social Center
Mather – The main cafeteria on campus
The Long Walk – The walk along Seabury and Jarvis dorm connecting the north side of campus to the south side
The Lower Long Walk – The walk on the east side of the main quad connecting The Bistro to the library

Plaque on the Long Walk
There is a plaque on the Long Walk that commemorates a visit FDR made to Trinity. It says something in Latin, but nobody will say exactly what, since each year there is a contest as to which student can translate it correctly. FDR stood on that spot to make a speech, and the plaque was put in. There is a legend that if you walk on it after you matriculate, you won't graduate. However, if you do take a drunken stumble across it, or, if in a bleary haze after pulling an all-nighter, a friend pushes you across it, don't fear—during your senior year, if you throw up on the plaque, the curse from having walked across it will be removed. There is another rumor that if you have sex with a member of the senior class while standing on the plaque, the curse will be taken away, too. Guess there's only one way for you to find out if any of it is true.

Famous Trinity Alumni:

• Edward F. Albee '50
Three-time Pulitzer Prize Winner
Author of *Who's Afraid of Virginia Woolf?*
Major: Sociology and Education

• Timothy P. Horne '59
Chairman & CEO, Watts Industries, Inc.
Major: Romance Languages

• Thomas M. Chappell '66
Business Entrepreneur & Founder of Tom's of Maine
Major: English

• Robert W. Baker '66
Vice Chairman, AMR Corporation & American Airlines
Major: Economics

• Michael D. Loberg '69
CEO, NitroMed, Inc.
Major: Chemistry

• Elizabeth Alden '75
CEO & Chair, Alden Products Co.
Major: Philosophy

• Joseph H. Kluger '77
President & Chief Operating Officer, the Philadelphia Symphony Orchestra
Major: Music

• Joanna J. Scott '82
Acclaimed Novelist, Professor of English at the University of Rochester, Recipient of Guggenheim and Macarthur fellowships
Major: English

• Mary McCormack '91
Stage, Screen, & Television Actress
Major: Interdisciplinary

Finding a Job or Internship

The Lowdown
ON FINDING A JOB OR INTERNSHIP

Internship searches are always stressful, but Trinity's career center helps however they can. There are several finger-food parties throughout the year intended to let students mingle with alumni and network. There are conferences that students can attend that explain good strategies for finding a job, and individual appointments with Career Center staff that include resume assistance and interview training. Trinity also has a pretty good Website where potential employers can place ads for internships and summer jobs.

Career Center Resources & Services
This is the general Website for career services: www.trincoll.edu/depts/career/students/welcome.htm; It has a lot of different options and suggestions and is very helpful.

This Website is a sort of high-tech classified pages, listing a ton of jobs and internships, both summer and school year, offered to Trinity students: trincoll.erecruiting.com

The Best & Worst

The Ten BEST Things About Trinity:

1. The quad in the spring
2. The professors
3. The small campus
4. Thursday nights
5. The 1980s party
6. Tropical!
7. Late Night at the frats
8. Spring Weekend
9. School-free snow days
10. The friends you will make

The Ten WORST Things About Trinity:

1. The turnover of college presidents
2. The location (Hartford)
3. Parking
4. The campus food service
5. The awful weather
6. The flipped-up Polo shirt collars
7. The snotty social cliques
8. Charge to print
9. Student apathy towards athletics
10. Poor public transportation

Tufts University

Medford, MA 02155
www.tufts.edu
(617) 627-3170

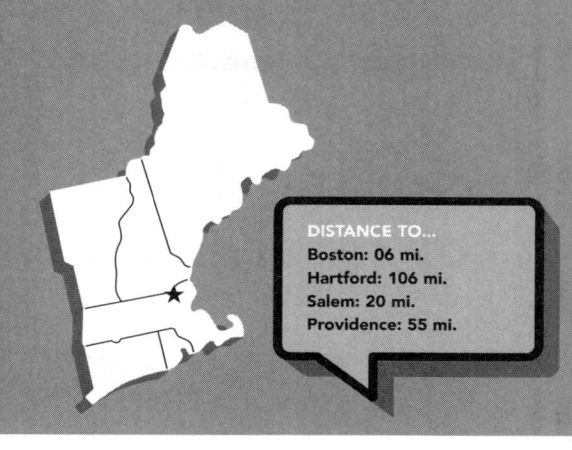

DISTANCE TO...
Boston: 06 mi.
Hartford: 106 mi.
Salem: 20 mi.
Providence: 55 mi.

"Tufts teeters on the fence between being a small New England liberal arts college and a large research institution."

Total Enrollment:
4,800

Acceptance Rate:
26%

Tuition:
$30,969

Top 10% of High School Class:
70%

SAT Range
Verbal	Math	Total
610 – 700	640 – 720	1250 – 1420

ACT Range
Verbal	Math	Total
N/A	N/A	27-31

SAT II Requirements
The SAT II writing test and two other subject tests determined by the applicant's field of interest.

Most Popular Majors:
13% Economics
10% Political Science and Government
9%   English Language and Literature

Students Also Applied To:*
Brown University, Harvard University, Cornell Univeristy, Dartmouth College
*For more school info check out www.collegeprowler.com

Table of Contents

Academics	327
Local Atmosphere	329
Safety & Security	330
Computers	332
Facilities	333
Campus Dining	335
Off-Campus Dining	336
Campus Housing	338
Off-Campus Housing	340
Diversity	341
Guys & Girls	343
Athletics	345
Greek Life	347
Drug Scene	348
Campus Strictness	350
Overall Experience	351
The Inside Scoop	352
Finding a Job or Internship	354
The Best & Worst	355

College Prowler Report Card

Academics	A-
Local Atmosphere	A-
Safety & Security	B+
Computers	B
Facilities	B
Campus Dining	B+
Off-Campus Dining	A
Campus Housing	B-
Off-Campus Housing	B-
Diversity	B-
Guys	C-
Girls	B-
Athletics	C-
Greek Life	C-
Drug Scene	B+
Campus Strictness	B+

Academics

The Lowdown
ON ACADEMICS

Degrees Awarded:
Bachelor, Master, Doctorate

Undergraduate Schools:
Arts and Sciences, Engineering University College of Citizenship, Public Service

Full-time Faculty:
411

Faculty with Terminal Degree:
99%

Student-to-Faculty Ratio:
8:1

Average Course Load:
4 or 5 classes

AP Test Score Requirements:
Possible credit for scores of 4 or 5 (exceptions in language)

IB Test Score Requirements:
Possible credit for scores of 5, 6, or 7

Special Degree Options
Five-year Bachelor of Music and Bachelor of Arts or Sciences from Tufts and New England Conservatory of Music

Five-year Bachelor of Arts and Bachelor of Fine Arts from Tufts and School of the Museum of Fine Arts

Five-year combined Bachelor and Master's Degree in Liberal Arts or Engineering

Six-year Bachelors and Master of Arts in Law and Diplomacy (M.A.L.D.) from Tufts and the Fletcher School of Law and Diplomacy

Early Notification Program for acceptance to Tufts School of Medicine

Nine-year, three-degree program with School of Engineering and Tufts School of Medicine

Nine-year, three-degree program with School of Engineering and Tufts School of Dental Medicine

ROTC

Sample Academic Clubs
The Economics Society, American Institute of Chemical Engineers (AIChE), American Medical Student Association (Pre-Med), American Society of Civil Engineers (ASCE), Child Development Association, Pre-Legal Society, Pre-Veterinary Society, Psychology Society, Public Health at Tufts (PHAT), Society of Collegiate Scholars (NSCS), Tau Beta Pi

Best Places to Study
Tisch Library Campus Center, President's Lawn

Did You Know?

You can take a class on anything from bugs to massage therapy at the Experimental College and get full credit.

Students Speak Out
ON ACADEMICS

The College Prowler Take
ON ACADEMICS

{ "The teachers at Tufts are so open and willing to help. Upper-level courses are designed to bring students' diversity and range of experiences into the classroom, making the material more tangible."

Q "**The teachers I had were all very unique**, interesting, and approachable. If I ever had a problem with anything, it was easy to e-mail them and they would respond, helpfully. Most teachers have high expectations of the kids, but are also very fair. I have no complaints about the teachers at Tufts, although I've heard some of the TAs are annoying. You run into TAs when you have a lab for a class, like science."

Q "**Professors are within your reach for extra help**, or just to chat. I met a couple mentors in my freshman year by just going up and seeing them in their office hours. They're generally very nice people, with the exception of a few. My chemistry professor throws parties in his own house every now and then, which is pretty rare for a professor. The best thing Tufts has going for it is the quality of its people, including the professors."

Q "The size of the class often determines the level of contact with professors, but generally, if you make the effort, **you'll get to know all your professors**. All offer office hours and are usually very accessible; they will always accept a phone call or a student who just drops in for help. For the most part, I've had luck with professors."

Q "It wasn't really until my junior year that I really liked all of my teachers and began to form relationships with them. Once you become comfortable with what you want to do, it is easier to relate to teachers and **take classes with the teachers you like** or have heard good things about."

As a top-level school, Tufts has an excellent faculty and academics that are some of the real newsmakers in modern philosophy, medicine, chemistry, and psychology, among other subjects. Classes are exactly what the students make of them, and so are the relationships with faculty. Students generally find Tufts' professors approachable, knowledgeable, and easygoing. Office hours are an excellent time to get to know a professor and find out about research opportunities and possible internships. They are also a good way to get some extra ideas outside of the classroom setting.

As for the classes, there are so many options that each semester starts with a "shopping period." Shopping for classes at Tufts is like shopping for a car. What you choose to take depends very much on both the subject and the instructor. Some professors are Porsches or convertibles, and, of course, there are always a few lemons. Don't be afraid to drop a class during the add-drop period if the professor bores you to tears, because there are plenty of other really exciting professors. With such a top-notch faculty, it's important to talk to friends, upperclassmen, and even other faculty members, to figure out what courses and teachers are best suited to your tastes. Tufts professors are really just grown-up students, and if you take the opportunity to get to know them outside of class, you will really enhance your college experience.

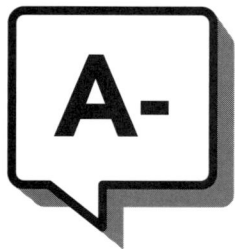

The College Prowler™ Grade on
Academics: A-

A high Academics grade generally indicates that professors are knowledgeable, accessible, and genuinely interested in their students' welfare. Other determining factors include class size, how well professors communicate, and whether or not classes are engaging.

Local Atmosphere

Students Speak Out
ON LOCAL ATMOSPHERE

"Boston is the biggest college town in the country. There are over 500,000 students in the city, so there are always things to do and people to go out and meet."

Q "**The town, itself, is just outside Boston**, and, although a little small, it's got some good restaurants, bars, and theaters. Overall, it's not Boston, and, although the city is only 20 minutes away, Tufts students rarely go there on a regular basis, even if the subway is an easy trip. Tufts is very campus-centered, and it's tough for students to get away from it sometimes, especially without a car."

Q "Tufts is like its own little world, but as soon as you hop on the T, the whole city of Boston appears on your doorstep. There are **endless restaurants, bars, clubs, shops, historical sites, and museums** to visit."

Q "**Tufts bridges together two towns**, Medford and Somerville. Tufts is on the border between Medford, a boring and old-fashioned, yet safe, suburban district, and Somerville, which has been growing at an exponential rate from an almost slummy area into the new, alternative district for college students."

Q "Tufts is in a small town and **there's not much to do**, but there are so many universities around. Harvard is the closest, then MIT, Boston University, and Boston College. It is definitely cool to go to their parties!"

Q "**You are really close to Boston**, and that proximity affords you great shopping, museums, bars, clubs, and touristy spots. Medford and Somerville are fine, and all of the merchants and locals that I've dealt with are always really nice. I would not walk around back alleys late at night by myself, but short of that, it's fine."

The Lowdown
ON LOCAL ATMOSPHERE

Region:
Northeast

City, State:
Medford and Somerville, Massachusetts

Setting:
Suburban (near Boston)

Distance from Montreal:
5 hours

Distance from New York:
3.5 hours

Points of Interest:
Museum of Fine Arts, Museum of Science, New England Aquarium, Paul Revere House, New England Quilt Museum, Franklin Park Zoo, Boston Ballet, Boston Pops, Boston Symphony Orchestra, Boston Lyric Opera

City Websites:
www.boston.com
www.bostonglobe.com

Major Sports Teams:
Patriots (NFL), Celtics (NBA), Bruins (NHL), Red Sox (MLB)

The College Prowler Take
ON LOCAL ATMOSPHERE

If you are venturing off campus for a night, chances are you'll take the T (subway) into Cambridge or Boston—but that doesn't mean that there isn't anything going on in Tufts' hometowns. Whether you pronounce them "Med-fuhd and Sumah-ville" or "Medford and Somerville," Tufts' local areas are your basic college towns.

Tufts has the advantage of being located just a 15-minute T-ride from the center of a city where there is plenty of nightlife, concerts, and shows to entertain the Tufts student body and those of the other 55 Boston-area schools. Although you won't find as many Tufts students in the city as you will in Medford and Somerville, it can make for much better variety in nightlife and activities.

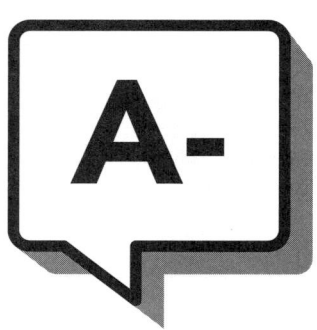

The College Prowler™ Grade on

Local Atmosphere: A-

A high Local Atmosphere grade indicates that the area surrounding campus is safe and scenic. Other factors include nearby attractions, proximity to other schools, and the town's attitude toward students.

Safety & Security

The Lowdown
ON SAFETY & SECURITY

Number of Tufts University Police:
58

Phone:
(617) 627-3030

Health Center Office Hours
Monday through Friday, 8 a.m. – 8 p.m.
Saturday, 10:30 a.m. – 5 p.m.

Safety Services
24-hour emergency response patrols, late-night transport/escort service, controlled dormitory access, security lighting, blue-light phones

Did You Know?

Health Services' massage therapist also teaches a class in the Ex College, where you can learn his trade.

The most common offense on campus, other than drug and liquor law issues, is burglary.

Students Speak Out
ON SAFETY & SECURITY

The College Prowler Take
ON SAFETY & SECURITY

"Although there are reports of petty crimes here and there, campus feels very safe. While I am wary of dangers as a girl, I am not nervous about walking home alone at night."

Q "**Tufts is a very safe place** with a large sense of community and courtesy. Most security violations come from local residents. Known as townies, they are not students of the University, but they come over to the campus on weekends and resent not being able to attend University functions and parties on campus."

Q "I never had an issue, as a man. When they first get to campus, some women are nervous about walking across at night, but I have never heard of an incident. **'Townies' sometimes cause trouble at house or frat parties** but rarely cause any trouble outside of that. I've heard of a couple of shouting matches and low-key brawls between guys from town and students, but nothing that would prevent me from feeling safe."

Q "**I have never felt unsafe, even late at night**. The campus police offer a self defense class for girls and have made many efforts to remind students that they aren't always as safe in the 'real world' as they are on campus. It's easy to take our safety for granted."

Q "I'm from New York City, so I feel really safe. You can't be anywhere on campus without being able to sprint to a dorm phone or a blue-light emergency phone because they're never more than, maybe, a hundred yards away. **We have a police station on campus** called the TUPD that's always open."

Q "Safety is not an issue. Campus is totally safe to walk around at night. I had a job off campus the first semester of my freshman year, and I felt fine walking home at night. **Dorms are always locked, but entrance is easy**. That may seem a bit unsafe, but it's never been a problem. You'll find that it's much nicer to have easy access to dorms and not have restrictions on who can stay over, like at other schools."

Tufts has gone to incredible lengths to make students feel safe on campus. With safety services like TEMS, police escorts, and a strong police presence on a well-lit campus, Tufts students feel safe walking around campus, even at night. Don't let the "you can't spell stupid without TUPD" jokes fool you—TUPD officers are always around campus and willing to help you. Every year, there are a few assaults, robberies, and hate crimes, but rarely are they committed by members of the Tufts community. Above all else, "townies" present the biggest threat around the Tufts area, and even this isn't something to worry about.

The College Prowler™ Grade on
Safety & Security: B+

A high grade in Safety & Security means that students generally feel safe, campus police are visible, blue-light phones and escort services are readily available, and safety precautions are not overly necessary.

Computers

Students Speak Out
ON COMPUTERS

"**The lab is fairly large, but a lot of coursework is online. Tack that on to all the writing that needs to be done for most courses, and the computer lab becomes impractical.**"

Q "**Computing on campus is really good**. The main lab is big, and there are usually enough computers to go around. Many buildings on campus also have wireless Internet, so that's a good perk to bring a laptop. Everyone has their own computers, so the lab is a good place to go to kill time midday or to do that last-minute paper in a less distracting environment."

Q "**Those students without their own computers will probably be at more of a social loss than an academic one**. The Tufts campus is split into uphill and downhill sections that are difficult to walk across on a whim. Therefore, plans are usually made beforehand. Plans are often made using chat programs such as AOL Instant Messenger, or by phone."

Q "**The computer network is really fast**. Be careful about getting caught using KaZaA. The computer labs are also good. They have plenty of computers, and they are rarely full. You should definitely bring a computer if you have one. It's so much more convenient."

Q "**Computer access can be problematic at times**. The labs are great if you go early, but you have to know when to use them. During midterms and finals you need to get to the lab five minutes before opening [8 a.m.] to get a computer. Your best bet is to bring a laptop."

Q "I would suggest bringing your own computer. **The labs are not really near the dorms**, so you have to walk in the snow or rain. But, they usually aren't crowded. I've never gone there and not been able to sit down immediately."

The Lowdown
ON COMPUTERS

High-Speed Network?
Yes

Wireless Network?
Yes

Number of Labs:
3

24-Hour Labs:
None

Charge to Print?
Yes, 10 cents per page.

Numbers of Computers:
2,008

Operating Systems:
Mac, Windows, Linux

The College Prowler Take
ON COMPUTERS

Tufts is a well-wired campus, and students don't complain about access to computer labs or the Internet from their dorm rooms. Over 80 percent of Tufts students bring their own computers to campus, and the campus is completely wired—meaning there is a huge social element to computers, as many use AOL Instant Messenger for all of their communication needs. There are three main computer labs in addition to computers in the library. Eaton is the main computing center, with two floors and over 260 computers. Students have recently enjoyed new, longer hours at the computer lab but are quick to complain about new printing charges. Though you can certainly survive without one, you'll be at a social (and possibly, academic) disadvantage at Tufts without your own computer.

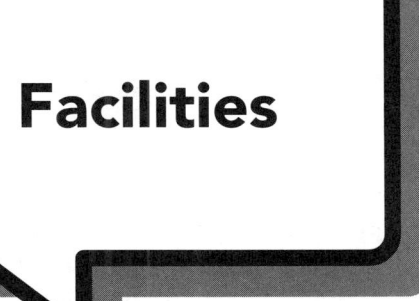

Facilities

The Lowdown
ON FACILITIES

Movie Theatre on Campus?
Film Series offers weekly movie showings.

Bowling on Campus?
No

Bar on Campus?
Hotung Café

Coffeehouse on Campus?
Brown & Brew, The Rez

Popular Places to Chill:
The Campus Center, the President's Lawn, dorm common rooms, Brown & Brew

The College Prowler™ Grade on
Computers: B

A high grade in Computers designates that computer labs are available, the computer network is easily accessible, and the campus' computing technology is up-to-date.

What Is There to Do?
The a cappella scene at Tufts is huge, and you'll see postings for shows for one, or a few, of the University's six groups throughout the semester. They kick off the year with the Orientation Show the night after students arrive back to campus in the fall.

Tufts' seasonal carnivals draw many new activities to the campus. There are all types of events going on in the Campus Center on these nights, including auctions, free massages, photo booths, Frisbee spin art, and one large attraction. In the past, they have turned the Campus Center into a mini golf course and a sumo wrestling pit.

Students Speak Out
ON FACILITIES

{ **"Facilities are nice and modern. The gym is one of the best around. The Campus Center can get overcrowded. It would be nice to have a larger community space."**

Q "Some of the facilities are a little on the older, 1970s side, but there are rarely complaints. **The athletics facility is brand new but too small**—in fact, many facilities are a little on the small side, with just not quite enough space to deal with all the students. But, I guess that happens at any college."

Q "The Campus Center is pretty cool. It's a good place for people to meet up, and there is a bunch of little study nooks and a couple big screen TVs with cable located upstairs. **The library is nice with its cozy armchairs**, but students beware, for they are known to lull studiers to sleep!"

Q "The facilities on campus are great. **The athletic facilities are wonderful, and we have good foreign language labs**. The student center isn't that big, but there are a couple of areas where they have some big TVs and lots of couches. You can even get discounted tickets for movies and stuff."

Q "**Some of the older places like the Campus Center could use renovations**, but the computer lab was remodeled last summer and a new athletic facility opened up a year ago. It's big enough to house an indoor track and tennis courts, and the school holds a lot of big functions there. We get speakers like Bill Clinton, Madeline Albright, and Al Gore."

Q "We have **brand new athletic and computer facilities**. Our student center is really nice and there is talk of expanding it. We have a brand new, gorgeous library and student services center, as well."

The College Prowler Take
ON FACILITIES

Tufts takes a lot of pride in its buildings, and they are always well-kept and maintained. There has been a flurry of construction over the last 10 years, with more new buildings and renovations every year. Still, students who wish that Tufts could compete with the facilities of larger, more well-endowed schools can always find room for complaint. Generally, students complain that the buildings are a little too small. There are minor problems with overcrowding, but with such a small student body to begin with, this is only noticeable during busy times.

The College Prowler™ Grade on
Facilities: B

A high Facilities grade indicates that the campus is aesthetically pleasing and well-maintained; facilities are state-of-the-art, and libraries are exceptional. Other determining factors include the quality of both athletic and student centers and an abundance of things to do on campus.

Campus Dining

The Lowdown
ON CAMPUS DINING

Freshman Meal Plan Requirement?
Yes

24-Hour On-Campus Eating?
No

Student Favorites:
Commons, Dewick, Brown & Brew

Meal Plan Average Cost:
$2,000

Did You Know?

Tufts Dining Services was once ranked as serving the second-best college food in the nation.

Points are the same as Dining Dollars, only better, because you can get MOPS delivery with them.

Students Speak Out
ON CAMPUS DINING

"We have awesome food. My parents were shocked. I swear the food is better than home-cooked."

Q "The food is amazing. Tufts ranked just behind the Cornell Hotel School in dining quality. **They care a lot about health and nutrition**, so there's a lot of fresh fruit and vegetables. We have 'special' nights like Belgian Waffle Night, Chicken Caesar Salad Night, Stir Fry Night, and cultural [and] ethnic theme nights. Dining halls aside, we have other eateries that offer sushi, smoothies, paninis, antipasti, and more. You can also order from off-campus restaurants on your meal plan."

Q "Food on campus is good, for mass-produced cafeteria food. **People complain about the tedium of it**, and many sophomores order in on 'points' instead of going to the dining halls. On campus, the Brown & Brew is a popular coffee and late-night study place, which closes at 1 a.m.. There's also a campus food mart, and the Campus Center has two different cafeteria-type places that accept cash and 'points.'"

Q "Your freshman year, **you are roped into getting the unlimited meal plan**. Every freshman has to get it. At some institutions, it would be worth complaining, but the dining hall food is so good at Tufts that it's nice to have freshman year."

Q "**I found the food to be disgusting**. You will be ordering in all the time."

Q "The food is nothing spectacular, although I have been to other places and their food stinks, so I guess that's a sign that Tufts' food is good. **There's plenty of variety**."

The College Prowler Take
ON CAMPUS DINING

The students don't lie. Most Tufts students will tell you that food on campus is great, and agree that they are lucky because it could have been a lot worse. There are always fresh vegetables and fruits in the dining halls, Campus Center eateries are generally packed, and Sunday brunch is a big social event. The one drawback is that the food can get monotonous after a while; but, fortunately, the MOPS program provides an opportunity to get a different flavor and order in, while still putting the bill on your meal plan.

The College Prowler™ Grade on
Campus Dining: B+

Our grade on Campus Dining addresses the quality of both school-owned dining halls and independent on-campus restaurants as well as the price, availability, and variety of food.

Off-Campus Dining

The Lowdown
ON OFF-CAMPUS DINING

Best Pizza:
Espresso's

Best Chinese:
Rose's

Best Breakfast:
SoundBites

Best Wings:
Wing Works

Best Health Food:
Blue Shirt Café

24-Hour Eating:
Dunkin' Donuts, Porter Square

Best Place to Take Your Parents:
Diva

Student Favorites:
SoundBites, Yoshi's, Jay's Deli, Rose's, Ana's Taqueria

Restaurants with Tufts Student Discounts:
Antonia's (20% on to go orders), Golden Light (10% all the time)

Fun Facts

Davis Square was once home to the first Bertucci's.

Store 24 in Davis Square isn't really open for 24 hours.

Students Speak Out
ON OFF-CAMPUS DINING

"The take out places, like Espresso's, are pretty decent. If you venture into Davis Square, there are some nice restaurants, like Joshua Tree, or sandwich places, like Blue Shirt Cafe."

Q "The restaurants off campus are pretty good. If you want to stay close to campus, Tasty Gourmet is really sweet. Then there are some yummy places in Davis Square and Porter Square. **If you want cheap, decent food, Espresso's is good.** Try to stay away from cheap Chinese food."

Q "**The off-campus restaurants are the highlight of Tufts**. We have some incredible food. SoundBites offers delicious breakfast brunches. Rose's offers incredible Chinese. Anna's Taqueria and Mexican Picante both offer Mexican food to die for, and Diva offers an incredible taste of Indian cuisine. There is a heavy Asian influence in the area as well, besides the usual Chinese take out. Asian options include many fine Thai and Vietnamese restaurants, as well as French Cambodian."

Q "The restaurants off-campus are good, and **in Boston they're amazing**. The standard ordering places are pretty good—but in Davis, there's a crepe place that I adore, an awesome old-school diner, and a bunch of other nice places with meals from five to 20 dollars."

Q "There are great take-out places—**Espresso's pizza is my personal favorite**. We have the usual cluster of delivery spots and the Tufts' meal plan you have to buy comes with 'points' that are good for delivery at three or four restaurants, which is useful for when you don't feel like walking."

Q "There are some decent places in Medford, but no really nice places—**it's kind of a crappy town**. The good places are not on the meal plan, so you have to pay for them—which is inconvenient and expensive."

The College Prowler Take
ON OFF-CAMPUS DINING

Dining off campus can be a great way to bring a little more excitement to your diet, and it's also a great way to explore the local communities. There are some restaurants already affiliated with Tufts on the MOPS program, and Medford and Somerville have some excellent dining options. If you want to trek a little further, Harvard Square and surrounding Boston—particularly the North End—are full of hundreds of different kinds of foods and local specialties. Students will often go out to big dinners, lunches, or brunches at local restaurants. You have to be careful though, because going out to dinner a lot can get expensive, so make sure to limit it to special occasions.

The College Prowler™ Grade on
Off-Campus Dining: A

A high Off-Campus Dining grade implies that off-campus restaurants are affordable, accessible, and worth visiting. Other factors include the variety of cuisine and the availability of alternative options (vegetarian, vegan, Kosher, etc.).

Campus Housing

The Lowdown
ON CAMPUS HOUSING

Undergrads on Campus:
80%

Number of Dormitories:
25

Number of University-Owned Special Living Units:
14

Room Types
Doubles, singles, triples, quads; two-person, three-person, four-person, six-person, and 10-person apartment-style suites

Special Features
For upperclassmen only: apartment-style which has common room, study lounges, kitchens, laundry, vending machines

Available for Rent
Mini-fridges

Cleaning Service?
Bathrooms and common rooms are cleaned by OneSource daily, except in on-campus apartments.

You Get
Bed, dresser, desk, desk chair, closet or wardrobe, T1 Ethernet connection (per person), phone jack (per room)

Bed Type
Twin extra-long mattress (39" x 80"); some lofts, some bunk-beds

Also Available
Cable television, special interest houses, healthy living options

Students Speak Out
ON CAMPUS HOUSING

> "The dorms are all pretty good, but Lewis, Carmichael, and Wren are boring for freshman. Most of the people who live there are upperclassman in singles, and they don't have the same community."

Q "No freshman has complained about all-freshman Tilton or Houston Hall, but I think that it is good to live and meet with sophomores when you first get to campus. **Some of my best friends are in the year above, or year below me** because I lived in the same dorms as them. Hanging out with all one class year limits you. Bush hall, where I lived for two years, is a great dorm. No one usually knows much about it because it is pretty small. But, it is right next to a dining hall and the Campus Center, and it's across the street from Tilton, so you can hang out with other freshmen. Also, Bush Hall is small enough that everyone on the floor usually becomes great friends."

Q "**All the dorms are fine**. Miller is probably the best one for freshmen, unless you want to live in the all-freshman dorm. I would try to avoid living in the O-zone [basement] of Wren or Haskell Hall, but I guess that you don't really have a choice."

Q "**I've seen better dorms**, but I've also seen dorms much worse than ours on other campuses. It's a conflict between uphill and downhill at Tufts: uphill are Miller and Houston, and the best downhill dorm is Bush. Tilton is the all-freshmen dorm, which is great for making friends. Haskell and Wren are generally considered the bad dorms; they're the oldest and 'dirtiest,' but they're honestly not that bad. If you live in Hogdon or Carmichael, you can get food in the dining hall without leaving, so you never have to change out of your PJs."

Q "You're assigned a room freshman year, so **you don't have any choice**. Most of the dorms are pretty nice, but the newer ones with nicer facilities have smaller rooms. Older ones with larger rooms have shadier bathrooms and other questionable facilities. Tufts is loosely split into two areas, creatively titled 'uphill' and 'downhill.' Uphill dorms are generally a little bigger, but the uphill dining hall, Carmichael, is not as good."

The College Prowler Take
ON CAMPUS HOUSING

Tufts dorm rooms aren't the biggest around, but they also aren't the smallest. Some dorms are slightly better than others, but most rooms are medium-sized, and living in any one of them is a similar experience. Students exhibit a preference for newer, or recently renovated dorms like South and Miller. West, Stratton, and Metcalf have the old, historic building style; this also means larger rooms. Overall, housing can't be too much of a concern for your first year, because you don't really have any control over it. The silver lining is that none of your classmates will either, and you'll all get at least two semesters to check out what areas you like the best before you pick housing for the years to come.

Want to find a dorm that best fits your personality? For a detailed listing of all dorms on campus, check out the College Prowler book on Tufts at www.collegeprowler.com.

The College Prowler™ Grade on
Campus Housing: B-

A high Campus Housing grade indicates that dorms are clean, well-maintained, and spacious. Other determining factors include variety of dorms, proximity to classes, and social atmosphere.

Off-Campus Housing

For Assistance Contact
Off-Campus Housing Resource Center
Web: *http://ase.tufts.edu/och/*
Phone: 617-627-5319
E-mail: och@tufts.edu

Students Speak Out
ON OFF-CAMPUS HOUSING

The Lowdown
ON OFF-CAMPUS HOUSING

"Many times, getting housing your junior year is in another class all by itself. Be sure to start early to find the best rentals, so you can live with your friends."

Q "**Living off-campus is amazing**. I moved off-campus after sophomore year, and I never want to move back. The off-campus houses are very close to campus. They are student houses, but they are nicer, and much bigger, than on-campus rooms and apartments."

Q "Unfortunately, housing off campus is often necessary after sophomore year. **Sophomores have among the worst lottery numbers** but are still guaranteed housing. Therefore, they often get the smallest rooms available. As for the junior class, they are always dealing with the threat of being homeless for the duration of junior year. There is no longer guaranteed housing after sophomore year, and the landlords around campus have come to realize it. A student will end up paying an exorbitant amount of money to stay on campus if they do not start looking for an off-campus house around the beginning of sophomore year."

Q "For me, it would not be convenient because it's very expensive. **I think it's better to live on campus, but it goes in cycles**. My junior year, everybody went off-campus. This year, there was a huge crunch. There are many funky little houses nearby that the University rents out. If you get organized with housemates early and go looking, it's no problem."

Undergrads in Off-Campus Housing:
20%

Average Rent for a One-Bedroom Apartment:
$900-$1,000/month

Average Rent for a Two-Bedroom Apartment:
$1,200-$1,800/month

Average Rent for a Three-Bedroom Apartment:
$1,800-$2,100/month

Average Rent for a Four-Bedroom Apartment:
$2,100-$3,000/month

Best Time to Look for a Place:
First semester of sophomore year

Popular Areas
College Avenue, Bromfield Road, Pearson Road, Sunset Avenue, Chetwynd Road, Powderhouse Boulevard, Boston Avenue

The College Prowler Take
ON OFF-CAMPUS HOUSING

Moving off campus is both a blessing and a curse. Every year, about 40 percent of the junior class goes abroad, mostly to experience a different culture and enrich their education, but also to avoid searching for an off-campus apartment. In other words, renting can be difficult. Utility bills are a hassle, you have to consider the safety of the area you choose, and dealing with the often greedy and unreasonable landlords out there is certainly no fun. However, many students enjoy the independence of having their own place, and living with friends off campus can add a whole new dimension to the Tufts experience.

The College Prowler™ Grade on
Off-Campus Housing: B-

A high grade in Off-Campus Housing indicates that apartments are of high quality, close to campus, affordable, and easy to secure.

Diversity

The Lowdown
ON DIVERSITY

African American: 7%

Asian American: 13%

Hispanic: 8%

Native American: 0%

White: 66%

International: 6%

Out-of-State: 75%

Minority Clubs

There are so many minority, cultural, and ethnic clubs on campus that they have their own Cultural Coordinating Committee (CCC) to coordinate activities. There is some debate in the student government as to whether these groups deserve special representation or not. *The Caribbean Club*, a South Asian Literary Magazine, and the Association of Latin American Students (ALAS) are very active on campus. The groups recruit minority students to campus, have mentoring programs in the community, and promote all different kinds of cultural activities on campus.

Most Popular Religions

There are a number of very active, religious communities on campus. Students are involved in a few different Christian organizations, and there's a very large and active Jewish community. The Islamic community on campus is growing; there are also numerous Eastern religions represented.

Political Activity

Tufts is a very politically-charged campus. Though most students would probably consider themselves centrist or leaning toward the left, the front pages of the campus newspaper are often covered with loud, public battles between a sect of radical liberals and a sect of reactionary conservatives.

Gay Tolerance

In past years, there were a few hate crimes each semester on campus, but those numbers have been dwindling. Except for a few isolated incidents, the campus is very tolerant, and most students are very supportive of the gay community. This community is very active, celebrating everything from Coming Out Day to Gay Pride Month. There is also a special living unit called the Rainbow House, where coed rooming is allowed. Every year, Tufts sponsors the Safe Colleges Conference for gay student movements all over the country, complete with a drag show.

Economic Status

Tufts students range from all economic levels, but since Tufts' endowment is somewhat miniscule for its tier, there are many students who are not receiving any financial aid. Thus, there is a huge population of very wealthy kids, many of them international students. There is also a huge population of students receiving financial aid. Students don't really discuss economic status—they focus more on academics, though many students say that they are simply surprised by the amount of money some of their classmates have when they first arrive on campus.

Students Speak Out
ON DIVERSITY

"I think the campus is pretty diverse. But, despite that, it seems that most people hang out with those of similar cultures or nationalities. There are cliques that are, to a certain extent, based on race."

Q "People complain a lot that the campus really isn't that diverse, but I think that, while it is diverse, **the different ethnic and racial groups tend to factionalize themselves a bit**. I think a lot of people do it, and it's understandable to a degree because you hang out with the people with whom you identify, but I think it tends to be divisive when it becomes exclusive."

Q "**The campus is fairly diverse**, though the administration does not seem to value diversity as much as it claims. We have had a number of hate crimes on campus in the last few years, and there has not been enough done, in my opinion, to counteract them. There is an active lesbian, gay, bisexual, and [transgender] group, and Tufts is a fairly friendly place for an alternative lifestyle."

Q "Tufts is progressively becoming more diverse. There are many clubs for different ethnic and cultural groups. I know **the Latino population has grown**, and I think the same goes for many of the minority groups. I would argue that diversity is the great strength of Tufts."

Q "**We have a very diverse student body**—it's something admissions is very aggressive about. There are lots of international students and students of different ethnic and religious backgrounds. There are all sorts of cultural clubs that provide a positive environment. As a white, upper-class, Anglo-Saxon, Protestant male, I think that the diversity of Tufts taught me more than anything else."

Q "Campus is diverse, but, like most colleges, **the disparate groups often don't interact well**. I don't feel bad in saying it since this is a problem common to almost every college, but I think the barrier can be broken if you want to hang out with different people."

The College Prowler Take
ON DIVERSITY

Looking around Tufts' campus on any given day, students may see a lot of diverse faces, but they may never actually interact with them during the year. This is one of the most unfortunate situations at Tufts, and increasing the admissions numbers will only help so much. Just as it happens at many schools, and indeed throughout much of life, people at Tufts tend to hang out with others of their own ethnic group, so there is a notable amount of self-segregation. These groups get along quite well but actually don't have that much interaction with the rest of campus. Despite this aspect of the social scene, however, Tufts does have students from every walk of life. Over a quarter of the student body is made up of minorities, and cultural groups on campus are very active. If you're open to meeting new people and learning from them, there are plenty of opportunities for a diverse and unique experience at Tufts.

The College Prowler™ Grade on
Diversity: B-

A high grade in Diversity indicates that ethnic minorities and international students have a notable presence on campus and that students of different economic backgrounds, religious beliefs, and sexual preferences are well-represented.

Guys & Girls

The Lowdown
ON GUYS & GIRLS

Women Undergrads: 52%

Men Undergrads: 48%

Birth Control Available?
Yes, from Health Services

Social Scene
While other prestigious schools nearby might be buried in their books, Tufts students, while still studious, like to say that they know how to leave their books behind and be "people people." There are parties going on every weekend, on every corner of campus (and off campus for that matter), and often students will take their parties into Boston or to Davis Square. There is a certain amount of camaraderie among students, and they are pretty willing to welcome any Tufts student into their parties. Though cliques may develop around certain extracurricular activities, no group is exclusive, and they are always looking for new people to join them. Since first-year students are all on the same meal plan and don't have so much homework yet, they tend to spend a lot of time hanging out in dining halls and common rooms. Sophomores, juniors, and seniors pretty much have their friends from their year, and parties get more exciting and more frequent with each year.

Hookups or Relationships?

Freshman year is dominated by a lot of "freshman lust" and consists mainly of hookups, except for those few couples who met the first week of school and stay together forever. Halfway through sophomore year, people begin to pair off and generally stay paired off. A lot of students complain that, by their third year, all the guys or girls worth being with at Tufts are taken. Fortunately, for those still unattached, Boston is overflowing with students from 55 other colleges.

Dress Code

Tufts students either have their own really unique style, or that standard New England, college look—collared shirts, visors, and jeans for the guys; tank tops, jeans or black pants, and tall black shoes for the girls.

Students Speak Out
ON GUYS & GIRLS

"It's a very diverse place, and guys and girls are different enough from one another to prevent general stereotyping. The people at Tufts seem friendly, interesting, and open-minded."

Q "**The girls at Tufts are definitely better looking than the guys**. Although, it's true that people don't really fix themselves up at Tufts as much as at schools, say, in the South. Girls, in general, dress more casual, except for the international folks, who are always dressed to the nines."

Q "I get really sick of this scene because **it can seem like a bunch of rich kids** at a good school who are here so they can be rich adults in the future. There's too much focus on material things, and too many spoiled kids who don't comprehend the value of their education because they haven't had to struggle to get here. There's also a lot of apathy about what is wrong in the world. There are many things I'm frustrated with, but, from what I hear, these problems exist at every elite private school."

Q "**There are a lot of nerds here**, but there are definitely a lot of people who are down to party, too. The people at Tufts aren't really good-looking, but there are so many college kids in Boston that it's not a problem. I prefer to chill with Boston University girls over Tufts, personally, but Tufts girls are really nice."

Q "**The school is notorious for having ugly girls**. It's a campus-wide joke that Tufts has the most hurt girls. If you're an attractive woman, you will have your choice of guys. The guys, mostly from the Midwest and East Coast, are pretty snobbish, arrogant, and stuck-up. These words come to mind: Abercrombie & Fitch, lacrosse, and beer."

Q "**Tufts is said to not be a very attractive campus**, but it's not that bad. There are some really good-looking guys and many sweet ones. One of my friends told me I should go to Tufts since the girls weren't all that attractive and I would have an easy time finding guys. This wasn't altogether true, but it does help to not go to school with a lot of supermodels."

The College Prowler Take
ON GUYS & GIRLS

You can generalize about Tufts guys and girls and still be fairly accurate. They aren't the best looking—usually a bit on the dorky side—and probably weren't super-popular in high school. They are pretty academic, but still really enjoy partying and socializing. Although it's not a huge school, there are enough students (and a relatively even mix of guys and girls) that you're sure to find some attractive coeds. As far as the dating scene goes, freshmen are generally single; about halfway through sophomore year, people begin pairing off. If you're still a loner by senior year, you'll probably find yourself surrounded by couples. Never fear, though—Boston has thousands upon thousands of college students passing through every year, so there is always hope, and plenty of opportunities, to meet new people.

The College Prowler™ Grade on
Guys: C-

A high grade for Guys indicates that the male population on campus is attractive, smart, friendly, and engaging, and that the school has a decent ratio of guys to girls.

The College Prowler™ Grade on
Girls: B-

A high grade for Girls not only implies that the women on campus are attractive, smart, friendly, and engaging, but also that there is a fair ratio of girls to guys.

Athletics

The Lowdown
ON ATHLETICS

Men's Varsity Teams:
Cross Country
Track
Football
Sailing
Soccer
Crew
Tennis
Baseball
Squash
Swimming
Basketball
Ice Hockey
Golf
Lacrosse

Women's Varsity Teams:
Cross Country
Track
Fencing
Field Hockey
Sailing
Soccer
Crew
Tennis
Volleyball
Squash
Swimming
Basketball
Softball
Golf
Lacrosse

Club Sports
Cycling (coed), skiing (coed), equestrian (coed), rugby (men, women), fencing (coed), volleyball (men), ultimate Frisbee (men, women), water polo (coed)

Intramurals (IMs)
Soccer (freshman league and other leagues) volleyball, three-on-three basketball, tennis

Most Popular Sports
Men's basketball, women's basketball, men's football, men's baseball, women's soccer, men's soccer, sailing

Athletic Division:
Division III

Conference:
New England Small College Athletic Conference (NESCAC)

Overlooked Teams:
Crew, ultimate Frisbee, women's volleyball

Fields:
Alumni Field, Ellis Oval, Fletcher Field

School Mascot:
Jumbo (P.T. Barnum's cherished elephant)

Students Speak Out
ON ATHLETICS

"Sports? Tufts has sports teams? Oh, that's what they were doing on that field! No, seriously, the best sports at Tufts are the club sports, like skiing and ultimate."

"Tufts is only a Division III school, and **nobody really watches the sports**. There are people who go to games, but they're not really Tufts students. There are a lot of older people coming to watch the games, and they just make parking worse on campus. School spirit has nothing to do with sports."

"Most sports are Division III. **Most Tufts teams are not very good**. But, if you choose to do a sport, it's a big time commitment. Intramural sports are a fun way to do a sport without the commitment. IM sports aren't huge, but they are easy to find if you are looking for them."

"**Lots of people are involved in sports**, but since it's a Division III school, the varsity games aren't anything like you see on TV. There are still a lot of people involved in the sports and a lot of intramural sports on campus. It's just tough figuring out when and where they are."

"Other than homecoming and the 'naked quad run,' which is what it sounds like, there really isn't much school spirit at Tufts. I wish there was more of it because the people are really great, and **the athletes are very talented**. IM sports are pretty big, but you have to be organized about it, or things just slip."

"**The teams are competitive, but school spirit is low**. It's one of Tufts' biggest flaws. The IM teams are pretty popular, though, since most people do not want to commit to varsity, or could not make the team or get enough playing time."

The College Prowler Take
ON ATHLETICS

The University certainly isn't known for its athletic bragging rights, which is why those who believe sports are the essence of college have probably never heard of Tufts. A little known fact, though, is that the first American college football game took place between Tufts and Harvard. Tufts has a long-standing tradition of athletics, but most students find that school spirit is not at all focused around sports.

The College Prowler™ Grade on
Athletics: C-

A high grade in Athletics indicates that students have school spirit, that sports programs are respected, that games are well-attended, and that intramurals are a prominent part of student life.

Greek Life

Students Speak Out
ON GREEK LIFE

"The frats are a fun place to go on the weekends, but they tend to be pretty quiet when they are not having a party. There are three sororities, but they aren't allowed to have parties, so frats basically make up for it."

The Lowdown
ON GREEK LIFE

Number of Fraternities: 11

Number of Sororities: 3

Percent of Undergrad Men in Fraternities: 15%

Percent of Undergrad Women in Sororities: 3%

Multicultural Colonies:
Alpha Kappa Alpha, Inc., Alpha Rho Lambda Sorority, Inc, Alianza de Raices Latinas, Alpha Phi Alpha Fraternity, Inc., La Unidad Latina, Lambda Upsilon Lambda Fraternity, Inc.

Q **"Greek life dominates much of the underclassmen social scene**, but that's because they have many beginning-of-the-year parties for people to get to know each other. Not many people are actually in the houses, but many people go to the parties."

Q **"The Greek life is very good.** I enjoy going to the frat parties, especially to meet people. I'm in a sorority, and I think joining was one of the best choices I made my freshman year at Tufts. The Greek life kind of dominates the social scene, but there are also other clubs that constantly give parties (such as the dance teams), that you can go to if the Greek system is not your thing."

Q "Greek life plays a big role in the social scene, especially when there's nothing huge elsewhere on campus. But, most people who go, go willingly. **I prefer house parties to frats**, but they're definitely available for those who want them. Greeks play a big role in the social scene, but it really depends on what kind of a good time you're looking for."

Did You Know?

The Tufts Chapter of Theta Delta Chi is the first one to exist, ever. Its address is 123 Professor's Row, which is why it is called 123.

The building that Zeta Psi inhabits has been a frat house for over 100 years.

Q "Greek life isn't dominant at all. The frats have parties, though the sororities aren't allowed to. It's easy to have a very active social life without ever setting foot in a frat. I've found that a lot of the people who do choose to get involved don't necessarily fit the usual stereotypes, and even though it's not really my thing, I have some friends who have had very good experiences with them. **Only about 14 to 15 percent of people pledge**."

The College Prowler Take
ON GREEK LIFE

The nice thing about the Greek system at Tufts is that they are always looking for new members, so almost all Tufts students get to sample what the system is like through open parties and other events. The pressure to join isn't strong, and if you choose not to, you won't be excluded. If you decide that Greek life is not your thing, it doesn't dominate the social scene; there are plenty of other things to do on and around campus.

The College Prowler™ Grade on
Greek Life: C-

A high grade in Greek Life indicates that sororities and fraternities are not only present, but also active on campus. Other determining factors include the variety of houses available and the respect the Greek community receives from the rest of the campus.

Drug Scene

The Lowdown
ON DRUG SCENE

Most Prevalent Drugs on Campus:
Alcohol, tobacco, marijuana, cocaine

Liquor-Related Referrals: 223

Liquor-Related Arrests: 0

Drug-Related Referrals: 43

Drug-Related Arrests: 1

Drug Counseling Programs
The Alcohol and Health Education Center
124 Professors Row
Phone: (617) 627-3861
Hours: Monday and Friday 9 a.m.-5 p.m.
Tuesday 1 p.m.-9 p.m.
Wednesday and Thursday 11 a.m.-7 p.m.
Additional evening hours available by appointment.

Many of the outreach programs take place in the evening in the residence halls. Watch for announcements in the campus paper and advertising flyers.

Students Speak Out
ON DRUG SCENE

The College Prowler Take
ON DRUG SCENE

{ *"There are certain circles where drugs are commonplace, but, overall, the only widespread substance use appears to be alcohol."*

Q *"If your thing is drugs, and you're from the West Coast, **prepare for a little culture shock**. A lot of people don't do drugs at Tufts, so the scene is really limited to a few groups who pretty much all know each other."*

Q *"**Drugs go around without dominating the social scene**. There aren't that many serious users here, but most drugs are available, if you want them."*

Q *"Pot is very big, as is ecstasy. **I hear about acid and coke**, but I've never seen it done, and I've never encountered anything."*

Q *"Druggies manage to keep themselves away from people that don't want them around, if that makes sense. People into the scene usually hang out with other people that are into it, and they do **a good job of hiding** what they do, to not affect the people around them."*

Q *"**If you want to do it, you can get it**, but, if you don't want to do it, there's not a lot of pressure. I lived in a frat house and never felt any. Just be your own person and do what you want to do."*

There isn't any social pressure at Tufts to use drugs, and you could probably go your entire college career without seeing anything more than alcohol and cigarettes. However, there is also no shortage of people using other substances. Generally, where there is smoking and drinking, marijuana isn't far away; there are also certain frats known for their coke habits. There's no need to use anything to fit in, and, in fact, the crowds that do use illegal substances are mostly isolated from the rest of the student body.

The College Prowler™ Grade on
Drug Scene: B+

A high grade on Drug Scene indicates that drugs are not a noticeable part of campus life; drug use is not visible, and no pressure to use them seems to exist.

Campus Strictness

The Lowdown
ON CAMPUS STRICTNESS

What Are You Most Likely to Get Caught Doing on Campus?
Smoking or drinking in a dorm room

Students Speak Out
ON CAMPUS STRICTNESS

"Police make sure everyone is safe. If you get caught, you aren't automatically kicked out of school—you just get put on probation, which isn't a big deal."

Q "**The campus police tend to be pretty lenient** about students partying. The police normally don't interrupt parties until about 2 a.m., and if they catch students drinking underage, they will just give them a warning. But, as long as students are not being disruptive while drinking, the police don't get involved."

Q "**Don't make them catch you with drugs**—they aren't trying to catch anybody because it's bad press. Likewise, they only bother about drinking if they have no choice, like if you are so drunk that you need medical attention. Parties get broken up at 2 a.m., though."

Q "The police seem pretty relaxed, but that's because **the scene is not really an issue**. If parties begin to bother other people, or look potentially dangerous, then police will step in. The worst I've heard happening is a $100 fine."

Q "The police are pretty lenient. A lot of the time **they begin busting frat parties when it starts getting late**, but you don't normally get in trouble for drinking if you're underage unless you get caught drinking drinking by police. Even then, you only get on Probation 1, which is only, like, a warning. The same goes if you are caught smoking pot, but that doesn't normally happen unless someone complains about it. For Probation 2, I think they tell your parents, and then on Probation 3, you're gone. I never got Probation 1, and I was caught drinking a few times."

The College Prowler Take
ON CAMPUS STRICTNESS

The campus police and RAs don't enjoy busting people for a couple of beer cans or a bong in their dorm room, but if you are stupid about it and people can smell what is going on in your room from far away, you don't really leave them any choice. When the policies are enforced, they can be quite strict, so once you are on probation, be super-careful. The consequences are bad if you get caught with anything else. Overall, however, authorities try to be lenient whenever possible.

The College Prowler™ Grade on
Campus Strictness: B+

A high Campus Strictness grade implies an overall lenient atmosphere; police and RAs are fairly tolerant, and the administration's rules are flexible.

Overall Experience

> "**Go anywhere but Tufts, or you'll regret it**. I left Tufts last year, and am going to UCLA as of this fall. I was pretty miserable after my first year—a popular sentiment among students, especially those from the West Coast."

> "**I have zero regrets**. I would probably have had a great time anywhere, after a slightly negative high school experience. It kind of stunk going cross-coast, as now I'm nowhere near any of my old friends, but it's great to experience another part of the country."

> "People are always impressed when I tell them I went to Tufts. **It's got a great reputation**, and our new president is awesome. I will miss my years at Tufts. You go to college to find out what kind of person you are, and in my opinion, Tufts allowed me to do that."

Students Speak Out
ON OVERALL EXPERIENCE

"I'm really happy at Tufts. Sometimes I wonder what would have happened if I went somewhere else, but I definitely feel that I made the right choice. I really like my friends, classes, and professors."

> "**Tufts is a solid, all-around school**. It doesn't have a lot going for it that would make you jump up and down for joy, but if you get involved, there's no reason you shouldn't have a good time and meet a lot of cool people. I'm glad I came to Tufts, although I kind of wish there was more of a character to the place, but that's tough when you're in a suburb. A lot of people like Tufts because it's just outside the city, but I'd rather be right in the center of things. It's a small place, so be prepared to know everybody, but it's big enough that you shouldn't feel claustrophobic."

> "I used to wish I were somewhere else, but not any more. I have been through many great things at Tufts and have had met many wonderful people. **I even got to go to Cuba**! College is definitely what you make of it, no matter where you go. Just be open-minded about things, and make sure that you look for the good things as opposed to the bad. When I did that, I saw that I was at a great school with a great reputation."

The College Prowler Take
ON OVERALL EXPERIENCE

Most of those who have chosen to attend Tufts are happy with their experience. As Tufts has so many programs and activities, it's impossible for one student to take advantage of everything the school has to offer in four short years; but, since there are so many different kinds of students at Tufts, all with different interests, there is definitely something for everyone. The most often reported difficulty by students is adjusting to the new lifestyle and environment, whether at the school itself or around Boston, in general.

The Tufts experience goes far beyond the classroom—it includes life in a dynamic part of the country, with a huge college presence. The combination of school opportunities and local culture gives Tufts its own distinctive flavor that allows students to grow in ways they never could have imagined. Most of the negative experiences that Tufts students report are also good growth experiences, and, overall, graduates are proud of their education. Students leave Tufts ready to enter the real world, or to move on to higher degrees with confidence and a diploma from a school that is making a name for itself.

The Inside Scoop

The Lowdown
ON THE INSIDE SCOOP

Tufts Slang:
Know the slang, know the school. The following is a list of things you really need to know before coming to Tufts. The more of these words you know, the better off you'll be.

A Cappella – Singing without accompaniment. Tufts has a huge scene with six different groups, many of which are award-winning. Not as dorky as it sounds.

CSL – Committee on Student Life

Dewick – (verb) When going to eat at Dewick, someone may ask you, "Do you want to Dewick it?"

Double-Jumbo – Someone who has attended Tufts both as an undergraduate and graduate or professional student

Downhill – Using the library steps as the dividing line, this refers to part of the hill below the library.

E – Short for "engineer" (i.e.: Chem. E = chemical engineer; EE = electrical engineer)

ELBO – Elections Board

Ex College – Experimental College, located in Miner Hall; a program that brings in outside experts to teach classes and coordinates many advising programs.

Flip Cup – A drinking game played by two teams. Each team lines up across a table and the game proceeds as a relay by first drinking the full cup as fast as you can and then trying to flip the cup until it stands.

Jackson College – The name of the Tufts college for women (from before the university became coed)

Joey – The popular name for the campus shuttle, named for the bus company Joseph's Transportation

JumboFOB – Electronic signal keys used to enter some dorms

Light on the Hill – A number of school traditions and songs derive from this phrase that initiated Tufts' creation, when Nathan Tufts vowed "to put a light on the hill."

O-zone – Where you live if you're on the basement level of a dorm

Pax Et Lux – Latin for "Peace and Light." These words are part of the Tufts symbol.

TEMS –Tufts Emergency Medical Service, the group of student-EMTs on call for emergency service.

The Hill – Walnut Hill, where Tufts is located

Uphill – Using the library steps as the dividing line, this is the part of the hill above the library.

Wren Bugs – The special species of bugs that live in and around Wren Hall.

Tufts Urban Legends
Direction of the Tufts Cannon
There is a replica of a U.S.S. Constitution cannon on the Tufts campus. It is said it points at Harvard, but no one really knows where it points.

Jumbo
If you can get a penny to land on the nose of the Jumbo statue, you're supposed to have good luck on your finals.

Rape Steps
These steps are behind the Hillel Center and lead down to Boston Avenue. It is said that the design of these steps was given to an engineering student as his final project. He was supposed to design them so that they would be easier for a woman to run up than a man if she were being chased, and that the steps were designed to match the exact stride of a woman, calculated from a number of biological factors.

Urban Legends (Continued...)

School Color Selection
In the first 30 years of Tufts' existence, the graduating class was allowed to pick their own school colors, and every year they changed. After 30 years, the administration decided it was time to settle on one set of colors. When the administration told the senior class that they would pick the school's colors for eternity, the class didn't believe them and thought it was a joke. That class picked the worst color combination they could come up with: baby blue and dark brown. Those remain Tufts' colors today. Tufts says the school colors represent earth and sky. We know the truth.

School Spirit
Students will go to homecoming and parents' weekend football games, and if a team is doing really well they will get excited about it; but Tufts school spirit extends further than sports. Despite the name sounding bad at first, almost all Tufts students are proud to be Jumbos. Most Tufts students express an affinity for Jumbo and could recite the story of how Jumbo came to be Tufts' mascot, and of the tragic fire that destroyed the real Jumbo. Most students are very happy at Tufts and proud of their school. In times of tragedy, the campus is able to come together very quickly and support each other as members of a community. No one knows the alma mater except the a cappella groups, and most students could only mutter a few syllables of the fight song, but on Tuftonia's Day (Tufts' birthday) everyone celebrates. School spirit is hard to avoid, since the Tufts Spirit Coalition is always cooking up something.

Traditions

Candle Ceremonies
There is a big candle-lighting ceremony during Freshman Orientation, and it is repeated during Senior Week, right before commencement. All these candle traditions are derived from the vow made by Nathan Tufts in 1852 to "put a light on the hill."

First Night
This is a new tradition: the first night of Freshman Orientation, the entire class gathers into the Gantcher Center for a huge dinner together. At this time, alumni tell them how wonderful they are for going to Tufts, and everyone learns the story of Jumbo. Watch out for indoor fireworks.

Frisbee Golf
Watch out for flying Frisbees! There is a Frisbee golf course on campus, only known to members of the ultimate Frisbee team. They aren't trying to hit you in the head with the Frisbee, they just want it to land on Jumbo's nose.

Naked Quad Run
In the 1960s, students in West Hall were living in the last all-male dorm on campus. They were told that women would be moving in next year, and they decided to protest. In the middle of winter, the men of West ran naked around the academic quad, and it has been a tradition ever since. Every year, the whole school turns out for this event, where about 200 brave students or so start out in West Hall and then run naked around the quad. The event traditionally takes place on the first night of reading period in December, usually with some amount of snow on the ground.

Pancake Breakfast
This used to happen after the Naked Quad Run, but now, due to a number of incidents of naked pancake throwing, the event has been moved to a study break during reading period in the spring semester.

Painting the Cannon
This is the best form of advertising on campus. Every night, students are allowed to paint the cannon, though painting may only be done in the dark. Students then guard the cannon until dawn. If you don't, it is free-game to anyone else to paint over.

Finding a Job or Internship

Things I Wish I Knew Before Coming to Tufts:

- Go to office hours and be sure to ask a lot of questions.
- Do not try to do everything on your own, sometimes you need help.
- Fill your math requirement freshman year.
- Do not dedicate your whole life to one activity right away, and shop around for a year before becoming super-involved.
- Bring your own computer.
- Get the 160-meal-plan, always, until you have your own kitchen.
- Go to the frat parties during orientation week—they are the best parties all year, especially ZBT Jello shots.

Tips to Succeed at Tufts:

- Go to office hours so some professors will know you well.
- Get involved in an organization and rise to a leadership role.
- Learn to write well.
- If a professor is bad, don't stick around. Drop the class and switch into something that will keep you interested.
- Check e-mail constantly.
- Don't even try to apply for an on-campus apartment before you are a senior, unless a senior is pulling you into an apartment.
- Study abroad so that you don't have to deal with finding junior-year housing.
- Look for sophomore-year housing in older dorms or Tufts-owned houses; they have the biggest rooms.
- First semester, take courses in very different subjects so you can find out what you like.
- Write a senior thesis, even though you don't have to.

The Lowdown
ON FINDING A JOB OR INTERNSHIP

Career Services probably won't be very helpful in actually putting you in contact with someone who could find you a job, but they do provide a number of workshops throughout your four years. Junior and senior year workshops have particularly good information on how to beef up your resume, interview for a job, and focus your skills toward various sectors of the economy.

Career Services is also very helpful with finding internships, and you can set up an appointment at any time to go over a cover letter or resume. A lot of students will do summer internships, and even internships during the semester, and Tufts has a lot of connections in Boston that can help students find out about these opportunities. There are a few internships for credit, but check with a department before you start looking so you know what you can get credit for.

Advice

Look for an internship well in advance. Some of the best internships have deadlines in November.

Have Career Services read over your cover letter and resume. They know what they're talking about.

Look through all the information on the Web, such as the Tufts Career Network and e-recruiting; these are all accessible from the Career Services Website.

Go to career fairs. Even if there is nothing you're interested in, at least you'll get a better handle on the job market and networking skills.

Career Center Resources & Services

Career Services
Tufts University
740 Dowling Hall
Medford, MA 02155
Phone: (617) 627-3299
Fax: (617) 627-3907
Career.Services@ase.tufts.edu
http://careers.tufts.edu/

Major Alumni Events

Homecoming
A chance for alumni of all ages to come back to the hill and hang out with organizations they were once a part of. The weekend is full of concerts, parades, barbecues, and football.

Alumni Weekend
Tufts alumni all come back to campus at the same time for five-year, 10-year, 25-year reunions, etc. These coincide with commencement.

Alumni Publications:
All graduates receive four free issues of *Tufts Magazine* each year to keep them tuned in with life on the hill.

Famous Tufts Alumni:

- Hank Azaria, actor
- Tracy Chapman, singer
- Pierre Omidyar, E-bay founder
- Bill Richardson, New Mexico Governor
- Guster, rock band
- Rob Burnett, *Ed TV* creator

The Best & Worst

The Ten BEST Things About Tufts:

1. The library roof
2. Getting to know your professors
3. A cappella groups
4. Spring Fling
5. Opportunities to do research
6. Free movies from Film Series
7. Sunday brunch at Dewick
8. Great speakers (two former U.S. Presidents!)
9. Location: six miles from Boston
10. The great reputation

The Ten **Worst** Things About Tufts:

1. Being called "Jumbo" all the time
2. Walking uphill to classes
3. Trying to make brown and blue match
4. Parking tickets
5. Elitists (students with "something to prove")
6. Revolting freshmen bathrooms
7. The crack-down on the Greek system
8. Ethnic cliques
9. Battles between liberals and conservatives
10. The small endowment

Wesleyan University

237 High Street, Middletown, CT 06459
www.wesleyan.edu   (860) 685-3000

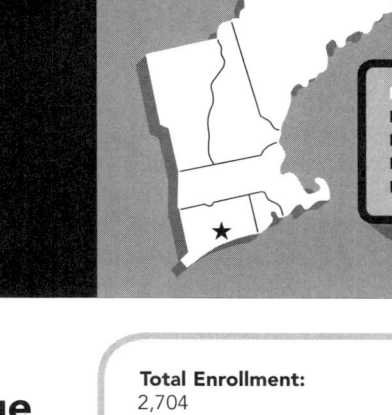

DISTANCE TO...
Boston: 115 mi.
Hartford: 17 mi.
New York: 112 mi.
Providence: 95 mi.

"Is it true they have naked parties? Is it true they do drugs? Is it true they sip foreign tea and talk about socialism? Yes, yes, and yes."

Total Enrollment:
2,704

Acceptance:
27%

Tuition:
$31,650

Top 10% of High School Class:
73%

SAT Range
Verbal	Math	Total
640 – 740	650 – 720	1290 – 1460

ACT Range
Verbal	Math	Total
28-33	27-32	28-32

SAT II Requirements
Sat II subject tests are recommended, however the ACT may be submitted in place of both SAT I and SAT II.

Most Popular Majors:
11% English Language and Literature
10% Psychology
7% Political Science and Government

Students Also Applied To:*
Brown University, Yale University, Columbia University, Amherst College
*For more school info check out www.collegeprowler.com

Table of Contents

Academics	358
Local Atmosphere	360
Safety & Security	361
Computers	363
Facilities	364
Campus Dining	366
Off-Campus Dining	368
Campus Housing	369
Off-Campus Housing	371
Diversity	372
Guys & Girls	374
Athletics	376
Greek Life	378
Drug Scene	379
Campus Strictness	381
Overall Experience	382
The Inside Scoop	383
Finding a Job or Internship	384
The Best & Worst	386

College Prowler Report Card

Academics	B+
Local Atmosphere	C-
Safety & Security	C+
Computers	B+
Facilities	B
Campus Dining	B
Off-Campus Dining	B
Campus Housing	A-
Off-Campus Housing	B
Diversity	B-
Guys	C
Girls	C
Athletics	C-
Greek Life	C
Drug Scene	B-
Campus Strictness	B

Academics

Special Degree Options
Pre-Professional Programs: Pre-Law, Pre-Dentistry, Pre-Medicine, Pre-Veterinary Science.

Combined-Degree Programs: 3-2 program with Columbia and Caltech for engineering.

Minors/Miscellaneous: Certificate in International Relations; Certificate in Environmental Studies; Certificate in Jewish and Israel Studies.

Sample Academic Clubs
Alternative Social Music Collective, Boogie Club, Desperate Measures Improve Comedy Group, Independent Student Film Production Co-Op, Muslim Students Association, Onomatopoeia A Cappella Group, Piccadilly Pow-Wow, Queer Social Club, Society of Classic Liberals, Trans/Gender Group, Wesleyan Film Series, WESU 88.1 FM, Zombie Arts Collective.

The Lowdown
ON ACADEMICS

Degrees Awarded:
Bachelor, Master, Doctorate

Full-time Faculty:
362

Faculty with Terminal Degree:
95%

Student-to-Faculty Ratio:
9:1

Average Course Load:
4 courses

AP Test Score Requirements:
Possible credit for scores of 4 or 5

IB Test Score Requirements:
Possible credit and/or placement

Best Places to Study:
Olin Library and the Science Library

Did You Know?

In 1953, Wesleyan first offered its Graduate Liberal Studies Program, the first ever liberal studies program for adults.

Students Speak Out
ON ACADEMICS

"For the most part, classes at Wesleyan are engaging. Also, teachers here are willing to go the extra mile. You can ask around and find out which profs to avoid. They might have you over for dinner."

Q "Most of the professors here are excellent. **Occasionally, there are some professors who are better suited to do their research, rather than actually teach**. All are invested in what they study, but not all are as inspiring in the classroom as others."

Q "**Almost every single one of my teachers has been amazing in their own way**. They're extremely knowledgeable and supportive. Most of the classes I've taken have been stellar, and I'm lucky to be enrolled in a university that offers a lot of classes that deal with subjects I'm passionate about."

Q "**The professors range from good to amazing**. I've had some wonderful experiences with the Russian department—none involving Smirnov vodka, I assure you! For the most part, professors teach their classes. There's not too much of that 'the TA will handle everything kind of stuff that you get at large state universities.'"

Q "**I wasn't overly impressed with the professors here**. There was definitely some condescension there. I think there's a bit of a snob thing going on at Wesleyan, and the professors feed into it. If you're not the typical Wes student, watch out!"

Q "Make friends with your professors. They want to talk to you. **Most of them will talk your ear off if you give them the chance**. Also, take advantage of office hours. I didn't my freshman year, and I paid the price for it. I'm a junior now, and I always meet with my profs In addition to being brilliant, they're really good people."

The College Prowler Take
ON ACADEMICS

Wesleyan has long been known to harbor some of the finest young intellectuals in the country, but believe it or not, there are plenty of party animals at Wesleyan, as well. One thing about Wesleyan is that everyone here likes to have a good time, but studies must come first. If you fall behind in one class, then it's only a matter of time before the domino effect kicks in and you fall behind in two or three others. Before you know it, you'll be placed on academic probation with little to no slack given by the administration (one more slipup and you're gone). As eccentric, or seemingly aloof, as the typical Wes student may seem, the majority of the student body is very serious about their academics. There are the occasional blow-off, general education requirement classes that many students show up to half the time and still get Bs. Many freshmen make the mistake of assuming that the remainder of their classes at Wesleyan will be this way (yeah, right).

While the workload is often tremendous (up to 150 pages of reading a day for some upper-level courses), Wesleyan allows for an unprecedented degree of academic freedom. The course load for the typical Wesleyan student is four classes per semester. For the most part, students wind up with the classes they desire. As far as academics at Wesleyan go, students get what they put in, and at a school where there's so much freedom and opportunity available, you'd only be cheating yourself if you did not give 100 percent.

The College Prowler™ Grade on
Academics: B+

A high Academics grade generally indicates that professors are knowledgeable, accessible, and genuinely interested in their students' welfare. Other determining factors include class size, how well professors communicate, and whether or not classes are engaging.

Local Atmosphere

Students Speak Out
ON LOCAL ATMOSPHERE

"Middletown has what you need and not much more. There are a couple nice restaurants and a movie theater, but students tend to stay on campus or go to New York on the weekends."

Q "**Middletown is not a college town. Period**. Even if I lost a couple of fingers in a mining incident, I could still count all the bars in town on one hand. The upside, however, is that this fact is irrelevant. The campus is lively enough. There's always something going on, and it's small enough that you can pretty much make your way anywhere without much hassle."

Q "Yale is about a half-hour drive away, but you wouldn't know it. I went there maybe twice in two years. The only downside is that, **without a car, there's really no way to get out of Middletown**. There's the bus, but it's inconvenient and expensive. You just have to make friends with people who have cars if you want to make it to the train station. There are a couple good restaurants. When six o'clock rolls around, though, Main Street has virtually nothing to offer."

Q "During the day, pretty much everywhere is safe. At night, however, you should **travel in groups** if you're planning on going into town. There's nothing going on in town at night anyway, aside from the movies, so this is generally not a problem."

Q "Stay away from Middletown. That's all you need to know. **This place is crawling with odd people**—and not the good kind of odd either. Most of them hate Wes students, so it's a good idea to avoid town altogether."

Q "**Middletown isn't great, but it's not a disaster either**. You could certainly go to school in worse neighborhoods. On the surface, the town looks pretty clean. There are some good places to eat. Some of them even accept Wesleyan meal points, and I guess more and more establishments will do so as time passes. Russell Library is fantastic, as well."

The Lowdown
ON LOCAL ATMOSPHERE

Region:
Northeast

City, State:
Middletown, Connecticut

Setting:
Urban/Suburban

Distance from Hartford:
30 minutes

Distance from Boston:
2 hours

Distance from New York:
2 hours

Points of Interest:
A.J.'s Putt-Putt, Broad Street Books, Center for the Arts, Connecticut aMAIZEing Maze, Foxwoods Resort Casino, Goodspeed Opera House, Harbor Park, Lyman Orchards, Mattabesett Blue Trail, Oddfellows Playhouse, Powder Ridge Ski Resort

Major Sports Teams:
Connecticut Wolves (soccer), The Hartford Wolf Pack (hockey), New Britain Rock Rats (baseball), Boston Red Sox (baseball), Boston Celtics (basketball), New York Yankees (baseball)

City Websites:
www.middletownct.com
www.cityofmiddletown.com

The College Prowler Take
ON LOCAL ATMOSPHERE

At first glance, Middletown appears to be a quaint riverside community detached from the hustle and bustle of Hartford and New Haven. The collection of old-fashioned diners, antique toy shops, and upscale restaurants along Main Street paint a picture not at all unlike a Norman Rockwell painting of a small town. In certain places, during certain hours of the day, this portrayal is not too far from the truth. However, at night, crime is prevalent in Middletown, especially immediately surrounding the University. An underlying tension between the town and the University occasionally rears its ugly head, as assaults on students by local gang members occur from time to time. The hard truth is that the students who decide to enroll here will eventually discover the very real and unromantic realities involving the surrounding community.

The College Prowler™ Grade on

Local Atmosphere: C-

A high Local Atmosphere grade indicates that the area surrounding campus is safe and scenic. Other factors include nearby attractions, proximity to other schools, and the town's attitude toward students.

Safety & Security

The Lowdown
ON SAFETY & SECURITY

Wesleyan Police Phone:
(860) 685-3000 (emergencies),
(860) 685-2345 (non-emergencies)

Health Center Office Hours:
Monday-Thursday 9 a.m.-7 p.m.
Friday 9 a.m.-5 p.m.
Saturday 12 p.m.-4 p.m.

Appointments can be scheduled:
Monday-Thursday 9 a.m.-6:30 p.m.
Friday 9 a.m.-4:30 p.m.
Saturdays 12 p.m.-3:30 p.m.
Closed during academic breaks and summer.

Safety Services:
Public safety escort/safety shuttle, blue-light emergency phones, whistle program, sexual assault awareness, identification cards, operation identification

Did You Know?
Wesleyan's Operation Identification program is working to reduce the rate of theft on campus.

 ## Students Speak Out
ON SAFETY & SECURITY

 ## The College Prowler Take
ON SAFETY & SECURITY

"There's an incident or two every year that gets people all riled up and talking about how they feel unsafe at Wesleyan. Honestly, though, I've never felt safer anywhere else."

Q "Sure, **there are some parts of campus that could be a little better lit**, but short of something commensurate to the Berlin Wall, Wesleyan's campus couldn't be any safer."

Q "I always feel safe on campus, but **there have been a few mugging incidents here**. One kid who had actually been mugged said that he felt that it was a freak incident and that he still feels safe."

Q "I personally feel extremely safe, **you can walk around campus alone at night and feel completely safe**. If you don't want to go somewhere alone at night then you can just call public safety and they will give you a ride."

Q "**Security is tight**."

Q "I feel pretty safe at Wesleyan. **There's a safety shuttle that you can take across campus after sunset**, but I never take it. Screw that! I think it'd be too embarrassing. Besides, if you walk in groups there's no reason to feel unsafe. Even by yourself you're usually fine. My sophomore year I trekked across campus every night to get to my friends house. I never felt too freaked out."

Q "Occasionally, P-Safe will bust up a wild party. **The Residential Advisors are in charge of keeping the peace in the individual dorms**, and they'll usually look the other way regarding things like drinking and drugs. If you piss them off, though, they'll call Public Safety and then you'll get SJB'd, which stands for Student Judicial Board. You certainly don't want that."

Campus security is a tense issue at Wesleyan. While the campus itself appears cleaner and more idyllic than many New England schools, there is a disturbingly high rate of crime in, and around, Wesleyan University. Very few of these crimes seem to be perpetrated by Wesleyan students, other than the occasional episode of "artistic vandalism" or civil disobedience. The simple fact is that Middletown is not a very safe place to live. The majority of Middletown residents are good, hardworking people. However, there is a criminal element that will occasionally find its way onto, or around, campus.

The College Prowler™ Grade on
Safety & Security: C+

A high grade in Safety & Security means that students generally feel safe, campus police are visible, blue-light phones and escort services are readily available, and safety precautions are not overly necessary.

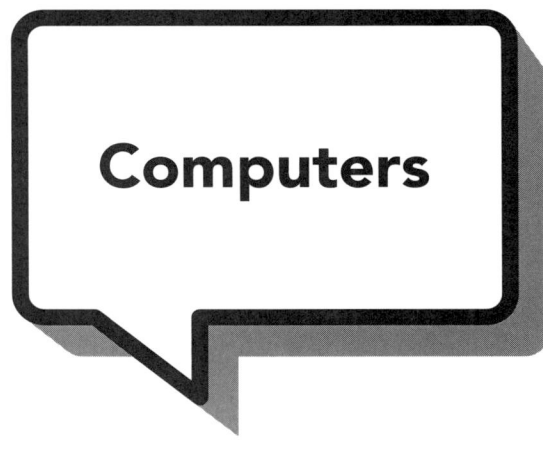

Computers

Students Speak Out
ON COMPUTERS

"**Computer labs are only crowded during reading week and exam week, when big papers are due. I've never had a problem finding a computer.**"

Q "**There are a huge number of computer labs on campus**, although some are more secret than others—like the one in the basement of the Science Tower. Most students have computers for the convenience of it, but anyone would be fine coming to school without one."

Q "I know very few people who don't have their own computer. I used the labs a good deal, though, for convenience's sake and because **they have lots of great software, scanners, and cool stuff like that**. But, forget about getting a computer around exams or when final papers are due."

Q "**Do bring your own computer**. The network's usually pretty good, but there were some problems with viruses last year. I know that's not a problem exclusive to Wesleyan, though."

Q "Bring your computer, definitely. **The Wesleyan network is a great way to trade music and movies** right in the comfort of your own room. I have friends who didn't have computers for awhile, but it's just silly not to bring one. There are computer labs, but it's a pain to walk across campus to get to one, especially when it's 2 a.m., freezing cold, and you still need to finish that psychology paper."

Q "**Computer labs are hell-on-earth during finals** and class registration. They're absolutely packed! People leave their stuff at a terminal for hours. It's called 'camping.' It's against the rules, but people do it anyway. The labs are good for emergencies, but I'd say definitely bring your own computer."

The Lowdown
ON COMPUTERS

High-Speed Network:
Yes

Wireless Network:
Yes

Number of Labs:
6

Number of Computers:
175

Charge to Print?
Black and white laser printing, five cents per page; color printing (only available at certain locations), 25 cents per page

Operating Systems:
PC, Mac

Free Software:
Virus protection and patch software, computer scans

The College Prowler Take
ON COMPUTERS

The good news for Wesleyan students is that computing on campus is pretty much a no-brainer. When your personal computer breaks down (which it will sooner or later), a very helpful and positive information technology staff is available to coach you through repairs over the phone, or for more serious problems, they will come to your residence. Computer labs are available all over campus, and most stay open until the wee hours of the night. However, during finals week, the labs are packed and it is not uncommon to see a line of stressed, computerless students waiting outside for a free terminal for hours at a time.

The College Prowler™ Grade on
Computers: B+

A high grade in Computers designates that computer labs are available, the computer network is easily accessible, and the campus' computing technology is up-to-date.

Facilities

The Lowdown
ON FACILITIES

Student Center
Yes, the Davenport Campus Center houses the student mailroom, ticket center, a multipurpose room, a game room, several dining options, and the only ATM on campus.

Athletic Center
Yes, the Freeman Athletic Center houses a pool, indoor and outdoor tracks, various game courts, and weight training facilities.

Libraries
Olin Library houses a collection of over a million titles. Olin also houses Wesleyan's music library, periodicals room, and various study halls and quiet rooms.

Movie Theatre on Campus?
The Wesleyan Film Series presents new and old films five days a week. The on-campus cinema charges $3 and usually features mainstream, second-run movies.

Bowling on Campus?
No

Bar on Campus?
No, however Middletown is home to a variety of bars of varying quality.

Coffeehouse on Campus?
Yes, the Pi Café recently opened on the first floor of the Science Tower and serves coffee and baked goods.

Popular Places to Chill
The Butterfield Quad, the Campus Center lawn, Foss Hill, the Hewitt Quad, Olin Library lawn, Pi Café, residential lounges, WestCo lawn

Students Speak Out
ON FACILITIES

Favorite Things to Do:
On any given Friday night, there's plenty to do on campus, no matter what your definition of a good time may be. The cinema and the Science Tower both show movies on the weekends, and these tend to draw large crowds. The fraternities on campus usually throw parties, as do many of the off-campus houses. Eclectic, one of Wesleyan's most popular theme houses, usually holds live concerts, as does Alpha Delt (Alpha Delta Theta), Wesleyan's only sorority.

The lecture series is great if you're in the mood for some fascinating academic conversation, as are the official University concerts, which include everything from Irish folk music to Gamelan. Several times a year, the theater department performs plays in the '92 Theater or the Center for the Arts Theater, and these performances are almost always fantastic. Visiting students are often surprised at how much time Wesleyan students actually spend in their room drinking tea and discussing world events. Big social events are always a blast, but more intimate gatherings are frequent. It is in these situations that you really get to know people and learn about some of the amazingly creative and unique individuals who attend Wesleyan.

"A lot of the facilities are under construction right now, so it's hard to say. I found that the gym was a little lacking in its fitness center, but this has already been addressed."

Q "Computer labs are all excellent. I think **the student center was fine,** but the University's decision to build a whole new one makes sense. We have a new theater right now, which is wonderful for student productions, and our new film center just got completed."

Q "I don't play sports, but I can say that **the exercise room at the gym is tiny—really, really tiny**. The libraries are wonderful. They're great places to hang out, work, and do just about anything. The libraries make up for what the student center lacks. The administration claims there'll be a new one in 2007, but it's too late for me."

Q "**There isn't enough space** to hang out, and what space they do have isn't utilized much."

Q "**The facilities at Wesleyan are fantastic**. The school is constantly building and renovating it's facilities, which means there's something new to look forward to every year. This year, they opened a brand new cinema for the film department that is huge and wonderful. There are a couple of great spaces for theater, like the '92 Theater. Crowell Music Hall is an excellent performance space for music and whatever else those crazy performance majors can think of."

Q "Facilities at Wesleyan aren't bad. They vary. **The Campus Center is not that great;** it's mostly a glorified cafeteria with a mailroom in the basement. The Center for the Arts is the best group of facilities on campus. That's where the cinema and theaters are located. The CFA is relatively new, so t is really state-of the-art. Wesleyan is an art-oriented school; so it makes sense that these are the best-kept facilities."

The College Prowler Take
ON FACILITIES

Wesleyan University's facilities, and the smorgasbord of events and shows that take place therein, are truly unique. While constantly expanding and adding newer and better structures to the campus' already considerable collection of theaters, dining areas, and concert halls, Wesleyan keeps its present structures clean and extremely well-maintained. Plans are currently underway to renovate the studio and update all the broadcasting equipment. One of the downsides to Wesleyan's constant expansion and renewal is the omnipresence of construction equipment on and around campus. There is a good deal of tension between the town and the University concerning the degree to which Wesleyan is gobbling up local land for its own use.

Campus Dining

The Lowdown
ON CAMPUS DINING

Freshman Meal Plan Requirement?
Yes

24-Hour On-Campus Eating?
No

Student Favorites
MoCon is the center of freshman life, particularly if your dorm is on Foss Hill, as is the case for the majority of first-year students. The lawn outside the Campus Center is a big hangout for upperclassmen during the warmer months, juniors and seniors also frequent the dining facilities located there. Summerfields is known for its late-night dining, however many students grumble that 2 a.m. is not late enough.

The College Prowler™ Grade on
Facilities: B

A high Facilities grade indicates that the campus is aesthetically pleasing and well-maintained; facilities are state-of-the-art, and libraries are exceptional. Other determining factors include the quality of both athletic and student centers and an abundance of things to do on campus.

Meal Plan Average Cost
$1,600

Meal plans are broken into individual meals, which may be used at certain locations, and points (or credits) available for use at WesShop, the on-campus store, and smaller dining facilities. Most meal plans consist of a combination of "meals" and "points." Additional points may be added at any time during the year in $25 increments.

Did You Know?
Wesleyan's MoCon houses the longest salad bar in the United States.

Students Speak Out
ON CAMPUS DINING

"The food is fine here. The freshman dining hall, MoCon, has gotten a lot better over the years, and it's a wonderful place to hang out and meet your new classmates."

Q "**Food on campus isn't all that bad.** It isn't great either. The real bonus is WesShop. It's basically a little corner store that operates in the middle of campus. The downside is that freshmen can't use it with their meal plan. So, basically, you suffer for a year, and then you're golden. On the other hand, there are a lot more options and better quality than when I was a frosh."

Q "MoCon is the main dining center. Definitely go there your freshman year. Even though there are those who will blanche at the thought of MoCon's cuisine, **it's definitely a stellar place to meet people**."

Q "I'm told that, **compared to other schools, Wesleyan food is great**. I'm not so sure though. There are plenty of vegan options, but that's not always a good thing. Cookies without real eggs are, well, not so good."

Q "**Wesleyan gouges you with their meal plans**. The food is extremely overpriced, and what's more, if you're a Wesleyan student, you must have a Wesleyan meal plan. This means that even if you're living in a program house and want to buy food for your kitchen, you more or less have to buy it from the school. It's a raw deal man—a raw deal."

Q "As a freshman, **your social life revolves around MoCon**. MoCon food is pretty good. There are usually lots of options—salad, sandwiches, pizza, and grilled food. However, after a few weeks, you start to realize how limited these options really are. Yes, you can always get a hamburger, but how many times can you have a hamburger in one school-year before you go totally nuts? The other dining options on campus leave much to be desired. The Campus Center isn't bad; it's mostly cafeteria-style food. I ate at the Kosher Kitchen a lot, which is smaller, but it has a great atmosphere, and the food is excellent."

The College Prowler Take
ON CAMPUS DINING

Spend some time on any college campus in America, and you're bound to hear students complaining about the food. This is no different at Wesleyan. In fact, no lunchtime conversation would be complete without one or two critical shots at campus food and campus food services. The truth, however, is that while Wesleyan's food is far from gourmet, it is very much above-average compared to most colleges and universities.

The College Prowler™ Grade on
Campus Dining: B

Our grade on Campus Dining addresses the quality of both school-owned dining halls and independent on-campus restaurants as well as the price, availability, and variety of food.

Off-Campus Dining

Fun Facts

Middletown is home to a fascinating cross-section of people and some of the most interesting work at restaurants. Chat up your waiter or waitress, and you're sure to get a few good stories. Though the service at Middletown restaurants tend to vary, sometimes the most endearing dining experiences occur at places where the service is terrible. The Neon Deli is famous for its cranky employees, but, with the right sense of humor, this trait can be a plus.

The Lowdown
ON OFF-CAMPUS DINING

Best Pizza:
Giuseppe's

Best Indian:
Haveli India

Best Breakfast:
The Athenian Diner

Best Wings:
First & Last Grill

Best Healthy:
It's Only Natural

Best Place to Take Your Parents:
The Tuscany Bar & Grill

Students Speak Out
ON OFF-CAMPUS DINING

"**Typhoon. Typhoon. Typhoon!** The owner is the sweetest woman in the world. Go to Mamoun's for falafel. Then, go to O'Rourke's at 5 a.m. for eggs and bacon."

"**Restaurants are one of Middletown's high points**. My favorite is Typhoon, a Thai restaurant where the staff will eventually get to know you and make custom dishes for you. There's also La Boca (Mexican), It's Only Natural (lots of vegetarian stuff, amazing sweet potato French fries), Thai Garden, Haveli (Indian), Giuseppe's (pizza, right near campus), and some Italian places."

"Middletown is not a great place to go out to eat. This is a small town, and there's not a lot to do. **Don't expect much in the way of fine cuisine.** There's not even a Chinese restaurant, I don't think—what's up with that?"

"**Thai Gardens is a big favorite in Middletown**. It used to accept Wesleyan meal points, but it stopped doing this in 2004. Mamoun's is another great spot for cheap food. You always see Wesleyan kids there. There are two great diners, as well: O'Rourke's and Athenian. Athenian is open 24 hours a day, which is splendid."

Student Favorites

Middletown is home to a collection of fantastic diners, and much cheaper than any place on campus. O'Rourke's, located on Main Street, is popular, as is the Athenian Diner, which is the only option for 24-hour dining in town. Klekolo World is a café a few blocks from campus that students frequent. However, the wait staff there tend to be anti-social and even a bit mean. Giuseppe's, a local pizza parlor, is another student favorite. The Neon Deli is open later than most on-campus facilities and, in addition to serving freshly made sandwiches, it's a great place to buy groceries. Prices there are much cheaper than at WesShop.

> "I wouldn't go to most of the restaurants in Middletown unless I was with my parents. The Tuscany Bar & Grill is that kind of place. **These are old people restaurants.** The Red and Black Café is located in Broad Street Books, Wesleyan's bookstore, and it's surprisingly good. Middletown's got the typical stuff, too, like ice cream, donuts, and more treats that will leave you plump."

The College Prowler Take
ON OFF-CAMPUS DINING

When asked what they think about Middletown, most Wesleyan students shrug and say "Well, there's a lot of good places to eat." Unless you're particularly imaginative, there is not a lot to do in Middletown other than eat. The upswing, however, is that the food tends to be very good, and the variety is amazing for such a small town. Middletown dining caters to just about every taste. From greasy, breakfast-style diners to high-end Italian restaurants, there's something for everyone.

The College Prowler™ Grade on
Off-Campus Dining: B

A high Off-Campus Dining grade implies that off-campus restaurants are affordable, accessible, and worth visiting. Other factors include the variety of cuisine and the availability of alternative options (vegetarian, vegan, Kosher, etc.).

Campus Housing

The Lowdown
ON CAMPUS HOUSING

Undergrads on Campus: 100%

Undergrads in Dormitories: 41%

Undergrads in University-Owned Apartments or Houses: 59%

Number of Dormitories: 6

Number of University-Owned Apartments: 14

Room Types
Residence halls include three types of rooms: single, double, and split-double. Singles are smaller, one-person rooms, only available in certain dorms. Doubles are standard two-person rooms, larger than singles, including two beds, two desks, and two dressers. A split-double is perhaps the most common style dorm room. The split-double is the same as two singles connected by a private door. In the split-double arrangement, only one room has access to the main hallway.

Available for Rent
Mini-fridge and microwave

Cleaning Service?
Public bathrooms and hallways are cleaned regularly, as are common rooms. Private housing is not cleaned, ever.

You Get
Bed, desk, closet or dresser, bookshelves, two chairs, window coverings, Internet access, free local and on-campus calling

Bed Type
Twin extra-long (39"x80"); some lofts, some bunk-beds

Also Available
Long-distance and cable TV are available for an extra cost.

Students Speak Out
ON CAMPUS HOUSING

"I think the dorms are great, mostly because there are a lot of singles, particularly in the Foss Hill dorms. WestCo has a wonderful sense of community."

Q "**All the dorms here are decent**; I'd recommend not living in the Butts [Butterfield dorms] freshman year, just because they're a little out of the way. When Summerfields, the restaurant in the Butts, is open, people in the Butts tend to hang out just with each other, and not with the rest of the campus. They are nice dorms, especially if you like it a little quieter."

Q "**The dorms are hideous, especially the ones on Foss Hill**, but what do you expect college dorms to look like? The rooms are pretty big in comparison to other universities. I had a single my freshman and sophomore year, and it was wonderful. Live in the Butts if you can. They're very social and sort of a community all unto themselves."

Q "I lived in Clark my freshman year and everyone called it 'The Children's Hospital' because it was so clean. **It was antiseptic in there**. But, I met some great people and made some friendships that lasted. It was a great place to live, despite it being made fun of all the time."

Q "**Most freshman start out on Foss Hill**, which is great because it's in the center of everything. WestCo is the big social dorm on the hill, though Hewitt and Nicholson aren't bad. Everything's pretty clean. Occasionally, someone will set off a fire alarm, but you'd get that kind of thing no matter where you went to school."

Q "**I lived in WestCo my freshman year, and it was incredible**. It's definitely the center of social life on Foss Hill. Occasionally, it drove me nuts; it was impossible to get to sleep at times, with all the yelling and banging. For the most part though, it was fantastic."

The College Prowler Take
ON CAMPUS HOUSING

For incoming freshman, social life is centered around Foss Hill, where all students are assigned rooms during their first year. Though the social scene changes from year to year, there is a definite personality or, in some cases, stigma attached to each dorm. The largest dorm on Foss Hill is called WestCo, short for West College, and it tends to be the epicenter of social interactions for underclassmen at Wesleyan. Friendships that form at WestCo tend to last through college and beyond.

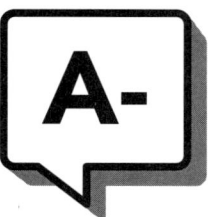

The College Prowler™ Grade on
Campus Housing: A-

A high Campus Housing grade indicates that dorms are clean, well-maintained, and spacious. Other determining factors include variety of dorms, proximity to classes, and social atmosphere.

Off-Campus Housing

For Assistance Contact

Web: www.wesleyan.edu/reslife/

Phone: (860) 685-3550

E-mail: reslife@wesleyan.edu

Students Speak Out
ON OFF-CAMPUS HOUSING

The Lowdown
ON OFF-CAMPUS HOUSING

Note: Wesleyan has a four-year residency requirement. So, technically, nobody lives "off campus." However, for the purposes of this guide, "off campus" refers to Wesleyan-owned housing facilities set apart from the main campus.

Undergrads in University-Owned Apartments, Houses:
59%

House (unfurnished single):
$5,966

House (unfurnished double):
$5,322

House (furnished single):
$6,610

House (furnished double):
$5,752

Rent for a One-Bedroom Apartment:
$6,044

Rent for a Two-Bedroom Apartment:
$5,518

Popular Areas:
High Street, Church Street, Court Street

Best Time to Look for a Place:
Beginning of second semester

"Get a house as soon as possible—trust me."

Q "With so many great on-campus options, **there's no need to go off campus**. Almost no one does it."

Q "There are lots of options and it's often cheaper, but **it's nice to be on campus** and to have the University take care of everything."

Q "**Ninety percent of the student body lives in University-owned housing**, and this ranges from dorms to old Victorian houses three blocks away from campus. If you want to actually rent your own apartment—one that isn't already owned by the school—you have to do it by special request, and there's all sorts of red tape involved. They really want you to live in the University housing all four years."

Q "The housing system at Wesleyan is a little screwy. When it comes time to choose housing for the upcoming year, there's an extremely complicated process everyone has to go through involving online registration, grouping, and all this other stuff that makes you want to pull your hair out. **It's sort of a crap shoot**. Some people end up with good housing and some don't."

Q "**Go for off-campus housing if you can get it**. Try to give yourself a balance. With the dorms, you get sort of a typical college experience, but it's great to move away from campus with your buddies during your junior year. That's what I did, and it was phenomenal."

Diversity

The College Prowler Take
ON DIVERSITY

The Lowdown
ON DIVERSITY

All freshman are required to live on campus and are usually relegated to either Foss Hill or the Butterfield dorms, the latter located one block away from MoCon, the main dining hall. The central location is definitely a plus, as it immerses the student in Wesleyan's academic and extracurricular life. Once they're a sophomore, a student can live wherever they want. However, it is usually best to stay on campus until junior year, when a wider selection of off-campus housing is available. When that time rolls around, the off-campus houses are a great way to live in an actual wood frame house with some of your closest buddies.

African American: 8%

Asian American: 8%

Hispanic: 6%

Native American: 0%

White: 72%

International: 6%

Out-of-State: 90%

The College Prowler™ Grade on
Off-Campus Housing: B
A high grade in Off-Campus Housing indicates that apartments are of high quality, close to campus, affordable, and easy to secure.

Minority Clubs
Students of Color, La Unidad Latina (Lamda Upsilon Lamda Fraternity)

Most Popular Religions
Programs are offered on campus for many different faiths, including Christianity, Judiasm, Islam, and Buddhism.

Political Activity

The 1994 film "PCU" (short for Politically Correct University) was written by Wesleyan alums Adam Leff and Zak Penn, and based on Wesleyan University. The film depicts the widely-held myth that Wesleyan is an extremely active, politically-oriented school. On the surface, protests and debate are prevalent, but for issues reaching beyond the boundaries of campus, Wesleyan is largely apathetic. In 2004, 300 Wesleyan students marched in Washington, DC for women's rights, but this was the extent of national political activism for the school that year. On the whole, while many Wes students pride themselves on bucking the system; very few students are actually involved in broader politics. Student apathy is the ugly underside of Wesleyan's activist façade.

Gay Tolerance

While the administration has been accused of being homophobic, the Wesleyan student body is extremely tolerant of gays. Wesleyan offers an undergraduate queer studies program, as well as a queer alum network. Also found on campus is the LGBTTQQFAGPBSDM organization (club motto: "No this is not a typo."), which represents every alternative gender/sexual choice including lesbian, gay, transgender, transsexual, queer questioning, flexural, and asexual. Each semester, this group organizes and advertises numerous events for the queer community both on and off campus. Other queer organizations on campus include the Queer Alliance, Spectrum, the Transgender Group, the Gay Café, Open House, and the Queer Task Force.

Economic Status

While Wesleyan promotes its "need blind" policy, it is, after all, a private school, and many lower-income students cannot afford to attend. While there certainly is a wide range of economic backgrounds, the majority of students falls into the middle- and upper-middle-class brackets.

Students Speak Out
ON DIVERSITY

"There are lots of different personalities, but not many different races. It's still primarily a white school with a bit of diversity."

"Let's be honest. **Wes is a semi-snooty, New England liberal arts college**. Diversity is not necessarily our strong point. On the other hand, we have a wide variety of people who regularly complain about how we're not diverse enough, which is a good place to start. Plus, in the context of other schools like us, we do pretty darn good."

"People always love to debate this. **We love to plug ourselves, apparently, as 'Diversity University,'** but then people like to complain that the campus is mostly white, which is true, but that doesn't mean it's not diverse. I know people from many different places, with different backgrounds, with different dreams. It's a very diverse and wonderful place."

"Racially, **we're more diverse than most New England colleges**. Politically, we're not diverse at all. People have slightly different opinions about things, but in most social circles on campus there are few conservatives."

"There are a lot of kids from Connecticut, and a lot of kids from New York. What can I say? It's a small school, so of course there's not going to be a very diverse background. **You get a good number of students from overseas**, but they're very much in the minority."

"**People rag on Wesleyan for not being very culturally diverse**, but, compared to a lot of New England schools, it very culturally diverse. This isn't a white-collar, Polo shirt, Ivy kind of a school. People are proud of where they come from, and they come from so many different places that it makes the school very diverse."

The College Prowler Take
ON DIVERSITY

Wesleyan prides itself on its diversity, hence the nickname "Diversity University." In actuality, Wesleyan is a primarily white, upper-middle-class school that pays particular attention to its minority groups. International students are as common at Wesleyan as at any other New England university. Other minority groups such as queer or interracial organizations are also available in moderation. However, where Wesleyan earns its nickname is in the welcoming atmosphere it provides to people of all persuasions. The queer community on campus frequently cites grievances with the administration that their voices are not heard, and, in certain respects, they are right. However, the student-based gay community is extremely vibrant, and all lifestyles—from queer to asexual to transgender—are extremely active in campus life.

The College Prowler™ Grade on
Diversity: B-

A high grade in Diversity indicates that ethnic minorities and international students have a notable presence on campus and that students of different economic backgrounds, religious beliefs, and sexual preferences are well-represented.

Guys & Girls

The Lowdown
ON GUYS & GIRLS

Women Undergrads:
52%

Men Undergrads:
48%

Birth Control Available?
Yes

Social Scene

As a rule, Wesleyan students are extremely extroverted, sometimes more than necessary. While the majority of Wes students probably did not sit at the popular lunch table in high school, many students here blossom into cheerful, well-liked individuals in their college years. Rather than struggling to find someone to talk to at a party, most visiting students wonder how to get their companions to shut up. Wes students love to talk, play, wrestle, joke, laugh, and horse around with one another. It's not uncommon to see two friends tackling one another on Foss Hill, or playing full-contact croquet on Andrus Field. Wesleyan students are friendly and genuinely want everyone around them to be as excited about life as they are. Certain niches of the social scene do have an element of snobbery, however. The theater and visual art departments, in particular, are known for having one or two snooty members per clique. Eclectic, one of the houses on campus, is extremely exclusive and self-contained. These tend to be exceptions to the rule, however, as most groups and organizations are extremely accepting of others.

Hookups or Relationships?

Part of the unpopular-in-high-school syndrome is a tendency toward casual sex in college. While the typical table at MoCon is home to two or three steady couples, more often than not, couplings tend to take place in back rooms and in stairwells, lasting about the same amount of time it takes to microwave a burrito. Also, upperclassmen are known to prey on freshmen.

Dress Code

Because of the eclectic and eccentric student body, on a given day, one can see anything from sweat pants to a full pin-striped suit. Wesleyan students tend to love bright, mismatched colors, traditional hippie attire (sweaters, flip-flops, and lots of hemp), or brooding semi-Gothic torn tops and leather. The T-shirt advertising some obscure product or rock star is always a staple, and, on a given day, accessories may include anything from cowboy hats to parakeets. Above all, Wesleyan students tend to dress to their mood and personality, which more often than not is showy and cheerfully bizarre.

Students Speak Out
ON GUYS & GIRLS

"Guys at Wes can be overly-sensitive, post-feminism types, but the girls often demand that. There seems to be a large lesbian contingency on campus, so I guess it's safe to say that guys don't make the grade."

Q "**If you're an athlete, you may not feel entirely welcome here**. However, if you weren't cool in high school, you might just have lots of company."

Q "**There's really no easy way to classify the guys and girls here**. Most of the guys are crazy. In the best possible way, of course. Same for the girls. Clearly we're all ridiculously hot. That goes without saying though—go Wes!"

Q "**The girls at Wesleyan are amazing**. Everything from tragically hip, to Gothic, to psycho cheerleader. There are very few ditsy girls here. They're all brilliant, which can be so attractive in itself. There's also lots of flowing scarves and pseudo-hippie garb. I love it."

Q "Guys at Wesleyan aren't great. Some of them are cute. Most of them are extremely fun to be around, but **I'm not sure how many of them I'd want to date**. I get the feeling a lot of Wesleyan kids were picked on in high school."

Q "Wesleyan's not that great, attractiveness-wise, but, **if you have interesting tastes, this could be the place for you**. People tend to dress in their own unique styles, which leads to some extremely attractive and alluring outfits, and some which are just putrid. Anyway, people continue to hook-up, so they must be doing something right."

The College Prowler Take
ON GUYS & GIRLS

Wesleyan is not widely recognized for the attractiveness of its student body. The stereotype, which only holds a certain amount of truth, is that all Wesleyan guys are bearded and barefoot, and all Wesleyan girls are unshaven and unwashed. In actuality, the student body presents a wide spectrum of body and personality types, some of which may be more desirable than others depending on your personal tastes. One thing that can be said with certainty, however, is that Wesleyan is an extremely open place, which basically means that there is a lot of free love going on. Although there is the occasional relationship drama that happens at any university, there is also a considerable 'no fuss, no muss' mentality. While drunken party hookups are not uncommon, candlelight and a full moon are also aphrodisiacs to the more poetically-minded Wesleyan students.

The College Prowler™ Grade on
Guys: C

A high grade for Guys indicates that the male population on campus is attractive, smart, friendly, and engaging, and that the school has a decent ratio of guys to girls.

The College Prowler™ Grade on
Girls: C

A high grade for Girls not only implies that the women on campus are attractive, smart, friendly, and engaging, but also that there is a fair ratio of girls to guys.

Athletics

The Lowdown
ON ATHLETICS

Club Sports:
Badminton
Cardinal Velo
Climbing Club
Club Ice Hockey
Club Soccer
Cricket Club
Croquet Club
Equestrian Team
Frisbee
Karate Kata
Kendo
Martial Arts
Rugby (women's/men's)
Water Polo

Intramurals (IMs):
Soccer
Inner Tube Water Polo
Singles Tennis Tournament
Squash
Basketball
Ice Hockey
Softball
Indoor Soccer
Doubles Tennis Tournament
Volleyball

Men's Varsity Teams:
Basketball
Ice Hockey
Fencing
Squash
Swimming
Wrestling
Indoor Track
Baseball
Crew
Football
Lacrosse
Rugby
Soccer
Cross Country
Diving
Tennis
Track & Field

Women's Varsity Teams:
Basketball
Ice Hockey
Volleyball
Squash
Swimming
Indoor Track
Crew
Field Hockey
Lacrosse
Rugby
Soccer
Softball
Cross Country
Diving
Golf
Tennis
Track & Field

Most Popular Sports
Baseball, football, lacrosse

Overlooked Teams
Volleyball, badminton, squash

Fields
Andrus Field, Fauver Field, softball field, North Field

School Mascot
The Cardinal

Athletic Division
NCAA Division III

Conference
New England Small College Athletic Conference

Getting Tickets
Except for tournament games, Wesleyan sporting events are free to Wesleyan students. There is a box office located in the Davenport Campus Center, but this is primarily for arts events.

Students Speak Out
ON ATHLETICS

The College Prowler Take
ON ATHLETICS

{ "IM sports are pretty big because a lot of people like to just run around and play and not be competitive. Varsity sports are only big for a small crowd of students we call 'jocks.'"

Q "You can find a good intramural team, if you'd like, and take it as seriously as you want. As for varsity sports, **I never see the football team** except on homecoming."

Q "The only thing you'll ever hear about varsity sports is athletes complaining about how **nobody knows they exist**. Who cares?"

Q "**People do play sports on campus**, but the big ones are the club sports. Girl's rugby is big. People turn out for the baseball games, but no one pays much attention. It's not really a sports school."

Q "**There's a huge Frisbee following at Wesleyan**. I've heard of one kid who actually majored in Frisbee. There are ultimate Frisbee teams—men's, women's, and coed."

Q "This really isn't a jock kind of school. Our sports teams aren't bad. **We end up playing schools like Amherst and Swarthmore.** People follow the big sports like football, baseball, and soccer. Otherwise, it's stuff like Frisbee and croquet and really not much else."

There is a running joke that Wesleyan harbors a secret underground legion of sports fanatics, the idea being that no one ever sees them because they hide in the weight room. Needless to say, the general consensus is that Wesleyan is not a sports-oriented school. The major intramural teams are often the butt of many campus jokes. In reality though, this good-natured ribbing probably stems from the fact that the Wesleyan student body is composed almost entirely of kids who were picked last in gym class. However, the lameness of Wesleyan sports is a bit of an exaggeration. While Wesleyan certainly is not part of Big Ten football or ACC basketball, it does feature an active and enthusiastic athletic scene. Certain club sports are very popular here. Intramural sports tend to be taken more seriously by those who participate in them than the quality of the teams ought to permit.

The College Prowler™ Grade on
Athletics: C-

A high grade in Athletics indicates that students have school spirit, that sports programs are respected, that games are well-attended, and that intramurals are a prominent part of student life.

Greek Life

The Lowdown
ON GREEK LIFE

Number of Fraternities: 5

Number of Sororities: 6

Percent of Undergrad Men in Fraternities: 5%

Percent of Undergrad Women in Sororities: 1%

Multicultural Colonies
La Unidad Latina, Latinas Promoviendo Comunidad, Lambda Pi Chi Sorority, Inc.

Did You Know?

Eclectic, formerly a fraternity, now is one of the most active houses on campus, hosting concerts and parties regularly.

Students Speak Out
ON GREEK LIFE

"**The frats are horrifically lame, and they most definitely don't dominate the social scene.**"

Q "I remember walking past parties at Beta—one of all-male frat houses—and wondering where they get all those girls from. **Did they truck them in from Trinity, like you might stock a pond with fish**? Who knows? After freshman year, I had no need for the frats, and I did just fine."

Q "I have successfully avoided setting foot in the frats too many times, and **you really aren't missing anything if you don't go to them**. I'd actually chalk it up to good taste."

Q "**I always thought the frats here were a little shady**. I almost got involved with one of the sororities on campus, and the whole secret handshake thing freaked me out. They're extremely exclusive and, if you're in one, it has to be your whole life. College is about finding yourself, not just joining a group and following a leader."

Q "**The frats get a bad rap on campus**. Yes, they drink. Yes, they have fun and party. However, they also do a huge amount of volunteer work for the campus. There's the community service aspect that gets overlooked. A lot of Wesleyan's student leaders came out of the fraternities. But of course, no one thinks about that."

Q "If you're the sort of person who's looking for a big Greek scene, Wesleyan isn't such a bad place to be. **The houses are immense and great places to live**, and the frat parties are always the best. If you're involved with the frat scene, you'll love it. Those who aren't usually haven't given it a fair shot."

The College Prowler Take
ON GREEK LIFE

Greek life is often compared to the sports scene at Wesleyan. Both are small and cliquish, both operate mostly outside the main Wesleyan social scene, and both are more or less mocked by the rest of the student body. As with Wesleyan athletics, some of these viewpoints are valid and some aren't. Wesleyan houses only a handful of frats and sororities, and these tend to take the major brunt of administrative badgering. Frats and sororities are constantly losing their privileges or getting kicked off campus, only sometimes rightfully. To most visiting students, the frat houses seem to hold the best parties on campus, complete with binge drinking, loud music, and rowdy, testosterone-pumping behavior. However, most Wes students tend to shy away from this kind of scene. Consequently, while there is nothing wrong with Greek life in principal, it doesn't really fit into the scheme of Wesleyan life.

Drug Scene

The Lowdown
ON DRUG SCENE

Most Prevalent Drugs on Campus:
Alcohol and marijuana are the most visible. Next come LSD and various amphetamines. The most underground but still present are hardcore drugs like cocaine and heroin, but those are far less frequent.

Liquor-Related Referrals:
120

Liquor-Related Arrests:
0

Drug-Related Referrals:
13

Drug-Related Arrests:
4

The College Prowler™ Grade on
Greek Life: C

A high grade in Greek Life indicates that sororities and fraternities are not only present, but also active on campus. Other determining factors include the variety of houses available and the respect the Greek community receives from the rest of the campus.

Drug Counseling Programs

Online resources; personal and group therapy sessions at the Office of Behavior Health; education about local 12 Step Programs; "WesFact" anti-drug abuse surveys.

 **Students Speak Out** ON DRUG SCENE

 **The College Prowler Take** ON DRUG SCENE

{ "Some people do drugs. Some don't. It's that simple."

Q "I've never come across any hardcore drug users at Wesleyan. I know of a few kids that have dabbled in the creative pharmaceuticals, but it's not generally the cool thing to do. A lot of students smoke a little pot, but **there are plenty of people who don't smoke at all**."

Q "Lots of drugs. **There are drugs everywhere**. It's a drug mentality. A lot of people smoke pot here. There's no way around that."

Q "**It depends on who you hang out with**. My friends weren't into drugs, so there was never any pressure on me to take them. There is a drug scene at Wesleyan, there's no denying that, but it's beneath the surface. Occasionally, at a party, you'll see someone light up a joint, but it's not like people are stumbling through the street tripping or anything like that."

Q "**I do drugs and I feel like the scene at Wesleyan is pretty tame**. There's a hardcore drug scene, but it's pretty subdued. You don't see it if you're not part of it. Most people smoke pot. Just about everybody drinks. Wesleyan is a very open place."

Q "**Most people have a 'live and let live' attitude at Wes**. Not everyone does drugs, but most people aren't really opposed to them, either. It's an individual choice, of course. The people who take drugs, they're not out there pushing them on anyone else. They want the drugs for themselves, after all."

Let's face it, at any environmentally conscious, extremely liberal, arts-centered university, you're going to find a large amount of drugs. The drug scene at Wesleyan includes everything from excessive amounts of caffeine to heroin. Most common is illegal, and excessive, consumption of alcohol, which is found at just about any large party or informal social gathering. While Wesleyan is not a "drinking school," students who have worked themselves to the brink of sanity during the week (a typical practice at Wesleyan) want to relax to the most extreme extent possible, and this usually includes getting drunk. Parties at the frats are known for having large amounts of alcohol. Illegal substances are not uncommon there, either. More covert is the hardcore drug scene, which includes cocaine and even heroin. The typical student who chooses not to partake in drugs could easily go all four years without ever coming across evidence of this underground network.

The College Prowler™ Grade on
Drug Scene: B-

A high grade on Drug Scene indicates that drugs are not a noticeable part of campus life; drug use is not visible, and no pressure to use them seems to exist.

Campus Strictness

> "**Public safety is pretty laid-back in general.** If they catch you red-handed, of course you're going to get in some trouble. Just don't be stupid about it. Don't stand on your balcony with a beer-bong in your hand!"

The College Prowler Take
ON CAMPUS STRICTNESS

The Lowdown
ON CAMPUS STRICTNESS

The consensus at Wesleyan is that public safety looks the other way when it comes to most student transgressions. Lately however, campus strictness has been heating up. This was certainly evident at 2003's Spring Fling. This annual, end-of-the-year bash is famous for its libations and public drinking akin to Mardis Gras. However, since 2003, all persons over the age of 21 (consuming alcohol openly) are now required to wear special armbands. The usually rampant underage drinking at this event is thus kept in check. When it comes to drugs and alcohol, residential advisors (RAs) will almost always leave you alone, as long as you're not being completely blatant about getting smashed. The best advice here is not to give the administration a reason to sink their teeth into you. Destruction of campus property, theft, vandalism, and other crimes are much more difficult to get away with. Serious offenses really get the administration's blood boiling, and convicted partiers are usually punished harshly. They won't hesitate to make an example out of you: don't give them a reason to.

What Are You Most Likely to Get Caught Doing on Campus?
Drunk and disorderly behavior, illegal consumption of drugs or alcohol, public nudity

Students Speak Out
ON CAMPUS STRICTNESS

"Generally, public safety looks the other way in regards to soft drugs and, though certainly not rampant, harder drugs can be found, just like anywhere else."

> "**Wesleyan public safety turns a blind eye to drinking most of the time**. I mean, there's no easy way to tell if someone is over 21. In other words, if public safety drives by a party where kids are drinking, they're not going to pull over and ask to see everyone's ID. There's only trouble when people get out of hand or if the party gets too loud. Otherwise, it's not really a big deal."

B

The College Prowler™ Grade on
Campus Strictness: B

A high Campus Strictness grade implies an overall lenient atmosphere; police and RAs are fairly tolerant, and the administration's rules are flexible.

Overall Experience

Q "I only wish the the lackluster atmosphere and sports teams at Wesleyan matched the school's academic intensity. Many times **I felt myself longing for that 'big school' feel**."

The College Prowler Take
ON OVERALL EXPERIENCE

What can one say about Wesleyan, except that it's an all-around great college. Make no mistake about it though, when you move into your dorm the first day of freshman year, you'll be petrified. You may very well be freaked out by the strange attire of your classmates, or by the angry protesters on Foss Hill. That you are plunging into a bizarre world of drugs, hippie-paranoia, and ultra-left-wing weirdness. Your first thought. You might even lock yourself in your room and refuse to come out, worried that those tree-hugging granola heads on campus might sacrifice you to their hemp god. These fears, of course, are unfounded, ridiculous, and are all part of becoming a college student (except maybe the part about the tree-hugging granola heads).

Wesleyan has a lot of reputations, and it lives up to some of them. It's often called "Diversity University." It has been portrayed as being extremely politically correct—too much so—in the movies "PCU." *The New York Times* has called the school "naively liberal." However, what you might not hear often enough—and what is the truest fact of all—is that Wesleyan is a wonderful, open, and stimulating place that will change your life forever. At Wes, one has room to try so many new things—and not just drugs either! There's music like you've never heard before, ideas you've never considered, people so fascinating and different from one another you can't believe they all exist in the same place. Wesleyan is for students with open minds, who love to think, who love art and music, theater, film, and experimentation. The feeling at Wesleyan is that life is short, and that now is the time for us to experience all that we can, learn all that we can, and in the end, come out so much larger than when we went in.

Students Speak Out
ON OVERALL EXPERIENCE

"**I graduated; mission accomplished. I can't imagine having a better college experience anywhere else. I think I'll show up during freshman orientation and do the whole thing again.**"

Q "I wasn't wild about Wesleyan at first. **Everyone I met was so eccentric and over-the-top**. I thought it couldn't be real. There are some fakers, but, for the most part, Wesleyan is filled with really wonderful people."

Q "**It's an incredible school, bottom line**. The degree to which you can control your own academics is fantastic. The school places all the power in your hands, and I really value that. The classes are amazing and so are the professors. I loved it."

Q "Wesleyan is not for everybody. **It's not a 'typical college,'** if there is such a thing. It's very eccentric and very artsy. It's a place for creative people, a place where they can grow and flourish. It's for open-minded people, people with a sense of humor. It's not for the faint of heart."

Q "Let's get one thing straight, Middletown is not your average college town. **It's not really the safest town**, either. Some students choose to transfer on that account alone."

The Inside Scoop

The Lowdown
ON THE INSIDE SCOOP

Wesleyan Slang:
Know the slang, know the school. The following is a list of things you really need to know before coming to Wesleyan. The more of these words you know, the better off you'll be.

The Butts: The Butterfield Dorms
MoCon: McConaughy Hall
The Hospital: Clark Residence Hall
PreFrosh: Prospective students, pre-freshmen
WestCo: West College Residence Hall
Nick: Nicholson Residence Hall
Elbow in the Air: A campus joke that nobody understands

Wesleyan Urban Legends
Several secret societies appear on campus, cropping up every few months to create mischief and the occasional episode of whimsical vandalism.

There is (truly) a network of tunnels beneath the school that gives the bold student access to just about every building on campus.

MoCon was originally designed to be an enormous aquarium.

School Spirit
While traditional school spirit, in the "Ra-Ra" banner-waving sense, is sparse at Wesleyan, the traditionally rebellious attitude of the student body exemplifies most enthusiasm for the school as an institution. However, most students at Wesleyan are deeply devoted to their university and see it as a completely unique school in a league of its own. While Wesleyan Cardinal T-shirts are rare, Wesleyan students are united by a sincere appreciation of the school.

The Douglas Cannon
Between South College and Memorial Chapel sits an empty gun mount that once held the Douglas Cannon. Throughout Wesleyan's history, the cannon itself (which is currently missing) has disappeared and reappeared periodically, often in very bizarre places. The tradition of stealing the cannon is a long-celebrated rite of passage in the Wesleyan community. In the past, the Douglas Cannon has surfaced in the office of the managing editor of *Life* magazine, been baked into an enormous cake, and presented as a gift to Richard Nixon.

The Wesleyan Cardinal
The Cardinal was adopted as Wesleyan's mascot and team name in the early 1930s. The Cardinal was originally inspired by a baseball captain named Walter W. Fricke, class of 1933, who purchased a baseball jacket with a Cardinal stitched on the breast pocket. Wesleyan, which was looking to replace "Methodists" as its official school nickname, soon adopted the Cardinal.

The Wesleyan Shield
The Wesleyan Shield is taken from the coat of arms of Wesleyan namesake and founder of Methodism, John Wesley. The shield is decorated with a cross and several scallop shells. The scallop shell is a symbol of pilgrimage, originally worn by early pilgrims on their way to the Holy Land.

Finding a Job or Internship

Things I Wish I Knew Before Coming to Wesleyan:

- Not all brilliant people are pretentious, and not all pretentious people are brilliant.
- Joining clubs is the fastest way to get involved with the school and make a name for yourself.
- WesFest does not accurately portray what normal life at Wesleyan is really like.
- Wesleyan has no journalism major.
- Many people (male and female) do not shave. Ever.
- The majority of bathrooms are coed.
- Many Wesleyan students can't tell the difference between "avant garde" and "just plain weird."
- The students at Wesleyan are some of the most fascinating and wonderful people you will ever meet.

Tips to Succeed at Wesleyan:

- Be yourself. Really. You'll eventually find your circle.
- Join lots of clubs and activities early on. It's a great way to meet new people and discover new interests.
- The Career Resource Center is a great way to fill your summer with exciting job or internship opportunities.
- If you live on Foss Hill, get a meal plan with fewer points. If you live in the Butterfields, get lots of points.
- Don't be intimidated by others' achievements or ability. Everyone has something different to offer.
- Try new things!
- Don't get sucked into the "protest everything" mentality.
- Chat up your professors. Most are genuinely interested in student input and output.

The Lowdown
ON FINDING A JOB OR INTERNSHIP

Already thinking about employment after college? The Wesleyan Career Resource Center is the place for you. They offer one-on-one counseling on everything from summer internships to graduate schools to full-time employment after school. The face time with these career counselors is really the greatest feature about the Career Resource Center. Each student is treated as an individual with unique talents and needs. They can help you land all sorts of interesting jobs and, if you're talented enough, maybe even a chance to write a college guidebook. Ha ha!

Advice

Check out the Career Resource Center as soon as you can. As a freshman, you've got three long summers ahead of you before graduation, and there's no reason to let them go to waste. The sooner you start looking for opportunities, the more fascinating ones you'll come across. Rather than flipping burgers, you could wind up in South Africa feeding the homeless, or shooting an independent film in Paris. Who knows? The Career Center is a wonderful resource that is far too under-utilized.

Career Center Resources & Services

Campus employment and work study, career counseling, placement advising, career workshops career resource center, graduate school advising, help with resumes, internships, etc., online alumni resources

Famous Wesleyan Alumni:

• Miguel Arteta, class of 1989—Film director ("Star Maps," "Chuck and Buck," "The Good Girl")

• Eric Asimov, class of 1979—Restaurant columnist and editor, *The New York Times*

• Gerald Baliles, class of 1963—Former governor of Virginia

• John Perry Barlow, class of 1969—Lyricist for the Grateful Dead, co-founder of the Electronic Frontier Foundation

• Michael Bay, class of 1986—Film director ("The Rock," "Armageddon," "Pearl Harbor")

• Bill Belichick, class of 1975—Head coach, New England Patriots, winner of 2002 and 2004 Super Bowls

Alumni Employment

Percentage of alumni who have entered these fields between 1999-2004:

Business: 22%

Graduate, Law, or Professional School: 22%

Education: 18%

Non-Profit or Philanthropy: 8%

Entertainment: 6%

Arts: 5%

Health, Medicine: 4%

Computers: 3%

Communications: 3%

Law: 3%

Life and Physical Science: 2%

Major Alumni Events

Sporting events are the biggest draw for alumni, as well as the Homecoming/Family Weekend. The Sons and Daughters Program allows alumni and other parents with sons and/or daughters applying to Wesleyan to learn more about the University. Reunion and Commencement Weekend takes place at the end of each year. New events are always being listed at *www.events.wesleyan.edu*.

Alumni Publications

Wesleyan Magazine

The Best & Worst

The Ten BEST Things About Wesleyan:

1. The amazing and unique student body
2. The beautiful campus
3. The exposure to all sorts of different ideas
4. The unique and talented professors
5. Academic freedom
6. The incredible film studies program
7. The Center for the Arts
8. Spring Fling!
9. The WestCo Café
10. Naked Parties

The Ten WORST Things About Wesleyan:

1. Pretentious artists and writers
2. The drug scene
3. The occasionally emotionless administration
4. The chaotic housing selection process
5. Mediocre campus security
6. Far distance from major cities
7. Constant construction and renovation
8. Frequent protests of all varieties
9. Angry and bitter townspeople
10. Naked Parties

Williams College

988 Main Street, Williamstown, MA 01267
www.williams.edu   (413) 597-2211

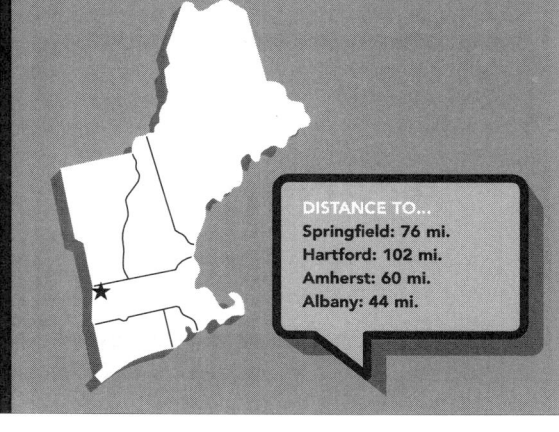

DISTANCE TO...
Springfield: 76 mi.
Hartford: 102 mi.
Amherst: 60 mi.
Albany: 44 mi.

"Williams is a place that shelters you from the world in many ways. It educates you in a thorough, but not necassarily practical, way."

Total Enrollment:
1,995
Acceptance:
21%
Tuition:
$29,990
Top 10% of High School Class:
87%
SAT Range
Verbal	Math	Total
650 – 760	660 – 750	1310 – 1510

SAT II Requirements
International students are required to take three SAT II subject tests. Students who are not native English speakers should take Writing as one of the three.

Most Popular Majors:
16% Psychology
15% Political Science and Government
13% English Language and Literature
12% Economics
10% Biology/Biological Sciences

Students Also Applied to:*
Amherst College, Bowdoin College, Dartmouth College, Harvard University,

*For more school info check out www.collegeprowler.com

Table of Contents

Academics	388
Local Atmosphere	390
Safety & Security	391
Computers	393
Facilities	394
Campus Dining	396
Off-Campus Dining	397
Campus Housing	398
Off-Campus Housing	400
Diversity	401
Guys & Girls	402
Athletics	403
Greek Life	405
Drug Scene	406
Campus Strictness	407
Overall Experience	408
The Inside Scoop	410
Finding a Job or Internship	411
The Best & Worst	411

College Prowler Report Card

Academics	A+
Local Atmosphere	C+
Safety & Security	A-
Computers	C+
Facilities	A-
Campus Dining	B
Off-Campus Dining	C+
Campus Housing	C
Off-Campus Housing	C-
Diversity	C
Guys	C-
Girls	C
Athletics	B
Greek Life	N/A
Drug Scene	A-
Campus Strictness	B+

Academics

Best Places to Study
Schow Library

Sample Academic Clubs
Phi Beta Capa, Sigma Xi

Did You Know?

In 1889, the first African American student graduated from Williams.

The Lowdown
ON ACADEMICS

Degrees Awarded:
Bachelor of Arts
Master of Arts in Art History
Master of Arts in Development Economics

Undergraduate Schools:
Humanities, Sciences, Social Sciences

Full-Time Faculty:
271

Faculty with Terminal Degree:
93%

Student-to-Faculty Ratio:
9:1

Average Course Load:
4 classes per semester

Special Degree Options:
Pre-Medical, Contract major, Self-devised major

AP Test Score Requirements:
Possible credit for scores of 4 or 5

IB Test Score Requirements:
Possible credit for scores of 4, 5, 6, or 7

Students Speak Out
ON ACADEMICS

"People at Williams expect us to be super-confident and ready to be in college. The truth is, when you come in as a freshman, you are just a kid, and many other students can be arrogant and stifling."

"When I came to Williams as a freshman, everybody kept telling me that the French professors weren't good. I had taken four years of French in high school and was intent on pursuing the language further. In four years, the department improved; they hired new professors and came up with new courses. I definitely don't regret majoring in French. I also know that many other majors here are even better than French, so I think that **no matter what you choose, you will learn a lot at Williams**. You shouldn't be declaring your major on the basis of a department's reputation but rather on your true interests. Departments change every semester, and there is a lot of student input influencing these changes."

Q "Professors at Williams are very friendly, helpful, and knowledgeable. Most are very hard graders, though, so you will have to sweat for that A-. In the end, you know you have learned a lot to earn your grade. At Williams, there isn't much pressure to have the highest GPA, so **professors are fair to their students, even though they set high standards**. I know that I need some pressure in order to work hard and stay motivated, so it was good for me to be around demanding profs."

Q "**Upper-level classes at Williams get very intense** because that's where you begin to spend lots of time with your professors. You do have to get through some boring introductory classes first. Most professors will be very welcoming and helpful in their office hours, even if you are one of 50 students in the class. It gets much better in 200- and 300- levels when class size decreases to 10 or so. You have to realize that you should be the one taking the initiative to meet your professors."

Q "I really liked the professors at Williams, but I think **they tolerate the jocks in the college and don't allow for a more intellectual climate**. Some people come to class in their gym clothes, chewing power bars and not bothering to do the reading or contribute to class. That attitude is really unfair and disrespectful to those of us who work hard, including the professors and teaching assistants who prepare for those classes."

Q "I feel like **some of the professors were too demanding** and assigned more homework than a normal person could handle. I am pretty hard-working, but I think it is wrong to deprive yourself of sleep all the time. I know many kids develop stress-related psych disorders because of trying to cope with all of the work and staying on top while not sleeping, eating, or socializing with friends. I think the school should try to make sure people stay healthy even though they are the ones who choose to work so hard. Maybe they just need to relax."

The College Prowler Take
ON ACADEMICS

True, you have to work hard at Williams, and As are hard to get. However, the amount of personal attention and the quality of instruction makes every bead of sweat worth it. Williams professors are accessible, articulate, and extremely erudite. Whatever their specific field, they share a commitment to encourage students to explore and learn both within and beyond the classroom. Williams professors are also willing to devote whatever time necessary to help a student learn. While the workload does vary with separate departments, students are constantly challenged to improve their skills and obtain new ones as well. They are also encouraged to share these achievements with others. Professors allow for each student to have his or her own style of learning and are supportive of everyone's individual learning process. Students have to work hard, but they enjoy help and inspiration from their professors every step of the way.

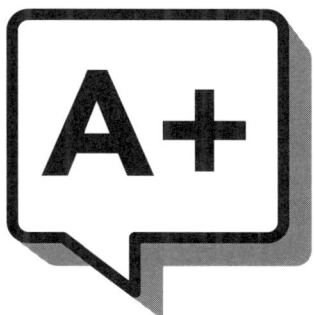

The College Prowler™ Grade on
Academics: A+

A high Academics grade generally indicates that professors are knowledgeable, accessible, and genuinely interested in their students' welfare. Other determining factors include class size, how well professors communicate, and whether or not classes are engaging.

Local Atmosphere

Students Speak Out
ON LOCAL ATMOSPHERE

"People in town are white, rich, and generally uninteresting. They won't get in your way at all, but if you are looking for fun beyond the school, get on the bus to New York."

Q "The **town is composed almost entirely of college students**, faculty, and other people related to Williams. So, while you won't meet any cool town people, you will always be surrounded by people who know how you're feeling."

Q "The **college and town buildings are gorgeous**; the lawns are so well-kept. What you see in those college catalogues is not enough to show the beauties of Williamstown. In the fall, when the leaves change color, it gets prettier than those pictures."

Q "I don't know how to describe the local atmosphere because there is no atmosphere. **Nothing ever happens in the town, except for college-related events**. If you come from NYC like myself, you might end up really bored. Breathing the clean air of the Berkshires is not enough sometimes, unless you spend most of your time in the library working."

Q "**Williamstown has a friendly, welcoming, and relaxing feel**. Even when you stress about work, a walk in the Hopkins Forest can lift your spirits. Nobody will intrude on your privacy ever; it's really nice."

Q "The **town is kind of dead in terms of social events**, so don't rely on locals for having an actual social life. It's beautiful, but there's nothing special about it except the fact that there's a church on every corner."

The Lowdown
ON LOCAL ATMOSPHERE

Region:
Northeast

City, State:
Williamstown, Massachusetts

Setting:
Berkshire Mountains

Distance from Boston:
1.5 hours

Distance from New York:
3 hours

Points of Interest:
MassMoca, North Adams,
Clark Museum, Williamstown

Major Sports Teams:
None

City Websites:
www.williamstown.net
www.wtfestival.org

The College Prowler Take
ON LOCAL ATMOSPHERE

Williamstown is not comparable to New York City as far as diversity, but, for a small town, it has a lot to offer both visitors and residents. A friendly, inviting, and intellectually-stimulating atmosphere, combined with peace and the beauty of nature, makes Williamstown more than attractive. The town is small, but if you are into the arts, it has a lot to offer. From the movie theater to the overall appearance of the town, Williamstown gives off an artsy aura. Though it is generally quiet, many students find it relaxing.

Safety & Security

The Lowdown
ON SAFETY & SECURITY

Number of Williams Police:
10 full-time officers, one part-time officer, 13 security office workers
Phone: (413) 597-4444

Health Center Office Hours:
9:00 a.m.-12:00 p.m. and 1:00 p.m.-5:00 p.m., Monday thru Friday

Safety Services:
Sexual Assault Network
Peer Health Advisors
Student Health Advisory Committee

The College Prowler™ Grade on

Local Atmosphere: C+

A high Local Atmosphere grade indicates that the area surrounding campus is safe and scenic. Other factors include nearby attractions, proximity to other schools, and the town's attitude toward students.

Did You Know?

Williams has an eating disorders team to combat problems with nutrition and body image.

Students Speak Out
ON SAFETY & SECURITY

The College Prowler Take
ON SAFETY & SECURITY

"**Security is a priority of the college, but I feel that a lot more could be done, especially at weekend parties when it's always too crowded and nobody really checks who's 21.**"

Q "**The security officers are very nice.** They help people a lot, and I really like that they offer to take you to your dorm after midnight— not that Williamstown isn't a safe place. It's comforting to know that they would do that."

Q "**Everything is great at Williams, except the fact that the Health Center closes on weekends,** and then security has to drive you to the hospital. I just feel it's not their job to do that because they are not doctors. The people who can't afford to call an ambulance have to rely on unprofessional people. One of my friends lost consciousness in class, and she refused to be taken care of because she knew her insurance could not cover it. This is ridiculous. It's not her fault that she passed out at a time when the Health Center was closed."

Q "**Williamstown is a small town, and it's safe.** The most you can do about your personal security is to make sure none of the other people in your dorm steal your shampoo in the bathroom, which they will anyway."

Q "**After 7 p.m. at Williams, random doors are locked up for random purposes.** This means people can't hand in papers and such. It's kind of ridiculous and annoying. The school hires way too many people to do stupid bureaucratic stuff like that, and our tuition money is spent on inane things like paying someone to lock a building that shouldn't be locked."

Q "The campus looks safe, but sometimes, **things go on at parties that should never happen** and that most people don't report. I think some more female security officers would be good for this campus."

There is no doubt that the town and the college of Williams are safe. Williams' security tries to make it safer by locking random doors and making fire alarms sensitive to the smell of fried onions. At the same time, the Health Center is closed on weekends when most college campus accidents occur, such as drinking problems and date rape. Overall, the security staff makes sure the campus is safe and that students have a reliable source for their safety needs. Known for their prompt and kind help, security officers on campus could ease off closing the libraries and be more attentive to drinking problems, but, all-in-all, they do a good job of making one feel safe at his/her home away from home.

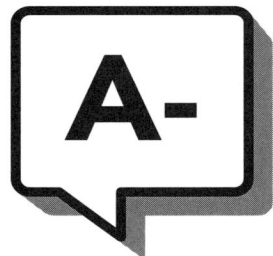

The College Prowler™ Grade on
Safety & Security: A-

A high grade in Safety & Security means that students generally feel safe, campus police are visible, blue-light phones and escort services are readily available, and safety precautions are not overly necessary.

Computers

Free Software
Acrobat 6, Amos, Canvas, ChemDraw, ChemOffice, Cindex, Command Anti-Virus, Director 8, Director MX, DNA Strider, Dreamweaver, EndNote, Fetch 4, Finale, Fireworks, Flash, Gauss, Illustrator, InDesign CS, Inspiration, JMP, KaleidaGraph, Key Server/Key Access, Labview, Lightwright, MacClade, MacVector, Mathmatica, Matlab, Max, Meeting Maker, Molecular Dynamics, PAUP, Peak2, Photoshop, Phylip 2.5, Pro Tools, Rats 6, Scientific SPSS, SHH Telnet, Strata, StatView, TrueBasic, VectorWorks

The Lowdown
ON COMPUTERS

Students Speak Out
ON COMPUTERS

"Printers are the real issue. The main computer building is equipped with about 10 of them, and not one works. They are either out of paper, sleeping, broken, jammed, or someone spilled Mountain Dew on them."

Q "The **Williams computer network is run by idiots**. The network is down every other day, people lose papers, and they can't tell if their e-mails got delivered. Every couple of months, your e-mail account is not accessible because you have to change your password. It sucks if this happens to be the day when you have a job application to mail that day."

High-Speed Network?
Yes

Wireless Network?
Yes

Number of Labs:
4 open labs, 6 specialty labs, 4 media labs, 8 computer classrooms

Numbers of Computers:
140 Macs, 112 PCs

24-Hour Labs:
Jesup Hall, Stetson Hall, Bronfman, Clark, Kellogg Matt Cole

Charge to Print?
None

Operating Systems:
Windows, Mac OS X

Q "The **labs aren't crowded**, and generally, you get do your work. E-mail might be a problem because there's always something wrong with the *williams.edu* server. Keep your Yahoo and Hotmail accounts activated."

Q "Computers work better than other places I have considered going to school. **Signing up for classes online and being able to see your grades, even when you are not on campus, can be very useful**. You have lots of space in your folder on the school server for keeping papers and downloading things."

Q "Williams has enough computers for those who didn't bring their own. **It is good to have a laptop on campus**. Don't trust any of the people that get paid by Williams to connect your laptop to the school network or to fix it. These people are likely to mess up big time."

Q "Computers function at Williams, and **tons of coursework is done online**, posted, and e-mailed to professors. It saves a lot of time and keeps people informed about everything. Most of us check our e-mail at least every hour to stay on top of schoolwork and extracurricular commitments, and it works."

The College Prowler Take
ON COMPUTERS

C++ and other programming languages often seem to be the only languages the Williams tech staff speaks. No one has been able to explain the daily network failures to us in actual English, so we can't say whose fault it is. Then again, the lost papers, job applications, and messages will never be retrieved, so why should we even know the reason for the failures? Williams computer facilities are truly wonderful, but with a network that falls apart every day, students cannot make full use of them. Students also feel that the tech staff is lacking in their knowledge of how to fix common problems.

The College Prowler™ Grade on
Computers: C+

A high grade in Computers designates that computer labs are available, the computer network is easily accessible, and the campus' computing technology is up-to-date.

Facilities

The Lowdown
ON FACILITIES

Movie Theatre on Campus? Yes

Bowling on Campus? No

Bar on Campus? Yes

Coffeehouse on Campus:
Coldspring Coffee, Eco Café in Schow Library, Goodrich Coffee Shop

Student Center:
In progress

Athletic Center:
Lasell Gym, Towne Field House, pool, Chanler Athletic Center, Squash Center, tennis courts, various outdoors fields

Libraries:
Schow Science Library, Sawyer Library, Chapin Library of Rare Books, Kellogg Library for Environmental Studies, Bronfman Math Library

Popular Places to Chill:
Baxter Snack Bar, Coldspring Coffee Shop, Goodrich

Favorite Things to Do:
Chill in the snack bar, walk in Hopkins Forest, swim in the pool between 5 and 7 p.m., play squash

Students Speak Out
ON FACILITIES

"The observatory is one of the most precious facilities at Williams. It's a space where you can learn a lot and admire the skies to the fullest."

Q "The **athletic facilities are amazing**, from the pool, to the squash center, to the indoor track and also the dance studio. Another strength of Williams are the labs and other science facilities that are always available to all and staffed by some of the friendliest people ever."

Q "Williams has truly amazing facilities. **Whatever they don't have, they are building**, such as the new theater. The old theater was fine, too, with its various stage and rehearsal spaces. But now it's going to be even better."

Q "Libraries are very important facilities for me. At Williams, I have always thought that looking for books and being in the library could never be more pleasant. **Schow library, in particular, catches the attention with its modern shapes**, high ceilings, and really, really good reading lights. Oh, I will miss the Schow lights when I leave."

Q "Art facilities at Williams are very inviting and cozy since few people use them, anyway. **I love the ceramics studio and the Spencer Art Building**. If you want to do ceramics, there are actual potter wheels and a very good kiln."

Q "I haven't thought much about Williams' facilities, which is probably because **I take them for granted**. I have to wake up at six for bio labs, so I don't think much about how well Williams labs are equipped, and they are. I am glad you asked me this question."

The College Prowler Take
ON FACILITIES

Want to have a special facility for basket weaving and knot-tying? Just ask. Williams will provide the space, the equipment, and the materials at once. Luckily, most Williams facilities support activities that are much more meaningful than the ones aforementioned. While many do argue that the quality of theater productions does not match the quality of the facility Williams is to building, it is reasonable to say that Williams students achieve good, if not excellent, results in many areas, including theater. The comfort of a well-designed and maintained facility helps people become better at what they do, whether it is playing the flute or kick-boxing.

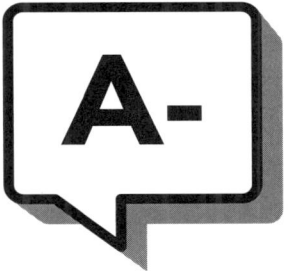

The College Prowler™ Grade on
Facilities: A-

A high Facilities grade indicates that the campus is aesthetically pleasing and well-maintained; facilities are state-of-the-art, and libraries are exceptional. Other determining factors include the quality of both athletic and student centers and an abundance of things to do on campus.

Campus Dining

The Lowdown
ON CAMPUS DINING

Freshman Meal Plan Requirement?
No

Student Favorites:
Brunch Night

24-Hour On-Campus Eating?
No

Meal Plan Average Cost:
$3,840

Students Speak Out
ON CAMPUS DINING

"I used to really like the food my freshman year, but then it got repetitive. Since then, I cook a lot. My dorm has a very nice kitchen, and we keep it clean, more or less."

Q "**Dining on campus should be open all the time**, not just between the hours of 5 p.m. and 7 p.m. because some of us have stuff to do then, and if you miss dinner, you wait on a long line to get your dinner points, or you just spend extra money on food."

Q "I like the **make-your-own omelette** bar, the waffle bar, and the bagels. Sunday brunch is usually pretty good in any of the dining halls."

Q "If you are a vegetarian, you might have consternation about the dining facilities. They've been trying to improve by adding some good soups and vegan cookies, but nothing for a sufficient meal just yet. I guess **as a vegetarian, not much can be expected** from a college dining service. I think it might be worth it for them to ask us about what they could add to the dining menu."

Q "**Food in Williams is generally good**, except in Baxter Dining Hall. I think in Baxter, they just make food for too many people, so they always mess up or run out of things. We have the Annual Lobster Dinner, though, which rocks, even in Baxter."

The College Prowler Take
ON CAMPUS DINING

While they may not make the best veggie pizza on earth, the campus dining facilities do an adequate job of allowing vegetarians and other individuals with special eating habits to stay satisfied. Most of the time, the food actually tastes good and is fresh. Many agree that the fruit and vegetable portion of the menu could use some work, but it could be a lot worse. Williams' on-campus dining has also been very successful in creating a pleasant atmosphere for enjoying your food, and they may surprise you from time to time with new recipes and touches.

The College Prowler™ Grade on
Campus Dining: B

Our grade on Campus Dining addresses the quality of both school-owned dining halls and independent on-campus restaurants as well as the price, availability, and variety of food.

Off-Campus Dining

The Lowdown
ON OFF-CAMPUS DINING

Best Pizza:
Hot Tomatoes

Best Chinese:
Chopsticks

Best Breakfast:
Papa Charlie's

Best Place to Take Your Parents:
Hobson's Choice

Student Favorites:
Hot Tomatoes, Chopsticks, Thai Garden, Papa Charlie's

24-Hour Eating:
No

Closest Grocery Stores:
Stop & Shop

Did You Know?

One of the waiters in the Spice Root Indian restaurant is fluent in Russian.

Students Speak Out
ON OFF-CAMPUS DINING

> "**It sucks because you always meet your classmates going on dates when you eat off campus. It's embarrassing. You can't eat in privacy.**"

> "There **aren't too many options for off campus food**, but the ones that we have are awesome. For a small town, we've done great. There are Indian, Thai, and Latin American places next to each other, and the owners of the sandwich shop are Greek. Well, there's also Subway."

> "I wish I didn't have to drive out of town for a good Chinese place, even though they deliver. Most **good restaurants are far from campus**, so when it's cold, snowing, or we have too much work, it's just not convenient."

> "Yeah, you can eat out, but **it's real expensive**. I like the sandwich shop, Papa Charlie's, because they have very original sandwiches and a nice atmosphere. Unfortunately, I can't eat there everyday."

> "Watch out with off-campus dining, or you will become like me—**totally addicted to the sandwich place on Spring Street**. They have very original sandwiches and awesome Greek salads and smoothies. Just down the street is a great ice cream place. I have to say that after spending three years in this town, I haven't gotten tired of any of them."

> "**There are many good restaurants in the area**, and some of my friends happen to have part-time jobs there, so we have tested those places, and they have great food."

The College Prowler Take
ON OFF-CAMPUS DINING

There could always be more variety in a small town. However, for its size, this town has a lot to offer when it comes to good food. It is true, though, that some of the restaurants are so expensive that you'll want to wait for your parents to visit and have them foot the bill. But fear not, there are several that are still affordable. There are also a couple of all-time favorites that no one even tries to grade anymore: they are just known to offer great quality and are frequented a lot by students.

Campus Housing

The Lowdown
ON CAMPUS HOUSING

Undergrads on Campus:
96%

Number of Dormitories:
42

Room Types:
Single, double, suite-style singles and doubles, co-op

Cleaning Service?
Cleaning of floor bathrooms, garbage removal

You Get:
Ethernet jacks, cable jack (cable is an additional cost), bed, desk, dresser

Also Available:
Cable TV in common rooms, kitchen shared by building

Bed Type:
Twin extra-long

The College Prowler™ Grade on
Off-Campus Dining: C+

A high Off-Campus Dining grade implies that off-campus restaurants are affordable, accessible, and worth visiting. Other factors include the variety of cuisine and the availability of alternative options (vegetarian, vegan, Kosher, etc.).

Students Speak Out
ON CAMPUS HOUSING

The College Prowler Take
ON CAMPUS HOUSING

"Williams dorms have been getting better and better during my time in the school. Some of the less convenient places were renovated, especially sophomore dorms."

Q "**You have to choose your dorm carefully** because things are very different from place to place. The overall quality of housing is good, but in some dorms, you have to share a bathroom with another five or six people, even more. Some do their laundry by hand, and you find their dirty socks in the sink. Others peel onions in the bathroom. And then others take an hour to shower. It's college life, but at Williams, you can avoid it if you pick into the right dorm with the right people."

Q "In my dorm, **there was always a line for the bathroom**, but never for the laundry. I guess one of the people in our dorm just took forever in the shower. In most dorms, you would do just fine, though."

Q "**Most dorm rooms in Williams are very big and nice**. Common room spaces are available, too, in most dorms, and many have a TV in them. Many dorms also have nice kitchens if you are into cooking at all. I also appreciate the pool tables and the laundry machines."

Q "Some Williams dorms and many buildings in general have horrible heating systems. **You can't control the heat from you room**, and it's so strong that the air gets really dry. People get nosebleeds, eye problems, and live in a furnace."

Q "You **can't rely on Williams housing to make a comfortable living situation**. You will buy your own chairs, blankets, pillows, and everything else you might need to make your room look nice."

Although some people do get lucky, most underclassmen are crammed in small rooms and bathrooms, and even upperclassmen sometimes end up in a room where they have to hear a drilling noise 10 hours a day. Relying on the buildings and grounds staff to help out with anything is not a good idea. They are more adept at creating more red tape and wasting people's time than anything else.

The College Prowler™ Grade on
Campus Housing: C

A high Campus Housing grade indicates that dorms are clean, well-maintained, and spacious. Other determining factors include variety of dorms, proximity to classes, and social atmosphere.

Off-Campus Housing

The Lowdown
ON OFF-CAMPUS HOUSING

Undergrads in Off-Campus Housing: 4%

Popular Areas:
Main Street, Water Street

Best Time to Look for a Place:
Applications are due February 7. Begin looking before this date, but you do not have to have a place lined up to apply for off-campus housing.

For Assistance Contact:
www.williams.edu/admin-depts/bg/housing/
Phone: (413) 597-2195
E-mail: housing@williams.edu

Students Speak Out
ON OFF-CAMPUS HOUSING

"You will live off campus for the rest of your life, so I just don't see what the advantages are of doing it now."

Q "**Living off campus is pointless** in a town as small as this. The school is the town. You will always be on campus, anyway."

Q "I gave up the thought of living off campus because **my dining hall is in my dorm now**, and I don't even need to go out in the cold to get food, do laundry, or play pool."

Q "I lived off campus last year, and **it was nice to know that I don't need my school ID** to get into the building. But paying bills, shopping, and having your own phone line set up is just too much trouble when you are also taking five classes at an academically-challenging school."

Q "**Living off campus can save you some money** if you are careful about where you shop and how much furniture you buy. It will make your life harder in other random ways, like dealing with a cranky landlord and a neighbor who hates loud music."

The College Prowler Take
ON OFF-CAMPUS HOUSING

Most students agree living off campus is not really an option. Because Williams is a small school, there is plenty of housing on campus. Williamstown is a small town, as well, and there are not many places to stay. The smallness of the town makes living on campus the most logical option. Some students choose to live off campus, though, and value the experience. Off-campus housing is near the campus, but the cost of renting can be pretty high. Many students enjoy the freedom of living on their own and getting to set their own rules. The housing policy regarding off-campus housing is rather tough. The number of students permitted to live off campus is limited, as are the options.

The College Prowler™ Grade on
Off-Campus Housing: C-

A high grade in Off-Campus Housing indicates that apartments are of high quality, close to campus, affordable, and easy to secure.

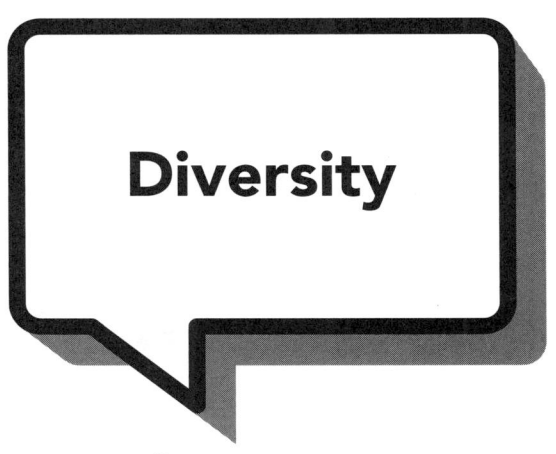

Diversity

Gay Tolerance
High, but recently some homophobic e-mails were sent out to the members of the Queer Student Union.

Economic Status
Wealthy and upper-middle-class

Students Speak Out
ON DIVERSITY

The Lowdown
ON DIVERSITY

African American: 9%

Asian American: 9%

Hispanic: 8%

Native American: 0%

White: 68%

International: 6%

Out-of-State: 80%

Minority Clubs
Black Student Union, VISTA, Asian American Students in Action (AASiA), the Harrison Morgan Brown Pre-Medical Society, the International Club, Koreans of Williams, SASA, QSU, Jewish Student Union.

Most Popular Religions
Protestant, Catholic

Political Activity
Liberal, MassPIRG

"Williams is okay for a small school. I think every school has a type of student they look for. We have mostly jocks, but it doesn't mean that the school is not diverse."

Q "I am one of not very many blacks on campus, and I know **from my own experience that the place is not really diverse**. You end hanging out with the same two or three people all the time, and they are just like you."

Q "Diversity is a state of mind, not a number of people. In this sense, Williams is diverse because all of [the students] have very open minds and are curious about other cultures. Here, **you can meet people from all over** America and the world if you take the time and make some effort."

Q "**Williams is not the most diverse place**, but there isn't pressure to be like the majority. If you aren't a jock, you won't be popular, but you would still have friends and no one will look down on you ever."

Q "Williams is boring and preppy. **Few interesting people spice up the scenes**; and you must find them as soon as you go to freshman orientation. If you wear polo shirts and J. Crew, though, you will fit right in."

Q "**There are a handful of international students** who always stick together and don't mix with the rest to of us. Minority students also stay in their own little group. I don't know how you can have diversity."

The College Prowler Take
ON DIVERSITY

To say that Williams tries hard to attract people from diverse backgrounds is just a euphemism for saying that Williams always ends up admitting people who belong to the same social group. One of the most pretty colleges in the country, Williams should not even try to argue that diversity is a top priority on the list of admissions officers. Too many students have parents who attended the school for this to be true. But if you are looking for diversity within a majority group of white, wealthy, preppy, and athletic, you might even find it.

The College Prowler™ Grade on
Diversity: C

A high grade in Diversity indicates that ethnic minorities and international students have a notable presence on campus and that students of different economic backgrounds, religious beliefs, and sexual preferences are well-represented.

Guys & Girls

The Lowdown
ON GUYS & GIRLS

Women Undergrads: 984

Men Undergrads: 985

Birth Control Available? Yes

Social Scene:
Everyone works very hard during the week and gets very, very drunk on the weekends. Then they go back to work on Sunday night. Many parties are run by athletic teams.

Hookups or Relationships?
Mostly hookups. Relationships do happen, but most people are not looking for a long-term commitment.

Dress Code:
Flip-flops, sweat pants, tank tops, Williams T-shirts

Students Speak Out
ON GUYS & GIRLS

"Guys at Williams are very immature. They drink too much and can be obnoxious at parties, trying to touch you. Many are good-looking, but it's not worth it."

Q "**Most guys are really hot** because they play sports and have gorgeous bodies, but they are not into committed relationships, which makes it hard if you don't go for one night stands."

Q "**Williams girls dress and act like guys**. I don't know how they think someone can be attracted to them. They look sloppy and don't take care of themselves."

Q "**There are some pretty hot girls at Williams**, on the track and tennis team in particular. They make you feel like you have a friend who can run, climb, or throw a Frisbee with you, not just go out for dinner all dressed up."

Q "Williams girls are cute and smart, but everyone has their little group of friends, and it's hard to meet other people and date. **Many people are too shy to even talk to each other**, and it's not like you can walk up to a girl in the dining hall and tell her you're attracted to her."

The College Prowler Take
ON GUYS & GIRLS

Guys and girls at Williams spend a lot of time complaining about each other, but the truth is that they are just like most college students. Williams students are good-looking, athletic, and like to have a lot of fun. Maturity might come to some of them well after college, if at all, but most create strong friendships, and those who wish to commit do form relationships. According to official statistics, 50 percent of Williams graduates marry another Williams student. Scary or not, this says a lot about whether we like each other.

The College Prowler™ Grade on
Guys: C-

A high grade for Guys indicates that the male population on campus is attractive, smart, friendly, and engaging, and that the school has a decent ratio of guys to girls.

The College Prowler™ Grade on
Girls: C

A high grade for Girls not only implies that the women on campus are attractive, smart, friendly, and engaging, but also that there is a fair ratio of girls to guys.

Athletics

The Lowdown
ON ATHLETICS

Men's Varsity	Women's Varsity
Baseball	Basketball
Basketball	Crew
Crew	Cross Country
Cross Country	Football
Football	Golf
Golf	Field Hockey
Ice Hockey	Ice Hockey
Lacrosse	Lacrosse
Alpine Skiing	Alpine Skiing
Nordic Skiing	Nordic Skiing
Soccer	Soccer
Squash	Squash
Swimming	Swimming
Diving	Diving
Tennis	Tennis
Track & Field	Softball
Wrestling	Volleyball

Club Sports

Aikikan, badminton. cycling, equestrian, figure skating, fencing, golf, gymnastics, martial arts, rugby, sailing, snowboarding, wiffleball, Ultimate Frisbee, volleyball, table tennis

Athletic Division:
Division III

Conference:
Little Three, NESCAC, ECAC, NCAA
Getting Tickets: Contact the Sports Information Director at (413) 597-4982.

Most Popular Sports:
Football, Basketball

Overlooked Teams:
Field Hockey, Tennis

School Mascot:
Purple Cow

Q "**It's amazing the money the college spends on building and renovating the sports facilities**. They are fantastic. I mean, I don't even swim that well, but I like being in the pool. It makes college life healthier. Instead of sleeping in the library, we actually exercise."

Q "**Athletics at Williams are on a very high level**, rivaling academics but not making it any less important. People at Williams are dedicated and able; they juggle more than one ball. There's no reason why you can't be a winner at sports and get good grades and learn from both."

Q "**Sports are really important** when you are in college, both for your physical health, but also your sanity when you are overworked like we tend to be on this campus. I am glad I was on a team during my college years because it helped me build wonderful personal relationships and develop a lot of character."

Students Speak Out
ON ATHLETICS

The College Prowler Take
ON ATHLETICS

"Athletics are great at Williams. You learn to be in a team and work with other people. I think it makes you a better person. However, it is a lot of really hard work."

Q "I am very involved in athletics and am on one intramural and one varsity team. I can tell you from experience that **the coaches at Williams are the nicest people on campus**, and they are really good at what they do. Also, the facilities are great. Williams is the place where you can do the sports that you like as much as you like, with people who share your passion."

Q "**If you are not on an athletic team at Williams, your social life sucks**. Teams have their own parties, which tend to exclude everybody else. They should put this in the college catalogue they send out because there are many schools out there where this is not the case. Plus, you have the right to know what you are getting into."

Athletics at Williams are for talented vets and amateurs, for devoted fans and new recruits, for everyone who loves sports, and even for those who might not be that athletic at all. The outstanding professionalism of the coaches and athletic staff makes the wonderful facilities on campus come alive with the spirit and effort of those who learn, teach, compete, or play to just have fun. The variety of sports classes and teams, both varsity and intramural, combined with the quality of the facilities, has made Williams stand out as a place where athletics thrive.

The College Prowler™ Grade on
Athletics: B

A high grade in Athletics indicates that students have school spirit, that sports programs are respected, that games are well-attended, and that intramurals are a prominent part of student life.

Greek Life

Students Speak Out
ON GREEK LIFE

"Not having to deal with fraternity life is part of the reason why I picked Williams over another school. I think I made the right choice."

Q "**I am glad there are no frats**, but sometimes I wish we had a way to build more community spirit and make friends for life. Everyone here is sort of by himself."

Q "**Frats were abolished to promote more interaction** between different types of students, but this is not really happening because we all just find our little niche, anyway."

Q "**Fraternities and hazing rituals are horrifying**. They are a thing of the past, and all schools should remove them."

Q "Sports teams are bad enough. They alienate other people and make you stick with one group. **We don't need fraternities for that in our school**."

Q "**Fraternities are a thing of the past and should be abolished everywhere**. I don't need a fraternity to make friends in college or feel safe because I am part of a group. We are all part of many groups here, whether it's a sports team, the Gospel Choir, a cultural club, or just sharing the same hobby with others. This is enough to make people feel like they're in a community that shares their interests."

The Lowdown
ON GREEK LIFE

Number of Fraternities: 0

Number of Sororities: 0

Multicultural Colonies:
Asian-American Students in Action, South Asian Student Association, Bisexual, Gay, Lesbian and Transgendered Union, Chinese American Student Organization, Koreans of Williams, Students of Mixed Heritage, VISTA, Williams Black Student Union, Williams Feminist Alliance, Minority Coalition

Williams features the Multicultural Center. Visit their Website at *www.williams.edu/MCC/welcome.html* for more information.

Other Greek Organizations:
Greek Council, Greek Peer Advisors, Interfraternity Council, Order of Omega, Panhellenic Council

Did You Know?

Fraternities were phased out at Williams in the 1960s. However, rumor has it that secret and very exclusive groups form on campus once in a while.

Like to party? Find out which frat or sorority is best for you by checking out the College Prowler book on Williams College available at *www.collegeprowler.com*.

The College Prowler Take
ON GREEK LIFE

Williams has no Greek life, and most students feel good about this. They find that a fraternity is not the kind of structure they want or need in order to have a fulfilling college life. Few would exercise a desire to bond with other students under the authority of a fraternity. The rumors about a secret fraternity remain a mystery. The idea that sports teams are a substitute for fraternities on campus is also highly debatable, but somewhat confirmed by the fact that teams are often able to live in the same dorm.

The College Prowler™ Grade on
Greek Life: N/A

A high grade in Greek Life indicates that sororities and fraternities are not only present, but also active on campus. Other determining factors include the variety of houses available and the respect the Greek community receives from the rest of the campus.

Drug Scene

The Lowdown
ON DRUG SCENE

Most Prevalent Drugs on Campus:
Marijuana, alcohol

Liquor-Related Referrals: 24

Liquor-Related Arrests: 0

Drug-Related Referrals: 10

Drug-Related Arrests: 0

Drug Counseling Programs:
Educational workshops offered by Health Center, individual counseling by appointment

Students Speak Out
ON DRUG SCENE

"I know people smoke weed at Williams, but not as much as many other colleges I have visited. I like that because nobody is pressured to do anything."

Q "At first, it seems that there is no drug scene at Williams, but if you look for it, you will find some interesting things, as well as **experienced mushroom fans**."

Q "Compared to other campuses I have visited, **Williams is almost drug-free**. Very few people smoke tobacco, which is great, even though I sometimes miss the smell of coffee and cigarettes that I grew up with."

Q "Let's face it: **two to three people sell weed on campus**, and everybody who wants some knows who they are. Not that many people want any, otherwise you would have more dealers for a crowd of over 2,000."

Q "I have to admit, I did my drugs in high school. **I came to Williams to study and have fun** and stay away from them. I have been really successful in doing this because most of my classmates here really are not into this kind of stuff. I am glad I ended up with them and not some different people."

The College Prowler Take
ON DRUG SCENE

As most students indicate, there hardly is a drug scene at Williams. Yet, there's always that voice in the corner saying that the drug scene is flourishing if you know where to look. That's why we are assigning a skeptical A- to this field, hoping that it is actually an A. Meanwhile, we know for a fact that no one would be pressured into doing drugs at Williams, and that those who wish to forget that drugs exist can do so easily on this campus.

The College Prowler™ Grade on
Drug Scene: A-

A high grade on Drug Scene indicates that drugs are not a noticeable part of campus life; drug use is not visible, and no pressure to use them seems to exist.

Campus Strictness

The Lowdown
ON CAMPUS STRICTNESS

What Are You Most Likely to Get Caught Doing on Campus?
Drinking, smoking in dorms

Students Speak Out
ON CAMPUS STRICTNESS

{ "The campus is not strict in general, but there is talk about banning Beirut games and hard alcohol. I don't know how I feel about that because people will want to keep doing those things."

Q "This is **not a very strict campus**. You can't keep candles in your room, but if you said you needed them for religious reasons, they'd let you do it. Many people have incense, too, and smoke in their rooms without having to put something over the smoke detector."

Q "**You can get drunk on this campus without worrying** about someone calling security or the police. Smoking is strictly prohibited, but some fire alarms inside older dorms do not pick up the smoke at all."

Overall Experience

Students Speak Out
ON OVERALL EXPERIENCE

Q "The custodial staff are actually strict, even mean. **You can't leave your shoes outside your dorm room** or have anything in the hallways. Storage rules suck, so if you are leaving Williams for the summer, think twice before you trust the housing office with anything that is of any value."

Q "I think the campus is as strict as it should be. There really is no reason to become paranoid about what students are going to do because **the regulations are in place**, and there are always going to be people who are willing to break them. At Williams, you do face the consequences of such actions for the most part, so don't get caught."

Q "This campus is a healthy space because strict rules are in place; at the same time nobody polices you, though, which also very important. I think **most people here are responsible** and know better than to do drugs, although Beirut games are not a harmless pleasure, either."

"Williams is a very liberal institution, and I'm not liberal, so I had a lot of scary thoughts in the beginning about keeping my opinions and expressing them. I now see that my convictions have changed, and this is good."

Q "After four years at Williams, I don't really feel ready for the real world, because Williams is not the real world. I had a very good time attending classes, hanging out with friends, and just being myself here because there was so little pressure to deal with the external reality of things. I know that Williams is also a place that tries to help you to find a job, but the range of jobs you can seek is limited. But, **I know that Williams has been excellent for me academically, and I always felt supported** and appreciated by people here."

Q "**Williams is great if you are white and rich**. The college has tried to make those of us who are not white and rich feel at home. I wish other students could have this in mind, not just the institution. Socially, I was always in a group of friends from the same race as mine. Maybe this was a good thing. But then I thought 'Gee, I'm supposed to be expanding my horizons.' So I am kind of confused about how college should work to make you more open by exposing you to different stuff. They expose you, but it doesn't mean you interact with others."

The College Prowler Take
ON CAMPUS STRICTNESS

Nobody could really tell us how strict this campus is. Strictness varied with the nature and seriousness of the situation. This statement can be frightening because it implies that the campus strictness is random. While Williams has many rules, and they may not be equally enforced at all times, most students do not find it difficult to follow the rules to begin with, so perhaps this is a moot point.

The College Prowler™ Grade on
Campus Strictness: B+

A high Campus Strictness grade implies an overall lenient atmosphere; police and RAs are fairly tolerant, and the administration's rules are flexible.

Q "Williams is better than Amherst. We all know that. It is better than many other schools, too. One of my friends thinks Williams gets all the Harvard rejects, but he is a Harvard reject himself, and I applied here for Early Decision. **I didn't choose the school because of the name, but for the beautiful campus**, and it just seemed like the right people were here for me. You're going to find out that this is the right place when you see how well they treat you and how much freedom they give for choosing classes. The core curriculum here is very flexible, and you really can design your own plan of what to do with four years of being among the brightest kids in the country. The professors are just awesome, too."

Q "Everything here is great, but **your social life sucks**; it's just so limited. I never had a relationship at Williams, and most of my friends didn't either. It can get very lonely and depressing. You have to do work all the time, and if you don't, there is nothing else to do. People care about their grades and their sports too much to notice others and be friends with them. If you are gay, your love life is extremely limited, and it doesn't get much better for the straight people, either. People look for sex, but not for any meaningful interaction. Most are too immature to appreciate another person."

Q "**Some of the people here are very selfish and arrogant, especially the jocks**, who can be very aggressive at parties and they think they just own this campus when they don't. The rest of us don't enjoy anything of what they get. They live in the best dorms and get drunk all the time and make too much noise for anyone to study, sleep, or just chill in their own room. People are very boring. Four years in a top school doesn't make them more open-minded, just more hypocritical and snobbish."

The College Prowler Take
ON OVERALL EXPERIENCE

It is very hard to get an A at Williams, so most are happy with a B+ or an A-. The same logic applies to what the school has to offer to students. Williams is amazing for its incredible academic and athletic programs. However, the lack of diversity among the student body is detrimental to students' social lives and personal growth. The students acknowledge that some of the weaknesses of the school, such as location and the nature of nightlife in Williamstown, are not fixable. They also agreed that Williams is working very hard on addressing other problematic issues. While the school changes with every class and every year, some positive and negative aspects of what it has to offer to the prospective student stand out as worth mentioning. These are not only conditions that can't be changed, like the weather, but also general features of Williams that many students criticize or praise.

No matter what the admissions office tries to tell you, the Williams campus is not particularly diverse. Many students of color feel very alienated here, and so do white students who don't necessary fit the typical preppy profile. Many blame the lack of diversity on the school's focus on athletics, but that just isn't fair to the Williams sports teams who do so much to promote the school's spirit. Choosing one group of people over another is a choice made by the admissions counsel. It is thought that maybe Williams lacks diversity because it has been thought of as a typically "white and preppy" school for so long. Besides admitting a fairly uniform and uninteresting student body, Williams has also placed them in a small and uninteresting town where their social life is limited to keg parties with the same group of people every weekend and occasional dancing to the same three songs. Although many complain about this, others do like those three songs, along with the beer, and don't require more options.

The Inside Scoop

The Lowdown
ON THE INSIDE SCOOP

School Spirit
Mucho Macho Moocow Marching Band is the cheering section at football games and a big provider to school spirit.

Traditions

The Mountains
The college alma mater, composed by Williams graduate Washington Gladden, puts the setting of Williams into words.

Ivy Planting
At graduation, a member of the graduating class plants ivy next to a wall or a building.

Watch Dropping
Also at graduation, a watch is dropped from the top of the college chapel. If the watch breaks, the graduating class will be lucky.

Class Banners
Each class designs a banner that will represent them while at school and at reunions in the future.

Things I Wish I Knew Before Coming to Williams:

- I wish I knew that Williamstown was so far from any place where you could go out at night. There are some sketchy bars in Pittsfield, which is a 30-minute drive, but, believe me, that's not where you want to go. And the college snack bar only makes burgers and fries.

- No matter what they tell you about the cold weather at Williams, you would always wish you knew more about how cold it actually can get. Most of us on campus have seen winter before, but not a seven-month winter with negative 40-degree wind chills that make your jeans freeze around your legs so you can't walk.

- I wish I knew more about the flimsy veil of political correctness behind which the school attempts to disguise a lot of very disturbing sentiments among the student body. Fortunately, the faculty and administration are pretty liberal people, but why should they try to disguise what someone else thinks? When a homophobic e-mail was sent to a gay person on campus, everyone tried to stifle the issue instead of make the person who did it think twice before they send out a hate message.

- Many students wish they knew more about the mind-boggling amount of work they are expected to do every week in almost all majors. High school is not the kind of place where you have to read 300 pages a week and be able to talk about them in class, and in many cases, write on them. Students in the social sciences and literature have to confront workloads that seem practically impossible, and someone has to tell them that beforehand, so they are spared some shock … and the feeling of being incapable of dealing with the work.

- Students need to be told that the Housing Office can put any move on them at any time, like kicking them out of their dorm during the week of finals because reconstruction is going on, or putting summer researchers for the math department in the most inconvenient dorm they could ask for, after previously telling them that they would get a different summer housing option.

Finding a Job or Internship

The Lowdown
ON FINDING A JOB OR INTERNSHIP

The Career Center offers programs for students and alumni. From resume writing to applying for jobs, the Career Center is ready to help students in their after-college pursuits. Many students feel that the OCC does not provide for all majors or career paths. However, they offer online resume posting and links to many job searches.

Career Center Resources & Services:
OCC, a career service center with very limited scope, caters mostly to economics majors heading to a career in finance.
www.williams.edu/resources/occ/

The Best & Worst

The Ten BEST Things About Williams:

1. Profs' willingness to give personal attention
2. The facilities
3. Being on a sports team
4. A very flexible core curriculum
5. Study abroad opportunities
6. Tutorials
7. The JA System
8. Extremely helpful administration
9. Rooms with windows and private bathrooms
10. Beautiful campus

The Ten WORST Things About Williams:

1. Lack of diversity
2. Limited social life due to geographic isolation
3. Transport to Williams
4. Heating in dorms
5. The computer network
6. Very cold weather
7. Limited selection of classes in departments
8. Overemphasizing few career opportunities
9. The Housing Office and the housing lottery
10. The swim requirement

Amherst College

Amherst College, PO Box 5000, Amherst, MA 01002
www.amherst.edu   (413) 542-2000

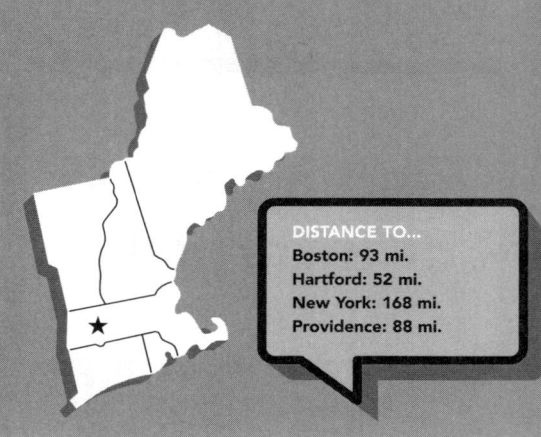

DISTANCE TO...
Boston: 93 mi.
Hartford: 52 mi.
New York: 168 mi.
Providence: 88 mi.

"With each passing year, Amherst College readjusts itself to meet new and constantly-changing personalities."

Total Enrollment:
1,618
Acceptance Rate:
18%
Tuition:
$31,360
Top 10% of High School Class:
86%
SAT Range
Verbal	Math	Total
660 – 770	660 – 770	1320 – 1540

ACT Range
Verbal	Math	Total
N/A	N/A	29-34

Most Popular Majors:
16% English Language and Literature
14% Economics
14% Psychology
11% Legal Professions and Studies
11% Political Science and Government

Students Also Applied To:*
Brown University, Harvard University, Princeton University, Williams College, Yale University

*For more school info check out www.collegeprowler.com

Table of Contents

Academics	413
Local Atmosphere	415
Safety & Security	416
Computers	418
Facilities	420
Campus Dining	421
Off-Campus Dining	423
Campus Housing	424
Off-Campus Housing	426
Diversity	427
Guys & Girls	429
Athletics	430
Greek Life	432
Drug Scene	433
Campus Strictness	434
Overall Experience	435
The Inside Scoop	436
Finding a Job or Internship	437
The Best & Worst	438

College Prowler Report Card

Academics	A-
Local Atmosphere	C
Safety & Security	A-
Computers	A
Facilities	A
Campus Dining	C+
Off-Campus Dining	B+
Campus Housing	B
Off-Campus Housing	D+
Diversity	B+
Guys	B
Girls	B
Athletics	B
Greek Life	D-
Drug Scene	B
Campus Strictness	A-

Academics

The Lowdown
ON ACADEMICS

Degrees Awarded:
Bachelor

Students with triple-majors:
0.7%

Undergraduate Schools:
School of the Arts and Sciences, School of Business, School of Communications, School of Education, School of Finance, School of Government, School of Health and Medicine, School of Law, School of Marketing and Sales, and School of Science and Technology

Full-time Faculty:
182

Faculty with Terminal Degree:
169

Student-to-Faculty Ratio:
8:1

Average Course Load:
4 courses

AP Test Score Requirements:
Possible credit for scores of 4 or 5

IB Test Score Requirements:
Possible credit for scores of 6 or 7

Special Degree Options

With the Five-College academic program (more on this in the pages ahead), Amherst students can major in the following areas (in addition to the majors offered by the college): International Relations; Coastal and Marine Studies; Latin American Studies; Native American Indian Studies; Logic; Culture, Health, and Science.

Two other Five-College programs are pending approval by Amherst College: Middle-Eastern Studies and Asian/Pacific/American Studies.

Best Places to Study

Frost Library, Computer Center, Keefe Campus Center, Keefe Science Library

Sample Academic Clubs

Debate Team, Mock Trial

Did You Know?

Amherst College sponsors an open curriculum, which literally means that there are absolutely no distribution requirements and that students can take however many classes they want in any department. The only class that Amherst requires all students to take is the First-Year Seminar, which is a one-semester course taken in the first semester of freshman year. These classes are small, from 10 to 20 students, and cover a wide array of topics. They are aimed at giving students proper coaching in college-level writing and discussion. Before the school year starts, all freshmen choose what seminars they would like to attend, and the college does its best to satisfy everyone's wishes.

A sample of the First-Year Seminars offered include Drugs: Society, History, and Culture; Terror; Performance; and the Art of Mathematical Thinking.

Students Speak Out
ON ACADEMICS

"In my time here, I've gotten close enough to three professors to the point where I feel free to e-mail or come see them to talk about any academic issue I might have."

Q "Professors are really accessible here. Some have even abandoned set office hours and will make themselves free for any students who wish to come and see them almost at any time. It's **great to be able to be lectured formally and then to come talk about the class with the professor one-on-one**. I feel more connected to the course material, since I know what the professor is trying to get at and what he or she wants to emphasize."

Q "I came to Amherst looking for lively discussion and academic rigor. **What I found was some degree of academic intensity**, but it's much more laid-back than I thought. Sometimes, discussion in class can get stagnated because people don't seem to want to speak. There is definitely a possibility to make your stay here an immersing, intellectual journey, but you'd generally be in the minority with that attitude towards school. People here are good students, but they're not overly driven."

Q "I think the best thing about the professors here is that they're human. They answer questions and ask them. **They teach and then they listen to your responses on what they've said**. They tell jokes and laugh at jokes. I feel very comfortable in class here—a kind of comfort that I don't think I would have had at other, larger schools. In the end, they expect a lot of effort from you, but professors do put a lot of their time in the classes."

Q "You can't really say that every professor here is a gifted orator. Some are, and so you sit in their classes and time just flies. Some aren't, and this makes their lectures a little tedious. And then, some have their good days and bad days. It's just like any other school in this sense. However, if you take classes that are interesting for you, and that you think you will enjoy, you should be fine regardless of who the professor is. **Every professor has a reputation** by now because this is such a small school. Some people actually choose their classes based on who is teaching them. However, the material in most of the classes here is very interesting, so looking at the college Website for reading lists and syllabi would help you a lot in choosing the classes you really want to take."

Q "What I think is great here is the fact that there is no core curriculum, and you can choose whatever classes you want. There is only one required course, which happens in the first semester of freshman [year], and this a First-Year Seminar. Mine was on a pretty interesting topic, and these seminars are small, so it was generally good discussion, but some of my friends told me they didn't enjoy their freshman seminar. **I've taken some hard courses and some easy ones**, to compensate my GPA. You're really in charge of selecting your courses here, which can be a little daunting. How can I know if Biology of Diseases will benefit me more than International Trade? It's hard. They do offer excellent academic assistance here, so you don't have to make those decisions on your own."

The College Prowler Take
ON ACADEMICS

Amherst is a small school that allows for complete freedom of course selection. It is also known for its amicable and chatty professors. The academic atmosphere is much different than other schools because the students have not been forced to take their class by a distribution requirement. Plus, there are no graduate students here to vie for the professors' attention. The college itself actively seeks student participation in planning its educational policies. When an academic position opens up, the relevant department will ask majoring students to both come and hear candidates lecture and then give feedback and sit in the selection committees.

The completely open curriculum requires that students have a certain level of self-discipline, since the truth about Amherst academics is that there is absolutely no pressure from professors on students to excel. If a student is passionate about a class and does all the work for it, he or she will assuredly enjoy a rewarding learning experience and, perhaps, even find a friend in the professor. On the other hand, students often get bored with a class they thought looked interesting in the course book, and then they end up doing only the minimum required in order to get a decent grade. Such a case is the bane of the teaching philosophy that Amherst supports, which, plainly put, is: "We'll give all the opportunities in the world, and all you have to do is take your pick."

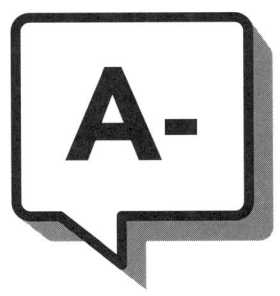

The College Prowler™ Grade on
Academics: A-

A high Academics grade generally indicates that professors are knowledgeable, accessible, and genuinely interested in their students' welfare. Other determining factors include class size, how well professors communicate, and whether or not classes are engaging.

Local Atmosphere

The Lowdown
ON LOCAL ATMOSPHERE

Region:
Northeast

City, State:
Amherst, Massachusetts

Setting:
Small town

Distance from New York City:
2 to 3 hours by car, 4 to 5 hours by bus

Distance from Boston:
90 minutes by car, about 2 hours by bus

Points of Interest:
Northampton, Hadley, The Big Y, Hampshire Mall, Holyoke, Holyoke Mall, Frat Row

City Websites:
http://www.city.northampton.ma.us
http://www.citysearch.com.

Students Speak Out
ON LOCAL ATMOSPHERE

"The schools around us are the best bet for interesting stuff to visit. There are museums, theaters, music, and amazing cultural events at Smith, Holyoke, and UMass. The Smith and Holyoke campuses are beautiful."

Q "Amherst is a **very small college town**. That has to be said. Even though UMass is a five-minute bus ride away, there is very little interaction between the two institutions."

Q "There is nothing to do in Amherst, really. There is a comic book store and a used CD store, CVS, and restaurants. Clearly, **it's a college town**."

Q "The town is small, and its **points of interest are few**. People definitely don't expect to find excitement outside of the college. I like to stay on campus during the weekends."

Q "People in town are ridiculously nice. There is a **variety of stores** and restaurants. That's pretty much it. Thank God the college has a lively social scene, otherwise I'd shoot myself."

Safety & Security

The Lowdown
ON SAFETY & SECURITY

The College Prowler Take
ON LOCAL ATMOSPHERE

There is not much in Amherst outside of the college. Amherst is the epitome of a college town. Main Street is right next the college, and there you'll find CVS, Starbucks, Fleet Bank, as well as various local shops for computer supplies, electrical appliances, and other gadgets and items, big and small, to equip to perfection your home away from home. The people are by and large nice to a degree that stupefies most students from New York City, and you can't walk down the street without a complete stranger nodding and saying hello, as if you had known each other since the days when all of this was naught but farmlands and a romantic dream. The place visibly caters to students, both those from UMass and Amherst.

Number of Amherst College Police Officers:
12 full-time officers
4 part-time officers

Emergency Phone:
(413) 542-2111

Health Center Office Hours:
Monday thru Friday, 8:30 a.m. to 5:30 p.m. when school is in session. It is located at the Keefe Health Center.

For urgent care call (413) 577-5000 or go to University Health Services at UMass, which is open 24 hours a day when school is in session.

When school is not in session, the only place providing medical care is University Health Services at UMass. It is open every day from 8 a.m. to midnight.

The College Prowler™ Grade on
Local Atmosphere: C

A high Local Atmosphere grade indicates that the area surrounding campus is safe and scenic. Other factors include nearby attractions, proximity to other schools, and the town's attitude toward students.

Safety Services

RAD (Rape Aggression Defense course), dorm talks, Operation Identification (permanent marking of personal valuable belongings with your social security number), bike registration, student security, Safe RIDE (rides back to dorms at night), Security Advisory Committee, Five-Colleges Sexual Assault Prevention and Intervention Committee

Did You Know?

There were 54 violent crimes reported in 2002 in Amherst, and 84 in 2003, in a population of approximately 35,000 people. From 1989 through 2001, there were no murders. Property crimes are by far the most common ones perpetrated at Amherst.

You can look at Amherst crime statistics at http://bjsdata.ojp.usdoj.gov/dataon-line/Search/Crime/Local/JurisbyJuris.cfm. Choose Massachusetts and then Amherst from the lists of states and municipalities.

Students Speak Out
ON SAFETY & SECURITY

"It seems very safe at Amherst, but I'm still afraid to walk alone at night, since the school is off of Route 9, which is a busy street."

"There were **some cases of property damage on campus**, but about half of the crimes I've heard of were perpetrated by students from one of the other schools nearby. Usually things don't get out of hand here. People don't get so drunk as to be violent, and campus police are always on alert and respond quickly to calls. I feel pretty safe going out on weekends here."

"In my opinion, the campus is **surprisingly secure**. There is not a huge number of thefts given the number of unlocked doors everywhere. People usually feel very secure. The campus police also maintain a very visible presence and are very quick to respond to calls, so safety is also very good."

"Amherst has got to be **one of the safest schools ever**. The town is so quiet, and the crime rate is relatively low. On campus, there's a kind of honor code among students. A lot of people don't bother locking their doors and leave their packs unattended in class. I have not had any of my stuff stolen."

"Campus police seems to be comprised of **officers who take their job seriously**. I think they have enough manpower to deal with such a small school. And it's not like their workload is heavy. People here are generally on the good side, behavior-wise."

"I don't really feel safe walking at night, but it's definitely safer here than where I come from. Sometimes **I see some shady-looking people walk down the streets** of the town. The college, however, is usually a sphere of its own, and hardly anyone but students are present at night."

The College Prowler Take
ON SAFETY & SECURITY

Along with the congeniality of the townsfolk, Amherst College has a certain homey atmosphere that drives away thoughts of crime. An alarming number of students feel comfortable leaving their room doors unlocked. Even still, cases of theft are rare. Both the college and the students are quite aware of maintaining a high level of security. Dorm front doors can only be opened with a personal code that only students and custodians possess. The Amherst College campus police patrol regularly during the day and night. Campus police also offer rides back to dorms at night to people who request them. Most people will tell you that Amherst is much safer than their hometown, and hardly anyone is afraid to walk alone at night when they're within the boundaries of the college.

The College Prowler™ Grade on
Safety & Security: A-

A high grade in Safety & Security means that students generally feel safe, campus police are visible, blue-light phones and escort services are readily available, and safety precautions are not overly necessary.

Computers

The Lowdown
ON COMPUTERS

High-Speed Network?
Yes

Wireless Network?
Yes

Number of Labs:
7

Numbers of Computers:
Over 100

Operating Systems:
PC and Mac

24-Hour Labs:
None

Charge to Print?
Five cents a page (taken out directly from your student account, so you don't have to carry around small change)

Free Software:
Acrobat 5, Acrobat Reader 5, AddressMagic, Aladdin, Dreamweaver 4, Dreamweaver MX, Endnote 6, Fetch 4, Fireworks 4, F-Secure SSH, Illustrator 9, KeyAccess, Netscape 4.79, Microsoft Office versions 2000 and 2001 (the Mac version), Pagemaker 7, Pagemill 3.0, Photoshop 7, Publisher 2000, SciFinder Scholar, Shockwave Player, SSH Secure Shell, Virex, Viruscan 4.5.1, WS_FTP

Did You Know?

The DailyJolt—remember the name—is the Website you'll most frequently visit while at Amherst. It is student-run and has everything you need to know: job listings, the lowdown on parties for the upcoming weekend, discussion forums, restaurant reviews, and procrastination games. It also sponsors "the professor quote of the day," to which students contribute funny, embarrassing, or kinky sentences they've heard their professors say in class. Let me tell you, I couldn't believe some of the stuff teachers said last year. You can visit it at *http://amherst.dailyjolt.com*.

There are Ethernet outlets in every dorm room, in the libraries, and in the Campus Center. Every student is connected to the college network, where there is access to free software for download and use.

Students Speak Out
ON COMPUTERS

"Definitely get a laptop, or bring your own PC or Mac. I know of very few people who don't have one, and it's not like they're severely hurt because of this, but it would've been so much easier for them if they had one."

Q "The Amherst network is pretty extensive and meets our needs adequately. More and more professors are using Blackboard, and this facilitates communication between professors and students. The e-mail and campus directories are handy, too. **Sometimes the network is down**, but usually not often and not for long periods of time."

Q "I bought a laptop before my first year, and it has proven to be essential. **The computer labs are definitely not overcrowded**, and you can find a free computer at almost any time, at almost any of the labs. Still, having a personal laptop means you can set your own studying schedule. That's very important here, because you're guaranteed to find yourself working on an essay at 2 a.m., even if you're a very organized person."

Q "The **computers here are state-of-the-art**, and I prefer using them to my beat-up, old laptop, even though I have to give up the luxury of working in my own room. It's fine, because the labs are definitely places where you can get work done, and people are respectful of each other's need for quiet. They have all the accessories you might need. Each computer has headphones, and some have microphones. There are also TVs and VCRs for student use. You can also choose between Macs and PCs, since there's a lot of each."

Q "The computer network is very organized. **A huge proportion of students have their own computers**, so the labs are very rarely crowded. There are people managing a help line 18 hours a day, and students can get personalized visits from trained students if necessary. The network managers are also very active in combating spam and viruses."

Q "We have a very nice network, and it facilitates a lot of the communication here. It's very helpful not to have to write down someone's e-mail in order to contact them. I can also view my grades and download course materials and assignments. **The DailyJolt, a student-run website, has a lot of helpful information, too**. I can find out anything from dining hall menus to job offerings. A relatively big group of students post comments in the forums, too."

The College Prowler Take
ON COMPUTERS

Computers for long-term student use are found in two locations on campus: Frost Library and the Computer Center. Frost Library is the main library and, as such, lies at the heart of the campus; there are two computer labs there. The Computer Center is a bit out of the way and has five labs. Both locations have Macs and PCs. **Two computer centers may seem too few at first, but there are more than enough computers for the 1,600 or so students who go here. What's more, the overwhelming majority of them bring their own computers, and every room is equipped with an Ethernet connector. The IT department is responsive to student needs and will send someone to your room to fix any problem you may have.**

The College Prowler™ Grade on
Computers: A

A high grade in Computers designates that computer labs are available, the computer network is easily accessible, and the campus' computing technology is up-to-date.

Facilities

Students Speak Out
ON FACILITIES

"The facilities are excellent at Amherst, both for athletics and computers. We have a very nice campus center, which makes me feel very cozy whenever I am there."

Q *"For a small college, **the facilities are very impressive and modern**. The Campus Center is very small, though, and is not really a place where too many people are prepared to hang out. The athletic and computer facilities are top-notch, and could cater to a lot more people than they currently do."*

Q *"All the facilities are really nice and up-to-date. The **library and Campus Center have wireless** and Ethernet cables available. The gym equipment is good, but the treadmills and Stairmasters are in high demand."*

Q *"All the facilities here are extremely well-kept. The bathrooms, floors, and furniture are almost always clean. In truth, we have a good variety of things to do—foosball, Ping-Pong, pool, and things like that. **The jukebox in the Campus Center is awesome**."*

Q *"The athletic facilities serve the college well. **The gym is well-equipped and is pleasing to the eye**. The squash courts are nice, and so are the tennis courts. It's a lot of fun to play sports or just work out in such a nice environment."*

Q *"I think the Campus Center is a little small, and it gets crowded around noontime, when everybody goes to check their mail. **The lecture/conference rooms are very nice**. The athletic facilities are great, although the gym is a little far away from everything. The computer labs have modern computers, and they are quiet and a good place to do your work."*

The Lowdown
ON FACILITIES

Student Center:
Keefe Campus Center

Athletic Center:
The Alumni Gymnasium

Libraries:
3—Frost Library, Keefe Science Library, and the Music Library

Movie Theatre on Campus?
The Campus Center offers screenings of newly-released films at no charge on weekends.

Bowling on Campus?
No

Bar on Campus?
No

Coffeehouse on Campus?
Schwemm's

Theater:
Kirby Theater

Music:
Buckley Recital Hall

Popular Places to Chill:
Schwemm's, the Campus Center's game room

The College Prowler Take
ON FACILITIES

As is the situation with the computer labs, at first glance, the sole coffeehouse, the lone theater, and the single gym may seem a bit insufficient. Still, for the relatively small number of students at Amherst, the variety of things you can do, and the number of places to do them, is overwhelming, and students regularly complain that they've missed out on some event or show because they just didn't have time. The architecture here is quaint and Victorian, but not in a huge, Gothic, makes-you-feel-tiny way. It is pleasant to walk outside and enjoy the simple beauty of the buildings. The Campus Center has just recently been renovated; it is all yellow on the outside, and all carpets and armchairs on the inside.

Campus Dining

The Lowdown
ON CAMPUS DINING

Freshman Meal Plan Requirement?
Yes

24-Hour On-Campus Eating?
No

Meal Plan Average Cost:
$3,590

The College Prowler™ Grade on
Facilities: A

A high Facilities grade indicates that the campus is aesthetically pleasing and well-maintained; facilities are state-of-the-art, and libraries are exceptional. Other determining factors include the quality of both athletic and student centers and an abundance of things to do on campus.

Did You Know?

Creative students make their own Thousand Island dressing in the dining hall with the cunning use of ketchup, mayonnaise, and mustard, with a French fry used for the mixing. Add black pepper for seasoning.

Creative students also give their favorite recipes to the dining hall, and, if the recipes are any good, these students can proudly get to see them incorporated in the menu. No royalties are paid.

The dining hall, upon request, will make you your very own birthday cake (when it's your birthday).

Students Speak Out
ON CAMPUS DINING

The College Prowler Take
ON CAMPUS DINING

"The food is nutritional, and there's a pretty good variety, particularly among the salad bar and cereals—if that's a big deal. The entrées are generally bland."

Q "A lot of people like to speak of the food with contempt, but I think that **most of them would admit that it's not that bad**. Home-cooked meals are definitely better, but after some getting used to, you'd be able to appreciate Val food, too."

Q "There is Valentine, whose dinner dining hours are not convenient [dinner is from 4:30 p.m. to 7:30 p.m.]. The **Campus Center serves sandwiches and other things until 2 a.m**.. Usually, people order off campus at night. There are a lot of places that stay open late, until 3 a.m.."

Q "Well, **the food in Val is pretty terrible most of the time**. I find myself ordering take out and going to restaurants more often than I want to. What I do like about Val is that everyone meets up there, and it's fun to meet your friends every day and eat together."

Q "The **food at Amherst is disgusting** all the way around."

Q "There is only one dining hall that caters for the whole student body, and even though it does a valiant catering job, there are **definitely times when it serves very unappealing food**. Then again, in a mass catering environment, people will always complain."

Central dining has a huge impact on the campus social life, in that it brings everybody together on a daily basis. You have to eat and so do your friends, and often people stay and chat hours after they've finished their meals. There's also something about the act of eating that makes people more talkative and jovial. The huge social plus to central dining almost compensates for what many students believe are serious flaws in the current dining system. Dining hours should be at least one hour later for every meal. Nobody gets up at 7:30 a.m. to eat breakfast, and many people would rather see dinner time continue past 7:30 in the evening. The food, itself, usually cannot shake the bland aftertaste that central dining halls have become infamous for. The variety of dishes, however, is impressive.

The College Prowler™ Grade on
Campus Dining: C+

Our grade on Campus Dining addresses the quality of both school-owned dining halls and independent on-campus restaurants as well as the price, availability, and variety of food.

Off-Campus Dining

Students Speak Out
ON OFF-CAMPUS DINING

"The restaurants at Amherst are good. Antonio's Pizza is amazing. Pasta E Basta and Bueno Y Sano are good, too. The Black Sheep is a great bakery and coffee place."

Q "Seeing as the town caters to students, **there are a number of coffee shops and fast food places** as well as restaurants. Favorites amongst the students include Antonio's, Bueno Y Sano, and The Black Sheep."

Q "There are many restaurants and different kinds of food to choose from. **The prices can be a little on the expensive side**, but they're mostly reasonable. It's a little spooky to go out into town at night because the streets are usually empty."

Q "Some restaurants and takeout places have become legendary around here. **Antonio's is one example, WINGS is another.** Overall, the selection and level of restaurants is great, and it compensates for the bland Valentine food."

Q "People love to order take out here. Just pick up the phone and call, and they'll show up in 10 minutes with tasty wings or pizza. **There's a lot of places that do deliveries**. I think this is mostly because of the large population of UMass students. You won't be disappointed if you decide to order take out. Too bad it's not healthy, because I really like the take out food."

Q "I like **Antonio's Pizza Parlor,** which is really popular. Also, Bart's Ice Cream Shop has good food and desserts. They also supply wireless Ethernet to dine-in customers. There are Mexican, Italian, and Chinese restaurants. Northampton, a nearby town, has plenty of restaurants to choose from."

The Lowdown
ON OFF-CAMPUS DINING

Best Pizza: Antonio's

Best Chinese: Panda East

Best Breakfast: Lord Jeffery Inn

Best Wings: WINGS

Best Healthy: The Black Sheep

Best Place to Take Your Parents: Lord Jeffery Inn

Student Favorites:
Antonio's, WINGS, Bueno Y Sano, Pinocchio's, Domino's, The Black Sheep, Bart's, Lord Jeffery Inn, Panda East, Rao's Coffee, Pasta E Basta

24-Hour Eating: None

Closest Grocery Stores:
CVS is a five-minute walk down Main Street. There is a cheap grocery store another five minutes away, if you continue in the same direction and turn right at the second turn after having passed Bart's.

The College Prowler Take
ON OFF-CAMPUS DINING

The tiny town of Amherst is disproportionately packed with restaurants. The vast selection is almost like the selection one would find in a big city, and Amherst students can thank the tens of thousands of UMass students and faculty who are potential customers. Many places stay open until 2 and 3 a.m., and the delivery is usually efficient, although deliveries from some restaurants that do not specialize in take out only may take a while. It's a common pastime to come back to the dorm after a party and order wings, providing something to chew on while the guys gather together to reflect on that blonde from Smith and her single friends. Overall, the restaurant selection and level of food are far better than what you would expect from a small town, and although the prices can be a little irritating in some places, they're never exorbitant.

The College Prowler™ Grade on
Off-Campus Dining: B+

A high Off-Campus Dining grade implies that off-campus restaurants are affordable, accessible, and worth visiting. Other factors include the variety of cuisine and the availability of alternative options (vegetarian, vegan, Kosher, etc.).

Campus Housing

The Lowdown
ON CAMPUS HOUSING

Undergrads on Campus:
Virtually all students live on campus.

Number of Dormitories:
36

Bed Type:
36"x80" (twin extra-long size)

Room Types:
Single, Double, Triple

Suite – a number of rooms connected by a common room (like a living room). Each person living in a suite usually has their own single. Suites often have bathrooms.

Available for Rent:
Nothing from the college, but fridges, TVs, microwaves and other electrical appliances are available at various stores near the campus.

Cleaning Service?
Custodians clean the bathrooms and the public areas in the dorms every weekday.

You Get:
Bed, desk, chair, closet, three or more bookshelves, dresser, windows coverings, cable TV jack, Ethernet connection, phone jacks, electricity outlets

Also Available:
Substance-free dorms and/or floors, single-sex floors, single-sex bathrooms

Language Houses

French House (Newport), Spanish House (Newport), German House (Porter), Russian House (Porter)

Lifestyle Houses

Health and Wellness House (substance-free) The dorms change every year, but usually it's in Morrow.

For more information on theme housing in Amherst visit www.amherst.edu/~dos/reslife/themehouses.

Students Speak Out
ON CAMPUS HOUSING

{ "The dorms are pretty nice. Freshman housing can get a little crowded, but that's changing. Amherst actually has very nice housing."

Q "The college is in the process of upgrading and renovating its dorms, so the outlook is definitely going to improve, especially seeing as there are also new dorms [King and Wieland] being constructed. **Most people live on campus**, so a lot of the upperclass housing is very spacious."

Q "The upperclass dorms are huge, and surprisingly in very good shape. The **college really takes care of the dorms** with regard to everyday maintenance and renovations."

Q "Most **freshmen dorms are pretty bad**, but I'd say Pratt is definitely the best."

Q "In my opinion, the **best dorms to live in are the Social Dorms**. There are really sociable people there, and it's never boring. It can become a little too noisy for studying on weekends, but I say what's college without a little partying every now and then?"

Q "Some dorms are considered better than others. For example, Tyler and Plimpton are usually thought of as too far away, and Williston is sometimes thought of as having very small rooms. However, **none of the dorms are bad**. Even the Mudds are okay; they're very social and are good for freshmen who are trying to get to know each other and find friends."

Q "When you're a sophomore, Room Draw can be quite cruel. A good way out is through **applying to a theme house**. Most theme housing is better than regular housing, at least for sophomores. Virtually all juniors and seniors have singles. For freshmen, the situation is notably worse."

The College Prowler Take
ON CAMPUS HOUSING

Most dorms have that New England look, brownstones and white windows and all, but they're not overly decorated with statues of winged lions and weeping angles, like some other universities. The newest dorms, King and Wieland (all singles), as well as some older ones, like Williston, have a more modern interior. Common social trends at Amherst include athletes and other partiers living in the Social Dorms, theme house members associating with their theme house neighbors, and quiet and studious people living in Cohan or Morrow. Of course, there are exceptions to all these trends, but they are worth keeping in mind.

The College Prowler™ Grade on
Campus Housing: B

A high Campus Housing grade indicates that dorms are clean, well-maintained, and spacious. Other determining factors include variety of dorms, proximity to classes, and social atmosphere.

Off-Campus Housing

Students Speak Out
ON OFF-CAMPUS HOUSING

"Living off campus is not worth it, unless you absolutely hate the dining hall or love to cook for yourself."

Q "Hardly anyone lives off campus. **You actually needs permission to do so**. It's definitely not worth it, because you miss out on most of the benefits of a small college if you does live off campus."

Q "**I don't see much reason in moving off campus**. If you dislike Valentine food that much, you can just cancel your meal plan. If you like cooking for yourself every day, you can do so by joining the Zu. It definitely ends up being way more expensive to live off campus on the whole than living in the dorms."

Q "Living off campus can be a good experience, especially in terms of feeling independent. **Financially, it's definitely not worth it**, but I can understand people who want a break from Amherst campus life. Life here can be suffocating sometimes."

Q "I don't know a lot about living off campus, but **I don't think it is worth it**. If you want, you can choose to live in dorms that are 10 minutes away from central campus. These dorms are basically in the town."

Q "I bet a lot of Amherst students don't even think of living off campus in all of their college years. The **campus is too vibrant and alive to leave**, and the town is too boring to live in."

The Lowdown
ON OFF-CAMPUS HOUSING

Undergrads in Off-Campus Housing:
Very few. Students must seek the approval of the Residential Life office to live off campus.

Average Rent for a Studio Apartment
Less than $250/month

Average Rent for a One-Bedroom Apartment:
Less than $300/month

Average Rent for a Two-Bedroom Apartment:
Less than $500/month

Popular Areas:
Main Street, North Pleasant Street, South Pleasant Street

Best Time to Look for a Place:
Towards the beginning of the academic year, landlords will usually jack up their prices, but you can avoid that by securing an apartment in the summer or the middle of the academic year.

For Assistance Contact:
The college does not assist in finding off-campus housing.
A popular private real-estate company, Aspen Square Management, has homes and apartments for rent. Contact them at *www.aspensquare.com* or (413) 256-0741.

Want to know where the best pads are off campus? Check out the College Prowler book on Amherst College available at *www.collegeprowler.com*.

The College Prowler Take
ON OFF-CAMPUS HOUSING

If UMass wasn't just around the corner, the market for apartments in Amherst would have probably gone bust decades ago. Although it takes some serious thinking to explain why this is so, the fact remains that Amherst students love their dorms. Hardly anyone lives off campus and, at the college, there isn't even an organized bulletin board of available apartments for rent. Although living in your own apartment offers a sense of independence to most college students, Amherst kids seem content with letting the college take care of them even as they slowly turn into mature men and women.

Diversity

The Lowdown
ON DIVERSITY

African American: 10%

Asian American: 12%

Hispanic: 8%

Native American: 0%

White: 64%

International: 6%

Out-of-State: 81%

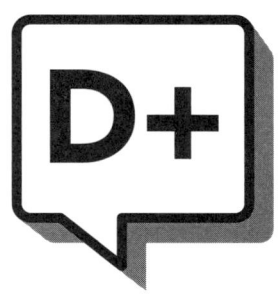

The College Prowler™ Grade on
Off-Campus Housing: D+

A high grade in Off-Campus Housing indicates that apartments are of high quality, close to campus, affordable, and easy to secure.

Minority Clubs

There are many organizations, as well as theme houses, at Amherst, which hold many fascinating cultural events during the academic year. Examples include AIKYA, the Asian Student Association, the Black Students Union, Chicano Caucus, International Student Association (ISA), Pacific Islander/South-East Asian Students (PISEAS), Asian Culture House (ACH), African, African American, and African Caribbean House (Drew House), La Casa.

Most Popular Religions

Christianity and Judaism. There is some religious activity on campus, and it is mostly characterized by a strong sense of community. The Amherst College Hillel is a large organization here, and its Shabbat diners are especially popular.

Political Activity

The campus is mostly very liberal, although the Amherst College Republicans are a very lively and combative organization. Many students like to complain about the student government, but the truth is that they have helpful and practical initiatives, such as arranging for free shuttles to the nearest airports and purchasing cardboard boxes for students to put their stuff in during breaks.

Gay Tolerance

The prevailing notion at Amherst is that a person's sexual orientation is their business. The campus is very accepting of gayness and lesbianism. Here are some student organizations concerned with gender and sexuality issues on campus: the Amherst College Pride Alliance (LBGTQA), Amherst Feminist Alliance, the Women's Center, Peer Advocates of Sexual Respect.

Economic Status

Most students come from wealthy families, and there is a considerable part of the student body that comes from a lower economic status. In any case, your economic background rarely comes into play at Amherst in any circumstance, social or otherwise.

Students Speak Out
ON DIVERSITY

{ "There are a lot of people from a lot of places, origins, backgrounds, faiths, and upbringings."

Q "I was **disappointed at the level of the diversity** when I came here. I think there should be more minorities. We have, in my opinion, too few international students as well, and one of the reasons I came here was to get to know people from different backgrounds and cultures."

Q "The **biggest minorities on campus are Asian Americans and African Americans**. Theme housing gives opportunity for people who want to learn more about different cultures."

Q "Amherst College belongs to that tier of schools that are both **selective and costly to attend**. Therefore, and sadly so, minorities here will not be strongly represented."

Q "The **international community is small but tight-knit**. Some internationals prefer to hang out mostly with American friends, but they always have a place to go if they want to. The International Student Association is the official international students' organization on campus, and it helps students out in various ways, from driving them to Holyoke to get registered with social security, to organizing meals when the dining hall is closed during school breaks."

The College Prowler Take
ON DIVERSITY

Whether Amherst is diverse enough is perhaps the most disputed question among the administration and the students. Many call for special programs to attract more minorities to the school, which suffers, as all New England private colleges do, from a stigma of being a WASP-only country club for young adults. The truth is that Amherst makes a considerable effort to make itself known to minorities and to make its expensive education more affordable. Still, many students feel that more should be done to have a more diverse student body. The current Amherst student body is far from being all white and will probably never be all white.

The College Prowler™ Grade on
Diversity: B+

A high grade in Diversity indicates that ethnic minorities and international students have a notable presence on campus and that students of different economic backgrounds, religious beliefs, and sexual preferences are well-represented.

Guys & Girls

Hookups or Relationships?
Both are options at Amherst, but it depends on the individual. Amherst students are generally calculated about their relationships—there may be times when they look strictly for hookups, and others when they look for something serious. In some cases, students opt to stay out of the market.

Dress Code
People feel free to put on whatever they like, and this results in some odd-looking creatures strolling the streets of Amherst. Most students dress casually—jeans, T-shirt, jacket, that kind of thing. Flip-flops are very popular in the summer and spring times. Overly flashy clothes and extravagant color combinations are usually considered bad taste. There is also a respectable crowd who prefer formal dress, and they can be detected by the nicer brands of pants they wear—no one wears a tie to the dining hall or to class.

The Lowdown
ON GUYS & GIRLS

Women Undergrads:
49%

Men Undergrads:
51%

Birth Control Available?
Yes

Sexual Assault Assistance:
The Peer Advocates of Sexual Respect is the organization entrusted with this mission on campus. Its staff consists of professionals as well as trained students, and they're available at all times of day or night.
The Amherst College Counseling Center is another option. Its staff consists of trained psychologists and psychiatrists. It is located on the third floor of Johnson Chapel, and its hours are from Monday to Friday 8:30 a.m. to 4:30 p.m..

Students Speak Out
ON GUYS & GIRLS

"Some guys are really cool. There are dateable people on both sides. The girls are simply gorgeous. Some guys are good-looking."

Q "There **isn't much of a dating scene on campus**. Maybe because it's a small place and people think it's unnecessary to go through the whole dating thing. Couples usually settle for hanging out in the dorms together, rather than going out to restaurants and movies."

Q "**Rumors spread very quickly in this small place**, and everyone's going to know who you hooked-up with last night by the next day. People like to attach stigmas, and it's very easy for a guy to get a reputation of being 'sketchy.' The girls here are alright, but don't expect anything spectacular. They're generally very interesting people, however, so if you're into conversing, and not just hooking up, then you should have a pretty good time."

Q "A lot of **guys complain about the shortage of hot women** at Amherst. I think they're mostly right. However, when you turn your eyes to the five-college area, you'll find some cool and hot women."

Social Scene
People are generally open to new social contacts, and this is true, especially at parties. Although students here hang out mostly with their close group of friends, most definitely dedicate time to meet new people. Some people, of course, are on the edges of the spectrum, being either hopelessly socially awkward at one extreme, or social butterflies on the other. You'll find very few unsocial nerds who care only about academics. Amherst students study a lot, but they definitely know how to have fun.

Q "The **guys are nothing special**. If you like the up-turned polo collar, though, you'll love it here. If you can't find what you want on campus, there's UMass and Hampshire College nearby."

The College Prowler Take
ON GIRLS & GUYS

The dating practices at Amherst can become downright weird. It's important to know who you're dealing with, because some gestures considered cute by one guy or girl can be thought of as stupid or embarrassing by others. On an optimistic note, both great couples and sizzling one-night stands have been known to flourish at Amherst, so don't worry about not finding your college sweetheart or eternal abstinence. You stand a decent chance at finding either one at Amherst. Contrary to what might be expected from a preppy Northeastern college, there are quite a few hookups at parties, and in general, if this is what you're interested in. Guys have more options than girls do, since Amherst is in close proximity to two all-women colleges, whose students do well at making their presence felt at Amherst parties. UMass students are also visible on weekends, but they are, in truth, less of a catch. A person's sexual preference and right to privacy are well-respected here. The prevailing opinion is that there should be no need for anyone to hide, or be ashamed of, their sexual orientation.

The College Prowler™ Grade on
Guys: B

A high grade for Guys indicates that the male population on campus is attractive, smart, friendly, and engaging, and that the school has a decent ratio of guys to girls.

The College Prowler™ Grade on
Girls: B

A high grade for Girls not only implies that the women on campus are attractive, smart, friendly, and engaging, but also that there is a fair ratio of girls to guys.

Athletics

The Lowdown
ON ATHLETICS

Men's Teams:
Football
Soccer
Tennis
Cross Country
Golf
Basketball
Ice Hockey
Squash
Swimming
Diving
Indoor Track
Baseball
Lacrosse
Outdoor Track

Women's Teams:
Soccer
Field Hockey
Volleyball
Tennis
Cross Country
Golf
Basketball
Ice Hockey
Squash
Swimming
Diving
Indoor Track
Softball
Lacrosse
Outdoor Track

Club Sports
Equestrian team, mountain biking, crew (Men and Women), fencing, rugby (Men and Women), sailing, skiing, ultimate Frisbee, water polo

Intramurals (IMs)
Soccer, softball, basketball, tennis

Fields
Memorial Field, Hitchcock Field, Pratt Field, Hills Field

Athletic Division:
NCAA Division III

Conference:
NESCAC

Most Popular Sports:
Basketball, football, soccer

Overlooked Teams:
Women's field hockey, women's lacrosse, cross country, indoor track, outdoor track, swimming, squash

School Mascot:
Lord Jeff

Students Speak Out
ON ATHLETICS

"There are 1,600 students, and a little over half of them play a sport. We are Division III in varsity sports. The IMs have about 20 to 40 people per team."

Q "A **large number of people are involved in varsity sports**, but the college doesn't revolve around sports at all. There is a ton of IM sports, but they don't draw huge numbers of entrants. Nonetheless, they are not very competitive and definitely focus on having fun and meeting friends."

Q "To an extent, **there's something for everyone here**. If you're interested in playing a mainstream sport, you should be able to find a place to do it and people to do it with. If you're interested in something less common, you'll probably have trouble because this is such a small campus."

Q "The basketball team is a favorite among students, and so is the football team of course. I've noticed that a lot of alums come and cheer in games, perhaps in attempt to relive old days of glory. There are many varsity sports, all of which are interesting to follow, because **there is real competition among the rival schools**."

Q "At first, it may seem strange that players in such a small and presumably insignificant school work so hard to win. But, I guess this is how most Amherst students take on challenges. **I like going to games when I have time**, and I wish more people would go."

Q "Though we're not Division I, we have our teams. With **40 percent of the student body involved in sports**, we are all a part of it. IM sports happen here every once in a while."

The College Prowler Take
ON ATHLETICS

For a college with such an academic reputation, surprisingly, Amherst maintains a highly-developed and competitive athletic regimen. Most student athletes simply love their teams, their teammates, their coaches, and the fact that they get to go out and compete. Students here have sports as a legitimate outlet for the competitiveness inherent in most Amherst students. Most intercollegiate games don't see capacity crowds, but loyal groups of alumni and parents keep things lively. Nonetheless, in big games, either in the postseason or against Williams College, seats are hard to find. Above all, students love their football and men's basketball teams. For those students who are not recruited, several more exotic sports are out there. Sailing, skiing, and ultimate Frisbee are all options, and even though these teams are generally not prone to the same adrenaline rushes that are prevalent in other varsity sports, they are still part of the social framework and still provide physical challenges to active Amherst students.

The College Prowler™ Grade on
Athletics: B

A high grade in Athletics indicates that students have school spirit, that sports programs are respected, that games are well-attended, and that intramurals are a prominent part of student life.

Greek Life

Students Speak Out
ON GREEK LIFE

"Actually, school-sponsored fraternities have been banned since around 1985, but there are two underground frats. They do not dominate the social scene; they add to it by having parties and events."

Q "The **underground frats hardly dominate the social scene**, and I think that's a good thing. It's not that bad people join those frats; I just think that there shouldn't be any kind of coercion on people to do stuff in order to be accepted."

Q "The frat scene at Amherst is virtually nonexistent, although there are a few underground ones out there. At UMass, however, **frats are huge**. On weekends, you can find some crazy parties going on down frat row [where UMass frats are located]. If you're looking for a frat party like in the movies, go to UMass, and you usually won't be disappointed. I think it's a good idea not to have frats here. I think frats cause people to feel constrained with regard to their social behavior."

Q "There are no school-recognized fraternities or sororities, and there have been none since the school banned fraternities in the mid 1980s. However, **there are a few fraternities that have purchased houses off campus** and function without school funding. These parties do not dominate the social scene on more than a few nights throughout the whole year. Generally, each fraternity throws two major parties a year. On those nights, those parties are the most popular, primarily because they are so rare. There is no obligation for males or females [Psi Upsilon accepts females] to participate in Greek life."

Q "I would never join a frat myself, and in my opinion, anyone who has joined a frat did so just to liven up his or her social life. The frats here don't really scream out legacy and honor. This is because **the school abolished frats,** and students here seem to support this decision. The frats here are more of a fun pastime, I think."

The Lowdown
ON GREEK LIFE

Number of Underground Fraternities:
2

Number of Sororities:
None

Percent of Undergrad Men in Fraternities:
Less than 5%

Percent of Undergrad Women in Sororities:
N/A

Multicultural Colonies:
Anyone can get into one of the frats on campus, and so all the frats are theoretically multicultural. In reality, most frat brothers are white.

Did You Know?

Amherst College followed many Ivy League and other elite schools and abolished frats and sororities.

Q "Greek life was officially ended at Amherst in the '80s. **There's always UMass within walking distance** if one needs frat parties. And despite this deficiency at Amherst, there is never a shortage of kegs and hard liquor."

The College Prowler Take
ON GREEK LIFE

Formally speaking, Amherst abolished fraternities and sororities some two decades ago, and the college will not tolerate frats on campus. In reality, you can still find a few "underground" frats (but not sororities) that are very much alive and kicking. The general public of Amherst students doesn't mind their existence, and in fact, they usually organize good parties, which are by no means exclusive to frat brothers and their entourages. Like frats at other colleges, being a member takes up considerable amounts of time and dedication and in return will give you a social center to which other people will inevitably gravitate.

The College Prowler™ Grade on
Greek Life: D-

A high grade in Greek Life indicates that sororities and fraternities are not only present, but also active on campus. Other determining factors include the variety of houses available and the respect the Greek community receives from the rest of the campus.

Drug Scene

The Lowdown
ON DRUG SCENE

Most Prevalent Drugs on Campus:
Alcohol, marijuana

Liquor related referrals: 171

Liquor related arrests: 0

Drug related referrals: 6

Drug related arrests: 0

Drug Counseling Programs:
The Amherst College Counseling Center provides psychological counseling to students when the need arises. In extreme cases, the college requests the student take a leave of a year or two, with the condition of returning to school after the student's completion of a private rehabilitation program.

Students Speak Out
ON DRUG SCENE

{ "You'll find drugs if you look for them, but it is not in your face. There's always alcohol available."

Q "It's **very easy to get weed here**, and many people smoke more than once a week. It's an acceptable pastime, and even most of the non-smoking students accept it as a fact of life."

Q "Most people **know their limits with respect to getting drunk**, and they know how to plan their time so that an occasional drinking binge will not interfere with their school work."

Q "I **haven't known anyone to have serious problems** with even the lightest drugs such as alcohol and marijuana."

Q "There is **a lot of marijuana on the campus**, but alcohol is abused far more. Other than that, I haven't encountered anything, other than occasional rumors of harder drugs."

The College Prowler Take
ON DRUG SCENE

Amherst nights—and for some, days too!—involve respectable amounts of alcohol. For many Amherst students, alcohol consumption is part of a weekly routine. It's common to get the lowdown on the weekend's parties and just go to the parties and drink, many times for free. Most of the time, this is due to generous seniors who pick up the tab for the poor underclassmen. When you're a senior, you'll probably do the same. Pot is the other popular substance, and, as is the case with alcohol, if you're into it, there's no problem getting it. Harder drugs are present, but are far less common. It is a near consensus among students that doing too many drugs will inevitably get in the way of academics and other activities.

The College Prowler™ Grade on
Drug Scene: B

A high grade on Drug Scene indicates that drugs are not a noticeable part of campus life; drug use is not visible, and no pressure to use them seems to exist.

Campus Strictness

The Lowdown
ON CAMPUS STRICTNESS

What Are You Most Likely to Get Caught Doing on Campus?
Holding an open container (cup, bottle, etc.) of alcohol while outdoors, underage drinking, holding an unauthorized party, parking illegally, smoking indoors

Students Speak Out
ON CAMPUS STRICTNESS

"**The campus police are way more serious about marijuana than they are about alcohol.**"

Q "The **college is strict if they find out you are having a party** without permission from the school. There are fines for every single rule violated. Underage drinkers are just warned."

Q "Some people have complaints about campus police, and some of them are justified. Overall, I think Amherst is one of the most open-minded colleges in the country. You can get away with stuff that you wouldn't in other places, generally because most kids here know when to stop. Therefore, the college doesn't have to be overly strict because they can sort of trust us."

Q "As for drinking, **it's okay as long as things are under control**. The campus police officers really don't like seeing drunken students stumbling and shouting in the streets."

Q "The **state police are much stricter about alcohol than campus police**. Students here get arrested for holding an open bottle of beer, even if they are of age. Campus police will usually just confiscate your alcohol."

Q "I respect the officers here because they realize that in college, **kids are going to party**, they are going to drink, and they are going to basically have fun on occasion. They understand that being unnecessarily strict will not help anyone."

The College Prowler Take
ON CAMPUS STRICTNESS

Amherst College, to the relief of those students who might find themselves disregarding the Massachusetts minimum drinking age, employs a small but adequate police force. The campus police officers are far more lenient than the Massachusetts state police officers are. Usually, the worst case scenario is that a college police officer reports you to the Dean of Students Office. The college, itself, seems to embrace the concept of a second chance. No one has yet been permanently expelled from Amherst for any reason other than blatant academic dishonesty, and if someone has, they must have done something so atrocious as to warrant jail time. If the college administration recognizes a disciplinary problem, usually that student will be suspended for a year. In cases of substance abuse, they will be asked to take part in a rehabilitation program.

The College Prowler™ Grade on
Campus Strictness: A-

A high Campus Strictness grade implies an overall lenient atmosphere; police and RAs are fairly tolerant, and the administration's rules are flexible.

www.collegeprowler.com

Overall Experience

Students Speak Out
ON OVERALL EXPERIENCE

"Amherst wasn't what I expected in terms of academics. The classes are challenging, and some of them are interesting, but the discussion can become stilted and unproductive."

Q "I really love the small, tolerant atmosphere at Amherst. **I am extremely happy here**, and even though there are some shortcomings, like the housing and the food, they are not crucial to your existence here. It is very easy to settle in and meet a huge portion of the people on campus—something you could never hope to do at a large university or college."

Q "Although I was somewhat disappointed [by] the academics, the interesting people more than made up for it, and, in the end, I'm happy to have gone to Amherst. It's not perfect. There are **plenty of things that I would have liked to see improved**. Ultimately though, I know that I'm having a great college experience, and, if I could turn back time, I probably wouldn't go anywhere else."

Q "I learned a lot, not only from classes, but from the people around me as well. **You just have to be willing to engage in conversations**. I know this is corny, but I love this place. I led a very stimulating life here, and I grew up a lot."

Q "I love Amherst, and **I'm glad that I'm here**. This place offers a perfect environment to learn and find out who I am and what I like to do. The open curriculum is incredible, because I take only the classes that I think are interesting and not the classes some random person who doesn't even know me thought were important to take."

The College Prowler Take
ON OVERALL EXPERIENCE

Students usually don't choose Amherst because of its academic reputation. Rather, students come here because of the promise of experiencing an eclectic array of stimulating peers, professors, classes, and activities. Some become disillusioned, not finding their niche within the abundance of opportunities and freedom. Freshman year can go by in a rush, with everyone immersed in the whole college experience alongside their freshmen friends and classmates. Sophomore year can be the most challenging, since a lot of people go through a "sophomore slump," which is usually a state of mild, or not-so-mild, depression caused by the sad fact their freshmen friends aren't living in the same dorm anymore and are now spread out in far corners of the campus. Also, many sophomore students are conflicted by the sudden need to decide on a major and get serious with their life. Junior and senior years are usually better and calmer, since most students have settled into a chosen major and formed a group of close friends.

The key to living here is perhaps keeping yourself open and receptive to new and unfamiliar experiences, opinions, and values. You'll gain a lot more if you communicate openly with that odd-looking and opinionated girl from Dallas or that too-cool-for-school guy from Philly, rather than being repulsed by them. A place like Amherst, with so many accomplished and bright people treading its grounds, is bound to have more oddities than the average university. Even though few people come to Amherst College for the sole purpose of meeting new people, most students do admit, however reluctantly, that Amherst is both fun and a unique learning and growing experience that can be found nowhere else.

The Inside Scoop

The Lowdown
ON THE INSIDE SCOOP

School Spirit
Some alumni are really proud of Amherst and the sports teams. In big games, the football field and the basketball court are filled to capacity. When the Amherst basketball team played in the national championship tournament last year, the school arranged for students and faculty to watch the game via a direct satellite feed. Current students in their time here become slowly, but surely, proud of their school, both in terms of athletics and otherwise.

Traditions
Go and cheer in the last football game of the season against arch rivals Williams College.

The same goes for basketball.

Slide down Memorial Hill on a dining hall tray on the first day of snow, with your shirt waiting for you at the bottom.

Things I Wish I Knew Before Coming to Amherst:
- That there is a true open curriculum. I would have planned my studies better.
- That there is absolutely no pressure from anyone here. You can do whatever you like, at whatever intensity. I would have come with better plan of how to spend my college years.
- How big music is here. I would have brushed up my guitar playing and joined one of the jazz combos on campus.
- How cold it is.

Finding a Job or Internship

The Lowdown
ON FINDING A JOB OR INTERNSHIP

When the academic year draws to a close, many seniors walk around with worried faces and whine to their friends about not having found a job yet, and what on earth they are going to do. In truth, most people that come out of this place get into the line of work, or into the grad school, of their choice.

Advice

The Amherst College Career Center has tremendous resources for you to exploit. Write your resume as soon as you get here and have it looked at and edited by Career Center Peer Career Advisors. Then you can post it on Experience, which is a network employers use to find potential workers and interns. This way, employers will have constant exposure to your resume.

In addition, big companies, especially financial services firms, come to the campus and hold information sessions, as well as interviews for internships and jobs. Consult the Career Center for dates and attend the information sessions; you'll come better prepared for the internship interviews.

Advice (Continued...)

The Amherst College Pre-Business Seminar offers a series of lectures and Q&A panels with business professionals from various fields such as investment banking, brokering, consulting, marketing, and public relations. The ACPB was initiated by students, and draws its participants from all the schools in the area. It is a week long, and at the end there is a job fair where you can find out information about hiring in various well-known firms. Attending the ACPB will give you basic knowledge about the various professions in the modern world and perhaps even give you a valuable connection that may prove helpful in years to come.

Career Center Resources & Services:

Experience Network – A network where students can advertise their résumés and cover letters and apply to jobs and internships online. Some of the largest companies in the United States recruit using this network.

Amherst Alumni Career Network – This allows you to receive advice, internship offers, and job offers from Amherst alumni.

Career Counseling – Deans and peer career advisors provide advice.

- Placement advising
- Internship workshops
- Career workshops
- Graduate school workshops
- Career, internships, and grad school Q&A Panels
- Job interview workshops
- Graduate school advising

The Best & Worst

The Ten BEST Things About Amherst:

1. Awesome people
2. Cream-of-the-crop academics
3. Great parties
4. Free alcohol everywhere
5. Highly-generous financial aid program
6. Friendly faculty and administration are
7. Awesome facilities and computer network
8. Valentine Dining Hall
9. Great career prospects
10. Awesome upperclassmen dorms

The Ten WORST Things About Amherst:

1. The town of Amherst
2. The weather
3. Valentine Dining Hall
4. Students who don't make an effort
5. Fake personalities
6. People are at times overly PC
7. The steep cost
8. Massachusetts state police
9. Shy guys and shy girls
10. Freshmen housing

Mount Holyoke College

50 College Street, South Hadley, MA 01075
www.mtholyoke.edu   (413) 538-2023

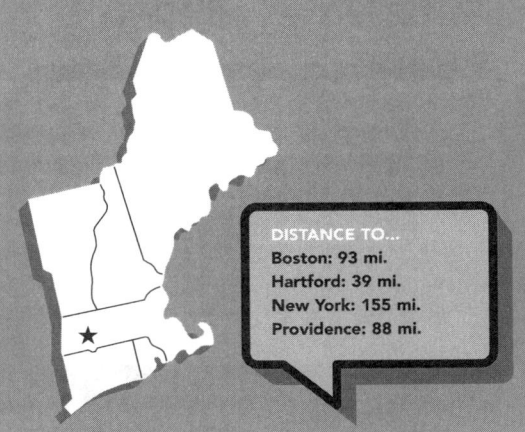

DISTANCE TO...
Boston: 93 mi.
Hartford: 39 mi.
New York: 155 mi.
Providence: 88 mi.

"The college is no longer a seminary, nor does it have any religious affiliation, but we take our traditions seriously."

Total Enrollment:
2,089

Acceptance Rate:
52%

Tuition:
$30,938

Top 10% of High School Class:
52%

Average GPA:
3.7

SAT Range
Verbal	Math	Total
620 – 700	590 – 670	1210 – 1370

ACT Range
Verbal	Math	Total
27-32	25-29	27-30

Most Popular Majors:
- 9% English Language and Literature/Letters
- 8% Biology/Biological Sciences/Psychology
- 7% Economics
- 6% International Relations and Affairs

Students Also Applied To:*
Barnard College, Bryn Mawr College
Smith College, Vassar College
Wellesley College

*For more school info check out www.collegeprowler.com

Table of Contents

Academics	440
Local Atmosphere	442
Safety & Security	444
Computers	446
Facilities	448
Campus Dining	450
Off-Campus Dining	452
Campus Housing	453
Off-Campus Housing	455
Diversity	457
Guys & Girls	459
Athletics	461
Greek Life	463
Drug Scene	464
Campus Strictness	466
Overall Experience	467
The Inside Scoop	468
Finding a Job or Internship	470
The Best & Worst	471

College Prowler Report Card

Academics	A-
Local Atmosphere	B+
Safety & Security	A-
Computers	B
Facilities	B
Campus Dining	B
Off-Campus Dining	B
Campus Housing	A-
Off-Campus Housing	C+
Diversity	B+
Guys	N/A
Girls	B
Athletics	C
Greek Life	N/A
Drug Scene	A
Campus Strictness	A-

Academics

The Lowdown
ON ACADEMICS

Degrees Awarded:
Bachelor, Master of Arts in Psychology

Certificates Awarded:
Postbaccalaureate Certificate of Achievement, Certificate for International Students

Full-time Faculty:
200

Faculty with Terminal Degree:
96%

Student-to-Faculty Ratio:
10:1

Average Course Load:
4 courses

AP Test Score Requirements:
Possible credit for scores of 4 or 5

IB Test Score Requirements:
Possible credit for scores of 5, 6, or 7

Best Places to Study:
Library, dorm common areas

Special Degree Options
Dual-Degree Programs: Engineering, Health Professions, Latin American Studies

Five College Certificate Programs
African Studies, Asian/Pacific/American Studies, Culture, Health, and Science, International Relations, Latin American Studies, Middle Eastern Studies

Teacher Licensure Programs
Early Childhood Education (grades PreK-2), Elementary Education (1-6), Biology Teacher (5-8 and 8-12), History Teacher (5-8 and 8-12), Mathematics Teacher (5-8 and 8-12), Earth Science (5-8 and 8-12), French (5-12), German (5-12), Italian (5-12), Spanish (5-12), Russian (5-12), Latin and Classical Humanities (5-12), Music (all levels), Political Science (5-8 and 8-12), Visual Art (PreK-8 and 5-12)

Sample Academic Clubs
American Sign Language Club, MHC Debate Society, Economics Club, Psi Chi Society (psychology), Sistahs in Science (women of color with an interest in science), Society of Physics Students, Students of Forensic Science

Did You Know?
Mount Holyoke students can take courses for credit at any of the other Five Colleges (Smith College, Amherst College, Hampshire College, and UMass Amherst) at no additional cost.

Approximately one-third of the junior class studies abroad each year.

Each year, a small group of incoming first-years are selected for participation in first-year tutorials. These are opportunities to work closely with a professor and a few other students in an area of interest. Tutorials may involve research or special projects and are two credits per semester. (Most tutorials go for the entire first year.)

Students Speak Out
ON ACADEMICS

"The visiting professors are usually pretty great since they're young and eager to please. The problem is that it's hard to form a relationship with a teacher when you know they aren't going to be there next year."

Q "I think the teachers are probably different for each department. I'm studying art history, so I'll discuss those teachers—I find them to be **engaging and passionate about their subjects**. Sometimes they can be traditionalists in their opinions, but I think that is a general trend in art history. There are only five or six full art history professors, but all of them are interesting, intelligent people."

Q "The teachers have been great. I didn't enjoy the FYS [First-Year Seminar] I took. I didn't enjoy the professor. But, other than that, **the teachers are always understanding and great**. They always make sure that you understand the material and are always willing to go out of their way to help you."

Q "Like any college, MHC has its boring and frustrating professors. But, I've found it also has more than its share of truly inspiring ones. All the faculty members I've worked with are **very concerned about the student's experience** and willing to go far out of their way to make sure you're getting what you need—you only need to ask. But more importantly, you can't have a good class unless your fellow students get involved, too, and MHC is packed with enthusiastic and interesting women that make seminars thought-provoking and enjoyable."

Q "The teachers are awesome; they generally facilitate class discussion rather than talking to the class, and they really know the material. Academics are really challenging, but there are also a lot of really interesting classes. For one class, I read a variety of legends about King Arthur and Joan of Arc, and for another, I worked in a preschool twice a week. **The teachers are really open and easy to talk to**, and they're really open to listening to ideas about alternative paper topics or just alternative ideas, in general."

Q "All my teachers were readily available if I needed to contact them, especially via e-mail. Of course I loved the classes for my majors, but a lot of the classes I took as distribution requirements were a lot of fun. **I'm glad that we had the distribution requirements**, because they really introduced me to areas that I, otherwise, might not have made time for, and they ended up being fun classes. Doing a double major was difficult because, after the requirements for both my majors and the distribution requirements, I didn't have very many classes free to take classes for fun."

Q "Professors at Mount Holyoke are very personable—they try to get to know their students, whether it's by something as simple as making themselves available after office hours or inviting students to their homes. I find that the professors are extremely passionate about the subjects they teach, thus making classes engaging. I know that **I had the hardest time choosing a major**, because after my first semester at Mount Holyoke, I loved my French, Italian, and politics courses and couldn't choose. Eventually I became an English major, because Professor Berek made Intro to Lit inviting and comfortable by encouraging me to talk when I was pretty shy about it, being interested in what I said, and pushing me to work my hardest. He is now my adviser and still pushes me to do my best!"

The College Prowler Take
ON ACADEMICS

Mount Holyoke's academics are top-notch. The workload is very intense, sometimes surprisingly so for students who thought they were going to a less high-profile school than, say, Yale or Harvard. Burnout is a very real possibility if you're not careful to balance your academic obligations with everything else you'll be tempted to do (extracurriculars, social time with friends, cultural events, and speakers on campus that are just too good an opportunity to pass up). However, the flip side of this is that you'll know you're getting one of the best educations possible. This is not a school where you can get away with not learning anything or slacking off because you will probably have to take at least one class in a subject that is outside your comfort zone. If you take it all in stride knowing that you will have some difficult moments, there will always be other students to commiserate with, and understanding professors to give you extensions (or at least moral support).

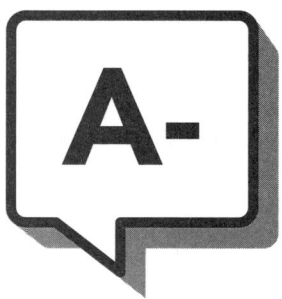

The College Prowler™ Grade on
Academics: A-

A high Academics grade generally indicates that professors are knowledgeable, accessible, and genuinely interested in their students' welfare. Other determining factors include class size, how well professors communicate, and whether or not classes are engaging.

Local Atmosphere

The Lowdown
ON LOCAL ATMOSPHERE

Region:
New England. (Specifically the Pioneer Valley, a section of Connecticut River Valley that runs through western Massachusetts.)

City, State:
South Hadley, Massachusetts

Setting:
Suburban

Distance from Boston:
90 minutes

Distance from New York:
3 hours

Points of Interest:
Village Commons, Amherst, Northampton, Skinner Park (hiking trails, skiing, water sports), Summit House on top of Mount Holyoke (the mountain for which the College was named), Atkins Farms Country Market, Emily Dickinson Homestead (Amherst), UMass Fine Arts Center, Iron Horse Music Hall (Northampton), Academy of Music (Northampton)

Major Sports Teams:
Bruins (NHL), Celtics (NBA), Patriots (NFL), Red Sox (MLB)

City Websites:
www.masslive.com
www.valleyadvocate.com
www.southhadleyguide.com
www.amherstguide.com

Students Speak Out
ON LOCAL ATMOSPHERE

"South Hadley is a very quiet town, which can be comforting and beautiful. Other schools are at least a 20- to 25-minute drive away. You definitely have to stay away from the local bars."

Q "The actual town is small but pleasant. **I find that a lot of students complain that there's nothing going on in South Hadley**, but the real issue is that the students don't bother going to the activities in the town, such as music concerts, book readings, and bake sales. Most students go to Amherst or Northampton when they get off campus. These towns offer an endless variety of activities for the college student, such as bars, cafes, used book shops, live music."

Q "There is nothing to do in the immediate town, unless you like to go to Subway for pleasure. However, **if you have a car, there is a lot of stuff to do on Route 33 down the road**, and of course there is always Amherst and Northampton. But, if you are looking for something to do around Mount Holyoke, expect to spend money to do it."

Q "**South Hadley isn't much of a town**. Students spend most of their time on campus. The bare basics are provided—a bookstore, a theatre, a grocery store a few miles down the road—but for any serious shopping, you'll be headed to Northampton or the Hampshire Mall on the free, but time-consuming, PVTA buses. There are some often-overlooked fun places to visit right on campus, including the botanical gardens, the art museum, and the forest trails near the Equestrian Center."

Q "South Hadley, itself, is small. There is a movie theater, coffee shops, a pizza place, a Chinese food place, and some knick-knack stores right across the street, and there's a grocery store a short drive away, as well as a few restaurants. However, the public transportation is great, and since we're part of the Five College System, **there's always something happening somewhere**."

Q "South Hadley is a rural town and pretty small, but as I came from a small town in the Midwest, it's not unlike my home. When South Hadley holds community events, MoHos are always welcome, and it's a friendly atmosphere. **Four other colleges are less than 15 minutes from us**: Smith, Hampshire, Amherst, and University of Massachusetts."

The College Prowler Take
ON LOCAL ATMOSPHERE

Because the immediate setting is suburban, when students think of places to go and do something, they think beyond South Hadley. As a result, the local area is not confined to a single city, but, instead, spans a section of towns in western Massachusetts known as the Pioneer Valley. This is a great area for hiking and other naturalistic, outdoor pursuits. The Skinner Mountain Range runs right through the Five College area and parts of it are easily accessible via the free bus. Amherst and Northampton also provide pockets of culture, being already set up to cater to college students, and you can always attend an event held at one of the other Five Colleges. Beyond that, however, there is little that is accessible if you don't have a car, which can be frustrating. Some students go off campus almost every weekend to Boston or New York, but this is definitely not necessary, and, in fact, most students will stick around and create their own fun.

The College Prowler™ Grade on

Local Atmosphere: B+

A high Local Atmosphere grade indicates that the area surrounding campus is safe and scenic. Other factors include nearby attractions, proximity to other schools, and the town's attitude toward students.

Safety & Security

Did You Know?

The Sexual Health Educators (better known as SHEs) are students who, supervised by the Office of Health Education, are on a mission to provide accurate information about sexual health issues to students. They also manage to make it fun, and hold yearly "Sex and Candy" dorm workshops.

The Department of Public Safety's staff instructor for RAD classes has been nationally recognized by the RAD program. She also helped develop their manual for key chain defense.

The Lowdown
ON SAFETY & SECURITY

Number of MHC Police:
21.total (9 Full-Time Officers, 3 Sergeants, 9 Part-Time On-Call Reserve Officers)

Phone:
(413) 538-2304 (non-emergencies)
1-911 (emergencies)

Health Center Office Hours:
Monday, Tuesday, Thursday: 9 a.m. - 7 p.m.
Wednesday and Friday: 9 a.m. - 4 p.m.

Safety Services:
Self-defense classes (RAD and karate), safety workshops, officer escort service (from campus parking lots or academic buildings to residence halls between 12:30 a.m. and dawn), emergency blue-light phones, 24-hour campus patrol, vehicle assistance, bicycle registration

Students Speak Out
ON SAFETY & SECURITY

"I feel absolutely safe walking around campus alone at night. Security is really good on the main part of campus, but not so good on the outskirts. The guards make an effort to get to know the students."

"**Public safety is a little bit too tough on students**. Actually, way too tough on students. They rigorously bust the tiny parties that spring up now and again, and I have found them to be quite a damper on most attempts to actually enjoy music with friends."

"Public safety, to me personally, is a little too much for the campus. **They are a bit too nosey**, but I guess some people find that as a comfort. They are always there driving around the campus, so if something does go wrong ,they will be there. There are also a few emergency buttons you can press if you're in danger and no one is around."

"Security is excellent—emergency 'blue-light' stations abound, **public safety is constantly on patrol**, and let's face it: an all-girls campus in a tiny rural Massachusetts town is an extremely uneventful place in terms of crime. I wouldn't be surprised if MHC was the safest campus in the country."

The College Prowler Take
ON SAFETY & SECURITY

Q "The campus is pretty safe—**I've never really felt unsafe walking around in the middle of the night** during the regular school year, although I do feel uncomfortable during breaks. Some areas could use a bit better lighting, but there isn't really much to worry about. Don't leave your wallet in an unattended bag, especially in the gym locker room, and it's a good idea to keep your door locked."

Q "There have been some problems; you can read about them in the public safety log. **The officers are nice and friendly** and hand out M&Ms in the library during finals. There have been minor thefts, such as clothing being stolen from the trunk room, people taking part of recently-delivered birthday cakes, people using other people's laundry detergent, things like that."

Q "**Public safety over-patrols in some areas and under-patrols in other areas**. However, I do appreciate the overall security and honor code on campus. The only complaint that I made with PS was a book stolen off my carrel, which was later recovered by a friend."

Any crime on campus tends to be petty, involving loss of or damage to belongings, but no threat to anyone's physical well being. Still, public safety is a very visible presence on campus, leading some to wonder just what it is they do all day (besides drive back and forth in their SUVs). Officers are generally friendly, and the department is well-stocked with accomplishments. This is one place where you literally do not have to worry about being alone at night, which gives much more flexibility in deciding, say, whether or not you want to study at the library until midnight. Dorm security is also very good. You can't get into any of the dorms without your OneCard (student ID), although you should still be careful to check who's behind you before you open the door for them. Overall, Holyoke maintains a very trusting atmosphere, regardless of the minor burglary.

Want the 411 on safety and security at Mount Holyoke? Check out the College Prowler book on Mount Holyoke College available at www.collegeprowler.com.

The College Prowler™ Grade on
Safety & Security: A-

A high grade in Safety & Security means that students generally feel safe, campus police are visible, blue-light phones and escort services are readily available, and safety precautions are not overly necessary.

Computers

Did You Know?
Student Web Technology Consultants (otherwise known as swebtechs) are available to provide assistance with computing. They also run regular instructional workshops.

Many places on campus, including Blanchard Student Center and some classrooms, have data ports for Internet access. Just plug in your laptop, and you're connected.

The Lowdown
ON COMPUTERS

High-Speed Network?
Yes

Wireless Network?
Yes

Number of Labs:
1 mini-lab in each of 18 residence halls, 7 public computing labs (including the Language Resource Center), 10 departmental labs

Numbers of Computers:
Over 40 in the library's Information Commons, approximately 5 in residence hall labs, 10-30 elsewhere

24-Hour Labs:
Residence hall labs

Charge to Print?
No

Operating Systems:
Windows XP and Mac OSX in most public labs, Windows NT, Sun, Unix, and Linux workstations available in departmental labs

Free Software:
Netscape, McAfee Viruscan Anti-Virus, Tera Term (telnet or ssh shell program, useful for connecting to MHC host computers)

Students Speak Out
ON COMPUTERS

"**The library can get crazy sometimes, but more often than not you can find a computer. There are also computers in all of the dorms, however, none of the printers work unless you go to the library.**"

Q "You should definitely bring your own computer—**the good labs close at midnight**, and the dorm lab computers are old. The computer labs aren't usually crowded, except during finals, but it's just better to have a computer of your own to save things on. All the rooms have Internet access via an Ethernet card, so make sure your computer already has one. I would also recommend downloading AOL Instant Messenger so you can chat with your friends all the time."

Q "The computer facilities at MHC are absolutely first-class. Vast computer labs await you, crammed to the brim with every techno-gadget imaginable. **Digital cameras and camcorders are available free from library services**, and it doesn't even have to be for an academic project—take advantage of that! All dorms have a small computer lab with slightly older, but perfectly serviceable models."

Q "**There's really absolutely no need to bring your own computer**, but you'll probably want to anyway—nearly everyone does. All dorm rooms are wired for super-fast Ethernet, and e-mail and IM are essential to campus communication. Plan to check your e-mail at least five times a day, so if walking downstairs to the computer lab that often would bug you, bring your own computer."

Q "You should definitely **bring your own computer** since dorm computers are often broken or taken by other students. The opportunity to use a school computer does arise, but, especially during finals and midterms, you are better off with your own."

Q "Bring your own computer because **dorm computers are often slow, the printers suck**, and they fill up fast. You don't want to always have to run to the computing center in the middle of a snowstorm to type up a midterm paper. Plus, it's good to have your own computer for those last-minute papers."

Q "I brought my own computer and one of the bonuses of doing so is that there is Internet in all the dorm rooms. When I use the computer labs, for the free printing, **I never have a problem finding a computer**, though they always seem busy. Our technology is up-to-date, and the tech staff is always willing to help you out with any computer problems."

The College Prowler Take
ON COMPUTERS

Mount Holyoke tries really hard to keep up with the latest technology—and it succeeds. All the software you should ever need for basic computing tasks, as well as some software that's just cool, is available on public computers. The people who work in Technology Support and Repair are competent and readily-available to answer student questions. You don't technically need your own computer, but many do bring their own if they can. If you have a laptop, you'll be able to take advantage of the new wireless network and various data ports around campus for a little more flexibility in where you work, but you'll also have to be more careful about thieves. (It is a bad idea to leave a laptop unattended, even in the library, and sometimes even in your room.) If you'd like to try the laptop lifestyle but don't have one of your own, you can rent one from the library's circulation desk.

The College Prowler™ Grade on
Computers: B

A high grade in Computers designates that computer labs are available, the computer network is easily accessible, and the campus' computing technology is up-to-date.

Facilities

The Lowdown
ON FACILITIES

Student Center:
Blanchard Student Center

Athletic Center:
Kendall Sports and Dance Complex

Movie Theatre on Campus?
No. Although the Film Board, a student organization, does show movies on a regular basis, (Friday and Saturday nights, for up to $2 per person), in various auditoriums around campus.

Bowling on Campus?
No

Bar on Campus?
No

Coffeehouse on Campus?
No, but if you're looking for open mic nights, go across the street to the Odyssey Bookstore, which holds one every month, along with other book-related events. There are poetry readings held on campus by a student organization, Revelations Poetry Collective, in Blanchard. Also, you can check out the Thirsty Mind, the coffeehouse across the street.

Libraries
2 (Williston Memorial Library is the main library, and attached to it is the Miles-Smith Science Wing. There is also the Music Library, located in Pratt Hall.)

Popular Places to Chill
Blanchard Student Center, Info Commons, Skinner Green

Favorite Things to Do
Take advantage of all the school-sponsored events that occur throughout the year, such as parties in Blanchard, Spring Weekend (often featuring inflatables and bounce houses on the Green, which are always fun), and No-Study Zone (held just before finals in the fall semester and hosted by Student Programs, this event features kids' toys and games that will help you relive your childhood), to name a few. Las Vegas Night, held every fall, is always popular, and students have fun coming up with the perfect outfit to wear while playing the role of a dealer or a gambler (or just a sophisticated lady or man) for a few hours. There is always at least one free concert a year. In the past, featured artists have included India Arie, Dar Williams, and Kanye West. In addition, there are other concerts that offer tickets at discounted prices (approximately $10) to MHC students. If you just want to hang out, try going for the pool table in Blanchard, or find a spot on the Green in nice weather and people-watch or chat with friends. There are Adirondack chairs scattered around the grassy areas in the center of campus, or you can bring a blanket. You can nearly always find someone on the computers in the Info Commons, but this isn't always the best place to be social, as others may be trying to work.

Students Speak Out
ON FACILITIES

{ "The facilities are great, and everything is maintained and kept in good condition. The gym is just big enough for any use a student might need to make of it and is usually not too crowded."

Q "The athletic center is open at most times during the day and has an indoor track, indoor tennis and squash courts, exercise machinery and weight equipment, a pool, basketball courts, and dance studios. **The student center was just remodeled**, and the new building has been completely renovated and added onto. Blanchard is definitely the center of student activity. It includes student organization offices, the campus store, mailboxes, a café, a full-service dining option, and a stage for student activities. There's something going on almost every weekend night, including a cappella concerts, and drama skits."

Q "I love Blanchard, the student union. Since it has been recently remodeled, the decor is warm but sophisticated. **The café offers a great selection of food options**, from the homemade pizzas, to the sub sandwiches, to the grilled food. The pool table and large screen TV bring a fun, entertaining atmosphere to the place. Blanchard is the place to go for mail, school memorabilia, concerts, eating, and even some of the school orgs, like *Mount Holyoke News*. Not to mention, some of your friends are bound to be hanging out there and, if not, it's a good place to meet new people!"

Q "The **athletic facilities are very nice, both for sports and personal exercise**. The student center was just remodeled and is a great place to meet with other students or go to the shows there. Everything on campus is kept clean, and given that many of the dorms are really old, that's pretty good!"

Q "The computer labs are nice, and the computers are all new. During finals the labs get very crowded, however. **Blanchard was recently revamped and, ever since, the students have been using it much more**. It's really nice, and is full of places to eat, hang out, or do a variety of other things. It's also a good place for hosting events."

Q "**I always appreciated the computer labs** being well-stocked whenever I had to print anything out. Loved the gym. It has everything I could ever have needed, except I wish it were open twenty-four-hours for those late-nights and early-morning times when I wanted to have a good workout."

The College Prowler Take
ON FACILITIES

For a small school, there's a decent amount that you can find to do here on any given day. True, there are not a lot of "hangout" places, so if you really want a social event on the spur of the moment that has more structure than going to Blanchard, finding some friends, and sitting down to watch the big screen TV, you'll have to go off campus. Mount Holyoke is bursting with cultural and educational opportunities. There are always many more speakers on campus in a week (on topics ranging from biology,to politics, to literature and beyond) than any student has time to see. The art museum (which often has special exhibits that are displayed for a limited time only) and the greenhouse are both excellent places to go if you just want to walk around and be entertained.

The College Prowler™ Grade on
Facilities: B

A high Facilities grade indicates that the campus is aesthetically pleasing and well-maintained; facilities are state-of-the-art, and libraries are exceptional. Other determining factors include the quality of both athletic and student centers and an abundance of things to do on campus.

Campus Dining

The Lowdown
ON CAMPUS DINING

Meal Plan Requirement?
Yes, for all full-time residential students

Meal Plan Cost:
Included in room and board fee

What You Get with Your Meal Plan:
21 meals a week in any open dining center, plus a Dining Dollar$ Account (a portion of the board fee that can be used to pay for guest meals or items from non-dining hall food locations—the exact amount is determined each school year, but it has been between $30 and $50 per semester). The MHCXpress Account can also be used for meals in various dining facilities and acts like a debit card. A certain amount of money can be put into the account, and it depletes after each use.

24-Hour On-Campus Eating?
No

Student Favorite:
Blanchard Café

Did You Know?

Wilder became a Kosher/Halal dining center in 2001. It offers special dining options that cater to Jewish and Muslim dietary needs, though anyone can eat here. Milk dishes and meat dishes are served on alternating days. You can find the freshest fruit and vegetables here.

Every Sunday, lunch is replaced by brunch in dining halls. Foods such as scrambled eggs, potatoes, bacon, and gourmet muffins are available. Each dining hall that serves brunch has a specialty. For example, Prospect has a made-to-order omelet and waffle bar, and The Rockies have fruit smoothies and assorted pastries.

Students Speak Out
ON CAMPUS DINING

"A lot of the dining halls have closed during the last few years, so the quality of dining options has gone down. Blanchard definitely is the place to go to get a quick, healthy meal."

"The food on campus can be weird sometimes. They offer vegetarian alternatives to mostly everything—I recall one time seeing Vegan Veggie Balls on the menu ... eeww. Since there are changes occurring this year with the dining services, there are fewer places to eat. **Prospect and The Rockies are always good**, Wilder is Kosher, and of course there is always Blanchard. The continental breakfasts in the dorms get really bland after a while."

"Compared to many college campuses, I think we have pretty good food. The worst option tends to be Blanchard Cafe, which is mostly fried food, but the other dining halls usually offer something nutritious. **There are vegetarian and vegan options at every meal,** and most of them tend to be more creative than pasta. We also have a Kosher dining hall with separate meat and dairy days."

> "**What is wonderful about food on campus is that there is such a good variety**: salad bar, hot food, bread table, desserts. And the menu varies depending on the dining hall, increasing the number of food choices. The best is Sunday brunch, where each dining hall has a different theme, whether it is the crepes in Abbey/Buck or the pastries in The Rockies—and the fried dough is amazing—everyone will find something that they like.

> "Each weeknight, right around the time when you need a break from studying, or right before your beloved sitcom comes on in the communal living room, **we have M&Cs [milk and cookies]**—in other words, a snack. It's a great time to catch up with the other women in your dorm and have a treat. It reminds me of the days when I was a kid having milk and cookies before bed."

> "It's a fact of life: wherever there are dining halls, there will be complaints about the food. **The food at MHC is actually very good**, though. Everything is usually very fresh and there is a wide variety of food options. So, it might not be what your mother makes at home; deal with it."

> "The food sucks except for the glorious bounty that is Sunday brunch. **Every Sunday we can choose from a variety of options** including omelets and special waffle things, crepes, and pastries, and smoothies, as well as traditional Sunday brunch-type food. Blanchard has better-tasting food than most of campus, but it offers a limited selection. There used to be a dining hall in every dorm, but they closed most of them, so now every dorm offers a different item that you can learn about on the menus, so there's usually something somewhere that's good. Our special bonus is of course M&Cs."

The College Prowler Take
ON CAMPUS DINING

It seems that the character of dining at MHC is changing and students are not sure yet whether it's for the better or not. In the spring of 2004, when it was announced that budget cuts in the dining services department necessitated cutting back some items, including making M&Cs every other night instead of every night, there was an uproar. Students banded together to save M&Cs and to have discussions about possible alternative cuts within the dining program because, as they put it, "it's not about the cookies, it's about the community." The felt sense of community that can be had around a dinner table, where you talk and relax with fellow residents of your dorm, versus the flexibility and choice offered by a more centralized dining atmosphere, is the issue here. Despite these problems, the food at MOUNT HOLYOKE is rated better than the food at other schools by those who've been to other colleges, so students count their blessings.

The College Prowler™ Grade on
Campus Dining: B

Our grade on Campus Dining addresses the quality of both school-owned dining halls and independent on-campus restaurants as well as the price, availability, and variety of food.

Off-Campus Dining

Students Speak Out
ON OFF-CAMPUS DINING

"I usually went to Veracruzana or Bueno y Sano in Amherst because I love Mexican food. However, the Chinese food here sucks."

Q "South Hadley restaurants are limited to pizza, Chinese, and one semi-nice restaurant—Fedora's, which serves quite decent food. Amherst and Noho are proper college towns and thus have all the funky ethnic restaurants you could ever wish for."

Q "In South Hadley, **you can usually get a good burger at Fedora's**, but for really good food, you have to drive to Northampton or Amherst for Judie's, the Teapot, and lots of other really good places."

Q "South Hadley has very few restaurants and I'm not really a fan of any of them. **When I eat off campus, I usually go to Northampton**, which has a huge variety of good food options. There are restaurants that offer Japanese, Chinese, Thai, Argentinean, vegetarian, Italian, Indian, Moroccan, organic and American cuisines."

Q "**Fedora's and Woodbridge's are across the street**; they are real good. Then Parthenon [Greek restaurant] is down the street and is still not bad. Various pizza places and Chinese food restaurants are in the area."

Q "Between South Hadley, Amherst, and Northampton, there are a ton of great restaurants for just about any kind of food you might want. **Pasta E Basta has excellent Italian food that's pretty cheap**. The Teapot in Northampton has great Chinese food. Main Moon, across from the college, delivers Chinese food, but it isn't the best."

The Lowdown
ON OFF-CAMPUS DINING

Best Pizza:
Antonio's

Best Chinese:
Taipei and Tokyo

Best Mexican:
Bueno Y Sano

Best Breakfast:
Karen's Kitchen

Best Wings:
Fedora's

Best Healthy:
Paul and Elizabeth's

Best Place to Take Your Parents:
Woodbridge's

Student Favorites:
Antonio's, Bueno Y Sano, Fedora's, Judie's, Main Moon, Tea Pot

The College Prowler Take
ON OFF-CAMPUS DINING

Campus Housing

There isn't much in the immediate area around the college, except for Fedora's, Main Moon, and Carmine's. Those are the places you'll want to go for a bite to eat that doesn't involve driving anywhere. If you have a car, you'll easily be able to get to Subway, Friendly's, Big Y for groceries, and a few other places that are a mile or less from campus. Most students, when they want a night out, take the bus or drive to Amherst or Northampton, where there are restaurants aplenty. Northampton in particular has a tremendous variety. Just walk down Main Street, and you're sure to find something that appeals to you.

The Lowdown
ON CAMPUS HOUSING

The College Prowler™ Grade on
Off-Campus Dining: B

A high Off-Campus Dining grade implies that off-campus restaurants are affordable, accessible, and worth visiting. Other factors include the variety of cuisine and the availability of alternative options (vegetarian, vegan, Kosher, etc.).

Undergrads on Campus:
95%

Number of Dormitories:
19

Number of University-Owned Apartments:
16 (including both apartments in residence halls and off-campus college-owned apartments)

Room Types:
Most residence hall rooms are singles or doubles. There are also some triples, a few quads, and a small number of suites (a combination of singles and doubles in an enclosed area, with a shared private bathroom).

Single rooms are reserved for juniors and seniors, with some available to sophomores who enter the singles lottery, which takes place towards the beginning of the school year. On-campus apartments, within residence halls, are also available to groups of three or four upper-class women. These include their own bathroom and kitchen facilities, plus at least two bedroom/living areas.

Available for Rent:
Micro-fridge (mini fridge with microwave), but only in dorms where this will not blow a fuse!

Hungry for something other than on-campus food? Check out the College Prowler book on Mount Holyoke College for a list of the best off-campus restaurants available at *www.collegeprowler.com*.

Cleaning Service?
There is a cleaning service provided in public bathrooms and common areas. Bathrooms are typically cleaned once a day on weekdays.

You Get
Bed, bookcase, desk and chair, mirror, dresser, window coverings, phone jack (on-campus calls only are free without a phone plan), Ethernet jack

Cable is available only with payment (about $100 per year, per room).

Bed Type
Twin (some bunkable with equipment available from Facilities Management)

Also Available
The college owns a few off-campus apartments, which require an application process to get into. They are located at 3 Park St., 24 Silver St., and 17 Morgan St.

Students Speak Out
ON CAMPUS HOUSING

"Safford is one of the best dorms. 1837 is definitely not a favorite since it's so far off campus. For the most part, the dorm rooms are comfortable and roomy enough."

Q "Many of the dorms are absolutely beautiful and offer a comfortable living environment. Personally, I tend to like the older dorms more than the newer ones. **My favorites are North Mandelle and Pearsons**. I also like Dickinson house because it is the only dorm with kitchens available 24-hours a day. The only problem is that they can become very messy if not properly cleaned every day."

Q "**Avoid North/South Mandelle**—it is too far away! Wilder is the most popular dorm because it just recently got restored. Avoid North/South Mandelle, and you should be good."

Q "I love the old dorms at MHC. They've got grand sitting rooms, old steam radiators, and funny little rooms that come in surprising shapes and sizes. And **MHC wasn't voted the prettiest campus in America umpteen years in a row for nothing**—the buildings are truly lovely. I personally think some of the newer dorms are eyesores (Torrey, Prospect, and 1837 are often avoided during dorm choosing), but none of the housing is truly hideous. Plus, you get a single when you're a senior!"

Q "**Dorm life is one of the best experiences of Mount Holyoke**. The older dorms are my favorite. I lived in Brigham junior year, which has hardwood floors, and—if you live on the fourth floor—sloped ceilings. The downstairs area was so homey, with a comfortable living room and TV room. You become very close to the women in your dorm and create your own 'home.' You get the closeness and sisterhood of a sorority but in a small dorm without all of the sorority fuss."

Q "There's a difference between a house and a home. Likewise, there's a difference between a dorm and a dorm. The main difference is people. You might be in a dorm you hate, but if you're with friends, then suddenly it isn't that bad. The whole issue is rather a moot point, though. **I don't think there are any bad dorms on campus**, just ones that don't suit certain people. If you like being close to the gym, for example, perhaps Torrey is the place for you. I like being a healthy distance away from the gym, and I like walking places, so I prefer the Mandelles. Likewise, if you like quirky architecture in the place you live, Abbey or The Rockies might be your thing. If architecture doesn't bother you, then live in Buckland. Each dorm has its good points and not-so-good points, but it's up to you to decide what they are and whether they make for a 'good' dorm or a 'bad' one."

The College Prowler Take
ON CAMPUS HOUSING

It's not for nothing that Mount Holyoke is said to have "dorms like palaces." While there are some dorms that are perpetually last to be chosen on dorm-choosing night, you're never going to find yourself living in a converted closet. Most rooms are spacious enough, except, perhaps, for some singles that have been converted into doubles. There are many beautiful dorms on campus and many older dorms that have their individual unique charms. This is a very residential campus with 95 percent of students living on campus or in college-owned apartments a few minutes away from campus.

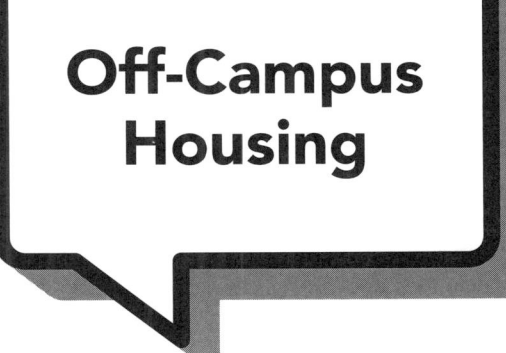

Off-Campus Housing

The Lowdown
ON OFF-CAMPUS HOUSING

The College Prowler™ Grade on
Campus Housing: A-

A high Campus Housing grade indicates that dorms are clean, well-maintained, and spacious. Other determining factors include variety of dorms, proximity to classes, and social atmosphere.

Undergrads in Off-Campus Housing:
5%

In general, living off campus is discouraged. Students who wish to must apply for special permission from the Office of Residential Life. (Frances Perkins students are exempted, as many of them do live off campus.)

Average Rent for a Studio Apartment:
$500/month

Average Rent for a One-Bedroom Apartment:
$625/month

Average Rent for a Two-Bedroom Apartment:
$750/month

Popular Areas:
Amherst, Granby, Northampton, South Hadley

Best Time to Look for a Place:
Beginning of second semester

Students Speak Out
ON OFF-CAMPUS HOUSING

"It's quite a selective lottery for off-campus housing, but to relieve the cost of room and board, it's definitely worth it."

"The **school tries to keep as many people as possible living on campus**. It is virtually impossible to get off-campus housing as a freshman or sophomore. As a junior or senior, it is very rare. I once tried to get an off-campus apartment, and they told me that only about 20 students are permitted to live off campus every year. Fortunately, there are many full-service apartments that are considered on-campus housing can be applied for. Some of them are actually located in big dorms, which means they are self-contained but still a part of the community."

"Living off campus is, generally, not done. The school really, really discourages it. Frankly, even had the option been there, I wouldn't have taken it. MHC is all about community; **living in residence halls really helps you meet your fellow classmates** of all classes. A lot of activities involve your hall, so if you live off campus, you'd be missing out."

"**If you have a car, living off campus is better** than living on campus because it is cheaper and you will have the opportunity to get HBO, Showtime, and the other cable movie channels. If you rely on the PVTA [public transportation], then you're screwed in the winter when the route between South Hadley and Amherst becomes nearly impassible."

"**Just about no one lives off campus**, but there is a lot of housing available in Amherst and Northampton (just a bus ride away), and some in South Hadley, as well. You have to apply to live off campus, and despite the housing crunch, not everyone is allowed."

The College Prowler Take
ON OFF-CAMPUS HOUSING

Only a very small number of people live off campus each year, and of those, not very many keep their own apartments. Some live with family; this is most common among FPs. Since the school actively discourages living off campus, only the most intrepid and/or fed up with dorm life will try it. Students are, in general, happy about this. The extremely residential character of the campus is part of its charm and definitely contributes to its sense of community. What would campus life be without cheesy floor activities? The only downside to this is that some students have really good reasons for wanting to live off campus and are still denied; some in this position have resorted to keeping a room on campus and paying for room and board, but actually living somewhere else.

The College Prowler™ Grade on
Off-Campus Housing: C+

A high grade in Off-Campus Housing indicates that apartments are of high quality, close to campus, affordable, and easy to secure.

Diversity

The Lowdown ON DIVERSITY

African American: 4%

Asian American: 10%

Hispanic: 4%

Native American: 1%

White: 66%

International: 15%

Out-of-State: 64%

Minority Clubs

There are a wide variety of cultural organizations on campus, ranging from AASIA (Asian American Sisters in Action), to the Bulgarian Club, to the Hawaii Club, to Liga Filipina (Philippine students), to MHACASA (Mount Holyoke African and Caribbean Student Association), with many more besides. These clubs are quite active, and some are also attached to cultural houses that provide a safe space for groups to get together.

Most Popular Religions

Catholicism boasts the highest representation on campus, but campus religious life has a distinctly multi-faith flavor. Those who don't prefer this atmosphere (and there are definitely some who don't) can select from many area churches and religious groups. Those who do prefer it will quickly find themselves involved with Eliot House, the center of campus religious life. From weekly interfaith prayer lunches to services in Abbey Interfaith Sanctuary, most campus religious activities, if they don't already include an offering from each of the nine active faith groups, are open to anyone who's curious, even if they have never experienced that tradition before. Those who join the "Eliot House community" often remain loyal for all four years, citing the warmth and support as reasons for coming back.

Political Activity

Mount Holyoke is well known as a liberal campus, although there is also a vocal minority of conservative groups. There are regular rallies held on the steps of Blanchard for such causes as solidarity with labor issues and anti-war speak-outs. The Student Coalition for Action, among other groups, is quite vocal, often running information campaigns that include placing flyers in bathroom stalls, tabling in Blanchard, and sometimes other more theatrical displays.

Gay Tolerance

There are a fair number of "out and proud" lesbians on campus, though by no means is the college comprised solely of lesbians. The Jeannette Marks house, located across the street near Dickinson Hall, is the designated safe space and community center for LGBTQQA (lesbian, gay, bi-sexual, transgender, queer, questioning, and allied) students. Its events are open to everyone. True Colors is the student organization allied to the house. In general, there is open acceptance of all forms of sexuality on campus.

Economic Status

One's economic class is generally not talked about. There is a whole range of students at Mount Holyoke, from those who are paying their own way, to those whose full tuition is paid by their parents. Most people don't think about class, which can lead some for whom class issues are very important to feel like a silenced minority.

Students Speak Out
ON DIVERSITY

The College Prowler Take
ON DIVERSITY

"I'd like to say it's very diverse because I have met so many women from all over the world, but the majority of students seem to be the white-bread, WASP type."

Q "Diversity is something that is emphasized on our campus. **We have hundreds of different cultures and backgrounds represented in our student body**, and I definitely think this is one strength of our community. Unfortunately, many people tend to stick with other people from similar backgrounds, and I wish there were more activities that were focused solely on getting to know people from other cultures."

Q "MHC has a very high percentage of international students and includes American students from all racial backgrounds. Whether or not you think it's diverse will depend on your background—some people say it's the 'whitest' place they've ever been; others say that it's far more diverse than their hometowns and high schools. **Some people complain that there is too little diversity of class**, but I haven't found that to be the case. I've met people from very diverse economic backgrounds."

Q "Some moments I am led to believe that Mount Holyoke is the very definition of diversity. In my first year at Mount Holyoke I had two roommates—one from Massachusetts, the other from Ghana—and I am from Iowa! We had different cultural and religious backgrounds, but that's what made it so great to live together. **I've met women from so many different states, countries, cultures and religions**. It has made me more open-minded. I feel like I have traveled the whole world over just by attending Mount Holyoke."

Q "In some ways it isn't diverse here. There are no men, few druggies, few renegades, and few lower-class students. However, **it is an ethnic, sexual orientation, and religious melting pot**. No one thinks twice about seeing a gay Catholic having lunch with a white Buddhist from Michigan."

As one student said, whether or not you see Mount Holyoke as diverse depends largely on where you've lived before. The school has a high percentage of international students, which creates many opportunities for those who haven't experienced a taste of many different cultures. Not everyone chooses to take advantage of these opportunities. Sometimes the cultural shows, put on by different cultural groups throughout the year and meant to showcase important aspects of those cultures, are poorly attended. It seems that some students are comfortable where they are and can't be bothered to learn about things that don't directly impact their studies and immediate social life, although this can sometimes be understandable given the often overwhelming array of events and activities that there are on any given weekend. Those who need to speak up about their views will find they have the space to do so. It's up to the students whether or not they will be heard.

The College Prowler™ Grade on
Diversity: B+

A high grade in Diversity indicates that ethnic minorities and international students have a notable presence on campus and that students of different economic backgrounds, religious beliefs, and sexual preferences are well-represented.

Guys & Girls

The Lowdown
ON GUYS & GIRLS

Women Undergrads: 100%

Men Undergrads: 0%

Birth Control Available?
Yes. The Health Center offers non-prescription items such as condoms, dental dams, and spermicides for a low price. It also offers prescription items including emergency contraception, oral and injectable contraceptives, and contraceptive patches and rings to students who have had a recent Pap smear.

Social Scene
For many students, the social scene does not include guys at all, or if it does, their role is limited to cameo appearances in a class that meets twice a week. However, for those who do want to meet guys, the places to look are at the three colleges in the area that have them: Hampshire, Amherst, and UMass. It is definitely possible to meet someone while at MHC (and for those students who prefer romance with women, it is more than definitely possible), although campus parties that attract mostly men looking to get drunk and possibly laid are not the best places to look for anyone who will make a lasting commitment. Social life on campus is mostly rather laid-back, which is good for those who want to avoid the wild side, but many do exercise their creativity in this area and host dorm room parties that rival anything you'll find somewhere else.

Hookups or Relationships?
If you're really looking for a random hookup, you can probably find one off campus, if not on campus. However, a lot of students are in serious relationships. Many come to college already attached to a long-distance relationship, and those who don't often find someone while at college. This happens to such an extent that one can begin to wonder whether anyone is still single.

Dress Code
There is no dress code. Many women feel comfortable wearing their pajamas to class. Some will dress up—not many, but enough so that those who do aren't stared at as if they were some sort of freak. Basically, you can wear anything you want, from cloaks and Renaissance dresses, to short skirts and makeup, to old sweatshirts and baseball caps, and it'll be fine. No worries about whether or not you have the latest fashions. Of course, most students you will see will be wearing the typical shirt and jeans, thrown on five minutes before going off to class, but that's because we're college students.

Students Speak Out
ON GUYS & GIRLS

"No guys. There are girls that look like guys, but no guys. It's lesbian heaven, but it's a complete hell if you're a woman who craves massive amounts of male testosterone."

Q "There are stereotypes about all the Five Colleges in the area. **It's easy to recognize a Mount Holyoke woman**, though. She's the one who is dressed nicely and carries an assignment calendar. And a Nalgene."

Q "Although we are an all-women's college, **there are almost always guys around**. Many of them tend to be boyfriends of current students, but there are others who take classes on campus through the Five College program or who just enjoy coming to our library to study. The lesbian population is strong on our campus, but I tend to think this is because we offer a more open-minded environment where students feel accepted no matter what their sexual orientation is."

Q "**There are many places in the Valley to meet other straight, gay, and bisexual people**, especially towns like Northampton and Amherst."

Q "The guys are nonexistent, but there are girls to suit anyone's tastes from the quiet and studious type, to the colorful hippie, from the lady who actually wears make-up every day, to the girl with the butch haircut and 20 piercings. **There's no typical Mount Holyoke girl**; our strength is in diversity. That includes a diversity of sexual orientations. The atmosphere is one of acceptance, whatever your orientation—the straight, the lesbian, the bisexual, and the undecided should all feel at home. There is no pressure to be anything you don't want to be. And yes, the girls are hot."

Q "We have plenty of hot women here! **The women of MHC are, for the most part, very liberal, good students, not big on parties**, independent, and high achievers. Most women at MHC will fit into most, if not all, of those categories. MHC women are also unusually friendly. The Five College men vary from the most drunken UMass frat boys to the yuppiest Amherst rich boys, but there really is a lot of variety. If you want to date a Five College man, the best way is to join a club or take a class at one of the other colleges."

Q "**The women are talented and goal-oriented**. About half are too ambitious, but I try not to let that influence me. In terms of looks, diversity is celebrated, and while crude jokes can run on *The Daily Jolt* about the number of 'fatties' here, there is definitely more openness towards bigger women, plainer-looking women, hairy women, and anyone else."

The College Prowler Take
ON GUYS & GIRLS

Well, it all depends on what you're looking for. Having a diverse range of "hotties" is not one of the main selling points of Mount Holyoke; rather, the academics and sense of community tend to take first place in one's choice to come here. So, the forging of a romantic relationship is somewhat of a secondary thing, though by no means do Mount Holyoke women turn off their hormones when they enter the gates. Romance is alive and well on campus, if kept somewhat subdued at a low steady hum. Because the student body is composed of all women and because of the open and somewhat experimental atmosphere on campus, there is perhaps more than average lesbian activity. Maybe it just seems that way, because, after all, there are no guys to gossip about (unless it's someone else's boyfriend or the random guy you met last weekend at a UMass party). Same-sex relationships gather all of the drama you'd expect to come with the possibility of love and breakups between floormates or classmates. But, if guys are what you're looking for, you can find them other places in the Pioneer Valley, most readily at the other three colleges in the area that have them.

The College Prowler™ Grade on
Guys: N/A

A high grade for Guys indicates that the male population on campus is attractive, smart, friendly, and engaging, and that the school has a decent ratio of guys to girls.

The College Prowler™ Grade on
Girls: B

A high grade for Girls not only implies that the women on campus are attractive, smart, friendly, and engaging, but also that there is a fair ratio of girls to guys.

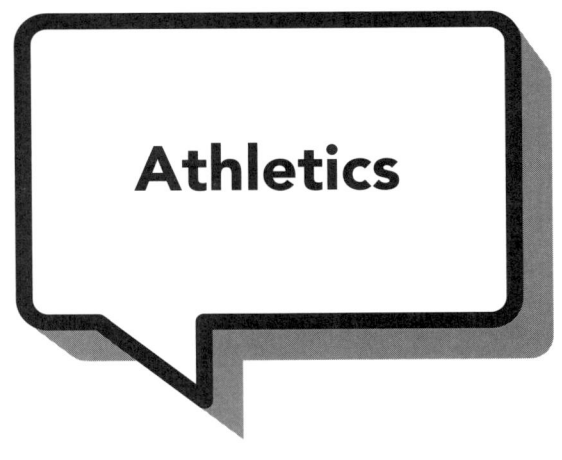

Athletics

Most Popular Sports
The rugby and crew teams are the most well-known, perhaps because of the extreme sacrifices team members must make. (Crewtons, as members of the crew team are called, must wake up hours before anyone else in order to make morning practice; the rugby team produces a T-shirt that says, "Give Blood. Play Rugby.") Other than that, each team, both intercollegiate and club, has its own following.

Fields
Kendall Sports and Dance Complex has six fields surrounding it.

The Lowdown
ON ATHLETICS

Men's and Women's

Basketball	Soccer
Crew	Squash
Cross Country	Swimming and Diving
Field Hockey	Tennis
Golf	Track and Field
Lacrosse	Volleyball
Riding	

Athletic Division:
NCAA Division III

Conference:
NEWMAC

Getting Tickets:
There is no need to get tickets. Anyone can come to watch a home event.

School Mascot:
Lyon

Club Sports
Basketball, Boots and Saddles (equestrian club), cheerleading, cycling, Dance Team, Dragonboat racing, dressage, fencing, ice hockey, ice skating, karate, Outing Club (hiking and camping), rugby, sailing, water polo

Intramurals (IMs)
Basketball, soccer, ultimate Frisbee, volleyball

Overlooked Teams
Mount Holyoke used to have a softball team, but because of budget cuts in the athletic department, the team no longer exists. Dedicated softball players made an effort to preserve the team through creating a student org for that purpose, but as of now, it looks like softball will have to become a club sport if it is to remain.

Did You Know?

Orchards Golf Course became famous in Summer 2004 when Mount Holyoke hosted the U.S. Women's Open here.

Students Speak Out
ON ATHLETICS

The College Prowler Take
ON ATHLETICS

"Sports, in my experience, aren't that popular on campus. A lot of women play sports, but I do not know about the turnout. I know I've never been to a game."

"Sports like crew and riding are really **popular** and get a lot of support from the school, as well as interest from the students."

"**MHC is not very big on sports.** I don't think sports matches are very well-attended, although I almost never go, so I wouldn't know. Intramural stuff is pretty low-key. The academic workload is intense, and while some people do manage to fit athletics into their schedules, many others can't be bothered."

"I don't think sports are that big. Although my roomie was on the volleyball team, and I knew a couple of water polo players, **I never went to any of the games and neither did any of my friends**. I know, I know, I know, I was such a bad roommate."

"While there are some great varsity sports, one can't forget the club sports. **One of the most popular sports on campus, rugby, is a club sport**. This allows for a lot more diversity in the sports offered, although club sports take a devoted group of students to keep them going. Sports, overall, while they all have their followings, are not especially big on campus, but they are important. So if you're into sports, there's a lot for you, and if you're not, you won't feel left out."

"A lot of women play both varsity and intramural sports, and some of the teams are really into it—crew and rugby come to mind—but while playing a sport is a central part of the athlete's life, it's not necessarily a big part of campus life. **We do offer a lot of both types of sports**, and team members of both groups tend to really enjoy them."

Let's just say this isn't a sports-oriented campus. There are those who faithfully participate in a sport all four years, but those who don't probably won't even come out to watch the games. It's not that you can't find sports if you're looking for them, but the latest basketball statistics probably won't be a hot topic of conversation around the dinner table (unless one of your friends is on the basketball team). That said, the facilities are there for some sports to really shine. Club sports differ widely in the level of commitment involved—since they are run through student programs, they are largely what the students who participate make of them. Unfortunately, club sports don't always get the funding they need, since the SGA (Student Government) that provides the funding to all clubs rarely has enough money to give every club what it asks for.

The College Prowler™ Grade on
Athletics: C

A high grade in Athletics indicates that students have school spirit, that sports programs are respected, that games are well-attended, and that intramurals are a prominent part of student life.

Greek Life

The Lowdown
ON GREEK LIFE

Number of Sororities: 0
As you may have gathered, Mount Holyoke doesn't have Greek life. If you're looking for fraternities or sororities, try UMass.

Students Speak Out
ON GREEK LIFE

"There is no Greek life at Mount Holyoke, but at UMass the frat parties dominate the first few days before school starts."

Q "We **don't have any Greek life**. Some people tried to start a sorority, but people felt like it would be too exclusive."

Q "Mount Holyoke is such a warm, welcoming community that it makes a 'Greek life' somewhat superfluous. **Sometimes it feels as though the entire campus is one big sorority**. I think that introducing a 'Greek life' to the campus would only create division, and what students want in a college, especially in a smaller one, is unity."

Q "Mount Holyoke doesn't have a Greek life, which is a fact I am eternally thankful for. I attended a large university a year before transferring to Mount Holyoke and rush week became hell week for non-Greeks. It most certainly dominated the social scene, and I don't think one body or group should do that on any campus. If you think Greek life is the only way to make close friends and a tight-knit group of people to live and study with, then you are wrong. **Mount Holyoke has the community feel and the 'sisterhood,' without all the negatives or cliquish** traits that Greek life can sometimes perpetuate."

Q "There is no Greek life—every slight attempt to start one has been squashed flat. **Students want to preserve the community on campus, not section it off**. Really, the whole school is like one giant sorority, even in the way the alumnae support their following classes. You don't need sorority sisters with these Mount Holyoke sisters."

Q "Instead of sorority pledging, we have Dis-O. **Dis-O does dominate the social scene**. I do not miss the fact that we do not have sororities. I consider the entire college an all-inclusive sisterhood, unlike a sorority which picks and chooses its members."

COLLEGE PROWLER

Want to party? Find out about the greek organizations on campus by checking out the College Prowler book on Mount Holyoke College available at *www.collegeprowler.com*.

The College Prowler Take
ON GREEK LIFE

There is no Greek life on campus—and with good reason, it seems. That kind of lifestyle just wouldn't work here. Many, many students have said that the entire campus feels like one big sorority and that's very true. One of the reasons cited in other places for the importance of Greek life is that it helps to create close bonds between people who might otherwise not have those bonds. At a large, coed school, this may be so (although there are, of course, other ways of bonding with one's peers that do not specifically require anything Greek to be involved), but at Mount Holyoke it seems that those types of bonds occur naturally, through living, working, and playing with one's fellow students. So, for the time being, those looking for the benefits of Greek life will have to look elsewhere.

Drug Scene

The Lowdown
ON DRUG SCENE

Most Prevalent Drugs on Campus:
Alcohol, marijuana, caffeine

Liquor-Related Referrals: 51

Liquor-Related Arrests: 5

Drug-Related Referrals: 9

Drug-Related Arrests: 10

Drug Counseling Programs
Alcohol and Drug Awareness Project (ADAP)
Pattie Groves Health Center, Room 110
Phone:
(413) 538-2616 (appointments)
(413) 538-2466 or (413) 538-3200
(educational services)

Services
Individual counseling and counselor-facilitated groups, peer support groups, network of recovering alumnae, workshops and other educational materials, referrals to local therapists and/or inpatient and outpatient chemical dependency treatment programs.

All services are free for Mount Holyoke students.

The College Prowler™ Grade on
Greek Life: N/A

A high grade in Greek Life indicates that sororities and fraternities are not only present, but also active on campus. Other determining factors include the variety of houses available and the respect the Greek community receives from the rest of the campus.

Students Speak Out
ON DRUG SCENE

{ "Not a lot of people do drugs on campus, and if they do, they usually get in trouble because everyone is pretty uptight about smoking or doing drugs in the room."

Q "MHC is pretty tame in terms of drugs. There is no substance-free housing for the simple reason that it isn't usually a problem. **Serious abuse of alcohol is rare**, especially compared to other campuses, and I personally haven't encountered any illegal drugs on campus."

Q "I didn't see much drug use while at school. Which, I suppose, says something in and of itself. Admittedly, I knew that there were drugs on campus, but if it's not part of your social circle, you don't have to deal with it. **It's not that visible**."

Q "**Lots of pot and coke if you know where to look**. Booze is a given. We all had at least a bottle of vodka or tequila hidden away—or out in the open—in our rooms."

Q "I remember when one girl got busted for having marijuana—the incident made college newspaper headlines. It just seemed so unthinkable that someone could do something that stupid and irresponsible on a campus known for attracting intelligent and responsible women. I don't want to say that no one on campus ever does drugs—perhaps some people do, but **you never hear about it** and none of your friends do it."

Q "Several of my roommates had pot in our rooms, and there were several times when I got stoned. However, **it generally seems to happen off campus**, and drug use is typically frowned upon."

The College Prowler Take
ON DRUG SCENE

Drugs exist on the MHC campus, but, in general, the drug scene is pretty tame. Yes, alcohol is ever-present (often hidden away in a secret stash), but, as one student said, serious abuse of any drug, including alcohol, is rare. There are far more liquor-related referrals than drug-related referrals, which tells you something right there. You won't find many hardcore drugs on this campus. It's also significant that there are many more referrals than arrests. Public safety is not likely to arrest you for alcohol use. Things just don't get that wild, although you can still get caught for excessive drinking, and then you'll probably get referred to a treatment program.

The College Prowler™ Grade on
Drug Scene: A

A high grade on Drug Scene indicates that drugs are not a noticeable part of campus life; drug use is not visible, and no pressure to use them seems to exist.

Campus Strictness

Q "The campus policies, from what I understand, are **fairly low-key**. Those who are caught with illegal substances have to go through some sort of drug therapy, but I don't know how much else they have to do."

Q "**Drugs are never tolerated**, but they're pretty lenient with drinking as long as it doesn't get out of hand."

The College Prowler Take
ON CAMPUS STRICTNESS

The Lowdown
ON CAMPUS STRICTNESS

What Are You Most Likely to Get Caught Doing on Campus?
Parking in the wrong place, holding a party that's too loud or too wild, underage or excessive drinking, having candles or other prohibited items in your room, stealing, harassing students via e-mail or phone

As can be seen from the student comments, there isn't much consensus on just what exactly public safety busts people for. Sure, there are the public safety logs, published faithfully every week in the *Mount Holyoke News* (the student-run newspaper), but those are filled mostly with accounts of suspicious males being escorted off campus, intoxicated or ill students being transported to the Health Center, and the occasional group of students who light a box on fire and then leave the area. Mount Holyoke does have a drug and alcohol policy, but few students take the time to read what it is, and many violations go unnoticed by public safety. If your party is too loud or otherwise attracts attention, you might get busted for underage drinking if they come to break it up, but otherwise, it's easy to not get caught.

Students Speak Out
ON CAMPUS STRICTNESS

"Public Safety claims to have a 'no tolerance' policy, but I've heard about people getting busted who got community service or got out of discipline somehow."

Q "Public safety is **overly strict** about drinking."

Q "There's a **policy** on drugs and alcohol?"

Q "Public safety is **too strict** sometimes."

The College Prowler™ Grade on
Campus Strictness: A-

A high Campus Strictness grade implies an overall lenient atmosphere; police and RAs are fairly tolerant, and the administration's rules are flexible.

Overall Experience

Students Speak Out
ON OVERALL EXPERIENCE

"I love MHC. While every now and then I did wonder about what life might've been like elsewhere, I never ever would've switched. I loved the sense of community, diversity, and all the traditions."

Q "Being a transfer student, I have experienced an entirely different social and academic scene from my previous school. **Mount Holyoke pushes me and is more academically rigorous** than my previous school, so even with all of the papers and projects, studying and stressing, I can't be thankful enough for being here. I have grown into a much more confident, self-assured, open-minded individual and accredit Mount Holyoke with a lot of that."

Q "Mount Holyoke is the best college in the world. It has its ups and downs like any place, but I would never, ever want to go anywhere else. **Being at a women's college rocks my tomorrow socks**—I like having a boyfriend, but it's so nice not to have to deal with guys. The women at Mount Holyoke are intelligent, creative, and able to do anything. There are no comparisons."

Q "I completely love MHC. It's a perfect fit for me, and I wouldn't want to be anywhere else. My life here is rich and full in all areas: academics, friendship, spirituality, and extracurricular interests. But, **MHC isn't for everyone**, so visit the campus, attend a few classes, and talk to as many students as you can to get a feel for the place before you enroll. A certain number of people do transfer out after their first year, mostly because they either didn't like the intense academic workload or because they wanted a campus with more parties and more boys. But, for the right person, MHC will become their beloved home, one that will challenge them and transform them and give them dozens of life-long friends."

Q "**I had a bad experience with roommates**, friends, and dorm location, so I was miserable most of the time. I did not spend a lot of time on campus, either. I am going to give the college another chance, but I may transfer."

Q "I am disappointed with the Study Abroad Office, the Registrar's Office, and the occasional bad professor, but that didn't ruin an otherwise great time at MHC. **I learned so much about different people and places and developed close friendships with the women I met**. Also, one of the great things about MHC is that it teaches you that you can do anything you put your mind to—that gender is not a hindrance. I have come into the 'real' world expecting people to be of that mind-set, and the professions that I am looking at are careers that have been traditionally male-dominated. Whether this or something else happens, my goal is to be an example for other women."

COLLEGE PROWLER

Curious about the overall atmosphere on campus? Read more student opinions in the College Prowler book on Mount Holyoke available at *www.collegeprowler.com*.

The College Prowler Take
ON OVERALL EXPERIENCE

It seems that students come to Mount Holyoke for the academics and stay for the community. Women who come here either quickly discover that they hate it and transfer out or fall in love with the school and become unable to imagine going anywhere else. The overall sense students have about this school is that it's more than just a school, more than a place to study for four years, get your diploma, and be set free. MHC becomes a second home. Its close-knit environment allows students to explore their own boundaries safely, perhaps try out a few lifestyle changes, and maybe even find a few that stick. You will undoubtedly be exposed to new influences during your time here, as you would at almost any college, but here you won't be afraid to call some of those new influences your friends—especially the ones who scared you at first.

Part of what's so wonderful and unique about this school is the sense that one is really cared about as an individual. Sure, it's an institution, and sure, there are the occasional oversights, like the registrar forgetting to record a grade, but most faculty and most staff are exceedingly helpful and willing to assist you with whatever difficulty you may be facing, whether it's a decision to apply to grad school or a mistake in your transcript. The atmosphere of care is catching—new students quickly catch it from older students, and so the tradition lives on. Things are changing for this institution, as it strives to keep up with modern times and with budget cuts resulting from a bad economy, but it still remains the school generations of women have known and loved, and alumnae still keep coming back to visit and reminisce.

The Inside Scoop

The Lowdown
ON THE INSIDE SCOOP

School Spirit

Mount Holyoke students have plenty of school spirit. Most of the time, it's not of the variety you'd find at large coed school football games, with people waving banners, cheering, and painting their faces with the school colors. It's more of a low-key, but constant, presence. MHC is unique in so many ways, and those who aren't turned off by it come to love the school with a passion. Loyalty runs strong. (This also applies to alumnae.) You'll see students actually buying and wearing overpriced items from the school store that have the school name on them. Even when criticizing aspects of the school, students are doing it because they love it and want it to be the best it can be.

Traditions

Big/Little Sisters

Juniors are paired with one or more first-years who become their "little sisters." There is an ice cream social planned for the very beginning of the school year at which the two classes are encouraged to mingle and, traditionally, juniors escort their little sisters to fall Convocation. A mentoring relationship may or may not ensue.

Canoe Sing

Part of the final days leading up to Commencement in the spring, this event is when seniors go out on Lower Lake in canoes and paddle around in different formations as their classmates sing from the bank. It is held at night with colored lanterns both strung from the canoes and on land. There are fireworks afterwards if the weather is good.

Traditions (Continued...)

Class Colors

Each class, upon entering, is assigned a class color and class mascot. These stay with the class all four years and only get "recycled" when the class graduates. The four mascots are: Blue Lion, Green Griffin, Red Pegasus, and Yellow Sphinx.

Disorientation

A sort of initiation for the first-years combined with a bit of dorm competition, this tradition is meant to provide a bonding opportunity for seniors and first-years. The seniors in each dorm plan activities for "their" firsties—activities that range from wearing their clothes inside out and backwards to stealing another's dorm's dorm banner. Dis-O lasts for a week in the fall beginning with a nighttime rally where seniors roust firsties from their beds to go out to the green and cheer, chant, and sing with dorm pride. Participation is voluntary and activities are never allowed to cross the line into hazing or outright destruction.

Elfing

This is the bonding opportunity for sophomores and first-years. Sophomores become "elves" for a week, while first-years become "elfees." Elves leave small gifts and notes for elfees during this time, along with placing magazine cutouts with original captions around the dorm. (On the first night, it's traditional to cover an elfee's door with newspaper, giving them a surprise when they try to leave the room in the morning!) At the end of the week, elves reveal themselves at a special M&Cs.

Faculty Show

A once-every-four-years event, this is a variety and comedy show that showcases the faculty's "talents." It, like Junior Show, makes fun of aspects of the school, but from the faculty's perspective.

Founder's Day

On Founder's Day (November 2), seniors gather at Mary Lyon's grave early in the morning, wearing their graduation robes, to eat ice cream served by the president and other faculty and staff. The day, which celebrates MHC's founder, culminates in a special dinner that features a special (though not necessarily tasty) dessert: Deacon Porter's Hat, named after one of Mary Lyon's good friends and a contributor to campus life in the first days of the Seminary, shaped like a top hat, and tasting like a not-very-sweet spice cake.

Traditions (Continued...)

Junior Show

Performed every year in the beginning of the spring semester, this is the juniors' chance to show off their school spirit while making fun of any and every aspect of the school. The show is entirely student-written and produced and features a number of skits starring juniors. It is performed on three separate nights: Faculty/Staff Night, when faculty and staff get in for a reduced price; Little Sister Night, when first-years get in for a reduced price; and Senior Night, when seniors get the reduced price. (Juniors always get in for free; sophomores can get in for free if they're willing to wear the juniors' class color!) Senior Night is notoriously raucous, with seniors writing their own versions of the skits and interrupting the performance in various ways.

Laurel Parade

Part of the Commencement/Reunion festivities held in late May, this tradition brings together alumnae from reuniting classes and the graduating class who become the newest alumnae. All classes dress in white with touches of their class color, except for graduating seniors, who wear only white. Each class parades through campus, holding signs and their class banner. Last of all come the seniors carrying a chain of laurel. When the beginning of the parade gets to Mary Lyon's grave, the alumnae part to form an aisle through which the seniors walk amidst cheers. Seniors then weave around the grave site until everyone surrounds the grave. They then place the laurel on the fence and sing "Bread and Roses," an old suffragette song, while the president places flowers on the grave.

Mountain Day

Once every fall, on a day that is meant to be unknown in advance, the president announces that classes have been cancelled. The Mary Lyon bell tolls for five minutes straight at seven in the morning; that's the signal that you really can go back to sleep. Everyone is free to do what they want for the day. It's tradition to climb Mount Holyoke, the mountain after which the college was named. If you're there at the right time, the president will be at the top with ice cream.

Finding a Job or Internship

Things I Wish I Knew Before Coming to MHC:

- Telnet commands!

- You don't need to bring a lot of stuff. You'll spend most of your time doing things, not sitting in your room.

- You will, however, want to bring a lot of posters to cover your walls with. Just make sure you also bring a hammer and some sturdy nails or tacks because those dorm room walls can be hard as a rock and quite often tape or other sticking methods won't survive the humidity.

- It is freaking cold in the winter. You will never regret that extra blanket or pair of gloves, except when they turn up the heat in the dorms. Then you'll be sleeping in a T-shirt and shorts in the middle of a snowstorm.

- Most MHC students are very friendly.

- Most MHC students change their major at least once. Some students graduate and still don't know what they want to do with their lives.

- The dining halls serve a lot of tofu (and various other items that are used as meat substitutes). You might actually start to like it, but, in general, stay away from anything called "seitan."

The Lowdown
ON FINDING A JOB OR INTERNSHIP

The Career Development Center is staffed with mostly friendly people who will do their best to introduce you to the resources the center has to offer and work with you on an individual basis to define your career goals, suggest directions you might want to take, and provide moral support. They won't do all the work for you, though, and students have reported that they sometimes feel at a loss when told to go into the CDC library and research internships, which can be found in a big folder marked "internships." Still, those students who do go regularly to the CDC are usually the ones who get the internships. You have to be somewhat self-motivated, even with the help of the staff, to wade through the many possibilities, and you have to have the patience to weed out the real opportunities from the ones that just aren't feasible.

It seems that the CDC has a greater focus on internships than on jobs for students, at least for undergrads. Technically, they are supposed to be a resource for on-campus jobs as well as off-campus and summer jobs, but most students get their on-campus jobs through word of mouth and asking around. For more "career-oriented" jobs, they are about as helpful as they are for internships, which is to say, average helpfulness. Students have reported being frustrated with the career counseling they have received, saying that they felt they were being pushed in a particular direction by the person they talked to. Though, on the good side, the CDC is very good about holding regular workshops on topics ranging from how to build up your resume to how to behave on that first interview.

Advice

Go early and go often to the Career Development Center. They have tons of resources to help you out, but you'll never know they're there unless you make the effort. The CDC has been slightly overlooked by students who view it as being out in no-man's land on the edge of campus (actually, it shares a building with the Health Center), but it can be your best friend when you're overwhelmed by all the options out there and you have no idea how to break into your field of choice. Do some research in the library; make an appointment to talk to one of the career counselors; utilize the CDC's online resources. If you start thinking about this when you're a first-year (even if you don't know quite yet what you want to do) you won't find yourself in the position of a second-semester senior who visits the CDC for the first time with a panic-stricken look on her face and absolutely no idea what she's going to do after graduation.

Career Center Resources & Services

- Career Counseling Appointments
- Library Resources (including books on choosing a career, on specific careers, folders with information on internship opportunities, and much more)
- Career and Job/Internship Search Skills Workshops
- Graduate School Advising
- Fellowship and Scholarship Advising
- Summer and January Term Internship Advising
- Student Job Board (for on-campus jobs)
- Recruiting Programs
- Recommendation and Credentials Services (the CDC will maintain copies of letters of recommendation you have placed on file with them and then will send them out to employers, graduate schools, or other places upon request)
- Alumnae Networking
- Online Resources (can be found at the CDC website: www.mtholyoke.edu/offices/careers/main/homepage.htm)

The Best & Worst

The Ten BEST Things About MHC:

1. The beauty of the campus
2. The sense of community
3. The inspiring and warm professors
4. The rigorous academics
5. Open, tolerant students
6. Having a good time without getting drunk
7. Women feel empowered here!
8. Free concerts with big name artists
9. Amherst and Northampton are really close
10. Strong alumnae connections

The Ten WORST Things About MHC:

1. Widespread academic burnout
2. The distance to the nearest grocery store
3. The lack of male perspective
4. The length of the winters
5. Lack of cultural variety
6. Inconvenient parking/frequent parking tickets
7. Housing crunch
8. Swarms of geese and ducks on Lower Lake
9. Forced full meal plan
10. Recent budget cuts

Smith College

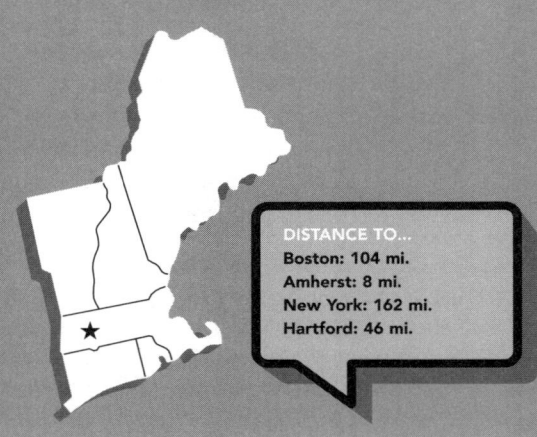

DISTANCE TO...
Boston: 104 mi.
Amherst: 8 mi.
New York: 162 mi.
Hartford: 46 mi.

7 College Lane, Northampton, MA 01063
www.smith.edu   (413) 585-2500

"Though some still think of Smith as a 'pearls and tea' school, it has shifted to a progressive, political student body."

Total Enrollment:
2,641
Acceptance Rate:
52%
Tuition:
$29,156
Top 10% of High School Class:
59%
Average GPA:
3.8
SAT Range
Verbal	Math	Total
580 – 700	570 – 670	1150 – 1370

ACT Range
Verbal	Math	Total
25-31	23-28	25-30

Most Popular Majors:
13% Economics
10% Political Science and Government
9%   English Language and Literature
7%   History

Students Also Applied To:*
Barnard College, Brown University, Bryn Mawr College, Mount Holyoke College, Wellesley College

*For more school info check out www.collegeprowler.com

Table of Contents

Academics	473
Local Atmosphere	475
Safety & Security	476
Computers	478
Facilities	479
Campus Dining	481
Off-Campus Dining	482
Campus Housing	484
Off-Campus Housing	485
Diversity	487
Guys & Girls	489
Athletics	490
Drug Scene	492
Campus Strictness	493
Overall Experience	494
The Inside Scoop	495
Finding a Job or Internship	496
The Best & Worst	497

College Prowler Report Card

Academics	A-
Local Atmosphere	C
Safety & Security	A-
Computers	B+
Facilities	A-
Campus Dining	B-
Off-Campus Dining	B+
Campus Housing	B+
Off-Campus Housing	D+
Diversity	C-
Guys	N/A
Girls	B+
Athletics	C
Greek Life	N/A
Drug Scene	C-
Campus Strictness	D

Academics

Sample Academic Clubs
Smith Chapter of the American Chemical Society, Smith College Investment Club, Smith Physics Club, Bad Seeds (botany club), Smith College Philosophical Society

Best Places to Study
Neilson Library has alcoves where students like to curl up and read. The Campus Center is also a popular place to study, though some students find all of the activity distracting.

The Lowdown
ON ACADEMICS

Did You Know?
Smith is the largest women's college in the United States.

Through the Five College Consortium (made up of Smith, Mount Holyoke College, Hampshire College, University of Massachusetts-Amherst, and Amherst College), students can take classes at any of the five colleges.

Smith's founder, Sophia Smith, was encouraged to leave her fortune to Amherst College. Instead, she stipulated in her will that the money be used "for the establishment and maintenance of an institution for the higher education of women." Smith opened in 1875 with 14 students and six professors.

Degrees Awarded:
Bachelor of Arts, Bachelor of Science (only for Engineering), Master of Arts (Italian, Biological Sciences, Music, Philosophy, Religion, Teaching), Master of Education, Master of Education of the Deaf, Master of Fine Arts in Dance, Playwriting, Master of Science in Exercise and Sports Studies, Doctor of Philosophy, Cooperative Ph.D. Program with the Five Colleges, Master/Ph.D. of Social Work

Full-time Faculty:
285

Student-to-Faculty Ratio:
9:1

Average Course Load:
4 courses

AP Test Score Requirements:
4 or 5 (can be used to count towards the degree or to accelerate within a department)

IB Test Score Requirements:
Final scores are reviewed and approved by the registrar.

Students Speak Out
ON ACADEMICS

"One of the best parts of Smith is the low faculty-to-student ratio; a lot of us take it for granted."

"My classes are so interesting. **One of my professors is one of the most intelligent people I've met**. She's the first Latina woman I've met that's in an important academic position. She's important to me personally and academically. The work that she focuses on is really relevant; it's not just abstract theory."

Q "I love my classes. I've had classes where every time I leave, **the world seems different because I've been so enraptured by what I've learned**. For instance, an East Asian literature class with the topic 'Gendered Fate' really focused a lot on women's studies and feminist theory that I've always believed in, and it helped me to articulate and vocalize my thoughts. By the end of the semester, I was able to process the literature on my own terms, which is the essence of education."

Q "The teachers are all very engaging and care about their students. Some of my friends at other schools have told me stories about professors who seem to be primarily interested in writing a book or having students help them with their research. Here at Smith, I feel that **teaching the students is the most important thing to the professors**."

Q "Most teachers are great, enthusiastic, and helpful, though some are not. Some classes are amazing, but **a few put me to sleep**."

Q "**Academics are intense**. You really have to figure out time management and prioritize. Sometimes that means not having a social life and coming home at 3 a.m. every night for two weeks. Professors sometimes think we're geniuses and give us way more than we can actually handle. In the end, though, it's worth it because it makes you know your stuff."

The College Prowler Take
ON ACADEMICS

The challenging and invigorating academic environment is what Smith is best known for. Academics here are Ivy League caliber, but the all-female environment makes it feel less competitive. The primary complaint of students when it comes to academics is that they are hard. There is no such thing as an "easy" class at Smith. Even exercise classes have required reading and writing assignments. Students at Smith work extremely hard. All-nighters are common, and no one gets enough sleep. Though the academics can be overwhelming at times, most say that Smith is challenging but not impossible.

The college's professors are consistently cited as one of the school's best attributes. Many go out of their way to make the material exciting. It is not unheard of for a professor to come to class in costume or armed with homemade cookies. Professors will always find time to meet with you after class or respond to your e-mails. The relationships are largely based on the amount of effort put in by the student. While it is possible to characterize the majority of the faculty as liberal, it would be a mistake to say that all faculty members bring their political opinions into their teaching. Though many express their views, very few, if any, are closed to hearing dissenting opinions. Professors are more committed to the academic material and making sure that students get the full picture than preaching their personal opinions.

The College Prowler™ Grade on
Academics: A-

A high Academics grade generally indicates that professors are knowledgeable, accessible, and genuinely interested in their students' welfare. Other determining factors include class size, how well professors communicate, and whether or not classes are engaging.

Local Atmosphere

The Lowdown
ON LOCAL ATMOSPHERE

Region:
New England

City, State:
Northampton, Massachusetts

Setting:
Suburb

Distance from Boston:
2 hours

Distance from New York City:
3.5 hours

Points of Interest:
The Words and Pictures Museum, Northhampton Film Festival, Connecticut River Greenway State Park, Norwottuck Rail Trail, The Northampton State Hospital

City Websites:
www.noho.com
www.city.northampton.ma.us

Students Speak Out
ON LOCAL ATMOSPHERE

"The town is too ritzy. It doesn't know the meaning of poverty, and it's very narrow-minded when it comes to socio-economic politics. Everything closes around 10 at night."

Q "Northampton is indescribable. You'll have to see it for yourself. I'd say **it's a funky town**, but it also has the feel of a safe, close-knit town. There are plenty of places to visit, and, of course, there's the Five College system, which provides more to do if one doesn't want to be in Northampton. Another thing I love about Northampton is that it's a small town but has three sushi places."

Q "Northampton is a wonderful town, **it's pretty artsy and almost 'too quaint.'** There are also some cool music venues like Pearl Street and the Iron Horse. Stay away from buying stuff at overpriced boutique stores on Main Street."

Q "NoHo is really laid-back. **There are street performers that engage passersby**. They are really cool. You're able to make eye contact and have conversations with people. There's pleasant human interaction that so often gets cut out of communities."

Q "I'm from D.C., so it's hard to compete with another city. They try really hard here. **It's 'bourgeoisie bohemian,'** low-key and intellectual with coffee shops and performers. But, it's not very diverse, and it seems a little contrived."

Q "It's cutesy, but coming from a big city, it was hard to adjust. But, it's not the small stereotype; **Northampton has a thriving cultural and political community**. Plus, it has a whole lot of smart, beautiful lesbians!"

The College Prowler Take
ON LOCAL ATMOSPHERE

The word most often used to describe the town is "quaint." Northampton is off-beat and has a bustling cultural atmosphere. It is "bourgeoisie bohemian"—that is, a predominantly liberal, white, and upper-middle-class suburb. It is not unusual to see middle-aged activists protesting on the street corners, waving signs and wearing Converse sneakers. Most of the stores are locally- owned shops. There are thrift shops, used-book stores, coffee shops, and funky boutiques.

Safety & Security

The Lowdown
ON SAFETY & SECURITY

The College Prowler™ Grade on
Local Atmosphere: C

A high Local Atmosphere grade indicates that the area surrounding campus is safe and scenic. Other factors include nearby attractions, proximity to other schools, and the town's attitude toward students.

Number of Public Safety Officers:
18

Phone for Smith College Public Safety:
Extension 800 (emergencies)
(413) 585-2490 (non-emergencies)

Health Center Office Hours:
8:30 a.m. – 4:30 p.m., Monday through Friday. However, there is a 24-hour nurse for urgent medical problems.

Safety Services:
Self defense classes, shuttle/escort van, emergency phones, disability van shuttle service

Want to know more about all the local hot spots around campus? Check out the College Prowler book on Smith at *www.collegeprowler.com*.

Students Speak Out
ON SAFETY & SECURITY

The College Prowler Take
ON SAFETY & SECURITY

{ "I feel very safe. In two years, I've never had an incident where I've been threatened or come into contact with a scary individual."

Q "Many of my friends in other schools, especially large universities, have to sign in their friends in order for them to get into the building. There are **no security cards here**. I never feel scared or worried walking around at night."

Q "I feel really safe on campus, but **I'm not a fan of Public Safety**. I feel that they don't really know what they're doing, and they don't do that much to begin with. I've also seen them harass students occasionally and not take their problems seriously."

Q "It's a safe school. But, it's so safe that campus security has too much time on their hands. **Public safety is really slow with little things like opening buildings**, and that's something that a lot of people complain about. Often, they give people the third degree when you just need to get a bag from a locked building. Also, they seem like they're always trying to get people in trouble."

Q "It is very safe. You can't say that it's 100 percent [safe], but **I have never felt threatened**, even when I was walking alone in the dark. It is one of the safest campuses I have been to. But Public Safety sucks."

Q "I've always felt pretty safe on campus. **It gets a little creepy late at night**, as all the lights are starting to go out and it gets very quiet. I think campus security is relatively efficient."

Students are in agreement that although there is occasional crime on and around campus, they feel secure and are not concerned about their safety. There is a general feeling of safety on campus that adds to a community of trust. In their houses, students leave their toiletries and towels in the bathrooms and often leave their doors unlocked. However, the feeling of safety and security on campus can lead students to take risks that they otherwise would not. Thefts have occurred when students have left their doors unlocked over the weekend or during a house party. While Smith is a very safe campus, it's not immune to random acts of theft. While there is 24-hour officer patrolling of the campus, the officers are rarely seen. Some students have also noted that often lights are out on campus, making it difficult to see people and the sidewalk. There are also insufficient emergency blue-lights.

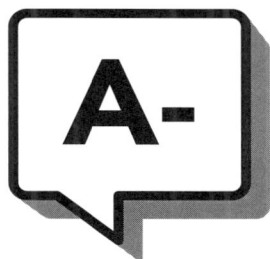

The College Prowler™ Grade on
Safety & Security: A-

A high grade in Safety & Security means that students generally feel safe, campus police are visible, blue-light phones and escort services are readily available, and safety precautions are not overly necessary.

Computers

Students Speak Out
ON COMPUTERS

"You can definitely get by without having a computer, especially if you live on the quad. There's a 24-hour computer lab in the basement of one of the houses."

Q "You can definitely survive without a computer at Smith. I find that the **library computer lab is almost always available in the evenings**. Some classes use the lab during the day. There are plenty of computers around campus to check e-mail on, and whatever else you may need. You don't really need a computer unless you'll be going off campus a lot."

Q "The computer labs have a lot of equipment, so there's space for people. They charge for printing now, though. It's also nice to have your own computer for privacy. They put up all of these firewalls so you can't download music or porn. I would recommend getting an Apple; **we get a lot of viruses**, and Apples never have to worry about them. It's a sweet deal if you get your computer from ITS [Information Technology Services] because it's insured the whole time I'm at Smith. They'll fix my computer for free."

Q "**You will never have a problem finding a computer on campus**. There are computer labs all over, so if you can't find one in one building, which is unlikely, just go to another. I have a computer because I like the privacy of typing in my room, but you don't need one."

Q "I recommend that a new student brings a computer, although it's certainly not needed. I think **I use my computer as much as I use the school lab computers**. They are new, clean, fast, and really nice. The labs are never crowded, and many of them are staffed in case you have a computer problem."

Q "**Computer labs are usually pretty available**, but it is nice to have one's own computer. Also, printing costs five cents a page, so a printer is good, too."

The Lowdown
ON COMPUTERS

High-Speed Network?
Yes

Wireless Network?
Yes

Number of Labs:
There are over 10 small labs, and each of the libraries has a computer station.

Numbers of Computers: About 500

24-Hour Labs:
2

Charge to Print?
Yes, five cents a page

Operating Systems:
Windows XP, Mac OSX, Red Hat Linux

Free Software:
Yes

The College Prowler Take
ON COMPUTERS

Smith is definitely a wired campus. Many classes utilize the Blackboard Website to post homework assignments and readings, as well as use message boards. Many Smithies are addicted to their computers to check their e-mail or *The Daily Jolt*. Most communication between people on campus is done through e-mail. Some people don't even have voicemail in their rooms because they use their phones so little. Whenever there is a problem with the network, which is more frequently than students would like, there is a minor campus crisis because students are so accustomed to constant Internet access. The campus has also been installing wireless connections; there are wireless zones in the libraries, Campus Center, and in some houses.

Facilities

The Lowdown
ON FACILITIES

Student Center:
The Campus Center

Athletic Center:
The Olin Fitness Center, a "mini-gym" in the basement of one of the quad houses

Movie Theatre on Campus?
No

Bowling on Campus?
No

Bar on Campus?
No

Libraries:
4

Museum:
Brown Fine Arts Center

Coffeehouse on Campus?
There is a coffee bar in the café of the Campus Center.

Popular Places to Chill:
Campus Center, anywhere outside when the weather permits

The College Prowler™ Grade on
Computers: B+

A high grade in Computers designates that computer labs are available, the computer network is easily accessible, and the campus' computing technology is up-to-date.

Favorite Things to Do

Every Tuesday and Thursday, many students go to see movies for free shown by the Recreation Council. There are multiple student- and faculty-directed plays and dance performances every semester. The Recreation Council has also brought musical acts like Pink, Busta Rhymes, and Ben Folds to perform. They also sponsored a talk from two former *Real World* cast members.

The academic emphasis at Smith is obvious by the number of lectures and panel discussions it sponsors. Most professors present their individual research and writing in lectures, and there are always outside speakers coming in. Though students are usually overwhelmed with work and commitments, most find a way to take a break and occasionally take in a lecture, play, or performance. The complaint is never that there isn't enough happening on campus; the tough part is balancing it with other commitments.

Students Speak Out
ON FACILITIES

"**The new athletic center is beautiful. It has motivated me to work out more often. The pool is also really nice. I'd say the facilities are top-notch.**"

Q "The facilities are great. **Some of the buildings look a little old**, but Smith has done a pretty good job of rebuilding things that need to be fixed. We have a new gym and a new campus center, which look great."

Q "I think the facilities are amazing. **The Campus Center is beautiful and functional**. It's the center of campus, and every time I'm there I see someone I know, which is the point. It's clean and modern; I think it's really comfortable and visually fun. I think it works wonderfully. It has the bookstore, café, post office, and offices."

Q "The facilities on campus are amazing. They are clean; some of them are even brand new. **The facilities that are older buildings are well-kept**. The student center is fantastic to get food, meet up with friends, purchase necessities from the school store, or shoot some pool."

Q "The gym is sweet. **Everything is brand new**. It's very pretty and has glass walls where you can look out over the campus. In a lot of the labs, the computers are brand new, and they usually have staff to help you out. The Campus Center is amazing! It's brand new, and really sunny and cheerful. A lot of people hang out there, including faculty, professors, and local high school students."

Q "I really like Campus Center because you run into people that you wouldn't normally run nto because of the way the housing and dining systems are set up. **The theater building is pretty extensive** in terms of sound and lighting technology, but it does need renovations."

The College Prowler Take
ON FACILITIES

In case you didn't notice, the Campus Center was cited as one of the only places to hang out on campus. There is really no other public space on campus for socializing. Before it opened, the only place for students to gather was in the Davis Student Center, a small, over-heated building that had a coffee bar and a grill, as well as tables, chairs, and several booths. Despite the fact that some buildings on campus are over 100 years old, the school works hard to keep its buildings and facilities clean and up-to-date. Students never have to complain that the facilities are poorly maintained. With the constant development of new projects—the museum, Campus Center, and Olin Fitness Center all opened within a year of each other—Smith ensures that its students learn and live with the best amenities possible!

The College Prowler™ Grade on
Facilities: A-

A high Facilities grade indicates that the campus is aesthetically pleasing and well-maintained; facilities are state-of-the-art, and libraries are exceptional. Other determining factors include the quality of both athletic and student centers and an abundance of things to do on campus.

Campus Dining

Students Speak Out
ON CAMPUS DINING

"I think the food needs to have a little bit more diversity. Mexican night needs to be more authentic, not Taco Bell night."

"The current dining system is wonderful. **Most houses have their own dining, and students really get to know the kitchen staff,** The staff works hard to give students the best service, and I love being able to ask for chocolate-chip pancakes for breakfasts!"

"There is a proposal that dining will be consolidated. **We already have consolidated dining on weekends**—meaning students go to eat at the larger houses—and it is ridiculously crowded, with few seats available in the whole room. The quality of the food is worse due to the quantity."

"The food is good. I love my kitchen. **I really like knowing my kitchen staff**. I feel that there really is a lot of choice here, considering that it's still a small school. The cooks are very accommodating, too. For instance, this morning they served scrambled eggs for breakfast. I was dying for some fried eggs, and one of the cooks made me fried eggs. That really made my morning!"

"The food tastes pretty good. I think one of the reasons is the fact that we have our own dining rooms. **Cooks don't usually have to make mass quantities of food, so it all tastes better**. Plus, you have the intimate dining room, which always makes mealtime more enjoyable. If you can't find what you like on campus, you can always go to the Campus Center or order from one of the many take out places."

"I think the food has gotten worse. The other day, we had tuna salad for dinner. **The food itself tastes good**, but the options are really bizarre. It felt like we weren't getting meals in the beginning of the semester."

The Lowdown
ON CAMPUS DINING

Freshman Meal Plan Requirement?
Yes. Because of the nature of the Smith dining system, all students who board in houses are automatically on the Smith meal plan. The exceptions to this are students who live in one of the co-ops, Hopkins or Tenney, or in Freidman apartments. These are equipped with their own kitchens, and students share the responsibility of food preparation.

24-Hour On-Campus Eating?
No

Did You Know?

Thursday is candlelight dinner night. The dining rooms are lit by candle and the food is generally more "gourmet." Before candlelight dinner, seniors in many houses have Senior Wine and Cheese, in which a senior hosts the other seniors in her house and serves them a wine and cheese of her choice.

The College Prowler Take
ON CAMPUS DINING

The decentralized dining system is one example of the fact that much of Smith life revolves around small, house-specific communities. Most houses have dining rooms and kitchens and students eat with their housemates. Many first-years work in the kitchens and, as a result, form strong bonds with the kitchen staff. Most people, in fact, form strong bonds with the workers in their kitchen. The workers become surrogate families, preparing soup and special dishes for students with specific dietary needs or for people who are sick.

Off-Campus Dining

The Lowdown
ON OFF-CAMPUS DINING

The College Prowler™ Grade on
Campus Dining: B-

Our grade on Campus Dining addresses the quality of both school-owned dining halls and independent on-campus restaurants as well as the price, availability, and variety of food.

Best Pizza: College Pizza

Best Chinese: Taipei & Tokyo

Best Breakfast: Jake's Diner

Best Healthy: Haymarket Cafe

Best Delivery:
CK's Late Night, (413) 587-3998, late night delivery exclusively for Smith College; everything from omelets and bagels, to nachos, to wraps, to cookies!

24-Hour Eating? No

Best Place to Take Your Parents:
Spoleto, Eastside Grill, Pizzeria Paradiso

Student Favorites:
La Veracruzana, Fresh Pasta Bistro, Taipei & Tokyo, India House

Students Speak Out
ON OFF-CAMPUS DINING

The College Prowler Take
ON OFF-CAMPUS DINING

{ "La Veracruzana is one of the last cheap restaurants to go to for quality food. The service is great, and it's a chill environment. Most of the restaurants are expensive for us college students."

Q "**Teapot is good for Chinese and Japanese**, Spoleto is expensive, but very good. Haymarket is good for salads and organic foods and great coffee and juice drinks. Fresh Pasta Bistro is delicious for Italian."

Q "There is an **amazing variety of restaurants**. Basically, they have any kind of food you want. My favorite spots are Vermont Country Deli, Haymarket, and Sylvester's."

Q "Coming from NYC, I've been to some great restaurants. I can confidently say that most of the restaurants in Northampton would survive just fine in the competitive environment of the NYC restaurant business. In short—**good food, good prices**."

Q "There are **a lot of good restaurants within walking distance** and even more in Amherst. India Palace and Fitzwilly's are great, but they're a little expensive. The many cafés downtown are great for less expensive, really good sandwiches. I particularly like Who's Next Café."

Q "Amherst has better restaurants. It's nice to get away and go to a different town for dinner. Also, **the Ground Round at Hampshire Mall is cheap** and easy to get to by the bus. Sometimes, my friends and I go there just to get away."

For a town of only 30,000 people, Northampton boasts a surprising array of restaurant and dining options. From coffee shops to gourmet restaurants, there's something for everyone. The downtown options offer choices for anyone looking to get off campus for a nice meal out. Students, however, say that they don't get to enjoy all of the restaurants Northampton has to offer because they're either too busy or too broke. Most of the restaurants (like many of the stores) don't cater to college students, and many are too pricey for regular eating out. Often, eating out is reserved for special occasions or when family is in town. There are plenty of cheap options, however, in the many diners and cafés.

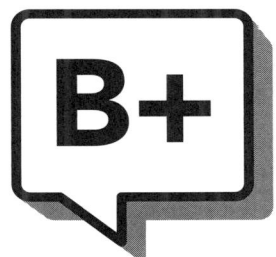

The College Prowler™ Grade on
Off-Campus Dining: B+

A high Off-Campus Dining grade implies that off-campus restaurants are affordable, accessible, and worth visiting. Other factors include the variety of cuisine and the availability of alternative options (vegetarian, vegan, Kosher, etc.).

Campus Housing

Students Speak Out
ON CAMPUS HOUSING

> "I love the housing, especially the bathroom situation. They're really clean. I love having a single, and a lot of people have singles their sophomore year."

Q "I like looking around the living room during house meetings and marveling over the fact that 70 women live in my house. **I like being in an environment where individual space** is respected and community space is treasured."

Q "I transferred in spring semester of my first year, so I was in Hubbard on Green Street. After returning from medical leave, I requested first floor elevator access. **I wanted to live on Green Street or Central Campus because I didn't want to walk on the ice**. But, unless you badger the administration, they aren't very accommodating. I found out the day before I left for school that they just gave me a room on the Quad. I felt like they didn't listen to me because I didn't yell and scream. That's something that a lot of people don't know; you have to be really aggressive to get what you want out of the housing system."

Q "I have lived in Wilder since first semester. It's far away from campus, though. **It's good to be away from the school buildings on the weekend, but it's a tough walk if it's cold or raining**. The good thing about the different areas of campus is that there's something for everyone. People in the Quad tend to be a bit louder and better partiers, although that doesn't mean we're not studious. Since we're away from the academic buildings on campus, it's easier for us to separate the school day and the social life. However, living closer to campus [Green Street or Elm Street] you can get to class and town faster; however, these houses tend to be smaller and a bit quieter."

The Lowdown
ON CAMPUS HOUSING

Undergrads on Campus:
2,500

Number of Dormitories:
36 houses

Room Types:
Single: Room for one student
Double: Room for two students (in some houses only first-years have doubles; in other houses, you can get stuck with a double up to junior year). Some of these have their own bathrooms.
Triple: A few of the houses have triples, which consist of a bathroom and two rooms.

Available for Rent:
Fridge rental (delivered to your room)

Cleaning Service?
Each house has a housekeeper who comes everyday and cleans the bathrooms, hallways, and common living areas.

You Get:
A bed, a desk, a bureau, a bookshelf, a chair, closet or wardrobe, cable TV jack, Ethernet Internet connection and cord, free campus and local phone calls

Bed Type: Standard twin

Q "The **housing system is great the way it is**. You are really able to build a house community, which is incredibly important. The other girls and the house staff become your family."

Q "**The Quad has the most diversity** and a party scene but it is a good 10- to 15-minute walk from classes. There are houses closer to campus. They tend to attract more artistic types but also quiet and borderline antisocial types."

The College Prowler Take
ON CAMPUS HOUSING

The houses are more like sorority houses than dormitories because of the community. Though the houses are not as different as people make them seem, it is important to find one that fits your personality. Some houses are quiet and not very social, which is difficult for students who want to go out every weekend. It is easy to switch houses and often once students find the house that fits them, they find that they never want to leave. While the housing system cultivates a great sense of community, it can be hard to make friends outside of your house. Also, if a student is stuck in a house which she doesn't feel fits her personality, it can be a really isolating experience.

Off-Campus Housing

The Lowdown
ON OFF-CAMPUS HOUSING

Undergrads in Off-Campus Housing:
2-3 percent

Average Rent for a Studio Apartment:
$650/month

Average Rent for a One-Bedroom Apartment:
$800/month

Average Rent for a Two-Bedroom Apartment:
$900/month

Popular Areas:
Nearby Florence and Deerfield are popular for students with cars because they are a lot cheaper than Northampton.

Best Time to Look For A Place:
No specific time, things open up all the time.

The College Prowler™ Grade on
Campus Housing: B+

A high Campus Housing grade indicates that dorms are clean, well-maintained, and spacious. Other determining factors include variety of dorms, proximity to classes, and social atmosphere.

For Assistance Contact
Web:
www.smith.edu/sao/reslife/lottery/speclottery.html
Phone: (413) 585–4940
E-mail: rshannon@smith.edu or housing@smith.edu

Students Speak Out
ON OFF-CAMPUS HOUSING

"First of all, living off campus totally rocks! But, it is kind of difficult to do. Rent in NoHo is pretty high, but if you do your homework, you can make it work out to be comparable to the Smith housing costs."

Q "The **housing committee does not make it easy**. Both of us—myself and my roommate—had pretty severe reasons to be granted permission to leave campus, and we still had to complain a lot. You have to be persistent, and there is quite a process to go through."

Q "I lived on my own for so long, it would have been really difficult for me to adjust to living with a bunch of people younger than I am—I'm an Ada. I have my own car and, as an Ada, I automatically get a spot in the Smith garage. Because I have a car, I can live farther away. **I live in Deerfield which is only about a 15-minute drive**, but it's a lot cheaper because it's more rural. When it snows, though, it can take a long time to get to school."

Q "It was pretty easy to find a place. For my first apartment, I just looked in *The Daily Hampshire Gazette*. I also asked around a lot and **people that I know were able to point me towards a place**. There are also postings all over towns and campus for available apartments or rooms. There is also a site on the UMass Website that posts available places to live."

Q "I already lived in Amherst before starting at Smith, so finding a place wasn't an issue for me—I'm an Ada. Originally, **I found the place using the classifieds in the newspaper**. It wasn't hard to find a place that I could afford and that I liked. Most of the neighborhoods are good, so finding a safe place isn't hard. I have a car, so transportation isn't bad. It's hard because I only come to campus once a day. That can be hard if I have to meet with a professor or a group about a project. Sometimes I'm stuck on campus for a long time. Once I leave to go home, I don't come back for events and things like that. Sometimes I feel like I miss out on a lot. But, I work and have friends in Amherst; my life just does not revolve around Smith like it does with most residential students."

Q "**Off-campus housing is a good option for people who don't necessarily want to live with a bunch of college students**. They also have more independence when it comes to living arrangements, like cleaning and cooking for themselves. Personally, I prefer to take advantage of the fact that I don't have to prepare my own meals. I also love being a part of the house communities and having all kinds of people around me all of the time."

Q "I think transportation is only an issue if the Smithie in question can only find an apartment across town. You know, sometimes you can't really bike in the winter, and it's a long walk if you're, say, close to the Cooley Dick Bridge. Costs are definitely prohibitive, but they're still less expensive than Smith. **My expenses for on-campus living were close to $1,000/month**, and now they're closer to $700, plus I can maintain my vegan diet without becoming anemic—Smith's vegan fare is not the best. If you want to live alone, the cheapest studio I've ever heard of in NoHo is $475. House shares are cheapest, and they're easy to find—check bulletin boards in Thornes and Paradise Copies."

The College Prowler Take
ON OFF-CAMPUS HOUSING

The growing off-campus population includes local women who have chosen to live at home during their time at Smith, as well as a number of women who have been granted permission to live off campus for special circumstances prior to their senior year. Off-campus status is usually granted by lottery to traditional-aged students who have lived in campus houses for at least two years and have a reason to live off campus, usually for senior year. Smith discourages students from living off campus because they see residential life as an integral part of the Smith experience. So, students have to apply to live off campus and their applications are not always approved.

Diversity

The Lowdown
ON DIVERSITY

African American: 6%

Asian American: 9%

Hispanic: 6%

Native American: 1%

White: 71%

International: 7%

Out-of-State: 76%

The College Prowler™ Grade on
Off-Campus Housing: D+

A high grade in Off-Campus Housing indicates that apartments are of high quality, close to campus, affordable, and easy to secure.

Cultural Heritage Groups
Many of the cultural heritage groups are present on campus and sponsor dances, dinners and concerts. They include: Prism ("Queer Students of Color"), Nosotras (Latina Organization), Asian Students Association, Black Students Alliance, EKTA (for students of South Asian heritage), International Students Organization, Native American Women of Smith, and Smith African Students Association.

Most Popular Religions
The most present religion on campus is Christianity, as evidenced by the numerous Christian groups. These include the Radical Catholic Feminists of Smith and the Ecumenical Christian Church.

Political Activity

Most students are politically and socially liberal. Though the campus has its share of protests, students are generally not outspoken about their political views. Many consider the student body to be generally apathetic.

Gay Tolerance

The gay community is one of the most vocal and present groups on campus. Though there are incidents of homophobia on campus, they are isolated incidents. Some students, however, complain that Smith is too accepting of the gay community, that the focus of Smith politics and social life is too often on the gay students.

Economic Status

Unlike many other schools, Smith students reflect the economic bell curve of the country. There is a small number of extremely upper and lower class students, with most students falling somewhere in between.

Students Speak Out
ON DIVERSITY

"**It's more diverse than a lot of other places. It could be a lot better, but it's more diverse than other schools.**"

"It depends on what you mean by 'diversity.' There's definite age diversity because of the Ada Comstock program which enrolls women who are not of traditional college-age. There is gender identification diversity. Racially, it's what you'd expect of a private, New England, liberal arts college. Politically-speaking, **it ranges from fairly conservative to radical-Marxist-separatist-lesbian**."

"It's **not the most diverse school** I've ever been to, but it's also not the least."

"The **campus is diverse in opinions and ideas** but not diverse in social life. There are limits on social activity that restrict people. There aren't enough options to bring people here and get us off campus. Smith has a snobby reputation, and a lot of people don't want to hang out with Smith girls."

"**It's very diverse in terms of sexuality**. It's somewhat diverse racially, but the races don't integrate as much as I would like. It's not too politically diverse."

The College Prowler Take
ON DIVERSITY

Students are divided on how diverse they feel the campus is. Some feel it is like many other private, liberal arts colleges in New England because it is too white. Smith is certainly a typical New England, private, liberal arts college in that it lacks racial diversity. Many students of color complain that they feel isolated and unwelcome because the culture (food, concerts, etc.) does not reflect what they are familiar with. Race is absolutely a tense issue on campus. Some students are eager to make it an issue and a topic of discussion, while others are happy to ignore it. Others complain that Smith is too liberal or too gay-oriented. The perspective varies based on the student's background and own identification.

The College Prowler™ Grade on
Diversity: C-

A high grade in Diversity indicates that ethnic minorities and international students have a notable presence on campus and that students of different economic backgrounds, religious beliefs, and sexual preferences are well-represented.

Guys & Girls

Dress Code
Most students dress however they want: it ranges from preppy, to crunchy, to punk. It's definitely a school where you can wear almost anything and that includes everything from homemade pants to Mohawks, to Steve Madden shoes. There is, however, a dominant "Smith look"—cuffed jeans, vintage T-shirts, trucker hats, and facial piercings.

Students Speak Out
ON GUYS & GIRLS

The Lowdown
ON GUYS & GIRLS

Birth Control Available?
Yes, oral contraceptives, Depo-Provera, diaphragm, cervical cap, morning-after pill

Social Scene
Due to the house system, students can find it hard to meet people who aren't in their houses. Therefore, many relationships and hookups, as well as friendships, tend to be centered around the student's house. However, through clubs, teams, classes, and parties, most students are able to meet people through a variety of social networks.

Hookups or Relationships?
For those Smithies interested in guys, they often stick with long-distance relationships or random, weekend hookups. There are many girls, however, who find nice boys from the surrounding area to date. For the gay community of Smith, the dating scene offers a few more options. There are a large number of people who develop serious relationships with people in their houses (which can lead to dramatic breakups). There are also a lot of random hookups, though many have learned the hard way that what felt random that night is not so random at a small school.

"**It's sparse for straight girls, and pretty good for the queer community, but there's not a lot of dating. Most people hook up or are in relationships.**"

Q "Well, **if you're a straight female, you're going to have to get out to other schools to meet guys**. It has definitely been difficult for me. It's not impossible, though. But, one of the reasons I came here was so I could get away from the dating scene for awhile and just focus on myself, my studies, and deciding where I want my life to go."

Q "It's a hormonal scene. People like each other and are attracted to each other, and there are relationships, but there's this hormonal excitement. **There's a lot of energy and everyone notices other people**. It's exciting to be in an atmosphere where you can appreciate being attracted to people and sometimes acting on it. But, it's not about objectification."

Q "If you're looking for girls, great. **If you're looking for guys, not so great**. The guys that come to the Smith parties usually are kind of annoying and just looking to get a Smith girl in bed. If you want to meet guys, you really have to go off campus, which isn't necessarily a bad thing. Sometimes it's good to break free from the Smith environment; you can feel like you're trapped here."

Q "**It appears to be very homosexual**. Although that doesn't mean that everyone identifies as a lesbian. There seems to be a lot of free love happening, as in no commitments. Some people are committed, but they seem to live on Green Street."

> "**Rarely will you see a boy that matches your preference**. The Boston and Worcester accents drive me nuts. There are not many college guys; it's mostly old, sketchy men. Beware of stalkers; they come in multitudes."

The College Prowler Take
ON GUYS & GIRLS

A lot of questions about dating focus on the trouble that girls have meeting guys. But, that's not the complaint of every Smithie. Some are perfectly content to take a break from dating and spend their college years connecting with friends and focusing on schoolwork. Others just like girls. For the gay student, being at a school with so many women offers dating opportunities that most coed schools do not. However, that does not mean that every gay student is happy with the dating scene. Relationships often occur between two people who have a lot of mutual friends or who live in the same house. So, when breakups happen, it can be difficult to get away from each other. For the straight girl who is looking for a relationship, it's hard. There is an informal straight-girl network, they go to parties together and try to introduce each other to guys. If one of them has guy friends at another school or (gasp!) a real boyfriend, she is expected to introduce her friends to his friends because, presumably, his friends won't be sketchy.

The College Prowler™ Grade on
Guys: N/A

A high grade for Guys indicates that the male population on campus is attractive, smart, friendly, and engaging, and that the school has a decent ratio of guys to girls.

The College Prowler™ Grade on
Girls: B+

A high grade for Girls not only implies that the women on campus are attractive, smart, friendly, and engaging, but also that there is a fair ratio of girls to guys.

Athletics

The Lowdown
ON ATHLETICS

Women's Varsity Sports

Basketball	Soccer
Crew	Softball
Cross Country	Squash
Equestrian	Swimming & Diving
Field Hockey	Tennis
Lacrosse	Track & Field
Skiing	Volleyball

Club Sports
Badminton, boxing, croquet, fencing, ice hockey, lifeguards (synchronized swimming), outing, riding, rugby, sailing, table tennis, ultimate Frisbee (Lunadisc), water polo

Most Popular Sports
Crew, softball, swimming & diving, rugby

Overlooked Teams
Ultimate Frisbee, synchronized swimming

Fields
25 acres of grass fields (they don't have names)

Athletic Division:
NCAA Division III

Conference:
NEWMAC (New England Women's and Men's Athletic Conference)

School Mascot:
Pioneers (it used to be the Unicorns, before that, it was the Virgins)

Students Speak Out
ON ATHLETICS

"A fair amount of students participate, but few students consider themselves more than fair-weather fans."

Q "A **lot of people either do club sports or varsity sports**. I wouldn't say that they're huge on campus, though. Very few people go to support the games. Rugby is a lot of fun, though, and it's not as time-consuming as other sports."

Q "Varsity sports are supported but not huge. **The team with the most support is the rugby team**, which is a club sport, but it is treated as a varsity sport because of all of the student support. The softball team also gets a lot of support."

Q "Smith athletics are pretty varied. I'm learning squash in an ESS [Exercise Sports Studies] class. I've been to cross country meets and the **people are full of Smith pride**."

Q "**Varsity sports are really big**. Club sports don't get enough respect or money that would provide coaches, referees, and goalposts. Club sports are thought of as merely social scenes that encourage drinking, as opposed to varsity sports, which are taken very seriously."

Q "In my opinion, **sports are one of Smith's last priorities**. There's so much else going on, people just don't notice sports. The people that play sports are really intense about their experience. Spectators really aren't a major presence, however."

The College Prowler Take
ON ATHLETICS

Athletics on campus are an important aspect of college life for the students who are involved in them. For athletes, sports are a major time commitment which their social lives often revolve around. Many club sports (particularly rugby) are known for the social life that comes along with joining the team. Usually, however, the people at games are there to cheer on their school and their friends, not because sports are a major part of Smith. However, more students get involved in more important games. Whenever Smith plays rival Mount Holyoke College, the Athletic Association gives out T-shirts that say "Official Holyoke Heckler" to the first 50 fans. Though sports are not a major aspect of Smith life, they certainly can be for those students that want them to be.

The College Prowler™ Grade on
Athletics: C

A high grade in Athletics indicates that students have school spirit, that sports programs are respected, that games are well-attended, and that intramurals are a prominent part of student life.

Drug Scene

Q "There are **a lot of drugs on campus**. If drugs are your thing, you can find most things. Mostly, it's weed and coke. A lot of people have money to spend on drugs."

Q "**Marijuana is prevalent**, as is alcohol, in the Quad. There is also some prescription—i.e. upper-middle-class—drug usage."

Q "There is **a huge underground cocaine scene**, which is surprising, but this is only if you get in the loop. There is definitely more pot smoking than drinking. Smith is a very herb-friendly."

Q "It's **moderately difficult to get marijuana**. I don't think I could get other drugs if I tried."

The Lowdown
ON DRUG SCENE

Most Prevalent Drugs on Campus:
Alcohol, marijuana, caffeine, Adderall, Ritalin, cocaine

Liquor-Related Referrals: 20

Liquor-Related Arrests: 2

Drug-Related Referrals: 10

Drug-Related Arrests: 0

Drug Counseling Programs:
The Office of Student Affairs
Phone: (413) 585-4940

Student Health Services
Phone: (413) 585-2830

Services: Alcohol Awareness workshops, Bodywide Peer Education, Peer Sexuality Educators, group therapy for self-cutting, eating disorders, and students with terminally ill family members

The College Prowler Take
ON DRUG SCENE

Though there is fairly significant usage of drugs on campus, it's mostly underground. People do drugs with other people that do drugs; no one is running around trying to sell drugs. If you want drugs, it's possible to get them, but it's not like dealers are announcing their presence. For some reason, cocaine is a fairly common drug on campus, though it is mostly underground. This is often attributed to the pockets of extremely wealthy students. There is more significant usage of softer drugs; alcohol and marijuana usage are highly-prevalent on campus. Non-users feel very little pressure to indulge in drugs, however, because of how insular the various drug-using groups are. Drugs are a dominant force on campus for the students that choose to be a part of that scene; those that want to stay away from it don't have a problem doing so.

The College Prowler™ Grade on
Drug Scene: C-

A high grade on Drug Scene indicates that drugs are not a noticeable part of campus life; drug use is not visible, and no pressure to use them seems to exist.

Students Speak Out
ON DRUG SCENE

{ "It's fairly simple to get drugs. Weed and alcohol are the most common, and they're very prevalent."

Campus Strictness

The Lowdown
ON CAMPUS STRICTNESS

What Are You Most Likely to Get Caught Doing on Campus?
Drinking, streaking, lewd conduct in a public location

Students Speak Out
ON CAMPUS STRICTNESS

"People have gotten into some serious problems with alcohol and pot. If you keep it concealed, you might be okay, but you're definitely taking a big risk."

Q "Recently, **our school has taken a conservative turn for the worse** in enforcing drug and alcohol policies. Generally, situations are ignored, but when you get caught it is blown way out of proportion."

Q "This year, the **drinking policies have gotten a lot stricter**. Public safety is enforcing alcohol policies a lot more."

Q "They **just started cracking down** this year on drugs. Be careful about smoking pot in your room. Drinking isn't that big a deal, most HRs don't care unless you do it in front of them."

Q "When it comes to drugs, people rarely get caught. But when they do, you're automatically turned over to the Northampton police. If you get caught drinking, **it's just a slap on the wrist**. They don't try to catch people; you usually get caught if your neighbors report you. That rarely happens, but sometimes it does. They won't come on their own, but they come if there's been a complaint. It's about respect. Some people are allergic to smoke, and when people smoke in their rooms, other people get sick. So, Public Safety has to be called. Usually, people talk to each other about it, but sometimes they'll report it."

Q "**House parties are overregulated**. But, enforcing regulations is totally dependent on individual Res Life staff."

The College Prowler Take
ON CAMPUS STRICTNESS

The drinking and drug policies on campus have been the source of a great deal of controversy on campus. In the fall of 2003, a new policy was implemented in which students that were caught with narcotics were immediately turned over to the Northampton police. While this policy change concerned the student body at first, it quickly became clear that not much had changed. The campus police do not become involved unless someone calls them or they happen to find someone outside who is breaking a rule. Generally, students deal with drug usage themselves, and campus security is never notified. If caught with drugs, however, the consequences can involve the police and getting kicked out of campus housing, depending on the severity of the situation.

The College Prowler™ Grade on
Campus Strictness: D

A high Campus Strictness grade implies an overall lenient atmosphere; police and RAs are fairly tolerant, and the administration's rules are flexible.

Overall Experience

> "One of the worst aspects of Smith is **the neglect of understanding socio-economic differences**; the way some people are privileged is different from the way other people are privileged, and that's not respected here. Everyone is privileged and they should share it. They're timid about talking about class; there's a lack of communication and discussion. Smith doesn't talk about it."

> "**I love that it's an all-female environment**. Everything caters to you; you're in an environment that depends not on how you look, but on your ideas, beliefs, and opinions. I'm straight, and I'm really glad that I'm here."

Students Speak Out
ON OVERALL EXPERIENCE

The College Prowler Take
ON OVERALL EXPERIENCE

{ "If you get bored easily, Smith may not be the school for you, unless you are looking for a highly academic, anti-'Animal House'/'Van Wilder' college experience." }

> "I had to decide between Smith and a coed school, and **I made the right choice**. There's a feeling of solidarity and security. Also, I think that it's an automatic control group. It's limited to females, and it makes you appreciate how different every individual is within the category 'female.' It's empowering to be one of those women and a part of this group that I admire."

> "I love the supportive, all-women community, and **I love being in classes without guys so that the professors can tailor to women's learning styles**. Especially in engineering; it's great to be in a class of 100 percent women instead of 15 percent, as is the case at many technical schools."

> "The **amazing financial aid and JYA** are what brought and kept me here. But, Smith is notorious for refusing to talk about its negative aspects. And there are negative aspects, like, the lesbian atmosphere. It's amazing and brings a lot to the school's diversity, but no one talks about sexual harassment. I've been grabbed at parties, and girls have tried to make out with me, and that's not okay. If that was some guy, it wouldn't have been okay, and it's not okay for girls to do it."

One thing is for sure: Smith is not for everyone. Talk to any student and you'll probably find that they have a love/hate relationship with the school. Some people cannot handle the single-sex environment, while others find it to be their favorite part of Smith. Some are miserable with the social scene, feeling limited in their options, while others are perfectly content. It's a college of extremes. One person's favorite part can be another's most hated aspect of the school. However, when it comes down to it, the education that you get while at Smith is top-notch. The small classes and wide range of academic opportunities ensure that students are engaged and challenged. Moreover, Smith is committed to providing opportunities that most students don't get until graduate school. Students are able to do independent research with professors in their first year, while others write theses that are on the graduate level.

It's not a huge party school, and it's not a stereotypical college experience, but, for most Smith students, that's exactly the way they like it. Though the campus can be claustrophobic at times, there is a tremendous sense of community. The comfort and security of the campus ensures that students have four years to discover themselves and really come into their own. Time and again, alums have told students that they are still very close to their friends from Smith. The campus community fosters tight bonds that last far beyond graduation.

The Inside Scoop

The Lowdown
ON THE INSIDE SCOOP

Traditions

Tea takes place every Friday afternoon at 4:00, when students gather in their house living rooms to enjoy pastries, fruit, and tea. It's a great time to relax at the end of a hard week and get caught up with people that you might not see every day. Occasionally, houses have teas with themes.

Convocation marks the formal beginning of the college year. The evening before classes begin, all members of the Smith community (including the faculty, dressed in caps and gowns) gather in John M. Greene Hall to listen to an opening address and a performance by the Glee Club. Each house dresses according to a common theme. The costumes range from togas and lingerie to outfits made entirely out of Saran Wrap.

Mountain Day is a welcome surprise break from classes. The president chooses a beautiful fall day and announces the holiday by ringing the college bells. All classes are cancelled for the day and students spend the day apple picking, boating on Paradise Pond, picnicking, and getting caught up on work!

Traditions (Continued...)

Celebration is a series of songs, skits, and readings. It takes place on the second Thursday of November and it is a time when students gather to celebrate female sexuality. It originated over 10 years ago as a candlelight vigil in response to a homophobic incident in one of the Quad houses. It has since evolved into a night of celebrating, dances, skits, and songs. There is a performance from each of the Quad houses, and then students move throughout campus where other houses have set up booths (everything from handing out hot chocolate, to head shaving, to a kissing line). The event culminates at the Campus Center where students dance and hang out.

Ivy Day and Illumination Night are traditional parts of Commencement Weekend. For Ivy Day, alumnae escort the seniors (who are dressed entirely in white) in a parade around campus. Then the seniors plant ivy to symbolize the connection between the college and its graduates. On Illumination Night, the campus is lit only by colored paper lanterns. The college basks in a soft glow, perfect for reminiscing on four years of Smith education and escapades.

Things I Wish I Knew Before Coming to Smith:
- It's harder to take classes off campus than it seems.
- There is a lot of work outside of classes, which is a hard adjustment coming from high school, where most of the work takes place in the classroom.
- The winters are frigid!
- The house you're in really shapes your experience.
- Girls drink a lot!
- Do a pre-orientation program.
- Buying your computer through the school ensures that you will have free access to technical assistance all four years.

Finding a Job or Internship

The Lowdown
ON FINDING A JOB OR INTERNSHIP

Career Development Office (CDO) -
http://sophia.smith.edu/cdo/

Advice

Use the CDO resources as much as possible before you're a senior. They offer services that can be of use to any student in any year. They give career counseling that can help you figure out not only what kind of job you want after you graduate, but what kind of internships and opportunities might be right for you. They also give great advice on cover letters and resumes.

Career Center Resources & Services

- Suit Yourself – lends students suits for interviews and formal events
- Interview Preparation
- Cover Letters and Resume Workshops
- Drop-in Hours – students can stop in without an appointment for a 15-minute consultation
- AlumNet – network of thousands of alums students can contact for job advice and to network within an industry
- Myers-Briggs Type Indicator (MBTI) - a personality profile students can take to help them in their job search
- Self-Assessment Tests
- Confidential Career Consultations
- Weekly Informational Sessions – recruiters speak to interested students about job opportunities
- Praxis – Students are awarded a $2,000 stipend when doing an unpaid summer internship

AVERAGE SALARY INFORMATION

The Lowdown:
The following statistics represent the national average starting salaries for graduates by major as reported by NACE (National Association of Colleges and Employers) in January.

Chemistry - $37,733
Economics - $39,438
Education - $39,438
Engineering - $41,669
English Language and Literature - $28,786
Foreign Languages and Letters - $31,048
Geology - $32,828
Government - $31,183
History - $31,862
Mathematics - $40,512
Physics - $42,365
Psychology - $27,683
Visual and Performing Arts - $28,982
Other Humanities - $29,694
Other Physical Sciences – $31,000
Other Social Sciences - $29,098

Want to know the ins and outs concerning jobs and internships at Smith? Check out the College Prowler book on Smith at *www.collegeprowler.com*.

The Best & Worst

The Ten BEST Things About Smith:

1. No guys
2. Great desserts
3. Beer is free at house parties
4. You don't have to shave your legs
5. Gorgeous living accommodations
6. Skating or boating on Paradise Pond
7. Lots of streaking
8. Five minutes from the only hospital in the area
9. Theme parties
10. Amazing, accessible professors

The Ten WORST Things About Smith:

1. No guys
2. Long winters
3. Bridge traffic
4. The stinky soy-sauce-like-substance they put down to melt the ice—it doesn't work well
5. Lack of acceptance of conservative students
6. Isolation from the other colleges
7. Highly-regulated parties
8. Conservative administration
9. Decentralized campus
10. Complaints from NoHo residents that live near houses

Brown University

45 Prospect Street, Providence, RI 02912
www.brown.edu   (401) 863-2378

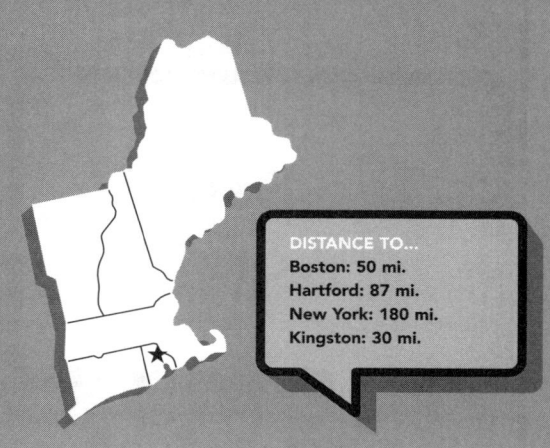

DISTANCE TO...
Boston: 50 mi.
Hartford: 87 mi.
New York: 180 mi.
Kingston: 30 mi.

"Brown's liberal nature and open curriculum exceed that of the average liberal arts school."

Total Enrollment:
5,660
Acceptance Rate:
16%
Tuition:
$31,334
Top 10% of High School Class:
87%
SAT Range
Verbal	Math	Total
640 – 750	650 – 750	1290 – 1500

ACT Range
Verbal	Math	Total
N/A	N/A	26-31

Most Popular Majors:
9% History
7% Biology
7% International Relations and Affairs
6% Business/Managerial Economics
5% Political Science and Government

Students Also Applied To:*
Cornell University, Harvard University, Princeton University, Stanford University, Yale University

*For more school info check out www.collegeprowler.com

Table of Contents

Academics	499
Local Atmosphere	501
Safety & Security	502
Computers	504
Facilities	505
Campus Dining	507
Off-Campus Dining	508
Campus Housing	510
Off-Campus Housing	511
Diversity	513
Guys & Girls	514
Athletics	516
Greek Life	517
Drug Scene	518
Campus Strictness	520
Overall Experience	521
The Inside Scoop	522
Finding a Job or Internship	523
The Best & Worst	524

College Prowler Report Card

Academics	A
Local Atmosphere	A-
Safety & Security	C+
Computers	B+
Facilities	B
Campus Dining	C-
Off-Campus Dining	A-
Campus Housing	B+
Off-Campus Housing	A-
Diversity	B
Guys	B+
Girls	B
Athletics	C+
Greek Life	C+
Drug Scene	B
Campus Strictness	B+

Academics

The Lowdown
ON ACADEMICS

Degrees Awarded:
Bachelor of Arts (B.A.), Bachelor of Science (Sc.B.), Master, Doctorate, Combined Degrees

Undergraduate Schools:
Applied Mathematics, Engineering, Biology and Medicine

Full-time Faculty:
573 (plus 168 adjunct and visiting)

Faculty with Terminal Degree:
97%

Student-to-Faculty Ratio:
8:1

Average Course Load:
4 courses

Sample Academic Clubs:
African Students Association, Asian American Student Association, Engineering Society, Women Students at Brown, Brown Film Society, Shakespeare on the Green, Pre-Med chapter AMSA (American Medical Student Association)

Special Degree Options
Brown's Program in Liberal Medical Education (PLME) is an eight-year program that combines a liberal arts education with medical school. Students are accepted to the college and medical school as freshmen and spend eight years at Brown completing their B.A. and M.D..

Brown also offers master's degrees in some departments for undergraduates who want to add on an additional year of study.

AP Test Score Requirements
Students might receive credit for scores of 4 or 5, but check the Brown Website for a complete list of accepted tests and scores. Typically, high AP test scores will get you placement in advanced classes but not course credit.

Best Places to Study
The John D. Rockefeller Library (The Rock) or the Sciences Library (Sci-Li), The Blue Room, coffee shops on Thayer Street, and dorm computer clusters and study rooms.

Did You Know?
Brown does not have any general course requirements. While you must complete a total of 30 courses and specific courses within a concentration (Brown's word for major), there are absolutely no course requirements. You'll never have to take another math class or English class if you don't want to. This system, known as the New Curriculum, started in 1969.

In line with this educational philosophy, most classes at Brown can be taken with a grade option of A/B/C/No Credit, or Satisfactory/No Credit.

An independent concentration is a course of study designed by the student with the guidance of professors and deans that combines classes from different concentrations to show relations and connections between different studies.

Students Speak Out
ON ACADEMICS

> "Many of my classes were interesting. Sometimes when taking many courses in the same department, I found that they were a bit repetitive."

> "Because there is no core curriculum, you aren't typically forced into any bad courses. The skills and styles of teachers at Brown vary widely, as they probably do everywhere. But Brown does tell you to judge for yourself. The **first several weeks of every semester are 'shopping periods'** during which you can try out as many classes as you can pack into your day. Most students shop at least a little. Shopping can be extremely useful for weeding out the incoherent mumblers and the digressive babblers, and for hunting down the best teachers."

> "Almost every semester, **I have taken at least one course that has had a profound impact** on my life. These classes have ranged from Early Modern Philosophy, to Intro to Object-Oriented Programming, to Seminar in the Teaching of Writing, to Intro to Neuroscience."

> "It took me a long time to figure out what I really wanted to concentrate in because **Brown really lets you explore whatever you want** when you get here. I wouldn't say that's a bad thing. I decided on visual arts, and I'm really happy about that. I knew I didn't want to go to an art school because I wanted to take more academic classes and have more of a background for my work, and that's exactly what Brown allowed me to do. I made my own experience out of it."

> "My experiences with graduate students as teachers have been really good. Freshman year, I took a philosophy class and the material was really good, but **the professor was horrible**. It was one of the few classes I've taken where a TA was in charge of teaching in a section, not just reviewing the material, and the TA was so much better than the professor."

> "I took a lecture and a seminar with my thesis advisor. At first, after the lecture, our relationship was distant. In the seminar, however, we had in-depth discussions and had **dinner at the professor's house with a guest lecturer** from the class, who was a big policy maker in his field."

> "A lot of classes I have taken in my first two years have been **taught by graduate students.** It's not that professors don't try to get to know you, but you have to take initiative and go to office hours to get to know them."

The College Prowler Take
ON ACADEMICS

At Brown, persistence and personal responsibility play a big role in defining the undergraduate career. Students are rewarded for learning to work within Brown's small and intimate academic departments. In other words, it is always possible to work the system. Students always have a good chance of getting into high-level classes even if they are outside their concentration. Many students come to Brown uncertain of their concentrations, and many switch their concentrations more than once in their undergraduate career. Brown's academic philosophy encourages exploration into new areas of study which can spark new interests or projects. In general, Brown believes that every student knows what's best for him or herself.

The College Prowler™ Grade on
Academics: A

A high Academics grade generally indicates that professors are knowledgeable, accessible, and genuinely interested in their students' welfare. Other determining factors include class size, how well professors communicate, and whether or not classes are engaging.

Local Atmosphere

Students Speak Out
ON LOCAL ATMOSPHERE

"**Providence is an ideal city for college.** The city is easily navigable, not overpowering, and still has plenty to do. Brown students have enough clout to influence city council elections."

Q "**Providence is what you make of it**. The town has a lot to offer—from parks to hang out in, to bars, clubs, and restaurants. Other universities are present, but aside from RISD [Rhode Island School of Design], there is little interaction between Brown students and other area university students. Check out the Waterfire and the mall on rainy days!"

Q "Personally, I can't imagine not going to school in a city. Brown, I would say, is in the perfect location for a school. It is on a hill, so it seems secluded, but just walking down the hill puts you in the center of downtown Providence. Providence is a small city, but it definitely has a city feel. There are **always things to do and places to go**. The Providence Place Mall, the largest mall in New England, is a 15-minute walk away."

Q "There is the Trinity Repertory Center, which shows Broadway-caliber plays, the Fleet Skating Center, the Providence Convention Center, Waterplace Park, and many restaurants and parks. **Providence can be considered a college town** since there is RISD, Providence College, and Johnston and Wales."

Q "The social options at Brown and in Providence are really very ideal. Many students become unhappy going to school in a small town where they are forced to stay on campus. Brown offers **a wide array of on-campus events**, but the city is so accessible if ever you are inclined to go off campus."

The Lowdown
ON LOCAL ATMOSPHERE

Region:
Northeast

City, State:
Providence, Rhode Island

Setting:
Urban

Distance from Boston:
50 miles

Distance from New York:
180 miles

Major Sports Teams:
New England Patriots (NFL)

Points of Interest:
The RISD Museum, The beaches in Newport, Waterplace Park, Roger Williams Zoo, Purgatory Chasm, the outdoor ice rink, downtown, Lupo's Heartbreak Hotel

City Websites:
www.Providenceri.com
www.brown.dailyjolt.com
www.oso.com

"It's nice that there is **a social life that revolves around the school**. I started college at a big university in New York, and I always felt like people were off doing their own things in their own world. Here, you really get to know the people in your class."

The College Prowler Take
ON LOCAL ATMOSPHERE

Safety & Security

Providence is a city, but it's not a big city. Sometimes the desire for the city to grow and incorporate new and exciting features is at odds with its efforts to maintain the small-town feel. If you want to go to a club one night, a museum the next day, a hip-hop show, and eat a few meals, you can cram it all into a weekend. Some Brown students never really explore the city, let alone the places less than an hour's drive in any direction from College Hill. There are beaches, state parks, ski areas, and vineyards close enough to make day-trips to, all surrounded by quaint New England towns. Students complain about the lack of a drive-in theater or an all-night diner, without realizing that there are several of both about 10 minutes away. The city simply has too much history, too many quirks, and too much to offer for the intrepid Brown student to find it boring.

The Lowdown
ON SAFETY & SECURITY

Number of Brown Police:
32

Additional Security Personnel:
16

Phone:
(401) 863-3103

Safety Services:
Blue-light phones, emergency e-mail notification, shuttle and escort service, Safewalk program

The College Prowler™ Grade on
Local Atmosphere: A-

A high Local Atmosphere grade indicates that the area surrounding campus is safe and scenic. Other factors include nearby attractions, proximity to other schools, and the town's attitude toward students.

Health Center Office Hours

Appointments for non-medical emergencies:

Monday and Friday:
8:30 a.m.-4.15 p.m.

Tuesday, Wednesday, and Thursday:
9:30 a.m.-4:15 p.m.

Students Speak Out
ON SAFETY & SECURITY

"I think that there are certain areas off campus that you should tend to avoid when you are walking alone, but you don't have to worry about much on campus."

Q "**My computer got stolen freshman year from my room**. I left my window cracked open, and someone crawled in. My roommate had her jewelry stolen at the same time. Still, I feel relatively safe on campus. I think security has improved since then. I walk home alone sometimes. I use the shuttles but not the Safewalk program."

Q "I never had a problem with security. They respond well when you lock yourself out of your room and don't hassle you too much when drinking is involved. However, **you have to watch your back at night** because there have been a lot of muggings, and security isn't everywhere. There has also been much dispute over arming Brown police with firearms."

Q "Safety is not one of Brown's strong points. It is, after all, located in the city. If you follow basic safety procedures, however, you should be fine. Walk in groups, and stay in well-lit areas. Personally, I have never had any problems with it, and I don't know anybody who has. **Providence is rated one of the safest cities in the United States**, but it's still a city. You just have to keep your wits about you when you're walking around."

Q "I think it's good that the University uses e-mail to keep us informed about crimes going on around campus, but I think **they are a little sensationalist**, and they also make it sound worse than the crime actually was. In some of the situations, I was actually part of the incident, but when I read the e-mails I knew they made it sound worse than it actually was. It's no worse than most other urban schools."

The College Prowler Take
ON SAFETY & SECURITY

Brown students receive an alert by e-mail every time there is a major crime committed on campus or the university perceives a specific safety threat. Over the last year, in response to a real and perceived increase in crime on and around campus, Brown increased the hours of campus police, hired security officers to patrol at night, and hired a private consulting firm to address the problems. The University tries very hard to inform the students about the status of crimes on campus and provides services to encourage smart and safe movement on campus at night. The shuttle runs on a route all the way around campus and comes approximately every five minutes until 3 am. The escort, which picks up and drops off students from off-campus housing to any location on campus, runs every night from 5 p.m. until 3 a.m..

The College Prowler™ Grade on
Safety & Security: C+

A high grade in Safety & Security means that students generally feel safe, campus police are visible, blue-light phones and escort services are readily available, and safety precautions are not overly necessary.

Computers

Did You Know?

Brown has a pioneering computer science department. One interesting ongoing project on campus is The Cave, an eight-foot cubicle where high-resolution stereo graphics are projected onto three walls and the floor to create a virtual-reality experience. The Cave is used for medical, archeological, artistic and creative writing projects.

The Lowdown
ON COMPUTERS

High-Speed Network?
Yes

Wireless Network?
Yes

Number of Computer Labs:
9

Number of Media Labs:
2

Numbers of Computers:
200+

24-Hour Labs:
Center for Information and Technology (CIT) Building

Charge to Print?
Not yet, but rumored to be happening pretty soon.

Operating Systems:
Mac, Windows, Unix

Free Software:
For a full listing visit www.brown.edu/Facilities/CIS/Software_Services/software/
Adobe CS, Cs ChemDraw, EndNote, Exceed, KaleidaGraph, Kedit, Dreamweaver, Mathematica, Matlab, PCTeX, ProDesktop, Scientific Word, SciFinder Scholar, Sigmaplot, SPSS, Tecplot

Students Speak Out
ON COMPUTERS

{ **"I think it's easy to use campus computers. I haven't needed to have my own in my three years here."**

Q "I brought my own computer, but I end up doing all my work at computer labs because I can't get anything done in my dorm. **I don't think it's essential to have a computer** because the facilities are pretty extensive. During finals, it could be hard without one."

Q "Brown has computer clusters in the main libraries and the CIT [Center for Information Technology]. It is not absolutely necessary to have a computer on campus. **There are enough computers** in the cluster to accommodate the 10 percent of students who do not have their own computers."

Q "The computer network is pretty good, and I believe it will get better. **Occasionally the network shuts down**, but they notify you ahead of time. It's best if you have a personal computer and printer because labs can get crowded at times."

Q "I think having a computer makes it a lot easier. **I don't know anyone without one**. I relied on the school's printers, but that's about it."

Facilities

> "Definitely bring your own computer. The computer clusters are **accessible and generally easy to use**, but, in college, everything depends on e-mail, and you need to be able to access it at any hour."

The College Prowler Take
ON COMPUTERS

Computers are a necessary tool at Brown. All papers, research, and communications revolve around having access to computers. The Center for Information Technology helps students adapt their own computers for use in the University network. Every Brown student has a university e-mail account, server space, and full access to most of the University's computer software and hardware. All of this is in addition to all the electronic research tools available through JOSIAH, the library Website server. The Center for Information Technology (CIT) also holds free group and individual training sessions to help students use specific software that the University makes available through their network. In general, Brown's computers offer more resources than most students could ever desire and the school continues to expand its computing facilities, taking advantage of new technology as it becomes available.

The Lowdown

Student Center:
Faunce House

Athletic Centers:
The Olney-Margolies Athletic Center (the OMAC), The Smith Swim Center, Pembroke Field, The Bear's Lair Athletic Center, Meehan Auditorium ice rink, Pizzitola Sports Center

Libraries:
The John D. Rockefeller Humanities Library (The Rock), The Sciences Library (The Sci-Li), Art Slide Library, The List Art Center, Orwig Music Library, John Hay Special Collections Library, Annemarie Brown Library, John Carter Brown Library

Popular Places to Chill:
Thayer Street, Wickenden Street, The Main Green, Faunce Steps, The GCB, The Bair's Lair, The Blue Room, the steps outside The Rock

The College Prowler™ Grade on
Computers: B+

A high grade in Computers designates that computer labs are available, the computer network is easily accessible, and the campus' computing technology is up-to-date.

Bowling on Campus?
No

Movie Theatre on Campus?
The Brown Film Society has movie marathons in the evenings and on the weekend in Carmichael Auditorium.

Bar on Campus?
Brown currently enjoys two on-campus bars. The Grad Center Bar, below the Grad Center Dorm, was recently named one of the 10 hippest college bars in the country. Known to students as the GCB, the bar donates thousands of dollars in profits to charity every year. The Underground, a bar and concert venue, is a favorite of underclassmen because of its lenient policies. Also, the bar is entirely student-staffed and -managed, offering some of the best on-campus jobs.

Coffeehouse on Campus?
The Upper Blue Room in Faunce House on the Main Green is home to the University's main coffee house, but the Rockefeller Library also has a small coffee and snack shop in the lobby. Similar snack/coffee shops are sprinkled all over campus, so you'll never be more that two minutes from an oasis that will accept your meal credits.

Students Speak Out
ON FACILITIES

{ "**The athletic facilities aren't the greatest or the newest, but they get the job done. The computer labs are pretty good.**"

Q "Nothing is crazy nice. They are doing better jobs on newer classrooms, but most of the buildings from the 1960s and '70s are pretty badly done, but **they are doing great things when they renovate halls**. The athletic center is all right, but weight room and nautilus machines could use a new layout."

Q "Brown **needs a better central place**, something like a student center or rec center."

Q "The computer clusters are nice, and there are a lot. I'm not an athlete, so **I don't know much about the athletic facilities**, but the student center consists of a café, a market and a bar, which is open almost every night and great if you can't muster the energy to go clubbing."

Q "Most things are fairly centralized, and the campus is fairly compact. The only thing is that the athletic center can be a little bit of a walk depending on where you are living. **Nothing is more than 10 minutes away**, though."

Q "The facilities are very nice. [They are] very **state-of-the-art and Ivy League-ish**. We don't have an official student center, but Faunce Hall acts as one, since it houses the Student Activities Office, the mail room, a mini-arcade, the Campus Market and various other things."

The College Prowler Take
ON FACILITIES

Brown's facilities reflect Brown students' needs; the average Brown student would tell you they spend much more time in the library than at the gym. Therefore, it makes sense that the libraries and computer centers are constantly renovated and updated, while other facilities may receive less attention. That being said, Brown is not completely lacking any facilities, but it is easy to see which interests are given priority. Most students have everything they need, though it might take them time to find it.

The College Prowler™ Grade on
Facilities: B

A high Facilities grade indicates that the campus is aesthetically pleasing and well-maintained; facilities are state-of-the-art, and libraries are exceptional. Other determining factors include the quality of both athletic and student centers and an abundance of things to do on campus.

Campus Dining

The Lowdown
ON CAMPUS DINING

Freshman Meal Plan Requirement?
Yes

24-Hour On-Campus Eating?
No

Meal Plan Average Cost:
$2,884

Student Favorites:
The Blue Room, The Ivy Room, Josiah's

Students Speak Out
ON CAMPUS DINING

Q "The meal plan is all right. The V-Dub has recently been renovated, and their food is consistently tasty. Food quality at the Ratty, the other dining hall, is less consistent. But, there is usually a decent selection."

Q "The main dining hall food is **below average to average cafeteria food**. Special snack bars are pretty good, and give you good variety."

Q "I stayed on the meal plan for all three years that I lived in the dorms. It was **great to get to see people in the dining halls**. There's usually something good to eat."

Q "I hated the meal plan when I was on it! The Ratty is the pits, but **I hear it got better**. The VW is a better option. Josiah's and the Blue Room are better alternatives if you have points, and the Gate is a good place to get pizza."

Q "The meal plan rips you off. **The Ratty was disgusting.** I was on the full meal plan. I'm definitely going off of it even though I'm living in a dorm without a real kitchen, which should tell you something. I think the V-Dub is a little better. Being off meal plan without a car might be a little difficult."

Q "**It would be cheaper if I went off the meal plan**, but there are trade-offs. Now that I'm off meal plan, I eat whatever comes my way. If you don't have a car or access to a car, it would be really frustrating to be off the meal plan."

Did You Know?
There is a Ratty Recipe Repository link off of Brown's DailyJolt Website which has student-invented recipes for meals using ingredients in the University's cafeteria. Recipes include Curry Chicken Salad, Fruity Desert Crepes, and Macaratty and Cheese.

COLLEGE PROWLER™

Got the munchies? Find out what the best camus dining spots are in the College Prowler book on Brown available at *www.collegeprowler.com.*

The College Prowler Take
ON CAMPUS DINING

While most schools have contracted Marriott or fast food companies for their dining needs, Brown prides itself on maintaining a University-run food service. Why exactly this is a source of pride is another question entirely. The main dining halls—the "Ratty" and the "V-Dub"—serve what can only be described as average food. Chances are you won't return home for the holidays demanding your mom cook more like Brown Food Services (BFS). In addition, there are basic restrictions on meal credit use that can be very frustrating. These include credits expiring daily, a lack of variety, and the inability to use credits in real restaurants close to campus. The Brown meal plan feels more like a middle-school lunch program than a welcomed dining experience.

Off-Campus Dining

The Lowdown
ON OFF-CAMPUS DINING

Best Pizza:
Antonia's on Thayer, Sicilia's on Federal Hill

Best Chinese:
Apsara, Dragon 2000

Best Healthy:
The Garden, Grill Café

Best Breakfast:
Louis' on Hope Street, Julian's

Best Wings:
Wes's Rib House, Wings to Go

Best Place to Take Your Parents:
Empire, Hemenway's, Mediterraneo

Student Favorites:
Spike's Junkyard Dogs, East Side Pockets, Sawadee, India Viva

The College Prowler™ Grade on
Campus Dining: C-

Our grade on Campus Dining addresses the quality of both school-owned dining halls and independent on-campus restaurants as well as the price, availability, and variety of food.

24-Hour Eating

There are not any 24-hour diners within walking distance of Brown, but the late-night diners are Haven Brothers, the Silver Top Diner, Wes's Rib House, Bickford's, and Fellini's.

Students Speak Out
ON OFF-CAMPUS DINING

"On my Brown application, I literally said that one reason I wanted to come here was for the great Italian food in the area."

Q "I've always been amazed at the variety of restaurants Providence has to offer. **My favorites are the Italian restaurants** and the Paragon burger. From diners, to 50$/head [restaurants], there is great variety … and Providence is small enough to try and digest most of them."

Q "The restaurants are great. Thayer and Wickenden streets are good and close. Paragon is great and cheap. Check out Sakura for sushi and Federal Hill for more expensive Italian food. Providence also has great Indian and Thai food. Just **steer clear of Chinese**."

Q "**Thayer Street is the 'college town' street of Brown.** There are lots of restaurants, small little sandwich shops, and chains. Paragon and Andrea's are nice sit-down places that are not too expensive. D'Angelo's, Au Bon Pain, Smoothie King, Ben and Jerry's, Johnny Rockets, Eastside Pockets, Antonio's pizza, and Kabob and Curry are the chains. Meeting Street Café has really great, mega-sized sandwiches and cookies; if it's your birthday they give you a free cookie."

Q "Off-campus food is spectacular. There is a ridiculous amount of really good restaurants in the area since Johnston and Wales serves up so many good local chefs. **Fast food type places are all over the place**; there's falafel, pizza, and pastries everywhere. You won't have to worry about having variety."

Q "There are so many good places that I feel like I need a full four years to try them all. When you get to school, **get an *Around and About Providence* book**; it has all the listings of restaurants in the area. There are really too many good ones to name, but generally, I eat on Thayer Street, on Wickenden Street, or downtown. Federal Hill, Providence's Italian district, is a short trolley ride away and has fantastic Italian food. There are also some great Thai and Indian places, if you like those types of food."

The College Prowler Take
ON OFF-CAMPUS DINING

Providence truly caters to the epicurean diner. One need not stray further than the College Hill and downtown areas to find all varieties of ethnic food, dining styles, and atmospheres. Without a doubt, Providence is host to an impressive number of off-campus restaurants that offer variety in terms of price and menus. Great food is truly one of Providence's greatest assets. Enough said.

The College Prowler™ Grade on
Off-Campus Dining: A-

A high Off-Campus Dining grade implies that off-campus restaurants are affordable, accessible, and worth visiting. Other factors include the variety of cuisine and the availability of alternative options (vegetarian, vegan, Kosher, etc.).

Campus Housing

The Lowdown
ON CAMPUS HOUSING

Undergrads on Campus:
80%

Number of Dormitories:
27

University-Owned Apartments:
40

Available for Rent
You can rent microwaves and small refrigerators from the Brown Student Agency. The same goes for towels and sheets.

Cleaning Service?
Most dorms have a custodial service that keeps hallways, bathrooms, and other public areas reasonably clean.

You Get
Every room has a phone jack, an Ethernet hub, and free cable with access to Brown's HBO-like movie channel. Rooms also come with a lamp or an overhead light, a desk, a dresser, a book shelf, and a bed.

Also Available
Although every dorm has laundry machines, laundry service is also available through the Brown Student Agency.

Did You Know?
Campus housing is the source of many of Brown's most popular rumors. There is a highly-mysterious tunnel system that connects a good deal of Wriston Quad around where the Greek and program houses are located. There are endless theories about the original intent of these tunnels, and rumor has it that they used to extend over a larger portion of the school. Brown is also said to have a few secret societies in addition to the well-publicized organizations; these societies are said to be located near campus in mysterious mansions. The most famous myth concerns the ominous Grad Center Dorm. It is rumored to have been designed in 1968 by prison architects as a fortress in case of riots. Regardless of the building's design intent, it is a fact that the imposing concrete spiral staircase was actually built in the incorrect orientation because the builders read the blueprints the wrong way.

Students Speak Out
ON CAMPUS HOUSING

"**All freshman dorms are fine. Don't worry if you get a so-called 'bad dorm' because you end up bonding with your dormmates over that.**"

Q "The dorms aren't bad, and many freshman rooms are actually very nice. As a freshman, **everyone is assigned a roommate and a dormitory**, so you have no say in either matter. However, in the follow years, you will enter a housing lottery where you can select housing. No matter what, housing is guaranteed for all four years."

Q "I am staying on campus senior year. I live in Slater Hall, right next to University Hall, and **I definitely don't want to move**. I can roll out of bed and into my classes. My room is large, with high ceilings, and I get a view of the sunset down College Hill."

> "Dorms are pretty decent. Some are much nicer than others, though. As a freshman, **you'd want to be in Keeney**—that's where most freshmen are, and it's located on the convenient side of campus."

> "I've stayed on campus all four years. I don't want to have to pay bills. I have the rest of my life to deal with real life. I feel like it's not worth it to buy a bed and furniture for a year... and **the senior dorms are nicer than a house off campus**, anyway. I don't see the point when the houses are right next door to the dorms."

Off-Campus Housing

The College Prowler Take
ON CAMPUS HOSSING

The Lowdown
ON OFF-CAMPUS HOUSING

Brown guarantees housing for four years if the student wants it. They also require students to live on campus for the first six semesters of their Brown career. Although many students complain about this policy, it makes life easier for rising sophomores and juniors and relieves a lot of the stress between freshman and junior year. Starting in the spring of freshman year, students are faced with a lot of choices in terms of housing. In addition to the lottery, all the program and Greek houses give students the choice of getting around the fickle lottery system. In addition to circumventing the lottery, special housing is one more chance to meet new people and have new experiences.

Undergrads in Off-Campus Housing:
19%

Average Rent for a Studio Apartment:
$600/month

Average Rent for a 1BR Apartment:
$800/month

Average Rent for a 2BR Apartment:
$1200/month

Popular Areas
Fox Point, around Governor Street, Wickenden Street Area, Brook and Cushing Streets, right off Thayer

Best Time to Look for a Place
For the best selection, look by no later than February; however, if you want the best prices, wait until late in the spring when the landlords are anxious to rent their spaces.

For Assistance Contact
Residential Life

www.brown.edu/Administration/ResLife/grapevine/offcampus.html

Phone: (401) 83-3500

E-mail: Res_Life@brown.edu

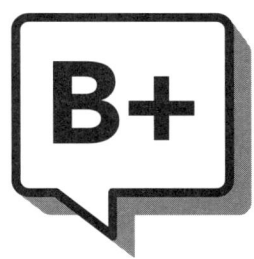

The College Prowler™ Grade on
Campus Housing: B+

A high Campus Housing grade indicates that dorms are clean, well-maintained, and spacious. Other determining factors include variety of dorms, proximity to classes, and social atmosphere.

Students Speak Out
ON OFF-CAMPUS HOUSING

The College Prowler Take
ON OFF-CAMPUS HOUSING

{ "Off campus is only available for seniors, but it is definitely the way to go if you can—just make sure your landlord and neighbors aren't too insane because that does happen."

Q "[It's] definitely worth it. **Most people live within a five- to 10-minutes walking distance** of campus. Then there are loft, warehouse, and other house [or] apartment options in the city if you want to pay less, have more space, and have more of a blank canvas to work with."

Q "I lived off campus one year, and **it was awesome**. I lived in Young Orchard the year before—that was a step down, but only a very small step."

Q "I lived off campus for two years. Off-campus living is totally better. The annoying thing was, I had to stay in dorms until my junior year. **I would have moved off earlier if I could have**."

Q "Off-campus housing can be extremely convenient; it's **as close to campus as a dorm**. Of course, the further away from campus you go, the cheaper it is. But, in general, students that live off campus find the walking commute to be minimal."

Q "I've never felt at home on campus. But, living off campus, I'm **not as likely to go to things on campus** late at night."

Brown guarantees housing for all four years, but most students opt to live on their own by senior year to gain more freedom, more space, or better facilities. Some years the University lets juniors live off campus, too, but officially only seniors are guaranteed permission. Students apply to the Office of Residential Life for off-campus permission in the early spring of their junior year, most having already signed a lease in the previous months. As a senior, getting permission is easy, but finding the perfect apartment can be a greater challenge. Within a mile radius of campus, there are endless housing options, but the best places are rarely advertised. Hit the pavement or ask friends if you want to find the best place. In general, students can find any kind of place they want—historic houses, new apartments, studios, or mansions.

Did You Know?

Like Boston, Providence is an attractive city for young professionals, with a growing market in technology. Providence, however, lacks Boston's exorbitant real estate prices and costs of living.

The College Prowler™ Grade on
Off-Campus Housing: A-

A high grade in Off-Campus Housing indicates that apartments are of high quality, close to campus, affordable, and easy to secure.

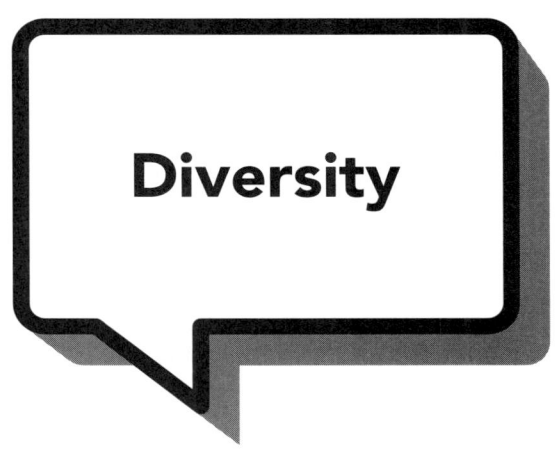

Diversity

The Lowdown
ON DIVERSITY

African American: 7%

Asian American: 14%

Hispanic: 7%

Native American: 1%

White: 65%

International: 6%

Out-of-State: 5%

Minority Clubs
The Third World Center at Brown was created in 1976 to meet the needs of all minority students and to promote racial and ethnic pluralism in the Brown community.

Political Activity
Brown is famed for its political activism and liberal atmosphere, but actual activism and demonstrations on campus have become more infrequent.

Most Popular Religions
Brown does not have a single predominant religion, and the majority of students claims to have no particular affiliation. However, some sources show that some religious minorities have particularly high numbers at Brown. The Chaplains' office provides services for students of all religions; they list Bahat, Buddhism, Christianity, Hinduism, Islam, Jainism, Judaism, and Sikhism the most popular Brown faiths.

Gay Tolerance
Brown students and faculty are extremely receptive and friendly to all people, and there have been very few incidences of discrimination or hate crimes related to sexual orientation. The effort to promote queer politics and acceptance is spearheaded by the Brown LGBTA (Lesbian-Gay-Bisexual-Transsexual Alliance). Twice a year, the organization hosts huge dances which are among the most popular campus parties.

Economic Status
Brown recently made a major admissions policy change to accept students on a "need-blind" basis in order to promote quality of scholarship and demonstrated ability above affluence. However, the average Brown student seems to come from the upper-middle-class.

Students Speak Out
ON DIVERSITY

"**Diverse compared to what? Compared to Berkeley, it's not diverse. Compared to Princeton, it's very diverse. I don't know; people have different opinions on this.**"

Q "It's not terrible. **We're doing okay by the percentages**. But, it's very hard to be here, and, for example, forget that you are in very white, very middle-class New England. I don't think it's an 'us versus them' environment, but the manifestations of [differences], either racial or class, exist."

Q "Brown has a diversity of opinions and political views, as well as students with all types of geographical, religious, racial, and educational backgrounds. If you want to meet people different from you, **you have to make an effort**."

Q "The campus is somewhat diverse. There are **a lot of people of Asian decent**, but other races and ethnicities are under-represented."

Q "There are two indications that race is still an issue around campus. One, there is still a lot of dialogue between the students and the administration on the subject, but also, there is an **overwhelming sense of mistrust** that most white students show when it comes to minorities."

The College Prowler Take
ON DIVERSITY

The University makes an honest effort to promote socioeconomic diversity in the student body; the recent change to need-blind admissions is just one example of this goal. While the hard numbers indicate that there is a good deal of racial and economic diversity at Brown, the day-to-day interactions between students are the real test of diversity and tolerance at Brown. There are very few outright problems, and public sentiment does not indicate any feeling that diversity is extremely lacking at Brown. In spite of this, however, the students, left to their own devices, do not necessarily diversify their own social circles.

The College Prowler™ Grade on
Diversity: B

A high grade in Diversity indicates that ethnic minorities and international students have a notable presence on campus and that students of different economic backgrounds, religious beliefs, and sexual preferences are well-represented.

Guys & Girls

The Lowdown
ON GUYS & GIRLS

Women Undergrads: 53%

Men Undergrads: 47%

Birth Control Available? Yes

Social Scene
Brown students generally can be put into two groups: social butterflies and social caterpillars. It makes for a great dynamic. Just when you think you've exhausted your social sphere, you meet someone in a class who, it turns out, lived down the hall from you for two years, but never left their room. That being said, freshman housing units are the basis for future social interaction at Brown. In freshmen housing units, personalities spill into the hallways and start friendships that may last a lifetime. At Brown, a smile really is all it takes to meet people.

Hookups or Relationships?
Brown is a school where hookups reign supreme. Most students would say that they are simply too busy and too involved to pursue a committed relationship. Brown also seems to attract many freshmen with little or no relationship experience. It's impossible to say what combination of factors lead to the two most common sentiments about Brown students and dating: "There is no dating at Brown," and "We're just friends ... with benefits."

Dress Code

Unshaved armpits and dreadlocks will always be a staple of the Brown hippie look, but Brown guys and girls exhibit the full range of styles and attitudes. Fake Prada and Louis Vuitton mix with real high-fashion looks. There's everything from boarding school kids who can't shake their preppy duds, to the dirty hippy garb that really makes you question whether all dorms are actually equipped with showers. Unfortunately, the cold weather can get the better of fashion during the winter months, but the dress code for those who care is either designer head-to-toe, or funky and artsy. In May, shorts and short skirts distinguish between those that spring-breaked in the Bahamas and those that stayed in to work on their thesis. The fashionable Brown guy looks a bit Euro, a bit bohemian, or just classic Abercrombie. For girls, there's everything from perfectly coiffured designer looks, to oblivious fashion victims. The fashionable Brown girl, above all, strives for her own unique style. Collectively, Brown kids definitely rock a style.

Students Speak Out
ON GUYS & GIRLS

{ "I'd have to say the guys at Brown are hotter than the girls. It's not exactly a big dating school, but people do date and hook up."

Q "I think the social life is fun. I don't think there is a ton of dating at Brown. There are plenty of attractive people here. Like everything at Brown, you have to be more persistent. It's nice **that there is a social life that revolves around the school**."

Q "I haven't had too much success with girls at Brown. Freshman year, I had a girlfriend. That was about it. **I meet most girls at parties**."

Q "No serious dating. Not here. I think there's a variety of guys. Some guys like to take girls out on dates. A lot of guys don't; they're more into the hookup thing. I think that there is **more going here than at most places**. It happens pretty often; it's definitely common."

Q "**Guys at Brown are flaky**. I've dated enough to know. I've met a lot of people that are socially awkward, but I think that's why we get along so well."

Q "Brown is one of those places where you meet really cool people, but there's **not so much casual dating going on**. You are either in a long-term relationship or single."

The College Prowler Take
ON GUYS & GIRLS

According to the rumors, the headshots Brown requires with every application are meant to ensure Brown's reputation for having most attractive Ivy League students. Whether or not you believe this rumor is entirely a matter of taste (and whether you consider "attractive Ivy League student" an oxymoron). In general, students tend to agree that the admissions office did a fabulous job choosing interesting and enjoyable classmates, but they are a little more critical when it comes to sharing anything more than intellectual curiosity with their peers. However, the truth of the matter is that the Brown student body is no more or less attractive than any other population of 20-year-old students; observers are just as likely to rave about the spectacular beauties lounging on the main green as they are to complain about the pale, four-eyed creatures that wander out of the library late at night.

The College Prowler™ Grade on
Guys: B+

A high grade for Guys indicates that the male population on campus is attractive, smart, friendly, and engaging, and that the school has a decent ratio of guys to girls.

The College Prowler™ Grade on
Girls: B

A high grade for Girls not only implies that the women on campus are attractive, smart, friendly, and engaging, but also that there is a fair ratio of girls to guys.

Athletics

The Lowdown
ON ATHLETICS

Men's Varsity Teams:

Baseball
Basketball
Crew
Equestrian
Golf
Football
Ice Hockey
Lacrosse
Soccer
Skiing

Wrestling
Water Polo
Squash
Swimming
Diving
Tennis
Track and Field
Cross Country
Fencing

Women's Varsity Teams:

Softball
Basketball
Ice Hockey
Field Hockey
Gymnastics
Golf
Lacrosse
Soccer
Skiing

Water Polo
Squash
Swimming
Diving
Tennis
Track and Field
Cross Country
Fencing

Club Sports
Sailing, men's rugby, men's volleyball, men's and women's Ultimate Frisbee

Intramurals
Football, volleyball, tennis, soccer, basketball, Frisbee, hockey, softball, squash

Most Popular Sports
Despite the fact that many Brown teams are highly ranked in any given season, there is a relatively low amount of student support for varsity athletic events. Big games against other Ivies, however, draw big crowds in ice hockey, football, and basketball. The intramural and club Frisbee, basketball, and football teams foster a lot of positive competition on campus.

Getting Tickets
It is only hard to get tickets for the biggest games of the year since most varsity athletic events are only moderately attended. In most cases, showing up to an event with your Brown ID is all you need to get in. For specific ticket information, call (401) 863-2773.

Students Speak Out
ON ATHLETICS

"Club sports offer a lot of fun without the pressure of varsity sports. There's a huge culture that revolves around the ultimate Frisbee teams."

"Intramurals are pretty popular. **Varsity sports are almost like a social scene**, and like all other social scenes, it's fractious and segregated from most other things. Part of the reason is less that there's a stigma for athletes and more that, physically, the sports complex is not in the center of campus."

"The only thing I don't like about Brown is the way the athletes are treated. I'm an athlete, and people assume I only got in because I'm an athlete and I'm in dumb-jock classes. **There's a lot of hostility toward athletes here**, not from the professors but sometimes from other students. I feel like the athletes do as well in classes, if not better, than non-athletes."

✏ "As far as professors go, at the beginning of each semester the professors let the athletes know that if there's a conflict they should let them know about it. They're willing to work with us, and **it's definitely supportive**."

The College Prowler Take
ON ATHLETICS

Brown is not an overly athletic school. Almost every student played some varsity sport in high school, but, for most students, academics and other extracurricular activities come before athletics. There are, however, a full range of varsity sports and less intense club and intramural sports. Many Brown students go for runs around campus, or find themselves playing catch or Frisbee on the Main Green. Sports are just one aspect of social life, but helps relieve stress from the academic rigors of the University. Brown has facilities for non-athletes to swim, work out, and play organized sports. Brown also has gifted student athletes who may go underappreciated despite winning records.

The College Prowler™ Grade on
Athletics: C+

A high grade in Athletics indicates that students have school spirit, that sports programs are respected, that games are well-attended, and that intramurals are a prominent part of student life.

Greek Life

The Lowdown
ON GREEK LIFE

Undergrads in Greek Houses:
Less than 10%

Number of Fraternities:
6

Number of Sororities:
2

Number of Coeds:
2

Students Speak Out
ON GREEK LIFE

"I think it's mostly a thing for freshman. It's not like other schools where it's cool to be in a sorority. Freshman year, I went to a lot of fraternity parties, but I haven't been to one since."

✏ "I'm in a fraternity. I never thought I would join one, but it turns out that I did. They definitely do not dominate, but **they do provide big parties** open to the whole campus that a lot of people find to be pretty fun—there's dancing, drinking, and usually some theme. There's usually always something else going on around campus, though, and bars are always open."

Q "I feel like only about six percent of people live in fraternities and sororities, so **it's a small part of the scene.** You really have to search pretty hard to find someone who is involved in them."

Q "Greek life is definitely there, but it in no way dominates the social scene. They have a lot of the parties on campus that can be fun, but **it is definitely avoidable** and not seen as being a big deal at all."

Q "I wasn't in a sorority, but I lived in a dorm that was partially joined with a Greek house. **They were very approachable**. It was intimidating at first, I thought they were going to be rowdy, but in the end it created a great dynamic."

Drug Scene

The College Prowler Take
ON GREEK LIFE

The Lowdown
ON DRUG SCENE

Greek life at Brown is about as minimized as it can be. This is due to the Greek system itself and the University's attempts to seamlessly integrate frats and sororities into daily campus life. All Greek houses are on campus and abide by the same rules and regulations as any other organization on campus. If a student never wants to see the Greek system, they can easily ignore it. On the flip side, if a student wants a real Greek experience, they can find it in one of the dozen houses that do exist. But if you want a school where who you are is defined by the three Greek letters printed on your T-shirt, Brown is simply not the place.

Liquor-Related Referrals:
103

Liquor-Related Arrests:
1

Drug-Related Referrals:
53

Drug-Related Arrests:
6

Most Prevalent Drugs on Campus:
Alcohol, marijuana, study drugs, speed, cocaine

The College Prowler™ Grade on
Greek Life: C+

A high grade in Greek Life indicates that sororities and fraternities are not only present, but also active on campus. Other determining factors include the variety of houses available and the respect the Greek community receives from the rest of the campus.

Drug Counseling Programs
Brown's Health Service provides information about substance abuse as well as other common health issues for college students through its Health Education Office, located on the third floor of Health Services. The phone number is (401) 863-2794. In addition, every freshman dorm has many undergraduate counselors who help students and provide a source of information on substance abuse issues.

Check out *Brown University—Off the Record* for more student responses on the presense and popularity of drugs. Get it at www.collegeprowler.com.

Students Speak Out
ON DRUG SCENE

"I think the policy is lax, and I like it. I got in trouble one time, but nothing came of it."

Q "Pot is the most used and accessible illicit drug at Brown. However, coke, acid, mushrooms, and ecstasy also seem to be around from time to time. The scene is avoidable if you so choose. **I haven't really heard anything about heroin … which is a good thing**."

Q "If you want to find the scene, you can find it pretty quickly. If you don't want to, you can stay away from it. **People are pretty open about their personal habits**."

Q "Yeah, most of my friends smoke and drink. I wouldn't date someone who doesn't smoke or drink. I think it's like that at most universities. I have friends outside of that group that I meet in class or at work to get a cup of coffee with, but **people kind of stick to their circles**."

Q "I've never been busted. You hear stuff like that happening. I think Brown is really cool. **They definitely give you a lot of responsibility**, and they're pretty hands off. They expect students to make the right decision."

Q "I would say **most students do drink**, but not a lot. I would say the average student would, at most, have fours drinks—I mean in a night, not in an hour."

The College Prowler Take
ON DRUG SCENE

While you can guarantee some exposure to drugs, it is by no means a social prerequisite. There is enough to do at Brown and in Providence to stave off the boredom that makes the drug scene thrive at other less entertaining schools. Brown students, like any college student body, look to drugs for both social and academic reasons. Many students drink and smoke cigarettes and pot casually. The effects that abuse will have on your work, and the threat of University and police action if you get caught, necessitate that students use drugs sensibly on campus. The most important thing to remember is that most Brown students are responsible and goal-driven kids. Drug use is more a by-product of college life than a main activity.

The College Prowler™ Grade on
Drug Scene: B

A high grade on Drug Scene indicates that drugs are not a noticeable part of campus life; drug use is not visible, and no pressure to use them seems to exist.

Campus Strictness

> "Campus was **too strict for me**. I couldn't wait to get off campus where there aren't people patrolling your lifestyle every day."

> "Many times, if you are caught drinking, the cops tell you to just pour it out and leave. **It's pretty laid-back.** Brown also doesn't have RAs in the normal sense, we have an MPC [minority peer counselor], a WPC [woman's peer counselor], and an RC [resident counselor]. Each of the three exists in your freshman unit, and they don't report you. Their job is to advise you to make good decisions."

The Lowdown
ON CAMPUS STRICTNESS

What Are You Most Likely to Get Caught Doing on Campus?
Smoking cigarettes or pot in the dorms

Students Speak Out
ON CAMPUS STRICTNESS

> "Where as most schools have RAs or proctors in the dormitories who play the disciplinary role regarding drugs and alcohol, Brown has residential councilors, but they do not play a disciplinary role at all."

> "Sometimes I felt like they were out to get me. We got busted once or twice, and then it seemed like **the cops made a habit of coming by my room**. We had some close calls, but we still got away with a lot."

> "They're not strict about drinking. **With smoking, they've buckled down a little but** not much—you will never go to jail, but maybe just get a dean's hearing."

> "Police generally don't look for people doing stuff. But, **it's not like they'll pretend they didn't see it** if they happen to come upon it."

The College Prowler Take
ON CAMPUS STRICTNESS

The Brown police are not unlike those cool parents you knew in high school; they let the kids have their parties and almost never checkout suspicious smells. While the police will nab students for any blatant displays of illegal behavior, they are unlikely to look for it unless staff or students notify them. These days, the main job of the Brown police is crime prevention and not student supervision. In addition, the counselor support system in the dorms provides a safe, open, and fun environment for the students, not a tool for the University to keep an eye on the students in their rooms. The University establishes safe, yet liberal, boundaries for students and uses security presence to protect, not police, the students.

The College Prowler™ Grade on
Campus Strictness: B+

A high Campus Strictness grade implies an overall lenient atmosphere; police and RAs are fairly tolerant, and the administration's rules are flexible.

Overall Experience

Students Speak Out
ON OVERALL EXPERIENCE

{ "Brown is an Ivy League school that places more emphasis on the quality of a liberal education than on the way they are perceived by other schools. Therefore, students at Brown are generally not competitive."

Q "Given the choice to do it over again, I would definitely come to Brown. Before I came to college, I never thought that the size of the school would be something really important to me. Now I know **I would never want to go to a school that was any bigger**. I think the size really lets you get to know a lot of people here. All my friends who just graduated are depressed that they're leaving. I have friends at other schools who are thrilled to be getting out after four years."

Q "I indulged my social life and my academic life. It was amazingly liberating. I think I'm leaving Brown **knowing who I am and where I want to go**. I don't have the specific plan, but I have the ability to deal with it. I think that's pretty specific to Brown. Everyone here has a good sense of themselves. They go through their life at Brown and after Brown being comfortable with themselves."

Q "My biggest qualm about Brown is the fact that **the University doesn't have a [large] endowment**. I know a lot of programs are in danger of being cut."

Q "Before I came to Brown, I didn't think there would be a big difference between the academics at the schools I was looking at. It is a big deal. The possibilities an open curriculum provides can be a big factor in your educational career. I took a lot of classes in a concentration I didn't end up pursuing. The switch wouldn't have been so easy if it wasn't for the open curriculum. It makes both the students and the professors care more. **Professors know you want to be in their classes**."

The College Prowler Take
ON OVERALL EXPERIENCE

Brown's reputation precedes it. As an Ivy League school, Brown carries the distinction that many students desire, even if they know little about what they need or want in a liberal arts education. In that sense, Brown's liberal nature and open curriculum exceed that of the average liberal arts school. Many students redefine and rediscover themselves in college, and Brown's biggest strength is that it promotes individual development and self-discovery over the course of the undergraduate career. Internally, you have a lot of chances to make mistakes, which the University calls "discoveries," in the course of your studies. It's easy to change your concentration in the fifth or even sixth semester.

Few people who choose Brown regret it. While it's not the school for everyone, almost anyone can find what they are looking for at Brown. Whether you are from New England or Siberia, there are clubs, organizations, and classes for you, and fellow students who share your academic and personal interests. Most people choose Brown for its liberal nature and its strong academic resources, and few are disappointed.

The Inside Scoop

The Lowdown
ON THE INSIDE SCOOP

School Spirit
School spirit at Brown is strong, but not necessarily reflected by the turnout at athletic events or other school functions. Although the bleachers may be empty and some people may not even know the school mascot is the Brown Bear, most people take advantage of other chances to show their school spirit. Brown students do attend political rallies, student rock shows, and other performances, art openings, and student film screenings to support other's work. The Brown school spirit is most strongly felt in the mutual admiration among students.

Traditions
ADOCH (A Day on College Hill)
All admitted students are invited to participate in ADOCH, a two day event in April where pre-frosh from all over the world come to check out the University and meet for the first time. While it's not required, it's the first chance for many students to meet their fellow classmates for the coming year. It's also when a lot of potential students decide to come to Brown.

The Van Winkle Gates
Every student walks through the main gates of the University exactly twice in the undergraduate career. The first week of freshman year, the gates are swung inwards towards University Hall, inviting the new University members to enter the Brown Campus. Years later, upon graduating, the gates are opened out, ushering the grads back into the world and ceremoniously ending their time at Brown.

The Freshman Ice Cream Social
The ice cream social on the terrace of Andrews Dorm during the first week of freshman year is a great chance for people to come out of their box-laden dorm rooms and meet other first-years.

Senior Week
The week before graduation is the last chance for seniors to celebrate before leaving the University. Underclassmen are invited to stick around in certain dorms while they work or party at the events, which include the Campus Dance and the commencement ceremonies, as well as special nights at clubs and bars, and some of the wildest parties of the year.

Spring Weekend
Usually timed to coincide with the burst of green that happens in late April, Spring Weekend promises a few solid rock or hip-hop shows, frat boys on couches on the greens, and girls wearing smiles, shorts, and bikinis. It's a chance to cut loose before final exams.

Things I Wish I Knew Before Coming to Brown:
- Most things can be bought at school for about what it costs to ship them, so don't be a pack rat when you are moving to campus.
- Upper-level courses are not necessarily harder than lower level ones. Don't be afraid to take upper-level classes as a freshman if you are interested in them.
- What you take freshmen year doesn't matter, but your grades do.
- Be careful of the credit/no credit grade option. Usually, you end up getting an A anyway, or you totally slack off and get nothing out of the class.

Tips to Succeed at Brown:
- Be very persistent, whether dealing with classes or other University services.
- Always seek the council of an advisor or a dean if you need questions answered or if you are having a hard time. Deans, especially, are there to protect you when things go wrong and can help improve your overall Brown experience.
- Make connections with professors or administrators who can provide you with good recommendations.

Finding a Job or Internship

The Lowdown
ON FINDING A JOB OR INTERNSHIP

Brown has the typical support to aid students looking for jobs and internships. The place to start is Career Services. Career Services tries to offer a full range of resources to students: a library with walls of books for researching internship, grant, program and job opportunities and services; a staff that will review and edit resumes, cover letters and perform mock interviews; and a few other specialized services, such as the dossier service which keeps recommendations on file for students, and a Website with job and internship listings.

In the end, however, most students use Career Services sparingly, if at all, and have, at best, limited results actually finding jobs through the network. Going to Career Services, however, can be a great way to get motivated or receive specific advice about cover letters or resumes.

Advice
There are a few good ways to get good work around the University. An easy and sure-fire option is to work for the University Food and Catering Service or the library system, both of which hire students for all shifts and give good hours with decent pay. For a slightly more academic job, most professors hire students as research or administrative assistants, depending on the department. These jobs are coveted, and students only get them by taking classes with the professor and demonstrating genuine interest and ability in the course, as well as developing a relationship with the professor.

Maddock Alumni Center
Located across from Wayland Arch on campus, the alumni center offers a place for alumni functions and administrative support services. The building serves as a nerve center for all of Brown's alumi.

Major Alumni Events
The biggest alumni events revolve around graduation week when alums are invited to come back to the University for a weekend to participate in class and University reunions.

Alumni Publications
BAM, Brown Alumni Magazine
BAM is published six times a year and is mailed to all alumni with active addresses.

B2B: Brown News for Brown Alumni
Sent monthly by e-mail, B2B offers headlines on campus news, alumni connections, sports, and other on campus events.

Alumni Services
Alumni Directory, Alumni College Advising, Career Networking, Alumni Medical and Home Insurance

Did You Know?
Famous Brown Alumni:
- Todd Haynes
- Charles Evans Hughes
- John F. Kennedy, Jr.
- Laura Linney
- Lisa Loeb
- Prince Nikolaos and Princess Alexandra or Greece
- John D. Rockefeller, Jr.
- Tom Scott and Tom First, founders of Nantucket Nectars
- Duncan Sheik
- Ted Turner

The Best & Worst

The Ten BEST Things About Brown:

1. The New Curriculum
2. The students
3. President Ruth Simmons
4. Thayer Street
5. College Greens
6. The restaurants off campus
7. Cheap rent
8. Close to Boston and New York
9. Providence
10. The classes and professors

The Ten WORST Things About Brown:

1. Eight channels on-campus cable
2. The paltry endowment
3. Winters
4. The meal plan
5. Providence parking laws
6. No liquor sales on Sunday!
7. No grocery stores within walking distance
8. Bars close at 2 a.m.
9. The stress of the housing lottery
10. Lots of rain

Dartmouth College

6016 McNutt Hall, Hanover, NH 03755
www.dartmouth.edu   (603) 646-2875

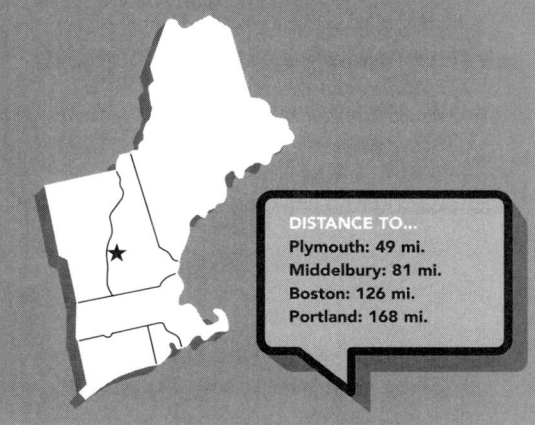

DISTANCE TO...
Plymouth: 49 mi.
Middlebury: 81 mi.
Boston: 126 mi.
Portland: 168 mi.

"Dartmouth is truly undergraduate. Professors teach every class and generally treat students like royalty."

Table of Contents

Academics	526
Local Atmosphere	528
Safety & Security	529
Computers	531
Facilities	532
Campus Dining	534
Off-Campus Dining	535
Campus Housing	537
Off-Campus Housing	538
Diversity	540
Guys & Girls	542
Athletics	544
Greek Life	546
Drug Scene	547
Campus Strictness	549
Overall Experience	550
The Inside Scoop	551
Finding a Job or Internship	553
The Best & Worst	554

Total Enrollment:
4,039

Acceptance Rate:
18%

Tuition:
$30,465

Top 10% of High School Class:
84%

Average GPA:
3.7

SAT Range
Verbal	Math	Total
660 – 760	670 – 770	1330 – 1530

ACT Range
Verbal	Math	Total
N/A	N/A	27-33

Most Popular Majors:
12% Economics
9%   Psychology
8%   History/Political Science and Government
7%   English Language and Literature

Students Also Applied To:*
Brown University, Harvard University
Princeton University, Stanford University
Yale University

*For more school info check out www.collegeprowler.com

College Prowler Report Card

Academics	A
Local Atmosphere	C-
Safety & Security	A+
Computers	A
Facilities	B
Campus Dining	B
Off-Campus Dining	C-
Campus Housing	B+
Off-Campus Housing	B
Diversity	B
Guys	A-
Girls	B-
Athletics	B+
Greek Life	A
Drug Scene	B
Campus Strictness	B

Academics

Best Places to Study
Novack Café, The Stacks, Baker Tower Room, Collis Center, dorm lounge/study spaces

Sample Academic Clubs
College Bowl
Mock Trial Society
Forensic Union
Daniel Webster Legal Society
Club of Dartmouth Entrepreneurs

The Lowdown
ON ACADEMICS

Degrees Awarded:
Bachelor, Post Bachelor certificate, Master, Doctoral, First Professional

Undergraduate Schools:
Students may also apply to Thayer School of Engineering.

Full-time Faculty:
644

Faculty with Terminal Degree:
82.7%

Student-to-Faculty Ratio:
8.5: 1

Average Course Load:
3 courses

Special Degree Options:
Combined Bachelor of Arts and Bachelor of Engineering

AP Test Score Requirements:
Possible credit for scores of 3, 4, or 5

IB Test Score Requirements:
Possible credit for scores of 6 or 7

Did You Know?

In need of luck during finals? Just rub the nose of Warner Bentley's bust in the Hopkins Center.

According to the Institute of International Education, Dartmouth has the highest percentage of students who study abroad (47 percent).

A perennial powerhouse, the Dartmouth Forensic Union policy debate team has won six national championships.

Students Speak Out
ON ACADEMICS

"The Student Assembly maintains a Website where students review classes they've taken (*http://sa.dartmouth.edu/guide*). It's a great way to see whether a course you're interested in is good or bad."

Q "**Academics at Dartmouth are unbeatable**. Since we aren't in the classroom very much compared to students at other schools, there is a lot of independent work, and it moves quickly. If you like to be challenged and move at a quick pace, you'll love Dartmouth."

Q "One nice thing is that, other than an English class that you can test out of and a freshman writing seminar, **there are no mandatory courses**. The distributive requirements are very general and give you a chance to take some really fun classes."

Q "**Small classes are a huge plus**. Intro courses that might have a few hundred students elsewhere have 50 at Dartmouth. While some social science departments are bigger, most upper-level classes have enrollments of a couple dozen or so."

Q "Honestly, there's not enough discourse in classes. **I've lost my ability to speak in groups from being out-of-practice in class**. Some professors are wonderful and have become mentors and friends, but on the whole, I'm disappointed by the academics. The history department is an exception—I've enjoyed 90 percent of the classes there. College courses are a waste of time."

Q "It's pretty easy to understand why Dartmouth is so alluring. **The student body has top-notch academics** available without any competition for resources from graduate students. With teaching-centered professors across the board, Dartmouth's academics are challenging, personal, and tailored for the intellectual development of individual students."

The College Prowler Take
ON ACADEMICS

Attending Dartmouth is a surefire way to avoid those troublesome TAs, as all classes are taught by professors. While there are some duds to be avoided, students consistently cite their profs as the most outstanding part of their academic experience. Professors are rarely sidetracked by research, and a low student-to-faculty ratio makes getting to know your instructors a breeze. Various study abroad programs are another student favorite—from strolling the hallowed halls of Oxford, to chasing sheep in New Zealand, Dartmouth presents plenty of options. The Dartmouth Plan facilitates taking a variety of exchange programs and terms abroad. Sophomore Summer (sounds better than summer school, right?) is a blast, but scattered off-terms are hard on amorous and platonic relationships alike.

As would be expected of an institution of Dartmouth's caliber, classes are challenging, professors are brilliant, and academic experiences are positive in the vast majority of cases. "Work hard, play hard" is an apt motto. While Dartmouth students let loose on weekends and remain surprisingly non-competitive when it comes to grades, most study more than they let on, particularly as finals draw near.

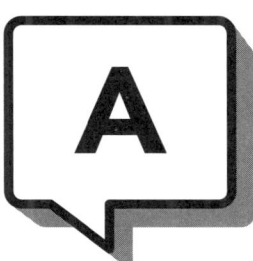

The College Prowler™ Grade on
Academics: A

A high Academics grade generally indicates that professors are knowledgeable, accessible, and genuinely interested in their students' welfare. Other determining factors include class size, how well professors communicate, and whether or not classes are engaging.

Local Atmosphere

Students Speak Out
ON LOCAL ATMOSPHERE

{ "The town life revolves around the college. This is one of the coolest things about Dartmouth—being immersed in an environment that is totally devoted to education."

The Lowdown
ON LOCAL ATMOSPHERE

Region:
Northeast

City, State:
Hanover, New Hampshire

Setting:
Small town

Distance from Boston:
2.5 hours

Distance from New York:
4.5 hours

Distance from Montreal:
4.5 hours

Points of Interest:
Quechee Gorge, Simon Pearce Glassblowing and Restaurant, Ben and Jerry's Factory, New England Transportation Museum, The Ledges

Major Sports Teams:
Boston Red Sox (MLB), Boston Celtics (NBA) Boston Bruins (NHL), New England Patriots (NFL)

City Websites:
www.hanovernh.org

Q "**Hanover is a quaint little college town**. If you want to get a good feel of what the campus is like without visiting, imagine the stereotypical 'college' atmosphere—large grassy lawns, distinguished brick buildings, a feeling of knowledge and history. Dartmouth is essentially the archetypical New England college, nestled into the almost unbearably picturesque Connecticut River Valley."

Q "**There's no culture in Hanover,** but, thankfully, Dartmouth brings culture to you. I think there's an average of three artistic events a day on campus, including movies. Best of all, everything's just five bucks for students."

Q "Dartmouth's atmosphere blends **New England architecture and history with Southern hospitality and West Coast relaxation** to create the perfect environment for a successful and happy college career. The city of Hanover has a fruitful partnership with Dartmouth, and the local atmosphere promotes friendly interpersonal interaction. While Hanover doesn't have the hustle and bustle of the Big Apple, it does have a pervasive 'feel good' atmosphere that is infectious."

Q "**There's really nothing except for some restaurants and stores**, just scenic New England stuff and a very pretty campus. There's not really anything to stay away from either. Dartmouth is 'in the sticks,' which can be pleasant, but it can also suck."

The College Prowler Take
ON LOCAL ATMOSPHERE

Hanover is unfailingly described as "small." However, with a full-service school like Dartmouth, who needs anything else? In fact, most Dartmouth students are so busy that they rarely ponder what's beyond Wheelock Street. Those who do are usually thrilled by their placid surroundings. Situated just across the Connecticut River from Vermont in the scenic Upper Valley, Hanover is consistently praised for its peaceful New England beauty. Unless you're satisfied donning apparel from the Gap, you'll have to hitch a ride to nearby West Lebanon or another of Hanover's less ritzy neighbors to find chain stores of any kind.

Safety & Security

The Lowdown
ON SAFETY & SECURITY

Number of Dartmouth Safety and Security Officers:
30

Phone:
(603) 646-2234

Health Center Office Hours:
8 a.m-4 p.m., seven days a week

Safety Services:
Bicycle registrations, BlitzMail bulletins, engraving of valuable items, escort service, Rape Aggression Defense, weapons storage

The College Prowler™ Grade on
Local Atmosphere: C-

A high Local Atmosphere grade indicates that the area surrounding campus is safe and scenic. Other factors include nearby attractions, proximity to other schools, and the town's attitude toward students.

Did You Know?

According to the FBI, Hanover is the safest town in New Hampshire, which is the safest state in the United States.

Students Speak Out
ON SAFETY & SECURITY

The College Prowler Take
ON SAFETY & SECURITY

"Dartmouth College is probably one of the safest colleges you will find, anywhere. Due to its location, there aren't exactly a lot of random, sketchy people wandering about, like you find on urban campuses."

Q "To be blunt, **security is really not an issue**. They put locks on the front doors of our dorms, and everybody thinks that it is a big joke. Virtually everyone leaves their doors unlocked all the time. College-sponsored Safety and Security officers patrol all the time and there are blue-light phones every twenty feet—at least it feels that way—but they're nearly always unneeded. I lost my key on the third day and never worried about [locking my door] again."

Q "Coming from the big city, it was quite a shock to be able to stroll around campus at the wee hours of the morning with impunity. **Many people don't even lock the doors to their rooms**. Neither myself nor anyone I know has ever felt threatened on campus, although the graveyard can be kind of spooky at night."

Q "**We have blue-light emergency phones all over the place**, and Safety and Security officers patrol the campus. There is also an escort service at night. The biggest cases usually deal with keg confiscation, inebriates, and the occasional bike theft. The crime scene at Dartmouth is minimal."

Q "As for security and safety, **don't worry**. The biggest crime at Dartmouth is bike theft, and [the perpetrators] usually return your bike when they're done with it. Dorms are always open; no one locks their doors. It's probably one of the safest campuses around, and even so, there is an awesome safety and security force that patrols and can help you out."

Because of Hanover's isolation and small size, most everyone on and around the campus is associated with Dartmouth. With no outside crime, occasional theft is virtually the only security concern. Blue-light safety phones are numerous in case you need a late-night escort or feel unsafe, and Safety and Security has a vigilant presence on campus just in case trouble arises. The campus evokes a simpler era, as students freely stroll campus at all hours; most rooms are left unlocked, and all dorms can be accessed with your student ID.

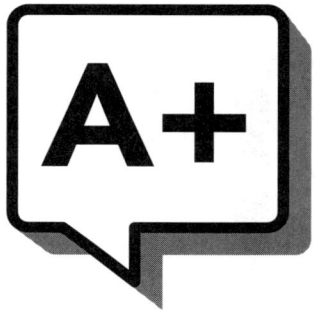

The College Prowler™ Grade on
Safety & Security: A+

A high grade in Safety & Security means that students generally feel safe, campus police are visible, blue-light phones and escort services are readily available, and safety precautions are not overly necessary.

Computers

Did You Know?

The first school to have a campus-wide wireless network, Dartmouth was named the nation's "Most Wired" campus by Yahoo! in 1998.

Students Speak Out
ON COMPUTERS

The Lowdown
ON COMPUTERS

High-Speed Network?
Yes

Wireless Network?
Yes

Number of Labs:
Four, plus departmental labs

Numbers of Computers:
100

24-Hour Labs:
Novack, in Berry Library

Charge to Print?
Every student is allowed to print 600 pages for free each term, with exceptions given to thesis writers. After that, every page costs five cents.

Operating Systems
Windows, Macintosh, UNIX

Free Software
Adobe Acrobat Reader, Adobe Photoshop, ArcView, BlitzMail, GreenPrint, Kerberos, QuickTime, Maple, Matlab, Mathematica, Netscape, SPSS 11, Stata 7

"**BlitzMail, our e-mail system, has basically taken over the role of the telephone for students. Everyone on campus uses it, and students check it practically 'round the clock.**"

Q "The computer access at Dartmouth is ridiculous. **I often wonder what we need so many computers** and so much technology for. We have every convenience and are spoiled rotten when it comes to this, so get excited!"

Q "They're everywhere. Literally. You can't walk down a hallway without finding public BlitzMail terminals that will soon dominate your life. Plus, **WiFi access everywhere** means that, with a laptop, the world is at your fingertips from the entire campus; doing research for a paper while sitting under a tree on The Green is not just an image plastered on brochures."

Q "**All students are required to have computers**, which are connected to one of the fastest Internet Ethernet connections in the country. There really aren't computer labs, but there are public computers all over campus."

Q "There are a handful of 24-hour machines by Novack Café, but **the college still lacks a central computer lab**. First floor Berry is the biggest, but it's impossible to get work done there with all the people traipsing through."

The College Prowler Take
ON COMPUTERS

Dartmouth's campus-wide wireless network is incredibly convenient and widely acclaimed, providing Internet and e-mail access everywhere from dorm lounges to The Green. Just don't let your professor catch you following your hometown team during class! All dorm rooms and many public spaces are equipped with Ethernet ports. Computers are used most often for the ubiquitous BlitzMail, and the Dartmouth Name Directory makes it easy to e-mail everyone from professors to that girl in your history class. All freshmen are to bring or purchase a computer, and most choose to buy one from the school for convenience. While the labs are too small and overcrowded, Dartmouth's online registration and public printing systems are both very easy to use.

Facilities

The Lowdown
ON FACILITIES

Student Center:
Collis

Athletic Center:
Alumni Gym, with the Kresge Fitness Center located inside

Libraries:
8

Popular Places to Chill:
Collis Commonground, The Green, Novack Café

Movie Theatre on Campus?
The Loew Auditorium

Bowling on Campus?
No, but there is a hot bowling alley in White River Junction, 10 minutes away

Bar on Campus?
Lone Pine Tavern

Coffeehouse on Campus?
Big Green Bean

The College Prowler™ Grade on
Computers: A

A high grade in Computers designates that computer labs are available, the computer network is easily accessible, and the campus' computing technology is up-to-date.

Favorite Things to Do

There's always an event going on at the Hopkins Center. Movies are popular, or you can rent your own from Jones Media Center in Berry Library. Students mob The Green when it's warm enough to be outside, particularly at the beginning of spring. Collis Commonground is home to everything from conferences, to volunteer fairs, to dance parties.

Did You Know?

Sanborn Library serves tea every weekday at 4 p.m..

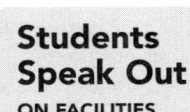

Students Speak Out
ON FACILITIES

"Everything's very nice and new. I have almost no complaints, and anything I would want to change is probably being renovated within the next few years."

"**The gym is really nice**. I work out often, so I'm there a bunch. Squash courts, basketball, tennis, swimming, weight lifting, and a whole lot more."

"On the whole, the infrastructure is a bit old, if well-maintained. **Most of the dorms date from the 1920s** and have not been changed much since. But, what is lost in modernity is made up for in charm."

"**Facilities are, for the most part, very good**. The gym is often criticized, but beyond that, the facilities here are top-notch. The great thing is that undergraduates have access to anything the college owns. If you want to do some research with the MRI Dartmouth owns, you don't need to wait 'til you're a med school student. You can sign up to use it."

"I don't know if this counts as facilities, but the college has two land grants. The Dartmouth Outing Club maintains hundreds of miles of trails as well as a bunch of cabins all over New Hampshire. The Skiway and the Connecticut River would be considered nice facilities, and **you can rent the stuff you need for either**."

"**A lot of people don't like Berry Library**, but I don't mind it. There are plenty of places to study, and be sure to check out the Tower Room when you visit. It's on the third floor of Baker and provides the most ideal Ivy League setting anywhere on campus."

The College Prowler Take
ON FACILITIES

Students are generally satisfied, but not thrilled, with Dartmouth's facilities. While Alumni Gym meets the needs of many, the cramped weight room, also known as Kresge Fitness Center, provides the perfect reason not to work out. The enormous Baker and Berry libraries, combined with satellite libraries, provide plenty of study space, although many students despise the antiseptic look of Berry's interior. While Dartmouth has poured millions into new buildings, including Berry and the adjacent Carson, the College is in need of more dorm space. While Collis is passable as a student center, with its dining options, TV room, and common space, Dartmouth lacks a true central gathering place for students once the Green is overcome by snow.

The College Prowler™ Grade on
Facilities: B

A high Facilities grade indicates that the campus is aesthetically pleasing and well-maintained; facilities are state-of-the-art, and libraries are exceptional. Other determining factors include the quality of both athletic and student centers and an abundance of things to do on campus.

Campus Dining

The Lowdown
ON CAMPUS DINING

Freshman Meal Plan Requirement?
Yes

24-Hour On-Campus Eating?
No

Student Favorites:
Food Court, Collis, Courtyard Cafe

Meal Plan Average Cost:
$2,400 per year

Did You Know?
The Pavilion serves Kosher-for-Passover meals during the Jewish holiday.

Students Speak Out
ON CAMPUS DINING

"There's the Hopkins Center, where most of the artsy people eat, since it's in the art building. There's also the main food court, and Homeplate, a healthier version of the regular stuff."

Q "The food is one of the best aspects of being a college student at Dartmouth. Dartmouth Dining Services [DDS] gives innumerable options about 20 hours a day. Inside Thayer dining hall alone, **there is a plethora of options**, including a grill [and] sandwich bar area, an exquisite Kosher dining section, an upscale specialized-entree section, a smoothie and juice bar, and a small college-owned convenience store. Food Court, the above mentioned 'grill [and] sandwich bar area,' is the most popular dining option for students, generally focusing American food, like cheeseburgers—and they are delicious burgers at that. The smoothie bar, The Blend, is also a tremendously popular option. Best of all, you can charge all food to your student card without having to worry about how many meals you have available."

Q "**Dartmouth is awesome**, as far as food goes! The food is honestly really good. Homeplate is probably my favorite. They have a great grill and sandwich bar and always have awesome hot meals and other stuff. There are a lot of good dining halls, though, not just that one. The food is pretty expensive but you just subtract money from your meal card, so you can eat whatever you want whenever you want, and you don't need cash. There are no set meal times or anything so you can just go grab some food whenever and subtract the price from your meal plan. It's a pretty cool system."

Q "**There's an abundance of greasy/fried food, if that's your thing**. Dining Services also does a good job of providing healthy meals, especially at the always-trendy Collis. What we seem to lack is the more 'normal' food. The new Kosher dining facility is great, though—never any lines and food of outstanding quality."

Q "**You're forced to get a meal plan by the college**, so you just have a card to eat at the various dining halls, and they subtract it from you account. It's kind of a rip-off, unless you shop smart. There is also a Dartmouth convenience store where you may also spend your meal plan dollars, but the prices are pretty high there."

Q "Aside from the fact that the food is overpriced, Dartmouth dining services offer more variety and higher quality food than most colleges do. **I've been happy so far, anyway**."

Off-Campus Dining

The College Prowler Take
ON CAMPUS DINING

The Lowdown
ON OFF-CAMPUS DINING

Dartmouth is that rare school where students speak fondly about their campus food. While all cafeteria offers are certain to get old, sumptuous options like the nutritious Homeplate or the greasy Courtyard Café will almost make you forget about mom's secret-recipe lasagna. **The food is expensive, and each item must be purchased individually, but savvy students know how to stretch their dollars.**

Best Pizza:
Ramunto's

Best Chinese:
Panda House

Best Breakfast:
Lou's Restaurant

Best Place to Take Your Parents:
Hanover Inn

Student Favorites:
EBAs, Ramunto's, Dirt Cowboy, Murphy's, Molly's

24-Hour Eating:
Fort Lou's in Lebanon, Food Stop on Main Street

The College Prowler™ Grade on
Campus Dining: B

Our grade on Campus Dining addresses the quality of both school-owned dining halls and independent on-campus restaurants as well as the price, availability, and variety of food.

Students Speak Out
ON OFF-CAMPUS DINING

The College Prowler Take
ON OFF-CAMPUS DINING

"Restaurants around here aren't bad. The campus runs right into Main Street, and there are a few good ones there. Molly's is my personal favorite, but Murphy's and 5 Olde Nugget are good, too."

Q "This is fairly limited, but considering Hanover is a small town in New Hampshire, we're not doing too badly. **Pretty much any type of food can be found**, and everything's open really late."

Q "If you have a car, you can drive to West Lebanon, where there's a McDonald's, a Burger King, and some good non-fast-food options. Without a car, you still have access to Subway, Ben and Jerry's, and a number of decent sit-down places. Most of them aren't usually that crowded. **There's some great pizza places**, too, but if you're from Chicago or New York City, you probably won't agree."

Q "It's severely limited for those without a car. Restaurants in Hanover are generally mediocre and expensive. **Only Murphy's On the Green is really worth it**. I'm salivating over their sweet potato fries right now."

Q "**This is one of the weaker aspects of Dartmouth life**, although thankfully the on-campus dining makes up for the shortcomings of off-campus dining. Ethnic food offerings are limited: there is one Japanese food option [Bamboo Garden], one Chinese food option [Panda House], two Indian food options [India Queen and Jewel of India], and a few other nearby restaurants, including an Italian restaurant in West Lebanon. The most notable restaurant in the area is Lou's Diner. Lou's has been serving Dartmouth students for over 50 years, and has perfected the art of huge portions and delicious food. Some students stay up until 6:00 a.m. and get an early breakfast at Lou's."

While the campus food is good enough to keep students eating in the dining halls, most of the time, one can only eat so many Food Court Double Burger Deals. When you finally venture off campus to sate your appetite, you'll find a surprisingly large selection of establishments for a town as small as Hanover. Everyone has their favorite restaurants, and they despise some, but there's always somewhere to take your parents or your date, should you be so lucky.

The College Prowler™ Grade on
Off-Campus Dining: C-

A high Off-Campus Dining grade implies that off-campus restaurants are affordable, accessible, and worth visiting. Other factors include the variety of cuisine and the availability of alternative options (vegetarian, vegan, Kosher, etc.).

Campus Housing

Did You Know?
All Dartmouth students receive free cable as well as free long-distance calls.

Students Speak Out
ON CAMPUS HOUSING

The Lowdown
ON CAMPUS HOUSING

Undergrads on Campus:
2,825 (70-80 percent)

Number of Dormitories:
32 (plus six Treehouses)

Room Types:
One-room singles
One-, two-, and three-room doubles
Two- and three-room triples
Three-room quads

Cleaning Service?
In public areas—Cleaning of rooms available only in East Wheelock

You Get:
Bed, desk, chair, bookshelf, dresser, closet, Ethernet port, cable jack

Not permitted:
Microwaves, pets

Bed Type:
Twin extra-long (39" x 80")

"Housing is amazing. I think that Residential Life works really hard to make living on campus a great experience, and it is. Most people choose to live on campus because it's a great deal."

"The dorms are, for the most part, really nice, but some really suck—**stay away from the river dorms and the Choates**. Otherwise, they're pretty sweet. Some have big rooms. I had a fireplace last year, and personal bathrooms are common."

"In terms of housing, the dorms are really nice. Most of them are **old buildings with a lot of character**. Some even have working fireplaces in the rooms. I lived in Wheeler last year in a small, one-room double with a fireplace. My room was probably the smallest out of all my friends', but it was in a great location. A lot of the rooms have two rooms for three people, so you can have a sleeping room and a common room."

"The River is the farthest away from campus—about a 10-minute walk, but that's about it. The **Choates aren't that great, but I think the dorms are generally nice**. A lot of them have extra amenities, bathrooms, carpeting, and fireplaces, so they can be really nice."

"**East Wheelock is the nicest dorm cluster** on campus; it's really like a three- or four-star hotel. The Choates, on the other hand, suck. They are an architectural nightmare, plain and simple; they are just ugly as all hell. The River is even worse—it's ugly and in the back of beyond. It is located behind the business and engineering schools."

The College Prowler Take
ON CAMPUS HOUSING

Of Dartmouth's residential clusters, the Choates and the River are uniformly regarded as the worst digs. However, the half of freshmen who are stuck there often say that the bonding experience of single-class housing makes up for the cramped quarters. Dartmouth's community is made stronger by the fact that almost all Dartmouth students, even seniors, live on campus in dorms or Greek houses. And, with the spacious size of most dorms, it's easy to see why. Most residence halls are of equal quality, and no one dorm is more than a 10-minute walk from anywhere on campus. However, while we can't guarantee you'll avoid the occasional roommate from hell, at least you'll have a large enough room that you can keep your distance from the fire and brimstone.

Off-Campus Housing

The Lowdown
ON OFF-CAMPUS HOUSING

Undergrads in Off-Campus Housing:
500-1,000 (12-25 percent)

Average Rent for a One-Bedroom Apartment:
$500-$700/month

Average Rent for a Two-Bedroom Apartment:
$600-$1,000/month

Average Rent for a Two-Bedroom Apartment:
$1,000+ month

Best Time to Look for a Place:
As early as possible, generally a year in advance

The College Prowler™ Grade on
Campus Housing: B+

A high Campus Housing grade indicates that dorms are clean, well-maintained, and spacious. Other determining factors include variety of dorms, proximity to classes, and social atmosphere.

Popular Areas
Close to campus—School Street and Lebanon Street. Hot spots include 8 School, 7 West, 30 Lebanon, The Red Barn, The Loveshack, and The Moontowers.

For Assistance Contact:
Dartmouth College Real Estate Office
Web: *www.dartmouthre.com*
Phone: (603) 646-2446

Students Speak Out
ON OFF-CAMPUS HOUSING

"I know a bunch of people that have moved off campus. **It seems pretty convenient, although I don't find it as practical as it would be at a big university. The dorms at Dartmouth are pretty good.**"

Q "Don't believe anyone who says there isn't a lot of it. **You can find housing in Hanover anywhere** as long as you're looking. I live off-campus now for Sophomore Summer, and it's been fabulous."

Q "**There really isn't much off-campus housing**, so most people live in the dorms all four years at Dartmouth. Some off-campus housing exists, of course, but nothing off campus is connected to the computer network, and that's a significant drawback."

Q "**It's great to live off campus and feel more independent**. You can cook your own meals, live with your closest friends, and get away from campus when things get stressful."

Q "If you want to live off campus, it is a definite possibility after your freshman year, but there is not a ton of housing in town, so **you have to plan early**. I actually have a house already for my junior year with nine other people. Usually off-campus housing is pretty nice—if you can get a place."

Q "There isn't a lot of housing off campus because there isn't a lot off campus. **Hanover is pretty darn small**. Cost will vary, convenience will vary, and landlords are generally rotten, but they vary, too."

The College Prowler Take
ON OFF-CAMPUS HOUSING

While many students live off campus for a term or two, there's no mass exodus from the dorms like at many other schools. The choice between the apartments adjacent to campus and the bigger houses deep in Hanover comes down to whether or not students want to drive to school every day.

Off-campus housing varies wildly in price and quality, as well as in distance from campus. The dorms are as nice as, or nicer than, most apartments and cost about the same on average. But, because of changes in the college's blocking policy, it is difficult to live with a group of friends in the same dorm after freshman year. That is the main appeal of off-campus housing; it's a chance to spend a lot of quality time with close friends in a secluded setting.

The College Prowler™ Grade on
Off-Campus Housing: B

A high grade in Off-Campus Housing indicates that apartments are of high quality, close to campus, affordable, and easy to secure.

Diversity

Most Popular Religions
There is a presence on campus for Catholics, Muslims, Jews, and Protestants of several denominations, while the non-denominational Tucker Foundation ensures that all faiths are respected and acknowledged. Only a small minority of Dartmouth students practice their religions fervently.

Political Activity
While the conservative Dartmouth Review is an established institution and the relatively new Dartmouth Free Press has added a liberal perspective to the campus debate, most students are apathetic. However, since New Hampshire is the first primary state, all Dartmouth students are guaranteed to get an up close view of at least one presidential election and a slew of visits from chief executive hopefuls, which generate a political buzz once every four years.

Gay Tolerance
Out students fare quite well, while those still in the closet often have a tougher time. Gays are becoming more prominent on campus, and acceptance is generally growing.

Economic Status
The fact that half of Dartmouth's students aren't on any financial aid speaks to the general wealth of the student body. But, despite the Ivy League prestige, there is little old money at Dartmouth—and few affluent students flaunt their wealth or act in an elitist manner. There are many middle-class students partially working their way through college.

The Lowdown
ON DIVERSITY

African American: 6%

Asian American: 12%

Hispanic: 6%

Native American: 3%

White: 68%

International: 5%

Out-of-State: 97%

Minority Clubs
AfriCaSO, Dartmouth Asian Organization, Dartmouth Chinese Culture Society, Hokupa'a, International Students Association, Japan Society, Korean American Students Association, La Alianza Latina, Movimiento Estudiantil Chicano/a de Aztlan, MOSAIC, Native Americans at Dartmouth, Shamis, Vietnamese Student Association

Students Speak Out
ON DIVERSITY

"Dartmouth is pretty diverse, but I think that after 200-plus years of being a predominantly white, heterosexual, male environment, the College still has some work to do on improving life for minorities."

Q "**People complain a lot about Dartmouth not being diverse**. In some ways, this complaint is completely justified. In others ways, I think people are missing what is around them. I have friends of all different races, ethnicities, and backgrounds, and diversity at Dartmouth has been essential to my positive experience here."

Q "This is a tough question to answer because even though the College is numerically very diverse, I think **the administration has gone about it in exactly the wrong way**. The notion is that I should make up for centuries of white male privilege by feeling guilty and being sensitive. While changing with the times certainly is in order, I think the college is really losing its identity in a sea of politically-correct mumbo jumbo."

Q "**Dartmouth is approaching a 40/60 percent minority/non-minority ratio and has improved in the area of diversity by leaps and bounds**. Despite a small natural minority recruiting pool—New Hampshire is one of the whitest states in the nation—Dartmouth has succeeded in bringing people of different races, ethnicities, religions, and perspectives together for an explosion of discourse. While racial self-segregation is a minor problem at the College, students consciously identify artificial barriers to relationships, like race, and act to overcome them. While very few people are 100-percent free of preconceived notions at Dartmouth, just as in most other areas of the world, Dartmouth students take advantage of their diversity in exploring new intellectual and personal areas together."

Q "As far as being gay at Dartmouth, **I find the school to be unacceptable**. I could talk about this for a while, but just know that, as a minority, I don't feel like Dartmouth is doing as much as they can for me. With the two-billion-dollar endowment that the school has, you'd think they could do more."

The College Prowler Take
ON DIVERSITY

As an Ivy League institution, Dartmouth's student body has traditionally been predominantly straight, white, and male. Despite fervent administration efforts to promote diversity, the "average" Dartmouth student is still a crusty New England type sporting Northface. But, special programs abound for traditionally underrepresented groups. Efforts to recruit Native Americans, whom Dartmouth was originally founded to educate, have been particularly vigorous. Students also report a sizable international population on campus. While women and minorities are now proportionally represented on campus, many still feel like outsiders in the rugged New Hampshire woods. Meanwhile, other students feel racial minorities frequently self-segregate into "affinity housing" and homogenous Greek houses. Despite occasional tension, a strong sense of school spirit often prevails over individual differences.

The College Prowler™ Grade on
Diversity: B

A high grade in Diversity indicates that ethnic minorities and international students have a notable presence on campus and that students of different economic backgrounds, religious beliefs, and sexual preferences are well-represented.

Guys & Girls

The Lowdown
ON GUYS & GIRLS

Women Undergrads:
48.9%

Men Undergrads:
51.1%

Birth Control Available?
Yes

Social Scene
With no notable divisions among its student body, Dartmouth has a vibrant social scene. While some students initiate love affairs with their laptops, and others go out every night of the week, most know when to hit the books and when to let loose—usually two or three nights a week. Students are usually very friendly in classes and extracurricular activities. As opportunities to meet others abound in daily interactions, and most students are linked by about two degrees of separation, building an ample social network is often as easy as lingering in the dining halls. While people usually associate by degrees of "coolness," and the strength of athletes' bonds tends to make them exclusive groups, most students do have a wide cross-section of friends.

Hookups or Relationships?
To the frustration of many guys and girls, commitment-free hookups are extremely prevalent. Those who enter relationships often do so seriously, to the point that casual dinner-and-movie relations are about as common as pterodactyls around campus. Many students enter Dartmouth with hometown significant others, but most of these relationships quickly fade away.

Dress Code
The protocol definitely calls for preppy, although with a North Woods twist. One glance at the Hinman Box mailroom indicates that J. Crew is the manufacturer of choice, but be sure to bring along that North Face or Columbia jacket for when the weather turns cold. While students may throw on jeans and a decent sweater for class, they don't overdo it. That goes for parties as well, over which guys and girls rarely fuss—and who could blame them, with a night of mucky basements ahead. Moreover, when it's time for one of many theme parties, dress codes go out the window. Color Dartmouth students "refined outdoorsy."

Students Speak Out
ON GUYS & GIRLS

"Everyone says the girls aren't that hot, but I think they are the same as at other colleges. They just wear more clothing because it is cold in Hanover a lot of the time."

"It's hard to generalize when it comes to looks. I think that the stereotypical Dartmouth male would be a beer-guzzling, football-playing frat boy, but you will find that **the guys are all very different**. I would consider myself to be as far from the 'typical' Dartmouth male as possible. The girls are the same way—the stereotypical girl would be a ditsy blonde sorority girl, but obviously they're not all that way. Both the guys and the girls are pretty attractive, I'd say. All in all, we have a good-looking campus."

Q "Supposedly **the guys are 'above average'** (I have had girls tell me this), and the girls are 'below average' (all the guys I know agree). The girls are not so hot, but then again, Dartmouth isn't a state school, so this is to be expected."

Q "Nice, cute, fun guys are everywhere, but the campus seems to fall into two categories when it comes to dating: random hookups that leave people confused, hurt, and make for awkward situations, but can be a lot of fun; and the married-since-they-met crowd, where couples end up living together. **There doesn't seem to be a middle ground of adult dating**. Meeting a guy through a friend, in class, or an activity seems to lead to more successful relationships than drunken hookups with near-strangers."

Q "Well, it's a mixed bag. **We tend to attract a ton of athletic girls**, so we get a mix of hyper-attractive athletes and relatively unattractive 'butch women.' The good thing is that they're generally all confident, smart, witty, and classy. Although dating can be difficult in the party-oriented atmosphere, it is comforting to know that it's easy to make friends with girls no matter what they look like."

Q "Dartmouth girls are regarded as **some of the ugliest in the Ivy League**. Lookers are few and tend to be snapped up by jocks and frat boys. The almost exactly equal gender ratio destroys any advantage guys would normally have in dating, and the result is almost cutthroat competition. Still, there are diamonds to be found in the rough."

The College Prowler Take
ON GUYS & GIRLS

Don't drop that high-school sweetheart just yet, but Dartmouth students seem to think they look all right. The disparity between guys and girls is very real, although recent female classes are quickly closing the gap, regardless of whether or not the Dartmouth Beautification Project actually exists. Hookups—drunken or otherwise—dominate a virtually nonexistent dating scene. With beer goggles or without, most students are able to locate a hottie or two. While Ivy Leaguers are known more for brain than brawn, Dartmouth students defy the stereotype. Students in general, and particularly freshman guys, sometimes complain about the slim pickings, but most everyone is relatively normal looking, not to mention in fantastic shape.

The College Prowler™ Grade on
Guys: A-

A high grade for Guys indicates that the male population on campus is attractive, smart, friendly, and engaging, and that the school has a decent ratio of guys to girls.

The College Prowler™ Grade on
Girls: B-

A high grade for Girls not only implies that the women on campus are attractive, smart, friendly, and engaging, but also that there is a fair ratio of girls to guys.

Athletics

The Lowdown ON ATHLETICS

Men's Varsity Teams:
Baseball
Basketball
Crew, Lightweight (plus freshman team)
Crew, Heavyweight (plus freshman team)
Cross Country (plus JV team)
Football (plus JV team)
Golf
Ice Hockey
Lacrosse
Skiing, Alpine and Cross Country
Soccer (plus JV team)
Squash
Swimming and Diving
Tennis
Track and Field, Indoor
Track and Field, Outdoor

Women's Varsity Teams:
Basketball
Crew (plus novice team)
Cross Country (plus JV team)
Field Hockey
Golf
Ice Hockey
Lacrosse
Skiing, Alpine & Cross Country
Soccer (plus JV team)
Softball
Squash
Swimming and Diving
Tennis
Track and Field, Indoor
Track and Field, Outdoor
Volleyball

Coed Teams:
Equestrian
Sailing

Club Sports:
Badminton
EMS
Fencing
Figure Skating
Ice Hockey
Rugby, Men's
Rugby, Women's
Snowboarding
Table Tennis
Tae Kwan Do
Tang Soo Doo
Ultimate Frisbee, Men's
Ultimate Frisbee, Women's
Volleyball, Men's
Water Polo, Men's
Water Polo, Women's

Intramurals (IMs):
Basketball
Eight Ball
Free Throw Shooting
Flag Football
Golf Handball
Ice Hockey
Lacrosse
Racquetball
Soccer
Softball
Table Tennis
Tennis/Team Tennis
Turkey Trot Fun Run
Volleyball
Wallyball
Water Polo
Whiffle Ball

Most Popular Sports
Men's rugby, football, and both ice hockey teams have the largest following. Rugby, crew, and ultimate Frisbee all have large squads.

Overlooked Teams
Women's basketball had a solid, yet overlooked, season, while, at the club level, the cycling team is fantastic.

Fields
Memorial Field, Sachem Field, Scully-Fahey Field

School Mascot
None

School Nickname
Big Green

Athletic Division
NCAA Division I (I-AA for men's football)

Conference
Eastern College Athletic Conference

Getting Tickets
All students receive free entry to all sporting events simply by flashing their IDs. Additional planning is unnecessary.

Students Speak Out
ON ATHLETICS

"**The varsity sports are not so big.** If you're looking for a school where athletics are an integral part of campus life, then Dartmouth isn't going to be your first choice. IM sports exist, but they aren't huge."

Q "**The main draws are football and hockey**, although we have great success in several other areas, including nationally-ranked lacrosse and crew teams. Our football team draws huge crowds, especially for the Homecoming and Harvard games. While our teams, as of late, have not been terribly successful, a good time is had by all. With hockey, on the other hand, Dartmouth has seen a great deal of success. Club and intramural sports are enormously popular, with nearly all students participating in some type of athletics."

Q "**Athletes are a dominant force on campus**. The resulting furor when the administration tried to cut the swim team far exceeded the mumbles of discontent over the closing of satellite libraries. While hockey comes close, there is no dominant sport on campus—but people here are always exercising. Sometimes I wonder if the admissions office specifically rejects obese people."

Q "**Some sports are better then others**, but no matter how badly the football team does, and it is usually bloody awful, there is always a big audience at games. IM sports are popular; most organizations have their own teams—College Bowl's basketball team or the 'God Squad' softball team, a combination of Aquinas House [Catholic organization] and Hillel."

The College Prowler Take
ON ATHLETICS

Very few students watch Dartmouth sporting events religiously, but don't let that fool you into thinking they can't distinguish between football and fútbol. This small school supports an amazing number of NCAA teams, meaning that a full half of Dartmouth students are varsity athletes. While basketball and football haven't fielded dominant teams for years, winter hockey games at Leverone Field House are a favorite. There is sometimes a divide between athletes and their egghead peers, but all the sweating that goes on at Dartmouth generally promotes a friendly atmosphere for the student-athlete.

The College Prowler™ Grade on
Athletics: B+

A high grade in Athletics indicates that students have school spirit, that sports programs are respected, that games are well-attended, and that intramurals are a prominent part of student life.

Greek Life

Students Speak Out
ON GREEK LIFE

"Most houses can be stereotyped, but there are many exceptions to each rule. Greeks provide most of the social space and programming on campus outside of college-sponsored events, which tend to be lackluster."

Q "**Frats make up the dominant social scene on campus.** You can find somewhere to party at any time on any night of the week. I nearly didn't come to Dartmouth because of the strength of the Greek system, but now I'm glad I did. While I came on to campus as a freshman vowing to never join a frat, I found out that their reputations are generally ill-deserved. While the parties are fun, the camaraderie and closeness that develops between members is incredible and well worth the disgust from looking at the floors of the basements. The Greek system is one of the last remnants of Old Dartmouth, the way that college life was supposed to be."

Q "It's not as bad as some would initially think. **Houses are vastly different from one another** and change every year. Sorority rush is awful, but it's worth the outcome of 50 to 80 potential new friends and a place that you're always welcome."

Q "It can be overwhelming and all-encompassing at times, but **it's a great social option if you choose to join a house or attend events**. There is a sense that everyone and anyone on campus is welcome, so openness is a positive feature."

Q "**Greek life on campus is very influential**, and many men and women decide to become affiliated with a Greek organization. Alcohol often plays a role in Greek life and activities. However, to say that this is a defining characteristic of Greeks is untrue. Greek houses frequently sponsor community service opportunities, concerts, speakers, and other community-oriented events. Greek life at Dartmouth also serves to foster community by increasing the support network available to students."

The Lowdown
ON GREEK LIFE

Number of Fraternities:
17

Number of Sororities:
10

Number of Coed Houses:
3

Number of Undergraduate Societies:
2

Percent of Undergrad Men in Fraternities:
28% of men, 37% of eligible men (non-freshmen)

Percent of Undergrad Women in Sororities:
22% of women, 30% of eligible women (non-freshmen)

The College Prowler Take
ON GREEK LIFE

As far as parties go, it's all Greek to me. While half of eligible students—those in their sophomore winter or later—pledge a fraternity or sorority, you don't have to be Greek to partake. Almost all frat parties are open to all students, and cheap beer—Keystone or Milwaukee's Best—flows freely to all. Liquor is less common, although invite-only "'tails" events are popular. And even for abstaining students, the parties on big weekends are truly a sight to behold. While a few students don't care for the frats and some upperclassmen grow weary of the monotonous scene, the Greek system is a binding tie for most. Three nights a week, most of the action can still be found on good ol' Webster Avenue.

Drug Scene

The Lowdown
ON DRUG SCENE

Most Prevalent Drugs on Campus:
Marijuana, cocaine, ecstasy

Liquor-Related Arrests:
Campus Safety and Security reported 247 cases of alcohol-related arrests in 2003.

Drug Counseling Programs
Counseling and Human Development

Phone: (603) 650-1442

Services: Assessment, individual counseling, group counseling

Students Speak Out
ON DRUG SCENE

"There's not much of a scene that I know of. If you want drugs, you can certainly get them, but it's not a huge deal at Dartmouth, and I think most students like it that way."

The College Prowler™ Grade on
Greek Life: A

A high grade in Greek Life indicates that sororities and fraternities are not only present, but also active on campus. Other determining factors include the variety of houses available and the respect the Greek community receives from the rest of the campus.

Q "**If you aren't into drugs, you won't know they're there**. If you want drugs, you'll always be able to find them."

Q "They're basically nonexistent. **There's a little weed here and there**, and a few other drugs, but you have to actively look for drugs other than pot to find them. I partied frequently last year and only saw alcohol, weed, and one piece of mushrooms. Nothing more."

Q "**The two biggest drugs are pot and ecstasy**. Quite a few people smoke up, but it's not a big deal. Personally, I don't smoke, and I have never been pressured into smoking."

Q "**The drug scene is pretty low-key**; but it does exist. Most people stick to alcohol, although I've seen tons of pot, and ecstasy is starting to become popular."

Q "Drugs are surprisingly present, despite the remoteness of Hanover. **Hard drugs are available**, though you won't witness much unless you specifically seek them, so it's easy to avoid. Most people aren't into it."

The College Prowler Take
ON DRUG SCENE

While the average student may run across quite a bit of pot, Dartmouth's drug scene has a very low profile. While ecstasy or the occasional bag of mushrooms might show up at parties, students generally pass on everything but the grass. People in the know claim that the hard drugs are out there, and certain fraternities at Dartmouth have a reputation as substance abuse hot spots. While it may not satisfy the authorities or your parents, you should know that most students are not bothered by the softer drugs they encounter.

The College Prowler™ Grade on
Drug Scene: B

A high grade on Drug Scene indicates that drugs are not a noticeable part of campus life; drug use is not visible, and no pressure to use them seems to exist.

Campus Strictness

The Lowdown
ON CAMPUS STRICTNESS

What Are You Most Likely to Get Caught Doing on Campus?
Public intoxication, drinking underage, having an unregistered keg, creating a fire hazard (read: leaving anything) in the hallway, keeping books from the reserve desk for too long, engaging in a vicious "blitz" war, streaking across The Green, speaking your politically-incorrect mind

Students Speak Out
ON CAMPUS STRICTNESS

{ "If you get really sick from drinking and have to go to the medical center, you won't get in trouble. I don't think they bust down on drugs very much because it would make Dartmouth look bad, heaven forbid that happen."

Q "**Lots of people get picked up by Safety and Security when they're drunk**, but it's not a big deal. Just make sure you don't get caught twice, and your parents will never know."

Q "**Punishment for drinking can be severe** depending on what campus police officer you get in trouble with. You aren't thrown in jail for underage drinking; everyone knows what goes on in frats, and campus police just needs to make sure no one is seriously in danger, or else they get in trouble. If you are caught for underage drinking, you must speak to the class dean, and they will possibly talk to your parents. You might get a fine, I don't know. I was never caught. Hanover police are a different story; they suck. They are far less frequent than the ubiquitous Dartmouth campus police, luckily."

Q "While frats aren't supposed to serve minors, **the wristband system they use is a joke**. When Safety and Security walks into a party, people just calmly put down their drinks until they leave. However, while rules aren't so strict for individuals, frats have to jump through a ridiculous number of administrative hurdles to throw a party and often get in trouble for minor violations."

Q "For the most part, there is not much strictness on campus. **Students generally do what they please**, within the bounds of the law, and have a great time doing it. Safety and Security usually stays out of students' business, except for when they're intervening for somebody's safety. While S&S has a bad rep in some quarters of campus, most people believe that S&S maintains a very low level of campus strictness while ensuring campus-wide safety."

Q "**I got fined for everything last year**. Leaving shoes outside my door, unspecified hall damage, turning in my practice-room key too late. It got to be rather ridiculous."

The College Prowler Take
ON CAMPUS STRICTNESS

Opinions are clearly mixed. But keep in mind that students most frequently encounter campus authorities while inebriated. Although visibly soused students are frequently detained, Safety and Security usually won't bug those who act sober. While they conduct walk-throughs at parties, S&S looks the other way at mass underage drinking, as long as containers are kept inside. Older students report that the increasing administration exercise of "*in loco parentis*" is just plain *loco* at this point and deprives Dartmouth of valuable traditions. While the administration rarely sweats the small stuff, fines for everything from parking violations to leaving shoes in the hall do occur.

The College Prowler™ Grade on
Campus Strictness: B

A high Campus Strictness grade implies an overall lenient atmosphere; police and RAs are fairly tolerant, and the administration's rules are flexible.

Overall Experience

Students Speak Out
ON OVERALL EXPERIENCE

"I love Dartmouth! I've seen so many schools. I guarantee that if you do decide to come, you'll enjoy the four years you have here and probably look back wishing they did not go by so quickly."

Q "Most college students like their colleges. Dartmouth students are often in love with their school. **My personal passion for Dartmouth has exceeded my own expectations**, and I have found myself enormously happy at Dartmouth, despite initial misgivings. The people, resources, and general campus activity have made my Dartmouth experience, so far, entirely successful, and I am utterly content at Dartmouth. I can't wait for my summer to end so I can get back!"

Q "Academically, I think I've learned a lot at Dartmouth. I went on their Foreign Study Program in Paris last winter, and that was amazing. I think that the professors are all really nice and really intelligent. **Dartmouth is definitely a giant step up from high school**."

Q "If you want to find out a little more about campus life, you can go to *www.thedartmouth.com*. **The school newspaper is pretty helpful with assessing what life is like** and how important frats are."

The Inside Scoop

Q "**The school honestly cares about the students' social lives**. The Dartmouth Outing Club program helped me meet a bunch of nice kids before school ever started. Then, from the moment I left the woods, they have been planning activities for us."

Q "I felt the campus was very safe. People were incredibly friendly. The dining hall food was pretty good compared to most other colleges, but, after I moved off campus when I finally had some money, **I ate out a lot because the local restaurants were great**."

The College Prowler Take
ON OVERALL EXPERIENCE

The Lowdown
ON THE INSIDE SCOOP

According to numerous surveys, Dartmouth students are among the happiest in the land. And with a gorgeous campus, great food, spacious dorms, and a vibrant party scene, why shouldn't they be? There are certainly a host of minor drawbacks to attending school in Hanover—things like isolation and no parking. However, unique positives like the study abroad programs, top-notch academics, and numerous outdoor opportunities blow these negatives out of the water.

Dartmouth students have, perhaps, the strongest love for their school of any college kids in the country. This passion and camaraderie motivates distant alums to trek to Hanover for big weekends and party like they're teenagers again—or at least try to! Dartmouth is a student-friendly, down-to-earth institution and provides the vast majority of its students with a genuine Ivy League experience along with a big-name diploma that will dazzle employers come adulthood—oh, the horror!

Dartmouth Slang:
Know the slang, know the school. The following is a list of things you really need to know before coming to Dartmouth. The more words you know, the better off you'll be.

AT: Appalachian Trail; runs through campus
Banner Student: Online Website containing personal academic information
Blitz: E-mail; can be used as any part of speech
CD: Community director; no one is sure what they do, except boss around the UGAs.
D, The: Student newspaper; the nation's oldest and, many allege, worst
DA$H: An account used for on-campus, non-food purchases; it's not real money.
Dick's House: Student health center
EBAs: Everything But Anchovies; they deliver until 2 a.m.
Free Press, The: Liberal, school-supported newspaper
Green, The: Huge grassy rectangle at the center of campus
HB: Hinman Box, where you pick up your mail; located in the Hop
H-Po: Hanover Police; really avoid when drunk
Hop, The: Hopkins Center; performing arts center of campus
HTH: Hometown honey, with whom you will break up shortly after arriving on campus
ORL: Office of Residential Life

Parkhursted: Suspended; named after the administration building, Parkhurst
Pong: Beer pong; played exclusively with handleless paddles
Review, The: Independent conservative student newspaper
Rocky: Rockefeller Center; government center
Senior Fence: Surrounds part of the Green; don't sit on it if you're not a senior.
'Shmenu: The Green Book; contains pictures of all the freshmen
'Shmob: The large group in which most freshmen travel.
Sketchy: All-purpose word to describe anyone or anything about which you are skeptical; use liberally.
SA Cash: Debit account that can be used in town
Sphinx: Large, tomb-like home to a secret society, located in the middle of campus
S&S: Safety and Security; avoid when drunk
Term: Used most often in place of "quarter;" saying "semester" will give you away as a newbie in a heartbeat.
Thayer: Dining hall and engineering school; pay attention to context clues.
Treehouses: Hastily-constructed and undesirable dwellings near the river
Tripee: Fellow member of your freshman trip
Webster Ave.: Fraternity (and sorority) row

Dartmouth Urban Legends

Any Native American admitted will receive full a scholarship to Dartmouth. (While this is untrue, Dartmouth has renewed its original commitment to Native Americans and now has more Native American students than the other Ivies combined.)

Students caught drinking during orientation, and before matriculation, will have their admission rescinded.

Playboy once ranked Dartmouth's guys the second-hottest in the country.

Beer pong was invented at Dartmouth; students believe their paddle version is a purer game than the oft-played Beirut.

School Spirit

Love for the college on the Hill extends far beyond the Dartmouth jock-wear most students are perpetually sporting. From freshman trips forward, Dartmouth students are imbued with a fierce love of their unique and historic institution. The college's small size fosters a single Dartmouth community, and students often make the trek to Hanover during their off terms. Dartmouth alumni are fiercely loyal and noted for being generous with pocketbooks and connections. However, there is a sense among even recent graduates that the school is being slowly transformed into a cookie-cutter research institution. But, for now at least, Hanover is filled with students who love their school and are sublimely happy.

Traditions
Homecoming

Freshmen are the focus of Homecoming weekend, as they are officially welcomed into the Dartmouth family. On Friday night, upperclassmen collect all the pea-greens during a "Freshman Sweep." Everyone marches en masse to the center of the Green, where a giant bonfire ensues. Freshmen run around it one hundred times plus the last two digits of their class year, while older students and alumni egg them on.

Winter Carnival

Back before Dartmouth was coeducational, the long winter was warmed on this weekend as hundreds of women were bused in from all over the country. Now that women have populated the Hanover campus for three decades, Winter Carnival focuses more on seasonal festivities. A variety of sporting contests are held, and brave souls leap into Occom Pond to partake in the Polar Bear Jump.

Green Key

With temperatures finally mild, Dartmouth students take to the great outdoors to celebrate. Green Key is arguably the biggest party weekend of the year, as students bask in the sun for three or four straight days. Barbecues and concerts abound, with some fraternities throwing annual parties.

Ledyard Challenge

Before graduation, students are supposed to swim naked across the Connecticut River to Vermont (where nudity is legal), and then scamper in the buff back across the Ledyard Bridge.

Finding a Job or Internship

Things I Wish I Knew Before Coming to Dartmouth:

- Orientation is by far the best time to meet people … and go to frat row.
- All that time I procrastinated could have been spent having fun.
- I only have time for two or three extracurricular activities.
- How few nice clothes I need and how many crazy clothes I could use.
- The Choates are nothing to worry about.
- How cold a New Hampshire winter is.
- How to ski … or camp.

Tips to Succeed at Dartmouth:

- Always go to class when midterms or finals are coming up.
- Take naps in the afternoon.
- Have at least one good friend in every class.
- Use distributive requirements to take fun classes.
- Avoid morning classes or Tuesday/Thursday classes all together.
- Plan a break or fun extracurricular activity into your schedule.
- Find two or three good study spots and move around.
- Don't let BlitzMail consume your life.

The Lowdown
ON FINDING A JOB OR INTERNSHIP

If your connections via Uncle Harold fail—or should you have none to begin with—seek out Career Services, which has a generally positive reputation around campus and provides comprehensive career help. Each fall, dozens of companies trek up to Dartmouth to woo seniors during Corporate Recruiting.

Advice
Career Services can be of help from the first summer onward, so attending a first-time users session immediately after arriving on campus can be especially helpful. Always keep a resume on file and monitor the Career Services BlitzMail Bulletin for interesting opportunities. Also, students interested in government should seek out the resources of the Rockefeller Center, which has a number of specific listings and internships.

Career Center Resources & Services
Job/Internship search workshops, job and internship listings (MonterTRAK), on-campus recruiting, Blitz Bulletin, graduate advising, electronic portfolio

Blunt Alumni Center

Blunt is located just northwest of the Green and often hosts alumni in a tent on big weekends.

Major Alumni Events

The three regular-year party weekends—Homecoming, Winter Carnival, and Green Key—bring a multitude of alums back to Hanover. Additionally, class reunions are held every five years during the week after commencement. Turnout for these reunions is very high, and the events raise a great deal of money for Dartmouth.

Alumni Publications

Dartmouth Alumni Magazine
(603) 646-2256
Alumni.Maganize@dartmouth.edu

Famous Dartmouth Alumni

Daniel Webster (Class of 1801), secretary of state under three Presidents

Robert Frost (Class of 1896), Pulitzer Prize-winning poet

Theodore ("Dr.") Seuss Geisel (Class of '25), world-famous children's author

Nelson Rockefeller (Class of '30), Vice-President under Gerald Ford

Dr. C. Everett Koop (Class of '37), U.S. surgeon general under President Reagan

(Mister) Fred Rogers (Class of '50), children's television entertainer

Louis Gerstner (Class of '63), former IBM CEO

H. Carl McCall (Class of '63), former New York comptroller and gubernatorial candidate

Paavo Lipponen (Class of '64), former Finnish prime minister

Robert Reich (Class of '68), U.S. secretary of labor under President Clinton

Paul Gigot (Class of '77), Pulitzer Prize-winning journalist

Dinesh D'Souza (Class of '83), political journalist and cultural critic

Jay Fiedler (Class of '94), quarterback for the Miami Dolphins

The Best & Worst

The Ten BEST Things About Dartmouth:

1. Tight-knit community
2. Beer Pong!
3. The D-Plan
4. Wireless everything
5. Outdoor opportunities
6. Big weekends
7. Three classes
8. Friendly professors
9. The Green on a beautiful day
10. EBAs at 2:15 a.m

The Ten WORST Things About Dartmouth:

1. Dark winter days
2. Isolation
3. The D-Plan
4. Wrangling over diversity
5. No parking!
6. Hefty fines (parking, drinking, etc.)
7. Lack of Hanover nightlife
8. Kresge Fitness Center on a crowded afternoon
9. Student apathy
10. Administration crackdown on the Greeks

Want to know more about the good, the bad, and the ugly on campus? Check out the College Prowler book on Dartmouth College available at www.collegeprowler.com.

Harvard University

University Hall, Cambridge, MA 02138
www.harvard.edu   (617) 495-1551

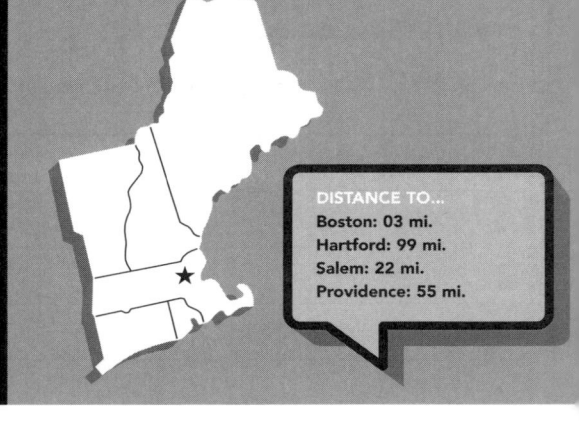

DISTANCE TO...
Boston: 03 mi.
Hartford: 99 mi.
Salem: 22 mi.
Providence: 55 mi.

"Harvard's reputation alone makes the school an attractive—and sometimes intimidating—place to earn a college education."

Total Enrollment:
6,591
Acceptance:
10%
Tuition:
$30,620
Top 10% of High School Class:
90%

SAT Range
Verbal	Math	Total
700 – 790	700 – 800	1400 – 1590

ACT Range
Verbal	Math	Total
30-35	30-35	31-34

SAT II Requirements
Any three subject tests.

Most Popular Majors:
14% Economics
11% Political Science and Government
8% Social Sciences
7% Psychology

Students Also Applied To:*
Princeton University, Yale University, Stanford University, MIT, Brown University

*For more school info check out www.collegeprowler.com

Table of Contents

Academics	557
Local Atmosphere	559
Safety & Security	560
Computers	562
Facilities	563
Campus Dining	565
Off-Campus Dining	566
Campus Housing	568
Off-Campus Housing	570
Diversity	571
Guys & Girls	573
Athletics	574
Greek Life	576
Drug Scene	578
Campus Strictness	579
Overall Experience	580
The Inside Scoop	582
Finding a Job or Internship	583
The Best & Worst	584

College Prowler Report Card

Academics	A
Local Atmosphere	A-
Safety & Security	B+
Computers	B
Facilities	B-
Campus Dining	D+
Off-Campus Dining	A
Campus Housing	A
Off-Campus Housing	F
Diversity	B+
Guys	B
Girls	B-
Athletics	C+
Greek Life	D+
Drug Scene	B+
Campus Strictness	A-

Academics

Special Degree Options
History and Literature, History and Science, MBB (Mind, Brain and Behavior), a diverse array of professional degrees from the professional schools

Best Places to Study
Lamont Library, House Dining Halls, in one of the many coffee shops around the square

Sample Academic Clubs
Model U.N., Women in Economics and Government, Harvard Venture Capital and Entrepreneurial Organization

The Lowdown
ON ACADEMICS

Degrees Awarded:
Bachelor, Master, Doctorate

Undergraduate Schools:
Harvard College

Full-time Faculty:
1,425

Faculty with Terminal Degree:
99%

Student-to-Faculty Ratio: 8:1

Average Course Load:
4 courses per semester

AP Test Score Requirements:
4 or 5 on AP Language Test exempts student from the one-year language requirement.

Four AP Test Scores of 4 or 5 allows student to enroll in Advanced Placement three-year degree program.

IB Test Score Requirements:
Advanced Placement for full IB diploma holders with three higher-level test scores of 6 or 7.

Did You Know?

The Harvard University library collection contains more than 14.6 million volumes. That makes it the second-largest library collection in the United States, falling behind only the Library of Congress.

Students Speak Out
ON ACADEMICS

"Most professors are terrific. Sure, there were a few I hated, but for the most part, they are excellent lecturers and make themselves available to all of their students."

Q "I've had some wonderful professors, some who were very dull, some who can't speak English, some who can't teach, and some who did not really care about us. It varies. You'll have some big classes and some really small ones, but you can usually pick good ones."

Q "**It all depends on what class**. Nearly all of my teachers this year were really amazing, except for my math teacher who was just horrid. You should definitely take foreign language classes—they rock—and if you take math, you should make sure your professor speaks English, unless you know another language."

Q "The teachers are amazing. **Some of them are a bit pompous and hard to deal with**, but they are all brilliant. With a little initiative, you can forge a strong relationship with a Nobel laureate in chemistry or whatever it is that you are interested in."

Q "Professors are good. The biggest piece of advice I can give you is to **pick classes based on the professors and not the subject material**. I didn't figure this out until my junior year and wasted a lot of time in bad classes. Ask around and read the CUE [Committee on Undergraduate Education] Guide, which is a student-compiled guide to courses that you'll get at the beginning of each year. There is also a two week 'shopping period' for classes. Again, student-professor contact is often hard to come by in larger classes, but I do know that the new president is very committed to changing that."

Q "**You're lucky if you ever meet your professor in almost every class**. Graduate students do the majority of the instruction. Some of them are good teachers, and some aren't. Classes can be interesting, but those are often the hardest ones. A lot of requirements are painful experiences, such as statistics."

The College Prowler Take
ON ACADEMICS

"Unparalleled," "world-class," and "exciting" are just a few of the words used to described the constellation of academic stars you will find leading class discussions and lecturing on a huge breadth of topics at Harvard. The school's unmatched resources and wide array of fields of study make it the ideal place to pursue nearly any academic interest. However, some students complain that professors are too far removed from undergraduate life and that teaching assistants are left with too much responsibility in some cases.

Despite a small number of complaints, Harvard University provides a fertile ground for intellectual growth. Renowned faculty, a treasure trove of resources, and undergraduate motivation all combine to make the Harvard a terrific place for higher education. Even if some students have trouble attaining "A" grades, the university passes with flying colors.

The College Prowler™ Grade on
Academics: A

A high Academics grade generally indicates that professors are knowledgeable, accessible, and genuinely interested in their students' welfare. Other determining factors include class size, how well professors communicate, and whether or not classes are engaging.

Local Atmosphere

Students Speak Out
ON LOCAL ATMOSPHERE

"I've loved it. The museums are great, and there's the symphony orchestra, the opera, and the ballet. Walking around Boston is wonderful. There are a lot of other schools around."

The Lowdown
ON LOCAL ATMOSPHERE

Region:
Northeast

City, State:
Cambridge, Massachusetts

Setting:
Major city

Distance from New York:
4-5 hours

Distance from Providence:
1 hour

Points of Interest:
Boston Common, Fenway Park, Quincy Market, Fanueil Hall

City Websites:
www.boston.com, www.bostonglobe.com

Major Sports Teams:
Boston Red Sox (MLB), Boston Celtics (NBA), Boston Bruins (NHL), New England Patriots (NFL)

Q "**Boston is neat, and it's all fairly accessible by subway**. There are a few bad areas, but it is a pretty safe city, overall. There are historic things, museums, sporting events—whatever you want—all about a 15-minute subway ride away from campus."

Q "I really like Cambridge as a city. **There's a good balance between feeling like you're in a city and not feeling too overwhelmed by it**. Then, of course, downtown Boston is nearby enough, which is nice. There are tons of other universities in the Boston area, including Boston University, Boston College, and Tufts."

Q "Boston has Boston University, Boston College, Tufts, Wellesley, Northeastern, and about 10 smaller schools. Right in Cambridge, one stop away, is MIT [Massachusetts Institute of Technology], filled with the techno-geniuses of tomorrow. **There are no places too dangerous to stay away from except Jamaica Plain**; but that's on the far side of Boston—you will never get close, unless you lose your mind."

Q "Cambridge is a great town. **Even in Harvard Square, there are tons of things to do**. My friend from Yale is always in awe of Harvard Square every time she comes to visit. I was in Princeton for several years, and I can tell you that Harvard Square is hands-down much livelier and more interesting. It also caters more to college students. Boston is also just a short train ride away; students go into the city all the time and hang out."

> "Boston is the best college city in the world. **BC, BU, Northeastern and Tufts are there, plus countless others**. The only problems are that the city shuts down at 2 a.m., and Cambridge is too high-class. Go downtown to Newbury Street, Quincy Market, the aquarium, and places like that when you have a chance."

Safety & Security

The College Prowler Take
ON LOCAL ATMOSPHERE

The Lowdown
ON SAFETY & SECURITY

The quintessential college area, Cambridge and Boston provide Harvard undergraduates with a variety of outlets for their creative, cultural, and social needs. Students laud the art museums and theatricals found throughout the city. Others find that Boston's four major sports teams make the city a haven for sports nuts—and over the past few years, this has been more true than ever. For the social animal in every college student, Boston also boasts numerous clubs and bars. Night owls, though, beware of the 2 a.m. closing time at all bars. Most students find nothing wrong with the local atmosphere, but all of Boston's vivacity does come at a price. And most students will find it at the cash register, as the city does tend to carry a rather hefty cost of living.

Number of Harvard Police:
50

Phone:
(617) 495-1215

Website:
www.hupd.harvard.edu/

Health Center Office Hours:
8:00 a.m. – 5:30 p.m. Monday – Friday; 24-hour Urgent Care, 7 days a week.

Safety Services:
Harvard University Police Department (HUPD), Cambridge Police Department (CPD)

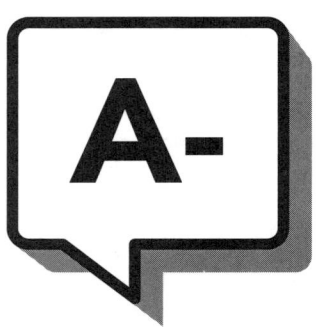

Did You Know?
To provide extra safety, the campus is littered with blue-light telephones that have direct lines to both emergency health and police response teams.

The College Prowler™ Grade on
Local Atmosphere: A-

A high Local Atmosphere grade indicates that the area surrounding campus is safe and scenic. Other factors include nearby attractions, proximity to other schools, and the town's attitude toward students.

Students Speak Out
ON SAFETY & SECURITY

"Incidents happen, and the lack of good lighting on campus pathways and the scarcity of patrolling HUPD officers make it less safe than it could be."

"Campus security is really good. The Harvard University Police Department is really dedicated, and the blue-light phone emergency system ensures that police can readily arrive to help any students in need. From personal experience, I've found the Harvard campus to be very safe. Surrounding Cambridge is also a pretty safe city, although just like anywhere else, **it's probably not the best idea to go walking alone late at night**. For the most part, though, I've felt very safe and comfortable."

"It's unsurpassed. The Harvard police are expertly trained. **Many are ex-marines and SWAT members**. They are extremely approachable and friendly. Also, the blue-light phone system is all over campus and very easy to use. Crime happens, but the HUPD prevents almost everything, and if they don't prevent it, they catch the criminals."

"I won't try and tell you that at Harvard no one gets robbed or mugged and crime doesn't happen; **students should always be mindful that Harvard is located in an urban area.** So, if you are like my roommate and had one too many drinks and hopped a ride with someone you didn't know, then you would probably end up getting mugged just like him. However, Harvard does a stellar job of protecting its students. Blue-light emergency phones litter the campus, allowing students to make a direct call to emergency response at any time. Additionally, all dorms require a keycard to gain access to the dorms, so prowling individuals rarely ever cause a disturbance."

"Unlike many colleges, **Harvard actually has its own police department**. It is still in a city, but safety is taken very seriously, and you are never out of sight of an emergency phone. Keycard access is still a bit of a problem, but they're pretty close to fixing that."

The College Prowler Take
ON SAFETY & SECURITY

Harvard students generally feel safe while roaming the streets of Cambridge, and they have good reason. The Harvard University Police Department and Cambridge Police Department do a commendable job of safeguarding the University's best assets—the students. Students also have access to multiple blue-light security phones on nearly every block and must swipe into dorms with keycards, preventing burglars from ever endangering students. However, Cambridge, like all cities, is not completely safe from crime. Students should always keep in mind they are in an urban setting, and they should be alert, especially when walking alone at night. In general, Harvard students rightly feel safe, but prospective students should not be lulled into believing Cambridge and Boston are crime-free.

The College Prowler™ Grade on
Safety & Security: B+

A high grade in Safety & Security means that students generally feel safe, campus police are visible, blue-light phones and escort services are readily available, and safety precautions are not overly necessary.

Computers

Did You Know?

Harvard College offers nearly 12,000 high-speed connections, including Ethernet and wireless. User assistants will also come to your dorm room to troubleshoot any computer problems you might have.

The Lowdown
ON COMPUTERS

Students Speak Out
ON COMPUTERS

"Bring your own computer. The labs aren't generally crowded at all, and they've got a great network, but they're way over in the Science Center and can be a pain to get to in the middle of the night."

High-Speed Network?
Yes

Wireless Network?
Yes

Number of Labs:
22

24-Hour Labs:
Each upperclass house has a small 24-hour lab and the Science Center's computer labs are open 24 hours as well.

Charge to Print?
Five cents per page if you print from computer lab printers

Operating Systems:
Mac OSX, Windows 2000, UNIX, and Linux

Free Software:
Acrobat, DreamWeaver, Eudora, Macafee Virus Scan, Photoshop, Telnet protocol, for e-mail access, course-relevant software also available

Q "I'd suggest that you bring your own computer if you have one. **All dorm rooms are wired with 24/7 high-speed and free Internet connections**. There are also labs in all houses, most freshman dorms, and several in the Science Center. Except for the peak hours—right around lunch—they generally aren't too crowded, but I think most people find it easier to write papers in their own rooms rather than in a lab."

Q "The network is fine. **There are occasional problems with connections**, but it works well for regular everyday purposes like e-mail, the Web, and AIM, of course. Computer labs are definitely available with both Macs and PCs, but the vast majority of people bring their own computers, just because it's a lot more convenient that way. I would definitely recommend bringing your own computer, and I've found a laptop to be the most convenient. If you'd rather not bring your own computer, though, the labs are definitely workable."

Q "I would definitely bring your own computer. Computer labs are abundant, but there is nothing like checking your e-mail in your own room. Plus, **many classes have their lectures and other course materials online**. Harvard also has tons of work, so the more access you have to a computer at all hours of the night, the better."

Q "You don't need your own computer, but it's very convenient. I never went in the computer lab because I never needed to. **Anything you ever have to do on campus could be done on the computer**."

Facilities

The Lowdown
ON FACILITIES

The College Prowler Take
ON COMPUTERS

Technology is increasingly important in today's colleges and universities, and Harvard certainly realizes that. Students have access to a number of computer labs, and every upperclass house has its own computer lab in the basement. Students benefit from a high-speed Ethernet network, as well as the recently installed Wi-Fi (wireless) network. The hardware is definitely available; just be patient and factor waiting time into your schedule if you plan on relying on Harvard's computer labs.

Student Center:
None

Athletic Center:
Yes, the Malkin Athletic Center (the MAC)

Libraries:
Over 90 collections, some open until 2 a.m. During exam periods, some open 24 hours

Popular Places to Chill:
Harvard Yard, the house courtyards

Movie Theatre on Campus?
Yes, Loews Harvard Square, 10 Church St.

Bowling on Campus?
No

Bar on Campus?
Yes, nearly a dozen sprinkled throughout Harvard Square

Coffeehouse on Campus?
Yes, nearly two dozen throughout Harvard Square

The College Prowler™ Grade on
Computers: A-

A high grade in Computers designates that computer labs are available, the computer network is easily accessible, and the campus' computing technology is up-to-date.

Favorite Things to Do
Run or bike along the Charles River, attend guest lectures at the Institute of Politics (located at the Kennedy School of Government)

 **Students Speak Out**
ON FACILITIES

 **The College Prowler Take**
ON FACILITIES

{ "The athletic facility is outdated and crowded. The facilities are old, but the technology is updated, and there's nice architecture if you ignore the few buildings built in the '70s."

Q "The facilities are nice, new, and **there are plans on the drawing boards for a new student center**. The center would have pool tables and the like, however social life on campus really focuses around our house system—something to definitely read up on, and something which makes Harvard so unique. They really are very successful at fostering a sense of community amongst the students at Harvard; it definitely made my first year really amazing."

Q "No student center. **Housing tries to make up for it, but doesn't always**. We need one. Athletic facilities are good and convenient."

Q "There are decent facilities for non-athletes. We don't really have a student center. Loker Commons, which is below the freshmen dining hall was intended to be a student center, but **not many people hang out there**. Student organization offices are all over campus."

Q "The facilities are nice. There can always be more—**more space for non varsity athletes to work out**, more dance studio space, and things like that."

Q "**Facilities are generally state-of-the-art**. Harvard has the nation's largest endowment, and most of the time it shows. Nearly all classrooms are equipped with amazing technology, some of which seems like it's never used but was added just so they could write about it in their admissions guide. However, the athletic facilities are pathetic. Unless you are a varsity athlete, you will be left to fight for one of the machines or stations at the Malkin Athletic Center."

Harvard's classrooms are equipped with state-of-the-art technology, and the Harvard library system is one of the largest in the world. For the most part, students wisely recognize these resources and praise the University for spending its enormous endowment on constantly improving existing facilities. There are always complaints, but regardless of that fact, Harvard receives high marks for providing top-notch facilities to aid undergraduates in their pursuit of improving the life of the mind, as well as the body.

The College Prowler™ Grade on
Facilities: B

A high Facilities grade indicates that the campus is aesthetically pleasing and well-maintained; facilities are state-of-the-art, and libraries are exceptional. Other determining factors include the quality of both athletic and student centers and an abundance of things to do on campus.

Campus Dining

Students Speak Out
ON CAMPUS DINING

"It's not bad, although there is only one meal plan option. Freshmen all eat together in Annenberg, which is a really impressive and huge dining hall. Each of the 12 upperclassmen houses has its own dining hall."

Q "**I'd say it's better than average dorm food.** I've had some pretty terrible cafeteria food in my life, and Harvard food is definitely better than that. It still comes down to being dorm food, though, so some of it is less than fantastic. But there are also days when it's actually pretty good."

Q "On campus, you're fairly limited, since you'll eat most meals in a dining hall. There is a restaurant in the Science Center called the Greenhouse, a pizza restaurant, Chick-fil-A, and a snack shop. There is also a place called Loker Commons, right underneath the freshman dining hall, which also has a few small restaurants. Within walking distance of The Yard, there are **literally hundreds of restaurants and cafes that cover just about every possible type of food**."

Q "All freshman—and only freshman, except at breakfast—eat in Annenberg Hall; it's a huge, beautiful building that looks much more like a church than a dining hall. Granted, **the building is more impressive than the food**, but the food is not bad at all. Plus, once you become a sophomore and you're living in your upperclassman house, the food is much better, because they are only cooking for about 200 people or so."

Q "I won't lie—freshman dining is awful. **Annenberg is rightly called 'Annenbarf.'** But, once you're assigned a house at the end of first year, the food is much better with all kinds of variety for vegetarians and meat-lovers alike."

The Lowdown
ON CAMPUS DINING

Freshman Meal Plan Requirement?
Yes

24-Hour On-Campus Eating?
Nothing, besides 7-11 (convenience store)

Student Favorites:
The Greenhouse, Loker Commons

Meal Plan Average Cost:
$2,520

Did You Know?

Through Harvard University Dining Services (HUDS), parents can send their children care packages that can be picked up at their house dining hall (or at Annenberg for freshmen).

Q "**First year food is tolerable.** Upperclassmen houses are a little better. You are stuck with the meal plan all four years, so you have to be able to accept it. The best dining hall is Adams House Dining Hall. They are bit pretentious there and let non-Adams residents eat there only at certain hours."

The College Prowler Take
ON CAMPUS DINING

Opinions on the quality of campus dining at Harvard run the gamut from total disgust to lavish praise. In general, students admire the beautiful architecture of Annenberg and most of the house dining facilities, but many students don't believe that the ambience of the dining halls makes up for the less-than-stellar cuisine served up by Harvard University Dining Services (HUDS). Most of the complaints about food quality come from first-years that are victims of Annenberg, where food is mass-produced to serve 1,600 freshmen. Upperclassmen note that food quality does improve after freshman year, and even though they love to complain about Harvard cuisine, the on-campus offerings are actually above average in the pantheon of college dining.

The College Prowler™ Grade on
Campus Dining: D+

Our grade on Campus Dining addresses the quality of both school-owned dining halls and independent on-campus restaurants as well as the price, availability, and variety of food.

Off-Campus Dining

The Lowdown
ON OFF-CAMPUS DINING

Best Pizza:
Pinocchio's Pizza

Best Chinese:
Hong Kong

Best Breakfast:
Henrietta's Table

Best Wings:
Tommy's Pizza

Best Healthy:
The Wrap and Smoothie Joint

Best Place to Take Your Parents:
Harvest or Henrietta's Table

24-Hour Eating:
7-11 on the corner of JFK and Mt. Auburn

Student Favorites: Pinocchio's, Tommy's House of Pizza, John Harvard's Brew House, Pho Pasteur

Fun Fact
Within a 10-minute walk from the center of campus, students can reach over 75 restaurants, offering every type of atmosphere and cuisine a student could ask for.

Students Speak Out
ON OFF-CAMPUS DINING

"There are some pretty good restaurants around Harvard Square. One of the favorites is called Spice, which is really good, relatively inexpensive Thai food."

Q "**We really benefit from the many amazing restaurants in Cambridge**. There are too many to name, but some of my favorites are Henrietta's Table, Mediterranean Skewers (which is now sadly closed), Border Cafe, Sandrine's, and Spice, not to mention the billion awesome restaurants in the North End of Boston, especially Little Italy."

Q "There are great restaurants in Harvard Square. Some popular choices for college students are Spice (Thai), Bombay Club (Indian), John Harvard's [brew pub], and Redline (a chic new bar/bistro which readily opened). Off campus, **there are just so many**."

Q "Food outside of the dining hall is really good too—particularly at Border Cafe and the Hi Rise Bakery—but **I find it hard to justify spending money out when the dining hall food is pretty good and already paid for**."

Q "The restaurants off campus offer an unmatched diversity, a smattering of price levels, and a wide range of quality. **Campus favorites include Pinocchio's Pizza, home to possibly the best pizza I've ever eaten**. Most Harvard students would agree."

The College Prowler Take
ON OFF-CAMPUS DINING

Though Harvard's on-campus dining sometimes lacks the zest that most students find necessary to completely satisfy their appetites, the cities of Cambridge and Boston provide a richly diverse environment to fulfill any gastronomic craving. It is certainly a treat to have the opportunity to indulge the fine cuisine of a major cosmopolitan center such as Boston.

The diversity of Harvard's off-campus dining opportunities provides cuisine and price ranges that are certain to satisfy even the most picky appetites and wallets. The off-campus dining more than makes up for the slim pickings on campus.

The College Prowler™ Grade on
Off-Campus Dining: A

A high Off-Campus Dining grade implies that off-campus restaurants are affordable, accessible, and worth visiting. Other factors include the variety of cuisine and the availability of alternative options (vegetarian, vegan, Kosher, etc.).

Campus Housing

Also Available
In addition to the 12 traditional upperclass houses, another option is the Dudley Co-op. This do-it-yourself house is home to about 32 undergraduates who share the duties of cooking and cleaning. They pay about half what other students pay for room and board.

Did You Know?

You can search the past inhabitants of every freshman dorm room at www.hcs.harvard.edu/~dorms/.

The Lowdown
ON CAMPUS HOUSING

Undergrads on Campus:
95%

Number of Dormitories:
13 upperclass houses
16 freshman dorms

Number of University-Owned Apartments:
2,500 apartments available, but only a limited number available to undergraduates.

Room Types:
Everything from singles to 10-person suites

Available for Rent:
On-campus rooms are not available for rent

Cleaning Service?
Weekly cleaning of all bathrooms

Bed Type:
Twin extra-long

You Get
Rooms vary widely, but many include fireplaces and large common areas, while others offer larger bedrooms but smaller common rooms. Harvard provides each student with a bed, a dresser, a desk, a bookcase, some closet space, and an Ethernet connection.

Students Speak Out
ON CAMPUS HOUSING

"The dorms, overall, are probably the best anywhere. There are a few that are sort of ugly and institutional, but most are old brick buildings with large, comfortable suites."

"I think that Harvard has some of the best dorms around. **There are very few that aren't, in relative dorm terms, spacious and nice.** There are many different arrangements, but almost everyone I know likes their dorm and develops a good deal of house pride! All of the freshmen live in Harvard Yard [or close by, in the Union] for their first year. After that, you're able to choose a group of seven other people [collectively, called a blocking group] who you want to live with for the following years, and all of you are assigned to the same upperclass house—you don't get to choose. I think it's a pretty good system."

"**Dorm rooms are amazing.** Just check out the Web and see pictures of some of the rooms. Most people live in suites with common rooms as freshmen, and many people even have private bathrooms. Nobody can complain about Harvard housing."

Q "You'll have no choice in dorms. All the freshman ones are great, if only for their location in The Yard. **Once you're moved into upperclassmen houses, you'll have a one-in-four chance of drawing a Quad House**. These are farther from The Yard than the others—about a 20-minute walk, as opposed to five—but they are also a bit more ornate and have great private libraries."

Q "Harvard students are spoiled by how nice the living arrangements are. **The worst of Harvard housing is amazing in comparison to most other schools**. You cannot really avoid dorms because all housing is random. However, the overflow housing as upperclassman is spacious, carpeted, and has a kitchen and cable, but some complain that you lose the house feel by living there."

Q "Harvard's unique housing system does not allow students to preference any particular dorm. At some point during the August before your freshman year, you will get your rooming assignment. Nearly all the freshman live in what is known as **Harvard Yard, the University's historic central hub that has witnessed over 350 years of history**. You will spend the next three years in your house. Students tend to develop a sense of house pride, mainly because you eat your meals with, and participate in a number of events, with the people in your house."

The College Prowler Take
ON CAMPUS HOUSING

When 95 percent of undergraduates at Harvard prefer to live on campus, you know there must be something attractive about the housing opportunities. From its rich history and beautiful architecture, to the close-knit house communities and central location, Harvard campus housing is matched by few, if any, universities in the country. Freshmen live in the Old Yard and the Union, while upperclassmen move towards the Charles River and out towards the Quad after their first year. But, regardless of location, Harvard's rooms tend to be spacious and almost all rooms feature common rooms and private bathrooms.

The College Prowler™ Grade on
Campus Housing: A

A high Campus Housing grade indicates that dorms are clean, well-maintained, and spacious. Other determining factors include variety of dorms, proximity to classes, and social atmosphere.

Off-Campus Housing

Students Speak Out
ON OFF-CAMPUS HOUSING

"I wouldn't want to live off campus. Living on campus, and in Kirkland, is the best part of my Harvard experience."

Q "**Almost nobody lives off campus because the dorms, for the most part, are really good**, and Cambridge housing is both expensive and difficult to find. However, during the summer, a lot of students stay around Cambridge doing various things and are able to find cheap and nice sublet apartments. During the year, though, I would definitely advise college housing."

Q "Usually, they make you live on campus the first year. I personally prefer to live off campus because **I can get more work done** and don't have to deal with the constant dormitory melodrama."

Q "Like Cambridge and Oxford in England, **Harvard has a house system**. More than 90 percent of students stay in the houses all four years. Those who don't are rich and can afford the high housing prices. But, the houses are great, and the community is friendly."

Q "**There is no reason to live off campus**. Ninety-eight percent of Harvard kids live on campus because housing off campus is so expensive and the Harvard rooms are so nice."

Q "**Housing off campus is farther away from classes than on-campus housing** and tends to be ridiculously expensive. Additionally, hardly anyone chooses off-campus housing options because their affinity towards their house satisfies nearly all students."

The Lowdown
ON OFF-CAMPUS HOUSING

Undergrads in Off-Campus Housing:
5%

Average Rent for a Studio Apartment:
$1,200 per month

Average Rent for a One-Bedroom Apartment:
$1,425 per month

Average Rent for a Two-Bedroom Apartment:
$1,750 per month

Popular Areas:
Central Square, Porter Square, Somerville

Best Time to Look for a Place
Start looking early—try during the summer if you're looking for term-time housing and by spring break if you're searching for a summer spot.

Contact For Assistance
The Harvard Housing Office (HHO)
Web: www.fas.harvard.edu/%7Euho/offcampus.htm
Phone: (617) 495-1942
E-mail: uho@fas.harvard.edu

The College Prowler Take
ON OFF-CAMPUS HOUSING

With a housing system that offers the best location and rooms in the Cambridge and Boston area, few students choose to live off campus. Most students complain that off-campus housing is too expensive and nearly impossible to find anywhere near Harvard Square.

If you absolutely must live off campus, then plan ahead, be open-minded, and take advantage of the Harvard Housing Office and tips (or hand-me-downs) from fellow students.

Diversity

The Lowdown
ON DIVERSITY

The College Prowler™ Grade on
Off-Campus Housing: F
A high grade in Off-Campus Housing indicates that apartments are of high quality, close to campus, affordable, and easy to secure.

African American: 8%

Asian American: 16%

Hispanic: 7%

Native American: 1%

White: 60%

International: 8%

Out-of-State: 80%

Minority Clubs
Undergraduate minority students have the opportunity to join many clubs and organizations that are focused on improving the status of and fostering community among minority students on campus. Most notable are the Black Students Association (BSA) and the Bisexual, Gay, Lesbian, Transgender and Supporters Allliance (BGLTSA).

Most Popular Religions

Harvard is certainly a secular university, and no one religion dominates. Christianity and Judaism appear to be the most represented religions.

Political Activity

Largely liberal political base, but conservative political groups do make their presence felt. Nearly every student has an informed opinion and the Institute of Politics provides an excellent forum for discussion and debate of current political topics.

Gay Tolerance

Harvard is tolerant of homosexuality, and the Bisexual, Gay, Lesbian, Transgender and Supporters Allliance (BGLTSA) is constantly rallying to increase tolerance for homosexuality on campus.

Economic Status

The economic status of Harvard students ranges the entire spectrum. Some students work their way through school, while others never worry about finances. Most students probably come from upper-middle-class homes.

Students Speak Out
ON DIVERSITY

"It depends on where you're coming from. For me, it was much more diverse than my high school, but I've heard other people say that it's not as diverse as theirs was."

Q "I think that the campus is diverse. There are people from all over the world and of every different race and religion. **Some people think that minorities are still underrepresented here**, but I think that it's full of tons of different cultures that make Harvard a very exciting place to be."

Q "**Harvard's diversity is one of its biggest assets**. I have friends from every imaginable racial, ethnic, and geographical group."

Q "Harvard is ethnically very diverse. But **financially, the students at Harvard are not so diverse**. In terms of political views of students, the extremes do not have a large presence."

Q "**The campus is incredibly diverse in more ways than just race**. One night on my way to a party, I found out that a guy I was walking with was previously in the circus. We passed a piano and learned that another guy was a concert pianist, and then another got drunk and started speaking Hindi. You never know what you're gonna get."

The College Prowler Take
ON DIVERSITY

Harvard undergraduates thrive on diversity because it presents alternate approaches and opinions on topics ranging from politics and religion, to culture and sexuality. Harvard students tend to be among the most open-minded in higher education. Students of all races, backgrounds, and beliefs will find a forum in which they can express and discuss their opinions. Despite the wealth of diversity, some students do complain that most of the undergraduates come from a very narrow socioeconomic bracket. But, overall, if diversity is a must for you, then Harvard is certainly the right fit. For close-minded souls, however, culture shock will certainly await you around every corner.

The College Prowler™ Grade on
Diversity: B+

A high grade in Diversity indicates that ethnic minorities and international students have a notable presence on campus and that students of different economic backgrounds, religious beliefs, and sexual preferences are well-represented.

Guys & Girls

Students Speak Out
ON GUYS & GIRLS

"I'm a guy, and I would say most girls aren't that hot, but there is a fair share of cute girls. It's pretty much the same situation at any top-15 school, I think."

Q "Dorks. However, the women in Boston have impressed me. **The guys are jerks**."

Q "**There are some 'beautiful people,'** though I'd say all of the Ivies have more than their share of people that could stand to get out of the library a little more."

Q "The people here, in general, are really great. Of course, **there are the occasional people I dislike**, but the group of students, as a whole, is a great one. If you're worried about people constantly talking about their academic accomplishments or something, don't worry; it doesn't happen here."

Q "**There are some very hot Harvard girls**, but there are also some really unattractive girls. Trust me, you'll find your own group, and regardless of appearances, the students are definitely Harvard's biggest asset."

Q "**We have the full range of the human spectrum**. Most people are very interesting, though, regardless of their other physical traits. It's what's inside that counts, and the guys and girls at Harvard have a lot inside!"

The Lowdown
ON GUYS & GIRLS

Female Undergrads: 48%

Male Undergrads: 52%

Birth Control Available?
University Health Services provides free condoms, and physicians will provide prescriptions for various methods of birth control.

Hookups or Relationships?
Random hookups do happen on the weekends (and weekdays see their share as well). However, most people are extremely busy and often are so focused on their work that relationships either die out or become serious within a short period of time. This isn't to say you'll never see lasting relationships; annoyingly cute couples walk The Yard surprisingly often. And the *Harvard Magazine*—the alumni pub—is always filled with news of Harvard newlyweds.

Dress Code
On the weekends, most people dress up to go out, but during weekday study breaks or hangout sessions, most anything goes. (Though throughout the winter, dress code really doesn't matter because everyone is so bundled up to keep warm.) In general, Harvard tends to be a bit more formal than average.

The College Prowler Take
ON GUYS & GIRLS

Don't let "Van Wilder" or "Girls Gone Wild" give you any crazy ideas about college and what girls and guys will look like at Harvard. If physical attractiveness is important to you, then you might want to steer clear of Harvard College. Though most students believe that the student body is of average attractiveness, very few report a significant number of hot guys or girls on campus. Additionally, girls tend to accept the male population as average or better, while guys have a less positive outlook towards the female population. But for those who believe looks are not everything, then Harvard students' individuality should provide plenty of options.

The College Prowler™ Grade on
Guys: B

A high grade for Guys indicates that the male population on campus is attractive, smart, friendly, and engaging, and that the school has a decent ratio of guys to girls.

The College Prowler™ Grade on
Girls: B-

A high grade for Girls not only implies that the women on campus are attractive, smart, friendly, and engaging, but also that there is a fair ratio of girls to guys.

Athletics

The Lowdown
ON ATHLETICS

Men's Varsity Teams:
Baseball
Basketball
Crew
Cross Country
Fencing
Football
Golf
Ice Hockey
Track
Lacrosse
Sailing
Skiing
Soccer
Squash
Swimming
Tennis
Volleyball
Water Polo
Wrestling

Women's Varsity Teams:
Basketball
Crew
Cross Country
Fencing
Field Hockey
Golf
Ice Hockey
Indoor Track
Lacrosse
Outdoor Track
Sailing
Skiing
Soccer
Softball
Squash
Swimming
Tennis
Volleyball
Water Polo

Intramurals (IMs)

Basketball (men's and women's Leagues), Charles River Run, crew (men's and women's teams), flag football, soccer (men's and women's leagues), ice hockey, pool tournament, table tennis tournament, tennis tournament (men's and women's brackets), fencing tournament, volleyball (men's and women's leagues), squash

Getting Tickets
Tickets are easily accessible from Harvard Box Office locations in the Holyoke Center and near the stadium.

Fields
Harvard Stadium (football), Jordan Field (lacrosse and field hockey), Club Sports Field (rugby, ultimate Frisbee, and intramurals)

Athletic Division:
NCAA Division I

Conference:
Ivy League

Most Popular Sports:
Football and Men's Ice Hockey

Overlooked Teams:
Men's Rugby and Women's Basketball

School Mascot:
The Crimson

Students Speak Out
ON ATHLETICS

"Varsity is not too big, except within the team. IM sports are big among people who do them. It's all relative, but you don't hear much about either unless you're really into them."

"**We offer dozens of sports and play over a thousand IM games per year**. Freshmen play in their own league, and upperclassmen houses compete against each other. Harvard has more varsity teams than any other school, and many survive on 'amateurs,' so if you want to play a varsity sport, it is much more open than other D-1 schools. Attendance at athletic events is, unfortunately, fairly light."

"Varsity sports can be big, depending on the sport and the team. **Attendance is very poor, except for 'The Game,'** which is the annual football rivalry with Yale. Hockey is also mildly popular, and basketball draws some as well. We have a ton of varsity teams, so if you do want to play competitively, chances are Harvard offers it."

"If you would rather compete in a more relaxed setting, **Harvard IMs offer a variety of sports in a much more friendly setting**. Many people use them as a way to meet other people, but there are some fairly competitive teams."

"**We are definitely lacking in the team spirit department**, however we still get big crowds at some football and basketball games. Rowing is really popular, and our teams are always pretty good. IMs are very popular, which is another great side effect of the house system. Men's IMs get more participation and are more competitive than the women's, but even the women's teams are really fun."

"Varsity athletes aren't revered like at other places. **Athletes do tend to be the more social students**. Hockey and football games get decent turnouts. And sports like crew and squash are among the best in the nation. Harvard offers a lot of intramural sports. They're well-organized, and there's a lot of variety such as crew, fencing, softball, Frisbee, football, volleyball, basketball, and running. People of all skill levels can join, and many students do."

The College Prowler Take
ON ATHLETICS

Originally founded as an athletic league, the Ivy League, including Harvard, has lost its reputation as an athletic powerhouse in major sports. However, Harvard is home to more varsity sports than any other institution in the nation. Additionally, Harvard offers an array of club sport opportunities that will satisfy the desires of any wannabe rugby, fencing, or Frisbee players, to name just a few. And for those not interested in organized sports or their accompanying time commitments, Harvard offers intramural sports that often generate heated battles and spawn a number of house rivalries. However, Harvard does lose points because of the lack of support for its varsity programs. Overall, the school offers the resources for just about any level of activity.

Greek Life

The Lowdown
ON GREEK LIFE

Number of Fraternities:
4

Number of Sororities:
3

Percent of Undergrad Men in Fraternities:
less than 1%

Percent of Undergrad Women in Sororities:
less than 1%

Multicultural Colonies:
None

The College Prowler™ Grade on
Athletics: C+

A high grade in Athletics indicates that students have school spirit, that sports programs are respected, that games are well-attended, and that intramurals are a prominent part of student life.

Did You Know?

Fraternities and sororities are not officially recognized on campus, although, in recent years, Greek life has been unofficially gaining a stronger presence.

Students Speak Out
ON GREEK LIFE

"There are no official fraternities, but there are finals clubs, which are the same thing, and they throw really fun parties. But, by no means are they the dominating thing on campus."

Q "There are a few off-campus fraternities and sororities, but they definitely do not dominate the campus. There are also all-male finals clubs and all-female societies that are sort of Greek-like, but none of these are sanctioned by the college. I went through four years perfectly happily without joining any of these, although I have several good friends in one of the off-campus fraternities."

Q "There isn't any official Greek life at Harvard. Instead, there are finals clubs, which kind of work like frats minus a house. Actually, some sororities are getting started just in recent years, and they're growing in popularity, I think. But it's not nearly enough to dominate the social scene."

Q "With very few frats and sororities, the Greek life is completely avoidable. Finals clubs are a little harder to hide from if they're not your things, but after freshmen year, they don't have as big of a presence if you're not in one. The finals club parties are great for freshman girls, but bad for everyone else not in the club."

Q "The Greek life is minor at Harvard because the frats and sororities are relatively new additions to campus that have been initiated in the hopes of creating a fuller social scene. Greeks have to rent out spaces to throw their functions, so they are shadowed in comparison to older establishments with their own space such as the finals clubs. However, some frats do throw a mean party."

Q "Fraternities and sororities exist unofficially at Harvard and really have no major presence on campus. There's no Greek week or crazy frat parties. Instead, Harvard features final clubs, which are an upscale version of fraternities. These clubs are over 100 years old, and members meet in multi-million dollar clubhouses around campus. These clubs are also unofficial, but they throw a good number of parties and tend to be late-night hangouts for people once the bars close at 2 a.m.."

The College Prowler Take
ON GREEK LIFE

Enamored of the ridiculous antics of the frat boys from "Animal House?" If so, then Harvard probably is not the place for you. Fraternities and sororities are not officially recognized on campus, though in recent years they have increased their presence as unofficial organizations. Without houses, these organizations do not have the ability to throw the parties one expects of a healthy Greek system, although they occasionally rent out Boston clubs or take over dorm rooms to throw enormous bashes. In place of a Greek system, Harvard has the controversial institution known as the "finals club." These clubs are often criticized as the remnants of the "old boys" network of Harvard days of yore. They selectively offer membership after a student's freshman year and serve an important role in an otherwise lean on-campus social scene.

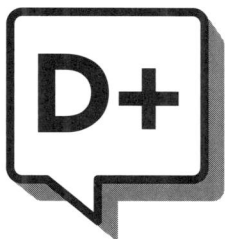

The College Prowler™ Grade on
Greek Life: D+

A high grade in Greek Life indicates that sororities and fraternities are not only present, but also active on campus. Other determining factors include the variety of houses available and the respect the Greek community receives from the rest of the campus.

Drug Scene

Q "I know some drugs are there, but it kind of seems like the kind of thing where, **if you're looking for it, you can find it, but if you aren't, it's not going to be something you'll notice**. I wouldn't say it's a big thing."

Q "**People smoke a lot of weed**, but still not very much compared to national or even high school scenes. Although other drugs are around, they're not everywhere."

Q "**Harvard certainly has its fair share of weed smokers**, but it is not that prevalent. I also know that some people do cocaine and other hard drugs, but I doubt Harvard's drug habits are that much different from any other college or university."

The Lowdown
ON DRUG SCENE

Most Prevalent Drugs on Campus:
Alcohol, marijuana

Liquor-Related Referrals:
123 (2003)

Liquor-Related Arrests:
12

Drug-Related Referrals:
3

Drug-Related Arrests:
9

The College Prowler Take
ON DRUG SCENE

Drugs have a very small presence at Harvard. Marijuana is certainly the most prevalent, while harder drugs such as cocaine are often rumored to be the drug of choice for a small minority. However, these tend to be rumors and should not be trusted completely. The overwhelming majority of students avoid all drug use and enjoy the ability to engage in a drug-free social life. Overall, Harvard receives high marks for its ability to keep drug use to a minimum and facilitate an academic and social life that is not inhibited by drugs.

Students Speak Out
ON DRUG SCENE

"I know people that smoke weed, and I've heard of people doing cocaine, but my friends aren't really into it, so I don't know much about the drug scene here at Harvard."

The College Prowler™ Grade on
Drug Scene: B+

A high grade on Drug Scene indicates that drugs are not a noticeable part of campus life; drug use is not visible, and no pressure to use them seems to exist.

Campus Strictness

The Lowdown
ON CAMPUS STRICTNESS

What Are You Most Likely to Get Caught Doing on Campus?
Drinking underage, parking illegally, public urination or indecency, smoking marijuana, making too much noise in your dorm

Students Speak Out
ON CAMPUS STRICTNESS

Q "**The official campus drug and alcohol policy is very strict**. [Repeated] violations usually result in a forced year away from Harvard or expulsion, but I don't know of anybody who that's happened to.'

Q "Campus police are not strict at all. **Even if you call them at 4 a.m. because you are drunk and locked yourself out**, they will still be super nice and understanding."

Q "**Harvard University police do not care about drinking at all**. Often times they will break up parties that are too rowdy. Even while busting the parties, the HUPD tend to be quite jovial and only care about quieting down the party, not about busting people. As a prime example, after Harvard won the Ivy League championship in football, a couple cops even showed up to joke around at the football team's keg party. Sometimes, an officer will try to scare an underage drinker by taking their name and ID number down, but rarely will they actually bust anyone. They are there to protect the students, not to get them in trouble."

{ "I don't know, but the HUPD are really, really cool and helpful, and they honestly care about the students. Get in trouble with Ad Board, though, and it can get ugly."

Q "**I never had a problem with how the HUPD handled parties or drinking**. I didn't ever drink or do drugs, however, but my friends did, and they haven't had any problems."

Q "Drugs obviously get you in trouble if you get caught, but **you can pretty much get around anything**, if you are smart."

The College Prowler Take
ON CAMPUS STRICTNESS

Other than freshmen, Harvard students have few worries about campus strictness. University police are present to protect the safety of students, not detain or punish every underage drinker or noisy reveler. Most students feel free from punishment because almost all students are given at least one warning before any official disciplinary actions are taken. For those unfortunate students who frequently abuse school policy, punishments can range from probation to expulsion; however, the University is reluctant to expel a student and often grants them readmission after a certain amount of time. Students should just keep in mind that with independence comes responsibility and that frequent abuse of the rules does not come without punishment at Harvard.

Overall Experience

Students Speak Out
ON OVERALL EXPERIENCE

"The class sizes are often too large, but every now and then a professor will prove to be human and make himself accessible outside of class. I like the campus, as it is very alive and very well-kept."

Q "**In one word: unimaginable**. In every sense, Harvard has fulfilled my highest expectations. The academics, people, resources, and opportunities are unbeatable. I wouldn't go anywhere else. But, a word of warning, and this kind of depends on your concentration—you do have to do a good amount of work if you want to do well. You can't really fail out, but you have to work hard to do well and get anywhere above a B- or B average."

Q "I love it at Harvard. It can be challenging at times, but **the resources and people available to you are unmatched**. I would not want to be anywhere else. The best part of the school is your peers—the students you are here with are some of the most amazing individuals, yet very few are cocky, too proud, or conceited. Everyone is really on level ground here, and it's great. You'll learn a lot in your classes, but you'll learn even more from your peers. And who knows, you might make friends with a future president, CEO, or actor."

The College Prowler™ Grade on
Campus Strictness: A-

A high Campus Strictness grade implies an overall lenient atmosphere; police and RAs are fairly tolerant, and the administration's rules are flexible.

Q "I love it. **The things I thought I would look for in a school—a lot of school spirit, good professor-to-student ratio, prestige—ended up not mattering at all**. What is important is the location and the people. Harvard has the best of both."

Q "My advice to prospective students—state school. **State school students have less work and more fun**. As one of my friends said, state school girls are cooler, hotter, and have fewer inhibitions. Classes at Harvard are hard."

Q "Yes, I hate the weather and I think the students can be a bit pretentious and too career-oriented, but overall, it is simply amazing. Professors and courses are thought-provoking and creative. Even though I might not have individual conversations with most of my professors, **they are generally the experts in their field** and simply listening to them is quite engaging. While binge drinking can be fun, Harvard's student theatre productions, speaker events on campus and Boston's various attractions offer opportunities to enjoy yourself, no matter what your idea of fun is."

The College Prowler Take
ON OVERALL EXPERIENCE

Challenging, rigorous, and positive all describe students' overall experience at Harvard. The academic challenge initially seems daunting to many students, but the intellectual growth facilitated by this academic powerhouse leaves students pleasantly surprised. The social life of most Harvard students acts as a counterbalance to the intellectual challenge, and not surprisingly, students forge lifetime memories and friends throughout their four years at Harvard.

The Harvard experience leaves most students yearning for more. The University provides undergraduates with a rich history, unparalleled cultural diversity, and intellectual rigor that challenges each student to fulfill every ounce of their potential. Students leave Harvard satisfied and prepared for life—and as a stronger, more aware global citizen than ever.

The Inside Scoop

The Lowdown
ON THE INSIDE SCOOP

Harvard Slang:
Know the slang, know the school. The following is a list of terms you really need to know before coming to Harvard. The more of these words you recognize, the better off you'll be.

Af-Am—Afro-American Studies

B-School—Harvard Business School

Concentration—Harvard's word for "major"

Coop—The Harvard Cooperative Society, the bookstore located at Harvard Square; Pronounced like "chicken coop"

Crimson Cash—A declining debit account system that uses your Harvard ID. You can put cash on electronically in order to purchase copies, food, and other sundries.

Div School—Harvard Divinity School

Ed School—Also known as HUGSE (Harvard University Graduate School of Education)

FAS—Faculty of Arts and Sciences, composed of Harvard College, the Graduate School of Arts and Sciences, and the Division of Continuing Education

Head of the Charles—The annual October regatta held on the Charles River

HOLLIS—Harvard libraries' online catalog and now also a directory to the suite of electronic resources that the libraries make available

House—The residences of sophomores, juniors, and seniors. Harvard Houses were modeled on the college systems of England's Oxford and Cambridge Universities.

KSG—Kennedy School of Government

Let's Go—The series of travel books written and published by Harvard students

MAC—Malkin Athletic Center

Masters—Faculty members who lead and administer each undergraduate house

MIT—Massachusetts Institute of Technology. The other university in Cambridge

Pit—The area immediately surrounding the Harvard Square T stop, one of the Square's hubs of street entertainment

Proctors—Graduate students or officers of the university who live among freshmen, serve as academic advisors, and direct the events and programs of an entryway

Reading Period—That 10-day period of anxiety in which students prep for finals

Resident Tutors—Graduate students or faculty members who live in the houses with students, and provide them with a range of informal advice and counsel

Shopping Period—The first five or so days of an academic term at Harvard, before Study Cards are submitted for formal enrollment in a course; when students can visit classes, sit in on lectures, and review syllabi and readings

Statue of 3 Lies—The John Harvard Statue (see Urban Legends below)

TF—Teaching fellow (like other colleges' TAs)

UHS—University Health Services

Veritas—The Harvard motto; Latin for "truth"

The Yard—Most universities have a quadrangle, but Harvard has its Yard, divided into two parts. The freshman dormitories border the Old Yard; Widener Library and Memorial Church border the New Yard

Harvard's Urban Legends

The John Harvard Statue is a statue of the founder of the University. In reality, the story of this statue contains three lies. Lie #1: John Harvard didn't found Harvard (the Massachusetts Bay Colony government did). Lie #2: Harvard started in 1636 not 1638. Lie #3: It's not even John Harvard. No one knows what he looked like since there are no surviving portraits of the man. Daniel Chester French, the sculptor, used a 19th century undergraduate for his model.

School Spirit

Harvard students are proud, almost snobbishly arrogant, when it comes to the University's reputation, though athletics receive little support, if any. Students wear their colors proudly, especially on the weekend of the Harvard-Yale football game. However, after freshman year, students find themselves wearing less and less apparel with the Harvard name or crest, though the color crimson becomes increasingly present in students' wardrobes. Overall, student spirit brims high when it comes to University reputation.

Traditions

According to tradition, there are two things that every undergraduate must do before they graduate from the college:

- Every student must urinate on the John Harvard statue found in the Old Yard.
- Every student should run Primal Scream at least once.

> **Things I Wish I'd Known Before Coming to Harvard:**
> - Harvard students are diverse in every way, and no matter who you are, you will find people similar to you.
> - Even though Cambridge is the quintessential town for college students, it is extremely expensive.
> - Do not be scared away from Harvard because you think you won't be smart enough or because you think the classes will be too difficult.
> - All Harvard students think its tough and think everyone else is smarter than ,they are. The college offers plenty of study groups and tutoring services, so that even if you are struggling, there is a place to which to turn.
>
> **Tips to Succeed at Harvard:**
> - Motivation, hard work, and organization will have a larger impact on success than sheer brainpower. (Keep this in mind.)
> - Pick classes you actually like.
> - Actually go to class.
> - Get advice from upperclassmen.
> - Check your final exam dates before you register for classes.
> - Join study groups if at all possible.

Finding a Job or Internship

The Lowdown
ON FINDING A JOB OR INTERNSHIP

Placing the Harvard name on your resume certainly gives you an advantage for applying to jobs or internships. However, it's not an automatic acceptance. The Harvard name is more like a foot in the door and your success at the college can help determine whether you ultimately find the job that you want.

Advice

If you are interested in finding jobs or internships, then stop by the Office of Career Services. At OCS you can meet with one of the many career counseling experts who will help you search out the perfect job match, help edit your resumes and even review your interview technique through videotaped mock interviews.

Career Center Resources & Services

The Office of Career Services offers a number of resources and services to help you figure out what you plan to do with your college education. The following list is just a sampling of the numerous opportunities to be found at OCS:

- Career Self-Assessment, resume, interview, and networking workshops, and case-studies
- Career Library with books and guides to finding summer and full-time careers

Career Center Resources & Services
(Continued...)

• Professional Connection – Links alumni with undergraduates pursuing similar fields

• Online job listing sites such as MonsterTRAK.

• For a complete listing of resources and opportunities at the Office of Career Services check out their Website at:

www.ocs.fas.harvard.edu/index.htm

AVERAGE SALARY INFORMATION

The Office of Career Services and the Harvard Alumni Association does not maintain data on average salary information of Harvard College graduates. But, the salary of Harvard undergraduates just out of college varies enormously. A number of students pursue high-paying, six figure salaries in consulting or investment banking, while other students earn very little monetary compensation while pursuing graduate degrees or public service opportunities.

The only information available related to salaries for Harvard graduates come from the Harvard Business School. The business school offers a two-year MBA program that places graduates into many of the most competitive jobs in the country. A general overview of what a Harvard Business School student might expect for salary in their first year after graduation is below:

Average starting-base salary (excluding bonuses) for the class of 2003:
$95,012

Median starting-base salary (excluding bonuses) for the class of 2003:
$93,050

Average first-year signing bonus:
$21,779

Median first-year signing bonus:
$20,000

Job-accepting graduates who received a signing bonus:
86%

The Best & Worst

The Ten BEST Things About Harvard:

1. Access to the best minds of our time
2. Contagious student motivation and ambition
3. The opportunity to pursue any interest at all
4. Alumni are eager to help undergraduates
5. The wonderful city of Boston
6. Harvard housing is among the best in the nation
7. The Harvard Library system (largest in the world)
8. An open and diverse campus
9. State-of-the-art technology in all facilities
10. R-E-S-P-E-C-T

The Ten WORST Things About Harvard:

1. Lots of pressure (losing track of enjoying college)
2. Tracking professors down is sometimes difficult
3. Classes are very hard and time-consuming
4. So much work ... and then some
5. The weather
6. Tough Massachusetts liquor laws
7. Hearing all your HS friends' wild college stories
8. Getting accepted into the school is hard
9. Student body has a snobby reputation
10. Having to last all four years

Yale University

New Haven, CT 06520
www.yale.edu   (203) 432-9300

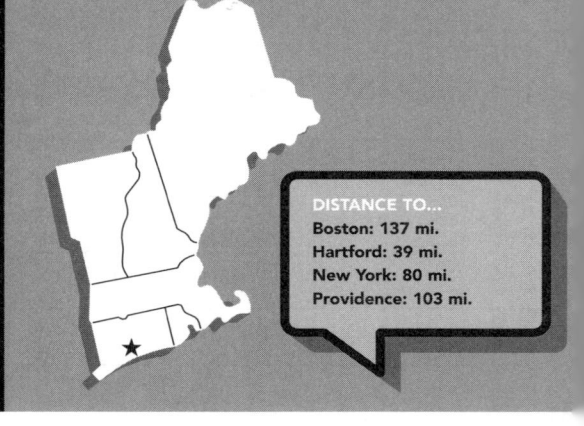

DISTANCE TO...
Boston: 137 mi.
Hartford: 39 mi.
New York: 80 mi.
Providence: 103 mi.

"Yale University is a brand name that inspires instant recognition, confidence, and esteem."

Total Enrollment:
5,292
Acceptance Rate:
11%
Tuition:
$29,820
Top 10% of High School Class:
99%

SAT Range
Verbal	Math	Total
690 – 790	690 – 790	1380 – 1580

ACT Range
Verbal	Math	Total
N/A	N/A	30-34

SAT II Requirements
Any three SAT II subject tests.

Most Popular Majors:
15% History
11% Political Science and Government
9%   Economics
8%   English Language and Literature
7%   Psychology

Students Also Applied To:*
Harvard University, Stanford University, Princeton University, Brown University
*For more school info check out www.collegeprowler.com

Table of Contents

Academics	587
Local Atmosphere	589
Safety & Security	590
Computers	592
Facilities	593
Campus Dining	595
Off-Campus Dining	596
Campus Housing	598
Off-Campus Housing	600
Diversity	601
Guys & Girls	603
Athletics	604
Greek Life	606
Drug Scene	608
Campus Strictness	609
Overall Experience	611
The Inside Scoop	612
Finding a Job or Internship	614
The Best & Worst	615

College Prowler Report Card

Academics	A
Local Atmosphere	C-
Safety & Security	B-
Computers	A
Facilities	A-
Campus Dining	C+
Off-Campus Dining	B+
Campus Housing	A-
Off-Campus Housing	B
Diversity	B
Guys	B
Girls	B+
Athletics	C
Greek Life	D+
Drug Scene	B+
Campus Strictness	A

Academics

Best Places to Study
Local coffeehouses (Koffee, Starbucks, Atticus, etc.), Sterling Memorial Library, Yale Center for British Art

Sample Academic Clubs
The Yale College Bioethics Society, Yale Psychological Society, Objectivist Study Group, Yale Entrepreneurial Society, Yale Film Society, Yale Political Union

The Lowdown
ON ACADEMICS

Did You Know?
Seventy-five percent of Yale courses enroll fewer than 20 students. Twenty-nine percent of courses enroll fewer than 10 students.

During finals, a group of very naked Yale students runs through the libraries and distribute candy to stressed studiers.

Degrees Awarded:
Bachelor, Master, Doctorate, Combined Degrees

Undergraduate Schools:
Yale College

Full-time Faculty:
836

Faculty with Terminal Degree:
91%

Student-to-Faculty Ratio:
7:1

Average Course Load:
4 or 5 courses

Special Degree Options:
Joint BA/MA programs for exceptional students

Students Speak Out
ON ACADEMICS

"Yale is known for its undergraduate focus, and all professors are required to teach undergrads. This is a huge advantage since, either way, you are paying for their salaries. You might as well have access to them."

"I haven't seen much competition at Yale. I think **the sciences tend to be the hardest classes**, so those students have a slightly harder time. But, nothing is impossible, and everyone is very supportive. I know a lot of people who study or do problem sets together."

The College Prowler Take
ON ACADEMICS

Q "**I honestly haven't been thrilled with my professors or my classes** this year. I really liked three out of the nine classes I took. This really surprised me because, well, it's Yale. But, I really think that it will get better as I get into the more advanced courses."

Q "As an English major, I have been lucky to love almost all of my professors, as well as the seminar leaders. Several stand out—in particular, my professor who was about 70 years old and came to lectures wearing short tight miniskirts with knee-high, black leather, four-inch heel, stiletto boots. She would comfortably lean against a table at the front of the lecture hall, or perhaps perch herself on the table, and then talk to us, rather than at us. **It was a highly intellectual environment, yet simultaneously laid-back and comfortable.** I loved her!"

Q "As a pre-med student, **the science classes I have taken have, for the most part, been strong**—well-taught and structured—and I have learned an immense amount of material. Unfortunately, the classes are all large, and therefore they are inevitably more impersonal. You have to make a fairly big effort to get to know the professor—ha, even to get him to know you exist."

Q "Most professors are excellent equally as scholars and teachers. **They communicate effectively, engagingly, and with authority.** It's hard to construct a schedule that isn't mostly composed of classes taught by great professors. That said, there is the occasional professor who is incoherent, either due to limited command of English or poor organizational skills. Those professors can be identified, and easily avoided, thanks to Yale's 'shopping period.'"

Although students seem happy with their education at Yale, most realize that a successful course load depends not only on the professors and the material, but also on the careful selection of classes. There are amazing lectures and seminars in every department, but there are also those few professors and classes that will be disappointing. The key is to choose the right class for you. Some people soon realize they love lectures but not seminars. Some students don't like to deal with TAs. Some want professors who dominate the class, while others want to interact with the material more directly. Once you figure out what you want, Yale becomes filled with opportunities to learn.

Most students come to Yale for a "name brand" education, hoping the school's reputation will be enough to carry them smoothly into their future. What these students might not realize is that they must choose to make the name stand for something. If you talk to students here, some will say Yale is a breeze, and some will say it's the most challenging experience of their lives. This difference of opinion is not based on the students' intelligence or the easiness or difficulty of their majors; it has to do with how many opportunities to challenge themselves they are willing to accept.

The College Prowler™ Grade on
Academics: A

A high Academics grade generally indicates that professors are knowledgeable, accessible, and genuinely interested in their students' welfare. Other determining factors include class size, how well professors communicate, and whether or not classes are engaging.

Local Atmosphere

The Lowdown
ON LOCAL ATMOSPHERE

Region:
Northeast

City, State:
New Haven, Connecticut

Setting: Urban

Distance from New York City: 1-2 hours

Distance from Boston: 2.5 hours

Points of Interest: Chapel Street, Yale University Art Gallery, Peabody Museum of Natural History, New Haven Green, Wooster Square, East Rock State Park

Major Sports Teams:
Ravens (baseball), Knights (hockey), Ninjas (arena football)

City Websites:
www.cityofnewhaven.com

Students Speak Out
ON LOCAL ATMOSPHERE

Q "Even though people sometimes say that New Haven is dangerous, I haven't had any trouble. There is an escort service available to walk you back to your dorm when you're at the library late and have a laptop with you or if you just feel a little nervous. **I haven't felt uncomfortable walking around at night** as long as there's someone else with me. I guess New Haven isn't as much of a city as some places, but it is still great."

Q "**New Haven has started to become more of a college town**, so the parts closest to the colleges are really nice. You have to walk for a bit to get into the rougher parts, and no one really goes there because there's nothing there for us. Overall, it's fine."

Q "**Yale students' lives are centered around Yale**, which has enough variety and things to do to keep you busy for years. And I like that, for a university, it's really pretty close-knit; we're all about Yale. I think that's great. Stuff to stay away from: sketchy neighborhoods, of course—but that's really it. There are tons of things to do. There is stuff for everyone."

Q "New Haven tends to get a bad rap among high school students considering elite universities, but I think the city has a lot to offer. **It has plenty of stores and restaurants to cater to student needs.** Beyond that, there's a substantial amount of cultural and other resources in the city for students to take advantage of. Yes, New Haven isn't as antiseptic and shiny as Princeton, New Jersey. But, it's a 'real' city, with real issues and real potential for students to get involved in the community in a meaningful way."

Q "I love New Haven, despite the bad reputation it sometimes gets. Actually, **the only people who say negative things about the city are people who don't actually live here**. Once you move in, though, you realize that—like any city—you need to take precautions and use common sense, but if you do then you are totally safe. New Haven has so much going on—from the repertory theaters to the arts festivals, and there are little, unknown blues and jazz cafes within walking distance—so much stuff, you'd never be able to get around to it all."

{ "Yale is redeveloping lots of the surrounding neighborhoods. We have a Broadway with our bookstore, Urban Outfitters, J.Crew, pizza places, and a bunch of other shops."

The College Prowler Take
ON LOCAL ATMOSPHERE

New Haven is unlike any other place in the world. Yale, a bastion of wealth and privilege, is surrounded by an urban and impoverished area. Although Yale tries to hide this element (while urging that they help to fix it), this atmosphere can still be depressing, especially on cold, gray days. On a different note, the area immediately around Yale is a great, bohemian, college town. The shop fronts look more like SoHo than Connecticut; the restaurants are mostly ethnic; and sometimes there are small street fairs. The college is not contained in one place—the dorms and classrooms are pretty scattered, but within walking distance. Everywhere you go there are Yalies, but rarely students from other colleges. Yale has an amazing art gallery that is often overlooked by the students, even though it is free to the public and very close. Across the street is the British Art Center, which is a great space in which to study, but sometimes a bore to visit for its art. At Yale, there is a real range of things to do—just not enough time to do them all!

The College Prowler™ Grade on
Local Atmosphere: C-

A high Local Atmosphere grade indicates that the area surrounding campus is safe and scenic. Other factors include nearby attractions, proximity to other schools, and the town's attitude toward students.

Safety & Security

The Lowdown
ON SAFETY & SECURITY

Number of Yale University Police:
35

Phone:
(203) 432-4400

Health Center Office Hours:
Urgent Care is open 24 hours a day.

Safety Services:
Blue-light Phones, Night Escorts, Minibus Service

Students Speak Out
ON SAFETY & SECURITY

{ "I personally haven't had any problems, and I leave my door unlocked and open most of the time."

Q "Security is good. **There are always campus police officers on their bikes or just standing around**, and I guess their presence makes us feel safe. I feel very safe on campus and in the area around campus, but if you stray too far, you probably should walk in a small group of people rather than by yourself, as with any other unfamiliar city."

Q "Be careful. **Buy mace**. Don't walk alone. But that goes for anywhere. New Haven isn't in that bad of an area at all."

Q "**It is necessary to have common sense when you're on campus**. School is pretty much contained, but New Haven is also a regular city, so I guess you could say one must have a sense of 'street smarts.' There were about two incidents of students in the various schools being mugged—they weren't harmed, but their wallets were taken—but the people were apprehended, and those people were also walking by themselves pretty late at night. That's never a good idea."

Q "There are countless blue phones all around campus, from which you can dial a friend or security. There are panic buttons on each phone, and you can also get in touch with security to come pick you up. I feel safe on campus, but **I usually try to walk with someone wherever I go late at night**. All you need is common sense on any urban campus. The minibus will pick you up from certain locations, but I walk everywhere."

Q "The campus is really safe. **You need to have an ID card and keys to get into dorms** and onto the freshman part of campus after hours. Yale Police are always around, and they are very friendly. You can always call the minibus to take you back to campus if it's late and you don't feel safe. Or you can call for an escort. They're really on-point about that. Also, there are blue phones everywhere, which will immediately connect you to security."

The College Prowler Take
ON SAFETY & SECURITY

Although New Haven is an urban setting with its share of crime, students agree that they generally feel safe on campus and in town. Because of the area, it is easy to end up in a bad part of town simply by walking three blocks in the wrong direction. But, you quickly learn what and where these places are, and when to avoid them. Yale has its own police force, separate from the New Haven Police Department, and its presence is felt. There are also many services for student safety, such as police escorts to walk you home after late-night study sessions. As long as you use common sense, there is rarely a reason to feel in danger.

The College Prowler™ Grade on
Safety & Security: B-

A high grade in Safety & Security means that students generally feel safe, campus police are visible, blue-light phones and escort services are readily available, and safety precautions are not overly necessary.

Computers

Students Speak Out
ON COMPUTERS

"Most kids I know bring their own. Yale has a cool deal with Dell to subsidize. I've never heard of the computer labs being crowded."

Q "Computer labs can get crowded during midterms and finals period, so **it would probably be better to bring your own computer**. There is usually one that is available to use, but it's just easier and more convenient to have your own."

Q "I always think everyone should bring their own computer! Again, I've only used the G4s in the art building at Yale and **a couple of dinosaur PCs in the library**, but the labs were never crowded. It's probably safe to say that they get crowded during finals."

Q "Bring your own computer if at all possible. You will be glad not to have to leave the room to work. **Each residential college dorm at Yale has computer labs**, but who wants to stay up all night in a place with fluorescent lighting, when you could be lounging in your pajamas with a cup of hot chocolate? It's much easier to concentrate that way."

Q "**I think the computer labs here are adequate**; I've never had a problem getting a computer when I've needed one. But, there's a bit of an e-mail culture here, so I've found it very convenient to have my own computer in my room."

Q "I love having a laptop. **Having your own computer gives you the freedom** to work wherever you feel comfortable, and bringing your laptop to the library is helpful. The computer clusters are useful but typically crowded. I use them to print sometimes, but it's easier to link to a roommate's printer."

The Lowdown
ON COMPUTERS

High-Speed Network?
Yes

Wireless Network?
Yes

Number of Labs:
11 open clusters, 12 restricted access (one in each residential college)

24-Hour Labs:
All labs are open 24 hours

Charge to Print?
Black laser printing: 7 cents per page
Color laser printing: 50 cents per page

Operating Systems:
PC, UNIX, and Macintosh

Free Software
Yale offers a variety of free software ranging from Norton Antivirus to statistics programs.

The College Prowler Take
ON COMPUTERS

Students agree that although it is convenient to have a personal computer, it is unnecessary. Everywhere you look there is a computer kiosk or lab, and every residential college has its own computer lab. Very rarely is it impossible to find a computer to work on or check e-mail (except during the chaos of midterms or finals). As a plus, labs provide a quiet place—away from roommates and your television—where work can actually be done. Also, every residential college has a team of computer assistants available to fix your computer for free practically anytime. This is an invaluable resource that comes in handy at the beginning of the year when you have to install Yale software, or if you tragically lose a paper the night before it is due.

The College Prowler™ Grade on
Computers: A

A high grade in Computers designates that computer labs are available, the computer network is easily accessible, and the campus' computing technology is up-to-date.

Facilities

The Lowdown
ON FACILITIES

Student Center:
No

Athletic Center:
Payne Whitney Gymnasium; also, most residential colleges have their own gyms

Libraries:
There are eight major libraries, as well as one in each residential college.

Theatre on Campus?
Yes

Bowling on Campus?
No

Bar on Campus?
GYPSY; also many bars near campus— Rudy's, The Anchor, BAR

Coffeehouse on Campus?
There are many near campus ranging from Starbucks to the local mainstay, Koffee.

Favorite Things to Do

Yale theater can often rival most off-Broadway shows, offering an astounding amount of talent for little or no money. If you want to experience a slightly more upscale evening, there are often art show openings where you can rub elbows with Yale's "artsy" crowd while drinking wine and looking at amazing artwork. If you feel like relaxing during the week, you can always see an independent film at the York Square Cinemas.

Popular Places to Chill

Koffee, East Rock State Park, New Haven Green

Students Speak Out
ON FACILITIES

"The library is gorgeous, and the gym is huge. There are computers everywhere—even outside the dining halls. The facilities are definitely up to par."

Q "Our facilities are great. **We have a gigantic gym**, seriously. It's one of the biggest, or the biggest; although I can't really remember, since there's a sort of competition to be the world's biggest gym. The computer clusters are up-to-date, available, etc. I don't think we really have a 'student center,' though."

Q "The facilities are decent. I don't have much to compare them to. The gym is huge. **Each residential college has some special features**, and some are better than others."

Q "**The buildings are hundreds of years old** and incredible to look at, let alone live in and use."

Q "Awesome. **There's no real student center**, but that's not a problem; there are tons of places to gather and do stuff."

Q "The facilities are pretty nice, especially in the renovated colleges. **Payne Whitney Gym is the scariest place on campus because it is large and intimidating**, but the smaller residential college gyms are user-friendly. Each residential college has special features. For example, Saybrook College has a darkroom, and Branford College has squash courts. Each college has its own buttery, kitchen, TV room, gym, laundry room, common room, dining hall, and library."

The College Prowler Take
ON FACILITIES

Most students agree that the facilities at Yale are pretty nice. The residential colleges are beautiful architectural wonders, and those that have been renovated are equally beautiful on the inside. The classroom buildings are often as picturesque as cathedrals, affording students the opportunity to learn amidst stained glass and Gothic stonework. There is no student center at Yale, but students agree that the lack of such a place is rarely, if ever, noticed. Each residential college has a common room for meetings or just hanging out, as well as a library (or two in the case of Davenport), dining hall, TV room, laundry room, and features such as private gyms, kitchens, darkrooms, or music rooms. Essentially, they are self-contained units.

The College Prowler™ Grade on
Facilities: A-

A high Facilities grade indicates that the campus is aesthetically pleasing and well-maintained; facilities are state-of-the-art, and libraries are exceptional. Other determining factors include the quality of both athletic and student centers and an abundance of things to do on campus.

Campus Dining

The Lowdown
ON CAMPUS DINING

Freshman Meal Plan Requirement?
Yes

Meal Plan Average Cost:
$3,222–$4,120

24-Hour On-Campus Eating?
No

Student Favorites:
The Law School Dining Hall, Berkeley

Students Speak Out
ON CAMPUS DINING

"Campus food is not good. Unless you go to one of the newer residential colleges, then you'll get some fresh stuff. Stay away from JE at all costs. We can also transfer and eat at the med school, law school, or SOM."

Q "**We have many dining halls, and the food is pretty good**. You will have a meal plan that allows you to eat at Commons, which is our main dining hall, and 12 residential colleges—each has its own dining hall. There are 'Pangeos' stations at each college that prepare things like wraps, pasta, and Asian food right in front of you."

Q "The newly-renovated colleges seem to have better food. Branford, Saybrook, and Berkeley seem good. **I like eating at Commons because it's open longer**. Each college has its own personality, and it shows in its dining halls. You can also have a different meal plan that gives you Flex Dollars to spend at local places like Au Bon Pain and Yorkside Pizza."

Q "The food on campus is decent and probably as good as you can expect out of a college dining hall. **Some days are better than others**, of course, but there's a pretty wide selection, so you can always find something."

Q "Food on campus is fine, but I'm not picky. It's obviously not the highest quality, but there's a ton of choice. **Don't worry about it**. The dining halls all serve the same food; you'll slowly find out about little differences."

Q "**The dining hall food is mediocre at best**. The food is repetitive and fattening. Its main downfall is self-serve, unlimited portions, so students have a tendency to consume mass quantities of food at each meal. The vegetables and fruits are usually not very fresh, and a limited selection is available. For late-night snacking, each residential college has a buttery, where fried foods and other treats can be purchased for cheap prices."

Q "Dining halls are dining halls. It's nothing special, but it's fine. **The School of Management is great**, well worth the trek halfway up Science Hill. And there are about a trillion great off-campus places, particularly Thai and Indian. Although, my favorite places to go are still the Educated Burgher and The Whole Enchilada, this amazing health-food Mexican place on Whitney."

The College Prowler Take
ON CAMPUS DINING

The dining-hall food at Yale is surprisingly decent, with a large selection of entrees every day and a salad bar and sandwich bar if all else fails. There are dining halls in each college, and they are all beautiful, decorated with crystal chandeliers, stained glass windows, and portraits of famous Yalies of the past (including Bill Clinton and George Bush). Furthermore, because most people take most of their meals in their residential college, the students and staff become a makeshift family. No matter how many options a dining hall presents, it can still be monotonous day in and day out. Moreover, the limited hours can be inconvenient for busy students whose schedules might be a bit unorthodox. All-in-all, dining-hall food is still the most convenient option, and often it is pretty good.

The College Prowler™ Grade on
Campus Dining: C+

Our grade on Campus Dining addresses the quality of both school-owned dining halls and independent on-campus restaurants as well as the price, availability, and variety of food.

Off-Campus Dining

The Lowdown
ON OFF-CAMPUS DINING

Best Pizza:
Pepe's or Sally's

Best Chinese:
It is hard to find good Chinese around Yale. Your best bet is Main Garden.

Best Breakfast:
Copper Kitchen

Best Wings:
The Anchor Bar

Best Healthy:
Claire's

Best Place to Take Your Parents:
Scoozi

Student Favorites:
Thai Taste, Claire's, and Yorkside

Students Speak Out
ON OFF-CAMPUS DINING

The College Prowler Take
ON OFF-CAMPUS DINING

"It's great. There's Thai food, Italian, and everything else. Good places include Pad Thai, Sally's, Abate, Clarie's, and Hot Tomatoes. There are too many to name."

Q "There are a bunch of great restaurants in the area. I'd recommend Hot Tomatoes, Roomba, a personal favorite, and Thai Taste, another personal favorite, to name a few."

Q "We usually just go to an organic grocery store called Out of the Woods. I've been to a few restaurants, none of which I remember. There's a place that we affectionately call 'Basement Thai' that is across the street from the art building at 1156 Chapel. Also, a bookstore and cafe called Book Trader has used books for sale as well as coffee and sandwich-type stuff."

Q "The restaurants around campus are great! There are tons of Thai restaurants that are all great. There is such a variety—Japanese, Chinese, cafés, pizza places, grills, Mexican, Ethiopian, and Indian. Some names of some good spots include Samurai, Thai Taste, Rainbow Café, Yorkside Pizza, Naples, Hot Tomatoes, and Ivy Noodle. There are so many places. New Haven is famous for pizza, so there are a bunch of those types of places."

Q "New Haven has an amazing food scene! For every budget, there is a restaurant that has great food. The upscale, atmospheric restaurants with fabulous food include Zinc, Roomba, and Miso. For fantastic pizza, try BAR—they also brew their own beer on the premises—or the infamous Wooster Square pizzerias: Sally's and Pepe's. Chapel Street has Thai restaurants across from each other as well as Rainbow Café for the informal BYOB crowd. Naples has cheap pizza to go by the slice but does not serve liquor anymore. Wonderful Indian, Ethiopian, Malaysian, and Japanese eateries also line the elm streets."

Sometimes, you might want to get away from the "Yale" atmosphere or catch a meal between dining-hall hours. Students agree there are many reasonably-priced places walking distance from Yale, particularly for pizza, Thai food (Thai Taste is best), or Indian food. If you feel like taking a longer walk or a cab ride, New Haven has the two "best" pizza places in America—Pepe's and Sally's—both less than a block away from each other. If ethnic food is your thing, New Haven will be like food heaven, but if your palate is a bit more sedate or if you like fast food, it is a little more difficult to find good food.

The College Prowler™ Grade on
Off-Campus Dining: B+

A high Off-Campus Dining grade implies that off-campus restaurants are affordable, accessible, and worth visiting. Other factors include the variety of cuisine and the availability of alternative options (vegetarian, vegan, Kosher, etc.).

Campus Housing

Did You Know?

The residential college system is the foundation of Yale's social structure, fostering a sense of community and creating a vibrant social and intellectual environment on a manageable scale.

Students are randomly assigned to their residential colleges. However, if one of your relatives was/is in a particular residential college, you can choose to be or not to be assigned to that college.

The Lowdown
ON CAMPUS HOUSING

Students Speak Out
ON CAMPUS HOUSING

Undergraduates living on-campus:
86%

Number of Dormitories:
20

Room Types:
Suites, singles

Suites:
Students live in singles or doubles that surround a main common room.

Singles:
A student has his or her own private room, but there is no common room.

Bed Type:
Twin extra-long

Available for Rent:
Mini-Refrigerators

Cleaning Service?
In public areas only (i.e., bathrooms, hallways, laundry rooms, etc.)

You Get:
Bed, dresser, desk, basic cable, Internet access, phone line with voicemail

"I was in Bingham; it has a huge tower for one entryway and nine stories! It has an elevator and an 'off-limits' roof with an amazing view—we had barbecues up there."

Q "My dorm this year was superb. **Durfee is on Old Campus; it's an excellent dorm** with huge windows and a great view of Old Campus for all sorts of activities. Dorms, in general, are really good. Morse's dorm rooms are also huge. Other dorms are not as huge, and you might not get singles until later on, but you get other perks, as well, for being in that college."

Q "You're assigned randomly to your residential college, so **you don't really get to choose your new identity**, although you can switch to another one after an application process. There's a random lottery process where you pick your future dorm rooms, but your freshman year dorm room is randomly assigned. Lanman Wright on Old Campus is known to be small, but the others are nice."

Q "The dorms are really nice—some more than others. There are 12 residential colleges, and **you're assigned to one 'randomly.'** Freshman year, you'll be on Old Campus unless you're in Silliman or TD, but it might be different next year because one of the dorms, Vanderbilt, has recently been renovated."

Q "All the dorms on Old Campus are nice except for Lanman-Wright—those rooms are a little small, but they're in a great location. **They've been renovating each of the colleges**—one per year. They've renovated four now, and those are obviously the nicest—Saybrook, Branford, Berkeley, and TD."

Q "They assign you to one of 12 residential colleges—**it's like your home for the next four years**. Each college is like a little community, so they have their own master, a professor who lives there and is responsible for ensuring good social life; and a dean, a professor responsible for overseeing academic matters. These two adults generally know everyone in the college and are there to help you. The houses also contain a dining hall, computer cluster, kitchen, and a TV room. You also play intramural sports for your college and participate in special house events."

Q "**I consider the college housing system one of Yale's most important assets**. Which college you end up in isn't really so important. My college house is usually considered one of the 'ugly' ones, but I've had a wonderful experience with the dean, master, and most importantly, the students. There are about 100 students per year in each college, so over the course of Yale you get to know them pretty well. Since most people at Yale are busy doing lots of different activities, it's really nice to have a home base of 'dorm friends' that are always familiar faces in the dining hall even if you don't spend all of your time with them."

Q "You don't really have much choice over where you're living since you're randomly assigned to a college freshman year and **you live there all four years**, unless you move off campus. I transferred colleges, but in general that is fairly difficult."

The College Prowler Take
ON CAMPUS HOUSING

Most students agree that Yale's residential college system provides students a place to live and learn that surpasses any other dorm experience. By combining social activities, extracurriculars, and academics, colleges become real homes for students for the four years they are at Yale. Each college is a microcosm of the University, creating the feel of a small college within a larger institution. The residential colleges are beautiful on the outside, mostly Gothic structures, but some are Georgian and more modern. On the inside, however, many colleges are in disrepair and have frequent power outages and plumbing problems. Most students live in suites with three to 12 students, although there are some singles.

The College Prowler™ Grade on
Campus Housing: A-

A high Campus Housing grade indicates that dorms are clean, well-maintained, and spacious. Other determining factors include variety of dorms, proximity to classes, and social atmosphere.

Off-Campus Housing

Students Speak Out
ON OFF-CAMPUS HOUSING

> "It depends on how much you want to spend. Some apartments are right across from dorms; some are four or more blocks away."

Q "There are lots of people who live off campus, and **it seems pretty convenient to me**. I personally like on-campus housing because it's more of a central social space. But, if you plan to live away from campus, it's pretty easy to find a nice space that's nearby."

Q "Off-campus housing is pretty convenient. There are some houses and apartments that are popular spots. **Most people stay on campus**, since the housing is really nice."

Q "You will not want off-campus housing. On-campus housing is excellent, and residential college life is at the center of the Yale experience. If you're not a part of residential college life, **you'll be more isolated from fellow students**."

Q "**Housing off campus is abundant but pricey**. The closer to Yale and New Haven, the more expensive or potentially dangerous is can be at night. It's better if you can get a group together that can share a place. A lot of places offer student pricing or have places reserved. The more people you have, the better things are in terms of out-of-pocket expenses."

Q "A lot of my friends think it is worth it to live off campus, and I love their places—most live in the Chapel Street area or on High Street. It's not that expensive, and you can get huge apartments, but I wanted to be on campus because I like the college atmosphere and the camaraderie of living with my class. Plus, **it's nice to pad down to brunch in PJs and slippers** on the weekends, and to have laundry right downstairs!"

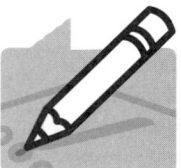

The Lowdown
ON OFF-CAMPUS HOUSING

Undergrads in Off-Campus Housing:
14%

Average Rent for a Studio Apartment:
$700/month

Average Rent for a One-Bedroom Apartment:
$850/month

Average Rent for a Two-Bedroom Apartment:
$1,100/month

Popular Areas:
Chapel Street, Broadway, Science Hill

Best Time to Look for a Place:
Spring semester

For Assistance Contact
University Properties
E-mail: rental.feedback@yale.edu

The College Prowler Take
ON OFF-CAMPUS HOUSING

While students admit that off-campus housing is available and close to campus, most choose to stay on campus for all four years. Because students must house on campus until their junior year, by the time they have the opportunity to move, they have made connections to their college and enjoy the social scene it creates. The decision to move off campus means separation from the Yale community. You don't have Ethernet, and you do have more responsibility. That being said, those who choose to move off campus are usually very happy with their decision. It is a personal decision to live off campus or on. The pluses of off-campus living include no more meal plan, more privacy, and a break from the academic environment.

Diversity

The Lowdown
ON DIVERSITY

African American: 8%

Asian American: 13%

Hispanic: 6%

Native American: 1%

White: 63%

International: 9%

Out-of-State: 87%

The College Prowler™ Grade on
Off-Campus Housing: B
A high grade in Off-Campus Housing indicates that apartments are of high quality, close to campus, affordable, and easy to secure.

Minority Clubs
There is a club for almost every minority group on campus, ranging from the African American House to Kasama: Filipino Students at Yale.

Most Popular Religions
Almost all religions are present and supported by the Yale community. There are a few vocal Christian associations, as well as a Jewish cultural center (Slifka). At Yale, students are free to pursue their private beliefs, alone or within associations.

Political Activity
Most students at Yale are politically and socially liberal, and often there are protests and active movements. However, there is a small but vocal conservative scene that sometimes dominates the floor at the Yale Political Union.

Gay Tolerance
Yale is a very gay-friendly campus with lots of gay/lesbian/transsexual associations. The sizable gay community is vocal and known for throwing the best parties.

Economic Status
Every economic status is represented at Yale. However, there is a large proportion of wealthy students, especially legacies.

Students Speak Out
ON DIVERSITY

"One of the best things about Yale is the diversity and open-mindedness. This is another good reason to be in the residential colleges—you will meet people from all walks of life, all cultures, and all backgrounds."

Q "The 'Yale part' of New Haven is quite radically different from the 'New Haven part' of New Haven. Basically, the Yale campus and immediate surroundings are primarily wealthy and primarily white. The rest of New Haven is quite poor, and it's primarily people of color. It's quite an astonishing separation."

Q "New Haven is like a mini New York at times. It's very much the melting pot, although Mediterranean cultures seem to be predominant here, as well as the Irish. For the most part, everything is just mixed. There is also a large number of Brazilians."

Q "I think Yale is a diverse place, but that diversity isn't always apparent. There's a noticeable tendency for students to self-segregate a little bit according to racial, ethnic, or religious background. I don't mean that everyone has friends exactly like themselves—more that there's a strong sense of shared cultural identity, fostered by clubs and other programs, that has a visible effect on the friendships that people form when they come here."

The College Prowler Take
ON DIVERSITY

Yale prides itself on its diversity and the freedom of expression on campus, and most students agree that the student body is really diverse racially, ethnically, religiously, and geographically. Not only does this diversity make student life more exciting, it also makes classes much more interesting. Everyone brings in a totally new perspective, so class often becomes more like a heated debate than a boring lecture. In addition, every element of the student body is represented in clubs and associations. Unfortunately, students note that while the campus is diverse, sometimes people stay in factions or cliques rather than branching out.

The College Prowler™ Grade on
Diversity: B

A high grade in Diversity indicates that ethnic minorities and international students have a notable presence on campus and that students of different economic backgrounds, religious beliefs, and sexual preferences are well-represented.

Guys & Girls

The Lowdown
ON GUYS & GIRLS

Women Undergrads: 49%

Men Undergrads: 51%

Birth Control Available?
Yes, Yale University Health Services.

Social Scene
The residential college system at Yale makes it easy to make connections between students. By transforming Yale into smaller social units, the colleges make interactions less overwhelming and intimidating, and by sponsoring social activities (like study breaks, dances, etc.), they provide opportunities to make new friends. In addition, campus organizations provide a place to meet people of similar interests.

Hookups or Relationships?
Because students at Yale are so focused on their academics and activities, hookups are more convenient and more popular than relationships. However, some people do develop these random encounters into serious relationships.

Dress Code
There's no official style at Yale. Everybody does his own thing, from punk to trendy to preppy. The only time there's a more uniform look is during finals, when most people walk around in their pajamas or sweats.

Students Speak Out
ON GUYS & GIRLS

"I'm not wealthy, and I was afraid of that infamous, 'Ivy league/private school atmosphere,' of over-privileged kids, but everyone at Yale seems so nice and not at all snobby."

Q "Well, are they hot? Hmmm … they're okay. I mean, **all the guys seem hot at first, but then it sort of dies down**. It depends on your standards, though. Most of them are really nice, fun, and cool. I love all the friends I've made at school; they're great. For the most part, everyone is very friendly and easy to get along with. Also, people aren't usually too cliquey. You know how girls can be kind of catty? The girls at Yale totally aren't at all; you can walk into any party or room and make some new friends."

Q "The guys are very nice—chivalrous, too. People hold the door for each other all the time. And when I started doing that in other places, people sort of stared at me. **There are many hot guys**, but you have to make sure they're straight. The gay, lesbian, bi, trans scene is out there and open. The girls are also very nice. Are girls hot? I wouldn't really know; my friends who are lesbians are happy here. I think the people here are the friendliest, most amazingly smart, and modest people ever!"

Q "I'm being perfectly honest: the common rhetoric is that the dating scene at Yale stinks. Some people do date, and some do have boyfriends or girlfriends, but mostly, **people like to complain about the dating scene** and say that it's usually more random hookups. I don't know how much this is true; I know a large number of people in every category. As always, there are the hotties, and there are the not-so-hotties. I'd say we're pretty average in the looks department."

Q "**I guess guys range from 'average' to 'not bad.'** Some are ugly, and some might be hot, though my preference runs towards women. The women are on the same range, but I would say that, for the most part, they are 'good' to 'hot.' They range from all around the world and in a variety of features. Whatever your preference, you won't be disappointed."

The College Prowler Take
ON GUYS & GIRLS

Students agree that Yale is a pretty attractive school. While many students do not have the time to put into primping (makeup, clothes selection, shaving), the rumor that beauty is inversely proportional to intelligence is proven wrong at Yale. Not only are many guys and girls hot, they are talented, smart, funny, and interesting to boot. Unfortunately, Yale students are also busy—too busy to have relationships. Instead, most of them partake in random hookups that occur during drunken blurs. To many, hooking up is just another kind of stress relief. But for those who are looking for love, there is hope. Some students do find real love; some even get married!

The College Prowler™ Grade on
Guys: B

A high grade for Guys indicates that the male population on campus is attractive, smart, friendly, and engaging, and that the school has a decent ratio of guys to girls.

The College Prowler™ Grade on
Girls: B+

A high grade for Girls not only implies that the women on campus are attractive, smart, friendly, and engaging, but also that there is a fair ratio of girls to guys.

Athletics

The Lowdown
ON ATHLETICS

Men's Varsity Teams:
Basketball
Cross Country
Fencing
Golf
Ice Hockey
Lacrosse
Soccer
Squash
Swimming
Tennis
Track
Sailing
Football
Crew
Baseball

Women's Varsity Teams:
Basketball
Cross Country
Fencing
Golf
Ice Hockey
Lacrosse
Soccer
Squash
Swimming
Tennis
Track
Volleyball
Softball
Gymnastics
Field Hockey
Crew

Fields
Yale Bowl, Johnson Field, Smillow Field Center, DeWitt Family Field, Baseball Stadium

Getting Tickets
For most events (except for the Harvard-Yale football game), there is no need to purchase tickets in advance. Tickets are usually inexpensive.

Athletic Division:
NCAA Division I

Conference:
Ivy League

Most Popular Sports:
Football, crew

Overlooked Teams:
Women's Fencing (Yale fencer Sada Jacobson is #1 in the world!)

School Mascot:
"Handsome Dan" (Bulldog)

Want to find a club sport that best fits your personality? For a detailed listing of all club sports on campus, check out the College Prowler book on Yale at *www.collegeprowler.com*.

Students Speak Out
ON ATHLETICS

"It's all about what you're into. Varsity is big if we're winning. Football is always big. Harvard-Yale games are ridiculously fun. Intramurals (IMs) are big if you're into them. I'm not, but I have friends who definitely are."

Q "**Varsity sports are not that big**. Yeah, you can probably make out the jocks because they are always wearing sports gear, sweatpants, and Yale gear. The football game against Harvard is obviously huge. Other than that, it's not that big. We had a good men's basketball season, so that gained some attention. IM sports depend on your college. Saybrook and Calhoun try hardcore to win, but others such as Trumbull don't really try."

Q "Varsity sports and IM sports are very popular. I don't participate in either one of them because I have my own activities that keep me busy, but **if you want to join, definitely go for it**!"

Q "Varsity sports are as big as you can expect at an Ivy League school. I am actually on the varsity golf team, and it's definitely growing and improving, but **it does not compare to a big state school**. When our basketball team tied for Ivy League champions, everyone got really excited and pumped up about that. It almost felt like we went to a big basketball school. It was fun. IM sports are pretty big. A lot of people play them, and they sound like they're fun and somewhat competitive."

Q "Varsity sports are pretty big, but **it's not like everyone goes to every game**. The big ones, like Harvard-Yale, are packed, and important games and playoffs are well-attended. IM sports are also cool and are played between the residential colleges. There are even club sports, which are not as rigorous as varsity sports but more intense than the mostly-for-fun IMs. I play a club sport, which if you're interested, is awesome; you need no experience at all. It's so great; you should really check it out!"

Greek Life

The College Prowler Take
ON ATHLETICS

The Lowdown
ON GREEK LIFE

For a school with such a strong academic reputation, Yale has a pretty strong athletic program. From IMs to varsity sports, Yale offers options for every level of athlete. Our varsity sports often do reasonably well, and most colleges compete actively in IMs. However, some students don't even know sports exist—it is Yale! Essentially, sports are as important as most other activities at Yale, such as volunteer projects, a cappella, drama, and the newspaper. It is in no way privileged. The great thing is that there are so many interests to pursue, and they are all seen as important.

Number of Fraternities: 8

Number of Sororities: 3

Did You Know?
Delta Kappa Epsilon is famous for Butthole Week in which its new pledges walk around campus, unwashed, performing degrading tasks.

Students Speak Out
ON GREEK LIFE

"There's not really a Greek life at Yale. Social activities mostly center around clubs and residential colleges."

The College Prowler™ Grade on
Athletics: C

A high grade in Athletics indicates that students have school spirit, that sports programs are respected, that games are well-attended, and that intramurals are a prominent part of student life.

Q "We have fraternities and some sororities, but most of the time, **you probably wouldn't even know they existed**. They do throw popular parties at their houses. Some have houses, some don't. But there's just so much to do on and off campus that Greek life is insignificant. In fact, I think that the a cappella scene sort of replaces that. If you're looking for parties, there are plenty of parties that are advertised by signs or by e-mail that are not Greek. Social life is really what you make of it."

Q "Sororities are almost nonexistent; you hardly know anyone in one. As for frats, **they're bigger if you want them to be**. There are maybe four houses that consistently throw parties, but it tends to be the same crowd at these parties. If it's your thing, it's really cool, if not, there is plenty more to do around here."

Q "**The Greek system is kind of small** and does not dominate the social scene. I am actually in a sorority, but it is very low-key and just another social outlet. It's nice, though, since everyone is very supportive and fun. The fraternities are mostly associated with certain sports. DKE is mostly football and baseball players. There is always a frat party on Thursday, Friday, and Saturday, and sometimes they have big parties with themes and fun drinks."

Q "Greek life does not dominate the social scene; it is a minority, although **you can find 'Greeks' if you look**. It took me until my senior year to make a friend who happened to be into the Greek scene and attend a few parties. There's definitely no pressure to be a part of that, although there are some nice sorority and fraternity houses near campus."

The College Prowler Take
ON GREEK LIFE

With the exception of a few frat parties, the Greek scene at Yale is almost nonexistent. For those few who are involved, it is mostly seen as another social activity, a place where you can hang out and find some support. The fraternity scene is more prominent than the sororities (there are eight fraternities, but only three sororities), mostly because they serve as clubs for varsity athletes.

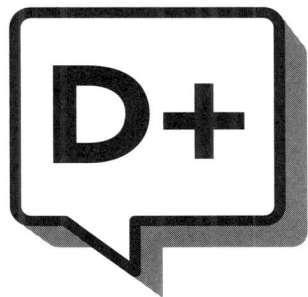

The College Prowler™ Grade on
Greek Life: D+

A high grade in Greek Life indicates that sororities and fraternities are not only present, but also active on campus. Other determining factors include the variety of houses available and the respect the Greek community receives from the rest of the campus.

Drug Scene

Students Speak Out
ON DRUG SCENE

"I know people who smoke marijuana, but I can't comment on anything harder than that. The drug scene is not very big around here."

Q "I'm not a part of it, so I wouldn't know a thing about it. The pot smokers have to get their pot somewhere, but I don't know where. **They get it somehow, so it must exist.**"

Q "**The drug scene isn't huge**, but you've definitely got your group of stoners and druggies. I feel like few people do things beyond smoking weed, though. I know some people who do coke occasionally."

Q "**Pot is easy to get and easy to smoke**. That's about my level of involvement in the drug scene, I don't know about anything else."

Q "I guess as in any place, if you're looking for them, you'll find them. **I've never been pressured** or exposed to them."

Q "Some people at Yale use drugs. I'm just guessing here, but I think most Yale students either have never used drugs, or have used pot socially a few times. **There are some more serious drug-users**, of course. But, even among those, I think you often find very serious students who do great academic work and contribute to the community here. I think the quality of the experience you have here has very little to do with whether or not you choose to use drugs."

The Lowdown
ON DRUG SCENE

Most Prevalent Drugs on Campus:
Alcohol, marijuana, stimulants (Ritalin, Adderall, cocaine), ecstasy

Liquor-Related Referrals:
2

Liquor-Related Arrests:
0

Drug-Related Referrals:
1

Drug-Related Arrests:
3

Drug Counseling Programs:
Substance Abuse Counseling (Mental Hygiene Department)

The College Prowler Take
ON DRUG SCENE

The drug scene on campus is surprisingly prevalent. Many of the students have the money to support a thriving drug habit and the stress to warrant one. Furthermore, the administration is very lax about their drug policies and punishments. The most popular drugs on campus are marijuana, which seems easily attained if you want it, and stimulants (cocaine, speed, and Ritalin), which are becoming more and more prevalent as study drugs. However, while the drug scene exists, it is easily avoided. It is generally present within certain cliques. If you don't interact with the members, you might never even encounter drugs on campus. Students certainly do not have to negotiate "peer pressure."

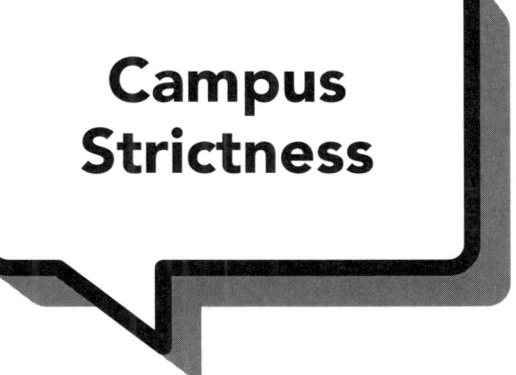

Campus Strictness

The Lowdown
ON CAMPUS STRICTNESS

What Are You Most Likely to Get Caught Doing on Campus?
Drinking underage, public urination or indecency, parking illegally, making too much noise in your dorm, downloading copyrighted materials, sending unsolicited e-mail (spam), running around on rooftops of buildings, having candles and incense sticks in your dorm

The College Prowler™ Grade on
Drug Scene: B+

A high grade on Drug Scene indicates that drugs are not a noticeable part of campus life; drug use is not visible, and no pressure to use them seems to exist.

Students Speak Out
ON CAMPUS STRICTNESS

"Basically, Yale's policy is 'we know you're going to drink, so please do it safely and on campus.' They pay for kegs for the quad parties; it's pretty amazing."

Q "I would say that the campus police are not very strict on drinking and drugs, or at least **they're not as strict as they could be**. There's a lot of drinking on campus, and I do know a few pot smokers, but I wouldn't want to jump to conclusions about how well they're doing their job. Maybe we just slip by."

Q "The campus police are not strict at all. You really can't get in trouble for any of that. **Yale just doesn't want you to die or get sick**. They usually never break apart parties or anything. When my friend who goes to a state school visited, she was shocked at how the alcohol was roaming around so freely. It's cool, though, because you don't have to worry about getting in trouble for having some fun."

Q "**Yale really has no big policy against drinking**. My college actually had a cookout, and there was a keg and wine. Yalies, for the most part, are responsible, so the school doesn't really have to worry about anything. There is also a place where you can go if you think you or your friend has had too much to drink—the Undergrad Department of Health—and they take care of you, and your parents don't know. Your parents only find out if you get really sick and have to go to the Yale-New Haven hospital."

Q "They have some type of policy on drugs, but to be honest, I really don't know about it because drugs aren't really big here. Marijuana is really the biggest drug here, and **no one seems to be out of hand with it**, so there aren't any problems."

Q "It's not very strict. **The Yale police are there to protect you from the New Haven police**. Drinking is pretty big, although if you don't want to, there is really no pressure. A decent amount of students smoke pot, but other than that, I don't think there's much of anything."

The College Prowler Take
ON CAMPUS STRICTNESS

As long as illegal things aren't done unabashedly and publicly, the campus police are completely willing to look the other way. Police do not usually raid houses unless there are noise complaints or fighting. Underage drinking is ignored by the administration, which even allows alcohol at public social events within the college. Yale treats its students as adults who are capable of taking care of themselves and making wise decisions. Essentially, the campus police follow the spirit of the law, not the letter of the law; they care only about the students' safety. In fact, the campus police officers often protect students from getting caught by the "real" police—i.e., if a student is walking down the street with an open beer can (this is illegal in New Haven), they will warn them.

The College Prowler™ Grade on
Campus Strictness: A

A high Campus Strictness grade implies an overall lenient atmosphere; police and RAs are fairly tolerant, and the administration's rules are flexible.

Overall Experience

Students Speak Out
ON OVERALL EXPERIENCE

{ "I have great friends, inspirational classes, and great photos to prove it. My friends all love Yale—they're all down-to-earth, quirky people who have exceptional talents and interesting perspectives on life."

Q "I've read somewhere that **Yale was described as 'intense,' and it really is**. There's so much to do here that you really have to sit down and think about what to do the next day to make the most of your time. I recommend coming to Yale because of the people and the amazing academic experience."

Q "I've had a great experience at school, both socially and academically. **I think there's a place for everyone at Yale**, since the University offers so much and is so diverse. We're not completely cutthroat either. It's much more laid-back than some Ivy League schools, but it's still competitive. There's a good balance. And the people are great. You'll meet so many interesting, fun, quirky, and cool people. You'll get a great academic experience, but the people you meet and your friends will complete the entire experience."

Q "I enjoyed aspects of Yale. **A lot depends on which program you're interested in** and what your study interests are. Some programs are great. You will find that there is a certain level of depersonalization present at any large university. I came from a small liberal arts high school and was used to a lot of individual personal attention—you will most likely have to fight for that."

Q "I like practically every single person I've met at Yale. They're all very smart, of course, but they're also down-to-earth. We all understand that there's something bigger than ourselves and that we're not the center of the universe. **There's more to life than studying all the time and trying to knock others down**. All I've heard from Yalies is praise. I personally adore the school and would recommend that anyone who gets in should go there."

The College Prowler Take
ON OVERALL EXPERIENCE

Students are enthusiastic about their love for Yale. Some even claim that they have never been happier in their lives. Although students often complain about their piles of work or their small dorm rooms, in the end, all these problems fade into the background of the overall picture. Instead, all they see are the gorgeous buildings, amazing classes, brilliant faculty, and endless list of cool things to do and achieve.

When it comes down to it, however, students are most in love with the people they have had the opportunity to meet. Students at Yale are smart, down-to-earth, dynamic, fun, interesting, and amazingly talented. When they get together, they have fascinating discussions and produce incredible work. At Yale, you have the opportunity to grow not only academically, but personally as well. Most Yalies agree that this personal development is the most important and rewarding part of their college experience.

The Inside Scoop

The Lowdown
ON THE INSIDE SCOOP

Yale Slang:
Know the slang, know the school. The following is a list of things you really need to know before coming to Yale. The more of these words you know, the better off you'll be.

Blue Book: This Bible of class listings and descriptions is your shopping guide to academics.

Bursar: A method of charging bookstore goods, food, and miscellaneous Yale services to your ID card. The Bursar and your parents should become good friends because this bill gets sent home!

CCL: Cross Campus Library. This is the underground home of weenie bins and lots of '70s furniture.

Couch Duty: There are two people in your bedroom and you are not one of them. Guess where you get to sleep? Also known as "sexile."

Gut: An easy class that takes the pressure off a busy schedule and fulfills distributional requirements—i.e. *Listening to Music*, better known as *Clapping for Credit*.

Legacy: A Yalie who is here because his or her parent or other miscellaneous relative went here.

Machine City: A subterranean oasis connecting CCL and Sterling. It's a common place for study groups and TA meetings, and is home to vending machines that fulfill your wildest junk-food fantasies.

Reading Period: A week with no classes where students supposedly prepare for their finals. You'll party, you'll goof off, and you'll cry when finals come around on Monday.

Science Hill: The location of most science classes. A half-mile from Old Campus, this is God's way of punishing physics and bio-chemistry majors who would otherwise get no exercise.

The Stacks: Not only is this the dusty tower where you can get lost looking for books, it is also the location for Yale's famous stab at pornographic film.

Weenie Bin: Similar to isolation tanks, the weenie bins are study carrels in CCL.

The Whale: Purportedly a hockey rink, but it looks like a whale.

Yale Urban Legends

The movie "The Skulls" is based on Yale's secret society, Skull and Bones (whose past members include President George W. Bush and his father).

The basic idea for Federal Express was submitted as a term paper at Yale—and only got a C.

Campus pundits Porn 'n Chicken (a club devoted to watching pornography and eating fried chicken) made the first Ivy League pornographic film. "The Staxxx" is set in Sterling Memorial Library's Stacks (home to millions of dusty books) and has a cast comprised of Yale students.

School Spirit

School spirit is strong at Yale. When you walk down the street, you see students parading in Yale clothing and accessories. This might be because there are few clothing stores near campus, but it still creates a sense of solidarity amongst the student body. Students are proud of the Yale name and are willing to defend it to the death against Harvard and Princeton. This becomes most apparent during the Harvard-Yale weekend. In preparation for this surge of school spirit, students buy shirts with insults such as "Harvard sucks, and Princeton doesn't matter," and they party for their school. Alumni flock, and practically the entire student body goes to the game to cheer the football team to victory in New Haven or Boston.

Traditions

Yale is a school steeped in tradition. In fact, there is a sense of the people who have come before you in almost every activity, from walking down the street to drinking a cup at Mory's. These traditions become most apparent during age-old ceremonies, such as Commencement and Class Day. However, Yale's real tradition is having traditions and creating new traditions. For example, during Class Day (the ceremony the day before Commencement) it is tradition for students to smoke a special tobacco blend out of a clay pipe and to wave good-bye to Yale with a white handkerchief. Today, students do this while wearing the silliest hats imaginable. Now, this is a new tradition.

Things I Wish I Knew Before Coming to Yale:

- During the winter, New Haven can get colder than one thought possible ... ever!

- No matter how much you like a class, odds are you won't go if it is before 9:30 am..

- Don't pack too much. You do not need your entire ballerina figurine collection! But, you will need lots of lamps (Yale has very bad overhead lighting), a shower basket, rugs, posters, and lots of underwear (no one wants to laundry!).

- Yale students aren't that intimidating.

- Don't buy sheets or lamps from Yale. In the end, they are rip-offs.

- Most importantly, you can do anything you want at Yale. If you want a class that is restricted to juniors and seniors, plead your case and beg if you have to, your enthusiasm will win you a spot. If you want to travel abroad but do not have the money, just apply for all grants or ask financial aid creatively.

Tips to Succeed at Yale:

- Explore different majors before committing to your (parents') dream of becoming a doctor, lawyer, or engineer. There are so many options out there, and Yale is a great place to discover some of them.

- Don't take on too much. As freshman, the temptation is to do everything because everything seems so darn cool. But in the end, no matter how cool all 15 of your extracurricular activities are, they will eventually seem like the bane of your existence.

- Try to quickly learn what type of class structure suits you best. Do you like large lectures, or do you crave personal interaction with your professors? Do you want to talk or listen? Do like to take tests or write papers?

- See your freshman counselor as the resource he or she is. This senior knows the ins and outs of Yale, and can give you advice on everything from good classes to take to where to take your parents when they come. They also remember what it is like to be a freshman and truly want to help you through it.

- Go to Master's Teas. These opportunities to spend the afternoon drinking tea and eating little sandwiches while listening to great and famous people speak is invaluable. Some recent guests include singer/songwriter Carole King, actor Bronson Pinchot, writer Tobias Wolff, and political commentator Arianna Huffington.

- Don't party too much. Freedom is great, but just because you can go out and get wasted every night it does not mean you should.

- That said, don't study all the time. Yale is a strong academic school, but it is also so much more. What you can learn about life is often just as valuable as what you can learn about astronomy. Remember, there is only so much information your brain can retain at once.

Finding a Job or Internship

Career Center Resources & Services
Individual counseling appointments, Career Resource Library, workshops, panels, and career fairs, practice interviews, on-campus interview program, resume referral program, internship/summer job listings, graduate/professional school information

Major Alumni Events
The biggest events for alumni are the Yale-Harvard football game and class reunions. The game takes place usually the weekend before fall recess and alternates between Yale's campus and Harvard's. Class reunions take place year-round. Information can be found on the alumni Website.

Alumni Publications
Yale Alumni Magazine

The *Yale Alumni Magazine* covers the entire University, including research, University policy, and student affairs. Being both separate and inseparable from Yale, the magazine's writers create a unique perspective on current campus affairs.

The Lowdown
ON FINDING A JOB OR INTERNSHIP

Finding a summer job, internship, or career (gasp!) can be an incredibly overwhelming experience, especially when you have no idea what you want to or can do. This is where Undergraduate Career Services steps in. While they can't do the deciding for you, they offer a variety of resources, from personal guidance appointments, to access to job databases, to career fairs and on-campus interview programs. There is no reason to struggle alone; they are there to help.

Famous Yale Alumni
- Angela Bassett (Class of '80)
- President George H.W. Bush (Class of '48)
- President George W. Bush (Class of '68)
- President Bill Clinton (Class of '73)
- Senator Hillary Clinton (Class of '73)
- Jodie Foster (Class of '84)
- Senator Joseph Lieberman (Class of '64)
- Ed Norton (Class of '91)
- Meryl Streep (Class of '75)
- President William Howard Taft (Class of 1878)
- Sigourney Weaver (Class of '74)

Advice
Although as competitive students we are eager to use every opportunity to add padding to our resume, it is important to take some time off to travel or just relax. Many students choose to do a painful unpaid internship the summer after freshman year, but the benefits are outweighed by a summer of suffering. As freshmen, it is very difficult to get a worthwhile internship (most good ones are reserved for sophomores or higher), so they usually end up standing by a photocopier all summer without being paid or learning. This early experience is unexceptional in the long run. Most are better off resting or traveling.

However, once it's time to decide your real future post-graduation, it is important to start at the beginning of senior year (if not earlier), when most early applications for jobs and graduate schools are accepted.

The Best & Worst

The Ten BEST Things About Yale:

1. Shopping Period
2. Master's Teas
3. Brilliant professors
4. Beautiful architecture
5. Yale in London (study abroad program)
6. Residential College System
7. Pepe's and Sally's Pizza
8. Computer Clusters
9. Yale University Art Gallery
10. Toad's Place

The Ten WORST Things About Yale:

1. The weather
2. Bad New Haven neighborhoods
3. Lack of time for social activities
4. Meal plan requirement
5. Weenie bins
6. Stuck-up legacies
7. Finals on Sunday
8. The Group IV (math & science) requirements
9. No parking
10. The dating scene (or lack thereof)

Babson College

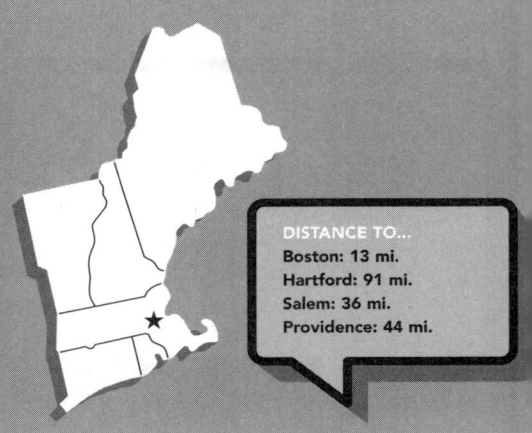

DISTANCE TO...
Boston: 13 mi.
Hartford: 91 mi.
Salem: 36 mi.
Providence: 44 mi.

231 Forest Street, Babson Park, MA 02457-0310
www.babson.edu   (800) 488-3696

"A majority of students at Babson might own summer and winter cars, but most students here are not as stuck-up as they may seem."

Total Enrollment:
1,717
Acceptance Rate:
37%
Tuition:
$28,832
Top 10% of High School Class:
50%
SAT Range
Verbal	Math	Total
560 – 640	610 – 680	1170 – 1320

ACT Range
Verbal	Math	Total
24-28	26-31	24-30

Most Popular Majors:
Babson is exclusively dedicated to Business Managagement and Administration, offering B.S., M.B.A., and custom M.S. degrees.

Students Also Applied To:*
Bentley College, Boston College, Boston University, New York University, University of Pennsylvania

*For more school info check out www.collegeprowler.com

Table of Contents

Academics	617
Local Atmosphere	619
Safety & Security	620
Computers	622
Facilities	623
Campus Dining	625
Off-Campus Dining	626
Campus Housing	628
Off-Campus Housing	629
Diversity	631
Guys & Girls	632
Athletics	634
Greek Life	635
Drug Scene	636
Campus Strictness	637
Overall Experience	638
The Inside Scoop	639
Finding a Job or Internship	640
The Best & Worst	641

College Prowler Report Card

Academics	B
Local Atmosphere	C+
Safety & Security	A-
Computers	A-
Facilities	B+
Campus Dining	C-
Off-Campus Dining	C+
Campus Housing	B-
Off-Campus Housing	C
Diversity	B+
Guys	B-
Girls	C+
Athletics	B-
Greek Life	B-
Drug Scene	B
Campus Strictness	C+

Academics

Best Places to Study
If you're looking for a quiet place to study, you're best bets will be the library and the Reynolds Campus Center.

Sample Academic Clubs
Student Government Association, Campus Activities Board, Communications Club, Investment Banking Club, Financial Management Association, Real Estate Club

The Lowdown
ON ACADEMICS

Did You Know?
A weak economy did not deter Babson's first-year students from earning big profits from their fledgling businesses. Some 400 freshmen, running 14 campus ventures, raised $45,283.33 in profits this year for donation to community service.

"The goal of the program is to give students a real-life learning experience in lessons about teamwork, problem-solving, and the importance of community service in their business lives," says Robert Major, associate director of the Undergraduate Foundation Program. "Their earnings reflect a strong commitment to community. Babson students also volunteer their time on a weekly basis to their selected charity."

The founder of Home Depot and current owner of the Atlanta Falcons, Arthur M. Black, graduated from Babson in 1963.

The current president of Babson, Brian M. Barefoot, may be the first president to truly understand what it is like to be a student here. He graduated from Babson in 1966.

Contrary to popular belief, the inventor of the magnetic strip on credit cards does not teach at Babson.

Degrees Awarded:
Bachelor, Master, Post Master Certificate

Undergraduate Schools:
Babson College

Full-time Faculty:
89%

Faculty with Terminal Degree:
77%

Student-to-Faculty Ratio:
14:1

Average Course Load:
5 courses

AP Test Score Requirements
Possible credit for scores of 4 or 5

IB Test Score Requirements
Possible credit for scores of 6 or 7

Special Degree Options:
Accelerated program, cross-registration, independent study, internships, Liberal Arts/Career combination, ROTC, Semester at Sea, student-designed major, study abroad, visiting/exchange student program

Students Speak Out
ON ACADEMICS

The College Prowler Take
ON ACADEMICS

{ **"The faculty is very personable. I've only had wonderful experiences. The classes that deal with business are very interesting, but the liberal arts classes aren't as great."**

Q "In general, classes that revolve around solid concepts like economics, marketing, and accounting are very well-taught and interesting. Things like organizational behavior (OB) and literature are **quite dry and not inspiring**. Faculty are very available to students and are passionate about the subjects they teach, which rubs off on the students."

Q "Faculty and teachers, for the most part, are very enthusiastic and truly want their students to do well. At times, it seems like they do not communicate with each other and all **decide to assign the most work at the same time**. This is being looked into by Babson, however. Most of my classes are interesting, and I intentionally picked two of my professors from last semester because I enjoyed their classes."

Q "Yes, the classes are interesting; **the faculty is very knowledgeable** as far as business classes are concerned. Science teachers are terrible, and interesting liberal arts classes are far and few in between."

Q "After being at Babson for three years, I think that I've learned a lot in class about general management and gained **expertise in the specific business areas** such as marketing, finance, and accounting. I was extremely shy when I first came to Babson, but with the help of my professors and their yearning to make each student an affective speaker, I became one of the top voices in my classes. Communication is something that I believe is extremely important in the business field, and Babson does a great job instilling and perfecting that quality in each student."

The competitive business atmosphere is felt at all times by the students and the teachers at Babson. The teachers take their work seriously and almost never miss a class or a meeting with a student. They work almost as hard as the students on trying to teach them the basics of business in the business-oriented classes (and even in some liberal arts ones). This approach isn't exactly necessary, although class participation is—it has gone up to as far as being 20 percent of your total class average!

The exceptional entrepreneurial education is the reason most students decide to enroll at Babson. This school is known for its First Year Management Program (FME), where students attempt to start their own businesses. From the start, everyone strives to learn how to effectively work with a group of people and to be led not only by the professors, but by the CEOs of their businesses as well. In addition to this experience, the industry-specific business classes provide a well-rounded, creative education. And when professors start sharing their work experiences in certain business fields, students listen attentively and hope to someday achieve status in the business world. With this school being so business-oriented, liberal arts classes tend to be put aside because they seem boring to most students. The business curriculum is what students here enjoy most and concentrate on. Altogether, students should expect a different approach to teaching from their professors at Babson, and they will have to be ready to work their butts off!

The College Prowler™ Grade on
Academics: B

A high Academics grade generally indicates that professors are knowledgeable, accessible, and genuinely interested in their students' welfare. Other determining factors include class size, how well professors communicate, and whether or not classes are engaging.

Local Atmosphere

Students Speak Out
ON LOCAL ATMOSPHERE

"**Wellesley is not a friendly place. There's a ton of traffic, and many local businesses there do not like dealing with college students. Needham is just as close, and it has many better places to visit.**"

Q "Wellesley is a rich and conservative town. It's a good place to walk around during the day and a great place not to be during the night. **There is no alcohol in Wellesley**, and all shops close down early. Wellesley College is nearby, but I personally don't like going there. I have friends at Babson and love it."

Q "Wellesley is a very small town, so **I prefer to travel into Boston if I want to get away** from the college atmosphere here. There is much more to do in the city. The clubbing and the bar scenes are great, and it's only 15 minutes away. I remember walking around Wellesley a couple of times—once to get a hair cut, and once to stop by a convenience shop to get some nail-polish remover. I also visit the Stop & Shop once in a while on the weekends, but I eat on campus, so I don't go there too often."

Q "Wellesley is **a very upscale suburb**. Downtown consists of pretty nice restaurants, retail stores, and specialty shops. Wellesley College and Olin College are there too, so there are plenty of college students to hang out with and make friends [with]."

Q "The surrounding area, including Wellesley, is considered to be 'dry' because alcohol is prohibited from being sold in restaurants, shops, or any other places except liquor stores. We are fortunate that our school provides us with our own pub, the only one in the surrounding area. So many students hang out there on Thursdays and go into Boston on the weekends, for the most part, because **the local atmosphere in Wellesley is very quiet** and limited to restaurants, coffee shops, and sandwich stores."

The Lowdown
ON LOCAL ATMOSPHERE

Region:
Northeast

City, State:
Wellesley, Massachusetts

Setting:
Medium-sized town

Distance from Boston:
25 minutes

Distance from New York City:
3.5 hours

Points of Interest:
New England Aquarium, Boston Harbor, Museum of Fine Arts (Huntington Avenue), Institute of Contemporary Art, Copley Place (connects to Prudential), Prudential Center, Fenuil Hall (Government Center T-Stop), Fenway Park, Freedom Trail, Comedy Connection, North End, Il Panino

Major Sports Team:
Red Sox (MLB), New England Patriots (NFL), Celtics (NBA), Bruins (NHL)

City Websites:
http://ci.wellesley.ma.us, http://wellesleyma.areaguides.net/google.html, www.city-data.com/city/Wellesley-Massachusetts.html

> "There's Boston, which is everything you could ever want. **Wellesley is a sweet town** and a nice place to just get away from campus, but it is a little too expensive."

The College Prowler Take
ON LOCAL ATMOSPHERE

Wellesley is not exactly a "college town," but Boston is. In Wellesley, the local atmosphere revolves around pastry shops, some decent restaurants, very expensive retail clothing stores, and a few movie theatres. With such slim pickings as far as things to do, most students tend to stay on campus or travel to the neighboring towns—and Boston of course. Framingham and Natick are popular student destinations, where you can spot a group of Babsonians in the Natick Mall or in Loews Movie Theatre. This being said, the small suburb is also just miles outside one of the largest college-populated cities in the nation. There are over 40 colleges in and around Boston, making it a "must-see" destination for all students, tourists, parents, and even locals. The 20 minutes that it takes to drive into the city is very much worth your time.

The College Prowler™ Grade on
Local Atmosphere: C+

A high Local Atmosphere grade indicates that the area surrounding campus is safe and scenic. Other factors include nearby attractions, proximity to other schools, and the town's attitude toward students.

Safety & Security

The Lowdown
ON SAFETY & SECURITY

Phone:
(781) 239-5555 (emergencies)
(781) 237-8164 (non-emergencies)

Health Center Office Hours:
Open Monday through Friday,
8 a.m. - 6 p.m.; during the academic year

Safety Services:
Electronic card readers, Rape Defense, Training (RAD) classes, emergency phones, Community Advisory program, safety escort service

Students Speak Out
ON SAFETY & SECURITY

> "The security is very good, but there could be more emergency buttons around campus. All of the officers are very worried about us, but they always give us the chance to take care of ourselves."

Q "I feel safer at Babson than at any other place I've lived. The student body is generally respectful of others' belongings, and the campus police are very responsive to calls. **I've never heard of anything unusual happening** in terms of a security breach, except one time we got an e-mail from public safety telling the campus that someone had been walking around damaging cars in the Trim parking lot."

Q "The BABO [Babson police] are **on friendly terms with students** and do not intervene unless they get a call with a noise complaint. I've heard of incidents where people complain to the BABO about an argument or a fight, but these are usually arguments between friends."

Q "Security seems pretty relaxed; it is easy to enter most buildings on campus, and **there's often no police call box in sight** when you are walking outside. Despite this, Babson College does not seem like an unsafe place to be."

Q "I always feel very safe on campus. Generally, the campus is **pretty well-lit during the night**, and even the lacrosse fields have bright lights on when it's dark. If I'm walking alone through the fields after a Knight Party, I still feel safe although I'm far away from the residence halls."

Q "The BABO do feel present. **It stinks when they break up parties**, but they make you feel safe walking around the campus at night."

The College Prowler Take
ON SAFETY & SECURITY

The public safety team (the BABO) is well-accepted by most students and seen as a helpful agent in crime prevention, campus security, and argument mending. "BABO," the friendly nickname used for the Babson Public Safety personnel, exemplifies students' accepting attitude towards the officers. The campus, itself, feels secure because it is so well lit everywhere, and it's in a safe town where crime is not an issue. Everyone knows the rules and policies here, but since it is college, students do get out of control and happen to break a law or two on the way. When incidents occur, it's best to be very cooperative with the BABO. They will usually be very considerate and helpful, and they do everything in their power to avoid making a student feel worse than necessary. They also try to avoid doling out harsh punishments, unless absolutely necessary. The Babson police should be congratulated for maintaining such a highly-visible presence and for giving the campus a general feeling of security.

Did You Know?
Electronic card readers control access to residence halls and access is available to all authorized users via their Babson ID (the OneCard).

Police logs can be read online at: www3.babson.edu/offices/public_safety/

The College Prowler™ Grade on
Safety & Security: A-

A high grade in Safety & Security means that students generally feel safe, campus police are visible, blue-light phones and escort services are readily available, and safety precautions are not overly necessary.

Computers

The Lowdown
ON COMPUTERS

High-Speed Network?
Yes

Wireless Network?
Yes

Charge to Print?
No

Numbers of Computers:
300

Number of Labs:
Six, plus departmental labs and work stations

Operating Systems
PC, IBM, OWA, and IMAP

24-Hour Labs
Yes, the 24-hour Multimedia Lab is located on the first floor of the Horn Library.

Free Software
Microsoft Office 2003, Minitab14, Precision Tree, @Risk, Symantec Antivirus, Palisade Decision Tools, NetSupport School, Clementine 8.5, and Intervideo. Also, SPSS, SAS, and Visual Studio.net are available upon faculty request.

Did You Know?

All Babson dorms have wireless Internet access and a second connection to improve Internet speed.

New IBM T42 laptops will be distributed to first-year freshmen in the fall.

A major new addition to the library's collection is "Ebrary," which has 13,000 electronic books that can be read and searched online. Babson's NETLibrary is designed to give students the tools they need to locate, evaluate, and effectively use the information they need.

Students Speak Out
ON COMPUTERS

"Since we get our own laptops, I have never been to the computer lab. Now, we have wireless in all of the dorms, but it would be nice if we got wireless in the classroom."

"The computer network is excellent. Babson **recently upgraded Internet service with an additional server**. Bringing a computer would be stupid—Babson gives them to you as part of your tuition. Almost everyone has the same version or the upgraded IBM ThinkPad, and this is useful for in-class work assignments because these computers are upgraded with the software used for homework assignments."

"The network itself is very reliable and quick. The computer **labs aren't usually that crowded** because each student has his or her own computer. People usually use these labs for printing material, for research projects, and long essay assignments."

Q "Babson provides a large array of computers and is always updating them. The library has **a lot of different resources available online** in the labs. You do not need to bring a desktop, because Babson provided state-of-the-art IBM laptops and has an ITSD service to fix the computers if something should break."

Q "Computers are **absolutely accessible anywhere, anytime**, with wireless access and printers. There are never any problems with computer accessibility in this school."

The College Prowler Take
ON COMPUTERS

Technology is a very important aspect in any business school, and Babson's got the newest computers, software, and other hardware. Babson makes sure to educate students about information technology in their first-year classes and gives them the option to take more advanced classes on management information systems (classes that emphasize how to build a Web page or set up a managerial computer program). The installation of the wireless Internet access in all dorms has improved not only the social college life, but also the academic aspect of life at Babson. Students no longer have to worry about finding an outlet for their Internet cable. From classroom use, to instant messaging friends, technology is extremely important here. It is also great that your laptop only weighs about as much as a textbook and can fit into your backpack like one, too!

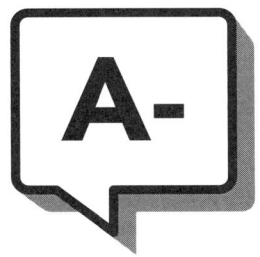

The College Prowler™ Grade on
Computers: A-

A high grade in Computers designates that computer labs are available, the computer network is easily accessible, and the campus' computing technology is up-to-date.

Facilities

The Lowdown
ON FACILITIES

Student Center:
Reynolds Campus Center

Athletic Center:
Webster Athletic Center

Libraries:
Horn Library

Movie Theatre on Campus?
Sorenson Center for the Arts

Bowling on Campus?
No

Bar on Campus?
Roger's Pub

Coffeehouse on Campus?
Woody's Coffee Bar, Reynolds Center

Popular Places to Chill
Reynolds Campus Center, Roger's Pub, and Woody's Coffee Bar

Favorite Things to Do
Many students are very familiar with the Sorenson Center because this is the place where plays, movies, and dance shows entertain the Babson crowds daily.

Students Speak Out
ON FACILITIES

> "The athletic center needs more machines, while the student center is a good place to do work, hang out with friends, or hold meetings."

Q "Everything is so **clean and modern**. Overall, most buildings are well-kept, although Webster is a little behind the times but still nice. Compared to other college campuses, this one is very classy and nicely decorated."

Q "Webster is nice. It's usually available, although sometimes there are scheduling conflicts where students don't have access to the pool, for example. **The library and computer centers are serviceable**, nothing special, although the access to Bloomberg on some of the computers is very nice. The campus center is beautiful, though having it closed on weekends isn't very student friendly. Trim Dining Hall has decent food with horrible hours. Closing at seven or eight is not smart."

Q "The athletic center and the computer center are decent, but not as good as they could be, and **the student center is nice**. Reynolds Center is probably the most modern-looking building on campus, with its glass windows and spacious atmosphere."

Q "Most of the classrooms are nice, with state-of-the-art technology. Classrooms vary from lecture, to stadium-style seating, to a standard floored room. **The athletic center is a great facility**, but at rush hour there is a line to use some of the cardio machines. The gym doesn't offer amenities like towels or shampoo."

Q "Babson is constantly renovating its offices and updating its technology. The working crew just recently finished **a complete renovation of the Alumni Office**. Although this building is far away from the rest of the facilities, it's very important for incoming perspective students to feel comfortable. Forest Hall, Putney Hall, and Publishers are others places where I've seen minor renovations."

The College Prowler Take
ON FACILITIES

Reynolds Center is located in the middle of campus, with Trim Hall on one side and the Sorenson Center of Fine Arts on the other. It contains the Crossroads Café, Woody's Coffee Bar, and the Campus Bookstore. Students feel like they are in charge of their monetary arrangements here, with free access to the Credit Union and a Fleet Bank/Bank of America ATM. Athletic facilities provide students with a wide range of exercise equipment, including racquetball and squash courts. A group of very dedicated rock-climbers are even in the process of building a climbing wall next to the varsity weight room. The campus consists of rolling hills, clusters of woods, and carefully-landscaped grounds. Altogether, the campus is very well-kept, with the custodians and gardeners working day and night.

The College Prowler™ Grade on
Facilities: B+

A high Facilities grade indicates that the campus is aesthetically pleasing and well-maintained; facilities are state-of-the-art, and libraries are exceptional. Other determining factors include the quality of both athletic and student centers and an abundance of things to do on campus.

Campus Dining

The Lowdown
ON CAMPUS DINING

Freshman Meal Plan Requirement?
Yes

Meal Plan Average Cost:
$1,720

24-Hour On-Campus Eating?
No

Student Favorites:
Crossroads Food Court and The Snack Bar at Olin Hall

Students Speak Out
ON CAMPUS DINING

"Food has gotten worse in the past year. There are a lot of lines and our main dining hall has been changing the things that are good. I enjoy our Reynolds Café, but it is expensive."

Q "The dining hall food **gets boring, very quick**. The lines are long and the halls are crowded. There are many great restaurants around Babson, in both Wellesley and Needham, many of which deliver. Ordering food is sometimes a better option than what is offered at Trim, and probably about as healthy."

Q "As with most colleges, campus food gets old. But in comparison to other schools, **Babson has quite good food**. Reynolds is good, although we can only eat there a limited amount during the year with only a certain amount of money allocated to the OneCard, depending on the meal plan."

Q "The food is very good at Reynolds. **I prefer Reynolds more than Trim**, because it offers sushi and freshly-made wraps. It takes forever to get through the sandwich line at Trim, while at Reynolds, the wraps are pre-made and take seconds to grab."

Q "You'll get bored with dining halls just like at any other campus, but the food is good, as far as cafeterias go. There is **a request sheet for students** to jot down what they like and don't like about Trim food, but mostly the food doesn't change even if it's requested."

Q "There is a large variety of food to pick from, but it doesn't seem very nutritious to me because I like cooking homemade food. Trim does try to provide variety for students by organizing festive dinners about once every two weeks. Examples from the past include Mardi Gras, Chinese, Russian, Indian, and Hawaiian homestyle food. **The cheesecake at Trim is delicious**, but most of the other desserts are not on my favorites list. Sodexo Services is a very prestigious catering group, but I wish that they offered more variety on a daily basis."

Did You Know?

Babson College even offers Gifts From Home packages that students can order for their friends or loved ones. These may be expensive, but they have a variety of options, including Healthy Snack Attack, Pizza Party, Cookie Basket, Get Well Basket, and Birthday Package.

The College Prowler Take
ON CAMPUS DINING

The dining facilities in Babson are not too shabby, with the exception of the negative student opinions of the Trim Dining Hall. But, even with all the incessant complaints about long lines, nutrition, and food variety, everyone admits that the food options here are the best when compared to any other college. A relevant issue that some students bring up is that all resident students are required to be on the meal plan. With the average meal plan costing $1,720 per semester, it is reasonable for some students to be upset. Overall, if a student is not satisfied with the meal plan options, he or she can also eat in the Olin Hall (where Babson Bucks may also be used), eat off campus, or order delivery. The food at Trim isn't really bad; it just gets boring after a while.

Off-Campus Dining

The Lowdown
ON OFF-CAMPUS DINING

Best Pizza:
Bertuccis Brick Oven Pizzeria

Best Chinese:
Wok

Best Breakfast:
Cheesecake Factory and S.E. Olson Uptown Gourmet

Best Wings:
Domino's Pizza

Best Healthy:
Au Bon Pain

Best Place to Take Your Parents:
Not Your Average Joe's

24-Hour Eating:
Bickfords and IHOP

Student Favorites:
Bertuccis Brick Oven Pizzeria, Not Your Average Joe's, Cheesecake Factory, Amarin of Thailand, Vinny Testas, Figs

Late-Night Food Specials:
Domino's Pizza, Nicks Pizza, Peter's Pizza Palace

The College Prowler™ Grade on
Campus Dining: C-

Our grade on Campus Dining addresses the quality of both school-owned dining halls and independent on-campus restaurants as well as the price, availability, and variety of food.

Fun Facts

The Multicultural Food Festival is held annually at Babson College. Its festivities include Asian, Russian, Mexican, Indian, and Hawaiian food dishes, dancing, and different types of performances by international clubs at Babson.

Students Speak Out
ON OFF-CAMPUS DINING

"There are lots of good 'mom and pop' shops around, plus the famous pizza joints. Bertuccis is my favorite!"

"Figs, Not Your Average Joe's, and Anna's Taqueria are some of my favorites. Anna's Taqueria is **one of the best burrito places in the Boston area**, although El Pelon Taqueria by Fenway Park definitely beats any Mexican food places around."

"Other than Bertuccis and some pizza joints, Wellesley doesn't have much to offer in terms of restaurants. However, a short 15-minute drive down Route 9 to Framingham will land you with **more restaurant choices than you could hope.** The Lotus Flower and Naked Fish restaurants are some of my favorites around that area."

"Bertuccis and the Olive Garden are my favorite restaurants here, and Bertuccis is right down the road! We sometimes go for team dinners to the Olive Garden, because it's **so spacious and comfy.**"

"Bertuccis is really close, and Domino's always delivers, which is important. Several other local pizza and sub places are near as well, so there are **plenty of food choices in the Wellesley area**. Domino's delivery service seems like they personally know me, because they have a computer system that picks up people who made previous orders. It's cool that they have such a close tie to Babson, because it saves time ordering food."

"Wellesley has lots of family restaurants. And if what you're looking for isn't in Wellesley, you can find **almost any other type of dining** in neighboring towns—Needham and Framingham, for example."

The College Prowler Take
ON OFF-CAMPUS DINING

With their busy schedules, most Babson students can only find time for off-campus dining on the weekends. To relax and enjoy a day at the mall and an awesome lunch, students head to the Atrium Mall on Route 9 East. This cute plaza contains clothes store options like Abercrombie & Fitch and J. Crew, as well as the famous Cheesecake Factory restaurant. The monotony of campus dining can drive anyone to stop enjoying the food at college. The need for diversity of food should make even the most studious student try at least some of the numerous places in Wellesley, Boston, and on Route 9 between the two. Students should start by exploring the local dining area because there are many tasty options, and it's not too far from campus.

The College Prowler™ Grade on
Off-Campus Dining: C+

A high Off-Campus Dining grade implies that off-campus restaurants are affordable, accessible, and worth visiting. Other factors include the variety of cuisine and the availability of alternative options (vegetarian, vegan, Kosher, etc.).

Campus Housing

Did You Know?
There is track lighting in some towers and suites, and all dorms are currently equipped with wireless, high speed Internet access.

The Lowdown
ON CAMPUS HOUSING

Students Speak Out
ON CAMPUS HOUSING

"The dorms are wireless and heated. The best dorms are McCullough, as they just were revamped over the summer with new furniture, windows, and carpeting for students to throw up on."

Undergrads on Campus:
1,735

Number of Dormitories:
19

University-Owned Apartments:
1

Available for Rent:
Safes and fridges

Also Available:
Smoke-free living option, special-interest housing, theme housing

Q "It depends on the dorm. I am in a single that has air conditioning, and it is wonderful. **Other dorms are not air conditioned**, so people have to get their own fans before school starts, since it's deathly hot in early September, especially on the top floors."

Q "Dorms aren't great. Often times there are some **obscure problems like fire alarms going off** in the middle of the night for two weeks straight or mold because of humidity."

Q "All dorms are pretty much the same. McCullough and Pietz are the dorms where the parities usually happen because they are made up of suites. **Many teams live in those dorms**, and there is at least one team party on the weekends in either one."

Q "The dorms are okay. The closer you are to the center of campus, the worse the dorm is, but it's also more convenient and social. **Farther out, the rooms get bigger and cleaner**, but you are farther away from the party scene and all the other facilities."

Cleaning Service?
The cleaning service crew works on all public areas from 7 a.m. to 11 p.m., except in Webster Center, where they work from 11 p.m. to 7 a.m. To get help with broken furniture, fixing a light bulb, etc., students may call (781) 239-4444 or e-mail workorder@babson.edu.

You Get
Bed, desk and chair, drawers or closet, bookshelf, trash basket, window shades, cable, Ethernet, and broadband Internet connections. Most dorms are equipped with air conditioning and free campus phone calls for on-campus students.

Q "Dorms are okay. The suites are great, and so are the upper-campus dorms. **The Park Manors are good**. I would avoid Forest, (although that is a designated dorm), Publishers, and Bryant (because it's so far away from everything). The grounds crew does a great job keeping the garbage changed and the bathrooms clean."

The College Prowler Take
ON CAMPUS HOUSING

The majority of freshmen live in Forest Hall, which is good because of its close proximity to Trim Hall. But, many freshmen quickly find out that they are not only far away from other halls, but also from virtually any place except Trim Hall and the BABO, who are located next door. Life there is great, especially for completing school assignments and holding small room parties. The beds at Babson are extremely uncomfortable, and some look unsanitary. Room size is another issue, because most dorms have low ceilings and very small floor space. This makes it hard for people to find room for everything, so they loft their bed to fit a fridge, some drawers, and even a desk. Room cleanliness is not a problem at Babson, but lighting and ample room space is sometimes a small hindrance to enjoying life on campus.

The College Prowler™ Grade on
Campus Housing: B-

A high Campus Housing grade indicates that dorms are clean, well-maintained, and spacious. Other determining factors include variety of dorms, proximity to classes, and social atmosphere.

Off-Campus Housing

The Lowdown
ON OFF-CAMPUS HOUSING

Undergrads in Off-Campus Housing:
5%

Best Time to Look for a Place:
At the end of the last semester

Average Rent for a Studio Apartment:
$1,000 per month

Average Rent for a 1BR Apartment:
$1,250 per month

Average Rent for a 2BR Apartment:
$1,700 per month

Popular Areas
Linden Street, Commonwealth Avenue

For Assistance Contact
Web: *www.babson.edu/offices/campuslife*
Phone: (781) 239-4438
E-mail: campuslife@babson.edu

Students Speak Out
ON OFF-CAMPUS HOUSING

The College Prowler Take
ON OFF-CAMPUS HOUSING

{ "Living off campus is great! I like driving to school and going back home to be with my family. Nothing beats mom's home-cooking!"

Q "There is so much homework here that has to be done in groups. I don't think there would be time to travel to my house if I didn't live in the dorms. **It's a pain to have someone in your study group that lives off campus**, because they're never on time for meetings."

Q "Off-campus housing isn't very convenient, because **it's really expensive**, but most of the students here are wealthy and can probably afford it."

Q "**Most students live on campus because it's more convenient**. A lot of students are in clubs or on sports teams, so it would be hard to make it to all the meetings and find time for traveling. There are lots of speakers that come to campus, too, so it would be hard to attend those if one has to travel back and forth."

Q "I know that the Office of Campus Life offers housing options off campus. And by researching their Website, I found that housing is very expensive in Wellesley. I can't afford it, but some of my friends live off campus. **It's great to have friends who live off campus** who I can always visit and hang out with."

Q "Students who live off campus are all **wicked rich and have nice apartments**, usually with their friends. TKE is a frat that had an off-campus house last year, and the parties there were fun. I'm not in that frat though, so I wouldn't know about living there."

Whoever decides to live off campus should have a car and could rent an apartment on Washington or Linden Streets in Wellesley. But with the very expensive rent, the student should also consider the time it'll take to travel back and forth for group meetings and other activities. Another problem with off-campus housing is the availability of it. Students are encouraged to start looking for fall housing as early as spring or early summer. There are many restrictions that accompany rent in the Wellesley area; one of them is age. And, overall, the Boston housing option is overrated and is disliked by many of those who have tried it.

The College Prowler™ Grade on
Off-Campus Housing: C

A high grade in Off-Campus Housing indicates that apartments are of high quality, close to campus, affordable, and easy to secure.

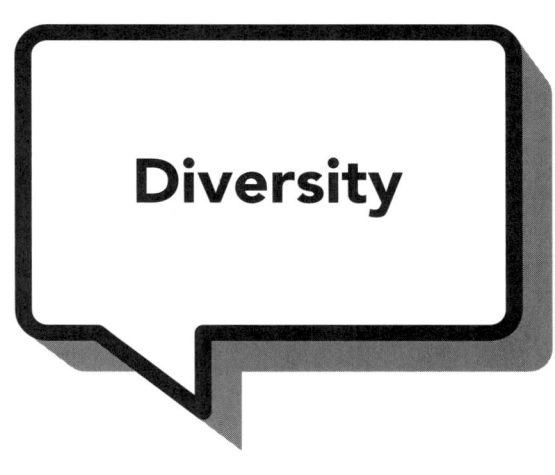

Diversity

The Lowdown
ON DIVERSITY

African American: 3%

Asian American: 8%

Hispanic: 4%

Native American: 0%

White: 66%

International: 19%

Out-of-State: 55%

Most Popular Religions
There is a Christian Fellowship group on campus that holds meetings and goes to church on Sundays. Overall religious affiliation is low on campus, but the group does a good job relating their events to the Babson community. The Babson-Olin Catholic Association is another religious group that brings together students from the neighboring Olin College of Engineering and Babson College students.

Political Activity
The political atmosphere at Babson College is not as liberal as most other campuses. Students are generally not outspoken about their political views, although some politicians have come to speak at Babson. Many consider the student body to be on the Republican side, but most students are really just apathetic.

Gay Tolerance
The campus is generally accepting of its gay students and has an on-campus organization, the Gay-Lesbian-and-Everybody-Else (GLEE) Club. This club provides students with an environment that is free from prejudice, hate, and stereotyping.

Economic Status
Babson College has a very diverse student body, with students coming from different countries and states, but it is apparent that students from wealthy backgrounds dominate. Many students also comment that the international student population is considerably wealthier than many American-born students. Some students categorize the international population as "BISO," the Babson International Student Organization, a fictional name passed down through generations.

Students Speak Out
ON DIVERSITY

{ *"Ethnically, the campus is very diverse; students come from all over the world and a significant percent of the student body is international."*

Q *"I went to a diverse high school, but I've never met so many different people in one place. **Babson's a very cultural place**, and it's good to have such diversity surrounding you daily."*

Q *"In terms of race, Babson is not diverse at all; it's very preppy and white. In terms of nationality, there is **a high percentage of international students,** but they either live off campus or in Van Winkle, which is far away from campus's center."*

Q "Well, the campus is quite diverse. There are white people, and there are whiter people. But seriously, there is not a lot of diversity in terms of race, but quite a bit of thought diversity, which is more important. There is **a campus Republicans club and a College Democrats club**. There is everything from the Black Student Union to the Russian Club."

Q "Babson has about 20 percent international students, but it **does not feel diverse**. Many people have similar upbringings. and there is very, very little racial diversity."

Q "There are many international students. It is interesting to meet other people who come from all over the world, and each year there are **always many more new faces**."

Guys & Girls

The Lowdown
ON GUYS & GIRLS

The College Prowler Take
ON DIVERSITY

Women Undergrads: 60%

Men Undergrads: 40%

More than 70 countries are represented in Babson's undergraduate student body. This statement alone shows that Babson is very culturally diverse. With the international population making up close to 20 percent of undergraduates, it is interesting to observe their visible impact on student life. This diversity gives students valuable experience, especially because students are able to practice their foreign languages right on campus. If one wants to find international students, they are not hard to spot. Different cultural backgrounds make up this school's atmosphere, which is unique from many other colleges.

Social Scene
Most students don't have a problem interacting socially with each other; both guys and girls have a tendency to be very confident in and out of class. This confidence does not stand in the way of meeting people at a Saturday night party, but it does have a direct effect on interaction on a day-to-day basis with people. This is not a social dilemma, because much socializing occurs at the Trim Dining Hall, where most students come to eat breakfast, lunch, and dinner. You can see almost the entire school by watching the circular staircase that leads into the hall.

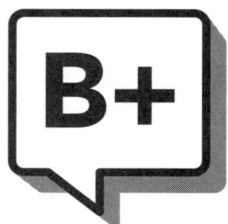

The College Prowler™ Grade on
Diversity: B+

A high grade in Diversity indicates that ethnic minorities and international students have a notable presence on campus and that students of different economic backgrounds, religious beliefs, and sexual preferences are well-represented.

Hookups or Relationships?
Between the tough workload and the 60-40 ratio of girls to guys, relationships are not very common between Babson students. Although girls find guys attractive, they are constantly worried about their reputation in such a close-knit community. Guys tend to avoid relationships with Babson girls, but they do form very close friendships. Therefore, hookups tend to happen frequently, especially after a Saturday Knight Party or a Thursday Pub Night.

Dress Code

Many wear either very fashionable or business-casual clothes to class, but Abercrombie & Fitch is the weekend style (for a lot of guys especially). Dressing up for class is very important not only for your social life but also for your in-class professionalism grade that the professor distributes. Some athletes, however, are brave enough to wear sports-clothes to class, but most do so sparingly and only if they have a game that they need to leave early for.

Birth Control Available?

Yes. Health Services offers all forms of birth control; pills, patches, and the shot. They also provide free condoms inside the facility as well as outside by the Health Services entrance.

Students Speak Out
ON GUYS & GIRLS

{ "Girls tend to be snobby, and guys are all the same. Everyone acts the same. I would like to meet someone more alternative, but I don't think that'll happen at Babson."

Q "The guys seem to be **very confident** and so do the girls. This can be a good thing and a bad thing all at once. For example, it's one thing to act confident in front of the class, but another to be that way because you want to show off."

Q "People here are very fashionable, kind, and interesting. But there's not enough balance, the 60-40 ratio messes up any hope for a relationship. That's why **most guys go to Wellesley to hang out with girls**, and a lot of girls go into Boston to meet guys."

Q "I would say that Babson kids are the same as kids in other colleges. We have a lot of foreign students and a lot of wealthy students. The kids can sometimes be **competitive and as a result a little less friendly**, but this is not always true. The girls are getting better looking with every year; I guess the guys are attractive. Most of the people here are pretty smart. The foreign students are usually more fashionable than the rest, but because most of the people have money here, they tend to look okay."

Q "On pure attractiveness, **Babson does very well**. However, the self-centered mindset that comes with a business outlook makes it not the best place for finding a boyfriend or girlfriend. It's great for partying and casual interaction, but not great on serious relationships."

Q "Guys and girls on campus are **definitely sub-par in the looks department**, compared to state schools. But hey, they are going to work for us someday."

The College Prowler Take
ON GUYS & GIRLS

The average Babson student looks well-groomed, well-dressed, and very intimidating to an outside observer—and to some students as well. But most people understand that the reason for such attire is purely to impress the professors who are in charge of giving out grades for professionalism. If one gets below the surface of the facade, they will probably find shared interests and even similarities in their personal lives. Most guys and girls, however, don't entirely understand each other and most don't want to put the time in to understanding. Therefore, most guys and girls meet up at on-campus parties or in classroom study groups. The problem is that people who meet at parties don't really get the true version of the opposite sex, because they are either intoxicated or just want to hook-up with each other.

The College Prowler™ Grade on
Guys: B-

A high grade for Guys indicates that the male population on campus is attractive, smart, friendly, and engaging, and that the school has a decent ratio of guys to girls.

The College Prowler™ Grade on
Girls: C+

A high grade for Girls not only implies that the women on campus are attractive, smart, friendly, and engaging, but also that there is a fair ratio of girls to guys.

Athletics

Most Popular Sports

On the varsity level, basketball games have the largest presence on campus. Volleyball and basketball are the intramural favorites on this campus, while club sports are gaining popularity in men's rugby. Rugby guys are known for their infamous parties before and after almost each game, which attract friends and newcomers to watch them battle the opposing teams.

Athletic Division:
NCAA Division III

Conference:
UAA

School Mascot:
The Beaver

The Lowdown
ON ATHLETICS

Men's Varsity Teams:
- Alpine Skiing
- Baseball
- Basketball
- Cross Country
- Golf
- Ice Hockey
- Lacrosse
- Soccer
- Swimming
- Tennis
- Track & Field

Women's Varsity Teams:
- Alpine Skiing
- Baseball
- Cross Country
- Field Hockey
- Lacrosse
- Soccer
- Softball
- Swimming
- Tennis
- Track & Field
- Volleyball

Club Sports
Wrestling, golf, Boston Marathon, women's ice hockey, men's ice hockey outdoor, women's rugby, men's rugby

Intramurals
Basketball, ultimate Frisbee, racquetball, squash, tennis, floor hockey, soccer, volleyball, Hot Shot, flag football

Students Speak Out
ON ATHLETICS

"Our school is Division III, so pretty much anyone can find some varsity sport to join. Intramural sports are also getting very popular, especially coed basketball and volleyball."

Q "Basketball is probably the most popular sport on campus because they usually compete for the division title. Men's baseball is also very successful. There are also **many intramural sports**, and every student can find something in which to participate."

Q "**Sports are so small here.** I am a huge fan of sports, and I have no idea what goes on with sports. I feel that this is a huge determination of just how unimportant sport is at Babson."

Q "Sports are huge on campus, **they are almost like fraternities**. They foster good attitudes, competitiveness, and teamwork."

Q "Varsity and intramural sports are so much fun at Babson. Students love to work hard and play hard. Basketball and baseball have great reputations, and many of the other programs score big during their seasons. It's great to be a part of a team physically running or batting or throwing because it only enhances your Babson experience. **You really get to feel at home with your team** and they become a support system all four years."

Q "Many people do not attend sporting events at Babson, but **plenty of people seem to participate in a sport**. There are many different intramurals to choose from for those who don't wish to compete on a varsity level."

The College Prowler Take
ON ATHLETICS

Varsity sports are very competitive, contrary to popular belief that because Babson is in the Division III category, it cannot be competitive. In terms of popularity, it is true that few students attend games, but it's not true that few students play them. Considering the small-school atmosphere, neither the game attendance nor athletic involvement can possibly be compared to other Division III giants. **Sports are very important to the athletes that play them, and they put a considerable amount of time into practice and into their meets, games, and races. Intramural sports involvement is slowly increasing, with more and more teams deciding to play.**

The College Prowler™ Grade on
Athletics: B-

A high grade in Athletics indicates that students have school spirit, that sports programs are respected, that games are well-attended, and that intramurals are a prominent part of student life.

Greek Life

The Lowdown
ON GREEK LIFE

Number of Fraternities:
3

Number of Sororities:
2

Undergrad Men in Fraternities:
9%

Undergrad Women in Sororities:
9%

Students Speak Out
ON GREEK LIFE

"Campus is only 10 percent Greek, so it doesn't dominate the social scene. However, as a member of a fraternity since my freshman year, I can honestly say that it is the best organization I have joined since coming to Babson."

Q "The Greek life is small on our campus, but if you want to be part of a group of friends, it is **a good social group** to be a part of."

Q "Greek life, even though I'm not a participant in any sorority, is **really a top-notch part of the social scene**. They're not exclusive and throw parties for the whole campus to really unite the student body. I feel accepted by them and comfortable to participate in their events."

Q "Greek life is **practically nonexistent at Babson**. There are frats and sororities, but they make up a very small percentage."

Q "Greek life apparently is pretty popular at Babson, however, when it comes down to it, **I'm never able to find good parties**. Maybe that is my fault though. TKE seems to be the only frat who offers real parties, but those are only two times a year."

The College Prowler Take
ON GREEK LIFE

Greek life doesn't dominate the social scene at Babson like it would on larger campuses; there are only three fraternities at Babson and only two that live on campus. This secretive—but not really secretive because the campus is so small that everyone knows about everything!—atmosphere makes some people curious about joining a fraternity or sorority. Most of the activities that Greeks participate in are not open to the rest of campus, except their parties, and those are primarily the works of the Sigma Phi Epsilon (SigEp) fraternity. These parties are relatively fun because you can see a diversity of students there. Although Greeks don't dominate the social scene, they are an integral part of this small, close-knit community.

The College Prowler™ Grade on
Greek Life: B-

A high grade in Greek Life indicates that sororities and fraternities are not only present, but also active on campus. Other determining factors include the variety of houses available and the respect the Greek community receives from the rest of the campus.

Drug Scene

The Lowdown
ON DRUG SCENE

Liquor-Related Referrals: 0

Liquor-Related Arrests: 1

Drug-Related Referrals: 0

Drug-Related Arrests: 0

Most Prevalent Drugs on Campus:
Alcohol, marijuana, caffeine, Ritalin, and Adderall

Human Relations Services (HRS)
11 Chapel Place
Wellesley Hills, MA 02481
(781) 235-4950

Services: HRS is available for confidential counseling. HRS may be contacted directly or through the Health Services to set up appointments.

Students Speak Out
ON DRUG SCENE

"A decent amount of people do coke, prescriptions, and marijuana. It's not as noticeable because nobody talks about it."

Q "In my experience, the drug scene basically consists of marijuana. **I haven't come across any hard drugs** in my time here. Marijuana isn't widespread, but it is definitely a presence on campus."

Q "Like any school campus, you can find people who abuse all types of drugs. **It is underground** and you don't really see any of it unless you seek it out."

Q "I've never witnessed any drug worse than weed being used on campus. That doesn't mean that drug use doesn't happen, but it does mean that **it isn't everywhere** and that it isn't obvious."

Campus Strictness

The College Prowler Take
ON DRUG SCENE

It's not too hard to find a dealer on campus, but nobody wants people to know that they actually want to find one. Marijuana has been seen in rooms and people have gotten caught smoking it in residence halls, but those incidents are few and far between. It's rare that students would rat out their peers, especially when it comes to drug use on campus. The people that do drugs on campus keep it on the down-low and don't ever talk about it with anyone but their close friends. Therefore, just like in any other place with a high student population, there is some drug use, but it's not prevalent. It's about being able to distinguish who does drugs and who doesn't; nobody really knows unless they're told about it, and that rarely happens.

The Lowdown
ON CAMPUS STRICTNESS

What Are You Most Likely to Get Caught Doing on Campus?
Unauthorized partying in residential hall rooms, smoking marijuana in residential hall rooms, running around the campus naked after the League Championships, downloading copywrighted materials, walking around with an open container, making too much noise, illegal parking, playing drinking games, fighting

Students Speak Out
ON CAMPUS STRICTNESS

"Campus police are very hot and cold. Sometimes it seems that they're breaking up every room with a stereo on when there's a DJ blasting music outside with public drinking."

The College Prowler™ Grade on
Drug Scene: B

A high grade on Drug Scene indicates that drugs are not a noticeable part of campus life; drug use is not visible, and no pressure to use them seems to exist.

> "The campus police are **very strict about drugs, drinking, and law enforcement**, and they go around to check up on parties quite often."

> "This school does not tolerate any drugs on campus. In many cases, **BABO will be easy on you in regards to drinking** and provide you with several warnings before you get in big trouble."

> "Usually **they treat each situation differently**. They are pretty reasonable about drinking, though they know when things are out of hand and try to stop them."

> "BABO is not very strict; **I've never had a problem**. Maybe ask someone who is always carrying a Keystone Light around."

The College Prowler Take
ON CAMPUS STRICTNESS

If you are a freshman here and you get caught, expect the officer to be much stricter with you than with your senior buddy. It's good advice to get to know as many BABO as you can and as soon as you can. BABO mostly treats everyone like mature adults unless things get out of control. Freshmen are generally at a high risk of getting caught and being given a strike, not just by BABO, but also by their RA. The party scene is not a raging one, and if one gets caught, the best thing to do is be very polite and honest. This technique will almost always help to get you off the hook and even meet a new friend—a BABO.

The College Prowler™ Grade on
Campus Strictness: C+

A high Campus Strictness grade implies an overall lenient atmosphere; police and RAs are fairly tolerant, and the administration's rules are flexible.

Overall Experience

Students Speak Out
ON OVERALL EXPERIENCE

> "It was a little tough to get used to, but once I fit in, I didn't want to leave. **The challenging academics, along with solid, extracurricular activity and strong social life make me not want to ever leave.**"

> "Sometimes **I wish I had gone to a bigger school** either in the city, out west, or down south. I've lived in the New England area my entire life, so I am tired of the atmosphere. The friends I met at Babson were the main reason I decided not to transfer."

> "Babson is great for academics, and the social scene is better than expected. We're **number one in entrepreneurship**, and that's why I'm here—I love it."

> "I love Babson. It is not a college for those who wish to do no work, not attend class, or just party. It is a school for people who want to do well in life. **Babson trains people for the rigorous business world**. I would not rather be at any other college. The education here is priceless, especially because much of it is 'hands-on,' and I feel it's good practice for my future career."

> "Sometimes I wish I was somewhere else, but overall, it's **a great place for a stellar education**. The only thing I would really change about Babson is that I would relocate it to Boston."

"Sometimes I wish I had gone to a bigger school, but I think the education would not have been as good. **I've had a great time here**, and I don't really have any regrets."

The College Prowler Take
ON OVERALL EXPERIENCE

The Inside Scoop

The Lowdown
ON THE INSIDE SCOOP

The best way to describe Babson is to say that, at first, you'll feel like a fish thrown out of your fishbowl, but as time goes on you somehow survive and become a lizard with tougher skin. No matter how hard you think your high school was, nothing can prepare you for the incredible and challenging academic life of a Babson freshman. Most students agree that the workload is far larger than they initially expected. And although it takes a while to get used to the curriculum, students feel that the impeccable education is worth it.

Students that are unhappy with their education here are usually just not used to it yet. Many say that the school is too small and they get bored walking around campus and seeing the same people all the time. Voicing the fact that this college is smaller than many high schools is not uncommon here. Some students also complain that too many of the students come from the same economic backgrounds, even though the campus is so diverse in other aspects. The social scene, however, is better than expected for the most part, although it's not a party school at all. Students here are very serious about their education and many are very competitive. School size is also directly proportional to the faculty-to-student ratio, and that's where Babson wins in comparison to the larger business schools. This ratio is important for the special attention that students receive from faculty, which most take for granted. Professors here are very well-educated and try their best to impart their knowledge to the young Babsonians. Although the workload can be shocking to students at first, it gets better with time. Most enjoy the challenges and hurdles of life here and believe that the education is excellent.

Things I Wish I Knew Before Coming to Babson:
- Get the largest possible meal plan.
- Go to McCullough parties.
- Go to the Pub on Thursdays.
- Skip Playfair during Orientation.
- The workload is going to be heavy.
- Cell phones are a necessity.
- Computers are more than a necessity. They will be your lifeblood.
- Time management is key.
- Check your e-mail daily, or even twice daily. No, make that three times daily. Just check it a lot.

Tips to Succeed at Babson:
- Research professors before choosing your classes. Having a professor who knows about his subject and, more importantly, cares about his students makes all the difference.
- Don't fall behind in the business classes.
- Get on Instant Messenger if you're not on yet.
- Ask teachers tons of questions.
- Dispute bad grades if you think they are unfair.
- Don't pick the advanced classes before completing the ones below those.
- Don't be shy.

School Spirit

Although students don't want to admit it, they are proud that they got into Babson. They are also swelling with pride after they finish their first year. In-classroom competition is where the spirit really kicks in. There, the overconfident students add fun and interesting dynamics to some of the less-entertaining classes. Finance and accounting majors feel exceptionally proud to be at Babson; they regard themselves as tougher and smarter than all other majors. Babson clothing and gifts are also seen all over campus, showing that students are proud to be at Babson and like to purchase these products. These things are even said to be the highest-margin goods at the Babson Bookstore. Although sports events are not too popular, they are recognized by faculty and the student body through online posting on the athletics Website. When a team wins a championship, the news travels fast and most everyone knows the game score. School spirit at this school is a bit underrated because of the poor sports attendance, but that doesn't necessarily mean that students don't care for school spirit—they are just trying to manage their time better.

Traditions
The BDE Performance

The Babson Dance Ensemble is recognized for its amazingly choreographed dances and awesome lighting. Shows consist of everything ranging from ballet to hip-hop, with a large number of students performing in multiple dances. Their shows are usually very entertaining and are held once a semester, in the fall and the spring.

The Multicultural Festival

The festival consists of student organizations and clubs, most of whom cook food and present it to the Babson public. In the past, this cultural gathering even consisted of a kata performance by the martial arts club and has been open to other sports clubs on campus.

Mr. and Mrs. Babson Competitions

These typically friendly contests allow anyone to enter and try to obtain the Babson crown and the large amount of money that is the main prize. Students compete on the basis of their looks, smarts, and talents. This competition is usually held in the over-filled Knight Auditorium and is one of the favorites among students.

Finding a Job or Internship

The Lowdown
ON FINDING A JOB OR INTERNSHIP

Babson's Center for Career Development (CCD) is helpful in providing Babson graduate and undergraduate students with useful resources. The staff is very educated and often offers great advice and help with career planning. They are also very involved in helping students find internships and jobs.

Advice

Start looking for a job as soon as possible—don't wait until the last minute when searching for a job or an internship. It's better to be the first rather than the last person whose resume a manager looks at when it is time to hire. It's also important to update your resume and get it edited and approved not only by the CCD but also by other people in your field of study. The CCD is a very good resource for guiding students through the right steps to successfully getting a job. This way, you have numerous opinions and can decide for yourself what is best based on the job for which you are applying.

Did You Know?

Daniel Gerber, founder of Gerber baby foods, graduated in the class of 1919. Gerber Hall was dedicated in his honor.

The Best & Worst

The Ten BEST Things About Babson:

1. The academic program
2. Alumni connections
3. Movie nights at Sorenson rock
4. Technology
5. Internet in classrooms
6. The Pub; enough said
7. Late-night parties in the suites
8. BDE Performances
9. The ability to balance studies and fun
10. Intramural sports

The Ten WORST Things About Babson:

1. Liberal arts programs
2. Difficulty understanding some professors
3. The oversensitive fire alarms
4. A lot of people smoke
5. There aren't enough guys to go around
6. The weather
7. Trim Hall
8. Unreasonable amounts of homework
9. Lack of 24-hour eateries
10. Lack of air-conditioning in dorms

Bentley College

175 Forest Street, Waltham, MA 02452-4705
www.bentley.edu   (781) 891-2244

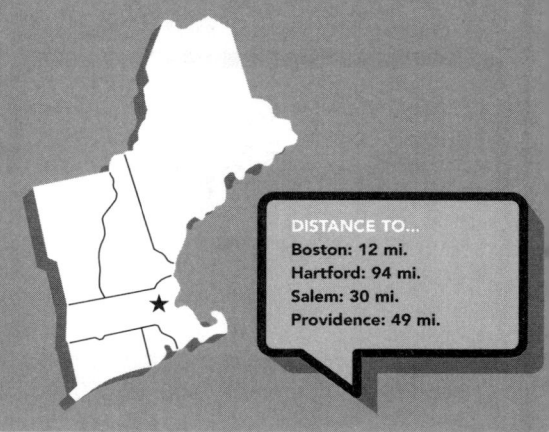

DISTANCE TO...
Boston: 12 mi.
Hartford: 94 mi.
Salem: 30 mi.
Providence: 49 mi.

"Bentley is the real deal. It's a true business school for the information age."

Total Enrollment:
3,932
Acceptance Rate:
46%
Tuition:
$25,544
Top 10% of High School Class:
37%
SAT Range
Verbal	Math	Total
530 – 610	570 – 660	1100 – 1270

ACT Range
Verbal	Math	Total
N/A	N/A	22-28

Most Popular Majors:
85% Business
11% Computer and Information Sciences
2%   Multi/Interdisciplinary Studies
1%   Liberal Arts
1%   Mathematics and Statistics

Students Also Applied To:*
Babson College, Boston College, Boston University, Northeastern University, University of Massachusetts–Amherst

*For more school info check out www.collegeprowler.com

Table of Contents

Academics	643
Local Atmosphere	645
Safety & Security	646
Computers	648
Facilities	649
Campus Dining	651
Off-Campus Dining	652
Campus Housing	653
Off-Campus Housing	654
Diversity	655
Guys & Girls	657
Athletics	658
Greek Life	660
Drug Scene	661
Campus Strictness	662
Overall Experience	664
The Inside Scoop	665
Finding a Job or Internship	666
The Best & Worst	667

College Prowler Report Card

Academics	B
Local Atmosphere	C+
Safety & Security	B+
Computers	A-
Facilities	B+
Campus Dining	C+
Off-Campus Dining	A-
Campus Housing	B+
Off-Campus Housing	C
Diversity	C
Guys	B+
Girls	B
Athletics	B-
Greek Life	C
Drug Scene	B+
Campus Strictness	C

Academics

Did You Know?

Each semester, on the night of the last day of classes, students celebrate the beginning of finals with food, music, and fun during Breakfast by Moonlight.

The Lowdown
ON ACADEMICS

Students Speak Out
ON ACADEMICS

> "Teachers are knowledgeable and always willing to help you whenever possible. Most classes are interesting, and professors often share their real-life experiences."

Degrees Awarded:
Bachelor, Master

Full-time Faculty:
260

Faculty with Terminal Degree:
83%

Student-to-Faculty Ratio:
13:1

Sample Academic Clubs:
Economics and Finance Society, National Association of Black Accountants, Bentley Investment Group, Bentley Marketing Association, Bentley Adamian Law Club

Best Places to Study:
Library, Student Center, Smith Center, dorm study rooms

Special Degree Options
Five Year Bachelor's/Master's Program

AP Test Score Requirements
Possible credit for scores of 3 or 4

Q "The teachers are decent, but every teacher varies. I haven't had one that was terribly bad or extremely good. **My classes so far aren't really all that interesting**, but I think that's because I am a freshman and am taking filler courses instead of classes related to my major."

Q "The core curriculum is great because it gives you **some background in liberal arts and several aspects of business**. Most of my teachers have been great and are very accessible; although I've had a couple of duds that made me wonder why they were hired."

Q "I've had all good experiences with the teaching staff here at Bentley. I find them all very reasonable and supportive. Some of the classes have been **boring from time to time**, but since you can pick the topics of most of your classes, its kind of up to you."

Q "During freshmen and sophomore year, the professors are not that good; often times they are young and inexperienced. However, **the professors in junior and senior year are excellent**. They really build relationships with their students."

The College Prowler Take
ON ACADEMICS

“Many of my professors do little or nothing to get students involved in the classroom. With the exception of my GB classes, **professors just lecture for an hour and 15 minutes** and then the students get up and leave. Classes are very boring, which causes little or no interest in the coursework and makes college feel like an extension of high school.”

During your first two years, you will most likely be busy taking required classes and won't actually meet a professor in your major until junior year. However, this is not to be seen as a drawback because even professors outside your major are generally knowledgeable in their field and always available for consultation or extra help. One thing is certain: Bentley professors do not want to see anyone fail and are willing to go out of their way so that it doesn't happen.

Because of the strong emphasis on a complete real-world business education, some of Bentley's professors may not actually be professors at all. There is a large percentage of instructors who are retired businesspeople who have already made their life's fortune and now use teaching as a way to supplement their lifestyle. The teaching styles vary from having only a traditional midterm and final exam, to writing journal entries every night, to offering extra credit for watching "The Apprentice," but you can expect group work as a standard in any class.

Get by-the-numbers admission information and expanded student quotes from *Bentley College—Off the Record*, available at www.collegeprowler.com.

The College Prowler™ Grade on
Academics: B

A high Academics grade generally indicates that professors are knowledgeable, accessible, and genuinely interested in their students' welfare. Other determining factors include class size, how well professors communicate, and whether or not classes are engaging.

Local Atmosphere

The Lowdown
ON LOCAL ATMOSPHERE

Region:
Northeast

City, State:
Waltham, Massachusetts

Setting:
Small metropolitan city

Distance from Boston:
15-20 minutes

Distance from Providence:
45 minutes

Points of Interest:
Harvard Square (Cambridge), Museum of Fine Arts, Fenway Park, North End, Newbury Street, Faneuil Hall, Boston Public Library, Arnold Arboretum, Beacon Hill, Isabella Stewart Gardner Museum, Public Garden

Major Sports Teams:
Red Sox (MLB), Patriots (NFL), Celtics (NBA), Bruins (NHL)

City Websites:
www.city.waltham.ma.us
www.waltham-community.org
www.walthamchamber.com
www.discoverwaltham.com

Students Speak Out
ON LOCAL ATMOSPHERE

"Brandeis is here in Waltham, but Boston is two seconds away, so there are a million and one things to do all the time. It's also not a far drive to the beach, New Hampshire, Maine, or Rhode Island."

Q "There are a few other universities in the area. Many clubs and bars around tend to be '18 and over' (to get in, not to drink!), which is great. It makes it somewhat easy to switch it up on weekends so you aren't always on campus. Waltham is an okay town. However, having **Cambridge and Boston only a few minutes away** puts Bentley College at a great location."

Q "Waltham is a nice town. It is busy, but not too busy. For those who crave craziness, Boston is right next door, where the possibilities are endless. There are many other colleges and universities in the area, so **if you need a change, just visit Boston College, Northeastern, or Harvard**."

Q "There is not much to do in the town, but the free shuttle to Cambridge is convenient. Cambridge has **good shopping and restaurants**, and you can be in Boston in just a few minutes to get to clubs and other universities by taking the T."

Q "Waltham is pretty boring. There are so many universities around this town with Boston being only ten miles away. With this in this mind, its obvious **there's plenty to do**."

Q "Waltham is **kind of a sleepy town** minus the restaurants. Brandeis is really close, though I never go there. I would recommend the restaurant Fire and Ice in Harvard Square, it's a little expensive, but the food is so good."

The College Prowler Take
ON LOCAL ATMOSPHERE

If you were to take Bentley out of Waltham, the school dynamic wouldn't change that much, and the city wouldn't be upset for very long. There is a strange, yet often unspoken, love/hate relationship between Waltham and Bentley. Waltham loves to boast on its city Websites how it has a rich academic tradition, yet it does little to nothing to encourage college students to become part of the community. Unlike other colleges in suburban cities, local Waltham businesses do not offer a student discount on things like food and school supplies. Many schools located directly in Boston have partnerships with restaurants that enable students to use their meal plan outside the college cafeteria, but this is an unheard of concept here. The major thing to remember about Waltham is that it is an up-and-coming Boston suburb, and it deserves a chance to be recognized for what it's worth, even though it doesn't always seem to treat students that way!

Safety & Security

The Lowdown
ON SAFETY & SECURITY

Number of Bentley Police:
22

Phone:
(781) 891-3131 (emergencies)
(781) 891-2201 (non-emergencies)

The College Prowler™ Grade on
Local Atmosphere: C+

A high Local Atmosphere grade indicates that the area surrounding campus is safe and scenic. Other factors include nearby attractions, proximity to other schools, and the town's attitude toward students.

Health Center Office Hours
Monday 8 a.m. - 5 p.m.
Tuesday 8 a.m. - 7 p.m.
Wednesday 8 a.m. - 5 p.m.
Thursday 8 a.m. - 5 p.m.
Friday 8 a.m. - 4:30 p.m.

Safety Services
Rape Aggression Defense class (RAD), dorm hall safety programs, CPR and first aid training, escort service

Students Speak Out
ON SAFETY & SECURITY

"Security seems pretty tight here on campus. I've never felt threatened or unsafe when walking on campus alone at night."

Q "I always feel very safe on campus because there is **a large campus police force** and you always see them driving around. The campus police are also friendly."

Q "This campus is very safe, but it is **not annoyingly strict by any means**. The campus police let us have our fun with barely any problems, but they are right there in case of emergency and handle serious matters extremely well."

Q "It's pretty good for the most part. **I do feel uncomfortable walking around on the weekend by myself late at night**, but that is mostly due to the large abundance of male students, and the peer pressures of getting intoxicated to the point of vomiting each and every weekend."

Q "I feel fine, but **there are no cameras in parking lots**. If your car gets hit while parked, campus police can't do anything about it."

Q "**Campus police can be annoying**, especially with speeders and such, so if you are habitually late for class, living on campus is a must."

The College Prowler Take
ON SAFETY & SECURITY

If there is one negative aspect about the security on campus, it is the fact that no matter where you are on campus, you can't avoid running into the campus police (CP). Most students understand that the strong police presence isn't necessarily a bad thing, but the joke is often, "Don't they have something better to do with their time?" The truth is, no, they don't. The campus is extremely safe, with the exception of the usual weekend stupid drunken incident or two, and students can walk around late at night without worry. CP doesn't take safety for granted, though: they offer various self-defense workshops for students and provide ongoing training to the officers.

Due to the lack of real crime on campus, the officers are left with a lot of free time. The overall attitude towards campus police is negative, which is unfortunate, but students know that, in the event of an emergency, CP will be there in record time ready to handle the situation, whether it's an incident of vandalism, a fight, or a fire alarm set off by burnt popcorn.

The College Prowler™ Grade on
Safety & Security: B+

A high grade in Safety & Security means that students generally feel safe, campus police are visible, blue-light phones and escort services are readily available, and safety precautions are not overly necessary.

Computers

Students Speak Out
ON COMPUTERS

The Lowdown
ON COMPUTERS

High-Speed Network?
Yes

Wireless Network?
Yes

Number of Labs:
8

Numbers of Computers:
328

24-Hour Labs:
None

Charge to Print:
No

Operating Systems:
PC

"The computer network here is amazing. There are computer labs in the library. as well as in Lindsay Hall near the computer resource center."

Q "Everyone has their own laptop and sometimes we are required to bring them to class. **The school's choice of laptops is good**. This year, we have IBMs with CD burners and DVD-ROM drives. The Internet connection is fast from the dorms, and the newer laptops also have wireless Internet access."

Q "Since they give you a computer, bringing your own is not necessary. The computer lab in the library is always busy, so it's best just to bring your own there. As for the network, **I am very happy with Bentley's hard work** to always remain connected."

Q "The computer network is awesome! Very high-tech with wireless Internet in all the newest laptops and **Internet ports in almost every classroom**. The classrooms are high-tech with video projectors and other cool stuff."

Free Software
Software standard on Bentley-issued laptops include Black Board classroom, Connected Network Backup, Lotus Notes, Internet Explorer, Symantec Antivirus and Windows XP

The College Prowler Take
ON COMPUTERS

Bentley's computer network is cutting-edge and very sophisticated. The state-of-the-art technology is visible no matter where you are on campus, which makes it hard to forget where all your tuition money goes. There is at least one computer in each classroom, yet many are equipped with computer consoles for each student. The laptop requirement is not forgotten in the classroom; in fact, there are power and network ports for each individual student's laptop in about half of the classrooms on campus. One thing is for sure—every Bentley student, no matter what major, will graduate with an advanced knowledge of the latest computer software and networks that will place them above the rest of college graduates across the country.

The College Prowler™ Grade on
Computers: A-

A high grade in Computers designates that computer labs are available, the computer network is easily accessible, and the campus' computing technology is up-to-date.

Facilities

The Lowdown
ON FACILITIES

Libraries
Soloman R. Baker Library

Student Center
The Student Center
LaCava Campus Center

Athletic Center
The Dana Center

Bowling on Campus?
No

Movie Theatre on Campus?
No, but every Sunday CAB shows not-in-theater-but-not-yet-on-DVD movies in the Student Center.

Bar on Campus?
Yes, the 1917 Tavern, or "Pub," in the Student Center.

Coffeehouse on Campus?
Yes, The Brookside Deli & Coffeehouse in the bottom of Collins Hall.

Popular Places to Chill
Coffeehouse, Student Center "Ski Lodge," and Smith study rooms

Students Speaks Out
ON FACILITIES

The College Prowler Take
ON FACILITIES

Q "The gym is gross. Smaller, less reputable schools have a better gym. The computers and student center are pretty nice."

Q "Everything is nice. The athletic center is older, but they are keeping up with it. **Rumor has it that there will be a new rec center** with a new gym."

Q "Athletic facilities are nice, but athletics, overall, are not really a main focus on the campus. Although very successful, the administration does not put a lot of emphasis on them. Computers are good and up-to-date. The student center is **up-to-date**."

Q "The facilities all seem new and in great condition. **Everything always feels clean**. Gardens are gorgeous—we have a fund set up by an alumnus which makes sure that the landscaping on Bentley campus is completely immaculate at all times."

Q "The facilities for the most part are new and up-to-date. I have found the weight room very advantageous; however I can not say the same for other things. There are racquetball courts being used for storage, and **the basketball courts are rarely open**."

Q "Facilities here are really nice. **The student center is a new multi-million dollar building**. Computers are new and up-to-date. The gym has many prime machines to work out on, as well as an indoor swimming pool that has open swim hours."

The hub of student activity on campus can be found in the Student Center, located behind the Rhodes and Boylston apartments. Opened in 2002, the Student Center has quickly replaced the smaller, outdated, former student center, LaCava, to become the mecca of anything related to student life. Students refer to the unnamed student center as the highly unoriginal, "Stu," which is mostly used by freshmen. With student organization offices on the third floor that overlook the Seasons Dining Hall on the second floor, there is an open, sunny feel to the building that makes it unique and unlike any other building on campus. Another exclusive feature is the study lounge, (also dubbed "Ski Lodge") on the second floor, characterized by high ceilings and a year-round working electric fireplace. With each building, both old and new, constructed mainly of brick, the campus has a uniform and professional look that never goes out of style.

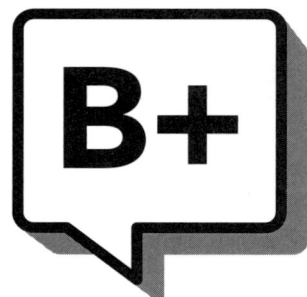

The College Prowler™ Grade on
Facilities: B+

A high Facilities grade indicates that the campus is aesthetically pleasing and well-maintained; facilities are state-of-the-art, and libraries are exceptional. Other determining factors include the quality of both athletic and student centers and an abundance of things to do on campus.

Campus Dining

Q "I don't mind the food on campus. All of the fattening food is very good, and some of the healthier stuff is good as well. **There's always a Panera down the street** if you get sick of it."

Q "There is a lack of options; the only places you can go to eat are the main dining hall, which prepares **low-quality food for the hefty price of the meal plan**; the deli, which has basic subs and wraps that are nothing to rave about; and the lower cafe, which generally has the same offering as the main cafeteria—wraps, grill items, and pizza."

The Lowdown
ON CAMPUS DINING

Freshman Meal Plan Requirement?
Yes

24-Hour On-Campus Eating?
No

Meal Plan Average Cost:
$4,000 annual

Student Favorites:
Seasons Dining Hall,
Brookside Coffeehouse

The College Prowler Take
ON CAMPUS DINING

For on-campus food, the main option and place to go is Seasons Dining Hall. Even though students love to complain about it, the truth is that the cafeteria is not really all that bad. Compared to other local college cuisine, Bentley has it pretty darn good. Sodexho, the company in charge of all campus eateries, is constantly changing meal plan options based on student feedback surveys. Recent additions to the Seasons Dining Hall include a wrap station and increased vegetarian options, which were requested by students. The one complaint about on-campus dining that cannot be ignored is the hefty price the required meal plan carries. While the food is good, it's not that good.

Students Speak Out
ON CAMPUS DINING

"The food on campus is not too bad. The best place to eat is the lower cafe, but the deli is an excellent choice for a late-night snack."

Q "Food on campus is **nothing special**. It gets old very soon. Restaurants in the surrounding area, however, are worth a look."

Q "Food is pretty good. The deli is nice because it's open until 2 a.m. and has warm food, but it **could use a bit more variety**."

The College Prowler™ Grade on
Campus Dining: C+

Our grade on Campus Dining addresses the quality of both school-owned dining halls and independent on-campus restaurants as well as the price, availability, and variety of food.

Off-Campus Dining

> "There are **a lot of nice restaurants in Harvard Square**. Bombay Club is good for Indian food, and Border Cafe is good for Mexican food. There's also a Bertuccis, and Pizzeria Uno."

> "There are many restaurants that deliver right to your door. Some other fun spots, when you want to get out of your room, like Fire and Ice and Border Café, are in Harvard Square, which is **only a shuttle ride away**."

> "Students in the dorms are inundated with takeout menus for Chinese, Italian, and wings. The food is decent, but not great, though it's sometimes **a nice change from the cafeteria**."

The Lowdown
ON OFF-CAMPUS DINING

Best Pizza: Angelo's

Best Chinese: Absolutely Asia

Best Breakfast: Wilson's

Best Wings: Bison County

Best Healthy: So-Cal Restaurant

Best Place to Take Your Parents:
Not Your Average Joe's, Watch City Brewing Company, Solea

Late-Night: Wendy's

24-Hour Eating:
IHOP, Brighton

Student Favorites:
Wilson's, Panera Bread, Margaritas

The College Prowler Take
ON OFF-CAMPUS DINING

Students don't get off campus enough to enjoy the plethora of quality restaurants in Waltham. Students are drawn to the dining experience in Harvard Square due to the allure and ease of the free college shuttle, but, in reality, Waltham has double the amount of restaurant options. The diversion away from Waltham establishments starts early, since freshmen are not allowed to have cars on campus, thus making the shuttle to Harvard Square very appealing. By the time you are allowed to have a car on campus, you will find you will be stuck in the routine of continuing to go into Harvard Square to eat out and won't explore your local community.

Students Speak Out
ON OFF-CAMPUS DINING

"There are good restaurants off campus on Moody Street and around that area, but many students don't get off campus to experience them."

A-

The College Prowler™ Grade on
Off-Campus Dining: A-

A high Off-Campus Dining grade implies that off-campus restaurants are affordable, accessible, and worth visiting. Other factors include the variety of cuisine and the availability of alternative options (vegetarian, vegan, Kosher, etc.).

Campus Housing

Did You Know?

All buildings are smoke-free.

All campus residents get free cable and access to Bentley's movie channel.

Living in Collins Hall or the Orchard Apartments means you agree to have other students living in your room during winter break.

The Lowdown
ON CAMPUS HOUSING

Students Speak Out
ON CAMPUS HOUSING

Undergrads on Campus:
80%

Number of Dormitories:
26

University-Owned Apartments:
1

You Get:
Bed, desk, chair, closest, dresser, window coverings, cable, TV jack, Ethernet, free campus and local phone calls

Cleaning Service?
Shared and public bathrooms are cleaned daily by staff. Suites and apartments are not cleaned.

Room Types:
Houses on campus are typically for those with special housing needs.

"The dorms are okay; Trees has small rooms, and it's far away from everything, but there are a lot of people there—probably most of the freshman class."

Q "The dorms are good. They have air conditioning and heat that you control, clean carpets, and clean bathrooms. No building is bad; **some are louder then others**, but you can pick where you want to be after your first year."

Q "The freshman housing at Bentley consists of small rooms that are either doubles, triples, or quads. They aren't great, but they aren't terrible; they are typical dormitory-style rooms. **For upperclassmen, there are suites and apartments**—suites do not have full kitchens; apartments do. Those are all generally nice. The ones on south campus are newer, which is the only big difference."

Q "**The dorms are okay**. The good ones are the apartments in Falcone, Collins, Boylston, and Orchard. There is also a huge dorm that is supposed to be very nice—tall windows, big rooms, nice view—called Fenway."

> "The dorms aren't bad. We have **beautiful new dorms on lower campus,** but that's usually reserved for second-year housing. There really aren't apartments and houses next to campus, so most students end up staying in on-campus housing for the four years."

> "The dorms are good overall, apart from the **ridiculous meal plan requirement** in most buildings. Falcone apartments are the best, while the new Fenway suites and recently built Copley suites are hotel-like."

Off-Campus Housing

The College Prowler Take
ON CAMPUS HOUSING

The Lowdown
ON OFF-CAMPUS HOUSING

After the mandatory struggle of living in the freshmen dorms, life will get much sweeter sophomore year as you make the choice between one of the three new suites on lower campus. Junior and senior year bring independent living to a new level as you begin your stay in an on-campus apartment. The major change happens after your time in the Trees, Miller, or Slade, when you move into one of the Copleys or the brand new Fenway. After sharing a bathroom with 20 other people, having your own personal bathroom inside your suite is well worth the hassle of cleaning it yourself. While most students live on campus all four years, it's because they choose to, not simply because of the lack of off-campus options. The small-school feel of Bentley can be alienating to someone who lives off campus. On-campus housing is where friends and bonds are often made, whether at late-night study sessions, or by hanging out in the student lounge.

Undergrads in Off-Campus Housing:
5%

Best Time to Look for a Place:
July/August

Average Rent for a Studio Apartment:
$950/month

Average Rent for a 1BR Apartment:
$1,100/month

Average Rent for a 2BR Apartment:
$1,300/month

Popular Areas:
Moody Street, Windsor Village, Brighton Allston

The College Prowler™ Grade on
Campus Housing: B+

A high Campus Housing grade indicates that dorms are clean, well-maintained, and spacious. Other determining factors include variety of dorms, proximity to classes, and social atmosphere.

Students Speak Out
ON OFF-CAMPUS HOUSING

> "It's better to stay on campus; you miss a lot if you move off campus. It's also much more expensive to live off, because housing in Boston is costly."

Q "Housing off campus is **not worth it** because the people who live off campus become out of touch with the people who live on campus."

Q "Bentley no longer offers off-campus housing. You used to be able to get housing through the Windsor Village, two minutes away, but the college no longer sponsors that. Now students have to go through Windsor directly, but I still feel this is a better deal than living on campus because it is cheaper and **you don't have to deal with all the rules the college enforces**."

Q "I don't think it's worth it; living off campus seems **too out of the way** and makes people anti-social from campus, but I haven't tried it."

The College Prowler Take
ON OFF-CAMPUS HOUSING

The choice to live off campus is not very popular; however, finding nearby accommodations is fairly easy. Bentley does not offer apartment search assistance, but this is not a problem as there are plenty of options that students use year after year. Living in a Waltham apartment can enable you to still feel connected to the Bentley nightlife and social scene; however, living anywhere beyond Waltham automatically makes you a commuter student. There is little to no interaction between commuters and on-campus residents. The closer to the city you get, the more expensive the rent, and it becomes necessary to either be financially stable or have multiple roommates to split the costs. The best-kept secret in finding an off-campus apartment is to check out http://boston.craigslist.org for sublets, roommate searches, and to find the abode of your off-campus dreams.

The College Prowler™ Grade on
Off-Campus Housing: C

A high grade in Off-Campus Housing indicates that apartments are of high quality, close to campus, affordable, and easy to secure.

Diversity

The Lowdown
ON DIVERSITY

African American: 3%

Asian American: 7%

Hispanic: 4%

Native American: 0%

White: 78%

International: 8%

Out-of-State: 43%

Minority Clubs
After the Campus Activities Board, NABA (National Association of Black Accountants) is the largest club on campus. African American students in NABA are a highly-respected and vocal force.

Most Popular Religions
There are a variety of active Christian groups. A Sacred Space was created in the Student Center for all religions to share. After 9/11, there is a stronger feeling of spirituality on campus.

Political Activity
Being a business school, most students are fairly conservative, and those with more liberal ideas do not feel as comfortable sharing their opinions.

Gay Tolerance

PRIDE, Bentley's gay, lesbian, and transgendered club, is one of the best known, yet under-appreciated, organizations on campus. There is a shift happening right now at Bentley towards increasing acceptance and tolerance of all minority groups, and it is starting with the gay community. An active student who is "out" on campus usually advocates education and understanding for those unfamiliar with what it's like being gay.

Economic Status

Designer clothes and the attitudes to go with it are far too common. If you don't have the money to buy Gucci or Prada, you aren't necessarily looked down upon, but once you realize the economic divide that exists here, it's hard to ignore.

Students Speak Out
ON DIVERSITY

"The student population is predominantly white and from the New England area, but there are also many international students."

"It's not extremely diversified among students from the U.S., however, there is **a lot of diversity in terms of international kids**."

"Minorities are definitely represented. However, as far as mingling with other races goes, well, it just doesn't happen. It's very frustrating because **everyone judges everyone else**."

"There are many international students here on campus, but **they tend to exclude themselves** by living off campus with each other. They don't put much effort into getting to know people who live here on campus."

"The campus is diverse, but **the school does little to facilitate interaction between ethnic groups**. They sponsor events, mainly for international students and students with different ethnic backgrounds to meet each other, not white students."

"It's not very diverse, **the white-hat crowd** is predominant—lots of jock and frat types."

The College Prowler Take
ON DIVERSITY

The issue of diversity at Bentley is divided; some think there is diversity here, but many do not. Most students agree that Bentley is more diverse than their high school was, but it's not as diverse as other local colleges. If you're American, you might very well be quite similar to the other students on campus from the United States—of course, you also might not be. The international student population is very diverse; over 50 countries are represented. In order to make friends with someone from a different country, culture, or background than yourself, take the personal initiative to break the barrier that exists between you. You see, unfortunately, while the school's diversity may be apparent as you look around at the faces of your classmates, this doesn't usually carry over to situations outside the classroom, where interaction between international and American-born students often seems forced and unnatural. But, with the right attitude, this can, and will, change.

The College Prowler™ Grade on
Diversity: C

A high grade in Diversity indicates that ethnic minorities and international students have a notable presence on campus and that students of different economic backgrounds, religious beliefs, and sexual preferences are well-represented.

Guys & Girls

Social Scene
Get ready for high school all over again. The number of cliques on campus can be intimidating to the shy computer information systems major, but don't worry, you will find your clique soon enough and the social order will continue without a hitch. The social elite at Bentley can often be seen in fraternity or sorority members, but are also present in the varsity sport scene. You may have to look hard to find people you get along with, or you may find your best friend on your floor freshmen year; really, it's all about luck.

Hookups or Relationships?
Go to any party and this question can easily be answered. There are lots of random hookups, mostly occurring under the influence, which will be forgotten (if need be) the next day. The smallness of the school is virtually impossible to ignore. If you want a hookup to remain a secret, good luck—there's no six degrees of separation here, try three degrees instead. Most people in relationships are involved with other Bentley students. This can be disgustingly cute in the early stages of relationships when canoodling couples are seen holding hands on the way to class and kissing in the hallway.

The Lowdown
ON GUYS & GIRLS

Women Undergrads: 42%

Men Undergrads: 58%

Birth Control Available?
Condoms are available at Health Services for free. Female students can have an exam at Health Services but need to have their prescription filled at a local pharmacy. Sometimes, if it is the first time a female is going on birth control, the nurse will give her a free pack of pills.

Dress Code
A quick survey of a typical Bentley classroom will reveal a number of students who came to class "dressed to impress" in their Gucci suits or Armani pants, mixed in with those who prefer American duds like Polo by Ralph Lauren. You never have to worry about whether you think you're overdressed for class—chances are, someone will top you. Many international students love the designer look, and any girl in the sorority DPhiE can be seen wearing Tiffany's jewelry and outfits straight out of "Sex and the City." If you want comfort, keep those sweats handy, but only wear them to the gym to avoid strange looks walking up the stairs. There are plenty of cliques on campus that continue wearing their Abercrombie uniforms from high school, however, chances are, it's only a matter of time before they give in and buy a Prada purse or Burberry scarf.

Students Speak Out
ON GUYS & GIRLS

"**If you're a girl looking for a guy, this is the perfect school for you. The ratio of girls to boys is roughly 40 percent to 60 percent. And, yes, the guys are all really attractive.**"

Q "Most guys here fit the same mold. Girls are a little bit different; they tend to hang out in groups where they all dress and look alike. There are **plenty of attractive people here**."

Q "Everyone seems like rich, spoiled, preppy people with too much money who only hang out in their clique. There are **not enough homey, down-to-earth kind of people**."

Athletics

Q "I have had a few different girlfriends since I have been here. There are a few girls here that are real nice and down-to-earth. There is also a crowd that thinks they are elite and above the rest of the world. There is also a large crowd that dresses very provocatively and acts as if they are very promiscuous; they're actually just teases and end up being let-downs when you really get to know them. The guys here are all over the spectrum. **Some are too rich and snobby, and others are like high schoolers for the rest of their life**. Overall, though, there is a good crowd of down-to-earth guys."

The College Prowler Take
ON GUYS & GIRLS

The Lowdown
ON ATHLETICS

This is a campus filled with pretty people, and most of them know it. It's unfortunate, but the prettier girls do get stuck in the stereotype of being bitchy and high-maintenance. There are always large groups of girls walking to class together, and it is very common to remain friends with that same large group throughout your four years. The guys are generally laid-back in a social setting but can also be ruthless in a business meeting. Some frat guys get the bad rep of being pigs and preying on freshman girls, and while those guys do exist, not all males give off the shady vibe. However, once cliques are formed, it can be very hard to become friendly with someone in another established clique. "Hooking-up" on campus can refer to anything from making out to having sex, and caution is necessary when using this term if trying to be discrete.

Men's Varsity Teams:

Baseball	Indoor Track
Basketball	Lacrosse
Cross Country	Outdoor Track
Football	Soccer
Golf	Swimming
Hockey (Division I)	Tennis

Women's Varsity Teams:

Basketball	Soccer
Cross Country	Softball
Field Hockey	Swimming
Indoor Track	Tennis
Lacrosse	Volleyball
Outdoor Track	

The College Prowler™ Grade on
Guys: B+

A high grade for Guys indicates that the male population on campus is attractive, smart, friendly, and engaging, and that the school has a decent ratio of guys to girls.

The College Prowler™ Grade on
Girls: B

A high grade for Girls not only implies that the women on campus are attractive, smart, friendly, and engaging, but also that there is a fair ratio of girls to guys.

Athletic Division:
NCAA Division II

Conference:
Northeast-10

School Mascot:
Falcon

Getting Tickets
Tickets are not required for Bentley students to attend Bentley sporting events.

Most Popular Sports
The 2001 field hockey team was Bentley's first-ever NCAA Division II National Championship, and the team has reached the national championship game each of last four years. Women's basketball has had 10 appearances in the Elite Eight and holds a NCAA Division II record with 21 NCAA Division II tournament berths.

Overlooked Teams
Both the men's and women's rugby teams have been dominating their opponents in club play for the past few years; it won't be long before they are officially recognized as a varsity sport and considered a formidable team in their division.

Students Speak Out
ON ATHLETICS

"Varsity sports are big. Contests and prizes are offered to students who attended varsity games. Intramural sports seem to be pretty big, but I don't really know much about them."

Q "There are some teams that stand out. There is **a good crowd at most of the events.** We have a super-fan program on campus that gets people to the events and gives out lots of free stuff. Intramurals are big, too. Over 50 percent of the people here are involved."

Q "Intramural sports are huge here and a lot of fun. Varsity sports are good, too. Football is the biggest. I know that **I never missed a home game**, and there are always fun activities beforehand, like tailgating parties."

Q "Sports are pretty big on campus. We're mostly Division II, but men's ice hockey is Division I. The College has **a great IM [intramural] program**."

Q "Varsity sports are a joke on campus. **Some of the athletes walk around campus as if they are amazing**, but everyone else, including many of them themselves, know that it is not a big deal and that they are not going to continue on after college. A decent turnout of students to a sporting event only happens when they advertise to give out free tuition or a big TV or some other great prize."

Q "**No one follows varsity sports here**. The teams are D2 so no one cares, and the D1 hockey team plays off campus at a terrible arena. IM sports are completely unorganized."

The College Prowler Take
ON ATHLETICS

There is a harsh stereotype that exists at Bentley regarding student athletes: if a student is good in their sport, it means they would have never gotten into Bentley for their grades. Varsity athletes are not exactly taken seriously by the rest of the population but are given significant academic leeway if a game or practice interrupts or overlaps into a class period. The football stadium isn't packed on the weekends with fans cheering wildly, but games are used as a way of "pre-gaming" for a party later on that night. The biggest up and coming sport on campus is hockey, which recently moved up to Division I play but is still struggling as it gets used to the tougher competition. In a few years, the Bentley/Army hockey game will be one hot ticket. Bentley simply is not a school you go to hoping to be drafted into any sort of professional sport; rather, it has excellent high school athletes looking to continue their passion and stay in shape.

The College Prowler™ Grade on
Athletics: B-

A high grade in Athletics indicates that students have school spirit, that sports programs are respected, that games are well-attended, and that intramurals are a prominent part of student life.

Greek Life

Students Speak Out
ON GREEK LIFE

> "Only a small percent of the campus is involved with Greek life. The others tend to like the people involved but laugh at the actual idea of joining a frat or sorority."

Q "Greek life here is small. I wouldn't say it dominates the social thing, but **the frats throw the most bashes**. I hate Greek life and think it's stupid. It's just there so people can buy their friends."

Q "It definitely doesn't dominate the social scene, but it does play its role. During rushing time, fliers are everywhere, and people are pledging until all hours of the night. **The frat parties are pretty fun**."

Q "**It is a joke**. They are another group that segregates themselves from the rest of the community. They do not get involved with much outside of the Greek life programs."

Q "Greek life sucks at Bentley. There are a few fraternities and sororities, but it's nothing like any other college I have been to. **Bentley does not have on-campus fraternity or sorority houses,** so if this is of importance to you, don't come to Bentley."

Q "Greek life exists, but **it's not very popular**. Most people agree that you don't have to pledge to a frat or sorority to have friends and fun on campus."

The Lowdown
ON GREEK LIFE

Number of Sororities:
4

Number of Fraternities:
3 national, 3 local

Undergrad Men in Fraternities:
13%

Undergrad Women in Sororities:
13%

Multicultural Colonies
Bentley has the historical black organizations Delta Sigma Theta (sorority) and Phi Beta Sigma (fraternity).

Get chapter listings and inside information on campus greek life from the Bentley College guidebook, available at www.collegeprowler.com.

The College Prowler Take
ON GREEK LIFE

The Greek scene at Bentley, which, by the way, is not ever actually referred to as "the Greek scene" by any student, is slightly non-traditional when compared to other local universities. There are no fraternity or sorority houses on campus, and only a few frats have brothers who rent a house off campus for the purpose of having parties. With 26 percent of the student population in a fraternity or sorority, they are a visible force on campus, but mostly serve a social purpose. The events and fundraisers run by the Greeks are something to be proud of, however, their main function is to appeal to those who have a compelling need for sisterhood or brotherhood.

The College Prowler™ Grade on
Greek Life: C

A high grade in Greek Life indicates that sororities and fraternities are not only present, but also active on campus. Other determining factors include the variety of houses available and the respect the Greek community receives from the rest of the campus.

Drug Scene

The Lowdown
ON DRUG SCENE

Most Prevalent Drugs on Campus:
Alcohol, marijuana

Liquor-Related Referrals:
481

Liquor-Related Arrests:
0

Drug-Related Referrals:
104

Drug-Related Arrests:
3

Students Speak Out
ON DRUG SCENE

{ "Some people smoke pot, but I'd say we're more an alcohol-drinking school rather than a drug-doing school."

Q "The drug scene is much like at any other campus, far less than at some. Campus police crack down on anyone doing stupid stuff outside, but if drugs are your thing, I'm sure you could get away with it, much like anywhere else. But if what you really want to know is how clean the campus is, I would say there's **not that much of a negative influence**."

Q "Drugs are accessible but not prevalent at parties. If people are going to do them, then they do it on their own or in small groups. **They don't bring it to a party** and do it there."

Q "There is **an abundance of marijuana on campus**, and you can pretty much call a number of individuals on any given night and pick up a nice bag. This is a big plus because there isn't usually much to do on week nights other than get high."

Q "I know where they're at when or if I want them, but the opportunities are probably **pretty darn small compared to most colleges**. Then again, we're in New England and we all smoke weed here."

The College Prowler Take
ON DRUG SCENE

If the campus police log is any indication of which drug is the most prevalent, it would appear there are a lot of stupid pot smokers who don't put a towel under their door, and get busted not only for the smell, but also for possession. Alcohol use is widespread, and it's not highly uncommon for students to start drinking Thursday night and go until Monday night. The peer pressure to indulge can be stronger in larger cliques such as sports teams and fraternities, but if you choose not to booze it up, just be prepared to pitch in a helping hand when your roommates come back from a party and can't make it to the trash can fast enough. As with most schools, it you want drugs, you will find a way to get them. Don't expect to be at an on-campus party and have someone offer you questionable pills or powder, because it won't happen. People either know there are drugs here or they don't.

The College Prowler™ Grade on
Drug Scene: B+

A high grade on Drug Scene indicates that drugs are not a noticeable part of campus life; drug use is not visible, and no pressure to use them seems to exist.

Campus Strictness

The Lowdown
ON CAMPUS STRICTNESS

What Are You Most Likely to Get Caught Doing on Campus?
Cheating on exams or papers, drinking underage, destruction of campus property, parking illegally, making too much noise in your room, downloading copyrighted materials, hanging up unregistered posters in buildings, having too many people at an unregistered party, having drug paraphernalia in your dorm room

Students Speak Out
ON CAMPUS STRICTNESS

"**Drugs can be big trouble if you are caught. If you're drinking and under control, or if you are 21, you are fine. People who get in trouble are the ones throwing the large parties.**"

Q "They aren't that strict here. It's not that hard to drink, but they do have penalties for drinking and are harder on drug violators than drinkers. Don't worry, **Bentley is a party school**!"

Q "It's not strict at all. They say you are kicked out for marijuana, but nobody ever really does get kicked out for it. **They just charge high fines** for drug and alcohol violations, which is useless because it doesn't teach anyone a lesson or deter them from doing it again."

Q "Campus police are not people you want to deal with. **They are trained to be intimidating, and the majority of them are idiots**. Avoid them as much as possible. They are very strict, and the school will fine the crap out of you for minor infractions."

Q "RAs say that if they see it, they have to write you up, but if they just hear about it, and you don't make it obvious, they let it slide. **Cops have little tolerance, though**—as usual."

Q "They are pretty strict, but they are also pretty cool. I hurt myself once during a night of heavy drinking, went to CP to get them to take me to the ER, and they were cool about it. I guess they **figured I already learned my lesson**."

The College Prowler Take
ON CAMPUS STRICTNESS

If campus police can help you out, they will. They always want to help you get out of potential trouble first; only if you talk back to them will you receive punishment. It's not an unusual sight for an officer to pull up next to a student carrying a thirty-pack to their dorm and ask to see the student's ID. If the student freaks out and starts complaining about how his constitutional rights are being violated, chances are, he will end up being escorted to the station and given a fine. However, if you do find yourself in this situation and are underage, don't be stupid, just accept the fact that you were caught. Give the officer the beer politely and you most likely won't have to show them any ID, thus avoiding being written up, which can be worth the cost of the beer. The presence of campus police officers is hard to ignore, and, generally, students like the idea of being safe and protected.

Did You Know?

Bentley College has a Balcony Policy! According to the college, "Balconies on the buildings are cosmetic only and were not built to accommodate people. Standing, sitting, or storing anything on balconies is prohibited. Offenders of this policy are subject to judicial action up to and including suspension and expulsion from the residence halls."

The College Prowler™ Grade on
Campus Strictness: C

A high Campus Strictness grade implies an overall lenient atmosphere; police and RAs are fairly tolerant, and the administration's rules are flexible.

Overall Experience

Students Speak Out
ON OVERALL EXPERIENCE

{ "Things need to be shaken up at Bentley. Overall, the student body is pretty conformist and conservative. There is a strong Republican group. You won't find anyone with blue hair or a pierced chin at Bentley."

Q "Bentley has a good image. It is getting better and better. **Socially you meet a lot of great kids**. Nightlife tends to get repetitive, but if you go into Boston and other schools on occasions to switch it up, it's a good time. Overall, I like Bentley a lot."

Q "I am not particularly fond of Bentley College. If you are looking for a large social scene with many diverse students, don't come here. The student body consists of **primarily middle-to-upper-class white kids**, and there is very little to do in order to entertain yourself on campus. I definitely wish that I would have visited more colleges before choosing Bentley because I wish I never came here."

Q "**My experience has been awful**. The people who work for Bentley are not customer service oriented. I went to a very large school for undergrad. And there, I never had this problem. Yet, at Bentley, I feel like a number, not an individual."

Q "I love Bentley; I got into Northeastern, BU, Suffolk and a few other schools in the area, and I had to choose Bentley. The teachers are very friendly, the workload gets tougher towards senior year, but the material is all extremely relevant to the real world. **Go to Bentley if you want to know business**, that's all there is to it."

Q "I'm definitely not smart enough—nor rich enough, to be here. I don't feel so alone, though, because a good majority of the athletes are neither so rich nor so smart. And, there are lots of geeky kids who never partied or did anything other than play on their computers and read books. I would and would not like to be somewhere else. I'd like to be somewhere else because **this really isn't a normal college experience**, it's pretty lame. At the same time though, I'm glad I'm here because I'm getting a practically free, really expensive education, and I will most likely get a great job after graduating from here."

The College Prowler Take
ON OVERALL EXPERIENCE

The Bentley experience is hardly a normal college experience. From day one, you will be set on a track to receive a unique business education. Hard work and effort are mandatory, but the rewards are endless. Students who are unhappy with their Bentley experience can likely attribute some of their issues to their own introverted nature, which may keep them from exploring Waltham and Boston and the events, concerts, and meetings the school offers. Other factors, such as the disconnect in the concept of diversity and the inability to form a relationship with local businesses, are out of control from a student perspective.

The opportunity to interact with professors who are leaders in the field, to learn from renowned companies in the classroom, and have access to the latest technology, is so distinctive that Bentley is in a class of its own as a business university. If, when you reflect upon your college experience, you want to be able to say that you received an excellent real-world business education, were exposed to state-of-the-art technology, and had a good time while doing it, then Bentley College is for you.

The Inside Scoop

The Lowdown
ON THE INSIDE SCOOP

School Spirit

Despite having division stars in hockey, football, and women's basketball, Bentley students are not oozing blue and gold. Because of the size, when students do watch a sporting event, they will most likely know at least one person on the team and that is the main reason why they are there. The bookstore has started to carry more fashionable clothing bearing the Bentley name, which students are beginning to integrate into their wardrobe. Chances are, you won't hear someone say, "I'm so proud to be a Falcon!" but in their own apathetic way, they'll muster up a, "Yeah, Bentley is better than Babson," which is their way of saying, "Yay! Go Bentley!"

Traditions
Spring Day

Get ready for a day filled with music, food, activities, and lots of beer, as every student on campus congregates on the Greenspace for Spring Day—the last Saturday before finals start at the end of the Spring semester. As long as you and your guests (bring your friends from other local colleges along!) have wristbands and keep your alcoholic beverage in a covered cup, you will not get in trouble for drinking underage. If the idea of getting drunk at 9 a.m. isn't your thing, then enjoy the music (usually a totally rad 1980s cover band), design your own trucker hat, or throw around a Frisbee. This is a guaranteed awesome time you won't forget.

Business Bowl

An event for the true business student! Held each spring, students compete in teams of five on various real-world business models and cases. Freshmen, sophomores, and juniors compete against each other, while seniors and graduate students go head-to-head. The teams have several hours to come up with the best solution to the business problems and then present their findings to a panel of judges. It is a highly-recognized event in the local business community, and students are able to interact and network with business professionals, practitioners, and college administrators. Of course, cash prizes are awarded to the top teams in each class.

Black United Body Fashion Show

Each Spring, the BUB fashion show showcases the hottest styles from local stores and boutiques. The music is kickin' and the models are flawless at this unique event.

Things I Wish I Knew Before Coming to Bentley:
- Meet as many people as possible during First Week.
- It's not a good school for people uncommitted to studying business.
- There is a large emphasis on group projects.
- Get out and explore Waltham as soon as possible.
- How to manage my time better.
- Don't call Boston "Beantown."

Tips to Succeed at Bentley:
- Take an elective to balance out the heavy business course load.
- Research your professors before choosing your classes.
- Actually go to class!
- Don't wait to take your unrestricted electives until senior year.
- Do your homework yourself so you actually understand the material.
- Always dispute grades you disagree with.
- Don't get stuck doing all the work for a group project.
- Use your first two years to figure out what you want to major in.
- Know how AP credits can affect your class standing.

Finding a Job or Internship

The Lowdown
ON FINDING A JOB OR INTERNSHIP

The Career Services office at Bentley is perhaps one of the most under-appreciated departments on campus. The staff is constantly making themselves available for resume critique and job search techniques, while running various job fairs and workshops throughout the semester. Most students will find an internship or promising job lead with the help of Career Services.

Advice

Attend as many workshops and employer info sessions as possible in order to gain an idea of what type of internship you are interested in so that you can plan your academic courses accordingly. Make sure to register for Bentley's MonsterTrak Website, where employers specifically post jobs for Bentley students.

Office of Career Services Resources & Services:
Campus employment, individual career advising, resume assistance, workshops, panels & alumni networking events, campus recruiting, career fairs, interview preparation, Career Handout series, MonsterTRAK

Alumni Services
Online Directory
The online directory allows alumni to search for information on their old classmates.

Clubs and Chapters
In order to stay in touch with alumni if you are from outside New England, various alumni clubs and chapters are set up across the country and internationally so there is always a way to stay connected with Bentley.

Alumni ID
An alumni ID card is the way to receive the many benefits and services available for graduates. To receive your alumni ID card or alumni parking sticker, call the Office of Alumni Relations at (800) 5-BENTLEY.

Insurance Discount
Bentley is partnered with Liberty Mutual to offer a special savings for Alumni Association members. The Group Savings Plus program provides a discount of up to 10 percent on the company's competitive auto and home insurance rates. The program also features 24-hour claims service, emergency roadside assistance to auto policy holders, and convenient billing options. For more information, visit: *www.libertymutual.com/lm/bentleyaa.*

Career Services
The Miller Center for Career Services is available to alumni no matter what stage of the job search process they are in. The resources, strategies, and opportunities such as skills workshops, networking events, and online job postings are available to alumni for life.

E-mail Forwarding
By establishing a free alumni e-mail account, you can take advantage of college e-mail services that include automatic message forwarding.

The Best & Worst

The Ten BEST Things About Bentley:

1. State-of-the-art technology at your fingertips
2. Recognized leader in business education
3. Proximity to Boston and free shuttle
4. Greedy Bingo
5. Real life experience many professors bring to the table
6. Ability to work with real companies in classes
7. Sarlary value of a Bentley diploma
8. Spring Day
9. On-campus concerts
10. The Greenspace on nice days

The Ten WORST Things About Bentley:

1. Intense business focus
2. Cliques
3. Walking up the hill to class
4. Requirement to take (and pass) economics and finance classes
5. Science professors
6. Parking
7. Group projects
8. Lack of recognition from Waltham businesses
9. Apathetic students
10. Construction and renovations all around

Boston College

140 Commonwealth Ave., Chestnut Hill, MA 02467
www.bc.edu   (617) 552-3100

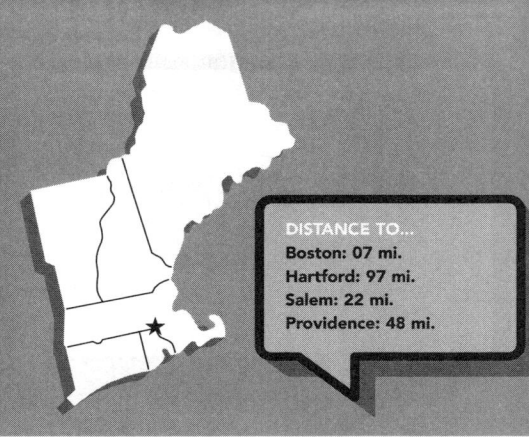

DISTANCE TO...
Boston: 07 mi.
Hartford: 97 mi.
Salem: 22 mi.
Providence: 48 mi.

"Boston College professors are extremely capable. More often than not, they're ridiculously intelligent."

Total Enrollment:
8,851

Acceptance Rate:
31%

Tuition:
$29,396

Top 10% of High School Class:
73%

SAT Range
Verbal	Math	Total
600 – 690	630 – 710	1230 – 1400

SAT II Requirements
Writing, Math I or II, and a third subject of the applicant's choosing are required for all classes.

Most Popular Majors:
11% Communications
10% English Language and Literature
9%   Finance
7%   History
7%   Psychology

Students Also Applied To:*
Boston University, Georgetown University, Harvard University, Tufts University, University of Pennsylvania

*For more school info check out www.collegeprowler.com

Table of Contents

Academics	669
Local Atmosphere	671
Safety & Security	672
Computers	674
Facilities	675
Campus Dining	677
Off-Campus Dining	678
Campus Housing	680
Off-Campus Housing	681
Diversity	683
Guys & Girls	684
Athletics	686
Greek Life	687
Drug Scene	688
Campus Strictness	689
Overall Experience	691
The Inside Scoop	692
Finding a Job or Internship	692
The Best & Worst	693

College Prowler Report Card

Academics	A-
Local Atmosphere	A
Safety & Security	A+
Computers	B+
Facilities	B+
Campus Dining	B
Off-Campus Dining	A
Campus Housing	B
Off-Campus Housing	B+
Diversity	D-
Guys	B+
Girls	A
Athletics	A
Greek Life	N/A
Drug Scene	B+
Campus Strictness	C

Academics

Special Degree Options
B.A. – M.A. Degree Option: In five years, students can receive both their bachelor's and master's degrees.

Did You Know?
There are no fewer than six factions of the student government at BC: CSOM Government, CSON Senate, LSOE Senate, Student Alumni Council, Undergraduate Government of Boston College, and Woods College of Advancing Studies Student Senate.

The 120 Jesuits living on the Boston College campus make up the largest Jesuit community in the world. About half are actively involved in the University's faculty and administration. Twenty-two are graduate students from 10 foreign countries.

The Lowdown
ON ACADEMICS

Degrees Awarded:
Bachelor, Master, Post Master, Doctorate, First Professional

Undergraduate Schools:
Carroll School of Management, The Lynch School of Education, Arts and Sciences The Connell School of Nursing

Full-time Faculty:
660

Faculty with Terminal Degree:
97%

Student-to-Faculty Ratio:
14:1

Average Course Load:
Five courses (three credits each)

Sample Academic Clubs:
Accounting Academy, Information Technology Club, Another Choice on Campus, Bellarmine Pre-Law Council, Black Law Students Association, Gold Key National Honor Society, Intellectual Property and Technology Forum, Political Science Association, Students for Corporate Citizenship

AP Test Score Requirements
Possible credit for scores of 4 or 5

IB Test Score Requirements
Possible credit for scores of 6 or 7

Students Speak Out
ON ACADEMICS

"The teachers, for the most part, are fairly willing to accommodate students' needs. Most teachers take their jobs very seriously, and they're dedicated to challenging the students in their classes."

"I am a biology major, and my introductory classes in the first year or two were rather large. **You'll have to go out of your way to get to know the professors**. They're always willing to help you, though, and as you focus in on your major, the classes become much smaller and you definitely get to know some professors very well. I've even had dinner at two of my professors' houses."

Q "I have had a bunch of bad teachers in the computer science department, but **the teachers here are usually pretty varied**."

Q "A few teachers know how to teach, but most are there for a paycheck, **to hear themselves talk**, or to fill quotas. Out of 38 classes at Boston College, I probably found a dozen, or so, interesting."

Q "The professors here are absolutely wonderful! Most of mine have reached out and really tried to get to know me as a person. Sometimes it is a good idea to attend their mandatory office hours so that they get to know you one-on-one, especially near grading time. However, **most of the professors genuinely want to get to know their students**, and many give out their home phone numbers in case we ever have burning questions."

Q "I've met some of the most amazing professors this year, but there's also been some crappy ones. The best way to get good professors is to go to www.ugbc.org and click on PEPs, which are **student evaluations of professors**. It really helps for course selections."

The College Prowler Take
ON ACADEMICS

It's fair to say that most, if not all, Boston College professors are extremely capable, and more often than not, they're ridiculously intelligent. However, competency and good nature don't necessarily always go hand in hand. Some of the professors are here just because it's their job, and some care but just don't know how to teach or help confused students understand better. There are also professors who are so eager for you to learn everything possible that they are very harsh graders and try to force you to know practically everything in order to get a decent grade. Luckily, bad or misdirected professors are in the minority. Most of the professors at Boston College are passionate and extremely intelligent individuals who inspire their students to follow the BC motto "ever to excel."

Of course, there are a few bad apples that just can't seem to relate to their students, typically because of an age gap that can span decades. Unfortunately, many of these professors are tenured, so there's little to no chance that they are leaving BC anytime soon. If the professor makes you queasy on the first day, then drop the class and add something else as soon as possible. To increase your chances of finding a good professor or interesting class, go to www.ugbc.org and check out the professor evaluations, where previous students have chimed in with their two cents regarding the teacher's aptitude. The professor evaluations (PEPs) are usually right on target describing the positive and negative attributes of the teacher. There are plenty of great professors at BC, and there's no reason you should have to remain in a class where you feel hesitant to shine.

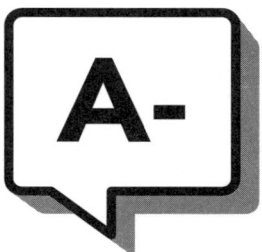

The College Prowler™ Grade on
Academics: A-

A high Academics grade generally indicates that professors are knowledgeable, accessible, and genuinely interested in their students' welfare. Other determining factors include class size, how well professors communicate, and whether or not classes are engaging.

Local Atmosphere

The Lowdown
ON LOCAL ATMOSPHERE

Region:
New England

City, State:
Chestnut Hill, Massachusetts

Setting:
Suburban town

Distance from Philadelphia:
5 hours

Distance from New York:
3.5 hours

Points of Interest:
Fenway Park, Freedom Trail, Boston Public Gardens

Major Sports Team:
Red Sox (MLB), Patriots (NFL), Bruins (NHL)

City Websites:
www.enjoyma.com
www.boston.com
www.boston-online.com

Students Speak Out
ON LOCAL ATMOSPHERE

"Our campus is perfectly situated in a suburban town, right next to Boston. The T, Boston's version of the subway, is located right at the foot of campus, and it is even called the 'Boston College Line.'"

Q "Boston is a college town, and anywhere you go you will see people your age. There are literally **some 50 colleges within a 15-mile radius**. Though we are technically in Chestnut Hill, we are only a half-hour train ride from Boston. There are many historic sites in close proximity, like Fenway Park, the Boston Public Gardens, Quincy Market, and Faneuil Hall."

Q "BC's partial isolation from downtown Boston is a wonderful thing. I was truly able to enjoy campus life, while also benefiting from the advantages of the city. It's a perfect balance. There are tons of other universities and **plenty of ways to satisfy your alternative interests in the city**. Go to Boston frequently, and avoid the kids on campus with visors, bleached tips, and Abercrombie sportswear."

Q "I think Boston is one of the greatest places to go to college, and **BC is ideal because it's not exactly in the heart of the city**. It's actually in a neighboring town, but the city is only a T ride away. This way you get the real college campus experience, since your campus isn't in the middle of a busy city, but you're close enough to the city that you don't feel like you're in the middle of nowhere. Sometimes you fall into a trap whereby you never make the effort to go into the city, which happened to me this year, but that's more of a personal choice."

Q "**The atmosphere in Chestnut Hill is chill**. It's 10 minutes from the city, but the town is beautiful and everywhere you go, whether it's across the street to Maddies, or to Newton Center, you're bound to run into classmates. We're close to BU, Northeastern, Harvard, Babson, Bentley and a bunch of other smaller schools. The only thing I'd stay away from would be the cops."

Q "Every year, from September through May, Boston plays home to thousands of 18- to 22-year-olds. **There are many, many schools in Boston**. There are theatres, museums and historic sites. It has everything and anything."

The College Prowler Take
ON LOCAL ATMOSPHERE

Boston is a wonderful city with loads of American history on pretty much every corner. It is also chock-full of college-aged people, so the area definitely has that youthful, alive feel that a lot of places don't. Boston is fairly clean and efficient, and it absolutely bursts with character. Boston College is located right on the outskirts of the Boston metropolis, which gives BC students a mix of low-key suburbia and thrilling city living. Harvard, Northeastern, and Tufts are all fairly close to BC, as are many other colleges. However, that doesn't mean you'll ever actually see or talk to a student at one of these universities, as some BC students tend to find friends only on Chestnut Hill. There is so much character to Boston, but you have to be willing to venture out and experience something more than just the few blocks that circle Boston College.

The College Prowler™ Grade on
Local Atmosphere: A

A high Local Atmosphere grade indicates that the area surrounding campus is safe and scenic. Other factors include nearby attractions, proximity to other schools, and the town's attitude toward students.

Safety & Security

The Lowdown
ON SAFETY & SECURITY

Boston College Police:
43 full-time police

Phone:
(617) 552-4444 (emergencies)
(617) 552-4440 (non-emergency)

Health Center Office Hours:
Monday-Friday, 8 a.m.-5 p.m.

Safety Services:
Eagle Escort, emergency blue-lights, RAD Training, Eagle Eye on Crime, Victim's Resource Manual, safety notices

Students Speak Out
ON SAFETY & SECURITY

"Security and safety are outstanding. I had a summer class that ended at 8 p.m., and I parked off campus. I never even gave it a second thought."

Q "Chestnut Hill is a quaint town, so there's not much to worry about walking through campus at night. Certain areas around campus are **sometimes dangerous late at night**, but actual on-campus safety is really good at BC."

Q "Our campus is extremely safe. It is located in **one of the wealthiest suburban areas around**, and we're not directly in the city. We have our own police force and escorts who will travel with you if you ever think you might need them. I have never felt scared walking alone at night since there are always people around."

Q "The campus is not overwhelmingly large, but it can be somewhat frightening for a freshman walking alone at night. As a result, **BC has an extremely reliable escort service** that will take a student to and from any destination on campus or within close proximity. Also, there are bright blue-light call stations everywhere that a student can utilize at any time to immediately contact the police. Word to the wise: never hit the blue button unless it's a real emergency!"

Q "Boston College is ridiculously safe. The **Boston College police force is notorious for being everywhere**, much to the students' annoyance and the parents' relief. The very first week of school, freshmen are required to attend a safety-information assembly, one that gives such disturbing national statistics that departing seniors still recall the frightening facts presented at the meeting. As a result, students are keenly aware of the dangers that are possible, yet with the BCPD [Boston College Police Department] around, they know that they're highly unlikely to ever occur."

Q "I feel that campus is pretty safe. The Boston College Police Department is always patrolling and making sure things are going well. There are also blue-lights and emergency call boxes located all around campus. **The BCPD has a very quick response time**, and the officers are very polite. Also, the dorms use key cards, which only allow access into certain dorms. For instance, one person's ID works only for the Newton campus dorms, and another person's ID works only for the College Road dorms, so strangers can't get into the dorms very easily."

Did You Know?

The BCPD (Boston College Police Department) officers are granted police authority while on campus by the Commonwealth of Massachusetts. They also have deputy sheriff powers for off-campus situations.

The College Prowler Take
ON SAFETY & SECURITY

Boston College is an extremely safe place for students to go to school. During the first week of school, mandatory meetings give students the emergency and non-emergency information on locating and contacting the police. Incoming students are made aware of the potential dangers around them and are told about the best ways to avoid being victimized in any way. Also, police officers are always extremely friendly and helpful. Since it is such a safe environment, no one is ever too busy to tend to whatever small concern you might have. If something were to go wrong, the BCPD would come to your rescue immediately and do everything they could to help you. When you leave campus, though, you should probably be a little more careful. Boston is a pretty safe city, but you do need to be a little more cautious there than you would just walking around our little town.

The College Prowler™ Grade on
Safety & Security: A+

A high grade in Safety & Security means that students generally feel safe, campus police are visible, blue-light phones and escort services are readily available, and safety precautions are not overly necessary.

Computers

Did You Know?

If you go to the lab and forget to bring your floppy to save your work, you're not out of luck. There are floppy disc vending machines for your convenience.

The Lowdown
ON COMPUTERS

Students Speak Out
ON COMPUTERS

High-Speed Network?
Yes

Wireless Network?
Yes

Number of Labs:
1

24-Hour Labs:
No

Charge to Print?
No

Number of Computers:
29 Macs, 118 PCs

Operating Systems:
Windows XP Professional, Mac OS X

Free Software:
Adobe Acrobat Reader, Apple QuickTime Player, McAfee Virex for Macintosh, McAfee VirusScan for Windows, Microsoft Internet Explorer, Microsoft Outlook Express, Netscape Mail, Netscape Navigator, Nortel Contivity VPN Client, Oracle CorporateSync Palm, Campus Time, Oracle CorporateTime, RealOne Player, Tera Term Pro for Windows, TN3270, WinImage, WinZip

"Having your own computer is essential at BC. The labs aren't open 24 hours a day and you won't have the freedom that you will with your own laptop or PC."

Q "I would suggest bringing your own computer if you have one. Each person gets their own Internet hook-up and phone line in the dorms. But, if you don't bring one, there is **a perfectly good computer lab** that generally isn't very crowded. So, it's up to you."

Q "**The network is kind of slow compared to other places**, but it is still significantly better than a modem. It is comparable to the cable modem that I have at home. I don't really visit the computer lab too often, except to print stuff, but it doesn't get too crowded. I would suggest your own computer if you can bring one. You basically need it as a word processor and for recreational Internet activity."

Q "I would recommend bringing your own computer, although one could survive without. **The computer labs are often crowded**, particularly when you need one most. I don't spend much time on the computer, but I never had much trouble with the network. It is prone to temporary shutdowns, but nothing too bad."

Q "Our computer lab is a great resource, but most students bring their own computers. BC sends out information about buying their brand of computer, the IBM ThinkPad, over the summer before freshman year. If you buy that computer through BC, they will fix it for no charge if there's ever a problem. However, it's not necessary that you have your own computer since **the computer lab is always available**. It's simply more convenient to have your own."

Q "The computer labs are pretty good. I use them a lot just because I get too easily distracted in my own room around my friends. The labs are not usually crowded, unless it's finals time. But, **I would bring your own computer** just for the convenience, even though it's not necessary."

The College Prowler Take
ON COMPUTERS

Boston College maintains an efficient and up-to-date computer lab that is only marginally crowded during exams. Even when the labs are crowded, or you have some kind of computer problem, the lab employees are generally very helpful. Despite the general accessibility of the labs, most students have their own computers. Most of the people at BC frequently check their e-mail and use Instant Messenger, so the convenience of having a personal computer in your own room can't be beat. The lab is a noteworthy resource and can be useful but most students agree that having a computer of your own is preferable.

The College Prowler™ Grade on
Computers: B+

A high grade in Computers designates that computer labs are available, the computer network is easily accessible, and the campus' computing technology is up-to-date.

Facilities

The Lowdown
ON FACILITIES

Athletic Center:
Conte Forum

Libraries:
Bapst Library and O'Neil Library

Movie Theatre on Campus?
No

Bowling on Campus?
No

Bar on Campus?
No

Coffeehouse on Campus?
Starbucks

Popular Places to Chill:
Hillside, The Quad

Student Center
There's no specific student center building; McElroy Commons is the closest thing.

Favorite Things to Do
Students love to go to sporting events, which also generally includes going to a party before or after the game—or sometimes both! There is no real student union for students to hang out in, but they make up for it by creating their own fun. Go into Boston for a movie or shopping. Go ice skating, sledding, or bowling.

 **Students Speak Out** ON FACILITIES

 **The College Prowler Take** ON FACILITIES

{ "The Plex could be better. You have to sign up for machines early in the morning if you want to get one for later in the day. Yet, it is a vast improvement from how it was!"

Q "The athletic facility on campus, which is called The Plex, is pretty nice. The roof of The Plex is an eyesore, but on the plus side, it has an indoor track, pool, weights, cardio equipment, basketball, tennis, racquetball and squash courts, and aerobic classes like step and yoga, all of which are free. **There's no official student center as of yet**, another campus joke, but McElroy is kind of like BC's version of a student center."

Q "The BC facilities are, for the most part, fine. **The dormitories are actually quite nice**. The Plex, which is the gym, is kind of small given the size of the school's population. It is always overcrowded and insanely hot in the late afternoons. A lot of people work out outside."

Q "When they built the new student center, it shockingly, coincided with my departure. The athletic facility has to be **the worst recreational center in all of Division I colleges**. It doesn't seem fair to pay $35,000 to share a weight machine with 9,000 other students."

Q "Some facilities are state-of-the-art, while others need some work. For example, the football, basketball and hockey facilities [Alumni Stadium and Conte Forum] are great, but **the recreation complex is terrible**. The computer center is nice and fairly efficient. We have the worst student center I have seen in all the colleges I have visited!"

Q "Upper campus just had a major remodeling job, so many of the dorms are updated and connected, which adds to a sense of community for the freshmen. These new conglomerations of buildings have **really nice study rooms** with vending machines; some have laundry rooms in the basement."

Throughout the last few years, the school has undergone a complete campus beautification program, and the results are awesome. Two entire new buildings were added, as well as a new dining hall and new routes for walking through campus. The athletic center for the athletes is excellent, or so the non-athletes are told. As great as it is, only a small portion is campus is allowed to use it, and students gave mixed reviews of the ordinary fitness facility, The Plex. It's much better than it used to be, and it offers a lot to do, but it still can feel dark, dingy, and crowded. The campus itself, on the other hand, is beautiful. Its Gothic architecture and newer buildings are certainly praiseworthy. With the exception of the virtually nonexistent student union and the small, ugly athletic facility for non-athletes, the facilities on campus are great.

The College Prowler™ Grade on Facilities: B+

A high Facilities grade indicates that the campus is aesthetically pleasing and well-maintained; facilities are state-of-the-art, and libraries are exceptional. Other determining factors include the quality of both athletic and student centers and an abundance of things to do on campus.

Campus Dining

The Lowdown
ON CAMPUS DINING

Freshman Meal Plan Requirement?
Yes

Meal Plan Average Cost:
$1,825 (flat rate without buying any extra Eagle Bucks)

24-Hour On-Campus Eating?
No, but late-night begins at 9 p.m. on Lower campus.

Student Favorites:
Chicken fingers at The Rat, make-your-own Belgium waffles at Lower, muffins at McElroy, The New England Classic at Hillside

Students Speak Out
ON CAMPUS DINING

Q "The only food on campus is the dining halls, unless you get a Chi Chi sausage after the bar on Thursday, Friday, or Saturday night. But other than that, if you want to eat on campus, it's going to be in a dining hall. The dining halls aren't bad, but not great. There are **a million places all around campus where you can order food for delivery**. You can always find something you like to eat in Boston."

Q "Although I don't really have a basis for comparison, I understand that the food on campus is great. The exorbitant price aside, the food has never posed a problem for me. **I really enjoyed the posh and cozy Hillside Café**, complete with made-to-order sandwiches and Starbucks."

Q "I live on Newton campus, and the food is okay at Stuart dining hall at first, but there's not much of a selection and **you get sick of it after a while**. I think that's the case at every school, though. If you live on the Upper campus, the food is better, and there's more of a selection at the McElroy dining hall."

Q "There are basically three major dining halls and three smaller ones. McElroy is where freshmen primarily eat (or at Stuart on Newton Campus), and Lower is where upperclassmen eat, both of which have just about everything. Chicken, pasta, salads, and sandwiches are pretty much the standard at both places. Breakfasts are awesome at BC, but the omelet line can be super long. For lunch, **a lot of people like The Rat for fast food type meals** and the Eagle's Nest for sandwiches, salads, or soup. Hillside has been a very popular addition to BC, and they have awesome sandwiches and a Starbucks as well. Watch out for the lines!"

Q "**The meal card is such a huge convenience at BC** because you never realize how expensive some of the food is that you're eating because it just gets deducted from your meal points. However, now that our meal cards can be used at Flatbreads, Pizzeria Uno on Harvard Avenue, and Maddies, you might never need to eat at a dining hall again!"

{ "The food is actually really good, although any campus food gets a little monotonous. Go visit your friends at other schools, and you will appreciate BC food so much more."

The College Prowler Take
ON CAMPUS DINING

The food at Boston College is excellent, but it can just feel monotonous after a while. Dietary concerns are very important at BC, and the school does its best to make concessions for all the students and provide a nice variety of foods for those students with special or specific dietary needs. The freshmen eat at either Stewart or McElroy, and most seem to prefer the former to the latter. The Rat is the fast food spot on campus, with the best French fries and chicken fingers in the world, or at least as far as we're concerned. Any student can eat at any dining hall. Some are just closer to certain dorms than others, and therefore attract certain students. Whether it's on or off campus, you'll be able to find food that tickles your taste buds and can be paid for with your meal plan.

Off-Campus Dining

The Lowdown
ON OFF-CAMPUS DINING

Best Pizza:
Pino's in Cleveland Circle

Best Chinese:
Lucky Wah

Best Breakfast:
Moogies, Eagle's Deli

Best Wings:
Wing It

Best Healthy:
Fresh City

Best Place to Take Your Parents:
The Cheesecake Factory

24-Hour Eating?
Yes, especially in Boston, but generally only in chains like Denny's that are known for being open all night.

The College Prowler™ Grade on
Campus Dining: B

Our grade on Campus Dining addresses the quality of both school-owned dining halls and independent on-campus restaurants as well as the price, availability, and variety of food.

Students Speak Out
ON OFF-CAMPUS DINING

"The restaurants around BC are excellent. Citysides, The Cheesecake Factory, Figs, Tasca, Fugakyu, and Kaya are just a few options!"

Q "Boston is a great city for food, but **you'd better have a lot of money** because off-campus dining gets really expensive. Most people eat in the dining halls."

Q "The good thing about Boston College is that you're in Boston, or at least close enough to be considered to be in the city, and there are thousands of places to eat at or order from. Roggie's is the best pizza. Definitely go to Vinny Testa's for Italian food, and if you can make it to the Cheesecake Factory, it is definitely worth your while—they don't serve just cheesecake, they have a huge menu of all sorts of foods, all excellent, though it's a little expensive. **You can also get Domino's on your meal card if you sign up for dining bucks**, so that's pretty nice."

Q "**Restaurants in Boston are awesome**! You can get coupon books near McElroy dining hall's lobby where you'll find tons of discounts on restaurants. You can also use it as a directory to find good spots. Some of the most popular restaurants with the students are Bangkok Bistro, Anna's Taqueria, Cheesecake Factory, Ginza, and Vinny Testa's. There are really way too many to name. Definitely go all around Chestnut Hill, Allston and Brighton area, Newton, and Cleveland Circle."

Q "You must hit up Bagel Rising on Commonwealth Avenue at the intersection of Harvard Avenue! The people that work there are hilarious, and the Tequila Sunrise is the best breakfast sandwich in the area. **The coffee is excellent**. Watch out for lines around noon."

Q "Boston has everything! Check out Fire and Ice at either Harvard Square in Cambridge or at the downtown Boston location. **It's an experience**. The Mexican food at the Border Café is phenomenal and reasonably priced. Also, the Big A deli in Brighton has the most incredible chicken Parmesan sandwich."

The College Prowler Take
ON OFF-CAMPUS DINING

If you're an avid eater, then you'll find more than your fair share of scrumptious eateries in Boston. Plant eaters take note that vegan, vegetarian, and sushi restaurants aren't available at the students' beck and call, as in California or New York. Incredible seafood, surprisingly flavorful Mexican, and incredible Italian food can be found within walking distance or a short drive from campus. Commonwealth Avenue runs adjacent to campus—there you can find a couple of above-average eateries for those who don't want to travel far. Travel a few minutes on the T down to Cleveland Circle, or perhaps even walk, and you'll pass a number of delicious off-campus dining establishments.

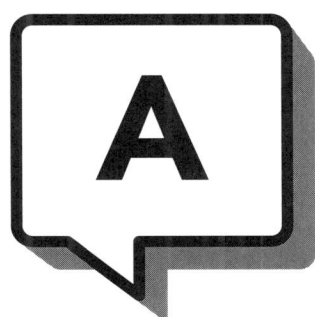

The College Prowler™ Grade on
Off-Campus Dining: A

A high Off-Campus Dining grade implies that off-campus restaurants are affordable, accessible, and worth visiting. Other factors include the variety of cuisine and the availability of alternative options (vegetarian, vegan, Kosher, etc.).

Campus Housing

The Lowdown
ON CAMPUS HOUSING

Undergrads on Campus:
73%

Number of Dormitories:
25

University-Owned Apartments:
6

Cleaning Service?
Yes, but only in public areas.

Also Available:
Special interest housing

You Get:
Bed, desk, chair, cable hookup, telephone hookup, Internet hookup, closet, window shade

Students Speak Out
ON CAMPUS HOUSING

"**Dorms are decent at Boston College, and they are getting better, as there have been many renovations in the past few years. All dorms are coed.**"

Q "They are coed by floor freshman year and by room every year after that. There are **communal bathrooms**, and the girls' bathrooms are always locked. Upperclassmen live in suite-style housing, some with kitchens. All seniors have kitchens."

Q "You don't get much of a choice as a freshman, and you are basically put where you're put. There are two main areas where freshmen live: Upper campus and Newton campus. You have to take a bus to get to Newton, which is a major pain, so I'm told, but both places are decent. Upper is definitely better, though. **You could also ask for substance-free housing**, which is on Upper and is all doubles. But, be advised: if you get caught drunk or high in there, you get kicked out of housing."

Q "As a freshman, I lived on Upper campus, which is the best place for first-years to live. I lived in Walsh as a sophomore, which is huge, and nicer than it looks. **We have a cute, eight-person suite**, which is nice and perfectly fine for a year. Even though others brag about Vanderslice, Walsh is practically the same on the inside and has a better setup. It's just not as close to the Lower Dining Hall, which is all of, like, a hundred or so steps away."

Q "Avoid Newton campus! As a freshman you get somewhat of a choice between the Upper and Newton campuses. **Newton campus is a 10-minute bus ride away from the main campus** and is composed of isolated freshmen. I strongly recommend Upper campus. Other than that, I think that most of the dorms on Upper campus are the same."

Q "As an incoming freshman you will either be placed on Upper campus, which is really nice and where I lived as a freshman, or on Newton campus, which is being done over, so all of the dorms on Newton will be brand new except Hardy/Cushing. The only catch to living on Newton is that you have to take a bus to the main campus where your classes are. Here's a hint: if you are interested in specialty housing, like substance-free housing—which isn't really substance free—or the music floor, then you will **automatically get a double on Upper**."

Q "On Lower campus, they have Edmonds, where I lived sophomore and junior year. It is good to live there for those years. **Walsh doesn't have kitchens**, but Edmond's does. Also, there are Ninety and Vanderslice, which are pretty new. They don't have kitchens either and are made for six or more people. Edmonds is for four people, and Walsh is for four or more people. Sixty-six is a singles or doubles dorm, but it's kind of scary there. There is another singles dorm off campus called Greycliff. Ignacio and Rubenstein are for seniors and are for six people. They have kitchens."

Q "**Voute and Gabelli are the nicest dorms** and are for four people. They both have townhouses, which have two floors, but only the lucky people get those through the lottery. Those dorms have kitchens, too. Then there are the infamous Mods for seniors. They don't have a full kitchen, but they have a yard. It is basically just a party area for the seniors, but the Mods are crappy."

Off-Campus Housing

The Lowdown
ON OFF-CAMPUS HOUSING

The College Prowler Take
ON CAMPUS HOUSING

The living arrangements at Boston College are very comfortable, mostly modern, and very well-kept. The main downside to BC's housing is the fact that the freshman dorms have communal bathrooms. If you're one of those people who absolutely cannot shower with others while wearing flip-flops, then you might want to pick another school with newer dorms that offer private bathrooms. BC's dorms offer less privacy because most of the buildings are old, but the flip side to that is that buildings are much more attractive and roomy than your average college dormitory.

Undergrads in Off-Campus Housing:
27%

Best Time to Look for a Place:
Early September

Average Rent for a Studio Apartment:
$500-$600 a month

Average Rent for a 1BR Apartment:
$600-$800 a month

Average Rent for a 2BR Apartment:
$1,000-$1,300 a month

Popular Places to Rent:
Cleveland Circle, Commonwealth Avenue

For Assistance Contact
Boston College's Off-Campus Housing Office
Web: *www.bc.edu/offices/reslife/offcampus*
Phone: (617) 552-3075

The College Prowler™ Grade on
Campus Housing: B

A high Campus Housing grade indicates that dorms are clean, well-maintained, and spacious. Other determining factors include variety of dorms, proximity to classes, and social atmosphere.

Students Speak Out
ON OFF-CAMPUS HOUSING

"Boston is the land of apartments. My roommates and I found one in two days with a realtor, but they're very expensive. There is no way to escape that. It's Boston."

Q "It's worth living off campus, if even for just a year. Most people have to move off because they are only given three years of on-campus housing. **Start looking for places to live nine months before you want to live there** because it's a race."

Q "A majority of BC juniors are forced to live off campus for their entire junior year. It helps BC's overcrowded housing issue, but also allows local rent prices to be ridiculously jacked up due to the supply and demand curve. If they charge it, you will have to come. Warning: **don't live above restaurants unless you're really interested in getting up close and personal with a variety of daring rodents.**"

Q "Off-campus housing tends to be conveniently close to the campus but can be difficult to find sometimes. BC does not have any of its own off-campus housing, so **each student is on their own to find an off-campus residence**. However, there never seems to be a big problem with off-campus housing. Most students live in Cleveland Circle, which is about a mile and half down the road."

Q "Usually, freshman, sophomores, and seniors live on campus. Most people, unless they are in the top five percent of the incoming class, a nursing student, or a varsity athlete, are only given three years of on-campus housing. So, juniors usually live off campus up and down Commonwealth Avenue and on the little side streets. **Apartments are very expensive.**"

Q "I live off-campus now, and **I like it so much better than living on campus**, but it is really expensive. When you break it down, though, it can be cheaper than paying BC for housing, depending on how much the monthly rent is."

The College Prowler Take
ON OFF-CAMPUS HOUSING

Boston College simply does not have enough allocated housing to accommodate all of its students. Most students are given only three years of housing, so living off campus becomes a necessity. If you are one of those students, then the best advice is simply to plan ahead. Start looking for an apartment early. The longer you put off looking, the harder it will be. You will certainly be able to find an apartment no matter what, but the cheapest apartments are the ones that get taken first. You will literally pay the price if you procrastinate. Having an apartment in Boston can be extremely expensive, as you usually have to pay for so much more than you bargained for, like maintenance. You might also want to make sure that the people you're living with are responsible enough to have an apartment. No one wants to live with someone who's constantly late with the rent or sticks you with the whole electric bill.

The College Prowler™ Grade on
Off-Campus Housing: B+

A high grade in Off-Campus Housing indicates that apartments are of high quality, close to campus, affordable, and easy to secure.

Diversity

The Lowdown
ON DIVERSITY

African American: 5%

Asian American: 9%

Hispanic: 6%

Native American: 0%

White: 78%

International: 2%

Out-of-State: 72%

Minority Clubs
AHANA, an acronym to describe individuals of African American, Hispanic, Asian, or Native American descent, is a student group that has implemented programs to foster the diversity at Boston College for over 20 years. From extracurricular to academic, AHANA makes a huge impact on the lives of all students at BC. There are also other organizations on campus specifically for certain cultures or nationalities.

Most Popular Religions
Around 70 percent of campus identifies as Catholic, which makes it obviously the most popular religion on campus. Other types of Christianity are also very popular on campus, but pretty much every religion is represented somewhere on campus.

Economic Status
Most students are middle- to upper-class.

Political Activity
Students are pretty politically active on both the Republican and Democratic side, although with the school being as conservative as it is, more students are Republicans.

Gay Tolerance
There are a couple organizations on campus, but only one, Allies of Boston College, is recognized by the school, and its constitution states that it is there to provide support, but not advocacy. It is very much rooted in Catholic beliefs and is really just a place to discuss sexuality. Another organization, GLBC, is a more active, liberally-minded organization, but it has repeatedly been denied status as a recognized student organization. Still, they are active on campus. Most students are tolerant of the GLBT community, but as a whole, BC isn't incredibly welcoming towards people with sexual orientations other than heterosexual.

Students Speak Out
ON DIVERSITY

"Sadly, this campus is not all that diverse. Though BC is trying desperately to diversify, it's probably my least favorite aspect of the school. It's not a very accepting and open-minded campus, either."

Q "The problem with BC is that, since **there aren't many minorities represented on campus right now**, not many minorities are going to want to come to Chestnut Hill and be one of the few exceptions to the typical BC student. It's the chicken and the egg problem."

> "I thought Boston College was **plenty diverse**. I didn't really find any problems with it."

> "Students that come from different nations end up hanging out mostly with only students from their home countries. You could go through all four years of school and never know that someone from Puerto Rico, or any other country, went to BC as well. **It can get pretty cliquey at BC**, but that's probably expected."

The College Prowler Take
ON DIVERSITY

Cultivating a more diverse student body at Boston College may currently be the school's largest problem. The majority of students are Caucasian and middle- to upper-class. Walking across campus, that's probably all you'll see. A lot of students feel that it's not the school's fault that many of the people it attracts hail from similar backgrounds. Yet, BC is diligently working towards drawing individuals from different upbringings and social demographics, and the other students are becoming more accepting of what diversity it does have. Hopefully, this will help increase BC's diversity in the future. Overall, the school is aware of the lack of diversity on campus and is working to rectify the problem. **Many students are not the least bit uncomfortable with the demographics represented at the school, and others may press the issue.**

The College Prowler™ Grade on
Diversity: D-

A high grade in Diversity indicates that ethnic minorities and international students have a notable presence on campus and that students of different economic backgrounds, religious beliefs, and sexual preferences are well-represented.

Guys & Girls

The Lowdown
ON GUYS & GIRLS

Women Undergrads: 52%

Men Undergrads: 48%

Birth Control Available?
Because of the religious affiliation of the college, University Health Services does not provide birth control to students.

Social Scene
The social scene at Boston College is hectic for the first couple of years. On-campus drinking can be impossible, with the BCPD making their stern presence known loud and clear. Students don't want to run the risk of getting written up or getting slapped with housing probation that can shadow a student throughout his entire academic career. Boston College doesn't encourage drinking, and it certainly doesn't foster or tolerate underage drinking. Needless to say, many students find a way to play hard anyway.

Hookups or Relationships?
Hookups are way more popular since most of us are just looking to have fun. If you're looking for a relationship, you'll be able to find other people that are as well, but it's definitely easier to just date around.

Dress Code

The dress code at Boston College is widely known to be preppy. At times, it can seem that BC is the sole entity that keeps Abercrombie & Fitch in business. Many women like to dress up for class and show off their cute new outfits, whereas only a few guys bring out their exclusive wardrobes for an 11 a.m. seminar. Sweats and fleeces make appearances in many a class, especially the courses that start at 9 a.m.. Many BC students, when asked, could care less about their appearance. It is refreshing that the student body isn't entirely filled with Barbie and Ken dolls.

Students Speak Out
ON GUYS & GIRLS

"Students are mostly preppy, like at any private college. There aren't many 'alternative-looking' people, and everyone basically blends in. If you are looking for a lot of diversity, don't go to BC."

"We have a beautiful campus, and I'm not talking about the Gothic buildings. I personally believe the guys are hotter than the girls. **BC isn't really a dating school**, though. There are so many really attractive people that most people tend not to settle down and seriously date. That's not to say that I don't know a few couples, but there are many more single people running around than non-singles."

"A high emphasis is placed on appearance at BC, so many people just use whatever they have been blessed with to the best of their ability. It seems like **no one really experiments with looks**, so if you have originality, you will stand out on campus, for better or worse!"

"I personally think that we have a good-looking population. There are lots of pretty girls and the guys aren't too shabby either. It does seem like **everyone has the same look**, though. The girls are all into J. Crew and Abercrombie and a lot of the guys have come from private, Catholic, preppy schools, so most of them are boring dressers, too."

"The chicks here are hot, and there are more girls than guys. BC is **a very fit place**, so you don't see many overweight people here. On average, I think both the guys and the girls at BC are better looking than the ones at a lot of other schools that I have visited."

"Everyone looks the same for the most part. Girls are very fit and are usually perfectionists. Guys are usually of average height, and have **little fashion sense**. There is even something called a 'BC haircut' that guys can receive at local barber shops. It's just a basic short cut with spiky bangs."

The College Prowler Take
ON GUYS & GIRLS

Overall, Boston College is a remarkably attractive campus, although very homogenous. The girls are typically gorgeous (if by gorgeous you mean blonde, thin, wealthy, and smart). On the other hand, several students commented that BC guys, for whatever reason, are short and not very socially adept, though there are a few notable exceptions to this rule. Most students place a lot of emphasis on appearance, for better or for worse, so be prepared. This is not the kind of place where you walk around in ripped jeans and flip-flops, or come to class still in your pajamas. In some ways it's nice that everyone makes such an effort to look good, but it can also put pressure on you to look just as good, even when you have an early class and stayed up all night finishing a paper.

The College Prowler™ Grade on
Guys: B+

A high grade for Guys indicates that the male population on campus is attractive, smart, friendly, and engaging, and that the school has a decent ratio of guys to girls.

The College Prowler™ Grade on
Girls: A

A high grade for Girls not only implies that the women on campus are attractive, smart, friendly, and engaging, but also that there is a fair ratio of girls to guys.

Athletics

The Lowdown
ON ATHLETICS

Men's Varsity Teams:
- Baseball
- Basketball
- Cross Country
- Fencing
- Football
- Golf
- Ice Hockey
- Sailing
- Skiing
- Soccer
- Swimming and Diving
- Tennis
- Track and Field

Women's Varsity Teams:
- Basketball
- Cross Country
- Fencing
- Field Hockey
- Golf
- Ice Hockey
- Lacrosse
- Rowing
- Sailing
- Skiing
- Soccer
- Softball
- Swimming and Diving
- Tennis
- Track and Field
- Volleyball

Club Sports:
- Cheerleading
- Crew
- Cycling
- Karate
- Men's Lacrosse
- Men's Rugby
- Men's Soccer
- Men's Ultimate Frisbee
- Men's Volleyball
- Skiing and Snowboarding
- Women's Field Hockey
- Women's Lacrosse
- Women's Rugby
- Women's Soccer
- Women's Ultimate Frisbee
- Women's Water Polo

Men's Intramurals:
- Basketball
- Ice Hockey
- Racquetball
- Softball
- Squash
- Tennis
- Touch Football
- Volleyball

Women's Intramurals:
- Basketball
- Ice Hockey
- Racquetball
- Squash
- Tennis
- Touch Football
- Volleyball

Co-ed Intramurals:
- Doubles Racquetball
- Doubles Tennis
- Road Racing
- Softball
- Volleyball

School Mascot
Eagle

Athletic Division
Division I

Conference
Big East Conference

Getting Tickets
You will need tickets to go to the games, and almost everyone gets season tickets. To buy tickets, call (617) 552-GoBC.

Students Speak Out
ON ATHLETICS

"There are over 800 varsity athletes at Boston College. Intramural sports are also considerable. On the day of intramural sign ups, people get to the office to get in line at 9 a.m., and sign ups don't start until 4 p.m."

"Social life centers around the sports teams. Our big rivalry weekend, when we play against Notre Dame in football and hockey, is our biggest party weekend of the year."

Q "Make sure you get season tickets for football, hockey, and basketball games. Even if you can't go to a game, someone will buy the ticket from you. Everyone goes to games. My freshman year, **I didn't have tickets and felt very left out** when everyone I knew was at the football game. IM [intramural] sports are big, too. There are lots of sports to choose from and lots of people join them."

Q "Everyone goes to the football games and they are **usually all day events.** The other games are really fun as well. There are a bunch of IM sports including Frisbee, rugby, basketball, and softball which seem to be pretty popular."

The College Prowler Take
ON ATHLETICS

Sports are huge at BC! The one recent area of interest is the Atlantic Coast Conference, and the fact that BC is not in it. Much debate has revolved around the strength of the Big East Conference now that Miami has joined the ACC. Nevertheless, football, basketball, and hockey are the big three sports at BC, and pretty much everyone is in tune to how the teams are doing. Tailgating for football games is the highlight of many BC students' experiences. The spirit in the stadium is palpable and a total rush for any sports fan. BC prides itself on its athletic program, so you're bound to catch a solid basketball, hockey, or football season. If you're not into sports, BC might not be a great place for you. You don't have to get into sports, but you might feel a little left out as everyone revs up for game day and you don't really care.

The Lowdown
ON GREEK LIFE

Number of Fraternities: 0

Number of Sororities: 0

Students Speak Out
ON GREEK LIFE

"There is no Greek life at Boston College. I like to think that it's because we all just party together!"

Q "There are no fraternities and sororities on campus. At first I wasn't happy about this, but now that I'm older, **the idea of cliques, like sororities, seems really stupid**. At BC there are no 'cool' groups and no social hierarchies, which is a nice change from high school."

Q "There is no Greek life. **Jesuit schools don't have fraternities or sororities**. There are, however, plenty of off-campus parties to make up for that. Just walk up Commonwealth Avenue and you'll find plenty of parties, most of which you can just walk into and pay five dollars for a plastic cup for the keg."

The College Prowler™ Grade on
Athletics: A

A high grade in Athletics indicates that students have school spirit, that sports programs are respected, that games are well-attended, and that intramurals are a prominent part of student life.

> "We do not have frats or sororities, which I love. No one is 'cooler' or 'better' than anyone else, it's a really even social scene. And **it's not like we don't still have raging parties**!"

> "Boston College doesn't have any fraternities because it's a Catholic school and we're not allowed. But don't worry; **we still have a good time**. Most all of the juniors live off campus so they're always having parties, and I've been to quite a few frat parties at other schools around BC like Tufts and BU, and honestly, I wasn't that impressed. They're crowded, the people are trashy, and the guys are sleazy. We also have a huge emphasis on sports, so the teams, which are kind of our mini-version of frats, have parties a lot. Seniors that live on campus have good parties in the Mods, which is also a great place to tailgate before football games—another huge part of BC social life."

The College Prowler Take
ON GREEK LIFE

The lack of Greek life on campus will most likely not affect your overall experience at BC (unless you are into that sort of thing). At times, it can feel like there is a Greek life, especially if you take into consideration the Newton campus versus Upper campus allegiances and rivalries. Students from these two sections can get inexplicably territorial. Nevertheless, not having a Greek life is a positive asset of Boston College in many ways. Cliquish behavior, paying dues, and hazing are not areas that Boston College is in favor of promoting. Social interaction and mixing with groups should be encouraged, but Greek life, at times, runs the risk of alienating individuals.

The College Prowler™ Grade on
Greek Life: N/A

A high grade in Greek Life indicates that sororities and fraternities are not only present, but also active on campus. Other determining factors include the variety of houses available and the respect the Greek community receives from the rest of the campus.

Drug Scene

The Lowdown
ON DRUG SCENE

Most Prevalent Drugs on Campus:
Alcohol, marijuana

Liquor-Related Referrals: 0

Liquor-Related Arrests: 38

Drug-Related Referrals: 0

Drug-Related Arrests: 1

Drug Counseling Programs
Alcohol and Drug Education is a service run by the Office of the Dean for Student Development. This program helps students do personal assessments and find referral programs when necessary. They also help students find support groups or 12-step programs. For more information, go to: www.bc.edu/offices/ade/.

Students Speak Out
ON DRUG SCENE

> "**Police are overly strict concerning alcohol. They treat it like manslaughter, but they brush all drug violations under the rug, which is mighty convenient for the growing number of coke-heads on campus.**"

Q "The only hard drug use I have seen is marijuana, if that is even considered hard. **BC isn't a drug school**, it's a drinking school."

Q "The drug scene is not really big, although it depends on who you hang out with. If people are doing drugs, they're usually just smoking. **Drinking is a much more popular activity**."

Q "There's the usual amount of weed on campus. I'm not sure about the hard stuff, but I don't know anybody who does those things. There are **a couple of people who roll** sometimes, but other than that, it's not prominent."

Q "**The hardest thing I've seen on campus is weed**, though I'm sure that there are people doing harder things."

The College Prowler Take
ON DRUG SCENE

Alcohol is where it's at for BC. Whether it's house parties, the bar, or football games, people on campus love to drink. It can be difficult when you're under 21, because it seems like everyone is drinking but you, which might not be that far from the truth. The illicit drug scene is not at all out in the open. It fluctuates in its popularity, but is usually very quiet and not center stage (as alcohol is). While there are definitely people to see and places to go for any kind of drug under the sun, this type of activity isn't usually widespread or popular with the majority of students. The school and its officials do not condone drug use of any kind, under any circumstances, period.

The College Prowler™ Grade on
Drug Scene: B+

A high grade on Drug Scene indicates that drugs are not a noticeable part of campus life; drug use is not visible, and no pressure to use them seems to exist.

Campus Strictness

The Lowdown
ON CAMPUS STRICTNESS

What Are You Most Likely to Get Caught Doing on Campus?
Underage drinking, drugs, being rowdy

Students Speak Out
ON CAMPUS STRICTNESS

"What you can get away with really depends on your RA. Mine was great, so we got away with murder, but I know some others who really weren't cool at all."

Q "Campus police are extremely strict on drugs. If you're caught with marijuana, you will most likely be thrown out. They aren't too strict about drinking, but they're not lenient. If you get caught drinking, you will get some sort of punishment. By your second or third punishment, you will most likely be told to live off campus for the next semester or to take AA classes. If a BCPD officer sees you extremely drunk on campus, he will **take you to St. Elizabeth's hospital for the night**. Your parents and the school will be notified and you will get in trouble. I haven't found this campus too strict with drinking, though."

Q "The police force can be pretty strict about underage drinking and drug use. First-time offenders get a letter sent home, and second- and third-time offenders are in danger of losing their housing. **It's pretty serious if you get caught,** so my best advice is to do everything discreetly and not to be obnoxious about it. If you're going to drink then drink, but don't start advertising keg parties in your room. You will get busted!"

Q "BC is kind of known as a drinking school. There aren't many drugs just because everyone drinks so much. But, drugs are there to some extent; I guess it just depends on who you hang out with, like it would anywhere. I've never gotten in trouble for drinking or anything, but **they aren't exactly lenient**. I mean, if you get caught very obviously drunk, you'll probably get in trouble, and if you get caught in the act of drinking, you'll probably get in trouble as well, unless you're somewhere where seniors live because they're 21, like the Mods. Off campus at the juniors' parties you don't get in trouble either."

Q "It's not too hard to get liquor or to drink it. I guess you just can't be too obvious about it. Don't walk around campus stumbling because the police will take you to the infirmary and write you up. And if you're in your room, don't be too crazy. **How crazy you can be all depends on your RA.**"

Q "The police are semi-strict. I drink every weekend and have never been caught, but I know plenty who have been. It's all a matter of luck. The first time they catch you, **it's not bad at all, just a letter home**. I think it's three strikes and you're out of housing policy, but there are always parties on and off campus that never get busted."

The College Prowler Take
ON CAMPUS STRICTNESS

The BCPD are definitely strict about underage drinking and drug use, so you'll have to learn the ropes if you ever want to participate in the social scene. However, "work hard, play hard" is a BC motto, so serious fun certainly can and does occur. The first few months of every semester are always deemed "lock down," where the BCPD goes overboard in the strictness department. Usually it tapers off after a couple of weeks, so sit tight and drink quietly in your room. Keep the Beirut tournaments at a less than audible level, watch out for RAs, and try not to make any foolish mistakes. The campus usually maintains a level of strictness not unlike that of a federal penitentiary. Well, not quite that strict, but you get the picture.

Drug counseling information is available in *Boston College—Off the Record.* Find it at www.collegeprowler.com.

The College Prowler™ Grade on
Campus Strictness: C

A high Campus Strictness grade implies an overall lenient atmosphere; police and RAs are fairly tolerant, and the administration's rules are flexible.

Overall Experience

Students Speak Out
ON OVERALL EXPERIENCE

"Overall, it's a good school, as long as you meet the right people. I've had a hard time finding people that I click with, so my experience hasn't been as good as that of others."

"I love BC. There are obvious downsides that may tip the scales a different way for you in making your decision, but I think that **BC is the place I was meant to be**. I'm so happy here. I would never think of transferring."

"As a recent BC grad, the only place that I wish I were now is back there. The connections and relationships that you form while at a school like BC define the greatness that the University embodies. Unlike most schools in this country, your BC experience does not end after graduation. It follows you in everything you do, in every town or city you find yourself in. There will always be a BC grad looking to help you out, wanting to talk about how the campus is changing and what the football team's schedule looks like. It's a sensation that is unparalleled, and something that will truly **make you proud to say that you graduated from Boston College**."

"I loved BC. I had some good and bad experiences, but overall, I'm glad I came to BC and made the friends that I did. **I'm sure you'll have a good experience, too, if you choose BC**. It just depends on what you make of it and the friends you make. Just join a lot of activities and study hard, but remember to have fun."

"I have had **the best two years so far** at BC. I absolutely love it here. The teachers are great, and the classes are very interesting. The city has offered so many opportunities. I'm glad I'm here, and I don't want to be anywhere else."

"I don't think I'd be this happy anywhere else. **I absolutely love BC**. I'm not just trying to sell the school to you because, really, what would I get from that? I'm just telling you how I feel, and there are probably a lot of people at BC that don't like it as much as I do. All I know is that out of all of my friends from home that went away to school, I am the happiest and having the best time."

The College Prowler Take
ON OVERALL EXPERIENCE

The general feeling seems to be that Boston College is a wonderful school and an incredible experience. However, the first few years can be tough, as you may not be prepared for the enormity of the college experience. If you're from a very diverse high school, you will certainly be shocked by the very different atmosphere that will surround you at BC. Yet, staying the course is absolutely worth it, as Boston College is a wonderful institution with many dynamic people that will truly challenge and amaze you. If you give the school a little time to grow on you, it certainly will, and you'll be really glad you gave it a chance.

Keep in mind, even if you feel a little socially disoriented at first, that parties and tailgating are fun but they are not all that college is about. Remember that you are going to college to receive a college education, and Boston College will certainly deliver that and then some. Friendships flourish, enriching academics abound, and you will walk away a changed person.

The Inside Scoop

The Lowdown
ON THE INSIDE SCOOP

Things I Wish I Knew Before Coming to Boston College:
It doesn't always click right away for everyone. Give yourself time to adjust if you don't fall in love with Boston College during the first week.

> **Tips to Succeed at Boston College:**
>
> - Expand your friendship circles! Just because people live in your hall doesn't mean there aren't thousands of other very cool individuals to form relationships with.
> - "Study hard, play hard" actually does work.
> - Go away for spring break, either on service trips or somewhere tropical. You can see your hometown friends during the summer
> - Always check the PEPs before class selection.
> - Expand your friendship circles!

School Spirit
Students at BC have a lot of pride in their school. Come to a football game and you'll see what I mean.

Traditions
Most of our traditions center around sports. Students at BC go to games to cheer for their team. They tailgate before and party after. They also know every word of the fight song.

Finding a Job or Internship

The Lowdown
ON FINDING A JOB OR INTERNSHIP

> The Career Center is extremely helpful and contains many resources for you at pretty much every point in your college career, from choosing a major to picking a grad school or looking for your first real job.

Advice
If you are uncertain about anything, go talk to the people at the Career Center. They'll help you find the job or internship that's right for you. Also, don't think you're too young for career advice. Even as a freshmen, you can benefit from talking to them and making sure that you're on the right path to get where you want to be in the future.

Career Center
Southwell Hall
38 Commonwealth Avenue
Chestnut Hill, MA 02467
Fax: (617) 552-2584
Phone: (617) 552-3430
E-mail: careerc@bc.edu
http://careercenter.bc./edu

Career Center Resources & Services:
Internship placement, job advice, help choosing a major, grad school advising, interview skills, resume writing

Alumni Office
Boston College Alumni Association
825 Centre Street
Newton, MA 02458-2527
(617) 552-4700
(800) 669-8430
Fax: (617) 552-4626
E-mail: alumni.comments@bc.edu

Boston College graduates are your most valuable resource for establishing a career network, which is why the BC Alumni Career Network is so invaluable. These alumni have volunteered to provide career information, but not actual jobs. In short, you can ask them any career related question except, "Can I have a job?" But, their advice can be helpful.

The Alumni House
The Alumni House is located on Center Street in Newton Campus. It is home to the Boston College Alumni Association.

Alumni Welcome Center
The Alumni Welcome Center is located on the first floor of Vanderslice Hall. It is another place that alumni can go for more information on campus.

The Best & Worst

The Ten BEST Things About BC:

1. Gorgeous campus
2. Excellent education
3. Awesome athletics
4. Knowledgeable professors
5. Jesuit teaching
6. Beautiful people
7. Incredible atmosphere
8. Major history and tradition
9. New dorms
10. Senior Week

The Ten WORST Things About BC:

1. Minimal diversity
2. Depressing weather
3. Bad jeans on guys
4. Newton residents can be aggravating
5. Conceited, arrogant students
6. Some dorms need makeovers (Edmonds)
7. Overly-selective volunteer organizations
8. The BCPD are strict
9. Rude, unwelcoming administration officials
10. Moving in and out of dorms

Boston University

121 Bay State Road, Boston, MA 02215
www.bu.edu   (617) 353-2300

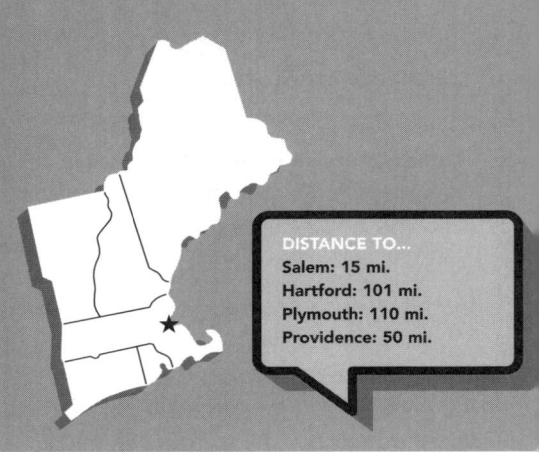

DISTANCE TO...
Salem: 15 mi.
Hartford: 101 mi.
Plymouth: 110 mi.
Providence: 50 mi.

"The most renowned professors aren't very accessible, and they have graduate assistants that do all the grading."

Total Enrollment:
16,248
Acceptance Rate:
52%
Tuition:
$30,402
Top 10% of High School Class:
60%
Average GPA:
3.5
SAT Range

Verbal	Math	Total
600 – 690	620 – 690	1220 – 1380

ACT Range

Verbal	Math	Total
25-30	25-29	25-30

SAT II Requirements
Writing and a foreign language test are strongly recommended for all applicants.
Most Popular Majors:
19% Social Sciences
18% Communications
17% Business
Students Also Applied To:*
NYU, Boston College, Northeastern University, Tufts University
*For more school info check out www.collegeprowler.com

Table of Contents

Academics	695
Local Atmosphere	697
Safety & Security	698
Computers	700
Facilities	702
Campus Dining	704
Off-Campus Dining	705
Campus Housing	707
Off-Campus Housing	709
Diversity	711
Guys & Girls	713
Athletics	715
Greek Life	717
Drug Scene	718
Campus Strictness	720
Overall Experience	721
The Inside Scoop	722
Finding a Job or Internship	724
The Best & Worst	725

College Prowler Report Card

Academics	B+
Local Atmosphere	A
Safety & Security	A
Computers	B+
Facilities	B+
Campus Dining	A+
Off-Campus Dining	A+
Campus Housing	C-
Off-Campus Housing	B+
Diversity	B-
Guys	C+
Girls	B+
Athletics	C+
Greek Life	D+
Drug Scene	C-
Campus Strictness	B

Academics

The Lowdown
ON ACADEMICS

Degrees Awarded:
Bachelor, Master, Doctorate

Undergraduate Schools:
School of Education, Goldman School of Dental Medicine, School of Hospitality Administration, School of Management, School of Medicine, College of Fine Arts, College of Arts and Sciences, College of Communication, College of Engineering, College of General Studies, Sargent College of Health and Rehabilitation Sciences, University Professors Program

Full-time Faculty:
2,350

Total Faculty:
More than 3,400

Faculty with Terminal Degree:
42.6%

Student-to-Faculty Ratio:
15:1

Average Course Load:
16 credits
(4 courses)

Special Degree Option

Several dual degrees are offered as double majors within colleges of the University: BUCOP—The Boston University Collaborative Degree Program (dual degrees awarded between colleges within the University); five-year B.A./M.A. program in the College of Arts and Sciences; five-year M.B.A. program in the School of Management; seven-year liberal arts/medical education program offers the B.A. and M.D.; and a seven-year liberal arts/dental education program offers the B.A. and D.M.D.; the College of Arts and Sciences and the School of Medicine jointly offer the eight-year Modular Medical Integrated Curriculum (MMEDIC), leading to a B.A. and M.D.

AP Test Score Requirements

Possible credit for scores of 3, 4, or 5, depending on specific requirements of the program.

IB Test Score Requirements

Possible credit for scores of 5 or better; call (617) 353-4492 for more information on IB.

Best Places to Study

The George Sherman Union is always a favorite place. Of course, we mourn the loss of the smoking lounge, which has fallen casualty to a more health-conscious nation. The "BU Beach," which acquired its name due to the sound of the "rushing" traffic against the "shore," is one of the few grassy areas on campus, and is always filled with students during good weather.

Did You Know?

The Core Curriculum Program is an option for the top candidates entering the College of Arts and Sciences department and is an excellent opportunity for those of us lacking specific direction or major. Core consists of eight historically-based, integrated courses providing an in-depth study of classic works in the humanities, natural sciences, and social sciences.

Students Speak Out
ON ACADEMICS

{ **"The chemistry department is awesome, but I didn't like my first taste of the biology department. The lectures are large, but other classes, such as my French and writing classes, were about 20 people."**

Q "A lot of classes are lectures, so you don't have any one-on-one time with your professors, but if you go to their office hours, they usually love to meet the students and help you out. **Some professors aren't so much interested in teaching as in hearing themselves talk**, but it's like that at all colleges, unfortunately."

Q "I hear that BU has some of the top professors around—**Elie Wiesel, for example, teaches classes in University Professors, theology, and core**—but the most renowned professors aren't very accessible and they have graduate assistants that do all the grading. It's a big school, and that's just the way it is. But, I have had some excellent professors who really care about their students and are very available. And some of the grad students aren't that bad either. They can be very good resources."

Q "**Freshman year, you'll have at least one class that is small**—a writing class that has 15 to 25 people in it. Other than that, most of the 100-level classes are large. The TFs [teaching fellows] are always glad to help out, but they don't teach the class and sometimes they don't speak English very well."

Q "The professors are mostly the same; they all love learning about their subject, and some even like teaching it, too. Usually it's the same deal, but **at least once a year, you'll find a great teacher**. Furthermore, most people would assume that taking required classes sucks, and yes, in fact, it does suck, but fortunately they're at least somewhat appealing—sometimes even fascinating—even if you don't care for the subject."

Q "Honestly, I think the whole idea of a core curriculum is generally whack, but ironically, **my core classes really weren't that bad**. And even though I didn't really do too well on the test—I'm a bad test taker, though, seriously!—I still enjoyed most of the classes overall, and I'd say I learned a lot of interesting things, too."

Q "What's most important about enjoying a class and professor at BU is getting past the 101 and introductory classes—most of them are so darn broad, and they pretty much suck. **Once you get more specific with regards to your personal interests, classes become much more enjoyable**. I found it difficult, though, to get a good rapport with professors that I enjoyed and respected because the majority of the classes were so huge."

The College Prowler Take
ON ACADEMICS

As with any university, the nature of any particular class is hugely dependent on the professor that is teaching it. Everyone seems to agree that the best way to choose a class is by first learning about the professor's teaching style from other students. While some professors fall into anonymity after the last day of class, some directly influence the course of your education. Don't get frustrated with your 100-level introductory classes; they are universally described as "a waste of time," "boring," and "impersonal." Get through your requirements, but just keep in mind that the best classes are the upper-levels.

The College Prowler™ Grade on
Academics: B+

A high Academics grade generally indicates that professors are knowledgeable, accessible, and genuinely interested in their students' welfare. Other determining factors include class size, how well professors communicate, and whether or not classes are engaging.

Local Atmosphere

The Lowdown
ON LOCAL ATMOSPHERE

Region:
Northeast

City, State:
Boston, Massachusetts

Setting:
Major City

Distance from New York City:
5 hours

Points of Interest:
Fenway Park, Boston Commons, Boston Public Gardens, Freedom Trail, Quincy Market and Faneuil Hall Marketplace, the North End, Newbury Street, the Charles River, Chinatown, Boston Symphony Orchestra, Boston Pops, Museum of Fine Arts, Museum of Science, the Institute for Contemporary Art, Isabella Stewart Gardner Museum, New England Aquarium (with IMAX).

Major Sports Teams:
Red Sox (MLB), Bruins (NHL), Celtics (NBA), Patriots (NFL)

City Website:
www.boston.com

Students Speak Out
ON LOCAL ATMOSPHERE

"There are tons of schools in the area: Boston College, Emerson, Simmons, and Northeastern, to name a few. Boston is also much different from, say, New York, because it is very student-oriented."

Q "**Boston is a college Mecca**. There are thousands of colleges in Boston alone, from BC and Emerson, to Berklee College of Music and Northeastern. There's Southie and Back Bay, and Copley is great. The Prudential and Newbury Streets are great for shopping. Chinatown is shady, but it has lots of little shops and great food."

Q "Boston is the place to be if you're a college student. **There are so many things you can do and visit**. There are shopping malls, nice restaurants, clubs, 'Broadway' shows, sporting events, and museums. Plus, the city is so rich with history. You learn a lot about the city in your first year. There are so many other colleges around BU. According to BU, there are about 88 other colleges in the city: Harvard, Boston College, MIT, Babson, Tufts, Brandeis, Northeastern, the University of Massachusetts, and others."

Q "Boston is such a college town. There are other colleges all over the place, and **the city has tons of culture**: museums, theater, opera, symphonies, concerts, and beautiful sites like the Public Gardens. There's a lot of historical stuff, too, as I'm sure you can imagine. A lot is nearby. New York is less than four hours away—great for long weekend road trips."

Q "Boston's one of those cities that's got a lot of different aspects. First off, everybody and their mother goes to school in Boston at one of the many colleges throughout the city and the outside suburbs. Also, **BU has so many darn people**, you meet a new friend, you see a new teacher, a new student, a new RA, and a new jerk, all in one day."

Q "**The vibe in Boston is chill if you are in the right area**; otherwise, you may find that the people are a bit on the conservative end, which is restricting at times. I advise you to search far and wide for the right atmosphere because it can be hard to find. Don't worry, it is there, and it is looking for you."

Safety & Security

The Lowdown
ON SAFETY & SECURITY

The College Prowler Take
ON LOCAL ATMOSPHERE

Boston is a city that is populated by thousands of students, due to the number of universities and colleges in the area. This is described by most students as one of the greatest benefits of attending BU. There is no reason to be stuck on campus. The best way to have a good experience at BU is to take full advantage of the city, itself.

Number of BU Police:
53

Number of BU Security Staff:
57

Number of Emergency Phones:
50

BU Police Phone:
(617) 353-2121

Health Center Office Hours
Walk-ins are available from 9 a.m. to 4:30 p.m. every day during the academic year, but the center is closed on University holidays. Mental Health is open from 9 a.m. to 5 p.m., during the academic year, with 24-hour emergency mental health care at (617) 353-3569 (or 3575). The infirmary is open 24 hours a day during the academic year, with visitation from 1 p.m. to 6 p.m. The Crisis Intervention counselors are available 24 hours at (617) 353-2121.

Safety Services
BU escort service, blue-light phones, red phones, Rape Hotline, Crisis Intervention Hotline, and self-defense classes, BU security staff, and BUPD

The College Prowler™ Grade on
Local Atmosphere: A

A high Local Atmosphere grade indicates that the area surrounding campus is safe and scenic. Other factors include nearby attractions, proximity to other schools, and the town's attitude toward students.

Did You Know?

The office of the vice president and dean of students, located in the GSU (George Sherman Union), distributes *The Lifebook*, which provides information about the details of daily life. This book is a helpful guide to security procedures and information on campus.

Students Speak Out
ON SAFETY & SECURITY

"BU has its own police force, the BUPD. They are real police officers, not just security guards, but we have those, too, in the dorms."

Q "**Security is a major issue at Boston University. It is very strict,** which is good and bad. It's good because you always feel safe and know no one is going to just stroll up and be let into your dorm; it's bad when it's 12:05 a.m. and you really need to sign someone in but you can't because you can only sign people in until midnight. You cannot just swipe into any of the dorms whenever you want, and the overnight guest policy is very strict: You have to hand in a signed form, from yourself and your roommate, 24 business hours in advance if it's a same sex visitor, and if it's an opposite sex visitor, then you must have a member of the opposite sex on your floor 'host' your visitor. But the RAs usually let your visitor stay with you, anyway."

Q "Boston University is very strict about who can and cannot enter dorms, and this is one of the biggest issues at Boston University that people get upset about. There are many dorms on campus, but unless it is a mealtime, you can only get into a dorm other than your own if you are signed in by someone who lives there. **After certain times, you can't sign anyone in**. So, while this helps keep the dorms safe, it can also get really annoying."

Q "The police have real cop cars and guns—the whole bit. There is also a 24-hour number you can **call to get free rides on campus** if you don't want to have to walk somewhere alone. Security here is very important since it is a major city, and it makes you feel very safe."

Q "**Security is structured completely backwards**. They spend so much time making sure security is as tight as possible in the freshmen dorms that the rest of BU seems to be completely overlooked. I don't think BU police patrol the streets where the majority of BU students live."

Q "**Since there really is no BU 'campus,' you're pretty much just getting around in the city**. If you're from a big city, then Boston seems pretty safe. As far as dorm safety, it's pretty much over-the-top. You definitely don't have to worry about strange bums coming into the dorms, but you also might have a big problem trying to get someone you met at the bar to stay with you overnight. Better make other plans, hot stuff."

The College Prowler Take
ON SAFETY & SECURITY

There is no question, students feel safe on campus. Most people even report feeling perfectly comfortable roaming the area alone at night. The overwhelming presence of campus security, however, does put a significant strain on student life in the dorms. Avoiding the larger on-campus housing options is universally suggested to decrease problems with the stringent guest policies and curfews enforced at BU.

The College Prowler™ Grade on
Safety & Security: A

A high grade in Safety & Security means that students generally feel safe, campus police are visible, blue-light phones and escort services are readily available, and safety precautions are not overly necessary.

Computers

Did You Know?

If you don't log out after a session on any of the campus computers, you are at risk. Your personal user name and password are necessary to gain access to your records. If you do not sign out of your session, it is possible for another individual to acquire this personal information about your academic status. The moral of the story? Don't forget to log out.

The Lowdown
ON COMPUTERS

Students Speak Out
ON COMPUTERS

Number of Labs:
37

24-Hour Labs:
ACS (UNIX cluster and central e-mail server) Help Desk, Campus Network, and Information Technology Computer Lab

High-Speed Network?
Yes. Boston University Campus Network (supporting up to 100 million bits per second).

Wireless Network?
Yes. Access is currently available in a growing number of locations, including Mugar Memorial Library, Science and Engineering Library, and the School of Law.

Operating Systems:
PC, Mac, Linux, and UNIX

Free Software:
ACS, Ethernet Campus Network

Charge to Print?
Each student receives up to 500 free pages per semester at the main computer lab on Cummington Street and most others on campus. At some of the smaller labs (CAS), the fee is 10 cents per page. You can use your BU ID card to print at a limited number of local photocopying businesses in the immediate area.

"One of the really nice things about college is the fast Internet connection, so you can download every song you ever wanted."

Q "The network at BU is great, and **every room has an Ethernet set up** for each person—the Ethernet is amazing. I would definitely bring your own computer, just for convenience, but the computer lab in my dorm, Rich Hall, was never crowded."

Q "The computer network is really fast, and it's cool because **people put stuff onto the network that is shared by everybody**, like music, and movies. I don't know what your major is, but if you can possibly get a computer to bring to school you should, even if it's just a really basic one. You'll probably be doing a lot of typing throughout the year, and having Internet access is really important for a lot of classes. There are computer labs near every dorm, if not in them, so if you don't have a computer don't freak out. But, I would definitely recommend one, even if only for the purpose of using Instant Messenger."

Q "Computer labs are pretty good, but usually pretty crowded. **When it comes time to write papers, midterms, and finals, it's crazy in the labs**. Your own computer is a really good idea. You just need to buy an Ethernet card; there is a connection in just about every part of campus. So it's well worth it."

Q "There's always a computer to be used. **My laptop broke, and I was too lazy to fix it for five months, but I still found a computer to use any time I needed one**. There are multiple computer labs, and all your friends will have them, too. Nevertheless, a personal computer is always preferable, but again, you don't need one. On the other hand, if you have your own, you'll usually have a fast connection to download music, games, programs, porn, notes, homework, cheat sheets—whatever you need—at a good speed."

Q "**The computer network is addictive**. That was definitely the only thing I was craving when I moved off campus. There are always tons of people in the main computer lab, and it's most crowded around lunchtime. But, besides the computer in your dorm, if you choose to bring one—which you should—there are other places that you can go to get onto the network."

Q "If you can afford it, get the computer. If not, there are plenty of facilities on campus, at a variety of locations that will be able to accommodate your Internet needs. **Prepare yourself for 20 to 40-minute waits when printing** at the main computer lab on Cummington Street. Here is a tip: go the printing center in Warren Towers during daytime hours. All campus facilities, in the spirit of socialism, have high-speed Internet."

The College Prowler Take
ON COMPUTERS

If you have the means to do so, bringing your own computer will save you a lot of hassle. The University provides Ethernet in all of the dorms, and it is pretty cheap to set up high-speed Internet even off campus. Almost all the facilities on campus are equipped with Internet connections, so a laptop is probably your best bet. If you do need to use campus computers, there are always people to help out, and printing is free at most locations. Unfortunately, the only major 24-hour computer lab tends to get really crowded, and if you're in a hurry, it can be frustrating—so leave yourself plenty of time. If you do bring your own computer, it will quickly become your most important asset. Not only is it a good tool for your academics, but it also allows you to stay in constant contact with friends from home and at school.

The College Prowler™ Grade on
Computers: B+

A high grade in Computers designates that computer labs are available, the computer network is easily accessible, and the campus' computing technology is up-to-date.

Facilities

Student Center
The George Sherman Union (GSU)

Athletic Center
The Case Athletic Center

Libraries
23 (2.3 million volumes; 29,389 periodicals; 4.1 million microfilm units)

Popular Places to Chill
The BU Beach, the GSU, the West Campus area/Nickerson Field, Marsh Chapel Plaza, Espresso Royale Café, and the Charles River Esplanade.

The Lowdown
ON FACILITIES

Movie Theatre on Campus?
The Nickelodeon (Nic), which recently shut down, was located on Cummington Street. It was used by BU to hold classes, but also operated as a fully functioning theatre. While there is currently no other theatre on campus, the rumor is that the Nic will be reopened within the next few years.

Bowling on Campus?
No bowling on campus, but bowling is available nearby.

Bar on Campus?
Yes. The notorious BU Pub is the only bar located on campus that is officially affiliated with the University. There are several other bars located on the Commonwealth stretch, including T's Pub, the Paradise Lounge, and several sports bars.

Coffeehouse on Campus?
Yes. The most popular café that attracts BU students (aside from the Starbucks' located in a variety of the buildings on campus) is Espresso Royale Café, or the ERC. This is a really chill place to study or socialize. Local artists display their contemporary work on the walls, amidst low lighting and comfy couches. Because BU students and professors hang out here it is a typical meeting ground for people of all ages.

Favorite Things to Do:

I spent nearly every day of my four years of college in the George Sherman Union smoking lounge. It was my study place, my meeting grounds, and my lunch break. Unfortunately, the smoking lounge is no more. During freshman year, I also hung out a lot outside at West Campus. Most of my activities occurred off BU grounds; that is sometimes your best bet.

Students Speak Out
ON FACILITIES

"The athletic center, Case, was recently renovated because it used to be small and crowded. The George Sherman Union is a big hangout and study center."

"Right now BU is building a lot of buildings. **They are constructing all new athletic facilities which should be really, really nice**, though who knows when they'll be done. The current ones are okay. There are a lot of gyms to work out at or play basketball in, and they have lots of fitness classes that you can take. There are some nice computer labs around, too, with a lot of computers. The student union is cool. Its main feature is the food court. The classrooms range from being really, really nice to kind of crappy."

Q "Certain colleges have older building than others. **Our sports center has been around for a while, but it's been well kept**. We have a swimming pool, ice rink, and a bunch of different courts in just one building. Our student center is pretty much just the George Sherman Union [the food court] or lounges in your individual dorms. If you're looking for a school with a strong sense of community, then you don't want this place. We're spread throughout the city, all within walking distance, but you don't get that community sense."

Q "The gym sucks, but it's being renovated and expanded soon. A lot of people go to the gym. **All the computer labs have Dell desktops, and they got a bunch of new ones last year**. The student center [GSU] is always filled with students. It's a nice place to eat dinner, watch a sports game, and get together with your friends."

Q "Everything on BU's campus is very nice. **It's either new or it's old but architecturally beautiful**. But, I will say that Commonwealth Avenue is the main road on campus, and it is a city campus, so it's very concrete-looking; no big fields of green grass like other places."

Q "Well, I wasn't one to exercise, but if you want a nice gym to work out in, Case Gym is the one to go to. It gets really crowded around and after dinner time, and you might have to fight people off for a turn on the elliptical machine. **The GSU—oh Lord, the GSU—was one of my favorite places to be**. I loved the smoking lounge, but because of the recent smoking law, it doesn't exist for your smoking 'n studying pleasure."

The College Prowler Take
ON FACILITIES

Recently, the administration has put a lot of money and effort into the improvement of the student facilities on campus. While students have noticed the improvements, no one seemed to be especially moved by the change. In comparison with other schools in the area, the university certainly has a large amount of money to play with, and most buildings are up-to-date and well-equipped for student needs.

The College Prowler™ Grade on
Facilities: B+

A high Facilities grade indicates that the campus is aesthetically pleasing and well-maintained; facilities are state-of-the-art, and libraries are exceptional. Other determining factors include the quality of both athletic and student centers and an abundance of things to do on campus.

Campus Dining

Did You Know?

Dining Services offers a variety of special events throughout the year, including a Visiting Chef Series; lobster, shrimp scampi, and prime rib dinners; a fondue festival; North End Dessert tour; and holiday meals.

The Lowdown
ON CAMPUS DINING

Freshman Meal Plan Requirement?
Yes

Meal Plan Average Cost: $3,358

24-Hour On-Campus Eating?
Just the Store 24s along Commonwealth Avenue and a couple Dunkin' Donuts off campus.

Student Favorites:
The GSU accepts BU dining points and convenience points at their food court, which is comprised of several independently-operating eateries, including Burger King, Aesop's Bagels, Jamba Juice, Starbucks, Caprizzi, Copper Kettle (soup), Cranberry Farms (Thanksgiving-style food year round), D'Angelo's Subs, and Tuscan Oven Pizza. There is also a salad bar, fruit bar, yogurt, sushi, and snacks. Ferretti's is another popular place for on-campus eating. They have really good sandwiches that are fashioned similarly to Au Bon Pain, bagels, gourmet coffee, fruit salad, scones, and muffins.

Students Speak Out
ON CAMPUS DINING

"Dorm food is so-so. It tastes good at first then gets old, fast! I think this is typical of all schools, though. I like our meal plan, where you use a 'meal' and then it's all-you-can-eat."

Q "The food is really good. It does however get repetitive in the dining halls, and that's when the student union comes in handy. The University gives you a certain amount of 'dining points' that you use there. **Cash is a thing of the past**. The student union has Burger King, D'Angelo's subs, Pasta Works, Country Kitchen (really good homestyle food), and Tuscan Oven (pizza and calzones)."

Q "BU's dining halls are, by far, some of the best in the country. **My favorite dining hall is in the Towers, which is a mostly freshman dorm**. If you have the choice, I definitely recommend living there. Besides the dining halls, there are tons of places around campus with all different types of cuisine. My favorite is Angora Café. It has salads, sandwiches, and it's cheap!"

Q "Food isn't really all that bad. Of course it's going to be somewhat bad—it's dorm food. However, **they make a good effort to meet the dietary needs of everyone**, and the food is decent because they have to feed wealthy international students."

Q "My preference is definitely West Campus. **The dining hall there is set up like a restaurant more than a cafeteria**. The smaller dorms are also nice, like Shelton and Myles. Warren really isn't that bad, and it's open until 12 a.m. for late-night eating, so if you live in Warren, and most freshmen do, it's really not as bad as it's made out to be."

Q "**On-campus food is actually pretty good**. They have annual lobster nights—that's when the line is out the door."

Q "While you'll hear all the students complain, **the food is actually very good compared to all the other universities and colleges around**. Just about every dorm has its own dining hall where you can get breakfast, lunch and dinner."

Off-Campus Dining

The College Prowler Take
ON CAMPUS DINING

While it is not uncommon to hear complaints about the food, all students will agree that BU is actually pretty hooked-up in that department. There is a lot of variety and tons of places to use your meal plan around campus. The big suggestions for getting your money's worth are to check out the specialty nights and the smaller eateries on campus. The presentation is very well done, too, so even if it doesn't taste right, it looks like it should. After four years, though, monotony sets in, and you won't care how good the food is supposed to be—it all looks the same after a while.

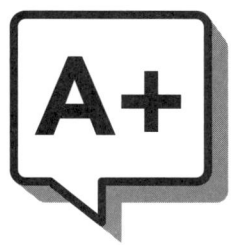

A+

The College Prowler™ Grade on
Campus Dining: A+

Our grade on Campus Dining addresses the quality of both school-owned dining halls and independent on-campus restaurants as well as the price, availability, and variety of food.

The Lowdown
ON OFF-CAMPUS DINING

Best Pizza:
The Upper Crust

Best Chinese:
P.F. Chang's

Best Breakfast:
Cookin' Café

Best Wings:
Wing It

Best Healthy:
Angora's Café

Best Place to Take Your Parents:
Any of the restaurants in the North End (Bella Vista is a favorite).

Student Favorites:
T-Anthony's is like *90210*'s Peach Pit. It is practically encrusted with BU paraphernalia and students and located at the central location in West Campus. T's serves pizza, subs, and pretty decent Italian food. They also have really good smoothies and breakfast foods. If the BU crowd makes you lose your appetite, this isn't the place to be.

24-Hour Eating:
Boston is definitely lacking in the 24-hour department. There is only one 24-hour diner, and it is way downtown.

Late-Night Snacking

For late-night munchies, hit up a Store 24 or a Dunkin Donuts. Drew and Greg's late-night cookies delivers hot, freshly baked cookies to your door, but only until midnight (1-866-EAT-LATE). BU offers Late-Night Cafes around campus at all of the traditional dining halls. Late-Night usually offers quesadillas, stir-fry, fried food, cookies, beverages, and the ever-popular giant rice crispy treats.

Students Speak Out
ON OFF-CAMPUS DINING

"Off campus, Boston offers plenty of restaurants. The possibilities are truly endless, so it depends on what kind of food you want. Vinny Testa's is great to start with; it is Italian food with huge portions."

Q "The Elephant Walk is a really good, kind of pricey, French and Cambodian place. It sounds weird, but it's really good. **The restaurants on Newbury Street, (the popular shopping and eating street) are all pretty good and semi-pricey**. The North End is all Italian food—really good and kind of pricey. California Pizza Kitchen is good and Legal Sea Foods is good for seafood, which is very popular in the New England area."

Q "You can find lots of stuff on Commonwealth Avenue, where BU is situated. **Clio is one of the hot spots, and so is the Thai House**. If you want to go off Commonwealth Avenue, then you can hop the green line to Newbury Street or the Prudential."

Q "Boston has a lot of good restaurants—Ginza for Japanese, Angora's for wraps and really good fro-yo. **If you go to BU, then you eat pizza at T's**, and go to Rangoli's for Indian, Sunset Grill for like five-million beers on tap, Cheesecake Factory in the Copley Mall, P.F. Chang's for really good Chinese, and the Middle East for excellent—guess—middle eastern food; it's also a venue that usually has some pretty good, cheap shows."

Q "Boston has a good selection of restaurants; I should know, I eat out all the time. **If you like the vegetarian ordeal, hit up Buddha's Delight**, either in Brookline or in Chinatown. If not, Grasshopper isn't bad either. If you are down for the deli, this city isn't going to satisfy your needs, unless you go to Rubin's or Zaftigs, which are both on Harvard Avenue in Brookline. For Italian, you can always be sure to get a good meal in a little trattoria in the North End. I always liked to eat at the Pour House on Boylston Street because it is really cheap and has a good atmosphere. Near campus, try An Tua Nua—there is good music, good food and drinks, good prices, and good people."

Fun Fact

Try Chinatown for a night out—not only is it home to the best Chinese food in Boston, but most restaurants serve alcohol without requesting identification. Depending on your situation, this is a very desirable scenario!

The College Prowler Take
ON OFF-CAMPUS DINING

Students all have suggestions and favorite restaurants for just about every type of cuisine you can imagine. There are virtually no complaints regarding the food in Boston. Restaurants off campus present as much variety as the city itself—they offer pretty much everything. Going out to eat is definitely a popular activity, and the prices actually tend to be pretty reasonable, especially around campus.

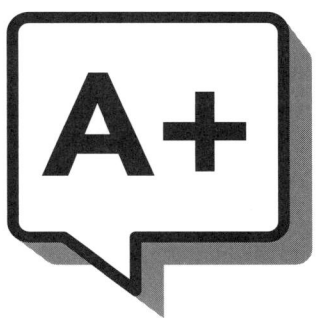

The College Prowler™ Grade on
Off-Campus Dining: A+

A high Off-Campus Dining grade implies that off-campus restaurants are affordable, accessible, and worth visiting. Other factors include the variety of cuisine and the availability of alternative options (vegetarian, vegan, Kosher, etc.).

Campus Housing

The Lowdown
ON CAMPUS HOUSING

Number of Dormitory Residents:
10,776

Undergrads on Campus:
68%

Number of Dormitories:
13

University-Owned Apartments:
The majority are located in the South Campus area, along Buswell Street, Arundel Street, Mountfort Street, St. Mary's Street, and Park Drive. There are also some on Bay State Road, Commonwealth Avenue, at the Hamilton House, and at the student residence on Buick Street.

Available for Rent
Micro-fridges

Cleaning Service?
The Physical Plant takes care of all of the cleaning services at BU. Public spaces are kept clean daily, as are communal bathrooms in the large dormitories. There is no private room cleaning service that is provided by BU.

Bed Type:
Twin extra-long for all beds. In some of the dorms, there are bunk-beds available. BU also sells "Rack Raisers," available in various sizes to loft your bed.

You Get

Dormitories: Each student receives a bed, desk (with storage space), chair, closet, dresser, Ethernet port, phone line, and mirror.

Apartments: Each student receives a bed, kitchen facilities, bathrooms, living area furnishings, desk chair, eating table and chairs, closet space, dresser, Ethernet port, telephone line, and mirrors.

Room Types

- Double, triple, and quad room (standard minimum fee).
- Multiple occupancy room in suite.
- Suite in 1019 Commonwealth Ave. and Shelton Hall.
- Single without private bath.
- Single with private bath.
- Apartment with two or more students.
- Single room in an apartment, including student residence at 10 Buick St.
- Apartment with one student.

Did You Know?

The new Student Village was just completed about three years ago. While the complex is by far the most "luxurious" on-campus living on BU campus, be warned: The Village gives the overwhelming sensation of life in a sanitarium. The entire complex works on central air and heat. For safety reasons, all of the "windows" are sealed shut. Now try to picture five people squeezed in a bathroom, attempting in vain to aim the smoke from their after-school activities up towards the ventilation duct on the ceiling for it to be re-circulated throughout the building. If fresh air is your thing, stay away.

Students Speak Out
ON CAMPUS HOUSING

"Dorm life is no fun. It's honestly horrible. Security guards just make living in the dorms a drag, a big fat drag. We hate them, and they hate us. It's a well-known fact."

Q "**Definitely avoid Warren Towers**. It's where most freshmen get put, but it's a hellhole. Regardless, it is the best for freshmen because it's small and you get to know everyone on your floor really well. Also, there are the brownstones, which are renovated and are very nice. It's kind of hard to make a lot of friends if you start out there, and it's hard to get into them, but if you can, go for it! West Campus is really far away from the main campus, unless you're in the College of General Studies."

Q "The dorms are decent. Warren Towers is okay, but very convenient due to its location. Plus, you can make a lot of new friends since its three towers are connected together and house about 1,400 students in all. **If you're lucky, you can get an awesome view of the Boston skyline**. All the nice dormitories are located in West Campus, but you'd be pretty far from your school, at least a 15-minute walk from the main part of the campus. The Towers are not coed by floor. All of the girls are on one floor, and all guys are on another."

Q "**Dorm life sucks**. Get out of the dorms as soon as you can. BU dorms are the worst on the planet, so my advice is not to give them more money than you already are. Get off campus, where you can be a real person once again."

Q "The dorms that you will likely get as a freshman [Warren Towers or West Campus] are like most freshman dorms—**small and cramped**. I guess they are part of the college experience, though. Some of the nicer ones that you could later get into are Shelton, Myles, and the best one by far, the Student Village—but most people have no chance of getting into it, ever."

Q "Dorm life is normal I guess. But you should always avoid stumbling in when you're not conscious of what you are doing. Otherwise, **it can be a mess. Trust me**, I've seen it. For freshmen, the dorms stink; you get tiny rooms with a lot of people all stuffed together. I mean come on, the hallways are wider than the rooms themselves, and doesn't that mean anything? Anything!"

Q "**Dorm life is exciting at first**, and then it starts to suck after you go visit friends who already moved off; then you get jealous. I had a great time in West Campus; it gives you that campus feel that you can't ordinarily get from BU. I guess Warren is a great place if you're a freshman, because you meet lots of people. Myles is nice, Shelton has great rooms, but I haven't been to Danielson cause it's too darn far away!"

Off-Campus Housing

The Lowdown
ON OFF-CAMPUS HOUSING

Undergrads in Off-Campus Housing: 30%

Average Rent for a Studio Apartment: $950 per month

Average Rent for a One-Bedroom Apartment: $1,100 per month

Average Rent for a Two-Bedroom Apartment: $1,500 per month ($750 per person)

Average Rent for a Four-Bedroom Apartment: $2,800 per month ($700 per person)

Popular Areas: Allston/Brighton, Brookline, Boston, Cambridge

Best Time to Look for a Place
Everyone starts apartment hunting really early, and the good stuff goes fast. Get yourself organized around February to ensure a spot in a nice place. Luckily, subletting is rampant in this city—if you are stuck without a place to live, it is always possible to find a room. The BU campus is littered with flyers requesting roommates.

For Assistance Contact
Web: *www.bu.edu/orientation/och/index.html*
Phone: (617) 353-3523
E-mail: *oocs@bu.edu*

The College Prowler Take
ON CAMPUS HOUSING

Freshmen are usually relegated to Warren Towers or West Campus. There are loads of complaints about both, but you will be able to make the most of either. Warren Towers is conveniently located, and the sheer number of people crammed together basically guarantees that you will make interesting friends. West Campus can also be a great place to live freshman year. It is not as conveniently located, but, on the other hand, its distance from the rest of campus means you can escape the incessant motion of daily life there—which is often a very good thing! It is also the only area with a grassy spot to hang out on. Kids are often hanging out outside, playing the guitar, smoking, talking, and generally interacting with one another—a sight rarely seen in city campus life.

The College Prowler™ Grade on
Campus Housing: C-

A high Campus Housing grade indicates that dorms are clean, well-maintained, and spacious. Other determining factors include variety of dorms, proximity to classes, and social atmosphere.

Students Speaks Out
ON OFF-CAMPUS HOUSING

{ "Many places are right down Commonwealth Avenue and close to the T stops. BU is a large campus, and everything is a little bit of a walk, but you get used to it quickly!"

Q "**Most people don't move off campus until junior year**. Apartments are usually rundown and very expensive. There are decent on-campus choices, especially the newer buildings that have been popping up."

Q "It's expensive, I'll tell you that. **The best place to get an apartment off campus, in my opinion, is Brookline**. It's a five-minute T ride from campus, and it's a great neighborhood, but like I said, it's expensive. I'm paying around $700 a month for a four-person apartment—that's per person! Get out early if you're looking for rooms, though, because there is always a rush for off-campus housing."

Q "Off-campus housing seems easy to find. **Real estate in Boston is pretty expensive**, though. It's fairly convenient because BU isn't really a campus, so you can live in off-campus housing and still be on campus."

Q "Honestly, I think **you'd be a fool to think that living on campus is better**. First off, living almost anywhere except for BU dorms is usually cheaper. You've saved some money, yeah!"

Q "**Off-campus housing also includes the conveniences of no security guards, or security tapes** for that matter. And of course, the RAs; they'll undoubtedly piss you off, but if you get off-campus, you're good to go. So concerning the question as to whether it is worth it or not to move off campus, it would definitely be worth it; in fact, it'd be stupid not to move off campus, unless you have to stay for financial aid or a scholarship, but that's just another BU control mechanism."

Q "Personally, I wanted to stay on campus for my sophomore year because I was still meeting my friends and getting into the swing of things. I definitely would have wanted to move off by junior year. **Rent is pretty expensive, but so is living on campus**, so you can convince your parents with a bunch of numbers you threw together for your monthly budget that it's actually cheaper to live off—who knows if it is, really, but it's definitely worth it. But, if you move off and decide you don't like it and want to come back on, BU gets very upset with you and you'll probably have a tough time. Odds are, though, that you'll want to stay off."

The College Prowler Take
ON OFF-CAMPUS HOUSING

The consensus is that campus life is a benefit to your social life for freshman year. After that, it is time to move out. If freedom is an issue, and you intend to have visitors from off campus for overnight stays, the visitor policies can be really stifling. Partying is notoriously difficult in on-campus living, and if you are looking for privacy, off-campus housing is the only way to go. Bear in mind though, it is very expensive!

The College Prowler™ Grade on
Off-Campus Housing: B+

A high grade in Off-Campus Housing indicates that apartments are of high quality, close to campus, affordable, and easy to secure.

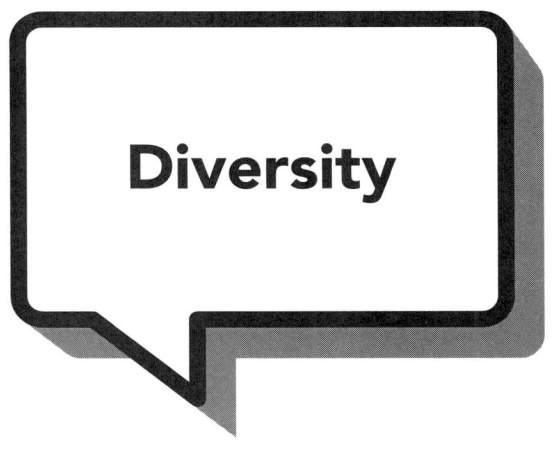

Diversity

Political Activity
There are a bunch of political groups on campus. They tend to be most prevalent on campus during times of political distress in the world beyond BU. Due to the recent events in the United States and abroad, the political scene has dramatically increased in visibility. The GSU held several events this past year, including an open public debate and discussion about the issues surrounding the situation in Israel and Palestine.

Gay Tolerance
In general, there sometimes seems to be more gay men on campus than straight ones. The lesbian scene is slightly more concealed, but definitely prevalent. And Boston tends to be extremely tolerant to all forms of sexuality. There are several gay clubs in Boston, and most of them are more fun than the typical club scene.

Economic Status
The Boston University student body spans a wide range of economic backgrounds; however, the majority of students are middle- to upper-class.

The Lowdown
ON DIVERSITY

African American: 2%

Asian American: 12%

Hispanic: 5%

Native American: 0%

White: 74%

International: 7%

Out-of-State: 78%

Minority Clubs
There is a club or organization working to represent nearly every minority group on campus. While some are certainly more visible than others, the amount of activity is the result of the effort put forth by the members of the individual group. Due to the size of the University, there is literally something for everyone.

Most Popular Religions
Catholic: 38.8%; Protestant: 23.8%; Jewish: 12.5%; other: 9.0%; none: 19.4%

Students Speak Out
ON DIVERSITY

"Campus diversity is one of the things that drew me to BU. I believe that there is a mixture of students here from all different backgrounds and classes. Gay, straight, white, black, Asian—we have everyone here."

Q "There are so many international students, and they are so nice. **My roommate was from Venezuela**, and one of my best friends was from Argentina. There is someone for everyone at this school."

Q "BU is internationally diverse, but **it's only around three percent African American**. There is a large Asian population. In general, the student body is fairly liberal and accepting of all races, ethnicities, and varieties of sexual orientation."

Q "There are two kinds of people on campus—**the children of rich parents, and those who can't stand the children of rich parents**. There is BU's diversity. Practically the only minorities at the University are the international students, who tend toward the School of Management and BMWs. Coming from New York City, diversity is something I miss at BU."

Q "**The campus is very diverse in both culture and personality**. Many foreign students from Europe, Asia, and the Middle East attend. BU greatly opened my eyes to these cultures and to new ways of looking at things and thinking about such issues on my own. No one should have a problem finding their niche—there is a group for everyone to run with."

Q "BU is not as diverse as the University purports, but if you take the right classes you will find that diverse opinions certainly abound. Also, in the last few years more and **more eclectic personalities have come to BU**— that means the kids who listen to the hip music, the club music, the rap, the rock, the Phish hits, the classical—yeah, they are all here. As for ethnicity, most of the kids are white, but there are a lot of international kids, depending on what school or classes you are in. SMG [School of Management] attracts many international students because of its renowned programs. If you take an African American studies class, chances are that you will be in a class with a lot of African Americans—the same goes for Asian studies classes."

The College Prowler Take
ON DIVERSITY

According to statistics, the majority of Boston University is white, middle- to upper-class students. Nevertheless, many individuals that I spoke to regarding diversity on campus reported a large amount of personal exposure to minority groups on campus. Due to the size of the University, even small percentages of students may seem like a whole lot of people. Depending on your classes, your participation in campus events, and choice of social scene, you may or may not feel the effects of the comparatively low percentages of minority groups at BU.

The College Prowler™ Grade on
Diversity: B-

A high grade in Diversity indicates that ethnic minorities and international students have a notable presence on campus and that students of different economic backgrounds, religious beliefs, and sexual preferences are well-represented.

Guys & Girls

The Lowdown
ON GUYS & GIRLS

Women Undergrads: 66%

Men Undergrads: 34%

Birth Control Available?
There is a Planned Parenthood in West Campus on Commonwealth Avenue. Planned Parenthood offers gynecological exams, all forms of birth control presently available (including free condoms), the emergency contraceptive pill (without an appointment), STD testing, abortion services, and family planning. For more information, you can call Planned Parenthood at (617) 616-1600.

Social Scene
Surprisingly, there is a lot less interaction in classrooms and around campus than you might hope. It is generally not the place to meet people. On any given day, students are usually clumped together, in prepackaged social circles. It is much easier to meet people off campus, and after academic hours.

Hookups or Relationships?
Freshman year is a sexual explosion. Hooking up is the only way to go. After that, and especially once you start finding your scene, people tend to pair off—at least for a while. But most people date individuals that they met outside of campus life.

Hookups or Relationships? (Continued....)
By graduation, relationships either last or they don't. Either way, you can expect drama. With all of the moving around and general dispersal of your social circle, it is not easy to deal with a serious relationship.

Dress Code
Sitting along the sidewalk of Commonwealth Avenue can often feel like a model runway. As soon as the winter breaks, no matter what the temperature, the girls and guys on campus shed their layers and expose their recent acquisitions from the French Connection, Prada, Gucci, D&G, and Armani Exchange. For those who are less materialistic, try out this favorite activity: on a sunny day in spring, sit on Commonwealth Avenue, directly in front of a dip or crack in the cement—for good results, try the one to the left of the Tsai Center at the College of Arts and Sciences. Due to the fact that over half of the student body clip-clops around in high heels, this provides for an exciting afternoon. There is nothing better than watching some self-enraptured BU chick trip in heels and then pretend like nothing happened. Try it!

Students Speak Out
ON GUYS & GIRLS

"There are lots of hot guys and girlies, but there are lots of snobs, too. Expect to get looked down upon if you're on financial aid or if you're not a trust fund baby."

Q "The girls on and around BU are pretty stuck-up. **Sorry for the stereotype, but it's so true**. If you don't know what I mean—they dress in expensive clothes and wear high heels all the time. They are constantly on their cell phones, they take three hours to get ready, they're annoying as hell, and they wear a lot of perfume. But that's just my opinion."

Q "**The campus is 60 percent girls**, 40 percent guys. So for us guys, it's nice. The females, for the most part, are hot, yet some can be stuck-up. Overall, we are an attractive campus."

"The guys and girls vary. **Some are really hot, and some are really not**. However, a lot of the women are Prada-wearing Gucci pushers, and the guys are pretty much the same. However, you do find your niche; there are so many people, that it doesn't really matter. One thing is there are more women than men, and a good number of the men are gay. I have been told there is a drought of good straight men—keep that in mind."

"**There are lots of girls, and way too few guys**. Of course, it is very easy to hook-up; it is college after all, and the boys are seemingly just going nuts. Suitable mates, on the other hand, are definitely more difficult to come by. The effects of the low population of males as compared to females is felt, but [it's] not the end of the world. There are plenty of places to go to seek out members of the opposite sex; just step outside."

"Supposedly, there are more girls in the Boston area than guys. **There are so many different colleges, universities, and programs in Boston**—however, there are so many different types of people who are drawn to the area. It is not hard to meet someone with your interests—you just have to know where to look."

The College Prowler Take
ON GUYS & GIRLS

If you are a guy, and you have just a glimmer of personality, intelligence, or looks, you are way ahead. There are girls to go around, and around again. The student body is notoriously described by those both on and off campus as shallow and materialistic. This is obviously not universally accurate, but BU certainly serves up its fair share of these sorts of individuals. And, as the University populated by nearly 70 percent females, the selection of suitable males is certainly slim. If the good ones aren't taken, they are usually gay. In fact, many of your relationships may end up being with people you meet off campus—yet another benefit of city living. Overall, finding people at such a huge university is easy; finding your niche, however, takes some time.

The College Prowler™ Grade on
Guys: C+

A high grade for Guys indicates that the male population on campus is attractive, smart, friendly, and engaging, and that the school has a decent ratio of guys to girls.

The College Prowler™ Grade on
Girls: B+

A high grade for Girls not only implies that the women on campus are attractive, smart, friendly, and engaging, but also that there is a fair ratio of girls to guys.

Athletics

The Lowdown
ON ATHLETICS

Getting Tickets
The ticket office is located in the Case Athletic Center. For information on ticket sales, call (617) 353-3838.

Fields
BU Softball Field: A grass field that is used for various team practices.

Nickerson Field: Acts as the facility for the men's and women's soccer and women's lacrosse teams. It is a 10,412-seat "FieldTurf" facility. The former football field of Boston University was also once the field of the Boston Braves National League baseball club, until it was purchased. Nickerson Field is also home to the Boston Breakers, which is the city's first professional women's soccer team.

Men's Varsity Teams:
Basketball
Crew
Golf
Cross Country
Ice Hockey
Track
Soccer
Softball
Swimming
Tennis
Wrestling

Women's Varsity Teams:
Basketball
Crew
Golf
Cross Country
Track
Soccer
Softball
Swimming
Tennis
Field Hockey
Lacrosse

Athletic Division:
Division I

Conference:
America East, Hockey East (hockey), Colonial Athletic Association (wrestling)

Most Popular Sports:
Hockey is definitely the most popular sport at BU.

School Mascot:
Rhett, the Boston Terrier (for those of you not up on your dog breeding information, the Boston Terrier is, quite simply, a little, yippy dog).

Club Sports
Badminton, baseball, cycling, dance team, equestrian, fencing, figure skating, gymnastics, ice hockey, in-line hockey, Kung Fu, lacrosse, rugby

Intramurals
Three-on-three basketball, five-on-five basketball, beach volleyball, flag football, floor hockey, ice broomball, indoor soccer, innertube water polo, outdoor soccer, softball, swimming, tennis, volleyball

Students Speaks Out
ON ATHLETICS

"Varsity hockey is great. I haven't missed a home game yet, especially considering that we are nationally-ranked and most of our starting players go on to the NHL."

Q "BU is not known really for sports. **We don't have a football team, they got rid of it over six years ago**; our major sport is hockey. We are awesome at hockey and win the Beanpot (a competition between Harvard, Northeastern, Boston College and BU) almost every year, but that's about it. Intramurals are big, and most of my friends are on some kind of team."

Q "**All varsity sports are Division I, but hockey gets the largest turnout** in terms of fans who actually attend the games. Basketball would be the second largest, and we also have soccer teams. Our school spirit isn't on the level of UNC or Duke, but if you enjoy watching sports you can attend all games for free. IM [intramural] sports are available as well and offer pretty much anything you might want to play. You have to attend an informational meeting where you sign up to play on a team."

Q "Who said varsity sports? **I am not to keen on the whole Abercrombie jock world**. There isn't too much of one anyhow. I know there is a soccer team, but they are far from varsity. Nice guys, though. I know them. Really, I even have an autograph."

Q "Sports are pretty much negligible at BU, unless you are part of some genetic upper caste. **The people that I have come across who play sports decided to do so out of necessity, usually scholarships**, and later despised it. They did not have time to associate with, let alone befriend, those people who lacked the physical prowess to run around with balls and wrestle one another in loosely fitting Speedos."

Q "**BU is humongazoid, there are so many different social circles to roam in**, so the answer is it is big in some social realms of the school—there will always be 'jocks' when there are universities to recruit them. If you want to establish a community within BU, sports is one venue to do it in. Hockey is the major attraction. Case Gym can be the place to pick up some hotties. However, for those on campus who prefer not to engage in sports, you will not be ostracized or considered a dork if you do not join the cheerleading squad or pep team."

The College Prowler Take
ON ATHLETICS

About half of the students interviewed were totally unaware of the athletic scene at BU. The remaining students pretty much agreed that there are a decent amount of athletic opportunities for those who are interested. The athletic facilities are rapidly improving with the new addition of the Tennis and Track Center at the Student Village. There seems to be more attention being paid to BU athletics by the administration over the past two years. Hockey is, by far, the most celebrated varsity sport at BU. While BU is not a huge sports Mecca, pretty much everything is offered: Frisbee, golf, basketball, snowboarding, even sailing, and lots, lots more. But—and this is a very big but—there is no football team, so if that is your thing, your best bet is to look elsewhere.

The College Prowler™ Grade on
Athletics: C+

A high grade in Athletics indicates that students have school spirit, that sports programs are respected, that games are well-attended, and that intramurals are a prominent part of student life.

Greek Life

The Lowdown
ON GREEK LIFE

Number of Fraternities:
8

Number of Sororities:
9

Percent of Undergrad Men in Fraternities:
3%

Percent of Undergrad Women in Sororities:
4%

Students Speak Out
ON GREEK LIFE

"Greek life is seven percent of the student body, which is not very dominating at all. Frat parties are lame. Sororities are there if you like them, but there are no houses because of Massachusetts state law."

Q "**Greek life is approximately 10 percent of the population**. I myself am in a sorority, and it is a great way to meet tons of people all at once. Formal rush is in January for freshmen. There are eight sororities and about just as many fraternities."

Q "**The Greek life is there if you want it**, but it definitely does not dominate the social scene. I think that is true for most urban schools. You will have plenty to do off campus, and a lot of people prefer to explore Boston's nightlife instead of the frats. If you want Greek life it's there, and those who attend [the parties] on a regular basis enjoy them. It's not really my scene, though."

Q "Boston University and the student population in the Boston area are both so large that the **Greek life definitely gets lost in the mix**. Those who seek it out will find it, and others who steer clear of that sort of thing will have no problem avoiding it. Unless you consciously choose to become involved with the Greek system, you normally never hear about it."

Q "**Greeks are present at BU, but not overwhelming**. I would say you really need to look around to find a frat. You are certainly not obligated to be in one to have friends, but people seem to be pretty close with their brothers. Mostly, the frat houses are just places to go and party on weekends."

Q "Greek is not life on campus. It is for a small percentage of students, but it is not considered to be the coolest or best kind of student organization to get involved with. Other organizations and kids throw parties that are just as good, if not exponentially better than the Greeks. Also, **many of the Greeks follow the dumb stereotypes of the MTV reality shows**—keep that in mind when pledging. It dominates the scene for the unimaginative."

The College Prowler Take
ON GREEK LIFE

For those that are looking for it, Greek life does exist on campus. It does not, however, dominate the social scene as it tends to do at other U.S. colleges. For many students attending BU, the lack of a prevalent Greek scene on campus is a welcomed benefit for student life. The truth is that Boston offers far more outside of campus grounds, and an overwhelming Greek population would have little influence on the dispersed student body. Greek life is the alternative to a real social life.

Drug Scene

The Lowdown
ON DRUG SCENE

The College Prowler™ Grade on
Greek Life: D+

A high grade in Greek Life indicates that sororities and fraternities are not only present, but also active on campus. Other determining factors include the variety of houses available and the respect the Greek community receives from the rest of the campus.

Most Prevalent Drugs on Campus:
Alcohol, pharmaceuticals, marijuana, ecstasy, cocaine

Liquor-Related Referrals:
468 on campus; 9 on public property

Liquor-Related Arrests:
10 on campus; 8 in dormitories; 35 on public property

Drug-Related Referrals:
19 on campus; 8 on public property

Drug-Related Arrests:
15 on campus; 7 in dormitories; 9 on public property

Drug Counseling Programs

The Danielson Institute
185 Bay State Rd.
(617) 353-3047
daninst@bu.edu

Student Health/Mental Health Services
881 Commonwealth Ave.
(West entrance)
(617)353-3575

Students Speak Out
ON DRUG SCENE

The College Prowler Take
ON DRUG SCENE

{ "You will definitely encounter drugs at BU. Many kids seem to be into them and experiment with all sorts of things—be careful, as I have seen it both screw people up and open their minds to new things."

Q "I never saw a lot of drugs. **I know weed is common**, but I don't smoke, so I don't know where to get it or who to get it from. If you don't choose to hang around it, you probably won't see it. As far as anything else, if you don't look for it, you probably won't see it."

Q "I don't do it, but it's the usual. Alcohol is big of course. **Weed is the biggest of the drugs, then I would say E [ecstasy], coke, and K [ketamine]**. Everything is there; it is a city. The University and the police are very strict, though, so party hearty, but safely and smart."

Q "Drug scene—I prefer alcohol myself, but **BU has plenty of people who enjoying smoking weed once in a while** and plenty of people who don't. I have a lot of friends who smoke on a regular basis and a lot of friends who have never touched the stuff. There is also a contingent of kids at BU who to do E and coke, but for the most part, alcohol and weed are the two main drugs."

Q "Honestly, I can say that **I know more kids that use drugs recreationally than those that do not**. Never, however, have I witnessed someone being forced to try something that they did not want to do themselves. If drugs are something that you wish to do, they are not hard to come by."

Q "**Not many people do drugs**, but I might not know a lot about it because I lived on the pre-med floors of Warren. There is some drug use, but not much."

Ah, yes, the drug scene. It is pretty readily agreed upon by most students that drugs are certainly a prevalent and available source of recreation on campus and off. No one, however, felt that this sort of activity was so rampant that it put a strain on campus life. The drug scene, while visible, is easily avoidable. Students stressed the ability to choose your scene. It is really easy to find people who are into—or not into—just about everything. The drugs that were most readily seen on campus were alcohol, marijuana, cocaine, and ecstasy. Many also noted that pharmaceuticals are often considered a "useful tool" for completing schoolwork, or else simply for recreation. To be brief, various social circles have their various social vices. Pick and choose as you see fit.

The College Prowler™ Grade on
Drug Scene: C-

A high grade on Drug Scene indicates that drugs are not a noticeable part of campus life; drug use is not visible, and no pressure to use them seems to exist.

Campus Strictness

Q "**You're screwed if you're caught with either drugs or alcohol**, but if you're 21, you can have a certain amount of liquor in your room. If they catch you, you get a judicial hearing, and you might get kicked out of housing. People do smoke pot and drink in the dorms though; it's common."

Q "In my experiences with the campus police and security guards, **I have found them to be extremely strict** as compared with other schools that my friends attend. Security seems to be ever-present. They are always around and come equipped with 'magic noses.'"

The Lowdown
ON CAMPUS STRICTNESS

What Are You Most Likely to Get Caught Doing on Campus?
Smoking pot, burning incense or smoking cloves in dorm rooms, drinking underage, public urination, noise violation, violating the guest policy

The College Prowler Take
ON CAMPUS STRICTNESS

Playing it smart seems to be the best bet. Stick to your limits, stay far from University buildings when you expect to party, and if things tend to get out of control, make sure you are not in the dorms when they do. Getting caught with drugs—or alcohol, if you are underage—may result in academic probation or removal from housing on campus. What you get away with depends largely on your housing assignment. Rules vary in strictness from dorm to dorm, and from RA to RA. Be extra careful early on in the academic year. BU tends to try to "send a message" to students before things even get rolling.

Students Speak Out
ON CAMPUS STRICTNESS

"BU is very strict about marijuana. You can get kicked out of housing if two resident advisors smell it; it is a pretty strict rule. Everyone who drinks gets away with it if they are smart about it."

Q "**The drinking policy isn't too tight**. Most people get an alcohol violation at some point or another, but it isn't a big deal. The drug policy is pretty strict, though."

Q "If you use drugs or drink alcohol and get caught, **you will be written up**, have a letter sent to your parents, and possibly get kicked out of housing. More likely, you'll get put on probation."

The College Prowler™ Grade on
Campus Strictness: B

A high Campus Strictness grade implies an overall lenient atmosphere; police and RAs are fairly tolerant, and the administration's rules are flexible.

Overall Experience

Students Speak Out
ON OVERALL EXPERIENCE

"Overall, it has been a good experience. Some people fit in better than others. It can be hard to find 'the real friends,' but as long as you're outgoing and open to meeting new people, you should be fine."

Q "I have really enjoyed BU so far. Some people form a negative opinion of it based on the administrative policies like the guest policy, but there are ways around it and hopefully it will be changed soon—there have been lots of protests about it. **I have made a ton of good friends at BU and have gotten involved in a lot of activities** such as writing a column for the student newspaper, *The Daily Free Press*, and writing for BUTV shows."

Q "Boston is great, and my boring town of Bloomfield, Connecticut seems 10 times more boring after living in Boston. There is a lot to do, and **it is an exciting place to be**. I don't know what you want to major in, but the communications program at BU was one of the main reasons I went there, because it is known as a really good program, and so far I have been happy with it."

Q "I always wish I was somewhere else. But, Boston is really great for a college experience. **It isn't as big and overwhelming as New York**, but it definitely isn't a small town either. You can find yourself here, or you can just look for your lost soul in vain. In any case, I am having a pleasant experience that I would exchange for nothing else."

Q "I left Boston University during the fall semester of my junior year, but **BU gave me many things I carried with me the rest of my life**—a drug addiction, depression, and an overall sense of what I do not want from life. For the latter, I thank it, and for the two former, well, we all need to be challenged, right?"

Q "It was rough at first, and at the end, but the middle—well, it was like a sandwich, you know? Overall, **I would not choose BU if I had the choice to do it over again** because I found the environment to be limiting for the type of person I have found myself to be. I did, however, make some amazing friends, and I wouldn't change them for the world."

Q "I love BU; **there are great people here**. Talk to the teachers; they have connections in the field, and will help you out. You will mature here. Also, Bostonians are some of the best people in the world to know, but you have to give them a chance, and they will soon warm up. However, you must venture outside of the Commonwealth Avenue area. The area is nearly exclusively comprised of college kids that don't give an accurate representation of Boston. In fact, not going outside of the area is probably the main reason that people at BU say that they don't like Boston. They don't know it."

The College Prowler Take
ON OVERALL EXPERIENCE

While BU certainly has its downfalls, most of which are due to the sheer size of the University, there are plenty of opportunities to take full advantage of all that it has to offer. For the resourceful and motivated individual, a little effort will go a long way. The most important thing is to utilize your professors to your advantage. It is their job to be available to their students. While some are certainly more attentive than others, you will not be turned away by a professor if you truly seek out their support.

Take full advantage of what BU has to offer. Keep busy, stay well-organized, choose a course of study that truly stimulates your intellectual interests, and you will be well on your way to having a successful experience at BU. Try to work with your environment. Do not stay inside for too long; do not drink away your college years; make school a priority; and meet personally with your professors—they are the best resource you have. Boston is a huge city with a really large population of young people. If you are looking for a taste of city life and think that you would be able to establish yourself at a big school in a high-paced atmosphere, it is definitely possible to find your niche here at BU. You may very well find that by the time graduation rolls around, leaving it all behind is the last thing you want to do.

The Inside Scoop

The Lowdown
ON THE INSIDE SCOOP

BU Slang:
Know the slang, know the school. Absolutely everything is abbreviated at BU. The following is a list to help you catch on fast:

BUCOP: BU Collaborative Degree Program
Cam-Co: Campus Convenience
CAS: College of Arts and Sciences
CFA: College of Fine Arts
CGS: College of General Studies
COM: College of Communications
ENG: College of Engineering
EOP: Center for English Language and Orientation Program (CELOP)
GMS: Graduate Medical Sciences
GRS: Graduate School of Arts and Sciences
GSM: Graduate School of Management
GSU: George Sherman Union
PDP: Physical Department Program
SAR: Sargent College of Health and Rehabilitation
SED: School of Education
SDM: Henry M. Goldman School of Dental Medicine
SMG: School of Management
SPH: School of Public Health
SSW: School of Social Work
STH: School of Theology
SUM: Summer Term Program
UNI: University Professors
XRG: Cross Registration

BU Urban Legends

The third floor of the Mugar Library at BU has supposedly been rated number two in the country for places to pick up good-looking college girls.

The top floor of the Photonics Building at BU (which is not accessible to students, as it requires a code for entry) is rumored to be guarded by armed security. It is said to be a federally protected area that engages in the production of "military technology."

It is said that if you walk across the seal on Marsh Chapel Plaza, you won't graduate. Don't try it!

School Spirit

BU truly lacks a strong base of students who care about university life. While there are certainly select circles that pursue the betterment of student life, it is really hard to get a good turnout at both on- and off-campus events. Occasionally, the students will surprise you, but for the most part, apathy is rampant. The student response to the war in Iraq displayed the general lack of unity at BU. There have been several war protests, sit-ins, teach-ins, speakers, and debates. However, the attendance at most of these events tended to be disheartening, particularly to those that spent hours putting them together.

Traditions

Midnight Madness occurs on the hockey rink at Case Athletic Center to celebrate the beginning of the season. Everyone gathers to be introduced to each player on the BU varsity team, often in a drunken frenzy.

The free concert that is "partially funded by your undergraduate student fee" (a phrase often joked about by anyone paying full tuition to attend BU), usually gets a lot of attention from students. A few years ago, BU held a free Bob Dylan concert, with tickets available on a first-come, first-served basis.

Senior Week occurs each year between final exams and graduation. It is basically comprised of a bunch of events to which seniors and their guests may purchase cheap tickets to participate in. These include trips to Six Flags New England, trips to the Cape, "booze-cruises" at the pier, clambakes, Red Sox games, and formal dances at popular Boston venues.

Things I Wish I Knew Before Coming to BU:

- The extremely high cost of living. This is especially difficult for your first taste of off-campus living.

- The city closes down at 2 a.m.. This is quite a culture shock, even for someone coming from a small town. I went to high school in upstate New York, and there were plenty of 24-hour diners around for late night socializing. Be prepared for early nights out; most after-hours partying takes place at off-campus apartments or at home.

- BU is extremely conservative, especially considering the liberal student body. The former president of the University, John Silber, despite being a Democrat, seems as right-wing as they come regarding policies. When petitioning for more lenient visitation rules, students were surprised to hear this widely-published response: "It is not our job to provide a 'love nest' for our students."

Tips to Succeed at BU:

- Talk to your professors. This is the number one piece of advice for any student at BU. Do not wait until the panicked need for recommendations forces you to become your professor's best friend—take the initiative early, and develop lasting relationships.

- Stay off campus as much as you can. While the University provides plenty of opportunities for meeting other students, it is not the only place to do so—or necessarily the best. There are so many people in Boston; do not make the mistake of limiting yourself to the occasionally homogenous BU crowd.

- Use the BU Job Board. Quickie Jobs are perfect for making easy and fast cash.

Finding a Job or Internship

The Lowdown
ON FINDING A JOB OR INTERNSHIP

The truth is that it is very difficult to find a "real" job in this city. Because of the high concentration of students, part-time work is not easy to come by, and to get a good job, with good pay, you really have to know someone. Now, to be fair, you are taking advice from an individual (namely, me) who hates part-time work. My last job, which I stuck with, was a tutoring position in the writing center at BU. While it didn't pay too much, I only had to work about nine hours a week, and I could schedule my appointments around my school schedule. Your best bet is to try to find a job on campus. This will save you time, money, and effort traveling back and forth around the city. BU offers a really good service to help students find work (be it part-time, full-time, on campus or off). Check out the job board online at the Student Link at *www.bu.edu/studentlink*, or stop by the office on the second floor of 881 Commonwealth Avenue to get yourself oriented.

Advice
It is extremely difficult to live in Boston without a fairly consistent source of funds. Unlike life in a small town, money is necessary for just about everything, and you really can't do much without it, unless you prefer quiet evenings at home—many, many quiet evenings. Those of us who often find ourselves without cash are doomed to suffer socially. Your best bet is to get a job, even if it doesn't pay much, because a little money is better than none. When in doubt, the GSU Union Court is always hiring food service employees. You do not even have to apply if you are a BU student. The pay is minimal, but the hours are flexible and easy to come by. Another option that is always guaranteed is the Shaw's Market on Commonwealth Avenue. It is right on campus, and they do mass hiring every Tuesday. Just show up. Most students typically find themselves working at one of the two places listed above for a few weeks to earn some quick cash.

Career Center Resources & Services
While the Job Board resource will provide you with just about all you need to know to find a job in Boston, there is also a fully-functioning Career Center located in Kenmore Square at 19 Deerfield St., on the third floor. You can call for more information at (617) 353-3590, e-mail at future@bu.edu, or visit the Website at *www.bu.edu/careers*.

The Career Center for BU holds events year-round and claims to provide students with countless opportunities to improve their chances of choosing, finding, and maintaining a career. Unfortunately, the truth is, these sessions tend to provide more common sense information than anything else.

Famous BU Alumni
Martin Luther King Jr. is certainly the most celebrated alum from BU. Noted celebrities Howard Stern, Jason Alexander, and Bill O'Reilly have also studied at BU.

The Best & Worst

The Ten BEST Things About BU:

1. Fine professors
2. Boston is a great college town.
3. A wide variety of courses
4. Using "convenience points" at Domino's
5. Lots of opportunities for undergrad research
6. Great food (off campus and on)
7. The "semi-campus" feel West Campus
8. The way the BU Beach looks at night
9. High-energy, intellectual atmosphere
10. Virtually no Greek life

The Ten WORST Things About BU:

1. The ultra-conservative administration
2. Large class sizes (some are over 400 students!)
3. Boston shuts down at 2 a.m.
4. Snobby rich kids
5. An absolutely impenetrable bureaucracy
6. When campus security goes overboard
7. Blatant student body apathy
8. Everything is overpriced
9. No smoking … anywhere!
10. Starting classes earlier and ending later than all other Boston area universities

Brandeis University

415 South Street, Waltham, MA 02454
www.brandeis.edu   (800) 622-0622

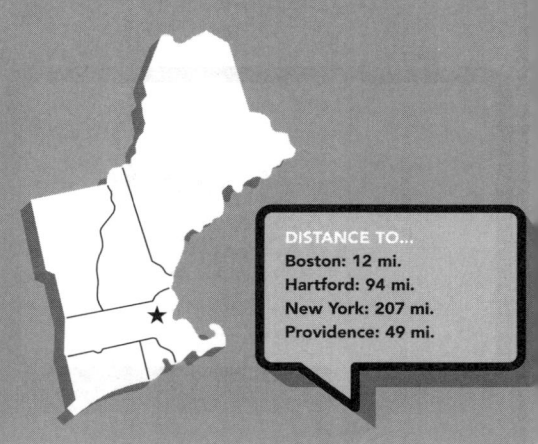

DISTANCE TO...
Boston: 12 mi.
Hartford: 94 mi.
New York: 207 mi.
Providence: 49 mi.

"The administration has been taking great strides to make sure that 'Deis' is a diverse institution, especially internationally."

Total Enrollment:
3,137
Acceptance Rate:
44%
Tuition:
$31,072
Top 10% of High School Class:
69%

SAT Range
Verbal	Math	Total
620 – 720	630 – 720	1250 – 1440

ACT Range
Verbal	Math	Total
28-33	26-32	28-33

Most Popular Majors:
17%   Economics
16%   Biology
8%   Political Science
8%   Sociology
7%   Psychology

Students Also Applied To:*
Boston University, Brown University, Cornell University, New York University, Tufts University

*For more school info check out www.collegeprowler.com

Table of Contents

Academics	727
Local Atmosphere	729
Safety & Security	730
Computers	732
Facilities	733
Campus Dining	734
Off-Campus Dining	736
Campus Housing	737
Off-Campus Housing	739
Diversity	740
Guys & Girls	742
Athletics	743
Greek Life	745
Drug Scene	746
Campus Strictness	747
Overall Experience	748
The Inside Scoop	749
Finding a Job or Internship	751
The Best & Worst	752

College Prowler Report Card

Academics	A-
Local Atmosphere	B
Safety & Security	A
Computers	A-
Facilities	B
Campus Dining	C+
Off-Campus Dining	A-
Campus Housing	B
Off-Campus Housing	B+
Diversity	C-
Guys	C
Girls	C+
Athletics	C
Greek Life	C-
Drug Scene	B+
Campus Strictness	A-

Academics

Special Degree Options
Tufts University School of Medicine Early Acceptance Program, Columbia University Law School's Accelerated Program in Interdisciplinary Legal Education, Columbia University School of Engineering Combined Degree Program, International Business School BA/MA Program

AP/ IB Test Score Requirements
For information on credit for scores, please visit www.brandeis.edu/registrar/bulletin/ and click on the most recent bulletin.

The Lowdown
ON ACADEMICS

Degrees Awarded:
Bachelor, Post-Bachelor Certificate, Master, Doctorate

Full-time Faculty:
326

Faculty with Terminal Degree:
98%

Student-to-Faculty Ratio:
9:1

Average Course Load:
16 credits (4 classes)

Best Places to Study:
Shapiro Campus Center, Library, Lounges, and Java City

Did You Know?
If you don't see a major you like, you can make up your own major. There are new ones being developed and implemented every year.

Students Speak Out
ON ACADEMICS

"**I enjoy classes. All of the teachers are intelligent, and the workload is challenging but not too heavy.**"

"While the teachers here are generally knowledgeable and interesting, **I think they're overrated**. I definitely don't think most of them are that stimulating, and I question why students constantly laud their professors because I don't feel as passionately about them as they do."

"I enjoyed my classes. Most of my teachers seemed to be really interested in both the lives of the students, as well as the subject that they were teaching. Aside from my USEM, all of the **classes were interesting and useful**."

The College Prowler Take
ON ACADEMICS

Q "The professors here are very attentive to student needs, and thet are available for meetings. They are all highly qualified in their fields and have an intimidating amount of knowledge about their subject. The courses taught are all very interesting; however, some classes can be a little slow at points. **Large lectures are rare and tend to get boring** the fastest."

Q "I have had very positive experiences with practically every one of my professors. Some classes have been more interesting than others. University requirements aren't as much fun to take as things in your major. I have never had any problems with professors. I'd say, if anything, **my experience has been very positive** compared to friends at other schools. I feel that teachers here try to know their students and are very accessible."

Most students at Brandeis are happy with their classes and the professors. Classes are usually small, and they are generally interesting rather than boring. Several factors, including course topic, professor, and the style in which the class is taught, affect the interest level of the class. Professors at Brandeis are highly skilled in their respective areas and make themselves available to assist students. Brandeis offers the opportunity to learn from well-known professors such as Robert Reich. These opportunities are open to undergraduates, as well as graduates.

The small population makes one-on-one interaction with professors not the exception but the rule. It is this closeness that allows for great student-professor relationships to form. Brandeis is growing into one of the top academic universities in the country thanks to the personal relationships with professors very skilled in their fields and some of the best and brightest students in the country.

Want more info about majors or professors at Brandeis? Visit www.collegeprowler.com for the detailed student insider's guide on Brandeis University.

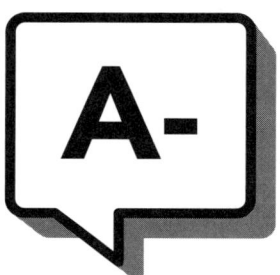

The College Prowler™ Grade on
Academics: A-

A high Academics grade generally indicates that Professors are knowledgeable, accessible, and genuinely interested in their students' welfare. Other determining factors include class size, how well professors communicate, and whether or not classes are engaging.

Local Atmosphere

Students Speak Out
ON LOCAL ATMOSPHERE

"Brandeis is kind of isolated because it is self-contained, but Moody Street is a great place to have a nice meal, and if you have a car, anything is within five minutes."

Q "Waltham is practically in Boston/Cambridge, so the atmosphere is comparable. There is a ridiculous number of other universities in the area. **Exploring Boston and the surrounding region is a must** for any student wanting to fully experience New England."

Q "Waltham is quiet and small, but I enjoy it. **It's just the right distance from Boston** so that we're close to a big city but not immersed directly in it. There are two other smaller universities, but there is little to no interaction between all of them."

Q "The town is like any normal small town with a pretty laid-back feeling. **There are a lot of good restaurants**. Other schools exist in the area, but we don't really interact with them. Lizzy's Ice Cream is the place to go for ice cream."

Q "The atmosphere is very peaceful. I have only been to one other college once, and it was quite the insignificant experience, though I like the fact that **the neighborhood has a lot of colleges**. There is nothing I can think of that one should stay away from in Waltham, but Moody Street is definitely a place to visit often! The Embassy, the movie theater in Waltham, shows great independent films."

Q "The town has not been very receptive to the college in the past, but it is improving. The restaurants are getting better, and **the bars seem to love us**. Bentley College is in Waltham, too, but neither college seems to admit that the other exists. Make sure to hit up Moody Street for dinner because there are some cool places there."

The Lowdown
ON LOCAL ATMOSPHERE

Region:
Northeast

City, State:
Waltham, Massachusetts

Setting:
Suburban

Distance from Boston:
20 minutes

Distance from NYC:
3.5 hours

Points of Interest:
Moody Street

Sports Teams:
Boston Red Sox (baseball), Boston Bruins (hockey), Boston Celtics (basketball), New England Patriots (football)

City Websites:
www.boston.com, www.city.waltham.ma.us

The College Prowler Take
ON LOCAL ATMOSPHERE

Right around the Brandeis campus is the residential town of Waltham. The immediate town is not exactly the most exciting place in the universe, but does include some bars, a supermarket, and other stores essential to college life. Less than a mile and a half from campus is Moody Street, which provides much more excitement for Brandeis students. Full of restaurants from every ethnic group, plus bars, a movie theater, Lizzy's Ice Cream, and even a porn shop, Moody Street provides many opportunities to get out and do something.

If one is not satisfied enough by this selection, Boston and Cambridge, home of Harvard, are extremely close. Both are reachable by the Brandeis shuttle on the weekends, the Commuter Rail located right off main campus, the T-line (Boston's subway system) that is about a 10-minute drive away, or by car, itself. Boston provides every type of entertainment you could want.

Safety & Security

The Lowdown
ON SAFETY & SECURITY

Number of Brandeis Police:
23

Phone:
(781) 736-3333

Safety Services:
24-hour foot and vehicle patrols, late-night transport/escort service, 24-hour emergency telephones, lighted pathways/sidewalks, controlled dormitory access including key and security card.

Health Center Office Hours:
Weekday 8 a.m. to 8 p.m., Weekends and holiday 10 a.m. to 4 p.m., Summer hours Monday – Friday: 10 a.m. to 4 p.m., Hours change during break and holidays.

The College Prowler™ Grade on
Local Atmosphere: B

A high Local Atmosphere grade indicates that the area surrounding campus is safe and scenic. Other factors include nearby attractions, proximity to other schools, and the town's attitude toward students.

Students Speak Out
ON SAFETY & SECURITY

"While Brandeis seems to be in its own secure bubble away from the world, security on campus isn't always trusted. Dorms are easy to get into, and anyone can come and go."

Q "There are no big problems, and in general, I feel safe. I know many people who leave the door to their suite and room unlocked. Of course, **you'll have your incidents**, but those students will always fall through the cracks no matter what school a person attends."

Q "The **campus has a pretty low crime rate**, so security is not necessary. Like every other school, we have the 'blue light system,' but I doubt that it's utilized very much."

Q "I have always felt perfectly safe on campus, even walking at night. Basically, **it boils down to using common sense** and trying your best to be safe. But, Brandeis has a generally low key, safe campus, so I wouldn't worry too much about it."

Q "Brandeis is incredibly safe. There are those blue-post thingies all over the place, and **the security makes regular rounds** because the campus is so small."

Q "I think there's a false sense of security. **It is an open campus**. No, I don't always feel safe; the Brandeis cops are sort of a joke."

The College Prowler Take
ON SAFETY & SECURITY

Although not located in the most affluent or nicest of towns, Brandeis has a surprisingly safe campus. While the rent-a-cop police officers seem incompetent, they actually do their job well. They don't have much crime to deal with on campus, and their main purpose is to give parking tickets and break up parties. Campus police patrols the campus 24-hours. Even though students may leave their doors unlocked, there is always the chance for theft. Better safe than sorry.

The blue-light system, which most colleges employ, makes sure that, if there is a problem, students are able to get help quickly. The College provides late-night transport and escort service for students who feel uncomfortable walking around at night or who may just need a ride. And if the provided transportation is not enough for you, you can call the police, and they will drive you back if you're out late at the Campus Center or at a friend's dorm. Overall, it's a very safe and secure campus, as long as you're smart and use common sense.

The College Prowler™ Grade on
Safety & Security: A

A high grade in Safety & Security means that students generally feel safe, campus police are visible, blue-light phones and escort services are readily available, and safety precautions are not overly necessary.

Computers

Q "It's a great system where **everyone has his own Ethernet connection**, so it's very easy. I don't generally use the computer labs, but others do and don't have a problem. I think it's probably good to bring a computer for convenience."

Q "Bringing your own computer isn't necessary, but it is a definite convenience. There are several computer clusters on campus, but they do fill up at times. **Many places on campus are now being set up with a wireless network**, so a laptop might be a good idea if you enjoy working outside of your room."

Q "Definitely bring your own computer because it's extraordinarily convenient to check e-mail and use AIM to talk to friends. **You can usually find an open computer** in the Campus Center or library, but I prefer to stay in my room."

The Lowdown
ON COMPUTERS

High-Speed Network?
Yes

Wireless Network?
Yes

Number of Labs:
8

Number of Computers:
235

24-Hour Labs:
Shapiro Campus Center

Charge to Print:
Yes

The College Prowler Take
ON COMPUTERS

The Brandeis network is awesome. The administration has taken no stance on file sharing and actually has made access easier to file share within the Brandeis network. The only exception is if you download an excessive amount for three weeks straight. Then, Brandeis will kick you off the network to preserve network bandwidth that rivals any school out there. Brandeis has a Website called Boogle which allows students to search for files on other students' computers, so file sharing becomes really easy. And with the quickness that the Brandeis network allows you to transfer files, music and movies are on your computer before you can blink.

Students Speak Out
ON COMPUTERS

"You definitely want to bring your own computer, purely for the sake of convenience. There are plenty of computers, but having your own is usually most helpful."

The College Prowler™ Grade on
Computers: A-

A high grade in Computers designates that computer labs are available, the computer network is easily accessible, and the campus' computing technology is up-to-date.

Facilities

Favorite Things to Do
Go to a dance, see an a capella concert, go to a party, hang out at Chum's

Students Speak Out
ON FACILITIES

{ **"Brandeis has a beautiful campus. The student center is a very popular place to hang out, work, get coffee, and hold meetings."**

Q **"Brandeis' campus has a lot to offer.** The new dorm is fantastic, as is the Shapiro center. I love the gym as well. All three of these buildings are extremely state-of-the art. The rest of the dorms are a little less desirable."

Q "The facilities are amazing, beautiful, and spacious. We have a **great gym**, ok computer lounges, great study halls, a student center with a coffee shop, and study rooms that are noise-proof."

Q "The facilities are fairly nice, especially the fairly-new student center and residence hall, which looks more like a hotel. **The gym is always crowded**, so don't count on getting to use a machine, especially around 3 p.m.."

Q "The facilities for the sciences and the graduate schools are very nice. But, it seems that **Brandeis has ignored the rest of the campus**. The Humanities Quad is in dire need of renovations. For a school that doesn't seem to pay attention to sports, Brandeis has beautiful sports facilities. The new student center is also great, minus the 'Emerald City' exterior."

Q "The facilities are pretty nice. The campus center is new, and there are **decent computers available** in the library. Gosman is a fantastic place with a solid weight room."

The Lowdown
ON FACILITIES

Student Center:
Shapiro Campus Center and Usdan Student Center

Libraries:
Two main libraries and a science library

Athletic Center:
Gosman Sports Center

Popular Places to Chill:
Chum's, dorm rooms, suite common rooms, the Campus Center

Movie Theater on Campus?
No

Bar on Campus?
Alcohol served at "The Stein" which is right above Sherman dining hall

Coffee on Campus?
Yes, Cholmondeley's (usually called Chum's) located in the Castle

The College Prowler Take
ON FACILITIES

Brandeis has a relatively small endowment, and sometimes the facilities reflect that. While many schools with more money in their pockets are better able to update facilities and pay for the upkeep, Brandeis has more problems. They are always in constant capital projects, trying to get money to improve existing buildings or build new ones. The Shapiro Campus Center has added a great element to the campus. The Village is a new dorm. Expansion continues to be made to classrooms, but unfortunately, it seems it's been more for the graduate schools. The place that Brandeis needs to put their money is into the dorms. The Castle has been there since before Brandeis was founded and is in need of renovation.

Campus Dining

The Lowdown
ON CAMPUS DINING

Freshman Meal Plan Requirement?
Yes

Meal Plan Average Cost:
$ 2,850-$4094

Student Favorites:
The Stein, Java City, and The Boulevard

The College Prowler™ Grade on
Facilities: B

A high Facilities grade indicates that the campus is aesthetically pleasing and well-maintained; facilities are state-of-the-art, and libraries are exceptional. Other determining factors include the quality of both athletic and student centers and an abundance of things to do on campus.

Students Speak Out
ON CAMPUS DINING

"**The food leaves something to be desired. It's not absolutely terrible, but it's close sometimes.**"

"There are only two dining halls. One is buffet and has a Kosher side and non-Kosher side. The other is à la carte. **The à la carte has better food**, but if you keep kosher, you'd probably prefer the buffet."

Q "Food is actually really good compared with most other schools. **There are a lot of healthy options**, which is really nice. The new food station, Balance, is really good, as is the salad bar. Brandeis is a relatively vegetarian/vegan-friendly campus. There are some good food options that still provide lots of protein."

Q "Food is actually good—**a little repetitive, but good**. The Stein is great; it has waitress service. Usdan has good food and is open later."

Q "Usdan Café is definitely better than the other dining halls. The food is actually quite good, and relatively varied. Though one would probably still hear me complaining about the food, mainly because **it gets monotonous after a while**."

Q "For college food, Brandeis does very well. It is repetitive, but that's what you're going to get. **Stay away from Sherman**, unless you want to spend the night in the bathroom."

The College Prowler Take
ON CAMPUS DINING

The food at Brandeis is edible, but it's nothing to rave about. Brandeis dining is broken down into only a couple of options. There's Sherman, broken down into Kosher and non-Kosher sides, which is all-you-can-eat. The food here is only good if you keep Kosher, if you're really hungry, or if you have meals instead of points as a dining plan. Usdan is an à la carte dining area that is open during breakfast, lunch, and dinner. Upstairs from Usdan is the Boulevard, which is open until midnight, Sunday through Thursday. The food here is good, but the selection rarely, if ever, changes. Aramark, who runs the dining services, is very hesitant once they get our money to make improvements that will cost them. The last dining area is The Stein, which is an on-campus restaurant. This is definitely the best option on campus, but only is worth it if you have points. All in all, most students find the dining a rip off but say the food is okay.

Want to know more about where to get the best food on campus? Visit www.collegeprowler.com for the Brandeis University guidebook.

The College Prowler™ Grade on
Campus Dining: C+

Our grade on Campus Dining addresses the quality of both school-owned dining halls and independent on-campus restaurants as well as the price, availability, and variety of food.

Off-Campus Dining

Did You Know?

You don't need to go to Boston for Zagat-rated restaurants. There is a number in Waltham, and some are very, very expensive.

The Lowdown
ON OFF-CAMPUS DINING

Students Speak Out
ON OFF-CAMPUS DINING

Best Pizza: Franca's

Best Chinese: Lily's Kitchen

Best Breakfast: Bickford's

Best Wings: Pete's Pizza and Wings

Best Healthy: So Cal Restaurant

Best Place to Take Your Parents: Naked Fish

Late-Night, Half-Price Food Specials: Late-night Bickford runs are always popular.

Student Favorites: Cappy's, Bison County, Lizzy's, Watch City Brewery, Asian Grill, Pete's Pizza and Wings

Closest Grocery Stores:
Victory Supermarket
836 Main St
Waltham, MA 02451

Salem Food Store
468 Moody St
Waltham, MA 02453

"Cappy's Pizza is right nearby; it's a great restaurant. Most of the restaurants on Moody Street are good. Lily's Kitchen is the best for Chinese take-out."

"Basically, most of the good restaurants are on Moody Street in Waltham. Tom Can Cook is good pan-Asian, Erawan of Siam is good Thai food, **Solea is a good Tapas bar**, and there are about 100 Indian restaurants."

"The restaurants in Waltham are very good. There are many types of food: Asian, American, Indian, Mexican, etc., and **the dishes are well-priced**. Some places to try are: Tom Can Cook, Margarita's, Lizzie's, Asian Grill, Bickford's and Watch City."

"Waltham, Boston, and Cambridge have thousands of restaurants in every conceivable cuisine. **They are relatively easy to get to**, and students often go out to eat."

"There are **tons of great restaurants** off campus like the Asian Grill, Carambola, and tons of Indian restaurants."

"The restaurants are great! **Moody Street is the place to be for food if in Waltham**, but the neighboring area has some great places, too, such as Boston and Cambridge. Waltham has several ethnic food places, and most are a really good and reasonably-priced."

The College Prowler Take
ON OFF-CAMPUS DINING

Off-campus dining makes up for sometimes sub-par, on-campus dining. Waltham's Moody Street is not just popular for Brandeis students and has some Zagat-rated restaurants. Most of these places in Waltham and on Moody Street won't break your piggy bank. If you're looking for a nice night out with friends, especially for birthdays, you have two main options. You can try out Moody Street, or you can go to Boston.

Boston provides many more options for food. Harvard Square and the Prudential Building area are the two most popular places for people to go for a dinner. For a big appetite, Vinny Testa's or Fire and Ice are the best places. For smaller appetites, Dick's Last Resort or The Cheesecake Factory are certainly great places to go for dinner. Just know that if you go to dinner in Boston, you are going to either have to make reservations or wait a very long time.

Campus Housing

The Lowdown
ON CAMPUS HOUSING

Undergrads on Campus:
84%

Number of Dormitories:
11

Number of College-Owned Apartments:
5

Room Types:
Single, Double, Natural Triple, Unnatural Triple, Suite

Bed-Type:
Twin extra-long

You Get:
Bed, dresser, Internet, phone, desk

Cleaning Service?
Laundry rooms are cleaned weekly or biweekly, depending on where you live. Bathrooms are cleaned weekly. Students in Castle E Tower, Rosenthal, Ridgewood, and Ziv are provided with a bathroom cleaning kit and toilet paper. Students in other apartment or suite housing must clean their own bathrooms.

The College Prowler™ Grade on
Off-Campus Dining: A-

A high off-campus dining grade implies that off-campus restaurants are affordable, accessible, and worth visiting. Other factors include the variety of cuisine and the availability of alternative options (vegetarian, vegan, Kosher, etc.).

 ## Students Speak Out
ON CAMPUS HOUSING

 ## The College Prowler Take
ON CAMPUS HOUSING

> "The dorms are okay. Upperclassmen usually live in on-campus suites, which are really nice. The campus is very squished together, so all the dorms are close to each other."

Q "There is a castle, which is cool. **I've had only good experience with dorms.** As long as you like communal living, Rosenthal and Ziv are nice. The Village, the newest residence hall, is nice for upperclassmen, singles, and doubles. For first-year housing, Massell is a beautiful quad, and the residence life staff was very nice."

Q "Some dorms are great; others are barely standing. **Freshmen dorms are average**, with most people preferring North Quad. Most upperclassmen live in suites, which are all pretty nice. Ridgewood Quad is falling apart."

Q "Many students prefer suites over dorm halls. Kitchens are certainly a plus. **The newer buildings have central air**, which is heavily desired. Ziv, Rosenthal, and The Mods are top choices. The village is expensive but gorgeous for a college dorm."

Q "I don't think there are too many 'bad' dorms. I live in the most notorious one [East] this year, and I love it. **It's just a matter of where your friends are.**"

Q "The dorms are pretty standard. The rooms are decent sized, with decent bathrooms—nothing spectacular, but **a nice place to hang your hat**. Shapiro dorm is the best for freshmen because it is coed."

The quality and experience of on-campus Brandeis housing really depends on whom you speak to. Most people agree that East is the worst of the dorms, but many people who live there end up loving it. It's all about where your friends live. If you live in a single across campus from all your friends, you're probably going to be miserable. But if you live in a hall or a suite with all of your friends, you will probably have a great time no matter which dorm it is. The problem is that it is not as easy at it seems to live with your friends, and wherever you live, there will still be complaints with the building. Every building on campus has positives and negatives.

The College Prowler™ Grade on
Campus Housing: B

A high Campus Housing grade indicates that dorms are clean, well-maintained, and spacious. Other determining factors include variety of dorms, proximity to classes, and social atmosphere.

Off-Campus Housing

The Lowdown
ON OFF-CAMPUS HOUSING

Undergrads in Off-Campus Housing:
16%

Best Time to Look for a Place:
Before the housing lottery numbers come out

Average Rent for an Apartment:
$550/month

Popular Areas:
Any place around campus; Dartmouth Street for fraternities or people who like to party

Students Speak Out
ON OFF-CAMPUS HOUSING

"Everyone wants to live on campus; it is easier and nice with lots of suites. Living off-campus just wouldn't be fun."

"Most of the students who want to remain on campus can do so all four years. I actually believe that **on-campus housing all four years will soon be guaranteed**. It's definitely worth it to stay on campus. It adds to the dynamic of the community when the seniors are involved."

"I've never lived off campus, so I can't answer this really. I know from having friends off campus, that **it is a pain if you don't have a car**. And you're a bit isolated from the rest of your friends and other social things."

"Many people find the experience 'priceless,' even if **it costs more money than on-campus living**. Many times this is not the case. Regardless, it is somewhat inconvenient."

"It is very difficult to be a Brandeis student without a car off campus. Many people do enjoy it, but **I can't imagine having to manage transportation**, and it would be harder socially as well."

"**Housing is guaranteed the first two years**, but it is becoming harder to get for juniors and seniors. Most people have no problem finding a place off campus, if necessary."

The College Prowler Take
ON OFF-CAMPUS HOUSING

Some students choose to live off campus so they don't have to deal with a meal plan. Others choose to live off campus because they want to see how living on their own is. Others are forced to do so after they lose out in the housing lottery. But, everyone who lives off campus seems to love it. Very few people live off campus junior year and then move back on campus senior year.

There are two main problems with off-campus housing. One is that Brandeis does nothing to help people find off-campus housing. The other is the lack of parking on campus for commuter students. For many months of the year, it is way to cold to walk every day. But then again, some students swear by it, so living off campus can't be all that bad.

Diversity

The Lowdown
ON DIVERSITY

African American: 2%

Asian American: 8%

Hispanic: 3%

Native American: 0%

White: 80%

International: 7%

Out-of-State: 76%

Minority Clubs
The BBSO (Brandeis Black Students Organization) and other Asian and Indian groups have great weight on campus.

Most Popular Religions
If there was a campus religion, it would be Judaism and it is definitely the strongest religion. Christian and Muslim groups are also prevalent on campus.

Political Activity
Brandeis is a highly-liberal campus, but recently, a conservative spark has been lit. Brandeis used to be, and is again becoming a very politically-active campus.

The College Prowler™ Grade on
Off-Campus Housing: B+
A high grade in Off-Campus Housing indicates that apartments are of high quality, close to campus, affordable, and easy to secure.

Gay Tolerance

The Brandeis gay community is tremendously strong. It is a very comfortable place for people to come out. The gay community also throws some of the best parties at Brandeis.

Economic Status

Brandeis happens to be very economically diverse. Add to that the fact that so many people are so cheap, it definitely means you won't be running into J. Crew on every student you meet.

Students Speak Out
ON DIVERSITY

{ "The campus feels very diverse at multicultural events. At other points, I cannot help but wonder if everyone on campus is Jewish."

Q "The campus is supposed to be very diverse, but it always feels like we are mostly Jewish. **Christian students are definitely a minority**, and many of the international students are Jewish."

Q "The student body still remains **over 50 percent Jewish**, which predominates the cultural feel of the campus. Minorities on campus sometimes feel unsupported and insolated."

Q "It's no secret that **Brandeis is a historically Jewish school**, and the presence is definitely there. But, the school is trying to become more diverse, and I think they are doing a fair job."

Q "There is increasing focus on diversity at Brandeis with each incoming class. **There have definitely been some big conflicts concerning diversity**, but in general, Brandeis is a very accepting environment where all types of people seem to get along and understand each other."

The College Prowler Take
ON DIVERSITY

Diversity is probably the biggest hot button on the Brandeis campus. We've had many things happen over the past few years that have had people readdressing diversity initiatives on the Brandeis campus. The administration has made promises to address diversity not only in the student body, but in the administration and the faculty. The thing is that Brandeis is a lot more diverse than most people think. We have about 15 percent students of color, and we have representatives from almost every state and from many countries. People meet so many different people in their freshman year that they can't help but feel that Brandeis is diverse. It may not be a black and white issue, but you may have a roommate who is gay and from Pennsylvania, and across the hall find a Hispanic girl from Rhode Island, a Christian girl from Massachusetts, and a Jewish girl from Israel. Some people disagree. It all depends on how you look at it. More often than not, people look around Brandeis and see white, Jewish people.

The College Prowler™ Grade on
Diversity: C-

A high grade in Diversity indicates that ethnic minorities and international students have a notable presence on campus and that students of different economic backgrounds, religious beliefs, and sexual preferences are well-represented.

Guys & Girls

Dress Code

The dress at Brandeis varies greatly. Some people are dressed to the nines every day; some people dress very casually in pajamas. For the most part, Brandeis could be seen in a Gap commercial because that's the most common theme in clothing. One guy wears suits every day he has a test for good luck; another guy doesn't wear shoes. But for the most part, every guy at Brandeis seems to be in jeans and a hoody, and every girl seems to be in jeans and some sort of top you can find at the Gap.

The Lowdown
ON GUYS & GIRLS

Women Undergrads:
56%

Men Undergrads:
44%

Birth Control Available?
Yes, at the Student Sexuality Information Service (SSIS) or the Health Center.

Social Scene
Although Brandeis students may claim not to have fun, they are still social. It is a very friendly campus. Of course, there is a small number of people who stick to themselves. But, for the most part, Brandeis students are very friendly and enjoy hanging out together. It is not unusual to see big groups of Brandeis students wherever you go off campus.

Hookups or Relationships?
It's hit or miss at Brandeis. Some people meet someone and stay with them for a very long time. Otherwise, it's just a casual relationships. There are a lot of random hookups, especially at the beginning of freshman year.

Students Speak Out
ON GUYS & GIRLS

"There are a few winners in both the guys and the girls, but Brandeis isn't exactly known for its hotness factor."

Q "This is definitely **not a campus known for hot girls**. But each year, the freshman class gets more and more good-looking. So hopefully, someday, this will change."

Q "The hotness level at Brandeis has skyrocketed in the past few years. My sister went to Brandeis from 1994-98, and back then, it was not an attractive campus. Now, I have to say that **the student population is getting increasingly better looking**, both for men and women."

Q "**People say that Brandeis is 'an ugly school**,' but I don't think it's true. There are plenty of good-looking people here, probably just as many as any other school, but it depends on your taste."

Q "Brandeis has a reputation for being an ugly campus. While there are cute guys here, they're not falling into your lap. However, **I like the ugly guys**."

The College Prowler Take
ON GUYS & GIRLS

To really talk about Brandeis guys and girls, you need to know your standards. There are some very attractive people on the Brandeis campus, but most of them are with the other attractive people. That leaves a lot of people without someone. Since a lot of people worth dating get into long-term relationships, there aren't always a lot of couples at Brandeis. Sometimes it seems that the gay community has better success in finding people than the straight community.

Many people come into Brandeis as virgins and seem to leave the same way. But some people certainly open up when they come to Brandeis and become more outgoing and promiscuous. An article in the Brandeis weekly newspaper, *The Justice*, claimed that the amount of emergency contraceptive pills given out in a recent school year were almost double that of the previous one (two years ago).

Athletics

The Lowdown
ON ATHLETICS

Men's Varsity Teams:
Baseball
Basketball
Cross-country
Fencing
Golf
Soccer
Swimming and diving
Tennis
Track and field (indoor)
Track and field (outdoor)

Women's Varsity Teams:
Basketball
Cross-country
Fencing
Soccer
Softball
Swimming and diving
Tennis
Track and field (indoor)
Track and field (outdoor)
Volleyball

The College Prowler™ Grade on
Guys: C

A high grade for Guys indicates that the male population on campus is attractive, smart, friendly, and engaging, and that the school has a decent ratio of guys to girls.

The College Prowler™ Grade on
Girls: C+

A high grade for Girls not only implies that the women on campus are attractive, smart, friendly, and engaging, but also that there is a fair ratio of girls to guys.

Fields
Gordon Field, Marcus Field, Chapels Field

Getting Tickets
Tickets are free or not required for sporting events at Brandeis.

Athletic Division:
UAA (University Athletic Association)

Conference:
ECAC (NCAA Division III)

Most Popular Sports:
Men's and women's basketball, baseball, ultimate Frisbee

Overlooked Teams:
Women's basketball and fencing

School Mascot:
Ollie the Owl

Students Speak Out
ON ATHLETICS

"Basketball is probably the biggest sport. IM sports are popular, but Brandeis isn't a very sports-centered school at all."

Q "Sports are non-existent. **Brandeis is known for its fencing team**, I guess, which is its third-best team, right after benching and the ballroom dance team (if you don't get the joke, you will). Some IM and club sports are great—rugby, frisbee, ballroom dance team, and crew. There are different levels of intensity, but there's a lack of presence at most basketball games."

Q "**IM sports can be a lot of fun** and offer a great way to meet people and enjoy yourself on campus. The more organized sports receive little support from the student body, but if you're expecting that, I've heard they are enjoyable, as well."

Q "Varsity sports are there, but **no one pays attention**. Most of the teams aren't very good, except for women's basketball and fencing. IM sports seem to get a decent response."

Q "Basketball games are becoming more of a '**Brandeis event**,' and can be lots of fun. IM is becoming very popular and fun, too."

Q "I love our basketball team. We have great games throughout the season. In the spring, **it's really nice to watch soccer and baseball games**. Sports aren't huge here, but they definitely exist."

The College Prowler Take
ON ATHLETICS

Athletics may not be Brandeis' selling point, but some sports programs here are starting to rise to the point of respectability. In 2004, the women's basketball team won the ECAC tournament and finished 18th in the country in the final women's poll. The lack of a football team puts focus on normally less popular sports. However, there has not been much in the way of supporting athletics at Brandeis. While sports do exist, they are not much of a big deal and not a main attraction. South Street separates the sporting complex from the main campus, but sometimes the gap seems much wider. Recently, Brandeis has made great strides in recruiting more and more talented athletes to play for their teams. As the teams continue to improve, so will the school spirit and the outlook on athleticism at Brandeis. If you are into sports, Brandeis offers a wide selection, including intramurals. You are sure to find something you like to do.

The College Prowler™ Grade on
Athletics: C

A high grade in Athletics indicates that students have school spirit, that sports programs are respected, that games are well-attended, and that intramurals are a prominent part of student life.

Greek Life

The Lowdown
ON GREEK LIFE

Number of Fraternities:
4

Number of Sororities:
2

Undergrad Men and Women in Fraternities or Sororities:
200

Students Speak Out
ON GREEK LIFE

"Greek life does not dominate the social scene at all. It's there if you want it, but it's not very big. People attend parties both at frats and hosted by other random people."

Q "It isn't big at all. There are about four frats, and they sometimes have parties. **They're generally nice guys** and their parties are okay. Sororities aren't big at all."

Q "**Greek life does not dominate the social scene**, and it's common to make fun of people who join frats. However, the good thing about frat life here is that the brothers/sisters actually have friends outside of the Greek system."

Q "Greek life is great. **The greeks are really cool and have a great time with one another**. The frats aren't allowed on campus, so the scene is kept more or less on the down-low, but there is always a great turnout at parties and events."

The College Prowler Take
ON GREEK LIFE

With four fraternities and two sororities, Brandeis does have some semblance of Greek Life, but it is not what students at Penn State or Indiana University are used to. The frat houses are just small, off-campus houses that have large basements for parties. Usually, only one or two frat members actually live at the house. When they throw parties, they are some of the better off-campus parties thrown. "Rush period" always produces the best parties as fraternities and sororities are trying recruit new members. There are certainly other parties, but Greek Life definitely helps dictate the party scene when they decide to throw one. Aside from the parties, the Greek scene is pretty quiet on campus. Although they are trying to get more recognition by the campus, Greek Life seems like it will be underground for many years to come.

The College Prowler™ Grade on
Greek Life: C-

A high grade in Greek Life indicates that sororities and fraternities are not only present, but also active on campus. Other determining factors include the variety of houses available and the respect the Greek community receives from the rest of the campus.

Drug Scene

The Lowdown
ON DRUG SCENE

Most Prevalent Drugs on Campus:
Marijuana

Liquor-Related Referrals:
82

Liquor-Related Arrests:
0

Drug-Related Referrals:
47

Drug-Related Arrests:
0

Drug Counseling Programs
Drug and Alcohol Counseling is provided by the Health Center
www.brandeis.edu/health/counseling.html

Students Speak Out
ON DRUG SCENE

"Drugs are there if you want them. Weed is pretty prevalent, but harder drugs aren't that popular, in my own experience."

Q "I'd say that **Brandeis has a bit of everything**, as all college campuses do. There are definitely people who drink and do drugs, but I'd say we're a good bunch of kids—for the most part anyway."

Q "There is quite a bit of pot being smoked all over campus. **The school doesn't really do much to prevent it**. Drinking is prevalent, but that's everywhere. I wouldn't say there's an extraordinary amount of alcohol consumption. I would say there's a lot more pot being smoked than at the average school. As for harder drugs, though, not as much."

Q "Marijuana is the Brandeis drug of choice, and **many people have tried it at least once**."

Q "People definitely smoke pot a lot, and **some do shrooms**. Not that many do more 'hardcore' drugs, although I know people who have."

Q "**Marijuana is readily available**. I'm not friends with anyone who does more drugs than that."

Q "The drug scene is pretty typical. A lot of people smoke pot, and I've heard rumors about cocaine and other things. **Opium is also pretty popular**, as well as concentration drugs for people pulling all-nighters."

The College Prowler Take
ON DRUG SCENE

Marijuana seems like it's everywhere, especially on the weekends. You can certainly avoid it if that's not your scene, but if you want it, it is there to be had. About half of the Brandeis population smokes weed at least once in their four years at Brandeis. The other half took D.A.R.E. very seriously and believes that drugs are really bad, and so are the people who use them.

As for more hardcore drugs, look to other colleges. There are hardcore drugs at Brandeis, but only a small population uses them. Even less use them now after one very popular Brandeis senior stabbed himself after tripping on 'shrooms. There are the few people who love to experiment, try acid, and snort Ritalin, Vicodin or whatever they can get their hands on. But, most people who use drugs stick to weed. Most of those people don't consider it a drug.

The College Prowler™ Grade on
Drug Scene: B+

A high grade in the Drug Scene indicates that drugs are not a noticeable part of campus life; drug use is not visible, and no pressure to use them seems to exist.

Campus Strictness

The Lowdown
ON CAMPUS STRICTNESS

What Are You Most Likely to Get Caught Doing on Campus?
Drinking alcohol, smoking pot

Students Speak Out
ON CAMPUS STRICTNESS

"They're not that strict, they usually give a warning or just look the other way, but sometimes they choose to make an example out of someone."

Q "I don't think the police are strict at all. Obviously, they need to bust people every now and then to validate themselves and prove to the administration that they are worth paying, but they don't do it unnecessarily. I'm not sure if they are more or less strict, relative to other schools, but **I don't find them to be too strict here**. In other words, it is pretty easy to use drugs or drink without being caught."

Q "Brandeis is **too strict**! Brandeis is too stringent and seems to not let students have any harmless fun."

> "**Campus police seem to look the other way** when it comes to pot because most people do it in their rooms. Parties get broken up very early, though."

> "The police tend to **turn a blind eye to drugs and alcohol** on campus."

> "The campus police are pretty lax. Some people get busted and get off with a slap on the wrist, or they have to meet with a drug and alcohol counselor—**nothing too severe** at all."

The College Prowler Take
ON CAMPUS STRICTNESS

Almost every student has been at a Brandeis party that has been broken up by the police. The consequences for those types of violations are usually very small. The police basically drive around breaking up parties, and giving parking tickets. Only the parking tickets actually pay for their salary, so when they break up parties, they usually aren't too crazy about prosecuting the people who held them.

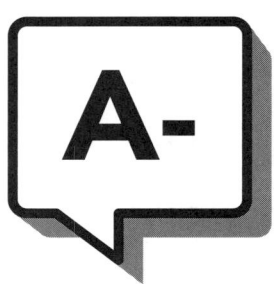

The College Prowler™ Grade on
Campus Strictness: A-

A high Campus Strictness grade implies an overall lenient atmosphere; police and RAs are fairly tolerant, and the administration's rules are flexible.

Overall Experience

The Lowdown
ON OVERALL EXPERIENCE

"I'm very happy at Brandeis. It's really easy to get involved, and it's a very active campus, so you'll have your hand in things. It's is definitely a great, friendly place to be. I love it!"

> "I actually really love being at Brandeis. **I have met some of the best people I've ever encountered** at Brandeis, and the friendships I've made are invaluable. I originally came to Brandeis for financial reasons, but I think that I made the right choice."

> "I've had a great time at Brandeis. But, **the school is not for everyone**. I am happy here and can't say I wish I was somewhere else."

> "I love it here. My friends and the Brandeis community in general, among a million other things, make this place worth it. Academics get progressively harder with the year, which sucks. **I want to be a freshman again**! And no, I don't wish I was elsewhere, however, I wish I had applied to NYU."

> "Overall, this is the best place for me when you combine everything together. I wish people were smarter. **I think admissions standards should be raised**. I expected that a top school would be more challenging. It would definitely make me happier to have a more academic environment."

> "**I love Brandeis**. I've made amazing friendships, learned an enormous amount, and decided what I want to do with my life. I feel that, on a day to day basis, I'm happy and lucky to be where I am."

The Inside Scoop

The College Prowler Take
ON OVERALL EXPERIENCE

They may complain a lot, but Brandeis students on the whole seem to be content at Brandeis. More than half of the students seem to be bitter when they first get to Brandeis; it was their third or fourth choice. But, after a little time, that bitterness usually turns to happiness. There are so many opportunities out there, you just need to be willing to put forth the effort to get the most out of them. If you sit in your room and do nothing, you will get nothing out of your experience here.

The administration and faculty sometimes seem to have the position that the cheapest way to do it is the best. In addition, poor diversity, parking, and weather, along with a lack of good-looking people and a social scene are some of the things people complain about. Regardless, there are many ways to get around that and have a good time. Many people come in and have no clue what to expect, and many people leave with memories that will last them a lifetime. The academics are gaining in strength, and when I look back on my decision to go to Brandeis, I realize I definitely made the right decision.

The Lowdown
ON INSIDE SCOOP

Brandeis Slang:

'Deis – Short for Brandeis.

Kosher – Food that is prepared in conformity with the requirements of the Jewish law. On the most basic level, someone who keeps Kosher cannot mix meat and cheese, cannot eat pork or shellfish, and can only eat meat killed and prepared a certain way.

Oy! – An exclamation one makes when they are either surprised or disgusted by something.

Pre-game – Getting drunk before going out to a party, club or dance.

Shomer – A religious Jew who is not supposed to touch someone of the opposite sex.

Brandeis Urban Legends

Friends

The creators of *Friends* went to Brandeis, and they formed Central Perk, the coffeehouse on the show, after their experience at Chum's, Brandeis' coffeehouse.

NASA

NASA operates from Brandeis and is located under the Rabb steps. They do special experiments there.

Football

Brandeis had a football team, but it was stopped. There are three myths that are most associated with this. One is that the Gosmans, who donated the sports complex, had a son die from playing football and would only give money for the gym if they stopped playing football at Brandeis. Another is that Jewish law and football law have discrepancies. And the third is that "Jews are no good at football."

The Castle

Middlesex College used to own The Castle before Brandeis, and it was used as a dormitory for the all-girls veterinary school that was there. Some say in the 1920s, before its use a dormitory, it was used as lab rooms; some say The Castle housed the morgue. Other myths about The Castle say that there are secret passageways and underground tunnels.

School Spirit

School spirit is few and far between, and it stems from a lack of sporting prowess. Although in the same conference as NYU, Washington University, and Emory, Brandeis fails to be able to provide the same sporting experience as any of those schools. One thing that hurts Brandeis a lot is the lack of football team. Another is the lack of administrative backing for sports. But overall, school spirit is way down at Brandeis but has been coming up as sports have recently begun to improve.

Traditions

Bronstein Weekend

One of the best weekends of the year which occurs in the spring and features a couple of concerts and lots of camp-like activities. Also right around the time that all the admitted students come to visit.

Traditions *(Continued...)*

Midnight Buffet

Happens twice a year, both during finals time, and involves lots of food (pizza, soda, bagels, donuts, ice cream, fruit, vegetables, and popcorn) and lots of giveaways (T-shirts, hats, Frisbees, etc.). It is one of the best times during finals.

School Spirit

Modfest

Modfest is a big alcoholic block party that goes on in the senior housing twice a year. The whole campus gets drunk and goes to this party and drinks some more. There's lots of music and lots of people, which equals lots of fun.

Things I Wish I Knew Before Coming to Brandeis:

- A winter in Boston is not as easy at it might seem.
- The education is comparable to many top-notch schools, but so is the price. Financial aid says they'll help, but most students are stuck paying out of pocket.
- Verizon Wireless is the best plan to have in the Boston area.
- Brandeis does a sub-par job at helping students find jobs and internships.

Tips to Succeed at Brandeis:

- Don't be intimidated by all the Jewish people.
- Open up your mind.
- Get involved early and often, but do not overextend yourself.
- Take classes with friends, and take classes at times you like.
- If you're a morning person, schedule early classes. If you aren't, do not schedule a 9 a.m. because of temptation to skip.
- Find your niche. Everyone does, and if you search for it, you can find it.

Finding a Job or Internship

The Lowdown
ON FINDING A JOB OR INTERNSHIP

Brandeis does a mediocre job at helping graduates find jobs and students find internships. Many graduates are going out into the world without a job. Many have to attend graduate school because Brandeis does such a poor job at setting people up with jobs. Brandeis is a relatively young school and many of the graduates are yet to reach back to the school to help out the seniors who are looking for jobs. Once in a while people get lucky and land a killer job or internship through an alumnus; but those cases are few and far between. Mostly they just leave you out on your own.

Did You Know?
Famous Brandeis Alumni include:

Mitch Albom (class of '79), started the book *Tuesdays with Morrie* in order to help the family of Morrie Schwartz offset extraordinary medical expenses stemming from his long-term home care. It has spent over four years on *The New York Times* Bestseller List. Thomas L. Friedman (class of '75), award-winning author and columnist for *The New York Times*.

Gary David Goldberg, the creator and producer of *Spin City*.

Marshall Herskovitz (class of '73), the producer/screenwriter for "The Last Samurai" starring Tom Cruise. In 2000, Herskovitz produced "Traffic," winner of two Golden Globe Awards and four Academy Awards.

Marta Kauffman (class of '78) and David Crane (class of '79), co-creators of *Friends*.

Roderick MacKinnon (class of '78), the 2003 recipient for the Nobel Prize in Chemistry.

Debra Messing, (class of '90), star on NBC's *Will and Grace*.

Shen Tong (class of '91), established the Olympic Institute that became a cornerstone of the 1989 Tiananmen Square demonstrations.

Michael Walzer (class of '56), one of the foremost "thinkers" of our time.

Advice

Make connections on your own and use every connection you have. Also, ask professors and department heads if they know of any openings. Also, ask your parents, your relatives, or your friends' parents because there's bound to be something out there for you.

Career Center Resources & Services

Hiatt Career Center, (781)-736-3618

The Best & Worst

The Ten BEST Things About Brandeis:

1. Close to Boston
2. Student activities
3. Tons of stuff to do in the area
4. Boston is truly a college town
5. Professors are top in their fields
6. Academics
7. The Castle on campus.
8. Modfest and Midnight Buffet
9. Two spring breaks!
10. Friendliest people ever

The Ten WORST Things About Brandeis:

1. Unattractive student body
2. Lacking party scene
3. Greek life is borderline-pathetic
4. Parking
5. "Brandeis Mondays"
6. Bitterly cold weather
7. Rain for days at a time
8. Cost of tuition
9. The career center is not the best.
10. Monotonous people and food

College of the Holy Cross

1 College Street, Worcester, MA 01610
www.holycross.edu   (800) 442-2421

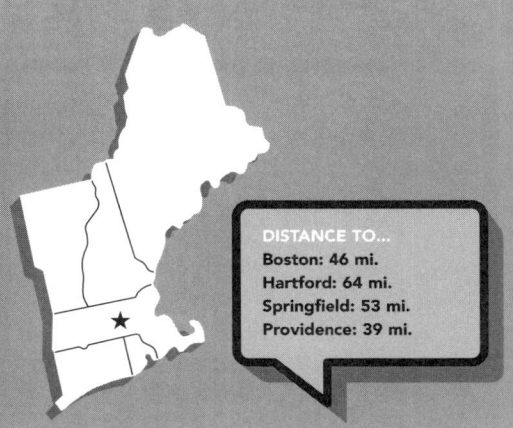

DISTANCE TO...
Boston: 46 mi.
Hartford: 64 mi.
Springfield: 53 mi.
Providence: 39 mi.

"The strong sense of community not only infuses the campus, but it goes beyond the campus gates."

Total Enrollment:
2,748

Acceptance Rate:
42%

Tuition:
$29,686

Top 10% of High School Class:
68%

SAT Range
Verbal	Math	Total
580 – 680	630 – 670	1210 – 1350

SAT II Requirements
Three SAT IIs are required for consideration, one of which must be the SAT II writing test. The applicant may choose the other two scores to submit.

Most Popular Majors:
49% Social Sciences
13% Psychology
12% English Language and Literature/Letters
7% Languages, Literature, and Linguistics
6% Biological and Biomedical Sciences

Students Also Applied To:*
Boston College, Fairfield University, Georgetown University, Providence College, Villanova University

*For more school info check out www.collegeprowler.com

Table of Contents

Academics	754
Local Atmosphere	756
Safety & Security	757
Computers	759
Facilities	760
Campus Dining	761
Off-Campus Dining	762
Campus Housing	764
Off-Campus Housing	765
Diversity	766
Guys & Girls	768
Athletics	769
Greek Life	770
Drug Scene	771
Campus Strictness	772
Overall Experience	773
The Inside Scoop	774
Finding a Job or Internship	775
The Best & Worst	776

College Prowler Report Card

Academics	B+
Local Atmosphere	D
Safety & Security	A-
Computers	B
Facilities	B
Campus Dining	C+
Off-Campus Dining	B+
Campus Housing	B
Off-Campus Housing	C+
Diversity	D-
Guys	B+
Girls	A-
Athletics	B+
Greek Life	N/A
Drug Scene	B
Campus Strictness	B-

Academics

The Lowdown
ON ACADEMICS

Degrees Awarded:
Bachelor of Arts (B.A.)

Undergraduate Schools:
Holy Cross is a solely undergraduate institution. There are no separate colleges within the school.

Student-to-Faculty Ratio: 11:1

Average Course Load:
3 courses

Full-time Faculty:
228

Part-Time Faculty:
59

Total Faculty:
287

Full-Time Faculty with Terminal Degree:
95%

AP/IB Test Score Requirements

There is not an institutional policy for AP/IB test score acceptance. These decisions are made by each individual department. Check with the registrar or department chairs for more specific information.

Distribution Requirements

Holy Cross requires all students to take 12 courses in seven different subject areas. Although the subject area is mandated, students are free to choose any course within that subject area. All students must take two foreign language courses; two arts and literature courses (one class in each discipline); two religion and philosophy courses (one class in each discipline); two courses in math and natural science (either one course in each discipline or two natural science classes); two social science classes; one history class; and one cross-cultural course.

Best Places to Study

For light reading, Cool Beans and Crossroads in Hogan provide the best mix of sociability and studying. The atmosphere is relaxed, chatty, and genial. Cool Beans is at the heart of campus in the Campus Center, so familiar faces are constantly wandering past.

For more intense studying—when it's important to focus on a tough-to-digest textbook—any one of the college's libraries provides an excellent place to quietly focus on work. Dinand Library is by far the largest and the most popular library. Dinand has individual study carrels placed throughout the stacks, group large tables in the Main Reading Room, and small tables in the Blue Room (talking and noise are permitted here). The Science Library, or the SciLi, (officially the O'Callahan Library, in Swords Hall) also provides a quiet environment in which to study or write. Additionally, each dorm also has a study room in its basement.

Sample Academic Clubs

Spanish Club, American Sign Language Club, Biology Society, the Society of Physics Students, French Club, German Club, Russian Club. Many other academic clubs also serve as departmental honor societies.

Did You Know?

When it comes to the number of students going on to earn doctorates, Holy Cross falls in the top three percent of four-year colleges.

Students Speak Out
ON ACADEMICS

The College Prowler Take
ON ACADEMICS

{ "The teachers at Holy Cross are great! They are always willing to provide students with extra help if it is needed. They love students to come and see them."

Q "The **teachers at Holy Cross are passionate** about what they do and truly cater to the students' needs. The majority of my classes have been interesting, especially my upper-level classes."

Q "The teachers at Holy Cross are caring and always available. **They really take pride in their jobs and are genuinely concerned for their students**. The classes offered touch on a wide range of topics within each discipline. There are definitely certain professors and classes you should steer clear of, but the vast majority is great."

Q "The professors at HC are continuously the brightest part of my college education. **I count many of my teachers as good friends**. Professors within my major, as well as professors external to it, have always been both well-prepared to teach their subjects and extremely accessible and personable outside of class. My experience has been that the opportunity to interact closely with students is a chief factor in most of my professors' decisions to teach at HC."

Q "Most professors really want to be at Holy Cross, where they can teach and help students, and be a vital part of a campus community. **Professors are always accessible**—they are required to have office hours each week—and many truly have gone above and beyond the call of duty in order help me, and most other students, succeed. Nearly every student has a story of at least one professor who went especially out of his or her way to give the student the help he needed."

Q "Based on my experience, overwhelmingly I have an excellent opinion of the faculty. **Nearly every one of them is highly intelligent and caring**; I've never heard of one refusing to give a student a break or an extension, and they always leave home numbers and ways to reach them in case of emergencies if need be."

The students almost unanimously praise their professors for their interest in course material and their efforts to make potentially boring classes interesting. Professors at Holy Cross are true educators. They all want to see their students develop not only into informed individuals, but men and women with the ability to truly think critically. Professors' passion for their subject matter carries through into the classroom, where students are inspired by, and therefore enjoy, their classes.

Since this is a small institution with a caring faculty, students are not just numbers. Many professors seek out personal relationships with their students that last beyond the end of the semester. Professors often go out of their way to ensure the success of their students, and it is this kind of personal, caring, and nurturing environment that is the hallmark of a Holy Cross education. The professors make themselves readily available to all of their students. If a student isn't doing well in a subject, the option is always available for the student to talk things over with the professor. There is no question that Holy Cross gives its students a truly first-rate, first-class education.

The College Prowler™ Grade on
Academics: B+

A high Academics grade generally indicates that professors are knowledgeable, accessible, and genuinely interested in their students' welfare. Other determining factors include class size, how well professors communicate, and whether or not classes are engaging.

Local Atmosphere

Students Speak Out
ON LOCAL ATMOSPHERE

"Worcester is a very industrial town and not very friendly. Although, there are many other colleges, it is definitely a town made for college students."

Q "The **atmosphere in Worcester is kind of dull**. Since freshmen and sophomores are not allowed to have cars, it is hard to go downtown without paying for a cab. However, many of the upperclassmen love Worcester. It is just a city that you need to explore for yourself. There are some great 24-hour diners. There are many universities in Worcester, which means there are tons of college kids."

Q "Worcester has a terrible reputation, but, as cliché as it sounds, **Worcester is 'what you make of it.'** Most everything is within a 15-minute drive, although taking cabs is a pain. Cab drivers don't seem to particularly like Holy Cross students. There are other universities present, but I never went to them."

Q "Worcester is not exactly a thriving metropolis. The **city offers little for the college-aged kid to do**. The atmosphere is like that of a plague-ridden medieval city: dark, depressing, and dull. There are a few clubs in town but nothing to write home about. They are only bearable because everyone there is from Holy Cross."

Q "Worcester is definitely an acquired taste. At first, pretty much everyone complains about its dirtiness and lack of things to do, but once you start exploring, **Worcester has tons of clubs, stores, museums, and events**. It is certainly not Boston, but it has its own charms. Beyond that, Worcester is surrounded by Auburn, Shrewsbury, Sturbridge, and other quaint cities with lots of history and beauty."

Q "Like any other city, **there are some dangerous parts of Worcester**. Basically, being off campus at night is never a great idea unless you are with a group of people. There was an attempted car-jacking last semester at a late-night Dunkin' Donuts, so the important thing is to remain with a group of people at night. If you play it safe and don't walk alone at night, you should be fine."

The Lowdown
ON LOCAL ATMOSPHERE

Region:
New England

City, State:
Worcester, Massachusetts

Setting:
Small city

Distance from Boston:
45 miles

Distance from Providence:
40 miles

Distance from New York:
170 miles

Major Sports Teams:
None

City Websites:
www.ci.worcester.ma.us
www.worcester.ma.us
www.Worcester.org

Points of Interest:
The Worcester Art Museum, on Institute Road, houses a remarkably good collection of art, from ancient to modern. The Higgins Armory Museum, located in the Greendale neighborhood, houses one of the best collections of medieval armor in the United States. The Eco-Tarium, in Worcester, combines a planetarium with animals and environmental education.

The College Prowler Take
ON LOCAL ATMOSPHERE

Worcester is not the most college-friendly city. Unlike colleges in Boston, where the city is a real selling point for the school, Worcester has to deal with a less stellar reputation. It is spread-out and tough to navigate without a car, and the locals are not always the friendliest toward Holy Cross students. The city hit its heyday in the 1920s and has been in steady decline since The Great Depression. Although there approximately 10 other colleges in Worcester, few establishments cater to the college-age community, most likely due to Worcester's sprawling geography. There is plenty to do in Worcester. Unlike New York or Boston though, where trendy bars, restaurants, and stores beckon from almost every corner, Worcester's hot spots need to be carefully discovered, and this can only be properly done with a car.

Safety & Security

The Lowdown
ON SAFETY & SECURITY

The College Prowler™ Grade on
Local Atmosphere: D

A high Local Atmosphere grade indicates that the area surrounding campus is safe and scenic. Other factors include nearby attractions, proximity to other schools, and the town's attitude toward students.

Number of Holy Cross Public Safety Officers:
14

Phone:
(508) 793-2224 (ext. 2224) for regular, non-emergency calls.
Extension 2222 can be dialed from anywhere on campus in case of emergency.

Health Center Office Hours:
Monday-Friday: 7:30 a.m.-8 p.m.
Saturday-Sunday: 10 a.m.-4 p.m.

Safety Services:
Emergency phones are placed strategically throughout campus. Public Safety also runs an escort program to drive students home late at night if they feel unsafe.

Students Speak Out
ON SAFETY & SECURITY

{ *"Safety and security on campus are slightly overbearing. They concern themselves with issues that need not be bothered with."*

Q *"The **campus is very safe**—Public Safety's Gestapo tactics ensure that. But watch out! They have been known to run down a student or two with their Public Safety vans."*

Q *"Security on campus is pretty good. **We have Public Safety minivans**, an 'unmarked' Crown Victoria, and a few bike cops. There are call-boxes all around campus."*

Q *"Public Safety sucks. They are not there to help the students, but have their own agenda—though I have never been able to figure out what that agenda is. **I never really felt that my safety was threatened** on campus, but I don't attribute that to Public Safety. I attribute that to the iron fence surrounding campus."*

Q *"**Security and safety on campus is almost not an issue**. We have a good Department of Public Safety. In my four years here, I can't remember hearing of one rape incident, and besides petty theft—like wallets being stolen from unlocked lockers in the gym—there were no major burglaries."*

Q *"Holy Cross is in a very working-class neighborhood of Worcester, but luckily it is not afflicted with the inner-city problems that have plagued other Worcester institutions in the past. **There is a system of call-boxes throughout campus** that allow students to call for help if needed. Additionally, Public Safety will provide students with rides to anywhere on campus after dark, should they feel unsafe."*

The College Prowler Take
ON SAFETY & SECURITY

The lack of crime at Holy Cross is almost comical. An incident such as the theft of a watch or wallet from an unlocked gym locker generates campus-wide safety alerts and a Herculean investigation from Public Safety. This lack of true crime leaves Public Safety officers to spend time dealing with quality-of-life issues, such as alcohol and parking violations, which seem to be students' main complaints about Public Safety. Woe betide the underclassman who parks his unregistered car on campus—it will soon be ticketed. The fact that Public Safety is able to focus so much energy on quality-of-life issues shows that Holy Cross is an extraordinarily safe school. It's true that Public Safety could do to ease up a little with their over-enforcement of certain campus policies,' they have done a superb job in keeping the campus crime-free.

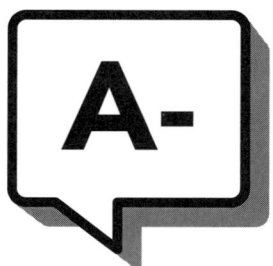

The College Prowler™ Grade on
Safety & Security: A-

A high grade in Safety & Security means that students generally feel safe, campus police are visible, blue-light phones and escort services are readily available, and safety precautions are not overly necessary.

Computers

Number of Labs
There are at least seven main computer labs, but there are computers at 21 locations throughout campus.

24-Hour Labs
O'Kane Lab (more than 30 computers)

Free Software
When computers are bought through Holy Cross, all programs are included (including MS Office Suite and all e-mail programs). When bringing your own computer, Holy Cross provides network and Holy Cross-related software, but the student is responsible for all hardware and non-network-related software.

Students Speak Out
ON COMPUTERS

"**The computer network is great. There are several T3 lines, and ITS [Information Technology Services] usually keeps things running smoothly.**"

Q "The computer network isn't bad, but I wouldn't say it's great. The **network is never down; it is just slow**. The school has put a ban on downloading music until, like, 11 p.m., which has really helped the network speed up."

Q "My biggest complaint is with **the lack of public computers on campus**. The computer lab in O'Kane is always packed, and I do recommend bringing your own computer."

Q "The labs generally aren't overcrowded, but **printing electronic reserves can be tough** because there aren't enough printers available. You don't need your own computer, but it does make things easier!"

Q "Definitely **buy the computer through Holy Cross**. I brought a laptop from home and it was difficult to configure it to the Holy Cross network. I eventually gave in and bought a school computer!"

Q "I would **recommend bringing your own computer**, but you can get by without one. I don't have a computer and find it inconvenient at times, but it wasn't something that I couldn't deal with. I would sometimes get frustrated when I saw students in the computer lab who I knew had computers themselves!"

The Lowdown
ON COMPUTERS

High-Speed Network?
Yes

Numbers of Computers:
457

Charge to Print?
No

Operating Systems:
Windows

Wireless Network?
Currently only in the Cool Beans area of Hogan and the Main Reading Room of Dinand Library, but it will be expanded in coming years.

The College Prowler Take
ON COMPUTERS

The Holy Cross computer network receives mixed reviews from the student body. It usually runs pretty well; however, during periods of high use it tends to slow down. Music downloading was a problem that the administration identified as contributing to the sluggishness of the network, so a ban was put on downloading music from 7 a.m. through 11 p.m., which sped up the network somewhat. ITS is constantly working to upgrade the school's Internet connections, and while having to wait an extra two seconds for a Website to load is annoying, it is by no means the end of the world. The network is pretty good, and the services available on the Internet are exactly what students (and professors) need. However, the network can be somewhat sluggish, and the school should consider investing in more computers for computer labs.

The College Prowler™ Grade on
Computers: B

A high grade in Computers designates that computer labs are available, the computer network is easily accessible, and the campus' computing technology is up-to-date.

Facilities

The Lowdown
ON FACILITIES

Student Center:
Hogan Campus Center

Athletic Center:
Hart Center

Libraries:
There are four libraries on campus: the Dinand Library, the O'Callahan Science Library, Fenwick Music Library, and Rehm Library.

Movie Theatre on Campus?
Yes, Kimball

Bowling on Campus?
No

Bar on Campus?
Yes, The Pub

Coffeehouse on Campus?
Cool Beans

Popular Places to Chill:
Cool Beans, Crossroads, Hogan Couches (in front of the Student Programs office on Hogan), East Street (the street in front of the underclassman dorms), Kimball Quad (in front of the dining hall)

Students Speak Out
ON CAMPUS DINING

Campus Dining

"Most are nice, but a few of the school's facilities need updating. The Hart Center definitely needs more cardio machines!"

Q "The **facilities definitely suit the needs of the average student**. However, the campus center tends to be more of an administrative center than a student center."

Q "All the facilities are nice and well-maintained. The **campus is always impeccably trimmed** and manicured. At times when the weather and classes suck—the one thing that can pull you through is how nice the campus is—it really makes a difference."

The Lowdown
ON CAMPUS DINING

The College Prowler Take
ON FACILITIES

The facilities on campus are pretty good. Although the Wellness Center at the gym is often crowded, it is a completely new, state-of-the art facility—it was opened in 1997. The buildings on campus, many dating from the 1890s to 1920s era, have been adapted to modern use and really don't show their age. It would be difficult to find a bathroom on campus containing any off-odors or writing on the walls. In all, the campus facilities are great, though some could be altered a bit to fit the needs of the current student body.

Freshman Meal Plan Requirement?
Yes

24-Hour On-Campus Eating?
No

Student Favorites:
Upper

Meal Plan Average Cost:
$4,430 for all freshmen

The College Prowler™ Grade on
Facilities: B

A high Facilities grade indicates that the campus is aesthetically pleasing and well-maintained; facilities are state-of-the-art, and libraries are exceptional. Other determining factors include the quality of both athletic and student centers and an abundance of things to do on campus.

Students Speak Out
ON CAMPUS DINING

"Surprisingly, the food at Holy Cross really isn't that bad. I'd even go so far as to call it good most of the time. The main dining hall is called Kimball and was built in 1843."

Q "The **food is not horrible, but it's not great**, either. If you know what to eat, and what to stay away from, then you can definitely get by without a problem. Kimball is one of the largest dining halls in the country, I think, so its sheer size makes meals interesting."

Q "The food on campus is decent—pretty standard, **run-of-the-mill college food**. Crossroads offers a greater variety. It's better than Upper Kimball."

Q "The food is pretty average. **Upper Kimball has all-you-can-eat**, which is great. Lower and Crossroads are just a la carte."

Q "**It's tolerable** and, at times, enjoyable. Crossroads is the best place to go if you're not a freshman. Upper Kimball has its good days and its bad days."

Q "The campus food is okay—it's nothing special. **Kimball is edible**; it could be better, but it could also be much worse! Lower Kimball and Crossroads are much better than Upper, but they mainly have greasy foods."

The College Prowler Take
ON CAMPUS DINING

Holy Cross is pretty average in terms of food. Most respondents seemed to agree that while the food isn't anything fantastic, it isn't toxic, either—although one student did say that the food was great! Dining options on campus are fairly limited, with only three dining halls (and only two for freshmen). There is always something edible in each place—even if it is just a salad or a bowl of Cheerios. Compared to other, larger colleges, the food at Holy Cross is definitely different—there are no fast food or national chains on campus. The dining at Holy Cross (especially at Upper Kimball) is rather idiosyncratic and therefore more personal and charming.

The College Prowler™ Grade on
Campus Dining: C+

Our grade on Campus Dining addresses the quality of both school-owned dining halls and independent on-campus restaurants as well as the price, availability, and variety of food.

Off-Campus Dining

The Lowdown
ON OFF-CAMPUS DINING

Best Pizza:
Pizzeria Delight (before 10 p.m.)
Blue Bird (any time)

Best Chinese:
King Chef

Best Breakfast:
Kimball Brunch or any of the diners

Best Wings:
Brew City

Best Place to Take Your Parents:
111 Chophouse

Late-Night/24-Hour Eats:
Any of the diners are great. Green Island, The Kenmore, and The Boulevard are the most popular.

 **Students Speak Out**
ON OFF-CAMPUS DINING

 **The College Prowler Take**
ON OFF-CAMPUS DINING

Q "The good, off-campus restaurants are 111 Chophouse, Sole Proprietor, Flying Rhino, Northworks Grille, and Portobello. Most of the restaurants on Shrewsbury Street are really good."

Q "**Worcester has tons and tons of diners**, which are especially popular in the wee hours of the morning after a party, a night out at the bar, or an all-nighter. Everybody, however, has a diner that they are particularly partial toward—mine is the Kenmore—and, after a few drunken or late-night visits, the wait staff begins to call you by name."

Q "The restaurants along Shrewsbury Street are very nice. If you just want to hang out, **go to Café Dolce**. If it's for dinner, try Flying Rhino. Piccadilly Pub is fairly standard, but it is enjoyable. The best restaurant in the city is Sole Proprietor, but it is expensive. 111 Chophouse is good, too."

Q "Dining definitely does not suck in Worcester! The **city has great restaurants**. Starting off in the immediate vicinity of Holy Cross, Fitzy's Market makes some of the best and most creative sandwiches. Restaurants along Shrewsbury Street are great—especially 111 Chophouse, Flying Rhino, and Brew City. As for Mexican, try Tortilla Sam's or Cactus Pete's. However, O'Connors has the best food for your money, hands down."

Q "The **restaurants off campus range from standard to awesome**. For a generic experience, there's always Piccadilly Pub, Friendly's, Chili's, Applebee's, Papa Gino's, and McDonald's. However, you need a car to get there!"

Q "One thing Worcester does have in abundance is good restaurants. **Shrewsbury Street is the restaurant district** and is a quick drive [or] cab ride away. Brew City is a favorite among students, as are a slew of Italian restaurants on Shrewsbury, although there isn't any restaurant that's really a Holy Cross student hangout like the Maxx on 'Saved by the Bell.'"

Off-campus dining is difficult at Holy Cross. With the exception of Wendy's, there are no restaurants within walking distance of campus, and even Wendy's is not an extremely popular option. Nobody listed it (or any fast food restaurants) among their favorites, and all of the restaurants mentioned are ones to which it is fine to bring parents. The off-campus dining situation, like so much else at Holy Cross, depends on the availability of an automobile. Because underclassmen are not allowed to have cars and going out to eat entails at least a 10-minute drive, the majority of dining out is done only when parents or other relatives come to visit. None of the restaurants cater to an exclusively student crowd, and some of the restaurants are places that you would only go with parents.

The College Prowler™ Grade on
Off-Campus Dining: B+

A high Off-Campus Dining grade implies that off-campus restaurants are affordable, accessible, and worth visiting. Other factors include the variety of cuisine and the availability of alternative options (vegetarian, vegan, Kosher, etc.).

Campus Housing

Students Speak Out
ON CAMPUS HOUSING

"The dorms are great and clean—the cleaning ladies are awesome! I wish there was better housing for sophomores than the standard two-man room."

The Lowdown
ON CAMPUS HOUSING

Undergrads on Campus:
2,232

Number of Dormitories:
10

Bed Type:
Nearly all are doubles

Cleaning Service?
Yes

Number of University-Owned Apartments:
One

Q "All of **the dorms are pretty much the same**. They are decent-sized with two beds, two desks, and two closets. The new apartments are awesome because they have a kitchen and living room. Wheeler should be avoided because the rooms are a bit smaller and further away from the other dorms."

Q "Dorms are **nice and pretty big for freshmen**. Once you hit junior year, the situation gets dicey. The school is making improvements, though, and recently built new apartments."

Q "All of the dorms are nice and well-maintained. **Some are more social than others**. Wheeler tends to have the best social atmosphere and is a big hangout for freshmen and sophomores."

Q "Dorms are all right, though not particularly modern. **Carlin and Alumni are good dorms**, but they suck for senior housing. The 'Hill Dorms' are awful. The bathrooms are disgusting, and the rooms are cramped. Loyola is the best to live in, if you feel like bearing the stigma of living in the 'substance-free dorm.'"

Q "The dorms are nothing special. **Freshmen and sophomores live in fairly basic dorms**—two-man rooms with a bathroom down the hall. As you get older, the dorms get better. The school just built a new apartment-style dorm which is really nice! I can't wait to live in it senior year!"

Room Types

Generally, freshmen and sophomores get doubles. There are a few triples and a few singles on campus, as well. For juniors and seniors, most on-campus housing is in four- or six-person suites or in campus apartments.

The College Prowler Take
ON CAMPUS HOUSING

All students seemed to agree that Holy Cross housing is good for underclassmen, but decidedly lacking for upperclassmen. At the beginning of the 2003-2004 school year, a new apartment-style dorm opened and was designed to keep upperclassmen on campus—so far, this option has proven very popular. Dorm cleanliness depends on those who live on your hall. One or two inconsiderate slobs could turn an entire hallway or bathroom into a pigsty. Overall, the living experience at Holy Cross should be improving. Housing is guaranteed for all four years, so there is no worry about being shut out of on-campus housing.

Off-Campus Housing

The Lowdown
ON OFF-CAMPUS HOUSING

The College Prowler™ Grade on
Campus Housing: B

A high Campus Housing grade indicates that dorms are clean, well-maintained, and spacious. Other determining factors include variety of dorms, proximity to classes, and social atmosphere.

Undergrads in Off-Campus Housing:
133 males, 135 females

Average Rent for a One-Bedroom Apartment:
$1,300 per month

Average Rent for a Two-Bedroom Apartment:
$1,500 per month

Popular Areas:
College Hill, Autumn Chase, Cambridge Street

Best Time to Look for a Place:
Apartments are always available. The best apartments are sometimes rented a year in advance, but housing can be found at all times. Rents in the vicinity of Holy Cross tend to be more expensive than in non-college neighborhoods of Worcester.

Students Speak Out
ON OFF-CAMPUS HOUSING

"There are a lot of houses and apartments off campus. Some houses are really nice, while others are completely ghetto and falling apart."

- Q "There are **some nice places to live** off campus, but, then again, there are definitely some real dumps."

- Q "Off-campus housing consists of two things: **old neighborhood housing and two apartment complexes**. The old three-deckers have the most character and are closest to campus. Cambridge and Autumn Chase are cool, but they're a hike."

- Q "Off campus is closer to the academic buildings than some dorms, and it's a cheaper option. The **off-campus scene consists of mostly seniors and a few juniors**. The houses aren't the Ritz, but they're definitely livable."

- Q "**Don't live off campus**! The houses are disgusting, and there are too many break-ins! Holy Cross just built new apartments for seniors on campus which have everything, plus the security and safety of campus."

Diversity

The Lowdown
ON DIVERSITY

The College Prowler Take
ON OFF-CAMPUS HOUSING

African American: 3%

Asian American: 4%

Hispanic: 5%

Native American: 0%

White: 87%

International: 1%

Out-of-State: 65%

Virtually no freshmen or sophomores live off campus. Traditionally, about one-third of the junior class chose to live off campus and about two-thirds of seniors, though this has changed with the construction of the new on-campus apartments. As evidenced by the student comments, living off campus is not for everyone. Living on campus is definitely easier—there are no worries about cooking, cleaning, and paying bills on time—but it's much less independent. Although off campus is not unsafe, it is not as safe as on campus, and there are a few burglaries each semester.

The College Prowler™ Grade on
Off-Campus Housing: C+

A high grade in Off-Campus Housing indicates that apartments are of high quality, close to campus, affordable, and easy to secure.

Political Activity
Although there are active chapters of the College Democrats and College Republicans, the student body on the whole tends to be apathetic—though issues concerning the Catholic Church and its policies (such as the pro-life argument) tend to cause much debate on campus, with some students taking the orthodox Catholic view and others breaking with the Church's teachings.

Most Popular Religion
Catholicism

Gay Tolerance

Holy Cross is the first Jesuit institution to support a club for homosexual students, and the Chaplain's Office sponsors a special group for gay students. Although the campus is not overtly homophobic, there is an underlying culture of homophobia, and there are one or two instances of anti-gay hate crimes on campus each year. "Rainbow Alliance Week," a week dedicated to raising awareness and tolerance about homosexuality, is held every year.

Economic Status

Most students come from upper-middle-class or privileged backgrounds.

Students Speak Out
ON DIVERSITY

{ "There isn't much ethnic or economic diversity, but there is a lot of geographic and political diversity."

Q "There are **three African American females in my class of 700**. I think that says a lot."

Q "If you're white, Irish, Catholic, and from a poor family in North Dakota, **you are the diversity!**"

Q "Most students who go to Holy Cross are very white. The school would do well to diversify. It seems as if all male black students are recruited for sports, instead of admitted on merit. I think the admissions office would do well to admit more minority students on merit. Also, because of the large white population, there tends to be a segmenting of the population. Whites hang out with whites, blacks with blacks, and Hispanics with Hispanics. **There are definitely students who do not fit this mold**, but I fear that too many do."

Q "A typical **Holy Cross student is Irish Catholic**. Racial diversity is an issue the school is trying to work on, but minority students are slow to attend a school that's been associated with Irish Catholics for so long."

The College Prowler Take
ON DIVERSITY

The fact that Holy Cross is not diverse is no secret, and most students agree that "the campus is not very diverse." Although Admissions is trying to make the campus more multicultural, it is difficult to attract minority students to a school that is already so overwhelmingly white and Catholic. So, even though the school's administration really has been trying to attract more students from different backgrounds, they haven't met much success, and Holy Cross remains overwhelmingly white. The average student is probably Irish, Catholic, from the greater New York or New England area, and fairly preppy. However, the Office of Admissions is still at work, never tiring, and trying to diversify the student body here at Holy Cross. Good luck.

The College Prowler™ Grade on
Diversity: D-

A high grade in Diversity indicates that ethnic minorities and international students have a notable presence on campus and that students of different economic backgrounds, religious beliefs, and sexual preferences are well-represented.

Want to find out more about cultural diversity on campus? Check out the College Prowler book on College of the Holy Cross available at *www.collegeprowler.com*.

Guys & Girls

The Lowdown
ON GUYS & GIRLS

Women Undergrads: 52.6%

Men Undergrads: 47.4%

Birth Control Available? No

Social Scene
The social scene centers around alcohol. During the week, students tend to go out to bars, especially on Tuesday and Thursday nights. On weekends, parties dominate. Sundays are usually spent recuperating from Saturday night and getting work done.

Hookups or Relationships?
Random hookups are the norm; there is no such thing as casual dating.

Dress Code
Although there isn't a dress code at school, the student body is overwhelmingly preppy. Pajamas are okay to wear to class so long as it's early in the morning. Otherwise, most students are dressed fairly well and look put-together for class. Observations that students look like they just stepped out of a J. Crew or Abercrombie catalog are right on target.

Students Speak Out
ON GUYS & GIRLS

"This is a hookup campus. As with any other institution, some guys are hot and others not so much. A lot of the girls try to look good at all times."

Q "On the whole, **HC is a clean-cut campus**. Everyone looks like they just stepped out of an Abercrombie or J. Crew catalogue. Some people are attractive, but 99 percent are preppy."

Q "The guys and girls are all pretty homogenous. There is a lot of **good-looking, preppy guys** who drink a lot of beer."

Q "They're pretty blah. Once **I saw a kid with a Mohawk**, and another bleached his hair, but that definitely isn't the norm here."

Q "The major problem with the girls here is their attitude—up until senior year, they all think they are a lot hotter than they are. This inflated ego is the guys' fault. **Freshman year, guys go for anything**, and the mediocre-looking girl gets a supermodel's ego. It also doesn't help that the girls—and guys—here are pretty rich."

The College Prowler Take
ON GUYS & GIRLS

Given the general lack of diversity at Holy Cross, it's not surprising that most of the guys and girls are "cut from the same mold," as one student put it. The campus as a whole is extremely preppy, and most students seem to be from upper-middle-class backgrounds, so comparisons to catalogs are particularly apt. The majority of guys and girls are good-looking in a clean-cut, preppy way. There are a few guys and girls who are particularly hot, and a few who are strikingly hideous, but for the most part, the average Holy Cross student is above average in terms of looks.

The College Prowler™ Grade on
Guys: B+
A high grade for Guys indicates that the male population on campus is attractive, smart, friendly, and engaging, and that the school has a decent ratio of guys to girls.

The College Prowler™ Grade on
Girls: A-
A high grade for Girls not only implies that the women on campus are attractive, smart, friendly, and engaging, but also that there is a fair ratio of girls to guys.

Athletics

Athletic Division:
I-A

Conference:
Patriot League

Most Popular Sports:
Football, basketball (men's and women's).

Overlooked Teams:
Baseball, hockey

School Mascot:
The Crusader

The Lowdown
ON ATHLETICS

Men's Teams:
Baseball
Basketball
Football
Golf
Ice Hockey
Lacrosse
Rowing
Soccer
Swimming
Tennis
Track & Field

Women's Teams:
Basketball
Field Hockey
Golf
Ice Hockey
Lacrosse
Rowing
Soccer
Softball
Swimming
Tennis
Track & Field
Volleyball

Students Speak Out
ON ATHLETICS

"**Nobody cares about any of the sports, except basketball.** There's usually minor interest in the football team at the beginning of the year, but it dissipates after they lose."

Q "**Football is huge despite the fact that we stink**. Basketball is also very popular, and we've been doing well for the past few years. Intramural sports are not big at all—in fact, I have never heard of any before."

Q "The only sport that's big on campus is basketball! This is really the only sport we are good at. We made it to the NCAA tournament for a few years. **Just about everyone on campus will show up to the basketball games**. Intramural sports are not that big on campus, however, I've participated in just about every sport. My favorite so far has been ultimate Frisbee!"

Q "Holy Cross in not Notre Dame, but **varsity sports are not ignored**. The basketball teams—both women's and men's—are at the top of their class and quite competitive. The football team draws a crowd, but this is basically because of tradition's sake and the tailgating—the stands grow sparse after halftime. The soccer team is always solid, as is the women's tennis team."

Fields

Fitton Field (football): Constructed 1924, renovated 1986. Seats 23,500.

Fitton Field (baseball): Not part of the football stadium. Seats 1,000.

Hart Center, constructed 1975: Basketball arena (3,600); hockey rink (1,600); pool (500).

Getting Tickets

Tickets can be purchased the day of football and basketball games, unless the game is particularly important. In cases such as this, reservations can be made. Tickets are generally free for students.

Q "On the whole, HC is a very athletic campus. Most students were varsity athletes in high school. **A lot of students participate in varsity, intramural**, and club sports. There is never a lack of athleticism!"

Q "**Intramural sports are present but not huge.** There is usually a softball club in the spring and a basketball league in the winter. There didn't seem to be a real organized structure to these leagues; people interested in starting one generally contacted the Student Programs office and had a campus-wide e-mail sent out."

Greek Life

The College Prowler Take
ON ATHLETICS

The Lowdown
ON GREEK LIFE

There is no question that basketball is the most popular sport on campus. Holy Cross is in the Patriot League, the champion of which is guaranteed a place in the NCAA tournament. Although Holy Cross hasn't won the tournament since 1948, the school is now focusing on strengthening both its men's and women's programs. Club and intramural sports at Holy Cross are somewhat spotty and generally operate on student interest. Football is also popular, but, as a few students said, it's mostly about the tailgating. Although Holy Cross hasn't fielded a competitive team in about 30 years, alumni flock to football games and tend to stick around for the first half—while there is still a chance of a Crusader victory—and leave once defeat is imminent.

Number of Fraternities: 0

Number of Sororities: 0

The College Prowler Take
ON GREEK LIFE

The College Prowler™ Grade on
Athletics: B+

A high grade in Athletics indicates that students have school spirit, that sports programs are respected, that games are well-attended, and that intramurals are a prominent part of student life.

The College Prowler™ Grade on
Greek Life: N/A

A high grade in Greek Life indicates that sororities and fraternities are not only present, but also active on campus. Other determining factors include the variety of houses available and the respect the Greek community receives from the rest of the campus.

Drug Scene

Q "**Pot is easy to come by; pills aren't**. There is some coke, but not much."

Q "**I've heard that there's a drug scene**, but I've never seen it or participated in it."

Q "**The only drug I've ever seen at HC is pot**. I don't even know how popular that is."

The Lowdown
ON DRUG SCENE

Most Prevalent Drugs on Campus:
Alcohol, marijuana, cocaine

Drug Counseling Programs:
Drug and alcohol hotline: 1-800-327-5050
Alcohol Awareness Program

The College Prowler Take
ON DRUG SCENE

With the exception of marijuana and a little cocaine, there is virtually no drug scene at Holy Cross. Pot, too, is not used as widely as it is at other colleges and is often difficult to find. Students prefer to drink, rather than smoke, their problems away. Ecstasy, heroin, and meth are practically unheard of on campus. Holy Cross, as stated before, is a drinking school, and alcohol is the drug of choice. Although drugs are out there, you really have to make an effort to find them, and there is no pressure to use drugs.

Students Speak Out
ON DRUG SCENE

"I haven't encountered any drugs here. I know a few people who smoke pot, but it doesn't seem to dominate the culture like drinking does."

Q "There are definitely those who use drugs, but they are in the great, great minority. I have never seen any at parties. **Holy Cross is a drinking school**. Cocaine is present but never done openly, and you can count the number of people who have done it."

Q "Excluding weed, **I haven't seen anything except a little coke**—definitely nothing hardcore. Even weed is kind of hard to come by here at Holy Cross."

B

The College Prowler™ Grade on
Drug Scene: B

A high grade on Drug Scene indicates that drugs are not a noticeable part of campus life; drug use is not visible, and no pressure to use them seems to exist.

Campus Strictness

"I have never had an encounter with campus police, but I do know that underage drinking and any kind of drug use is not permitted under any circumstance, and **campus police will take action if you're caught**."

"Since **Holy Cross is obviously a Catholic institution** they are very strict with their rules about drinking and drugs. Underage drinking is just not tolerated and HC communicates with the Worcester Police to punish anyone who is arrested off campus. Anyone caught on campus is sent to judicial advisors to receive punishment. Drug offenses are punishable by expulsion, and the College definitely enforces its policies."

The Lowdown
ON CAMPUS STRICTNESS

What Are You Most Likely to Get Caught Doing on Campus?
Drinking

The College Prowler Take
ON CAMPUS STRICTNESS

Some students find Public Safety's enforcement of rules oppressive; others find it extremely lax. It seems pretty safe to say that as long as you don't openly flaunt the rules, you won't run into trouble. On campus, students under 21 are prohibited from having alcohol in their rooms, while students over 21 can have a case of beer or one half-gallon of liquor per person. The former rule is more enforced than the latter. However, as long as alcohol is kept responsibly—i.e., not displayed prominently or not part of loud and crazy goings on—you generally won't be harassed for having it in your room if you're underage. The only problem is getting it.

Students Speak Out
ON CAMPUS STRICTNESS

"**Campus police are lax.** Unless you openly drink in a public area or refuse to quiet down after being told to do so, you won't get in trouble."

"The **campus police are pretty strict** about drugs and drinking. Every weekend you hear of someone you know who got written up. It all depends on the RAs on duty."

"**Public Safety isn't too bad about alcohol.** I mean, if you're 21, you are allowed to have a 30-pack in your room! I've never seen them break up parties for having alcohol, just for having too much noise."

"**Campus police are too strict.** People are going to drink and do drugs regardless of what the campus police do. They should back off and realize that students are more responsible than they think."

The College Prowler™ Grade on
Campus Strictness: B-

A high Campus Strictness grade implies an overall lenient atmosphere; police and RAs are fairly tolerant, and the administration's rules are flexible.

Overall Experience

The College Prowler Take
ON OVERALL EXPERIENCE

Students were mixed, though generally positive, in their responses here. The social scene seems to be the victim of most criticism. There is no question that Holy Cross provides all its students with a first-rate education. Most students are friendly, outgoing, and fun, and making friends is not a problem. However, some students do complain about the school's homogeneity. Few students seem to want to do anything that is outside of the norm. All in all, most students are very happy at Holy Cross, as evidenced by the school's high retention rate.

Students Speak Out
ON OVERALL EXPERIENCE

"I love it—anyone could find their niche at HC. I wouldn't want to be anyplace else right now, but four years is definitely enough."

Q "I think **I'm getting the best education money can buy**, but the social life here is really stifling and really boring, especially if you don't want to follow the crowd."

Q "I enjoy HC and would not want to be anywhere else. Overall, **it's a great academic institution** where you will make friends, have fun, and freeze in the winter."

Q "I love HC and can't picture myself anywhere else. The school is perfect for me, and **I really feel that it's like my second home**."

Q "Overall, **I'm happy with my HC experience**. The friends I have made are really great. I'm sure I could be happy somewhere else, too, but I'm here!"

Q "Holy Cross wasn't my first choice, but **I'm really happy I ended up here**. I couldn't have asked for a better school. It's the perfect size, and I can tell the teachers really care about me as a person and my education. Now, I can't picture myself anyplace else."

COLLEGE PROWLER

Want to know more about what to expect at Holy Cross? Check out the College Prowler book on College of the Holy Cross available at *www.collegeprowler.com*.

The Inside Scoop

The Lowdown
ON THE INSIDE SCOOP

Traditions

Holy Cross has a rich store of traditions, some practically as old as the school itself, some more recent. The traditional rivalry with Boston College is still strong, despite the fact that the two schools haven't competed athletically since the 1980s. The Catholic Church provides many traditions, such as the Mass of the Holy Spirit, which welcomes freshmen to the college (and provides parents with a way to say good-bye) and the Baccalaureate Mass at graduation. The college also has a strong tradition of community service and volunteering within the Worcester community.

In terms of more tangible traditions, Spring Weekend (the first weekend in May) is an excuse for the campus to celebrate spring. The school sponsors a carnival held on the Hart Lawn, and most off-campus houses have huge parties. As an institution with a large population of Irish American students, St. Patrick's Day celebrations are also a long-standing tradition.

School Spirit

Holy Cross has a lot of school spirit. There's even one day a year—Purple Pride Day—that's dedicated to enlivening it. School spirit is most evident at athletic events, particularly football and basketball games. The every-other-year away football game at Harvard always attracts a large Holy Cross crowd. The bleachers at basketball games are usually filled with a sea of students wearing purple T-shirts. Most students sport at least one piece of Holy Cross garb—usually, either a sweatshirt or a baseball hat. For a small school, Holy Cross has tons of spirit.

Tips to Succeed at Holy Cross:
- Work hard.
- Take advantage of personal relationships with professors.
- Don't feel bad about staying in on a Friday to do work—everyone does it once in a while.
- Have fun!

Finding a Job or Internship

The Lowdown
ON FINDING A JOB OR INTERNSHIP

Holy Cross has an amazing network of high-placed alumni, many of whom are eager to help out a fellow Crusader. The Career Planning Office (located in Hogan) provides excellent counseling opportunities and helps put students on a track to landing a job after graduation.

Career Planning also sponsors the Summer Internship Program, which is truly superb. Using the Holy Cross network of alumni, parents, and friends, internships have been developed that are earmarked and designed specifically for Holy Cross students. Although students must apply to this program, the benefits of the program far outweigh the work and effort it takes to put the application together. This is not to imply that the only internships offered by Holy Cross come through the Summer Internship Program. On the contrary, there are hundreds of other internship opportunities available through other Holy Cross alumni and connections.

Advice

Visit Career Services early and often! It can't hurt to stop into the office freshman or sophomore year and begin getting advice about internship opportunities or a specific career field.

Career Center Resources & Services

The career center is wonderful about helping students identify a career path and giving them the tools they need to find a job in that field. Career Planning offers frequent workshops and tutorials in a variety of different areas, including resume writing, cover letter composition, job seeking, interview skills, and table manners. Career Planning staff have even been known to help students decide what to wear on an interview!

The career center offers many resources to students, including career advising (drop-in hours are Monday through Friday, 1 p.m. to 4 p.m.), individual career counseling, a broad spectrum of self-help materials, mock interviews, and career fairs, just to name a few.

For more information, please visit the Career Planning Website at:

www.holycross.edu/departments/dos/website/career_planning/index.htm

The Best & Worst

The Ten BEST Things About CHC:

1. The campus is beautiful.
2. The students are very friendly.
3. The professors are friendly and helpful.
4. The parties are great.
5. Springtime, when it finally comes, is beautiful.
6. The facilities on campus are great.
7. The staff is always willing to help.
8. It's size—you're always bumping into somebody you know.
9. It's a great education for a great price.
10. It's less than an hour from Boston.

The Ten WORST Things About CHC:

1. Worcester is awful.
2. The Worcester police.
3. A lot of the students can be close-minded.
4. The campus is extremely homogenous.
5. The school's drinking policies are draconian.
6. It's a small school, so the gossip is atrocious.
7. The social scene needs to be improved—it can get a little stale!
8. The extremely long winters!
9. Lack of diversity.
10. Bland cafeteria food.

Emerson College

120 Boylston Street, Boston, MA 02116-4624
www.emerson.edu   (617) 824-8600

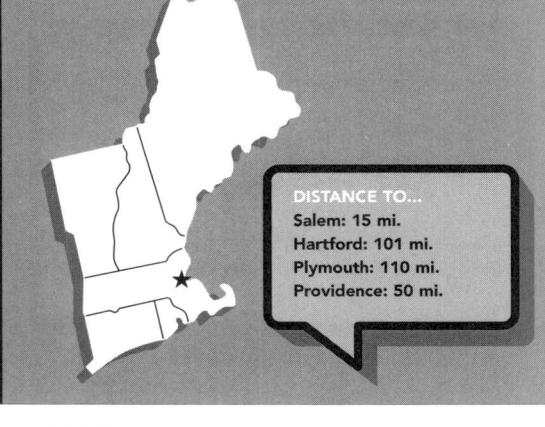

DISTANCE TO...
Salem: 15 mi.
Hartford: 101 mi.
Plymouth: 110 mi.
Providence: 50 mi.

"Emerson has limited majors, but those that it does have are very specialized and definitely cool."

Total Enrollment:
2,947

Acceptance Rate:
48%

Tuition:
$23,380

Top 10% of High School Class:
34%

Average GPA:
3.5

SAT Range
Verbal	Math	Total
570 – 660	540 – 640	1110 – 1300

ACT Range
Verbal	Math	Total
24-30	22-28	24-28

Most Popular Majors:
17% Cinematography/Drama
14% Creative Writing
12% Journalism
12% Radio, Television, & Digital Communication

Students Also Applied To:*
Boston University, Ithaca College,
New York University, Northeastern University,
Syracuse University

*For more school info check out www.collegeprowler.com

Table of Contents

Academics	778
Local Atmosphere	780
Safety & Security	781
Computers	783
Facilities	784
Campus Dining	786
Off-Campus Dining	787
Campus Housing	788
Off-Campus Housing	790
Diversity	791
Guys & Girls	793
Athletics	794
Greek Life	796
Drug Scene	797
Campus Strictness	798
Overall Experience	799
The Inside Scoop	800
Finding a Job or Internship	801
The Best & Worst	802

College Prowler Report Card

Academics	B+
Local Atmosphere	A
Safety & Security	B+
Computers	B
Facilities	B
Campus Dining	B+
Off-Campus Dining	A
Campus Housing	A-
Off-Campus Housing	B+
Diversity	D
Guys	B
Girls	A-
Athletics	D+
Greek Life	D+
Drug Scene	B
Campus Strictness	A-

Academics

Best Places to Study
Take advantage of Emerson's unique setting when you need to study and head to the Boston Common. Or, if you're not up for that, there's always the library.

Sample Academic Clubs
Communication and Political Law Association (CPLA), Emerson Communication (EmComm), National Broadcasting Society/ Alpha Epsilon Rho (NBS/AERho), Public Relations Student Society of America (PRSSA), Radio-Television News Directors Association (RTNDA), Society of Professional Journalists (SPJ), the Undergraduate Writers' Network

The Lowdown
ON ACADEMICS

Degrees Awarded:
Bachelor, Master

Undergraduate Schools:
School of the Arts
School of Communication

Full-time Faculty:
128

Part-time Faculty:
247

Faculty with Terminal Degree:
71%

Student-to-Faculty Ratio:
15:1

Average Course Load:
4 courses

Special Degree Options:
Emerson allows students to design their own majors and has a teacher certificate program.

AP Test Score Requirements:
Possible credit for scores of 3, 4, or 5, except English Language, Literature, and Composition exams, which require scores of 4 or 5.

IB Test Score Requirements:
Possible credit for scores of 4, 5, 6, or 7, with the exception of Language A/English, for which a score of 6 or 7 is required.

Students Speak Out
ON ACADEMICS

"**The teachers at Emerson can be a bit spacey, but many are seasoned professionals who are willing to help eager students.**"

Q "**Teachers are on both ends of the spectrum**. They are either engaging, excellent, and teach fun, interesting courses, or they are boring, painful to listen to, and don't seem to have much knowledge in the subject."

Q "That daunting red line between student and teacher is often blurred to the point where, despite the teacher's position behind the desk, there's an air of camaraderie. But, they don't blow smoke either; I've been in more than one workshop where the teacher has, in so many words, told the student that he or she was wasting the class's time. It may seem harsh, but the world is harsh, the job market competitive, and the sooner that's made clear, the better. **Emerson is not a school for people looking to half-ass their way to a degree**; if you come, come all the way or not at all. The teachers won't have it any other way."

Q "Most of the professors are at least competent and securely-educated in their subject matter. I have also **had my share of arrogant, pompous professors** who I would recommend staying away from. As for the classes, a lot of times I was surprised at how interesting I found them to be, but I was also disappointed at times. Overall, the good outweigh the bad."

Q "It's an art school. I came here expecting a teaching roster full of beret donning, chain-smokers sipping whiskey-laced coffee and extolling the virtues of Dadaism. What you have instead, for the most part, are **well-educated individuals who are serious about teaching their craft** to students who are serious about learning it."

Q "**The faculty is pretty diverse**; there are the stuffed-shirts, the pipe-smoking grand wizards of tenure, who, from time to time, will snap off some wry comment that lets you know they weren't always like this. There are a lot of young teachers, too—people who are on top of the now, who know what's really taking off in their fields, and have a lot of contacts that they are more than willing to put you in touch with. They aren't the fresh-out-of-the-meat-grinder types, with tags still dangling from tweed blazers, hoping to make enough money teaching so they can pay their bills and focus on their true passion. I think for a lot of them, teaching is the passion. Many professors encourage students to come by their office, if not to ask questions about the class, then just to chat."

Q "Talk to upperclassmen about professors because **it's a real gamble**. Some of the teachers here are amazing and totally dedicated to their students. Some are just professionals, teaching on the side. The writing, literature, and publishing department is great. I recommend Peter Shippy and Kevin Miller. They are hot tickets. For the most part, you'll get back what you put into a class."

The College Prowler Take
ON ACADEMICS

Emerson is perfect for students who have always wanted to be on stage, behind a camera, writing the next best seller, editing a magazine, or studying communication disorders. Classes are generally small. Very few are lecture size, and you'll never be in class with hundreds of students, as can happen at larger universities. That, coupled with the opportunity to start taking classes within your major concentration during your first semester, makes Emerson great for giving students a running start.

Emerson has plenty of stellar professors. Unfortunately, many are adjunct faculty, which means that they aren't guaranteed job security. Students often complain about Emerson's inability to keep great professors around for long, due to the lack of sufficient contracts. Even so, there are plenty of part-time professors, who stick around because they love it, and full-time professors who are well worth their salaries. When it comes to majors, don't come to Emerson without one. Though, the College does allow students to enter freshman year as undeclared, Emerson is so specialized that it doesn't make sense to come here without a strong specific area of interest or dream to pursue.

The College Prowler™ Grade on
Academics: B+

A high Academics grade generally indicates that professors are knowledgeable, accessible, and genuinely interested in their students' welfare. Other determining factors include class size, how well professors communicate, and whether or not classes are engaging.

Local Atmosphere

Did You Know?

Boston goes wild about St. Patrick's Day. South Boston and Cambridge celebrate for the whole week. Green beer is the drink of choice.

The Lowdown
ON LOCAL ATMOSPHERE

Region:
Northeast

City, State:
Boston, Massachusetts

Setting:
City

Distance from Providence:
41 miles, 1 hour

Distance from New York City:
190 miles, 4 hours

Points of Interest:
Museum of Fine Arts, Boston Symphony Orchestra, Freedom Trail, Old North Church, Museum of Science, Harvard Museum of Natural History, the Institute of Contemporary Art, Charles River Esplanade, Franklin Park Zoo, Arnold Arboretum, Faneuil Hall, Fogg Art Museum, Harvard Square, John Hancock Conservatory, Museum of Afro American History, Fenway Park, Boston Commons, the Charles River

Major Sports Teams:
Patriots (NFL), Red Sox (MLB), Bruins (NHL), Celtics (NBA)

City Websites:
www.boston.com
www.cityofboston.gov
www.boston.citysearch.com

Students Speak Out
ON LOCAL ATMOSPHERE

"Boston is beautiful when you first move here. I know plenty of people who still love it; but for me, three years in this college town has been too many."

Q "**Cambridge is a lot more relaxed than Boston** will ever be. Massachusetts Avenue is a plethora of fun, with all the music venues and mixes of people. Shops like Pearl Art and Harvest Co-op draw an artsy, young crowd that keeps the area fresh."

Q "Being in downtown Boston is awesome, and Emerson has one of the best, if not the best, locations of any Boston higher education institution. We are situated around the Commons, which is gorgeous every season of the year and offers a respite from the busy city streets. **Boston has a great blend of historic beauty and metropolitan chic**. There definitely are seedy areas; one is Chinatown, which is right next door to Emerson, but normal street smarts will keep you safe in these areas. You probably won't have any problems in this relatively safe urban setting."

Q "**Boston consists almost entirely of places of higher learning**. It would be safe to say that no one over the age of 22 lives here. Unless, of course, they're alumni who graduated years ago and are now distributing subway tokens, or working at a video store asking for your card number while glancing up at the TV playing 'Army of Darkness.'"

Q "Boston is an amazing city to go to college in. **It is a small, historic, beautiful city with a lot of young people** and things for students to do because of the number of colleges in such a small area."

Q "Emerson is seated in the **heart of Boston's downtown area**, right at the edge of the Boston Commons—a kind of Central Park Jr.—which has become Emerson's unofficial campus and a haven for underclassmen."

Safety & Security

The College Prowler Take
ON LOCAL ATMOSPHERE

The Lowdown
ON SAFETY & SECURITY

Interested in moving to a small city with big ideas? Then Boston's for you. Filled to the city limits with colleges, Boston offers everything imaginable for entertainment. Because of the high numbers of young people, *Forbes.com*'s **2003 survey rated the city number three in its list of best singles cities. The survey also voted Boston number one for best culture. From theater to live music, from sports to art, there is plenty to keep you occupied in this city. Just make sure to bring your wallet or purse. Having fun in Boston can get expensive if you like to live it up every night.**

Number of EC Police:
16

Phone:
Police Emergency (617) 824-8888
Police Business (617) 824-8555

Safety Services:
Emerson safety consists of 24-hour foot and vehicle patrols, shuttle service, emergency phones, controlled residence hall access, and educational programs about acquaintance rape and sexual assault.

Center for Health and Wellness
Phone: (617) 824-8666

Health Center Office Hours:
The Center for Health is available for walk-ins and appointments, Monday through Friday, during the school year.

The College Prowler™ Grade on
Local Atmosphere: A

A high Local Atmosphere grade indicates that the area surrounding campus is safe and scenic. Other factors include nearby attractions, proximity to other schools, and the town's attitude toward students.

Students Speak Out
ON SAFETY & SECURITY

"The building security guards don't seem to do anything. You just need to know not to walk through the Boston Commons at night."

"The **dorms at Emerson are pretty well-guarded**, and no one will be getting in without a valid resident ID or guest sign-in. I always felt safe at the school, but the police officers who work downstairs in the Little Building have been known for being rude and hard to approach. That is definitely a department within Residence Life that needs revision."

"The **security guards at 100 Beacon Street definitely get plenty of sleep** while on duty overnight, but the doors are locked, so nobody who doesn't belong will get in."

"I **always felt safe**, even when it seemed like everyone was getting mugged and I had to cross the Commons every night."

"Emerson is really safe. **There are locks where there should be**, desk-sitters where there should be, and no random people coming into the dorms off the street."

"I think the safety measures taken by Emerson are more than adequate. When we faced the Democratic National Convention, **the school took a lot of effort to make sure that the facilities were secure.**"

The College Prowler Take
ON SAFETY & SECURITY

Despite the fact that Emerson is located in the heart of a city, the campus is quite safe. Emerson Police are visible on campus and respond quickly to complaints and emergencies. Of course, students should be aware of their surroundings, especially at night, and take care when walking through the park after dark. Dorms are secure with sign-in procedures in operation 24 hours a day. Students must swipe their IDs before accessing residence floors, and all guests must be signed in and out. Though the campus is relatively safe from non-Emerson mischief-makers, crime does occasionally take place. Keeping yourself safe and your belongings secure usually doesn't take much more than using your common sense.

The College Prowler™ Grade on
Safety & Security: B+

A high grade in Safety & Security means that students generally feel safe, campus police are visible, blue-light phones and escort services are readily available, and safety precautions are not overly necessary.

Computers

Students Speak Out
ON COMPUTERS

The Lowdown
ON COMPUTERS

High-Speed Network?
Yes

Wireless Network?
Yes

Number of Labs:
9

Numbers of Computers:
310

24-Hour Labs:
None

Charge to Print?
Students automatically receive $5 for printing on their student IDs each semester. Additional pages may be printed for 10 cents per black and white page, and 50 cents per color page.

Operating Systems:
PC and Mac

Free Software:
None

"I'm not a computer person, so everything I need is there in the labs. But, I hear that there are lots of cool film editing programs from my technology-savvy friends."

Q "Computer **labs are crowded**. You can usually get a computer pretty fast, but bringing your own computer is a good idea, if you have one—though the computers are excellent and have all the programs you'll need."

Q "I absolutely hate using the computer lab in the library. **It seems like there is always a wait**, except in the summer for obvious reasons, and there are always people obnoxiously gabbing on their cell phones."

Q "The labs are actually pretty good. Programs are prevalent, and there are computers designated for various majors so you can almost always find a free space. **Bringing your own stuff does help** when you get lazy and don't want to leave the house but have work to do."

Q "There are a few **computer networks available that are equipped with all kinds of useful programs**. There are usually a few computers available, and the tech department has always been extremely helpful. Having your own computer is ideal of course, but you can just rely on the labs if you need to."

Q "**Avoid the computer labs during midterm and finals times.** Otherwise, it's a good resource. The lab assistants can range from helpful, to condescending, to clueless. So if you need help, it's a gamble. My suggestion is to make friends with a nice boy on the technology floor of the Little Building."

The College Prowler Take
ON COMPUTERS

Does Emerson have what you need to compose, process, and develop your project? Most likely. Are you always guaranteed the opportunity to work on it when you want? Not a chance. The computer lab in the library is usually packed, especially during weekday evenings, finals, and days that your personal computer crashes. The lab at 100 Beacon Street is small, but very convenient for those who live on campus. Occupancy of the other labs fluctuates based on classes that may be taught in them. Students often complain about the availability of computers in the library, forgetting that there are other labs that can be used to print and work from. Each classroom is also hooked up with at least one network connection. The wireless network reaches into the Commons, the cafeteria, and some classrooms.

Facilities

The Lowdown
ON FACILITIES

Student Center:
Yes

Athletic Center:
No

Libraries:
Emerson College Library

Movie Theatre on Campus?
No

Bowling on Campus?
No

Bar on Campus?
Not in Boston (though The Tam is just across the street). There is a lounge that serves wine and beer in the residence hall in the Netherlands campus.

Coffeehouse on Campus?
Yes

Radio Stations:
2

Popular Places to Chill:
Emerson students can usually be found relaxing outside any of the College's buildings or off-campus apartments

The College Prowler™ Grade on
Computers: B

A high grade in Computers designates that computer labs are available, the computer network is easily accessible, and the campus' computing technology is up-to-date.

Did You Know?

Emerson's library has the only computer lab on campus that is food-friendly. Cell phones are strongly discouraged.

Students Speak Out
ON FACILITIES

{ "I really like our gym. It's definitely tiny compared to a lot of schools, but there also aren't as many people working out here."

Q "The facilities are new and pretty, but small. The **gym sucks**. The facilities are feeling the crunch of bigger incoming classes, but they still manage. I'm sure it will be updated with the uber-pricey tuition."

Q "The **Student Union is beautiful**, and it will be sad when Emerson sells the Back Bay buildings, because they really provide a warmer atmosphere than the new sterile buildings going up on Boylston and Tremont Streets."

Q "The facilities on campus are all pretty great. From the gym, to the theatres, to the editing rooms, **most of Emerson's facilities cater to what Emerson students need**. Everything has been updated in recent years, and offers modern technology that enhances both students' learning experiences and lifestyle."

Q "I haven't checked out the gym, which as far as I know, is the only real athletic facility on campus. The computers in labs are pretty good, but **the kiosks are terrible**. So are the ones in the front of the library."

Q "**You have to pay to join the gym**, which is ridiculous since the school is so expensive. But overall, the facilities are really nice, with computers and great camera equipment."

The College Prowler Take
ON FACILITIES

As you may know by now, Emerson does not have a traditional campus. The college claims that the city is their campus. What does this really mean? Well, there aren't any superfluous buildings standing around. And by superfluous I mean a recreational center or other fun facilities where enjoyment is the name of the game. Yes, there is a student union, but because of its location (across campus from where the classes are located), it's more for business than socializing. Though Emerson doesn't have as many amenities as other colleges might, it does offer the facilities that will help you with what you're here for. And, if you ask Emerson students what they're here for, they most likely won't say "to work on my pecs." Overall, the facilities are useful, but undersized.

The College Prowler™ Grade on
Facilities: B

A high Facilities grade indicates that the campus is aesthetically pleasing and well-maintained; facilities are state-of-the-art, and libraries are exceptional. Other determining factors include the quality of both athletic and student centers and an abundance of things to do on campus.

Campus Dining

The Lowdown
ON CAMPUS DINING

Freshman Meal Plan Requirement?
Yes

24-Hour On-Campus Eating?
No

Meal Plan Average Cost:
$4,098

Students Speak Out
ON CAMPUS DINING

"The dining hall is the best I've been to of all the cafeterias I visited. The selection is always great, and the food is of good quality."

Q "Try not to eat on campus—seriously. I'm amazed that, despite being two blocks away from Chinatown, students rarely go there for good food."

Q "The food is good if you eat it every once in a while. **There's a lot of variety**. There's food for vegans, vegetarians, and carnivores. But when it's lunch and dinner everyday, you tire of it very quickly."

Q "The **food is very good compared to other schools**. You will definitely get sick of it after living there for a semester, but Aramark is pretty good at giving us a wide selection. If you're a vegetarian or vegan, they give a lot of alternative choices."

Q "The dining hall really isn't that bad. I think **people like to complain about it** because Emerson students just like to complain. I enjoy the food and will even beg an on-campus friend to let me have a guest meal every now and then."

Q "**Individual meals are very expensive**. It makes more sense to eat at one of the restaurants over in Chinatown if you just need to grab lunch or dinner. The salad bar is also good for a quick, healthy meal."

The College Prowler Take
ON CAMPUS DINING

Plenty of students gripe about the dining hall, but that might be because Emerson students like to complain. The meal plans are generous, and few students who choose the block meal plan can complain of not getting enough food. The dining hall operates on an all-you-can-eat basis, which means that if you do run out of meals by the end of the semester, you can always stay in the dining hall all day and keep eating, for the price of one meal. Eating in the dining hall for three or four months straight can get to be nauseating, but the same goes for any school. Overall, the on-campus eating situation is a good one.

The College Prowler™ Grade on
Campus Dining: B+

Our grade on Campus Dining addresses the quality of both school-owned dining halls and independent on-campus restaurants as well as the price, availability, and variety of food.

Off-Campus Dining

Did You Know?
There are 80 Dunkin' Donuts within a five-mile radius of Emerson's Little Building.

Students Speak Out
ON OFF-CAMPUS DINING

The Lowdown
ON OFF-CAMPUS DINING

Best Pizza:
New York Pizza, Upper Crust

Best Chinese:
Buddha's Delight

Best Breakfast:
Sorella's

Best Wings:
The Pour House

Best Healthy:
Other Side Cosmic Café

Best Place to Take Your Parents:
Mother Anna's, Legal Seafood

Late-Night, Half-Price Food Specials:
McCormick & Schmick's, The Pour House

24-Hour Eating:
South Street Diner, Bova's Bakery

Student Favorites:
Grasshopper, New York Pizza, Middle East, Other Side Cafe, Trident Cafe

"I never go out. I can't afford to eat anything except the stale and moldy leftovers that my roommates leave in the fridge."

Q "Everything that delivers in Boston is either pizza and subs or Chinese. The **Chinese food in this city is the worst**. Do not eat the Chinese food, unless you only eat vegetables, in which case, the broccoli is usually good no matter where you call."

Q "There are **lots of great restaurants**. Don't be afraid to go far to find good food."

Q "Buddha's Delight is delicious. As for pizza, there is no better place than Upper Crust. And you can't forget about the **$2 happy hour menu at McCormick and Schmick's**. Other than that, I am too poor to eat out very often. Oh yeah, the sandwich shop down the alley by 120 Boylston is amazing, if pricey."

Q "The **Chinatown cafeteria has a few different restaurants** located in one building, and they are all relatively cheap and really good to eat."

Q "My favorite places to eat are **Grasshopper and the Italian restaurants in the North End**. But, while I'm at school, the only place I have time to patronize is the Dunkin' Donuts."

The College Prowler Take
ON OFF-CAMPUS DINING

Taking the time to go off campus to eat is well worth the trip and money. Unfortunately, there aren't many restaurants within sprinting distance of Emerson, which means many students don't take the time to dine between classes. When there is a long break between classes, or students have the time to travel, there are tons of great restaurants to try. Many students complain that the best restaurants are out of the immediate vicinity of Emerson. Pricing also becomes a concern for many students. School is expensive, and city-eating can definitely add to an expense account quickly. The bottom line is that you can find any kind of food you want in Boston; hopefully you have the time and the resources to go and get it.

The College Prowler™ Grade on
Off-Campus Dining: A

A high Off-Campus Dining grade implies that off-campus restaurants are affordable, accessible, and worth visiting. Other factors include the variety of cuisine and the availability of alternative options (vegetarian, vegan, Kosher, etc.).

Campus Housing

The Lowdown
ON CAMPUS HOUSING

Undergrads on Campus:
46%

Number of Dormitories:
4

Number of University-Owned Apartments: 0

Room Types:
Emerson offers singles, doubles, triples, and suite rooms.

Available for Rent:
Emerson does not have any appliances available for rent.

Cleaning Service?
Common bathrooms are cleaned daily; semi-private and in-room bathrooms are not cleaned by Emerson staff.

You Get:
A bed, desk, chair, dresser, wardrobe or closet, Ethernet hookup, window coverings, bookshelf, telephone and cable TV jacks, phone number, free on-campus calling, local and long distance options

Bed Type:
Twin extra-long (39"x 80"); some lofted, some bunked, some regular

Also Available:
Specialized learning communities

Did You Know?

With the exception of the few single gender floors, all floors are coed. In the older residence halls, specifically 100 Beacon, bathrooms connect some rooms, which means that you'll get to know your neighbors (whether they're guys or girls) really fast.

Because of the electrical system constraints in the older dorms, microwaves are not permitted in 100 Beacon, 132 Beacon, or 6 Arlington, and mini-refrigerators are not allowed in 132 Beacon or 6 Arlington. Both appliances are allowed in 80 Boylston.

"The **Little Building is nice, if you've always wanted to live in a completely self-contained environment** right out of some bleak sci-fi flick, set sometime in the near future where your entire life is lived vertically, [and] you occasionally venture down in one of the starkly-lit elevators to the cafeteria or convenience store for sustenance, then back up to your room, which looks exactly like every other one on the floor, where the windows don't open more than six inches."

"There's something about the **Little Building that makes it really easy to get sick in the winter**. I think it's all of the people living in one building, coupled with the fact that they recycle the air from floor to floor."

The College Prowler Take
ON CAMPUS HOUSING

The dorms at Emerson quickly become the students' home and pride. The best part about the dorms is that they provide a community, and new friends give freshmen a leg to stand on in an otherwise, overwhelming new experience. You might want to try to get housing in the older dorms, just to experience life on Beacon Street. Unless your daddy's rich, you won't be able to afford living there again for a long, long time. Dorms are equipped with an Internet hookup for each resident and enough furniture for your comfort. The suites are pretty nice, but, unfortunately, only available in the Little Building. Overall, residence life is good while it lasts, but few tears are shed when moving out.

Students Speak Out
ON CAMPUS HOUSING

"The residential campus is divided between the Little Building and those 'across campus' living in 6 Arlington or 100 Beacon. I lived in the LB for two years and loved it."

"The dorms that are located in **old brownstones are homey and comfortable**, but with the school relocating all the classes across campus, across the Commons, it is much easier to live in the Little Building, since everything is right there."

"The **Little Building feels like an asylum** after a while. It's big enough to allow students not to leave it for entire weekends. It has a dining hall and fitness center, and can be damaging to students. I'm not going to say they're cannibals, but LB people are pretty crazy sometimes."

"It depends on what you like. The older dorms, like 6 Arlington and 100 Beacon, have originality because they are older buildings. **The Little Building is newer and cleaner**, but all the rooms look the same."

The College Prowler™ Grade on
Campus Housing: A-

A high Campus Housing grade indicates that dorms are clean, well-maintained, and spacious. Other determining factors include variety of dorms, proximity to classes, and social atmosphere.

Off-Campus Housing

Students Speak Out
ON OFF-CAMPUS HOUSING

{ "It's always a challenge to find housing in Boston. There are good places, people, and prices, but it's not easy to have all three at once."

Q "Housing is cheaper when you live off campus. It gives you a head start on life, such as learning how to budget, make dinner, and all those sorts of things you get under your belt before some other college folks do. You also **get the benefit of being able to do whatever you wish**—whether it's lighting a candle or lighting a bong."

Q "After two years of the dorms, **most of the students move off campus** to get the other college experience. Boston offers a series of pockets, each with a different atmosphere. You can choose the experience you want: Cambridge, Somerville, Jamaica Plain, Fenway, Allston, or Brighton. Each has its own pulse, its own rhythm, and its own strengths and weaknesses. Students have the rare opportunity to really tailor their college experience, based on the place they decide to live."

Q "You've just finished your sophomore year, and you decide to move off campus; you want to live somewhere with a good party scene, a good choice of bars close by, so you chose Fenway. You live there for a year and have a blast, but decide you'd like to spend your senior year someplace a little quieter, a little less hectic, so you go out to Brighton, a quieter area at the end of the B Line, about a 30-minute train ride from school. It's still all there, all the bars, clubs, parties, but **you can get away from it if you want**."

Q "The idea of not having guaranteed housing after sophomore year scared me, but after living on campus for two years, I decided, along with most of the students in my class, to live off campus. **It's very easy to find housing** in Boston, and most of your friends will probably want to move off campus as well, so it's easy to find a roommate. Off-campus student housing services are helpful with the whole process."

The Lowdown
ON OFF-CAMPUS HOUSING

Undergrads in Off-Campus Housing:
54%

Average Rent for a Studio Apartment:
$800–$1,500 per month

Average Rent for a One-Bedroom Apartment:
$1,300–$2,000 per month

Average Rent for a Two-Bedroom Apartment:
$1,300–$1,700 per month

Popular Areas:
Allston, Brighton, Mission Hill, North End, and Jamaica Plain

Best Time to Look for a Place:
February or March

For Assistance Contact
Off-Campus Student Services
www.emerson.edu/offcampus_housing
Phone: (617) 824-7863
E-mail: ocss@emerson.edu

Q "**Renting is expensive**, and don't forget about the bills. The apartment market is finally opening up. Move outside of downtown Boston. Look in Somerville and Brookline."

Q "Emerson has a Website where you can hook up with other off-campus kids who are looking for housing. It's **pretty convenient**."

The College Prowler Take
ON OFF-CAMPUS HOUSING

Because of the lack of housing at Emerson, few students stay in the dorms until they graduate. In fact, students are not guaranteed housing after freshman year. Some students worry about getting kicked out after their first year, but in the long run, they appreciate the early start on living in the real world. It's true that living off campus is vastly different from living on the same floor with at least a dozen other people. Living in an off-campus apartment provides students with more freedom, virtually no rules, and a fair share of responsibility. Boston is a pricey place to live, but Emerson's expensive room and board rates provide little excuse to stick around in the dorms. Though Boston has some of the highest rents in the country, it is definitely possible to find housing that ends up being cheaper than the dorms.

The College Prowler™ Grade on
Off-Campus Housing: B+

A high grade in Off-Campus Housing indicates that apartments are of high quality, close to campus, affordable, and easy to secure.

Diversity

The Lowdown
ON DIVERSITY

African American: 2%

Asian American: 4%

Hispanic: 5%

Native American: 0%

White: 85%

International: 4%

Out-of-State: 65%

Minority Clubs
Despite the glaring "whiteness" shown in the Emerson's diversity statistics, minority clubs on campus such as ASIA, Amigos, and EBONI are abundant, active, and throw some of the best events.

Most Popular Religions
Emerson students are known for fearing holy water and all things religious. A few religious groups, such as Hillel and the Islamic Community of Emerson, exist on campus, but they don't make much noise.

Political Activity

Most students and faculty are politically and socially liberal. Both are generally outspoken about politics and politically active.

Gay Acceptance

The campus welcomes gay and lesbian students. The Office of Gay, Lesbian, Bisexual, and Transgender (GLBT) Student Life works to improve the quality of life for all students. The Office of GLBT Student Life works closely with the student organization Emerson's Alliance for Gays, Lesbians, and Everyone (EAGLE). For more information visit www.emerson.edu/student_life, and click on GLBT Student Life.

Economic Status

Let's just say that the phrase, "Do you know who her father/uncle/mummy/brother is?" isn't uncommon. Emerson students are loaded.

Students Speak Out
ON DIVERSITY

{ "I think the admissions office thinks the college is very diverse, but there seem to be very few black students and not many other minorities."

Q "There are a lot of international students who all seem to be quite wealthy, and I never felt as if they really contributed to the 'diversity' of the classroom because of their socioeconomic status. **There is a thriving, strong, and open gay community** on campus, which is cool."

Q "The campus is **not very diverse** at all. I have heard many a complaint that the Emerson student population is made up of rich white kids who pretend to be in the minority by going against the mainstream. A lot of students dress differently, get piercings, and/or dye their hair just to appear rebellious, when they are just conforming to what they think a defiant person would look like. In terms of racial minorities, African Americans and Hispanics are barely represented, for whatever reason."

Q "Emerson **isn't very diverse**. We are mostly white, rich, liberal-minded, possibly gay, and into indie rock or hip-hop. Yes, there are exceptions, but unfortunately there aren't a lot of people who bring different political, socio-economic, or racial elements to the school."

Q "Like, **does the campus include people from both the East Coast and the West Coast**? Then, yes, it's definitely diverse. I'm from Vermont, and I had a class with someone all the way from Portland. Portland, Oregon, that is. Er, wait. Maybe that was Portland, Maine."

The College Prowler Take
ON DIVERSITY

The admissions office at Emerson prides the school on the diversity of its students, but anyone who looks at the numbers quickly gathers that the school is predominantly white. African Americans, Hispanics, and other minorities are barely represented at Emerson. Anyone who attends a class learns that the school is mostly comprised of liberal students and faculty. The exceptions to these, of course, exist and are refreshing. The college does have a sizable gay community, which is well-supported and positively contributes to the diversity of the school. Emerson is also home to many international students. Overall, many Emerson students complain about the overwhelmingly white, liberal, wealth of the campus. But, as a student, you will be exposed to many different people, and really, who cares what they look like?

The College Prowler™ Grade on
Diversity: D

A high grade in Diversity indicates that ethnic minorities and international students have a notable presence on campus and that students of different economic backgrounds, religious beliefs, and sexual preferences are well-represented.

Guys & Girls

The Lowdown
ON GUYS & GIRLS

Women Undergrads: 61.3%

Men Undergrads: 38.7%

Social Scene
There is no social hierarchy on campus. There are groups that can be generalized based on style of dress or major, but you'll find that those generalizations don't hold up very long. Emerson students are very social and don't keep to a small group of friends.

Hookups or Relationships?
There are a fair amount of people in relationships, a relatively large amount of those are long distance, too. Of course, there are plenty of students who are looking for non-committal nights on the town.

Dress Code
Emerson does not dress like your high school (most likely). Here, the students look like the kids who dressed weird and went to your high school—and lots of them. Yes, there are plenty of well-dressed students. Yes, there are some preppy kids. But, please expect more tight pants, Clash T-shirts, studded belts, Mohawks, dyed hair, and leather than you are used to.

Students Speak Out
ON GUYS & GIRLS

"It seems like there are definite 'types' of people at Emerson, as far as styles go. There are mod kids, hip-hop kids, and indie rock kids. Okay, mostly indie rock kids."

Q "The **guys are gay for a large part**, and the girls like to hang out with them and date guys from other schools and graduate students. The remaining guys are lonely or have girlfriends from back home. And the film majors and theatre majors, while hard to avoid, are easy to stay separated from, which is nice."

Q "As a girl, my opinion may be a little biased, but I think the girls are way better looking than the guys on this campus. It's very cliché to say that most of the guys that attend this school are gay, and it is true that we probably **have a higher homosexual male population then most schools**, but there are some straight guys here—just not very good ones. The decent ones are few and far between. But, it's not like we're in the middle of nowhere and limited to Emerson's selection. Most guys come with some kind of quirky personality, and you won't find too many Type-A personalities, but that goes for most of the Emerson population."

Q "What is truly unique about the student body is that it's not compartmentalized; you're likely to walk by a circle of kids hacking out in front of one of the dorms and see the kid with the three-foot spiked blue Mohawk handing a cigarette to the kid with the rugby sweater and Birkenstocks. It **can be a little trendy at times**, and a bit of conforming to the rebellion, but I think most of it is in earnest."

Q "The **guys are gay**—I'm just kidding. Both sexes are super trendy, and have some sort of definitive style, but almost everyone thinks they are wildly unique and somehow manage to not see that all of their friends look and act just like them."

> "Revel in the absence of all things jock. The guys at Emerson are mostly emo types—the tight black Ramones T-shirt, studded belt, fitted jeans, Chuck Jones-thing. It's like a music video. Nerd-rock and skinny is cool, and there are cardigans everywhere. Mohawks aren't uncommon, neither is dyed or spiked hair, facial piercings, or tattoos. The girls, ah the girls. **There's a lot of the pixie types, the spiky hair, no make-up, natural beauty**. The Goth movement is well-represented; the girl with raven hair, black mascara, pale skin, pouting lips. There are straight-up punked-out chicks, too—leather, steel-studded bracelets, Doc Martin's, wallet chains. Or, there's the Lisa Loeb types, with the nerdy glasses and cute smiles."

The College Prowler Take
ON GUYS & GIRLS

Emerson students will probably tell you that their campus is pretty attractive. It's most likely because whoever you ask looks a lot like everyone else. Emerson's population likes to look good, though "good" is a subjective term. There are some really well-dressed rich kids, who look good by anyone's standards, and some interesting styles that are attractive in their own unique way. On the whole, Emerson isn't a campus of slobs who roll out of bed and trudge to class, but this is probably because most students don't live on campus. Some describe the general look as "art school-esque," and find comfort in the fact that they may seem to fit in here. But, please don't make a decision based on looks. Emerson students have more depth than that, and so should you.

The College Prowler™ Grade on
Guys: B

A high grade for Guys indicates that the male population on campus is attractive, smart, friendly, and engaging, and that the school has a decent ratio of guys to girls.

The College Prowler™ Grade on
Girls: A-

A high grade for Girls not only implies that the women on campus are attractive, smart, friendly, and engaging, but also that there is a fair ratio of girls to guys.

The Lowdown
ON ATHLETICS

Men's Teams:
Basketball
Baseball
Cross Country
Lacrosse
Soccer
Tennis
Volleyball

Women's Teams:
Basketball
Cross Country
Lacrosse
Softball
Soccer
Tennis

Overlooked Teams
Plenty of Emerson students don't know about the school's sports teams. There is virtually no following of Emerson teams, aside from the friends and roommates of the players.

Fields
Because Emerson does not own any fields or courts, the college rents play space from nearby schools and the city to field their teams. Rotch Playground was reopened in March of 2005 and the new Emerson College Gymnasium is part of the new residence and student life building that is currently being built. The gym is slated to open in January of 2006.

Getting Tickets
Sports events are free, just show up.

Athletic Division:
NCAA Division III

Conference:
Eastern College Athletic Conference (ECAC) and Great Northeast Athletic Conference (GNAC)

School Mascot:
Lion

Students Speak Out
ON ATHLETICS

"Sports aren't big here. There are some great athletes who have clearly chosen academics over sports by attending Emerson."

Q "As far as I know, **sports aren't big at all** on campus. The last that I heard, the basketball team held practice in the gym of a local high school, but maybe things have changed."

Q "**Lacrosse and soccer for guys** are the only sports I've ever heard anything about. But I am sure they exist somewhere."

Q "Varsity sports are not very popular at all on campus. A few of my friends played sports here, but they mostly did it because they had played in high school and missed it, not because they were good. **My roommate played volleyball, and you have to be very dedicated**. But, don't expect anyone from the Emerson community to come out and support because rarely anyone goes to any games."

Q "There is **not much to say about Emerson sports**. We have them, and some people play them. Nobody really cares, though."

Q "I think **I'm actually one of the few people at Emerson who wishes we had some intramural sports clubs going on**. The only real sporting experience I've had here is an attempt to create a kickball game freshmen year in the dorms."

The College Prowler Take
ON ATHLETICS

The average student doesn't play varsity sports at Emerson, and chances are his or her friends don't either. In fact it's possible that the average student doesn't even know that Emerson has sports teams. Though team members and their roommates, friends, and parents might attend Emerson's varsity sports events, there is very little awareness and much less support on campus. As for playing sports non-competitively, Emerson doesn't have many options. Your best bet would be to try to organize a group to meet in the Commons and play Frisbee. Perhaps after Emerson completes its move to the east side of campus, and the new facilities have been built, there will be more opportunities for sports. But, knowing the typical Emerson student, the interest for intramural teams isn't likely to grow.

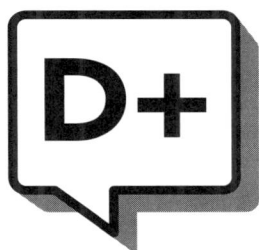

The College Prowler™ Grade on
Athletics: D+

A high grade in Athletics indicates that students have school spirit, that sports programs are respected, that games are well-attended, and that intramurals are a prominent part of student life.

Want to find a club sport that'll get you going? Check out the complete College Prowler book on Emerson available at *www.collegeprowler.com*.

Greek Life

Q "Greek life is present on campus, but you probably will have to make an effort to find it. **There are only a few sororities and fraternities**. They host a few of the off-campus parties, but anyone can get into them, so why bother going through all the hassle of rushing? There are enough clubs to get involved in that will actually help your career."

Q "Greek life exists at Emerson, but **very few students participate**. In my two years here I haven't met one person that was in either a frat or sorority. It's just not that kind of school."

Q "I didn't know that we had frats until my junior year. **I don't think they are what you'd expect at big universities**. The frats here don't have official housing, and I think they are mostly professional and involved in providing services, rather than socially-oriented."

The Lowdown
ON GREEK LIFE

Number of Fraternities:
4

Number of Sororities:
3

Percent of Undergrad Men in Fraternities:
12%

Percent of Undergrad Women in Sororities:
12%

The College Prowler Take
ON GREEK LIFE

The few frats and sororities available for membership at Emerson are not popular; and in contrast to the societies at bigger universities, the goal for Emerson Greeks is not just to party. Emerson fraternities and sororities are designed for community service and professional networking. They do not rule the social scene. In fact, you might not even know they exist, unless you visit the Student Union and take a peak at their bulletin board, or go to the Organizational Fair and get recruited. The fraternities and sororities do throw an occasional party, but unless you're in the know, you'll probably miss it.

Students Speak Out
ON GREEK LIFE

{ "I think Emerson Greek life may actually have more to do with the 'foundations' of Greek life than the movie version of the frat party."

Q "**Who cares about Greek life**? There are frats, but even those involved don't seem to be crazy about it."

The College Prowler™ Grade on
Greek Life: D+

A high grade in Greek Life indicates that sororities and fraternities are not only present, but also active on campus. Other determining factors include the variety of houses available and the respect the Greek community receives from the rest of the campus.

Drug Scene

> "The drug scene is mostly **limited to alcohol and marijuana**. You can find the crowd that goes further, but if you're not looking for it, it probably won't be thrown in your face."

> "I didn't really **know much about Emerson's particular drug scene** until I read an article in *Boston Magazine*."

> "I **don't do drugs**. The cool thing about Emerson is that there are enough people who are straight-edge or rarely ever drink, that you can find some people to hang out with who want to stay sober."

The Lowdown
ON DRUG SCENE

Most Prevalent Drugs on Campus:
Marijuana, alcohol

Liquor-Related Referrals:
127

Liquor-Related Arrests:
4

Drug-Related Referral:
75

Drug-Related Arrest:
43

Drug Counseling Services:
The Counseling Center
Phone: (617) 824-8595
Services: Emerson offers contact information for local support groups, crisis intervention, outside referrals, and therapy groups.

The College Prowler Take
ON DRUG SCENE

Emerson is not a haven for drug dealers or addicts. This, of course, is not to say that there aren't the occasional pot smokers and alcoholics. But what school isn't that way? Alcohol is readily available at Emerson parties (which, it should be noted, are parties that occur off campus at Emerson students' houses; there aren't really any on-campus parties to speak of). While living in the dorms, it is very easy to avoid drugs. On the other hand, if you're looking for weed, you'll most likely be able to find it. As the students tell it, there are a few students who use cocaine and other serious drugs, but this is not prevalent, nor thrown in anyone's face.

Students Speak Out
ON DRUG SCENE

"The drug scene is definitely more prominent than the Greek scene, but you have to go off campus to do anything of that sort."

The College Prowler™ Grade on
Drug Scene: B

A high grade on Drug Scene indicates that drugs are not a noticeable part of campus life; drug use is not visible, and no pressure to use them seems to exist.

Campus Strictness

Students Speak Out
ON CAMPUS STRICTNESS

"**I know someone who got a note sent home to his parents once. But, if you really screw up, it can be as extreme as being kicked out of the dorm.**"

Q "Emerson **doesn't seem to be strict at all.** People on my floors were always drunk or high, and I never heard of anyone getting in trouble for it."

Q "Depending on how strict your resident assistant is, **you can get by with drinking in your dorm room pretty easily**, as long as you're not stupid about it. If you do get caught; you will get written up, but alcohol penalties are not that severe unless you get caught more then once. For smoking pot, the consequences are a lot higher. It is possible to smoke in your dorm room, but you might as well go out to the park where cops will just slap you on the wrist, rather then get caught in your room where your living situation could be jeopardized."

Q "**I got an alcohol violation, and it sucked**. The worst part was that I was the only person I knew who actually got caught. Don't get caught. Don't be a sucker."

Q "It seems like **Emerson is stricter about little things**, such as having candles in your dorm and bringing lattes into the computer labs, than about stuff like smoking and drinking. I guess it depends on your luck and the RA you're dealing with."

Q "I think that Emerson is **pretty lax** about minor offenses. The thing that really gets me is, that every single time you bring a drink into the computer lab, it's like someone pops out of the ceiling or CD drive to reprimand you for it."

The Lowdown
ON CAMPUS STRICTNESS

What Are You Most Likely to Get Caught Doing on Campus?
Smoking marijuana or cigarettes in your dorm room, bringing food or drinks into computer labs, having candles or incense in your dorm room, smoking cigarettes in the doorway to the Little Building, underage drinking, moving your dorm furniture into the hallway, plagiarism, losing your keys, illegally downloading copyrighted materials, making too much noise in your dorm room at night, chaining your bike to fences in front of dorms

Did You Know?

Alcohol is permitted in dorm rooms of students who are at least 21 years of age.

The College Prowler Take
ON CAMPUS STRICTNESS

Emerson Police clearly aren't state troopers. They are visible on campus, but it's usually the same two or three cops that you always see, and they aren't looking to throw the book at somebody. The cops are generally around to keep the students safe from other suspicious activity that may happen on campus. They work to protect the campus from outsiders more than from itself. Basically, if students use common sense, as well as some genuine consideration for others, they can all get a long just fine. And most of the time, they do.

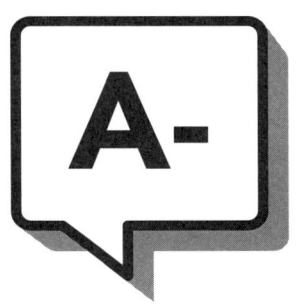

The College Prowler™ Grade on
Campus Strictness: A-

A high Campus Strictness grade implies an overall lenient atmosphere; police and RAs are fairly tolerant, and the administration's rules are flexible.

Want the 411 on campus strictness? Check out the complete College Prowler book on Emerson College available at www.collegeprowler.com.

Overall Experience

The Lowdown
ON OVERALL EXPERIENCE

"Sometimes I wish I were elsewhere, but that would involve motivation, and I am a broken human being."

Q "Overall, I think I made the right choice in coming to Emerson. I knew **I wanted a city school that was small and a bit creative**, and I think Emerson has all of those elements. I have love for the people who I have met here so far because of their great personalities and eclectic style. The Castle Program was the most amazing semester of my life, and I'm very grateful that Emerson gives their students that opportunity to explore the world and to get to know each other in such an amazing setting. I'm excited for my next two years here and hope they work out for the best."

Q "My experience at Emerson has obviously **had its ups and downs**, but, overall, I have enjoyed my time here. For the cost of tuition, you better enjoy it here, too. I think that people who leave regretting the experience are foolish for not transferring. Emerson has so much to offer, but you have to be willing to take advantage of everything to get your money's worth. You must make strong relationships with faculty in your department. You must take advantage of the opportunities to get involved in the student organizations, or create your own."

Q "**I really enjoyed Emerson**. I just graduated and feel like Emerson really prepared me for the real world. It was much more interesting and creatively-stimulating than the state school I transferred here from."

Q "Emerson is a great academic experience. Financially, **I could have made wiser decisions about college**. My funding sucks. It often feels as if people are just trying too hard socially, and that is irritating, but I would imagine that the 'traditional' college social scene would have been more maddening."

The Inside Scoop

The College Prowler Take
ON OVERALL EXPERIENCE

Most Emerson students are thrilled with the access they have at Emerson. From the professors, to the production equipment, to the classes, many students feel that they are being well-prepared for the real world. At Emerson, students have more internship opportunities, more well-known industry professionals as professors, and more quality classes than some larger schools. Because Emerson students come with fervor to learn their trade, they end up bolstering each other in workshops and projects. Some students gripe about the long lines and difficulty of dealing with the administrative aspects at Emerson, such as the Financial Aid office and the Registrar. These experiences can obscure the positive parts of the educational experience, but most students agree that something very exciting and positive is going on at Emerson.

Emerson students are unmatched in their excitement to learn, create, and get involved in activities that will better them academically and in character. Though it's common to boo-hoo about the unpredictable weather, the dismal parking and driving situation, and the early curfews in Boston, most Emerson students love their temporary home. The chance to work with award-winning faculty is one-of-a-kind, as are the students. Emerson isn't perfect, but it is a fantastic place for students who are willing to learn and work hard for what they care about. Your time spent at Emerson will certainly not be soon forgotten.

The Lowdown
ON THE INSIDE SCOOP

School Spirit

Emerson students have a quiet way of showing school spirit. In fact, for many, the way is silence. But, just because sports events don't rally school spirit, that doesn't mean that Emerson students aren't proud of their education and the opportunities they have to get their hands dirty in their particular field.

Traditions

The Evvys is an annual awards ceremony that is held in the spring to honor students who submit creative works.

Things I Wish I Knew Before Coming to Emerson:

- Sell that graphing calculator because I probably won't need to take any math classes.
- Buy textbooks online; it's often much, much cheaper.
- Most things at orientation aren't really mandatory.
- Go to the Organization Fair in September.
- I'm not going to be drafted for the WNBA from Emerson's basketball team.
- It's not a good school for people who are undecided about their major.
- Procrastination doesn't work.

Finding a Job or Internship

The Lowdown
ON FINDING A JOB OR INTERNSHIP

Career Services does a great job of helping students who want help finding a job. There are a number of services and resources that Career Services offers. While they can help you copyedit your cover letter or polish your resume, remember that it's your charm, wit, and know-how that will land the job.

Advice

Use Emerson's Career Services to the max. They are there to help you get a job or an internship, which is why you're going to school, right? Check out their Website www.emerson.edu/career_services and keep an ear out for events and workshops that they host.

Career Center Resources & Services:

Resume and cover letter critique, mock interviews, individual career advising, information on job search strategies, self-assessment tools, networking resources, job boards, CareerFinder (Emerson's site for students to post profiles and establish connections with alumni), workshops, recruiting services

AVERAGE SALARY INFORMATION

The Lowdown:
Emerson does not record average salaries for its graduates. The following annual salaries are 2002's median figures for occupations related to Emerson's majors. The information below is from the *Occupational Outlook Handbook* provided by the U.S. Department of Labor's Bureau of Statistics (www.bls.gov).

Occupation	Salary
Actors	$23,470
Advertising and Promotions	$57,130
Art directors	$61,850
Audio and video technicians	$31,110
Broadcast technicians	$27,760
Choreographers	$29,470
Dancers	$21,100
Desktop publishers	$31,620
Directors and producers	$46,240
Editors	$41,170
Fine artists	$35,260
Marketing managers	$78,250
Marketing research analysts	$53,810
Multimedia artists and animators	$43,980
News analysts, and reporters	$30,510
Photographers	$24,040
Public relations managers	$75,040
Public relations specialists	$41,710
Sound engineering technicians	$36,970
Special education teachers	$42,690
Speech-language pathologists	$49,450
Technical writers	$50,580
TV, video, motion picture	$32,720
Writers and authors	$42,790

The Best & Worst

The Ten BEST Things About Emerson:

1. Student organizations. There are tons of them at Emerson, and they give you real-life experience to contrast your classroom drudgery.

2. Video didn't kill all of the radio stars. WERS-FM keeps Emerson listeners entertained.

3. Emerson students are creative, and they show it in student films and theater productions.

4. It's nice to be at a school that makes the transition from learning to working so easy. Emerson has plenty of internship opportunities.

5. The Castle and L.A. programs give students a chance to see the world in a different light.

6. The professors at Emerson really know what they are talking about and aren't afraid to help students out.

7. Most classes are available for students who don't put off registering until the last minute.

8. Sometimes, all you can do is laugh. The comedy troupes on campus try to make that all the time.

9. Even though tuition is sky-high, the College does have some nice financial aid packages.

10. The Senior "Booze" Cruise. So long, it's been a nice trip.

The Ten WORST Things About Emerson:

1. There's a definite lack of organization in administrative offices. This becomes a problem when you need to register or contact a specific administrator.

2. Sometimes you get shafted out of a class because honors students get first dibs on registration.

3. The comedy troupes just aren't funny sometimes.

4. Boston's weather leaves much to be desired. It's rainy and windy. It's cold and grey.

5. Parking and driving in Boston can't be better than anywhere in the world.

6. Students have to pay for the fitness center.

7. Some people were never meant for the stage. These people always find their way to open-mic nights. You've been warned.

8. The Little Building has poor air circulation.

9. The computer labs get crowded during finals and midterms.

10. When I woke up this morning, I had money in my wallet. Now it's not there. Yup, that's tuition for you. It takes and it takes and it takes.

MIT

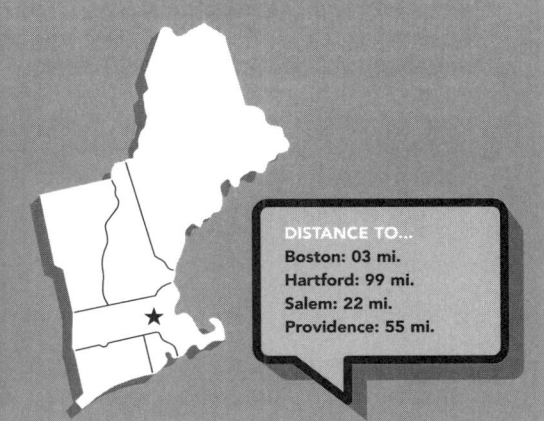

DISTANCE TO...
Boston: 03 mi.
Hartford: 99 mi.
Salem: 22 mi.
Providence: 55 mi.

77 Massachusetts Avenue, Cambridge, MA 02139
web.mit.edu   (617) 253-4791

"It's unquestionably one of the most respected colleges in the nation. Its alumni are among the most respected in the entire world."

Total Enrollment:
4,070
Acceptance Rate:
16%
Tuition:
$30,800
Top 10% of High School Class:
97%
Average GPA:
3.9
SAT Range
Verbal	Math	Total
680 – 760	730 – 800	1410 – 1560

ACT Range
Verbal	Math	Total
N/A	N/A	30-34

Most Popular Majors:
40% Engineering
13% Computer Science
9% Business/Commerce
8% Mathematics/Biology/Biological Sciences

Students Also Applied To:*
Cornell University, Harvard University, Princeton University, Stanford University, Yale University

*For more school info check out www.collegeprowler.com

Table of Contents

Academics	804
Local Atmosphere	806
Safety & Security	807
Computers	809
Facilities	810
Campus Dining	812
Off-Campus Dining	813
Campus Housing	814
Off-Campus Housing	816
Diversity	817
Guys & Girls	818
Athletics	820
Greek Life	821
Drug Scene	823
Campus Strictness	824
Overall Experience	825
The Inside Scoop	827
Finding a Job or Internship	828
The Best & Worst	828

College Prowler Report Card

Academics	A+
Local Atmosphere	A
Safety & Security	B
Computers	A+
Facilities	B+
Campus Dining	B-
Off-Campus Dining	A
Campus Housing	B+
Off-Campus Housing	D-
Diversity	A
Guys	C+
Girls	C-
Athletics	C+
Greek Life	A-
Drug Scene	B+
Campus Strictness	B-

Academics

Sample Academic Clubs

American Medical Student Association, Asian Business Club, Biomedical Engineering Society, BioPharma Business Club, Finance Club, Management Consulting Club, Marketing Club, National Society of Black Engineers, Society of Physics Students

Did You Know?

Eleven current faculty members have been awarded the Nobel Prize in subjects such as physics, physiology of medicine, economics, and chemistry.

Every January, MIT holds its Independent Activities Period (IAP), during which students can stay on campus for four weeks to take part in activities that are not offered during the regular school year. During IAP, workshops, independent research projects, field trips, and lecture series are given based on subjects ranging from figure skating and vegetarian cooking, to neuro-anatomy and robot design.

The Lowdown
ON ACADEMICS

Degrees Awarded:
Bachelor, Master, Doctorate

Undergraduate Schools:
School of Architecture and Planning, School of Engineering, School of Humanities, Arts and Social Sciences, Sloan School of Management, School of Science

Full-time Faculty:
956

Faculty with Terminal Degree:
96%

Student-to-Faculty Ratio:
7:1

Average Course Load:
4 courses

AP Test Score Requirements:
Possible credit for scores of 4 or 5

IB Test Score Requirements:
Possible credit for scores of 6 or 7

Best Places to Study:
Reading room, Lewis Music Library, Barker Engineering Library, Hayden Library

Students Speak Out
ON ACADEMICS

"Some of the classes are interesting. I think the ones that everyone needs to take to fulfill the GIRs [General Institute Requirements] are not as interesting as the higher-level courses you take within your major."

"I've liked most of the teachers that I've had. **There are some really great teachers here**—both professors and teaching assistants—and some really bad ones. One of the important things is to talk to upperclassmen and ask which classes and professors are good."

Q "**Teachers are the best in their fields**, often having discovered, developed, or decoded the subject they are teaching. This makes them incredibly knowledgeable—although not always the best teachers. Classes and assignments are not very interactive, although they are intensely difficult."

Q "At MIT, **you will find that professors are very much occupied with research**. There are some who are really good at teaching, and I've built a lot of good, strong relationships over the years. However, I have to admit that I miss my high school teachers and the ones who really took the time to be involved in my life. I am impressed with how much they know, but once you get to college, everything's hard. I place a higher value on their commitment to my learning and interest in my personal life over their commitment to research, however, that's not how you get tenure if you're a professor."

Q "The big difference in teaching comes in the selection of a smaller school versus a bigger one, and it also depends on whether you'll be doing science or humanities. That's important to know. **If you're going to study English, don't come to MIT**."

Q "There are two types of classes—those you get to talk in and those you fall asleep in. I feel like the best classes are the ones where you feel like you can approach the professor anytime. **Most teachers are scary at first** since they're so distinguished, but you get used to it."

The College Prowler Take
ON ACADEMICS

The academics at MIT are top-notch. Classes are designed so that you learn as much as possible. But learning at MIT doesn't mean just memorizing a formula and plugging in numbers. Tests at MIT are designed so that, not only do you have to know the formula, you also have to know what it means, how to derive it, and how to manipulate it in all sorts of ways. Most introductory classes are a combination of lectures taught by professors and recitations taught by TAs. In fact, a large number of classes in general are taught this way. For the large classes, however, students are allowed to change their recitations. You should take advantage of this! Try to go to as many recitations as you can at the beginning of the term to find out which TA suits you best. Trust me, the extra time you spend looking for a recitation in the beginning will save you hours of struggling later.

Not only are the classes rigorous, academic opportunities outside the classroom are endless. One of the best academic programs at MIT is the Undergraduate Research Opportunities Program (UROP). Landing a UROP simply starts with approaching a professor with your interest. Given the culture of MIT, expect to do a lot of work. The things that you can accomplish within, and beyond, the classroom at MIT are miles above anything you could do anywhere else. This sets MIT apart as one of the best academic institutions in the country.

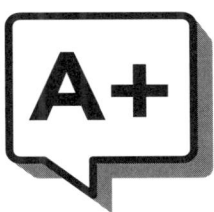

The College Prowler™ Grade on
Academics: A+

A high Academics grade generally indicates that professors are knowledgeable, accessible, and genuinely interested in their students' welfare. Other determining factors include class size, how well professors communicate, and whether or not classes are engaging.

Local Atmosphere

Students Speak Out
ON LOCAL ATMOSPHERE

"Boston rocks! The only downside is that shops close at, like, 5 p.m. and restaurants at 10 p.m., so there is not that much, besides bars and clubs, to do at night."

Q "Since the Boston and Cambridge area is filled with colleges—Harvard, Boston University, Boston College, Wellesley, Tufts, etc.—it is a definitely a city with a collegiate atmosphere. Around MIT, **there are great places to eat food from different countries**, shopping places, and more."

Q "Boston is a college city. It is well known for being home to more than 50 colleges and universities within the city and its surrounding suburbs. Harvard is down the street, Boston University is across the river, and many other schools are easily accessible by either bus or subway. **Boston businesses cater to the college crowd**, with distinctive shopping areas and restaurants that are upbeat and modern."

Q "There are many museums and galleries (find them on or around Newbury Street) nightlife venues, and sports arenas to keep you on your toes. With so much to do, and so much to see, the atmosphere in Boston is vibrant and colorful. Dance the night away at one of the hip clubs on Landsdowne Street, **catch a Red Sox game at Fenway Park**, satisfy your taste buds with delicious Italian food in the North End, or listen to live music on the streets of Harvard Square—your options are endless."

Q "**MIT is a blend of work and play**. It is in the heart of Cambridge/Boston, where a ton of other colleges are present. Throughout the week, MIT students rarely experience the world outside our campus due to work. However, on most weekends, the fun begins. Students from surrounding colleges like to come to the frat parties. Things to see: the Museum of Science, ice-skating at the Frog Pond in the winter, Walden Pond in the fall—[you'll] need a car—and Salem, famous for the Salem Witch Trials."

The Lowdown
ON LOCAL ATMOSPHERE

Region:
Northeast

City, State:
Cambridge, Massachusetts

Setting:
Urban

Distance from Boston:
10 minutes

Distance from New York City:
4 hours

Points of Interest:
Fenway Park, Freedom Trail and related Boston Historic Sites, Boston Public Library, Boston Symphony Orchestra, Museum of Fine Arts, Public Garden

Major Sports Teams:
Boston Celtics (NBA), Boston Red Sox (MLB), New England Patriots (NFL), Boston Bruins (NHL)

City Websites:
http://boston.sidewalk.com
www.boston.com
www.boston-online.com

Q "**Boston is probably the best city to be in as a college student**. There is so much to do. The shopping is great, and there is no sales tax. There is a lot of history, yet at the same time, there are so many colleges nearby that the city doesn't seem old and outdated. Boston University is right across the river, Harvard is down the street; girls from Wellesley take the bus into town all the time; Northeastern, Boston College, Simmons, and Tufts are all nearby. You should also check out Boston Symphony Orchestra concerts, Blue Man Group, and the Boston Ballet."

Q "You can visit downtown Boston, which has museums, the Symphony Hall—where MIT students get a discount—shopping outlets, and food places. **There's a mall within walking distance**—there is a shuttle that goes to it from MIT—the MIT museum, the Museum of Science, and anything you could ever want."

Safety & Security

The Lowdown
ON SAFETY & SECURITY

The College Prowler Take
ON LOCAL ATMOSPHERE

Number of MIT Police:
55 sworn officers

Phone:
100, from any campus phone

Health Center Office Hours:
8:30 a.m. to 5 p.m., Monday through Friday; emergency medical care is also available 24 hours a day, 7 days a week

Safety Services:
Blue-light emergency phones, emergency medical services, late-night transportation, SafeRide

MIT is located in Cambridge, Massachusetts, about a 10-minute walk from Boston. In fact, a large percentage of students actually live in Boston in the various MIT-sponsored FSILGs (Fraternities, Sororities, and Independent Living Groups). Sandwiched between Harvard and Boston University, MIT is in the hub of the ultimate college city. With so many high-quality schools in the area, Boston is a city that is driven by young, hip, and ambitious students. Concerts, clubs, restaurants, and malls are everywhere. Unfortunately, at MIT, some students get so wrapped up in their schoolwork that the only problem with living in Boston is finding the time to enjoy it.

The College Prowler™ Grade on

Local Atmosphere: A

A high Local Atmosphere grade indicates that the area surrounding campus is safe and scenic. Other factors include nearby attractions, proximity to other schools, and the town's attitude toward students.

Students Speak Out
ON SAFETY & SECURITY

"It's fairly safe, but it could be better. At night, SafeRide shuttles allow students to get from the academic buildings to their residences safely and conveniently."

The College Prowler Take
ON SAFETY & SECURITY

Q "MIT's campus is very safe. Despite being surrounded by heavy urban areas, **MIT tends to have a fairly isolated feeling**, and a small woman can walk across campus at 4 a.m., half-asleep, without feeling unsafe. There are places to avoid at certain times of day, sure, but they're easy to avoid if you want to."

Q "Campus security is great, though it is rarely needed. **On this campus, nothing happens**. There has never been a time when I feared for my life or was even too scared to walk to my dorm at 4 a.m.—yes, I was up doing work that late. My female friends say the same thing. They never fear that anything will happen. Though that is the case, and although I said nothing happens, there are situations at times (burglaries, harassment, etc.), but they are few and far between. There was an article written in our school newspaper stating how low crime is here and how it recently went down to an even lower point. If you should ever need campus police, they are always ready to help. There are blue emergency phones all over campus if you should ever need one."

Q "MIT has a very safe campus. Unlike other larger universities, MIT's small size makes it pretty cozy, and **I feel safe even when I am walking around late at night**. All the dorms have security at the door. Use your ID cards when entering your dorm, but you must phone the front desk if you wish to visit another dorm. Some people find it a hassle, but I like the fact that MIT really takes the safety of its students seriously. At night, there are security guards that patrol the floors of each dorm, and police cruisers make rounds throughout the campus. Emergency telephone booths were also recently put in as an additional safety feature."

Q "For the most part, it is relatively safe on campus. However, **it's important that you are always cautious, especially late at night**, because we do go to school near a large city. The dorms are pretty safe, but it doesn't hurt to always lock your door."

MIT provides several services in the interest of increasing campus security. First, student IDs are required at every dorm, and your ID gives access only to the dorm you live in. Just remember that security in some dorms is better than in others. Next, MIT runs a shuttle service after 6 p.m. called SafeRide from campus to various student living groups in Boston. Additionally, the campus police provide nighttime transportation for any student who requests it. Finally, MIT has installed blue emergency phones all over campus that dial 911 services. Walking around the campus late at night is not an issue. However, students should know better than to walk around the city late at night by themselves. If you're going out at night, make sure to take someone with you.

The College Prowler™ Grade on
Safety & Security: B

A high grade in Safety & Security means that students generally feel safe, campus police are visible, blue-light phones and escort services are readily available, and safety precautions are not overly necessary.

Computers

The Lowdown
ON COMPUTERS

High-Speed Network?
Yes

Wireless Network?
Yes

Charge to Print?
No

Operating Systems:
UNIX based Athena

Number of Labs:
19

Numbers of Computers:
Over 600

24-Hour Labs:
All

Free Software:

Adobe Reader 6.0, BrioQuery 5.5.6, ESRI, Eudora 5.2.1, Dreamweaver, Host Explorer 6.0.2, iPassConnect 2.40, Maple, Netscape 7.02, Oracle 9i Client Core, VirusScan Enterprise 7.0, WinZephyr 1.1 (beta), and X-Win32 5.4.2, just to name a few. For a full list check out MIT's Website at http://web.mit.edu/software.

Students Speak Out
ON COMPUTERS

"**Given that MIT is one of the most technologically-advanced schools in the world, its network is quick. At times, when a lot of people are using it, it tends to slow down, but for the most part, you never have to wait.**"

Q "Almost all students have their own personal computers—a mix of desktops and notebooks. It is possible to get by without one, though I don't recommend it. Athena is the campus network operating system, **clusters are everywhere and open 24 hours a day**. The campus is quickly becoming equipped with wireless networks, so having a laptop with a wireless card is an asset."

Q "I've never been unable to find a space in the Athena clusters, but I try to stay away during finals time. It's a nice way to avoid having to buy a printer, although **the computers are amazingly slow**."

Q "There are lots of public labs. **They're only crowded during the middle of the day**. The network is generally fine, though the dorm networks are congested. MIT recommends that you bring a computer, though it certainly isn't necessary. I didn't bring one, and didn't get one until my senior year. You might wait until you come to see if you really want one since it doesn't take long if you order from Dell, Gateway, Compaq, or whatever."

Q "I'd guess that **95 percent of MIT students, if not higher, own their own computers**. It's not because the computer labs are always crowded, but it's just because it's MIT, and with a fast T3 connection, you'll be downloading MP3s, surfing the Web, checking e-mail, and IM-ing, often. These are very necessary tools for all college students. Computer labs are not always crowded; we have a million of them."

Q "As a 'tech' school, MIT has computer clusters and computer quick stations all over campus open 24 hours a day. Wireless Ethernet was also installed in many of the dorms and academic buildings. **The largest computer cluster is located on the top floor of our student center**. While most students bring their own computers to school, many often prefer to work at one of the computer clusters for better concentration or for access to more sophisticated software applications. During exam weeks, these clusters are guaranteed to be crowded, so having your own computer will be convenient then."

Facilities

The College Prowler Take
ON COMPUTERS

The Lowdown
ON FACILITIES

Considering MIT's reputation, it should come as no surprise that computers are everywhere on campus. There are a large number of computer labs (commonly known as "clusters"), as well as various "quick stations" (one or two computers primarily used for checking e-mail) set up all around campus. The network, known as Athena, was designed in the mid 1980s, long before network computing was commonplace. Today, students use public workstations to check e-mail, download music, finish papers, analyze data, and much more. Also, finding an available workstation is usually very easy, although you should avoid the main clusters the day before large computer science classes have projects due, and also around finals time. In fact, it's always good to know where a few of the smaller clusters are in order to avoid crowds.

Student Center:
Yes, Stratton Student Center

Athletic Center:
Yes, Zesiger Center, Johnson, Dupont Athletic Center

Libraries:
Yes, 11 around campus

Movie Theatre on Campus?
No, but a group on campus called MIT Lecture Series Committee (LSC) regularly shows movies in 10-250 and 26-100. Go to http://lsc.mit.edu/schedule/current/index.html for details.

Bowling on Campus?
No

Bar on Campus?
Yes, The Thirsty Ear in Ashdown and the Muddy Charles in Walker Memorial

Coffeehouse on Campus?
Yes, one in the student center, one in building four, and one in lobby seven

Popular Places to Chill:
Fifth floor of the student center, first floor lounge in the student center, steps of the student center when the weather is nice

The College Prowler™ Grade on
Computers: A+

A high grade in Computers designates that computer labs are available, the computer network is easily accessible, and the campus' computing technology is up-to-date.

Students Speak Out
ON FACILITIES

"The student center is where we go for late-night snacks, to meet up with friends for lunch or after classes, or to watch a band performance on the front steps."

Q "**MIT is undergoing this huge renovation**, improving everything from the fitness center to the lab for computer science. The facilities are good, and the food services are slowly improving. The only mild complaint would be the eclectic architecture of some buildings."

Q "The student center holds a coffeehouse which used to be open 24 hours, but now they've cut back to only 18 hours. **There's also a convenience store**, although there is a grocery store within walking distance that's on campus."

Q "**The Z-Center, the athletic center, is awesome**. It features two floors of machines and weights, as well as an Olympic-sized pool and a diving pool. The student center has nice couches, a convenience store, four dining places with a variety of foods, a campus store, a bank, and many rooms where activities are held throughout the year."

Q "In terms of **places to study, there is a reading room**, where almost everyone convenes for a quiet place to study for midterms and finals. There is also a computer lab. Besides all of that, there are conference rooms where groups often hold meetings."

Q "The facilities on campus are really nice. **The athletic center is awesome**. You can go swimming or use the machines on the second floor. The student center has basically everything you need. There's LaVerde's, a market, as well as a dry cleaners, a barbershop, a post office, and a Fleet bank."

The College Prowler Take
ON FACILITIES

The highlight of MIT's facilities is the gorgeous new athletic facility, the Zesiger Center. Opened in fall 2002, the Z-Center features two pools, six squash courts, an indoor track, and multi-activity courts for basketball, volleyball, and other sports. Students have access to this state-of-the-art facility, free of charge. Moreover, students also have access to personal trainers and certain other services at a premium. The other main student facility is the Stratton student center. Although the building itself has not undergone any major renovations recently, the various shops and restaurants inside are constantly improving. Because dorms and living groups are so spread out, students often choose to meet in the student center to eat, work, and socialize. Overall, most facilities on campus offer students their own preferred places to hang out, study, or make themselves comfortable.

The College Prowler™ Grade on
Facilities: B+

A high Facilities grade indicates that the campus is aesthetically pleasing and well-maintained; facilities are state-of-the-art, and libraries are exceptional. Other determining factors include the quality of both athletic and student centers and an abundance of things to do on campus.

Campus Dining

The Lowdown
ON CAMPUS DINING

Freshman Meal Plan Requirement?
Minimums depend on which dorm you live in. Dorms with dining halls include a meal plan charge of about $200. Students who pay this get discounted meals in the dorm dining halls.

Meal Plan Average Cost:
Anywhere from $200-$1,400

24-Hour On-Campus Eating?
No

Students Speak Out
ON CAMPUS DINING

"Arrow Street Crepes is good, but it's a bit expensive. Meals are pricey, and they're not buffet-style. Baker dining is good, but the selection is limited. At least they offer veggie options."

Q "The **dining halls aren't too good**. Lots of people that I know cook for themselves since many dorms have kitchens and there is a supermarket nearby."

Q "It's **horrible**. But, the dorms all have kitchens, and the off-campus and delivery food is decent—some of it's even pretty cheap."

Q "Food on campus is fair quality and kind of expensive. Most students have a declining balance on their ID card that they use to purchase food. **LaVerde's is good for pretty much whatever** you need, and is sort of like a small grocery store with a sub counter and lots of prepackaged meals. The student center also has a bagel cafe, a crepe bar, and a full dining hall that is open only for lunch."

Q "Well, it's campus dining. **There are some new changes going on**—hopefully, they should improve the current dining situation."

Q "So maybe campus dining isn't MIT's best quality, but the **food here is actually pretty decent**. Dormitory dining halls recently switched caterers, so the options are getting better. Baker and Simmons have the best selection and taste."

The College Prowler Take
ON CAMPUS DINING

One of the best things about MIT dining is that there are no required "meals" that you have to buy. Instead, you (and your parents) decide how much money to credit to your student ID. Then you can spend the money however you like on campus. The most common complaint that students have is the lack of food selection at the regular dining halls. Because various dining halls are only open for lunch or dinner, your options at any given time can vary widely. Students can suggest meals or even comment on prices, and usually the staff will do what they can to help.

The College Prowler™ Grade on
Campus Dining: B-

Our grade on Campus Dining addresses the quality of both school-owned dining halls and independent on-campus restaurants as well as the price, availability, and variety of food.

Off-Campus Dining

The Lowdown
ON OFF-CAMPUS DINING

Best Place to Take Your Parents:
Charley's Eating & Drinking Saloon

Late-Night, Half-Price Food Specials:
The Pour House: Half-off burgers on Saturday, half-off chicken on Tuesday, half- off Mexican on Thursday

24-Hour Eating:
IHOP in Brighton

Students Speak Out
ON OFF-CAMPUS DINING

Q "There are lots of restaurants of all kinds near campus. **There is pizza, Chinese, Italian, Indian, and more**. There are plenty of cheap places that are good for normal occasions and a couple of nicer places, as well."

Q "The Pour House is on Boylston in Boston and is relatively close to campus. On half-off nights you can get a meal for about $3. **Thursdays is half-off Mexican food**. Charley's is an upscale prime-rib place on Newbury Street; they have the best warm Apple Crisp. LA Burdick's is in Harvard Square and they make the best hot chocolate. It's an adorable chocolate store. Finale is a dessert restaurant where the food looks like art. There is one in Harvard Square, and one in the Theater District. If you want to buy your own fruits and vegetables, go to the Haymarket by Quincy Market. You can get them really cheap, and it's a really fun, outdoor market."

Q "There are **tons of great restaurants close to campus**. The closest ones—that deliver!—include Thailand Cafe, Ankara's (deli style), and Cinderella's (authentic Italian). Harvard Square is also just a few T stops away with a great pizza place in the Garage and Pho Pasteur, an awesome Vietnamese restaurant. Boston is also right across the bridge with cute restaurants on Newbury where you can shop and eat at the same time."

Q "There are a lot of good restaurants in Boston and in Harvard Square. **I go into Boston more than I go into Harvard Square**, but there's a lot of good places within walking distance, such as The Pour House, Vinny Testas, and The Cheesecake Factory."

Q "There are some **good spots for outside food**. The Chinese ones include Nan Ling and Quan's Kitchen. The good Italian places are Cinderella's and Bertucci's."

"There are so many restaurants, you'll never eat at them all. I recommend Chinatown, The Middle East, Mary Chung's, and for late-night dining, La Marché at The Prudential Center. There aren't a lot of diners, but IHOP isn't far if you can get a ride."

The College Prowler Take
ON OFF-CAMPUS DINING

No matter what you want to eat, you can find it in Boston. Restaurants range from the very cheap fast food joints to more expensive fine dining. A great thing about off-campus dining in Boston and Cambridge is the variety of ethnic foods that you can find. From authentic Italian dining and historic restaurants such as the Union Oyster House in the North End, to dim sum in Chinatown, you can find anything you're craving. Given all the hard work that students do during the week, going out on the weekends is a fun break. But, remember that almost everything in Boston shuts down at 2 a.m.. If you're hungry after that, you're basically out of luck.

Campus Housing

The Lowdown
ON CAMPUS HOUSING

The College Prowler™ Grade on
Off-Campus Dining: A

A high Off-Campus Dining grade implies that off-campus restaurants are affordable, accessible, and worth visiting. Other factors include the variety of cuisine and the availability of alternative options (vegetarian, vegan, Kosher, etc.).

Undergrads on Campus:
97%

Number of Dormitories:
11 undergraduate halls

Room Types:
Singles, Doubles, Triples, Quads

Cleaning Service?
Some dorms have housekeeping for public spaces.

You Get:
All dorms have Athena stations, study areas, lounges, and computer quick stations.

Bed Type:
Twin extra-long

Students Speak Out
ON CAMPUS HOUSING

> "Baker is the most social. Next isn't far behind, and Burton Conner and Simmons are not quite as social. MacGregor and McCormick are pretty quiet."

Q "Depending on your personality, I don't know which dorm to recommend or to tell you to stay away from. Usually, **people stay away from East Campus, Senior House, Bexley Hall, and Random Hall**. It's not to say that these are bad places to live, some of them have the biggest rooms, but a lot of the people usually stereotype them as the 'geek dorms.' That's where the stereotypical MIT student lives. I personally live in a newer dorm, Simmons Hall. I love it. It's so different from any dorm I have ever seen. Each dorm has something to offer."

Q "Each dorm at MIT has a unique personality. Incoming freshmen get to choose which dorm they want to live in after orientation. Some dorms, like Burton Connor, are a little run-down and may appear cramped. New House and Next House are better furnished, though they're located farther from classes than most other dorms. Simmons, the newest dorm, is spacious and spacey. **Baker House, known as the 'most social dorm on campus'** is a long brick building that hosts many barbecues, floor/lounge parties, and roof deck excursions. The all-female dorm, McCormick is nice for those girls who want their own space. Bexley Hall, the closest dorm to campus, is right off Massachusetts Avenue, across from the main building. East Campus is famous for its eclectic mix of residents, who often choose to paint and decorate their rooms in funky fashion. Senior House and Random House are a bit apprehensive to outsiders, but they look like interesting places to live."

Q "I really liked the dorm that I lived in (East Campus). **There's some time when you get here to go visit the dorms** and meet people there. You should definitely do that before you decide where to live."

Q "It depends what kind of person you are. **McCormick is all women, very clean, quiet, and kind of boring**. Baker is very social, pretty new, kind of loud, and party-ish. Burton Conner has suites, and it's social; people cook here. MacGregor has all singles, and sometimes it's considered antisocial; it depends on what entry you live on. There are also ethnic houses like the French house, Russian house, and German house. Next House has great community spirit. Simmons is a new dorm, so its culture is not yet defined. East Campus has lots of drugs, is eccentric, and has really big rooms. Senior House also has lots of drugs and is eccentric; it was recently renovated."

Q "Each dorm holds a personality of its own, so it's to each student's individual taste as to how they like their living arrangements. While **some dorms are older and perhaps more run-down**, they may be more convenient. The nice dorms, by my tastes, are Simmons, McCormick, Baker, and Bexley."

The College Prowler Take
ON CAMPUS HOUSING

The dorms at MIT are as varied as the students. Each dorm has its own culture and reputation, but don't go on stereotypes alone. Try to ask some current students for their opinions. However, MIT housing has recently changed due to freshmen being required to live on campus. In the end, the best thing you can do is try to go visit all the dorms you find interesting.

The College Prowler™ Grade on
Campus Housing: B+

A high Campus Housing grade indicates that dorms are clean, well-maintained, and spacious. Other determining factors include variety of dorms, proximity to classes, and social atmosphere.

Off-Campus Housing

Students Speak Out
ON OFF-CAMPUS HOUSING

{ *"The only thing I know about off-campus housing is that it is really, really expensive."*

Q *"Almost all undergraduates live on campus all four years. Frats house brothers, and some sororities have housing for sisters, but very few people actually move into apartments as an undergraduate. Independent housing is expensive in the area, and transportation is a hassle if you don't have a car. Plus, most people stay on campus so they can take advantage of all that MIT has to offer."*

Q *"**Most undergrads live on campus** because off-campus housing is just not convenient in terms of affordability and location."*

Q *"It is expensive. **People don't generally live off campus in Boston** all that much. Typical housing is $600 or more per month, and that's a really good price, too."*

Q *"**You don't want to live off campus**. The dorms are great, and if you can find one bedroom to rent in a shared apartment in Cambridge for less than $600 month, you're a miracle worker."*

Q *"If it isn't in a fraternity or sorority, **avoid off-campus housing** like the plague until you're very, very rich. Cambridge is more expensive than Manhattan."*

The Lowdown
ON OFF-CAMPUS HOUSING

Undergrads in Off-Campus Housing:
3%

Average Rents:
For Cambridge:
Studio: $1,082/month
One-bedroom: $1,394/month
Two-bedroom: $1,758/month
Three-bedroom: $2,172/month

For Boston:
Studio: $1,025/month
One-bedroom: $1,394/month
Two-bedroom: $1,856/month
Three-bedroom: $2,133/month

Rents vary by location and number of rooms. For additional areas around MIT, check out *http://web.mit.edu/housing/och/rents.html*.

Best Time to Look for a Place:
September rental—mid to late July/ January rental—late November/ Summer rental—April and early May

For Assistance Contact:
Off Campus Housing Service:
http://web.mit.edu/housing/och/index.html
Phone: (617) 253-1493
E-mail: eleonore@mit.edu.

The College Prowler Take
ON OFF-CAMPUS HOUSING

For MIT students, off-campus housing means not living in a dorm or FSILG (Fraternities, Sororities, and Independent Living Groups). Although FSILGs aren't exactly on-campus housing, they are affiliated with MIT. Most houses are in Boston. Only four percent of MIT students live in what we would consider true off-campus housing. True off-campus housing means living in an apartment or house that is not affiliated with MIT. And the bottom line is: don't do it. Not only is rent expensive, but actually finding an apartment is a hassle. Off-campus housing also means you will be farther away from your classes and almost all your friends. Save the apartment for post-graduation.

The College Prowler™ Grade on
Off-Campus Housing: D-
A high grade in Off-Campus Housing indicates that apartments are of high quality, close to campus, affordable, and easy to secure.

Diversity

The Lowdown
ON DIVERSITY

African American: 6%

Asian American: 28%

Hispanic: 12%

Native American: 2%

White: 44%

International: 8%

Out-of-State: 91%

Students Speak Out
ON DIVERSITY

"There are lots of different ethnicities and viewpoints on campus. It's great because everyone can find somewhere they belong."

"Personally, I think **the campus is very diverse**. I know that is one thing the admissions office strives for. I am a black student at MIT, and I have to say that I am impressed with how many underrepresented minorities attend MIT."

> "MIT is very ethnically diverse, but it doesn't mix well. You'll find this problem at any college campus. **MIT generates high diversity in international population and ethnic races.** There are lots of Asians; sometimes it feels like 70 percent of people here are Asian because all the white kids live across the river in frats."

> "MIT is one giant melting pot. Of all the colleges I have visited, **MIT is definitely the most diverse**. With kids from 50 states and dozens of countries worldwide, you will see people of all sorts on campus. Although MIT's campus is extremely diverse, some students do tend to self-segregate."

> "**MIT draws in students from very different parts** of the world. The student body is quite diverse economically, socially, and ethnically."

The College Prowler Take
ON DIVERSITY

The MIT admissions office strives to find brilliant and unique students. By the numbers, MIT is one of the most diverse campuses in the nation. This diversity extends beyond race to religion, background, and beliefs. In fact, despite the large number of applicants, MIT still manages to create a student body where no two people are exactly alike. There are student groups and clubs for every possible interest, including political groups, cultural groups, religious groups, and a variety of combinations in between. The point is, that, although no two students at MIT are exactly alike, people still want to bond over the things that they share in common. If you welcome diversity, new experiences, and open exchange of ideas and beliefs, you will be very comfortable here at MIT.

The College Prowler™ Grade on
Diversity: A

A high grade in Diversity indicates that ethnic minorities and international students have a notable presence on campus and that students of different economic backgrounds, religious beliefs, and sexual preferences are well-represented.

Guys & Girls

The Lowdown
ON GUYS & GIRLS

Women Undergrads: 41%

Men Undergrads: 59%

Birth Control Available?
Yes

Hookups or Relationships?
Both. It depends on what you're looking for.

Dress Code
The truth is, after the first round of midterms, nobody has the time to make themselves look great every day. So, don't worry too much about what you need to wear. Besides, MIT has so many different kinds of people, that no matter what you wear, you won't look weird. Trust me.

Students Speak Out
ON GUYS & GIRLS

The College Prowler Take
ON GUYS & GIRLS

"It doesn't seem like there are many hotties. Those who are hotties are so arrogant that they aren't hot anymore."

Q "There are **all kinds here—hot, not, geek, preppy, whatever**. All are intelligent, though. If you're into geeky guys who think that handmade electronic teddy bears and hand-painted war game miniatures are romantic, this is definitely a good place to start. But, there're plenty of more normal guys and girls out there, and plenty are interested in playing the field if you're into that sort of thing."

Q "MIT is definitely underrated in terms of the aesthetics of its populace. Like anywhere else, there are 'hot' people. **If you're having problems, there are schools all over the Boston area**. Or you can drink."

Q "As far as the people go, there's **the whole social spectrum** here. Take the top three percent or so from all over the world, make it a given that all your peers are smart, a lot of them smarter than you, and redistribute the 'scene' from high school—you've got the nerds, the jocks, and the cool kids. There's anything and everything, not to mention cultures from all over the planet."

Q "It's way too varied. **Remember, beauty truly lies within**. I've met the most 'beautiful' people at MIT and I wouldn't have if I was simply concerned with hotness."

Q "MIT is **apparently pretty ugly compared to other colleges**. I don't seem to notice anymore, though."

In terms of pure physical attractiveness, MIT isn't at the top of any list. And, although the men outnumber the women, the ratio between eligible men and women tends to be fairly even. Why is this? Because a good percentage of MIT men are more interested in computers, "Star Wars," and classes than they are in women. Don't worry, though, there are definitely standouts from both genders. There's even a list of the hottest guys at MIT floating around somewhere. For the most part, many students try to meet people from other schools. Lots of guys will date girls from Boston University or Wellesley College. In fact, a lot of MIT girls have a tendency to be bitter towards the Wellesley girls who always show up at parties.

The College Prowler™ Grade on
Guys: C+

A high grade for Guys indicates that the male population on campus is attractive, smart, friendly, and engaging, and that the school has a decent ratio of guys to girls.

The College Prowler™ Grade on
Girls: C-

A high grade for Girls not only implies that the women on campus are attractive, smart, friendly, and engaging, but also that there is a fair ratio of girls to guys.

Athletics

Fields
One Astroturf field, outdoor track, and football field

Getting Tickets
Games are free.

Athletic Division:
NCAA Division III

Conference:
New England

Most Popular Sports:
One of the most popular activities students do for fun is ultimate Frisbee.

Overlooked Teams:
Most varsity sports

School Mascot:
Beaver

The Lowdown
ON ATHLETICS

Men's Teams:
Baseball
Basketball
Crew HWT
Crew LWT
Cross Country
Football
Golf
Gymnastics
Ice Hockey
Lacrosse
Soccer
Swimming
Tennis
Track and Field
Volleyball
Wrestling

Women's Teams:
Basketball
Crew LWT
Crew OWT
Cross Country
Field Hockey
Gymnastics
Ice Hockey
Lacrosse
Soccer
Softball
Swimming
Tennis
Track and Field
Volleyball

Club Sports:
The Aikido Club
The Archery Club
Badminton
Boxing
Cheerleading Club
Crew
Cricket
Cycling
Dance Troupe
Fencing
Field Hockey (Coed)
Ice Hockey (Women)
Kokikai
Women's Rugby
Sailing
The Scuba Club
Shotokan Karate
SKA Karate
Snowboard Team
Table Tennis
Ultimate Frisbee
Unihoc
Volleyball
Water Polo

Students Speak Out
ON ATHLETICS

"**IM sports definitely dominate over varsity sports.** There are so many sports, from football and soccer to the smaller, but still competitive, table tennis and bowling."

"**Varsity sports don't draw in large crowds**, because, on the whole, MIT sports rarely excel. IM sports are more popular because they are dorm/FSILG/club-organized and there is no demand for practice time—it's just a bunch of people taking an hour out of the week to go out and have fun."

"People who play varsity think it's a big deal but it **tends to be overlooked** by the general population. Many people do IM, though, because you don't have to be good and it's so much fun."

Q "Varsity sports are big here in the sense that **lots of people play sports** and it doesn't take over your life. But, in terms of spectators, almost no one watches games. MIT offers over 40 sports, so there's a pretty big variety. It can be as competitive as you want it to be. You can try something totally new and be successful at it. Some of our sports teams aren't so great since we're pretty big nerds."

Q "There are lots of sports teams that people play on. **IM sports are also pretty big.** Most people who play sports do it because they want something to do that's not academic, not because they're a hardcore athlete."

The College Prowler Take
ON ATHLETICS

Although MIT is obviously not one of the most competitive schools in terms of sports, many people are interested in athletics. In fact, according to the NCAA, MIT offers one of the broadest intercollegiate athletic programs in the country. Even if MIT isn't necessarily winning championships, there are definitely more than enough sports for people to get involved in. Some varsity sports will take you even if you have never played before; just be prepared to put in the work. Joining a varsity team means that you have to practice at least two hours a day. That's two hours less study time. As a result of the time they put into practices, though, athletes tend to be fairly good with time management. MIT also offers a wide variety of club and IM sports. The great thing about IMs is that games are fairly infrequent and a lot of fun.

The College Prowler™ Grade on
Athletics: C+

A high grade in Athletics indicates that students have school spirit, that sports programs are respected, that games are well-attended, and that intramurals are a prominent part of student life.

Greek Life

The Lowdown
ON GREEK LIFE

Number of Fraternities:
27

Number of Sororities:
5

Percent of Undergrad Men in Fraternities:
38%

Percent of Undergrad Women in Sororities:
24%

Living Group Organizations:
Dormitory Council, Interfraternity Council; MIT Living Group Council, MIT Panhellenic Association

Students Speak Out
ON GREEK LIFE

"Greek life here is not the stereotypes you see on TV! You don't have to pay to get into parties. Frats have lots of parties with DJs and stuff, so it's fun."

Q "Greek life is pretty cool. There's a lot going on if you want to be involved in it and plenty of other things to do if you don't. I'm dating a frat boy right now, so I spend a fair amount of time at the fraternities—**the guys are pretty great** and know how to throw really good parties."

Q "It **doesn't dominate the social scene** because there isn't just one social scene; there are several. How much you get involved in them depends entirely on your preferences. MIT Greeks are non-standard, by the way. Some are stereotypical frats and sororities, but we also have an assortment of non-standard fraternities and independent living groups. Many of those are dry, and they frequently have their own style. Check out Epsilon Theta, Pika, Fenway House, and WILG for an idea."

Q "**Everyone who comes to MIT is a nerd**, and that's the bottom line. Frat guys can act like they're all hardcore, but they're really not. There's no way to describe MIT Greek life; it just isn't typical. It's more like another option for living rather than a system that dominates the social scene."

Q "The Greek life is pretty big at MIT. **The frats and sororities don't follow the typical stereotypes at other schools**. For the most part, they have a very positive impact on campus. Sometimes it feels like it dominates the social scene, but there is still a lot to do without getting involved in Greek life. MIT is basically in Boston, so everybody can find something they like to do."

Q "Very popular. The frats here are different than other places, though they still like to party. **They mostly live off campus in gorgeous brownstones**. The sororities are huge—like 100 people—and most have housing. Smaller percentages live in the house. They're a lot of fun and not catty like that MTV show."

The College Prowler Take
ON GREEK LIFE

As with everything else at MIT, the personalities of the fraternities and sororities vary widely. Everyone who wants to join can usually find some place where they feel comfortable. With 27 fraternities and five sororities, MIT has an incredibly vibrant Greek system. Greek life at MIT revolves more around academics and building friendships than purely social activities. Many community service events are sponsored or attended by Greek houses, and Greeks hold many leadership positions as well. The Greek system at MIT is unlike what most people would expect based on other schools. That is why many of the people who go Greek at MIT are people who never even would have considered it at any other school.

The College Prowler™ Grade on
Greek Life: A-

A high grade in Greek Life indicates that sororities and fraternities are not only present, but also active on campus. Other determining factors include the variety of houses available and the respect the Greek community receives from the rest of the campus.

Want to get down with a frat or sorority? For a detailed listing of all the greek organizations on campus, check out the College Prowler book on MIT available at www.collegeprowler.com.

Drug Scene

Students Speak Out
ON DRUG SCENE

"**Most people are discreet. I've tried drugs. I know people who've tried drugs. No one really pressures you into it.**"

Q "I cannot comment on the drug scene because **I am not a part of it**. I do have friends that are, but not heavily. There are drugs here at MIT, but they don't rule everyone's life. As far as I know, MIT has never really had much of a problem with drug abuse."

Q "**It's as big as you want it to be**—if you want to get drugs, you can, but if you want to avoid them, its just as easy."

Q "Alcohol is definitely the most prevalent drug on campus, if you choose to classify it as one. Aside from that, pot would come in second. I know people who are involved in that and some other people who deal with heavier drugs, but **most do not let their habits affect their schoolwork**. For a lot of people who do drugs, it's merely a social routine."

Q "As far as drugs, alcohol, or anything else goes, **it's all there**. Sure, it's college, but it's not in your face. If you like it, you can find it; if you don't, you don't ever have to deal with it."

Q "There are **actually several users scattered through a couple of dorms**. Just ask when you get here; it's one of those open secrets. There are people who will strongly discourage harder drugs, but the soft ones are quite common."

The Lowdown
ON DRUG SCENE

Most Prevalent Drugs on Campus:
Marijuana

Drug Counseling Services:
AA – Alcoholics Anonymous
Open to the public.
Monday (Women's Group), 5:30 p.m.-6:30 p.m. in Room E23-364.
Tuesday, noon-1:00 p.m. in Room E23-364.
Thursday, noon-1:00 p.m. in Room E23-364.
Call (617) 253-4911 for more information.

Al-Anon
Open to the public
Friday, noon – 1:00 p.m. in Room E25-101.
Call Alise at (617) 253-4911 for more information.

Alcohol Support Group
MIT students only
Wednesday, 7:30 a.m. – 9:00 a.m. in Room E23-364. Call (617) 253-4911 to make an appointment before attending this group.

Counseling and Support Services:
(617) 253-4861

Narcotics Anonymous Helpline:
(617) 884-7709

The College Prowler Take
ON DRUG SCENE

Some people do use drugs at MIT. A surprising number of students have at least tried marijuana or use it occasionally. It is the most widely-used drug, and users have an easy enough time getting their hands on it. After all, MIT is right in Boston, and, as with any other urban area, drugs are there for those who want them. But, one of the unique aspects of the drug scene at MIT is that even those people who use drugs tend to know when they need to do work. The bottom line at MIT is that students are given a large amount of freedom to make their own decisions and take responsibility for the consequences.

The College Prowler™ Grade on
Drug Scene: B+

A high grade on Drug Scene indicates that drugs are not a noticeable part of campus life; drug use is not visible, and no pressure to use them seems to exist.

Campus Strictness

The Lowdown
ON CAMPUS STRICTNESS

What Are You Most Likely to Get Caught Doing on Campus?
Campus police are most likely to bust fraternity parties for noise complaints and various alcohol-related problems.

Students Speak Out
ON CAMPUS STRICTNESS

"In light of the death of a student in 1995 due to drinking, administrators are strict on alcohol. But if you want to get wasted, it's still very easy."

Q "Campus police, or **CPs, crash parties frequently to ensure that facilities are not overcrowded** and that minors are not consuming alcohol. In my experience, CPs have never arrested anyone or gotten anyone in serious trouble with drugs or drinking. I have seen people get taken away in ambulances for their own safety."

Q "Campus **police are generally stricter on fraternities** than dorms in terms of drinking. I have never heard of any students getting busted for drugs. Don't expect to be able to bring a handle to class, but it's definitely within easy access if you want to get trashed."

Q "The **campus police are very strict** when it comes to drugs and drinking. If you are found using drugs, or if you are underage and drunk or found consuming alcohol, you will face disciplinary action. I don't know how far they would go with the punishments because I have never seen it happen in my one-and-a-half years here. I do know that they state the policy and print it in the school material if you do decide to come here. There is also a CD sent to you that deals with alcohol, although it's mainly for your parents."

The College Prowler Take
ON CAMPUS STRICTNESS

Any discussion of campus strictness at MIT has to include the fact that a freshman died in an alcohol-related incident several years ago. Since this death, the MIT administration has made many changes to policies regarding freshmen, housing, and alcohol. As a result, penalties and punishments for alcohol and drug-related infractions can be harsh. But, the MIT administration generally doesn't punish individuals. Instead, MIT will try to punish the living group where the student was drinking or taking the drugs. The punishments can be anything from alcohol being prohibited at the house to the loss of the actual housing license. Therefore, living groups, especially fraternities, tend to try to be as careful as possible. The campus police can be strict, or not, depending on the living group. If you're an underage student consuming alcohol, just avoid the CPs and you'll have no trouble. Definitely be cautious at parties, and practice common sense at all times.

The College Prowler™ Grade on
Campus Strictness: B-

A high Campus Strictness grade implies an overall lenient atmosphere; police and RAs are fairly tolerant, and the administration's rules are flexible.

Overall Experience

Students Speak Out
ON OVERALL EXPERIENCE

"When you come here, you'll be doing a lot more studying than you did in high school. Know that there may not always be time to party when you have a problem set due and need to spend a lot of time working on it."

Q "I have **enjoyed almost every moment of my experience** at MIT. Despite all the work and stress, my two years at this crazy institute of learning have been tremendously rewarding. Living on my own and supporting myself through school has taught me a lot about life as well. The people I have met at MIT have been amazing. I wouldn't want to be anywhere else."

Q "It's been an incredible experience: **challenging academics, wonderful people, and actually some fun occasionally**. There are a few days each term where you say to yourself, 'If I had gone to state school, I would be partying instead of studying right now.' But, despite the stress, I can't picture myself anywhere else. This is where I belong."

Q "It rocks. It's really tough—you'll hate it, but you'll love it. IHTFP is the local motto—it has a double meaning of 'I have truly found paradise' and **'I hate this #$%-ing place,'** and we mean every word of it. The culture around here tends to subdivide somewhat; the vast majority of students are friendly, but the pressure creates smaller, close-knit groups."

Q "I love MIT because of the people I've met, but **I've struggled with my original decision to come here** after spending four years studying something I don't like. I should've gone somewhere else, but I chose MIT because of the people and the environment and because I wanted to be all hardcore. Sigh. Silly me."

Q "We get our hands dirty, we work together, and, sometimes, we fail together. **I think you'll have a much greater chance of figuring out who you really are** and what you really want to do with yourself if you come here. Honestly, I can't imagine being anywhere else."

The College Prowler Take
ON OVERALL EXPERIENCE

MIT students have a love/hate relationship with the school. They love the people and the atmosphere, and they hate the work. Correction, some people like the work and learning things, but most people hate the sheer volume of work. Most of the students who attend MIT had a tough decision to make about schools. For example, "Should I go to Harvard or MIT?" or, "Should I go to this in state school with a full scholarship and a free computer, or go to MIT?" And every student, at some point, will think that they made the wrong decision. But, it's the fact that these people made the decision to attend MIT that sets them apart. Whether they knew what the school was like or not, students here were willing to take the chance. And as a result, the people at MIT are some of the most creative, helpful, brilliant, and unique in the world. MIT admissions doesn't admit people accidentally (no matter how dumb you may feel when you fail your first exam). Everyone at MIT is incredibly down-to-earth, and everyone has the potential to do great things, even if we are all deprived of sleep. It's okay; some of the best work happens between 3 and 5 a.m..

MIT will teach you how to survive on your own in the real world. It will teach you more about yourself, too. Don't expect to be babied. MIT is one of the most challenging schools in the country, but it is also one of the most rewarding. It is an opportunity that few are given, so don't waste your time. You will form some lifelong relationships, and, if you survive, you will thrive anywhere.

COLLEGE PROWLER™

Want to know what to expect from MIT? For more student opinions, check out the College Prowler book on MIT available at www.collegeprowler.com.

The Inside Scoop

The Lowdown
ON THE INSIDE SCOOP

School Spirit
When it comes to school spirit, most students have a love/hate relationship with MIT, and spirit is focused more within housing communities. Students have a fierce pride in their living groups.

Traditions
Bad Taste – An annual concert held by the Chorallaries, an MIT singing group. The concert occurs late at night to accommodate its reputation for being in "bad taste."

CPW – Campus Preview Weekend; a weekend for prospective freshmen to come visit MIT.

Hacks – Look for them around campus. Some of the most famous include an MIT balloon inflating in the middle of the field during and Harvard/Yale football game, a cow on top of the dome, a house on top of the dome, and many others.

IAP – Independent Activities Period; the month between semesters where MIT students have the chance to do what they want.

Killian Kickoff – The traditional kickoff for FSILG rush. It used to be held right at the end of orientation, but with rush being moved, it is now held later.

Spring Weekend – One of the last weekends in April featuring an International Fair, a concert, and many other activities.

Steer Roast – A weekend-long event held at Senior House, including bands, mud wrestling, body painting, and (of course) roasting a steer.

Tips to Succeed at MIT:

- Do a pre-orientation program. The people who do these always end up knowing the campus better and have a built-in group of friends before orientation even starts. You're just a step ahead if you do this. FLP is one of the largest, most popular programs.

- Check www.mit411.com for students selling their old textbooks. Note: If the same teacher is teaching, you should buy the old course notes. They rarely (if ever) change. Also, if the book being sold is one edition too old, still buy it. The changes between editions are usually tiny.

- Realize that you might not be the best anymore. You're actually being compared to people who are just as smart, if not smarter, than you are. Don't be disappointed; be content that you are truly in a group of your peers.

- Start your work as early as possible. There's nothing worse than having to pull a last-minute all-nighter before something is due. By doing your work in little increments, you'll actually end up with more free time. And studying for tests will be easier, because you've been working at it frequently.

- Sometimes, you just can't do all the work that you are assigned perfectly. Learn to prioritize. Better yet, learn to deal.

- Work in groups. Sure, you'll get more glory if you do everything by yourself, but you also might end up in a padded room.

- Meet as many people as possible during orientation and the first month. The campus is really vibrant and friendly up until the first round of tests during the third and fourth weeks.

- Don't believe everything you hear. Sometimes a rumor is just a rumor.

Finding a Job or Internship

The Best & Worst

The Lowdown
ON FINDING A JOB OR INTERNSHIP

At the end of your four years, all your hard work will earn you an MIT degree. This, in itself, will make your job search infinitely easier. However, that doesn't mean that the jobs will automatically come to you. Even MIT students have to work a little to find the jobs they want.

Advice
Start early, and don't get discouraged. Make your resume as soon as possible, and take it to the Career Services Office—they offer free critiques. Post it on MonsterTRAK. Check MonsterTRAK often. Don't be afraid to pick up the phone and call certain companies. Even more than that, don't be afraid to contact alumni. MIT has a great alumni network that you should take advantage of. You may be worried that alumni will get annoyed with a lot of people calling and e-mailing them, but the truth is that few students actually do this. Therefore, if you do, you will be showing great initiative.

Career Center Resources & Services
Office of Career Services and Pre-Professional Advising
12-170
(617) 253 - 4733
http://web.mit.edu/career/www

The Ten BEST Things About MIT:

1	Outstanding professors
2	Student-faculty research opportunities
3	Athena
4	The truly wonderful student body
5	The city of Boston and all its resources
6	Killian Kickoff
7	Fabolous museums
8	Campus is very safe and secure
9	The Pour House
10	An abundance of Greek organizations

The Ten WORST Things About MIT:

1. GIRs
2. The Intense Workload
3. Not enough hot, single women on campus
4. Bland campus food
5. Realizing that you might not be the smartest anymore
6. Campus police busting up frat parties
7. Students who think they're better than others
8. Student apathy toward varsity sports
9. Strict alcohol policies
10. Getting over the whole MIT stigma

Northeastern University

360 Huntington Avenue, Boston, MA 02115
www.northeastern.edu   (617) 373-2200

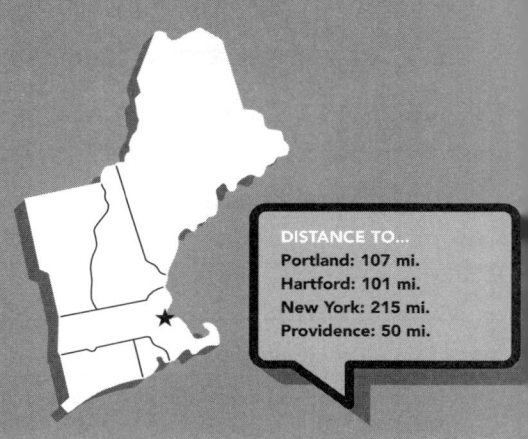

DISTANCE TO...
Portland: 107 mi.
Hartford: 101 mi.
New York: 215 mi.
Providence: 50 mi.

"We have something here called co-op. It's very unique and a big draw to NU."

Table of Contents

Academics	831
Local Atmosphere	833
Safety & Security	834
Computers	836
Facilities	837
Campus Dining	839
Off-Campus Dining	840
Campus Housing	842
Off-Campus Housing	843
Diversity	845
Guys & Girls	846
Athletics	848
Greek Life	849
Drug Scene	851
Campus Strictness	852
Overall Experience	853
The Inside Scoop	853
Finding a Job or Internship	854
The Best & Worst	855

Total Enrollment: 14,492
Acceptance Rate: 47%
Tuition: $26,990
Top 10% of High School Class: 35%

SAT Range
Verbal	Math	Total
550 – 640	570 – 660	1120 – 1300

ACT Range
Verbal	Math	Total
N/A	N/A	23-28

Most Popular Majors:
29% Business
14% Engineering
9% Health Professions
8% Security and Protective Services
5% Communications

Students Also Applied To:*
Boston University, George Washington University, Syracuse University, University of Connecticut, University of Massachusetts
*For more school info check out www.collegeprowler.com

College Prowler Report Card

Academics	B
Local Atmosphere	A
Safety & Security	B
Computers	B+
Facilities	A-
Campus Dining	A-
Off-Campus Dining	B+
Campus Housing	A-
Off-Campus Housing	B+
Diversity	C
Guys	B+
Girls	A-
Athletics	B-
Greek Life	C-
Drug Scene	B+
Campus Strictness	B-

Academics

Undergraduate Schools:
Bouve College of Health Sciences
College of Arts and Sciences
College of Business Administration
College of Computer and Information Services
College of Criminal Justice
College of Engineering
School of Law
School of Professional and Continuing Studies

The Lowdown
ON ACADEMICS

Degrees Awarded:
Bachelor, Post-Bachelor Certificate, Master, Post-Master Certificate, First Professional, Doctorate

Average Course Load:
4 classes a semester

Full-time Faculty:
830

Faculty with Terminal Degree:
80%

Student-to-Faculty Ratio:
16 to 1

AP Test Score Requirements:
Possible credit for scores of 3,4,5

IB Test Score Requirements:
Possible credit for scores of 3, 4, 5

Did You Know?

Former presidential candidate (and Massachusetts governor) Michael Dukakis works here. He teaches public policy, state, and local government. Jack Levin, a well-known sociologist (he's appeared on Oprah!) teaches criminology.

The Snell Library opened in 1990 and is a $35 million Resource Center. Spatially, it is the largest academic library in Boston and has shelving for 1.2 million volumes and seats 2,800 users. The library houses 3 microcomputer labs and has over 300 computer workstations for students.

COLLEGE PROWLER

For in-depth information about classes and professors, check out the College Prowler guide to Northeastern at *www.collegeprowler.com*.

Special Degree Options
BS in Engineering, MS in Nursing

Best Places to Study
Snell Library, Curry Student Center

Students Speak Out
ON ACADEMICS

{ *"Some classes are educational; it all depends on the topic. If you're taking a class that covers a subject you're passionate about, then you'll enjoy it that much more."*

Q *"It really varies on the class or subject matter. I would say that most classes have been pretty interesting.* **Some of the professors here are very impressive**—*such as Michael Dukakis and Alan Schroeder."*

Q *"***Overall, the teachers at Northeastern are pretty good***. Some are more caring than others. The classes are usually interesting—if you choose to be in a major, you should be interested in at least some of the classes you are taking. Some are really boring, and some are really difficult, however, some could also be really easy A's."*

Q *"I think the teachers are, for the most part, very educated, but it depends on whom. You can't really generalize because it's a very individual thing. I think* **most of my classes are interesting** *because, overall, I am interested in the content of my major."*

Q *"On the whole, academics are on the easy side—at least as far as liberal arts goes. Northeastern specializes in the techie fields, so these majors are more difficult (I hear the engineering majors never sleep). Granted, some classes are universally difficult: middle-year writing ain't no walk in the park—even for us English majors—and the* **core requirements will stretch your brain in places it may not like**. *I opted for a calculus class for math majors to fulfill my math credit and am quite relieved I will never have to find the derivative of anything, ever again."*

The College Prowler Take
ON ACADEMICS

Since Northeastern is actively trying to build its reputation, I have seen the average SAT score rise about 100 points and the students seem to be smarter and better students. This was not the case when I applied and entered the school in the fall of 2002. Of course I'm happy that when I graduate from Northeastern in 2006, it will mean more to have graduated from this institution. What I did not know was that I would feel less than average in some of my classes. When you choose a college or university, you want to make sure that it fits with your academic capabilities. Just because you are accepted somewhere does not mean that it is right for you, academically. Northeastern students are very different from each other. Some are huge slackers who never go to class and some are diligent and hard working, never settling for below an A-.

The professors here can seem inconsistent. Almost all of the math and science teachers are foreign, which can be hard if they are not comfortable with English. However, we do have some professors who are experts in their fields, such as former presidential candidate Michael Dukakis and criminologist, Jack Levin. Our professors have won scholarly honors, written books, and appeared on television.

The College Prowler™ Grade on
Academics: B

A high Academics grade generally indicates that Professors are knowledgeable, accessible, and genuinely interested in their students' welfare. Other determining factors include class size, how well professors communicate, and whether or not classes are engaging.

Local Atmosphere

Five Fun Facts about Boston:

1. Boston built the first subway system in the United States in 1897.
2. The Boston Tea Party reenactment takes place in Boston Harbor every December 16th.
3. The first church of Christian Science was founded here by Mary Baker Eddy.
4. There are duckling statuettes in Boston Commons (park) from the book *Make Way for Ducklings*.
5. The restaurant from the TV show *Cheers* is a real place. Go there to eat and drink.

The Lowdown
ON LOCAL ATMOSPHERE

Students Speak Out
ON LOCAL ATMOSPHERE

Region:
Northeast

City, State:
Boston, Massachusetts

Setting:
Urban

Distance from New York City:
4.5 hours

Distance from New Hampshire:
About less than an hour to the border

Points of Interest:
Museum of Fine Arts, Aquarium, Prudential Center, Boston Symphony, The Charles River, Fenway Park, Boston Commons, The North End, Downtown Crossing, Faneuil Hall

Sports Teams:
Boston Red Sox, New England Patriots, Celtics, Bruins

Closest Shopping Malls or Plazas:
The Prudential Center, Copley Mall, Cambridgeside Galleria

"**Boston is positively the best college town.** There are numerous colleges and universities in the city. It's a definite tourist spot, as well. I feel pretty safe wherever I go."

Q "**Boston has a good atmosphere, clean city**, and a good amount to do. It has many universities and lots of students. Stay away from Lansdowne Street, it is so generic. Go to Whiskey Park, Aria, and Rumor. You will meet cool people and even Derek Jeter!"

Q "**Boston is well known for its culture and education.** The NU campus is located along the Avenue of the Arts, which is another way of saying 'the section of Huntington Avenue where the Museum of Fine Arts is located.' The museum is right across the street and has wonderful exhibits (which cost a little extra, but NU students get free general admission)."

Q "The atmosphere is fast-paced in Boston. It is a great place to attend college because Boston is populated mainly by young people (under the age of 30), and there are tons other schools in our area, including Boston College, Boston University, Harvard, Tufts, Emerson, etc. There are **so many places to go, so many things to do**, but it does get expensive."

The College Prowler Take
ON LOCAL ATMOSPHERE

Two words explain it all—college town! Boston is the ultimate place to be for a college student. There are countless ways to spend your time, be it Boston Commons in the springtime, taking in a concert at the Paradise Rock Café, or going on tourist attractions such as Duck Tours! I'm from a big city, but I have never thought of Boston as particularly small. Why would I? It's not like I have run out of things to do here during my three years at Northeastern. It's true that once you turn 21, more doors open up for you. But until you reach that crossroads, you can certainly get into many other clubs, if that's your thing. There are many fabulous restaurants, shops, and, best of all, neighborhoods to wander around.

No matter what you enjoy seeing, doing, or eating, the city of Boston and its suburbs have so much to offer that it's impossible to think of going to college anywhere else.

The College Prowler™ Grade on

Local Atmosphere: A

A high Local Atmosphere grade indicates that the area surrounding campus is safe and scenic. Other factors include nearby attractions, proximity to other schools, and the town's attitude toward students.

Safety & Security

The Lowdown
ON SAFETY & SECURITY

Phone for the NU Police:
(540) 865-3434

Safety Services:
Escort Services
(617) 373-2121
Student Patrols, 24 hour foot and vehicle patrols, 24 hour emergency telephones, lighted pathways, controlled dorm access.

Health Services:
Physicals, allergy testing, birth control, gynecology, HIV testing

Health Center Office Hours:
Monday, Tuesday, Thursday, Friday 9 a.m.-7 p.m.
Wednesday 11 a.m.-7 p.m.
Saturday 9 a.m.-1 p.m.

Did You Know?

The *Northeastern News*' Crime Log is one of the most well-read sections of the paper.

Students Speak Out
ON SAFETY & SECURITY

{ "There is great security here. We have police patrolling 24 hours a day and lots of guards outside of campus buildings. We can also get a hold of security at any time."

Q "Security on campus is pretty good. If you press the button in one of the boxes where the blue lights are located, police will be there within a minute. **The NU Escort service is pretty easy to use and reliable**. A police car will come pick you up and bring you where you need to go, within a mile of campus. The number for NU Escort is (617) 373-2121."

Q "Campus is pretty safe. However, most recently, there have been cases of criminal activity. NU is right on the edge between a very nice area in Boston, and a somewhat questionable area. When you're here, **you pretty much know where, and where not, to wander**."

Q "**Security seems to be pretty good.** I feel safe, anyways. I do read the NU News and the crime log always has crazy things in it. But I was never worried that anything would happen to me in my room, such as a break-in or anything like that. Most halls have 24-hour security, which makes me feel much safer."

Q "Despite this visual sense of security, Northeastern is nestled in the heart of a city, up against some of the grittier sections of it, I might add. When the Patriots made an encore performance at the Super Bowl this year, riots erupted all over Boston, and Northeastern was no exception. Six cars were overturned and one student was killed in a hit-and-run accident. In the last year, two students have been killed in unsavory incidences in their off-campus apartments. However, **security on campus is pretty tight**. Use common sense and remember that wandering off campus, means you apply city rules, not campus ones."

The College Prowler Take
ON SAFETY & SECURITY

Any city is going to be dangerous in some areas and intimidating at night If you're not familiar with your surroundings. Boston is no exception. However, the NUPD makes a huge effort to ensure our safety. Exterior doors to student residence halls are locked at 11 p.m. Public Safety patrols a one mile radius around Northeastern. There is a seven day a week security and escort service. NU is a well-lit campus, equipped with emergency call-boxes. The Public Safety Division also works with the Boston Police Department.

The best advice I can give is to leave if you are uncomfortable somewhere. There is always a way out of a situation before it turns into a sticky one.

The College Prowler™ Grade on
Safety & Security: B

A high grade in Safety & Security means that students generally feel safe, campus police are visible, blue-light phones and escort services are readily available, and safety precautions are not overly necessary.

Computers

Students Speak Out
ON COMPUTERS

"The cable network is very good. There are so many accessible computers on campus, though I have only been to the computer labs a couple of times. I recommend bringing your own computer. It's just easier."

The Lowdown
ON COMPUTERS

High-Speed Network?
Yes

Wireless Network?
Yes

Number of Wired Connections (places where you can bring your laptop):
644

Numbers of Computers:
1,993

24-Hour Labs:
InfoCommons in Snell Library

Charge to Print?
Not at InfoCommons but in the Library.

Q "Although Northeastern says that students don't need to have their own computer, I can't imagine surviving college without one. The computer laps are pretty crowded on average, but I've never had a problem finding one. I think the best part about **the labs is the free printing service**."

Q "**The network is good in the dorms**, but the computer labs are always full, so you really do need your own computer."

Q "There are also kiosks to check your NEU email account spread out all over campus, although you can't access anything outside of the Northeastern network (like hotmail, yahoo mail, or any other kind of mail). For us non-NU-email users, **there are several internet cafes** (Snell, Shillman, and the Curry Student Center)."

Q "The computer lab in the new computer science building is really nice. **There are lots of machines, both Linux and Windows**. I have yet to see that place even half filled. However I believe it is only available for students with a CCIS account. Whenever I happen to go to InfoCommons it is always a mob scene and I try to avoid that place at all costs. I guess it depends on where you go."

Q "Get a laptop. The network is amazing--**200 megabytes per second**."

Did You Know?

Since the library went pay for print, the amount of printing in InfoCommons has gone up drastically.

The College Prowler Take
ON COMPUTERS

Since this is the Information Age, a college student really benefits from having his or her own computer. You can find relatively cheap models because computers are getting updated every day, and the older versions go on sale. However, our system here at Northeastern is really magnificent. We have state-of-the-art computers in our labs—every student will be able to find one that he or she feels comfortable using. NU professors are finally starting to use the Blackboard system to post assignments and document class discussions so it is quite necessary to have access to the internet at all times. With a few computers in just about every campus building, you can pretty much always check your email, even if you can't surf the Web.

I doubt you'll find a college guidebook that says you shouldn't bring your own computer. Whether you're going on AOL Instant Messenger or www.thefacebook.com, students rely on their own personal machine to connect with other students and research and study for class. So do yourself a favor and ask for your graduation gift to be a sparkling new computer.

The College Prowler™ Grade on
Computers: B+

A high grade in Computers designates that computer labs are available, the computer network is easily accessible, and the campus' computing technology is up-to-date.

Facilities

The Lowdown
ON FACILITIES

Student Center:
Curry Student Center

Athletic Center:
Marino Athletic and Recreation Center. The Cabot Gym. Squashbusters, Matthews Arena

Libraries:
1 on campus and the Boston Public Library

Movie Theatre on Campus?
No, but films can be watched in the Media Center on the second floor of Snell Library and films are sometimes shown in classrooms when arranged by a club or a professor.

Bowling on Campus?
No

Bar on Campus?
No, but there are many within places walking distance.

Coffeehouse on Campus?
Yes, afterHOURS is on the lower level of the Curry Student Center.

Popular Places to Chill
Krentzman Quad, Centennial Quad, afterHOURS, Curry Student Center

Students Speak Out
ON FACILITIES

> "There's a 24-hour gym, a 24-hour Cybercafe, and plenty of food around campus, including brick oven pizza and stir fry. I'd say it's a pretty good deal."

Q "Our facilities are very nice. **You can definitely see where your tuition money goes**! The Marino Center is very high tech and has a lot to offer the students. It's nice—we're in a big city, but unlike many city colleges, NU definitely has a campus so you won't miss out on the college experience."

Q "Just check out the pictures of our amazing campus. **Everything is new and sparkling**. The main gym has three floors with basketball courts, machines, weights, and an elevated running track. The gym across the street has an indoor soccer field and a pool. The Student Center is beautiful, as well. Not only does it have a ton of great restaurants (that accept our Husky Card), but it also has computers, TVs, and a lounge."

Q "I think the gym is great. I heard that now it is open 24/7 and I think that it is a bit much, but whatever. On the other hand **the student center is not open enough**. It might have just been summer hours, but that place always seems to be closed. I hate the bookstore because it's always so crowded."

Q "I think that the facilities are **very nice and state-of-the-art**. This campus is filled with great places for students to be. I never find myself without something to do."

Q "Our facilities that serve everyone are great; although some of the more specialized facilities (practice rooms, labs) are **not up to par**."

The College Prowler Take
ON FACILITIES

Our facilities get better every year. Last year there was a lot of construction going on, but this year it has clearly paid off. There are brand new classrooms, dorms, and even the dining hall has been revamped with eight plasma TV screens. We have the Cabot center, where students can swim and teams meet for practice. The Marino Center, as you've read, is open almost all day and night. The Student Center, although shabby in appearance, serves its purpose and students meet there a lot, whether it's for a study group, a meeting, or just to get some cheap eats in the food court area. The Ballroom hosts concerts, lectures, and Greek events. Blackman Auditorium hosts larger events, such as top comedians and theater productions. Northeastern also has something very unique—tunnels. Whether it's cold, snowy, raining, or you just feel like walking through them, most university buildings are attached by underground tunnels.

The College Prowler™ Grade on
Facilities: A-

A high Facilities grade indicates that the campus is aesthetically pleasing and well-maintained; facilities are state-of-the-art, and libraries are exceptional. Other determining factors include the quality of both athletic and student centers and an abundance of things to do on campus.

Campus Dining

Students Speak Out
ON CAMPUS DINING

"Amazingly, the food is amazing. Stetson West has brick oven pizza and stir fry, and Stetso East has a huge selection plus the old faithfuls—burgers, chicken, and hot dogs."

The Lowdown
ON CAMPUS DINING

Freshman Meal Plan Requirement?
Yes

Meal Plan Average Cost:
$4,740

24-Hour On-Campus Eating?
No

Student Favorites:
Chicken Lou's, Qdoba, The Wrap, Woody's Pizzeria, Espresso Royale Café, Au Bon Pain

Other Options

Out Takes is available if you're in need of a meal on the go. Items such as salad, roasted chicken, burgers, mashed potatoes, and desserts come in disposable packaging and you can get a few different foods equaling one meal.

Q "Our dining halls have, by far, **the best food I have ever had at any college**, beautiful dining halls, plasma TVs, and a great atmosphere. Everything from make-your-own waffles, to make-your-own stir-fry, to getting an omelet cooked for you, with whatever you want in it."

Q "I don't mind the dining halls so much. **They just remodeled Stetson West** so now they have the Xhibition kitchen where chefs come every few weeks to do demonstrations. The only problem is the stir-fry is so good, you have to wait a really long time for it! Stetson East is basic food like burgers, fries, chicken, salad, and omelets. Now they have kosher food for dinner seven nights a week which anyone can have as long as they sign up for it beforehand."

Q "The food is good compared to most universities. While it is not gourmet **it gets the job done**. The dining halls are very nice and provide the students with a large variety of things to eat based on their eating habits."

Q "The dining halls are delicious – both East and West Dining Halls have their own specific characteristics that each student learns to know. **East serves a full breakfast** complete with omelets, hash browns, bagels, fruit, sausage, etc. and is open until 2 p.m. every Saturday and Sunday, which is perfect for those of us who sleep late."

Did You Know?

There are 5 brand new plasma TVs in the Stetson West dining hall.

The Stetson West Dining Hall has a make your own stir fry option with a number of different meats and sauce options. Students would agree it is worth the wait!

The College Prowler Take
ON CAMPUS DINING

The food on campus is pretty good. There are healthy choices for the health conscious, and with two dining halls, students can mix up their meals so they don't get bored. As a freshman, you are required to have a meal plan if you're living in the residence halls. Since you won't have a kitchen your freshman year, you'll be spending a lot of time in the D-hall, as it's commonly known. It's fun to go with a group of friends and get waffles and omelets for brunch, or a grilled chicken sandwich and fries for lunch. Some people complain about the food, but they'd be hard pressed to find a college campus with much better options. This year there are some new additions such as the Xhibition Kitchen where they have food demonstrations.

Some students swear by the dining halls so much they'll even spend much of the day there, chatting with friends, doing homework, and of course eating! There are always the staples such as pizza, burgers, omelets, sandwiches, pasta, and salad. Tacos and Mexican food is often served, as well as roasted chicken with mashed potatoes and gravy.

The College Prowler™ Grade on
Campus Dining: A-

Our grade on Campus Dining addresses the quality of both school-owned dining halls and independent on-campus restaurants as well as the price, availability, and variety of food.

Off-Campus Dining

The Lowdown
ON OFF-CAMPUS DINING

Best Pizza:
Boston House of Pizza

Best Chinese:
P.F. Chang's China Bistro

Best Breakfast:
Sonsie's

Best Wings:
Wingit Foods

Best Healthy:
Whole Foods Market and Cafe

Best Place to Take Your Parents:
The Cheesecake Factory

Late-Night, Half-Price Food Specials:
The Pour House

24-Hour Eating
None

Closest Grocery Stores:
Wollaston's Market
369 Huntington Ave. (Boston)
Phone:
(617) 247-0011

Whole Foods
15 Westland Ave.
Boston
Phone:
(617) 375-1010

 **Students Speak Out**
ON OFF-CAMPUS DINING

 **The College Prowler Take**
ON OFF-CAMPUS DINING

"There is pretty much every kind of food in walking distance—American (Uno's), Mexican (Qdoba or El Pelon at Fenway), Chinese (Taste of Asia), and pizza places (Cappy's or BHOP)."

Q "Boston is a great city to dine in. Hit up Newbury Street (Stephanie's, Ciao Bella, Sonsie, Armani Café and Scoozi is cheaper but good), Abe and Louis on Boylston, Aujourd'Hui at The Four Seasons and Top of the Hub are all great. In Government Center, go to Houston's and on Arlington, **Bonfire has good steaks**. Via matta has good fish and overpriced pasta. These are all expensive places for the most part, so save them for a special occasion."

Q "The restaurants here are great. You can pretty much find any type of food that you could possibly dream of within a 10-mile radius. The Cheesecake factory is quite popular—huge portions, great food, but a bit pricey...at least you can take home leftovers and are guaranteed a good meal for the money. The North End (Boston's equivalent of New York's little Italy) is a fun place to go for good food also. **There are so many restaurants that are good**, I can't even begin to explain. Sonsie and also Stephanie's on Newbury are both really good, but expensive."

Q "It depends on where you go. **The North End has amazing Italian food**. The pizza is terrible in more areas of Boston except for Newbury Street."

Q "Two words: The Wrap. It's located on the first floor of the Marino Center gym, right next to Au Bon Pain. **I practically live on their grilled chicken burritos**."

The city of Boston, like most elite cities, is definitely not a place to find a bargain. Northeastern is located in a supremely expensive area and the restaurants off campus indicate this fact. However, if you go with a group of friends or have your parents take you out, you'll find that you will have many great dining experiences here. Every type of cuisine is at your fingertips, and the hardest part is deciding where to spend your dollars!

For birthdays, most of my friends like to take a large group to The Cheesecake Factory or TGI Friday's. For a more intimate setting, try Ciao Bella's or Legal Sea Food in the Prudential Center. Very special occasions could send you to the Top Of The Hub, know for its exquisite views of the city and high-priced food and drinks. Chinatown is known for its cheap Dim Sum brunches and grocers. The North End is known for Mike's Pastry and excellent Italian fare.

The College Prowler™ Grade on
Off-Campus Dining: B+

A high off-campus dining grade implies that off-campus restaurants are affordable, accessible, and worth visiting. Other factors include the variety of cuisine and the availability of alternative options (vegetarian, vegan, Kosher, etc.).

Campus Housing

Available for Rent
Mini Fridge with microwave

Cleaning Service?
Just in public areas like the common bathrooms in freshmen dorms. Once a day the garbage is disposed of and the showers/toilets are cleaned.

You Get
Bed, desk, chair, dresser, (dining table, chairs, and living room furniture if you are in an upperclassmen dorm)

Also Available
Quiet Hall, Wellness Hall, Criminal Justice Floor, International Hall, Honors Hall, Engineering, Living/Learning, Bouve, Computer Science

The Lowdown
ON CAMPUS HOUSING

Best Dorms:
West Village, Davenport Commons, Kennedy Hall

Worst Dorms:
Smith Hall, Melvin Hall, Light Hall

Undergrads on Campus:
7,126, 49%

Number of Dormitories:
34 and 18 Leased Properties

Number of University-Leased Apartments:
19

Bed Type:
Twin extra-long, some bunk beds

Did You Know?
New halls West Village G and H have wireless internet throughout the building.

You can have your laundry done for you with Husky Express in the new Speare Commons. There is also dry cleaning available. You can pay with your Husky Card.

Students Speak Out
ON CAMPUS HOUSING

"Dorms are typical dorms as freshmen, but if you can live in West Village after that, it's definitely worth it. Juniors and seniors are not guaranteed housing, but it's possible that you will get great housing every year."

"West Village dorms and **Davenport dorms are the best**. Willis is decent, and I think all the other ones suck."

Room Types
Residence Halls include standard double, economy double, standard triple, economy triple, and single rooms. Economy is a word we're trying to get rid of here at NU. It means that because of space constraints, a lofted bed and a bunk bed have been put into a room for two people so three people can live in it. It's crowded and definitely not ideal. It is cheaper though. In the suite style dorms, four to five students share a bathroom and a common living area.

Off-Campus Housing

Q "Dorms are typical dorms as freshmen, but if you can live in West Village after that, it's definitely worth it. **Juniors and seniors are not guaranteed housing**, but it's possible that you will get great housing every year. Avoid smaller dorms such as Burstein and Rubenstein."

Q "I enjoyed my time in the dorms, although I only stayed in them for my freshman year. **All of them have their positive and negative aspects**, but no matter where you end up your first year, keep in mind that it's the worst it's gonna get, because upperclassman housing is top of the line."

The College Prowler Take
ON CAMPUS HOUSING

The Lowdown
ON OFF-CAMPUS HOUSING

Campus housing at Northeastern is pretty great. We use a lottery system that is weighted by the year you are at Northeastern. We are guaranteed housing for three of our five years here, but if you get your housing form and deposit in on time you should have no problem getting housing for the last two years, as well. After freshman year, you can decide who you want to room with by entering the lottery with that person, or those people. A few weeks after that you will be assigned the same lottery number as the person/people you went in with. The lower the number, the better the housing. Lottery numbers are assigned randomly, but if you are a middler, you will be given a better number than a sophomore because of your year at NU.

Undergrads in Off-Campus Housing:
About half—7,000

Best Time to Look for a Place:
Early spring (February and March)

Average Rent for a Studio Apartment:
$1,000 per month

Average Rent for a One-Bedroom Apartment:
$1,200 per month

Average Rent for a Two-Bedroom Apartment:
$1,500 per month

Popular Areas:
Fenway, Back Bay, Jamaica Plain, Huntington, Hemenway, Allston

The College Prowler™ Grade on
Campus Housing: A-

A high Campus Housing grade indicates that dorms are clean, well-maintained, and spacious. Other determining factors include variety of dorms, proximity to classes, and social atmosphere.

Students Speak Out
ON OFF-CAMPUS HOUSING

The College Prowler Take
ON OFF-CAMPUS HOUSING

"Off-campus housing rocks. Personally, I would never go back; you're so much more on your own. You don't have to sign people in, and you don't have RAs monitoring you."

Q "I have never lived off campus, but I do know NU offers **'Apartment Hunting Workshops.'**"

Q "I think it's easier to live on-campus because you don't have to worry about getting your own furniture, cable, internet, etc. **It's just a whole lot easier**."

Q "Off-campus housing is very convenient and many find it to be worth it. **The price is not too expensive** compared to on campus."

Q "Housing is definitely worth it. **It isn't difficult to find a nice place for you and your friends**, as long as you look early on (for fall housing, start looking for apartments in the spring, and no later than May.)"

Never having lived off-campus, I did some research on the subject and found that there are some very good deals off-campus in the city of Boston and neighbor towns. I have a friend who pays $800/month for a studio on NU's side of Fenway park while I pay over $1,000/month to have my own room (very small) and share a bathroom, kitchen, and living room with three other girls. However, when you live off-campus, you end up paying extra for Internet connection and utilities bills. If you don't mind doing that, and you're tired of having to sign in guests and pay ridiculous amounts of money for campus dorms, then you might want to look into living off campus after freshman year.

While Boston is most certainly a college town, NU students can get the vibe that our adult neighbors would rather not have us around late on a Saturday night when the parties get going. If you live off campus, you'll need to remember that your neighbors are probably not college students, and the noise level has to be kept at a respectable level. Also, you start dealing with landlords which can be unsettling. But, all the students I know who are living, and have lived, off campus really enjoy the sense of freedom it gives them and they won't go back to campus living again.

The College Prowler™ Grade on
Off-Campus Housing: B+

A high grade in Off-Campus Housing indicates that apartments are of high quality, close to campus, affordable, and easy o secure.

Diversity

The Lowdown
ON DIVERSITY

- **African American:** 6%
- **Asian American:** 7%
- **Hispanic:** 5%
- **Native American:** 0%
- **White:** 77%
- **International:** 5%
- **Out-of-State:** 64%

Political Activity
The campus seems overwhelmingly democratic, but there are a few conservatives in the crowd.

Gay Tolerance
We have NuBiLaga, which is the group for bisexual, lesbian, and gay students. Being gay is no big deal at all here at NU or in Boston.

Most Popular Religions
There are a few Christian groups, but Hillel for Jewish students on campus is also popular and this year they were able to get kosher food served in the dining hall.

Minority Clubs
There are so many clubs at school that anyone can hold an event and people will go to it.

Economic Status
It's tough to say because Northeastern is such an expensive school, yet 73% of the student body is on financial aid.

Students Speak Out
ON DIVERSITY

"It's very diverse and one of the reasons I came here. Although, I do think people still tend to find themselves in cliques and hang with the same types all the time."

"**Campus is very diverse, which I love**. There are students and faculty from every race and ethnicity. We actually have a diversity requirement here where you must take at least two courses in order to graduate."

"The campus is quite diverse with all nationalities from all areas of the world. **You never know who you are going to meet**."

"The campus seems **whiter than anything else**, but I'll admit that it's more diverse than I expected it to be. I've never seen anyone disrespecting someone else's culture, and if people are rude it's because they're ignorant."

"I am white and I once lived in a really friendly building on campus, but **there were some black girls who gave me dirty looks** and would say awful things about me behind my back. I never knew why, and I was too nervous to confront them, but I hope things like that don't happen a lot to people here."

"Freshman year I had a roommate who was from New York City and she should've known about diversity. Instead, **she made offensive remarks about my Jewish customs** and observances and instead of sharing ideas with her I ended up keeping my mouth shut, which was a shame."

The College Prowler Take
ON DIVERSITY

Every person I've talked to embraces the diversity on campus, and it doesn't seem like most of the campus is white. If you walk from the quad to the library you will pass every kind of race and nationality. We also have exchange students that stay here for a semester. The area we live in is diverse, as well. There are really wealthy neighborhoods (like where John Kerry lives in Beacon Hill) and there are poor neighborhoods, like Dorchester. Sometimes groups on campus will team up and have a joint event. For example, recently there was a Jewish/Latin American night where we learned how to do salsa and Israeli dancing. Afterwards, we ate food from both cultures.

The Latino/a Student Cultural Center provides resources for academic and personal counseling, as well as professional mentoring. The center houses the Latino, Latin American, and Caribbean Studies minor. The center is equipped with a computer lab, a seminar room, a student office, a kitchen and a beautiful deck.

The College Prowler™ Grade on
Diversity: C

A high grade in Diversity indicates that ethnic minorities and international students have a notable presence on campus and that students of different economic backgrounds, religious beliefs, and sexual preferences are well-represented.

Guys & Girls

The Lowdown
ON GUYS & GIRLS

Women Undergrads:
7,219

Men Undergrads:
7,273

Birth Control Available?
Yes, at Lane Health Center on campus.

Most Prevalent STDs on Campus:
Genital warts, HPV

Social Scene
I find that most of the socially awkward kids around here are the ones who find boyfriends/girlfriends because they find people just like them to hang out with. NU is an extremely social campus because there are so many places to go. You don't have to sit in someone's apartment or dorm. You can walk down the street and meet a girl or guy in Store 24 or at afterHOURS.

Hookups or Relationships?
More and more I feel like NU is fast becoming a relationship school. Maybe it's because of the cold weather and the desire to cuddle up to someone. However, NU students are very attractive and are always meeting new prospects, even from neighbor schools. If you're looking for a relationship, it can seem a hopeless at times because all anyone wants to do is hookup.

Best Place to Meet Guys/Girls

There are a ton of places to meet guys and girls. Besides meeting someone through a friend or in your residence hall, NU students like to go out on the town and party it up. You can go to a bar or club nearby on Boylston and Newbury Street. A lot of students will go to Tiger Lily's in a big group because the scorpion bowls are strong, and it's easy to meet someone there for a nightcap. Another place to meet a prospect is at a party, although chances are, it won't be more than a one night thing.

Dress Code

The basic style is casual, but of course, some people get more dressed up. Since we are so close to major shopping areas of Boston, students will find any excuse to shop and pretty much always want to look their best.

The College Prowler Take
ON GUYS & GIRLS

Oh, the joys of being young and in college. NU is full of attractive people and most of them are just waiting to hook up. The problem is the communication. We need some sort of dating guide, it seems, because both girls and guys don't know how to treat each other properly. For every good relationship, I hear about ten bad ones. I must admit this is concerning, but then again, we're in college and it's all about fun. NU is a sexually open campus. We have events on sex (Sex Week) and we're always talking about who hooked up, who's a nasty slut, and who's still a virgin. Even if you came to school a virgin freshman year, chances are you didn't stay one for long.

I don't want to give you the wrong impression, though. I also have friends who really do want to be in a relationship, but haven't found the right girl or guy. It can be hard waiting around for love, but as Cher once said, "it doesn't mean you can't have a wonderful time with all the wrong men."

Students Speak Out
ON GUYS & GIRLS

{ "All different types of people from all parts of the world—you're pretty much guaranteed to find someone that you'll like to chill with. There are a lot of good-looking people."

Q "Some of the guys are gorgeous and some of the girls are very pretty, too. **Watch out for the fake bakers** and please don't ever become one. Keep your tan to a warm latte, please, for all our sakes."

Q "I guess the girls and guys here are okay. Like every other college, **it just depends on where you are** and how hard you're looking. Then again, Boston is a college town, so you'll pretty much find anything out here!"

Q "I think there is a large amount of diversity here so **you will run into many different kinds of people**. I think people here are anywhere from artsy, to intellectual, to athletic."

Q "*Playboy Magazine* ranked Northeastern **#1 for Hot Girls**. There's great night life, plenty of clubs and parties."

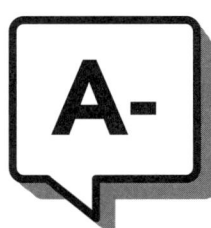

The College Prowler™ Grade on
Guys: B+

A high grade for Guys indicates that the male population on campus is attractive, smart, friendly, and engaging, and that the school has a decent ratio of guys to girls.

The College Prowler™ Grade on
Girls: A-

A high grade for Girls not only implies that the women on campus are attractive, smart, friendly, and engaging, but also that there is a fair ratio of girls to guys.

Athletics

Conference:
American East Conference (Division I); Atlantic 10 Conference (Division I, Football I-AA); Hockey East Association (Division I)

Most Popular Sports:
Football, Hockey

Overlooked Teams:
Field Hockey, Track, Women's Crew

School Mascot:
Huskies

The Lowdown
ON ATHLETICS

Men's Varsity Teams:
Baseball, Basketball, Crew, Cross-country, Football, Ice hockey, Soccer, Track and field (indoor), Track and field (outdoor)

Women's varsity Teams:
Basketball, Crew, Cross-country, Field hockey, Ice hockey, Soccer, Swimming and diving, Track and field (indoor), Track and field (outdoor), Volleyball

Club Sports:
Cycling, Figure skating, Inline hockey, Lacrosse, Goju Ryu Karate, Judo, Tae Kwon Do, Rugby, Ultimate frisbee, Volleyball, Wrestling

Fields
Parson's and Sweeney

Getting Tickets
Matthews Arena, Sports Pass. Tickets are not required for admission to soccer, volleyball, field hockey, swimming & diving, track & field, rowing or baseball games. For tickets to away games for football, hockey, and basketball call 617-373-4700. Group rate prices are available for any party of 15 or more, but must be purchased at least 48 hours in advance.

Students Speak Out
ON ATHLETICS

"Varsity sports are pretty big, but it's often difficult to get to the places where these events go on. Intramural sports are pretty big. Broomball is a fun one played in the ice hockey rink."

Q "The only varsity sports games I've ever attended are the Hockey games when we play our rivals Harvard, BU and BC. Other than that, **I don't pay much attention** to our team's stats, or whatever."

Q "With the exception of the Huskies Football team, I never hear about any of the athletic stuff here. I know we have it, but **it's so not a big part of college for me**."

Q "We have such awesome facilities that I think **we should have more awesome sports teams**."

💬 "I'm on the field hockey team and **we work hard, everyday**. It would be nice to get some more recognition for what we do."

💬 "I sometimes browse the sports pages of the *Northeastern News*, and **I'm happy when we win**, but I wouldn't exactly say I have school spirit when it comes to sports. I've been to, like, two games."

The College Prowler Take
ON ATHLETICS

Northeastern University is an integral part of the New England sports community, fielding 19 varsity teams in National Collegiate Athletic Association (NCAA) Division I sports, as well as other teams and individuals in national and international arenas. The university's teams, nicknamed the Huskies, are also some of the region's most successful.

NU plays host to some of the biggest collegiate events. Northeastern hosted the NCAA field hockey championship at Parsons Field in 1994 and 1999. Northeastern, along with Harvard, will host the 2006 NCAA Women's Basketball Final Four at the Fleet Center in Boston. The 2001 Women's Hockey National Championship semifinals and finals were played at Matthews Arena. NU and Matthews Arena hosted the 2002 America East Men's Basketball Championship and then co-hosted the 2003 event with Boston University at Walter Brown Arena. Yet, according to students, athletics aren't huge here, and although you can get a full scholarship if you're on a team, students don't look to athletics as a reason to come to Northeastern. Some students get involved in the intramurals, such as volleyball and broomball.

The College Prowler™ Grade on
Athletics: B-

A high grade in Athletics indicates that students have school spirit, that sports programs are respected, that games are well-attended, and that intramurals are a prominent part of student life.

Greek Life

The Lowdown
ON GREEK LIFE

Number of Fraternities:
9

Number of Sororities:
7

Percent of Undergrad Men in Fraternities:
4%

Percent of Undergrad Women in Sororities:
4%

Fraternities on Campus
Alpha Epsilon Pi, Alpha Kappa Sigma, Theta Delta Chi, Beta Gamma Epilon, Kappa Sigma, Pi Kappa Alpha, Phi Gamma Pi, Sigma Alpha Mu, Sigma Phi Epsilon

Sororities on Campus
Sigma Sigma Sigma, Alpha Epsilon Phi, Delta Phi Epsilon, Delta Zeta, Sigma Delta Tau, Sigma Gamma Rho, Zeta Phi Beta

Other Greek Organizations
Greek Council, Greek Peer Advisors, Interfraternity Council, Order of Omega, Panhellenic Council

Did You Know?

At the beginning of the year, the pledge class in each sorority puts on a show called Greek Follies and afterwards a winner is declared.

Students Speak Out
ON GREEK LIFE

"Greek life is limited. There are very few frat houses because we are in a city, and there are no sorority houses. But, it's a good way to get involved if you are into that sort of thing."

"**Go Greek**, trust me on this one."

"Screw Greek life. I hate it and **I would never become one of them**. I could never let someone run my life the way they do during pledge. It ruins your grades and your chance to meet all the other great people outside of your Greek community. I have lost touch with any of the Greek friends I made freshman year."

"Greek Life is a fun time for those involved. Most of the sororities and fraternities try to organize as many events, both together and separate, to help the community and get to know each other. **It definitely doesn't dominate the social scene**, however. There are no sorority houses due to the fact that Boston law states that no more than 6 unrelated girls may live under the same roof. The fraternity scene is located mostly away from campus, but is always a good time."

"The Greek life is **a very small part of the NU social scene**."

The College Prowler Take
ON GREEK LIFE

I haven't had any experience with Greek life except the occasional party. There are no houses for women because of the "Brothel Law" that Massachusetts passed years and years ago, making it illegal for more than 5 women to live together. All of the fraternities are on Mission Hill, which is about a mile away from campus. It's easy to get to but when it gets cold in the winter time, many students feel that it's not worth the hike for what could very well be a mediocre party. At the beginning of each semester, there is a rush week where students can visit with the different houses and they can place a bid for a student much like, I assume, it works at other schools.

The College Prowler™ Grade on
Greek Life: C-

A high grade in Greek Life indicates that sororities and fraternities are not only present, but also active on campus. Other determining factors include the variety of houses available and the respect the Greek community receives from the rest of the campus.

Drug Scene

Q "**I don't do drugs**, but I know people do get caught smoking weed in the dorms."

Q "You can go through college having never touched the stuff, or you could get it every weekend. **The choice is yours**."

Q "Northeastern has a very strict drug policy, making it a rarity to hear about, or see a lot of, drug usage on campus. Other than marijuana, which is popular no matter where you go, **there isn't a huge problem** with the consumption of illegal substances."

The Lowdown
ON DRUG SCENE

Most Prevalent Drugs on Campus:
Alcohol, marijuana, cocaine, caffeine, Ritalin, Adderall

Liquor-Related Referrals:
110

Liquor-Related Arrests:
133

Drug-Related Referrals:
62

Drug-Related Arrests:
81

Drug Counseling Programs:
None

The College Prowler Take
ON DRUG SCENE

I'd be lying if I said I haven't seen drugs on campus, but it really isn't hard to avoid. Just don't get caught if you're going to do them, which I do not advocate, by the way! There are harsh penalties in Massachusetts for Marijuana smoking. Other drugs are around I'm sure, but, again, I'm from New York City, so it seems pretty tame compared to there. Of course, if drugs are your scene, it doesn't seem to hard to find what you're looking for. Also, make sure your roommate knows your stance on drugs because I have seen many problems between roommates when it comes to that sort of thing. If you get caught, chances are your roommate will too, and visa versa.

The College Prowler™ Grade on
Drug Scene: B+

A high grade in the Drug Scene indicates that drugs are not a noticeable part of campus life; drug use is not visible, and no pressure to use them seems to exist.

Students Speak Out
ON DRUG SCENE

"I'm not in it, and it doesn't seem too overwhelming. It's not too difficult to avoid, though."

Campus Strictness

Q "NUPD is very strict about drugs, but **not as terrible about drinking**."

Q "If you aren't providing alcohol to minors or dealing large quantities of drugs, the policy is the basic three-strikes-you're-out method. **There is an online class to complete on the dangers of drugs and alcohol** and a fine to pay. On the last strike, you may lose the rights to attend the school and live on-campus."

The Lowdown
ON CAMPUS STRICTNESS

What Are You Most Likely to Get Caught Doing on Campus?
Drinking underage, public urination or indecency, making too much noise in your dorm, downloading copyrighted materials

The College Prowler Take
ON CAMPUS STRICTNESS

Last summer, 11 orientation leaders had to resign as the result of drinking underage at a party and serving alcohol to minors. These students were among Northeastern's finest and it was a classic case of being at the wrong place at the wrong time. A fellow student reported the orientation leaders and prompted the Student Government Association President to resign as well. This might say something about how strict our campus and our city is. Underage drinking is a big deal here and you will get written up and passed along to Judicial Affairs if you're not careful. My friends have had their fake IDs taken away at bars and clubs, too.

Students Speak Out
ON CAMPUS STRICTNESS

"I have never had a problem with underage drinking. You just have to be smart about it. Don't go walking down the street with a beer in one hand and a joint in the other."

Q "**Parties get broken up a lot**, so I don't usually go to them."

Q "**Campus is pretty strict**, but if you are smart, you won't get caught."

The College Prowler™ Grade on
Campus Strictness: B-

A high Campus Strictness grade implies an overall lenient atmosphere; police and RAs are fairly tolerant, and the administration's rules are flexible.

Overall Experience

Students Speak Out
ON OVERALL EXPERIENCE

"If you are an independent person and do not rely solely upon others for your happiness, you'll have a good time. Make the most of Boston—the experience is what you make of it."

Q "**I love it here**, I think it is a great town to go to college in and, even afterwards, I would certainly look into staying here."

Q "I have had a very good experience at NU. I am from Virginia, so I wasn't quite sure what to expect—but you meet a lot of people. It's a big school, so **everyone has a place**."

Q "I love it here. **I wouldn't trade it for anything** short of a professional baseball contract."

Q "Overall, **I am very happy with my choice to attend Northeastern**. I can't think of a better place to attend college than here."

The College Prowler Take
ON OVERALL EXPERIENCE

Students complain about Northeastern like they do at every college. The advisors don't care enough, people slack off in their jobs, etc., but when it comes down to it, I think most of us are happy to be here.

The Inside Scoop

Students Speak Out
ON THE INSIDE SCOOP

NU Slang:

Know the slang, know the school. The following is a list of things you really need to know before coming to NU. The more of these words you know, the better off you'll be.

AfterHours: Northeastern's on-campus lounge. There is food and good performances there. Gavin Degraw played there recently.

BHOP: Boston House of Pizza

Curry: Not food, but the Student Center

Middler: The year between sophomore and junior year

The T: Our subway/public transportation system. It's all we've got!

UHOP: University House of Pizza

Things I Wish I Knew Before Coming to NU:

- There's nothing I can think of because I really looked into the school beforehand, but my friends have said they wish they'd know more about their major because once you get here you really need to pick one, quickly.
- If the going gets tough, go to www.collegebellhop.com!
- If you're roommate is terrible, you can get a new room.

Tips to Succeed at NU:

- If you are having trouble in a class, don't wait until the last minute to make an appointment to see your professor (all profs have office hours), or go to the Peer Tutoring Center on the second floor on Snell Library and make an appointment.

NU Urban Legends

If you rub the husky statue's nose in the Krentzman Quad, you will have good luck!

School Spirit

People wear black and red, the school's colors, on Northeastern Day in May

Traditions

Every year we have Sex Week, The BeanPot (Ice Hockey tournament), SpringFest

Finding a Job or Internship

Advice

Northeastern University is a world leader in cooperative education with students coming from 50 United States and over 130 different countries to study.

Career Center Resources & Services:

Northeastern University has historically been guided by the conviction that the function of higher education is to prepare individuals for useful, productive, and satisfying lives. In 1909, the University introduced cooperative education into its traditional educational strategy, making work experience a structured part of the curriculum. The success of this educational model has distinguished Northeastern University from other institutions of higher education; cooperative education has become the University's signature program.

Dual Learning Settings

Through co-op, students alternate between semesters of learning in the classroom and semesters of learning in the workplace. The co-op work experiences are full-time, connected to the student's major and/or personal interests, and almost always paid. Co-op students test their skills in a variety of environments while undergraduates. They discover what they like and don't like, and understand the rich connections between theory and practice. Each learning experience informs the next.

Learning is facilitated through the preparation, activity, and reflection phases of the co-op process. Students work one-to-one with co-op faculty as they alternate periods of classroom study with planned, career-related work experience. In the work setting, students are evaluated by employers on an ongoing basis, and also have opportunities for self-evaluation. The co-op curriculum is designed to trigger change and growth within the student.

www.careerservices.neu.edu

The Best & Worst

The Ten BEST Things About NU:

1. It's getting better and more recognized every day.
2. There's a Dunkin' Donuts shop everywhere you look.
3. The Husky Card is better than gold.
4. Co-op
5. Diversity
6. Nightlife
7. Housing when you get a good lottery number
8. The new buildings
9. It's in Boston!
10. Shopping: Newbury Street/The Prudential Center/Copley

The Ten WORST Things About NU:

1. The cost
2. The NU Shuffle
3. The cold weather
4. Getting a bad lottery number
5. Profs who don't speak English and teach math and science
6. The construction noise with all the new buildings
7. People always leaving for co-op
8. People confusing us for that other school in Chicago with the similar name
9. Comcast rules our cable; they don't play nice
10. Forced triples and quads—rooms for two but they put three or four in!

Providence College

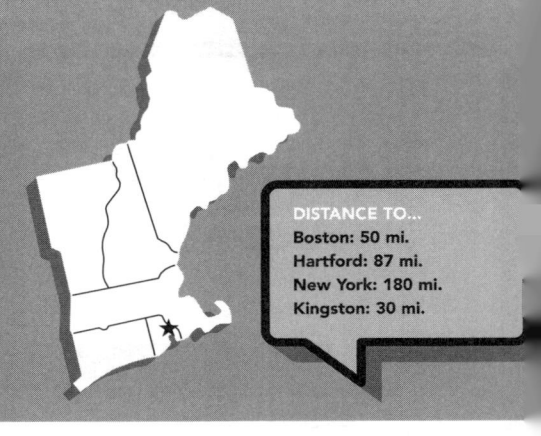

DISTANCE TO...
Boston: 50 mi.
Hartford: 87 mi.
New York: 180 mi.
Kingston: 30 mi.

549 River Avenue, Providence, RI 02918
www.providence.edu   (800) 721-6444

"The College's Catholic and Dominican traditions work to develop students into virtuous models of civility."

Total Enrollment:
3,714
Acceptance Rate:
53%
Tuition:
$23,639
Top 10% of High School Class:
42%
Average GPA:
3.4
SAT Range
Verbal	Math	Total
550–650	560–650	1110–1300

ACT Range
Verbal	Math	Total
N/A	N/A	23-28

Most Popular Majors:
11% Marketing/Marketing Management
9%   Business Administration and Management
9%   Special Education and Teaching
8%   Finance

Students Also Applied To:*
Boston College, College of the Holy Cross, Fairfield University, Stonehill College, Villanova University

For more school info check out www.collegeprowler.com

Table of Contents

Academics	857
Local Atmosphere	859
Safety & Security	860
Computers	862
Facilities	863
Campus Dining	865
Off-Campus Dining	866
Campus Housing	868
Off-Campus Housing	869
Diversity	871
Guys & Girls	872
Athletics	874
Greek Life	876
Drug Scene	877
Campus Strictness	878
Overall Experience	880
The Inside Scoop	881
Finding a Job or Internship	882
The Best & Worst	883

College Prowler Report Card

Academics	B+
Local Atmosphere	B+
Safety & Security	B-
Computers	B-
Facilities	B
Campus Dining	C+
Off-Campus Dining	A-
Campus Housing	B-
Off-Campus Housing	B+
Diversity	D-
Guys	B+
Girls	A-
Athletics	B+
Greek Life	N/A
Drug Scene	B+
Campus Strictness	B

Academics

Special Degree Options
Accelerated Master's Programs: Optometry, BS/BA/MBA

Intercollege Programs
3-2 Engineering/Physics Systems with Colombia University and Washington University in St. Louis

Sample Academic Clubs
Alpha Delta Mu, Alpha Epsilon Delta, Gamma Kappa Alpha, National Society of Collegiate Scholars, Amigos Unidos, Circolo Italiano, Law Society, Philosophy Club

The Lowdown
ON ACADEMICS

Students Speak Out
ON ACADEMICS

Degrees Awarded:
Certificate, Associate, Bachelor, Master

Full-time Faculty:
249

Faculty with Terminal Degree:
88%

Student-to-Faculty Ratio:
14:1

Average Course Load:
5 courses

AP Test Score Requirements:
Possible credit for scores of 4 or 5

IB Test Score Requirements:
Used for placement only

Best Places to Study:
Library, St. Dominic's Chapel, Slavin Center, Aquinas Lounge

"Some teachers are wonderful, enthusiastic, and completely interesting, while others can be ridiculously boring and hard to stay awake for."

Q "**The professors are usually incredibly friendly and helpful.** Many of them take an active interest in student life. I have seen professors show up to their students' athletic games and send out mass e-mails encouraging other students to also attend."

Q "I have found that all of my professors have been very passionate about their subject and also make themselves very accessible to the students. **PC's academic setting can be a very advantageous environment to the undeclared student**, as it is very encouraging of students to test the waters to discover subject matter that interests them before committing to a major."

Q "The Providence College faculty is made up of professors who have the highest degrees attainable in their particular fields. This definitely shows you that they are extremely qualified to teach the subjects that they do. Despite this fact, **some particular professors are not great teachers**: they lack personality, the ability to interact with students and even other faculty members, which makes the learning experience quite dull and uninspiring. But, a vast majority of the professors I have had thus far have been great."

Q "One of the best things about professors at PC is the fact that **they're always accessible**. They make it easy to contact them, often giving you their home phone numbers. I'd say that most of the classes are interesting, but I have to admit a professor can make or break the class."

Q "I feel the teachers can be anywhere from fairly liberal to extremely conservative. **I guess you can't expect too much from a Catholic school**. Some teachers are cold, boring and confusing, while others can be extremely interesting and fun."

The College Prowler Take
ON ACADEMICS

Professors at PC, although varying in teaching style, all possess a genuine concern for their students, often going above and beyond the average to make themselves accessible. Like all colleges, professors and their classes cover the entire spectrum, from liberal and eccentric to conservative and traditional; the trick is to try a little of both and discover what suits you best.

While most major courses are stimulating, core classes can be tedious and downright painful. A unique and central experience for the PC student is the Development of Western Civilization course (usually referred to simply as Civ.). Requiring you to attend class five days a week for four consecutive semesters can seem, at first, a legal means of torture that somehow slipped past the founding fathers when drafting the Bill of Rights. But the program is not some remnant of medieval torture passed down in the Dominican tradition since the time of St. Thomas Aquinas; rather, it is a comprehensive examination of Western Civilization since its dawn in Mesopotamia a millennia ago through the Modern Age. Although Civ. may be a challenge, it is one that every PCer is proud to have completed. Another boon of Providence academics is the notable lack of teaching assistants. A professor teaches every class, and students will find competing with difficult accents to be nearly nonexistent.

The College Prowler™ Grade on
Academics: B+

A high Academics grade generally indicates that professors are knowledgeable, accessible, and genuinely interested in their students' welfare. Other determining factors include class size, how well professors communicate, and whether or not classes are engaging.

Local Atmosphere

Students Speak Out
ON LOCAL ATMOSPHERE

"**Providence is wonderful! A student receives all the benefits of a city atmosphere while also feeling as if they are living in a suburb. There are several other colleges and universities in the area and lots of places to visit!**"

Q "**The immediate area is up-and-coming**, due largely in part to the community service of PC students. Downtown, there are tons of things to do. The mall is new, Thayer Street is kind of an eclectic shopping and eating district, [and] the beaches like Narragansett and Newport are within 45 minutes of campus. Basically anything and everything that you could want to do in a city is here. There are four additional colleges in Providence—Brown University, Johnson and Wales University, Rhode Island College, and Rhode Island School of Design. PC students don't tend to really hang around with these other schools, though; we're pretty much a self-contained campus."

Q "**The city of Providence is truly a Renaissance city.** In recent years, there has been much improvement to the city that has made it a beautiful, fun, wonderful place to attend college. There are bars, clubs, movies, coffee shops, and during the warmer months the city lights up the river in an event called WaterFire. Unfortunately, PC is not in the greatest area of Providence, so one must use caution when walking at night. However, I have not felt uncomfortable yet."

Q "I love the atmosphere in Providence. While there are other colleges around, **PC students tend to stick together for the most part** at the same off-campus areas. This establishes a familiarity within the student body."

The Lowdown
ON LOCAL ATMOSPHERE

Region:
Northeast

City, State:
Providence, Rhode Island

Setting:
Medium-Sized City

Distance from New York:
3 hours

Distance from Boston:
1 hour

Points of Interest:
Thayer Street, Providence Place Mall, Roger Williams Park Botanical Gardens, Roger Williams Park Zoo, WaterFire, Fleet Skating Center

Major Sports Teams:
Patriots (NFL), Red Sox (MLB), Bruins (NHL)

City Websites:
www.providnceri.com
www.jumptoprovidence.com

The College Prowler Take
ON LOCAL ATMOSPHERE

Pop! You have stepped off Huxley Avenue, popping the "PC bubble." The small, private, Catholic campus is encircled by poverty-stricken North Providence. While the area directly surrounding campus is one that anyone with common sense avoids, PC is also minutes away from downtown Providence. The heart of this cleaner, smaller version of Boston is home to numerous hot spots for college students. An eclectic mix of shops and restaurants can be found on Thayer Street, near Brown University. With numerous entertainment venues, from the Providence Performing Arts Center to the Dunkin' Donuts Center, Providence has something for everyone. Overall, Providence is a city that irradiates a vivacity and youthfulness that can mainly be attributed to the several nearby colleges and universities.

Safety & Security

The Lowdown
ON SAFETY & SECURITY

Number of PC Police:
27

Phone:
(401) 865-2391 (non-emergencies)
(401) 865-2222 (emergencies)

Fax:
(401) 865-1391

The College Prowler™ Grade on
Local Atmosphere: B+

A high Local Atmosphere grade indicates that the area surrounding campus is safe and scenic. Other factors include nearby attractions, proximity to other schools, and the town's attitude toward students.

Health Center Office Hours:
Monday through Friday, 8:30 a.m. - 4:30 p.m.
Gyn clinic (by appointment only)

Safety Services:
(RAD) Rape Defense Classes, Emergency Phones, Late-Night Shuttle/Escort Services, 24-Hour Foot and Vehicle Patrols, Lighted Pathways and Sidewalks, Student Patrols, Controlled Dorm Access, Silent Witness Report Program

Students Speak Out
ON SAFETY & SECURITY

{ "Security is tight, but it's still important to use street smarts on campus. Walk in groups, especially at night, and don't make yourself a target for crime by flashing expensive electronic equipment."

Q "**Security is stupid; anyone and everyone can get onto campus and in and out the dorms very easily**. It's nice not to have to worry about any sort of hassle getting friends from outside of school onto campus, but it's scary to think of all the things that could happen due to lack of security."

Q "**The security on campus, to be honest, is worthless**. Men in their nineties isn't my idea of security. Dunbar is the only useful security guard we have."

Q "Safety on campus is totally blown out of proportion. Many people site the neighborhood as a problem and think the residents are willing to come on to campus to harm unsuspecting college students, which is definitely not the case. **Campus is quite safe**, and security does a good job in maintaining this safety. I feel that many students might feel unsafe at times because they are unfamiliar with the neighborhood and the neighborhood is unfamiliar with them."

Q "The security on campus is pretty good. But it's like any other campus, there are going to be problems. It is important to remember that no place is 100-percent safe. **The safety on campus works best when students use common sense**. PC security is usually right on top of situations."

Q "Security and safety at school is something that in my three years thus far I am aware they have tried to beef up; yet, **there is still a lot of work needed to be done**."

The College Prowler Take
ON SAFETY & SECURITY

Ah! The age old question that haunts parents of collegiate-bound children: is my child going to be safe at school? Providence College takes safety and security seriously, as the numerous lectures on the matter during orientation and freshman year prove. While freshmen girls may feel that living in an all-girl dorm, which requires males to sign in, is like living in a prison, others consider the Huxley Avenue entrance a security joke. Overall, PC has put into place numerous security measures to ensure both student and parental peace of mind. The use of common sense and awareness of one's surroundings is the best preventative measure. General consensus relates, "I have never felt unsafe at PC." The administration excels in keeping students informed and posts occurrences and security concerns.

The College Prowler™ Grade on
Safety & Security: B-

A high grade in Safety & Security means that students generally feel safe, campus police are visible, blue-light phones and escort services are readily available, and safety precautions are not overly necessary.

Computers

Students Speak Out
ON COMPUTERS

"There are nine computer labs on campus; it's usually never hard to find a computer if need be. I find that most students have their own computer, but a lot of time it's for personal use."

Q "**I must say the Providence College network is one of the worst you can ever find**. It is slow, always littered with countless viruses, and not on the cutting edge of technology. Most computer labs can get crowded, but it depends on location, time of day, and time of year."

Q "There are plenty of computer labs on campus in the various buildings, and while **they tend to be in higher demand during midterm and final weeks**, there is still availability as long as one can be flexible."

Q "**The computer labs aren't usually very crowded, and the network usually runs pretty well**. But, I recommend that every student bring his or her own computer."

Q "Generally speaking, there are plenty of computers available, but **not bringing a computer is a big risk to take**, especially around finals time. I frequently make use of the printers in the library. All of the course registration is done online, so it goes very quickly, but there are often errors and delays in the system due to the high number of students accessing the network at once, on those days, the computer labs are flooded with students."

Q "The computer network is inconsistent. **At times it can be very fast and helpful**, but other times it can be slow and a burden."

The Lowdown
ON COMPUTERS

High-Speed Network?
Yes

Wireless Network?
Yes, in the library

Number of Labs:
8

Numbers of Computers:
219

24-Hour Labs:
None

Charge to Print:
No

Operating Systems:
PC, Mac, and UNIX

Free Software:
None

The College Prowler Take
ON COMPUTERS

At least three times a year, you will get an e-mail explaining that the network will be shut down for a period of about four hours "due to servicing." It's hard to maintain control of your emotions when you receive such news. What on earth will you do without AIM for four hours? The answer comes in a lightning-quick flash of insight: Snood! These two activities—AIM and Snood—are the real reason you'll want to bring your own computer to PC. The computer labs on campus are sufficient, but they can get crowded during midterms and finals. The network at PC is comparative to high-speed DSL and, more importantly, is free—music to any college student's ears! The degree of satisfaction supplied by the network varies from frustration to felicity.

The College Prowler™ Grade on
Computers: B-

A high grade in Computers designates that computer labs are available, the computer network is easily accessible, and the campus' computing technology is up-to-date.

Facilities

The Lowdown
ON FACILITIES

Movie Theatre on Campus?
No, but there are outdoor movies on Slavin lawn occasionally.

Bowling on Campus?
No

Bar on Campus?
McPhails

Coffeehouse on Campus?
No

Student Center:
Slavin Center

Athletic Center:
Peterson Recreation Center

Libraries:
Phillips Memorial

Popular Places to Chill:
McPhails, The Quad, Alumni Hall Cafeteria

Favorite Things to Do:
The artistically-inclined can check out the latest student masterpieces at the Hunt-Cavanaugh Gallery and the new Smith Center for the Fine Arts. The Guzman Chapel holds performances by the musically-gifted students of PC. Blackfriars theatre hosts the school's dramatic productions twice a year.

 **Students Speak Out** ON FACILITIES

 **The College Prowler Take** ON FACILITIES

"PC is just finishing a restoration and renovation period, so many of the facilities on campus are changing for the better. The library looks brand new and has added state-of-the-art computers."

Q "The athletic facilities are sometimes too crowded, and the weight room is extremely small. **As a Big East school, I had expected larger facilities** and better equipment."

Q "**The facilities are nice, open areas.** Especially with the recent addition of McPhails on our campus, it invites and accommodates more on-campus activity among students."

Q "For anyone who is looking at PC now, **the facilities are state-of-the-art**. There are several buildings which need updating when I looked at PC, but they are in the middle of a lot of renovations which have made the campus almost brand new."

Q "The athletic center isn't that great. **Sometimes you just want to go play basketball and you can't because they are using the courts for some other activity**. They are in desperate need of a new athletic facility. The computers in the labs are pretty good. The student center is very nice. We recently had a new campus bar and hangout built; it's a good place to go play pool, Ping-Pong, or watch a baseball game on the big screen television."

Q "PC's athletic facility is undergoing new additions of turf fields, aerobic rooms, and hopefully, in a few years, an outdoor track. Overall, the athletic department is budgeting multi-millions from fund-raising for all the new updates. **Some athletic facilities, such as Peterson, are only accessible to non-athletes.**"

The year of our Lord two thousand and four was a year of renewal for Providence College. Heretofore existing structures were deemed antiquated and obsolete, and have been undergoing renovations. Returning students to the PC campus eagerly anticipate the unveiling of these new edifices. Students have grown accustomed to the new restaurant-style look of Raymond Cafeteria, but the latest renovations bring another new addition to the dining hall. Not many people have seen the interior of the new Smith Center for the Fine Arts, but if it is anything like the outside, students can expect a fantastic new facility. Providence administration deserves a round of applause for addressing the needs of the student body and refurbishing the campus in so short a period of time. The campus will now be filled with the hustle and bustle of merry students rather than scaffolding, workmen, and the melody of heavy machinery.

The College Prowler™ Grade on
Facilities: B

A high Facilities grade indicates that the campus is aesthetically pleasing and well-maintained; facilities are state-of-the-art, and libraries are exceptional. Other determining factors include the quality of both athletic and student centers and an abundance of things to do on campus.

Campus Dining

Students Speak Out
ON CAMPUS DINING

"**Raymond Hall is our main dining facility on campus. You can get almost anything you want to eat, and it's open most of the day. The favorite meal of the week is weekend brunch.**"

Q "**Raymond Hall—eh, I've had better college food**. But, the good news is you can always find something to eat. 'Ray' is a great place to socialize! And it's all-you-can-eat and has good desserts. Oh yeah, and the staff is awesome! Slavin has much better food than Ray and is a little more expensive. It's a debit system. It's a great place to grab a snack at night or to meet with a study group."

Q "Food is not that great on campus, but it is not that bad. **Most people decide to eat off campus or order out to avoid the monotony of the dishes served at school**. It would be nice to actually have a restaurant on campus like I know other schools do."

Q "**It's all run by Sodexho**, which serves 90 percent of the schools in the United States, so it's going to be about the same wherever you go in this country."

Q "The food on campus is pretty good, **not as good as home cooking**, but good for college food. They have a huge variety, and personally, being a vegetarian, offered a lot of choices."

Q "**The food is getting better every year** I return to campus. The dining company has a wide variety of foods to choose from and has started to become more health conscious about what meals they are giving PC students."

The Lowdown
ON CAMPUS DINING

Freshman Meal Plan Requirement?
Yes

24-Hour On-Campus Eating?
No

Student Favorites:
The Grill, Theme Cuisine, The Pizzeria

Meal Plan Average Cost:
$4,250

Did You Know?

Some dorms have a kitchen if you're feeling up to the task of attempting a home-cooked meal.

The College Prowler Take
ON CAMPUS DINING

There are two sources of food on campus: Raymond Cafeteria and Alumni Food Court in the Slavin Center. Ray Café, the main cafeteria at PC and the one at which your meal plan applies, was refurbished in 2003. Although the decor was jazzed up with the addition of booths, swank lighting, and iron grating for the individual stations, Ray can leave a bitter taste in the mouth of some of PC's more finicky eaters. Those lacking an iron stomach and the courage needed to attempt the more exotic cuisine can take solace; Ray Café is the best place to eat if you want to keep it simple and stick to the basics.

Off-Campus Dining

The Lowdown
ON OFF-CAMPUS DINING

The College Prowler™ Grade on
Campus Dining: C+

Our grade on Campus Dining addresses the quality of both school-owned dining halls and independent on-campus restaurants as well as the price, availability, and variety of food.

Best Pizza:
Antonio's

Best Chinese:
Lili Wok

Best Breakfast:
Admiral Spa

Best Wings:
Joe's American Bar and Grille

Best Healthy:
La Creperie

Best Place to Take Your Parents:
Blue Grotto, Mediterraneo, Hemenway's

24-Hour Eating:
No

Student Favorites:
Golden Crust, Lili Wok, The Cheesecake Factory, Uno's, Sicilia's

Late-Night Food Specials:
Golden Crust, Union Station Brewery

Fun Facts

When ordering from Golden Crust, make sure to get blue cheese and throw in a side of golden fries.

Want more than just a regular slice? Antonio's specializes in gourmet pizza. Chicken pesto and tomato basil are to die for!

Meditterraneo's turns into a salsa club after hours on the weekend.

Students Speak Out
ON OFF-CAMPUS DINING

"**Federal Hill is less than 10 minutes away, and the food there is great.** If you're looking for something a little less pricey, the mall has great places like The Cheesecake Factory, Fire & Ice, and Uno's."

"If there is one thing that's great about the city of Providence, it's the restaurants. There is so much to choose from. **There's great Indian food and great Italian food.** There are so many little places to go and enjoy. There is something for everyone."

"**The Federal Hill area is amazing**—tons of fine Italian food. Blue Grotto and Mediterraneo are delicious; Cassarinos is more popular if you don't want to empty your bank account."

"**Two words: Fire & Ice**. Usually when you're going out to eat from school, you're going with a group of friends. Not only is Fire & Ice great food, but it's the easiest to split the bill. It's a buffet and runs about 15 dollars for dinner and even less for lunch. You personalize your own stir-fry plate and, most importantly, it's all you can eat!"

"The restaurants off campus are amazing. **On Thayer Street I would hit up Kartabar** [for] really interesting Mediterranean food, Phillipe's for really good wraps and sandwiches, or Café Paragon for a slightly nicer sit-down meal."

The College Prowler Take
ON OFF-CAMPUS DINING

Providence leaves residents and visitors with a plethora of dining choices. From upscale Italian on Federal Hill to the more eclectic flavors of Thayer Street, the city has something to offer every gourmet, except, of course, the indecisive. Certain local spots become staples in the PC collegiate dining experience. Many eateries do deliver, including Sicilia's on Federal Hill. A drawback to delivery is that, in the snow, it can take up to two hours. Some places, such as Mai Tai, accept credit cards for those running short on cash. Dining out and delivery are an excellent option when you've run out of Slavin money and Ray disappoints yet again. Offering a diverse selection of cuisine for all budgets, Providence restaurants subscribe to the old adage, "variety is the spice of life."

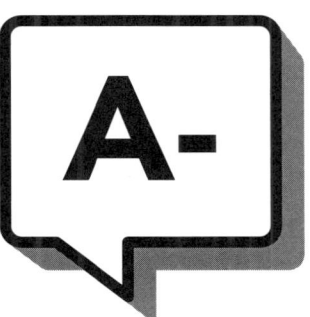

The College Prowler™ Grade on
Off-Campus Dining: A-

A high Off-Campus Dining grade implies that off-campus restaurants are affordable, accessible, and worth visiting. Other factors include the variety of cuisine and the availability of alternative options (vegetarian, vegan, Kosher, etc.).

Campus Housing

Did You Know?

Providence College has banned smoking in all of the dorms on campus. Smokers should be ready to stand outside.

Students Speak Out
ON CAMPUS HOUSING

The Lowdown
ON CAMPUS HOUSING

Number of Dormitories:
9

Number of Apartment/Suite Buildings:
5

Room Types:
Standard, apartment, suite

Available for Rent:
Micro-fridge with microwave

Cleaning Service?
In communal areas including community bathrooms. UNICO staff comes daily. Apartment bathrooms are not cleaned.

You Get:
Bed, desk, chair, dresser, closet or wardrobe, window shade, cable TV jack, Ethernet or broadband Internet connection, free campus and local phone calls

Bed Type:
Twin extra-long (39"x 80"), bunkable beds, lofting available in certain dorms

Also Available:
Special interest housing

"The dorms are a decent size. Compared to other colleges I've seen, they are average. If you are a freshman male and like to party and be loud, you want to live in Guzman; its opposite would be Fennell Hall."

Q "**The dorms aren't beautiful or anything incredible, but they are fun.** Living on the quad was the time of my life. Freshman year I recommend the normal frosh dorms just because you meet all the other freshmen."

Q "All the dorms are nice in their own way, but if you want to stay away from the traditional rowdy dorms or the fines that go along with them, I would **stay away from McDermott, Guzman, and St. Joe's**."

Q "**A couple of the dorms are extremely old-fashioned and basically falling apart—more specifically, Fennell and Dore**. These dorms are for those who like the quiet laid-back environment, but who are willing to go to upper campus to have fun."

Q "The dorm rooms are pretty big—especially now that they opened the new suites. It creates fewer beds in the rooms and makes it spacious. **The quad is still a must for sophomores**—a year on the quad is a year well spent."

Q "**The dorms are pretty standard**. The nicest dorm is Aquinas Hall. This hall is great because all of the rooms have sinks in them, which is a major convenience."

The College Prowler Take
ON CAMPUS HOUSING

Adequate is the best word to describe on-campus housing. Ranging from old and in need of repairs to brand new suites, on-campus housing covers the entire gamut of possibilities. Everyone recommends that first-years choose an all-freshman dorm to create solidarity with their class. Sophomore year on the quad is practically a necessity. The all-girl dorms—Raymond, Meagher, and McVinney—tend to be quieter and less prone to damages. Overall, the dorms at PC are not too big, not too small, but just right.

Off-Campus Housing

The Lowdown
ON OFF-CAMPUS HOUSING

The College Prowler™ Grade on
Campus Housing: B-

A high Campus Housing grade indicates that dorms are clean, well-maintained, and spacious. Other determining factors include variety of dorms, proximity to classes, and social atmosphere.

Undergrads in Off-Campus Housing:
15%

Average Rent for a Pinehurst House:
$900-$1,200 a month

Average Rent for an Oakland House:
$900-$1,200 a month

Average Rent for a Pembroke House:
$900-$1,200 a month

Popular Areas:
Pinehurst, Oakland, Pembroke. Rent varies depending on number of bedrooms, upgrades, and furnishings.

Best Time to Look for a Place:
Beginning of first semester junior year

For Assistance Contact:
Office of Off-Campus Living
Web: www.providence.edu/Student+Life/Living+at+PC/Off-Campus+Living
Phone: (401) 865-2420
E-mail: rkless@providence.edu

Students Speak Out
ON OFF-CAMPUS HOUSING

"I like living off-campus because there's much more freedom; but, I have to deal with bills and a landlord. Most houses are within a quarter mile from campus, so it's convenient, even if you don't have a car."

Q "Housing off-campus is easy to get, and **sometimes you can get a deal**, but you have to watch out for the landlords. Make sure the house you rent is registered with the Office of Off-Campus Living."

Q "I think living off-campus is great, and I highly encourage students to do so. There is a new policy for members of the upcoming junior class where **they have to obtain permission to move off** before they actually can—I think that is absurd."

Q "I personally don't think it's worth it, given the people I have talked to. **Many of the houses are old and not in the best locations**."

Q "**You need to be a junior or senior to live off-campus**, but it is definitely worth it. I lived right off-campus—a three-minute walk—both years and I loved it!"

Q "Money-wise **it's a little cheaper** and, hey, you can do whatever you want—but, with that, comes a lot of other responsibilities."

The College Prowler Take
ON OFF-CAMPUS HOUSING

If you're looking for a smoother transition to post-college life, off-campus housing may be the choice for you. While all the houses are on the streets immediately surrounding campus, making it onto campus for class in the bitter cold may take more motivation than some possess. Renting an off-campus house may seem like a rule-free college experience, but it comes equipped with its own set of worries—bills, landlords, and housemates, to name just a few. Some of the houses are poorly maintained, while others are newly renovated. Living off campus isn't for everyone, but those responsible enough to handle the bills and walking to campus seem to thoroughly enjoy the experience.

The College Prowler™ Grade on
Off-Campus Housing: B+

A high grade in Off-Campus Housing indicates that apartments are of high quality, close to campus, affordable, and easy to secure.

Diversity

Political Activity
The campus lacks political protests, although some members of the student body are extremely active in politics.

Gay Tolerance
PC is very accepting of its gay community and even has clubs such as SHEPARD to increase awareness, tolerance, and acceptance of gays. RAs usually participate in a SafeZone program as well.

Economic Status
PC students are typically from middle-class or higher economic backgrounds.

The Lowdown
ON DIVERSITY

African American: 2%

Asian American: 2%

Hispanic: 2%

Native American: 0%

White: 93%

International: 1%

Out-of-State: 80%

Minority Clubs
Although PC isn't very diverse, there is a club for just about every ethnicity on campus. African American Club and Gaelic Society are two noticeably active clubs on campus that sponsor events under the BMSA banner.

Most Popular Religions
Catholicism. Pastoral Services and the Chaplain's Office direct numerous programs on and off campus for multiple faiths.

Students Speak Out
ON DIVERSITY

> "I'm not going to lie, the campus isn't very diverse. Although, the students are very accepting and open-minded."

Q "Diversity is something PC acknowledges needs work. **Most of the students are Catholic**, and we're not very geographically diverse either."

Q "As a student of color, I came into Providence knowing that diversity might be a problem, but as a student, **it seems so unbelievably lacking that it seems as if it is deliberate**."

Q "We have the Balfour Center for Multicultural students and the Board of Multicultural Student Affairs, which promote the celebration of diversity on campus, but aside from this, **our student body is not very diverse**."

Q "**Economically, most students are middle- and upper-class**, and there is a small legion of blatant rich kids. The faculty is even less diverse than the student body."

Q "**The only 'minorities' we have in abundance are women**, who seem to be sweeping colleges across the country by storm."

The College Prowler Take
ON DIVERSITY

American Eagle or Abercrombie & Fitch? This fairly simple question sums up the extent of diversity at PC. The majority of the student body is Caucasian and Christian—and preppy. The lack of diversity at PC is noted by everyone. While some think this makes for comfortable surroundings, many long for a more diverse campus. There are numerous ethnic clubs on campus, such as the African American club, Asian club, Gaelic Society, and Amigos Unidos, which highlight the diversity PC does have.

Concern vocalized by the student body has spurred the administration to address the issue. The admissions office cites a 25 percent increase in African American, Hispanic, Asian, and Native American (AHANA) student applicant pool for the class of 2008. There was also an increase in the number of AHANA students invited to enroll at PC. But, even with these efforts, diversity remains poor at Providence College.

The College Prowler™ Grade on
Diversity: D-

A high grade in Diversity indicates that ethnic minorities and international students have a notable presence on campus and that students of different economic backgrounds, religious beliefs, and sexual preferences are well-represented.

Guys & Girls

The Lowdown
ON GUYS & GIRLS

Women Undergrads: 58.2%

Men Undergrads: 41.8%

Birth Control Available?
No, birth control is not available for sale at the Health Center.

Social Scene
PC is a hugely social school. With all the outgoing people, it is nearly impossible to walk to class without having a conversation with someone. Many students choose to get involved in at least one of the clubs, sports, or organizations at PC. Intermingling and networking are practically core requirements here at Providence College.

Hookups or Relationships?
Many PC students choose commitment-free hookups on the weekends. Although there are couples at PC, their numbers are diminishing and dating is suffering a slow, painful death. Many people date outside PC.

Dress Code
PC is definitely a preppy school—polo shirts, button-downs, khakis, the whole nine yards. Abercrombie & Fitch, American Eagle, and J. Crew all epitomize the PC look. Jeans and T-shirts are the basic staples. Be prepared to see flip-flops for the greater percentage of the year as well.

Students Speak Out
ON GUYS & GIRLS

{ "I like to think we're a pretty attractive campus, at least that's what I've found in the past! You could classify the campus as pretty preppy, but everyone has his or her own twist of style."

Q "There is something funny about PC students. **Everyone is good-looking and has a great smile**, and it's without effort. It's an all-American kind of look. The girls are really great, down to earth, and really kind. I have found my best girlfriends at PC. The guys are also great. They won't be the guys at the bar hitting on you, but the ones sticking up for you when that other guy visiting from elsewhere does. You'll notice everyone is always saying hello or waving to 10 people as they walk to and from classes. The students at PC are good-looking, incredibly kind, and know how to have a good time anywhere they're at."

Q "The guys and girls at this school are all the same, **dressed in Abercrombie and accessorized with a silver spoon in their mouths**. Though the guys and girls are, for the most part, attractive, they get kind of repetitive after a while."

Q "The guys can be anywhere from really cool, smart, and interesting, to dumb, mean, rude, and immature—the same goes for girls. **There are a lot of attractive people at PC**, but sometimes that's as far as it will go. There are a lot of people at PC who are just there to party and nothing else. There are a lot of cool people there; you just have to find them."

Q "On this matter **I would have to compare PC to a typical high school**. There are different cliques like jocks, and nerds. Girls are definitely hot, one better than the other. To sum it all up, I would call the majority of the people at PC typical 'New Englanders.'"

The College Prowler Take
ON GUYS & GIRLS

Caucasian and cute is how many here at Providence would define the "typical" PC student. While the campus, overall, subscribes to a preppy style, there are those who choose to wear things other than Abercrombie & Fitch. Sweats are not at all unusual for 8:30 a.m. classes. There is a significant dearth of males at PC, but the ones that are here are good-looking for the most part. Females of the attractive variety are available in abundance. Overall, everyone agrees that PC is a good-looking school, even if the look is slightly repetitive. One disheartening and noticeable trend is the demise of dating. Fewer couples grace the quad and drunken hookups—commitment-free of course—are the vanguard these days.

The College Prowler™ Grade on
Guys: B+
A high grade for Guys indicates that the male population on campus is attractive, smart, friendly, and engaging, and that the school has a decent ratio of guys to girls.

The College Prowler™ Grade on
Girls: A-
A high grade for Girls not only implies that the women on campus are attractive, smart, friendly, and engaging, but also that there is a fair ratio of girls to guys.

Athletics

The Lowdown
ON ATHLETICS

Most Popular Sports
Men's basketball and hockey are the most important sports at PC, drawing local fans as well as alumni. All of the IM sports are popular, especially volleyball, softball, basketball, and hockey.

Overlooked Teams
The women's rugby team is phenomenal. Their recent trip to nationals has definitely expanded their fan base.

Fields
Hendricken

Getting Tickets
Tickets for the men's basketball games are available through the ticket office in Peterson. They are also sold in Ray and Slavin during meal times.

Men's Varsity Teams:
Basketball
Ice Hockey
Cross Country
Lacrosse
Soccer
Swimming and Diving
Indoor Track and Field
Outdoor Track and Field
Baseball
Football

Women's Varsity Teams:
Basketball
Cross Country
Soccer
Softball
Swimming and Diving
Tennis
Track and Field
Volleyball
Cheerleading
Football
Golf

Athletic Division:
NCAA Division I

Conference:
Big East, Hockey East

School Mascot:
Friar

Students Speak Out
ON ATHLETICS

The College Prowler Take
ON ATHLETICS

{ "PC is a Division I school, so varsity sports are very popular. Basketball, hockey, and lacrosse are everyone's favorites, but all games have pretty good turnouts."

Q "All sports are played on campus and all are free, with the exception of men's basketball. **The men play downtown at the Dunkin' Donut's Center**, and it's $5 for transportation and admission. Even so, men's basketball is the most popular thing to go to here at PC. We're in the Big East—that means that we play the most competitive teams in the country."

Q "**There is more of a competitive nature among the IM sports**—the majority of students participated in varsity sports in high school and want to continue playing them in college."

Q "**Men's basketball and hockey are huge**. Our women's rugby team is amazing, but the guys probably have more fans. Competition on the IM level varies by team and by sport. Some are very competitive, but even beginners can play and have a blast."

Q "**Intramurals are out-of-control**; it's very competitive and lots of fun! Everyone wants to win but is definitely having a good time. To wear an IM championship shirt you have to be someone special, and everyone on the team will be sporting it the day after the big win."

Q "Varsity sports are huge, and intramurals are another way to help you stay in shape. But, **you won't be ostracized if you don't play any type of sport**."

The lights go out and a spotlight illuminates the door. The crowd is hyped, screaming, and counting down the seconds until midnight. Three, two, one and with a deafening roar the basketball season has officially begun. For all PC students, Late Night Madness (Formerly Midnight Madness) is one event you must attend. Being a Division I school in the Big East, men's basketball is by far the biggest sport at PC. Friar fanatics pack the Dunk or McPhails to watch the games. School spirit extends to hockey and lacrosse as well, and generally, all the sports have a decent turnout. Because most students won't compete on a Division I team, intramurals are huge; anyone of any degree of athleticism can play and have tons of fun.

The College Prowler™ Grade on
Athletics: B+

A high grade in Athletics indicates that students have school spirit, that sports programs are respected, that games are well-attended, and that intramurals are a prominent part of student life.

Greek Life

The Lowdown
ON GREEK LIFE

Number of Fraternities: 0

Number of Sororities: 0

Percent of Undergrad Men in Fraternities: 0%

Percent of Undergrad Women in Sororities: 0%

Students Speak Out
ON GREEK LIFE

"At first, I was a little hesitant about not having Greek life, but I love not having it at PC. Everyone is accepting of everyone else, and there aren't such drastic lines dividing students."

Q "**We don't need them**! There are so many different ways to meet people and have fun that Greek life would only make things complicated and less inclusive."

Q "There is no Greek life at PC. I find this to be a perk. But, **if you're looking for a Greek system as means for a social life, PC is not a school for you**. However, we have clubs on campus that do more for the school and community than a frat or sorority would."

Q "Being a private, Catholic institution, Providence College doesn't feel the need to have Greek life on campus. **T**he only fraternities on campus are academic societies. One thing that is great about going to school in Providence is that **you have the ability to pledge at other schools** in the area, which is an option often taken by PC students."

Q "While **there is no Greek life**, a lot of the different clubs and organizations on campus take on a Greek social life, having houses and 'welcoming parties.' It's a good time."

Q "There are no fraternities or sororities on campus. **I honestly think this is one of the best things about the school**. There is no rushing, and campus is usually pretty quiet compared to those with a Greek system."

The College Prowler Take
ON GREEK LIFE

There is no Greek scene at PC due to the Catholic nature of the college. Because of this policy, PC students mingle freely without respect to class years or any other restricting criteria. Many students like the absence of Greek life. Unofficially, a Greek scene comparison can be drawn to several clubs on campus whose extensive interview process may feel like rushing. Following tradition those who make the club are "initiated" with a night of silly, usually messy, fun.

The College Prowler™ Grade on
Greek Life: N/A

A high grade in Greek Life indicates that sororities and fraternities are not only present, but also active on campus. Other determining factors include the variety of houses available and the respect the Greek community receives from the rest of the campus.

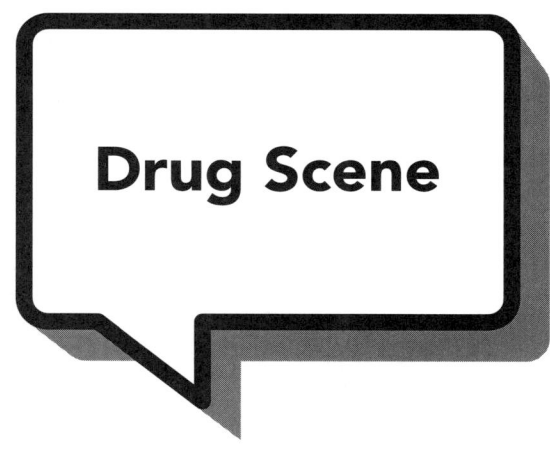

Drug Scene

Students Speak Out
ON DRUG SCENE

"Truthfully, I don't believe there is a lot of drug use on campus. I'm a very social person and have never come across any drugs besides marijuana."

Q "**I feel like the drug scene here is pretty mild**. Alcohol is much more prevalent on campus than any drug. I suppose pot would be the biggest drug used on campus, but it's never been as widespread as alcohol by any means. I've never been in a situation where anything more 'hardcore' than pot was being used either. There will always be kids that do it, but it's not as common as booze."

Q "Honestly, I don't know much about it. I know **its not overbearing**. It's a college campus, if you want to find drugs you will. But it really is not a huge problem at Providence College."

Q "Marijuana is usually the biggest drug on campus. But I sometimes **I hear of individuals taking Ecstasy and mushrooms**. The drug scene on campus, from what I see, isn't big but it is still evident."

Q "From what I know, I do not think the drug scene is too bad at PC compared to other colleges across the country. However, **there is heavy drinking all over campus**, and it is pretty much accepted as the norm."

Q "**I know a lot of people smoke weed**, and I have heard that the school has an underground cocaine scene, but as for seeing it and being associated with it, I cannot comment because I do know about it."

The Lowdown
ON DRUG SCENE

Most Prevalent Drugs on Campus:
Alcohol, marijuana

Liquor-Related Referrals:
181

Liquor-Related Arrests:
0

Drug-Related Referrals:
27

Drug-Related Arrests:
0

Drug Counseling Programs
The Personal Counseling Center
Phone: (401) 865-2343
Services: Early identification, assessment, and intervention, substance abuse counseling

Student Health Services
Phone: (401) 865-2422
Services: Works in cooperation with the Personal Counseling Center in assessing problems

The College Prowler Take
ON CAMPUS STRICTNESS

By far, the most widely-used drug at PC is alcohol. Binge drinking is a normal occurrence and one which every student cannot help but observe. The real drug scene is much more inconspicuous. While marijuana is the drug of choice, there are whispers about ecstasy, mushrooms, and a small coke scene. Drugs can be acquired at PC, like most colleges, but the scene is not so prevalent that it cannot be avoided. The low-key use of drugs makes PC a comfortable atmosphere for the students who don't use, while users should be satisfied. The drug scene could be far worse than it is, but drinking, not drugs, is really what PC is about.

Campus Strictness

The Lowdown
ON CAMPUS STRICTNESS

What Are You Most Likely to Get Caught Doing on Campus?
Drinking underage, breaking parietals, stealing mugs from Ray, making too much noise, parking illegally, fire code violations, opening fire doors, setting off fire alarms, propping doors, throwing things from the windows

The College Prowler™ Grade on
Drug Scene: B+

A high grade on Drug Scene indicates that drugs are not a noticeable part of campus life; drug use is not visible, and no pressure to use them seems to exist.

Students Speak Out
CAMPUS STRICTNESS

"They aren't going to look for it, but they also don't want to see it. Basically, if you're discreet, you can get away with drinking."

Q "It's your resident assistant's job to monitor the alcohol and drug use on campus. It does happen, and more often than not, **you'll get along with just a strict warning**. But, if it becomes a problem, chances are you will get written up. It's a hefty fine and probation."

Q "**The campus is strict on drugs and not so strict on drinking**. It is a wet campus and as long as you aren't causing problems it really is not overly strict on alcohol."

Q "My problem with campus police is that **they are not strict at all** when it comes to drugs or drinking. PC is far from being a dry campus, not because of the many bars surrounding, it but because campus police don't do a good job preventing it."

Q "The **drinking policy and drug policy are pretty strict** according to the written rules. As long as its use isn't seen and people aren't causing a problem, then it's usually not as strict as the rules suggest."

Q "I would say **fairly strict**; I mean if you are being blatantly obvious about something, they will punish you."

The College Prowler Take
ON CAMPUS STRICTNESS

Policies are in place to punish miscreants for everything from parking to drug use, however, enforcement of these policies varies. Campus security will hand out parking tickets without hesitation, but they very rarely conduct searches for suspected drug use. Usually, a warning is given before any penalties are assigned for offenses. If you are written up for an infraction, the fines are steep. A first time alcohol infraction is $100 and a meeting with your hall director. A transport to the hospital for an alcohol-related occurrence can be $1,000. **The best way to avoid fines and write ups is to not break the rules, but, if you are breaking the rules, avoid being blatant. Most agree that drinking is generally overlooked unless it is disturbing others.**

The College Prowler™ Grade on
Campus Strictness: B

A high Campus Strictness grade implies an overall lenient atmosphere; police and RAs are fairly tolerant, and the administration's rules are flexible.

Overall Experience

Students Speak Out
ON OVERALL EXPERIENCE

"I could not imagine myself anywhere but here. Socially, intellectually, and emotionally, I have grown so much in the past three years. I've met my absolute best friends in the entire world, without a doubt."

Q "I am in love with Providence College. I transferred after my first semester of freshman year at Virginia Tech. **PC offers so much in its well-rounded academics education** and its opportunities to meet other amazing students that attend PC. Under no circumstance do I wish I was somewhere else. I am sad to say I only have two years left, and I hope these years go by as slow as possible because the last year and a half have been the best time of my life."

Q "School is pretty good. The academic schedule at PC is very challenging, with **teachers who really push their students to the limit**, which is important for intellectual growth. Also, I have made long-lasting relationships with people on campus, so I really couldn't see myself anywhere else. Although I had the opportunity to go to tons of other schools with better varsity teams, Greek life, campuses, and maybe even better-looking girls, I think I made the right choice with Providence College."

Q "I've really enjoyed my time at PC. **There is a good party scene and a lot of young people who want to have fun**. However, it is also a good environment to get a solid, all-around education. There are also a lot of opportunities to get involved in the Providence College community. It all depends on how much you are willing to put into your experience. I feel I have been very active in my three years here, and because of that, I have thoroughly enjoyed my time at PC."

Q "**I never once for one second felt that I made a wrong decision choosing Providence**. There were hard moments at the beginning of freshman year—everyone has a breakdown now and then—but overall, I made the best friends I always heard that I would make in college. I want my future kids to go to PC!"

The College Prowler Take
ON OVERALL EXPERIENCE

Looking back on their time at PC leaves students glowing with fond memories. Most appreciate the stimulating academics and whirlwind social scene that PC offers. While the occasional bout of homesickness is unavoidable, no one remarked that they were unsatisfied with their experience at PC. The worst response is a feeling of mere adequacy, that they received all they would have received at another school. The overwhelming majority look on their time spent at PC as a phenomenal learning experience that has assisted in developing them into the intellectually, emotionally, and socially well-rounded people that they are today.

The brilliance of the education at PC is that it extends outside of the classroom as well. Your experience of PC can be anything that you want to make it. If you want to focus on academics, you can, and you will find a group of people who feel exactly the same way you do. If you want an education in socializing, or just want your college years to be the wild and crazy ones you've heard they can be, PC has that, too. Most students come to PC ready to work and ready to have fun; as long as you are open-minded, PC will give you everything you desire.

The Inside Scoop

The Lowdown
ON THE INSIDE SCOOP

PC Slang:
Know the slang, know the school. The following is a list of things you really need to know before coming to PC. The more of these words you know, the better off you'll be.

Angel: Internal Internet site used by teachers to post grades and assignments
Aquinas Chapel: No longer utilized chapel that is becoming a favorite place to study
BOP: Board of Programmers, who organize most of the on-campus events
Bursar: Where you go to get new ID cards
Fishbowl: The all-glass room in Slavin Center
The Fountain: Fountain/pond located on lower campus, hidden and discreet, there are rumors of "Boptisms" occurring here
Friars: Members of a club on campus that give tours, noted for their white blazers
Hollywood: Coolest security guard on campus
The Lion's Den: McDermott Residence Hall
The New Quad: Recently created on lower campus, the new quad in front of the Smith Fine Arts Center is going to be the place to be this year.
Ray: Raymond Hall cafeteria
The Scowl: The yearly April Fool's newspaper put out by the school newspaper, *The Cowl*
Slay: Slavin Center containing the student center, McPhails, and Alumni Food Court
The Tunnels: Intricate set of underground tunnels connecting buildings on lower campus
UA: Urban Action (service organization)

PC Urban Legends
The Dore basement is haunted.

Aquinas' fourth floor is haunted by the girls who died in the fire (no really, it is).

McDermott Hall is ranked as one of the most promiscuous dorms in the country.

School Spirit
Providence students are full of pep and vigor particularly when it comes to their school. There are blackout games where fans wear all black, and when it comes to men's basketball, anything goes. The new logo is definitely an improvement, and everyone owns a closet full of PC apparel. PCers are definitely united around their sports teams, although they show this school spirit when discussing the school itself. Although some are not as enthusiastic as others, the majority of students love PC and share that love with everyone.

Traditions
The Clam Jam
The Clam Jam is an annual event coordinated by BOP. Held on Hendickson field, there is food, games, and music. It is key to stop by the Clam Jam even if it is just en route to going out. There are alcoholic beverages for those with proper ID, but many get around that by pre-gaming before they go. It's a great way to start off the year, kick off the weekend, and spend a fun night on campus.

Mr. PC
Mr. PC isn't just like any other beauty pageant. It gives the women of PC, who do outnumber the men, a chance to ogle some of PC's finest male specimens. Each year, one male will be crowned Mr. PC after displaying casual style, a talent, formal wear, and answering a question put to them by the judges. Last year, Mr. PC was graciously hosted by Dennis Haskins, better known as Mr. Belding from "Saved by the Bell." Mr. PC always promises a few laughs, even if they aren't accompanied by a "Hey hey hey, what's going on here?" from television's favorite principal.

Midnight Madness
Midnight Madness marks the official start to the basketball season, which at PC is a big deal. The night is spent in the Mullaney gym awaiting the strike of 12, when the basketball team can officially begin practice sessions. Midnight Madness usually sports a variety of entertainment acts including games, music, free T-shirts, and the pep band. The cheerleaders and dance team both do a routine, although the latter is always better than the former. Since PC is so big on sports and school spirit, this is a must-attend event.

Finding a Job or Internship

Things I Wish I Knew Before Coming to PC:
- Get your housing form in ASAP.
- Do Urban Action your freshman year.
- It's cool to wear a white blazer and give tours.
- Don't buy bedding from the school catalog.
- It's a huge party school!
- Civ. sucks.
- Everyone runs for congress.
- The Newport trip really is important.

Tips to Succeed at PC:
- Schedule classes at times you'll actually go.
- Get all your work done in the afternoon, then nap so you can go out at night.
- Check your e-mail all the time.
- Get AIM + or Dead AIM.
- Don't be afraid to explore different subjects; you have to fulfill core anyway.
- Ask friends about professors before scheduling classes.
- Always have a back-up for your schedule choices.
- Smile and say hi—don't worry, we'll all wave back.

The Lowdown
ON FINDING A JOB OR INTERNSHIP

If finding a job after you graduate is a high priority concern, as it is for many PC students, assistance is available through a number of services from the Career Services Center. Taking advantage of PC's friendly social environment is always a great idea.

Advice
Career Services can assist anyone who is looking for career guidance. Utilizing their services is just as important freshman and sophomore year as it is junior and senior year. Conference notifications and career opportunities are often sent directly to your mailbox.

Career Center Resources & Services
Shadowing program, interviewing, resumes and correspondence, on-campus recruitment, internships, networking, career research, exploring majors, graduate school advising, career workshops, and employment fairs

The Best & Worst

The Ten BEST Things About PC:

1. Being in a city
2. Fabulous restaurants
3. Bars/ticket parties
4. Civ. Scream
5. Rejects on the rise
6. Movies on Slavin Lawn
7. Raymond Hall staff
8. Blackfriars theater
9. The renovated library
10. Cyberfriar registration

The Ten WORST Things About PC:

1. Lack of diversity
2. No parking
3. Ray food
4. Wind tunnels
5. Nautilus weight room
6. Civ.
7. Parietals
8. Male/female ratio (for females!)
9. Frumpy cheerleaders
10. Silver spoon students (snobby rich kids)

Rhode Island School of Design

2 College Street, Providence, RI 02903
www.risd.edu   (800) 364-7473

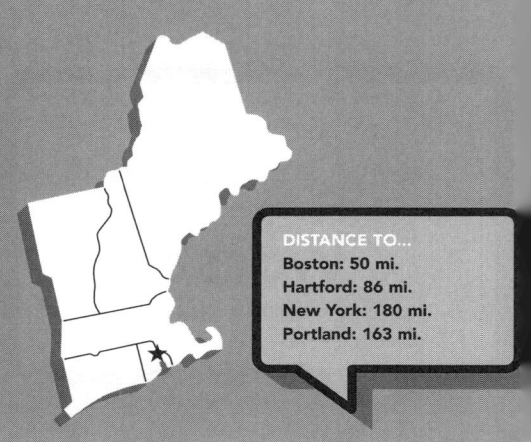

DISTANCE TO...
Boston: 50 mi.
Hartford: 86 mi.
New York: 180 mi.
Portland: 163 mi.

"Rhode Island School of Design is like the Harvard of art schools."

Table of Contents

Academics	885
Local Atmosphere	886
Safety & Security	888
Computers	889
Facilities	891
Campus Dining	892
Off-Campus Dining	894
Campus Housing	895
Off-Campus Housing	897
Diversity	898
Guys & Girls	899
Athletics	900
Greek Life	902
Drug Scene	903
Campus Strictness	904
Overall Experience	905
The Inside Scoop	906
Finding a Job or Internship	907
The Best & Worst	908

Total Enrollment:
1,920

Acceptance Rate:
35%

Tuition:
$27,975

Top 10% of High School Class:
34%

SAT Range
Verbal	Math	Total
540 – 650	550 – 660	1090 – 1310

Supplemental Forms
A portfolio of work is mandatory, along with three original drawings that satisfy certain specifications.

Most Popular Majors:
55% Fine and Studio Art
13% Commercial and Advertising Art
12% Architecture

Students Also Applied To:*
Cooper Union, Maryland Institute College of Art, Pratt Institute, Parsons School of Design, New School University, School of the Visual Arts
*For more school info check out www.collegeprowler.com

College Prowler Report Card

Academics	B
Local Atmosphere	B+
Safety & Security	B+
Computers	B
Facilities	B-
Campus Dining	B-
Off-Campus Dining	A-
Campus Housing	C-
Off-Campus Housing	B+
Diversity	C
Guys	C+
Girls	B
Athletics	D
Greek Life	D
Drug Scene	C+
Campus Strictness	A-

Academics

Best Places to Study
Library, local coffeehouses

Sample Academic Clubs
Mixed Media, the school newspaper and *Blackletter* literary magazine

Students Speak Out
ON ACADEMICS

The Lowdown
ON ACADEMICS

"My profs have been so helpful and professional. They really care about us as students."

Q "Some studio classes are interesting, but **most liberal arts classes are jokes**."

Q "Both **teachers and classes vary drastically**. They're both really wonderful and awe-inspiring, or they're terrible!"

Q "It's hard to generalize about such a diverse faculty and course offerings. I will say that I have had at least one really amazing teacher every semester as well as at least one interesting class. Overall I think that **the classes get more interesting as you go along** and can specialize more and have more freedom in choosing your own classes."

Q "Almost the only teachers that I have had that I would consider bad were in Foundation Year. Everything is less specialized and it doesn't seem they're quite as into the class. But, then again, **it really depends on what teachers you happen to get**."

Degrees Awarded:
BFA, MFA

Undergraduate Schools:
School of Design, School of Fine Art

Full-time Faculty:
176

Faculty with Terminal Degree:
79%

Student-to-Faculty Ratio:
11:1

Average Course Load:
12-15 credits (3 studios, 1 or 2 liberal arts)

Special Degree Options:
5-Year BARCH, BIA, BID, BGD, 3-Year MID, MIA, MARCH, MA, MAT, MLA

AP Test Score Requirements:
Possible credit for scores of 4 or 5

IB Test Score Requirements:
Possible credit for scores of 5, 6, and 7

For in-depth information about professors and classes, check out the College Prowler guide to RISD at *www.collegeprowler.com*.

The College Prowler Take
ON ACADEMICS

Academics at RISD are based on a number of variables, two of which being what major you choose, and whether you decide to "concentrate" in a liberal arts field. The differences in majors have to do with departmental budgets and resources, individual faculty members, and overall departmental philosophy. Each major has a different number of required major credits, with some allowing students to take more classes outside their major, and others almost taking up a student's entire studio course load. Regardless of major, studio classes are almost always challenging and enriching, and demand all of a student's resources to complete them successfully.

The faculty are the driving force behind RISD's strenuous and exiting classes. It is safe to say that while there might be the odd professor that does not meet the high standard students expect from their faculty, professors at RISD are professional, knowledgeable, and dedicated to their students and their field. When it comes to Liberal Arts, students may "concentrate," which is similar to having a minor, in English, Art History, or HPSS (History, Philosophy, Social Science). While it's true that some Liberal Arts courses may not be as rigorous, nearly all seminar courses, among others, are just as challenging as an equivalent class at almost any liberal arts university.

The College Prowler™ Grade on
Academics: B

A high Academics grade generally indicates that Professors are knowledgeable, accessible, and genuinely interested in their students' welfare. Other determining factors include class size, how well professors communicate, and whether or not classes are engaging.

Local Atmosphere

The Lowdown
ON LOCAL ATMOSPHERE

Region:
Northeast

City, State:
Providence, Rhode Island

Setting:
Urban

Distance from NY:
3 hours

Distance from Boston:
1 hour

Points of Interest:
Narragansett Bay, Local Galleries, Russian Submarine Museum, Waterplace Park/River Walk, Fleet Skating Center, RISD Museum, The Culinary History Museum, Slater Mill Museum, The John Brown House, Providence Repertory Company

Closest Movie Theatre:
National Amusements Providence Place 16
Providence Place Mall
5 Providence Place
(401) 270-4646

Major Sports Teams:
Boston Red Sox (baseball),
New England Patriots (football)

Five Fun Facts about Providence:

1. Most streets aren't labeled, which makes for crazy adventures.
2. Providence began as a haven for Puritans.
3. Due to a clerical error in the late 1800s, for a time, "Providence" was the official Rhode Island state bird.
4. Former Mayor, "Buddy" Cianci, has received the most votes for public office while serving probation or jail time since Eugene Debbs in WWI.
5. Providence was the birthplace of pulp horror novelist H.P. Lovecraft, and served as a temporary home to Edgar Allen Poe.

Students Speak Out
ON LOCAL ATMOSPHERE

"**Providence is a paper city—it's really weird. Go to '80s Night 'til it's boring, and go to shows in whatever warehouses are left.**"

Q "The atmosphere is ok, I guess. I don't really think there is one distinct atmosphere for the entire city. **There are bad areas**; ones to stay away from, but nothing close enough for a RISD student to really wander into."

Q "Providence is nice for being at college. **There's some stuff to do**, but not too much to get distracted. I thought I'd have more time to go to NY and Boston, though."

Q "**Providence is a weird, big college/colonial town**. Stay away from the downtown transit area. Visit Wickenden St., Thayer St., Brown University, and Downtown. Visit the old buildings and the capitol building."

Q "The East Side and College Hill are rather student friendly. It's not a large city, it's pretty small actually, but **it has the same kinds of benefits that a larger city has**. I wouldn't venture out into the South End of Providence alone at night."

The College Prowler Take
ON LOCAL ATMOSPHERE

Providence, Rhode Island is absolutely New England. It is the largest city in New England outside Boston and behaves accordingly. While Boston is culturally a big leap from Providence, there are things about the city that make it wonderful. Once such thing is the once-a-month celebration of Waterfire. This is a celebration of the art of Providence, which includes lighted piles of wood all along the canal and ambient music that fills the streets until midnight. While there is a definite city feel, Providence is not devoid of green space, and there are several parks within walking distance that give really pleasant views of the city and its waterfront.

The main activity in Providence is built on the colleges of RISD, Brown, and Johnson and Wales, so the town caters much of its business and attitude toward college students. The surrounding college neighborhoods are fairly quiet and pleasantly residential. If you're looking for a taste of the bigger city, New York is fairly close by, and a Commuter Rail train will take you to Boston during the week for six dollars. Providence does not have the same excitement and culture of New York, and it doesn't have the natural beauty of the American West, but rather sits in a perfect middle ground and will give you a little taste of both.

The College Prowler™ Grade on

Local Atmosphere: B+

A high Local Atmosphere grade indicates that the area surrounding campus is safe and scenic. Other factors include nearby attractions, proximity to other schools, and the town's attitude toward students.

Safety & Security

Students Speak Out
ON SAFETY & SECURITY

> "It seems like Brown kids get mugged more than us, but supposedly it happens to us, too."

> "We're in a city. We try to stay safe, and our **Public Safety officers do the best they can.** The only thing that has been not so effective is our SAFERIDE."

> "**Public Safety are constantly power tripping** and harassing kids, you will without a doubt have a run-in with a Public Safety officer."

> "**It's safe.** Providence is a city; muggings are a reality, but happen infrequently."

> "I think campus feels pretty safe, most of the time, but **I get a little skittish walking around at three in the morning.** I wouldn't walk around on parts other than Thayer St. and Wickenden St. by myself after dark. Definitely travel in groups after dark when off campus."

> "**Security is pretty good.** They're pretty strict about getting doors locked and who has access to rooms."

The Lowdown
ON SAFETY & SECURITY

Number of RISD Police:
42

Phone:
(401) 454-6376

Safety Services:
Campus foot patrol, emergency call-boxes, SafeWalk, SafeRide, key card access to certain buildings, strict building hours, self-defense classes

Health Services:
On-duty nurse and physician on call, some testing can be done by the physician during certain hours of the day. Basic psychological and counseling services.

Health Center Office Hours:
Monday – Friday 8:30 a.m. – 8:30 p.m.
Saturday 9 a.m. – 5 p.m.
Sundays and Holidays Noon – 7:30 p.m.

COLLEGE PROWLER™

Want to know more about safety and security at RISD? For a detailed listing of all safety and security procedures on campus, check out the College Prowler book on RISD available at *www.collegeprowler.com*.

The College Prowler Take
ON SAFETY & SECURITY

Even though Providence is a city, most students feel safe while they're on campus and the close surrounding areas. It goes without saying that it's not a good idea to go walking alone at night or to wander off into the farther parts of town alone. The blue emergency phones, Public Safety patrol, strict building access, and SafeRide system keep the feeling of on-campus safety high. RISD's SafeRide van system is in a partnership with Brown SafeRide. It provides shuttle service to RISD students from the hours of five in the evening to three in the morning and will take students from a residence to campus, or campus to residence. Students who live on-campus may catch the shuttle during its regular stops along a fixed route. Students living off campus may call for a specific pickup and will be reached within 15 minutes. While it is still in the process of being improved and refined, SafeRide is not completely satisfactory. There is a route that the shuttle adheres to which circumnavigates the area in which most students live. However, there are students who live outside of this area who have been left out of the SafeRide loop.

The College Prowler™ Grade on
Safety & Security: B+

A high grade in Safety & Security means that students generally feel safe, campus police are visible, blue-light phones and escort services are readily available, and safety precautions are not overly necessary.

Computers

The Lowdown
ON COMPUTERS

High-Speed Network?
Yes

Wireless Network?
Yes

Number of Labs:
Approx. 18

Numbers of Computers:
520

24-Hour Labs:
None

Charge to Print?
An 8.5"x 11" page costs 10 cents for black and white, $1.00 for color. These charges are made to pre-paid print cards, but they do not apply the same to Graphic Design students who print a mile a minute.

Students Speak Out
ON COMPUTERS

> "Bring your own computer if you can. The network is constantly down for long periods of time."

Q "The computer network is ok. **It depends on what you need it for**. Most of the computer-heavy departments have their own labs or require students to purchase their own laptops, so crowding in communal labs isn't a problem. Sometimes the lab hours aren't the best, or monitors fail to show up, but I wouldn't go so far as to recommend bringing a computer in order to avoid the labs."

Q "Bring your own computer and a printer to avoid hassle. If you're in a certain major, **they'll make you buy a laptop**."

Q "The network is good for e-mail, but it's difficult for online recourses (online storage is not always available). We need a Mac-based network so we wouldn't suffer from IBM viruses. **The labs are usually busy**. I use RISD-ROMEABOUT often."

Q "The computers situation is terrible! **The only help you can get is from other students**. Don't buy a computer if you're going into a major with the laptop program."

The College Prowler Take
ON COMPUTERS

It may sound surprising for an art school, but computers are actually a big part of most major curriculums at RISD. Many majors use CAD (Computer Assisted Design) programs in their curricula in order to prepare students for competitive job markets, as well as the different ways that they may approach their art on a personal level. If you already have your own computer and printer, they are extremely handy to have at school. However, there is a chance that you will enter a major that will require you to purchase a very expensive laptop package through the school, so it is a really bad idea to buy a computer before you come.

Aside from the more major-specific labs that have certain CAD programs on them, there are general labs that students may use to type and print papers and use the internet. These labs are equipped with several computer stations, usually two flatbed scanners and a negative scanner, and two laserjet printers, one color, one black and white. Students who sign in and are recognized by the network can print from any computer station and get their work within a matter of seconds. Overall, the network is fairly reliable, although it does go down from time to time. The computers in the labs are replaced every few years, and you will always have the newest versions of programs with fairly new computers. The lab resources are sufficient, and labs are rarely overcrowded.

The College Prowler™ Grade on
Computers: B

A high grade in Computers designates that computer labs are available, the computer network is easily accessible, and the campus' computing technology is up-to-date.

Facilities

Favorite Things to Do
Walk around, see independent films, shop, go to coffeehouses, hang out in a laid-back bar

Popular Places to Chill
The Beach, in front of Mem Hall, dorm lounges, The quad, The Met (main dining facility), in studio

Students Speak Out
ON FACILITIES

The Lowdown
ON FACILITIES

Movie Theatre on Campus?
No, but there are sometimes movie showings in the Auditorium and Tap Room.

Bowling on Campus?
No

Bar on Campus?
No

Coffeehouse on Campus?
Carr Haus, on the corner of Waterman St. and Benefit St., is a coffeehouse and café open only on the weekdays. Watermark Café, on the 2nd floor of the RISD Store in the Design Center at 30 North Main St., is open on the weekdays.

Student Center:
The Chace Center

Athletic Center:
Catanzaro Fitness Center
(RISD students may use all Brown athletic facilities.)

Libraries:
RISD Library, Nature Lab, Picture Collection
(RISD students may enter and sometimes check out material from all Brown libraries. RISD students may also use the Providence Athenaeum.)

"The studios are cool. The new computers are great, and the old ones are just ok. We need all Mac screens, but other than that, all of the peripheral supplies are awesome."

"The computers are fine; the gym is ok. Studios are fine, but be careful! They will say you can use any facilities, and it's a lie! **You need to know someone in that department**."

"Some departments are a lot nicer and newer than others as far as facilities. **The computers are all pretty new and fast**. The gym is mediocre, but we can use the very nice Brown gym instead."

"I honestly wish RISD had its own swimming pool! I wouldn't mind going swimming. I don't think there are enough athletic facilities on campus, but at the same time **it's nice that we get to share facilities with Brown**. Although RISD has a lot of computer labs located around campus, I honestly don't think they're well-maintained. I think RISD's studio facilities are really great, although I've encountered serious space issues in terms of the Textile department during my sophomore and junior years."

"Our athletic facilities are good, but I've heard Brown is nicer. Our color printers often fail, the studios are good, but people do not clean up after themselves. **The dorm studios are messy**, but it's nice that they're there."

"Printmaking studios are **crammed**."

The College Prowler Take
ON FACILITIES

This subject is a touchy one with a lot of people because when it comes to studio space, (the facility that students care most about) it's on a department-by-department basis. On the whole, people's needs are met one way or another. When it comes to athletic facilities, Brown makes up for what RISD lacks. When it comes to computers, the communal labs satisfy anyone who doesn't need extremely specific programs, and then certain majors have their own labs to fulfill those needs (an example of this would be the need for CAD programs in different departments). When it comes to studio space, most everyone has what they need to function.

The equipment that RISD students are privileged to have access to during their college experience is impressive. For example, there are approximately six wood shops on campus which grant access to different groups of students, and the Textiles department has one of two college-owned Jacquard looms in the country. Aside from these kinds of departmental resources, RISD's greatest resource is the museum. Admission is free to all RISD students, and sometimes events are planned specifically for them, such as the yearly showing of graduate student work and the winners of the contest "Sightings."

The College Prowler™ Grade on
Facilities: B-

A high Facilities grade indicates that the campus is aesthetically pleasing and well-maintained; facilities are state-of-the-art, and libraries are exceptional. Other determining factors include the quality of both athletic and student centers and an abundance of things to do on campus.

Campus Dining

The Lowdown
ON CAMPUS DINING

Freshman Meal Plan Requirement?
Yes

Meal Plan Average Cost:
Freshman plan is $3,000/year

24-Hour On-Campus Eating?
None

Student Favorites:
Carr Haus, Watermark Café

Other Options:
Eat off campus

Did You Know?
Carr Haus is student-run and student-employed.

You can bring The Met a recipe from home (within reason) and they'll serve it on the menu.

Students Speak Out
ON CAMPUS DINING

> "The Met is better than other schools, but that's not saying much."

> "The food on campus is improving. **The Met needs to offer more vegan options** and cashiers to avoid long lines."

> "For campus food, it's good. You get sick of it by the second half of freshman year, but it's still pretty good. There are always vegetarian and vegan options and lots of 'do-it-yourself' salad/sandwich stuff. **Carr Haus has good baked goods but vile coffee**. The new RISD Watermark Café is great quality, but pricey."

> "For vegans, it's pretty good, actually, very good. **The Watermark Café is good.**"

> "The food on campus is actually not so bad compared to the campus food at Brown. I personally like hanging out a lot in Carr Haus and The Pit, **they make good food**, and it's a great environment to stay in especially because they're more personal. I like Carr Haus a lot since that's where I go to meet people and friends who are out of my major."

> "The breakfast menu at the cafeteria never changes, and **the eggs aren't real**, but it's very sanitary."

The College Prowler Take
ON CAMPUS DINING

Students will always, always complain about school food. Anyone eating the same things every day for every meal is bound to get sick of them. However, if you ask freshmen in the first month of school, they'll tell you how great the food is. It's diverse, there are always vegetarian and vegan options, it's accessible, it's tasty, and it's healthy. Many of the cooks are Johnson and Wales graduates or interns, so there is a certain culinary flair to most dishes.

Also, to give some perspective, The Met, which is the main dining center, caters most school functions, so the administration must think the food is good. Most of the food in The Met is sold by weight, so you get what you pay for, and you're not charged for a "meal" if you just want to come in and get an apple and a drink. Except for Carr Haus, the food is fairly expensive for kids who are not on the meal plan, but if you are on the meal plan, it will give you enough points to eat comfortably. The Met also takes special care in trying to accommodate the foods that students may miss from home. There is always a suggestion box, so students can make requests or submit their favorite recipes.

The College Prowler™ Grade on
Campus Dining: B-

Our grade on Campus Dining addresses the quality of both school-owned dining halls and independent on-campus restaurants as well as the price, availability, and variety of food.

Off-Campus Dining

Students Speak Out
ON OFF-CAMPUS DINING

{ **"Restaurants off-campus are good, but they're expensive."**

Q "Restaurants off-campus are ok. **Antonio's Pizza is cheap**, by the slice. East Side Pocket has good falafel, too."

Q **"Providence is full of great restaurants** of all types. Antonio's and East Side Pockets are great for less money and dinner at midnight. Then there are too many more expensive excellent places to mention."

Q "There are lot of fantastic restaurants around. Lucky Garden, a Chinese restaurant on Smith Street, has great food and dim sum on weekends. I also like the little Thai restaurant located on Hope Street called Sawadee. **Lemi's Restaurant is my favorite**. It's where Reservoir Avenue is near Cranston. It serves great local Chinese food for cheap! Also King's Garden is a nice dim sum eatery place. I don't recommend going to Dragon Phoenix for dim sum; it's terrible."

Q "Gordito Burrito is **cheap and filling**."

Q "Sun and Moon Korean restaurant is decent. Sakura Japanese restaurant is **good, but it's very expensive**."

The Lowdown
ON OFF-CAMPUS DINING

Best Pizza:
Fellini's

Best Chinese:
Asian Paradise

Best Breakfast:
The Modern Diner, Brickway

Best Wings:
Wings To Go

Best Healthy:
Garden Grille

Best Place to Take Your Parents:
Paragon, The Blue Grotto

Student Favorites:
Sakura, Bombay Club, Spike's

Late-Night, Half-Price Food Specials:
None

24-Hour Eating:
None

Closest Grocery Stores:
Eastside Marketplace
165 Pitman St.
(401) 831-7771

Want to know more about off-campus dining? For a detailed listing of all off-campus favorites, check out the College Prowler book on RISD available at *www.collegeprowler.com*.

The College Prowler Take
ON OFF-CAMPUS DINING

Although most RISD kids stick pretty close to school, there is still a surprising variety of restaurants that are cheap enough for students that can be found on Main Street, Thayer Street, and Wickenden Street. Despite Providence's small size, there are surprising amounts of unique restaurants in the area. For instance, Thayer Street is one long chain of restaurants and shops that spans several blocks in the heart of the Brown/RISD radius. In one block, students will walk past Indian, Mexican, Pizza, Mediterranean, and Middle Eastern food, all of which are small unique restaurants. In fact, other than the occasional McDonald's downtown, you might have to go outside Providence proper to find a chain restaurant.

Because Johnson and Wales has a culinary academy, there is a wealth of interest and innovation in the immediate area that is constantly replenished, and there are always new and interesting places popping up. There is also a large Asian population, which feeds some of the best Asian and Indian restaurants in the area.

Campus Housing

The Lowdown
ON CAMPUS HOUSING

Room Types:
Single, double, triple, suite, apartment single, apartment double, apartment triple, studio, large studio

Best Dorms:
Colonial Apartments

Worst Dorms:
Farnum Hall

Undergrads on Campus:
34%

Number of Dormitories:
12

Number of University-Owned Apartments:
2

Bed Type:
Twin extra long, can be lofted upon request.

Also Available:
All housing is smoke free.

The College Prowler™ Grade on
Off-Campus Dining: A-

A high off-campus dining grade implies that off-campus restaurants are affordable, accessible, and worth visiting. Other factors include the variety of cuisine and the availability of alternative options (vegetarian, vegan, Kosher, etc.).

Available for Rent
Microwaves, mini-fridges

Cleaning Service?
Every day in Outer Houses and dorms. No service in Colonial Apartments and Dwight.

You Get
Bed, bureau, closet, night table, desk and chair, Internet access, lounge with cable TV, curtains, wastebasket, local telephone service

Students Speak Out
ON CAMPUS HOUSING

 "The dorms are ok, but you run into Public Safety way too much."

Q "East Hall is nice, South is quiet, **Homer is smelly**, and Nickerson has bedbugs."

Q "The dorms, freshmen especially, are uniformly awful. **Fake a medical condition to get a single** … that's about all you can do to make it any better."

Q "Our lottery system is **inept**."

Q "The freshman dorms are really fun, and the rooms are a fine size. There's enough space. **If you're a party kid go for Homer 5**, for upperclassmen, avoid Farnum."

Q "**One thing I hated about freshmen dorms are the mice running around**. They ate my Ramen noodles once and spat the Styrofoam pieces out and left their feces all over the place. I hated those nasty mice."

The College Prowler Take
ON CAMPUS HOUSING

It's true; you can't avoid dorm life if you come to RISD as a freshman. However, there are some definite pluses to living in the quad. You are right by food and studios, and there are always people around and awake to hang out with. Some of the dorms are suites, so you're not sharing a bathroom with an entire floor, and all the rooms are big enough to be comfortable. If you're not so lucky as to get a suite, the communal bathroom is only for a year. Once you're out of the freshman dorms, life gets better. Almost all of the dorms on campus are full of character and have a nice atmosphere and space to them. They are fairly small, so you get to know your house, and remain plugged into what's going on around campus without being smothered by it. If you stick it out a year or so in outer housing, then you will build up enough points to get yourself into Colonial Apartments, which is basically just as good as living off-campus, only slightly less homey.

RISD is currently in the process of answering the shortage of student housing. A new housing facility at 15 Westminster Street is in the process of opening and will be available to students for the 2005/2006 school year. This housing will not be open to freshmen, and now that there is enough space, RISD will be requiring that all sophomores live in school housing.

The College Prowler™ Grade on
Campus Housing: C-

A high Campus Housing grade indicates that dorms are clean, well-maintained, and spacious. Other determining factors include variety of dorms, proximity to classes, and social atmosphere.

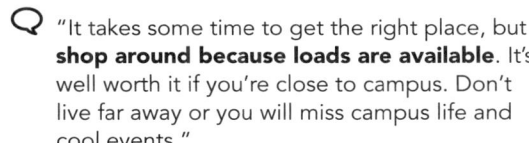

Off-Campus Housing

Q "It takes some time to get the right place, but **shop around because loads are available**. It's well worth it if you're close to campus. Don't live far away or you will miss campus life and cool events."

Q "Living off campus is more of a hassle. **They're building more housing for students** and if you can get in, then go for it. It's very close."

Q "A lot depends on your landlord and how close you are to school. It's important to **start looking early**, and try to rent from someone who you think takes care of their property."

The Lowdown
ON OFF-CAMPUS HOUSING

The College Prowler Take
ON OFF-CAMPUS HOUSING

Undergrads in Off-Campus Housing:
66%

Best Time to Look for a Place:
End of fall semester, Wintersession

Average Rent for a Studio Apartment:
$550/month

Average Rent for a One-Bedroom Apartment:
$700/month

Average Rent for a Two-Bedroom Apartment:
$1200/month

Most students who live off-campus swear that it's the only way to be, and those who are on campus note the convenience and proximity to school. When making the housing decision, it's important to remember that one can enter the housing lottery, withdraw, and only loose a small deposit.

Contrary to popular belief, it is generally cheaper to live off campus than in school housing. However, off-campus living costs can skyrocket if utilities are not included in the rent. Many students end up paying hefty heat bills in the winter, so it is important to talk to the previous tenants to get an idea of how the apartment is kept by the landlord and what kind of bills to expect. The downside is that the closer you want to be to campus, the more you'll have to pay.

Students Speak Out
ON OFF-CAMPUS HOUSING

"More campus housing is being built to accommodate students. Landlords are crooks in Providence; watch out!"

The College Prowler™ Grade on
Off-Campus Housing: B+

A high grade in Off-Campus Housing indicates that apartments are of high quality, close to campus, affordable, and easy to secure.

Diversity

> "The campus is somewhat diverse. It's hard because there's so little financial aid available for international students. **It's hard for any student that's not upper-class.**"

> "**RISD is very diverse**, provided you consider white and Asian diverse."

> "I think **there might be four black people**, maybe five."

> "Gender-wise, the female-to-male ratio is not as female dominated as I would have thought. Ethnically, **there is diversity among international students** although more than half seems to be Korean."

The Lowdown
ON DIVERSITY

African American: 2%
Asian American: 13%
Hispanic: 5%
Native American: 0%
White: 68%
International: 11%
Out-of-State: 90%

Political Activity
Most kids are pretty liberal.

Gay Tolerance
Extremely tolerant

Most Popular Religions
Christianity, Catholicism and Judaism

Economic Status
Middle- to upper-class

The College Prowler Take
ON DIVERSITY

Diversity at RISD is a tricky issue. It does not just call for non-white non-Americans, but a mixing of students from different backgrounds, socio-economic status, culture, and race. On the positive side, the diversity that does exist at RISD is made the most of, and most students benefit from learning about each other and how people from different cultures and artistic backgrounds approach art and design problems. Everyone gives their input based on their personal backgrounds, aesthetics, and beliefs.

By having a diverse range of students in these intimate situations, there is a great deal of aesthetic exchange, and many students are able to expand their understanding of what their art can be. Especially relevant conversations center on gender politics in art, cultural identity, and product design for a world market.

The College Prowler™ Grade on
Diversity: C

A high grade in Diversity indicates that ethnic minorities and international students have a notable presence on campus and that students of different economic backgrounds, religious beliefs, and sexual preferences are well-represented.

Students Speak Out
ON DIVERSITY

{ "There are minimal black kids but plenty of Asians at RISD."

Guys & Girls

The Lowdown
ON GUYS & GIRLS

Women Undergrads:
64.5%

Men Undergrads:
35.5%

Birth Control Available?
Yes, Free condoms are provided by Health Services and Planned Parenthood.

Most Prevalent STDs on Campus
Herpes, Chlamydia

Social Scene
Most students are friendly and fun-loving, but not terribly socially-minded. Everyone loves to cut loose. Some go to parties, some just chill with friends, but work always comes first. When the semester begins to get really stressful, you will notice people walking on opposite sides of the street, recognize each other, and then pretend that they didn't see each other. However, when the stress is off, especially during Wintersession and after graduation, well, that's when RISD kids tend to earn their wild reputations.

Hookups or Relationships?
Most girls date outside the school, and most relationships in general are fairly serious. There are not a lot of random hookups, especially after freshman year.

Best Place to Meet Guys/Girls
The best places to meet people are in bars, on "the Beach," at parties, and in class. Because most studio classes are not simple lectures where everyone is staring front and quiet, people get to know each other quite well. Most relationships at RISD are fairly mature, they may be casual, but there are less instances of randomly "hooking up," probably because it's a small campus and people get to know each other. It's not that it doesn't happen, but there is less a feeling of people being nameless and faceless, and more accountability.

Dress Code
To each his/her own. Some students dress punk, some hippy, some preppy, some expensively, some scary, most vintage-chic, all very unique.

Students Speak Out
ON GUYS & GIRLS

> "I'd be better off if I were a lesbian."

Q "The guys and girls are hot, fun, and smart. **There are too many gay guys**, bummer, but they make great friends. There are plenty of good girlfriends."

Q "Guys? **RISD is predominantly female**, completely so in some majors. I'm sure there are some hot guys out there. There are definitely lots of very attractive, stylish girls."

Q "RISD is **the sexiest place I've ever been**. Everyone is beautiful! It's shocking!"

The College Prowler Take
ON GUYS & GIRLS

It may sound like a lot of places, but it certainly doesn't sound like college—tons of young, beautiful women, surrounded by a small showing of fairly attractive, mostly gay men. That's art school. However, gay or straight, the RISD men are mostly kind, talented, and funny people, who, regardless of their other intentions, will gallantly offer to walk a girl home at night, no strings attached. Both the gay and straight dating scenes are vibrant and energetic, and there are plenty of clubs, bars, and coffeehouses for both. The women at RISD are smart, beautiful, and talented, and dating at RISD is often more inhibited by students' tight work schedules than by the students themselves.

At RISD, personality gets you the farthest. While there are some very beautiful women and some hot guys around, it's really all about the attitude. If you are unique and comfortable with yourself, you will become one of the sexiest students on campus. If you are looking for casual hookups, you can find them, but you may be better off going to Brown parties or to bars where Johnson and Wales kids hang out, because the intensity that comes with being at RISD and surrounding yourself with art, usually transfers to intensity in relationships as well.

The College Prowler™ Grade on
Guys: C+

A high grade for Guys indicates that the male population on campus is attractive, smart, friendly, and engaging, and that the school has a decent ratio of guys to girls.

The College Prowler™ Grade on
Girls: B

A high grade for Girls not only implies that the women on campus are attractive, smart, friendly, and engaging, but also that there is a fair ratio of girls to guys.

Athletics

The Lowdown
ON ATHLETICS

Men's Varsity Teams:
The Nads (ice hockey), The Balls (basketball)

Women's Teams:
The Jugs (soccer)

Club Sports: Soccer, Hockey, Basketball, Sailing, Bicycling, Rock Climbing

Getting Tickets
Most games are free and require no tickets. Every once in a while you might have to pay a dollar or two, but most times they give away prizes because they're grateful that someone actually showed up.

Athletic Division:
Small Art School (Cooper Union is our biggest rival)

Most Popular Sports:
Sprinting to class

Overlooked Teams:
Architecture's mental gymnastics

School Mascot:
Scrotie (7 ft. tall penis with balls and cape; the Nad's Mascot.)

Students Speak Out
ON ATHLETICS

The College Prowler Take
ON ATHLETICS

"Athletics aren't big, but they're fun. Go Nads!"

Q "Sports are not big at all. It's gotten better from the past. **The biggest thing is probably ice hockey**, The Nads, and maybe The Balls. Students are so busy getting their studio work done, I don't think they have time to do extra-curricular stuff. I tried fencing and Tai Chi on campus, and I had a lot of fun."

Q "**Athletics aren't very big here,** unless you count getting drunk to cheer on a giant foam rubber penis a sport."

Q "Sports are non-existent. **Some of them are fun clubs**. They're more like fun and loose get-togethers."

Q "Sports at RISD aren't big at all. I don't even know if they're fun. But, **they're definitely funny to watch**."

While serious athletics is pretty much out of the question at RISD, students definitely have fun with what they've got. Imagine, during parents' weekend, half the campus drunk and yelling obscenities at a team of completely bewildered ice hockey players while a giant penis in a cape leads cheers from the sidelines. Often the Jockstraps (cheerleading team) will rouse the RISD crowd into heckling some players so badly that fights ensue. Another rallying move is when Scrotie tries to ram the goalposts tip-first. (Some images really are worth a thousand words).

The Balls are a slightly different experience. There is no obscene mascot and profane cheerleading team, and mostly games appear to be fairly average, however the advertising is uniquely RISD. While walking across campus, you may encounter several posters of our beloved President Roger Mandle, nonchalantly cradling two basketballs to his chest, and solemnly urging the RISD community to "Support Your Balls." RISD sports? Should get an A for Amusement!

The College Prowler™ Grade on
Athletics: D

A high grade in Athletics indicates that students have school spirit, that sports programs are respected, that games are well-attended, and that intramurals are a prominent part of student life.

Greek Life

The Lowdown
ON GREEK LIFE

Number of Fraternities:
0

Number of Sororities:
1 (sort of)

Percent of Undergrad Men in Fraternities:
0

Percent of Undergrad Women in Sororities:
.002 (five or seven people)

Sororities on Campus:
Psi Phi Pi

Students Speak Out
ON GREEK LIFE

{ **"What on earth is a Greek life?"**

Q "Well, **we kind of have a fake Sorority**, Psi Phi Pi. But it's just funny. I don't think anybody around here could take something as stupid as frats too seriously."

Q "Some friends of mine made really terrible spanikopita one time. I'm a big fan of Homer and Sophocles. Actually **I do think I know a Greek kid.** He's named Kevin, he's from New Jersey. What?"

Q "I don't think the RISD community is big enough to actually have a Greek life. Also, I think **sororities and fraternities have a tendency to be exclusive**. I think there are enough drinking parties around campus (just in people's houses) that we don't need a frat. Also, RISD students are so busy with studio, I don't think we have time for that sort of thing. I think it's better if people join student clubs, since I personally find it more purposeful than joining a frat."

Q "**No Greek life**. People who are involved in Greek life are mindless sheep who deserve to be eaten."

The College Prowler Take
ON GREEK LIFE

It's no secret that RISD students revel in their uniqueness and make fun of those who they perceive to be unable to think for themselves. While many fraternities and sororities across the country are clearly not the stereotypes that we all see in movies, to RISD kids, they might as well be. Psi Phi Pi exists because a group of friends thought it would be funny. They host parties, and make parodies of matching outfits, but that's about as far as it goes at RISD. If someone came into RISD and offered to set up the whole Greek system, there might not be enough interested students to fill one house.

The College Prowler™ Grade on
Greek Life: D

A high grade in Greek Life indicates that sororities and fraternities are not only present, but also active on campus. Other determining factors include the variety of houses available and the respect the Greek community receives from the rest of the campus.

Drug Scene

> "**It's not a big thing here.** There is drinking, but not as much as most other colleges. There are drugs, too, but once again, not as much as many other places. I think most RISD people are too dedicated to their work to want to waste lots of time getting really messed up. Caffeine abuse, that's rampant, but everything else is limited."

> "**There's lots of pot** and a decent amount of mushrooms."

The Lowdown
ON DRUG SCENE

Most Prevalent Drugs on Campus:
Alcohol, marijuana

Liquor-Related Referrals:
Under 20 per year

Drug-Related Referrals:
Under 10 per year

Drug Counseling Programs:
Yes

The College Prowler Take
ON DRUG SCENE

The drug scene at RISD is something that exists behind closed doors. It's definitely around, and if you look hard enough, you can find what you want, but most people don't get mixed up in anything worse than pot. If there is some drug use at a party, unless you are participating, you probably won't even know about it because there are too many other students around dancing and talking without being under the influence of anything.

There is a manageable amount of drinking, but for most people, it's not for more than one night a week, if every week. There is also a small section of students who abuse caffeine and prescription drugs in order to stay awake and do work, but mostly that's during finals. The bottom line is that students work too hard to distract themselves with a lot of drugs and drinking. What they do is too important to them to throw away, and those students who have been more into recreational use, find themselves failing because they can't keep up in class.

Students Speak Out
ON DRUG SCENE

> "I have only seen some alcohol on campus during parties; however, no one got very drunk. There was lots of safe use."

> "There are a lot of people taking drugs and also smoking. I don't have contact with people who smoke up, so **I can't explain how serious the drug issue is**. It's quite amazing how some people can handle drugs and still be able to keep up with their school work."

The College Prowler™ Grade on
Drug Scene: C+

A high grade in the Drug Scene indicates that drugs are not a noticeable part of campus life; drug use is not visible, and no pressure to use them seems to exist.

Campus Strictness

> "It's weird, because if you live in an outer house, your house can vote to be a wet or dry house. If the majority votes dry, **you can get busted for having alcohol even if you're of legal age**. If the house is wet, you are not allowed to drink in the presence of anyone under 21. That's really the last nail in the coffin of enjoying a drink on campus."

The College Prowler Take
ON CAMPUS STRICTNESS

The Lowdown
ON CAMPUS STRICTNESS

The campus police are strict about some things and lax about others, and it is especially dependent on which officer you run into. Usually, if a student is caught drinking or doing drugs on campus, they're given one more shot. In severe cases, campus officers have been more concerned about the student's wellbeing than discipline.

What Are You Most Likely to Get Caught Doing on Campus?
Trying to stay in studio after the buildings are closed.

What campus police are extremely strict on is getting everyone out of studio after the buildings close and making sure that the monitored shops are closed at the appropriate times. This is an understandably important task because a sleepy student operating a table saw is clearly not safe, and it is the school's concern to be somewhat responsible for inhibiting tired students when operating dangerous machinery. This policy has been debated feverishly for several years. Students want 24-hour access, but the school wants to save on resources and encourage students to sleep. Until the school caves, campus police will be patrolling, yelling at kids to get out, and locking doors.

Students Speak Out
ON CAMPUS STRICTNESS

> "If they catch you drinking in the dorms, you get 'written up.' It's not a huge deal since most people live off campus, anyway."

> "I don't think it comes up that much. **People caught drinking in the dorms get a slap on the wrist**. Technically, there's no drinking in studio at all. Because most kids live off campus after freshman year outside the range of campus police, and everyone is so into their work, I don't consider it an issue."

> "Drinking is basically tolerated as long as you don't disturb people, but **drugs are less tolerated**. I know two people who were kicked out this year for smoking weed in the dorms."

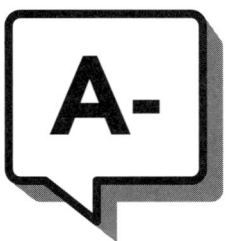

The College Prowler™ Grade on
Campus Strictness: A-

A high Campus Strictness grade implies an overall lenient atmosphere; police and RAs are fairly tolerant, and the administration's rules are flexible.

Overall Experience

Students Speak Out
ON OVERALL EXPERIENCE

> "RISD is a school that is rigorously challenging, both academically and personally."

Q "It's been a good one. **There have been downsides**, things I didn't enjoy, but nothing I think I could have necessarily avoided by going anywhere else (all the dorms I've seen are equally crappy)."

Q "Art school is the biggest joke and the best thing ever. **Don't take it too seriously**."

Q "I love RISD, and I can't imagine being in another school. Everyone is so nice and friendly. You can talk to random people out of your major and feel perfectly comfortable talking to them. **I was amazed at how much talent people have** and how much you can learn from each other. It's very inspiring to be around a group of talented people; you get new ideas from your peers. I have also branched out a lot and have many friends from other departments."

Q "I find it comforting to hang out with people from ID or Illustration or FAV or Architecture because they give you another perspective of how art can be done, and how their departments function. I also gained a great experience with extracurricular activities. **It trained me to think beyond, and outside of, RISD**. Also I learned a lot of leadership skills being involved with various activities."

Q "I think I'm meant to be here. Despite a couple of minor drawbacks, this school has helped me hone my technical knowledge and fine art capabilities. **A number of teachers have been life-alteringly inspirational**. It is an intense place, and I don't recommend attending unless you bring that same level of intensity with you."

The College Prowler Take
ON OVERALL EXPERIENCE

Many students love and hate RISD at the same time. The workload may be extremely demanding, but RISD students are not coming to receive the typical college experience. They are coming to get in touch with a community of artists that will enrich their understanding of art as a medium. Students who come to RISD are coming to gain access to an amazing amount of resources and equipment, which enable them to push their art form as much as possible.

RISD students work very hard and are rewarded in the end. Many feel they are prepared to enter some sort of job, or pursue a way to become active professionals in their field. In many ways, RISD is like boot camp for art, but it's also an amazing opportunity for students to make the work that they want to make and learn about themselves and their surroundings in the process. Once students let go of any ideas of what college is supposed to be, they will realize that what RISD offers is not only a completely unique and exhilarating experience, but a degree that holds a lot of weight in the professional world and skills that will serve the students for their entire lives. If you ask any student at RISD, they will say that as much as they complain, they would never go anywhere else.

The Inside Scoop

The Lowdown
ON THE INSIDE SCOOP

Things I Wish I Knew Before Coming to RISD:
- Only some majors offer the prospect of job stability.
- Sometimes following your gut is more important than listening to professors' specific opinions.
- It's not that easy to find the time to get up to Boston or down to New York.
- Drinking coffee is necessary.
- Some majors are very definitely oriented towards design, while others are oriented towards fine art.
- If you want to work in a medium other than your major, you'll need a friend in that major to help you.
- It is important to be self-directed because advising is lax and you have to look after yourself.

RISD Slang:
Know the slang, know the school. The following is a list of things you really need to know before coming to RISD. The more of these words you know, the better off you'll be.

The Beach: The patch of grass on the corner of Waterman St. and Benefit St.

Emo: Self-pitying and emotional

Pomo: Meaninglessly trendy, post-modernist

RISD Urban Legends
- Dunnel House is haunted.
- If you fall into the canal, it will dissolve your skin.
- Crooked former Mayor, Buddy Cianci, and RISD President, Roger Mandle, are like bread and butter.
- In connection with the mob activity and Cianci, there was a body found downtown without its thumbs.
- There are billboards in Korea advertising RISD.

Tips to Succeed at RISD:
- Be Yourself!
- Learn to love coffee.
- Don't wait for crossing lights, just go.
- Get good walking shoes.
- Confidence is key (a lot of people end up inhibiting themselves when they could be expanding themselves).
- You have to fail along the way, and if you stop failing, you'll never pass through it.

Finding a Job or Internship

The Lowdown
ON FINDING A JOB OR INTERNSHIP

Advice
The most important thing in finding a job or internship is one's portfolio, and the second-most important thing is a student's connections. It's important to keep in touch with your department head and see if she knows of jobs in the field that may be a good fit for you. Document your work as you progress through school so that you have a body of work to edit during your senior year.

Career Center Resources & Services
Alumni and Career Services, your department

Famous RISD Alumni
Dale Chihuly, Scott MacFarlane, David Macaulay, Liz Collins, Mark Pollack, Martin Mull, David Byrne (dropped out), Chris van Allsburg,

The ease of finding a job or internship comes at the mercy of one's major. Those in the design majors have an immediate one-up on the fine arts majors, but don't count the latter out. The main thing working in RISD students' favors is that a degree from RISD carries a lot of weight. Whether you're applying for a corporate job in architecture, or an assistant position to the head potter in a ceramics studio, when most employers hear that you are from RISD, it gets your foot in the door. One of RISD's shining attributes is that it works very hard to prepare its students for careers, and there are a lot of programs in place that give students access to invaluable information, whatever their major.

RISD Alumni and Career Services heads up most of the effort to find students and alumni internships, jobs, and information. They have a constantly updated database that may be searched for jobs or internships, based on your student status, major, and location. You may also make an appointment for more acute counseling. Alumni and Career Services also provides a seminar and workshop series which provides sessions for nearly every students' situation. These lectures are free and include programs such as "Prospering as a Creative Entrepreneur" or "The Art of Business," and include topics such as how to prepare a resume and portfolio, interview tips for design students, how to start one's own fine art studio, and how to start and run one's own gallery or business. The list goes on.

The Best & Worst

The Ten BEST Things About RISD:

1. Training and skill building
2. The art community
3. The professors
4. The Museum
5. Studio facilities
6. Preparation for making a living as an artist
7. Connection with Brown
8. Guest lectures
9. Student shows
10. Student sarcasm and sense of humor

The Ten WORST Things About RISD:

1. Lack of sleep
2. Lack of financial aid
3. No interdepartmental connections
4. The timid social scene
5. Wishy-washiness of some liberal arts classes
6. Lack of preparation for extra-curriculars
7. Restricted resources
8. Not a two-year program like most art schools
9. Not making enough money for hard work
10. Enduring horrible mispronunciations (It's RIZ DEE, not RISS DUH, RYZE DUH or RIZZED!)

Wellesley College

106 Central Street, Wellesley, MA 02481-8203
www.wellesley.edu   (781) 283-2270

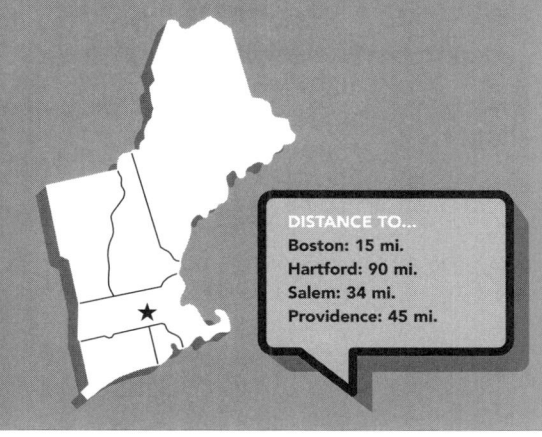

DISTANCE TO...
Boston: 15 mi.
Hartford: 90 mi.
Salem: 34 mi.
Providence: 45 mi.

"A community like Wellesley would be difficult to achieve in a coed environment. Living at Wellesley is like living with 2,300 sisters."

Total Enrollment:
2,219

Acceptance Rate:
41%

Tuition:
$29,796

Top 10% of High School Class:
75%

SAT Range
Verbal	Math	Total
639 – 730	630 – 720	1260 – 1450

ACT Range
Verbal	Math	Total
N/A	N/A	27-31

SAT II Requirements
3 SAT IIs required from applicants submitting SAT I scores, one must be SAT II Writing.

Most Popular Majors:
13% Economics
12% Psychology
10% English Language and Literature

Students Also Applied To:*
Harvard University, Brown University, Smith College, Tufts University, Boston University
*For more school info check out www.collegeprowler.com

Table of Contents

Academics	910
Local Atmosphere	912
Safety & Security	913
Computers	915
Facilities	916
Campus Dining	918
Off-Campus Dining	919
Campus Housing	921
Off-Campus Housing	923
Diversity	924
Guys & Girls	926
Athletics	928
Greek Life	929
Drug Scene	931
Campus Strictness	932
Overall Experience	934
The Inside Scoop	935
Finding a Job or Internship	937
The Best & Worst	938

College Prowler Report Card

Academics	A-
Local Atmosphere	C
Safety & Security	A-
Computers	B-
Facilities	B+
Campus Dining	B-
Off-Campus Dining	A-
Campus Housing	B+
Off-Campus Housing	D
Diversity	B+
Guys	N/A
Girls	B
Athletics	C
Greek Life	D
Drug Scene	A
Campus Strictness	D-

Academics

Special Degree Options
Double Degree Program with MIT: Students accepted to MIT as transfers (after completing junior year at Wellesley) earn a B.A. from Wellesley and an S.B. from MIT over the course of five years.

Sample Academic Clubs
Architectural Forum, ASTRO Club, Classics Club, Economic Students Association, German Club, Hippocratic Society, Investment Society, Italian Society, Japan Club, Marine Biology Club, Model United Nations, Philosophical Society, Pre-Business Association, Pre-Dental Society, Pre-Law Society, Psychology Club, Russian Club, Society of Physics Students, Wellesley Pre-Veterinary Society

The Lowdown
ON ACADEMICS

Degrees Awarded:
Bachelor

Undergraduate Schools:
Wellesley College

Full-time Faculty:
235

Faculty with Terminal Degree:
96%

Student-to-Faculty Ratio:
9:1

Average Course Load:
4 courses per semester

AP Test Score Requirements:
Possible credit for scores of 4 or 5 (3 if Math/BC)

IB Test Score Requirements:
Possible credit for scores of 5, 6, or 7

Best Places to Study:
One of the libraries, Schneider Student Center, or The Hoop

Students Speak Out
ON ACADEMICS

"Courses have great titles, and the information is interesting. However, never choose your classes based on the title and topic. The professors at Wellesley range from outstanding to terrible, to everything in between."

Q "I've had some really great teachers and a few really horrible ones. For the most part, the teachers go out of their way to help their students and form relationships with them. **Most teachers make their classes as interactive as possible.** I choose my classes based on the professor more then the topic because the quality of the teacher determines how the class is."

Q "The professors are, on the whole, extremely smart and engaging. They're also often **very accessible and interested in the students**; they seem to genuinely want to help us learn as much as possible. Most professors are engaging lecturers."

Q "I find my professors fascinating and brilliant. They've always been open to stopping class discussion to address questions or go on a tangent to explain something someone wants to explore more. **They've always had open-door policies and welcomed me in during office hours**—or beyond—as well as been willing to stop and chat. I cannot count the number of reading or activity recommendations I've received from them, and they're always ready to be mentors in unofficial capacities."

Q "It depends on the subject and the teacher; **I've had horribly boring ones and extremely exciting ones**. For the most part though, the classes are interesting because there are so few people in them that everyone really gets to participate, and if you don't pay attention, it's pretty obvious. I'd say the quality of classes is one of the largest advantages of Wellesley."

Q "One thing I have to say about Wellesley is that it has the most wonderful professors. The professors are there for you when you need to discuss the class work with someone, and you can always drop in when they are around their office to tell them about your personal life, experiences in other classes, or other topics of interest. In general, **I find most professors very approachable**."

Q "In terms of class material, some were interesting but others were not. I think how much you will enjoy a class **depends on your areas of interest and expertise**. Some class topics are inevitably boring, but, nevertheless, the professors will try their best to make the class more interesting. In long seminar classes especially, some professors will bring in food and video clips to keep the student awake."

The College Prowler Take
ON ACADEMICS

The typical Wellesley professor is willing to field hysterical eleventh-hour phone calls. She also spends hours in her office, meeting with whole parades of students—when the job calls for it! She is also likely willing to personally mentor students on intensive projects. Of course, quality and style vary individually and departmentally, but on the whole, Wellesley professors are excellent and extremely committed—and students are very appreciative. There are many who are exceptional lecturers, and of course a few who are incredibly boring, too. But, professors invariably prove to be very dynamic during office hours, and a more extensive relationship is almost always there to be forged if you are willing. Few students go through their Wellesley career without forming some kind of close relationship with a professor. Though sometimes one might wish Wellesley had a few more big-name professors (it's tough being near Harvard and MIT, with their celebrity profs), accessibility and dedication are more important. If you ask around and do your research, you can ensure some serious, and—believe it or not—exciting learning. Also, the school's e-mail system has an online conference where students can post questions about professors and get in-depth responses about professors' teaching styles. Everything from the professor's clothing to competence is fair game. Take advantage of this!

The College Prowler™ Grade on
Academics: A-

A high Academics grade generally indicates that professors are knowledgeable, accessible, and genuinely interested in their students' welfare. Other determining factors include class size, how well professors communicate, and whether or not classes are engaging.

Local Atmosphere

Students Speak Out
ON LOCAL ATMOSPHERE

"**The town is the biggest downside to Wellesley** because, unlike the campus, it is not diverse. The townspeople look down upon the students, and the students are unbelievably bored by the area."

Q "**Wellesley is very white and rich.** They do not seem to realize how lucky they are to live where they do and have the kind of money that they do. Of course, there is no diversity, and the town has not adapted for the college in any way. It can lead to inconvenience and boredom, but you eventually figure your way out of the town for almost everything."

Q "**The town of Wellesley is pretty lame.** There are very few independent businesses, and even fewer businesses that actually cater to the needs of college students. There isn't really anywhere for students to hang out, except maybe Starbuck's or Peet's Coffee, and these both close by 8 p.m.. Babson and Wellesley are in the same town, but you'd never know it, which is a shame, because having a bar, [which is] not happening [or a] 24-hour diner, coffee house, or even an independent movie theater or record store where students from both schools could mingle without the awkwardness of Wellesley society parties, would be incredibly beneficial."

Q "In a word, I think the Ville is boring. Unless you like hanging out at CVS, or any of half a dozen hairdressing salons. I do like the Wellesley Public Library, though. One plus: many people I know go to church in town, so **religious havens aren't far away if you're Christian**. Most other people I know see the Ville only in passing, while on the bus into Boston or Cambridge."

The Lowdown
ON LOCAL ATMOSPHERE

Region:
Northeast

City, State:
Wellesley, Massachusetts

Setting:
Small town/suburban

Distance from Boston:
20 minutes

Distance from New York:
4 hours

Points of Interest:
Faneuil Hall, Quincy Market, Boston Harbor, The Freedom Trail, Boston Common, Harvard Square, Newbury Street, The Museum of Fine Arts, The Prudential Center, the North End, Isabella Stewart Gardner Museum, Museum of Science, New England Aquarium, Downtown Crossing, Chinatown, The Fleet Center, The Charles River, Central Square

City Websites:
www.boston-online.com

Major Sports Teams:
Red Sox (MLB), Patriots (NFL), Bruins (NHL) Celtics (NBA), Revolution (MLS)

💬 "There is almost nothing for students to do in the town of Wellesley, except eat at overpriced restaurants and shop for handmade baby clothes at one of the many children's boutiques. However, **Boston is only a 45-minute drive**—less if you have a car—and there is plenty to do there: bars, restaurants, museums, and lots of other colleges."

The College Prowler Take
ON LOCAL ATMOSPHERE

The ladies are pretty much in accord here: the town of Wellesley is not there to cater to students. In fact, it often seems that the town's residents are trying to forget our existence. Wellesley is one of the richest communities in the country, and the shops and restaurants show it. Some students report that they feel uncomfortable in the Ville, while others feel they make townies uncomfortable. It's possible that the residents of Wellesley are all very normal with middle-class hearts, but sometimes the town has a bit of a "Leave It To Beaver" meets "Children of the Corn" ambience. Boston, for many students, is a beacon of hope (real life! parties! men!) that breaks through the hazy, money-drenched clouds of the suburbs.

The College Prowler™ Grade on
Local Atmosphere: C

A high Local Atmosphere grade indicates that the area surrounding campus is safe and scenic. Other factors include nearby attractions, proximity to other schools, and the town's attitude toward students.

Safety & Security

The Lowdown
ON SAFETY & SECURITY

Number of Wellesley Police:
18

Phone:
(781) 283-2121 (non-emergency);
(781) 283-5555 (emergency)

Health Center:
(781) 283-2810

Outpatient clinic:
Monday through Friday 8 a.m.-noon, and 1 p.m.-4 p.m. Emergencies only will be seen after 4 p.m. and on weekends.

Inpatient clinic:
Open 24 hours a day when classes are in session. Registered nurse on duty, physician and counselor on call.

Safety Services:
24-hour patrol, Campus Escort Program, Community-Policing Officer Program which assigns individual police officers to specific residence halls, self-defense class (PE credit), RAD (Rape Aggression Defense training), emergency blue-light phones.

 ## Students Speak Out
ON SAFETY & SECURITY

 ## The College Prowler Take
ON SAFETY & SECURITY

"I'd say the campus is safe. Campus police are receptive to safety suggestions, and I never feel nervous about leaving my door unlocked or walking around at night alone."

Q "Security is not very good. **Campus police are rarely seen**, except at events or giving out parking tickets. When things happen that show how lax our security is on campus, our college, instead of making everyone aware and doing more to avoid it in the future, ignores it."

Q "The campus feels safe, and, while I've heard of isolated incidents in the past few years, **there seems to be very little threat to the safety of students** on campus. Campus po' spend more time breaking up parties on weekends and handing out parking tickets than they do keeping anyone out of harm's way."

Q "One security hole that shouldn't exist is the Bells system. This is left over from the time when the dorms' front doors weren't locked, but now they are, and only people with student IDs can get in. Many people have suggested that this renders Bells unneeded, but the issue remains of people slipping in behind students and wandering around the dorms. **Bells coverage is spotty**, however, and usually only in action between nine and five, so the system doesn't actually keep anyone very safe."

Q "**We've had some strange things happen on our campus**, and when something strange happens, we are alerted to it by the chief of police. There are some things we don't hear about, but I don't think they happen extremely often. I feel like our campus is relatively safe, as long as one has common sense—don't walk around the lake by yourself at 2 a.m.."

Q "I have never had a problem with safety. Although, **it is scary to be walking alone at night**, I have never felt threatened. Wellesley's campus however, could definitely use some more lights on the walkways."

On the whole, Wellesley students feel very comfortable on their campus, largely due to the efforts of the campus police. The Bells system is under fire, however, both from those who say it's unnecessary, and those who argue that it is not strict enough. The Horizontal-Vertical Rule is supposed to keep unescorted guests from roaming from floor to floor, and while stray men are usually rounded up quickly, female guests can move without problems. Occasionally, a rash of thefts can occur, but serious crime is almost unheard of. Though Wellesley is very safe, prudence should not be abandoned just because you are inside the Wellesley Bubble.

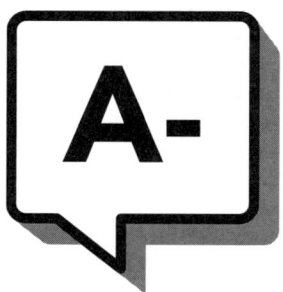

The College Prowler™ Grade on
Safety & Security: A-

A high grade in Safety & Security means that students generally feel safe, campus police are visible, blue-light phones and escort services are readily available, and safety precautions are not overly necessary.

Computers

Students Speak Out
ON COMPUTERS

"People here are way obsessed with e-mail, and computer labs are always crowded with girls having marathon e-mailchecks. I'd say bring a computer and a printer."

Q "**Wellesley has a very decent computer network** and there are usually enough computers in labs for anyone who might need one, unless you are doing a multimedia project, then labs get tight. I would recommend that people bring their own computers if they are able, if only for convenience. Most labs close around midnight, so if you wanted to work after that you would have limited options outside the dorm. The computer rooms in the dorms do fill up quickly and are not usually available for quick activities, like e-mail and such."

Q "Bring your own computer. **Computer labs are dirty and crowded**, and people like to hog computers even if they're not using them. The FirstClass network is very resourceful, but it can turn into a stalker weapon."

Q "The computer network is kind of annoying because **it crashes a lot**, but I get what I need. The computer labs are almost always full, so one should bring a computer. Make it a laptop, so you can bring it around campus."

Q "I work for information services, and I would say, follow their lead. They're very good with keeping students informed on computer purchases and provide support after you get here. Most people bring their own computers, but **there are approximately 150 public stations you can use** at any point, with free scanning, printing, and software, plus consultants to help you with FAQs. The network is fast, FirstClass is super-useful, though super-addictive, and we have tons of storage space online for files, papers, and presentations."

The Lowdown
ON COMPUTERS

High-Speed Network?
Yes

Wireless Network?
Yes, and it is being developed further.

Number of Labs:
6

Numbers of Computers:
370 public computers

24-Hour Labs:
In the Science Center

Charge to Print?
No

Operating Systems:
Windows XP, Macintosh OSX, Linux (in the computer science lab)

Free Software:
McAfee virus protection, Adaware, Dreamweaver, Fireworks, Photoshop, and more

> "**The computer network is great**—it's pretty fast [T3 connection], and each student has her own network drop in her dorm room. I think a very high percentage of students bring computers, so there are usually computers available in the labs."

> "Each residence hall has a computer lab, and there are many computers scattered around campus, so if you're savvy with scrounging around the crunch times, **you could probably make it without your own computer just fine**. However, it's loads easier with one's own computer and an occasional trip to Knapp to do special work, like scanning, PowerPoint, or Photoshopping."

The College Prowler Take
ON COMPUTERS

Students tend to think that computing at Wellesley is sufficient for their needs. True, around exam time, women stalk the aisles of Knapp breathing over the shoulders of those who look like they're about to leave, but for most of the semester, it is no trouble to get a public computer. FirstClass addiction may be a problem for some students, but it is a sign that our e-mail system is effective at keeping everyone in touch. While having a computer isn't necessary, it is a very good idea.

The College Prowler™ Grade on
Computers: B-

A high grade in Computers designates that computer labs are available, the computer network is easily accessible, and the campus' computing technology is up-to-date.

Facilities

The Lowdown
ON FACILITIES

Student Center:
Schneider Student Center

Athletic Center:
Keohane Sports Center

Libraries:
Clapp Library, Science Library, Music Library, Art Library

Popular Places to Chill:
Schneider, The Hoop, dorm rooms and living rooms, the dining halls

Movie Theatre on Campus?
Collins Cinema, Davis Museum Plaza

Bowling on Campus?
No

Bar on Campus?
Molly's Pub, Schneider Student Center

Coffeehouse on Campus?
El Table, Founders basement, The Hoop, Schneider Basement, Collins Café, Davis Museum Plaza

Favorite Things to Do:
During the week, students tend to run around from activity to activity all day, then eat a long, drawn-out dinner with friends, until the dining hall workers start putting up chairs around them. Late night brings nacho runs to The Hoop, complaint sessions in the PLTC about how much work you have to do, or movies or chats in friends' rooms. In their free time, students flow into Boston to shop or grab something to eat. SBOG and other clubs also organize activities such as film festivals, parties, and lectures, which can be interesting and fun to participate in.

Students Speak Out
ON FACILITIES

"The sports center isn't the best. There are few cardio machines, and the weight room's hours are limited. The computers are up-to-date, except our campus network has a tendency to crash at inconvenient times."

"The facilities are really nice. The athletic center could use some more workout equipment, but is otherwise very useful. **The pool is amazing, and the computer labs are great**. The new student center is spectacular as well."

"Facilities are, for the most part, gorgeous. **I find them to be better than most Ivy League colleges**, if not all. Our new student center is awesome and though I'm partial to the exterior aesthetics of the building, it's nice, considering how small and inadequate our current Schneider Center is. The athletic facilities are good, and we have new fields. However, if you live on the other side of campus from the fields, you probably won't be able to take advantage of them since it would take a lot of time to walk back and forth. There is also the question of whether the gym equipment will be available for use."

"**The facilities are nice; it's just hard to access them**. We have two dance studios, but they are hard to reserve for rehearsal space because aerobics classes get priority. There is rehearsal space in Jewett, the arts and music building, but those are hard to reserve as well because choir and school-sponsored activities get priority there. The weight rooms in the athletic center aren't open very often, and when they are, of course the sports teams take precedence. We have nice stuff; there just isn't enough to go around."

The College Prowler Take
ON FACILITIES

The computer labs are all very nice, and most are stocked with comfortable couches and armchairs. Classrooms in Pendleton and the Science Center tend to be well-laid-out and high-tech, though those in Founders are cramped and stuffed with Wellesley's signature big wooden straight-backed chairs. The Science Center is a love-it-or-hate-it affair, with its Mondrian-esque exterior, which encases the remains of the old brick Science Center inside. The campus is indisputably gorgeous, and walking up to Tower Great Hall or the quad can get your heart beating faster. The new dorms, on the other hand, may make you break out in a cold sweat, but they serve their purpose (and they're mostly hidden by trees, anyway).

The College Prowler™ Grade on
Facilities: B+

A high Facilities grade indicates that the campus is aesthetically pleasing and well-maintained; facilities are state-of-the-art, and libraries are exceptional. Other determining factors include the quality of both athletic and student centers and an abundance of things to do on campus.

Campus Dining

Students Speak Out
ON CAMPUS DINING

"The food sucks—it is industrial—and the administration will not let you off the meal plan, no matter how hard you try. There are some improvements underway, but they'll probably be insignificant and far off."

Q "The dining halls provide **a wide range of options**, thanks to the numerous halls, many of which have dietary specifications like Kosher, vegetarian, wellness and peanut-free. The meal plan is excellent; it is unlimited and not based on a points system. And for those wishing to spend a small amount for high-quality food, the student co-op cafe, El Table, offers healthy and delicious lunch and snacks."

Q "The food on campus is pretty good. Our meal plan allows you to **eat as much as you want**, and there are usually healthy options in the bigger dining halls. I'd steer clear of the smaller dining halls in the quad and head for the bigger ones in Stone-Davis or Tower for the most options. One bummer is that the school's contract with Sodexho, our food provider, doesn't allow many people to be off the meal plan, which is a little restrictive."

Q "I personally hate campus food, but from what I hear, Wellesley food isn't that bad on the grand scale of college cuisine. In my opinion, **breakfast is the only decent meal**, and I think that Bates serves the best. Stone-D has decent food for other meals if you do get hungry, although it is closed on weekends."

Q "The food isn't bad. Some dining halls are better than others. Some dining halls don't have very much variety. Beebe is great; it's the Wellness dorm, so **it's healthier eating**, but the staff is the nicest on campus. There's usually a line at 5:30 when it opens. Tower Court is good, too, but a lot of people eat there, so it's usually crowded. Pom is great for vegetarian meals and Kosher, and Stone-D has the most variety [salad bar, pizza, sandwich bar] if you don't like the entree."

The Lowdown
ON CAMPUS DINING

Freshman Meal Plan Requirement?
There is a gour-year meal plan requirement, unless you're on Lake House Meal Plan or other individual exceptions.

24-Hour On-Campus Eating?
No

Student Favorites:
Tower Court, Davis, The Hoop

Meal Plan Average Cost:
$4,540

Fun Facts
Each dining hall hosts one theme dinner a month. Examples include: Harry Potter Night, complete with bubbling cauldrons of soup; World Series Night, which features chili dogs, hot pretzels, and ice cream sandwiches; and Italian Night, adorned with checkered tablecloths and candles.

💬 "The food on campus is okay. I hear that, compared to other schools, it's fabulous. The six flavors of ice cream in every dining hall rocks. **Pom has better desserts than anywhere else** because the college gets them separately, since Pom is Kosher. Stone-D and Pom have the best salad bars."

💬 "The waffle bar is great if you don't mind gaining nine zillion pounds, as are the little personal pizzas in Schneids. **I'm obsessed with the milk shake machine in Stone-D.** The best thing about the meal plan is being able to eat as much as you want, whenever you want, and, being able to eat all your meals in your own dorm in your pajamas."

Off-Campus Dining

The College Prowler Take
ON CAMPUS DINING

The dining halls are, overall, pretty darn good. Everyone has her complaints, but it is possible to eat well at Wellesley (and compared to many colleges, to eat very well). Students really like dining-hall workers, and certain workers, such as Pasta Bob in Tower, have gained semi-celebrity status. Though the meal plan is very open in some ways, it can be equally as restrictive. **We can eat as much as we like at any time during the day and most dining halls don't keep track of guest meals, but we have no options other than the dining halls.**

The College Prowler™ Grade on
Campus Dining: B-

Our grade on Campus Dining addresses the quality of both school-owned dining halls and independent on-campus restaurants as well as the price, availability, and variety of food.

The Lowdown
ON OFF-CAMPUS DINING

Best Pizza:
Figs, Bertucci's

Best Chinese:
Shanghai Tokyo

Best Breakfast:
Vidalia's, Maugus Restaurant

Best Place to Take Your Parents:
Figs, Blue Ginger

Student Favorites:
Amarin, Figs

Fun Fact
Wellesley students are lucky to live near a city big enough to host hundreds of great restaurants. The North End is Boston's Little Italy, and Chinatown has several blocks packed with restaurants.

Students Speak Out
ON CAMPUS DINING

"There are several good places to eat: Maugus Restaurant is good for cheap diner-style breakfasts on weekends. Lemon Thai and Amarin are good for Thai food, but Lemon Thai is a little better, and cheaper."

Q "There are many good restaurants in the town of Wellesley, though **most are pricey**. Figs is excellent for Italian and bistro food. Blue Ginger and Amarin are also great for Asian food. And there are plenty of restaurants that deliver to the college, but after 11 p.m. or 12 a.m., the only option is Domino's."

Q "Vidalia's isn't too bad and there is Figs, but not very much in terms of restaurants in Wellesley. **I suggest Boston for great Chinese food**, Penang, The Cheesecake Factory and Legal Sea Foods, among others."

Q "There are some good places around, but **you need a car**. The Maugus restaurant in Wellesley Hills is the closest you'll get to a cheap diner, the town of Natick has a good farmers' market, and there are some good restaurants down Routes 9 and 135. The town of Wellesley has two ice cream parlors, as well as a pizza place and two Thai restaurants, of which Lemon Thai is the best option."

Q "Wellesley is a suburb, so **there really aren't that many places near campus**. Blue Ginger is good for fine dining and Vidalia's serves great breakfast and greasy hangover food. The two Thai places in the town center are okay. Delivery is hit-or-miss."

Q "They have great food in the town of Wellesley within walking distance, such as Figs [gourmet Italian], Amarin [Thai], and Vidalia's [gourmet diner-style food]. **In Boston, they have way too many good restaurants**."

The College Prowler Take
ON CAMPUS DINING

Boston is a foodie's paradise, and the town of Wellesley isn't too shabby, either. One advantage to being in the upscale 'burbs is access to well-known restaurants such as Blue Ginger and Figs. Between Boston, Cambridge, and (with a little bit of driving) even the fishing communities of the Massachusetts coast, you can satisfy cravings for every imaginable food. So, if you've got the dough, you can sample everything from haute cuisine to fantastic greasy pizza.

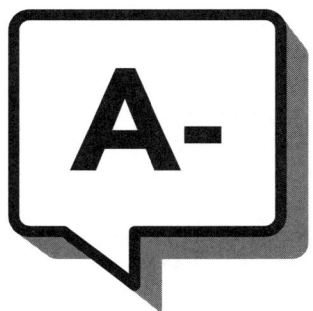

The College Prowler™ Grade on
Off-Campus Dining: A-

A high Off-Campus Dining grade implies that off-campus restaurants are affordable, accessible, and worth visiting. Other factors include the variety of cuisine and the availability of alternative options (vegetarian, vegan, Kosher, etc.).

Campus Housing

Also Available

Several apartments located in the dorms, offer kitchens, living rooms, and more independent living. Orchard Apartments, in Dower, and Hemlock Apartments, in McAfee, tend to go to upperclass women. Small-scale, special-interest housing is available by application to everyone except first-years. French House, located slightly off campus, is French-language housing; Cervantes House, near the Tower complex, is Spanish-language; Instead Feminist Co-op, on the east side of campus, is a feminist vegetarian cooperative.

There are also on-campus housing options for Davis Scholars in houses and dorms on the east side of campus.

The Lowdown
ON CAMPUS HOUSING

Undergrads on Campus:
94%

Number of Dormitories:
19

Number of University-Owned Apartments:
0

Room Types:
Singles, doubles, triples, two- to five-person suites (single-person rooms, shared bathroom).

Cleaning Service?
Public spaces are cleaned daily by staff.

Bed Type:
Twin extra-long; many can be bunked or lofted.

You Get:
It varies slightly based on dorm, but, generally, a desk, chair, lamp, bookcase, bed, chest of drawers, closet or wardrobe, window coverings, Ethernet and phone connection, free campus and local calls.

Students Speak Out
ON CAMPUS HOUSING

"If you plan to spend your days in the Science Center, the newer dorms [McAfee, Bates, Freeman] are closest to the Sci Center. If you want to live amongst old architecture, Tower Court has some great Gothic features."

"I think the dorms are really nice. They're all very different, and depending on what you're looking for, you can usually find one that's a good fit for you. **Most of the dorms have a campus personality** and everyone can find a place where they're happy to live. There are certain dorms that are quieter, some are known for partying, and other ones are known for their queer community. There's pretty much something for everyone."

Q "**Stone-D is the really quiet dorm**, so are the new dorms, but they are both relatively close to the town center. Munger doesn't have its own dining hall and isn't particularly close to anything. The dorms in the quad are fun, they have specialty dining halls—no peanuts and such. Your best bet if you want to be relatively close to everything and get a more social atmosphere, would be the Tower complex. Lake House is good if you are an upperclass woman and want to be off the meal plan."

Q "Avoid the new dorms because they're **psychotic and isolated**. I like the Tower dorms the best, because they're social and close to everything."

Q "**All of the dorms are nice** and have their own atmosphere, whether it be old-fashioned, with hardwood floors, or modern. I have lived in Beebe all of my college life, and I love it. Munger is bad for first-years, though, because the rooms are tiny and not made for two people—they are used for two people."

The College Prowler Take
ON CAMPUS HOUSING

Housing at Wellesley really is a matter of taste—the dorms all have different personalities, and just as many students would prefer a dank room in Munger over a lake view in Stone-Davis, and vice versa. Unfortunately, there is a limited number of suites. In general, Wellesley was designed to promote studiousness, not sociability. Even if you strike out, however, you can try for a room swap. A lake view lifts the spirits, as does being in a social dorm where people are likely to prop open their doors. So, although we've got beautiful, diverse housing, independent living is largely out, as is the more social setup that suites provide.

The College Prowler™ Grade on
Campus Housing: B+

A high Campus Housing grade indicates that dorms are clean, well-maintained, and spacious. Other determining factors include variety of dorms, proximity to classes, and social atmosphere.

Off-Campus Housing

The Lowdown
ON OFF-CAMPUS HOUSING

Undergrads in Off-Campus Housing:
6%

Popular Areas:
Natick, Allston

For Assistance Contact:
Web:
www.wellesley.edu/Housing/housing.html
Phone: (781) 283-2681
E-mail: studenthousing@wellesley.edu

Students Speak Out
ON OFF-CAMPUS HOUSING

"There's lots of student housing in Boston and maybe a place or two in neighboring towns, but Wellesley is way too expensive. You would definitely need a car, and very few people live off campus."

Q "There's no housing off campus. **Some Davis Scholars live off campus** with their families. The occasional student lives off campus, but it is not really a very common thing."

Q "**Wellesley is one of the richest suburbs of Boston**, so affordable housing within walking-distance of campus isn't an option. If you have a car, you can get somewhere in the surrounding area, but it's not cheap. Living in Boston requires a lot of patience with the transportation system. It can be inconvenient if you spend large amounts of time on campus."

Q "We have four-year, guaranteed housing, so **you might as well stay on campus** unless it's making you miserable, but I'd recommend getting off campus and maybe living in the city at an MIT frat if you're working in Boston over the summer."

Q "**It's extremely inconvenient to live off campus after freshman year**. The area around Wellesley is one of the wealthiest in the country—read: expensive—and there is a lot of traffic around, so it would be difficult to get to class. The dorms are nice enough, anyway."

Q "If you have a car and several friends that want to live with you, **you could live in Newton or Natick**, but it's pricey, and unless it's something you have your heart set on, living on campus is much more convenient, and guaranteed."

Q "**Virtually no one lives off campus**. The Newton and Wellesley area is really unaffordable for college students looking for off-campus housing and, in addition, living on campus is hugely responsible for forming the tight sense of community at Wellesley. Socially, it would probably be really difficult to feel like you're a part of things if you live off campus."

The College Prowler Take
ON OFF-CAMPUS HOUSING

Wellesley guarantees four years of housing, and most students can't think of a reason to live anywhere else. Apart from the unreasonable cost of off-campus living in the area, students also question whether its possible to really be a part of campus life while living somewhere else, and it is true that while meetings and activities can be scheduled in, large parts of the Wellesley experience are the chance chats in the dining hall that turn into long conversations, the all-house meetings that go on way too long, and the study breaks organized by RAs. There is a variety of dorm-related activities, and although first-years may seem perky and annoying to the jaded senior, living together is beneficial to everyone. People living off campus really miss out.

Diversity

The Lowdown
ON DIVERSITY

African American: 6%

Asian American: 26%

Hispanic: 5%

Native American: 0%

White: 55%

International: 8%

Out-of-State: 83%

The College Prowler™ Grade on
Off-Campus Housing: D

A high grade in Off-Campus Housing indicates that apartments are of high quality, close to campus, affordable, and easy to secure.

Minority Clubs
There are large amounts of minority clubs, including religious, cultural, and racial groups. Ethos and Mezcla have large memberships, and many performance groups are inspired by the minority cultures around campus.

Political Activity
Students tend to be very liberal, so much so that conservatives report that they often feel oppressed. Conservative views do tend to be shot down rather quickly in class, an interesting phenomenon in a community that prides itself on its open-mindedness.

Most Popular Religions

Wellesley has a very diverse mix of the religious, the spiritual, and the agnostic. Christian, Buddhist, Muslim, Jewish, and Pagan groups are very active.

Gay Tolerance

Wellesley is extremely tolerant; many straight students graduate as self-proclaimed "cultural gays." Dyke Ball is a Wellesley institution, and National Coming Out Day is practically a holiday, where a large portion of the school community—including students, faculty, and staff—share their support for the gay community.

Economic Status

Wellesley students run the gamut from high-society girls (even some royalty) to first-generation college students from low socioeconomic backgrounds.

Students Speak Out
ON OFF-CAMPUS HOUSING

"As the administration will tell you, it is incredibly diverse in terms of personalities, beliefs, race, sexual orientation, or whatever other criteria you could possibly imagine."

Q "Wellesley is definitely more diverse in terms of backgrounds than I, the product of a public school in the state of South Carolina, have experienced before. **There are students from all over the USA and the world**, and from all walks of life—from the incredibly affluent to those who had to scrape dimes to survive, some who must live with physical or mental disabilities, some who have been through incredibly trying times, and those who've led sheltered lives."

Q "Wellesley, regrettably, fails to be quite so diverse as it should: there are so many liberal voices on campus that **the dissenting conservatives are often drowned out** and ignored or—sometimes—unfairly ridiculed for their beliefs. As on many college campuses, there is a lot of PC-ness, which can sometimes be stifling."

Q "Wellesley is all about its diversity, and **we look good on paper**. There probably aren't as many African American or Native American students as one would hope. There are many Asian students. There are also supposedly a lot of international students, but this is misleading. Most of our international students come from the United World Colleges and therefore all received the same educational experience, so it's essentially as diverse as taking a bunch of students from the same high school, except this is from a high school in another country."

Q "Wellesley tries very hard to be diverse, which I know everyone appreciates. **It still has a long way to go**, though."

The College Prowler Take
ON OFF-CAMPUS HOUSING

The student who said that diversity is relative is right. Compared to other private colleges and universities, Wellesley is doing great. Compared to actual population sizes, Wellesley is not very diverse, at all. Yet because the school puts such a premium on racial and religious diversity, minority groups have quite a high on-campus profile (though perhaps not as high as they would like). Students worry that the desire not to offend anyone keeps frank discussions from taking place and forms cliques, further preventing students from educating one another. Meanwhile, the administration constantly reminds students, and anyone else who will listen, that Wellesley is as diverse as can be.

The College Prowler™ Grade on
Diversity: B+

A high grade in Diversity indicates that ethnic minorities and international students have a notable presence on campus and that students of different economic backgrounds, religious beliefs, and sexual preferences are well-represented.

Guys & Girls

The Lowdown
ON GUYS & GIRLS

Women Undergrads: 100%

Men Undergrads: 0%

Birth Control Available?
Health Services provides birth control, as well as STI tests. Oral contraceptives, the Ortho-Evra patch, Depo Provera, the Nuva ring, diaphragms, Lunelle and the morning after pill are available. Dorm Health Representatives and SHEs (Sexual Health Educators) give out free condoms.

Social Scene
Wellesley has several different social scenes. Some heterosexual students throw themselves into the MIT frat scene, while others keep a cynical distance and agonize over their lack of coed interaction. Most find their groove, however, whether it's lots of girls' nights out (or in), or alternative male contact through extracurricular activities, friends-of-friends, or chance meetings. Those who are, as one student put it, of "the girl-kissing persuasion," find a welcoming social community.

Hookups or Relationships?
Many students complain that while it is easy to find men to hook up with, it's not nearly so easy to make male friends or develop long-term relationships. And, despite jokes about lesbians' tendency to commit to a lifetime on the first date, many members of the queer community say the same thing. Nevertheless, it seems like Wellesley women do pretty well for themselves, and a good number are in committed relationships.

Dress Code
Classwear really varies: some wear pajamas (almost out of a feeling of obligation—it is a women's college, after all), while others dress up in Gucci. Most, however, stick to jeans and sweaters. There are jokes that the Science Center is the realm of the "Wolf Shirt Girl" (an official Wellesley type, replete with tapered, pleated jeans, Keds, long straggly hair, and an oversized T-shirt), while econ majors please the profs with sweater sets and pearls.

Students Speaks Out
ON GUYS & GIRLS

"The only guys are professors and some kitchen staff. A few of them are hot. There are a zillion 'types' of women at Wellesley; every kind of person is represented."

"**Guys? They don't exist**. Except for the token cross-exchange student from MIT, Olin, or Babson. Oh yeah, please call us women, not girls. Anyway, every sort of woman you can imagine attends Wellesley. Nice, not-quite-so-friendly, liberal, conservative, American, foreign, queer, straight, large, small, those with plenty o' common sense, those who attempt to bake cookies on a plastic tray from the dining hall, those who party at frats off campus, those who 'party' in the labs instead, overachievers, procrastinators, athletes, musicians, scientists, philosophers, some with ambition for politics, others for education, raising families, fashion, or law."

Q "There are a lot of girls here who are really immature, or **really anal and bitchy**—both are probably a result of a tunnel-vision approach to learning, just learning what needs to be learned to get an A and go to a good college. I wouldn't say those girls are hot. There are, however, a lot of really interesting, smart, engaged girls here, and once you find your niche, you're set. I guess the ladies here who are really intelligent and have a strong sense of themselves are hot."

Q "**Yeah, the girls are hot. Seriously**. Sometimes this place can induce complexes: everyone seems perfect and overachieving and brilliant. But, they also make good friends when they're not busy studying."

Q "**Guys at MIT generally have problems at being social**. Women at Wellesley tend to be extremely good-looking. When they go out, they put a lot of effort into looking good."

Q "My first year on campus, I felt secluded and uncomfortable. I do not think that Wellesley is the easiest campus at which you can make friends. However, **second year, I adjusted much better**, and found wonderful friends within my niche. It helps to have certain interests that you can share with people; you can bond through those interests."

The College Prowler Take
ON GUYS & GIRLS

While resisting the request to sum up the cool quotient of their fellow students, the Wellesley women did not hold back on their critiques of area men. Our dating pool tends to be guys from Boston-area schools, and so there's a range there as well. Wellesley has a T-shirt that sums up the common opinion of MIT guys (and Wellesley students claimed to have coined the phrase, though it's been seen elsewhere): "MIT: where the odds are good, but the goods are odd." Wellesley women also date men from Harvard, BC, BU, Northeastern, Berklee (a music school), Babson, or any number of the dozens of schools in the area. Lesbians seem to be happy with the dating pool, and heterosexuals seem thrilled with the friends they've made.

The College Prowler™ Grade on
Guys: N/A

A high grade for Guys indicates that the male population on campus is attractive, smart, friendly, and engaging, and that the school has a decent ratio of guys to girls.

The College Prowler™ Grade on
Girls: B

A high grade for Girls not only implies that the women on campus are attractive, smart, friendly, and engaging, but also that there is a fair ratio of girls to guys.

Athletics

Athletic Division:
Division III

Conference:
New England Women's and Men's Athletic Conference (NEWMAC)

Overlooked Teams:
Pretty much all of them

School Mascot:
No official mascot, though we are called the "Wellesley Blue."

The Lowdown
ON ATHLETICS

Students Speak Out
ON ATHLETICS

Varsity Sports:
Basketball
Crew
Cross Country
Fencing
Field Hockey
Golf
Lacrosse
Soccer
Softball
Squash
Swimming
Tennis
Volleyball

Club Sports:
Soccer
Lacrosse
Equestrian Club
Golf
Outing Club
Rugby
Snowboarding
Softball Club
Table Tennis
Tennis
Ultimate Frisbee
Volleyball
Water Polo
Ice Hockey

"Varsity sports are very big for those who play them, but there are virtually no spectators. This is mostly due to a lack of fan recruiting."

"**We have really dedicated teams at Wellesley**, but we're not a very sports-oriented school. Don't expect a massive cheering section if you play a varsity sport. Rugby and ultimate Frisbee are probably the two biggest IM [intramural] sports on campus."

"We have athletics. **The people who do them are involved and dedicated**, and maybe some people go to watch them and stuff, but most people I know would rather go see the Red Sox or Harvard than go watch a Wellesley game, although rugby has quite the following now."

"Varsity sports aren't big on campus. Also, they are not a priority for the school. I was on the cross country team. **Our uniforms were old, ugly, and did not fit**. We did not have any cross-training equipment for the team to prevent us from being injured. No school officials ever made it to our races, even though we had a home meet and our league championships were on our home course."

Fields
Field hockey and lacrosse field, soccer field, varsity softball field, PE recreation area

Getting Tickets
Getting tickets is certainly not a worry. The bigger problem, unless you know someone on the team, is finding out when the games are.

Most Popular Sports
Rugby, ultimate Frisbee

Q "I don't really know anything about the size of varsity sports on campus, but I know **crew seems to be pretty popular**, as both a varsity sport and an extracurricular/intramural activity."

Q "There is a big athletic crowd, but it is kind of creepy, like the mafia. **They do not really associate with the rest of the school**. Club sports are fun, though."

The College Prowler Take
ON ATHLETICS

No, sports are not big at Wellesley, but as any Division III athlete can attest, they're big for those who participate. Balancing intense academics with demanding athletics isn't an easy task, and so it's safe to say that Wellesley athletes are under-appreciated. Even when teams perform excellently, the college community at large rarely takes notice. It would be nice to have a team that drew all the students together, but for a D-III school whose main focus will always be academics, that probably isn't going to happen.

The College Prowler™ Grade on
Athletics: C

A high grade in Athletics indicates that students have school spirit, that sports programs are respected, that games are well-attended, and that intramurals are a prominent part of student life.

Greek Life

The Lowdown
ON GREEK LIFE

Number of Sororities:
None, though there are three societies, which are not part of any Greek system and technically are social/academic clubs.

Percent of Undergrad Women in Societies:
Less than 1%

Did You Know?
The three societies sponsor many of the lectures on campus. In addition to bringing speakers themselves, they contribute funding to academic departments and organizations that wish to hold lectures.

Students Speak Out
ON GREEK LIFE

The College Prowler Take
ON GREEK LIFE

{ "Wellesley masks its Greek life by calling its sororities 'societies,' but it does exist. It does not dominate the social scene, and all of its parties are open to the entire campus."

Q "Societies like ZA and TZE do a sort of rush thing called 'tea-ing.' They supposedly have purposes other than throwing parties, but I think that's what they are best known for on campus, and maybe off campus, too."

Q "There are three societies, only two of which are worth mentioning. TZE, the 'Arts and Music Society,' is very much for girls who aspire to be like Carrie on "Sex and the City," and want to meet boys. **They have a house and their parties are usually well-attended**, but some of the girls are a little spoiled and about as close as Wellesley gets to sorority girls. Art and music aren't so much the focus of TZE as shoes and champagne. ZA, the 'Literary Society,' is a little better than TZE. They do more with their academic theme, have book nights, and other cool stuff. They also have parties, which are fun, and are a bit more diverse in their membership than TZE."

Q "**The societies are basically a bunch of prissy girls** that are, for the most part, really fake and act like they're on some sort of reality show with the way they are so dramatic. The societies have parties, but they usually suck, and we only go to them because it's free booze and they're nearby. Other than that, they suck."

Q "There is no 'Greek life,' per se, but there are societies, which I guess is analogous. There are three: Tau Zeta Epsilon, or TZE, is Arts and Music; Zeta Alpha is Literary; and Phi Sigma is Lecture. The difference between a society at Wellesley and a full-out sorority is that, in my opinion at least, **societies have a much more legitimate purpose**."

Wellesley students view any kind of exclusive group with suspicion, especially a group whose acceptance process requires going to "teas" and shmoozing. And, though the stereotype of the Wellesley society girl doesn't really hold up, the societies end up with a bad rap because there are always a few token members who totter around campus in their Manolos while clutching their Saint Laurent bags. The societies aren't very popular on campus, but their parties are usually well-attended. First-years quickly figure out whether these parties are their scene or not, and upperclass women take advantage of the free booze. Though students may ridicule the societies as a whole, most society members have many friends outside their society.

The College Prowler™ Grade on
Greek Life: D

A high grade in Greek Life indicates that sororities and fraternities are not only present, but also active on campus. Other determining factors include the variety of houses available and the respect the Greek community receives from the rest of the campus.

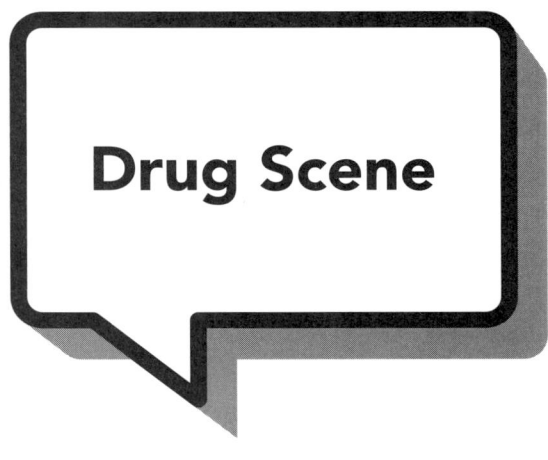

Drug Scene

Students Speak Out
ON DRUG SCENE

"Either the drug scene is much more widespread than they make it out to be, or I know every single drug user on campus. It's low-key, but it exists."

Q "Students do drugs at Wellesley, but definitely not more than at any other college, and definitely not to the point where it's a problem. **There's a lot more binge drinking at Wellesley than drugs**, I think, and this is probably more of an area of concern, as the extremely strict alcohol policy causes most students to drink a huge amount before a party in order to stay drunk the whole night, as the alcohol at parties is so regulated."

Q "On big party nights, like Tower Court or Dyke Ball, **a lot of underclassmen who don't know how to drink** get taken to Health Services."

Q "**Pot and alcohol are the biggest**, but you can get other stuff if you are looking for it. Most people are at Wellesley for the academics, but if you want to unwind, drinking and smoking are not uncommon."

Q "Pot, coke, and Ritalin seem to be the biggest drugs on campus. **People are pretty quiet about their drug habits** but drugs definitely do exist at Wellesley, it's just not part of the mainstream social scene."

Q "I don't see a lot of it, but I know **certain dorms are known for 'attracting' the few druggies we have**. I hear that a lot of people try more recreational drugs on occasion, and I'm sure a lot of people here are on uppers and downers of some kind—prescribed or not."

The Lowdown
ON DRUG SCENE

Most Prevalent Drugs on Campus
Marijuana, Adderall, caffeine, coke, Ritalin

Liquor-Related Referrals:
54

Liquor-Related Arrests:
0

Drug-Related Referrals:
22

Drug-Related Arrests:
0

Drug Counseling Programs
Wellesley doesn't have any specific drug counseling programs, but all of the residential staff are trained to deal with residents' varied problems. The best resource is the Stone Center, whose counseling services are free; their number is (781) 283-2839.

💬 "Yes, **drugs do exist on campus**. But, from what I gather, it's really only among a small, select group that they are used. I've also heard of drugs being taken to enhance academic performance, but know almost nothing about that other than yes, it happens occasionally."

The College Prowler Take
ON DRUG SCENE

Drugs are at Wellesley, just like everywhere else, and can be found if sought after, and forgot about if ignored. Depending on where they hang out and who their friends are, some students report never having smelled marijuana smoke wafting down the hall, while others see classmates toke up on a daily basis. Drugs that help people concentrate, from caffeine to Adderall and Ritalin, are both used and abused, but it's hard to determine how widespread this practice is.

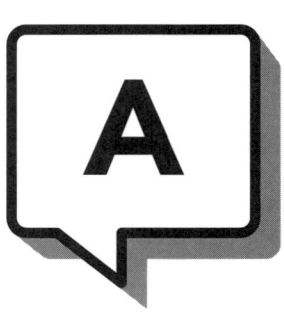

The College Prowler™ Grade on
Drug Scene: A

A high grade on Drug Scene indicates that drugs are not a noticeable part of campus life; drug use is not visible, and no pressure to use them seems to exist.

Campus Strictness

The Lowdown
ON CAMPUS STRICTNESS

What Are You Most Likely to Get Caught Doing on Campus?

Drinking underage or in common spaces (including your room if the door is open), being loud during "quiet hours," fire code violations (shoes or boxes left in hall, for example), having an unregistered party, parking illegally

Students Speak Out
ON CAMPUS STRICTNESS

"Campus policies about drinking and drugs are, in most cases, very strict. The alcohol policy is under constant revision with the help of student volunteers."

- "**Wellesley is ridiculously strict**. Even though Wellesley is one of the driest, safest colleges in the whole country, a very harsh, new alcohol policy was put into place a couple of years ago, probably because the administration is afraid of being sued if a student were to die."

- "**Alcohol violations are very popular** with campus police, but they usually give fair warning when they are going to bust a party."

- "They attempt to be strict on the alcohol policy, but **it's such a crock**. As for drugs, I don't hear a lot of stuff about people getting caught with them, so it's hush-hush. Campus police doesn't do anything about it, or they don't catch a lot of people in the act."

- "My friend got written up for drinking in her dorm. They had to acquit her, because at the 'trial,' they said she was a 110-pound blonde girl, and she's really about six feet tall and African American. I guess they're pretty tough on crime but **have really bad eyesight**."

- "Policies are extremely strict, sometimes to the point of being **too strict**, especially considering that this school has nowhere near an alcohol problem as big as other schools."

The College Prowler Take
ON CAMPUS STRICTNESS

For many students, the perceived strictness brings up issues of campus hypocrisy and suffocation. Why all the rhetoric about "independent women," if you're not going to let legal women drink in their own living rooms? Why assume we're responsible enough to take on complicated, important ideas and then make us sign up if we want to have a party? Why treat us like adults in the classroom but like children outside of it? Sometimes campus police and residential staff will pretend they don't know what's going on, but more often than not any violations of the extremely strict alcohol policy will get you a date to defend yourself before your peers and faculty on the Alcohol Hearing Board. It is, of course, a liability issue: were Wellesley to get slapped with a serious lawsuit, it would affect their ability to educate us.

The College Prowler™ Grade on
Campus Strictness: D-

A high Campus Strictness grade implies an overall lenient atmosphere; police and RAs are fairly tolerant, and the administration's rules are flexible.

Want to know more about campus drug & alcohol policies? Check out the College Prowler book on Wellesley available at *www.collegeprowler.com*.

Overall Experience

Students Speak Out
ON OVERALL EXPERIENCE

{ *"Most of the time, I'm happy to be at Wellesley. The skewed social scene makes me wonder if I'll be able to function normally after I graduate. But, you work with it."*

Q *"I would guess that **most every Wellesley student has seriously contemplated transferring**, probably a number of times. I needed to find good friends and places to feel comfortable before I was at all happy, but there will always be things I dislike about the school. It's nearly impossible to balance the work and stress with everything else going on, especially when everybody else around you usually feels overwhelmed. That said, the amazing classes definitely make it worth it, and my wonderful friends make it possible."*

Q *"I love Wellesley. It's not perfect, but it's certainly the best place for me, and I wouldn't want to go anywhere else. **The all-female environment allows girls to feel more comfortable with themselves and with each other**, both inside the classroom and out. The education you receive is wonderful, and the school does as much as possible for its students. The administration is very responsive to student wishes, and students are pretty much pampered."*

Q *"I don't wish I was somewhere else, but that has taken me two years to come to terms with. There were many times I considered transferring, but **I'm really grateful for Wellesley's financial resources**, which allow me to do things I have always wanted to do. For example, I was able to go to Costa Rica this summer, which probably would not have happened if not for Wellesley and the generous alumnae. The financial aid at Wellesley is great, unless you are an international student."*

Q *"My professors have been good and bad. However, the bad ones have always been compared to the amazing professors I've had who are extremely helpful and care about their students. Social life is what you make of it, and **don't expect to find a great social life from the Wellesley Bubble.** It definitely warrants getting off campus, which is unlike some other colleges, but you get used to it because you have to in order to make it through four years."*

Q *"I like Wellesley because it has great academic programs. I could have done without the all-girl atmosphere, but I also think that adds something to the experience because you do establish solid friendships that will last a long time. I have friends that I won't speak to for a year and then we'll get together again and it will be like old times. **Wellesley is really great if you want to go to an all-girls, Ivy League-quality school.** Wellesley is expensive, but if you're looking to get into the top law school or grad school, it's worth it. There are certainly problems with the campus and administration, but I think that the turmoil helps set you up for the 'real' world."*

Q *"I love Wellesley. Sometimes I love to hate it, but, overall, **I made the right decision in coming here**. I have grown intellectually and personally, met amazing people, and my outlook on life has changed completely. I feel more confident, and I have developed a passion for learning that I hope I'll continue to foster throughout my life."*

The College Prowler Take
ON OVERALL EXPERIENCE

So, the nightlife stinks, it's too darn strict, and students constantly battle the fear of four years of celibacy. Hold on, why do we love this place again? Oh, right: the academics rock, it's possible to make amazing friends, the campus is gorgeous, and graduates wind up with a prestigious name on their diploma. Some students might feel they're missing out by coming to Wellesley, while others feel they're gaining incredible resources as far as support, critical thinking, and endurance are concerned. Whether or not they're happy about it, this latter group is right.

A community like Wellesley would be difficult to achieve in a coed environment, because living at Wellesley is like living with 2,300 sisters: you bitch, you fight, and you talk about sex in ridiculously frank ways. You hate and love each other at the same time. Wellesley is intense and bizarre, both restrictive and liberating. But, students learn to adapt, and they learn to overcome. Some might apply for transfer after their first year, but, if they choose to stay, they will soon grow to love beautiful, infuriating, rewarding Wellesley.

The Inside Scoop

The Lowdown
ON THE INSIDE SCOOP

Wellesley Slang:
Know the slang, know the school. The following is a list of things you really need to know before coming to Wellesley. The more of these words you know, the better off you'll be.

BDOC: Big Dyke On Campus, voted on each year at Dyke Ball; an on-campus celebrity who makes even the straight girls swoon

Community: An online forum with the stated purpose of keeping the college community in touch; in reality, tends to disintegrate into flamewars (see below).

CWIS: College-Wide Information System, Wellesley's intranet system

CWS: Center for Work and Service, career-counseling office

Davis Scholars: Non-traditional, aged students

Flamewar: An online argument, usually conducted on a public forum, which degenerates into insults

F@#k Truck: The Senate Bus, the $1.75 weekend campus-to-campus bus that shuttles between Wellesley, Harvard, and MIT

Gen Judic: General Judiciary, the student, faculty and staff enforcement body of the Honor Code

Hoopies: Students who work at The Hoop, an on-campus café

Honor Code: Wellesley's trust-based code of conduct

LUG/BUG: Lesbian/Bisexual Until Graduation, a term illustrating some students relaxed approach to sexuality

Prospies: Prospective students

Quad: The Hazard residence complex, including Beebe, Caz, Pom, and Shafer Halls

Quint: The Quad, with the addition of Munger Hall

Sci Center: Science Center

Shakes: Shakespeare Society's Tudor house, where performances are held

Stalkernet, Stalkhernet: Online photo directory

Swells/Hells/Wells: Varyingly affectionate nicknames for Wellesley College.

Tunnelling: Going on an expedition into the series of campus steam tunnels

The Ville: Town of Wellesley

Wendy Wellesley: Used by the administration as the Wellesley version of "Jane Doe," used by students as "That" girl

Wellesley Urban Legends

- Almost every dorm at Wellesley has its own ghost story, and every story is told several different ways. There are lots of suicides and boarded-up rooms, roommate murders, and mysterious footsteps.

- In Tower Court, students reportedly hear the elevator go up and down the shaft all night; that's the maid who fell down the shaft early in the twentieth century.

- Claflin Hall's living room is supposedly decorated with an "Alice in Wonderland" theme in honor of a founder's daughter, Alice, who was crushed by a beam during construction; it's said she plays there still.

- The Beebe ghost, who many students claim to have sensed, is a former house president who either killed herself or was taken by a mysterious woman in black.

- The academic building, Founders Hall, is purportedly haunted by a Revolutionary War messenger boy who was killed in the woods that the campus now covers; he is said to wander the halls with an undelivered note in his hand.

School Spirit

For every student that walks around campus with an "I'm applying for transfer" scowl pasted on her face, there are two or three that are "And on the Eighth Day, She Created Wellesley"-T-shirt-wearing, rabid Wellesley Women. First year, the doubters and the fans are about equal in number; after four years, sentimental seniors can't say enough about the bizarre institution that has become their home. Despite sticking us in the 'burbs, sequestering us from men, working us till our brains are sore and making us pay ridiculous amounts of money for the privilege, students wind up loving Wellesley.

Carillon

The carillon, a kind of organ that plays bells, has a place of honor at the top of the Galen-Stone tower. Whenever a member of the Guild of Carillonneurs has a few minutes to spare, the campus is treated to unearthly versions of "the Pink Panther," "America the Beautiful" (written by a Wellesley alum), or even "Happy Birthday."

Traditions

Wellesley has a long list of traditions, from the obscure to the popularly observed.

Class Colors

There are four class colors: red, green, purple, and yellow. The class of 2004 was red, class of 2005 is green, 2006 purple, and so on. It may seem a trivial detail, but it determines the color of class T-shirts (and, in the mid-twentieth century, the color of the class beanies), the color of balloons at key events, like Spring Open Campus and Commencement, and the color of streamers when the graduating class decorates the campus (see Graduating Class Decorating, below). After a few years, the sight of a certain colored balloon bobbing in the Lake Waban breeze has a Pavlovian effect, conjuring up pride and sentimentality.

Class Tree

On Family and Friends Weekend every fall, the sophomore class holds a ceremonial tree planting. The elected Tree Mistress and chosen assistants plant the tree using a ceremonial shovel used since 1879. A plaque commemorates the tree, and so it is possible to walk around campus and find the tree of every class year.

Finding a Job or Internship

Things I Wish I Knew Before Coming to Wellesley:
- FirstClass use starts out innocuously, but it becomes an addiction by your sophomore year.
- 8:30 classes seem a lot earlier in college than they did in high school.
- Boston winters are absolutely inhumane.
- You'll have to justify your decision to go to a women's college to almost everyone you meet.
- Even women who feel like they've got a pretty good social life will occasionally despair and question whether they're still "normal."

Tips to Succeed at Wellesley:
- Don't kill yourself over your studies or grades; do your work, but don't despair if you don't get it done.
- Don't take on too many activities right away—be sure you can handle the normal workload.
- Don't give into the pressure of doing recruiting or internships—not everyone is made for investment banking or building houses in third-world countries.
- Get to know your professors.
- Everything really will be all right, but you're going to have to adjust your idea of what "all right" really means.

The Lowdown
ON FINDING A JOB OR INTERNSHIP

Wellesley has tons of resources to get you jobs, internships, and fellowships. Get hooked up with the Center for Work and Service (CWS) as soon as you can, and take advantage of their programs and library. The CWS also holds on-campus job fairs and recruitment programs every year, so sign up for their weekly e-mail notice.

Advice

Take advantage of the CWS's Summer Stipend program, as it's an excellent way to get job experience prior to graduation. There are hundreds of stipends—usually $1,500 or $3,000—to fund your summer internship of choice. Think about it: you can get paid to do pretty much any work you want! There are also established internship programs in Asia, Costa Rica, and Africa, in a variety of fields.

It's also a good idea to get plugged in to the Alumnae Career Advisory Network, an online resource of 20,000 alums who are willing to share career information and advice. The Shadow Program allows students to trail alums to their jobs.

Career Center Resources & Services

Career exploration, individual counseling, assessment and guidance, career development workshops, resume workshops, library with career, internship, fellowship and grant resources, recruiting not-for-profit networking fairs, alumnae career advisory network, MonsterTrak, Internet job bulletin, graduate school advising, fellowship advising, lifelong career advising

The Best & Worst

Famous Wellesley Alumni:

- Harriet Stratemeyer Adams, '14, author of *Nancy Drew* series under the pen name Carolyn Keene

- Madeleine Albright, '59, former Secretary of State

- Nora Ephron, '62, screenwriter; producer

- Lynn Scherr, '63, print/broadcast journalist

- Jean Kilbourne, '64, feminist/activist/writer

- Cokie Roberts ,'64, broadcast journalist, television producer, writer

- Linda Wertheimer, '65, radio journalist

- Diane Sawyer, '67, journalist

- Hillary Rodham Clinton, '69, Senator, former First Lady

The Ten BEST Things About Wellesley:

1. Gorgeous campus and buildings
2. Excellent professors and small class sizes
3. All on-campus activities are free
4. FirstClass: facilitates academics and social life
5. The all-women thing: strong sense of community
6. Strong alumnae network
7. Diversity of students, classes, and activities
8. Location: urban, along beautiful Lake Waban
9. The Wellesley name and reputation
10. Strong traditions

The Ten WORST Things About Wellesley:

1. The weather
2. The all-women thing: missing men, isolation, etc.
3. Limited nightlife
4. Location: in a rich area, 40 minutes from the city
5. No independent living options
6. Political correctness
7. FirstClass: addictive time-suck
8. Very strict campus
9. The Wellesley name and reputation
10. Stress upon stress

Wheaton College

East Main Street, Norton, MA 02766
www.wheatoncollege.edu   (800) 394-6003

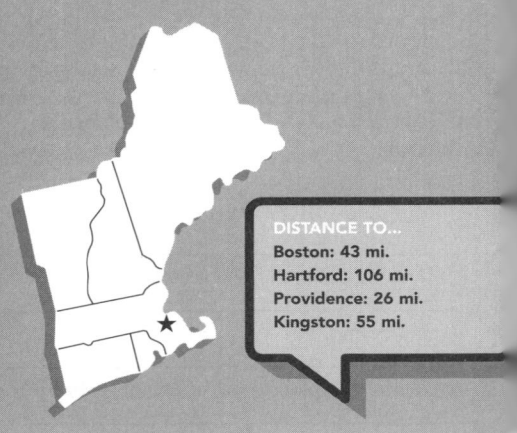

DISTANCE TO...
Boston: 43 mi.
Hartford: 106 mi.
Providence: 26 mi.
Kingston: 55 mi.

"Wheaton really focuses on personal growth rather than just the academic."

Table of Contents

Academics	941
Local Atmosphere	943
Safety & Security	944
Computers	946
Facilities	948
Campus Dining	949
Off-Campus Dining	951
Campus Housing	952
Off-Campus Housing	954
Diversity	955
Guys & Girls	956
Athletics	958
Greek Life	960
Drug Scene	961
Campus Strictness	963
Overall Experience	964
The Inside Scoop	966
Finding a Job or Internship	968
The Best & Worst	969

Total Enrollment:
2,354

Acceptance Rate:
43%

Tuition:
$30,580

Top 10% of High School Class:
43%

Average GPA:
3.5

SAT Range
Verbal	Math	Total
560 – 640	570 – 650	1130 – 1290

ACT Range
Verbal	Math	Total
N/A	N/A	25-28

Most Popular Majors:
19% Psychology
10% English Language and Literature
9% Economics
8% History
6% International Relations and Affairs

Students Also Applied To:*
Boston University, Clark University, Connecticut College, Mount Holyoke College, Skidmore College

College Prowler Report Card

Academics	B
Local Atmosphere	C-
Safety & Security	B-
Computers	B
Facilities	B
Campus Dining	B-
Off-Campus Dining	B-
Campus Housing	B+
Off-Campus Housing	D+
Diversity	D-
Guys	C+
Girls	B
Athletics	B+
Greek Life	N/A
Drug Scene	B-
Campus Strictness	B

Academics

Special Degree Options

Wheaton offers combined-degree programs with 12 other colleges and universities.

BA/MA Mass Communications/Communication Studies with Emerson, BA/BFA Studio Art with Museum of Fine Arts, BA/BS Engineering with George Washington University and WPI, BA/BEng with Dartmouth College, BA/MBA with Clark University and University of Rochester, BA/MA Religion with Andover Newton Theological BA/D, Optometry with New England College of Optometry

The Lowdown
ON ACADEMICS

Did You Know?
Most students at Wheaton register for their classes between 1:00 and 3:00—in the morning!

Degrees Awarded:
Bachelor

Full-time Faculty:
122

Faculty with Terminal Degree:
97%

Student-to-Faculty Ratio:
11:1

Average Course Load:
4 courses (16 credits)

AP Test Score Requirements:
Possible credit for scores of 4 or 5

IB Test Score Requirements:
Successful completion of an IB course can result in up to a year's worth of credit.

Best Places to Study:
Lyon's Den, The Dimple on a sunny day

Sample Academic Clubs:
Education Club, Anthropology Club, Art League, Spanish Club, Pre-Health Society, German Club

Students Speak Out
ON ACADEMICS

"Most of the teachers are cool. They thrive on providing individual attention, and that's an essential part of the environment because it's such a small school. It's great—a lot better than a lecture with a billion people in it."

Want to know which professors to take and which ones to avoid? Check out the College Prowler guide to Wheaton at *www.collegeprowler.com*.

> "**Critical thinking is very important to professors at Wheaton**, and though we may have our occasional disagreements, most of the faculty members I have encountered have all been extremely helpful in making sure their classes are fully understood by their students. In fact, at Wheaton, I have found that students frequently visit with their professors, even after classes have ended and new semesters have already begun."

> "In general, **Wheaton's faculty consists of dedicated professors who are more than willing and able to help their students**, not only with learning inside the classroom, but with support and ideas regarding outside projects, as well. Classes, as is the case in any learning environment, usually depend on your professor. Some professors just have a knack for making any subject interesting, and Wheaton has a lot of professors like that."

> "**The professors are one of the best things about Wheaton**. They take time to get to know who you are; they genuinely want you to develop as a student. There are some great professors at Wheaton who make lectures interesting, and the work is challenging, but still fascinating."

> "My classes are very interesting, even those that I wasn't originally interested in. **The teachers are young and innovative**, and their teaching styles make things interesting."

> "The teachers, from my experience, are a significant part of what makes Wheaton such a good school. With the exception of a few, **the majority of Wheaton professors I have had are extremely thought-provoking**, intellectual people who appear more concerned with teaching students how to think, more than simply what to think."

The College Prowler Take
ON ACADEMICS

One of the first things you will notice as a freshman is how excited and dedicated most of the students are about being at Wheaton. People are seriously interested in what they are learning, which is a big change from high school. There are some really brilliant people at Wheaton. Of course, there are also a lot of people that just party a lot. Basically, you can avoid doing too much work, if you want to, your first couple of years. But, due to the small class sizes, especially at the upper level, you have to stay on top of your work, and professors expect a lot from you.

The small class sizes and the personal attention from professors are the main reasons most prospective students set their sights on Wheaton. The professors are truly excellent; they make themselves incredibly available inside and outside of the classroom, and are always willing to give you extra help if you need it. But, what is most striking about the faculty at Wheaton is how much they are willing to help you determine your future after Wheaton, which is, after all, the point of attending college. Overall, the academics are very strong, particularly if you make the effort to make the most of all your resources.

The College Prowler™ Grade on
Academics: B

A high Academics grade generally indicates that professors are knowledgeable, accessible, and genuinely interested in their students' welfare. Other determining factors include class size, how well professors communicate, and whether or not classes are engaging.

Local Atmosphere

Students Speak Out
ON LOCAL ATMOSPHERE

"**Norton sucks. There's little to do here, but Providence and Boston are close and public transportation is easily accessible.**"

Q "**Norton is the epitome of a small town**. We have very little to do, aside from a CVS, many Chinese restaurants, a pizza place, and a few local bars. Norton locals don't appear to like us or hate us—we just coexist. Wheaton College is Norton, Massachusetts, and the locals know that. Aside from that, Norton is peaceful, and it is kind of nice to be close to the city, but in your own little bubble, sheltered from the scary, outside world. I feel like I get more done that way. There are things like a historical society and such in Norton, but I have not been to any of them. I find that anything fun I want to do is in North Attleboro, where the mall is, or in Boston or Providence."

Q "Norton is a town where **there isn't much to do**. Wheaton seems to be the center of this small town, and trips to CVS, Roche Brothers, Dunkin' Donuts, and Massive Video are about as exciting as Norton gets."

Q "**Norton sucks**. There's little to do here, but Providence and Boston are close, and public transportation is easily accessible. I think that the people of Norton don't like to consider it a college town, because it's so small. They don't really cater much to students, as in things to do and nightlife, but it's cool because the train station isn't far away, and you can go to Boston or Providence in less than an hour."

Q "**Norton, unfortunately, is probably the biggest downfall of Wheaton**. Aside from the local drug store, there is little in the town that is worthy of leaving campus for. Not too far away, however, are the cities of Providence and Boston. If students are willing to do a little bit of driving, there is plenty within a half-hour of travel time to make for quality weekend entertainment. But, as far as the town itself goes, a big thumbs down would probably be a good judgment of the locals and their own forms of entertainment."

The Lowdown
ON LOCAL ATMOSPHERE

Region:
Northeast

City, State:
Norton, Massachusetts

Setting:
Small town (Boonies)

Distance from Boston:
40 minutes

Distance from Providence:
20 minutes

Points of Interest:
The Museum of Fine Arts, Boston Commons, the Science Museum, The Patriot's Stadium in Foxboro, The Tweeter Center, Lupo's at the Strand, Harvard Square, Haymarket, Fenway Park, the Swan Boats in the Public Garden

Major Sports Teams:
The Red Sox (MLBl), The Patriots (NFL)
The Celtics (NBA), The Bruins (NHL)

City Websites:
www.nortonma.org,
www.topix.net/city/norton-ma

💬 "**Norton is a special place with special people in it.** The town has no more to offer than a CVS in close proximity, and a grocery store, which isn't too far if you have a car. Although, being equidistant from both Boston and Providence has its definite perks!"

The College Prowler Take
ON SAFETY & SECURITY

Norton isn't a bustling metropolis, but if you choose Wheaton, that's probably not what you're looking for, anyway. Luckily, we are so close to Boston and Providence that it isn't really an issue. There aren't any other universities in the immediate area, but Boston has more colleges and universities than any other city in the country, which makes for a lot of activity just a short ride away. Although people may complain about Norton and how small it is, this does have at least one benefit: it makes Wheaton a much more close-knit community, since people spend a lot more time on campus.

Safety & Security

The Lowdown
ON SAFETY & SECURITY

Number of Wheaton Police (public safety):
19

Phone:
(508) 286-8213

Health Center Office Hours
The Norton Medical Center works in conjunction with Wheaton College. Since Norton Medical also serves the surrounding area, Wheaton students can only go to the Health Center for free during certain hours. If these hours do not fit into your schedule or are booked, you can go at another time, but you or your insurance will have to pay.

The Wheaton Hours are as follows:
Monday, 1:30 p.m. - 4:30 p.m.
Tuesday, 1:30 p.m. - 4:30 p.m.
Wednesday, 1:30 p.m. - 4:30 p.m.
Thursday, 12:30 p.m. - 3:30 p.m.
Friday, 11 a.m. - 12 p.m. and 1 p.m. - 3 p.m.

Safety Services
(RAD) Rape Defense classes, Shuttle/Escort, Emergency Phones

www.wheatoncollege.edu/PublicSafety/

The College Prowler™ Grade on
Local Atmosphere: C-

A high Local Atmosphere grade indicates that the area surrounding campus is safe and scenic. Other factors include nearby attractions, proximity to other schools, and the town's attitude toward students.

Did You Know?

After participating in the RAD self-defense course for 20 dollars, you can take the class again later in your life as a refresher or go on to Advanced RAD for free, anywhere in the country that it is offered.

Students Speak Out
ON SAFETY & SECURITY

"A few officers are very understanding and chill, but others suck. The new alcohol policy sucks and is the source of most of the problems with Public Safety."

"**Public Safety is actually pretty lax, despite student complaints**. They are not always reliable when needed, but they do offer help through programs, such as their RAD rape defense course. Generally, they are pretty chill; if you have alcohol they ask you to pour it out, unless you are being belligerent, and that's when you will get written up. They aren't out to get you. They just make sure you aren't being an idiot, or endangering yourself or others, which I suppose is their job, so it's fine. You can avoid them easily just by turning down the music a little or remembering to close your shades if you are on a roadside room."

"**Security is tight enough for you to feel safe walking alone on campus**, although it seems Wheaton might be a little behind with dorm security technology, since we still use keys to get into each dorm. The quaintness of Norton definitely makes you feel safe in the town and on campus, and there're always people out and about, and considering Wheaton's size, it's probably someone you know."

"**There are call-boxes all over campus**, and Public Safety will pick you up or escort you if you don't feel safe, but I have heard of officers being bothered by it. Security can be tough or lax at times; it all depends on the officer and the situation."

"Public Safety patrols on a regular basis. It's an open campus, so **anyone can walk around**, but it's in a quiet town, so it never feels unsafe. If you get locked out of your room, however, you might have to wait all day for Public Safety to come let you in."

"Public Safety does a great job of keeping the students on campus safe. We have great events on campus, like dances and Spring Weekend, and they're always looking out for us, but not pushing people around. Also, if you come home late and have to park far away from your dorm, **call them on the call-box and they'll come give you a ride**. It's a safety precaution, and it makes a lot of us feel good knowing that we don't have to walk across dark areas alone really late at night."

The College Prowler Take
ON SAFETY & SECURITY

Students feel very safe on campus. They know how seriously the Public Safety department takes its job, and how much the officers genuinely care for the safety of the students. The officers are not there to bust you for things without good reason; they are there to keep you out of harm's way, and that is a reassuring feeling. Wheaton does, however, lack some of the newer technological security aspects that are present at other schools. For instance, we still use keys to get into our dorms rather than having the doors unlocked by swiping our ID cards—only one dorm on campus has this technology. (How twentieth-century!) Also, many of the doors still do not have alarms on them, so they are left propped for days on end so anyone could walk in.

Computers

The Lowdown
ON COMPUTERS

The College Prowler™ Grade on
Safety & Security: B-

A high grade in Safety & Security means that students generally feel safe, campus police are visible, blue-light phones and escort services are readily available, and safety precautions are not overly necessary.

High-Speed Network?
Yes

Wireless Network?
In the library, Beard Hall, Knapton Hall, and KACC

Number of Labs:
Two public labs, 35 other labs for students when not being used for class

Numbers of Computers:
Approximately 1,000

24-Hour Labs:
No, library and computer center open until 2 a.m.

Charge to Print?
No

Operating Systems:
Windows 98 and XP, Mac OS 9 and OS X

Did You Know?

The Computer Center gets unnaturally cold at all times of the year, so bundle up before you go do homework!

"Aside from the occasional virus, **computing at Wheaton is very easy**. The computer center has up-to-date computers and software, the network is fast and easy to hook into, and the help desk is, from my experience, very helpful. I would suggest bringing a computer, merely because the computers in the library and computer center are often in use, especially during finals, but it's far from a necessity."

Students Speak Out
ON COMPUTERS

The College Prowler Take
ON COMPUTERS

"It seems like the computer systems are always having failures or virus alerts. I think the network is generally fast, except when it needs to be shut down for repairs, which seems to be more often than it should."

"You should bring your own computer. There are several computer labs all over campus, but you won't want to walk to certain places for a computer, and **it is just easier to have one**. You don't need one, but it helps. If you can't afford one, the school definitely won't help you with that."

"I have honestly only visited the computer center once or twice, and that was for an errand my boss sent me to do. Generally, I think **it's a good idea to bring your own computer** to school. The computers in the library are a nice alternative to working in your room, but they're usually always taken, and I find it hard to get work done there."

"**Computers in the library are normally taken**, even more so around midterms and finals time. There are labs in the Science Center that aren't full, usually. It is definitely convenient to have your own computer, but you can get your work done without one."

Wheaton does a good job of keeping up with the times in terms of computers and technology, especially for a small campus, and it is a heavenly change to go back to school after being home all summer with just dial-up. Almost every aspect of college life these days involves computers—everything from class registration, Blackboard involvement with classes, and social life. Overall, Wheaton is appropriately wired for its liberal arts population, and having your own computer would simply be much more convenient, since most classes require you to log into Blackboard very often for class participation and assignment updates. And then, of course, there is the very important matter of keeping in touch with all of your new acquaintances.

The College Prowler™ Grade on
Computers: B

A high grade in Computers designates that computer labs are available, the computer network is easily accessible, and the campus' computing technology is up-to-date.

Facilities

Favorite Things to Do
On the weekends, Wheaton usually has dances in Balfour-Hood, or other planned events, sometimes put on by different clubs. If you're looking to catch some live music, bands frequently visit the Loft throughout the week. The Lyon's Den is a down-to-earth, little coffee shop that has a cyber café and also features live music.

The Lowdown
ON FACILITIES

Students Speak Out
ON FACILITIES

Student Center:
Balfour-Hood

Athletic Center:
Haas Athletic Center, Fitness Center

Libraries:
Madeleine Clark Wallace Library

Popular Places to Chill:
The Loft, The Lyon's Den, Balfour Cafe

Movie Theatre on Campus?
No, but movies are shown in Hindle Auditorium each weekend.

Bowling on Campus?
No

Bar on Campus?
The Loft serves a few different types of beer.

Coffeehouse on Campus?
The Lyon's Den

"A few classroom buildings have been remodeled and are very nice. I've heard complaints about the Science Center, though."

Q "**We definitely could use some more cool things for students**. The student center is all right but it only provides a place to get your mail, a small café, and a gym. The gym is okay, but the equipment was handed down from another college who was getting rid of it, so it could be better for sure. The Haas Athletic Center is awesome and was one of the reasons I came here. I was a huge track person, and the track and other equipment for the sports teams is up to par. That is one reason we have national track champions!"

Q "**Balfour, the student center, is really nice**. After three years at Wheaton, I consider it the trademark! That's where everything is located—Student Life, mail facilities, the gym, the dance studio, the radio station, the café, and, best of all, the Loft. It's pretty much the center of campus, because there are always things going on there!"

Q "Wheaton facilities are, for the most part, up to date and maintained well. Though honestly **there's nothing special about most of it**. And what's a student center? Do we even have one of those?"

Q "The majority of facilities on campus are very nice. The computer center is constantly updating its **arsenal of machines and software**, giving students the chance to use all the latest programs, ranging from those necessary for music making, film editing, and Web page building. The athletic department at Wheaton is also well-funded, and this is apparent in taking just a small walk through the Haas Athletic Center, which houses a track, an Olympic-sized pool, and indoor tennis courts, among other things."

Q "The student center is okay. **There's a crappy bar called The Loft that robs you blind**, a gym, game room, and a radio station. The atmosphere blows, but it serves its purpose."

Campus Dining

The College Prowler Take
ON FACILITIES

In the recent years, major renovations have been undertaken at Wheaton. The one place that many students complain about, the Science Center, with its rumored high mercury levels in the air, recently updated their facili a multi-million dollar overhaul—in fact, a completely new Science Center will be built. But until then, the Science Center at Wheaton is adequate, and has a lot of state-of-the-art technology, like the ICUC lab. Most of the buildings are modern, and those that aren't have that old-brick-and-ivy charm. And even the old buildings have computers and projectors in most of the classrooms; so, even though the exterior may seem old-fashioned, the interior is fully updated.

The Lowdown
ON CAMPUS DINING

Freshman Meal Plan Requirement?
Yes, it is required all four years.

Meal Plan Average Cost:
$3,580

24-Hour On-Campus Eating?
No

Student Favorites:
The Loft

Did You Know?

Several times a semester, breakfast is served at midnight in one of the dining halls.

The College Prowler™ Grade on
Facilities: B

A high Facilities grade indicates that the campus is aesthetically pleasing and well-maintained; facilities are state-of-the-art, and libraries are exceptional. Other determining factors include the quality of both athletic and student centers and an abundance of things to do on campus.

Students Speak Out
ON CAMPUS DINING

The College Prowler Take
ON CAMPUS DINING

{ "The food sucks, like most schools. The chicken is gristle-laden, and much of the main course is unidentifiable. But, sometimes, they surprise us with something good."

Q "As a freshman, Chase is better to go to because you have much more choices, it's probably closer to where you are living, and it is much more social. **Emerson is much more 'classy,' but there's much less choice in food**. We call Chase a 'black hole' because you sit there chatting for hours, which can be great, but not good if you have tons of work to do. The Café is great, too; they make yummy sandwiches that are expensive but good, and they have lunch specials that are affordable."

Q "The Loft is, by far, the best. **The popcorn chicken and smoothies are heavenly**. It is a great reward after a challenging week, or day, or whenever you just need to have some popcorn chicken. I highly recommend that, but go in moderation because you will find yourself adding more and more money onto your card before you know it. Chicken addictions can be expensive, keep that in mind."

Q "Well, the pre-made food in the dining halls is not always the best, but there are always other alternatives. We have the Lyon's Den, which is on the edge of campus. **It's our own cute little coffee place**. It's great, a quiet place to come and study while downing one caffeinated beverage after another."

Q "The food in the dining halls is not bad, although **by the end of the year it gets very tiresome**. The Loft is a place on campus that opens at 9 p.m. and has great popcorn chicken, but it is kind of expensive."

Q "**The dining halls aren't great**. A safe bet, on a night where you can't find anything good, is a bagel. In Chase the sauté is good, but don't overdo it. It gets old fast. The food is better at Emerson, and they have a nice salad bar."

No matter where you go, students will complain about the food in dining halls. This is especially true at Wheaton, just because there aren't many choices. There are two dining halls on campus: Emerson is located on Upper Campus and is smaller and somewhat fancier, while Chase is the dining hall for Lower Campus and tends to have more selection, though sometimes at the cost of quality. Other than that, there is The Café, which serves sandwiches and other snack items, and The Loft, which is open at night and has a variety of incredibly unhealthy food—the main staple of college life. What irks students the most is that they are required to be on the meal plan for all four years at Wheaton. The meal plan is all-you-can-eat style, but some slim girls complain that they don't eat nearly as much as the baseball players, so they shouldn't be charged as much. One thing is for sure, you will never go hungry at Wheaton, despite the quality at times.

The College Prowler™ Grade on
Campus Dining: B-

Our grade on Campus Dining addresses the quality of both school-owned dining halls and independent on-campus restaurants as well as the price, availability, and variety of food.

Off-Campus Dining

FUN FACTS

Jimmy's Pub is decorated with brewery artifacts, and all beverages are served in pint glasses. They have every beer imaginable.

There are hundreds of restaurants in Boston and Providence just half an hour away.

Students Speak Out
ON OFF-CAMPUS DINING

The Lowdown
ON OFF-CAMPUS DINING

"There are a few pizza places and Chinese restaurants within walking distance that deliver and have dine-in. Jeffrey's is good, but it takes forever to get your food."

Best Pizza:
Jeffrey's

Best Chinese:
Great Woods Mandarin

Best Breakfast:
The Old Colony Creamery

Best Wings:
Wendell's

Best Healthy:
Jimmy's Pub

Best Place to Take Your Parents:
Water's Edge Restaurant & Lil Pub

Late-Night, Half-Price Food Specials:
None

24-Hour Eating:
Cumberland Farms

Student Favorites:
Great Woods Mandarin, Jeffrey's, Jimmy's Pub

"Despite how unexciting the town of Norton is, **Wheaton is actually within close driving distance to a few good restaurants**. Some student favorites include Bertucci's, various Asian restaurants, and a small-town diner called Pattie's Place."

"They are okay, I suppose. **Norton has very little to offer besides Subway**, Chinese, and a pizza place. But, Attleboro and Providence have great places. In Providence, there are places like Antonio's Pizza, where you can get a pizza with anything you could imagine on it. There's also and T**he Cheesecake Factory, which is the most amazing place ever in the world to eat**. It is pricey, but for a special occasion it is really fun and delicious."

"There are a couple places in Norton to eat, but when I say a couple, I really mean a couple. There's a great pizza place called Jeffrey's, which is only a two- or three-minute walk from campus. But if it's not your taste, **Domino's delivers**! There's a tasty Chinese buffet right down the street in Great Woods Plaza called Great Woods Mandarin; the prices are great, and the food is fantastic. If you're going for something a little less fast-foodsy, try the Water's Edge. If you have the means to travel a little further, Attleboro has a few good restaurants—mostly chains."

> "Norton's restaurant reputation is not really the most renowned in all of New England. If you want a quick pizza, or some Chinese, then you've come to the right place. Aside from that, **North Attleboro has all the typical chain restaurants**, as do a few other neighboring towns. You can always trek out to Providence or Boston for a meal in the city."

The College Prowler Take
ON OFF-CAMPUS DINING

For such a small town, Norton does have its fair share of dining opportunities, probably attracted here because of the college itself. The pizza, Chinese, and other fast types of food are pretty good. The surrounding area is severely lacking in healthy options. If you are willing to drive off campus to an actual restaurant and spend a little more money, you can manage to find something healthier. There is no way a small town like Norton can compete with a larger city in terms of off-campus food, but, luckily, Wheaton is between two major cities, so plenty of good dining can be found there. But, in terms of nearby options, expect to find pizza, Chinese, or pizza.

The College Prowler™ Grade on
Off-Campus Dining: B-

A high Off-Campus Dining grade implies that off-campus restaurants are affordable, accessible, and worth visiting. Other factors include the variety of cuisine and the availability of alternative options (vegetarian, vegan, Kosher, etc.).

Campus Housing

The Lowdown
ON CAMPUS HOUSING

Undergrads on Campus:
99%

Number of Dormitories: 16

Number of Campus-Owned Houses: 10

Room Types:
Single, double, triple, quad, suite

Bed Type:
Twin extra-long (39"x 80"); some lofts, some bunk-beds

Available for Rent:
Nothing

Cleaning Service?
Yes, in public areas. Community bathrooms are cleaned by staff several times a week.

You Get:
Bed, desk and chair, bookshelf (in some rooms), closet or wardrobe, dresser, Ethernet, free campus and local phone calls

Also Available:
Special-interest housing

Did You Know?
All dorms on campus have recently been made smoke-free.

"All of the dorms are nice, for the most part, but it depends on what you're looking for in a living environment. Besides, the home away from home is what you make it, and the people you live with have a big impact on whether it's a pleasant living environment or not."

Students Speak Out
ON CAMPUS HOUSING

The College Prowler Take
ON CAMPUS HOUSING

"The dorms on Lower Campus are ugly and industrial, but they always have singles. The new dorms are nice, but you have to apply for them."

"**Upper Campus is much more desirable than Lower Campus**, but sadly, Lower Campus is where you will be freshman and definitely sophomore year. Meadows is the 'ghetto' of Wheaton. Try to avoid that dorm if you can, but it is hard."

"**Live on Lower Campus for freshman and sophomore year**. The rooms are smaller and not as nice, but the social atmosphere is much more inviting and friendly. Upper Campus is all seniors in singles who won't talk to you. Lower Campus is fun."

"Dorm rooms on Lower Campus don't have much to offer **when you first move into your stark, barren prison cell**. As far as I know, none of the rooms even have carpeting. But, if you get your creative juices flowing, it's easy enough to give your room some character and make it more livable. Most definitely, the difference between Upper and Lower Campus is what you make it."

"The rooms aren't great on Lower Campus, but the people are. **Everyone leaves their doors open and is friendly**. There are always parties going on and everyone hangs out together. I would recommend Meadows to freshman and sophomores, but Upper Campus is better for juniors and seniors who already have their group of friends."

Well, to understand the living situation at Wheaton, you should first know about the Upper Campus versus Lower Campus debate. There is, and probably always will be (even with the recent refurbishing of Lower Campus), a common belief that Upper Campus is by far the more desirable place to live. Upper Campus is the oldest and prettiest portion of campus, and includes The Dimple—a large grassy lawn with huge, beautiful elm trees. The Dimple is the site of much sunbathing and Frisbee in the early fall and spring, and mattress sledding in the winter when it snows, so proximity to The Dimple is highly-prized. However, you will be relegated to Lower Campus as a freshman and sophomore—but don't despair! This is the more social of the two halves of campus, and you'll enjoy getting to know all your classmates up close and personal. In fact, the cramped quarters will give you something to bond over.

The College Prowler™ Grade on
Campus Housing: B+

A high Campus Housing grade indicates that dorms are clean, well-maintained, and spacious. Other determining factors include variety of dorms, proximity to classes, and social atmosphere.

Off-Campus Housing

The Lowdown
ON OFF-CAMPUS HOUSING

Undergrads in Off-Campus Housing:
5%

Popular Areas:
Mansfield, Norton

Students Speak Out
ON OFF-CAMPUS HOUSING

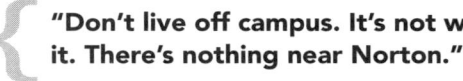

"Don't live off campus. It's not worth it. There's nothing near Norton."

Q "**Housing off campus isn't very convenient**, but housing on campus is guaranteed for all four years."

Q "Student Life doesn't do more than they're obligated to. They don't make it hard, but they also don't accommodate you as much as people living on campus. **You pretty much have to do it all on your own** and just tell them that you're not going to be on campus anymore, but I think it is a good thing to learn how to find an apartment, like many other students at other schools have to do."

Q "**It has been different living off campus**. I'm much less in touch with on-campus social events, but if you enjoy the time spent with the person (or people) you're living with off campus, it's worth it."

Q "It was not hard to find housing here in the apartment complex that I live in, but the rest of Norton is not so easy. **Once most of the landlords found out that we are college kids, they wanted nothing to do with us**. Wheaton offered no help in finding an apartment."

The College Prowler Take
ON OFF-CAMPUS HOUSING

Off-campus housing is not an easy thing to come by at Wheaton, mostly because the college makes it this way. On-campus housing is required for all four years, and if you want to live off campus, you have to go through a petition process and state why you want to leave. Despite being confined to just one room on campus, rather than having a whole apartment to call one's own, the majority of people decide to live on campus because of the feeling of community. You meet so many more people than you would if you lived elsewhere, separated from the campus. This creates a true social and learning environment—something that a smaller school like Wheaton can truly develop, unlike a larger school in a city.

The College Prowler™ Grade on
Off-Campus Housing: D+

A high grade in Off-Campus Housing indicates that apartments are of high quality, close to campus, affordable, and easy to secure.

Diversity

Political Activity
The majority of the population at Wheaton is liberal and accepting, both politically and socially. For the most part, though, students are fairly uninvolved and seem to be confined within the "Wheaton Bubble," where not much news of the outside world gets in.

Gay Tolerance
The campus is accepting of its gay students, and there are groups that organize events on campus every now and then to raise awareness.

Economic Status
Students come from all different backgrounds at Wheaton. There are a lot of students that can't afford the outrageous tuition, but there are also those who can.

The Lowdown
ON DIVERSITY

African American: 2%

Asian American: 7%

Hispanic: 2%

Native American: 0%

White: 88%

International: 1%

Out-of-State: 69%

Minority Clubs
Unity (Black Students Association)
MESA (Middle Eastern Students Association)
ASA (Asian Students Association)

Most Popular Religions
Most religious activity takes place off campus, and not much is seen on or around campus.

Students Speak Out
ON DIVERSITY

"**It can be difficult to be in a situation where you are the only minority student in the class and a sensitive subject comes up. We have all been there, but Wheaton embraces students of all races and nationalities.**"

"The campus is not that diverse, but **Wheaton is trying**. But, there are still very few ethnic people on campus."

"To be honest, Wheaton is not diverse at all. **There are a few minority organizations on campus**, but the students involved have a tendency to stick with one another, as do the white students, not allowing for much interracial mingling. Wheaton is not a school that I have ever found to be, in the least, racist or homophobic, but it's just difficult to get white and black students, for example, going to the same parties."

"Wheaton is definitely still a **predominantly white, upper-middle-class, private college**. It's also mostly girls, which is to be expected from Wheaton's semi-recent history of being an all-girls college. But as the years go by, Wheaton appears to be seeing more and more diversity among entering classes."

> "**It is not diverse at all**. There are clubs that include students from urban communities. Some of the classes try to promote diversity, but nothing has been too successful."

> "The school is located in a small town in New England, and the majority of the campus population is from New England, itself, which **isn't diverse to begin with**."

The College Prowler Take
ON GUYS & GIRLS

Wheaton tries hard and boasts about its diversity and international population, but, in reality, there is a very long way to go. Wheaton has a small international population, though they are trying hard to attract more students from around the world. Minority students are few and far between, so they tend to stick together in a group, which doesn't allow for as much interaction between all the various students as there should be. Despite their small numbers, though, Wheaton's minority and international students make their presence known through clubs, organizations, and events.

The College Prowler™ Grade on
Diversity: D-

A high grade in Diversity indicates that ethnic minorities and international students have a notable presence on campus and that students of different economic backgrounds, religious beliefs, and sexual preferences are well-represented.

Guys & Girls

The Lowdown
ON GUYS & GIRLS

Women Undergrads: 64%

Men Undergrads: 36%

Birth Control Available?
Yes. Prescriptions can be written at Norton Medical Center, but are filled at local drug stores. Norton Med offers help giving the shot and can write prescriptions for pills and patches.

Hookups or Relationships?
Girls far outnumber guys at Wheaton, so this drives many of the girls to off-campus relationships, if they can find one. Otherwise, the nights at Wheaton are filled with random, and not-so-random, hookups, but they rarely result in a solid relationship. Don't expect to find the love of your life at Wheaton; the odds just aren't in your favor.

Dress Code
There is a wide range of apparel on the Wheaton campus, ranging from those that are dedicated to their pajamas, to those that won't leave their rooms without a perfectly-crafted ensemble. Most Wheaties pride themselves on their appearance, in one way or another, whether it is in terms of hemp and back-to-the-earth clothes, or Abercrombie.

Students Speak Out
ON GUYS & GIRLS

The College Prowler Take
ON GUYS & GIRLS

"Most of the people I know are attractive. I have had my share of crushes around campus, so yeah, a lot of the guys are pretty hot."

"There are no guys here. I am a biology major and in most of my classes there have been one, or maybe two, guys. **There are a few hot guys, but they are either whores or taken by an equally cute girl**. Life is tough at Wheaton as a girl because there are a lot of rich, pretty girls and weird boys, with only a cute boy here and there."

"You know, one thing I have definitely noticed about Wheaton is the fact that **there are no goblins**. Even the most unattractive Wheaton students have a tendency to be far more attractive than some people I have seen at other colleges. I know this probably sounds like the most superficial statement ever, but it's just a truthful observation. Not all Wheaton students may be models, but our campus is one that is undeniably attractive, well-dressed, and concerned with personal appearance."

"**Currently, the ratio of men to women is 36 percent to 64 percent**, which has gotten smaller since my arrival—it used to be 40 percent to 60 percent. Many of the girls are high-maintenance, and the decent guys are taken. The population isn't exceptionally good-looking."

"**Most of the girls aren't too hot**, nor are most of the guys. The dumbest thing I've seen is when people get dressed up for campus parties, like I didn't see them in the dining hall that morning in their pajamas."

"**There is a range, just like anywhere else**. There are some dorky guys and some drop-dead gorgeous ones, and some ones in the middle, but most are pretty cute."

The ratio of boys to girls is horribly skewed at Wheaton, likely some sort of lingering malady from the days when Wheaton was an all-girls school. In any case, it does nothing but cause a lot of stress in the life of the busy female college student here, since much time is spent agonizing over the dearth of even slightly acceptable mates. Basically, there are way too many girls looking for a relationship, and a much smaller population of boys relishing their freedom to hook-up as they please—or, at least, so they hope. In any event, the disproportionate ratio certainly favors the boys, who have their pick of numerous, somewhat disheartened, girls.

The College Prowler™ Grade on
Guys: C+

A high grade for Guys indicates that the male population on campus is attractive, smart, friendly, and engaging, and that the school has a decent ratio of guys to girls.

The College Prowler™ Grade on
Girls: B

A high grade for Girls not only implies that the women on campus are attractive, smart, friendly, and engaging, but also that there is a fair ratio of girls to guys.

Athletics

Getting Tickets
No tickets needed.

Fields
Mirrione Stadium and Keefe Field, softball field, Sidell Stadium, outdoor tennis complex

Athletic Division:
Division III

Conference:
NCAA

Most Popular Sports:
Baseball, track, synchronized swimming

Overlooked Teams:
Basketball, swimming

School Mascot:
Lyon

The Lowdown
ON ATHLETICS

Men's Varsity Teams:
Lacrosse
Baseball
Soccer
Swimming/Diving
Cross Country
Track
Tennis
Basketball
Indoor Track & Field
Outdoor Track & Field

Women's Varsity Teams:
Field hockey
Lacrosse
Softball
Soccer
Swimming/Diving
Cross Country
Indoor Track & Field
Outdoor Track & Field
Tennis
Basketball
Synchronized Swimming
Volleyball

Students Speak Out
ON ATHLETICS

"Intramural sports are bigger than varsity sports, although soccer here is a huge deal."

COLLEGE PROWLER™

Need help choosing a sport? For a detailed listing of all sports teams on campus, check out the College Prowler book on Wheaton available at *www.collegeprowler.com*.

Q "**The track, basketball, soccer, and baseball teams are big**, and we also have a great synchronized swimming team. I have been to a few games, and school spirit is insane—we have a great Lyon as our mascot."

Q "**Sports people are kind of cliquey**, but they aren't considered gods or anything. Wheaton is very good in men's and women's soccer, and it's also known for synchronized swimming. There are intramural sports, but I don't know much about those."

Q "**A lot of people are into sports**, but the games are not a big thing on campus."

Q "The sports we have are **moderately big**. We have basketball, lacrosse, rugby, soccer, baseball, swimming, and others. I try not to follow sports, but despite my efforts, news of a big victory seems to reach me. We're proud of our athletes, but it's not like high school."

Q "I don't know too much about the sports programs at Wheaton, aside from seeing my friends devote an extremely large amount of their time to practice, games, and exercising. I have a friend on the softball team who likened being on a Wheaton sports team to joining a cult. According to her, **the devotion it takes is serious** and not for anyone who's not fully committed to being an excellent athlete."

The College Prowler Take
ON ATHLETICS

Wheaton allows you to be as involved or distanced from athletics as you want to be. The sports teams at Wheaton aren't an overwhelming presence, but their actions are still widely known and respected on campus. Sports teams are known to house many of the hotties on campus, as well as some dedicated party animals. If you are thinking about getting involved in any of the teams on campus, make sure you are ready to devote ridiculous amounts of time and wake up at hours that none of the rest of the campus ever sees while sober.

The College Prowler™ Grade on
Athletics: B+

A high grade in Athletics indicates that students have school spirit, that sports programs are respected, that games are well-attended, and that intramurals are a prominent part of student life.

Greek Life

The Lowdown
ON GREEK LIFE

What Greek Life?
Wheaton, like many small liberal arts colleges, doesn't have any fraternities or sororities on campus. In fact, when you come to Wheaton as a freshman, you must sign an "anti-hazing" contract, stating that you won't make people do any stunts typical of entering a fraternity. But, this doesn't stop many clubs and sports teams from taking on the roll of supplying parties for the campus.

Did You Know?
Wheaton's all-male a cappella group—The Gentleman Callers—have been referred to as one of Wheaton's fraternities. They host some of the best parties on campus in the past.

Sports teams sometimes take on the roll of fraternities, particularly the baseball team in recent years.

Students Speak Out
ON GREEK LIFE

"What Greek life?! We don't have frats or sororities on our campus!"

"There isn't any, thank God! **There are enough sorority-like girls anyway**; it would be horrible if there was a place where they could all congregate and form packs."

"The closest thing we have to Greek is food **served at the salad bar**."

"There isn't any, and **I don't know if there ever has been**. I don't know if there has been any pressure on the school to have Greek life."

"No fraternities, no sororities—technically—and **thank God**."

"I don't know, **I've hardly heard of anyone talking about Greek life** on campus."

The College Prowler Take
ON DRUG SCENE

Wheaton doesn't have any Greek life on campus, and, for the most part, students don't really miss it. Sure, huge scandalous parties aren't as likely to take place, but it eliminates the exclusivity that fraternities bring with them and allows for more open social interaction between all the students. It's never been an issue, and likely never will be, because Wheaton students find plenty of other ways to entertain themselves.

Drug Scene

The Lowdown
ON DRUG SCENE

Most Prevalent Drugs on Campus:
Alcohol, marijuana, caffeine, Ritalin, Adderall

Liquor-Related Referrals:
57

Liquor-Related Arrests:
0

Drug-Related Referrals:
10

Drug-Related Arrests:
0

The College Prowler™ Grade on
Greek Life: N/A

A high grade in Greek Life indicates that sororities and fraternities are not only present, but also active on campus. Other determining factors include the variety of houses available and the respect the Greek community receives from the rest of the campus.

Drug Counseling Programs
The Counseling Center: 42 Howard Street; (508) 286-3905; Monday-Friday, 3:30 a.m.- 4:30 p.m.

 ## Students Speak Out
ON DRUG SCENE

 ## The College Prowler Take
ON DRUG SCENE

{ "It's pretty chill. There isn't all that much drug use, and people that do use drugs don't make a huge deal out of it or pressure anyone to join them."

Q "Yeah, **it's something that isn't a huge problem**, but like anywhere, there will be the occasional report of a marijuana smell. Public safety tries as hard as they can to crack down on that sort of thing, and I feel happy and safe saying that it's not something you hear about as an everyday problem on campus. The drug problems that we have are about individual people who choose that lifestyle, and Wheaton doesn't welcome it. It's as simple as that."

Q "**I know many people on campus who smoke marijuana regularly**, but none who abuse it to the point of letting it interfere with their grades or extracurricular activities. I hate to keep comparing Wheaton to other schools, but at many other ones I have visited, such as the University of Massachusetts–Amherst, the smell of pot is practically commonplace on campus. The majority of pot-smoking, Wheaton students I know, however, use it for recreation when time and work allow."

Q "There's a lot of pot. **You can get other stuff if you want**, but it's not in your face."

Q "**It's there if you want it**. Suburban and middle-class kids seem to take more prescription drugs. I've noticed those coming from lower income brackets usually smoke weed if they do anything, but many people don't do it anything at all."

Q "**There's going to be a subculture anywhere you go**, but it's still your choice whether you get involved in it or not."

Like any college campus, drugs are going to be there whether you like it or not. Some people do like it, but they keep it to themselves. Those that don't want to be exposed to it can probably get through their entire four years without experiencing much more than an odd smell in the hallways every now and then. Wheaton students take their academics seriously, for the most part, and don't let drugs get in the way unless they have time and their workload isn't too heavy.

The College Prowler™ Grade on
Drug Scene: B-

A high grade on Drug Scene indicates that drugs are not a noticeable part of campus life; drug use is not visible, and no pressure to use them seems to exist.

Campus Strictness

"**Public Safety is very lax**; they don't really care unless you are being stupid, belligerent, or annoying. If you keep out of their way, they keep out of yours."

"Public Safety is strict enough to keep students from sitting outside smoking out of bongs, but cool enough to respect the privacy of students who are responsible. The general unspoken rule on campus is that, **as long as you're not a bonehead**, Public Safety, even if they catch you smoking up or underage drinking, will not give students too hard of a time."

"**They're becoming more and more strict**, from what I hear. Which is ironic because I remember my first Spring Weekend on campus, and reading the alcohol policy for the weekend which was issued by Public Safety. In short it stated, 'There is no alcohol policy. By the way, no Solo cups.' Wheaton's fight against underage drinking has its obvious positive points, but unfortunately those students on campus who are legally allowed to consume alcohol are also feeling the effects and consequences of the new alcohol policy. Fortunately, our campus has yet to turn dry, but it wouldn't surprise me if it did within the next few years."

"Campus police are stricter than a couple of years ago. If you and your friends are quiet, **Public Safety usually won't bother you**."

"They've been getting stricter. **It depends on the officer busting you**, but just cooperate with them and they'll usually be chill."

The Lowdown
ON CAMPUS STRICTNESS

What Are You Most Likely to Get Caught Doing on Campus?

Drinking underage, drinking outside without a closed container, making Jell-o shots in your room with the door open, running away from public safety officers, smoking marijuana in your dorm room, getting in a fight, having candles or incense burning in your dorm room, making too much noise in your dorm room, tapestries hanging from your ceiling or fire sprinkler

Students Speak Out
ON CAMPUS STRICTNESS

"Public Safety is strict about drugs and drinking. They are trying very hard to stop underage drinking; it is a problem that a lot of colleges have, and ours is no different from the rest."

The College Prowler Take
ON CAMPUS STRICTNESS

Generally, if you don't taunt the campus police, or run away from them while heavily intoxicated, you shouldn't have any problems. Those are pretty much the only times you will get in trouble, unless it is for something even dumber than that. Public Safety is fairly forgiving, as long as you are smart about your actions. There is, however, a recent move to come down harder on the student body concerning the alcohol policy, and Public Safety has no choice but to enforce the official college mandates. But, as of right now, strictness is pretty lax on campus. In terms of general rowdiness on campus, whether intoxicated or not, nobody really bothers you as long as you aren't damaging property. If you are smart about things, you shouldn't have any trouble. Now pass me that human slingshot!

The College Prowler™ Grade on
Campus Strictness: B

A high Campus Strictness grade implies an overall lenient atmosphere; police and RAs are fairly tolerant, and the administration's rules are flexible.

Overall Experience

Students Speak Out
ON OVERALL EXPERIENCE

"Sometimes I have a difficult time when I'm stressed out about work or something, but I've made friends here without whom I know I wouldn't be able to make it through college."

Q "**Sometimes I wish I was at a larger college so that I could have more choice in courses**, but the community here is awesome, and it feels like you are part of a family, rather than just another number. I think it is a fair trade, especially since there are ways to take courses at other colleges in the area, like through the 12 college exchange and interdepartmental classes in the sciences."

Q "The classes and teachers are interesting, and **the campus is beautiful**. It can get boring during weekends, but the weeks are busy with lots of events—movies, vendors, and fairs. Drinking and vandalism are problems, but I never feel unsafe. I'm glad I chose Wheaton."

💬 "**Wheaton, as a whole, is a wonderful place**. People on campus complain all the time about the institution's idiosyncrasies, but all one has to do is visit almost any other college in the region to recognize how great ours is. The campus is absolutely beautiful; the general student mentality is one that embraces the 'work hard, play hard' approach to academics; the food is far from bad; the professors are intellectually stimulating; and the community is one that is bonded very tightly. I can't think of much more anyone could ask for from a college, except possibly slightly lower tuition."

💬 "**I feel like I could get an equal education for a smaller dollar amount**, but I do feel like I am receiving a good education here. When I looked at myself in the future, I thought I would be in a relationship by now, but the boy scene is not good. I wish I was at a school where the ratio was more even, but it isn't enough to make me say that I wish I didn't come here. I have made great friends and have been academically successful."

💬 "Sometimes I hate it. **I like the smallness of the school and hate it at the same time**. Junior year abroad is probably a good idea to escape being on campus. I've had a great experience and learned a lot, but I bet I'd have a similar experience at other good small schools, maybe better. Or maybe not."

The College Prowler Take
ON OVERALL EXPERIENCE

Sometimes students may wonder what course their life would have taken had they attended a different school—a larger one in a city, perhaps. But, then they realize: they don't want to know, because it could not turn out any better than it does here at Wheaton. In the course of four years, Wheaton allows you to discover who you are and what you love in life, and that is far more valuable than being super competitive with classmates and always worrying about grades. Wheaton is competitive—don't get the wrong idea!—but there is an overall sense that there's more to life than just people passing through to earn a degree and get a job.

The school's motto is, "That they may have life and have it abundantly," and that truly does fit the school's character. Students aren't just a number on a sheet here. They are individuals who are looking for a path in life that will let them continue to learn, live, and love what they do. If that is your outlook, Wheaton may very well be the place for you.

The Inside Scoop

The Lowdown
ON THE INSIDE SCOOP

Wheaton Slang:
Know the slang, know the school. The following is a list of things you really need to know before coming to Wheaton. The more of these words you know, the better off you'll be.

The 12-Year-Old's Birthday Party: The Loft

44: The student house located on 44 Howard Street. If you hear someone say, "There's a party at 44," follow them.

Chapel Field: The field behind Cole Chapel. Good for Frisbee.

The Dimple: The large grassy lawn in the center of Upper Campus. It is the site of much sunbathing in the spring, and mattress sledding in the winter. Its official name is The Quad but no one calls it that.

Freshman 15: It is a rumor that you will gain 15 pounds during your freshman year at school. This may be true, depending on your activity level, how much you drink, and how many trips you make to The Loft each week.

Ghettos: Meadows, the largest dorm on Lower Campus

The Gym: For those that don't play sports and never go to Haas, "The Gym" is the Fitness Center.

Mad: Used interchangeably with wicked, as in, "This is a mad sandwich!"

"Meet me at Hebe": If someone says this to you, don't be alarmed. Just know that you should meet them by the statue that is in front of Metcalf and Kilham Halls.

The Pond Race: Each year during Spring Weekend, groups of students build and captain their own boats across the pond in a crazy race.

S.M.: Stands for Student Mentor, which is equal to an RA at other schools.

The Stone Thrones: A secret location in the woods, the site of many bonfires and parties, if weather permits.

Throw Down: A big party.

Wheat Thins: Another affectionate term for Wheaton students.

Wheaties: The affectionate term for Wheaton College students.

Wheatonstock: A large gathering of Wheaton bands, playing all night long.

YMCA: The quad of residence halls on Lower Campus: Young, Clark, McIntyre. I don't know what the A stands for, actually.

Yo: Exclamation or greeting along the lines of hey: "Yo! Wait, yo … no way, yo."

Traditions

Slype
Each semester, auditions are held for each of the a cappella groups on campus. Those that are accepted into the various groups are roused from their dorms in one of many ways (one of which is having a can of beer sprayed all over you in your sleep), and then taken to their first concert, which is held at the archway of Everett, called "Slype."

Boats
Each spring, students come together to craft what they affectionately call boats. These contraptions are then attempted to be sailed/paddled/desperately floated across the Peacock Pond in a race during Spring Weekend. Beer kegs have recently been outlawed as material for constructing the boats.

Boston Bash
Each fall, students grab their significant other or friends and get all fancy and go out for a night of dancing and drinks in Boston. This is held at a ritzy hotel, where students dance the night away.

Senior Disorientation
At the very end of the spring semester, seniors are taken on a special trip. They all pile into a bus and are driven to an undisclosed location, where they are given ridiculous amounts of alcoholic beverages, and then are driven home again in the wee hours of the morning. Previous Senior Disorientation locations have been breweries and casinos.

Traditions (Continued...)

Dining Hall Trays
Whatever you do, do not touch the dining hall trays. If you do, you will be forever marked as a dork, and no one will talk to you. Well, it's not really that bad, but seriously, don't use trays—it will mark you as a freshman for sure. Even if it takes you five trips to get all of your food—which it will—stay away from the tray.

Running to Class
Never run to class. Even if you are horribly late and your professor is known for her satanic tendencies, walk calmly but briskly. No one ever runs to class, and those that do are looked down upon as some strange freak of nature.

Wheaton Urban Legends
Peacock Pond Romance
Peacock Pond, located on Lower Campus, is rumored to bring love to young couples who walk around its edges. Historically, if a couple walks around the pond three times in a row and the man does not kiss the girl he's with by the end of the walk, she has the right to push him into the water.

Marriage and the Statue of Hebe
In the courtyard of Metcalf and Kilham Halls, the statue of Hebe, the legendary daughter of Zeus and Hara, can be seen. Before the 1980s, students used to gather on the steps of the library after graduation and then charge across campus to be the first to touch the statue. It was believed that the first one to touch the statue would be the first to get married.

School Spirit
Though students may complain a lot, deep down there is a very dedicated aspect to our school spirit. People will complain ruthlessly about the 10-minute walk to freshman parking, but then turn around and say they wouldn't want to be anywhere else. Those that find that they don't like the small-campus feel of Wheaton usually leave within the first year, so those that remain are generally very happy with the school. Students proudly sport all sorts of clothing with the Wheaton name, and though our sports teams aren't a huge force on campus, students still turn out to support their friends. Though the mutterings against Wheaton may get more vicious during finals time, the overall sense of community is what holds the campus together in the end.

Things I Wish I Knew Before Coming to Wheaton:
- It is imperative to have a car.
- It's way better to have a laptop than it is to have a desktop.
- How bad college food can get after months of the same selection.
- There's no need to bring enough Ramen noodles to feed an army—nine times out of 10 you'll end up bringing a full case of it back home at the end of the year.
- The "Freshman 15" is not a lie. Keep going to the gym from the start, or else you will wake up one day, months later, after having eaten hundreds of dollars of Loft food, and realize that it has become the Freshman 30.

Tips to Succeed at Wheaton:
- Get to know your professors, and when you find ones that you like, stick with them.
- Double-check everything your advisor tells you because it might not always be right.
- Get as involved as possible in clubs, organizations, or on-campus jobs.
- Make sure the professor of a class is right for you before taking it—you can read comments made by fellow students about your professor on Blackboard.
- If your rooming situation sucks, just move! A weekend of moving across campus will be well-worth avoiding a semester of misery.

Finding a Job or Internship

The Lowdown
ON FINDING A JOB OR INTERNSHIP

Finding a job or internship is a large emphasis in the Wheaton curriculum. In fact, a second transcript is required to graduate. The Filene Center for Work and Learning helps students find jobs and internships, and they require that one of your internships or jobs be documented and approved by them. Your second transcript is then submitted with your regular transcript anywhere you might apply after college, giving you an added edge over competition.

Advice
Make yourself known to services on campus—that way they can keep you current on opportunities that other students might miss. But, more important than that, you're the only one that can really make these things happen, despite what Wheaton has to offer. If you don't have the motivation, these services aren't going to help you.

Career Center Resources & Services:
The Filene Center (www.wheatonma.edu/Filene), second floor of Admissions Building; (508) 286-8211.

The Filene Center is the key resource on campus. They send out campus-wide newsletters about new part-time jobs opening up during the school year, and internships available in the summer. They can also help you get involved in the community by volunteering at a local animal shelter or something that interests you.

Academic advising, career workshops, campus employment, JobTrak (career service network for students and alums), 4WORK (allows students to view catalogs of internships according to interest or specialty)

For additional resources, visit the Filene Center Resources Web page:
www.wheatonma.edu/Filene/resource

Major Alumni Events
Commencement at the end of the year is probably the biggest event for alumni, mainly because their reunions are held at the same time. Every five years, each class has their reunion Commencement weekend, and alumni travel from around the world to join their old classmates.

Alumni Publications
The Wheaton Quarterly
The Wheaton Quarterly comes out four times a year and reaches all across the country and the world. It helps to keep alumni, parents of current students, and those interested in Wheaton up-to-date with what's going on around campus.

Famous Wheaton Alumni:
- Lesley Stall (Class of '63); Co-editor of *60 Minutes*
- Christie Todd Whitman (Class of '68); Former governor of New Jersey and EPA Administrator
- Trish Karter (Class of '77); Owner of Dancing Bear Bakery
- Catherine Keener (Class of '83); A famous actress, you can spot her in "Being John Malkovich" and "Full Frontal"

The Best & Worst

The Ten BEST Things About Wheaton:

1. Compassionate professors
2. Small class sizes
3. Opportunity for research
4. The Dimple
5. Upper Campus
6. Watson Fine Arts Center
7. Ten-Minute Play Festival
8. Spring Weekend
9. Close to Boston/Providence (if you have a car)
10. Slype at midnight

The Ten WORST Things About Wheaton:

1. Girl-to-boy ratio (for girls)
2. Tuition
3. Norton
4. Lack of diversity
5. Peacock Pond's "scent" on warm days
6. Dining hall food
7. The basement at Elms
8. Small, monotonous parties
9. Lack of elevators in dorms (when moving in)
10. Pond fountain mist (when it's hot)

New England Weather Map

With New England's humid summers and harsh winters, the weather can be hard to predict. You'll need to pack for all four seasons.

Portland:

	High	Low	Rainfall
Jan.	30°	11°	3.5"
Apr.	52°	34°	4.1"
Jul.	79°	58°	3.1"
Oct.	59°	38°	3.9"

Hartford:

	High	Low	Rainfall
Jan.	33°	16°	3.4"
Apr.	60°	38°	3.9"
Jul.	85°	62°	3.2"
Oct.	64°	41°	3.6"

Boston:

	High	Low	Rainfall
Jan.	36°	22°	3.6"
Apr.	56°	40°	3.6"
Jul.	82°	65°	2.8"
Oct.	63°	47°	3.3"

REPORT CARD SUMMARY
Academics

Academic Atmosphere
As many as one in four college students drop out after or during freshman year. One of the reasons for this trend is that many incoming freshman just aren't prepared for the enormous academic transition from high school to college; it's a huge change.

A+	MIT
A+	WILLIAMS COLLEGE
A	BOWDOIN COLLEGE
A	BROWN UNIVERSITY
A	DARTMOUTH COLLEGE
A	HARVARD UNIVERSITY
A	MIDDLEBURY COLLEGE
A	YALE UNIVERSITY
A-	AMHERST COLLEGE
A-	BATES COLLEGE
A-	BOSTON COLLEGE
A-	BRANDEIS UNVERSITY
A-	MOUNT HOLYOKE COLLEGE
A-	WELLESLEY COLLEGE
A-	SMITH COLLEGE
A-	TUFTS UNIVERSITY
B+	BOSTON UNIVERSITY
B+	COLBY COLLEGE
B+	COLLEGE OF THE HOLY CROSS
B+	CONNECTICUT COLLEGE
B+	EMERSON COLLEGE
B+	PROVIDENCE COLLEGE
B+	TRINITY COLLEGE
B+	WESLEYAN UNIVERSITY
B	BABSON COLLEGE
B	BENTLEY COLLEGE
B	NORTHEASTERN UNIVERSITY
B	RHODE ISLAND SCHOOL OF DESIGN
B	UNIVERSITY OF CONNECTICUT
B	UNIVERSITY OF MASSACHUSETTS
B	UNIVERSITY OF RHODE ISLAND
B	WHEATON COLLEGE
B-	UNIVERSITY OF NEW HAMPSHIRE
B-	UNIVERSITY OF VERMONT

REPORT CARD SUMMARY
Local Atmosphere

> **Around Town**
> When you're not studying, you'll probably want to be doing something other than sitting around. Every school offers different surroundings, and while visiting is important, hanging around for a few hours won't always give you all the information you'll need about what other students do for fun off campus.

A	BOSTON COLLEGE		**C+**	BOWDOIN COLLEGE
A	BOSTON UNIVERSITY		**C+**	MIDDLEBURY COLLEGE
A	EMERSON COLLEGE		**C+**	WILLIAMS COLLEGE
A	MIT		**C**	AMHERST COLLEGE
A	NORTHEASTERN UNIVERSITY		**C**	SMITH COLLEGE
A-	BROWN UNIVERSITY		**C**	UNIVERSITY OF MASSACHUSETTS
A-	HARVARD UNIVERSITY		**C**	WELLESLEY COLLEGE
A-	TUFTS UNIVERSITY		**C-**	BATES COLLEGE
A-	UNIVERSITY OF VERMONT		**C-**	COLBY COLLEGE
B+	MOUNT HOLYOKE COLLEGE		**C-**	CONNECTICUT COLLEGE
B+	PROVIDENCE COLLEGE		**C-**	DARTMOUTH COLLEGE
B+	RHODE ISLAND SCHOOL OF DESIGN		**C-**	TRINITY COLLEGE
B	BRANDEIS UNIVERSITY		**C-**	WESLEYAN UNIVERSITY
B	UNIVERSITY OF RHODE ISLAND		**C-**	WHEATON COLLEGE
B	UNIVERSITY OF NEW HAMPSHIRE		**C-**	YALE UNIVERSITY
C+	BABSON COLLEGE		**D+**	UNIVERSITY OF CONNECTICUT
C+	BENTLEY COLLEGE		**D**	COLLEGE OF THE HOLY CROSS

REPORT CARD SUMMARY
Safety & Security

Staying Safe and Secure
The presence of crime on campus is something you should strongly consider when choosing a college. Your chosen school may look like Pleasantville when the tour guide shows you around campus, but there may be more to the picture than what you're shown. Your safety and security should not be taken for granted.

- **A+** BOSTON COLLEGE
- **A+** BOWDOIN COLLEGE
- **A+** DARTMOUTH COLLEGE
- **A** BATES COLLEGE
- **A** BOSTON UNIVERSITY
- **A** BRANDEIS UNIVERSITY
- **A** UNIVERSITY OF NEW HAMPSHIRE
- **A-** AMHERST COLLEGE
- **A-** BABSON COLLEGE
- **A-** COLLEGE OF THE HOLY CROSS
- **A-** CONNECTICUT COLLEGE
- **A-** WELLESLEY COLLEGE
- **A-** MOUNT HOLYOKE COLLEGE
- **A-** SMITH COLLEGE
- **A-** UNIVERSITY OF CONNECTICUT
- **A-** UNIVERSITY OF RHODE ISLAND
- **A-** UNIVERSITY OF VERMONT
- **A-** WELLESLEY COLLEGE
- **A-** WILLIAMS COLLEGE
- **B+** BENTLEY COLLEGE
- **B+** COLBY COLLEGE
- **B+** EMERSON COLLEGE
- **B+** HARVARD UNIVERSITY
- **B+** RHODE ISLAND SCHOOL OF DESIGN
- **B+** TUFTS UNIVERSITY
- **B** MIT
- **B** NORTHEASTERN UNIVERSITY
- **B** UNIVERSITY OF MASSACHUSETTS
- **B-** PROVIDENCE COLLEGE
- **B-** WHEATON COLLEGE
- **B-** YALE UNIVERSITY
- **C+** BROWN UNIVERSITY
- **C+** WESLEYAN UNIVERSITY
- **C** TRINITY COLLEGE

REPORT CARD SUMMARY
Computers

- **A+** MIT
- **A** AMHERST COLLEGE
- **A** DARTMOUTH COLLEGE
- **A** YALE UNIVERSITY
- **A-** BABSON COLLEGE
- **A-** BENTLEY COLLEGE
- **A-** BRANDEIS UNIVERSITY
- **A-** HARVARD UNIVERSITY
- **B+** BATES COLLEGE
- **B+** BOSTON COLLEGE
- **B+** BOSTON UNIVERSITY
- **B+** BOWDOIN COLLEGE
- **B+** BROWN UNIVERSITY
- **B+** MIDDLEBURY COLLEGE
- **B+** NORTHEASTERN UNIVERSITY
- **B+** SMITH COLLEGE
- **B+** UNIVERSITY OF VERMONT
- **B+** WESLEYAN UNIVERSITY

Megabyte, Schmegabyte
College is becoming more dependent on technology every day. Don't get to school and kick yourself for leaving your computer at home. If the school has tiny computer labs packed with students, you might want to bring or buy your own machine (it'll make printing out assignments ten minutes before class much easier).

- **B** COLLEGE OF THE HOLY CROSS
- **B** EMERSON COLLEGE
- **B** MOUNT HOLYOKE COLLEGE
- **B** RHODE ISLAND SCHOOL OF DESIGN
- **B** TUFTS UNIVERSITY
- **B** UNIVERSITY OF CONNECTICUT
- **B** WHEATON COLLEGE
- **B-** COLBY COLLEGE
- **B-** PROVIDENCE COLLEGE
- **B-** TRINITY COLLEGE
- **B-** UNIVERISTY OF NEW HAMPSHIRE
- **B-** UNIVERSITY OF RHODE ISLAND
- **B-** WELLESLEY COLLEGE
- **C+** UNIVERSITY OF MASSACHUSETTS
- **C+** WILLIAMS COLLEGE
- **C** CONNECTICUT COLLEGE

REPORT CARD SUMMARY
Facilities

A Beautiful Campus
Okay, you've paid the school thousands of dollars. Now you expect them to give you a little something in return—nice buildings, up-to-date computer labs, a decent gym or two. In the College Prowler guidebooks, students speak out on the quality of the facilities each school has to offer.

A	AMHERST COLLEGE
A	MIDDLEBURY COLLEGE
A-	NORTHEASTERN UNIVERSITY
A-	SMITH COLLEGE
A-	UNIVERSITY OF CONNECTICUT
A-	UNIVERSITY OF RHODE ISLAND
A-	WILLIAMS COLLEGE
A-	YALE UNIVERSITY
B+	BABSON COLLEGE
B+	BENTLEY COLLEGE
B+	BOSTON COLLEGE
B+	BOSTON UNIVERSITY
B+	MIT
B+	UNIVERSITY OF NEW HAMPSHIRE
B+	UNIVERSITY OF VERMONT
B+	WELLESLEY COLLEGE
B	BOWDOIN COLLEGE
B	BRANDEIS UNIVERSITY
B	BROWN UNIVERSITY
B	COLBY COLLEGE
B	COLLEGE OF THE HOLY CROSS
B	CONNECTICUT COLLEGE
B	DARTMOUTH COLLEGE
B	EMERSON COLLEGE
B	HARVARD UNIVERSITY
B	MOUNT HOLYOKE COLLEGE
B	PROVIDENCE COLLEGE
B	TRINITY COLLEGE
B	TUFTS UNIVERSITY
B	WESLEYAN UNIVERSITY
B	WHEATON COLLEGE
B-	BATES COLLEGE
B-	RHODE ISLAND SCHOOL OF DESIGN
B-	UNIVERSITY OF MASSACHUSETTS

REPORT CARD SUMMARY
Campus Dining

Grade "F" Meat
The food a school offers probably doesn't seem particularly important, does it? When considering a school, students often fail to consider that they'll be living (and eating) at the mercy of the institution for at least the next four years.

- **A+** BOSTON UNIVERSITY
- **A** BOWDOIN COLLEGE
- **A-** COLBY COLLEGE
- **A-** MIDDLEBURY COLLEGE
- **A-** NORTHEASTERN UNIVERSITY
- **B+** CONNECTICUT COLLEGE
- **B+** EMERSON COLLEGE
- **B+** TUFTS UNIVERSITY
- **B+** UNIVERSITY OF VERMONT
- **B** BATES COLLEGE
- **B** BOSTON COLLEGE
- **B** DARTMOUTH COLLEGE
- **B** MOUNT HOLYOKE COLLEGE
- **B** UNIVERSITY OF NEW HAMPSHIRE
- **B** WESLEYAN UNIVERSITY
- **B** WILLIAMS COLLEGE
- **B-** MIT
- **B-** RHODE ISLAND SCHOOL OF DESIGN
- **B-** SMITH COLLEGE
- **B-** TRINITY COLLEGE
- **B-** UNIVERSITY OF CONNECTICUT
- **B-** WELLESLEY COLLEGE
- **B-** WHEATON COLLEGE
- **C+** AMHERST COLLEGE
- **C+** BENTLEY COLLEGE
- **C+** BRANDEIS UNIVERSITY
- **C+** COLLEGE OF THE HOLY CROSS
- **C+** PROVIDENCE COLLEGE
- **C+** UNIVERSITY OF MASSACHUSETTS
- **C+** UNIVERSITY OF RHODE ISLAND
- **C+** YALE UNIVERSITY
- **C-** BABSON COLLEGE
- **C-** BROWN UNIVERSITY
- **D+** HARVARD UNIVERSITY

REPORT CARD SUMMARY
Off-Campus Dining

> **Sick and Tired of the Cafeteria?**
> Face it. You will get tired of the cafeteria food very quickly. You're going to have to explore the surrounding area for great restaurants with affordable prices. Quotes in the College Prowler guidebooks come from the students who can tell you how to eat cheaply and well at the school of your choice.

- **A+** BOSTON UNIVERSITY
- **A** BOSTON COLLEGE
- **A** EMERSON COLLEGE
- **A** HARVARD UNIVERSITY
- **A** MIT
- **A** TUFTS UNIVERSITY
- **A-** BENTLEY COLLEGE
- **A-** BRANDEIS UNIVERSITY
- **A-** BROWN UNIVERSITY
- **A-** PROVIDENCE COLLEGE
- **A-** RHODE ISLAND SCHOOL OF DESIGN
- **A-** UNIVERSITY OF VERMONT
- **A-** WELLESLEY COLLEGE
- **B+** AMHERST COLLEGE
- **B+** COLBY COLLEGE
- **B+** COLLEGE OF THE HOLY CROSS
- **B+** NORTHEASTERN UNIVERSITY
- **B+** SMITH COLLEGE
- **B+** UNIVERSITY OF MASSACHUSETTS
- **B+** UNIVERSITY OF RHODE ISLAND
- **B+** TRINITY COLLEGE
- **B+** YALE UNIVERSITY
- **B** BOWDOIN COLLEGE
- **B** CONNECTICUT COLLEGE
- **B** MOUNT HOLYOKE COLLEGE
- **B** WESLEYAN UNIVERSITY
- **B-** MIDDLEBURY COLLEGE
- **B-** UNIVERSITY OF NEW HAMPSHIRE
- **B-** WHEATON COLLEGE
- **C+** BABSON COLLEGE
- **C+** BATES COLLEGE
- **C+** WILLIAMS COLLEGE
- **C** UNIVERSITY OF CONNECTICUT
- **C-** DARTMOUTH COLLEGE

REPORT CARD SUMMARY
Campus Housing

Dorm Atmosphere
Living in a dorm is going to be a huge part of your college life. Your living situation will influence almost everything about your four years in college. The people you live with and the comforts you're afforded will affect your personal and academic life.

A	BOWDOIN COLLEGE
A	HARVARD UNIVERSITY
A-	EMERSON COLLEGE
A-	MOUNT HOLYOKE COLLEGE
A-	NORTHEASTERN UNIVERSITY
A-	WESLEYAN UNIVERSITY
A-	YALE UNIVERSITY
B+	BENTLEY COLLEGE
B+	BROWN UNIVERSITY
B+	CONNECTICUT COLLEGE
B+	DARTMOUTH COLLEGE
B+	MIDDLEBURY COLLEGE
B+	MIT
B+	SMITH COLLEGE
B+	TRINITY COLLEGE
B+	UNIVERSITY OF CONNECTICUT
B+	UNIVERSITY OF NEW HAMPSHIRE
B+	WELLESLEY COLLEGE
B+	WHEATON COLLEGE
B	AMHERST COLLEGE
B	BATES COLLEGE
B	BOSTON COLLEGE
B	BRANDEIS UNIVERSITY
B	COLLEGE OF THE HOLY CROSS
B	UNIVERSITY OF VERMONT
B-	BABSON COLLEGE
B-	PROVIDENCE COLLEGE
B-	TUFTS UNIVERSITY
B-	UNIVERSITY OF MASSACHUSETTS
B-	UNIVERSITY OF RHODE ISLAND
C	WILLIAMS COLLEGE
C-	BOSTON UNIVERSITY
C-	COLBY COLLEGE
C-	RHODE ISLAND SCHOOL OF DESIGN

REPORT CARD SUMMARY
Off-Campus Housing

> **Moving Out of the Dorms**
> Are you really going to want to live in the dorms for four years? Some students say that one of the greatest experiences of a college career is moving out of your dorm and into a house with your friends. Living off campus is one step closer to the world beyond college, which is why students spoke out about the ins and outs of finding the perfect place.

- **A-** BROWN UNIVERSITY
- **A-** UNIVERSITY OF RHODE ISLAND
- **B+** BOSTON COLLEGE
- **B+** BOSTON UNIVERSITY
- **B+** BRANDEIS UNIVERSITY
- **B+** EMERSON COLLEGE
- **B+** NORTHEASTERN UNIVERSITY
- **B+** PROVIDENCE COLLEGE
- **B+** RHODE ISLAND SCHOOL OF DESIGN
- **B** DARTMOUTH COLLEGE
- **B** UNIVERSITY OF CONNECTICUT
- **B** UNIVERSITY OF VERMONT
- **B** WESLEYAN UNIVERSITY
- **B** YALE UNIVERSITY
- **B-** TUFTS UNIVERSITY
- **B-** UNIVERSITY OF NEW HAMPSHIRE
- **C+** COLLEGE OF THE HOLY CROSS
- **C+** MOUNT HOLYOKE COLLEGE
- **C** BABSON COLLEGE
- **C** BATES COLLEGE
- **C** BENTLEY COLLEGE
- **C** BOWDOIN COLLEGE
- **C** UNIVERSITY OF MASSACHUSETTS
- **C-** WILLIAMS COLLEGE
- **D+** AMHERST COLLEGE
- **D+** MIDDLEBURY COLLEGE
- **D+** SMITH COLLEGE
- **D+** WHEATON COLLEGE
- **D** COLBY COLLEGE
- **D** CONNECTICUT COLLEGE
- **D** TRINITY COLLEGE
- **D** WELLESLEY COLLEGE
- **D-** MIT
- **F** HARVARD UNIVERSITY

REPORT CARD SUMMARY
Diversity

The Melting Pot
College isn't just supposed to be high school with more buildings. It's supposed to be an experience that broadens your horizons, and it's hard to do that if you only meet people exactly like you.

- **A** MIT
- **B+** AMHERST COLLEGE
- **B+** BABSON COLLEGE
- **B+** HARVARD UNIVERSITY
- **B+** MOUNT HOLYOKE UNIVERSITY
- **B+** WELLESLEY COLLEGE
- **B** BROWN UNIVERSITY
- **B** DARTMOUTH COLLEGE
- **B** YALE UNIVERSITY
- **B-** BOSTON UNIVERSITY
- **B-** TUFTS UNIVERSITY
- **B-** WESLEYAN COLLEGE
- **C** BENTLEY COLLEGE
- **C** BOWDOIN COLLEGE
- **C** NORTHEASTERN UNIVERSITY
- **C** RHODE ISLAND SCHOOL OF DESIGN
- **C** WILLIAMS COLLEGE
- **C-** BRANDEIS UNIVERSITY
- **C-** SMITH COLLEGE
- **C-** UNIVERSITY OF MASSACHUSETTS
- **D+** COLBY COLLEGE
- **D** CONNECTICUT COLLEGE
- **D** EMERSON UNIVERSITY
- **D** MIDDLEBURY COLLEGE
- **D** TRINITY COLLEGE
- **D** UNIVERSITY OF CONNECTICUT
- **D** UNIVERSITY OF RHODE ISLAND
- **D** UNIVERSITY OF VERMONT
- **D-** BATES COLLEGE
- **D-** BOSTON COLLEGE
- **D-** COLLEGE OF THE HOLY CROSS
- **D-** PROVIDENCE COLLEGE
- **D-** UNIVERSITY OF NEW HAMPSHIRE
- **D-** WHEATON COLLEGE

REPORT CARD SUMMARY
Guys

> **Guys Gone Wild**
> College guys are different from the high school guys you're used to; they're a different breed. College should offer you an entirely new and engaging social scene, and with that comes members of the opposite (or same) sex who are not only attractive, but also fun and personable.

A-	BOWDOIN COLLEGE	B	YALE UNIVERSITY
A-	DARTMOUTH COLLEGE	B-	BABSON COLLEGE
A-	UNIVERSITY OF MASSACHUSETTS	B-	BATES COLLEGE
A-	UNIVERSITY OF RHODE ISLAND	B-	RHODE ISLAND SCHOOL OF DESIGN
B+	BENTLEY COLLEGE	B-	UNIVERSITY OF NEW HAMPSHIRE
B+	BOSTON COLLEGE	C+	BOSTON UNIVERSITY
B+	BROWN UNIVERSITY	C+	COLBY COLLEGE
B+	COLLEGE OF THE HOLY CROSS	C+	CONNECTICUT COLLEGE
B+	MIDDLEBURY COLLEGE	C+	MIT
B+	NORTHEASTERN UNIVERSITY	C+	WHEATON COLLEGE
B+	PROVIDENCE COLLEGE	C	BRANDEIS UNIVERSITY
B+	TRINITY COLLEGE	C	WESLEYAN UNIVERSITY
B+	UNIVERSITY OF CONNECTICUT	C-	TUFTS UNIVERSITY
B	AMHERST COLLEGE	C-	WILLIAMS COLLEGE
B	EMERSON COLLEGE	N/A	MOUNT HOLYOKE COLLEGE
B	HARVARD UNIVERSITY	N/A	SMITH COLLEGE
B	UNIVERSITY OF VERMONT	N/A	WELLESLEY COLLEGE

REPORT CARD SUMMARY
Girls

Pretty Woman
You're going to have a hard time enjoying your next four years if there just aren't any worthwhile people on campus. College should offer you an entirely new and engaging social scene, and with that comes members of the opposite (or same) sex who are not just attractive, but fun and personable as well. College Prowler guidebooks offer you a variety of student opinions about the girls on each campus.

- **A** BOSTON COLLEGE
- **A** UNIVERSITY OF RHODE ISLAND
- **A-** COLLEGE OF THE HOLY CROSS
- **A-** CONNECTICUT COLLEGE
- **A-** EMERSON COLLEGE
- **A-** MIDDLEBURY COLLEGE
- **A-** NORTHEASTERN UNIVERSITY
- **A-** PROVIDENCE COLLEGE
- **A-** UNIVERSITY OF MASSACHUSETTS
- **B+** BOSTON UNIVERSITY
- **B+** COLBY COLLEGE
- **B+** SMITH COLLEGE
- **B+** TRINITY COLLEGE
- **B+** UNIVERSITY OF VERMONT
- **B+** YALE UNIVERSITY
- **B** AMHERST COLLEGE
- **B** BATES COLLEGE
- **B** BENTLEY COLLEGE
- **B** BROWN UNIVERSITY
- **B** MOUNT HOLYOKE COLLEGE
- **B** RHODE ISLAND SCHOOL OF DESIGN
- **B** UNIVERSITY OF CONNECTICUT
- **B** UNIVERSITY OF NEW HAMPSHIRE
- **B** WELLESLEY COLLEGE
- **B** WHEATON COLLEGE
- **B-** DARTMOUTH COLLEGE
- **B-** HARVARD UNIVERSITY
- **B-** TUFTS UNIVERSITY
- **C+** BABSON COLLEGE
- **C+** BOWDOIN COLLEGE
- **C+** BRANDEIS UNIVERSITY
- **C** WESLEYAN UNIVERSITY
- **C** WILLIAMS COLLEGE
- **C-** MIT

REPORT CARD SUMMARY
Athletics

Be a Good Sport
Even if you're not a hardcore athlete, a school's athletics can still be important to you. School spirit can be an exhilarating feeling, and intramural sports offer you a social outlet and a break from the academic routine.

A	BOSTON COLLEGE		B-	UNIVERSITY OF VERMONT
A	UNIVERSITY OF CONNECTICUT		C+	BATES COLLEGE
A-	UNIVERSITY OF RHODE ISLAND		C+	BOSTON UNIVERSITY
B+	BOWDOIN COLLEGE		C+	BROWN UNIVERSITY
B+	COLLEGE OF THE HOLY CROSS		C+	COLBY COLLEGE
B+	DARTMOUTH COLLEGE		C+	HARVARD UNIVERSITY
B+	MIDDLEBURY COLLEGE		C+	MIT
B+	PROVIDENCE COLLEGE		C	BRANDEIS UNIVERSITY
B+	UNIVERSITY OF NEW HAMPSHIRE		C	MOUNT HOLYOKE COLLEGE
B+	WHEATON COLLEGE		C	SMITH COLLEGE
B	AMHERST COLLEGE		C	WELLESLEY COLLEGE
B	CONNECTICUT COLLEGE		C	YALE UNIVERSITY
B	UNIVERSITY OF MASSACHUSETTS		C-	TUFTS UNIVERSITY
B	WILLIAMS COLLEGE		C-	WESLEYAN UNIVERSITY
B-	BABSON COLLEGE		D	RHODE ISLAND SCHOOL OF DESIGN
B-	BENTLEY COLLEGE		D+	EMERSON COLLEGE
B-	NORTHEASTERN UNIVERSITY			
B-	TRINITY COLLEGE			

REPORT CARD SUMMARY
Greek Life

Going Greek
Whether or not you plan on joining a fraternity or sorority, it is possible that Greek life could still be a huge part of your college experience; Greek events are major social functions. You may discover that joining a Greek organization is a much more enriching and worthwhile experience than you'd ever expected (or much less).

A	DARTMOUTH COLLEGE
A-	MIT
B+	UNIVERSITY OF MASSACHUSETTS
B-	BABSON COLLEGE
B-	TRINITY COLLEGE
B-	UNIVERSITY OF CONNECTICUT
B-	UNIVERSITY OF VERMONT
C+	BROWN UNIVERSITY
C+	UNIVERSITY OF NEW HAMPSHIRE
C+	UNIVERSITY OF RHODE ISLAND
C	BENTLEY COLLEGE
C	WESLEYAN UNIVERSITY
C-	BRANDEIS UNIVERSITY
C-	NORTHEASTERN UNIVERSITY
C-	TUFTS UNIVERSITY
D+	BOSTON UNIVERSITY
D+	EMERSON COLLEGE
D+	HARVARD UNIVERSITY
D+	YALE UNIVERSITY
D	RHODE ISLAND SCHOOL OF DESIGN
D	WELLESLEY COLLEGE
D-	AMHERST COLLEGE
N/A	BATES COLLEGE
N/A	BOSTON COLLEGE
N/A	BOWDOIN COLLEGE
N/A	COLBY COLLEGE
N/A	COLLEGE OF THE HOLY CROSS
N/A	CONNECTICUT COLLEGE
N/A	MIDDLEBURY COLLEGE
N/A	MOUNT HOLYOKE COLLEGE
N/A	PROVIDENCE COLLEGE
N/A	SMITH COLLEGE
N/A	WHEATON COLLEGE
N/A	WILLIAMS COLLEGE

REPORT CARD SUMMARY
Drug Scene

Drugs, Drugs Everywhere
Drugs have been an issue ever since people discovered that they could grind up, inject, smoke, melt, or swallow various stuff to change the way they feel. College Prowler guidebooks address the prominence of the drug scene on campus, and the student attitudes, to let you know how visible the threat of drug use actually is at each school. Here, a high grade means that drugs are not a noticeable part of campus life.

A	MOUNT HOLYOKE COLLEGE
A	WELLESLEY COLLEGE
A-	UNIVERSITY OF CONNECTICUT
A-	WILLIAMS COLLEGE
B+	BENTLEY COLLEGE
B+	BOSTON COLLEGE
B+	BRANDEIS UNIVERSITY
B+	COLBY COLLEGE
B+	HARVARD UNIVERSITY
B+	MIT
B+	NORTHEASTERN UNIVERSITY
B+	PROVIDENCE COLLEGE
B+	TUFTS UNIVERSITY
B+	YALE UNIVERSITY
B	AMHERST COLLEGE
B	BABSON COLLEGE
B	BOWDOIN COLLEGE
B	BROWN UNIVERSITY
B	COLLEGE OF THE HOLY CROSS
B	DARTMOUTH COLLEGE
B	EMERSON COLLEGE
B	MIDDLEBURY COLLEGE
B-	CONNECTICUT COLLEGE
B-	TRINITY COLLEGE
B-	UNIVERSITY OF MASSACHUSETTS
B-	WESLEYAN UNIVERSITY
B-	WHEATON COLLEGE
C+	RHODE ISLAND SCHOOL OF DESIGN
C+	UNIVERSITY OF RHODE ISLAND
C+	UNIVERSITY OF VERMONT
C	BATES COLLEGE
C-	BOSTON UNIVERSITY
C-	SMITH COLLEGE
C-	UNIVERSITY OF NEW HAMPSHIRE

REPORT CARD SUMMARY
Campus Strictness

Don't Step Out of Line
You're going to have a lot more freedom as a college student. What you do with that freedom, though, isn't always up to you. Some schools don't seem to care; others impose curfews and lights-out policies. Every college is different—College Prowler guidebooks will give you the inside scoop. Here, a high grade implies an overall lenient atmosphere.

A	YALE UNIVERSITY
A-	AMHERST COLLEGE
A-	BRANDEIS UNIVERSITY
A-	EMERSON COLLEGE
A-	HARVARD UNIVERSITY
A-	MOUNT HOLYOKE COLLEGE
A-	RISD
A-	TRINITY COLLEGE
A-	UNIVERSITY OF MASSACHUSETTS
B+	BATES COLLEGE
B+	BOWDOIN COLLEGE
B+	BROWN UNIVERSITY
B+	CONNECTICUT COLLEGE
B+	MIDDLEBURY COLLEGE
B+	TUFTS UNIVERSITY
B+	WILLIAMS COLLEGE
B	BOSTON UNIVERSITY
B	DARTMOUTH COLLEGE
B	PROVIDENCE COLLEGE
B	WESLEYAN UNIVERSITY
B	WHEATON COLLEGE
B-	COLLEGE OF THE HOLY CROSS
B-	MIT
B-	NORTHEASTERN UNIVERSITY
B-	UNIVERSITY OF CONNECTICUT
B-	UNIVERSITY OF RHODE ISLAND
C+	BABSON COLLEGE
C	BENTLEY COLLEGE
C	BOSTON COLLEGE
C-	COLBY COLLEGE
C-	UNIVERSITY OF NEW HAMPSHIRE
D+	UNIVERSITY OF VERMONT
D	SMITH COLLEGE
D-	WELLESLEY COLLEGE

Financial Aid

This section of the books has advice and important information for funding your New England education.

FAFSA Deadline:
The application period opens January first for the following year, so if a class begins in September 2006, you could apply for aid as early as January 1, 2006. The application period closes in June, at the end of the academic year.

Federal Aid
The FAFSA (Free Application for Federal Student Aid) is the application you must complete to get federal aid. You can apply online or get an application at *www.fafsa.ed.gov/*.

Federal aid comes in two forms: grants and loans. Grants are awards with nothing to pay back, while federal loans need to be repaid down the road at a low (or zero) interest rate.

Federal Grants
Pell Grants are awarded to low-income students, while Federal Supplemental Educational Opportunity Grants (SOEG) are for low-income students with exceptional financial need.

Federal Loans
- Unsubsidized Stafford Loan—Available to any student regardless of financial need, but the student pays the interest.
- Subsidized Stafford Loan—A loan that is interest-free until six months after you graduate from college (the government pays the interest until that time). These are available to students who meet financial requirements and attend school more than half-time.
- Plus Loans—Available for the parents of students attending college.
- Perkins Loans—Administered by the college, these are for students with exceptional financial need.

New England Tuition Breaks

The New England Board of Higher Education offers the New England Regional Student Program, which provides a tuition break at New England public schools for students studying a major not offered by a public school in their home state. All 78 public colleges and universities in New England participate in the scheme, with programs available at all levels—associate, bachelor's, master's, certificate of advanced graduate study, master's, doctoral and first-professional. Majors are listed in the anual RSP catalog, which can be searched online at the New England Board of Higher Education's Website. Available majors are approved by the individual institutions.

www.nebhe.org/

Check with your Colleges

Outside of state and federal aid, colleges themselves offer financial aid money to students. Be sure to visit the financial aid Website of each school to which you plan on applying. Also, although every college requires you to fill out the FAFSA, some colleges will ask for additional forms, and each school will have its own deadline.

Students with Special Needs

Colleges and universities are required by federal law to meet certain physical and educational needs unique to those with disabilities. The degree to which schools accommodate both learning and physically challenged students varies. Schools often have a staff member especially knowledgeable of such issues who will best answer questions about access, education, and housing.

Amherst College

Contact:
Frances Tuleja
Associate Dean of Students
(413) 542-2529
fetuleja@amherst.edu

Is a smaller course load available? - **No**
Is more time given to finish your degree? - **No**
Is credit given toward the degree for remedial courses? - **No**
Services offered to students with learning disabilities: **other testing accommodations, tape recorders, note-taking services, readers, extended time for tests, tutors**
Services offered to students with physical disabilities: **note-taking services, tape recorders, special housing, tutors, reader services, Braille services, interpreters for hearing-impaired, talking books**
Is the campus accessible to students with physical disabilities? - **Yes**
Is housing available for disabled students? - **Yes**

Babson College

Contact:
Erin Evans
Coordinator of Disability Services
(781) 239-4508
eevans@babson.edu

Is a smaller course load available? - **Yes**
Is more time given to finish your degree? - **Yes**
Is credit given toward the degree for remedial courses? - **No**
Services offered to students with learning disabilities: **other testing accommodations, tape recorders, note-taking services, oral tests, readers, extended time for tests, tutors**
Services offered to students with physical disabilities: **note-taking services, tape recorders, special housing, tutors, adaptive equipment, reader services, talking books**
Is the campus accessible to students with physical disabilities? - **Partially**
Is housing available for disabled students? - **Yes**

Bates College

Contact:
N/A

Is a smaller course load available? - **No**
Is more time given to finish your degree? - **N/A**
Is credit given toward the degree for remedial courses? - **N/A**
Services offered to students with learning disabilities: **other testing accommodations, tape recorders, untimed tests, note-taking services, oral tests, readers, extended time for tests**
Services offered to students with physical disabilities: **note-taking services, special transportation, tape recorders, special housing, tutors, adaptive equipment, reader services, interpreters for hearing-impaired, talking books**
Is the campus accessible to students with physical disabilities? - **95%**
Is housing available for disabled students? - **N/A**

Bentley College

Contact:
Christopher Kennedy
Coordinator of Disability Services
(781) 891-2274
ckennedy@bentley.edu

Is a smaller course load available? - **Yes**
Is more time given to finish your degree? - **Yes**
Is credit given toward the degree for remedial courses? - **No**
Services offered to students with learning disabilities: **other testing accommodations, reading machines, tape recorders, note-taking services, oral tests, learning center, readers, extended time for tests, tutors, other**
Services offered to students with physical disabilities: **note-taking services, special transportation, tape recorders, special housing, tutors, braille services, interpreters for hearing-impaired**
Is the campus accessible to students with physical disabilities? - **Mostly**
Is housing available for disabled students? - **Yes**

Boston College

Contact:
Kathy Duggan
Assistant Director
(617) 552-8093
dugganka@bc.edu

Is a smaller course load available? - **Yes**
Is more time given to finish your degree? - **Yes**
Is credit given toward the degree for remedial courses? - **N/A**
Services offered to students with learning disabilities: **other testing accommodations, reading machines, tape recorders, note-taking services, learning center, readers, extended time for tests, tutors**
Services offered to students with physical disabilities: **note-taking services, special transportation, tape recorders, special housing, tutors, adaptive equipment, reader services, braille services, interpreters for hearing-impaired, talking books**
Is the campus accessible to students with physical disabilities? - **Mostly**
Is housing available for disabled students? - **Yes**

Boston University

Contact:
Lorraine Wolf
Clinical Director Office of Disability Services
(617) 353-3658
access@bu.edu

Is a smaller course load available? - **Yes**
Is more time given to finish your degree? - **Yes**
Is credit given toward the degree for remedial courses? - **No**
Services offered to students with learning disabilities: **reading machines, tape recorders, note-taking services, oral tests, learning center, readers, extended time for tests, tutors, other**
Services offered to students with physical disabilities: **note-taking services, tape recorders, tutors, adaptive equipment, reader services, braille services, interpreters for hearing-impaired, talking books**
Is the campus accessible to students with physical disabilities? - **90%**
Is housing available for disabled students? - **Yes**

Bowdoin College

Contact:
Joann E. Canning
Dir, Accommodations for Students with Disabilities
(207) 725-3866
jcanning@bowdoin.edu

Is a smaller course load available? - **No**
Is more time given to finish your degree? - **No**
Is credit given toward the degree for remedial courses? - **No**
Services offered to students with learning disabilities: **other testing accommodations, reading machines, tape recorders, note-taking services, oral tests, learning center, readers, extended time for tests, tutors**
Services offered to students with physical disabilities: **note-taking services, tape recorders, special housing, tutors, adaptive equipment, reader services, interpreters for hearing-impaired, talking books**
Is the campus accessible to students with physical disabilities? - **Mostly**
Is housing available for disabled students? - **Yes**

Brandeis University

Contact:
Alwina Bennett
Assistant Dean
Office of Student Life
Shapiro Campus Center 224
781-736-3600
alwina@brandeis.edu

Is a smaller course load available? - **No**
Is more time given to finish your degree? - **No**
Is credit given toward the degree for remedial courses? - **No**
Services offered to students with learning disabilities: **reading machines, tape recorders, diagnostic testing service, untimed tests, note-taking services, oral tests, extended time for tests, tutors, other**
Services offered to students with physical disabilities: **N/A**
Is the campus accessible to students with physical disabilities? - **Fully**
Is housing available for disabled students? - **Yes**

Colby College

Contact:
admissions@colby.edu

Is a smaller course load available? - **Yes**
Is more time given to finish your degree? - **Yes**
Is credit given toward the degree for remedial courses? - **No**
Services offered to students with learning disabilities: **other testing accommodations, reading mareading machines, tape recorders, note-taking services, readers, extended time for tests, tutors**
Services offered to students with physical disabilities: **note-taking services, tape recorders, tutors, reader services, interpreters for hearing-impaired, talking books, other**
Is the campus accessible to students with physical disabilities? - **Mostly**
Is housing available for disabled students? - **N/A**

College of the Holy Cross

Contact:
Dr. Matthew Toth
Asst. Dean of Students for Student Development Services
(508) 793-3693

Is a smaller course load available? - **No**
Is more time given to finish your degree? - **No**
Is credit given toward the degree for remedial courses? - **No**
Services offered to students with learning disabilities: **other testing accommodations, learning center, extended time for tests**
Services offered to students with physical disabilities: **tape recorders, special housing, reader services, other**
Is the campus accessible to students with physical disabilities? - **85%**
Is housing available for disabled students? - **Yes**

Connecticut College

Contact:
Susan L. Duques, Ph.D.
Director of Disability Services
(860) 439-5428
slduq@conncoll.edu

Is a smaller course load available? - **Yes**
Is more time given to finish your degree? - **Yes**
Is credit given toward the degree for remedial courses? - **No**
Services offered to students with learning disabilities: **note-taking services, extended time for tests, other**
Services offered to students with physical disabilities: **note-taking services, tape recorders, adaptive equipment, reader services, interpreters for hearing-impaired, talking books**
Is the campus accessible to students with physical disabilities? - **Mostly**
Is housing available for disabled students? - **Yes**

Dartmouth College

Contact:
Nancy Pompian
Student Disabilities Coordinator
(603) 646-2014
Nancy.Pompian@Dartmouth.edu

Is a smaller course load available? - **Yes**
Is more time given to finish your degree? - **Yes**
Is credit given toward the degree for remedial courses? - **N/A**
Services offered to students with learning disabilities: **other testing accommodations, learning center, other**
Services offered to students with physical disabilities: **note-taking services, special transportation, tape recorders, special housing, tutors, adaptive equipment, reader services, braille services, interpreters for hearing-impaired, talking books**
Is the campus accessible to students with physical disabilities? - **N/A**
Is housing available for disabled students? - **N/A**

Emerson College

Contact:
Dr. Anthony Bashir
Director of Learning Assistance Center
(617) 824-8415
dso@emerson.edu

Is a smaller course load available? - **Yes**
Is more time given to finish your degree? - **Yes**
Is credit given toward the degree for remedial courses? - **No**
Services offered to students with learning disabilities: **remedial math, remedial English, reading machines, remedial reading, note-taking services, learning center, tutors, other**
Services offered to students with physical disabilities: **N/A**
Is the campus accessible to students with physical disabilities? - **Partially**
Is housing available for disabled students? - **N/A**

Harvard University

Contact:
Louise H. Russell
Director, Student Disability Resource Center
(617) 496-8707
lrussell@fas.harvard.edu

Is a smaller course load available? - **N/A**
Is more time given to finish your degree? - **N/A**
Is credit given toward the degree for remedial courses? - **N/A**
Services offered to students with learning disabilities: **tape recorders, videotaped classes, untimed tests, readers, extended time for tests**
Services offered to students with physical disabilities: **note-taking services, tape recorders, tutors, note-taking services, special transportation, tape recorders, special housing, adaptive equipment, reader services, braille services, interpreters for hearing-impaired**
Is the campus accessible to students with physical disabilities? - **Mostly**
Is housing available for disabled students? - **Yes**

MIT

Contact:
Kathleen Monagle, Carol Clark
Program Specialist, Administrative Assistant
(617) 253-1674
monaglek@mit.edu, cclark@mit.edu

Is a smaller course load available? - **N/A**
Is more time given to finish your degree? - **N/A**
Is credit given toward the degree for remedial courses? - **No**
Services offered to students with learning disabilities: **reading machines, tape recorders, note-taking services, readers, extended time for tests**
Services offered to students with physical disabilities: **note-taking services, tape recorders, adaptive equipment, reader services, braille services, interpreters for hearing-impaired**
Is the campus accessible to students with physical disabilities? - **Partially**
Is housing available for disabled students? - **Yes**

Middlebury College

Contact:
Jodi E. Litchfield
ADA Coordinator
(802) 443-5936
litchfie@middlebury.edu

Is a smaller course load available? - **Yes**
Is more time given to finish your degree? - **Yes**
Is credit given toward the degree for remedial courses? - **N/A**
Services offered to students with learning disabilities: **reading machines, tape recorders, diagnostic testing service, note-taking services, oral tests, learning center, readers, extended time for tests, tutors, other**
Services offered to students with physical disabilities: **note-taking services, tape recorders, tutors, reader services**
Is the campus accessible to students with physical disabilities? - **Mostly**
Is housing available for disabled students? - **Yes**

Mount Holyoke College

Contact:
John Body III
Associate Dean of Learning Skills
(413) 538-2504
jbody@mtholyoke.edu

Is a smaller course load available? - **Yes**
Is more time given to finish your degree? - **Yes**
Is credit given toward the degree for remedial courses? - **No**
Services offered to students with learning disabilities: **other testing accommodations, diagnostic testing service, note-taking services, oral tests, readers, extended time for tests, tutors, other**
Services offered to students with physical disabilities: **other testing accommodations, diagnostic testing service, note-taking services, oral tests, readers, extended time for tests, tutors, other**
Is the campus accessible to students with physical disabilities? - **Mostly**
Is housing available for disabled students? - **N/A**

Northeastern University

Contact:
Debbie Auerbach
Service Coordinator
(617) 373-2675
d.auerbach@neu.edu

Is a smaller course load available? - **Yes**
Is more time given to finish your degree? - **Yes**
Is credit given toward the degree for remedial courses? - **No**
Services offered to students with learning disabilities: **remedial math, remedial English, reading machines, tape recorders, videotaped classes, diagnostic testing service, note-taking services, oral tests, learning center, readers, extended time for tests, tutors, other**
Services offered to students with physical disabilities: **note-taking services, tape recorders, special housing, adaptive equipment, reader services, braille services, interpreters for hearing-impaired, talking books, other**
Is the campus accessible to students with physical disabilities? - **95%**
Is housing available for disabled students? - **N/A**

Providence College

Contact:
Nicole Kudarauskas
Disability Support Services Coordinator
(401) 865-1121
nkudarau@providence.edu

Is a smaller course load available? - **No**
Is more time given to finish your degree? - **No**
Is credit given toward the degree for remedial courses? - **No**
Services offered to students with learning disabilities: **tape recorders, note-taking services, oral tests, learning center, readers, extended time for tests, tutors, other**
Services offered to students with physical disabilities: **note-taking services, tape recorders, tutors, reader services**
Is the campus accessible to students with physical disabilities? - **90%**
Is housing available for disabled students? - **Yes**

Rhode Island School of Design

Contact:
rmcmahon@risd.edu

Is a smaller course load available? - **Yes**
Is more time given to finish your degree? - **Yes**
Is credit given toward the degree for remedial courses? - **No**
Services offered to students with learning disabilities: **reading machines, untimed tests, note-taking services, oral tests, learning center, readers, extended time for tests, tutors**
Services offered to students with physical disabilities: **note-taking services, tape recorders, tutors, adaptive equipment, reader services**
Is the campus accessible to students with physical disabilities? - **Mostly**
Is housing available for disabled students? - **Yes**

Smith College

Contact:
Laura Rauscher
Disability Services Director
(413) 585-2071
lrausch@email.smith.edu

Is a smaller course load available? - **No**
Is more time given to finish your degree? - **No**
Is credit given toward the degree for remedial courses? - **No**
Services offered to students with learning disabilities: **other testing accommodations, reading machines, tape recorders, untimed tests, note-taking services, readers, extended time for tests, tutors, other**
Services offered to students with physical disabilities: **note-taking services, special transportation, tape recorders, special housing, tutors, adaptive equipment, reader services, braille services, interpreters for hearing-impaired, talking books**
Is the campus accessible to students with physical disabilities? - **85%**
Is housing available for disabled students? - **N/A**

Trinity College

Contact:
Fred Alford
Dean of Students
(860) 297-2157

Is a smaller course load available? - **No**
Is more time given to finish your degree? - **No**
Is credit given toward the degree for remedial courses? - **No**
Services offered to students with learning disabilities: **other testing accommodations, tape recorders, videotaped classes, diagnostic testing service, note-taking services, oral tests, readers, extended time for tests, tutors**
Services offered to students with physical disabilities: **note-taking services, special transportation, tape recorders, special housing, tutors, adaptive equipment, reader services, braille services, interpreters for hearing-impaired, talking books**
Is the campus accessible to students with physical disabilities? - **Partially**
Is housing available for disabled students? - **N/A**

Tufts University

Contact:
Sandra Baer
Disability Services Coordinator
(617) 627-2000

Is a smaller course load available? - **No**
Is more time given to finish your degree? - **No**
Is credit given toward the degree for remedial courses? - **No**
Services offered to students with learning disabilities: **tape recorders, note-taking services, oral tests, learning center, readers, extended time for tests, tutors**
Services offered to students with physical disabilities: **other**
Is the campus accessible to students with physical disabilities? - **Mostly**
Is housing available for disabled students? - **Yes**

University of Connecticut

Contact:
Joseph Madaus, PhD
Director, UPLD
(860) 486-0178

Is a smaller course load available? - **Yes**
Is more time given to finish your degree? - **Yes**
Is credit given toward the degree for remedial courses? - **No**
Services offered to students with learning disabilities: **other testing accommodations, reading machines, tape recorders, untimed tests, note-taking services, oral tests, readers, extended time for tests**
Services offered to students with physical disabilities: **note-taking services, special transportation, tape recorders, special housing, tutors, adaptive equipment, reader services, braille services, talking books, other**
Is the campus accessible to students with physical disabilities? - **80%**
Is housing available for disabled students? - **Yes**

University of Massachusetts - Amherst

Contact:
(413) 545-0892

Is a smaller course load available? - **Yes**
Is more time given to finish your degree? - **Yes**
Is credit given toward the degree for remedial courses? - **N/A**
Services offered to students with learning disabilities: **other testing accommodations, reading machines, tape recorders, untimed tests, note-taking services, oral tests, readers, extended time for tests, other**
Services offered to students with physical disabilities: **note-taking services, tape recorders, tutors,note-taking services, special transportation, tape recorders, special housing, tutors, adaptive equipment, reader services, braille services, interpreters for hearing-impaired**
Is the campus accessible to students with physical disabilities? - **100%**
Is housing available for disabled students? - **Yes**

University of New Hampshire

Contact:
Maxine Little
ACCESS Director
(603) 862-2607
tph2@cisunix.unh.edu

Is a smaller course load available? - **Yes**
Is more time given to finish your degree? - **Yes**
Is credit given toward the degree for remedial courses? - **No**
Services offered to students with learning disabilities: **reading machines, tape recorders, note-taking services, oral tests, readers, extended time for tests, other**
Services offered to students with physical disabilities: **note-taking services, special transportatnote-taking services, special transportation, tape recorders, special housing, adaptive equipment, reader services, interpreters for hearing-impaired, talking books, other**
Is the campus accessible to students with physical disabilities? - **80%**
Is housing available for disabled students? - **N/A**

University of Rhode Island

Contact:
Pamela Rohland
Asst Director, Office of Student Life
(401) 874-2098
rohland@uri.edu

Is a smaller course load available? - **Yes**
Is more time given to finish your degree? - **Yes**
Is credit given toward the degree for remedial courses? - **No**
Services offered to students with learning disabilities: **other testing accommodations, reading mareading machines, tape recorders, diagnostic testing service, note-taking services, special bookstore section, oral tests, learning center, readers, extended time for tests, other**
Services offered to students with physical disabilities: **note-taking services, tape recorders, tutors,note-taking services, special transportation, tape recorders, special housing, tutors, adaptive equipment, reader services, braille services, interpreters for hearing-impaired, talking books, other**
Is the campus accessible to students with physical disabilities? - **80%**
Is housing available for disabled students? - **Yes**

University of Vermont

Contact:
Margaret Ottinger
Assistant director, ACCESS
(802) 656-7853
Margaret.Ottinger@uvm.edu

Is a smaller course load available? - **Yes**
Is more time given to finish your degree? - **Yes**
Is credit given toward the degree for remedial courses? - **No**
Services offered to students with learning disabilities: **other testing accommodations, reading machines, tape recorders, other special classes, note-taking services, learning center, readers, extended time for tests, tutors**
Services offered to students with physical disabilities: **note-taking services, tape recorders, tutors, reader services, braille services, interpreters for hearing-impaired, other**
Is the campus accessible to students with physical disabilities? - **Mostly**
Is housing available for disabled students? - **N/A**

Wellesley College

Contact:
Barbara Boger - Director, Pforzheimer Learning & Teaching Center
(781) 283-2092
bboger@wellesley.edu

Is a smaller course load available? - **No**
Is more time given to finish your degree? - **N/A**
Is credit given toward the degree for remedial courses? - **N/A**
Services offered to students with learning disabilities: **other testing accommodations, tape recorders, note-taking services, learning center, extended time for tests**
Services offered to students with physical disabilities: **note-taking services, special transportation, tape recorders, special housing, adaptive equipment, reader services, braille services, interpreters for hearing-impaired, talking books, other**
Is the campus accessible to students with physical disabilities? - **Partially**
Is housing available for disabled students? - **N/A**

Wesleyan University

Contact:
Vancenia Rutherford
Dean for First-Year Students
(860) 685-2765
vrutherford@wesleyan.edu

Is a smaller course load available? - **No**
Is more time given to finish your degree? - **Yes**
Is credit given toward the degree for remedial courses? - **No**
Services offered to students with learning disabilities: **other testing accommodations, note-taking services, extended time for tests, tutors**
Services offered to students with physical disabilities: **N/A**
Is the campus accessible to students with physical disabilities? - **N/A**
Is housing available for disabled students? - **Yes**

Wheaton College (MA)

Contact:
Marty Bledsoe
Assistant Dean for College Skills
(508) 286-8215
mbledsoe@wheatoncollege.edu

Is a smaller course load available? - **Yes**
Is more time given to finish your degree? - **Yes**
Is credit given toward the degree for remedial courses? - **No**
Services offered to students with learning disabilities: **other testing accommodations, reading machines, tape recorders, note-taking services, oral tests, learning center, readers, extended time for tests, other**
Services offered to students with physical disabilities: **note-taking services, special housing, reader services, braille services, interpreters for hearing-impaired, talking books**
Is the campus accessible to students with physical disabilities? - **50%**
Is housing available for disabled students? - **N/A**

Williams College

Contact:
Charles Toomajian
Associate Dean for Student Services
(413) 597-4010
Charles.Toomajian@williams.edu

Is a smaller course load available? - **Yes**
Is more time given to finish your degree? - **N/A**
Is credit given toward the degree for remedial courses? - **N/A**
Services offered to students with learning disabilities: **other testing accommodations, tape recorders, note-taking services, extended time for tests, other**
Services offered to students with physical disabilities: **note-taking services, special transportation, tape recorders, special housing, tutors, adaptive equipment, reader services, other**
Is the campus accessible to students with physical disabilities? - **Partially**
Is housing available for disabled students? - **N/A**

Yale University

Contact:
N/A

Is a smaller course load available? - **No**
Is more time given to finish your degree? - **No**
Is credit given toward the degree for remedial courses? - **N/A**
Services offered to students with learning disabilities: **N/A**
Services offered to students with physical disabilities: **note-taking services, special transportation, tape recorders, special housing, tutors, reader services, braille services, interpreters for hearing-impaired**
Is the campus accessible to students with physical disabilities? - **Mostly**
Is housing available for disabled students? - **Yes**

New England Admissions Counseling

Source: Independent Educational Consultants Association

College Prowler Counseling
Our network of former college admissions officers use evaluation tools and methods employed by universities nationwide to provide you with an insider analysis of your admissions case. Learn more at *www.collegeprowler.com*.

There are also several local counselors registered in the New England area, which you'll find listed below. Don't forget to tell them College Prowler sent you!

Connecticut

Camille M. Bertram, CEP
Camille M. Bertram, Educational Consultants, LLC
120 Riders Lane
Fairfield CT 06824
203-255-2577
CMBert@cmbconsultants.com

Adrienne A. DuBois M.S.Ed., CEP
Adrienne A. DuBois Associates
15 E. Putnam Avenue
Greenwich CT 06830
203-629-2566
AADuBois@aol.co

William M. Morse Ph.D., CEP
William Morse Associates, Inc.
260 Riverside Avenue
Westport CT 06880-4804
203-222-1066

Massachusetts

Edward L. Bigelow, PHD
Dunbar Educational Consultants, Inc.
PO Box 248
Dedham MA 02027
781-329-1248
MOE9817@aol.com

Joan H. Bress LICSW, CEP
College Resource Associates
12 Southwood Road
Worcester MA 01609
508-757-8920
jbress@aol.com

Sarah M. McGinty Ph.D., CEP
McGinty Consulting Group
322 Marlborough Street
Boston MA 02116
617-262-3435
sarahmcginty@att.net

Bonny Musinsky M.A., CEP
Musinsky & Associates
49 Kendall Common Road
Weston MA 02493
781-899-5759
musin@attbi.com

New Hampshire

Peter P. Drake M.Ed.
Drake Associates Educational Planners, LLC
195 Old Dublin Road, PO Box 355
Hancock NH 03449
603-525-3232
ppdnhd@aol.com

Mei-Ling Henrichson CEP
Mei-Ling Henrichson Educ. Consulting
PO Box 138
Winchester NH 03470
603-239-8189
mlhedcon@ix.netcom.com

Rhode Island

Susan M. Hanflik M.Ed.
Educational Consultant
170 Summit Drive
Cranston RI 02920
401-944-4315
smhanflik@cox.net

C. Claire Law M.S., CEP
Educational Avenues
2358 South County Trail
Suite 100
E. Greenwich RI 02818
401-885-8611
Claire@eduave.com

Ruth Lipka M.A.
Academic Admissions Consultants, LLC
430 Old River Rd.
Lincoln RI 02838
401-762-3675

Vermont

Lora K. Block M.A., CEP
College Advisory Services
McIntosh Lane
Bennington VT 05201
802-447-0776
lblock@sover.net

Robert M. Kantar
Educational Resources
1041 Brown Farm Road
Lyndonville VT 05851
802-626-4620
Kantar@aol.com

Words to Know

Academic Probation – A student can receive this if they fail to keep up with their school's academic minimums. Those who are unable to improve their grades after receiving this warning can possibly face dismissal.

Beer Pong / Beirut – A drinking game with numerous cups of beer arranged in a particular pattern on each side of a table. The goal is to get a ping pong ball into one of the opponent's cups by throwing the ball or hitting it with a paddle. If the ball lands in a cup, the opponent is required to drink the beer.

Bid – An invitation from a fraternity or sorority to pledge their specific house.

Blue-Light Phone – Brightly-colored phone posts with a blue light bulb on top. These phones exist for security purposes and are located at various outside locations around most campuses. If a student has an emergency or is feeling endangered, they can pick up one of these phones (free of charge) to connect with campus police or an escort service.

Campus Police – Policemen who are specifically assigned to a given institution. Campus police are not regular city officers; they are employed by the university in a full-time capacity.

Club Sports – A level of sports that falls somewhere between varsity and intramural. If a student is unable to commit to a varsity team but has a lot of passion for athletics, a club sport could be a better, less intense option. If a club sport still requires too much commitment, intramurals often involve no traveling and a lot less time.

Cocaine – An illegal drug. Also known as "coke" or "blow," cocaine often resembles a white crystalline or powdery substance. It is highly addictive and dangerous.

Common Application – An application that students can use to apply to multiple schools.

Course Registration – The time when a student selects what courses they would like for the upcoming quarter or semester. Prior to registration, it is best to have an idea of several back-up courses in case a particular class becomes full. If a course is full, a student can place themselves on the waitlist, although this still does not guarantee entry.

Division Athletics – Athletics range from Division I to Division III. Division IA is the most competitive, while Division III is considered to be the least competitive.

Dorm – Short for dormitory, a dorm is an on-campus housing facility. Dorms can provide a range of options from suite-style rooms to more communal options that include shared bathrooms. Most first-year students live in dorms. Some upperclassmen who wish to stay on campus also choose this option.

Early Action – A way to apply to a school and get an early acceptance response without a binding commitment. This is a system that is becoming less and less available.

Early Decision – An option that students should use only if they are positive that a place is their dream school. If a student applies to a school using the early decision option and is admitted, they are required and bound to attend that university. Admission rates are usually higher with early decision students because the school knows that a student is making them their first choice.

Ecstasy – An illegal drug. Also known as "E" or "X," ecstasy looks like a pill and most resembles an aspirin. Considered a party drug, ecstasy is very dangerous and can be deadly.

Ethernet – An extremely fast internet connection that is usually available in most university-owned residence halls. To use an Ethernet connection properly, a student will need a network card and cable for their computer.

Fake ID – A counterfeit identification card that contains false information. Most commonly, students get fake IDs and change their birthdates so that they appear to be older than 21 (of legal drinking age). Even though it is illegal, many college students have fake IDs in hopes of purchasing alcohol or getting into bars.

Frosh – Slang for "freshmen."

Hazing – Initiation rituals that must be completed for membership into some fraternities or sororities. Numerous universities have outlawed hazing due to its degrading or dangerous requirements.

Sports (IMs) – A popular, and usually free, student activity where students create teams and compete against other groups for fun. These sports vary in competitiveness and can include a range of activities—everything from billiards to water polo. IM sports are a great way to meet people with similar interests.

Keg – Officially called a half barrel, a keg contains roughly 200 12-ounce servings of beer and is often found at college parties.

LSD – An illegal drug. Also known as acid, this hallucinogenic drug most commonly resembles a tab of paper.

Marijuana – An illegal drug. Also known as weed or pot; besides alcohol, marijuana is one of the most commonly-found drugs on campuses across the country.

Major –The focal point of a student's college studies; a specific topic that is studied for a degree. Examples of majors include physics, English, history, computer science, economics, business, and music. Many students decide on a specific major before arriving on campus, while others are simply "undecided" and figure it out later. Those who are extremely interested in two areas can also choose to double major.

Meal Block – The equivalent of one meal. Students on a "meal plan" usually receive a fixed number of meals per week. Each meal, or "block," can be redeemed at the school's dining facilities in place of cash. More often than not, if a student fails to use their weekly allotment of meal blocks, they will be forfeited.

Minor – An additional focal point in a student's education. Often serving as a compliment or addition to a student's main area of focus, a minor has fewer requirements and prerequisites to fulfill than a major. Minors are not required for graduation from most schools; however some students who want to further explore many different interests choose to have both a major and a minor.

Mushrooms – An illegal drug. Also known as "shrooms," this drug looks like regular mushrooms but are extremely hallucinogenic.

Off-Campus Housing – Housing from a particular landlord or rental group that is not affiliated with the university. Depending on the college, off-campus housing can range from extremely popular to non-existent. Those students who choose to live off campus are typically given more freedom, but they also have to deal with things such as possible subletting scenarios, furniture, and bills. In addition to these factors, rental prices and distance often affect a student's decision to move off campus.

Office Hours – Time that teachers set aside for students who have questions about the coursework. Office hours are a good place for students to go over any problems and to show interest in the subject material.

Pledging – The time after a student has gone through rush, received a bid, and has chosen a particular fraternity or sorority they would like to join. Pledging usually lasts anywhere from one to two semesters. Once the pledging period is complete and a particular student has done everything that is required to become a member, they are considered a brother or sister. If a fraternity or a sorority would decide to "haze" a group of students, these initiation rituals would take place during the pledging period.

Private Institution – A school that does not use taxpayers dollars to help subsidize education costs. Private schools typically cost more than public schools and are usually smaller.

Prof – Slang for "professor."

Public Institution – A school that uses taxpayers dollars to help subsidize education costs. Public schools are often a good value for in-state residents and tend to be larger than most private colleges.

Quarter System (sometimes referred to as the Trimester System) – A type of academic calendar system. In this setup, students take classes for three academic periods. The first quarter usually starts in late September or early October and concludes right before Christmas. The second quarter usually starts around early to mid–January and finishes up around March or April. The last quarter, or "third quarter," usually starts in late March or early April and finishes up in late May or Mid-June. The fourth quarter is summer. The major difference between the quarter system and semester system is that students take more courses but with less coverage.

RA (Resident Assistant) – A student leader who is assigned to a particular floor in a dormitory in order to help to the other students who live there. A RA's duties include ensuring student safety and providing guidance or assistance wherever possible.

Recitation – An extension of a specific course; a "review" session of sorts. Because some classes are so large, recitations offer a setting with fewer students where students can ask questions and get help from professors or TAs in a more personalized environment. As a result, it is common for most large lecture classes to be supplemented with recitations.

Rolling Admissions – A form of admissions. Most commonly found at public institutions, schools with this type of policy continue to accept students throughout the year until their class sizes are met. For example, some schools begin accepting students as early as December and will continue to do so until April or May.

Room and Board – This is typically the combined cost of a university-owned room and a meal plan.

Room Draw/Housing Lottery – A common way to pick on-campus room assignments for the following year. If a student decides to remain in university-owned housing, they are assigned a unique number that, along with seniority, is used to choose their new rooms for the next year.

Rush – The period in which students can meet the brothers and sisters of a particular chapter and find out if a given fraternity or sorority is right for them. Rushing a fraternity or a sorority is not a requirement at any school. The goal of rush is to give students who are serious about pledging a feel for what to expect.

Semester System – The most common type of academic calendar system at college campuses. This setup typically includes two semesters in a given school year. The "fall" semester starts around the end of August or early September and finishes right before winter vacation. The "spring" semester usually starts in mid-January and ends around late April or May.

Student Center/Rec Center/Student Union – A common area on campus that often contains study areas, recreation facilities, and eateries. This building is often a good place to meet up with fellow students and is most commonly used as a hangout. Depending on the school, the student center can have a huge role or a non-existent role in campus life.

Student ID – A university-issued photo ID that serves as a student's key to many different functions within an institution. Some schools require students to show these cards in order to get into dorms, libraries, cafeterias, and other facilities. In addition to storing meal plan information, in some cases, a student ID can actually work as a debit card and allow students to purchase things from bookstores or local shops.

Suite – A type of dorm room. Unlike other places that have communal bathrooms that are shared by the entire floor, a suite has a private bathroom. Suite-style dorm rooms can house anywhere from two to ten students.

TA (Teacher's Assistant) – An undergraduate or grad student who helps in some manner with a specific course. In some cases, a TA will teach a class, assist a professor, grade assignments, or conduct office hours.

Undergraduate – A student who is in the process of studying for their Bachelor (college) degree.

About the Authors

Nadav Klein—Amherst College
He hails from the distant and mysterious lands of Israel, where men are still men, women are still women, and sex is still sexy. He first heard English as an infant, watching in grief as the Transformers constantly defeated his beloved Decepticons. He went to Eshel Hanassi, an all Israeli high school with all Israeli teachers who, after observing how eloquently he articulated his arguments and how good he looked in a suit, told him with pride, "Nadav, you're going to be a great lawyer some day, and remember where you first heard it." In addition, and without direct logical connection, he once served in the Israeli Army and dreamed of becoming a pilot. Now, he is neither a pilot nor will he become a lawyer, and the Decepticons are still getting their butts kicked in re-runs.

I applied to U.S. schools while I was in the army, after having only casually inquired about the places I applied to. Now, I am living in a faraway country, trying to make sense of it all, trying to get to know who I really am, and having a ball doing it. I am humbled by the immense opportunities that Amherst has opened by admitting me, and I am, and always will be, eternally grateful to Amherst, both for having accepted an unusual person such as me, and for having supplemented the cceptance letter with enough financial aid to get me through four years. I truly believe that it's people like those found in Amherst College that create and mobilize all the great things of which the human race is capable.

Hopefully I'll amount to something special in my life, and so will you. Happy trails and e-mail me at nadavklein@collegeprowler.com with any questions, comments, or criticisms.

Anna Klimentievna Gatker—Babson College
I had a great time writing this book, and I would like to thank College Prowler for presenting me with such a unique opportunity! Having lived on campus for more than three years (this one being my fourth), I can honestly say that I enjoyed a well-rounded life at Babson College. By balancing social, educational, and extra-curricular activities I was able to mature in this fast-paced and exciting environment. As a result, I already know what Babson is all about and what it has to offer you throughout the years. However, being the curious person that I am, I really wanted to find out what other students thought about life here. That is the reason why the timing of this project was impeccable, making it an enjoyable piece of writing for me. First, I conducted some focus groups and surveyed the students. After reviewing everyone's responses, I found that a lot of people shared my opinions. But, by approaching this project as objectively as possible, I tried to paint a picture of Babson that was both educational and fun to read for an individual like you. I also like to see people laugh, so a bit of my humor is reflected in these writings. I hope you enjoy reading about my college as much as I enjoyed writing about it!

Lastly, I would like to thank my mother, father, sister, and grandpa for helping me with this project and my success at Babson. Also, big thanks to Kate Walsh, Natalie Ruppert, and Vince Framularo for being my best friends, and for their encouragement and help with this project.

annagatker@collegeprowler.com

Sarah Connell—Bates

Writing this book has been an amazing experience. Though I hope to go into publishing when I graduate, this is the first time I've ever worked on such an extensive project. Writing about Bates and seeing what other students had to say about the school also helped me get ready to return here, after having spent my junior year abroad in Cork, Ireland. I'm hoping to do my postgraduate studies at Cork next year and possibly live and work there, as well. When I graduate, I'll have degrees in English and Classics, and a Certificate in Irish Studies.

Bates was my first-choice college. It's a small, private liberal arts school with an excellent academic reputation and only about 50 miles from my home in New Hampshire. I've learned a lot while I've studied here, but probably the best part about going to Bates is the opportunity I've had to study abroad. In addition to spending a year in Ireland, I traveled to Budapest during Short Term my first year. I was able to go to 15 plays, ballets, and operas, and I also got the chance to perform in two plays myself. It was Bates' unique calendar that allowed me to go abroad in my very first year at school, and I really believe that traveling has been a vital part of my college experience.

I hope that you've gotten a more detailed picture of what living at Bates is like from reading what I, and other students, had to say about the school. If you are considering Bates, I urge you to visit the school and even spend a night here, if you can.

sarahconnell@collegeprowler.com

Jessica Low—Bentley College

For those of you who made it through the entire book to get to this final page, congratulations! Now is your chance to read about the person who wrote the guide that may or may not convince you that it is the school for you. As a marketing major, I held two different internships in Public Affairs and will soon be starting a career in public relations, hopefully with an agency in Boston. I have always enjoyed writing, for personal pleasure and as an integral part of my job function. The angle this particular College Prowler book was written from may be different than other guides because I was a second-semester senior reflecting back on my entire college life. I wanted to write this book because, as a senior, I felt I had the experience, knowledge, and resources to offer you a complete and thorough look inside campus life. It was my goal to offer an unbiased, insider's look at Bentley, and if I accomplished that, I hope to meet some of you at alumni events!

This was a tough last semester of college for me and if it wasn't for these special people, I couldn't have made it through with my sanity intact. Thank you Dad, Eric, Adam, Sandy, Gram, Loren, Amanda, Lynn, and the Barneys. I love you Mom.

jessicalow@collegeprowler.com

Caren M. Walker—Boston University

I certainly hope that this information, as well as my various personal experiences, have been at least somewhat useful in your decision-making process in choosing a school. The truth is, while being prepared and advised is extremely beneficial, the best way to check out BU is to check out BU. Come visit and hang out on your own for a bit. As soon as I arrived on campus I felt comfortable and confident that I could be both happy and productive in this environment. This does not mean, however, that it will feel the same to you.

So, what am I going to do now? Right after graduation, and the completion of my thesis, I moved to LA for about eight months. I had planned to do some quality "finding myself"—but spent most of it partying and hanging out in the desert. It was around the time that I felt my brain was atrophying that I decided to return to the East Coast. I am now working as a research assistant and study coordinator in the neuroscience department at MGH (a part of Harvard Medical School).

I am planning to hit up NYC for graduate school, but I have yet to decide on a direction for study. I intend to get my Ph.D. in something, perhaps evolutionary psychology, philosophy of mind, or cognition studies. I don't know. Remember, no matter how many friends, relatives, and complete strangers look at you and say, "So, what are you going to do?" it is okay to have no idea. I still don't. My long-term plan is to remain in an academic environment for a while. As long as my parents keep paying, I will keep going … indefinitely. I suggest you do the same. Do not rush into the mechanism. Feed your head.

I would like to thank the people at College Prowler for all of their help through this process, all of those at BU who offered their insight for the creation of this book, and anyone else who has provided me with little nuggets of wisdom. If you have any questions, need to talk, or if you suddenly engage in a personal revelation concerning the nature of the self and its relation to the physical world, don't hesitate to e-mail me. Good luck!

carenwalker@collegeprowler.com

Derrick S. Wong—Bowdoin College

This project has been a labor of love for me. It gave me the opportunity to learn nuances about Bowdoin, get to know my peers and administrators better, to be resourceful, and to discover my passion for journalism.

I am currently a sophomore at Bowdoin College. I serve in Student Government, write for the school newspaper (*The Orient*), and mentor local kids in Maine. I plan to major in government and history. My love for ice hockey, staying active, and coaching stems from attending a small, private high school in Vermont, my home state. I hope to one day pursue a career in journalism and business.

I'd like to thank all those who contributed to this book. Margaret Allen, Matthew O' Donnell, Lisa Randall, and James Westoff provided me support, input, and data to keep statistics and information about Bowdoin current. My mentor, John D. Moyers, gave me an unbiased perspective on life and offered his professional advice when necessary. Mary Branagan served as my partner in crime, whether as girlfriend or friend.

My guidance counselor Andrea Torello spent hours with me discussing the finer points of life and the college process. Thanks to Kevin Clark, my freshmen and junior year history teacher, for helping me discover Bowdoin and for listening to my ranting in and outside of class. Doreen Marquis and Joey Solomon, my sophomore and freshmen English teachers, showed me my potential and taught me to love writing.

Mary Beatty, Ann Kenney, Kelle Carmen, Judith Ring, Linda Barnes, and many more served as listening ears in high school. Jeffrey Nagle, Bernie Hershberger, Penny Martin, and others at Bowdoin College helped me adjust to the rigors of college.

My half-brother Andrew served as a reminder to do my best. My father and step-mother Annie never shied away from showing their concern and affection. I'd like to express my deepest appreciation for my step-father Bob for providing me a stable and nurturing environment to grow up in with unconditional love. Most importantly, I would like to thank my mother for her love and support, unwavering confidence, and constructive criticism—even when I didn't want to hear it. I could not be the person I am today without her.

I hope you felt entertained by my conversational commentaries and found insights into how four years at Bowdoin College could shape your life.

If you have any comments or questions, please contact me at derrickwong@collegeprowler.com

Andrew Katz—Brandeis University

Andrew Katz was born in 1983 in New York City. He grew up in Scarsdale, New York and attended Edgemont High School. In high school he got a hand in everything from being the class president, to serving as editor of the features section of the newspaper, to starting a volunteer tutoring group. In college, this same passion for getting involved continued as Andrew served as a senator while living in the Castle Quad. He has also served as a volunteer for admissions, worked in Hillel's social action wing Mitzvah Corps, and written for the Arts section of the school newspaper, *The Justice*. His favorite activities are writing his weekly sports column for *The Justice*, his sports talk radio show, his opportunities to broadcast basketball games, and tutoring.

As part of the Brandeis Class of 2006, Andrew was undecided as to what to major in when he first came to Brandeis. He threw around American Studies and Politics as possible majors, and Legal Studies and Near Eastern and Judaic Studies as possible minors. But he has finally decided on economics as a major with minors in business and journalism. He is not sure what he's going to do when he graduates Brandeis, but would like to go into a field where his love of sports can be expressed. Andrew is an avid sports fan and admits he goes to *ESPN.com* more times in a day than he visits the library in a year.

As a die-hard Yankees fan living in Red Sox country, Andrew would like to thank Aaron Boone for making his sophomore year a little more enjoyable. All joking aside, Andrew says that the real thanks go out to everyone who helped him write this book. Without their input, he would be lost. He would especially like to thank his girlfriend, Jess, who has been his biggest supporter. He would also like to thank Mom, Dad, and Gillian for putting up with him as he wrote this book—let's just say he wasn't in the mood to chit-chat most of those days.

Lastly he would like to thank the people who bought this book. Brandeis was about number four on Andrew's college list, but he admits he wouldn't go back and change his decision for anything. He's looking forward to his last two years at Brandeis and hopes that the people who read that book can experience the same enjoyment.

andrewkatz@collegeprowler.com

Matthew Kittay—Brown University

This book reflects a lot of time and effort, and I hope you find it as useful as I intended it to be. I picked up the project as a chance to reflect on my own experience at Brown and to learn even more about the university where I spent four years of my life. Upon graduating in May of 2003, I never expected to find myself writing a book the following summer.

I had a great time writing this edition of the guidebook to Brown, and I get a good deal of satisfaction knowing that people will know more about the University and what they can hope to find when they come to visit or study at the school. Brown is a great place and, like many of the students I interviewed, there's nowhere in the world I would rather call my alma mater than Brown University.

If you have any questions, feel free to e-mail me at matthewkittay@collegeprowler.com.

Allyson Rudolph—Colby College

Hi! I'm the author. While not writing college guidebooks, I actually go to college. I'm currently a sophomore at Colby. I think I am an English major, but that is subject to change on a minute-by-minute basis. I'm also a political junkie. At school I am the Arts and Entertainment editor for *The Echo*, the president of the League of Progressive Voters (like I said, political junkie), an HR, and a tour guide.

I have lived in northern Virginia, the western suburbs of Chicago, and now, Maine.

Thanks to my family, especially my parents. Thanks to my friends, who I will not list by name because I would probably forget somebody or put someone last and I don't want to do that. Thanks to the College Prowler. Thanks to my teachers. Thanks to you, dear reader, for putting up with my writing.

Good luck with the college search. If you have any comments about the guidebook, or questions about Colby, the application process, the meaning of life, etc., I enjoy receiving e-mails. They make me feel loved.

allysonrudolph@collegeprowler.com

Matthew Hayes— College of the Holy Cross

I am a graduate of the College of the Holy Cross, where I majored in history and minored in economics. I was raised in Sea Cliff, on Long Island, and currently reside in New York City, where I work at a textbook publishing company.

Unlike many other students at Holy Cross who grew up in households steeped in Holy Cross tradition or went to Catholic high schools where Holy Cross was a well-known name, I had never heard of the school until the summer before my senior year in high school. A colleague of my father's who serves on the College's Board of Trustees told me what an excellent school it was and highly suggested that I visit. A few weeks later, I did—and as soon as I saw the campus (and met the Public Safety officer who had an Irish brogue), I was in love. Although the decision process was arduous—I was deciding between Holy Cross and a number of other top-ranked liberal arts colleges—in the end I believe I made the right choice.

In most of the ways that matter, Holy Cross prepared me well for the real world. The school's tough academic policies ensured that I left school not only four years older, but four years wiser. Unlike the traditional stereotype of Catholic education—the rote learning model that is so often lampooned—the Jesuit tradition encourages free thinking and questioning, and obtaining knowledge through understanding. This thought process is the hallmark of a Holy Cross education, and I know that it has helped me immensely in my postgraduate career.

Please feel free to contact me at matthewhayes@collegeprowler.com

Brian Sendrowski—Connecticut College

Brian Sendrowski spent incredible years at Connecticut College studying English, a subject he had earlier vowed never to major in, because English majors tend not to find jobs until after they're dead. After graduating summa cum laude, he's pleased to report that he has discovered that they get them sooner than that. He currently resides in Ellington, Connecticut, not too far from his alma mater.

The author would like to thank everyone at College Prowler for the opportunity to write this book and all of the professors at Conn's English department with whom he had the pleasure to work. Special thanks go out to everyone at the Roth Writing Center, especially to Michael Reder for his inexhaustible enthusiasm for writing and teaching, Andrea Rossi for her service as a Faculty Adviser and constant stream of recommendation letters, and Beverly Matias for making each day at the center so much fun. And of course, never-ending thanks to Mom, Dad, Brendan, and Laura for all of your support over the years.

The author enjoys being called "the author," so if someone reading this happens to have any freelance writing jobs, feel free to e-mail him at BrianSendrowski@collegeprowler.com. Of course, comments and feedback are also welcome.

briansendrowski@collegeprowler.com

Scott Glabe—Dartmouth College

This book has given me the opportunity to fuse my passion for writing and the college search process. I deeply hope it has provided you with an insider's look at the college I have grown to love.

I am now a sophomore at Dartmouth, where I'm pursuing a double major in government and anthropology. I arrived in Hanover by way of Columbia, Missouri, where I was born and raised. I was a founding student of Columbia Independent School and one of four in the school's first graduating class. I am currently a contributor for The Dartmouth Review and am also active in Ivy Council and the Mock Trial Society. Other extracurricular interests include club rugby and the alto saxophone.

Big thanks go to Emily; to Mom, Dad, and Grant; to Sanders but not to Suhler. Thanks to the all the folks at College Prowler for making this dream possible and to you, the reader, for making it a success. For those involved in the college search, good luck, and I hope you enjoy what was one of the most exciting times of my life.

scottglabe@collegeprowler.com

Janos Marton (editor)—Dartmouth College

I remember the college search process as an extremely exciting time, and it's great to be able to help out future generations of (hopefully Dartmouth) students.

I graduated last year and recieved a degree in History. Born and raised in New York City, I came to Dartmouth on a whim but have loved my four years here. I'm serving my second term as Student Body President, am a staff writer for the Free Press, and a member of Chi Gamma Epsilon fraternity.

Best of luck to everyone—while I hope you find the best college for you, no matter where you end up, the next four years are going to be incredible.

janosmarton@collegeprowler.com

Jordan Ross—Emerson College

I decided to do this book because I wanted to gain experience working on a large writing project during my last summer of classes. It turns out that it was a lot of work, but well worth the effort. As I finish this book, I am getting ready to grab my degree and run (I've enjoyed my three years here, but am ready to leave Boston). I will miss my professors at Emerson; they have made all the difference in my experience.

Thanks for the opportunity for me to share some insight about Emerson with you. I hope this book has been useful in your college search. Your years at college should be a challenging, maturing, and fun experience. I wish you the best in finding the perfect school for you. Thanks to the professors who have encouraged and taught me so much: Jeff Seglin, Lisa Diercks, Kevin Miller, John Coffee, and Tim Weiskel. Much thanks to my parents, M.C., Leah, Taylor, Crystal, Kari, Ryan, Penny, Emily, Ethan, Shiny, Maggie, 45 Columbus, and everyone at College Prowler.

JordanRoss@collegeprowler.com

Dominic Hood—Harvard University

Originally born in San Antonio and raised in New Orleans, my transition to the New England culture and weather of Harvard University challenged me beyond my dreams. I'm now a junior at Harvard and concentrating in psychology, with my own emphasis on organizational behavior. I've been excited about writing this guide because I remember the challenge of selecting a college, and I wish I had found a guide like this to provide a realistic perspective on colleges instead of relying on the admissions office propaganda. This has been a great opportunity to sharpen my writing and editing skills.

I want to take this opportunity to especially thank my mother who has always supported my decisions and guided me in the right direction when I was uncertain of the right path. I also want to thank my father for instilling in me the sense of independence and motivation necessary to succeed in the ever-changing, fast-paced world. And finally, above all things I thank God, for without Him this book and wonderful universities like Harvard would not be possible.

If you have any questions or comments, please contact me: dominichood@collegeprowler.com

Susie Lee—
Massachusetts Institute of Technology

My name is Susie Lee, and I'm a rising junior at MIT. It's funny that I wrote this because I actually didn't want to go to MIT when I was a high school senior. I never would have bought a book like this because I just didn't care about it. In fact, I only applied because I was already applying to a dozen other schools (what was one more?). But plans change. three years later, here I am, and I am thankful everyday for my decision. My major is management and my double major and/or minor(s) change everyday. Other than that, I am active in my sorority, my research job, and the campus in general.

I am originally from Granger, Indiana, a small town near Notre Dame. Being from the Midwest, I had no idea what to expect from Boston or MIT. As I read everything that I have written, I realize that I knew almost none of the things in this book. Writing this book has caused me to re-examine my entire MIT experience at the exact time when I was starting to take everything for granted. There are so many tiny little things that no one knows unless they go here that I was more than happy to explain.

Aside from all this generic info, some of my favorite things include: good food, good books, Disney World, math, card games, Notre Dame college football, sleeping, and beautiful sunny weather.

There is a long list of people who I would like to thank. The most important people are my family. I am working as hard as I can in this life to make all the work my parents have done worthwhile. They are always proud and supportive of me in every way. Even though my picture won't end up on this page, I know my dad will buy 10 copies anyway. I also want to thank my sister, Cecile, for teaching me about the things that really matter in life and for always making me smile.

Other than that, I want to thank the following people: Dave for helping me understand who I am, Christy, Kathryn, Val, Michelle, and all the people at College Prowler for giving me this chance.

If you have any questions at all, e-mail me at: susie@collegeprowler.com

Thanks again!

Abbie Beane—Middlebury

Seems I've come a long way since writing R.L. Stine knockoffs and fabricating stories about my first published novel at college interviews. Writing a book of some sort has always been a dream, or borderline fantasy, of mine, and College Prowler has given me the chance to realize it even before graduation. Most things I do or say are for the sake of irony, or in the name of a spectacular story, but writing is the exception. I genuinely love language, possibly too much, judging by my prolix style, and hope to continue using it in constructive ways while my writing grows and develops.

I suppose failing out of physics was a blessing in disguise. You see, somewhere along the "tangent line" I smartly realized that most writers end up writhing in poverty and "decided" to be a scientist—a meteorologist, in fact. Yet, by my second Newtonian physics class we had covered all my high school material, and were delving into integral calculus. Not even toting my lucky Furby to the first test could save me from the dormancy of my left-brain. Lost in endless reels of mathematical jargon, daunting deltas, and formidable forces of friction, the only thing I began to re-weigh was my ostensible career path.

So that's when I started to write again—for the student newspaper, student humor magazine, and for College Prowler. Along the way, I also inadvertently joint-majored in French and nearly starved to death in Paris during my star-studded semester abroad. In plain terms, I already have experience coping with the lifestyle of a writer.

I do wish I had a book like this one to cart around campus from the get-go at Middlebury. Instead, I wandered aimlessly for two years feigning know-how before I fumbled my way into the upper echelons of college knowledge. My hope is that readers of this guide will be vaulted into that esteemed stratosphere more quickly and efficiently.

Thanks to all of those who provided quotes for this guide, made contributions to my effort, including allowing me to borrow a computer here and there, and to College Prowler for granting me this opportunity. To all those who mocked my ambitions and see no merit in becoming just another name in a sea of names at the bookstore, I'd like to send out to you a big, scary scowl with a red bow on it. Thanks again.

abbiebeane@collegeprowler.com

Jennifer Lewis—Mount Holyoke College

I am a lifelong native of central New Jersey, although, in the four years I spent at school, I came to love western Massachusetts. I graduated from Mount Holyoke this past May with a philosophy major and religion minor and am now contemplating the wide world beyond college. I don't know yet what I want to do, but I know it will involve writing. Currently, I am occupying myself by working at a bookstore, reading anything I can get my hands on, and teaching myself photography (I'm partial to landscapes). It was a pleasure to work on this guidebook, and even after four years, I learned a lot about my school. It's a beautiful place and I'll miss it, but I'll definitely be back for reunions. I'm proud to join the long lines of alumnae who have come before me.

Many thanks to my family and friends, and to all my fellow students who gave me valuable insights on life at MHC.

jenniferlewis@collegeprowler.com

Briyah A. Paley—Northeastern University

This book was a great experience for me because it brought me back to my freshman year of college when I didn't know anything about Northeastern, or where to go in Boston for a good time. I never thought I would be a published author at the age of 21! I'm a junior journalism major in the College of Arts and Sciences. I've been lucky to intern at *The New York Post*, *YM*, *Us Weekly*, and *Time Out New York*.

Coming from Manhattan, one might think I have a skewed view of other places in the country and, in part, it is true. But, living in Boston for almost three years has taught me to appreciate what each place has to offer. I'll always be a city girl at heart! Coming to college has only made me grow as a person, and I can't stress how important it is to really think about what is the best school for you. Through the ups and downs, Northeastern is the best school for me. I hope this book has helped you see what this place is all about.

I want to thank my roommate Joanna Old for answering all of my questions regarding this book. She is a great roommate and a good friend. I also want to thank my parents, Anny Dobrejcer and Michael Paley, for being supportive throughout my college search and learning with me every day. I'm grateful to my grandparents, Marjorie and Bertram Paley, for taking me out to dinner and letting me come over so much. You've helped me more than you know. I promise to do my work now! Also, a thank you goes out to Omid Gohari who had the faith that I would be able to write this guidebook.

briyahpaley@collegeprowler.com

Kathryn Treadway—Providence College:

When the opportunity to write this guidebook first entered my summer plans, it presented the irresistible charm that every worthwhile challenge does. I found myself drawn to it, and yet, dreading the work; so of course, I had to accept it. From that moment on, this project has directed the course of many weeks of my life—altering plans, creating stress, and if you know me, causing shaking. Through all the ups and downs, it has challenged me as a writer, forced me to scrutinize the place I call home eight months of the year, and has been a thoroughly rewarding experience, overall.

I hope this book is revealing and useful in your search for the right college. Now a junior at PC, I know, without a doubt, this is where I belong, studying English and minoring in history. I look forward to sharpening my writing skills as World News Editor on *The Cowl* and wish to pursue more publishing opportunities in the future. A native of Long Island, NY, I am eager to return to PC to begin my second year as an RA.

There are so many people that I must thank for their love, support, and help during this project. My family, for putting up with my cranky, dramatic self when things get stressful. Neil, for his enthusiasm in utilizing his numerous contacts. To my girls—Karen, Monica, Siobhan, Krissy, Meg—you are the champagne bubbles in my life; gabbing, giggling, and gossiping with you make my days, weeks, months, and years. To my friend, the Yale crew-rowing, gymnast and microeconomist (wink, wink); the person who by far makes me laugh more than anyone else. To all my friends, new and old, from Kellenberg, PC, and all the places in between, you are the ones who make my daily existence extraordinary; thank you for that. To Tarra for forcing me to take a much needed two-day vacation that ended up being one of the best weekends of the summer. I cannot forget to express my gratitude to Mrs. Von and Mr. Huggard for their continual literary inspiration. And lastly, to everyone at the College Prowler for extending this opportunity to me. Thank you.

kathryntreadway@collegeprowler.com

Brooke Ackerley— Rhode Island School of Design

It's been a very valuable experience compiling this information about RISD. As a senior, looking back has given me perspective and a newfound appreciation for what I have gone through and what I will be taking away with me. RISD has taught me that you can support yourself doing something that you love, and although parts of our society may not feel that art is important, I have found that it touches people in ways far more profound than can be simply expressed. The students and graduates of RISD are the eyes and hands of America; we keep the rest of the country and the world seeing beauty. It is our job to observe and display that beauty in every way we can, and that job is important.

I would like to thank the textiles and English departments for supporting me and teaching me so much, the students who took time out of their busy, busy lives to tell me about themselves, and the people at College Prowler for giving prospective students a chance to better understand what they are getting themselves into.

Brooke Ackerley is a Textile Design major, an English Concentrator (emphasis on poetry), and co-founder and editor of RISD's literary magazine *Blackletter*.

brookeackerley@collegeprowler.com

Megan Hebard McRobert—Smith College

I've always enjoyed writing, and I love talking to people about Smith and their college decision process, so I jumped at the opportunity to write a whole book about Smith. I love it here, and I don't want to be anywhere else. At the same time, I have friends here and at other schools who are unhappy with their colleges. I think that part of that dissatisfaction comes from the fact that students are unable to see a complete picture of a school. I tried to give as a complete a picture as possible; I even learned a few things myself! I hope that this book helps you figure out what's right for you. I am currently a junior (and a proud resident of Wilder House) pursuing a major in women's studies and a minor in international relations. One of the many activities I enjoy at Smith is writing an opinion column for our weekly newspaper, *The Sophian*. Eventually, I hope to put my political and writing backgrounds to use as a journalist.

There are a million people I would like to thank who have helped throughout this process and throughout my academic and writing careers. However, I would like to dedicate this book to the memory of my grandfather, George Hebard, who passed away a few days before I got this job. He always taught me to work towards my goals and offered me unconditional support.

If you have any questions or comments, please feel free to contact me at meganmcrobert@collegeprowler.com

Rachel Clark Unkovic—Trinity College

I really enjoyed writing this book, and I hope you've enjoyed reading it, or at least that it gave you some good pointers towards what to expect from Trinity. Writing the book has helped the summer homesickness I've been feeling for the college and my friends there. Next fall, I will be back on campus as a senior majoring in Creative Writing and Classical Civilization. After Trinity, I'll go to graduate school to pursue an M.F.A. in Prose Fiction Writing. In the meantime, I plan to make the most of my last year there, because I really do believe that college is mainly what you yourself make of it. The best advice I can give you is this: decide to have fun in college, and wherever you end up, most likely you will have a blast!

If you have any questions or comments, e-mail me: rachelunkovic@collegeprowler.com

Emily Chasan—Tufts University

I had a great time writing this book! I've just returned from a semester in Madrid, and it was really exciting to be able to delve into the world of Tufts all over again. I'm hoping that this will help me progress as a writer. I'm now a senior at Tufts University pursuing degrees in both international relations and economics while serving on the executive board of *The Tufts Daily*. I hope to use everything I've learned to work in business reporting in the future. Being from Philadelphia, Boston took a little getting used to, but going to Tufts has been a wonderful experience and now I know how to say "artery" like "ahtehy." I hope this book has been insightful for you, and I hope you learned what it is really like to live on the hill.

I'd like to give many people many thanks for supporting me while I attempted to work on this book. Thank you Mom, Dad, Alex, Grandma, George, Erika, Jon, Nick, Emily, Josh, Leah, Nico, Andrea, Naushin, Rachel, and everyone at College Prowler!

emilychasan@collegeprowler.com

Colin Megill—University of Connecticut

You know, when I got here, I realized that nowhere is there a place to tell you about the bathrooms on campus. So I'm going to tell you. They're clean, depending on how anal retentive your floor and janitor are about cleaning them. The showers are really nice, but you should bring flip flops, and ones without cloth, because it gets wet and that's annoying (In a shower? Gets wet he says? No way!). The best advice I ever got in regards to college were the fateful words "bring liquid soap." I'll pass those along. Also, because I think it'd be really funny for this to be published: the locks on the bathroom stalls (at least in Northwest) are made by a company called "Hiney Hiders."

Ok, onto the serious stuff. I have to thank all of my friends who let me completely ignore them for this book and classes, yet never stopped calling me or caring how it was going. Steve Wheeler, Brad, Dan, Dan, Dan (in order of which Dan I like best), Drew, Mike, Michealla, Jordan, Beth, John, Eric, Lindsey, Mr. Harvey, Kyle, Ryan, Ryan, Matt, Crazy Asian Cheng, Crazy Russian Alina, and the faithful roomie Travis—you're the best, this book is dedicated to you, and so am I. Dedicating a book to my parents wouldn't be enough to thank them for what they've given me in life—an opportunity to truly do whatever I want, and all the tools to do it with. For working so hard so that I can have a school to write about, my life is dedicated to you both.

So you're still reading this, maybe you're actually interested in who I am. I am now officially not afraid to call myself a writer, considering I have published numerous articles for the commentary section of *The Daily Campus*, UConn's student newspaper. I swam four years varsity in high school (Hi Mr. Murin), which afforded me the nickname "Brick," because I sank when I dove my freshman and sophomore years. I play the snare drum in the marching band, which afforded me the nickname "Helmet" because they thought I looked like Rick Moranis (except for him being ugly, and me being ravishingly handsome).

I strongly encourage you to contact me at colinmegill@collegeprowler.com. I promise to answer your e-mail and give you my instant messenger name so that we can communicate faster, because I'm completely addicted to it. Write with questions, feedback. I hope this book has helped, and I hope to see you at the UConn football games in the future. I'll be one of the ones making a lot of noise.

Seth Pouliot—University of Massachusetts

I graduated from UMass a few months ago, and writing this book was the first job I found. I'm originally from western Massachusetts, so going to UMass seemed like the next logical step in my life after high school. I spent my entire junior year of college at the University of Alaska, Southeast in Juneau, on a domestic exchange program. Although my degree is in business management, I've been interested in a career in writing for as long as I can remember.

I hope this book has been a useful resource for you. I approached this guidebook as objectively as possible, but of course every word I wrote will reflect the fact that my experince at UMass has been uniquely personal. Many people in my life have been in some way responsible for the quality of this book, leaving myself the only one to blame for any mistakes and shortcomings, so instead of a list, I woud like to say "Thank you, all."

If anyone has any questions for me, about anything, e-mail me at sethpouliot@collegeprowler.com.

"This isn't who it would be, if it wasn't who it is."
-Phish

Jeff Lewis—University of New Hampshire

My name is Jeff Lewis, and although I wish to bring peace to the world, I realize that I'm probably best off settling for just having a good time and enjoying the rest of my college career at UNH.

I was born and raised in Holderness, NH near Plymouth State College. Before you ask, I didn't go to Plymouth State College because, honestly, that is just a little too close to home. I thought UNH would be a better fit because of its size and variety of courses. I am currently pursing a major in journalism.

I particularly enjoyed writing this guidebook because I believe students should know the truth about the schools they are looking at. I believe UNH has a lot to offer to students who are not sure what direction they want to go in life. In parting, live life to the fullest and never stop exploring

jefflewis@collegeprowler.com

Jessica Pritz—
University of Rhode Island

Writing this guidebook was my first real step in becoming a writer. It was a great experience, and I had a lot of fun with it. I have had two other essays published in the past. I have always loved to write, and I hope to make a career out of it. Right now I'm in my fourth year at URI and will be graduating in 2006. Yes, it'll take me five years to graduate and I am in no rush to leave behind my college experience. I have decided to study journalism and I'm focusing on print and feature writing. I have no idea what lies in store for me as a journalist, just as long as I get to write and make some money doing it. I would love to find work in Rhode Island after I graduate. I would not want to have to return back to my hometown of Orange, Connecticut and move back in with my dad, (no offense dad). Anyway, I hope that you were able to learn something that you didn't otherwise know about URI.
Thanks everyone!

jessicapritz@collegeprowler.com

Kevin Jonas Lenfest—
University of Vermont

The University of Vermont has thus far lent me an extraordinary experience. Initially, I wanted to attend a small liberal-arts college, but after coming to UVM and settling in, I eventually found myself beyond happiness, despite its large size. For me, everything really started coming together during my sophomore year when I was more familiar with what the school and professors had to offer. I got to take more classes that I really wanted, and my real friendships were solidified. UVM rekindled my love of academics, and I am now looking forward to a possible future in the scholarly circle.

Writing this guidebook has been both a pleasure and an honor. I am currently entering my junior year at the University of Vermont, pursuing a double major in English and religion with a focus on philosophy. As a native Vermonter, I have come to appreciate UVM for the same reasons I love Vermont: its beautiful surroundings and endless opportunities and activities for those who cannot get enough of the outdoors. Cycling throughout the green mountains and skiing during the winters have both given me unique perspectives on this picturesque state. The University of Vermont has been an invaluable transitioning step toward achieving my goal of competing in cycling, as well as a working force in opening the doors to further study in graduate school. Whatever I end up doing, I know I will be passionate about it, as passion supercedes all other priorities and, in my opinion, provides the building blocks to happiness.

If given the choice, I would not wish to go any other place. Looking back on the people I've met and the opportunities I've seized, the classes I've had, and the places I've gone, I cannot see it any other way. The more I learned, the more I grew. I have changed in many different ways since high school, all for the better, and I credit much of this to the friends I've made and my personal experience with education, experience, and life. I will never turn back.

Thanks for reading.

kevynlenfest@collegeprowler.com

Genevieve Brennan—Wellesley College

This is my senior year at Swells and after a leave of absence junior year to be a fruit picker in New Zealand, and a summer on a Wellesley internship in Costa Rica, I've become the sentimental senior I never thought I'd be.

I'm an English major who's bitten off more than she can chew with a creative writing senior thesis, but I'm still looking forward to long nights at Molly's and midnight swims in Lake Waban. My future is obstinately undecided, but some kind of writing seems pretty unavoidable.

Though most students seem to toil away their time at Wellesley, I've become a bit of a hedonist. I've been in the improv comedy group Dead Serious since first year, and I manage my beloved co-op café, El Table.

Thanks to College Prowler, MaryAnn Hill, and all who contributed their opinions for this guide. Personal thanks to my family, friends from home, friends from my travels, and my Wellesley girls, who have always been there with what I needed, be it a back scratch or a beer.

genevievebrennan@collegeprowler.com

John Cusick—Wesleyan University

John Cusick is a student at Wesleyan University. His articles and short stories have appeared in *The Auburn News*, *The Worcester, Massachusetts Telegram & Gazette* and at *www.aboutteens.com*. He is a writer for the *Wesleyan Argus*, and co-hosts, co-produces and co-writes the Steve Kovacs Show on WESU 88.1 FM, Middletown. He is an occasional member in The Dead Poets Society, The Wesleyan Boogie Club, and The Atlas Thirteen Society. He is an avid fan of Steely Dan, funny hats, and drives much, much too fast.

The Author would like to thank, firstly, his girlfriend Claire, whom he loves very much and who has put up with him for nearly two years now. The author also thanks his parents for their constant badgering and merciless affection, as well as his good friend Adam, without whom he would never have heard of Wesleyan University. The author also thanks, in no particular order, his very, very good friends from Wesleyan who have taught him so much and kept him in the lifestyle to which he is slowly becoming accustomed. They are: Andrea, Ashraf, Kat, Liz, Rory, and many, many more. The author would also like to thank all the people that helped bring this book together, including the extremely plucky and enthusiastic summer interns who helped him to dig up so much of the information needed to complete this guide to Wesleyan. Lastly, the author thanks Richard, Tom, Hunter, Vladimir, Truman, George, Fyodor, Jack, Bill, F. Scott, J.D., Barbara, Mary, Annie, Ernest, David, and all the rest for their wit, wisdom, and companionship.

johncusick@collegeprowler.com

Alexandra Grashkina—Williams College

Alexandra Grashkina, known as Alex or Sasha, was born 06/06/1981 in Sofia, Bulgaria. She attended an American high school called ACS (American College of Sofia) and traveled to New York City as an exchange student when she was 16. Ever since, she decided that traveling was a good thing and packed her suitcase every four months or so.

Later on, she studied social sciences and languages in Williams College, Williamstown, in Fortaleza, Brazil, and in Geneva, Switzerland. Alex speaks English, Bulgarian, Russian, French, and Portuguese with very little difficulty and has intermediate knowledge of Spanish and Italian. She is now learning the Armenian alphabet.

To Williams College, Alex owes a lot, but her biggest achievement was overcoming her fear of water and learning to swim.

Currently, she works as a paralegal in civil litigation and is trying to stay out of trouble when not at work.

alexandragrashkina@collegeprowler.com

Melissa Doscher—Yale University

If I had to write this guide at any other time in my life, the result would have been different and biased by my perspective at the moment. But, now that I have just graduated and have had the time to reflect honestly and objectively, I can step back and see the experience for what it truly was—amazing. As an English major, I have had the opportunity to immerse myself in what I love, to read the words of geniuses, and to participate in their legacies. But, as a student at Yale, I have had the opportunity to grow as a person and to realize that I am not just a list of achievements or an academic machine—I am a human being. In my time at college, I have encountered people whose talents blow my mind, and whose life experiences could make me laugh until I cry, or cry until I laugh. These moments were some of the most important I experienced at Yale.

At this point, I feel prepared to enter my future, although, I am completely unsure of what it holds for me—graduate school, publishing work, writing? I hope that this guide proves helpful, whether it is assisting you in making a choice or informing you about your future. It is so exciting to be where you are, and I wish you the best of luck!

If you have any questions or comments, feel free to contact me at melissadoscher@collegeprowler.com.